America Votes™ 24

America Votes™ 24

A HANDBOOK OF CONTEMPORARY AMERICAN ELECTION STATISTICS

RICHARD M. SCAMMON
ALICE V. McGILLIVRAY
RHODES COOK

2000

CQ PRESS

A Division of Congressional Quarterly Inc.
Washington, D.C.

CQ Press
A Division of Congressional Quarterly Inc.
1414 22nd St. N.W.
Washington, D.C. 20037

(202) 822-1475; (800) 638-1710

www.cqpress.com

♾ The paper used in this publication meets the minimum requirements of the American National Standard for Information Sciences—Permanence of Paper for Printed Library Materials, ANSI Z39.48-1992.

Printed and bound in the United States of America

05   04   03   02   01   5   4   3   2   1

Electronic composition: Paul P. Pressau

Library of Congress Catalog Card Number: 56-10132
International Standard Book Number: 1-56802-600-5

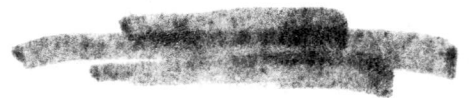

Richard M. Scammon

1915–2001

Richard M. Scammon, who died April 27, 2001, was for more than four decades America's leading expert on elections. Mr. Scammon, with his wife, Mary, created *America Votes* to present the results of U.S. elections in a comprehensive and orderly manner that would allow scholars, students of politics, reporters, and all citizens to study the building blocks of democracy. The first, *America Votes 1*, chronicled the 1954 elections. The volumes have continued to the present *America Votes 24*, with new editions published every two years in a series that is the longest and most complete and accurate record of federal and gubernatorial elections in existence. In addition, he created *America at the Polls*, now a two-volume work that provides detailed election data for presidential contests beginning in 1920. Both were published for many years by the Elections Research Center, which he established in Washington, D.C.

Mr. Scammon worked for the Army and the State Department before being named by President John F. Kennedy as director of the U.S. Census Bureau, a position he held from 1961 to 1964. During this period he served as chairman of the Presidential Commission on Regulation and Voting Participation. He also was for many years a consultant to NBC News, when television was emerging as the primary method of delivering election night returns. During his life he published hundreds of books and papers. One for which he is notably remembered is a volume written with Ben Wattenberg titled *The Real Majority*. The book gave a penetrating look at the dramatically changing electorate in the volatile 1960s, examining the opportunities those changes posed for Republicans and the serious challenges they presented for the increasingly divided Democrats.

Contents

Chicago, Detroit, Harris County (Houston), Los Angeles County, New York City, and Philadelphia data will be found in the appropriate state sections.

ERRATA

America Votes 23

The following corrections should be made in the previous edition of *America Votes,* covering the 1998 election cycle.

Page 7. In the chart of special elections, the victor in the Pennsylvania 1st, Robert A. Brady, should be designated as a Democrat.

Page 89. Democrat Jim Davis won the House election in the Florida 11th District in 1998 by a plurality of 39,086 votes.

Page 90. Republican Lincoln Diaz-Balart won the House election in the Florida 21st District by a plurality of 55,640 votes.

Page 127. The last election listed in the Illinois 17th should be 1992, not 1991.

Page 166. The victorious Democratic candidate in 1998 in the Louisiana 7th District was Chris John, not Chris Lundy.

Page 289. The section after "1998 General Elections" should read "1998 Primary Elections."

Pages 357 and 358. The percentage of the Total Vote and Major Party Vote received by Republican congressional candidates in 1992 is missing for a number of Texas districts. The Republican vote percentages should be as follows: District 2: Total 43.6%, Major 43.7%; District 4: Total 38.1%, Major 39.6%; District 10: Total 26.2%, Major 27.9%; District 11: Total and Major 32.6%; District 12: Total and Major 37.2%; District 13: Total and Major 39.7%; District 14: Total 27.3%, Major 28.6%; District 15: Total and Major 39.6%; District 16: Total and Major 48.1%; District 17: Total and Major 33.9%; District 19: Total and Major 77.4%; District 21: Total 72.2%, Major 75.2%; District 23: Total 59.1%, Major 60.6%; District 27: Total 42.6%, Major 43.4%.

Introduction

When once asked to describe himself, the legendary Huey Long supposedly responded: Just call me "sui generis." The same might be said about the election of 2000, one of the closest ever held for president, the Senate and the House of Representatives.

It was surely one of a kind. The presidential election was not settled until more than a month after the November balloting, and then after the intervention of the Supreme Court. The unusual 50–50 deadlock in the Senate (which lasted until the following June) was not confirmed until fully three weeks after the election, when the final recount of ballots was completed in Washington state.

The twenty-fourth volume of *America Votes* details in numerical form the sweep of this unique election cycle, from the three gubernatorial elections in 1999 in Kentucky, Louisiana and Mississippi, through the 2000 primary season, to the focus of this book, the November 2000 general election for president, Congress and a handful of governorships.

The 2000 election is already an instant classic for its almost impossible-to-resolve closeness.

For the first time since the election of 1888, there were different winners of the popular and electoral votes, albeit by narrow margins on both counts. Democrat Al Gore won the popular vote by roughly 540,000 votes out of more than 105 million ballots cast—the smallest margin in the popular tally since 1968. Republican George W. Bush won the all-important electoral vote by just five votes, the smallest margin in the Electoral College since 1876.

And that same degree of closeness was evident at the other end of Pennsylvania Avenue. The post-election breakdown of 221 Republicans, 212 Democrats and two independents was the smallest advantage that either party has had in the House of Representatives since 1952.

As for the 50–50 deadlock in the Senate, the election created a tie between Senate Democrats and Republicans for the first time since 1880.

Why was the election so close?

At the presidential level, there were strongly conflicting tides that, at the end, virtually cancelled each other out. Vice President Gore was boosted by the

2000: Democrats Inch Back

Republicans may have regained the White House in the 2000 election, but Democrats gained one governorship, a pair of House seats and four Senate seats, the latter creating a 50–50 tie. With Vice President Richard B. Cheney casting the tie-breaking vote, Republicans held nominal control of the Senate in the 107th Congress until June 2001, when Democrats gained the upper hand upon the shift of James M. Jeffords of Vermont from Republican to Independent.

The chart below reflects partisan totals immediately before and after the 2000 general election. The pre-election House totals include two vacancies—one seat previously held by the Democrats, one by the Republicans. They are credited to each party in the pre-election count.

	Pre-Election			Post-Election		
	Rep.	Dem.	Other	Rep.	Dem.	Other
Governor	30	18	2	29	19	2
Senate	54	46	0	50	50	0
House	223	210	2	221	212	2

nation's prosperity and high performance ratings for the Clinton administration, of which he was a part, factors borne out in presidential election models created by academics who were virtually unanimous in predicting a comfortable Gore victory.

Propelling Bush were Clinton's low personal ratings, a sentiment for change that often begins to work against the incumbent party at the eight-year mark and a liberal third-party candidate in Ralph Nader of the Green Party, who posed a much greater problem for Gore than conservative Patrick J. Buchanan did for Bush.

The presidential race also pitted two conflicting political eras against each other—a short-term Democratic period that twice elected Clinton in the 1990s, and a longer-term Republican era that had given the GOP victory in five of the six previous presidential elections from 1968 through 1988.

Counting the 2000 Vote

The closeness of the 2000 election was eye-catching, but not new. It marked the third straight election that neither party won a majority of the popular vote for president, and the third straight election that neither party won a majority of the ballots cast for the House of Representatives. In each of the last three presidential contests—1992, 1996 and 2000—Democrats received the most votes. In each of the last three contests for the House—1996, 1998 and 2000—Republicans drew the most votes. No blank or void ballots are included in the totals below. They are based on official results from 14 gubernatorial contests (11 held in 2000, three in 1999) and 34 races for the Senate, as well as two versions of the House vote. "All Races" feature the results from every district in which a vote was taken. "Contested Races" are those in which the Democrats and Republicans both fielded candidates.

Office	Total Vote	Republican	Democratic	Other	Rep.-Dem. Plurality	Percentage of Total Vote		
						Rep.	Dem.	Other
President	105,396,627	50,455,156	50,992,335	3,949,136	537,179 D	47.9%	48.4%	3.7%
Governor	15,868,945	7,271,361	8,056,020	541,564	784,659 D	45.8%	50.8%	3.4%
Senate	79,312,137	37,840,177	38,384,289	3,087,671	544,112 D	47.7%	48.4%	3.9%
House								
All Races	97,226,268	46,954,281	46,520,851	3,751,136	433,430 R	48.3%	47.8%	3.9%
Contested Races	85,705,246	41,527,049	41,722,989	2,455,208	195,940 D	48.5%	48.7%	2.9%

2000: Close House Races

A total of 25 House members were elected to a seat in the 107th Congress in November 2000 with less than 52 percent of the total vote in their district. That is a greater number of close elections of this sort than in 1998, but still represented only the tip of the iceberg when compared to the hundreds of House races that were won in 2000 with little or no competition at all. An asterisk (*) indicates candidates who won their first election to the House in November 2000.

Republicans	2000 Winning Percentage	Democrats	2000 Winning Percentage
Mark Kennedy, Minn. 2 *	48.1	Steve J. Israel, N.Y. 2 *	47.9
Steve Horn, Cal. 38	48.4	Betty McCollum, Minn. 4 *	48.0
Shelley Moore Capito, W.V. 2 *	48.5	Jane Harman, Cal. 36	48.4
Clay Shaw, Fla. 22	50.1	Rush Holt, N.J. 12	48.7
Heather A. Wilson, N.M. 1	50.3	Susan A. Davis, Cal. 49 *	49.6
Rob Simmons, Conn. 2 *	50.6	Bill Luther, Minn. 6	49.6
Ric Keller, Fla. 8 *	50.8	Dennis Moore, Kan. 3	50.0
Mike Pence, Ind. 2 *	50.9	James A. Traficant, Ohio 17	50.0
Samuel B. Graves, Mo. 6 *	50.9	Rick Larsen, Wash. 2 *	50.0
Mark Steven Kirk, Ill. 10 *	51.2	Mike Ross, Ark. 4 *	51.0
Dennis Rehberg, Mont. AL *	51.5	Tammy Baldwin, Wis. 2	51.4
Mike Ferguson, N.J. 7 *	51.6	Tim Roemer, Ind. 3	51.6
		Shelley Berkley, Nev. 1	51.7

In the House, Democrats had been inching back toward a position of parity since their loss of congressional control in 1994. But much of the closeness in the 2000 House balloting was due to the lack of competition, which kept partisan change to a minimum.

Although 435 seats were at stake, the playing field was really barely one-tenth that size. Well-heeled incumbents and the lack of galvanizing issues or presidential coattails all proved to be powerful forces promoting the status quo and deterring significant competition in most districts. In the end Democrats scored a net gain of two seats.

In the Senate the races were more competitive and Republicans had a larger proportion of seats to defend (19, to the Democrats' 15), factors that were reflected in the final results. The Democrats registered a net gain of four seats, picking off some of the more vulnerable members of the large GOP class of 1994—Rod Grams of Minnesota, Spencer Abraham of Michigan and John Ashcroft of Missouri. In one of the year's more bizarre results, Ashcroft lost to the state's late governor, Mel Carnahan, whose name remained on the ballot even though he had died in a plane crash several weeks earlier.

Ultimately each party did a good job of rallying its base in the 2000 election. Bush scored an electoral vote shutout

The House Since 1990: From Democrat To Republican

The House has gone from Democratic to Republican in the 1990s, fueled by the GOP upsurge in the South. But since winning control of the House in 1994, Republicans have steadily lost ground. After the 2000 election, Republicans held a majority of House seats in the South and Midwest, while Democrats held the larger number in the Northeast and West. Regions are defined below. "I" indicates Independent.

	South				West			Midwest			East				Total House			
	R	D	I		R	D		R	D		R	D	I		R	D	I	
1990	44	85	0	D	37	48	D	45	68	D	41	66	1	D	167	267	1	D
1992	52	85	0	D	38	55	D	44	61	D	42	57	1	D	176	258	1	D
1994	73	64	0	R	53	40	R	59	46	R	45	54	1	D	230	204	1	R
1996	82	55	0	R	51	42	R	55	50	R	39	60	1	D	227	207	1	R
1998	82	55	0	R	49	44	R	54	51	R	38	61	1	D	223	211	1	R
2000	81	55	1	R	43	50	D	57	48	R	40	59	1	D	221	212	2	R
Net Change in GOP Seats, 1990–2000	+37				+6			+12			–1				+54			

Note: Traditionally, Congressional Quarterly has defined the four regions as follows:

EAST—Connecticut, Delaware, Maine, Maryland, Massachusetts, New Hampshire, New Jersey, New York, Pennsylvania, Rhode Island, Vermont, West Virginia.
MIDWEST—Illinois, Indiana, Iowa, Kansas, Michigan, Minnesota, Missouri, Nebraska, North Dakota, Ohio, South Dakota, Wisconsin.
SOUTH—Alabama, Arkansas, Florida, Georgia, Kentucky, Louisiana, Mississippi, North Carolina, Oklahoma, South Carolina, Tennessee, Texas, Virginia.
WEST—Alaska, Arizona, California, Colorado, Hawaii, Idaho, Montana, Nevada, New Mexico, Oregon, Utah, Washington, Wyoming.

in presidential voting in the South, the basic building block of the modern Republican Party, while Gore just missed a clean sweep in the Democratic Northeast, where he lost only New Hampshire and West Virginia.

Gore swept many of the large urban centers of the Frost Belt and Pacific West by wider margins than Clinton did in his clear-cut victory over Bob Dole in 1996. Yet Bush dominated the vote in rural and small-town America, winning more than three-quarters of the nation's counties.

And the two tended to split the large suburban vote, with Gore holding the upper hand in the Frost Belt and Bush dominating across the Sun Belt.

Many Gore supporters blamed Nader for costing their candidate the election. The Green Party nominee took nearly 3 million votes nationally, including nearly 100,000 in Florida, where the vote was so close that disputed ballots and selected recounts extended the election for weeks.

Yet any snippiness by Democrats toward Nader would be moot if Gore had carried his home state of Tennessee and its 11 electoral votes. As it was, Gore was the first presidential candidate since George McGovern in 1972 to lose his home state.

The Methodology

The twenty-fourth volume of *America Votes* follows the general pattern used in previous editions of this series. There is an expanded introduction with tables designed to help tie together various aspects of the 2000 election cycle. As well, the front section contains tables with the state-by-state voter turnout and vote for president, Senate, House and governorships in the 2000 election cycle. There are also sections with the results of special elections held between the general elections of 1998 and 2000 to fill vacancies in the 106th Congress, and a listing of changes in congressional membership in the 107th Congress that occurred between the 2000 general election and early June 2001.

2000: Defeated Incumbents

One sitting governor, six senators and six House members were defeated in the November 2000 general election. In addition, three House members were beaten earlier in the year in their party's primary—Democrats Matthew G. Martinez of California and Michael P. Forbes of New York, and Republican Merrill Cook of Utah. Half of the defeated Senate incumbents were members of the Republican class of 1994. The bulk of the House losers were veteran members. The chart lists the incumbents defeated in the 2000 general election, the number of terms that they had served in that office before their loss in 2000, the percentage of the total vote they had received the previous time they had run for that office (1994 for senators, 1996 for governors, 1998 for House members) and their percentage of the total vote in 2000.

	Number of Terms	Previous Election Percentage	2000 Election Percentage
GOVERNORS			
(1 Republican)			
Cecil H. Underwood, R-W.V.	2	51.6	47.2
SENATORS			
(5 Republicans, 1 Democrat)			
Spencer Abraham, R-Mich.	1	51.9	47.9
John Ashcroft, R-Mo.	1	59.7	48.4
Slade Gorton, R-Wash.	3	55.7	48.6
Rod Grams, R-Minn.	1	49.1	43.3
Charles S. Robb, D-Va.	2	45.6	47.7
William V. Roth Jr., R-Del.	5	55.8	43.7
REPRESENTATIVES			
(4 Republicans, 2 Democrats)			
Brian P. Bilbray, R-Cal. 49	3	48.8	46.2
Jay Dickey, R-Ark. 4	4	57.5	49.0
Sam Gejdenson, D-Conn. 2	10	61.0	49.4
Steven Kuykendall, R-Cal. 36	1	48.9	46.5
David Minge, D-Minn. 2	4	57.0	48.0
James E. Rogan, R-Cal. 27	2	50.7	43.8

Following this introductory material is the heart of the volume, 50 chapters—one for each state. Each chapter begins with a profile sheet listing the current governor, senators and representatives, followed by tables of the statewide vote for president, governor and senator from 1946 or 1948 to the present. Following this information is a map of the state showing its counties and congressional districts for members of the House. Following the map are the county-by-county tables of presidential, gubernatorial and Senate elections. All these tables are for the 2000 general election except for the governorships in Kentucky, Louisiana and Mississippi, where voting was conducted in 1999.

The county tables for president feature a four-column format, with separate columns for Republican, Democrat, Green and Other, with the latter an aggregation of the vote for smaller third-party and write-in candidates. Although Nader received less than 3 percent of the nationwide vote as the Green Party candidate, his effect on the close 2000 election was considered enough to merit inclusion in the county tables.

Virtually all the other county tables for gubernatorial and Senate elections feature a three-column format (Republican, Democratic, Other). The only exceptions are for elections in which an independent or third-party candidate received at least 10 percent of the vote; in that case a column for the candidate's vote is also included. All the county tables include 2000 population numbers from the Census Bureau.

The county tables are followed by a listing of votes cast for candidates for the House of Representatives, arranged by congressional district. The implementation of the 1990 Census for redistricting purposes led to changes in all multimember states. Most states in 2000 were using the same lines that had been established for the 1992 election, although court-ordered changes have required several states to redraw their lines since then.

The redrawn maps for these states appear in this volume, and the election returns are for the altered congressional districts. Votes for House members are for the districts as defined for the 107th Congress, and in most states results are included back to 1992. Votes for districts before 1992 are not included except for states with a single member in the House.

The last pages of each state chapter consist of two parts. The first is the notes section containing a breakdown of votes cast in the general election for third-party, independent and write-in candidates. The second part provides official results for the primary elections for president, governor, Senate and House held in the 2000 election cycle.

Voting data also is provided in the appropriate state chapters for six large urban areas: Chicago, Detroit, Harris County (Houston), Los Angeles County, New York City and Philadelphia. In the chapters for New England states, tables that list the vote for president, governor and senator by larger cities and towns are also included. In Rhode Island the results are listed for all cities and towns.

The *America Votes* series is compiled from the final, official results obtained from election authorities in each state. The protracted postelection controversy over the casting and counting of ballots in Florida underscores that perfection, though always the goal, can sometimes prove elusive in a work such as this one. And it must be noted that on occasion states may belatedly report vote total changes that occur after publication of this volume. Any such changes will be noted in the next volume.

As always, there is the desire to make these reference volumes of maximum efficiency in meeting the needs of their users. Suggestions for new materials, together with any corrections of data, are welcome.

As in the preparation of *America Votes 23,* thanks are in order to Eileen J. Canavan of the Federal Election Commission, with whom the author consulted in an effort to reconcile discrepancies in vote totals.

And special thanks are due to the staff at CQ Press: David Tarr, the executive editor of CQ Press, whose continued good grace, keen eye and knowledge of the electoral process has for years steered these election volumes to a successful completion; Gwenda Larsen, senior production editor, who helped edit the book and who shepherded the day-to-day movement of copy with skill and good humor; and Paul Pressau, who once again assembled this mass of data into readable, published form.

And as a final note, the author would like to dedicate this edition to his stepmother, Ann Cook, who died in early June. Although she did not always understand what her stepson produced, she was a constant source of support and encouragement that was always appreciated.

Rhodes Cook
June 2001

VOTER TURNOUT IN 2000 ELECTIONS

State	2000 Voting Age Population	November 2000 Registration	Percentage Voting Age Registered	Presidential Vote	Presidential Vote as Percent of		U.S. House Vote	Senate Vote	Governor Vote
					Voting Age Population	Registered Voters			
Alabama	3,333,000	2,528,963	75.9%	1,666,272	50.0%	65.9%	1,438,994		
Alaska	430,000	473,648	110.2%	285,560	66.4%	60.3%	274,393		
Arizona	3,625,000	2,654,700	73.2%	1,532,016	42.3%	57.7%	1,465,656	1,397,076	
Arkansas	1,929,000	1,555,809	80.7%	921,781	47.8%	59.2%	632,765		
California	24,873,000	15,707,307	63.2%	10,965,856	44.1%	69.8%	10,437,665	10,623,614	
Colorado	3,067,000	2,858,239	93.2%	1,741,368	56.8%	60.9%	1,623,882		
Connecticut	2,499,000	2,031,626	81.3%	1,459,525	58.4%	71.8%	1,313,490	1,311,261	
Delaware	582,000	503,672	86.5%	327,622	56.3%	65.0%	313,171	327,017	323,688
Florida	11,774,000	8,752,717	74.3%	5,963,110	50.6%	68.1%	5,011,372	5,856,731	
Georgia	5,893,000	4,648,205	78.9%	2,596,645	44.1%	55.9%	2,416,622	2,428,510	
			0.0%						
Hawaii	909,000	637,349	70.1%	367,951	40.5%	57.7%	340,424	345,623	
Idaho	921,000	728,085	79.1%	501,621	54.5%	68.9%	492,835		
Illinois	8,983,000	7,117,449	79.2%	4,742,123	52.8%	66.6%	4,393,352		
Indiana	4,448,000	4,000,809	89.9%	2,199,302	49.4%	55.0%	2,156,744	2,145,209	2,179,413
Iowa	2,165,000	1,969,199	91.0%	1,315,563	60.8%	66.8%	1,275,934		
Kansas	1,983,000	1,623,623	81.9%	1,072,218	54.1%	66.0%	1,038,379		
Kentucky	2,993,000	2,556,815	85.4%	1,544,187	51.6%	60.4%	1,435,409		580,074
Louisiana	3,255,000	2,782,929	85.5%	1,765,656	54.2%	63.4%	1,202,171		1,295,205
Maine	968,000	947,189	97.9%	651,817	67.3%	68.8%	638,399	634,872	
Maryland	3,925,000	2,715,366	69.2%	2,020,480	51.5%	74.4%	1,926,764	1,946,898	
Massachusetts	4,749,000	4,000,218	84.2%	2,702,984	56.9%	67.6%	2,347,375	2,599,420	
Michigan	7,358,000	6,861,342	93.3%	4,232,711	56.6%	60.7%	4,069,736	4,167,685	
Minnesota	3,547,000	2,801,077	79.0%	2,438,685	68.8%	87.1%	2,363,738	2,419,520	
Mississippi	2,047,000			994,184	48.6%		986,139	994,144	763,938
Missouri	4,105,000	3,676,664	89.6%	2,359,892	57.5%	64.2%	2,325,788	2,361,586	2,346,830
Montana	668,000	698,260	104.5%	410,997	61.5%	58.9%	410,523	411,601	410,192
Nebraska	1,234,000	1,085,272	87.9%	697,019	56.5%	64.2%	683,071	692,344	
Nevada	1,390,000	878,970	63.2%	608,970	43.8%	69.3%	585,204	600,250	
New Hampshire	911,000	856,519	94.0%	569,081	62.5%	66.4%	556,417		564,953
New Jersey	6,245,000	4,710,768	75.4%	3,187,226	51.0%	67.7%	2,988,233	3,015,662	
New Mexico	1,263,000	928,931	73.5%	598,605	47.4%	64.4%	587,514	589,526	
New York	13,805,000	11,262,816	81.6%	6,821,999	49.4%	60.6%	5,823,850	6,779,839	
North Carolina	5,797,000	5,186,094	89.5%	2,911,262	50.2%	56.1%	2,779,800		2,942,062
North Dakota	477,000			288,256	60.4%		285,658	287,539	289,412
Ohio	8,433,000	7,537,822	89.4%	4,701,998	55.8%	62.4%	4,517,838	4,448,801	
Oklahoma	2,531,000	2,233,602	88.2%	1,234,229	48.8%	55.3%	1,087,515		
Oregon	2,530,000	1,950,902	77.1%	1,533,968	60.6%	78.6%	1,440,002		
Pennsylvania	9,155,000	7,781,997	85.0%	4,913,119	53.7%	63.1%	4,554,347	4,735,504	
Rhode Island	753,000	655,107	87.0%	409,047	54.3%	62.4%	384,127	391,537	
South Carolina	2,977,000	2,266,200	76.1%	1,382,717	46.4%	61.0%	1,321,312		
South Dakota	542,000	520,881	96.1%	316,269	58.4%	60.7%	314,761		
Tennessee	4,221,000	3,400,487	80.6%	2,076,181	49.2%	61.1%	1,854,378	1,928,613	
Texas	14,850,000	12,365,235	83.3%	6,407,637	43.1%	51.8%	5,985,763	6,276,652	
Utah	1,465,000	1,120,129	76.5%	770,754	52.6%	68.8%	758,754	769,704	761,806
Vermont	460,000	427,354	92.9%	294,308	64.0%	68.9%	283,366	288,500	293,473
Virginia	5,263,000	4,071,471	77.4%	2,739,447	52.1%	67.3%	2,421,729	2,718,301	
Washington	4,368,000	3,335,714	76.4%	2,487,433	56.9%	74.6%	2,382,411	2,461,379	2,469,852
West Virginia	1,416,000	1,067,822	75.4%	648,124	45.8%	60.7%	579,872	603,477	648,047
Wisconsin	3,930,000			2,598,607	66.1%		2,506,314	2,540,083	
Wyoming	358,000	220,012	61.5%	218,351	61.0%	99.2%	212,312	213,659	
District of Columbia	411,000	354,410		201,894	49.1%	57.0%			
	205,814,000	159,049,775	77.3%	105,396,627	51.2%	66.3%	97,226,268	79,312,137	15,868,945

Voting age population exluding states without registration 199,360,000 159,049,775

Sources: Registration figures - Committee for the Study of the American Electorate. Voting Age Population - U.S. Census Bureau

Wisconsin and North Dakota do not maintain registration systems. Figures for Mississippi were unavailable. Excluding these states, the percentage of voting age population that was registered was 79.8 percent. The presidential vote as a percent of voting age population was 50.9 and as a percent of registered voters was 63.8.

GUBERNATORIAL ELECTIONS 1999 AND 2000

| State | Total Vote | Republican | | Democratic | | Other Vote | Rep.-Dem. Plurality | Percentage | | | |
| | | Vote | Candidate | Vote | Candidate | | | Total Vote | | Major Vote | |
								Rep.	Dem.	Rep.	Dem.
Delaware	323,688	128,603	Burris, John M.	191,695	Minner, Ruth Ann	3,390	63,092 D	39.7%	59.2%	40.2%	59.8%
Indiana	2,179,413	908,285	McIntosh, David M.	1,232,525	O'Bannon, Frank L.	38,603	324,240 D	41.7%	56.6%	42.4%	57.6%
Kentucky[1]	580,074	128,788	Martin, Peppy	352,099	Patton, Paul E.	99,187	223,311 D	22.2%	60.7%	26.8%	73.2%
Louisiana[1]	1,295,205	805,203	Foster, Mike	382,445	Jefferson, Willilam J.	107,557	422,758 R	62.2%	29.5%	67.8%	32.2%
Mississippi[1]	763,938	370,691	Parker, Mike	379,034	Musgrove, Ronnie	14,213	8,343 D	48.5%	49.6%	49.4%	50.6%
Missouri	2,346,830	1,131,307	Talent, James M.	1,152,752	Holden, Bob	62,771	21,445 D	48.2%	49.1%	49.5%	50.5%
Montana	410,192	209,135	Martz, Judy	193,131	O'Keefe, Mark	7,926	16,004 R	51.0%	47.1%	52.0%	48.0%
New Hampshire	564,953	246,952	Humphrey, Gordon	275,038	Shaheen, Jeanne	42,963	28,086 D	43.7%	48.7%	47.3%	52.7%
North Carolina	2,942,062	1,360,960	Vinroot, Richard	1,530,324	Easley, Mike	50,778	169,364 D	46.3%	52.0%	47.1%	52.9%
North Dakota	289,412	159,255	Hoeven, John	130,144	Heitkamp, Heidi	13	29,111 R	55.0%	45.0%	55.0%	45.0%
Utah	761,806	424,837	Leavitt, Michael O.	321,979	Orton, Bill	14,990	102,858 R	55.8%	42.3%	56.9%	43.1%
Vermont	293,473	111,359	Dwyer, Ruth	148,059	Dean, Howard	34,055	36,700 D	37.9%	50.5%	42.9%	57.1%
Washington	2,469,852	980,060	Carlson, John	1,441,973	Locke, Gary	47,819	461,913 D	39.7%	58.4%	40.5%	59.5%
West Virginia	648,047	305,926	Underwood, Cecil H.	324,822	Wise, Bob	17,299	18,896 D	47.2%	50.1%	48.5%	51.5%
	15,868,945	7,271,361		8,056,020		541,564	784,659 D	45.8%	50.8%	47.4%	52.6%

[1] 1999 election

SENATE ELECTIONS 2000

| State | Total Vote | Republican | | Democratic | | Other Vote | Rep.-Dem. Plurality | Percentage | | | |
| | | Vote | Candidate | Vote | Candidate | | | Total Vote | | Major Vote | |
								Rep.	Dem.	Rep.	Dem.
Arizona	1,397,076	1,108,196	Kyl, Jon	—	—	288,880	1,108,196 R	79.3%		100.0%	
California	10,623,614	3,886,853	Campbell, Tom	5,932,522	Feinstein, Dianne	804,239	2,045,669 D	36.6%	55.8%	39.6%	60.4%
Connecticut	1,311,261	448,077	Giordano, Philip A.	828,902	Lieberman, Joseph I.	34,282	380,825 D	34.2%	63.2%	35.1%	64.9%
Delaware	327,017	142,891	Roth, William V.	181,566	Carper, Thomas R.	2,560	38,675 D	43.7%	55.5%	44.0%	56.0%
Florida	5,856,731	2,705,348	McCollum, Bill	2,989,487	Nelson, Bill	161,896	284,139 D	46.2%	51.0%	47.5%	52.5%
Georgia S	2,428,510	920,478	Mattingly, Mack	1,413,224	Miller, Zell	94,808	492,746 D	37.9%	58.2%	39.4%	60.6%
Hawaii	345,623	84,701	Carroll, John S.	251,215	Akaka, Daniel K.	9,707	166,514 D	24.5%	72.7%	25.2%	74.8%
Indiana	2,145,209	1,427,944	Lugar, Richard G.	683,273	Johnson, David L.	33,992	744,671 R	66.6%	31.9%	67.6%	32.4%
Maine	634,872	437,689	Snowe, Olympia J.	197,183	Lawrence, Mark		240,506 R	68.9%	31.1%	68.9%	31.1%
Maryland	1,946,898	715,178	Rappaport, Paul	1,230,013	Sarbanes, Paul S.	1,707	514,835 D	36.7%	63.2%	36.8%	63.2%
Massachusetts	2,599,420	334,341	Robinson, Jack E.	1,889,494	Kennedy, Edward M.	375,585	1,555,153 D	12.9%	72.7%	15.0%	85.0%
Michigan	4,167,685	1,994,693	Abraham, Spencer	2,061,952	Stabenow, Debbie	111,040	67,259 D	47.9%	49.5%	49.2%	50.8%
Minnesota	2,419,520	1,047,474	Gams, Rod	1,181,553	Dayton, Mark	190,493	134,079 D	43.3%	48.8%	47.0%	53.0%
Mississippi	994,144	654,941	Lott, Trent	314,090	Brown, Troy	25,113	340,851 R	65.9%	31.6%	67.6%	32.4%
Missouri	2,361,586	1,142,852	Ashcroft, John	1,191,812	Carnahan, Mel	26,922	48,960 D	48.4%	50.5%	49.0%	51.0%
Montana	411,601	208,082	Burns, Conrad	194,430	Schweitzer, Brian	9,089	13,652 R	50.6%	47.2%	51.7%	48.3%
Nebraska	692,344	337,967	Stenberg, Don	353,097	Nelson, Ben	1,280	15,130 D	48.8%	51.0%	48.9%	51.1%
Nevada	600,250	330,687	Ensign, John	238,260	Bernstein, Ed	31,303	92,427 R	55.1%	39.7%	58.1%	41.9%
New Jersey	3,015,662	1,420,267	Franks, Bob	1,511,237	Corzine, Jon	84,158	90,970 D	47.1%	50.1%	48.4%	51.6%
New Mexico	589,526	225,517	Redmond, Bill	363,744	Bingaman, Jeff	265	138,227 D	38.3%	61.7%	38.3%	61.7%
New York	6,779,839	2,915,730	Lazio, Rick A.	3,747,310	Clinton, Hillary Rodham	116,799	831,580 D	43.0%	55.3%	43.8%	56.2%
North Dakota	287,539	111,069	Sand, Duane	176,470	Conrad, Kent		65,401 D	38.6%	61.4%	38.6%	61.4%
Ohio	4,448,801	2,665,512	DeWine, Mike	1,595,066	Celeste, Ted	188,223	1,070,446 R	59.9%	35.9%	62.6%	37.4%
Pennsylvania	4,735,504	2,481,962	Santorum, Rick	2,154,908	Klink, Ron	98,634	327,054 R	52.4%	45.5%	53.5%	46.5%
Rhode Island	391,537	222,588	Chafee, Lincoln	161,023	Weygand, Bob	7,926	61,565 R	56.8%	41.1%	58.0%	42.0%
Tennessee	1,928,613	1,255,444	Frist, Bill	621,152	Clark, Jeff	52,017	634,292 R	65.1%	32.2%	66.9%	33.1%
Texas	6,276,652	4,082,091	Hutchison, Kay Bailey	2,030,315	Kelly, Gene	164,246	2,051,776 R	65.0%	32.3%	66.8%	33.2%
Utah	769,704	504,803	Hatch, Orrin G.	242,569	Howell, Scott N.	22,332	262,234 R	65.6%	31.5%	67.5%	32.5%
Vermont	288,500	189,133	Jeffords, James M.	73,352	Flanagan, Ed	26,015	115,781 R	65.6%	25.4%	72.1%	27.9%
Virginia	2,718,301	1,420,460	Allen, George F.	1,296,093	Robb, Charles S.	1,748	124,367 R	52.3%	47.7%	52.3%	47.7%
Washington	2,461,379	1,197,208	Gorton, Slade	1,199,437	Cantwell, Maria	64,734	2,229 D	48.6%	48.7%	50.0%	50.0%
West Virginia	603,477	121,635	Gallaher, David T.	469,215	Byrd, Robert C.	12,627	347,580 D	20.2%	77.8%	20.6%	79.4%
Wisconsin	2,540,083	940,744	Gillespie, John	1,563,238	Kohl, Herb	36,101	622,494 D	37.0%	61.5%	37.6%	62.4%
Wyoming	213,659	157,622	Thomas, Craig	47,087	Logan, Mel	8,950	110,535 R	73.8%	22.0%	77.0%	23.0%
	79,312,137	37,840,177		38,384,289		3,087,671	544,112 D	47.7%	48.4%	49.6%	50.4%

S - Short term

U.S. HOUSE OF REPRESENTATIVES ELECTIONS 2000

State	Seats Won Republican	Seats Won Democratic	Seats Won Independent	Total Vote	Republican	Democratic	Other	Rep.-Dem. Plurality	Percentage Total Vote Rep.	Total Vote Dem.	Major Vote Rep.	Major Vote Dem.
Alabama	5	2		1,438,994	849,229	485,660	104,105	363,569 R	59.0%	33.7%	63.6%	36.4%
Alaska	1			274,393	190,862	45,372	38,159	145,490 R	69.6%	16.5%	80.8%	19.2%
Arizona	5	1		1,465,656	854,715	557,849	53,092	296,866 R	58.3%	38.1%	60.5%	39.5%
Arkansas	1	3		632,765	277,146	355,366	253	78,220 D	43.8%	56.2%	43.8%	56.2%
California	20	32		10,437,665	4,446,295	5,407,163	584,207	960,868 D	42.6%	51.8%	45.1%	54.9%
Colorado	4	2		1,623,882	968,651	496,045	159,186	472,606 R	59.7%	30.5%	66.1%	33.9%
Connecticut	3	3		1,313,490	594,830	699,237	19,423	104,407 D	45.3%	53.2%	46.0%	54.0%
Delaware	1			313,171	211,797	96,488	4,886	115,309 R	67.6%	30.8%	68.7%	31.3%
Florida	15	8		5,011,372	2,851,623	1,976,189	183,560	875,434 R	56.9%	39.4%	59.1%	40.9%
Georgia	8	3		2,416,622	1,498,337	918,085	200	580,252 R	62.0%	38.0%	62.0%	38.0%
Hawaii		2		340,424	110,895	221,373	8,156	110,478 D	32.6%	65.0%	33.4%	66.6%
Idaho	2			492,835	332,655	142,345	17,835	190,310 R	67.5%	28.9%	70.0%	30.0%
Illinois	10	10		4,393,352	1,907,306	2,453,674	32,372	546,368 D	43.4%	55.8%	43.7%	56.3%
Indiana	6	4		2,156,744	1,140,554	953,167	63,023	187,387 R	52.9%	44.2%	54.5%	45.5%
Iowa	4	1		1,275,934	717,322	531,642	26,970	185,680 R	56.2%	41.7%	57.4%	42.6%
Kansas	3	1		1,038,379	657,978	328,194	52,207	329,784 R	63.4%	31.6%	66.7%	33.3%
Kentucky	5	1		1,435,409	824,915	561,752	48,742	263,163 R	57.5%	39.1%	59.5%	40.5%
Louisiana	5	2		1,202,171	747,115	359,668	95,388	387,447 R	62.1%	29.9%	67.5%	32.5%
Maine		2		638,399	203,437	422,606	12,356	219,169 D	31.9%	66.2%	32.5%	67.5%
Maryland	4	4		1,926,764	856,306	1,060,857	9,601	204,551 D	44.4%	55.1%	44.7%	55.3%
Massachusetts	0	10		2,347,375	343,498	1,967,942	35,935	1,624,444 D	14.6%	83.8%	14.9%	85.1%
Michigan	7	9		4,069,736	1,786,991	2,177,678	105,067	390,687 D	43.9%	53.5%	45.1%	54.9%
Minnesota	3	5		2,363,738	993,371	1,234,204	136,163	240,833 D	42.0%	52.2%	44.6%	55.4%
Mississippi	2	3		986,139	468,483	495,687	21,969	27,204 D	47.5%	50.3%	48.6%	51.4%
Missouri	5	4		2,325,788	1,135,724	1,136,020	54,044	296 D	48.8%	48.8%	50.0%	50.0%
Montana	1			410,523	211,418	189,971	9,134	21,447 R	51.5%	46.3%	52.7%	47.3%
Nebraska	3			683,071	486,513	178,071	18,487	308,442 R	71.2%	26.1%	73.2%	26.8%
Nevada	1	1		585,204	330,884	224,848	29,472	106,036 R	56.5%	38.4%	59.5%	40.5%
New Hampshire	2			556,417	303,190	238,754	14,473	64,436 R	54.5%	42.9%	55.9%	44.1%
New Jersey	6	7		2,988,233	1,384,170	1,532,240	71,823	148,070 D	46.3%	51.3%	47.5%	52.5%
New Mexico	2	1		587,514	274,017	299,841	13,656	25,824 D	46.6%	51.0%	47.7%	52.3%
New York	12	19		5,823,850	2,465,640	3,189,626	168,584	723,986 D	42.3%	54.8%	43.6%	56.4%
North Carolina	7	5		2,779,800	1,514,806	1,193,600	71,394	321,206 R	54.5%	42.9%	55.9%	44.1%
North Dakota		1		285,658	127,251	151,173	7,234	23,922 D	44.5%	52.9%	45.7%	54.3%
Ohio	11	8		4,517,838	2,203,086	2,067,441	247,311	135,645 R	48.8%	45.8%	51.6%	48.4%
Oklahoma	5	1		1,087,515	701,820	336,955	48,740	364,865 R	64.5%	31.0%	67.6%	32.4%
Oregon	1	4		1,440,002	607,098	790,365	42,539	183,267 D	42.2%	54.9%	43.4%	56.6%
Pennsylvania	11	10		4,554,347	2,229,057	2,279,227	46,063	50,170 D	48.9%	50.0%	49.4%	50.6%
Rhode Island		2		384,127	89,454	247,247	47,426	157,793 D	23.3%	64.4%	26.6%	73.4%
South Carolina	4	2		1,321,312	729,799	525,398	66,115	204,401 R	55.2%	39.8%	58.1%	41.9%
South Dakota	1			314,761	231,083	78,321	5,357	152,762 R	73.4%	24.9%	74.7%	25.3%
Tennessee	5	4		1,854,378	991,984	819,100	43,294	172,884 R	53.5%	44.2%	54.8%	45.2%
Texas	13	17		5,985,763	2,932,411	2,799,051	254,301	133,360 R	49.0%	46.8%	51.2%	48.8%
Utah	2	1		758,754	426,648	304,797	27,309	121,851 R	56.2%	40.2%	58.3%	41.7%
Vermont			1	283,366	51,977	14,918	216,471	144,141 I	18.3%	5.3%	77.7%	22.3%
Virginia	6	4	1	2,421,729	1,131,999	1,060,484	229,246	71,515 R	46.7%	43.8%	51.6%	48.4%
Washington	3	6		2,382,411	997,877	1,245,872	138,662	247,995 D	41.9%	52.3%	44.5%	55.5%
West Virginia	1	2		579,872	108,769	420,784	50,319	312,015 D	18.8%	72.6%	20.5%	79.5%
Wisconsin	4	5		2,506,314	1,311,447	1,187,866	7,001	123,581 R	52.3%	47.4%	52.5%	47.5%
Wyoming	1			212,312	141,848	60,638	9,826	81,210 R	66.8%	28.6%	70.1%	29.9%
	221	212	2	97,226,268	46,954,281	46,520,851	3,751,136	433,430 R	48.3%	47.8%	50.2%	49.8%

UNITED STATES

PARTY SWITCHES, SPECIAL ELECTIONS, AND POST-ELECTION CHANGES 1999–2000

Between the general elections of 1998 and 2000, there were four party switches in Congress—one in the U.S. Senate and three in the U.S. House.

PARTY SWITCHES

SENATOR

Sen. Robert C. Smith switched from Republican to Independent on July 13, 1999. Smith returned to the Republican Party on November 1, 1999.

REPRESENTATIVES

Rep. Michael P. Forbes of New York 1st switched from Republican to Democrat on July 17, 1999.

Rep. Virgil H. Goode Jr. of Virginia 5th, a Democrat, announced on January 24, 2000, that he would seek re-election as an Independent..

Rep. Matthew G. Martinez of California 31st switched from Democrat to Republican on July 26, 2000. Martinez had lost his bid for renomination in California's March 7 Democratic primary.

SPECIAL ELECTIONS TO THE 106th CONGRESS

Between the general elections of 1998 and 2000, two appointments were made to fill vacancies in the Senate and three special elections were held to fill vacancies in the House of Representatives. In addition, two House members died late in the 106th Congress, Herbert H. Bateman of the Virginia 1st District (on September 11, 2000) and Bruce F. Vento of the Minnesota 4th District (on October 10, 2000). In neither case was there a special election. The Senate appointments and House special elections held to fill vacancies in the 106th Congress are listed below.

SENATORS

GEORGIA

Paul Coverdell (R) died July 18, 2000. Former Gov. Zell Miller (D) was appointed July 24, 2000, to fill the vacancy.

RHODE ISLAND

John H. Chafee (R) died October 24, 1999. His son, Lincoln D. Chafee (R) , was appointed November 2, 1999, to fill the vacancy.

REPRESENTATIVES

CALIFORNIA 42nd CD

George E. Brown Jr. (D) died July 15, 1999. Joe Baca (D) was elected November 16, 1999, to fill out the remaining term for the 106th Congress.

September 21, 1999 Special Primary Election

12,089 Joe Baca (D); 11,571 Maria Macias Brown (D); 10,526 Elia Pirozzi; 1,676 David Eshleman (D); 735 Rob S. Guzman (R); 572 Hal J. Styles Jr. (R); 375 Rick Simon (Reform); 368 John "Scott" Ballard (Libertarian); 271 Bernard McClay (D); 78 Don Hubner (D).

6

UNITED STATES

SPECIAL ELECTIONS TO THE 106th CONGRESS

CALIFORNIA 42nd CD (Continued)

November 16, 1999 Special General Election

23,690 Joe Baca (D); 21,018 Elia Pirozzi (R); 1,198 Rick Simon (Reform); 956 John "Scott" Ballard (Libertarian).

GEORGIA 6th CD

House Speaker Newt Gingrich (R) resigned January 3, 1999, in the wake of a poorer-than-expected Republican showing in the 1998 congressional elections. Gingrich was never sworn in as a member of the 106th Congress. Johnny Isakson (R) was elected February 23, 1999, to fill the term for the 106th Congress. Since Isakson won a majority of the vote in the first-round balloting, no runoff election was held.

February 23, 1999 Special Election

51,548 Johnny Isakson (R); 20,115 Christina Jeffrey (R); 4,014 Gary "Bats" Pelphrey (D); 1,593 Barry Doublestein (R); 1,459 A. Leigh Baier (Independent); 478 Marco Longo (R); 6 Kelly Brown (Independent write-in). (The election was nonpartisan, and candidates were not identified on the ballot by party affiliation.)

LOUISIANA 1st CD

Bob Livingston (R) resigned February 28, 1999, after admitting to marital infidelity during the House debate on the impeachment of President Clinton in December 1998. Livingston was the would-be successor to Newt Gingrich as House Speaker. David Vitter (R) was elected May 29, 1999, to fill out the remaining term for the 106th Congress.

May 1, 1999 Special Election (First Round)

36,719 David Conner Treen (R); 31,741 David Vitter (R); 28,059 David Duke (R); 22,928 Monica Monica (R); 16,446 "Bill" Strain (D); 9,295 "Rob" Couhig (R); 720 Darryl P. Ward (D); 344 Patrick E. Landry (R); 246 S. J. LoCoco (R).

May 29, 1999 Special Election Runoff

61,661 David Vitter (R); 59,849 David Conner Treen (D).

HOUSE SPECIAL ELECTIONS: SUMMARY

District	Former Member	New Member	Date Elected	Percentage	Voter Turnout
California 42nd	George E. Brown Jr. (D)	Joe Baca (D)	November 16, 1999	50.6%	46,862
Georgia 6th	Newt Gingrich (R)	Johnny Isakson (R)	February 23, 1999	65.1%	79,213
Louisiana 1st	Bob Livingston (R)	David Vitter (R)	May 29, 1999	50.7%	121,510

Note: Results from this chart are from the decisive round of voting when the new member was elected to Congress.

CHANGES FOLLOWING THE 2000 ELECTION

Following the 2000 general election, and through June 5, 2001, the following changes occurred in the membership of the 107th Congress, including one party switch.

SENATORS

Missouri—Governor Roger Wilson (D) announced December 4, 2000, the appointment of Jean Carnahan (D) to fill the seat of her late husband, Mel Carnahan (D), who was killed in a plane crash October 17, 2000, but won the seat posthumously in the November general election. Mrs. Carnahan's two-year appointment took effect with the start of the 107th Congress.

UNITED STATES

CHANGES FOLLOWING THE 2000 ELECTION

Vermont—Senator James M. Jeffords announced May 24, 2001, that he would switch his party affiliation from Republican to Independent. The switch became effective June 5, 2001.

REPRESENTATIVES

California 32nd CD—Representative Julian C. Dixon (D) died December 8, 2000. Diane E. Watson (D) was elected June 5, 2001, to succeed him.

Florida 1st CD—Representative Joe Scarborough (R) announced May 25, 2001, that he would resign from the House on September 6, 2001. A special primary election was scheduled for July 24, 2001, with the special election on October 16, 2001.

Massachusetts 9th CD—Representative John Joseph Moakley died on May 28, 2001. A special election was scheduled for later in 2001.

Pennsylvania 9th CD—Representative Bud Shuster (R) resigned February 3, 2001, citing health reasons. His son, Bill Shuster (R), was elected May 15, 2001, to succeed him.

Virginia 4th CD—Representative Norman Sisisky (D) died March 29, 2001. A special election was scheduled for June 19, 2001, to fill the seat.

PRESIDENT 2000

In New York the Republican figures include Conservative and the Democratic figures include Liberal and Working Families.

In Minnesota the Democratic candidate appears on the ballot as Democratic-Farmer-Labor. In many states various non-major party candidates appeared on the ballot with variations of the party designations, were carried with entirely different party labels, or were listed as "Independent". The state Notes sections list the party labels used by the minor party candidates.

The candidates listed below include all who appeared on the ballot in at least one state. Write-in votes for minor party candidates are credited to their total below. See the minor party chart on page 10 for details.

50,455,156	George W. Bush and Richard B. Cheney	Republican
50,992,335	Al Gore and Joseph I. Lieberman	Democratic
2,882,738	Ralph Nader and Winona La Duke	Green
449,077	Pat Buchanan and Ezola Foster	Reform
384,429	Harry Browne and Art Olivier	Libertarian
98,020	Howard Phillips and J. Curtis Frazier	Constitution
83,525	John Hagelin and Nat Goldhaber	Natural Law
7,378	James E. Harris, Jr. and Margaret Trowe	Socialist Worker
5,775	L. Neil Smith and Vin Suprynowicz	Arizona Libertarian
5,602	David McReynolds and Mary Cal Hollis	Socialist
4,795	Monica Moorehead and Gloria La Riva	Workers World
1,606	Cathy Gordon Brown and Sabrina R. Allen	Independent
1,044	Denny Lane and Dale Wilkinson	Vermont Grassroots
535	Randall Venson and Gene Kelly	Independent
208	Earl F. Dodge and W. Dean Watkins	Prohibition
161	Louie G. Youngkeit and Robert Leo Beck	Unaffiliated

UNITED STATES

PRESIDENT VOTE BY STATE 2000

State	Electoral Vote Rep.	Electoral Vote Dem.	Electoral Vote Other	Total Vote	Republican	Democratic	Green (Nader)	Other	Rep.-Dem. Plurality		Percentage Rep.	Percentage Dem.	Percentage Reform
Alabama	9			1,666,272	941,173	692,611	18,323	14,165	248,562	R	56.5%	41.6%	1.1%
Alaska	3			285,560	167,398	79,004	28,747	10,411	88,394	R	58.6%	27.7%	10.1%
Arizona	8			1,532,016	781,652	685,341	45,645	19,378	96,311	R	51.0%	44.7%	3.0%
Arkansas	6			921,781	472,940	422,768	13,421	12,652	50,172	R	51.3%	45.9%	1.5%
California		54		10,965,856	4,567,429	5,861,203	418,707	118,517	1,293,774	D	41.7%	53.4%	3.8%
Colorado	8			1,741,368	883,748	738,227	91,434	27,959	145,521	R	50.8%	42.4%	5.3%
Connecticut		8		1,459,525	561,094	816,015	64,452	17,964	254,921	D	38.4%	55.9%	4.4%
Delaware		3		327,622	137,288	180,068	8,307	1,959	42,780	D	41.9%	55.0%	2.5%
Florida	25			5,963,110	2,912,790	2,912,253	97,488	40,579	537	R	48.8%	48.8%	1.6%
Georgia	13			2,596,645	1,419,720	1,116,230	13,273	47,422	303,490	R	54.7%	43.0%	0.5%
Hawaii		4		367,951	137,845	205,286	21,623	3,197	67,441	D	37.5%	55.8%	5.9%
Idaho	4			501,621	336,937	138,637	12,292	13,755	198,300	R	67.2%	27.6%	2.5%
Illinois		22		4,742,123	2,019,421	2,589,026	103,759	29,917	569,605	D	42.6%	54.6%	2.2%
Indiana	12			2,199,302	1,245,836	901,980	18,531	32,955	343,856	R	56.6%	41.0%	0.8%
Iowa		7		1,315,563	634,373	638,517	29,374	13,299	4,144	D	48.2%	48.5%	2.2%
Kansas	6			1,072,218	622,332	399,276	36,086	14,524	223,056	R	58.0%	37.2%	3.4%
Kentucky	8			1,544,187	872,492	638,898	23,192	9,605	233,594	R	56.5%	41.4%	1.5%
Louisiana	9			1,765,656	927,871	792,344	20,473	24,968	135,527	R	52.6%	44.9%	1.2%
Maine		4		651,817	286,616	319,951	37,127	8,123	33,335	D	44.0%	49.1%	5.7%
Maryland		10		2,020,480	813,797	1,140,782	53,768	12,133	326,985	D	40.3%	56.5%	2.7%
Massachusetts		12		2,702,984	878,502	1,616,487	173,564	34,431	737,985	D	32.5%	59.8%	6.4%
Michigan		18		4,232,711	1,953,139	2,170,418	84,165	24,989	217,279	D	46.1%	51.3%	2.0%
Minnesota		10		2,438,685	1,109,659	1,168,266	126,696	34,064	58,607	D	45.5%	47.9%	5.2%
Mississippi	7			994,184	572,844	404,614	8,122	8,604	168,230	R	57.6%	40.7%	0.8%
Missouri	11			2,359,892	1,189,924	1,111,138	38,515	20,315	78,786	R	50.4%	47.1%	1.6%
Montana	3			410,997	240,178	137,126	24,437	9,256	103,052	R	58.4%	33.4%	5.9%
Nebraska	5			697,019	433,862	231,780	24,540	6,837	202,082	R	62.2%	33.3%	3.5%
Nevada	4			608,970	301,575	279,978	15,008	12,409	21,597	R	49.5%	46.0%	2.5%
New Hampshire	4			569,081	273,559	266,348	22,198	6,976	7,211	R	48.1%	46.8%	3.9%
New Jersey		15		3,187,226	1,284,173	1,788,850	94,554	19,649	504,677	D	40.3%	56.1%	3.0%
New Mexico		5		598,605	286,417	286,783	21,251	4,154	366	D	47.8%	47.9%	3.6%
New York		33		6,821,999	2,403,374	4,107,697	244,030	66,898	1,704,323	D	35.2%	60.2%	3.6%
North Carolina	14			2,911,262	1,631,163	1,257,692	—	22,407	373,471	R	56.0%	43.2%	—
North Dakota	3			288,256	174,852	95,284	9,486	8,634	79,568	R	60.7%	33.1%	3.3%
Ohio	21			4,701,998	2,350,363	2,183,628	117,799	50,208	166,735	R	50.0%	46.4%	2.5%
Oklahoma	8			1,234,229	744,337	474,276		15,616	270,061	R	60.3%	38.4%	—
Oregon		7		1,533,968	713,577	720,342	77,357	22,692	6,765	D	46.5%	47.0%	5.0%
Pennsylvania		23		4,913,119	2,281,127	2,485,967	103,392	42,633	204,840	D	46.4%	50.6%	2.1%
Rhode Island		4		409,047	130,555	249,508	25,052	3,932	118,953	D	31.9%	61.0%	6.1%
South Carolina	8			1,382,717	785,937	565,561	20,200	11,019	220,376	R	56.8%	40.9%	1.5%
South Dakota	3			316,269	190,700	118,804	—	6,765	71,896	R	60.3%	37.6%	—
Tennessee	11			2,076,181	1,061,949	981,720	19,781	12,731	80,229	R	51.1%	47.3%	1.0%
Texas	32			6,407,637	3,799,639	2,433,746	137,994	36,258	1,365,893	R	59.3%	38.0%	2.2%
Utah	5			770,754	515,096	203,053	35,850	16,755	312,043	R	66.8%	26.3%	4.7%
Vermont		3		294,308	119,775	149,022	20,374	5,137	29,247	D	40.7%	50.6%	6.9%
Virginia	13			2,739,447	1,437,490	1,217,290	59,398	25,269	220,200	R	52.5%	44.4%	2.2%
Washington		11		2,487,433	1,108,864	1,247,652	103,002	27,915	138,788	D	44.6%	50.2%	4.1%
West Virginia	5			648,124	336,475	295,497	10,680	5,472	40,978	R	51.9%	45.6%	1.6%
Wisconsin		11		2,598,607	1,237,279	1,242,987	94,070	24,271	5,708	D	47.6%	47.8%	3.6%
Wyoming	3			218,351	147,947	60,481	4,625	5,298	87,466	R	67.8%	27.7%	2.1%
District of Columbia		2	1	201,894	18,073	171,923	10,576	1,322	153,850	D	9.0%	85.2%	5.2%
United States	271	266	1	105,396,627	50,455,156	50,992,335	2,882,738	1,066,398	537,179	D	47.9%	48.4%	2.7%

UNITED STATES

PRESIDENT 2000 MINOR PARTIES

State	Minor Party Total	Buchanan	Browne	Phillips	Hagelin	Other Candidates and Scattered Write-ins
Alabama	14,165	6,351	5,893	775	447	699
Alaska	10,411	5,192	2,636	596	919	1,068
Arizona	19,378	12,373		110	1,120	5,775
Arkansas	12,652	7,358	2,781	1,415	1,098	—
California	118,517	44,987	45,520	17,042	10,934	34
Colorado	27,959	10,465	12,799	1,319	2,240	1,136
Connecticut	17,964	4,731	3,484	9,695	40	14
Delaware	1,959	777	774	208	107	93
Florida	40,579	17,484	16,415	1,371	2,281	3,028
Georgia	47,422	10,926	36,332	140		24
Hawaii	3,197	1,071	1,477	343	306	—
Idaho	13,755	7,615	3,488	1,469	1,177	6
Illinois	29,917	16,106	11,623	57	2,127	4
Indiana	32,955	16,959	15,530	200	167	99
Iowa	13,299	5,731	3,209	613	2,281	1,465
Kansas	14,524	7,370	4,525	1,254	1,375	—
Kentucky	9,605	4,173	2,896	923	1,533	80
Louisiana	24,968	14,356	2,951	5,483	1,075	1,103
Maine	8,123	4,443	3,074	579		27
Maryland	12,133	4,248	5,310	919	176	1,480
Massachusetts	34,431	11,149	16,366		2,884	4,032
Michigan	24,989	2061	16,711	3,791	2,426	—
Minnesota	34,064	22,166	5,282	3,272	2,294	1,050
Mississippi	8,604	2,265	2,009	3,267	450	613
Missouri	20,315	9,818	7,436	1,957	1,104	—
Montana	9,256	5,697	1,718	1,155	675	11
Nebraska	6,837	3,646	2,245	468	478	—
Nevada	12,409	4,747	3,311	621	415	3,315
New Hampshire	6,976	2,615	2,757	328		1,276
New Jersey	19,649	6,989	6,312	1,409	2,215	2,724
New Mexico	4,154	1,392	2,058	343	361	—
New York	66,898	31,599	7,649	1,498	24,361	1,791
North Carolina	22,407	8,874	12,307			1,226
North Dakota	8,634	7,288	660	373	313	—
Ohio	50,208	26,721	13,473	3,823	6,181	10
Oklahoma	15,616	9,014	6,602			—
Oregon	22,692	7,063	7,447	2,189	2,574	3,419
Pennsylvania	42,633	16,023	11,248	14,428		934
Rhode Island	3,932	2,273	742	97	271	549
South Carolina	11,019	3,519	4,876	1,682	942	—
South Dakota	6,765	3,322	1,662	1,781		—
Tennessee	12,731	4,250	4,284	1,015	613	2,569
Texas	36,258	12,394	23,160	567		137
Utah	16,755	9,319	3,616	2,709	763	348
Vermont	5,137	2,192	784	153	219	1,789
Virginia	25,269	5,455	15,198	1,809		2,807
Washington	27,915	7,171	13,135	1,989	2,927	2,693
West Virginia	5,472	3,169	1,912	23	367	1
Wisconsin	24,271	11,446	6,640	2,042	878	3,265
Wyoming	5,298	2,724	1,443	720	411	—
District of Columbia	1,322		669			653
Total	1,066,398	449,077	384,429	98,020	83,525	51,347

UNITED STATES

POPULAR VOTE FOR PRESIDENT 1920 TO 2000

Year	Total Vote	Republican Vote	Republican Candidate	Democratic Vote	Democratic Candidate	Other Vote	Plurality	Percentage Total Vote Rep.	Percentage Total Vote Dem.	Percentage Major Vote Rep.	Percentage Major Vote Dem.
2000	105,396,627	50,455,156	Bush, George W.	50,992,335	Gore, Al	3,949,136	537,179 D	47.9%	48.4%	49.7%	50.3%
1996	96,277,872	39,198,755	Dole, Bob	47,402,357	Clinton, Bill	9,676,760	8,203,602 D	40.7%	49.2%	45.3%	54.7%
1992	104,425,014	39,103,882	Bush, George	44,909,326	Clinton, Bill	20,411,806	5,805,444 D	37.4%	43.0%	46.5%	53.5%
1988	91,594,809	48,886,097	Bush, George	41,809,074	Dukakis, Michael S.	899,638	7,077,023 R	53.4%	45.6%	53.9%	46.1%
1984	92,652,842	54,455,075	Reagan, Ronald	37,577,185	Mondale, Walter F.	620,582	16,877,890 R	58.8%	40.6%	59.2%	40.8%
1980	86,515,221	43,904,153	Reagan, Ronald	35,483,883	Carter, Jimmy	7,127,185	8,420,270 R	50.7%	41.0%	55.3%	44.7%
1976	81,555,889	39,147,793	Ford, Gerald R.	40,830,763	Carter, Jimmy	1,577,333	1,682,970 D	48.0%	50.1%	48.9%	51.1%
1972	77,718,554	47,169,911	Nixon, Richard M.	29,170,383	McGovern, George S.	1,378,260	17,999,528 R	60.7%	37.5%	61.8%	38.2%
1968	73,211,875	31,785,480	Nixon, Richard M.	31,275,166	Humphrey, Hubert H.	10,151,229	510,314 R	43.4%	42.7%	50.4%	49.6%
1964	70,644,592	27,178,188	Goldwater, Barry M.	43,129,566	Johnson, Lyndon B.	336,838	15,951,378 D	38.5%	61.1%	38.7%	61.3%
1960	68,838,219	34,108,157	Nixon, Richard M.	34,226,731	Kennedy, John F.	503,331	118,574 D	49.5%	49.7%	49.9%	50.1%
1956	62,026,908	35,590,472	Eisenhower, Dwight D.	26,022,752	Stevenson, Adlai E.	413,684	9,567,720 R	57.4%	42.0%	57.8%	42.2%
1952	61,550,918	33,936,234	Eisenhower, Dwight D.	27,314,992	Stevenson, Adlai E.	299,692	6,621,242 R	55.1%	44.4%	55.4%	44.6%
1948	48,793,826	21,991,291	Dewey, Thomas E.	24,179,345	Truman, Harry S.	2,623,190	2,188,054 D	45.1%	49.6%	47.6%	52.4%
1944	47,976,670	22,017,617	Dewey, Thomas E.	25,612,610	Roosevelt, Franklin D.	346,443	3,594,993 D	45.9%	53.4%	46.2%	53.8%
1940	49,900,418	22,348,480	Willkie, Wendell	27,313,041	Roosevelt, Franklin D.	238,897	4,964,561 D	44.8%	54.7%	45.0%	55.0%
1936	45,654,763	16,684,231	Landon, Alfred M.	27,757,333	Roosevelt, Franklin D.	1,213,199	11,073,102 D	36.5%	60.8%	37.5%	62.5%
1932	39,758,759	15,760,684	Hoover, Herbert C.	22,829,501	Roosevelt, Franklin D.	1,168,574	7,068,817 D	39.6%	57.4%	40.8%	59.2%
1928	36,805,951	21,437,277	Hoover, Herbert C.	15,007,698	Smith, Alfred E.	360,976	6,429,579 R	58.2%	40.8%	58.8%	41.2%
1924	29,095,023	15,719,921	Coolidge, Calvin	8,386,704	Davis, John W.	4,988,398	7,333,217 R	54.0%	28.8%	65.2%	34.8%
1920	26,768,613	16,153,115	Harding, Warren G.	9,133,092	Cox, James M.	1,482,406	7,020,023 R	60.3%	34.1%	63.9%	36.1%

For detail of Other Vote, see Notes sections included with each U.S. summary table that follows.

ELECTORAL COLLEGE VOTE 1920 TO 2000

Year	Total	Republican	Democratic	Other	
2000	538	271	266	1	
1996	538	159	379	—	
1992	538	168	370	—	
1988	538	426	111	1	BENTSEN
1984	538	525	13	—	
1980	538	489	49	—	
1976	538	240	297	1	REAGAN
1972	538	520	17	1	LIBERTARIAN
1968	538	301	191	46	AIP
1964	538	52	486	—	
1960	537	219	303	15	BYRD
1956	531	457	73	1	JONES
1952	531	442	89	—	
1948	531	189	303	39	SR
1944	531	99	432	—	
1940	531	82	449	—	
1936	531	8	523	—	
1932	531	59	472	—	
1928	531	444	87	—	
1924	531	382	136	13	PROGRESSIVE
1920	531	404	127	—	

PRESIDENT 1996

In New York the Republican figures include Conservative, Freedom, and Right to Life votes and the Democratic figures include Liberal votes.

In Minnesota the Democratic candidate appears on the ballot as Democratic-Farmer-Labor. In many states various non-major party candidates appeared on the ballot with variations of the party designations, were carried with entirely different party labels or listed as "Independent". The state note sections list the party labels used by the minor party candidates.

The candidates listed below include all those who appeared on the ballot in at least one state. Write-in votes for minor party candidates are credited to their total below. See the minor party vote chart on page 14 for details.

47,402,357	Bill Clinton and Al Gore	Democratic
39,198,755	Bob Dole and Jack Kemp	Republican
8,085,402	Ross Perot and Pat Choate	Reform
685,040	Ralph Nader and Winona LaDuke	Green
485,798	Harry Browne and Jo Jorgensen	Libertarian
184,658	Howard Phillips and Herbert W. Titus	U.S. Taxpayers
113,668	John Hagelin and Mike Tompkins	Natural Law
29,083	Monica Moorehead and Gloria La Riva	Workers World
25,332	Marsha Feinland and Kate McClatchy	Peace and Freedom
8,930	Charles Collins and Rosemary Giumarra	Independent
8,476	James Harris and Laura Garza	Socialist Workers
5,378	Dennis Peron and Arlin D. Troutt Jr.	Grassroots
4,706	Mary Cal Hollis and Eric Chester	Socialist
2,438	Jerome White and Fred Mazelis	Socialist Equality
1,847	Diane Beall Templin and Gary Van Horn	American
1,298	Earl F. Dodge and Rachel B. Kelly	Prohibition
1,101	A. Peter Crane and Connie Chandler	Independent
932	Ralph Forbes and "Pro-Life" Anderson	America First
787	John Birrenbach and George McMahon	Independent Grassroots
752	Isabell Masters and Shirley Jean Masters	Looking Back
408	Steve Michael and Ann Northrop	Independent

In addition to the votes listed above, 25,118 scattered write-in votes were reported from various states, and 5,608 votes were cast for "None of these Candidates" in Nevada.

UNITED STATES

PRESIDENT 1996

State	Electoral Vote Rep.	Electoral Vote Dem.	Electoral Vote Other	Total Vote	Republican	Democratic	Reform	Other	Plurality		Percentage Rep.	Percentage Dem.	Percentage Reform
Alabama	9			1,534,349	769,044	662,165	92,149	10,991	106,879	R	50.1%	43.2%	6.0%
Alaska	3			241,620	122,746	80,380	26,333	12,161	42,366	R	50.8%	33.3%	10.9%
Arizona		8		1,404,405	622,073	653,288	112,072	16,972	31,215	D	44.3%	46.5%	8.0%
Arkansas		6		884,262	325,416	475,171	69,884	13,791	149,755	D	36.8%	53.7%	7.9%
California		54		10,019,484	3,828,380	5,119,835	697,847	373,422	1,291,455	D	38.2%	51.1%	7.0%
Colorado	8			1,510,704	691,848	671,152	99,629	48,075	20,696	R	45.8%	44.4%	6.6%
Connecticut		8		1,392,614	483,109	735,740	139,523	34,242	252,631	D	34.7%	52.8%	10.0%
Delaware		3		271,084	99,062	140,355	28,719	2,948	41,293	D	36.5%	51.8%	10.6%
Florida		25		5,303,794	2,244,536	2,546,870	483,870	28,518	302,334	D	42.3%	48.0%	9.1%
Georgia	13			2,299,071	1,080,843	1,053,849	146,337	18,042	26,994	R	47.0%	45.8%	6.4%
Hawaii		4		360,120	113,943	205,012	27,358	13,807	91,069	D	31.6%	56.9%	7.6%
Idaho	4			491,719	256,595	165,443	62,518	7,163	91,152	R	52.2%	33.6%	12.7%
Illinois		22		4,311,391	1,587,021	2,341,744	346,408	36,218	754,723	D	36.8%	54.3%	8.0%
Indiana	12			2,135,842	1,006,693	887,424	224,299	17,426	119,269	R	47.1%	41.5%	10.5%
Iowa		7		1,234,075	492,644	620,258	105,159	16,014	127,614	D	39.9%	50.3%	8.5%
Kansas	6			1,074,300	583,245	387,659	92,639	10,757	195,586	R	54.3%	36.1%	8.6%
Kentucky		8		1,388,708	623,283	636,614	120,396	8,415	13,331	D	44.9%	45.8%	8.7%
Louisiana		9		1,783,959	712,586	927,837	123,293	20,243	215,251	D	39.9%	52.0%	6.9%
Maine		4		605,897	186,378	312,788	85,970	20,761	126,410	D	30.8%	51.6%	14.2%
Maryland		10		1,780,870	681,530	966,207	115,812	17,321	284,677	D	38.3%	54.3%	6.5%
Massachusetts		12		2,556,785	718,107	1,571,763	227,217	39,698	853,656	D	28.1%	61.5%	8.9%
Michigan		18		3,848,844	1,481,212	1,989,653	336,670	41,309	508,441	D	38.5%	51.7%	8.7%
Minnesota		10		2,192,640	766,476	1,120,438	257,704	48,022	353,962	D	35.0%	51.1%	11.8%
Mississippi	7			893,857	439,838	394,022	52,222	7,775	45,816	R	49.2%	44.1%	5.8%
Missouri		11		2,158,065	890,016	1,025,935	217,188	24,926	135,919	D	41.2%	47.5%	10.1%
Montana	3			407,261	179,652	167,922	55,229	4,458	11,730	R	44.1%	41.2%	13.6%
Nebraska	5			677,415	363,467	236,761	71,278	5,909	126,706	R	53.7%	35.0%	10.5%
Nevada		4		464,279	199,244	203,974	43,986	17,075	4,730	D	42.9%	43.9%	9.5%
New Hampshire		4		499,175	196,532	246,214	48,390	8,039	49,682	D	39.4%	49.3%	9.7%
New Jersey		15		3,075,807	1,103,078	1,652,329	262,134	58,266	549,251	D	35.9%	53.7%	8.5%
New Mexico		5		556,074	232,751	273,495	32,257	17,571	40,744	D	41.9%	49.2%	5.8%
New York		33		6,316,129	1,933,492	3,756,177	503,458	123,002	1,822,685	D	30.6%	59.5%	8.0%
North Carolina	14			2,515,807	1,225,938	1,107,849	168,059	13,961	118,089	R	48.7%	44.0%	6.7%
North Dakota	3			266,411	125,050	106,905	32,515	1,941	18,145	R	46.9%	40.1%	12.2%
Ohio		21		4,534,434	1,859,883	2,148,222	483,207	43,122	288,339	D	41.0%	47.4%	10.7%
Oklahoma	8			1,206,713	582,315	488,105	130,788	5,505	94,210	R	48.3%	40.4%	10.8%
Oregon		7		1,377,760	538,152	649,641	121,221	68,746	111,489	D	39.1%	47.2%	8.8%
Pennsylvania		23		4,506,118	1,801,169	2,215,819	430,984	58,146	414,650	D	40.0%	49.2%	9.6%
Rhode Island		4		390,284	104,683	233,050	43,723	8,828	128,367	D	26.8%	59.7%	11.2%
South Carolina	8			1,151,689	573,458	506,283	64,386	7,562	67,175	R	49.8%	44.0%	5.6%
South Dakota	3			323,826	150,543	139,333	31,250	2,700	11,210	R	46.5%	43.0%	9.7%
Tennessee		11		1,894,105	863,530	909,146	105,918	15,511	45,616	D	45.6%	48.0%	5.6%
Texas	32			5,611,644	2,736,167	2,459,683	378,537	37,257	276,484	R	48.8%	43.8%	6.7%
Utah	5			665,629	361,911	221,633	66,461	15,624	140,278	R	54.4%	33.3%	10.0%
Vermont		3		258,449	80,352	137,894	31,024	9,179	57,542	D	31.1%	53.4%	12.0%
Virginia	13			2,416,642	1,138,350	1,091,060	159,861	27,371	47,290	R	47.1%	45.1%	6.6%
Washington		11		2,253,837	840,712	1,123,323	201,003	88,799	282,611	D	37.3%	49.8%	8.9%
West Virginia		5		636,459	233,946	327,812	71,639	3,062	93,866	D	36.8%	51.5%	11.3%
Wisconsin		11		2,196,169	845,029	1,071,971	227,339	51,830	226,942	D	38.5%	48.8%	10.4%
Wyoming	3			211,571	105,388	77,934	25,928	2,321	27,454	R	49.8%	36.8%	12.3%
Dist. of Col.		3		185,726	17,339	158,220	3,611	6,556	140,881	D	9.3%	85.2%	1.9%
United States	159	379		96,277,872	39,198,755	47,402,357	8,085,402	1,591,358	8,203,602	D	40.7%	49.2%	8.4%

UNITED STATES

PRESIDENT 1996 MINOR PARTIES

State	Other	Nader	Browne	Phillips	Hagelin	Moorehead	Feinland	Other Candidates and Scattered Write-ins
Alabama	10,991		5,290	2,365	1,697			1,639
Alaska	12,161	7,597	2,276	925	729			634
Arizona	16,972	2,062*	14,358	347*	153*			52
Arkansas	13,791	3,649	3,076	2,065	729	747		3,525
California	373,422	237,016	73,600	21,202	15,403		25,332	869
Colorado	48,075	25,070	12,392	2,813	2,547	599		4,654
Connecticut	34,242	24,321	5,788	2,425	1,703			5
Delaware	2,948	156*	2,052	348	274			118
Florida	28,518	4,101*	23,965		418*			34
Georgia	18,042		17,870	145*				27
Hawaii	13,807	10,386	2,493	358	570			
Idaho	7,163		3,325	2,230	1,600			8
Illinois	36,218	1,447*	22,548	7,606	4,606			11
Indiana	17,426	895*	15,632	291*	118*			490
Iowa	16,014	6,550	2,315	2,229	3,349			1,571
Kansas	10,757	914*	4,557	3,519	1,655			112
Kentucky	8,415	701*	4,009	2,204	1,493			8
Louisiana	20,243	4,719	7,499	3,366	2,981	1,678		
Maine	20,761	15,279	2,996	1,517	825			144
Maryland	17,321	2,606*	8,765	3,402	2,517			31
Massachusetts	39,698	4,565*	20,426		5,184	3,277		6,246
Michigan	41,309	2,322*	27,670	539*	4,254	3,153		3,371
Minnesota	48,022	24,908	8,271	3,416	1,808			9,619
Mississippi	7,775		2,809	2,314	1,447			1,205
Missouri	24,926	534*	10,522	11,521	2,287			62
Montana	4,458		2,526	152*	1,754			26
Nebraska	5,909		2,792	1,928	1,189			
Nevada	17,075	4,730	4,460	1,732	545			5,608
New Hampshire	8,039		4,237	1,346				2,456
New Jersey	58,266	32,465	14,763	3,440	3,887	1,337		2,374
New Mexico	17,571	13,218	2,996	713	644			
New York	123,002	75,956	12,220	23,580	5,011	3,473		2,762
North Carolina	13,961	2,108*	8,740	258*	2,771			84
North Dakota	1,941		847	745	349			
Ohio	43,122	2,962*	12,851	7,361	9,120	10,813		15
Oklahoma	5,505		5,505					
Oregon	68,746	49,415	8,903	3,379	2,798			4,251
Pennsylvania	58,146	3,086*	28,000	19,552	5,783			1,725
Rhode Island	8,828	6,040	1,109	1,021	435	186		37
South Carolina	7,562		4,271	2,043	1,248			
South Dakota	2,700		1,472	912	316			
Tennessee	15,511	6,427	5,020	1,818	636			1,610
Texas	37,257	4,810*	20,256	7,472	4,422			297
Utah	15,624	4,615	4,129	2,601	1,085	298		2,896
Vermont	9,179	5,585	1,183	382	498			1,531
Virginia	27,371		9,174	13,687	4,510			
Washington	88,799	60,322	12,522	4,578	6,076	2,189		3,112
West Virginia	3,062		3,062					
Wisconsin	51,830	28,723	7,929	8,811	1,379	1,333		3,655
Wyoming	2,321		1,739		582			
Dist. of Col.	6,556	4,780	588		283			905
United States	1,591,358	685,040	485,798	184,658	113,668	29,083	25,332	67,779

An asterisk to the right of a candidate's vote indicates write-in.

The vote, including write-ins, for other minor party candidates who were listed on the ballot in at least one state: 8,930 Collins (Arizona, Arkansas, California, Colorado, Georgia, Idaho, Kansas, Maryland, Mississippi, Missouri, Montana, Tennessee, Utah, Washington; 8,476 Harris (Alabama, California, Colorado, Connecticut, Florida, Georgia, Iowa, Minnesota, New Jersey, New York, North Carolina, Utah, Vermont, Washington, Wisconsin, District of Columbia; 5,378 Peron (Minnesota, Vermont); 4,706 Holllis (Arkansas, Colorado, Florida, Maryland, Massachusetts, Montana, Oregon, Texas, Utah, Vermont, Wisconsin); 2,438 White (Michigan, Minnesota, New Jersey); 1,847 Templin (Colorado, Utah); 1,298 Dodge (Arkansas, Colorado, Illinois, Massachusetts, Tennessee, Utah); 1,101 Crane (Utah); 932 Forbes (Arkansas); 787 Birrenbach (Minnesota); 752 Masters (Arkansas, California, Maryland); 408 Michael (Tennessee). The Other Candidates and Scattered Write-ins column includes 5,608 votes cast in Nevada for "None of these Candidates" and 25,118 scattered write-ins.

UNITED STATES

1996 TURNOUT

State	1996 Census Voting Age Pop. Est.	November 1996 Registration	Percentage Voting Age Registered	Total Valid Vote President	Percentage Voting Age Voted	Percentage Registered Voted
Alabama	3,218,000	2,470,766	76.8%	1,534,349	47.7%	62.1%
Alaska	425,000	414,817	97.6%	241,620	56.9%	58.2%
Arizona	3,094,000	2,244,672	72.5%	1,404,405	45.4%	62.6%
Arkansas	1,860,000	1,396,459	75.1%	884,262	47.5%	63.3%
California	23,133,000	15,662,075	67.7%	10,019,484	43.3%	64.0%
Colorado	2,843,000	2,285,503	80.4%	1,510,704	53.1%	66.1%
Connecticut	2,468,000	1,975,000	80.0%	1,392,614	56.4%	70.5%
Delaware	547,000	419,695	76.7%	271,084	49.6%	64.6%
Florida	11,043,000	8,077,877	73.1%	5,303,794	48.0%	65.7%
Georgia	5,396,000	3,811,284	70.6%	2,299,071	42.6%	60.3%
Hawaii	882,000	544,916	61.8%	360,120	40.8%	66.1%
Idaho	845,000	700,430	82.9%	491,719	58.2%	70.2%
Illinois	8,764,000	6,663,301	76.0%	4,311,391	49.2%	64.7%
Indiana	4,369,000	3,484,033	79.7%	2,135,842	48.9%	61.3%
Iowa	2,138,000	1,776,433	83.1%	1,234,075	57.7%	69.5%
Kansas	1,898,000	1,436,418	75.7%	1,074,300	56.6%	74.8%
Kentucky	2,924,000	2,396,086	81.9%	1,388,708	47.5%	58.0%
Louisiana	3,137,000	2,539,240	80.9%	1,783,959	56.9%	70.3%
Maine	939,000	1,001,292	106.6%	605,897	64.5%	60.5%
Maryland	3,811,000	2,587,977	67.9%	1,780,870	46.7%	68.8%
Massachusetts	4,623,000	3,459,193	74.8%	2,556,785	55.3%	73.9%
Michigan	7,067,000	6,688,893	94.6%	3,848,844	54.5%	57.5%
Minnesota	3,412,000	2,730,505	80.0%	2,192,640	64.3%	80.3%
Mississippi	1,961,000			893,857	45.6%	
Missouri	3,980,000	3,339,852	83.9%	2,158,065	54.2%	64.6%
Montana	647,000	590,749	91.3%	407,261	62.9%	68.9%
Nebraska	1,208,000	1,015,056	84.0%	677,415	56.1%	66.7%
Nevada	1,180,000	778,298	66.0%	464,279	39.3%	59.7%
New Hampshire	860,000	713,236	82.9%	499,175	58.0%	70.0%
New Jersey	6,005,000	4,320,866	72.0%	3,075,807	51.2%	71.2%
New Mexico	1,210,000	837,794	69.2%	556,074	46.0%	66.4%
New York	13,579,000	10,162,156	74.8%	6,316,129	46.5%	62.2%
North Carolina	5,499,000	4,315,723	78.5%	2,515,807	45.8%	58.3%
North Dakota	473,000			266,411	56.3%	
Ohio	8,358,000	6,879,687	82.3%	4,534,434	54.3%	65.9%
Oklahoma	2,419,000	1,979,017	81.8%	1,206,713	49.9%	61.0%
Oregon	2,396,000	1,962,155	81.9%	1,377,760	57.5%	70.2%
Pennsylvania	9,196,000	6,799,637	73.9%	4,506,118	49.0%	66.3%
Rhode Island	750,000	602,692	80.4%	390,284	52.0%	64.8%
South Carolina	2,777,000	1,814,777	65.4%	1,151,689	41.5%	63.5%
South Dakota	530,000	476,422	89.9%	323,826	61.1%	68.0%
Tennessee	4,021,000	3,097,336	77.0%	1,894,105	47.1%	61.2%
Texas	13,622,000	10,520,379	77.2%	5,611,644	41.2%	53.3%
Utah	1,323,000	1,050,452	79.4%	665,629	50.3%	63.4%
Vermont	441,000	385,328	87.4%	258,449	58.6%	67.1%
Virginia	5,089,000	3,322,740	65.3%	2,416,642	47.5%	72.7%
Washington	4,122,000	3,081,971	74.8%	2,253,837	54.7%	73.1%
West Virginia	1,414,000	970,745	68.7%	636,459	45.0%	65.6%
Wisconsin	3,824,000			2,196,169	57.4%	
Wyoming	352,000			211,571	60.1%	
District of Columbia	435,000	361,419	83.1%	185,726	42.7%	51.4%
Total	196,507,000	144,145,352	73.4%	96,277,872	49.0%	66.8%

Registration Source: Committee for the Study of the American Electorate. Those states without numbers do not maintain formal voter registration systems or had no figures readily available. Excluding these four states, the percentage of the voting age population registered in the remaining states was 75.9%, and the percentage of registered that voted was 64.3%.

PRESIDENT 1992

In New York the Republican figures include Conservative and Right to Life votes and the Democratic figures include Liberal votes.

In Minnesota the Republican candidates appear on the ballot as Independent-Republican, the Democratic as Democratic-Farmer-Labor. In many states various non-major party candidates appeared on the ballot with variations of the party designations, were carried with entirely different party labels or listed as "Independent". The state note sections list the party labels used by the minor-party candidates. In several states minor party Vice-Presidential candidates were different from those listed below.

The candidates listed below include all those who appeared on the ballot in at least one state. Where identified by state authorities, write-in votes for minor party candidates are credited to their total below. See page 18 for details.

44,909,326	Bill Clinton and Albert Gore, Jr.	Democratic
39,103,882	George Bush and J. Danforth Quayle	Republican
19,741,657	Ross Perot and James Stockdale	Independent
291,627	Andre V. Marrou and Nancy Lord	Libertarian
107,014	James Gritz and Cyril Minett	America First
73,714	Lenora B. Fulani and Maria E. Munoz	New Alliance
43,434	Howard Phillips and Albion W. Knight	Taxpayers
39,179	John Hagelin and Mike Tompkins	Natural Law
27,961	Ron Daniels and Asiba Tupahache	Peace and Freedom
26,333	Lyndon H. LaRouche and James L. Bevel	Economic Recovery
23,096	James Warren and Willie Mae Reid	Socialist Workers
4,749	Drew Bradford and no Vice Presidential candidate	Independent
3,875	Jack Herer and Derrick P. Grimmer	Grassroots
3,057	J. Quinn Brisben and Barbara Garson	Socialist
3,050	Helen Halyard and Fred Mazelis	Workers League
2,199	John Yiamouyiannis and Allen C. McCone	Take Back America
1,149	Delbert L. Ehlers and Rick Wendt	Independent
961	Earl F. Dodge and George Ormsby	Prohibition
956	Jim Boren and Will Weidman	Apathy
405	Eugene A. Hem and Joanne Roland	Third Party
339	Isabell Masters and Walter Masters	Looking Back
292	Robert J. Smith and Doris Feimer	American
181	Gloria LaRiva and Larry Holmes	Workers World

In addition to the votes listed above, 14,041 scattered write-in votes were reported from various states and 2,537 votes were cast for "None of these Candidates" in Nevada.

UNITED STATES

PRESIDENT 1992

State	Electoral Vote Rep.	Electoral Vote Dem.	Electoral Vote Other	Total Vote	Republican	Democratic	Perot	Other	Plurality		Percentage Rep.	Percentage Dem.	Percentage Perot
Alabama	9			1,688,060	804,283	690,080	183,109	10,588	114,203	R	47.6%	40.9%	10.8%
Alaska	3			258,506	102,000	78,294	73,481	4,731	23,706	R	39.5%	30.3%	28.4%
Arizona	8			1,486,975	572,086	543,050	353,741	18,098	29,036	R	38.5%	36.5%	23.8%
Arkansas		6		950,653	337,324	505,823	99,132	8,374	168,499	D	35.5%	53.2%	10.4%
California		54		11,131,721	3,630,574	5,121,325	2,296,006	83,816	1,490,751	D	32.6%	46.0%	20.6%
Colorado		8		1,569,180	562,850	629,681	366,010	10,639	66,831	D	35.9%	40.1%	23.3%
Connecticut		8		1,616,332	578,313	682,318	348,771	6,930	104,005	D	35.8%	42.2%	21.6%
Delaware		3		289,735	102,313	126,054	59,213	2,155	23,741	D	35.3%	43.5%	20.4%
Florida	25			5,314,392	2,173,310	2,072,698	1,053,067	15,317	100,612	R	40.9%	39.0%	19.8%
Georgia		13		2,321,125	995,252	1,008,966	309,657	7,250	13,714	D	42.9%	43.5%	13.3%
Hawaii		4		372,842	136,822	179,310	53,003	3,707	42,488	D	36.7%	48.1%	14.2%
Idaho	4			482,142	202,645	137,013	130,395	12,089	65,632	R	42.0%	28.4%	27.0%
Illinois		22		5,050,157	1,734,096	2,453,350	840,515	22,196	719,254	D	34.3%	48.6%	16.6%
Indiana	12			2,305,871	989,375	848,420	455,934	12,142	140,955	R	42.9%	36.8%	19.8%
Iowa		7		1,354,607	504,891	586,353	253,468	9,895	81,462	D	37.3%	43.3%	18.7%
Kansas	6			1,157,335	449,951	390,434	312,358	4,592	59,517	R	38.9%	33.7%	27.0%
Kentucky		8		1,492,900	617,178	665,104	203,944	6,674	47,926	D	41.3%	44.6%	13.7%
Louisiana		9		1,790,017	733,386	815,971	211,478	29,182	82,585	D	41.0%	45.6%	11.8%
Maine		4		679,499	206,504	263,420	206,820	2,755	56,600	D	30.4%	38.8%	30.4%
Maryland		10		1,985,046	707,094	988,571	281,414	7,967	281,477	D	35.6%	49.8%	14.2%
Massachusetts		12		2,773,700	805,049	1,318,662	630,731	19,258	513,613	D	29.0%	47.5%	22.7%
Michigan		18		4,274,673	1,554,940	1,871,182	824,813	23,738	316,242	D	36.4%	43.8%	19.3%
Minnesota		10		2,347,948	747,841	1,020,997	562,506	16,604	273,156	D	31.9%	43.5%	24.0%
Mississippi	7			981,793	487,793	400,258	85,626	8,116	87,535	R	49.7%	40.8%	8.7%
Missouri		11		2,391,565	811,159	1,053,873	518,741	7,792	242,714	D	33.9%	44.1%	21.7%
Montana		3		410,611	144,207	154,507	107,225	4,672	10,300	D	35.1%	37.6%	26.1%
Nebraska	5			737,546	343,678	216,864	174,104	2,900	126,814	R	46.6%	29.4%	23.6%
Nevada		4		506,318	175,828	189,148	132,580	8,762	13,320	D	34.7%	37.4%	26.2%
New Hampshire		4		537,943	202,484	209,040	121,337	5,082	6,556	D	37.6%	38.9%	22.6%
New Jersey		15		3,343,594	1,356,865	1,436,206	521,829	28,694	79,341	D	40.6%	43.0%	15.6%
New Mexico		5		569,986	212,824	261,617	91,895	3,650	48,793	D	37.3%	45.9%	16.1%
New York		33		6,926,925	2,346,649	3,444,450	1,090,721	45,105	1,097,801	D	33.9%	49.7%	15.7%
North Carolina	14			2,611,850	1,134,661	1,114,042	357,864	5,283	20,619	R	43.4%	42.7%	13.7%
North Dakota	3			308,133	136,244	99,168	71,084	1,637	37,076	R	44.2%	32.2%	23.1%
Ohio		21		4,939,967	1,894,310	1,984,942	1,036,426	24,289	90,632	D	38.3%	40.2%	21.0%
Oklahoma	8			1,390,359	592,929	473,066	319,878	4,486	119,863	R	42.6%	34.0%	23.0%
Oregon		7		1,462,643	475,757	621,314	354,091	11,481	145,557	D	32.5%	42.5%	24.2%
Pennsylvania		23		4,959,810	1,791,841	2,239,164	902,667	26,138	447,323	D	36.1%	45.1%	18.2%
Rhode Island		4		453,477	131,601	213,299	105,045	3,532	81,698	D	29.0%	47.0%	23.2%
South Carolina	8			1,202,527	577,507	479,514	138,872	6,634	97,993	R	48.0%	39.9%	11.5%
South Dakota	3			336,254	136,718	124,888	73,295	1,353	11,830	R	40.7%	37.1%	21.8%
Tennessee		11		1,982,638	841,300	933,521	199,968	7,849	92,221	D	42.4%	47.1%	10.1%
Texas	32			6,154,018	2,496,071	2,281,815	1,354,781	21,351	214,256	R	40.6%	37.1%	22.0%
Utah	5			743,999	322,632	183,429	203,400	34,538	119,232	R	43.4%	24.7%	27.3%
Vermont		3		289,701	88,122	133,592	65,991	1,996	45,470	D	30.4%	46.1%	22.8%
Virginia	13			2,558,665	1,150,517	1,038,650	348,639	20,859	111,867	R	45.0%	40.6%	13.6%
Washington		11		2,288,230	731,234	993,037	541,780	22,179	261,803	D	32.0%	43.4%	23.7%
West Virginia		5		683,762	241,974	331,001	108,829	1,958	89,027	D	35.4%	48.4%	15.9%
Wisconsin		11		2,531,114	930,855	1,041,066	544,479	14,714	110,211	D	36.8%	41.1%	21.5%
Wyoming	3			200,598	79,347	68,160	51,263	1,828	11,187	R	39.6%	34.0%	25.6%
Dist. of Col.		3		227,572	20,698	192,619	9,681	4,574	171,921	D	9.1%	84.6%	4.3%
United States	168	370		104,425,014	39,103,882	44,909,326	19,741,657	670,149	5,805,444	D	37.4%	43.0%	18.9%

UNITED STATES

PRESIDENT 1992 MINOR PARTIES

State	Other	Marrou	Gritz	Fulani	Phillips	Hagelin	Daniels	LaRouche	Warren	Other Candidates and Scattered Write-ins
Alabama	10,588	5,737		2,161		495		641	831	723
Alaska	4,731	1,378	1,379	330	377	433		469		365
Arizona	18,098	6,759	8,141	923		2,267		8*		
Arkansas	8,374	1,261	819	1,022	1,437	764		762		2,309
California	83,816	48,139	3,077*		12,711	836*	18,597	180*	115*	161
Colorado	10,639	8,669	274*	1,608		47*		20*		21
Connecticut	6,930	5,391	72*	1,363	20*	75*		4*	5*	
Delaware	2,155	935	9*	1,105	2*	6*		9*	3*	86
Florida	15,317	15,079				214*				24
Georgia	7,250	7,110	78*	44*	7*				9*	2
Hawaii	3,707	1,119	1,452	720		416				
Idaho	12,089	1,167	10,281	613		24*		1*		3
Illinois	22,196	9,218	3,577	5,267		2,751			1,361	22
Indiana	12,142	7,936	1,467*	2,583		126*		14*		16
Iowa	9,895	1,076	1,177	197	480	3,079	212	238	273	3,163
Kansas	4,592	4,314	79*	10*	55*	77*				57
Kentucky	6,674	4,513	47*	430	989	695				
Louisiana	29,182	3,155	18,545	1,434	1,552	889	1,663	1,136		808
Maine	2,755	1,681		519	464					91
Maryland	7,967	4,715	41*	2,786	22*	191*	167*	18*	25*	2
Massachusetts	19,258	9,024		3,172	2,218	1,812		1,027		2,005
Michigan	23,738	10,175	168*	21*	8,263	2,954		14*		2,143
Minnesota	16,604	3,374	3,363	958	733	1,406		622	990	5,158
Mississippi	8,116	2,154	545	2,625	1,652	1,140				
Missouri	7,792	7,497	180*	17*		64*	12*	13*	6*	3
Montana	4,672	986	3,658	8*		20*				
Nebraska	2,900	1,340		846		714				
Nevada	8,762	1,835	2,892	483	677	338				2,537
New Hampshire	5,082	3,548		512		292				730
New Jersey	28,694	6,822	1,867	3,513	2,670	1,353	1,996	2,095	2,011	6,367
New Mexico	3,650	1,615		369	620	562			183	301
New York	45,105	13,451	23*	11,318		4,420	385*	20*	15,472	16
North Carolina	5,283	5,171		59*		41*			12*	
North Dakota	1,637	416		143		240		642	193	3
Ohio	24,289	7,252	4,699	6,413		3,437		2,446	32*	10
Oklahoma	4,486	4,486								
Oregon	11,481	4,277	1,470*	3,030		91*				2,613
Pennsylvania	26,138	21,477		4,661						
Rhode Island	3,532	571	3*	1,878	215	262	1*	494		108
South Carolina	6,634	2,719		1,235	2,680					
South Dakota	1,353	814		110		429				
Tennessee	7,849	1,847	756	727	579	599	511	460	277	2,093
Texas	21,351	19,699	505*	301*	359*	217*		169*		101
Utah	34,538	1,900	28,602	414	393	1,319	177	1,089	200	444
Vermont	1,996	501		429	124	315			82	488
Virginia	20,859	5,730		3,192				11,937		
Washington	22,179	7,533	4,854	1,776	2,354	2,456	1,171	855	515	665
West Virginia	1,958	1,873	34*	6*	2*	2*			6*	35
Wisconsin	14,714	2,877	2,311	654	1,772	1,070	1,883	633	390	3,124
Wyoming	1,828	844	569*	270	7*	11*				127
Dist. of Col.	4,574	467		1,459		230	1,186	260	105	867
United States	670,149	291,627	107,014	73,714	43,434	39,179	27,961	26,333	23,096	37,791

An asterisk to the right of a candidate's vote indicates write-in.

The vote, including write-ins, for minor party candidates who received less than 5,000 votes is as follows: 4,749 Bradford (on the ballot in New Jersey); 3,875 Herer (on the ballot in Iowa, Minnesota and Wisconsin); 3,057 Brisben (on the ballot in Tennessee, Utah, Wisconsin and DC); 3,050 Halyard (on the ballot in Michigan and New Jersey); 2,199 Yiamouyiannis (on the ballot in Arkansas, Iowa, Louisiana and Tennessee); 1,149 Ehlers (on the ballot in Iowa); 961 Dodge (on the ballot in Arkansas, New Mexico and Tennessee); 956 Boren (on the ballot in Arkansas); 405 Hem (on the ballot in Wisconsin); 339 Masters (on the ballot in Arkansas); 292 Smith (on the ballot in Utah); 181 LaRiva (on the ballot in New Mexico). The other vote column also includes 2,537 votes cast in Nevada for "None of these Candidates" and 14,041 scattered write-ins.

UNITED STATES

1992 TURNOUT

State	Resident Voting Age Population	November 1992 Registration	Total Valid Vote President	Percentage Voting Age Registered	Percentage Voting Age Voted	Percentage Registered Voted
Alabama	3,056,000	2,367,972	1,688,060	77.5%	55.2%	71.3%
Alaska	395,000	315,058	258,506	79.8%	65.4%	82.1%
Arizona	2,749,000	1,964,949	1,486,975	71.5%	54.1%	75.7%
Arkansas	1,768,000	1,317,944	950,653	74.5%	53.8%	72.1%
California	22,668,000	15,101,473	11,131,721	66.6%	49.1%	73.7%
Colorado	2,501,000	2,003,375	1,569,180	80.1%	62.7%	78.3%
Connecticut	2,535,000	1,955,268	1,616,332	77.1%	63.8%	82.7%
Delaware	525,000	342,088	289,735	65.2%	55.2%	84.7%
Florida	10,586,000	6,541,825	5,314,392	61.8%	50.2%	81.2%
Georgia	4,950,000	3,177,061	2,321,125	64.2%	46.9%	73.1%
Hawaii	889,000	464,495	372,842	52.2%	41.9%	80.3%
Idaho	740,000	611,121	482,142	82.6%	65.2%	78.9%
Illinois	8,568,000	6,600,358	5,050,157	77.0%	58.9%	76.5%
Indiana	4,176,000	3,180,157	2,305,871	76.2%	55.2%	72.5%
Iowa	2,075,000	1,703,532	1,354,607	82.1%	65.3%	79.5%
Kansas	1,836,000	1,365,849	1,157,335	74.4%	63.0%	84.7%
Kentucky	2,779,000	2,076,263	1,492,900	74.7%	53.7%	71.9%
Louisiana	2,992,000	2,292,129	1,790,017	76.6%	59.8%	78.1%
Maine*	944,000		679,499		72.0%	
Maryland	3,719,000	2,463,010	1,985,046	66.2%	53.4%	80.6%
Massachusetts	4,607,000	3,351,918	2,773,700	72.8%	60.2%	82.7%
Michigan	6,923,000	6,147,083	4,274,673	88.8%	61.7%	69.5%
Minnesota	3,278,000	3,138,901	2,347,948	95.8%	71.6%	74.8%
Mississippi	1,861,000	1,640,150	981,793	88.1%	52.8%	59.9%
Missouri	3,858,000	3,067,955	2,391,565	79.5%	62.0%	78.0%
Montana	586,000	529,822	410,611	90.4%	70.1%	77.5%
Nebraska	1,167,000	951,395	737,546	81.5%	63.2%	77.5%
Nevada	1,013,000	649,913	506,318	64.2%	50.0%	77.9%
New Hampshire	852,000	660,985	537,943	77.6%	63.1%	81.4%
New Jersey	5,943,000	4,059,472	3,343,594	68.3%	56.3%	82.4%
New Mexico	1,104,000	706,966	569,986	64.0%	51.6%	80.6%
New York	13,609,000	9,193,391	6,926,925	67.6%	50.9%	75.3%
North Carolina	5,217,000	3,817,380	2,611,850	73.2%	50.1%	68.4%
North Dakota*	458,000		308,133		67.3%	
Ohio	8,146,000	6,542,931	4,939,967	80.3%	60.6%	75.5%
Oklahoma	2,328,000	2,302,279	1,390,359	98.9%	59.7%	60.4%
Oregon	2,226,000	1,774,449	1,462,643	79.7%	65.7%	82.4%
Pennsylvania	9,129,000	5,993,002	4,959,810	65.6%	54.3%	82.8%
Rhode Island	776,000	554,664	453,477	71.5%	58.4%	81.8%
South Carolina	2,672,000	1,537,140	1,202,527	57.5%	45.0%	78.2%
South Dakota	502,000	448,292	336,254	89.3%	67.0%	75.0%
Tennessee	3,783,000	2,726,449	1,982,638	72.1%	52.4%	72.7%
Texas	12,524,000	8,440,143	6,154,018	67.4%	49.1%	72.9%
Utah	1,142,000	965,211	743,999	84.5%	65.1%	77.1%
Vermont	429,000	383,371	289,701	89.4%	67.5%	75.6%
Virginia	4,842,000	3,054,662	2,558,665	63.1%	52.8%	83.8%
Washington	3,818,000	2,814,680	2,288,230	73.7%	59.9%	81.3%
West Virginia	1,350,000	956,172	683,762	70.8%	50.6%	71.5%
Wisconsin*	3,669,000		2,531,114		69.0%	
Wyoming	322,000	234,260	200,598	72. 8%	62.3%	85.6%
Dist. of Col.	459,000	340,953	227,572	74.3%	49.6%	66.7%
United States	189,044,000	132,827,916	104,425,014	70.3%	55.2%	78.6%

*Maine registration figures not available; North Dakota has no formal registration system; Wisconsin has no statewide registration system.

20

PRESIDENT 1988

In West Virginia one Democratic elector voted in the Electoral College for Lloyd Bentsen for President and Michael S. Dukakis for Vice President.

In New York the Republican figures include Conservative votes and the Democratic figures include Liberal votes.

In Minnesota the Republican candidates appear on the ballot as Independent-Republican, the Democratic as Democratic-Farmer-Labor. In many states various non-major party candidates appeared on the ballot with variations of the party designations given here, were listed as "Independent" or were carried with entirely different party labels.

In several states minor party Vice-Presidential candidates were different from those listed below. The full list of candidates for President and Vice President was:

48,886,097	George Bush and J. Danforth Quayle	Republican
41,809,074	Michael S. Dukakis and Lloyd Bentsen	Democratic
432,179	Ron Paul and Andre V. Marrou	Libertarian
217,219	Lenora B. Fulani and Joyce Dattner	New Alliance
47,047	David E. Duke and Floyd C. Parker	Populist
30,905	Eugene J. McCarthy and Florence Rice	Consumer
27,818	James C. Griffin and Charles J. Morsa	American Independent
25,562	Lyndon H. LaRouche and Debra H. Freeman	National Economic Recovery
20,504	William A. Matra and Joan Andrews	Right to Life
18,693	Ed Winn and Barry Porster	Workers League
15,604	James Warren and Kathleen Mickells	Socialist Workers
10,370	Herbert Lewin and Vikki Murdock	Peace and Freedom
8,002	Earl F. Dodge and George Ormsby	Prohibition
7,846	Larry Holmes and Gloria LaRiva	Workers World
3,882	Willa Kenoyer and Ron Ehrenreich	Socialist
3,475	Delmar Dennis and Earl Jeppson	American
1,949	Jack Herer and Dana Beal	Grassroots
372	Louie G. Youngkeit with no Vice-Presidential candidate	Independent
236	John G. Martin and Cleveland Sparrow	Third World Assembly

The candidates listed above include all those who appeared on the ballot in at least one state. Republican, Democratic and New Alliance candidates appeared on the ballot in all fifty-one jurisdictions. The Libertarian nominees were on the ballot in all save four. Where identified by state authorities, write-in votes for minor party candidates are credited to their total above and listed in the individual state note sections. In addition to the votes listed, 21,041 scattered write-in votes were reported from various states and 6,934 votes were cast for "None of these Candidates" in Nevada.

UNITED STATES

PRESIDENT 1988

State	Electoral Vote Rep.	Electoral Vote Dem.	Electoral Vote Other	Total Vote	Republican	Democratic	Other	Plurality		Percentage Total Vote Rep.	Percentage Total Vote Dem.	Percentage Major Vote Rep.	Percentage Major Vote Dem.
Alabama	9			1,378,476	815,576	549,506	13,394	266,070	R	59.2%	39.9%	59.7%	40.3%
Alaska	3			200,116	119,251	72,584	8,281	46,667	R	59.6%	36.3%	62.2%	37.8%
Arizona	7			1,171,873	702,541	454,029	15,303	248,512	R	60.0%	38.7%	60.7%	39.3%
Arkansas	6			827,738	466,578	349,237	11,923	117,341	R	56.4%	42.2%	57.2%	42.8%
California	47			9,887,065	5,054,917	4,702,233	129,915	352,684	R	51.1%	47.6%	51.8%	48.2%
Colorado	8			1,372,394	728,177	621,453	22,764	106,724	R	53.1%	45.3%	54.0%	46.0%
Connecticut	8			1,443,394	750,241	676,584	16,569	73,657	R	52.0%	46.9%	52.6%	47.4%
Delaware	3			249,891	139,639	108,647	1,605	30,992	R	55.9%	43.5%	56.2%	43.8%
Florida	21			4,302,313	2,618,885	1,656,701	26,727	962,184	R	60.9%	38.5%	61.3%	38.7%
Georgia	12			1,809,672	1,081,331	714,792	13,549	366,539	R	59.8%	39.5%	60.2%	39.8%
Hawaii		4		354,461	158,625	192,364	3,472	33,739	D	44.8%	54.3%	45.2%	54.8%
Idaho	4			408,968	253,881	147,272	7,815	106,609	R	62.1%	36.0%	63.3%	36.7%
Illinois	24			4,559,120	2,310,939	2,215,940	32,241	94,999	R	50.7%	48.6%	51.0%	49.0%
Indiana	12			2,168,621	1,297,763	860,643	10,215	437,120	R	59.8%	39.7%	60.1%	39.9%
Iowa		8		1,225,614	545,355	670,557	9,702	125,202	D	44.5%	54.7%	44.9%	55.1%
Kansas	7			993,044	554,049	422,636	16,359	131,413	R	55.8%	42.6%	56.7%	43.3%
Kentucky	9			1,322,517	734,281	580,368	7,868	153,913	R	55.5%	43.9%	55.9%	44.1%
Louisiana	10			1,628,202	883,702	717,460	27,040	166,242	R	54.3%	44.1%	55.2%	44.8%
Maine	4			555,035	307,131	243,569	4,335	63,562	R	55.3%	43.9%	55.8%	44.2%
Maryland	10			1,714,358	876,167	826,304	11,887	49,863	R	51.1%	48.2%	51.5%	48.5%
Massachusetts		13		2,632,805	1,194,635	1,401,415	36,755	206,780	D	45.4%	53.2%	46.0%	54.0%
Michigan	20			3,669,163	1,965,486	1,675,783	27,894	289,703	R	53.6%	45.7%	54.0%	46.0%
Minnesota		10		2,096,790	962,337	1,109,471	24,982	147,134	D	45.9%	52.9%	46.4%	53.6%
Mississippi	7			931,527	557,890	363,921	9,716	193,969	R	59.9%	39.1%	60.5%	39.5%
Missouri	11			2,093,713	1,084,953	1,001,619	7,141	83,334	R	51.8%	47.8%	52.0%	48.0%
Montana	4			365,674	190,412	168,936	6,326	21,476	R	52.1%	46.2%	53.0%	47.0%
Nebraska	5			661,465	397,956	259,235	4,274	138,721	R	60.2%	39.2%	60.6%	39.4%
Nevada	4			350,067	206,040	132,738	11,289	73,302	R	58.9%	37.9%	60.8%	39.2%
New Hampshire	4			451,074	281,537	163,696	5,841	117,841	R	62.4%	36.3%	63.2%	36.8%
New Jersey	16			3,099,553	1,743,192	1,320,352	36,009	422,840	R	56.2%	42.6%	56.9%	43.1%
New Mexico	5			521,287	270,341	244,497	6,449	25,844	R	51.9%	46.9%	52.5%	47.5%
New York		36		6,485,683	3,081,871	3,347,882	55,930	266,011	D	47.5%	51.6%	47.9%	52.1%
North Carolina	13			2,134,370	1,237,258	890,167	6,945	347,091	R	58.0%	41.7%	58.2%	41.8%
North Dakota	3			297,261	166,559	127,739	2,963	38,820	R	56.0%	43.0%	56.6%	43.4%
Ohio	23			4,393,699	2,416,549	1,939,629	37,521	476,920	R	55.0%	44.1%	55.5%	44.5%
Oklahoma	8			1,171,036	678,367	483,423	9,246	194,944	R	57.9%	41.3%	58.4%	41.6%
Oregon		7		1,201,694	560,126	616,206	25,362	56,080	D	46.6%	51.3%	47.6%	52.4%
Pennsylvania	25			4,536,251	2,300,087	2,194,944	41,220	105,143	R	50.7%	48.4%	51.2%	48.8%
Rhode Island		4		404,620	177,761	225,123	1,736	47,362	D	43.9%	55.6%	44.1%	55.9%
South Carolina	8			986,009	606,443	370,554	9,012	235,889	R	61.5%	37.6%	62.1%	37.9%
South Dakota	3			312,991	165,415	145,560	2,016	19,855	R	52.8%	46.5%	53.2%	46.8%
Tennessee	11			1,636,250	947,233	679,794	9,223	267,439	R	57.9%	41.5%	58.2%	41.8%
Texas	29			5,427,410	3,036,829	2,352,748	37,833	684,081	R	56.0%	43.3%	56.3%	43.7%
Utah	5			647,008	428,442	207,343	11,223	221,099	R	66.2%	32.0%	67.4%	32.6%
Vermont	3			243,328	124,331	115,775	3,222	8,556	R	51.1%	47.6%	51.8%	48.2%
Virginia	12			2,191,609	1,309,162	859,799	22,648	449,363	R	59.7%	39.2%	60.4%	39.6%
Washington		10		1,865,253	903,835	933,516	27,902	29,681	D	48.5%	50.0%	49.2%	50.8%
West Virginia		5	1	653,311	310,065	341,016	2,230	30,951	D	47.5%	52.2%	47.6%	52.4%
Wisconsin		11		2,191,608	1,047,499	1,126,794	17,315	79,295	D	47.8%	51.4%	48.2%	51.8%
Wyoming	3			176,551	106,867	67,113	2,571	39,754	R	60.5%	38.0%	61.4%	38.6%
Dist. of Col.		3		192,877	27,590	159,407	5,880	131,817	D	14.3%	82.6%	14.8%	85.2%
United States	426	111	1	91,594,809	48,886,097	41,809,074	899,638	7,077,023	R	53.4%	45.6%	53.9%	46.1%

PRESIDENT 1984

In New York the Republican figures include Conservative votes and the Democratic figures include Liberal votes.

In Minnesota the Republican candidates appear on the ballot as Independent-Republican, the Democratic as Democratic-Farmer-Labor. In many states various non-major party candidates appeared on the ballot with variations of the party designations given here, were listed as "Independent" or "Non-Party", or were carried with entirely different party labels.

The Workers World candidate for President was Gavrielle Holmes in Ohio and Rhode Island; in several states minor party Vice-Presidential candidates were different from those listed below.

The full list of candidates for President and Vice President was:

54,455,075	Ronald Reagan and George Bush	Republican
37,577,185	Walter F. Mondale and Geraldine A. Ferraro	Democratic
228,314	David Bergland and James A. Lewis	Libertarian
78,807	Lyndon H. LaRouche and Billy M. Davis	Independent
72,200	Sonia Johnson and Richard Walton	Citizens
66,336	Bob Richards and Maureen Salaman	Populist
46,868	Dennis L. Serrette and Nancy Ross	Alliance
36,386	Gus Hall and Angela Davis	Communist
24,706	Mel Mason and Matilde Zimmermann	Socialist Workers
17,985	Larry Holmes and Gloria LaRiva	Workers World
13,161	Delmar Dennis and Traves Brownlee	American
10,801	Ed Winn and Helen Halyard	Workers League
4,242	Earl F. Dodge and Warren C. Martin	Prohibition
1,486	John B. Anderson and Grace Pierce	National Unity
892	Gerald Baker and Ferris Alger	Big Deal
825	Arthur J. Lowery and Raymond L. Garland	United Sovereign Citizens

The candidates listed above are those who appeared on the ballot in at least one state. Where identified by state authorities, write-in votes for minor party candidates are credited to their total above and listed in the individual state note sections. In addition to the votes listed, 13,623 scattered write-in votes were reported from various states and 3,950 votes were cast for "None of these Candidates" in Nevada.

UNITED STATES

PRESIDENT 1984

State	Electoral Vote Rep.	Electoral Vote Dem.	Electoral Vote Other	Total Vote	Republican	Democratic	Other	Plurality		Percentage Total Vote Rep.	Percentage Total Vote Dem.	Percentage Major Vote Rep.	Percentage Major Vote Dem.
Alabama	9			1,441,713	872,849	551,899	16,965	320,950	R	60.5%	38.3%	61.3%	38.7%
Alaska	3			207,605	138,377	62,007	7,221	76,370	R	66.7%	29.9%	69.1%	30.9%
Arizona	7			1,025,897	681,416	333,854	10,627	347,562	R	66.4%	32.5%	67.1%	32.9%
Arkansas	6			884,406	534,774	338,646	10,986	196,128	R	60.5%	38.3%	61.2%	38.8%
California	47			9,505,423	5,467,009	3,922,519	115,895	1,544,490	R	57.5%	41.3%	58.2%	41.8%
Colorado	8			1,295,380	821,817	454,975	18,588	366,842	R	63.4%	35.1%	64.4%	35.6%
Connecticut	8			1,466,900	890,877	569,597	6,426	321,280	R	60.7%	38.8%	61.0%	39.0%
Delaware	3			254,572	152,190	101,656	726	50,534	R	59.8%	39.9%	60.0%	40.0%
Florida	21			4,180,051	2,730,350	1,448,816	885	1,281,534	R	65.3%	34.7%	65.3%	34.7%
Georgia	12			1,776,120	1,068,722	706,628	770	362,094	R	60.2%	39.8%	60.2%	39.8%
Hawaii	4			335,846	185,050	147,154	3,642	37,896	R	55.1%	43.8%	55.7%	44.3%
Idaho	4			411,144	297,523	108,510	5,111	189,013	R	72.4%	26.4%	73.3%	26.7%
Illinois	24			4,819,088	2,707,103	2,086,499	25,486	620,604	R	56.2%	43.3%	56.5%	43.5%
Indiana	12			2,233,069	1,377,230	841,481	14,358	535,749	R	61.7%	37.7%	62.1%	37.9%
Iowa	8			1,319,805	703,088	605,620	11,097	97,468	R	53.3%	45.9%	53.7%	46.3%
Kansas	7			1,021,991	677,296	333,149	11,546	344,147	R	66.3%	32.6%	67.0%	33.0%
Kentucky	9			1,369,345	821,702	539,539	8,104	282,163	R	60.0%	39.4%	60.4%	39.6%
Louisiana	10			1,706,822	1,037,299	651,586	17,937	385,713	R	60.8%	38.2%	61.4%	38.6%
Maine	4			553,144	336,500	214,515	2,129	121,985	R	60.8%	38.8%	61.1%	38.9%
Maryland	10			1,675,873	879,918	787,935	8,020	91,983	R	52.5%	47.0%	52.8%	47.2%
Massachusetts	13			2,559,453	1,310,936	1,239,606	8,911	71,330	R	51.2%	48.4%	51.4%	48.6%
Michigan	20			3,801,658	2,251,571	1,529,638	20,449	721,933	R	59.2%	40.2%	59.5%	40.5%
Minnesota		10		2,084,449	1,032,603	1,036,364	15,482	3,761	D	49.5%	49.7%	49.9%	50.1%
Mississippi	7			941,104	582,377	352,192	6,535	230,185	R	61.9%	37.4%	62.3%	37.7%
Missouri	11			2,122,783	1,274,188	848,583	12	425,605	R	60.0%	40.0%	60.0%	40.0%
Montana	4			384,377	232,450	146,742	5,185	85,708	R	60.5%	38.2%	61.3%	38.7%
Nebraska	5			652,090	460,054	187,866	4,170	272,188	R	70.6%	28.8%	71.0%	29.0%
Nevada	4			286,667	188,770	91,655	6,242	97,115	R	65.8%	32.0%	67.3%	32.7%
New Hampshire	4			389,066	267,051	120,395	1,620	146,656	R	68.6%	30.9%	68.9%	31.1%
New Jersey	16			3,217,862	1,933,630	1,261,323	22,909	672,307	R	60.1%	39.2%	60.5%	39.5%
New Mexico	5			514,370	307,101	201,769	5,500	105,332	R	59.7%	39.2%	60.3%	39.7%
New York	36			6,806,810	3,664,763	3,119,609	22,438	545,154	R	53.8%	45.8%	54.0%	46.0%
North Carolina	13			2,175,361	1,346,481	824,287	4,593	522,194	R	61.9%	37.9%	62.0%	38.0%
North Dakota	3			308,971	200,336	104,429	4,206	95,907	R	64.8%	33.8%	65.7%	34.3%
Ohio	23			4,547,619	2,678,560	1,825,440	43,619	853,120	R	58.9%	40.1%	59.5%	40.5%
Oklahoma	8			1,255,676	861,530	385,080	9,066	476,450	R	68.6%	30.7%	69.1%	30.9%
Oregon	7			1,226,527	685,700	536,479	4,348	149,221	R	55.9%	43.7%	56.1%	43.9%
Pennsylvania	25			4,844,903	2,584,323	2,228,131	32,449	356,192	R	53.3%	46.0%	53.7%	46.3%
Rhode Island	4			410,492	212,080	197,106	1,306	14,974	R	51.7%	48.0%	51.8%	48.2%
South Carolina	8			968,529	615,539	344,459	8,531	271,080	R	63.6%	35.6%	64.1%	35.9%
South Dakota	3			317,867	200,267	116,113	1,487	84,154	R	63.0%	36.5%	63.3%	36.7%
Tennessee	11			1,711,994	990,212	711,714	10,068	278,498	R	57.8%	41.6%	58.2%	41.8%
Texas	29			5,397,571	3,433,428	1,949,276	14,867	1,484,152	R	63.6%	36.1%	63.8%	36.2%
Utah	5			629,656	469,105	155,369	5,182	313,736	R	74.5%	24.7%	75.1%	24.9%
Vermont	3			234,561	135,865	95,730	2,966	40,135	R	57.9%	40.8%	58.7%	41.3%
Virginia	12			2,146,635	1,337,078	796,250	13,307	540,828	R	62.3%	37.1%	62.7%	37.3%
Washington	10			1,883,910	1,051,670	807,352	24,888	244,318	R	55.8%	42.9%	56.6%	43.4%
West Virginia	6			735,742	405,483	328,125	2,134	77,358	R	55.1%	44.6%	55.3%	44.7%
Wisconsin	11			2,211,689	1,198,584	995,740	17,365	202,844	R	54.2%	45.0%	54.6%	45.4%
Wyoming	3			188,968	133,241	53,370	2,357	79,871	R	70.5%	28.2%	71.4%	28.6%
Dist. of Col.		3		211,288	29,009	180,408	1,871	151,399	D	13.7%	85.4%	13.9%	86.1%
United States	525	13		92,652,842	54,455,075	37,577,185	620,582	16,877,890	R	58.8%	40.6%	59.2%	40.8%

PRESIDENT 1980

In New York the Republican figures include Conservative votes and in a number of states candidates appeared on the ballot with variants of the party designations listed below, without any party designation, or with entirely different party names.

In several cases Vice-Presidential nominees were different from those listed for most states and the Socialist Workers party nominee for President varied from state to state.

43,904,153	Ronald Reagan and George Bush	Republican
35,483,883	Jimmy Carter and Walter F. Mondale	Democratic
5,720,060	John B. Anderson and Patrick J. Lucey	Independent
921,299	Edward E. Clark and David Koch	Libertarian
234,294	Barry Commoner and LaDonna Harris	Citizens
45,023	Gus Hall and Angela Davis	Communist
41,268	John R. Rarick and Eileen M. Shearer	American Independent
38,737	Clifton DeBerry and Matilde Zimmermann	Socialist Workers
32,327	Ellen McCormack and Carroll Driscoll	Right to Life
18,116	Maureen Smith and Elizabeth Barron	Peace and Freedom
13,300	Deirdre Griswold and Larry Holmes	Workers World
7,212	Benjamin C. Bubar and Earl F. Dodge	Statesman
6,898	David McReynolds and Diane Drufenbrock	Socialist
6,647	Percy L. Greaves and Frank L. Varnum	American
6,272	Andrew Pulley and Matilde Zimmermann	Socialist Workers
4,029	Richard Congress and Matilde Zimmermann	Socialist Workers
3,694	Kurt Lynen and Harry Kieve	Middle Class
1,718	Bill Gahres and J.F. Loughlin	Down With Lawyers
1,555	Frank W. Shelton and George E. Jackson	American
923	Martin E. Wendelken with no Vice-Presidential candidate	Independent
296	Harley McLain and Jewelie Goeller	Natural Peoples

In addition to these votes, 13,185 scattered write-in votes were reported from various states, 6,139 votes were cast in Minnesota for American party electors without designated national nominees, and 4,193 votes were cast for "None of these Candidates" in Nevada.

UNITED STATES

PRESIDENT 1980

State	Electoral Vote Rep.	Dem.	Other	Total Vote	Republican	Democratic	Other	Plurality		Percentage Total Vote Rep.	Dem.	Major Vote Rep.	Dem.
Alabama	9			1,341,929	654,192	636,730	51,007	17,462	R	48.8%	47.4%	50.7%	49.3%
Alaska	3			158,445	86,112	41,842	30,491	44,270	R	54.3%	26.4%	67.3%	32.7%
Arizona	6			873,945	529,688	246,843	97,414	282,845	R	60.6%	28.2%	68.2%	31.8%
Arkansas	6			837,582	403,164	398,041	36,377	5,123	R	48.1%	47.5%	50.3%	49.7%
California	45			8,587,063	4,524,858	3,083,661	978,544	1,441,197	R	52.7%	35.9%	59.5%	40.5%
Colorado	7			1,184,415	652,264	367,973	164,178	284,291	R	55.1%	31.1%	63.9%	36.1%
Connecticut	8			1,406,285	677,210	541,732	187,343	135,478	R	48.2%	38.5%	55.6%	44.4%
Delaware	3			235,900	111,252	105,754	18,894	5,498	R	47.2%	44.8%	51.3%	48.7%
Florida	17			3,686,930	2,046,951	1,419,475	220,504	627,476	R	55.5%	38.5%	59.1%	40.9%
Georgia		12		1,596,695	654,168	890,733	51,794	236,565	D	41.0%	55.8%	42.3%	57.7%
Hawaii		4		303,287	130,112	135,879	37,296	5,767	D	42.9%	44.8%	48.9%	51.1%
Idaho	4			437,431	290,699	110,192	36,540	180,507	R	66.5%	25.2%	72.5%	27.5%
Illinois	26			4,749,721	2,358,049	1,981,413	410,259	376,636	R	49.6%	41.7%	54.3%	45.7%
Indiana	13			2,242,033	1,255,656	844,197	142,180	411,459	R	56.0%	37.7%	59.8%	40.2%
Iowa	8			1,317,661	676,026	508,672	132,963	167,354	R	51.3%	38.6%	57.1%	42.9%
Kansas	7			979,795	566,812	326,150	86,833	240,662	R	57.9%	33.3%	63.5%	36.5%
Kentucky	9			1,294,627	635,274	616,417	42,936	18,857	R	49.1%	47.6%	50.8%	49.2%
Louisiana	10			1,548,591	792,853	708,453	47,285	84,400	R	51.2%	45.7%	52.8%	47.2%
Maine	4			523,011	238,522	220,974	63,515	17,548	R	45.6%	42.3%	51.9%	48.1%
Maryland		10		1,540,496	680,606	726,161	133,729	45,555	D	44.2%	47.1%	48.4%	51.6%
Massachusetts	14			2,524,298	1,057,631	1,053,802	412,865	3,829	R	41.9%	41.7%	50.1%	49.9%
Michigan	21			3,909,725	1,915,225	1,661,532	332,968	253,693	R	49.0%	42.5%	53.5%	46.5%
Minnesota		10		2,051,980	873,268	954,174	224,538	80,906	D	42.6%	46.5%	47.8%	52.2%
Mississippi	7			892,620	441,089	429,281	22,250	11,808	R	49.4%	48.1%	50.7%	49.3%
Missouri	12			2,099,824	1,074,181	931,182	94,461	142,999	R	51.2%	44.3%	53.6%	46.4%
Montana	4			363,952	206,814	118,032	39,106	88,782	R	56.8%	32.4%	63.7%	36.3%
Nebraska	5			640,854	419,937	166,851	54,066	253,086	R	65.5%	26.0%	71.6%	28.4%
Nevada	3			247,885	155,017	66,666	26,202	88,351	R	62.5%	26.9%	69.9%	30.1%
New Hampshire	4			383,990	221,705	108,864	53,421	112,841	R	57.7%	28.4%	67.1%	32.9%
New Jersey	17			2,975,684	1,546,557	1,147,364	281,763	399,193	R	52.0%	38.6%	57.4%	42.6%
New Mexico	4			456,971	250,779	167,826	38,366	82,953	R	54.9%	36.7%	59.9%	40.1%
New York	41			6,201,959	2,893,831	2,728,372	579,756	165,459	R	46.7%	44.0%	51.5%	48.5%
North Carolina	13			1,855,833	915,018	875,635	65,180	39,383	R	49.3%	47.2%	51.1%	48.9%
North Dakota	3			301,545	193,695	79,189	28,661	114,506	R	64.2%	26.3%	71.0%	29.0%
Ohio	25			4,283,603	2,206,545	1,752,414	324,644	454,131	R	51.5%	40.9%	55.7%	44.3%
Oklahoma	8			1,149,708	695,570	402,026	52,112	293,544	R	60.5%	35.0%	63.4%	36.6%
Oregon	6			1,181,516	571,044	456,890	153,582	114,154	R	48.3%	38.7%	55.6%	44.4%
Pennsylvania	27			4,561,501	2,261,872	1,937,540	362,089	324,332	R	49.6%	42.5%	53.9%	46.1%
Rhode Island		4		416,072	154,793	198,342	62,937	43,549	D	37.2%	47.7%	43.8%	56.2%
South Carolina	8			894,071	441,841	430,385	21,845	11,456	R	49.4%	48.1%	50.7%	49.3%
South Dakota	4			327,703	198,343	103,855	25,505	94,488	R	60.5%	31.7%	65.6%	34.4%
Tennessee	10			1,617,616	787,761	783,051	46,804	4,710	R	48.7%	48.4%	50.1%	49.9%
Texas	26			4,541,636	2,510,705	1,881,147	149,784	629,558	R	55.3%	41.4%	57.2%	42.8%
Utah	4			604,222	439,687	124,266	40,269	315,421	R	72.8%	20.6%	78.0%	22.0%
Vermont	3			213,299	94,628	81,952	36,719	12,676	R	44.4%	38.4%	53.6%	46.4%
Virginia	12			1,866,032	989,609	752,174	124,249	237,435	R	53.0%	40.3%	56.8%	43.2%
Washington	9			1,742,394	865,244	650,193	226,957	215,051	R	49.7%	37.3%	57.1%	42.9%
West Virginia		6		737,715	334,206	367,462	36,047	33,256	D	45.3%	49.8%	47.6%	52.4%
Wisconsin	11			2,273,221	1,088,845	981,584	202,792	107,261	R	47.9%	43.2%	52.6%	47.4%
Wyoming	3			176,713	110,700	49,427	16,586	61,273	R	62.6%	28.0%	69.1%	30.9%
Dist. of Col.		3		175,237	23,545	131,113	20,579	107,568	D	13.4%	74.8%	15.2%	84.8%
United States	489	49		86,515,221	43,904,153	35,483,883	7,127,185	8,420,270	R	50.7%	41.0%	55.3%	44.7%

PRESIDENT 1976

In Washington one Republican elector voted in the Electoral College for Ronald Reagan for President and Robert Dole for Vice-President.

In New York the Republican figures include Conservative votes and the Democratic figures include Liberal votes; in Vermont the Democratic figures include votes cast on the Independent Vermonters party ticket.

In a number of states candidates appeared on the ballot with variants of the party designations listed below and in several cases with entirely different party names.

The ballot designations for electors for Eugene J. McCarthy for President varied from state to state, as did the names of Vice-Presidential candidates running with him. In New Jersey the Maddox Vice-Presidential candidate was Edmund O. Matzal.

The full list of candidates for President and Vice President was:

40,830,763	Jimmy Carter and Walter F. Mondale	Democratic
39,147,793	Gerald R. Ford and Robert Dole	Republican
756,691	Eugene J. McCarthy with various Vice-Presidential candidates	Independent
173,011	Roger L. MacBride and David D. Bergland	Libertarian
170,531	Lester G. Maddox and William D. Dyke	American Independent
160,773	Thomas J. Anderson and Rufus Shackelford	American
91,314	Peter Camejo and Willie Mae Reid	Socialist Workers
58,992	Gus Hall and Jarvis Tyner	Communist
49,024	Margaret Wright and Benjamin Spock	People's
40,043	Lyndon H. LaRouche and R.W. Evans	United States Labor
15,934	Benjamin C. Bubar and Earl F. Dodge	Prohibition
9,616	Julius Levin and Constance Blomen	Socialist Labor
6,038	Frank P. Zeidler and J.Q. Brisben	Socialist
361	Ernest L. Miller and Roy N. Eddy	Restoration
36	Frank Taylor and Henry Swan	United American

In addition to these votes, 39,861 scattered write-in votes were reported from various states and 5,108 votes were cast for "None of these Candidates" in Nevada.

UNITED STATES

PRESIDENT 1976

State	Electoral Vote Rep.	Dem.	Other	Total Vote	Republican	Democratic	Other	Plurality		Percentage Total Vote Rep.	Dem.	Major Vote Rep.	Dem.
Alabama		9		1,182,850	504,070	659,170	19,610	155,100	D	42.6%	55.7%	43.3%	56.7%
Alaska	3			123,574	71,555	44,058	7,961	27,497	R	57.9%	35.7%	61.9%	38.1%
Arizona	6			742,719	418,642	295,602	28,475	123,040	R	56.4%	39.8%	58.6%	41.4%
Arkansas		6		767,535	267,903	498,604	1,028	230,701	D	34.9%	65.0%	35.0%	65.0%
California	45			7,867,117	3,882,244	3,742,284	242,589	139,960	R	49.3%	47.6%	50.9%	49.1%
Colorado	7			1,081,554	584,367	460,353	36,834	124,014	R	54.0%	42.6%	55.9%	44.1%
Connecticut	8			1,381,526	719,261	647,895	14,370	71,366	R	52.1%	46.9%	52.6%	47.4%
Delaware		3		235,834	109,831	122,596	3,407	12,765	D	46.6%	52.0%	47.3%	52.7%
Florida		17		3,150,631	1,469,531	1,636,000	45,100	166,469	D	46.6%	51.9%	47.3%	52.7%
Georgia		12		1,467,458	483,743	979,409	4,306	495,666	D	33.0%	66.7%	33.1%	66.9%
Hawaii		4		291,301	140,003	147,375	3,923	7,372	D	48.1%	50.6%	48.7%	51.3%
Idaho	4			344,071	204,151	126,549	13,371	77,602	R	59.3%	36.8%	61.7%	38.3%
Illinois	26			4,718,914	2,364,269	2,271,295	83,350	92,974	R	50.1%	48.1%	51.0%	49.0%
Indiana	13			2,220,362	1,183,958	1,014,714	21,690	169,244	R	53.3%	45.7%	53.8%	46.2%
Iowa	8			1,279,306	632,863	619,931	26,512	12,932	R	49.5%	48.5%	50.5%	49.5%
Kansas	7			957,845	502,752	430,421	24,672	72,331	R	52.5%	44.9%	53.9%	46.1%
Kentucky		9		1,167,142	531,852	615,717	19,573	83,865	D	45.6%	52.8%	46.3%	53.7%
Louisiana		10		1,278,439	587,446	661,365	29,628	73,919	D	46.0%	51.7%	47.0%	53.0%
Maine	4			483,216	236,320	232,279	14,617	4,041	R	48.9%	48.1%	50.4%	49.6%
Maryland		10		1,439,897	672,661	759,612	7,624	86,951	D	46.7%	52.8%	47.0%	53.0%
Massachusetts		14		2,547,558	1,030,276	1,429,475	87,807	399,199	D	40.4%	56.1%	41.9%	58.1%
Michigan	21			3,653,749	1,893,742	1,696,714	63,293	197,028	R	51.8%	46.4%	52.7%	47.3%
Minnesota		10		1,949,931	819,395	1,070,440	60,096	251,045	D	42.0%	54.9%	43.4%	56.6%
Mississippi		7		769,361	366,846	381,309	21,206	14,463	D	47.7%	49.6%	49.0%	51.0%
Missouri		12		1,953,600	927,443	998,387	27,770	70,944	D	47.5%	51.1%	48.2%	51.8%
Montana	4			328,734	173,703	149,259	5,772	24,444	R	52.8%	45.4%	53.8%	46.2%
Nebraska	5			607,668	359,705	233,692	14,271	126,013	R	59.2%	38.5%	60.6%	39.4%
Nevada	3			201,876	101,273	92,479	8,124	8,794	R	50.2%	45.8%	52.3%	47.7%
New Hampshire	4			339,618	185,935	147,635	6,048	38,300	R	54.7%	43.5%	55.7%	44.3%
New Jersey	17			3,014,472	1,509,688	1,444,653	60,131	65,035	R	50.1%	47.9%	51.1%	48.9%
New Mexico	4			418,409	211,419	201,148	5,842	10,271	R	50.5%	48.1%	51.2%	48.8%
New York		41		6,534,170	3,100,791	3,389,558	43,821	288,767	D	47.5%	51.9%	47.8%	52.2%
North Carolina		13		1,678,914	741,960	927,365	9,589	185,405	D	44.2%	55.2%	44.4%	55.6%
North Dakota	3			297,188	153,470	136,078	7,640	17,392	R	51.6%	45.8%	53.0%	47.0%
Ohio		25		4,111,873	2,000,505	2,011,621	99,747	11,116	D	48.7%	48.9%	49.9%	50.1%
Oklahoma	8			1,092,251	545,708	532,442	14,101	13,266	R	50.0%	48.7%	50.6%	49.4%
Oregon	6			1,029,876	492,120	490,407	47,349	1,713	R	47.8%	47.6%	50.1%	49.9%
Pennsylvania		27		4,620,787	2,205,604	2,328,677	86,506	123,073	D	47.7%	50.4%	48.6%	51.4%
Rhode Island		4		411,170	181,249	227,636	2,285	46,387	D	44.1%	55.4%	44.3%	55.7%
South Carolina		8		802,583	346,149	450,807	5,627	104,658	D	43.1%	56.2%	43.4%	56.6%
South Dakota	4			300,678	151,505	147,068	2,105	4,437	R	50.4%	48.9%	50.7%	49.3%
Tennessee		10		1,476,345	633,969	825,879	16,497	191,910	D	42.9%	55.9%	43.4%	56.6%
Texas		26		4,071,884	1,953,300	2,082,319	36,265	129,019	D	48.0%	51.1%	48.4%	51.6%
Utah	4			541,198	337,908	182,110	21,180	155,798	R	62.4%	33.6%	65.0%	35.0%
Vermont	3			187,765	102,085	80,954	4,726	21,131	R	54.4%	43.1%	55.8%	44.2%
Virginia	12			1,697,094	836,554	813,896	46,644	22,658	R	49.3%	48.0%	50.7%	49.3%
Washington	8		1	1,555,534	777,732	717,323	60,479	60,409	R	50.0%	46.1%	52.0%	48.0%
West Virginia		6		750,964	314,760	435,914	290	121,154	D	41.9%	58.0%	41.9%	58.1%
Wisconsin		11		2,104,175	1,004,987	1,040,232	58,956	35,245	D	47.8%	49.4%	49.1%	50.9%
Wyoming	3			156,343	92,717	62,239	1,387	30,478	R	59.3%	39.8%	59.8%	40.2%
Dist. of Col.		3		168,830	27,873	137,818	3,139	109,945	D	16.5%	81.6%	16.8%	83.2%
United States	240	297	1	81,555,889	39,147,793	40,830,763	1,577,333	1,682,970	D	48.0%	50.1%	48.9%	51.1%

PRESIDENT 1972

In Virginia one Republican elector voted in the Electoral College for the Libertarian candidates for President and Vice-President.

In New York the Republican figures include Conservative votes and the Democratic figures include Liberal votes. In Alabama the Democratic figures include votes cast on the National Democratic Party of Alabama ticket, and in South Carolina include United Citizens Party votes.

In certain states candidates appeared on the ballot under party names other than those used below; for the Socialist Workers party the votes listed for Jenness and Pulley were actually cast for substitute candidates (Reed and DeBerry) or without named candidates in several states.

The Democratic Vice-Presidential candidate originally was Senator Thomas F. Eagleton; on his withdrawal shortly after the party convention, R. Sargent Shriver was named by the Democratic National Committee as candidate.

The full list of candidates for President and Vice-President was:

47,169,911	Richard M. Nixon and Spiro T. Agnew	Republican
29,170,383	George S. McGovern and R. Sargent Shriver	Democratic
1,099,482	John G. Schmitz and Thomas J. Anderson	American
78,756	Benjamin Spock and Julius Hobson	People's
66,677	Linda Jenness and Andrew Pulley	Socialist Workers
53,814	Louis Fisher and Genevieve Gunderson	Socialist Labor
25,595	Gus Hail and Jarvis Tyner	Communist
13,505	E. Harold Munn and Marshall E. Uncapher	Prohibition
3,673	John Hospers and Theodora Nathan	Libertarian
1,743	John V. Mahalchik and Irving Homer	America First
220	Gabriel Green and Daniel Fry	Universal

In addition to the above, 34,795 scattered votes were reported from various states.

Vice President Agnew resigned in October 1973 and Representative Gerald R. Ford of Michigan was nominated by President Nixon to fill the vacancy. In November (Senate) and December (House of Representatives) this action was approved by Congress.

In August 1974 President Nixon resigned and was succeeded by Vice President Ford. In the same month Nelson A. Rockefeller, former Governor of New York, was nominated to be Vice President and was confirmed by Congress in December 1974.

UNITED STATES

PRESIDENT 1972

State	Electoral Vote Rep.	Electoral Vote Dem.	Electoral Vote Other	Total Vote	Republican	Democratic	Other	Plurality		Percentage Total Vote Rep.	Percentage Total Vote Dem.	Percentage Major Vote Rep.	Percentage Major Vote Dem.
Alabama	9			1,006,111	728,701	256,923	20,487	471,778	R	72.4%	25.5%	73.9%	26.1%
Alaska	3			95,219	55,349	32,967	6,903	22,382	R	58.1%	34.6%	62.7%	37.3%
Arizona	6			622,926	402,812	198,540	21,574	204,272	R	64.7%	31.9%	67.0%	33.0%
Arkansas	6			651,320	448,541	199,892	2,887	248,649	R	68.9%	30.7%	69.2%	30.8%
California	45			8,367,862	4,602,096	3,475,847	289,919	1,126,249	R	55.0%	41.5%	57.0%	43.0%
Colorado	7			953,884	597,189	329,980	26,715	267,209	R	62.6%	34.6%	64.4%	35.6%
Connecticut	8			1,384,277	810,763	555,498	18,016	255,265	R	58.6%	40.1%	59.3%	40.7%
Delaware	3			235,516	140,357	92,283	2,876	48,074	R	59.6%	39.2%	60.3%	39.7%
Florida	17			2,583,283	1,857,759	718,117	7,407	1,139,642	R	71.9%	27.8%	72.1%	27.9%
Georgia	12			1,174,772	881,496	289,529	3,747	591,967	R	75.0%	24.6%	75.3%	24.7%
Hawaii	4			270,274	168,865	101,409		67,456	R	62.5%	37.5%	62.5%	37.5%
Idaho	4			310,379	199,384	80,826	30,169	118,558	R	64.2%	26.0%	71.2%	28.8%
Illinois	26			4,723,236	2,788,179	1,913,472	21,585	874,707	R	59.0%	40.5%	59.3%	40.7%
Indiana	13			2,125,529	1,405,154	708,568	11,807	696,586	R	66.1%	33.3%	66.5%	33.5%
Iowa	8			1,225,944	706,207	496,206	23,531	210,001	R	57.6%	40.5%	58.7%	41.3%
Kansas	7			916,095	619,812	270,287	25,996	349,525	R	67.7%	29.5%	69.6%	30.4%
Kentucky	9			1,067,499	676,446	371,159	19,894	305,287	R	63.4%	34.8%	64.6%	35.4%
Louisiana	10			1,051,491	686,852	298,142	66,497	388,710	R	65.3%	28.4%	69.7%	30.3%
Maine	4			417,042	256,458	160,584		95,874	R	61.5%	38.5%	61.5%	38.5%
Maryland	10			1,353,812	829,305	505,781	18,726	323,524	R	61.3%	37.4%	62.1%	37.9%
Massachusetts		14		2,458,756	1,112,078	1,332,540	14,138	220,462	D	45.2%	54.2%	45.5%	54.5%
Michigan	21			3,489,727	1,961,721	1,459,435	68,571	502,286	R	56.2%	41.8%	57.3%	42.7%
Minnesota	10			1,741,652	898,269	802,346	41,037	95,923	R	51.6%	46.1%	52.8%	47.2%
Mississippi	7			645,963	505,125	126,782	14,056	378,343	R	78.2%	19.6%	79.9%	20.1%
Missouri	12			1,855,803	1,153,852	697,147	4,804	456,705	R	62.2%	37.6%	62.3%	37.7%
Montana	4			317,603	183,976	120,197	13,430	63,779	R	57.9%	37.8%	60.5%	39.5%
Nebraska	5			576,289	406,298	169,991		236,307	R	70.5%	29.5%	70.5%	29.5%
Nevada	3			181,766	115,750	66,016		49,734	R	63.7%	36.3%	63.7%	36.3%
New Hampshire	4			334,055	213,724	116,435	3,896	97,289	R	64.0%	34.9%	64.7%	35.3%
New Jersey	17			2,997,229	1,845,502	1,102,211	49,516	743,291	R	61.6%	36.8%	62.6%	37.4%
New Mexico	4			386,241	235,606	141,084	9,551	94,522	R	61.0%	36.5%	62.5%	37.5%
New York	41			7,165,919	4,192,778	2,951,084	22,057	1,241,694	R	58.5%	41.2%	58.7%	41.3%
North Carolina	13			1,518,612	1,054,889	438,705	25,018	616,184	R	69.5%	28.9%	70.6%	29.4%
North Dakota	3			280,514	174,109	100,384	6,021	73,725	R	62.1%	35.8%	63.4%	36.6%
Ohio	25			4,094,787	2,441,827	1,558,889	94,071	882,938	R	59.6%	38.1%	61.0%	39.0%
Oklahoma	8			1,029,900	759,025	247,147	23,728	511,878	R	73.7%	24.0%	75.4%	24.6%
Oregon	6			927,946	486,686	392,760	48,500	93,926	R	52.4%	42.3%	55.3%	44.7%
Pennsylvania	27			4,592,106	2,714,521	1,796,951	80,634	917,570	R	59.1%	39.1%	60.2%	39.8%
Rhode Island	4			415,808	220,383	194,645	780	25,738	R	53.0%	46.8%	53.1%	46.9%
South Carolina	8			673,960	477,044	186,824	10,092	290,220	R	70.8%	27.7%	71.9%	28.1%
South Dakota	4			307,415	166,476	139,945	994	26,531	R	54.2%	45.5%	54.3%	45.7%
Tennessee	10			1,201,182	813,147	357,293	30,742	455,854	R	67.7%	29.7%	69.5%	30.5%
Texas	26			3,471,281	2,298,896	1,154,289	18,096	1,144,607	R	66.2%	33.3%	66.6%	33.4%
Utah	4			478,476	323,643	126,284	28,549	197,359	R	67.6%	26.4%	71.9%	28.1%
Vermont	3			186,947	117,149	68,174	1,624	48,975	R	62.7%	36.5%	63.2%	36.8%
Virginia	11		1	1,457,019	988,493	438,887	29,639	549,606	R	67.8%	30.1%	69.3%	30.7%
Washington	9			1,470,847	837,135	568,334	65,378	268,801	R	56.9%	38.6%	59.6%	40.4%
West Virginia	6			762,399	484,964	277,435		207,529	R	63.6%	36.4%	63.6%	36.4%
Wisconsin	11			1,852,890	989,430	810,174	53,286	179,256	R	53.4%	43.7%	55.0%	45.0%
Wyoming	3			145,570	100,464	44,358	748	56,106	R	69.0%	30.5%	69.4%	30.6%
Dist. of Col.		3		163,421	35,226	127,627	568	92,401	D	21.6%	78.1%	21.6%	78.4%
United States	520	17	1	77,718,554	47,169,911	29,170,383	1,378,260	17,999,528	R	60.7%	37.5%	61.8%	38.2%

PRESIDENT 1968

In North Carolina one Republican elector voted in the Electoral College for the American Independent candidates for President and Vice President.

In New York the Democratic figure includes Liberal votes and in Alabama the Democratic vote is the total of the Alabama Independent Democratic and National Democratic Party of Alabama vote. In certain states candidates appeared under variants of the party name used below and in most states the Vice-Presidential candidate of the American Independent party was listed as Marvin Griffin rather than Curtis E. LeMay.

The full list of candidates for President and Vice President was:

31,785,480	Richard M. Nixon and Spiro T. Agnew	Republican
31,275,166	Hubert H. Humphrey and Edmund S. Muskie	Democratic
9,906,473	George C. Wallace and Curtis E. LeMay	American Independent
52,588	Henning A. Blomen and George S. Taylor	Socialist Labor
47,133	Dick Gregory	Peace and Freedom, with various Vice-Presidential candidates
41,388	Fred Halstead and Paul Boutelle	Socialist Workers
36,563	Eldridge Cleaver	Peace and Freedom, with various Vice-Presidential candidates
25,552	Eugene J. McCarthy	Under various titles and written-in, but without indication of Vice-Presidential candidates
15,123	E. Harold Munn and Rolland E. Fisher	Prohibition
1,519	Ventura Chavez and Adelicio Moya	People's Constitutional
1,075	Charlene Mitchell and Michael Zagarell	Communist
142	James Hensley and Roscoe B. MacKenna	Universal
34	Richard K. Troxell and Merle Thayer	Constitution
7	Kent M. Soeters and James P. Powers	Berkeley Defense Group

In the vote listed above for Eldridge Cleaver, two states are included (California and Utah) in which only the party Vice-Presidential candidate appeared on the ballot.

In addition to these votes, 12,430 were cast for elector tickets for which there were no formal Presidential or Vice-Presidential candidates, and 11,192 scattered votes were reported from various states.

UNITED STATES

PRESIDENT 1968

State	Electoral Vote Rep.	Electoral Vote Dem.	Electoral Vote Other	Total Vote	Republican	Democratic	AIP	Other	Plurality		Percentage Rep.	Percentage Dem.	Percentage AIP
Alabama			10	1,049,922	146,923	196,579	691,425	14,995	494,846	A	14.0%	18.7%	65.9%
Alaska	3			83,035	37,600	35,411	10,024		2,189	R	45.3%	42.6%	12.1%
Arizona	5			486,936	266,721	170,514	46,573	3,128	96,207	R	54.8%	35.0%	9.6%
Arkansas			6	619,969	190,759	188,228	240,982		50,223	A	30.8%	30.4%	38.9%
California	40			7,251,587	3,467,664	3,244,318	487,270	52,335	223,346	R	47.8%	44.7%	6.7%
Colorado	6			811,199	409,345	335,174	60,813	5,867	74,171	R	50.5%	41.3%	7.5%
Connecticut		8		1,256,232	556,721	621,561	76,650	1,300	64,840	R	44.3%	49.5%	6.1%
Delaware	3			214,367	96,714	89,194	28,459		7,520	R	45.1%	41.6%	13.3%
Florida	14			2,187,805	886,804	676,794	624,207		210,010	R	40.5%	30.9%	28.5%
Georgia			12	1,250,266	380,111	334,440	535,550	165	155,439	A	30.4%	26.7%	42.8%
Hawaii				236,218	91,425	141,324	3,469		49,899	D	38.7%	59.8%	1.5%
Idaho	4	4		291,183	165,369	89,273	36,541		76,096	R	56.8%	30.7%	12.5%
Illinois	26			4,619,749	2,174,774	2,039,814	390,958	14,203	134,960	R	47.1%	44.2%	8.5%
Indiana	13			2,123,597	1,067,885	806,659	243,108	5,945	261,226	R	50.3%	38.0%	11.4%
Iowa	9			1,167,931	619,106	476,699	66,422	5,704	142,407	R	53.0%	40.8%	5.7%
Kansas	7			872,783	478,674	302,996	88,921	2,192	175,678	R	54.8%	34.7%	10.2%
Kentucky	9			1,055,893	462,411	397,541	193,098	2,843	64,870	R	43.8%	37.6%	18.3%
Louisiana			10	1,097,450	257,535	309,615	530,300		220,685	A	23.5%	28.2%	48.3%
Maine		4		392,936	169,254	217,312	6,370		48,058	D	43.1%	55.3%	1.6%
Maryland		10		1,235,039	517,995	538,310	178,734		20,315	D	41.9%	43.6%	14.5%
Massachusetts		14		2,331,752	766,844	1,469,218	87,088	8,602	702,374	D	32.9%	63.0%	3.7%
Michigan		21		3,306,250	1,370,665	1,593,082	331,968	10,535	222,417	D	41.5%	48.2%	10.0%
Minnesota		10		1,588,506	658,643	857,738	68,931	3,194	199,095	D	41.5%	54.0%	4.3%
Mississippi			7	654,509	88,516	150,644	415,349		264,705	A	13.5%	23.0%	63.5%
Missouri	12			1,809,502	811,932	791,444	206,126		20,488	R	44.9%	43.7%	11.4%
Montana	4			274,404	138,835	114,117	20,015	1,437	24,718	R	50.6%	41.6%	7.3%
Nebraska	5			536,851	321,163	170,784	44,904		150,379	R	59.8%	31.8%	8.4%
Nevada	3			154,218	73,188	60,598	20,432		12,590	R	47.5%	39.3%	13.2%
New Hampshire	4			297,298	154,903	130,589	11,173	633	24,314	R	52.1%	43.9%	3.8%
New Jersey	17			2,875,395	1,325,467	1,264,206	262,187	23,535	61,261	R	46.1%	44.0%	9.1%
New Mexico	4			327,350	169,692	130,081	25,737	1,840	39,611	R	51.8%	39.7%	7.9%
New York		43		6,791,688	3,007,932	3,378,470	358,864	46,422	370,538	D	44.3%	49.7%	5.3%
North Carolina	12		1	1,587,493	627,192	464,113	496,188		131,004	R	39.5%	29.2%	31.3%
North Dakota	4			247,882	138,669	94,769	14,244	200	43,900	R	55.9%	38.2%	5.7%
Ohio	26			3,959,698	1,791,014	1,700,586	467,495	603	90,428	R	45.2%	42.9%	11.8%
Oklahoma	8			943,086	449,697	301,658	191,731		148,039	R	47.7%	32.0%	20.3%
Oregon	6			819,622	408,433	358,866	49,683	2,640	49,567	R	49.8%	43.8%	6.1%
Pennsylvania		29		4,747,928	2,090,017	2,259,405	378,582	19,924	169,388	D	44.0%	47.6%	8.0%
Rhode Island		4		385,000	122,359	246,518	15,678	445	124,159	D	31.8%	64.0%	4.1%
South Carolina	8			666,978	254,062	197,486	215,430		38,632	R	38.1%	29.6%	32.3%
South Dakota	4			281,264	149,841	118,023	13,400		31,818	R	53.3%	42.0%	4.8%
Tennessee	11			1,248,617	472,592	351,233	424,792		47,800	R	37.8%	28.1%	34.0%
Texas		25		3,079,216	1,227,844	1,266,804	584,269	299	38,960	D	39.9%	41.1%	19.0%
Utah	4			422,568	238,728	156,665	26,906	269	82,063	R	56.5%	37.1%	6.4%
Vermont	3			161,404	85,142	70,255	5,104	903	14,887	R	52.8%	43.5%	3.2%
Virginia	12			1,361,491	590,319	442,387	321,833	6,952	147,932	R	43.4%	32.5%	23.6%
Washington		9		1,304,281	588,510	616,037	96,990	2,744	27,527	D	45.1%	47.2%	7.4%
West Virginia		7		754,206	307,555	374,091	72,560		66,536	D	40.8%	49.6%	9.6%
Wisconsin	12			1,691,538	809,997	748,804	127,835	4,902	61,193	R	47.9%	44.3%	7.6%
Wyoming	3			127,205	70,927	45,173	11,105		25,754	R	55.8%	35.5%	8.7%
Dist. of Col.		3		170,578	31,012	139,566			108,554	D	18.2%	81.8%	
United States	301	191	46	73,211,875	31,785,480	31,275,166	9,906,473	244,756	510,314	R	43.4%	42.7%	13.5%

PRESIDENT 1964

In New York the Democratic figure includes Liberal votes.

The full list of candidates for President and Vice President was:

43,129,566	Lyndon B. Johnson and Hubert H. Humphrey	Democratic
27,178,188	Barry M. Goldwater and William E. Miller	Republican
45,219	Eric Hass and Henning A. Blomen	Socialist Labor
32,720	Clifton DeBerry and Edward Shaw	Socialist Workers
23,267	E. Harold Munn and Mark R. Shaw	Prohibition
6,953	John Kasper and J.B. Stoner	National States Rights
5,060	Joseph B. Lightburn and T.C. Billings	Constitution
19	James Hensley and John O. Hopkins	Universal

In addition, 210,732 votes were cast in Alabama for an unpledged Democratic elector ticket and 12,868 scattered votes were reported from various states.

UNITED STATES

PRESIDENT 1964

State	Electoral Vote Rep.	Electoral Vote Dem.	Electoral Vote Other	Total Vote	Republican	Democratic	Other	Plurality		Percentage Total Vote Rep.	Percentage Total Vote Dem.	Percentage Major Vote Rep.	Percentage Major Vote Dem.
Alabama	10			689,818	479,085		210,733	479,085	R	69.5%		100.0%	
Alaska		3		67,259	22,930	44,329		21,399	D	34.1%	65.9%	34.1%	65.9%
Arizona	5			480,770	242,535	237,753	482	4,782	R	50.4%	49.5%	50.5%	49.5%
Arkansas		6		560,426	243,264	314,197	2,965	70,933	D	43.4%	56.1%	43.6%	56.4%
California		40		7,057,586	2,879,108	4,171,877	6,601	1,292,769	D	40.8%	59.1%	40.8%	59.2%
Colorado		6		776,986	296,767	476,024	4,195	179,257	D	38.2%	61.3%	38.4%	61.6%
Connecticut		8		1,218,578	390,996	826,269	1,313	435,273	D	32.1%	67.8%	32.1%	67.9%
Delaware		3		201,320	78,078	122,704	538	44,626	D	38.8%	60.9%	38.9%	61.1%
Florida		14		1,854,481	905,941	948,540		42,599	D	48.9%	51.1%	48.9%	51.1%
Georgia	12			1,139,335	616,584	522,556	195	94,028	R	54.1%	45.9%	54.1%	45.9%
Hawaii		4		207,271	44,022	163,249		119,227	D	21.2%	78.8%	21.2%	78.8%
Idaho		4		292,477	143,557	148,920		5,363	D	49.1%	50.9%	49.1%	50.9%
Illinois		26		4,702,841	1,905,946	2,796,833	62	890,887	D	40.5%	59.5%	40.5%	59.5%
Indiana		13		2,091,606	911,118	1,170,848	9,640	259,730	D	43.6%	56.0%	43.8%	56.2%
Iowa		9		1,184,539	449,148	733,030	2,361	283,882	D	37.9%	61.9%	38.0%	62.0%
Kansas		7		857,901	386,579	464,028	7,294	77,449	D	45.1%	54.1%	45.4%	54.6%
Kentucky		9		1,046,105	372,977	669,659	3,469	296,682	D	35.7%	64.0%	35.8%	64.2%
Louisiana	10			896,293	509,225	387,068		122,157	R	56.8%	43.2%	56.8%	43.2%
Maine		4		380,965	118,701	262,264		143,563	D	31.2%	68.8%	31.2%	68.8%
Maryland		10		1,116,457	385,495	730,912	50	345,417	D	34.5%	65.5%	34.5%	65.5%
Massachusetts		14		2,344,798	549,727	1,786,422	8,649	1,236,695	D	23.4%	76.2%	23.5%	76.5%
Michigan		21		3,203,102	1,060,152	2,136,615	6,335	1,076,463	D	33.1%	66.7%	33.2%	66.8%
Minnesota		10		1,554,462	559,624	991,117	3,721	431,493	D	36.0%	63.8%	36.1%	63.9%
Mississippi	7			409,146	356,528	52,618		303,910	R	87.1%	12.9%	87.1%	12.9%
Missouri		12		1,817,879	653,535	1,164,344		510,809	D	36.0%	64.0%	36.0%	64.0%
Montana		4		278,628	113,032	164,246	1,350	51,214	D	40.6%	58.9%	40.8%	59.2%
Nebraska		5		584,154	276,847	307,307		30,460	D	47.4%	52.6%	47.4%	52.6%
Nevada		3		135,433	56,094	79,339		23,245	D	41.4%	58.6%	41.4%	58.6%
New Hampshire		4		288,093	104,029	184,064		80,035	D	36.1%	63.9%	36.1%	63.9%
New Jersey		17		2,847,663	964,174	1,868,231	15,258	904,057	D	33.9%	65.6%	34.0%	66.0%
New Mexico		4		328,645	132,838	194,015	1,792	61,177	D	40.4%	59.0%	40.6%	59.4%
New York		43		7,166,275	2,243,559	4,913,102	9,614	2,669,543	D	31.3%	68.6%	31.3%	68.7%
North Carolina		13		1,424,983	624,844	800,139		175,295	D	43.8%	56.2%	43.8%	56.2%
North Dakota		4		258,389	108,207	149,784	398	41,577	D	41.9%	58.0%	41.9%	58.1%
Ohio		26		3,969,196	1,470,865	2,498,331		1,027,466	D	37.1%	62.9%	37.1%	62.9%
Oklahoma		8		932,499	412,665	519,834		107,169	D	44.3%	55.7%	44.3%	55.7%
Oregon		6		786,305	282,779	501,017	2,509	218,238	D	36.0%	63.7%	36.1%	63.9%
Pennsylvania		29		4,822,690	1,673,657	3,130,954	18,079	1,457,297	D	34.7%	64.9%	34.8%	65.2%
Rhode Island		4		390,091	74,615	315,463	13	240,848	D	19.1%	80.9%	19.1%	80.9%
South Carolina	8			524,779	309,048	215,723	8	93,325	R	58.9%	41.1%	58.9%	41.1%
South Dakota		4		293,118	130,108	163,010		32,902	D	44.4%	55.6%	44.4%	55.6%
Tennessee		11		1,143,946	508,965	634,947	34	125,982	D	44.5%	55.5%	44.5%	55.5%
Texas		25		2,626,811	958,566	1,663,185	5,060	704,619	D	36.5%	63.3%	36.6%	63.4%
Utah		4		401,413	181,785	219,628		37,843	D	45.3%	54.7%	45.3%	54.7%
Vermont		3		163,089	54,942	108,127	20	53,185	D	33.7%	66.3%	33.7%	66.3%
Virginia		12		1,042,267	481,334	558,038	2,895	76,704	D	46.2%	53.5%	46.3%	53.7%
Washington		9		1,258,556	470,366	779,881	8,309	309,515	D	37.4%	62.0%	37.6%	62.4%
West Virginia		7		792,040	253,953	538,087		284,134	D	32.1%	67.9%	32.1%	67.9%
Wisconsin		12		1,691,815	638,495	1,050,424	2,896	411,929	D	37.7%	62.1%	37.8%	62.2%
Wyoming		3		142,716	61,998	80,718		18,720	D	43.4%	56.6%	43.4%	56.6%
Dist. of Col.		3		198,597	28,801	169,796		140,995	D	14.5%	85.5%	14.5%	85.5%
United States	52	486		70,644,592	27,178,188	43,129,566	336,838	15,951,378	D	38.5%	61.1%	38.7%	61.3%

PRESIDENT 1960

Senator Harry Flood Byrd received 15 votes for President in the Electoral College; these were the votes of 6 of the 11 Democratic electors in Alabama, all 8 unpledged Democratic electors in Mississippi, and one of the 8 Republican electors in Oklahoma. The Alabama and Mississippi electors also cast 14 votes for Senator Strom Thurmond for Vice President; the single Oklahoma elector voted for Senator Barry M. Goldwater for Vice President.

In New York the Democratic figure includes Liberal votes.

The full list of candidates for President and Vice President was:

34,226,731	John F. Kennedy and Lyndon B. Johnson	Democratic
34,108,157	Richard M. Nixon and Henry Cabot Lodge	Republican
47,522	Eric Hass and Georgia Cozzini	Socialist Labor
46,203	Rutherford L. Decker and E. Harold Munn	Prohibition
44,977	Orval E. Faubus and John G. Crommelin	National States Rights
40,165	Farrell Dobbs and Myra Tanner Weiss	Socialist Workers
18,162	Charles L. Sullivan and Merritt B. Curtis	Constitution
8,708	J. Bracken Lee and Kent H. Courtney	Conservative
4,204	C. Benton Coiner and Edward J. Silverman	Conservative
1,767	Lar Daly and B.M. Miller	Tax Cut
1,485	Clennon King and Reginald Carter	Independent Afro-American
1,401	Merritt B. Curtis and B.M. Miller	Constitution

In addition, 169,572 votes were cast in Louisiana for Independent electors and 116,248 in Mississippi for an unpledged Democratic elector ticket. Another 539 votes were cast in Michigan for an Independent American ticket and 2,378 scattered votes were reported from various states.

UNITED STATES

PRESIDENT 1960

State	Electoral Vote Rep.	Electoral Vote Dem.	Electoral Vote Other	Total Vote	Republican	Democratic	Other	Plurality		Percentage Total Vote Rep.	Percentage Total Vote Dem.	Percentage Major Vote Rep.	Percentage Major Vote Dem.
Alabama		5	6	570,225	237,981	324,050	8,194	86,069	D	41.7%	56.8%	42.3%	57.7%
Alaska	3			60,762	30,953	29,809		1,144	R	50.9%	49.1%	50.9%	49.1%
Arizona	4			398,491	221,241	176,781	469	44,460	R	55.5%	44.4%	55.6%	44.4%
Arkansas		8		428,509	184,508	215,049	28,952	30,541	D	43.1%	50.2%	46.2%	53.8%
California	32			6,506,578	3,259,722	3,224,099	22,757	35,623	R	50.1%	49.6%	50.3%	49.7%
Colorado	6			736,236	402,242	330,629	3,365	71,613	R	54.6%	44.9%	54.9%	45.1%
Connecticut		8		1,222,883	565,813	657,055	15	91,242	D	46.3%	53.7%	46.3%	53.7%
Delaware		3		196,683	96,373	99,590	720	3,217	D	49.0%	50.6%	49.2%	50.8%
Florida	10			1,544,176	795,476	748,700		46,776	R	51.5%	48.5%	51.5%	48.5%
Georgia		12		733,349	274,472	458,638	239	184,166	D	37.4%	62.5%	37.4%	62.6%
Hawaii		3		184,705	92,295	92,410		115	D	50.0%	50.0%	50.0%	50.0%
Idaho	4			300,450	161,597	138,853		22,744	R	53.8%	46.2%	53.8%	46.2%
Illinois		27		4,757,409	2,368,988	2,377,846	10,575	8,858	D	49.8%	50.0%	49.9%	50.1%
Indiana	13			2,135,360	1,175,120	952,358	7,882	222,762	R	55.0%	44.6%	55.2%	44.8%
Iowa	10			1,273,810	722,381	550,565	864	171,816	R	56.7%	43.2%	56.7%	43.3%
Kansas	8			928,825	561,474	363,213	4,138	198,261	R	60.4%	39.1%	60.7%	39.3%
Kentucky	10			1,124,462	602,607	521,855		80,752	R	53.6%	46.4%	53.6%	46.4%
Louisiana		10		807,891	230,980	407,339	169,572	176,359	D	28.6%	50.4%	36.2%	63.8%
Maine	5			421,767	240,608	181,159		59,449	R	57.0%	43.0%	57.0%	43.0%
Maryland		9		1,055,349	489,538	565,808	3	76,270	D	46.4%	53.6%	46.4%	53.6%
Massachusetts		16		2,469,480	976,750	1,487,174	5,556	510,424	D	39.6%	60.2%	39.6%	60.4%
Michigan		20		3,318,097	1,620,428	1,687,269	10,400	66,841	D	48.8%	50.9%	49.0%	51.0%
Minnesota		11		1,541,887	757,915	779,933	4,039	22,018	D	49.2%	50.6%	49.3%	50.7%
Mississippi			8	298,171	73,561	108,362	116,248	34,801	D	24.7%	36.3%	40.4%	59.6%
Missouri		13		1,934,422	962,221	972,201		9,980	D	49.7%	50.3%	49.7%	50.3%
Montana	4			277,579	141,841	134,891	847	6,950	R	51.1%	48.6%	51.3%	48.7%
Nebraska	6			613,095	380,553	232,542		148,011	R	62.1%	37.9%	62.1%	37.9%
Nevada		3		107,267	52,387	54,880		2,493	D	48.8%	51.2%	48.8%	51.2%
New Hampshire	4			295,761	157,989	137,772		20,217	R	53.4%	46.6%	53.4%	46.6%
New Jersey		16		2,773,111	1,363,324	1,385,415	24,372	22,091	D	49.2%	50.0%	49.6%	50.4%
New Mexico		4		311,107	153,733	156,027	1,347	2,294	D	49.4%	50.2%	49.6%	50.4%
New York		45		7,291,079	3,446,419	3,830,085	14,575	383,666	D	47.3%	52.5%	47.4%	52.6%
North Carolina		14		1,368,556	655,420	713,136		57,716	D	47.9%	52.1%	47.9%	52.1%
North Dakota	4			278,431	154,310	123,963	158	30,347	R	55.4%	44.5%	55.5%	44.5%
Ohio	25			4,161,859	2,217,611	1,944,248		273,363	R	53.3%	46.7%	53.3%	46.7%
Oklahoma	7		1	903,150	533,039	370,111		162,928	R	59.0%	41.0%	59.0%	41.0%
Oregon	6			776,421	408,060	367,402	959	40,658	R	52.6%	47.3%	52.6%	47.4%
Pennsylvania		32		5,006,541	2,439,956	2,556,282	10,303	116,326	D	48.7%	51.1%	48.8%	51.2%
Rhode Island		4		405,535	147,502	258,032	1	110,530	D	36.4%	63.6%	36.4%	63.6%
South Carolina		8		386,688	188,558	198,129	1	9,571	D	48.8%	51.2%	48.8%	51.2%
South Dakota	4			306,487	178,417	128,070		50,347	R	58.2%	41.8%	58.2%	41.8%
Tennessee	11			1,051,792	556,577	481,453	13,762	75,124	R	52.9%	45.8%	53.6%	46.4%
Texas		24		2,311,084	1,121,310	1,167,567	22,207	46,257	D	48.5%	50.5%	49.0%	51.0%
Utah	4			374,709	205,361	169,248	100	36,113	R	54.8%	45.2%	54.8%	45.2%
Vermont	3			167,324	98,131	69,186	7	28,945	R	58.6%	41.3%	58.6%	41.4%
Virginia	12			771,449	404,521	362,327	4,601	42,194	R	52.4%	47.0%	52.8%	47.2%
Washington	9			1,241,572	629,273	599,298	13,001	29,975	R	50.7%	48.3%	51.2%	48.8%
West Virginia		8		837,781	395,995	441,786		45,791	D	47.3%	52.7%	47.3%	52.7%
Wisconsin	12			1,729,082	895,175	830,805	3,102	64,370	R	51.8%	48.0%	51.9%	48.1%
Wyoming	3			140,782	77,451	63,331		14,120	R	55.0%	45.0%	55.0%	45.0%
Dist. of Col.													
United States	219	303	15	68,838,219	34,108,157	34,226,731	503,331	118,574	D	49.5%	49.7%	49.9%	50.1%

2000 PRESIDENTIAL PRIMARIES

In 2000 42 states and the District of Columbia held presidential primaries, in which at least one of the parties held contests where voters balloted directly for candidates or for a statewide slate of delegates that was pledged to a candidate. In addition, there was a Republican primary in New York where delegates were elected on a congressional district basis.

The list below, alphabetical by state, lists primary vote totals for all candidates. The tables on pages 42 and 44 give a chronological list of the primary votes for those candidates in the Democratic and Republican parties who received at least 100,000 votes nationwide.

Republican candidates on the ballot in at least one state were: James Attia, Gary Bauer, Samuel H. Berry Jr., George W. Bush, Kenneth A. Capalbo, Steve Forbes, Mark "Dick" Harnes, Orrin G. Hatch, Lawrence L. Hornung, Alan Keyes, Andy Martin, John McCain, John R. McGrath, Timothy Lee Mosby, Tom Oyler, Richard C. Peet, Chuck See, Charles Bass Urban, Dorian Yeager, and James T. Zanon.

Democratic candidates on the ballot in at least one state were: Bill Bradley, Charles Buckley, Willie F. Carter, Thomas Coos, Randolph "Randy" W. Crow, John B. Eaton, Al Gore, Mark Greenstein, Vincent S. Hamm, Heather Harder, Lyndon H. LaRouche Jr., Angus Wheeler McDonald, Nathaniel Thomas Mullins, Edward T. O'Donnell Jr., Jeffrey B. Peters, Pat Price, Michael Skok, and Jim Taylor.

ALABAMA JUNE 6

Republican   171,077 Bush; 23,394 Keyes; 8,608 Uncommitted.

Democratic   214,541 Gore; 48,521 Uncommitted; 15,456 LaRouche.

ARIZONA

Republican (February 22)   193,708 McCain; 115,115 Bush; 11,500 Keyes; 1,211 Forbes; 637 Hatch; 239 McGrath; 177 Bauer; 54 Zanon; 28 See.

Democratic (March 11)   67,582 Gore; 16,383 Bradley; 1,439 No Preference; 1,358 Harder.

ARKANSAS MAY 23

Republican   35,759 Bush; 8,814 Keyes.

Democratic   193,750 Gore; 53,150 LaRouche.

CALIFORNIA MARCH 7 (SEE PAGE 86)

Republican   1,725,162 Bush; 988,706 McCain; 112,747 Keyes; 8,449 Forbes; 6,860 Bauer; 5,997 Hatch.

Democratic   2,155,321 Gore; 482,882 Bradley; 15,911 LaRouche.

COLORADO MARCH 10

Republican   116,897 Bush; 48,996 McCain; 11,871 Keyes; 1,197 Forbes; 1,190 Bauer; 504 Hatch.

Democratic   63,384 Gore; 20,663 Bradley; 3,867 Non-committed; 821 LaRouche.

2000 PRESIDENTIAL PRIMARIES

CONNECTICUT MARCH 7

Republican   87,176 McCain; 82,881 Bush; 5,913 Keyes; 1,242 Forbes; 1,222 Uncommitted; 373 Bauer; 178 Hatch.

Democratic   98,312 Gore; 73,589 Bradley; 5,400 Uncommitted.

DELAWARE

Republican
(February 8)   15,250 Bush; 7,638 McCain; 5,883 Forbes; 1,148 Keyes; 120 Bauer; 21 Hatch.

Democratic
(February 5)   6,377 Gore; 4,476 Bradley; 288 LaRouche.

FLORIDA MARCH 14

Republican   516,263 Bush; 139,465 McCain; 32,354 Keyes; 6,553 Forbes; 3,496 Bauer; 1,372 Hatch.

Democratic   451,718 Gore; 100,277 Bradley.

GEORGIA MARCH 7

Republican   430,480 Bush; 179,046 McCain; 29,640 Keyes; 1,962 Bauer; 1,647 Forbes; 413 Hatch.

Democratic   238,396 Gore; 46,035 Bradley.

IDAHO MAY 23

Republican   116,385 Bush; 30,263 Keyes; 11,798 None of the Names Shown.

Democratic   27,025 Gore; 5,722 None of the Names Shown; 2,941 LaRouche.

ILLINOIS MARCH 21

Republican   496,685 Bush; 158,768 McCain; 66,066 Keyes; 10,334 Forbes; 5,068 Bauer.

Democratic   682,932 Gore; 115,320 Bradley; 11,415 LaRouche.

INDIANA MAY 2

Republican   330,095 Bush; 76,569 McCain.

Democratic   219,604 Gore; 64,339 Bradley; 9,229 LaRouche.

KENTUCKY MAY 23

Republican   75,783 Bush; 5,780 McCain; 4,337 Keyes; 2,408 Bauer; 1,829 Uncommitted; 1,186 Forbes.

Democratic   156,966 Gore; 32,340 Bradley; 26,046 Uncommitted; 4,927 LaRouche.

LOUISIANA MARCH 14

Republican   86,038 Bush; 9,165 McCain; 5,900 Keyes; 1,041 Forbes; 768 Bauer.

Democratic   114,942 Gore; 31,385 Bradley; 6,127 LaRouche; 5,097 Crow.

2000 PRESIDENTIAL PRIMARIES

MAINE MARCH 7

Republican   49,308 Bush; 42,510 McCain; 2,989 Keyes; 1,038 Uncommitted; 455 Forbes; 324 Bauer.

Democratic   34,725 Gore; 26,520 Bradley; 2,634 Uncommitted; 208 LaRouche; 192 Epstein.

MARYLAND MARCH 7

Republican   211,439 Bush; 135,981 McCain; 25,020 Keyes; 1,678 Forbes; 1,328 Bauer; 588 Hatch.

Democratic   341,630 Gore; 144,387 Bradley; 16,935 Uncommitted; 4,510 LaRouche.

MASSACHUSETTS MARCH 7

Republican   324,708 McCain; 159,534 Bush; 12,630 Keyes; 1,744 Bauer; 1,407 Forbes; 1,292 No Preference; 262 Hatch; 374 Write-in.

Democratic   341,586 Gore; 212,452 Bradley; 11,281 No Preference; 2,135 LaRouche; 2,620 Write-in.

MICHIGAN FEBRUARY 22

Republican   650,805 McCain; 549,665 Bush; 59,032 Keyes; 8,714 Uncommitted; 4,894 Forbes; 2,733 Bauer; 905 Hatch; 22 Schriner (Write-in).

Democratic   31,655 Uncommitted; 13,195 LaRouche.

MISSISSIPPI MARCH 14

Republican   101,042 Bush; 6,478 Keyes; 6,263 McCain; 588 Forbes; 475 Bauer; 133 Hatch.

Democratic   79,408 Gore; 7,621 Bradley; 1,573 LaRouche.

MISSOURI MARCH 7

Republican   275,366 Bush; 167,831 McCain; 27,282 Keyes; 2,044 Forbes; 1,345 Uncommitted; 1,038 Bauer; 363 Hatch; 94 Hornung.

Democratic   171,562 Gore; 89,092 Bradley; 3,364 Uncommitted; 906 LaRouche; 565 Price.

MONTANA JUNE 6

Republican   88,194 Bush; 20,822 Keyes; 4,655 No Preference; 2 John McCain (Write-in).

Democratic   68,420 Gore; 19,447 No Preference.

NEBRASKA MAY 9

Republican   145,176 Bush; 28,065 McCain; 12,073 Keyes; 444 Write-in.

Democratic   73,639 Gore; 27,884 Bradley; 3,191 LaRouche; 557 Write-in.

2000 PRESIDENTIAL PRIMARIES

NEW HAMPSHIRE FEBRUARY 1

Republican   115,606 McCain; 72,330 Bush; 30,166 Forbes; 15,179 Keyes; 1,640 Bauer; 163 Hatch; 98 Yeager; 81 Martin; 61 Berry; 51 Capalbo; 41 Mosby; 34 Harnes; 23 Peet; 14 Oyler; 2,719 Write-in.

Democratic   76,897 Gore; 70,502 Bradley; 322 Buckley; 192 Harder; 156 Peters; 134 Eaton; 124 LaRouche; 87 Taylor; 75 Greenstein; 35 Mullins; 35 O'Donnell; 30 Carter; 29 Crow; 22 Hamm; 19 Koos; 18 Skok; 5,962 Write-in.

NEW JERSEY JUNE 6

Republican   201,209 Bush; 39,601 Keyes.

Democratic   358,951 Gore; 19,321 LaRouche.

NEW MEXICO JUNE 6

Republican   62,161 Bush; 7,619 McCain; 4,850 Keyes; 600 Uncommitted delegates.

Democratic   98,715 Gore; 27,204 Bradley; 3,298 Uncommitted delegates; 3,063 LaRouche.

NEW YORK MARCH 7

Republican   Voting by congressional districts for delegates. See p. 326.

Democratic   639,417 Gore; 326,038 Bradley; 9,008 LaRouche.

NORTH CAROLINA MAY 2

Republican   253,485 Bush; 35,018 McCain; 25,320 Keyes; 5,383 No Preference; 3,311 Gary Bauer.

Democratic   383,696 Gore; 99,796 Bradley; 49,905 No Preference; 11,525 LaRouche.

OHIO MARCH 7

Republican   810,369 Bush; 516,790 McCain; 55,266 Keyes; 8,934 Forbes; 6,169 Bauer.

Democratic   720,311 Gore; 241,688 Bradley; 16,513 LaRouche.

OKLAHOMA MARCH 14

Republican   98,781 Bush; 12,973 McCain; 11,595 Keyes; 1,066 Forbes; 394 Bauer.

Democratic   92,654 Gore; 34,311 Bradley; 7,885 LaRouche.

OREGON MAY 16

Republican   292,522 Bush; 46,764 Keyes; 10,545 Write-in.

Democratic   300,922 Gore; 38,521 LaRouche; 15,151 Write-in.

2000 PRESIDENTIAL PRIMARIES

PENNSYLVANIA APRIL 4

Republican   472,398 Bush; 145,719 McCain; 16,162 Forbes; 8,806 Bauer; 7,100 Keyes (write-in); 1,624 Write-in.

Democratic   525,306 Gore; 146,797 Bradley; 32,047 LaRouche; 3,840 Write-in.

RHODE ISLAND MARCH 7

Republican   21,754 McCain; 13,170 Bush; 923 Keyes; 114 Uncommitted; 89 Forbes; 35 Bauer; 35 Hatch; 23 Write-in.

Democratic   26,801 Gore; 19,000 Bradley; 844 Uncommitted; 199 LaRouche; 235 Write-in.

SOUTH CAROLINA FEBRUARY 19

Republican   305,998 Bush; 239,964 McCain; 25,996 Keyes; 618 Bauer; 449 Forbes; 76 Hatch.

Democratic   No presidential primary.

SOUTH DAKOTA JUNE 6

Republican   35,418 Bush; 6,228 McCain; 3,478 Keyes; 155 Attia.

Democratic   No Democratic primary.

TENNESSEE MARCH 14

Republican   193,166 Bush; 36,436 McCain; 16,916 Keyes; 1,623 Uncommitted; 1,305 Bauer; 1,018 Forbes; 252 Hatch; 75 Write-in.

Democratic   198,264 Gore; 11,323 Bradley; 4,407 Uncommitted; 1,031 LaRouche; 178 Write-in.

TEXAS MARCH 14

Republican   986,416 Bush; 80,082 McCain; 43,518 Keyes; 9,570 Uncommitted; 2,865 Forbes; 2,189 Bauer; 1,324 Hatch; 793 Urban.

Democratic   631,428 Gore; 128,564 Bradley; 26,898 LaRouche.

UTAH MARCH 10

Republican   57,617 Bush; 19,367 Keyes; 12,784 McCain; 859 Forbes; 426 Bauer.

Democratic   12,527 Gore; 3,160 Bradley.

VERMONT MARCH 7

Republican   49,045 McCain; 28,741 Bush; 2,164 Keyes; 616 Forbes; 293 Bauer; 496 Write-in.

Democratic   26,774 Gore; 21,629 Bradley; 355 LaRouche; 525 Write-in.

VIRGINIA FEBRUARY 29

Republican   350,588 Bush; 291,488 McCain; 20,356 Keyes; 852 Bauer; 809 Forbes.

Democratic   No Democratic primary.

2000 PRESIDENTIAL PRIMARIES

WASHINGTON FEBRUARY 29

Republican   284,053 Bush; 191,101 McCain; 11,753 Keyes; 1,749 Forbes; 1,469 Bauer; 1,023 Hatch.

Democratic   202,456 Gore; 93,375 Bradley; 1,170 LaRouche.

WEST VIRGINIA MAY 9

Republican   87,050 Bush; 14,121 McCain; 5,210 Keyes; 1,733 Forbes; 1,290 Bauer.

Democratic   182,403 Gore; 46,710 Bradley; 19,374 McDonald; 4,823 LaRouche.

WISCONSIN APRIL 4

Republican   343,292 Bush; 89,684 McCain; 48,919 Keyes; 5,505 Forbes; 3,452 Uninstructed Delegation; 1,813 Bauer; 1,712 Hatch; 1,392 Write-in.

Democratic   328,682 Gore; 32,560 Bradley; 4,105 Uninstructed Delegation; 3,743 LaRouche; 2,106 Write-in.

DISTRICT OF COLUMBIA MAY 2

Republican   1,771 Bush; 593 McCain; 69 Write-in.

Democratic   18,621 Gore; 796 LaRouche.

2000 REPUBLICAN PREFERENCE PRIMARIES

Date		State	Total Vote	Bush	Forbes	Keyes	McCain	Other
Feb.	1	New Hampshire	238,206	72,330	30,166	15,179	115,606	4,925
				30.4%	**12.7%**	**6.4%**	**48.5%**	**2.1%**
Feb.	8	Delaware	30,060	15,250	5,883	1,148	7,638	141
				50.7%	**19.6%**	**3.8%**	**25.4%**	**0.5%**
Feb.	19	South Carolina	573,101	305,998	449	25,996	239,964	694
				53.4%	**0.1%**	**4.5%**	**41.9%**	**0.1%**
Feb.	22	Arizona	322,669	115,115	1,211	11,500	193,708	1,135
				35.7%	**0.4%**	**3.6%**	**60.0%**	**0.4%**
Feb.	22	Michigan	1,276,770	549,665	4,894	59,032	650,805	12,374
				43.1%	**0.4%**	**4.6%**	**51.0%**	**1.0%**
Feb.	29	Virginia	664,093	350,588	809	20,356	291,488	852
				52.8%	**0.1%**	**3.1%**	**43.9%**	**0.1%**
Feb.	29	Washington	491,148	284,053	1,749	11,753	191,101	2,492
				57.8%	**0.4%**	**2.4%**	**38.9%**	**0.5%**
March	7	California	2,847,921	1,725,162	8,449	112,747	988,706	12,857
				60.6%	**0.3%**	**4.0%**	**34.7%**	**0.5%**
	7	Connecticut	178,985	82,881	1,242	5,913	87,176	1,773
				46.3%	**0.7%**	**3.3%**	**48.7%**	**1.0%**
	7	Georgia	643,188	430,480	1,647	29,640	179,046	2,375
				66.9%	**0.3%**	**4.6%**	**27.8%**	**0.4%**
	7	Maine	96,624	49,308	455	2,989	42,510	1,362
				51.0%	**0.5%**	**3.1%**	**44.0%**	**1.4%**
	7	Maryland	376,034	211,439	1,678	25,020	135,981	1,916
				56.2%	**0.4%**	**6.7%**	**36.2%**	**0.5%**
	7	Massachusetts	501,951	159,534	1,407	12,630	324,708	3,672
				31.8%	**0.3%**	**2.5%**	**64.7%**	**0.7%**
	7	Missouri	475,363	275,366	2,044	27,282	167,831	2,840
				57.9%	**0.4%**	**5.7%**	**35.3%**	**0.6%**
	7	New York	See page 326					
	7	Ohio	1,397,528	810,369	8,934	55,266	516,790	6,169
				58.0%	**0.6%**	**4.0%**	**37.0%**	**0.4%**
	7	Rhode Island	36,143	13,170	89	923	21,754	207
				36.4%	**0.2%**	**2.6%**	**60.2%**	**0.6%**
	7	Vermont	81,355	28,741	616	2,164	49,045	789
				35.3%	**0.8%**	**2.7%**	**60.3%**	**1.0%**
	10	Colorado	180,655	116,897	1,197	11,871	48,996	1,694
				64.7%	**0.7%**	**6.6%**	**27.1%**	**0.9%**
	10	Utah	91,053	57,617	859	19,367	12,784	426
				63.3%	**0.9%**	**21.3%**	**14.0%**	**0.5%**
	14	Florida	699,503	516,263	6,553	32,354	139,465	4,868
				73.8%	**0.9%**	**4.6%**	**19.9%**	**0.7%**
	14	Louisiana	102,912	86,038	1,041	5,900	9,165	768
				83.6%	**1.0%**	**5.7%**	**8.9%**	**0.7%**
	14	Mississippi	114,979	101,042	588	6,478	6,263	608
				87.9%	**0.5%**	**5.6%**	**5.4%**	**0.5%**
	14	Oklahoma	124,809	98,781	1,066	11,595	12,973	394
				79.1%	**0.9%**	**9.3%**	**10.4%**	**0.3%**
	14	Tennessee	250,791	193,166	1,018	16,916	36,436	3,255
				77.0%	**0.4%**	**6.7%**	**14.5%**	**1.3%**
	14	Texas	1,126,757	986,416	—	43,518	80,082	16,741
				87.5%	**—**	**3.9%**	**7.1%**	**1.5%**
	21	Illinois	736,921	496,685	10,334	66,066	158,768	5,068
				67.4%	**1.4%**	**9.0%**	**21.5%**	**0.7%**
April	4	Pennsylvania	651,809	472,398	16,162	7,100	145,719	10,430
				72.5%	**2.5%**	**1.1%**	**22.4%**	**1.6%**
	4	Wisconsin	495,769	343,292	5,505	48,919	89,684	8,369
				69.2%	**1.1%**	**9.9%**	**18.1%**	**1.7%**

2000 REPUBLICAN PREFERENCE PRIMARIES

Date		State	Total Vote	Bush	Forbes	Keyes	McCain	Other
May	2	District of Columbia	2,433	1,771			593	69
				72.8%	**—**	**—**	**24.4%**	**2.8%**
	2	Indiana	406,664	330,095			76,569	
				81.2%	**—**	**—**	**18.8%**	**—**
	2	North Carolina	322,517	253,485		25,320	35,018	8,694
				78.6%	**—**	**7.9%**	**10.9%**	**2.7%**
May	9	Nebraska	185,758	145,176		12,073	28,065	444
				78.2%	**—**	**6.5%**	**15.1%**	**0.2%**
	9	West Virginia	109,404	87,050	1,733	5,210	14,121	1,290
				79.6%	**1.6%**	**4.8%**	**12.9%**	**1.2%**
May	16	Oregon	349,831	292,522	10,545	46,764		
				83.6%	**3.0%**	**13.4%**	**—**	**—**
May	23	Arkansas	44,573	35,759		8,814		
				80.2%	**—**	**19.8%**	**—**	**—**
	23	Idaho	158,446	116,385		30,263		11,798
				73.5%	**—**	**19.1%**	**—**	**7.4%**
	23	Kentucky	91,323	75,783	1,186	4,337	5,780	4,237
				83.0%	**1.3%**	**4.7%**	**6.3%**	**4.6%**
June	6	Alabama	203,079	171,077		23,394		8,608
				84.2%	**—**	**11.5%**	**—**	**4.2%**
	6	Montana	113,673	88,194		20,822	2	4,655
				77.6%	**—**	**18.3%**	**—**	**4.1%**
	6	New Jersey	240,810	201,209		39,601		
				83.6%	**—**	**16.4%**	**—**	**—**
	6	New Mexico	75,230	62,161		4,850	7,619	600
				82.6%	**—**	**6.4%**	**10.1%**	**0.8%**
	6	South Dakota	45,279	35,418		3,478	6,228	155
				78.2%	**—**	**7.7%**	**13.8%**	**0.3%**
			17,156,117	**10,844,129**	**129,509**	**914,548**	**5,118,187**	**149,744**

2000 DEMOCRATIC PREFERENCE PRIMARIES

Date	State	Total Vote	Bradley	Gore	LaRouche	Other
Feb. 1	New Hampshire	154,639	70,502 **45.6%**	76,897 **49.7%**	124 **0.1%**	7,116 **4.6%**
Feb. 5	Delaware	11,141	4,476 **40.2%**	6,377 **57.2%**	288 **2.6%**	— **—**
Feb. 22	Michigan	44,850	— **—**	— **—**	13,195 **29.4%**	31,655 **70.6%**
Feb. 29	Washington	297,001	93,375 **31.4%**	202,456 **68.2%**	1,170 **0.4%**	— **—**
March 7	California	2,654,114	482,882 **18.2%**	2,155,321 **81.2%**	15,911 **0.6%**	— **—**
7	Connecticut	177,301	73,589 **41.5%**	98,312 **55.4%**	— **—**	5,400 **3.0%**
7	Georgia	284,431	46,035 **16.2%**	238,396 **83.8%**	— **—**	— **—**
7	Maine	64,279	26,520 **41.3%**	34,725 **54.0%**	208 **0.3%**	2,826 **4.4%**
7	Maryland	507,462	144,387 **28.5%**	341,630 **67.3%**	4,510 **0.9%**	16,935 **3.3%**
7	Massachusetts	570,074	212,452 **37.3%**	341,586 **59.9%**	2,135 **0.4%**	13,901 **2.4%**
7	Missouri	265,489	89,092 **33.6%**	171,562 **64.6%**	906 **0.3%**	3,929 **1.5%**
7	New York	974,463	326,038 **33.5%**	639,417 **65.6%**	9,008 **0.9%**	— **—**
7	Ohio	978,512	241,688 **24.7%**	720,311 **73.6%**	16,513 **1.7%**	— **—**
7	Rhode Island	47,079	19,000 **40.4%**	26,801 **56.9%**	199 **0.4%**	1,079 **2.3%**
7	Vermont	49,283	21,629 **43.9%**	26,774 **54.3%**	355 **0.7%**	525 **1.1%**
10	Colorado	88,735	20,663 **23.3%**	63,384 **71.4%**	821 **0.9%**	3,867 **4.4%**
10	Utah	15,687	3,160 **20.1%**	12,527 **79.9%**	— **—**	— **—**
11	Arizona	86,762	16,383 **18.9%**	67,582 **77.9%**	— **—**	2,797 **3.2%**
14	Florida	551,995	100,277 **18.2%**	451,718 **81.8%**	— **—**	— **—**
14	Louisiana	157,551	31,385 **19.9%**	114,942 **73.0%**	6,127 **3.9%**	5,097 **3.2%**
14	Mississippi	88,602	7,621 **8.6%**	79,408 **89.6%**	1,573 **1.8%**	— **—**
14	Oklahoma	134,850	34,311 **25.4%**	92,654 **68.7%**	7,885 **5.8%**	— **—**
14	Tennessee	215,203	11,323 **5.3%**	198,264 **92.1%**	1,031 **0.5%**	4,585 **2.1%**
14	Texas	786,890	128,564 **16.3%**	631,428 **80.2%**	26,898 **3.4%**	— **—**
21	Illinois	809,667	115,320 **14.2%**	682,932 **84.3%**	11,415 **1.4%**	— **—**
April 4	Pennsylvania	707,990	146,797 **20.7%**	525,306 **74.2%**	32,047 **4.5%**	3,840 **0.5%**
4	Wisconsin	371,196	32,560 **8.8%**	328,682 **88.5%**	3,743 **1.0%**	6,211 **1.7%**
May 2	District of Columbia	19,417	— **—**	18,621 **95.9%**	796 **4.1%**	— **—**
2	Indiana	293,172	64,339 **21.9%**	219,604 **74.9%**	9,229 **3.1%**	— **—**

2000 DEMOCRATIC PREFERENCE PRIMARIES

Date		State	Total Vote	Bradley	Gore	LaRouche	Other
	2	North Carolina	544,922	99,796	383,696	11,525	49,905
				18.3%	**70.4%**	**2.1%**	**9.2%**
May	9	Nebraska	105,271	27,884	73,639	3,191	557
				26.5%	**70.0%**	**3.0%**	**0.5%**
	9	West Virginia	253,310	46,710	182,403	4,823	19,374
				18.4%	**72.0%**	**1.9%**	**7.6%**
May	16	Oregon	354,594	—	300,922	38,521	15,151
				—	**84.9%**	**10.9%**	**4.3%**
May	23	Arkansas	246,900	—	193,750	53,150	—
				—	**78.5%**	**21.5%**	—
	23	Idaho	35,688	—	27,025	2,941	5,722
				—	**75.7%**	**8.2%**	**16.0%**
	23	Kentucky	220,279	32,340	156,966	4,927	26,046
				14.7%	**71.3%**	**2.2%**	**11.8%**
June	6	Alabama	278,527	—	214,541	15,465	48,521
				—	**77.0%**	**5.6%**	**17.4%**
	6	Montana	87,867	—	68,420	—	19,447
				—	**77.9%**	—	**22.1%**
	6	New Jersey	378,272	—	358,951	19,321	—
				—	**94.9%**	**5.1%**	—
	6	New Mexico	132,280	27,204	98,715	3,063	3,298
				20.6%	**74.6%**	**2.3%**	**2.5%**
			14,045,745	**2,798,302**	**10,626,645**	**323,014**	**297,784**

ALABAMA

GOVERNOR
Don Siegelman (D). Elected 1998 to a four-year term.

SENATORS
Jeff Sessions (R). Elected 1996 to a six-year term.

Richard C. Shelby (R). Re-elected 1998 to a six-year term. Previously elected 1992, 1986. Changed party affiliation from Democrat to Republican in November 1994.

REPRESENTATIVES
1. H. L. Callahan (R)
2. Terry Everett (R)
3. Bob Riley (R)
4. Robert B. Aderholt (R)
5. Bud Cramer (D)
6. Spencer Bachus (R)
7. Earl F. Hilliard (D)

POSTWAR VOTE FOR PRESIDENT

| | | Republican | | Democratic | | Other | | Percentage | | | |
| | | | | | | | | Total Vote | | Major Vote | |
Year	Total Vote	Vote	Candidate	Vote	Candidate	Vote	Plurality	Rep.	Dem.	Rep.	Dem.
2000**	1,666,272	941,173	Bush, George W.	692,611	Gore, Al	32,488	248,562 R	56.5%	41.6%	57.6%	42.4%
1996**	1,534,349	769,044	Dole, Bob	662,165	Clinton, Bill	103,140	106,879 R	50.1%	43.2%	53.7%	46.3%
1992**	1,688,060	804,283	Bush, George	690,080	Clinton, Bill	193,697	114,203 R	47.6%	40.9%	53.8%	46.2%
1988	1,378,476	815,576	Bush, George	549,506	Dukakis, Michael S.	13,394	266,070 R	59.2%	39.9%	59.7%	40.3%
1984	1,441,713	872,849	Reagan, Ronald	551,899	Mondale, Walter F.	16,965	320,950 R	60.5%	38.3%	61.3%	38.7%
1980**	1,341,929	654,192	Reagan, Ronald	636,730	Carter, Jimmy	51,007	17,462 R	48.8%	47.4%	50.7%	49.3%
1976	1,182,850	504,070	Ford, Gerald R.	659,170	Carter, Jimmy	19,610	155,100 D	42.6%	55.7%	43.3%	56.7%
1972	1,006,111	728,701	Nixon, Richard M.	256,923	McGovern, George S.	20,487	471,778 R	72.4%	25.5%	73.9%	26.1%
1968**	1,049,922	146,923	Nixon, Richard M.	196,579	Humphrey, Hubert H.	706,420	494,846 A	14.0%	18.7%	42.8%	57.2%
1964**	689,818	479,085	Goldwater, Barry M.		Johnson, Lyndon B.	210,733	268,353 R	69.5%		100.0%	
1960	570,225	237,981	Nixon, Richard M.	324,050	Kennedy, John F.	8,194	86,069 D	41.7%	56.8%	42.3%	57.7%
1956	496,861	195,694	Eisenhower, Dwight D.	280,844	Stevenson, Adlai E.	20,323	85,150 D	39.4%	56.5%	41.1%	58.9%
1952	426,120	149,231	Eisenhower, Dwight D.	275,075	Stevenson, Adlai E.	1,814	125,844 D	35.0%	64.6%	35.2%	64.8%
1948**	214,980	40,930	Dewey, Thomas E.		Truman, Harry S.	174,050	130,513 SR	19.0%		100.0%	

In 2000 the other vote column includes 18,323 votes cast for Green (Nader). In 1996 the other vote column includes 92,149 votes cast for Perot. In 1992 the other vote column includes 183,109 votes cast for Perot. In 1980 the other column includes 16,481 votes for Independent (Anderson). In 1968 other vote was 691,425 American Independent (Wallace); 10,960 American Independent of Alabama; 4,022 Prohibition and 13 scattered. In 1964 and 1948 the national Democratic candidates were not represented on the ballot. In 1964 other vote was 210,732 Unpledged Democratic and 1 scattered. In 1948 other vote was 171,443 States Rights; 1,522 Progressive and 1,085 Prohibition.

ALABAMA

POSTWAR VOTE FOR GOVERNOR

Year	Total Vote	Republican Vote	Republican Candidate	Democratic Vote	Democratic Candidate	Other Vote	Rep.-Dem. Plurality	Total Vote Rep.	Total Vote Dem.	Major Vote Rep.	Major Vote Dem.
1998	1,317,842	554,746	James, Forrest H.	760,155	Siegelman, Don	2,941	205,409 D	42.1%	57.7%	42.2%	57.8%
1994	1,201,969	604,926	James, Forrest H.	594,169	Folsom, James E.	2,874	10,757 R	50.3%	49.4%	50.4%	49.6%
1990	1,216,250	633,519	Hunt, Guy	582,106	Hubbert, Paul R.	625	51,413 R	52.1%	47.9%	52.1%	47.9%
1986	1,236,230	696,203	Hunt, Guy	537,163	Baxley, Bill	2,864	159,040 R	56.3%	43.5%	56.4%	43.6%
1982	1,128,725	440,815	Folmar, Emory	650,538	Wallace, George C.	37,372	209,723 D	39.1%	57.6%	40.4%	59.6%
1978	760,474	196,963	Hunt, Guy	551,886	James, Forrest H.	11,625	354,923 D	25.9%	72.6%	26.3%	73.7%
1974	598,305	88,381	McCary, Elvin	497,574	Wallace, George C.	12,350	409,193 D	14.8%	83.2%	15.1%	84.9%
1970**	854,952		—	637,046	Wallace, George C.	217,906	637,046 D		74.5%**		100.0%
1966	848,101	262,943	Martin, James D.	537,505	Wallace, Mrs. George C.	47,653	274,562 D	31.0%	63.4%	32.8%	67.2%
1962	315,776		—	303,987	Wallace, George C.	11,789	303,987 D		96.3%		100.0%
1958	270,952	30,415	Longshore, W. L.	239,633	Patterson, John	904	209,218 D	11.2%	88.4%	11.3%	88.7%
1954	333,090	88,688	Amernethy, Tom	244,401	Folsom, James E.	1	155,713 D	26.6%	73.4%	26.6%	73.4%
1950	170,541	15,127	Crowder, John S.	155,414	Persons, Gordon		140,287 D	8.9%	91.1%	8.9%	91.1%
1946	197,324	22,362	Ward, Lyman	174,962	Folsom, James E.		152,600 D	11.3%	88.7%	11.3%	88.7%

In 1970 other vote was 125,491 National Democratic Party of Alabama (Cashin); 75,679 Independent (Shelton); 9,705 Prohibition (Couch); 3,534 Independent (Walter) and 3,497 Whig (Watts).

POSTWAR VOTE FOR SENATOR

Year	Total Vote	Republican Vote	Republican Candidate	Democratic Vote	Democratic Candidate	Other Vote	Rep.-Dem. Plurality	Total Vote Rep.	Total Vote Dem.	Major Vote Rep.	Major Vote Dem.
1998	1,293,405	817,973	Shelby, Richard C.	474,568	Suddith, Clayton	864	343,405 R	63.2%	36.7%	63.3%	36.7%
1996	1,499,393	786,436	Sessions, Jeff	681,651	Bedford, Roger	31,306	104,785 R	52.5%	45.5%	53.6%	46.4%
1992	1,577,799	522,015	Sellers, Richard	1,022,698	Shelby, Richard C.	33,086	500,683 D	33.1%	64.8%	33.8%	66.2%
1990	1,185,563	467,190	Cabaniss, Bill	717,814	Heflin, Howell	559	250,624 D	39.4%	60.5%	39.4%	60.6%
1986	1,211,953	602,537	Denton, Jeremiah	609,360	Shelby, Richard C.	56	6,823 D	49.7%	50.3%	49.7%	50.3%
1984	1,371,238	498,508	Smith, Albert L.	860,535	Heflin, Howell	12,195	362,027 D	36.4%	62.8%	36.7%	63.3%
1980	1,296,757	650,362	Denton, Jeremiah	610,175	Folsom, James E., Jr.	36,220	40,187 R	50.2%	47.1%	51.6%	48.4%
1978	582,025		—	547,054	Heflin, Howell	34,971	547,054 D		94.0%		100.0%
1978S	731,614	316,170	Martin, James D.	401,852	Stewart, Donald W.	13,592	85,682 D	43.2%	54.9%	44.0%	56.0%
1974	523,290		—	501,541	Allen, James B.	21,749	501,541 D		95.8%		100.0%
1972	1,051,099	347,523	Blount, Winston M.	654,491	Sparkman, John J.	49,085	306,968 D	33.1%	62.3%	34.7%	65.3%
1968	912,708	201,227	Hooper, Perry	638,774	Allen, James B.	72,707	437,547 D	22.0%	70.0%	24.0%	76.0%
1966	802,608	313,018	Grenier, John	482,138	Sparkman, John J.	7,452	169,120 D	39.0%	60.1%	39.4%	60.6%
1962	397,079	195,134	Martin, James D.	201,937	Hill, Lister	8	6,803 D	49.1%	50.9%	49.1%	50.9%
1960	554,081	164,868	Elgin, Julian	389,196	Sparkman, John J.	17	224,328 D	29.8%	70.2%	29.8%	70.2%
1956	330,191		—	330,182	Hill, Lister	9	330,182 D		100.0%		100.0%
1954	314,459	55,110	Guin, J. Foy	259,348	Sparkman, John J.	1	204,238 D	17.5%	82.5%	17.5%	82.5%
1950	164,011		—	125,534	Hill, Lister	38,477	125,534 D		76.5%		100.0%
1948	220,875	35,341	Parsons, Paul G.	185,534	Sparkman, John J.		150,193 D	16.0%	84.0%	16.0%	84.0%
1946S	163,217		—	163,217	Sparkman, John J.		163,217 D		100.0%		100.0%

The 1946 election and one of the 1978 elections were for short terms to fill vacancies.

ALABAMA

Districts Established March 27, 1992

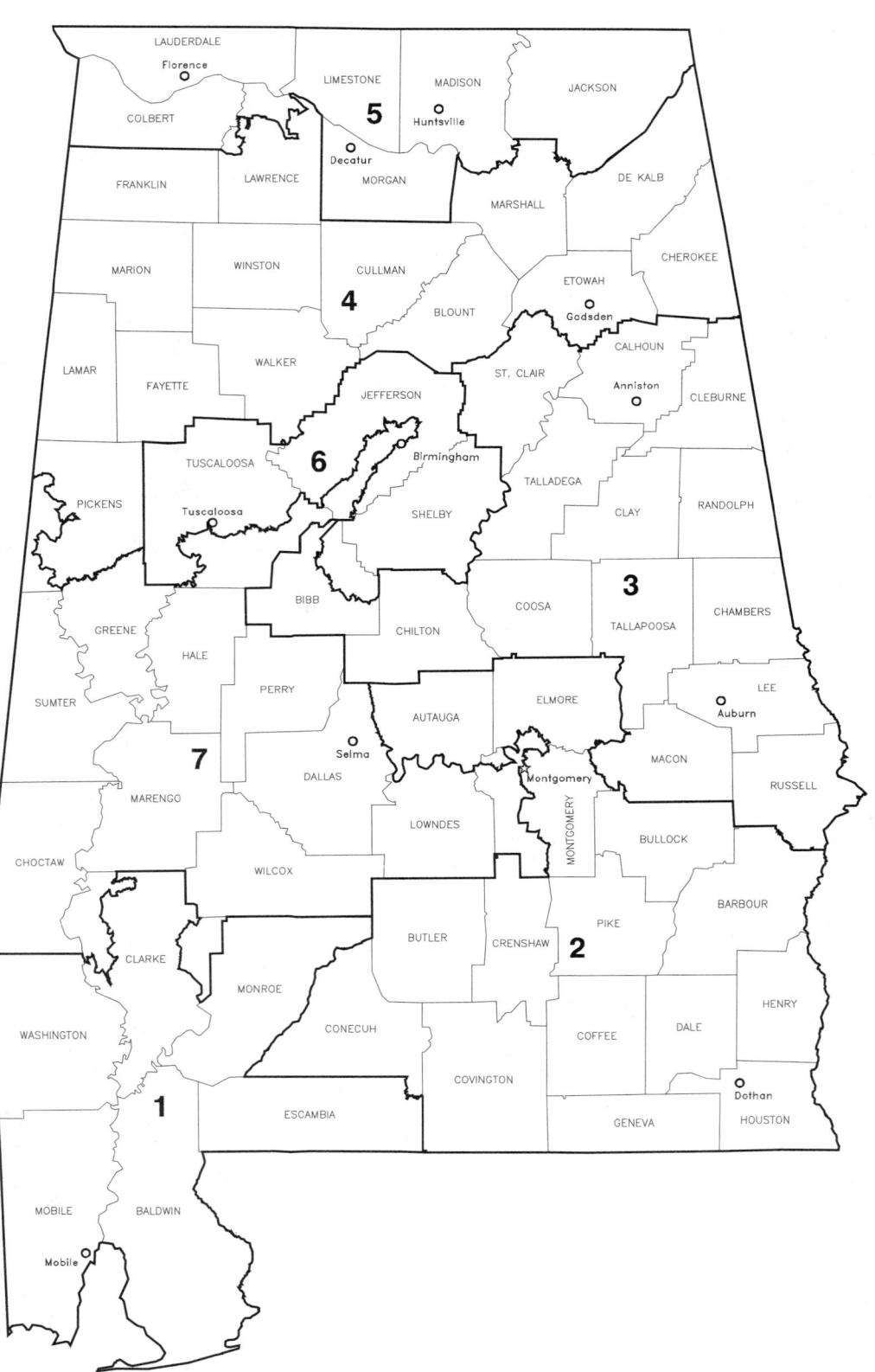

ALABAMA

PRESIDENT 2000

2000 Census Population	County	Total Vote	Republican	Democratic	Green (Nader)	Other	Rep.-Dem. Plurality	Percentage of Total Vote		
								Rep.	Dem.	Green
43,671	AUTAUGA	17,208	11,993	4,942	160	113	7,051 R	69.7%	28.7%	0.9%
140,415	BALDWIN	56,480	40,872	13,997	1,033	578	26,875 R	72.4%	24.8%	1.8%
29,038	BARBOUR	4,116	1,860	2,197	20	39	337 D	45.2%	53.4%	0.5%
20,826	BIBB	7,101	4,273	2,710	52	66	1,563 R	60.2%	38.2%	0.7%
51,024	BLOUNT	17,973	12,667	4,977	154	175	7,690 R	70.5%	27.7%	0.9%
11,714	BULLOCK	4,904	1,433	3,395	24	52	1,962 D	29.2%	69.2%	0.5%
21,399	BUTLER	7,803	4,127	3,606	36	34	521 R	52.9%	46.2%	0.5%
112,249	CALHOUN	38,909	22,306	15,781	481	341	6,525 R	57.3%	40.6%	1.2%
36,583	CHAMBERS	11,834	6,037	5,616	95	86	421 R	51.0%	47.5%	0.8%
23,988	CHEROKEE	7,823	4,154	3,497	77	95	657 R	53.1%	44.7%	1.0%
39,593	CHILTON	15,092	10,066	4,806	92	128	5,260 R	66.7%	31.8%	0.6%
15,922	CHOCTAW	7,374	3,600	3,707	33	34	107 D	48.8%	50.3%	0.4%
27,867	CLARKE	10,752	5,988	4,679	33	52	1,309 R	55.7%	43.5%	0.3%
14,254	CLAY	5,883	3,719	2,045	52	67	1,674 R	63.2%	34.8%	0.9%
14,123	CLEBURNE	5,092	3,333	1,664	39	56	1,669 R	65.5%	32.7%	0.8%
43,615	COFFEE	15,434	9,938	5,220	155	121	4,718 R	64.4%	33.8%	1.0%
54,984	COLBERT	21,532	10,518	10,543	208	263	25 D	48.8%	49.0%	1.0%
14,089	CONECUH	5,551	2,699	2,783	35	34	84 D	48.6%	50.1%	0.6%
12,202	COOSA	4,567	2,382	2,104	34	47	278 R	52.2%	46.1%	0.7%
37,631	COVINGTON	13,613	8,961	4,440	123	89	4,521 R	65.8%	32.6%	0.9%
13,665	CRENSHAW	4,795	2,793	1,934	40	28	859 R	58.2%	40.3%	0.8%
77,483	CULLMAN	29,525	19,157	9,758	282	328	9,399 R	64.9%	33.0%	1.0%
49,129	DALE	15,806	10,593	4,906	188	119	5,687 R	67.0%	31.0%	1.2%
46,365	DALLAS	18,464	7,360	10,967	63	74	3,607 D	39.9%	59.4%	0.3%
64,452	DE KALB	20,285	12,827	7,056	175	227	5,771 R	63.2%	34.8%	0.9%
65,874	ELMORE	23,804	16,777	6,652	212	163	10,125 R	70.5%	27.9%	0.9%
38,440	ESCAMBIA	11,660	6,975	4,523	78	84	2,452 R	59.8%	38.8%	0.7%
103,459	ETOWAH	39,348	21,087	17,433	435	393	3,654 R	53.6%	44.3%	1.1%
18,495	FAYETTE	7,808	4,582	3,064	60	102	1,518 R	58.7%	39.2%	0.8%
31,223	FRANKLIN	11,103	6,119	4,793	72	119	1,326 R	55.1%	43.2%	0.6%
25,764	GENEVA	9,559	6,588	2,769	97	105	3,819 R	68.9%	29.0%	1.0%
9,974	GREENE	4,396	850	3,504	24	18	2,654 D	19.3%	79.7%	0.5%
17,185	HALE	7,731	2,984	4,652	43	52	1,668 D	38.6%	60.2%	0.6%
16,310	HENRY	6,932	4,054	2,782	48	48	1,272 R	58.5%	40.1%	0.7%
88,787	HOUSTON	32,057	22,150	9,412	257	238	12,738 R	69.1%	29.4%	0.8%
53,926	JACKSON	17,906	8,475	9,066	184	181	591 D	47.3%	50.6%	1.0%
662,047	JEFFERSON	273,763	138,491	129,889	3,393	1,990	8,602 R	50.6%	47.4%	1.2%
15,904	LAMAR	7,249	4,470	2,653	57	69	1,817 R	61.7%	36.6%	0.8%
87,966	LAUDERDALE	32,137	17,478	13,875	354	430	3,603 R	54.4%	43.2%	1.1%
34,803	LAWRENCE	12,185	5,671	6,296	63	155	625 D	46.5%	51.7%	0.5%
115,092	LEE	38,264	22,433	14,574	895	362	7,859 R	58.6%	38.1%	2.3%
65,676	LIMESTONE	23,634	14,204	8,992	193	245	5,212 R	60.1%	38.0%	0.8%
13,473	LOWNDES	6,243	1,638	4,557	18	30	2,919 D	26.2%	73.0%	0.3%
24,105	MACON	8,831	1,091	7,665	31	44	6,574 D	12.4%	86.8%	0.4%
276,700	MADISON	113,318	62,151	48,199	1,885	1,083	13,952 R	54.8%	42.5%	1.7%
22,539	MARENGO	9,608	4,690	4,841	40	37	151 D	48.8%	50.4%	0.4%
31,214	MARION	11,756	6,910	4,600	125	121	2,310 R	58.8%	39.1%	1.1%
82,231	MARSHALL	27,989	17,084	10,381	256	268	6,703 R	61.0%	37.1%	0.9%
399,843	MOBILE	139,745	78,162	58,640	1,585	1,358	19,522 R	55.9%	42.0%	1.1%
24,324	MONROE	8,951	5,153	3,741	25	32	1,412 R	57.6%	41.8%	0.3%
223,510	MONTGOMERY	80,328	38,827	40,371	677	453	1,544 D	48.3%	50.3%	0.8%
111,064	MORGAN	42,681	25,774	16,060	450	397	9,714 R	60.4%	37.6%	1.1%
11,861	PERRY	5,787	1,732	4,020	18	17	2,288 D	29.9%	69.5%	0.3%
20,949	PICKENS	8,540	4,306	4,143	39	52	163 R	50.4%	48.5%	0.5%
29,605	PIKE	10,544	6,058	4,357	75	54	1,701 R	57.5%	41.3%	0.7%
22,380	RANDOLPH	7,919	4,666	3,094	60	99	1,572 R	58.9%	39.1%	0.8%
49,756	RUSSELL	14,775	6,198	8,396	109	72	2,198 D	41.9%	56.8%	0.7%
64,742	ST. CLAIR	24,090	17,117	6,485	221	267	10,632 R	71.1%	26.9%	0.9%
143,293	SHELBY	62,128	47,651	13,183	812	482	34,468 R	76.7%	21.2%	1.3%
14,798	SUMTER	6,088	1,629	4,415	20	24	2,786 D	26.8%	72.5%	0.3%

ALABAMA

PRESIDENT 2000

2000 Census Population	County	Total Vote	Republican	Democratic	Green (Nader)	Other	Rep.-Dem. Plurality	Percentage of Total Vote		
								Rep.	Dem.	Green
80,321	TALLADEGA	25,451	13,807	11,264	184	196	2,543 R	54.2%	44.3%	0.7%
41,475	TALLAPOOSA	16,253	9,805	6,183	153	112	3,622 R	60.3%	38.0%	0.9%
164,875	TUSCALOOSA	60,114	34,003	24,614	1,007	490	9,389 R	56.6%	40.9%	1.7%
70,713	WALKER	25,641	13,486	11,621	264	270	1,865 R	52.6%	45.3%	1.0%
18,097	WASHINGTON	7,596	4,117	3,386	26	67	731 R	54.2%	44.6%	0.3%
13,183	WILCOX	5,126	1,661	3,444	6	15	1,783 D	32.4%	67.2%	0.1%
24,843	WINSTON	9,318	6,413	2,692	88	125	3,721 R	68.8%	28.9%	0.9%
4,447,100	TOTAL	1,666,272	941,173	692,611	18,323	14,165	248,562 R	56.5%	41.6%	1.1%

ALABAMA

CONGRESS

CD	Year	Total Vote	Republican		Democratic		Other Vote	Rep.-Dem. Plurality	Percentage			
									Total Vote		Major Vote	
			Vote	Candidate	Vote	Candidate			Rep.	Dem.	Rep.	Dem.
1	2000	165,669	151,188	CALLAHAN, H. L.			14,481	151,188 R	91.3%		100.0%	
1	1998	113,564	112,872	CALLAHAN, H. L.			692	112,872 R	99.4%		100.0%	
1	1996	205,417	132,206	CALLAHAN, H. L.	69,470	WOMACK, DON	3,741	62,736 R	64.4%	64.4%	64.4%	64.4%
1	1994	153,767	103,431	CALLAHAN, H. L.	50,227	WOMACK, DON	109	53,204 R	67.3%	32.7%	67.3%	32.7%
1	1992	214,204	128,874	CALLAHAN, H. L.	78,742	BREWER, WILLLIAM A.	6,588	50,132 R	60.2%	36.8%	62.1%	37.9%
2	2000	222,636	151,830	EVERETT, TERRY	64,958	WOODS, CHARLES	5,848	86,872 R	68.2%	29.2%	70.0%	30.0%
2	1998	189,669	131,428	EVERETT, TERRY	58,136	FONDREN, JOE	105	73,292 R	69.3%	30.7%	69.3%	30.7%
2	1996	209,793	132,563	EVERETT, TERRY	74,317	GAINES, BOB E.	2,913	58,246 R	63.2%	35.4%	64.1%	35.9%
2	1994	169,213	124,465	EVERETT, TERRY	44,694	DOWLING, BRIAN	54	79,771 R	73.6%	26.4%	73.6%	26.4%
2	1992	228,160	112,906	EVERETT, TERRY	109,335	WALLACE, GEORGE C., JR.	5,919	3,571 R	49.5%	47.9%	50.8%	49.2%
3	2000	169,519	147,317	RILEY, BOB			22,202	147,317 R	86.9%		100.0%	
3	1998	175,217	101,731	RILEY, BOB	73,357	TURNHAM, JOE	129	28,374 R	58.1%	41.9%	58.1%	41.9%
3	1996	195,047	98,353	RILEY, BOB	92,325	LITTLE, T.D. "TED"	4,369	6,028 R	50.4%	47.3%	51.6%	48.4%
3	1994	147,745	53,757	HAND, BEN	93,924	BROWDER, GLEN	64	40,167 D	36.4%	63.6%	36.4%	63.6%
3	1992	197,604	73,800	SLEDGE, DON	119,175	BROWDER, GLEN	4,629	45,375 D	37.3%	60.3%	38.2%	61.8%
4	2000	231,106	140,009	ADERHOLT, ROBERT	86,400	FOLSOM, MARSHA	4,697	53,609 R	60.6%	37.4%	61.8%	38.2%
4	1998	188,476	106,297	ADERHOLT, ROBERT	82,065	BEVILL, DONALD	114	24,232 R	56.4%	43.5%	56.4%	43.6%
4	1996	205,917	102,741	ADERHOLT, ROBERT	99,250	WILSON, ROBERT T. "BOB"	3,926	3,491 R	49.9%	48.2%	50.9%	49.1%
4	1994	121,262			119,436	BEVILL, TOM	1,826	119,436 D		98.5%		100.0%
4	1992	230,523	66,934	STRICKLAND, MICKEY	157,907	BEVILL, TOM	5,682	90,973 D	29.0%	68.5%	29.8%	70.2%
5	2000	209,514			186,059	CRAMER, BUD	23,455	186,059 D		88.8%		100.0%
5	1998	193,490	58,536	AUST, GIL	134,819	CRAMER, BUD	135	76,283 D	30.3%	69.7%	30.3%	69.7%
5	1996	205,547	86,727	PARKER, WAYNE	114,442	CRAMER, BUD	4,378	27,715 D	42.2%	55.7%	43.1%	56.9%
5	1994	175,693	86,923	PARKER, WAYNE	88,693	CRAMER, BUD	77	1,770 D	49.5%	50.5%	49.5%	50.5%
5	1992	244,133	77,951	SMITH, TERRY	160,060	CRAMER, BUD	6,122	82,109 D	31.9%	65.6%	32.8%	67.2%
6	2000	241,917	212,751	BACHUS, SPENCER			29,166	212,751 R	87.9%		100.0%	
6	1998	215,582	154,761	BACHUS, SPENCER	60,657	SMALLEY, DONNA WESSON	164	94,104 R	71.8%	28.1%	71.8%	28.2%
6	1996	254,859	180,781	BACHUS, SPENCER	69,592	BATES, MARY LYNN	4,486	111,189 R	70.9%	27.3%	72.2%	27.8%
6	1994	196,222	155,047	BACHUS, SPENCER	41,030	FORTENBERRY, LARRY	145	114,017 R	79.0%	20.9%	79.1%	20.9%
6	1992	280,139	146,599	BACHUS, SPENCER	126,062	ERDREICH, BEN	7,478	20,537 R	52.3%	45.0%	53.8%	46.2%
7	2000	198,633	46,134	MARTIN, ED	148,243	HILLIARD, EARL F.	4,256	102,109 D	23.2%	74.6%	23.7%	76.3%
7	1998	139,181			136,431	HILLIARD, EARL F.	2,750	136,431 D		98.0%		100.0%
7	1996	192,113	52,142	POWELL, JOE	136,651	HILLIARD, EARL F.	3,320	84,509 D	27.1%	71.1%	27.6%	72.4%
7	1994	151,117	34,814	MIDDLETON, ALFRED J.	116,150	HILLIARD, EARL F.	153	81,336 D	23.0%	76.9%	23.1%	76.9%
7	1992	207,773	36,086	JONES, KERVIN	144,320	HILLIARD, EARL F.	27,367	108,234 D	17.4%	69.5%	20.0%	80.0%

ALABAMA

GENERAL AND PRIMARY ELECTIONS

2000 GENERAL ELECTIONS

President Other vote was 6,351 Independent (Buchanan); 5,893 Libertarian (Browne); 775 Independent (Phillips); 447 Independent (Hagelin); 699 scattered write-in. (Nader was also listed on the ballot as Independent.)

Congress Other vote was: CD 1: 14,031 Libertarian (Coffee), 450 scattered write-in; CD 2: 4,111 Libertarian (McGahan), 1,737 scattered write-in; CD 3: 21,119 Libertarian (Sophocleus), 1,083 scattered write-in; CD 4: 3,519 Libertarian (Goodrich), 1,178 scattered write-in; CD 5: 22,110 Libertarian (Barksdale), 1,345 scattered write-in; CD 6: 28,189 Libertarian (Reagin), 977 scattered write-in; CD 7: 3,829 Libertarian (Hager), 427 scattered write-in.

2000 PRIMARY ELECTIONS

Primary June 6, 2000 **Registration** (as of June 2000) 2,420,075 No Party Registration

Primary Type Open—Any registered voter could vote in either the Democratic or Republican primary.

Note: An asterisk (*) denotes incumbent. The names of unopposed candidates do not appear on the ballot; therefore, no votes are cast for these candidates.

	REPUBLICAN PRIMARIES			DEMOCRATIC PRIMARIES		
President	George W. Bush	171,077	84.2%	Al Gore	214,541	77.0%
	Alan Keyes	23,394	11.5%	Uncommitted	48,521	17.4%
	Uncommitted	8,608	4.2%	Lyndon H. LaRouche Jr.	15,465	5.6%
	TOTAL	203,079		TOTAL	278,527	
Congressional District 1	H. L. "Sonny" Callahan*	Unopposed		No Democratic candidate		
Congressional District 2	Terry Everett*	Unopposed		Charles Woods	Unopposed	
Congressional District 3	Bob Riley*	Unopposed		No Democratic candidate		
Congressional District 4	Robert B. Aderholt*	Unopposed		Marsha Folsom	Unopposed	
Congressional District 5	No Republican candidate			Robert E. "Bud" Cramer*	Unopposed	
Congressional District 6	Spencer Bachus*	Unopposed		No Democratic candidate		
Congressional District 7	Ed Martin	3,018	61.1%	Earl F. Hilliard*	36,249	50.1%
	Milton Bethune	1,923	38.9%	Arthur Davis	30,973	42.8%
				Wayne Sowell	5,155	7.1%
	TOTAL	4,941		TOTAL	72,377	

ALASKA

GOVERNOR

Tony Knowles (D). Re-elected 1998 to a four-year term. Previously elected 1994.

SENATORS

Frank H. Murkowski (R). Re-elected 1998 to a six-year term. Previously elected 1992, 1986, 1980.

Ted Stevens (R). Re-elected 1996 to a six-year term. Previously elected 1990, 1984, 1978, 1972, and in 1970 to fill out term vacated by the death of Senator E. L. Bartlett; had been appointed December 1968 to fill this vacancy.

REPRESENTATIVE

At-Large. Don Young (R)

POSTWAR VOTE FOR PRESIDENT

| | | Republican | | Democratic | | Other | | Percentage | | | |
| | | | | | | | | Total Vote | | Major Vote | |
Year	Total Vote	Vote	Candidate	Vote	Candidate	Vote	Plurality	Rep.	Dem.	Rep.	Dem.
2000**	285,560	167,398	Bush, George W.	79,004	Gore, Al	39,158	88,394 R	58.6%	27.7%	67.9%	32.1%
1996**	241,620	122,746	Dole, Bob	80,380	Clinton, Bill	38,494	42,366 R	50.8%	33.3%	60.4%	39.6%
1992**	258,506	102,000	Bush, George	78,294	Clinton, Bill	78,212	23,706 R	39.5%	30.3%	56.6%	43.4%
1988	200,116	119,251	Bush, George	72,584	Dukakis, Michael S.	8,281	46,667 R	59.6%	36.3%	62.2%	37.8%
1984	207,605	138,377	Reagan, Ronald	62,007	Mondale, Walter F.	7,221	76,370 R	66.7%	29.9%	69.1%	30.9%
1980**	158,445	86,112	Reagan, Ronald	41,842	Carter, Jimmy	30,491	44,270 R	54.3%	26.4%	67.3%	32.7%
1976	123,574	71,555	Ford, Gerald R.	44,058	Carter, Jimmy	7,961	27,497 R	57.9%	35.7%	61.9%	38.1%
1972	95,219	55,349	Nixon, Richard M.	32,967	McGovern, George S.	6,903	22,382 R	58.1%	34.6%	62.7%	37.3%
1968	83,035	37,600	Nixon, Richard M.	35,411	Humphrey, Hubert H.	10,024	2,189 R	45.3%	42.6%	51.5%	48.5%
1964	67,259	22,930	Goldwater, Barry M.	44,329	Johnson, Lyndon B.		21,399 D	34.1%	65.9%	34.1%	65.9%
1960	60,762	30,953	Nixon, Richard M.	29,809	Kennedy, John F.		1,144 R	50.9%	49.1%	50.9%	49.1%

In 2000 the other vote column includes 28,747 votes cast for Green (Nader). In 1996 the other vote column includes 26,333 votes cast for Perot. In 1992 the other vote column includes 73,481 votes for Perot. In 1980 the other column includes 11,155 votes for Independent (Anderson). Alaska was formally admitted as a state in January 1959.

POSTWAR VOTE FOR GOVERNOR

| | | Republican | | Democratic | | Other | Rep.-Dem. | Percentage | | | |
| | | | | | | | | Total Vote | | Major Vote | |
Year	Total Vote	Vote	Candidate	Vote	Candidate	Vote	Plurality	Rep.	Dem.	Rep.	Dem.
1998	220,177	39,331	Lindauer, John	112,879	Knowles, Tony	67,967	73,548 D	17.9%	51.3%	25.8%	74.2%
1994	213,435	87,157	Campbell, James O.	87,693	Knowles, Tony	38,585	536 D	40.8%	41.1%	49.8%	50.2%
1990**	194,750	50,991	Sturgulewski, Arliss	60,201	Knowles, Tony	83,558	15,520 I	26.2%	30.9%	45.9%	54.1%
1986	179,555	76,515	Sturgulewski, Arliss	84,943	Cowper, Steve	18,097	8,428 D	42.6%	47.3%	47.4%	52.6%
1982	194,885	72,291	Fink, Tom	89,918	Sheffield, Bill	32,676	17,627 D	37.1%	46.1%	44.6%	55.4%
1978**	126,910	49,580	Hammond, Jay S.	25,656	Croft, Chancy	51,674	23,924 R	39.1%	20.2%	65.9%	34.1%
1974	96,163	45,840	Hammond, Jay S.	45,553	Egan, William A.	4,770	287 R	47.7%	47.4%	50.2%	49.8%
1970	80,779	37,264	Miller, Keith	42,309	Egan, William A.	1,206	5,045 D	46.1%	52.4%	46.8%	53.2%
1966	66,294	33,145	Hickel, Walter J.	32,065	Egan, William A.	1,084	1,080 R	50.0%	48.4%	50.8%	49.2%
1962	56,681	27,054	Stepovich, Mike	29,627	Egan, William A.		2,573 D	47.7%	52.3%	47.7%	52.3%
1958	48,968	19,299	Butrovich, John	29,189	Egan, William A.	480	9,890 D	39.4%	59.6%	39.8%	60.2%

In 1990 Walter J. Hickel, the Alaskan Independence candidate, polled 75,721 votes (38.9% of the total vote) and won the election with a 15,520-vote plurality. In 1978 other vote was 33,555 Walter J. Hickel (write-in); 15,656 Tom Kelly (Alaskans for Kelly) and 2,463 Donald R. Wright (Alaskan Independence).

ALASKA

POSTWAR VOTE FOR SENATOR

Year	Total Vote	Republican		Democratic		Other Vote	Rep.-Dem. Plurality	Percentage			
								Total Vote		Major Vote	
		Vote	Candidate	Vote	Candidate			Rep.	Dem.	Rep.	Dem.
1998	221,807	165,227	Murkowski, Frank H.	43,743	Sonneman, Joseph	12,837	121,484 R	74.5%	19.7%	79.1%	20.9%
1996**	231,916	177,893	Stevens, Ted	23,977	Obermeyer, Theresa	30,046	153,916 R	76.7%	10.3%	88.1%	11.9%
1992	239,714	127,163	Murkowski, Frank H.	92,065	Smith, Tony	20,486	35,098 R	53.0%	38.4%	58.0%	42.0%
1990	189,957	125,806	Stevens, Ted	61,152	Beasley, Michael	2,999	64,654 R	66.2%	32.2%	67.3%	32.7%
1986	180,801	97,674	Murkowski, Frank H.	79,727	Olds, Glenn	3,400	17,947 R	54.0%	44.1%	55.1%	44.9%
1984	206,438	146,919	Stevens, Ted	58,804	Havelock, John E.	715	88,115 R	71.2%	28.5%	71.4%	28.6%
1980	156,762	84,159	Murkowski, Frank H.	72,007	Gruening, Clark S.	596	12,152 R	53.7%	45.9%	53.9%	46.1%
1978	122,741	92,783	Stevens, Ted	29,574	Hobbs, Donald W.	384	63,209 R	75.6%	24.1%	75.8%	24.2%
1974	93,275	38,914	Lewis, C. R.	54,361	Gravel, Mike		15,447 D	41.7%	58.3%	41.7%	58.3%
1972	96,007	74,216	Stevens, Ted	21,791	Guess, Gene		52,425 R	77.3%	22.7%	77.3%	22.7%
1970S	80,364	47,908	Stevens, Ted	32,456	Kay, Wendell P.		15,452 R	59.6%	40.4%	59.6%	40.4%
1968	80,931	30,286	Rasmuson, Elmer	36,527	Gravel, Mike	14,118	6,241 D	37.4%	45.1%	45.3%	54.7%
1966	65,250	15,961	McKinley, Lee L.	49,289	Bartlett, E. L.		33,328 D	24.5%	75.5%	24.5%	75.5%
1962	58,181	24,354	Stevens, Ted	33,827	Gruening, Ernest		9,473 D	41.9%	58.1%	41.9%	58.1%
1960	59,978	21,937	McKinley, Lee L.	38,041	Bartlett, E. L.		16,104 D	36.6%	63.4%	36.6%	63.4%
1958S	49,525	23,462	Stepovich, Mike	26,063	Gruening, Ernest		2,601 D	47.4%	52.6%	47.4%	52.6%
1958S	48,837	7,299	Robertson, R. E.	40,939	Bartlett, E. L.	599	33,640 D	14.9%	83.8%	15.1%	84.9%

In 1996 Green Party candidate Jed Whittaker finished second with 29,037 votes, a total of 148,856 behind Stevens. The 1970 election was for a short term to fill a vacancy. The two 1958 elections were held to indeterminate terms and the Senate later determined by lot that Senator Gruening would serve four years, Senator Bartlett two.

54

ALASKA
One At Large
Election Districts Established June 29, 1992

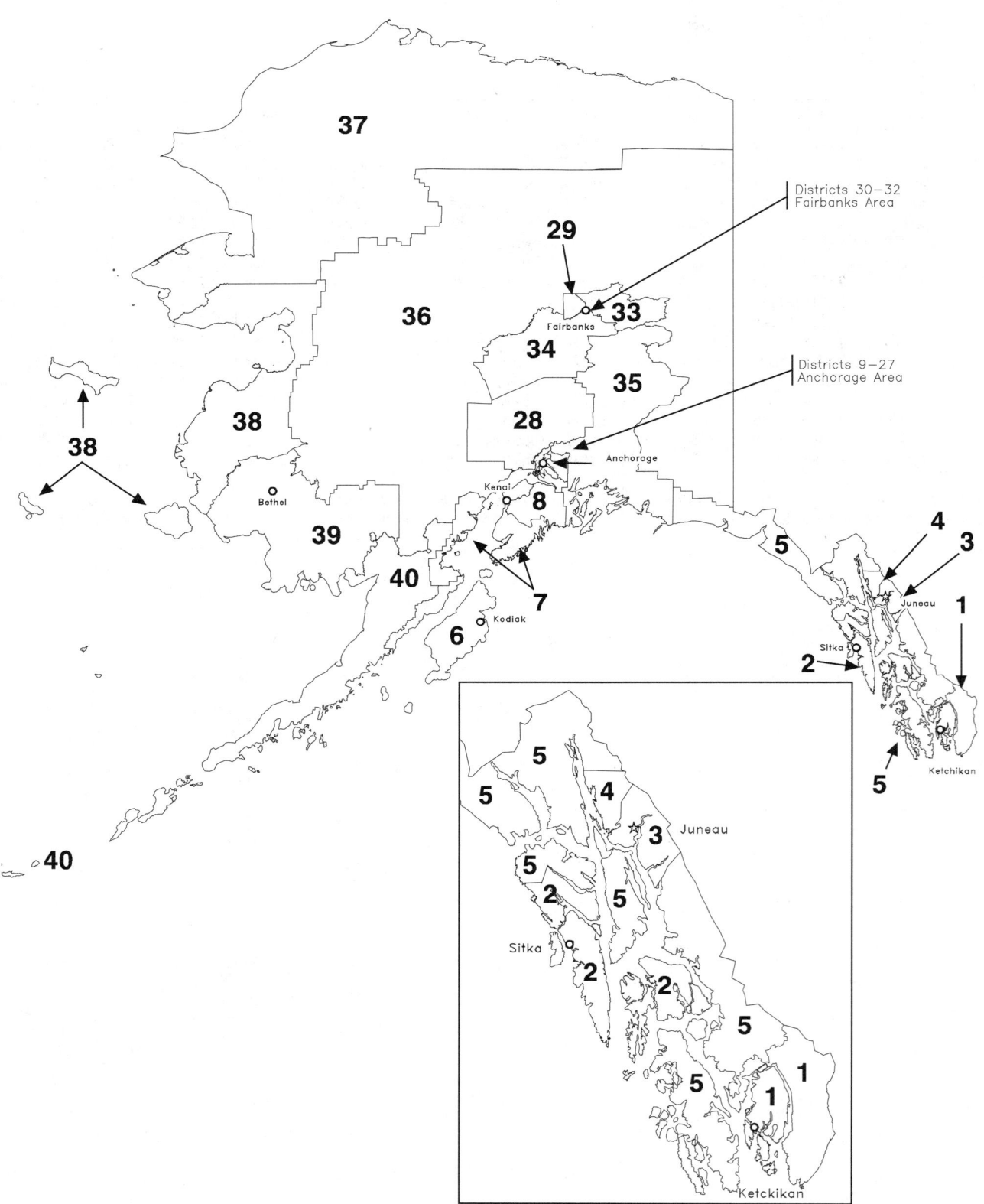

ALASKA

PRESIDENT 2000

2000 Census Population	District	Total Vote	Republican	Democratic	Green (Nader)	Other	Rep.-Dem. Plurality	Percentage of Total Vote		
								Rep.	Dem.	Green
14,199	DISTRICT 1	6,656	4,681	1,284	475	216	3,397 R	70.3%	19.3%	7.1%
14,679	DISTRICT 2	7,388	4,235	2,081	846	226	2,154 R	57.3%	28.2%	11.5%
15,201	DISTRICT 3	8,225	3,135	3,693	1,161	236	558 D	38.1%	44.9%	14.1%
15,589	DISTRICT 4	7,823	4,127	2,715	768	213	1,412 R	52.8%	34.7%	9.8%
13,286	DISTRICT 5	6,437	3,545	1,931	751	210	1,614 R	55.1%	30.0%	11.7%
13,913	DISTRICT 6	6,100	3,862	1,542	494	202	2,320 R	63.3%	25.3%	8.1%
16,904	DISTRICT 7	8,677	4,868	1,893	1,563	353	2,975 R	56.1%	21.8%	18.0%
16,752	DISTRICT 8	7,978	5,371	1,498	809	300	3,873 R	67.3%	18.8%	10.1%
15,810	DISTRICT 9	6,800	4,789	1,203	478	330	3,586 R	70.4%	17.7%	7.0%
16,497	DISTRICT 10	8,884	5,673	2,194	803	214	3,479 R	63.9%	24.7%	9.0%
14,906	DISTRICT 11	6,980	3,960	2,043	743	234	1,917 R	56.7%	29.3%	10.6%
16,568	DISTRICT 12	7,601	4,626	2,051	691	233	2,575 R	60.9%	27.0%	9.1%
15,204	DISTRICT 13	7,973	3,853	2,661	1,230	229	1,192 R	48.3%	33.4%	15.4%
14,558	DISTRICT 14	5,868	3,750	1,626	342	150	2,124 R	63.9%	27.7%	5.8%
15,359	DISTRICT 15	5,870	2,453	2,106	1,068	243	347 R	41.8%	35.9%	18.2%
16,471	DISTRICT 16	4,685	1,980	1,969	530	206	11 R	42.3%	42.0%	11.3%
20,153	DISTRICT 17	7,704	4,564	2,230	641	269	2,334 R	59.2%	28.9%	8.3%
16,033	DISTRICT 18	9,882	5,421	2,739	1,484	238	2,682 R	54.9%	27.7%	15.0%
18,537	DISTRICT 19	7,951	4,619	2,350	728	254	2,269 R	58.1%	29.6%	9.2%
14,537	DISTRICT 20	6,963	3,648	2,259	839	217	1,389 R	52.4%	32.4%	12.0%
15,618	DISTRICT 21	6,629	3,263	2,309	810	247	954 R	49.2%	34.8%	12.2%
16,522	DISTRICT 22	8,525	4,910	2,656	697	262	2,254 R	57.6%	31.2%	8.2%
12,433	DISTRICT 23	4,630	2,961	1,282	283	104	1,679 R	64.0%	27.7%	6.1%
16,420	DISTRICT 24	7,915	5,063	1,985	631	236	3,078 R	64.0%	25.1%	8.0%
15,700	DISTRICT 25	8,201	5,489	1,697	743	272	3,792 R	66.9%	20.7%	9.1%
17,897	DISTRICT 26	8,590	5,869	1,608	715	398	4,261 R	68.3%	18.7%	8.3%
21,751	DISTRICT 27	10,438	6,714	2,199	1,014	511	4,515 R	64.3%	21.1%	9.7%
24,441	DISTRICT 28	11,040	7,113	2,116	1,100	711	4,997 R	64.4%	19.2%	10.0%
15,911	DISTRICT 29	8,823	4,054	2,806	1,628	335	1,248 R	45.9%	31.8%	18.5%
12,715	DISTRICT 30	6,083	3,622	1,698	538	225	1,924 R	59.5%	27.9%	8.8%
13,638	DISTRICT 31	5,965	3,326	1,831	535	273	1,495 R	55.8%	30.7%	9.0%
13,554	DISTRICT 32	6,033	4,178	1,389	285	181	2,789 R	69.3%	23.0%	4.7%
15,314	DISTRICT 33	8,712	5,804	1,765	789	354	4,039 R	66.6%	20.3%	9.1%
13,767	DISTRICT 34	7,154	5,243	1,300	407	204	3,943 R	73.3%	18.2%	5.7%
12,769	DISTRICT 35	6,382	4,278	1,208	588	308	3,070 R	67.0%	18.9%	9.2%
13,564	DISTRICT 36	5,577	3,007	1,945	383	242	1,062 R	53.9%	34.9%	6.9%
15,453	DISTRICT 37	5,028	2,725	1,821	255	227	904 R	54.2%	36.2%	5.1%
15,744	DISTRICT 38	4,976	2,467	2,015	267	227	452 R	49.6%	40.5%	5.4%
17,322	DISTRICT 39	5,188	2,321	2,282	383	202	39 R	44.7%	44.0%	7.4%
11,243	DISTRICT 40	3,226	1,831	1,024	252	119	807 R	56.8%	31.7%	7.8%
626,932	TOTAL	285,560	167,398	79,004	28,747	10,411	88,394 R	58.6%	27.7%	10.1%

ALASKA

CONGRESS

CD	Year	Total Vote	Republican		Democratic		Other Vote	Rep.-Dem. Plurality	Total Vote		Major Vote	
			Vote	Candidate	Vote	Candidate			Rep.	Dem.	Rep.	Dem.
AL	2000	274,393	190,862	YOUNG, DON	45,372	GREENE, CLIFFORD	38,159	145,490 R	69.6%	16.5%	80.8%	19.2%
AL	1998	223,300	139,676	YOUNG, DON	77,232	DUNCAN, JIM	6,392	62,444 R	62.6%	34.6%	64.4%	35.6%
AL	1996	233,700	138,834	YOUNG, DON	85,114	LINCOLN, GEORGIANNA	9,752	53,720 R	59.4%	36.4%	62.0%	38.0%
AL	1994	208,240	118,537	YOUNG, DON	68,172	SMITH, TONY	21,531	50,365 R	56.9%	32.7%	63.5%	36.5%
AL	1992	239,116	111,849	YOUNG, DON	102,378	DEVENS, JOHN S.	24,889	9,471 R	46.8%	42.8%	52.2%	47.8%
AL	1990	191,647	99,003	YOUNG, DON	91,677	DEVENS, JOHN S.	967	7,326 R	51.7%	47.8%	51.9%	48.1%
AL	1988	192,955	120,595	YOUNG, DON	71,881	GRUENSTEIN, PETER	479	48,714 R	62.5%	37.3%	62.7%	37.3%
AL	1986	180,277	101,799	YOUNG, DON	74,053	BEGICH, PEGGE	4,425	27,746 R	56.5%	41.1%	57.9%	42.1%
AL	1984	206,437	113,582	YOUNG, DON	86,052	BEGICH, PEGGE	6,803	27,530 R	55.0%	41.7%	56.9%	43.1%
AL	1982	181,084	128,274	YOUNG, DON	52,011	CARLSON, DAVE	799	76,263 R	70.8%	28.7%	71.2%	28.8%
AL	1980	154,618	114,089	YOUNG, DON	39,922	PARNELL, KEVIN	607	74,167 R	73.8%	25.8%	74.1%	25.9%
AL	1978	124,187	68,811	YOUNG, DON	55,176	RODEY, PATRICK	200	13,635 R	55.4%	44.4%	55.5%	44.5%
AL	1976	118,208	83,722	YOUNG, DON	34,194	HOPSON, EBEN	292	49,528 R	70.8%	28.9%	71.0%	29.0%
AL	1974	95,921	51,641	YOUNG, DON	44,280	HENSLEY, WILLIAM L.		7,361 R	53.8%	46.2%	53.8%	46.2%
AL	1972	95,401	41,750	YOUNG, DON	53,651	BEGICH, N. J.		11,901 D	43.8%	56.2%	43.8%	56.2%
AL	1970	80,084	35,947	MURKOWSKI, FRANK H.	44,137	BEGICH, N. J.		8,190 D	44.9%	55.1%	44.9%	55.1%
AL	1968	80,362	43,577	POLLOCK, HOWARD W.	36,785	BEGICH, N. J.		6,792 R	54.2%	45.8%	54.2%	45.8%
AL	1966	65,907	34,040	POLLOCK, HOWARD W.	31,867	RIVERS, RALPH J.		2,173 R	51.6%	48.4%	51.6%	48.4%
AL	1964	67,146	32,556	THOMAS, LOWELL	34,590	RIVERS, RALPH J.		2,034 D	48.5%	51.5%	48.5%	51.5%
AL	1962	58,591	26,638	THOMAS, LOWELL	31,953	RIVERS, RALPH J.		5,315 D	45.5%	54.5%	45.5%	54.5%
AL	1960	59,063	25,517	RETTIG, R. L.	33,546	RIVERS, RALPH J.		8,029 D	43.2%	56.8%	43.2%	56.8%
AL	1958	48,647	20,699	BENSON, HENRY A.	27,948	RIVERS, RALPH J.		7,249 D	42.5%	57.5%	42.5%	57.5%

ALASKA

GENERAL AND PRIMARY ELECTIONS

2000 GENERAL ELECTIONS

President   Other vote was 5,192 Reform (Buchanan); 2,636 Libertarian (Browne); 919 Natural Law (Hagelin); 596 Constitution (Phillips); 1,068 scattered write-in.

Congress   Other vote was 22,440 Green (Anna Young); 10,085 Alaskan Independence (Dore); 4,802 Libertarian (Karpinski); 832 scattered write-in.

2000 PRIMARY ELECTIONS

Primary	August 22, 2000	**Registration** (as of Aug. 22, 2000)		
		Republican	113,636
		Democratic	75,081
		Alaskan Independence	18,777
		Libertarian	6,537
		Green	3,681
		Republican Moderate	1,918
		Other	4,950
		Non-Partisan	75,997
		Undeclared	161,249
		TOTAL	461,826

ALASKA

GENERAL AND PRIMARY ELECTIONS

Primary Type   There were two primary ballots. One listed only Republican candidates, and to participate a voter had to be a registered Republican, undeclared (may be affiliated with a party but does not declare it), or non-partisan (not affiliated with a party), although voters could change their registration at the polls. The other primary was open to all candidates from other parties and any registered voter could participate in it. The nominations went to the candidate in each party with the highest vote.

Note: An asterisk (*) denotes incumbent.

	REPUBLICAN PRIMARY			OPEN PRIMARY (Including Democrats)		Overall Percentage	Democratic Percentage
Congressional At-large	Don Young*	33,792	100.0%	Clifford Greene (D)	11,688	32.5%	55.1%
				Anna C. Young (Green)	7,198	20.0%	
				Jim Dore (Alaskan Independence)	5,725	15.9%	
				Dae Miles (D)	5,430	15.1%	25.6%
				Frank Vondersaar (D)	4,095	11.4%	19.3%
				Leonard Karpinski (Libertarian)	1,862	5.2%	
	TOTAL	33,792		TOTAL	35,998		

ARIZONA

GOVERNOR

Jane Dee Hull (R). Elected 1998 to a four-year term. Had succeeded Fife Symington (R) in September 1997 after his conviction on fraud charges.

SENATORS

Jon Kyl (R). Re-elected 2000 to a six-year term. Previously elected 1994.

John McCain (R). Re-elected 1998 to a six-year term. Previously elected 1992, 1986.

REPRESENTATIVES

1. Jeff Flake (R)
2. Ed Pastor (D)
3. Bob Stump (R)
4. John Shadegg (R)
5. Jim Kolbe (R)
6. J. D. Hayworth (R)

POSTWAR VOTE FOR PRESIDENT

| | | Republican | | Democratic | | | | Percentage | | | |
| | | | | | | | | Total Vote | | Major Vote | |
Year	Total Vote	Vote	Candidate	Vote	Candidate	Other Vote	Plurality	Rep.	Dem.	Rep.	Dem.
2000**	1,532,016	781,652	Bush, George W.	685,341	Gore, Al	65,023	96,311 R	51.0%	44.7%	53.3%	46.7%
1996**	1,404,405	622,073	Dole, Bob	653,288	Clinton, Bill	129,044	31,215 D	44.3%	46.5%	48.8%	51.2%
1992**	1,486,975	572,086	Bush, George	543,050	Clinton, Bill	371,839	29,036 R	38.5%	36.5%	51.3%	48.7%
1988	1,171,873	702,541	Bush, George	454,029	Dukakis, Michael S.	15,303	248,512 R	60.0%	38.7%	60.7%	39.3%
1984	1,025,897	681,416	Reagan, Ronald	333,854	Mondale, Walter F.	10,627	347,562 R	66.4%	32.5%	67.1%	32.9%
1980**	873,945	529,688	Reagan, Ronald	246,843	Carter, Jimmy	97,414	282,845 R	60.6%	28.2%	68.2%	31.8%
1976	742,719	418,642	Ford, Gerald R.	295,602	Carter, Jimmy	28,475	123,040 R	56.4%	39.8%	58.6%	41.4%
1972	622,926	402,812	Nixon, Richard M.	198,540	McGovern, George S.	21,574	204,272 R	64.7%	31.9%	67.0%	33.0%
1968	486,936	266,721	Nixon, Richard M.	170,514	Humphrey, Hubert H.	49,701	96,207 R	54.8%	35.0%	61.0%	39.0%
1964	480,770	242,535	Goldwater, Barry M.	237,753	Johnson, Lyndon B.	482	4,782 R	50.4%	49.5%	50.5%	49.5%
1960	398,491	221,241	Nixon, Richard M.	176,781	Kennedy, John F.	469	44,460 R	55.5%	44.4%	55.6%	44.4%
1956	290,173	176,990	Eisenhower, Dwight D.	112,880	Stevenson, Adlai E.	303	64,110 R	61.0%	38.9%	61.1%	38.9%
1952	260,570	152,042	Eisenhower, Dwight D.	108,528	Stevenson, Adlai E.		43,514 R	58.3%	41.7%	58.3%	41.7%
1948	177,065	77,597	Dewey, Thomas E.	95,251	Truman, Harry S.	4,217	17,654 D	43.8%	53.8%	44.9%	55.1%

In 2000 the other vote column includes 45,645 votes cast for Green (Nader). In 1996 the other vote column includes 112,072 votes cast for Perot. In 1992 the other vote column includes 353,741 votes cast for Perot. In 1980 the other column includes 76,952 votes for Independent (Anderson).

ARIZONA

POSTWAR VOTE FOR GOVERNOR

Year	Total Vote	Republican Vote	Republican Candidate	Democratic Vote	Democratic Candidate	Other Vote	Rep.-Dem. Plurality	Total Vote Rep.	Total Vote Dem.	Major Vote Rep.	Major Vote Dem.
1998	1,017,616	620,188	Hull, Jane Dee	361,552	Johnson, Paul	35,876	258,636 R	60.9%	35.5%	63.2%	36.8%
1994	1,129,607	593,492	Symington, Fife	500,702	Basha, Eddie	35,413	92,790 R	52.5%	44.3%	54.2%	45.8%
1990**	940,737	492,569	Symington, Fife	448,168	Goddard, Terry		44,401 R	52.4%	47.6%	52.4%	47.6%
1986**	866,984	343,913	Mecham, Evan	298,986	Warner, Carolyn	224,085	44,927 R	39.7%	34.5%	53.5%	46.5%
1982	726,364	235,877	Corbet, Leo	453,795	Babbitt, Bruce	36,692	217,918 D	32.5%	62.5%	34.2%	65.8%
1978	538,556	241,093	Mecham, Evan	282,605	Babbitt, Bruce	14,858	41,512 D	44.8%	52.5%	46.0%	54.0%
1974	552,202	273,674	Williams, Russell	278,375	Castro, Raul H.	153	4,701 D	49.6%	50.4%	49.6%	50.4%
1970**	411,409	209,522	Williams, John R.	201,887	Castro, Raul H.		7,635 R	50.9%	49.1%	50.9%	49.1%
1968	483,998	279,923	Williams, John R.	204,075	Goddard, Sam		75,848 R	57.8%	42.2%	57.8%	42.2%
1966	378,342	203,438	Williams, John R.	174,904	Goddard, Sam		28,534 R	53.8%	46.2%	53.8%	46.2%
1964	473,502	221,404	Kleindienst, Richard	252,098	Goddard, Sam		30,694 D	46.8%	53.2%	46.8%	53.2%
1962	365,841	200,578	Fannin, Paul	165,263	Goddard, Sam		35,315 R	54.8%	45.2%	54.8%	45.2%
1960	397,107	235,502	Fannin, Paul	161,605	Ackerman, Lee		73,897 R	59.3%	40.7%	59.3%	40.7%
1958	290,465	160,136	Fannin, Paul	130,329	Morrison, Robert		29,807 R	55.1%	44.9%	55.1%	44.9%
1956	288,592	116,744	Griffen, Horace B.	171,848	McFarland, Ernest W.		55,104 D	40.5%	59.5%	40.5%	59.5%
1954	243,970	115,866	Pyle, Howard	128,104	McFarland, Ernest W.		12,238 D	47.5%	52.5%	47.5%	52.5%
1952	260,285	156,592	Pyle, Howard	103,693	Haldiman, Joe C.		52,899 R	60.2%	39.8%	60.2%	39.8%
1950	195,227	99,109	Pyle, Howard	96,118	Frohmiller, Ana		2,991 R	50.8%	49.2%	50.8%	49.2%
1948	175,767	70,419	Brockett, Bruce	104,008	Garvey, Dan E.	1,340	33,589 D	40.1%	59.2%	40.4%	59.6%
1946	122,462	48,867	Brockett, Bruce	73,595	Osborn, Sidney P.		24,728 D	39.9%	60.1%	39.9%	60.1%

The term of office for Arizona's Governor was increased from two to four years effective with the 1970 election. In 1986 other vote was Bill Schulz (Independent). In 1990 neither major-party candidate won an absolute majority, therefore a runoff election was held February 26, 1991; the vote above is for the February runoff.

POSTWAR VOTE FOR SENATOR

Year	Total Vote	Republican Vote	Republican Candidate	Democratic Vote	Democratic Candidate	Other Vote	Rep.-Dem. Plurality	Total Vote Rep.	Total Vote Dem.	Major Vote Rep.	Major Vote Dem.
2000	1,397,076	1,108,196	Kyl, Jon	—		288,880	1,108,196 R	79.3%		100.0%	
1998	1,013,280	696,577	McCain, John	275,224	Ranger, Ed	41,479	421,353 R	68.7%	27.2%	71.7%	28.3%
1994	1,119,060	600,999	Kyl, Jon	442,510	Coppersmith, Sam	75,551	158,489 R	53.7%	39.5%	57.6%	42.4%
1992	1,382,051	771,395	McCain, John	436,321	Sargent, Claire	174,335	335,074 R	55.8%	31.6%	63.9%	36.1%
1988	1,164,539	478,060	DeGreen, Keith	660,403	DeConcini, Dennis	26,076	182,343 D	41.1%	56.7%	42.0%	58.0%
1986	862,921	521,850	McCain, John	340,965	Kimball, Richard	106	180,885 R	60.5%	39.5%	60.5%	39.5%
1982	723,885	291,749	Dunn, Pete	411,970	DeConcini, Dennis	20,166	120,221 D	40.3%	56.9%	41.5%	58.5%
1980	874,238	432,371	Goldwater, Barry M.	422,972	Schulz, Bill	18,895	9,399 R	49.5%	48.4%	50.5%	49.5%
1976	741,210	321,236	Steiger, Sam	400,334	DeConcini, Dennis	19,640	79,098 D	43.3%	54.0%	44.5%	55.5%
1974	549,919	320,396	Goldwater, Barry M.	229,523	Marshall, Jonathan		90,873 R	58.3%	41.7%	58.3%	41.7%
1970	407,796	228,284	Fannin, Paul	179,512	Grossman, Sam		48,772 R	56.0%	44.0%	56.0%	44.0%
1968	479,945	274,607	Goldwater, Barry M.	205,338	Elson, Roy L.		69,269 R	57.2%	42.8%	57.2%	42.8%
1964	468,801	241,089	Fannin, Paul	227,712	Elson, Roy L.		13,377 R	51.4%	48.6%	51.4%	48.6%
1962	362,605	163,388	Mecham, Evan	199,217	Hayden, Carl		35,829 D	45.1%	54.9%	45.1%	54.9%
1958	293,623	164,593	Goldwater, Barry M.	129,030	McFarland, Ernest W.		35,563 R	56.1%	43.9%	56.1%	43.9%
1956	278,263	107,447	Jones, Ross F.	170,816	Hayden, Carl		63,369 D	38.6%	61.4%	38.6%	61.4%
1952	257,401	132,063	Goldwater, Barry M.	125,338	McFarland, Ernest W.		6,725 R	51.3%	48.7%	51.3%	48.7%
1950	185,092	68,846	Brockett, Bruce	116,246	Hayden, Carl		47,400 D	37.2%	62.8%	37.2%	62.8%
1946	116,239	35,022	Powers, Ward S.	80,415	McFarland, Ernest W.	802	45,393 D	30.1%	69.2%	30.3%	69.7%

The Democratic Party did not run a candidate in the 2000 Senate election.

ARIZONA

Districts Established May 6, 1992

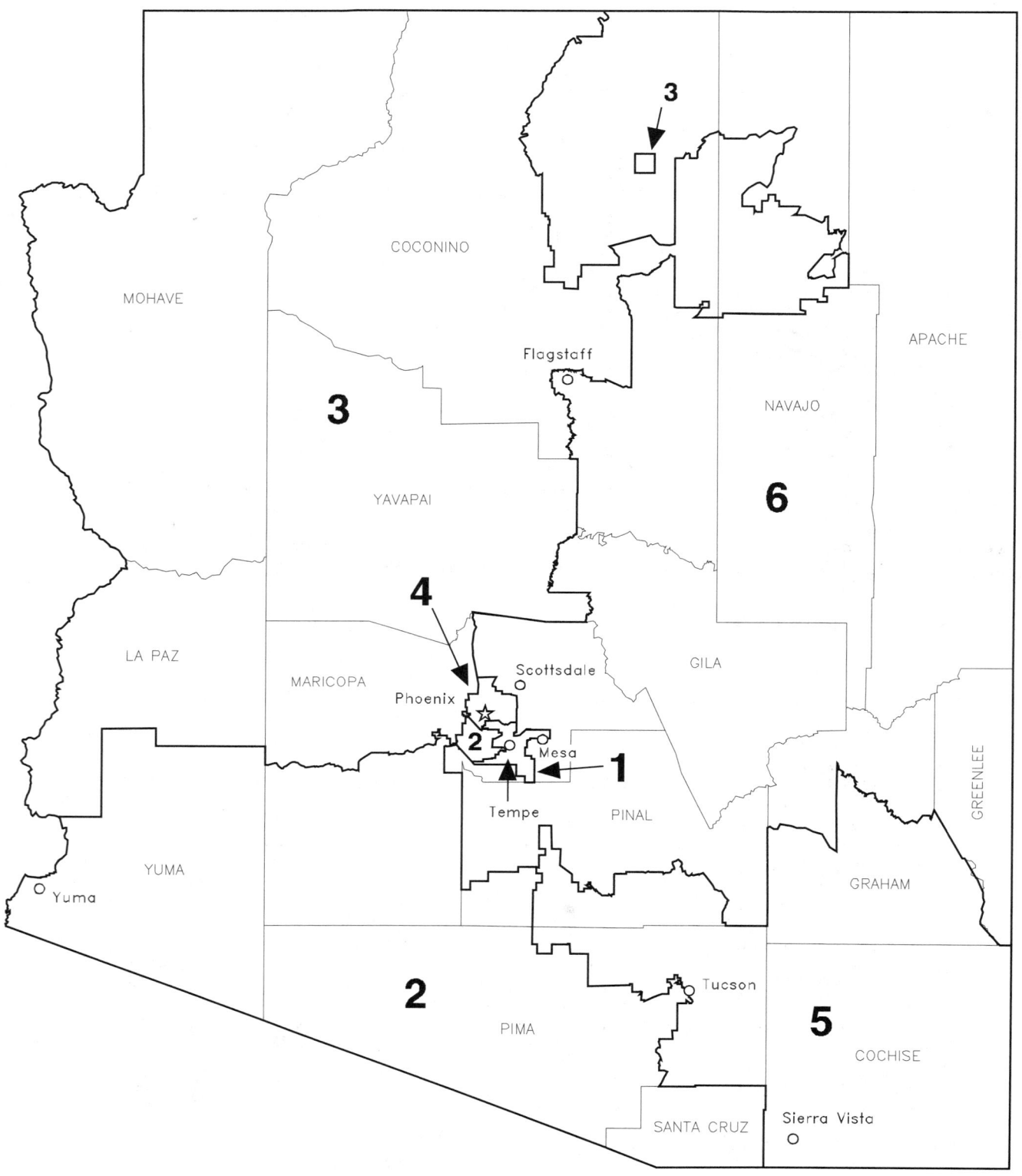

ARIZONA

PRESIDENT 2000

2000 Census Population	County	Total Vote	Republican	Democratic	Green (Nader)	Other	Rep.-Dem. Plurality	Percentage of Total Vote		
								Rep.	Dem.	Green
69,423	APACHE	19,433	5,947	13,025	245	216	7,078 D	30.6%	67.0%	1.3%
117,755	COCHISE	33,204	18,180	13,360	1,113	551	4,820 R	54.8%	40.2%	3.4%
116,320	COCONINO	40,883	17,562	20,280	2,478	563	2,718 D	43.0%	49.6%	6.1%
51,335	GILA	17,736	9,158	7,700	497	381	1,458 R	51.6%	43.4%	2.8%
33,489	GRAHAM	9,664	6,007	3,355	144	158	2,652 R	62.2%	34.7%	1.5%
8,547	GREENLEE	2,960	1,619	1,216	68	57	403 R	54.7%	41.1%	2.3%
19,715	LA PAZ	4,483	2,543	1,769	91	80	774 R	56.7%	39.5%	2.0%
3,072,149	MARICOPA	899,808	479,967	386,683	22,465	10,693	93,284 R	53.3%	43.0%	2.5%
155,032	MOHAVE	44,141	24,386	17,470	1,323	962	6,916 R	55.2%	39.6%	3.0%
97,470	NAVAJO	25,147	12,386	11,794	517	450	592 R	49.3%	46.9%	2.1%
843,746	PIMA	287,640	124,579	147,688	12,355	3,018	23,109 D	43.3%	51.3%	4.3%
179,727	PINAL	41,290	20,122	19,650	904	614	472 R	48.7%	47.6%	2.2%
38,381	SANTA CRUZ	8,893	3,344	5,233	217	99	1,889 D	37.6%	58.8%	2.4%
167,517	YAVAPAI	68,082	40,144	24,063	2,733	1,142	16,081 R	59.0%	35.3%	4.0%
160,026	YUMA	28,652	15,708	12,055	495	394	3,653 R	54.8%	42.1%	1.7%
5,130,632	TOTAL	1,532,016	781,652	685,341	45,645	19,378	96,311 R	51.0%	44.7%	3.0%

ARIZONA

SENATOR 2000

2000 Census Population	County	Total Vote	Republican	Democratic	Other	Rep.-Dem. Plurality	Percentage			
							Total Vote		Major Vote	
							Rep.	Dem.	Rep.	Dem.
69,423	APACHE	16,134	9,857		6,277	9,857 R	61.1%		100.0%	
117,755	COCHISE	30,901	24,766		6,135	24,766 R	80.1%		100.0%	
116,320	COCONINO	37,885	25,512		12,373	25,512 R	67.3%		100.0%	
51,335	GILA	16,693	13,549		3,144	13,549 R	81.2%		100.0%	
33,489	GRAHAM	8,808	7,520		1,288	7,520 R	85.4%		100.0%	
8,547	GREENLEE	2,627	2,135		492	2,135 R	81.3%		100.0%	
19,715	LA PAZ	4,244	3,484		760	3,484 R	82.1%		100.0%	
3,072,149	MARICOPA	818,097	663,756		154,341	663,756 R	81.1%		100.0%	
155,032	MOHAVE	40,947	32,686		8,261	32,686 R	79.8%		100.0%	
97,470	NAVAJO	24,203	18,671		5,532	18,671 R	77.1%		100.0%	
843,746	PIMA	261,314	198,266		63,048	198,266 R	75.9%		100.0%	
179,727	PINAL	38,178	30,134		8,044	30,134 R	78.9%		100.0%	
38,381	SANTA CRUZ	7,876	5,753		2,123	5,753 R	73.0%		100.0%	
167,517	YAVAPAI	63,337	50,815		12,522	50,815 R	80.2%		100.0%	
160,026	YUMA	25,832	21,292		4,540	21,292 R	82.4%		100.0%	
5,130,632	TOTAL	1,397,076	1,108,196		288,880	1,108,196 R	79.3%		100.0%	

Note: The Democratic Party did not run a candidate in the 2000 Senate election.

ARIZONA

CONGRESS

CD	Year	Total Vote	Republican Vote	Republican Candidate	Democratic Vote	Democratic Candidate	Other Vote	Rep.-Dem. Plurality	Total Vote Rep.	Total Vote Dem.	Major Vote Rep.	Major Vote Dem.
1	2000	229,971	123,289	FLAKE, JEFF	97,455	MENDOZA, DAVID	9,227	25,834 R	53.6%	42.4%	55.9%	44.1%
1	1998	152,948	98,840	SALMON, MATT	54,108	MENDOZA, DAVID		44,732 R	64.6%	35.4%	64.6%	35.4%
1	1996	225,372	135,634	SALMON, MATT	89,738	COX, JOHN		45,896 R	60.2%	39.8%	60.2%	39.8%
1	1994	180,867	101,350	SALMON, MATT	70,627	BLANCHARD, CHUCK	8,890	30,723 R	56.0%	39.0%	58.9%	41.1%
1	1992	254,789	113,613	RHODES, JOHN J., III	130,715	COOPERSMITH, SAM	10,461	17,102 D	44.6%	51.3%	46.5%	53.5%
2	2000	122,605	32,990	BARENHOLTZ, BILL	84,034	PASTOR, ED	5,581	51,044 D	26.9%	68.5%	28.2%	71.8%
2	1998	84,363	23,628	BARRON, ED	57,178	PASTOR, ED	3,557	33,550 D	28.0%	67.8%	29.2%	70.8%
2	1996	126,101	38,786	BUSTER, JIM	81,982	PASTOR, ED	5,333	43,196 D	30.8%	65.0%	32.1%	67.9%
2	1994	100,446	32,797	MACDONALD, ROBERT	62,589	PASTOR, ED	5,060	29,792 D	32.7%	62.3%	34.4%	65.6%
2	1992	137,378	41,257	SHOOTER, DON	90,693	PASTOR, ED	5,428	49,436 D	30.0%	66.0%	31.3%	68.7%
3	2000	301,970	198,367	STUMP, BOB	94,676	SCHARER, GENE	8,927	103,691 R	65.7%	31.4%	67.7%	32.3%
3	1998	204,623	137,618	STUMP, BOB	66,979	STARKY, STUART MARC	26	70,639 R	67.3%	32.7%	67.3%	32.7%
3	1996	263,445	175,231	STUMP, BOB	88,214	SCHNEIDER, ALEXANDER		87,017 R	66.5%	33.5%	66.5%	33.5%
3	1994	207,335	145,396	STUMP, BOB	61,939	SPRAGUE, HOWARD L.		83,457 R	70.1%	29.9%	70.1%	29.9%
3	1992	258,503	158,906	STUMP, BOB	88,830	HARTSTONE, ROGER	10,767	70,076 R	61.5%	34.4%	64.1%	35.9%
4	2000	219,497	140,396	SHADEGG, JOHN	71,803	JANKOWSKI, BEN	7,298	68,593 R	64.0%	32.7%	66.2%	33.8%
4	1998	158,822	102,722	SHADEGG, JOHN	49,538	EHST, ERIC	6,562	53,184 R	64.7%	31.2%	67.5%	32.5%
4	1996	225,343	150,486	SHADEGG, JOHN	74,857	MILTON, MARIA ELENA		75,629 R	66.8%	33.2%	66.8%	33.2%
4	1994	193,902	116,714	SHADEGG, JOHN	69,760	CURE, CAROL	7,428	46,954 R	60.2%	36.0%	62.6%	37.4%
4	1992	264,066	156,330	KYL, JON	70,572	MYBECK, WALTER R.	37,164	85,758 R	59.2%	26.7%	68.9%	31.1%
5	2000	287,609	172,986	KOLBE, JIM	101,564	CUNNINGHAM, GEORGE	13,059	71,422 R	60.1%	35.3%	63.0%	37.0%
5	1998	201,473	103,952	KOLBE, JIM	91,030	VOLGY, TOM	6,491	12,922 R	51.6%	45.2%	53.3%	46.7%
5	1996	260,898	179,349	KOLBE, JIM	67,597	NELSON, MORT	13,952	111,752 R	68.7%	25.9%	72.6%	27.4%
5	1994	220,771	149,514	KOLBE, JIM	63,436	AUERBACH, GARY	7,821	86,078 R	67.7%	28.7%	70.2%	29.8%
5	1992	259,813	172,867	KOLBE, JIM	77,256	TOEVS, JIM	9,690	95,611 R	66.5%	29.7%	69.1%	30.9%
6	2000	304,004	186,687	HAYWORTH, J.D.	108,317	NELSON, LARRY	9,000	78,370 R	61.4%	35.6%	63.3%	36.7%
6	1998	201,537	106,891	HAYWORTH, J.D.	88,001	OWENS, STEVE	6,645	18,890 R	53.0%	43.7%	54.8%	45.2%
6	1996	255,287	121,431	HAYWORTH, J.D.	118,957	OWENS, STEVE	14,899	2,474 R	47.6%	46.6%	50.5%	49.5%
6	1994	196,068	107,060	HAYWORTH, J.D.	81,321	ENGLISH, KARAN	7,687	25,739 R	54.6%	41.5%	56.8%	43.2%
6	1992	234,372	97,074	WEAD, DOUG	124,251	ENGLISH, KARAN	13,047	27,177 D	41.4%	53.0%	43.9%	56.1%

ARIZONA

GENERAL AND PRIMARY ELECTIONS

2000 GENERAL ELECTIONS

President   Other vote was 12,373 Reform (Buchanan); 5,775 Libertarian (Smith); 1,120 Natural Law (Hagelin); 110 write-in (Phillips). (L. Neil Smith was the Libertarian candidate in Arizona, while Harry Browne was the party's standard-bearer elsewhere.)

Senator   Other vote was 109,230 Independent (Toel); 108,926 Green (Hansen); 70,724 Libertarian (Hess).

Congress   Other vote was: CD 1: 9,227 Libertarian (Burroughs); CD 2: 3,169 Libertarian (Weber), 2,412 Natural Law (Shelor); CD 3: 8,927 Libertarian (Carlson); CD 4: 7,298 Libertarian (Hancock); CD 5: 9,010 Green (M. J. Green), 4,049 Libertarian (Nost); CD 6: 9,000 Libertarian (Duncan).

ARIZONA
GENERAL AND PRIMARY ELECTIONS

2000 PRIMARY ELECTIONS

Primary	February 22, 2000 (Republican President) March 11, 2000 (Democratic President) September 12, 2000 (Congress)	**Registration** (as of Sept. 12, 2000)	Republican Democratic Libertarian Green Reform Natural Law Other	905,205 797,090 12,425 2,714 1,530 89 323,409
			TOTAL	2,042,462

Note: The Democratic presidential primary was conducted by the party. The others were conducted by the state.

Primary Type   Only registered Democrats and Republicans could vote in their party's presidential primary. But the September congressional primaries were also open to voters who were not members of a recognized political party.

Note: An asterisk (*) denotes incumbent.

	REPUBLICAN PRIMARIES			DEMOCRATIC PRIMARIES		
President	John McCain	193,708	60.0%	Al Gore	67,582	77.9%
	George W. Bush	115,115	35.7%	Bill Bradley	16,383	18.9%
	Alan Keyes	11,500	3.6%	No Preference	1,439	1.7%
	Steve Forbes	1,211	0.4%	Heather Harder	1,358	1.6%
	Orrin G. Hatch	637	0.2%			
	John R. McGrath	239	0.1%			
	Gary Bauer	177	0.1%			
	James T. Zanon	54				
	Chuck See	28				
	TOTAL	322,669		TOTAL	86,762	
Senator	Jon Kyl*	255,659	100%	*No Democratic candidates were listed on the ballot. Write-in vote was as follows: Stuart Starky, 3,245 (67.7%); Ronald E. Maynard, 1,545 (32.3%).*		
	TOTAL	255,659				
Congressional District 1	Jeff Flake	16,745	31.8%	David Mendoza	15,573	100.0%
	Sal Diciccio	12,490	23.7%			
	Susan Bitter Smith	11,763	22.3%			
	Tom Liddy	10,898	20.7%			
	Bert Tollefson	764	1.5%			
	TOTAL	52,660		TOTAL	15,573	
Congressional District 2	Bill Barenholtz	10,730	100.0%	Ed Pastor*	26,354	100.0%
	TOTAL	10,730		TOTAL	26,354	
Congressional District 3	Bob Stump*	60,143	82.9%	Gene Scharer	20,471	100.0%
	Dick Hensley	12,427	17.1%			
	TOTAL	72,570		TOTAL	20,471	
Congressional District 4	John Shadegg*	35,985	100.0%	Ben Jankowski	11,413	100.0%
	TOTAL	35,985		TOTAL	11,413	
Congressional District 5	Jim Kolbe*	35,263	78.8%	George Cunningham	23,388	52.5%
	Joseph Sweeney	9,477	21.2%	Mary Judge Ryan	21,201	47.5%
	TOTAL	44,740		TOTAL	44,589	
Congressional District 6	J. D. Hayworth*	46,743	100.0%	Larry Nelson	24,257	57.1%
				Kevin B. Harris	18,231	42.9%
	TOTAL	46,743		TOTAL	42,488	

ARKANSAS

GOVERNOR
Mike Huckebee (R). Elected 1998 to a four-year term. Had become Governor in July 1996 upon the resignation of Governor Jim Guy Tucker (D) who was convicted on fraud and conspiracy charges.

SENATORS
Blanche Lincoln (D). Elected 1998 to a six-year term.

Tim Hutchinson (R). Elected 1996 to a six-year term.

REPRESENTATIVES
1. Marion Berry (D)
2. Vic Snyder (D)
3. Asa Hutchinson (R)
4. Mike Ross (D)

POSTWAR VOTE FOR PRESIDENT

| | | Republican | | Democratic | | Other | | Percentage | | | |
| | Total | | | | | | | Total Vote | | Major Vote | |
Year	Vote	Vote	Candidate	Vote	Candidate	Vote	Plurality	Rep.	Dem.	Rep.	Dem.
2000**	921,781	472,940	Bush, George W.	422,768	Gore, Al	26,073	50,172 R	51.3%	45.9%	52.8%	47.2%
1996**	884,262	325,416	Dole, Bob	475,171	Clinton, Bill	83,675	149,755 D	36.8%	53.7%	40.6%	59.4%
1992**	950,653	337,324	Bush, George	505,823	Clinton, Bill	107,506	168,499 D	35.5%	53.2%	40.0%	60.0%
1988	827,738	466,578	Bush, George	349,237	Dukakis, Michael S.	11,923	117,341 R	56.4%	42.2%	57.2%	42.8%
1984	884,406	534,774	Reagan, Ronald	338,646	Mondale, Walter F.	10,986	196,128 R	60.5%	38.3%	61.2%	38.8%
1980**	837,582	403,164	Reagan, Ronald	398,041	Carter, Jimmy	36,377	5,123 R	48.1%	47.5%	50.3%	49.7%
1976	767,535	267,903	Ford, Gerald R.	498,604	Carter, Jimmy	1,028	230,701 D	34.9%	65.0%	35.0%	65.0%
1972	651,320	448,541	Nixon, Richard M.	199,892	McGovern, George S.	2,887	248,649 R	68.9%	30.7%	69.2%	30.8%
1968**	619,969	190,759	Nixon, Richard M.	188,228	Humphrey, Hubert H.	240,982	50,223 A	30.8%	30.4%	50.3%	49.7%
1964	560,426	243,264	Goldwater, Barry M.	314,197	Johnson, Lyndon B.	2,965	70,933 D	43.4%	56.1%	43.6%	56.4%
1960	428,509	184,508	Nixon, Richard M.	215,049	Kennedy, John F.	28,952	30,541 D	43.1%	50.2%	46.2%	53.8%
1956	406,572	186,287	Eisenhower, Dwight D.	213,277	Stevenson, Adlai E.	7,008	26,990 D	45.8%	52.5%	46.6%	53.4%
1952	404,800	177,155	Eisenhower, Dwight D.	226,300	Stevenson, Adlai E.	1,345	49,145 D	43.8%	55.9%	43.9%	56.1%
1948**	242,475	50,959	Dewey, Thomas E.	149,659	Truman, Harry S.	41,857	98,700 D	21.0%	61.7%	25.4%	74.6%

In 2000 the other vote column includes 13,421 votes cast for Green (Nader). In 1996 the other vote column includes 69,884 votes cast for Perot. In 1992 the other vote column includes 99,132 votes cast for Perot. In 1980 the other column includes 22,468 votes for Independent (Anderson). In 1968 other vote was American (Wallace). In 1948 other vote was 40,068 States Rights; 1,037 Socialist; 751 Progressive and 1 Prohibition.

ARKANSAS

POSTWAR VOTE FOR GOVERNOR

Year	Total Vote	Republican Vote	Republican Candidate	Democratic Vote	Democratic Candidate	Other Vote	Rep.-Dem. Plurality	Total Vote Rep.	Total Vote Dem.	Major Vote Rep.	Major Vote Dem.
1998	706,011	421,989	Huckabee, Mike	272,923	Bristow, Bill	11,099	149,066 R	59.8%	38.7%	60.7%	39.3%
1994	716,840	287,904	Nelson, Sheffield	428,936	Tucker, Jim Guy		141,032 D	40.2%	59.8%	40.2%	59.8%
1990	696,412	295,925	Nelson, Sheffield	400,386	Clinton, Bill	101	104,461 D	42.5%	57.5%	42.5%	57.5%
1986**	688,551	248,427	White, Frank D.	439,882	Clinton, Bill	242	191,455 D	36.1%	63.9%	36.1%	63.9%
1984	886,548	331,987	Freeman, Woody	554,561	Clinton, Bill		222,574 D	37.4%	62.6%	37.4%	62.6%
1982	789,351	357,496	White, Frank D.	431,855	Clinton, Bill		74,359 D	45.3%	54.7%	45.3%	54.7%
1980	838,925	435,684	White, Frank D.	403,241	Clinton, Bill		32,443 R	51.9%	48.1%	51.9%	48.1%
1978	528,912	193,746	Lowe, A. Lynn	335,101	Clinton, Bill	65	141,355 D	36.6%	63.4%	36.6%	63.4%
1976	726,949	121,716	Griffith, Leon	605,083	Pryor, David H.	150	483,367 D	16.7%	83.2%	16.7%	83.3%
1974	545,974	187,872	Coon, Ken	358,018	Pryor, David H.	84	170,146 D	34.4%	65.6%	34.4%	65.6%
1972	648,069	159,177	Blaylock, Len E.	488,892	Bumpers, Dale		329,715 D	24.6%	75.4%	24.6%	75.4%
1970	609,198	197,418	Rockefeller, Winthrop	375,648	Bumpers, Dale	36,132	178,230 D	32.4%	61.7%	34.4%	65.6%
1968	615,595	322,782	Rockefeller, Winthrop	292,813	Crank, Marion		29,969 R	52.4%	47.6%	52.4%	47.6%
1966	563,527	306,324	Rockefeller, Winthrop	257,203	Johnson, James D.		49,121 R	54.4%	45.6%	54.4%	45.6%
1964	592,113	254,561	Rockefeller, Winthrop	337,489	Faubus, Orval E.	63	82,928 D	43.0%	57.0%	43.0%	57.0%
1962	308,092	82,349	Ricketts, Willis	225,743	Faubus, Orval E.		143,394 D	26.7%	73.3%	26.7%	73.3%
1960	421,985	129,921	Britt, Henry M.	292,064	Faubus, Orval E.		162,143 D	30.8%	69.2%	30.8%	69.2%
1958	286,886	50,288	Johnson, George W.	236,598	Faubus, Orval E.		186,310 D	17.5%	82.5%	17.5%	82.5%
1956	399,012	77,215	Mitchell, Roy	321,797	Faubus, Orval E.		244,582 D	19.4%	80.6%	19.4%	80.6%
1954	335,176	127,004	Remmel, Pratt C.	208,121	Faubus, Orval E.	51	81,117 D	37.9%	62.1%	37.9%	62.1%
1952	391,592	49,292	Speck, Jefferson W.	342,292	Cherry, Francis	8	293,000 D	12.6%	87.4%	12.6%	87.4%
1950	317,087	50,309	Speck, Jefferson W.	266,778	McMath, Sidney S.		216,469 D	15.9%	84.1%	15.9%	84.1%
1948	249,301	26,500	Black, Charles R.	222,801	McMath, Sidney S.		196,301 D	10.6%	89.4%	10.6%	89.4%
1946	152,162	24,133	Mills, W. T.	128,029	Laney, Ben T.		103,896 D	15.9%	84.1%	15.9%	84.1%

The term of office for Arkansas' Governor was increased from two to four years effective with the 1986 election.

POSTWAR VOTE FOR SENATOR

Year	Total Vote	Republican Vote	Republican Candidate	Democratic Vote	Democratic Candidate	Other Vote	Rep.-Dem. Plurality	Total Vote Rep.	Total Vote Dem.	Major Vote Rep.	Major Vote Dem.
1998	700,644	295,870	Boozman, Fay	385,878	Lincoln, Blanche	18,896	90,008 D	42.2%	55.1%	43.4%	56.6%
1996	846,183	445,942	Hutchinson, Tim	400,241	Bryant, Winston		45,701 R	52.7%	47.3%	52.7%	47.3%
1992	920,008	366,373	Huckabee, Mike	553,635	Bumpers, Dale		187,262 D	39.8%	60.2%	39.8%	60.2%
1990**	494,735		—	493,910	Pryor, David H.	825	493,910 D		99.8%		100.0%
1986	695,487	262,313	Hutchinson, Asa	433,122	Bumpers, Dale	52	170,809 D	37.7%	62.3%	37.7%	62.3%
1984	875,956	373,615	Bethune, Ed	502,341	Pryor, David H.		128,726 D	42.7%	57.3%	42.7%	57.3%
1980	808,812	330,576	Clark, Bill	477,905	Bumpers, Dale	331	147,329 D	40.9%	59.1%	40.9%	59.1%
1978	522,239	84,722	Kelly, Tom	399,916	Pryor, David H.	37,601	315,194 D	16.2%	76.6%	17.5%	82.5%
1974	543,082	82,026	Jones, John H.	461,056	Bumpers, Dale		379,030 D	15.1%	84.9%	15.1%	84.9%
1972	634,636	248,238	Babbitt, Wayne H.	386,398	McClellan, John L.		138,160 D	39.1%	60.9%	39.1%	60.9%
1968	591,704	241,739	Bernard, Charles T.	349,965	Fulbright, J. W.		108,226 D	40.9%	59.1%	40.9%	59.1%
1966**					McClellan, John L.		D				
1962	312,880	98,013	Jones, Kenneth	214,867	Fulbright, J. W.		116,854 D	31.3%	68.7%	31.3%	68.7%
1960**			—		McClellan, John L.		D				
1956	399,695	68,016	Henley, Ben C.	331,679	Fulbright, J. W.		263,663 D	17.0%	83.0%	17.0%	83.0%
1954	291,058		—	291,058	McClellan, John L.		291,058 D		100.0%		100.0%
1950	302,582		—	302,582	Fulbright, J. W.		302,582 D		100.0%		100.0%
1948	216,401		—	216,401	McClellan, John L.		216,401 D		100.0%		100.0%

In 1990 Senator Pryor's vote was not canvassed in seven counties due to the fact that he was unopposed. Senator McClellan was re-elected in 1966 and in 1960, but his vote was not canvassed in many counties.

ARKANSAS

Districts Established April 10, 1991

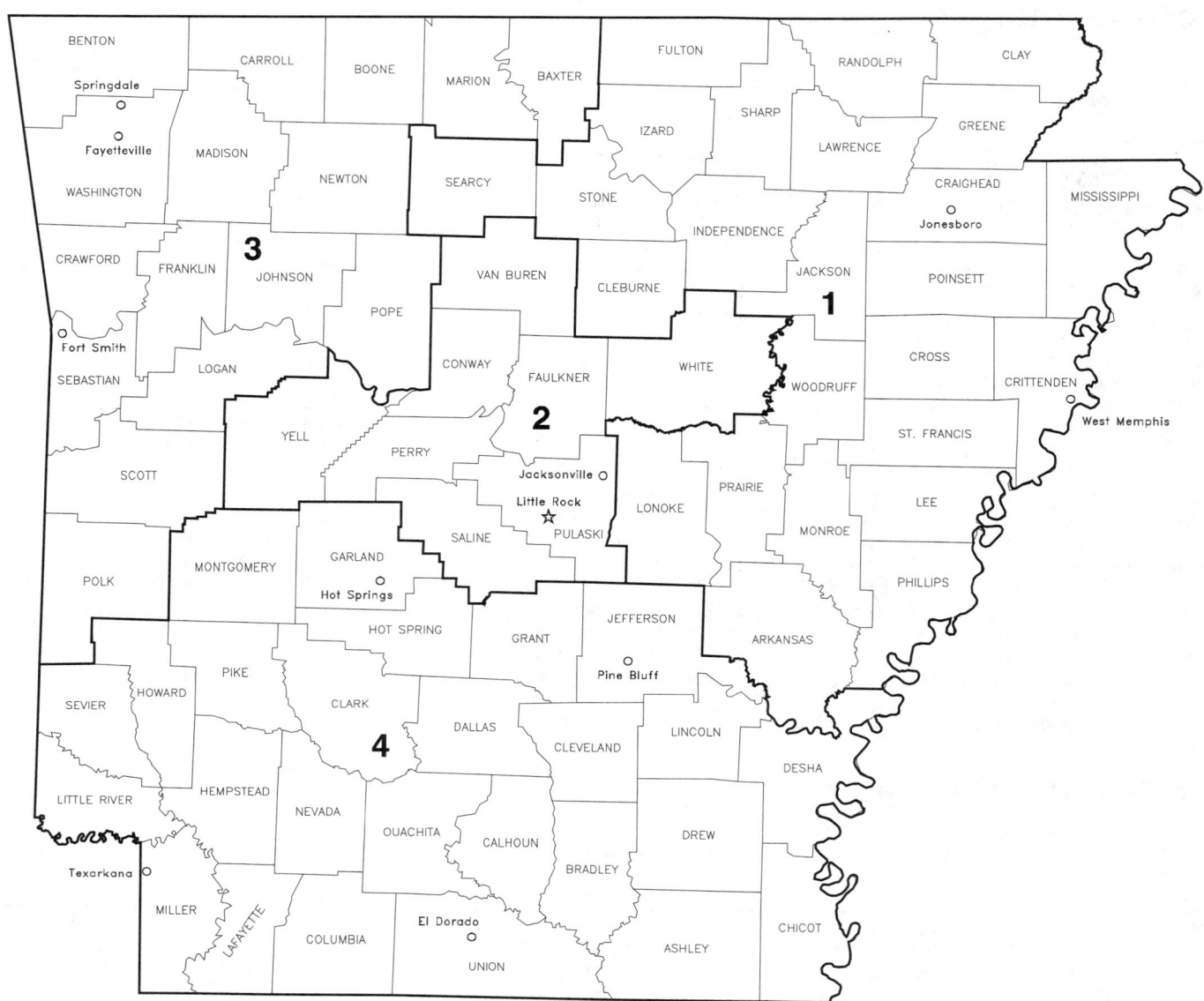

ARKANSAS

PRESIDENT 2000

2000 Census Population	County	Total Vote	Republican	Democratic	Green (Nader)	Other	Rep.-Dem. Plurality	Percentage of Total Vote		
								Rep.	Dem.	Green
20,749	ARKANSAS	6,372	3,353	2,877	65	77	476 R	52.6%	45.2%	1.0%
24,209	ASHLEY	8,271	3,876	4,253	61	81	377 D	46.9%	51.4%	0.7%
38,386	BAXTER	16,708	9,538	6,516	429	225	3,022 R	57.1%	39.0%	2.6%
153,406	BENTON	53,646	34,838	17,277	862	669	17,561 R	64.9%	32.2%	1.6%
33,948	BOONE	13,635	8,569	4,493	289	284	4,076 R	62.8%	33.0%	2.1%
12,600	BRADLEY	3,979	1,793	2,122	34	30	329 D	45.1%	53.3%	0.9%
5,744	CALHOUN	2,185	1,128	1,017	19	21	111 R	51.6%	46.5%	0.9%
25,357	CARROLL	9,590	5,556	3,595	301	138	1,961 R	57.9%	37.5%	3.1%
14,117	CHICOT	4,452	1,564	2,820	26	42	1,256 D	35.1%	63.3%	0.6%
23,546	CLARK	8,626	3,776	4,661	103	86	885 D	43.8%	54.0%	1.2%
17,609	CLAY	5,900	2,254	3,527	73	46	1,273 D	38.2%	59.8%	1.2%
24,046	CLEBURNE	10,207	5,730	4,120	183	174	1,610 R	56.1%	40.4%	1.8%
8,571	CLEVELAND	3,181	1,678	1,414	30	59	264 R	52.8%	44.5%	0.9%
25,603	COLUMBIA	9,307	5,018	4,003	70	216	1,015 R	53.9%	43.0%	0.8%
20,336	CONWAY	7,234	3,545	3,496	84	109	49 R	49.0%	48.3%	1.2%
82,148	CRAIGHEAD	25,157	12,158	12,376	409	214	218 D	48.3%	49.2%	1.6%
53,247	CRAWFORD	17,625	10,804	6,288	223	310	4,516 R	61.3%	35.7%	1.3%
50,866	CRITTENDEN	13,234	5,857	7,224	97	56	1,367 D	44.3%	54.6%	0.7%
19,526	CROSS	6,215	3,033	3,096	38	48	63 D	48.8%	49.8%	0.6%
9,210	DALLAS	3,325	1,571	1,710	21	23	139 D	47.2%	51.4%	0.6%
15,341	DESHA	4,495	1,603	2,776	38	78	1,173 D	35.7%	61.8%	0.8%
18,723	DREW	5,922	2,756	3,060	47	59	304 D	46.5%	51.7%	0.8%
86,014	FAULKNER	29,216	16,055	11,950	513	698	4,105 R	55.0%	40.9%	1.8%
17,771	FRANKLIN	6,140	3,277	2,674	100	89	603 R	53.4%	43.6%	1.6%
11,642	FULTON	4,108	2,036	1,976	51	45	60 R	49.6%	48.1%	1.2%
88,068	GARLAND	35,935	19,098	15,840	566	431	3,258 R	53.1%	44.1%	1.6%
16,464	GRANT	6,013	3,285	2,535	88	105	750 R	54.6%	42.2%	1.5%
37,331	GREENE	12,484	5,831	6,319	205	129	488 D	46.7%	50.6%	1.6%
23,587	HEMPSTEAD	7,289	3,257	3,937	50	45	680 D	44.7%	54.0%	0.7%
30,353	HOT SPRING	10,981	5,042	5,527	202	210	485 D	45.9%	50.3%	1.8%
14,300	HOWARD	4,459	2,326	2,063	50	20	263 R	52.2%	46.3%	1.1%
34,233	INDEPENDENCE	11,594	6,145	5,146	171	132	999 R	53.0%	44.4%	1.5%
13,249	IZARD	5,032	2,301	2,587	76	68	286 D	45.7%	51.4%	1.5%
18,418	JACKSON	6,072	2,280	3,651	77	64	1,371 D	37.5%	60.1%	1.3%
84,278	JEFFERSON	27,201	8,765	17,716	361	359	8,951 D	32.2%	65.1%	1.3%
22,781	JOHNSON	7,161	3,657	3,270	109	125	387 R	51.1%	45.7%	1.5%
8,559	LAFAYETTE	3,383	1,538	1,806	27	12	268 D	45.5%	53.4%	0.8%
17,774	LAWRENCE	6,040	2,626	3,255	87	72	629 D	43.5%	53.9%	1.4%
12,580	LEE	4,121	1,351	2,727	18	25	1,376 D	32.8%	66.2%	0.4%
14,492	LINCOLN	3,546	1,526	1,957	21	42	431 D	43.0%	55.2%	0.6%
13,628	LITTLE RIVER	5,263	2,283	2,883	50	47	600 D	43.4%	54.8%	1.0%
22,486	LOGAN	8,096	4,487	3,283	124	202	1,204 R	55.4%	40.6%	1.5%
52,828	LONOKE	17,943	10,606	6,851	237	249	3,755 R	59.1%	38.2%	1.3%
14,243	MADISON	5,628	3,387	2,055	88	98	1,332 R	60.2%	36.5%	1.6%
16,140	MARION	6,015	3,402	2,233	220	160	1,169 R	56.6%	37.1%	3.7%
40,443	MILLER	13,745	7,276	6,278	100	91	998 R	52.9%	45.7%	0.7%
51,979	MISSISSIPPI	12,586	5,199	7,107	110	170	1,908 D	41.3%	56.5%	0.9%
10,254	MONROE	3,293	1,329	1,910	29	25	581 D	40.4%	58.0%	0.9%
9,245	MONTGOMERY	3,739	2,128	1,438	101	72	690 R	56.9%	38.5%	2.7%
9,955	NEVADA	3,738	1,796	1,867	42	33	71 D	48.0%	49.9%	1.1%
8,608	NEWTON	3,927	2,529	1,205	112	81	1,324 R	64.4%	30.7%	2.9%
28,790	OUACHITA	10,395	4,739	5,464	100	92	725 D	45.6%	52.6%	1.0%
10,209	PERRY	4,007	2,114	1,648	61	184	466 R	52.8%	41.1%	1.5%
26,445	PHILLIPS	9,313	3,154	6,018	75	66	2,864 D	33.9%	64.6%	0.8%
11,303	PIKE	3,971	2,275	1,604	45	47	671 R	57.3%	40.4%	1.1%
25,614	POINSETT	7,235	2,988	4,102	87	58	1,114 D	41.3%	56.7%	1.2%
20,229	POLK	7,193	4,600	2,315	130	148	2,285 R	64.0%	32.2%	1.8%
54,469	POPE	18,422	11,244	6,669	259	250	4,575 R	61.0%	36.2%	1.4%
9,539	PRAIRIE	3,507	1,862	1,563	29	53	299 R	53.1%	44.6%	0.8%
361,474	PULASKI	127,151	55,866	68,320	1,756	1,209	12,454 D	43.9%	53.7%	1.4%

ARKANSAS

PRESIDENT 2000

2000 Census Population	County	Total Vote	Republican	Democratic	Green (Nader)	Other	Rep.-Dem. Plurality	Percentage of Total Vote Rep.	Dem.	Green
18,195	RANDOLPH	5,877	2,673	3,019	84	101	346 D	45.5%	51.4%	1.4%
29,329	ST. FRANCIS	8,496	3,414	4,986	42	54	1,572 D	40.2%	58.7%	0.5%
83,529	SALINE	32,391	18,617	12,700	533	541	5,917 R	57.5%	39.2%	1.6%
10,996	SCOTT	3,981	2,399	1,444	48	90	955 R	60.3%	36.3%	1.2%
8,261	SEARCY	4,058	2,610	1,229	83	136	1,381 R	64.3%	30.3%	2.0%
115,071	SEBASTIAN	40,159	23,483	15,555	503	618	7,928 R	58.5%	38.7%	1.3%
15,757	SEVIER	4,293	2,111	2,095	55	32	16 R	49.2%	48.8%	1.3%
17,119	SHARP	7,126	3,698	3,236	115	77	462 R	51.9%	45.4%	1.6%
11,499	STONE	4,860	2,623	2,043	98	96	580 R	54.0%	42.0%	2.0%
45,629	UNION	15,609	8,647	6,261	130	571	2,386 R	55.4%	40.1%	0.8%
16,192	VAN BUREN	6,984	3,485	3,202	153	144	283 R	49.9%	45.8%	2.2%
157,715	WASHINGTON	51,459	28,231	21,425	1,208	595	6,806 R	54.9%	41.6%	2.3%
67,165	WHITE	22,150	13,170	8,342	243	395	4,828 R	59.5%	37.7%	1.1%
8,741	WOODRUFF	2,651	898	1,699	19	35	801 D	33.9%	64.1%	0.7%
21,139	YELL	6,479	3,223	3,062	78	116	161 R	49.7%	47.3%	1.2%
2,673,400	TOTAL	921,781	472,940	422,768	13,421	12,652	50,172 R	51.3%	45.9%	1.5%

ARKANSAS

CONGRESS

			Republican		Democratic				Percentage			
		Total					Other	Rep.-Dem.	Total Vote		Major Vote	
CD	Year	Vote	Vote	Candidate	Vote	Candidate	Vote	Plurality	Rep.	Dem.	Rep.	Dem.
1	2000	199,956	79,437	MYSHKA, SUSAN	120,266	BERRY, MARION	253	40,829 D	39.7%	60.1%	39.8%	60.2%
1	1998					BERRY, MARION		D				
1	1996	199,450	88,436	DUPWE, WARREN	105,280	BERRY, MARION	5,734	16,844 D	44.3%	52.8%	45.7%	54.3%
1	1994	178,437	83,147	DUPWE, WARREN	95,290	LAMBERT, BLANCHE		12,143 D	46.6%	53.4%	46.6%	53.4%
1	1992	214,176	64,618	HAYES, TERRY	149,558	LAMBERT, BLANCHE		84,940 D	30.2%	69.8%	30.2%	69.8%
2	2000	220,649	93,692	THOMAS, BOB	126,957	SNYDER, VIC		33,265 D	42.5%	57.5%	42.5%	57.5%
2	1998	173,071	72,737	WYRICK, PHIL	100,334	SNYDER, VIC		27,597 D	42.0%	58.0%	42.0%	58.0%
2	1996	219,389	104,548	CUMMINS, BUD	114,841	SNYDER, VIC		10,293 D	47.7%	52.3%	47.7%	52.3%
2	1994	170,053	72,473	POWELL, BILL	97,580	THORNTON, RAY		25,107 D	42.6%	57.4%	42.6%	57.4%
2	1992	208,924	53,978	SCOTT, DENNIS	154,946	THORNTON, RAY		100,968 D	25.8%	74.2%	25.8%	74.2%
3	2000			HUTCHINSON, ASA				R				
3	1998	191,697	154,780	HUTCHINSON, ASA			36,917	154,780 R	80.7%		100.0%	
3	1996	246,132	137,093	HUTCHINSON, ASA	102,994	HENRY, ANN	6,045	34,099 R	55.7%	41.8%	57.1%	42.9%
3	1994	191,683	129,800	HUTCHINSON, TIM	61,883	SEITZ, BERTA		67,917 R	67.7%	32.3%	67.7%	32.3%
3	1992	249,494	125,295	HUTCHINSON, TIM	117,775	VAN WINKLE, JOHN	6,424	7,520 R	50.2%	47.2%	51.5%	48.5%
4	2000	212,160	104,017	DICKEY, JAY	108,143	ROSS, MIKE	4,126	4,126 D	49.0%	51.0%	49.0%	51.0%
4	1998	160,540	92,346	DICKEY, JAY	68,194	SMITH, JUDY		24,152 R	57.5%	42.5%	57.5%	42.5%
4	1996	198,347	125,956	DICKEY, JAY	72,391	TOLLIVER, VINCENT		53,565 R	63.5%	36.5%	63.5%	36.5%
4	1994	168,839	87,469	DICKEY, JAY	81,370	BRADFORD, JAY		6,099 R	51.8%	48.2%	51.8%	48.2%
4	1992	215,927	113,009	DICKEY, JAY	102,918	MCCUEN, W. J.		10,091 R	52.3%	47.7%	52.3%	47.7%

ARKANSAS

GENERAL AND PRIMARY ELECTIONS

2000 GENERAL ELECTIONS

President Other vote was 7,358 Reform (Buchanan); 2,781 Libertarian (Browne); 1,415 Constitutional (Phillips); 1,098 Natural Law (Hagelin).

Congress Other vote was: CD 1: 253 write-in (Moody).

2000 PRIMARY ELECTIONS

Primary May 23, 2000 **Registration** 1,527,453 No Party Registration
Primary Runoff June 13, 2000 (as of May 23, 2000)

Primary Type Open—Any registered voter could vote in either the Democratic or Republican primary, though if they voted in one party's primary they could not participate in a primary runoff of the other.

Note: An asterisk (*) denotes incumbent. The names of unopposed candidates do not appear on the primary ballot; therefore, no votes are cast for these candidates.

	REPUBLICAN PRIMARIES			DEMOCRATIC PRIMARIES		
President	George W. Bush	35,759	80.2%	Al Gore	193,750	78.5%
	Alan Keyes	8,814	19.8%	Lyndon H. LaRouche Jr.	53,150	21.5%
	TOTAL	44,573		TOTAL	246,900	
Congressional District 1	Susan Myshka	3,250	64.1%	Marion Berry*	Unopposed	
	Jason Sutfin	1,820	35.9%			
	TOTAL	5,070				
Congressional District 2	Bob Thomas	6,330	58.8%	Vic Snyder*	Unopposed	
	Rod Martin	4,427	41.2%			
	TOTAL	10,757				
Congressional District 3	Asa Hutchinson*	Unopposed		No Democratic candidate		
Congressional District 4	Jay Dickey*	Unopposed		Mike Ross	41,668	44.7%
				Dewayne Graham	20,575	22.1%
				Judy Smith	20,341	21.8%
				Bruce Carleton Harris	10,539	11.3%
				TOTAL	93,123	
				PRIMARY RUNOFF		
				Mike Ross	28,286	58.1%
				Dewayne Graham	20,392	41.9%
				TOTAL	48,678	

CALIFORNIA

GOVERNOR
Gray Davis (D). Elected 1998 to a four-year term.

SENATORS
Barbara Boxer (D). Re-elected 1998 to a six-year term. Previously elected 1992.

Dianne Feinstein (D). Re-elected 2000 to a six-year term. Previously elected 1994 and 1992 to fill the remaining two years of the term vacated when Senator Pete Wilson (R) was elected Governor in November 1990.

REPRESENTATIVES

1. Mike Thompson (D)
2. Wally Herger (R)
3. Doug Ose (R)
4. John T. Doolittle (R)
5. Robert T. Matsui (D)
6. Lynn Woolsey (D)
7. George Miller (D)
8. Nancy Pelosi (D)
9. Barbara Lee (D)
10. Ellen O. Tauscher (D)
11. Richard W. Pombo (R)
12. Tom Lantos (D)
13. Fortney Stark (D)
14. Anna G. Eshoo (D)
15. Mike Honda (D)
16. Zoe Lofgren (D)
17. Sam Farr (D)
18. Gary A. Condit (D)
19. George Radanovich (R)
20. Calvin Dooley (D)
21. William M. Thomas (R)
22. Lois Capps (D)
23. Elton Gallegly (R)
24. Brad Sherman (D)
25. Howard P. McKeon (R)
26. Howard L. Berman (D)
27. Adam Schiff (D)
28. David Dreier (R)
29. Henry A. Waxman (D)
30. Xavier Becerra (D)
31. Hilda Solis (D)
32. Diane E. Watson (D)
33. Lucille Roybal-Allard (D)
34. Grace F. Napolitano (D)
35. Maxine Waters (D)
36. Jane Harman (D)
37. Juanita Millender-McDonald (D)
38. Steve Horn (R)
39. Ed Royce (R)
40. Jerry Lewis (R)
41. Gary Miller (R)
42. Joe Baca (D)
43. Ken Calvert (R)
44. Mary Bono (R)
45. Dana Rohrabacher (R)
46. Loretta Sanchez (D)
47. Christopher Cox (R)
48. Darrell Issa (R)
49. Susan A. Davis (D)
50. Bob Filner (D)
51. Randy Cunningham (R)
52. Duncan L. Hunter (R)

POSTWAR VOTE FOR PRESIDENT

Year	Total Vote	Republican Vote	Republican Candidate	Democratic Vote	Democratic Candidate	Other Vote	Plurality	Total Vote Rep.	Total Vote Dem.	Major Vote Rep.	Major Vote Dem.
2000**	10,965,856	4,567,429	Bush, George W.	5,861,203	Gore, Al	537,224	1,293,774 D	41.7%	53.4%	43.8%	56.2%
1996**	10,019,484	3,828,380	Dole, Bob	5,119,835	Clinton, Bill	1,071,269	1,291,455 D	38.2%	51.1%	42.8%	57.2%
1992**	11,131,721	3,630,574	Bush, George	5,121,325	Clinton, Bill	2,379,822	1,490,751 D	32.6%	46.0%	41.5%	58.5%
1988	9,887,065	5,054,917	Bush, George	4,702,233	Dukakis, Michael S.	129,915	352,684 R	51.1%	47.6%	51.8%	48.2%
1984	9,505,423	5,467,009	Reagan, Ronald	3,922,519	Mondale, Walter F.	115,895	1,544,490 R	57.5%	41.3%	58.2%	41.8%
1980**	8,587,063	4,524,858	Reagan, Ronald	3,083,661	Carter, Jimmy	978,544	1,441,197 R	52.7%	35.9%	59.5%	40.5%
1976	7,867,117	3,882,244	Ford, Gerald R.	3,742,284	Carter, Jimmy	242,589	139,960 R	49.3%	47.6%	50.9%	49.1%
1972	8,367,862	4,602,096	Nixon, Richard M.	3,475,847	McGovern, George S.	289,919	1,126,249 R	55.0%	41.5%	57.0%	43.0%
1968	7,251,587	3,467,664	Nixon, Richard M.	3,244,318	Humphrey, Hubert H.	539,605	223,346 R	47.8%	44.7%	51.7%	48.3%
1964	7,057,586	2,879,108	Goldwater, Barry M.	4,171,877	Johnson, Lyndon B.	6,601	1,292,769 D	40.8%	59.1%	40.8%	59.2%
1960	6,506,578	3,259,722	Nixon, Richard M.	3,224,099	Kennedy, John F.	22,757	35,623 R	50.1%	49.6%	50.3%	49.7%
1956	5,466,355	3,027,668	Eisenhower, Dwight D.	2,420,135	Stevenson, Adlai E.	18,552	607,533 R	55.4%	44.3%	55.6%	44.4%
1952	5,141,849	2,897,310	Eisenhower, Dwight D.	2,197,548	Stevenson, Adlai E.	46,991	699,762 R	56.3%	42.7%	56.9%	43.1%
1948	4,021,538	1,895,269	Dewey, Thomas E.	1,913,134	Truman, Harry S.	213,135	17,865 D	47.1%	47.6%	49.8%	50.2%

In 2000 the other vote column includes 418,707 votes cast for Green (Nader). In 1996 the other vote column includes 697,847 votes cast for Perot. In 1992 the other vote column includes 2,296,006 votes cast for Perot. In 1980 the other column includes 739,833 votes for Independent (Anderson).

CALIFORNIA

POSTWAR VOTE FOR GOVERNOR

Year	Total Vote	Republican		Democratic		Other Vote	Rep.-Dem. Plurality	Percentage			
		Vote	Candidate	Vote	Candidate			Total Vote		Major Vote	
								Rep.	Dem.	Rep.	Dem.
1998	8,385,196	3,218,030	Lungren, Dan	4,860,702	Davis, Gray	306,464	1,642,672 D	38.4%	58.0%	39.8%	60.2%
1994	8,665,375	4,781,766	Wilson, Pete	3,519,799	Brown, Kathleen	363,810	1,261,967 R	55.2%	40.6%	57.6%	42.4%
1990	7,699,467	3,791,904	Wilson, Pete	3,525,197	Feinstein, Dianne	382,366	266,707 R	49.2%	45.8%	51.8%	48.2%
1986	7,443,551	4,506,601	Deukmejian, George	2,781,714	Bradley, Tom	155,236	1,724,887 R	60.5%	37.4%	61.8%	38.2%
1982	7,876,698	3,881,014	Deukmejian, George	3,787,669	Bradley, Tom	208,015	93,345 R	49.3%	48.1%	50.6%	49.4%
1978	6,922,378	2,526,534	Younger, Evelle J.	3,878,812	Brown, Edmund G., Jr.	517,032	1,352,278 D	36.5%	56.0%	39.4%	60.6%
1974	6,248,070	2,952,954	Flournoy, Houston I.	3,131,648	Brown, Edmund G., Jr.	163,468	178,694 D	47.3%	50.1%	48.5%	51.5%
1970	6,510,072	3,439,664	Reagan, Ronald	2,938,607	Unruh, Jess	131,801	501,057 R	52.8%	45.1%	53.9%	46.1%
1966	6,503,445	3,742,913	Reagan, Ronald	2,749,174	Brown, Edmund G.	11,358	993,739 R	57.6%	42.3%	57.7%	42.3%
1962	5,853,270	2,740,351	Nixon, Richard M.	3,037,109	Brown, Edmund G.	75,810	296,758 D	46.8%	51.9%	47.4%	52.6%
1958	5,255,777	2,110,911	Knowland, William F.	3,140,076	Brown, Edmund G.	4,790	1,029,165 D	40.2%	59.7%	40.2%	59.8%
1954	4,030,368	2,290,519	Knight, Goodwin J.	1,739,368	Graves, Richard P.	481	551,151 R	56.8%	43.2%	56.8%	43.2%
1950	3,796,090	2,461,754	Warren, Earl	1,333,856	Roosevelt, James	480	1,127,898 R	64.8%	35.1%	64.9%	35.1%
1946**	2,558,399	2,344,542	Warren, Earl	—		213,857	2,344,542 R	91.6%		100.0%	

In 1946 the Republican candidate won both major party nominations.

POSTWAR VOTE FOR SENATOR

Year	Total Vote	Republican		Democratic		Other Vote	Rep.-Dem. Plurality	Percentage			
		Vote	Candidate	Vote	Candidate			Total Vote		Major Vote	
								Rep.	Dem.	Rep.	Dem.
2000	10,623,614	3,886,853	Campbell, Tom	5,932,522	Feinstein, Dianne	804,239	2,045,669 D	36.6%	55.8%	39.6%	60.4%
1998	8,314,953	3,576,351	Fong, Matt	4,411,705	Boxer, Barbara	326,897	835,354 D	43.0%	53.1%	44.8%	55.2%
1994	8,514,089	3,817,025	Huffington, Michael	3,979,152	Feinstein, Dianne	717,912	162,127 D	44.8%	46.7%	49.0%	51.0%
1992	10,799,703	4,644,182	Herschensohn, Bruce	5,173,467	Boxer, Barbara	982,054	529,285 D	43.0%	47.9%	47.3%	52.7%
1992S	10,782,743	4,093,501	Seymour, John	5,853,651	Feinstein, Dianne	835,591	1,760,150 D	38.0%	54.3%	41.2%	58.8%
1988	9,743,598	5,143,409	Wilson, Pete	4,287,253	McCarthy, Leo	312,936	856,156 R	52.8%	44.0%	54.5%	45.5%
1986	7,398,549	3,541,804	Zschau, Ed	3,646,672	Cranston, Alan	210,073	104,868 D	47.9%	49.3%	49.3%	50.7%
1982	7,805,538	4,022,565	Wilson, Pete	3,494,968	Brown, Edmund G., Jr.	288,005	527,597 R	51.5%	44.8%	53.5%	46.5%
1980	8,327,481	3,093,426	Gann, Paul	4,705,399	Cranston, Alan	528,656	1,611,973 D	37.1%	56.5%	39.7%	60.3%
1976	7,472,268	3,748,973	Hayakawa, S. I.	3,502,862	Tunney, John V.	220,433	246,111 R	50.2%	46.9%	51.7%	48.3%
1974	6,102,432	2,210,267	Richardson, H. L.	3,693,160	Cranston, Alan	199,005	1,482,893 D	36.2%	60.5%	37.4%	62.6%
1970	6,492,157	2,877,617	Murphy, George	3,496,558	Tunney, John V.	117,982	618,941 D	44.3%	53.9%	45.1%	54.9%
1968	7,102,465	3,329,148	Rafferty, Max	3,680,352	Cranston, Alan	92,965	351,204 D	46.9%	51.8%	47.5%	52.5%
1964	7,041,821	3,628,555	Murphy, George	3,411,912	Salinger, Pierre	1,354	216,643 R	51.5%	48.5%	51.5%	48.5%
1962	5,647,952	3,180,483	Kuchel, Thomas H.	2,452,839	Richards, Richard	14,630	727,644 R	56.3%	43.4%	56.5%	43.5%
1958	5,135,221	2,204,337	Knight, Goodwin J.	2,927,693	Engle, Clair	3,191	723,356 D	42.9%	57.0%	43.0%	57.0%
1956	5,361,467	2,892,918	Kuchel, Thomas H.	2,445,816	Richards, Richard	22,733	447,102 R	54.0%	45.6%	54.2%	45.8%
1954S	3,929,668	2,090,836	Kuchel, Thomas H.	1,788,071	Yorty, Samuel W.	50,761	302,765 R	53.2%	45.5%	53.9%	46.1%
1952**	4,542,548	3,982,448	Knowland, William F.	—		560,100	3,982,448 R	87.7%		100.0%	
1950	3,686,315	2,183,454	Nixon, Richard M.	1,502,507	Douglas, Helen	354	680,947 R	59.2%	40.8%	59.2%	40.8%
1946	2,639,465	1,428,067	Knowland, William F.	1,167,161	Rogers, Will	44,237	260,906 R	54.1%	44.2%	55.0%	45.0%

One of the 1992 elections was for a short term to fill a vacancy. The 1954 election was for a short term to fill a vacancy. In 1952 the Republican candidate won both major party nominations.

CALIFORNIA

Districts Established January 28, 1992

SAN FRANCISCO BAY AREA
CONGRESSIONAL DISTRICTS

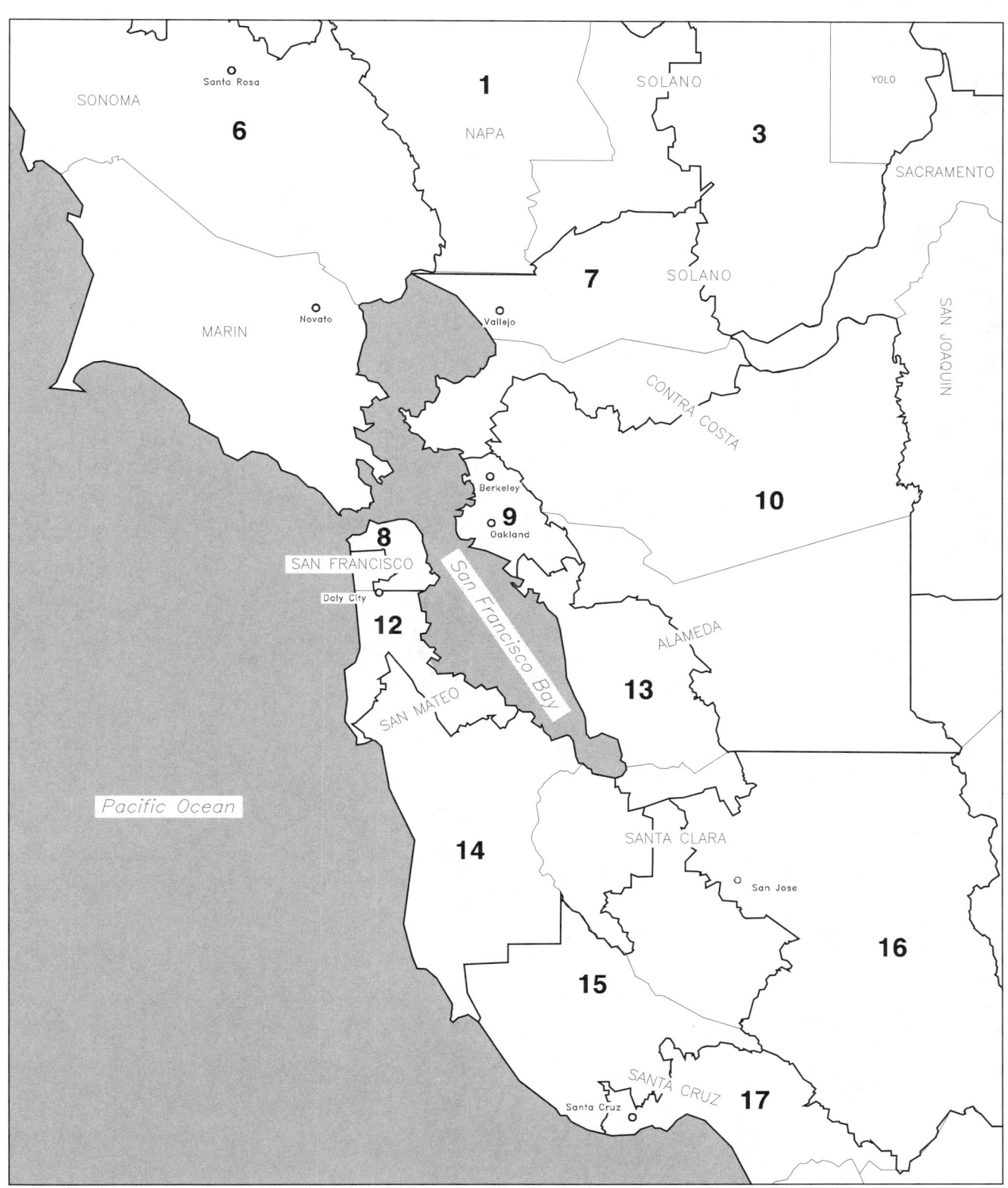

LOS ANGELES COUNTY AREA
CONGRESSIONAL DISTRICTS

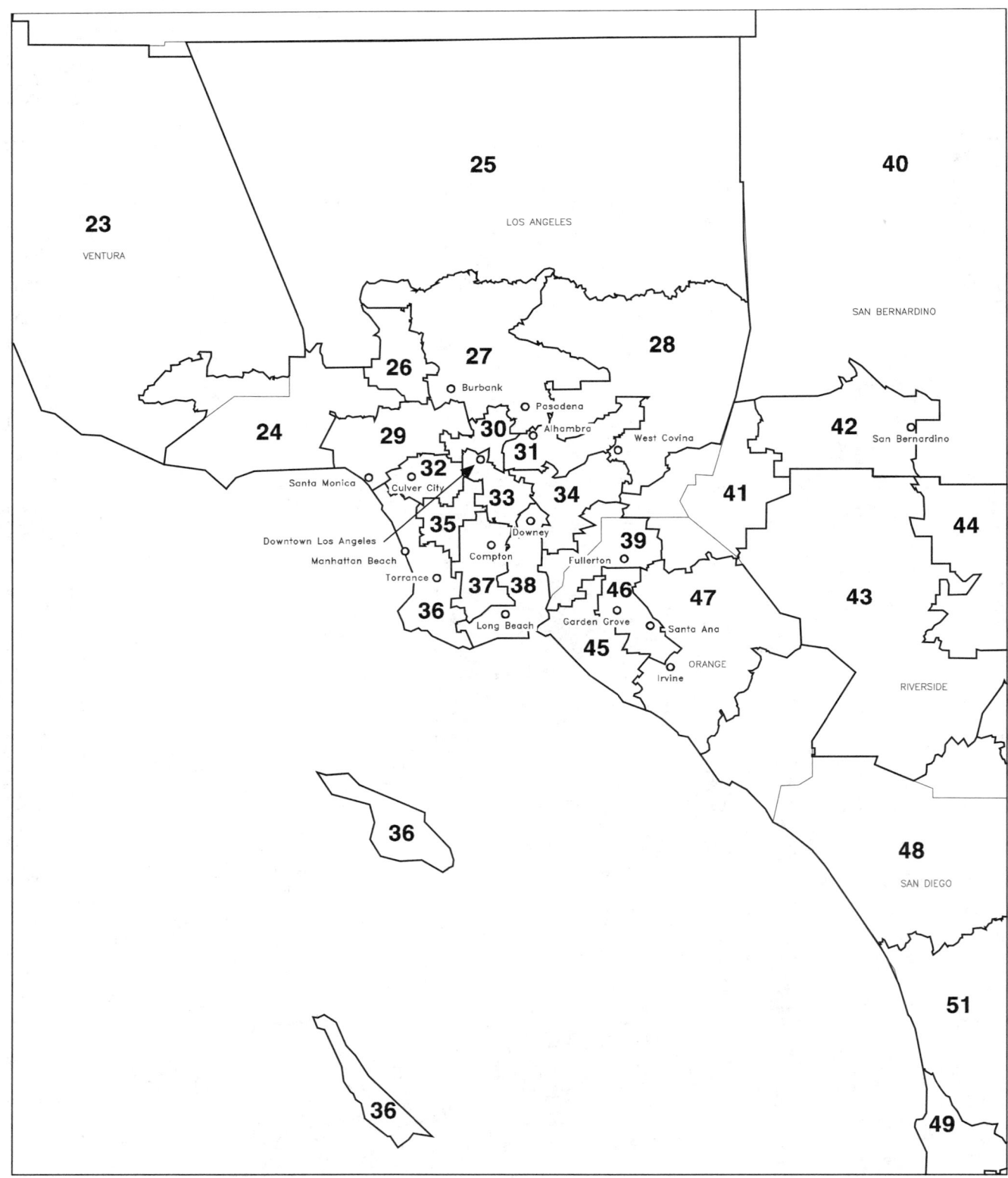

LOS ANGELES COUNTY

ASSEMBLY DISTRICT BOUNDARIES

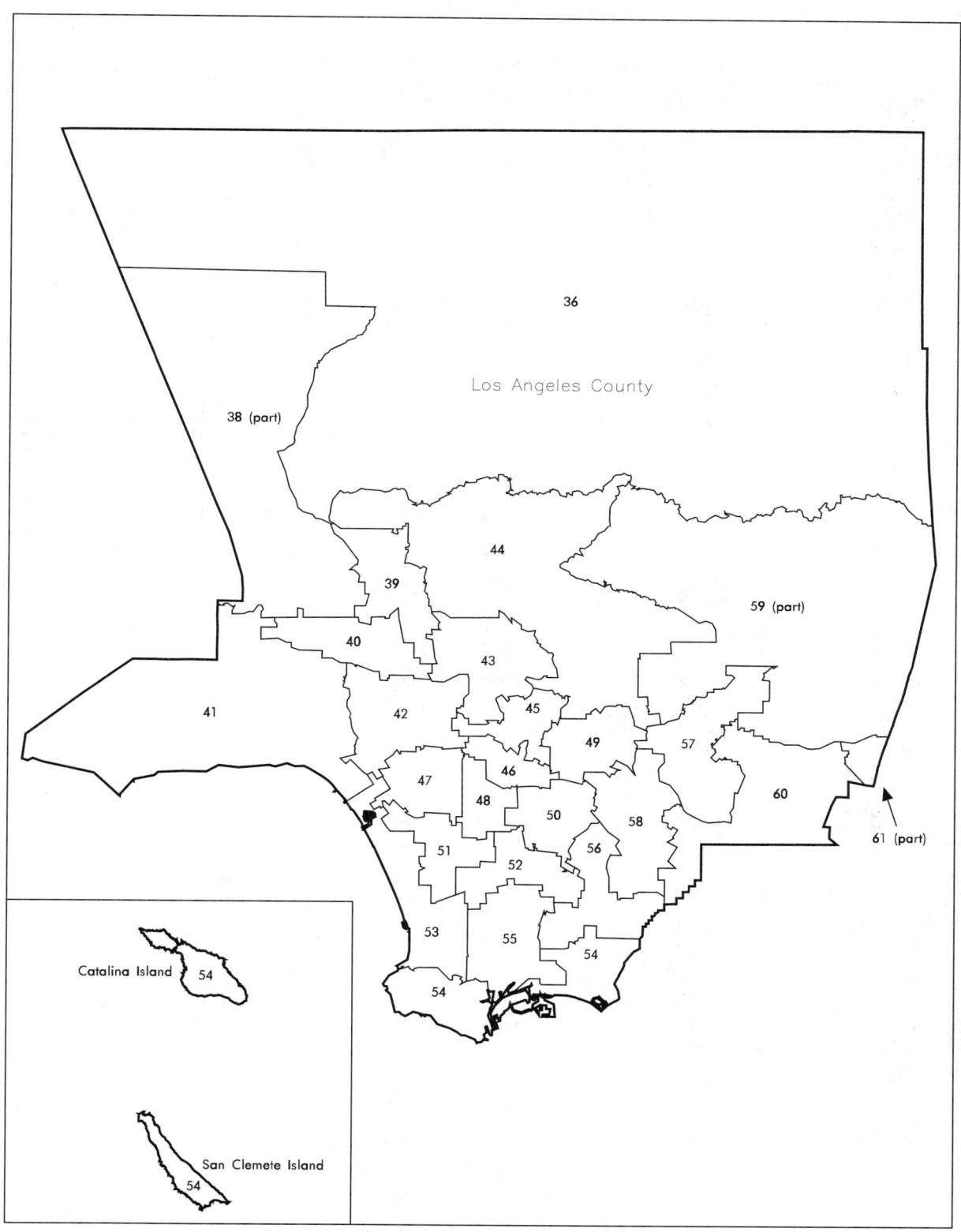

Los Angeles County

36

38 (part)

44

39

59 (part)

40

43

41

42

45

49

57

47

46

60

48

50

58

61 (part)

51

56

52

53

55

54

54

Catalina Island 54

San Clemete Island 54

CALIFORNIA

PRESIDENT 2000

2000 Census Population	County	Total Vote	Republican	Democratic	Green (Nader)	Other	Rep.-Dem. Plurality	Percentage of Total Vote		
								Rep.	Dem.	Green
1,443,741	ALAMEDA	494,336	119,279	342,889	27,499	4,669	223,610 D	24.1%	69.4%	5.6%
1,208	ALPINE	586	281	265	25	15	16 R	48.0%	45.2%	4.3%
35,100	AMADOR	15,464	8,766	5,906	584	208	2,860 R	56.7%	38.2%	3.8%
203,171	BUTTE	83,721	45,584	31,338	5,727	1,072	14,246 R	54.4%	37.4%	6.8%
40,554	CALAVERAS	18,876	10,599	7,093	863	321	3,506 R	56.2%	37.6%	4.6%
18,804	COLUSA	5,590	3,629	1,745	151	65	1,884 R	64.9%	31.2%	2.7%
948,816	CONTRA COSTA	381,478	141,373	224,338	13,067	2,700	82,965 D	37.1%	58.8%	3.4%
27,507	DEL NORTE	8,294	4,526	3,117	485	166	1,409 R	54.6%	37.6%	5.8%
156,299	EL DORADO	72,136	42,045	26,220	3,013	858	15,825 R	58.3%	36.3%	4.2%
799,407	FRESNO	220,835	117,342	95,059	6,541	1,893	22,283 R	53.1%	43.0%	3.0%
26,453	GLENN	8,711	5,795	2,498	268	150	3,297 R	66.5%	28.7%	3.1%
126,518	HUMBOLDT	55,972	23,219	24,851	7,100	802	1,632 D	41.5%	44.4%	12.7%
142,361	IMPERIAL	28,937	12,524	15,489	608	316	2,965 D	43.3%	53.5%	2.1%
17,945	INYO	7,815	4,713	2,652	344	106	2,061 R	60.3%	33.9%	4.4%
661,645	KERN	182,308	110,663	66,003	3,474	2,168	44,660 R	60.7%	36.2%	1.9%
129,461	KINGS	28,335	16,377	11,041	567	350	5,336 R	57.8%	39.0%	2.0%
58,309	LAKE	20,919	8,699	10,717	1,265	238	2,018 D	41.6%	51.2%	6.0%
33,828	LASSEN	10,586	7,080	2,982	339	185	4,098 R	66.9%	28.2%	3.2%
9,519,338	LOS ANGELES	2,695,154	871,930	1,710,505	83,731	28,988	838,575 D	32.4%	63.5%	3.1%
123,109	MADERA	33,395	20,283	11,650	1,080	382	8,633 R	60.7%	34.9%	3.2%
247,289	MARIN	123,155	34,872	79,135	8,289	859	44,263 D	28.3%	64.3%	6.7%
17,130	MARIPOSA	8,074	4,727	2,816	379	152	1,911 R	58.5%	34.9%	4.7%
86,265	MENDOCINO	34,410	12,272	16,634	5,051	453	4,362 D	35.7%	48.3%	14.7%
210,554	MERCED	50,418	26,102	22,726	1,166	424	3,376 R	51.8%	45.1%	2.3%
9,449	MODOC	4,107	2,969	945	122	71	2,024 R	72.3%	23.0%	3.0%
12,853	MONO	4,371	2,296	1,788	230	57	508 R	52.5%	40.9%	5.3%
401,762	MONTEREY	117,534	43,761	67,618	5,059	1,096	23,857 D	37.2%	57.5%	4.3%
124,279	NAPA	51,724	20,633	28,097	2,471	523	7,464 D	39.9%	54.3%	4.8%
92,033	NEVADA	47,479	25,998	17,670	3,287	524	8,328 R	54.8%	37.2%	6.9%
2,846,289	ORANGE	970,905	541,299	391,819	26,833	10,954	149,480 R	55.8%	40.4%	2.8%
248,399	PLACER	117,799	69,835	42,449	4,449	1,066	27,386 R	59.3%	36.0%	3.8%
20,824	PLUMAS	10,401	6,343	3,458	456	144	2,885 R	61.0%	33.2%	4.4%
1,545,387	RIVERSIDE	451,127	231,955	202,576	11,678	4,918	29,379 R	51.4%	44.9%	2.6%
1,223,499	SACRAMENTO	431,550	195,619	212,792	17,659	5,480	17,173 D	45.3%	49.3%	4.1%
53,234	SAN BENITO	16,831	7,015	9,131	535	150	2,116 D	41.7%	54.3%	3.2%
1,709,434	SAN BERNARDINO	454,893	221,757	214,749	11,775	6,612	7,008 R	48.7%	47.2%	2.6%
2,813,833	SAN DIEGO	958,634	475,736	437,666	33,979	11,253	38,070 R	49.6%	45.7%	3.5%
776,733	SAN FRANCISCO	319,786	51,496	241,578	24,828	1,884	190,082 D	16.1%	75.5%	7.8%
563,598	SAN JOAQUIN	167,239	81,773	79,776	4,195	1,495	1,997 R	48.9%	47.7%	2.5%
246,681	SAN LUIS OBISPO	108,886	56,859	44,526	6,523	978	12,333 R	52.2%	40.9%	6.0%
707,161	SAN MATEO	259,399	80,296	166,757	10,433	1,913	86,461 D	31.0%	64.3%	4.0%
399,347	SANTA BARBARA	154,974	71,493	73,411	8,664	1,406	1,918 D	46.1%	47.4%	5.6%
1,682,585	SANTA CLARA	548,129	188,750	332,490	19,072	7,817	143,740 D	34.4%	60.7%	3.5%
255,602	SANTA CRUZ	108,350	29,627	66,618	10,844	1,261	36,991 D	27.3%	61.5%	10.0%
163,256	SHASTA	66,544	43,278	20,127	2,131	1,008	23,151 R	65.0%	30.2%	3.2%
3,555	SIERRA	1,847	1,172	540	86	49	632 R	63.5%	29.2%	4.7%
44,301	SISKIYOU	19,819	12,198	6,323	872	426	5,875 R	61.5%	31.9%	4.4%
394,542	SOLANO	131,735	51,604	75,116	3,869	1,146	23,512 D	39.2%	57.0%	2.9%
458,614	SONOMA	197,006	63,529	117,295	14,324	1,858	53,766 D	32.2%	59.5%	7.3%
446,997	STANISLAUS	128,267	67,188	56,448	3,398	1,233	10,740 R	52.4%	44.0%	2.6%
78,930	SUTTER	26,564	17,350	8,416	594	204	8,934 R	65.3%	31.7%	2.2%
56,039	TEHAMA	20,854	13,270	6,507	697	380	6,763 R	63.6%	31.2%	3.3%
13,022	TRINITY	5,797	3,340	1,932	396	129	1,408 R	57.6%	33.3%	6.8%
368,021	TULARE	89,818	54,070	33,006	1,834	908	21,064 R	60.2%	36.7%	2.0%
54,501	TUOLUMNE	23,727	13,172	9,359	949	247	3,813 R	55.5%	39.4%	4.0%
753,197	VENTURA	282,692	136,173	133,258	10,235	3,026	2,915 R	48.2%	47.1%	3.6%
168,660	YOLO	61,436	23,057	33,747	4,107	525	10,690 D	37.5%	54.9%	6.7%
60,219	YUBA	16,127	9,838	5,546	507	236	4,292 R	61.0%	34.4%	3.1%
33,871,648	TOTAL	10,965,856	4,567,429	5,861,203	418,707	118,517	1,293,774 D	41.7%	53.4%	3.8%

LOS ANGELES COUNTY

PRESIDENT 2000

Assembly District	Total Vote	Republican	Democratic	Green (Nader)	Other	Rep.-Dem. Plurality	Percentage of Total Vote		
							Rep.	Dem.	Green
District 36	152,115	84,973	61,369	3,895	1,878	23,604 R	55.9%	40.3%	2.6%
District 38	92,681	39,742	49,060	2,790	1,089	9,318 D	42.9%	52.9%	3.0%
District 39	73,952	17,934	53,287	1,767	964	35,353 D	24.3%	72.1%	2.4%
District 40	109,021	29,849	73,873	3,991	1,308	44,024 D	27.4%	67.8%	3.7%
District 41	181,820	58,755	114,193	7,065	1,807	55,438 D	32.3%	62.8%	3.9%
District 42	166,662	33,873	124,223	7,083	1,483	90,350 D	20.3%	74.5%	4.2%
District 43	127,993	49,022	71,753	5,709	1,509	22,731 D	38.3%	56.1%	4.5%
District 44	156,181	64,540	83,547	6,367	1,727	19,007 D	41.3%	53.5%	4.1%
District 45	74,224	13,409	56,355	3,601	859	42,946 D	18.1%	75.9%	4.9%
District 46	41,961	6,576	33,682	1,199	504	27,106 D	15.7%	80.3%	2.9%
District 47	130,954	17,522	108,561	3,771	1,100	91,039 D	13.4%	82.9%	2.9%
District 48	63,394	3,187	59,023	724	460	55,836 D	5.0%	93.1%	1.1%
District 49	88,300	23,028	62,206	2,096	970	39,178 D	26.1%	70.4%	2.4%
District 50	55,901	8,377	46,346	792	386	37,969 D	15.0%	82.9%	1.4%
District 51	96,876	17,793	76,319	1,921	843	58,526 D	18.4%	78.8%	2.0%
District 52	74,227	8,905	63,759	947	616	54,854 D	12.0%	85.9%	1.3%
District 53	172,097	73,129	89,650	7,111	2,207	16,521 D	42.5%	52.1%	4.1%
District 54	148,290	62,439	78,041	6,161	1,649	15,602 D	42.1%	52.6%	4.2%
District 55	82,920	18,082	62,366	1,524	948	44,284 D	21.8%	75.2%	1.8%
District 56	126,974	50,924	71,158	3,256	1,636	20,234 D	40.1%	56.0%	2.6%
District 57	84,107	24,858	56,830	1,673	746	31,972 D	29.6%	67.6%	2.0%
District 58	103,799	30,121	70,210	2,426	1,042	40,089 D	29.0%	67.6%	2.3%
District 59	148,856	73,102	69,330	4,699	1,725	3,772 R	49.1%	46.6%	3.2%
District 60	128,254	58,321	65,690	2,830	1,413	7,369 D	45.5%	51.2%	2.2%
District 61	13,592	3,469	9,674	333	116	6,205 D	25.5%	71.2%	2.4%
9,519,338 TOTAL	2,695,154	871,930	1,710,505	83,731	28,988	838,575 D	32.4%	63.5%	3.1%

Note: The countywide totals for "Total Vote" and "Other" include 3 write-in votes for McReynolds that are not included in the results by assembly district.

CALIFORNIA

SENATOR 2000

2000 Census Population	County	Total Vote	Republican	Democratic	Other	Rep.-Dem. Plurality	Percentage			
							Total Vote		Major Vote	
							Rep.	Dem.	Rep.	Dem.
1,443,741	ALAMEDA	485,299	109,517	328,355	47,427	218,838 D	22.6%	67.7%	25.0%	75.0%
1,208	ALPINE	580	242	253	85	11 D	41.7%	43.6%	48.9%	51.1%
35,100	AMADOR	15,212	7,502	6,671	1,039	831 R	49.3%	43.9%	52.9%	47.1%
203,171	BUTTE	82,173	38,961	34,117	9,095	4,844 R	47.4%	41.5%	53.3%	46.7%
40,554	CALAVERAS	18,558	8,986	7,852	1,720	1,134 R	48.4%	42.3%	53.4%	46.6%
18,804	COLUSA	5,467	2,936	2,250	281	686 R	53.7%	41.2%	56.6%	43.4%
948,816	CONTRA COSTA	376,788	125,188	232,109	19,491	106,921 D	33.2%	61.6%	35.0%	65.0%
27,507	DEL NORTE	8,172	3,672	3,670	830	2 R	44.9%	44.9%	50.0%	50.0%
156,299	EL DORADO	70,933	36,684	28,873	5,376	7,811 R	51.7%	40.7%	56.0%	44.0%
799,407	FRESNO	214,175	86,502	113,228	14,445	26,726 D	40.4%	52.9%	43.3%	56.7%
26,453	GLENN	8,596	4,664	3,282	650	1,382 R	54.3%	38.2%	58.7%	41.3%
126,518	HUMBOLDT	54,884	19,882	25,788	9,214	5,906 D	36.2%	47.0%	43.5%	56.5%
142,361	IMPERIAL	28,375	9,666	15,937	2,772	6,271 D	34.1%	56.2%	37.8%	62.2%
17,945	INYO	7,712	4,397	2,711	604	1,686 R	57.0%	35.2%	61.9%	38.1%
661,645	KERN	179,549	90,564	77,676	11,309	12,888 R	50.4%	43.3%	53.8%	46.2%
129,461	KINGS	27,639	12,246	13,402	1,991	1,156 D	44.3%	48.5%	47.7%	52.3%
58,309	LAKE	20,843	7,826	11,410	1,607	3,584 D	37.5%	54.7%	40.7%	59.3%
33,828	LASSEN	10,330	5,618	3,673	1,039	1,945 R	54.4%	35.6%	60.5%	39.5%
9,519,338	LOS ANGELES	2,605,254	743,872	1,677,668	183,714	933,796 D	28.6%	64.4%	30.7%	69.3%
123,109	MADERA	32,433	15,810	14,123	2,500	1,687 R	48.7%	43.5%	52.8%	47.2%

CALIFORNIA

SENATOR 2000

2000 Census Population	County	Total Vote	Republican	Democratic	Other	Rep.-Dem. Plurality		Percentage			
								Total Vote		Major Vote	
								Rep.	Dem.	Rep.	Dem.
247,289	MARIN	121,721	32,077	79,421	10,223	47,344	D	26.4%	65.2%	28.8%	71.2%
17,130	MARIPOSA	7,890	3,837	3,195	858	642	R	48.6%	40.5%	54.6%	45.4%
86,265	MENDOCINO	33,301	10,503	16,981	5,817	6,478	D	31.5%	51.0%	38.2%	61.8%
210,554	MERCED	48,975	19,612	25,426	3,937	5,814	D	40.0%	51.9%	43.5%	56.5%
9,449	MODOC	3,964	2,414	1,221	329	1,193	R	60.9%	30.8%	66.4%	33.6%
12,853	MONO	4,272	2,037	1,818	417	219	R	47.7%	42.6%	52.8%	47.2%
401,762	MONTEREY	116,284	41,113	67,401	7,770	26,288	D	35.4%	58.0%	37.9%	62.1%
124,279	NAPA	50,939	18,442	28,884	3,613	10,442	D	36.2%	56.7%	39.0%	61.0%
92,033	NEVADA	46,742	23,095	19,354	4,293	3,741	R	49.4%	41.4%	54.4%	45.6%
2,846,289	ORANGE	943,728	471,410	403,123	69,195	68,287	R	50.0%	42.7%	53.9%	46.1%
248,399	PLACER	115,184	60,182	47,169	7,833	13,013	R	52.2%	41.0%	56.1%	43.9%
20,824	PLUMAS	9,998	5,122	4,075	801	1,047	R	51.2%	40.8%	55.7%	44.3%
1,545,387	RIVERSIDE	435,436	195,085	210,235	30,116	15,150	D	44.8%	48.3%	48.1%	51.9%
1,223,499	SACRAMENTO	421,959	163,343	228,992	29,624	65,649	D	38.7%	54.3%	41.6%	58.4%
53,234	SAN BENITO	16,660	6,545	9,170	945	2,625	D	39.3%	55.0%	41.6%	58.4%
1,709,434	SAN BERNARDINO	408,241	177,158	200,558	30,525	23,400	D	43.4%	49.1%	46.9%	53.1%
2,813,833	SAN DIEGO	908,531	370,287	466,461	71,783	96,174	D	40.8%	51.3%	44.3%	55.7%
776,733	SAN FRANCISCO	308,318	47,072	222,787	38,459	175,715	D	15.3%	72.3%	17.4%	82.6%
563,598	SAN JOAQUIN	164,722	67,907	86,731	10,084	18,824	D	41.2%	52.7%	43.9%	56.1%
246,681	SAN LUIS OBISPO	106,293	49,055	47,976	9,262	1,079	R	46.2%	45.1%	50.6%	49.4%
707,161	SAN MATEO	254,958	76,273	165,216	13,469	88,943	D	29.9%	64.8%	31.6%	68.4%
399,347	SANTA BARBARA	150,914	60,417	75,357	15,140	14,940	D	40.0%	49.9%	44.5%	55.5%
1,682,585	SANTA CLARA	537,429	187,953	320,400	29,076	132,447	D	35.0%	59.6%	37.0%	63.0%
255,602	SANTA CRUZ	107,164	32,537	60,853	13,774	28,316	D	30.4%	56.8%	34.8%	65.2%
163,256	SHASTA	65,226	35,884	24,027	5,315	11,857	R	55.0%	36.8%	59.9%	40.1%
3,555	SIERRA	1,818	980	666	172	314	R	53.9%	36.6%	59.5%	40.5%
44,301	SISKIYOU	19,470	10,048	7,476	1,946	2,572	R	51.6%	38.4%	57.3%	42.7%
394,542	SOLANO	123,970	41,449	74,414	8,107	32,965	D	33.4%	60.0%	35.8%	64.2%
458,614	SONOMA	194,303	57,244	118,455	18,604	61,211	D	29.5%	61.0%	32.6%	67.4%
446,997	STANISLAUS	125,637	55,919	60,610	9,108	4,691	D	44.5%	48.2%	48.0%	52.0%
78,930	SUTTER	26,133	14,394	10,326	1,413	4,068	R	55.1%	39.5%	58.2%	41.8%
56,039	TEHAMA	20,563	10,859	7,870	1,834	2,989	R	52.8%	38.3%	58.0%	42.0%
13,022	TRINITY	5,717	2,771	2,307	639	464	R	48.5%	40.4%	54.6%	45.4%
368,021	TULARE	88,124	41,587	40,117	6,420	1,470	R	47.2%	45.5%	50.9%	49.1%
54,501	TUOLUMNE	23,339	11,385	10,028	1,926	1,357	R	48.8%	43.0%	53.2%	46.8%
753,197	VENTURA	276,439	118,463	138,836	19,140	20,373	D	42.9%	50.2%	46.0%	54.0%
168,660	YOLO	60,490	19,528	35,193	5,769	15,665	D	32.3%	58.2%	35.7%	64.3%
60,219	YUBA	15,790	8,131	6,345	1,314	1,786	R	51.5%	40.2%	56.2%	43.8%
33,871,648	TOTAL	10,623,614	3,886,853	5,932,522	804,239	2,045,669	D	36.6%	55.8%	39.6%	60.4%

LOS ANGELES COUNTY
SENATOR 2000

Assembly District	Total Vote	Republican	Democratic	Green (Nader)	Other	Rep.-Dem. Plurality		Percentage of Total Vote Rep.	Dem.	Green
District 36	147,154	73,282	63,401	10,471	9,881	R	49.8%	43.1%	53.6%	46.4%
District 38	89,722	35,044	48,925	5,753	13,881	D	39.1%	54.5%	41.7%	58.3%
District 39	71,779	14,346	51,506	5,927	37,160	D	20.0%	71.8%	21.8%	78.2%
District 40	105,332	26,159	70,457	8,716	44,298	D	24.8%	66.9%	27.1%	72.9%
District 41	176,272	53,943	110,609	11,720	56,666	D	30.6%	62.7%	32.8%	67.2%
District 42	161,289	31,324	117,555	12,410	86,231	D	19.4%	72.9%	21.0%	79.0%
District 43	122,078	40,830	71,295	9,953	30,465	D	33.4%	58.4%	36.4%	63.6%
District 44	151,105	54,969	85,684	10,452	30,715	D	36.4%	56.7%	39.1%	60.9%
District 45	71,508	11,098	52,531	7,879	41,433	D	15.5%	73.5%	17.4%	82.6%
District 46	40,396	5,259	31,902	3,235	26,643	D	13.0%	79.0%	14.2%	85.8%
District 47	126,983	15,368	102,896	8,719	87,528	D	12.1%	81.0%	13.0%	87.0%
District 48	61,386	2,621	56,080	2,685	53,459	D	4.3%	91.4%	4.5%	95.5%
District 49	83,806	17,977	59,665	6,164	41,688	D	21.5%	71.2%	23.2%	76.8%
District 50	54,101	5,952	44,685	3,464	38,733	D	11.0%	82.6%	11.8%	88.2%
District 51	94,636	14,497	75,466	4,673	60,969	D	15.3%	79.7%	16.1%	83.9%
District 52	72,315	6,993	61,743	3,579	54,750	D	9.7%	85.4%	10.2%	89.8%
District 53	166,663	63,488	90,240	12,935	26,752	D	38.1%	54.1%	41.3%	58.7%
District 54	143,638	54,617	78,997	10,024	24,380	D	38.0%	55.0%	40.9%	59.1%
District 55	80,203	14,249	61,033	4,921	46,784	D	17.8%	76.1%	18.9%	81.1%
District 56	122,413	42,743	71,791	7,879	29,048	D	34.9%	58.6%	37.3%	62.7%
District 57	81,242	19,631	55,752	5,859	36,121	D	24.2%	68.6%	26.0%	74.0%
District 58	100,856	23,530	70,437	6,889	46,907	D	23.3%	69.8%	25.0%	75.0%
District 59	143,587	63,613	69,910	10,064	6,297	D	44.3%	48.7%	47.6%	52.4%
District 60	123,645	49,631	65,774	8,240	16,143	D	40.1%	53.2%	43.0%	57.0%
District 61	13,145	2,708	9,334	1,103	6,626	D	20.6%	71.0%	22.5%	77.5%
TOTAL (9,519,338)	2,605,254	743,872	1,677,668	183,714	933,796	D	28.6%	64.4%	30.7%	69.3%

CALIFORNIA
CONGRESS

CD	Year	Total Vote	Republican Vote	Republican Candidate	Democratic Vote	Democratic Candidate	Other Vote	Rep.-Dem. Plurality	Total Vote Rep.	Total Vote Dem.	Major Vote Rep.	Major Vote Dem.
1	2000	239,335	66,987	CHASE, RUSSEL J.	155,638	THOMPSON, MIKE	16,710	88,651 D	28.0%	65.0%	30.1%	69.9%
1	1998	196,772	64,622	LUCE, MARK	121,713	THOMPSON, MIKE	10,437	57,091 D	32.8%	61.9%	34.7%	65.3%
1	1996	222,118	110,242	RIGGS, FRANK	96,522	ALIOTO, MICHAELA	15,354	13,720 R	49.6%	43.5%	53.3%	46.7%
1	1994	200,673	106,870	RIGGS, FRANK	93,717	HAMBURG, DAN	86	13,153 R	53.3%	46.7%	53.3%	46.7%
1	1992	251,206	113,266	RIGGS, FRANK	119,676	HAMBURG, DAN	18,264	6,410 D	45.1%	47.6%	48.6%	51.4%
2	2000	255,856	168,172	HERGER, WALLY	72,075	MORGAN, STAN	15,609	96,097 R	65.7%	28.2%	70.0%	30.0%
2	1998	205,367	128,372	HERGER, WALLY	70,837	BRADEN, ROBERTS A.	6,158	57,535 R	62.5%	34.5%	64.4%	35.6%
2	1996	238,333	144,913	HERGER, WALLY	80,401	BRADEN, ROBERTS A.	13,019	64,512 R	60.8%	33.7%	64.3%	35.7%
2	1994	214,809	137,864	HERGER, WALLY	55,959	JACOBS, MARY	20,986	81,905 R	64.2%	26.1%	71.1%	28.9%
2	1992	256,556	167,247	HERGER, WALLY	71,780	FREEDMAN, ELLIOT R.	17,529	95,467 R	65.2%	28.0%	70.0%	30.0%
3	2000	230,182	129,254	OSE, DOUG	93,067	KENT, BOB	7,861	36,187 R	56.2%	40.4%	58.1%	41.9%
3	1998	192,006	100,621	OSE, DOUG	86,471	DUNN, SANDIE	4,914	14,150 R	52.4%	45.0%	53.8%	46.2%
3	1996	221,737	91,134	LEFEVER, TIM	118,663	FAZIO, VIC	11,940	27,529 D	41.1%	53.5%	43.4%	56.6%
3	1994	195,157	89,964	LEFEVER, TIM	97,093	FAZIO, VIC	8,100	7,129 D	46.1%	49.8%	48.1%	51.9%
3	1992	238,685	96,092	RICHARDSON, H. L.	122,149	FAZIO, VIC	20,444	26,057 D	40.3%	51.2%	44.0%	56.0%

CALIFORNIA

CONGRESS

CD	Year	Total Vote	Republican Vote	Republican Candidate	Democratic Vote	Democratic Candidate	Other Vote	Rep.-Dem. Plurality	Total Vote Rep.	Total Vote Dem.	Major Vote Rep.	Major Vote Dem.
4	2000	311,423	197,503	DOOLITTLE, JOHN T.	97,974	NORBERG, MARK A.	15,946	99,529 R	63.4%	31.5%	66.8%	33.2%
4	1998	248,224	155,306	DOOLITTLE, JOHN T.	85,394	SHAPIRO, DAVID	7,524	69,912 R	62.6%	34.4%	64.5%	35.5%
4	1996	271,315	164,048	DOOLITTLE, JOHN T.	97,948	HIRNING, KATIE	9,319	66,100 R	60.5%	36.1%	62.6%	37.4%
4	1994	236,323	144,936	DOOLITTLE, JOHN T.	82,505	HIRNING, KATIE	8,882	62,431 R	61.3%	34.9%	63.7%	36.3%
4	1992	283,365	141,155	DOOLITTLE, JOHN T.	129,489	MALBERG, PATRICIA	12,721	11,666 R	49.8%	45.7%	52.2%	47.8%
5	2000	214,059	55,945	PAYNE, KEN	147,025	MATSUI, ROBERT T.	11,089	91,080 D	26.1%	68.7%	27.6%	72.4%
5	1998	181,838	47,307	DINSMORE, ROBERT S.	130,715	MATSUI, ROBERT T.	3,816	83,408 D	26.0%	71.9%	26.6%	73.4%
5	1996	202,460	52,940	DINSMORE, ROBERT S.	142,618	MATSUI, ROBERT T.	6,902	89,678 D	26.1%	70.4%	27.1%	72.9%
5	1994	182,596	52,905	DINSMORE, ROBERT S.	125,042	MATSUI, ROBERT T.	4,649	72,137 D	29.0%	68.5%	29.7%	70.3%
5	1992	230,560	58,698	DINSMORE, ROBERT S.	158,250	MATSUI, ROBERT T.	13,612	99,552 D	25.5%	68.6%	27.1%	72.9%
6	2000	283,118	80,169	MCAULIFFE, KEN	182,116	WOOLSEY, LYNN	20,833	101,947 D	28.3%	64.3%	30.6%	69.4%
6	1998	232,981	69,295	MCAULIFFE, KEN	158,446	WOOLSEY, LYNN	5,240	89,151 D	29.7%	68.0%	30.4%	69.6%
6	1996	253,836	86,278	HUGHES, DUANE C.	156,958	WOOLSEY, LYNN	10,600	70,680 D	34.0%	61.8%	35.5%	64.5%
6	1994	236,840	88,940	NUGENT, MICHAEL J.	137,642	WOOLSEY, LYNN	10,258	48,702 D	37.6%	58.1%	39.3%	60.7%
6	1992	291,786	98,171	FILANTE, BILL	190,322	WOOLSEY, LYNN	3,293	92,151 D	33.6%	65.2%	34.0%	66.0%
7	2000	208,789	44,154	HOFFMAN, CHRISTOPHER A.	159,692	MILLER, GEORGE	4,943	115,538 D	21.1%	76.5%	21.7%	78.3%
7	1998	164,132	38,290	REECE, NORMAN H.	125,842	MILLER, GEORGE		87,552 D	23.3%	76.7%	23.3%	76.7%
7	1996	190,917	42,542	REECE, NORMAN H.	137,089	MILLER, GEORGE	11,286	94,547 D	22.3%	71.8%	23.7%	76.3%
7	1994	166,601	45,698	HUGHES, CHARLES V.	116,105	MILLER, GEORGE	4,798	70,407 D	27.4%	69.7%	28.2%	71.8%
7	1992	217,982	54,822	SCHOLL, DAVE	153,320	MILLER, GEORGE	9,840	98,498 D	25.1%	70.3%	26.3%	73.7%
8	2000	215,428	25,298	SPARKS, ADAM	181,847	PELOSI, NANCY	8,283	156,549 D	11.7%	84.4%	12.2%	87.8%
8	1998	172,462	20,781	MARTZ, DAVID J.	148,027	PELOSI, NANCY	3,654	127,246 D	12.0%	85.8%	12.3%	87.7%
8	1996	207,760	25,739	RAIMONDO, JUSTIN	175,216	PELOSI, NANCY	6,805	149,477 D	12.4%	84.3%	12.8%	87.2%
8	1994	168,171	30,528	CHEUNG, ELSA C.	137,642	PELOSI, NANCY	1	107,114 D	18.2%	81.8%	18.2%	81.8%
8	1992	232,691	25,693	WOLIN, MARC	191,906	PELOSI, NANCY	15,092	166,213 D	11.0%	82.5%	11.8%	88.2%
9	2000	214,650	21,033	WASHINGTON, ARNEZE	182,352	LEE, BARBARA	11,265	161,319 D	9.8%	85.0%	10.3%	89.7%
9	1998	169,895	22,431	SANDERS, CLAIBORNE	140,722	LEE, BARBARA	6,742	118,291 D	13.2%	82.8%	13.7%	86.3%
9	1996	200,976	37,126	WRIGHT, DEBORAH	154,806	DELLUMS, RONALD V.	9,044	117,680 D	18.5%	77.0%	19.3%	80.7%
9	1994	178,875	40,448	WRIGHT, DEBORAH	129,233	DELLUMS, RONALD V.	9,194	88,785 D	22.6%	72.2%	23.8%	76.2%
9	1992	228,467	53,707	HUNTER, G. WILLIAM	164,265	DELLUMS, RONALD V.	10,495	110,558 D	23.5%	71.9%	24.6%	75.4%
10	2000	304,819	134,863	HUTCHISON, CLAUDE B. JR.	160,429	TAUSCHER, ELLEN O.	9,527	25,566 D	44.2%	52.6%	45.7%	54.3%
10	1998	237,809	103,299	BALL, CHARLES	127,134	TAUSCHER, ELLEN O.	7,376	23,835 D	43.4%	53.5%	44.8%	55.2%
10	1996	283,183	133,633	BAKER, BILL	137,726	TAUSCHER, ELLEN O.	11,824	4,093 D	47.2%	48.6%	49.2%	50.8%
10	1994	234,241	138,916	BAKER, BILL	90,523	SCHWARTZ, ELLEN	4,802	48,393 R	59.3%	38.6%	60.5%	39.5%
10	1992	280,429	145,702	BAKER, BILL	134,635	WILLIAMS, WENDELL H.	92	11,067 R	52.0%	48.0%	52.0%	48.0%
11	2000	208,607	120,635	POMBO, RICHARD W.	79,539	SANTOS, TOM Y.	8,433	41,096 R	57.8%	38.1%	60.3%	39.7%
11	1998	155,449	95,496	POMBO, RICHARD W.	56,345	FIGUEROA, ROBERT L.	3,608	39,151 R	61.4%	36.2%	62.9%	37.1%
11	1996	181,096	107,477	POMBO, RICHARD W.	65,536	SILVA, JASON	8,083	41,941 R	59.3%	36.2%	62.1%	37.9%
11	1994	159,814	99,302	POMBO, RICHARD W.	55,794	PERRY, RANDY A.	4,718	43,508 R	62.1%	34.9%	64.0%	36.0%
11	1992	198,490	94,453	POMBO, RICHARD W.	90,539	GARAMENDI, PATRICIA	13,498	3,914 R	47.6%	45.6%	51.1%	48.9%
12	2000	212,556	44,162	GARZA, MIKE	158,404	LANTOS, TOM	9,990	114,242 D	20.8%	74.5%	21.8%	78.2%
12	1998	173,212	36,562	EVANS, ROBERT H. JR.	128,135	LANTOS, TOM	8,515	91,573 D	21.1%	74.0%	22.2%	77.8%
12	1996	207,913	49,278	JENKINS, STORM	149,052	LANTOS, TOM	9,583	99,774 D	23.7%	71.7%	24.8%	75.2%
12	1994	175,636	57,228	WILDER, DEBORAH	118,408	LANTOS, TOM		61,180 D	32.6%	67.4%	32.6%	67.4%
12	1992	228,407	53,278	TOMLIN, JIM	157,205	LANTOS, TOM	17,924	103,927 D	23.3%	68.8%	25.3%	74.7%
13	2000	183,146	44,499	GOETZ, JAMES R.	129,012	STARK, FORTNEY PETE	9,635	84,513 D	24.3%	70.4%	25.6%	74.4%
13	1998	142,787	38,050	GOETZ, JAMES R.	101,671	STARK, FORTNEY PETE	3,066	63,621 D	26.6%	71.2%	27.2%	72.8%
13	1996	175,539	53,385	FAY, JAMES S.	114,408	STARK, FORTNEY PETE	7,746	61,023 D	30.4%	65.2%	31.8%	68.2%
13	1994	150,642	45,555	MOLTON, LARRY	97,344	STARK, FORTNEY PETE	7,743	51,789 D	30.2%	64.6%	31.9%	68.1%
13	1992	205,516	64,953	TEYLER, VERNE	123,795	STARK, FORTNEY PETE	16,768	58,842 D	31.6%	60.2%	34.4%	65.6%

CALIFORNIA

CONGRESS

| | | | Republican | | Democratic | | | | Percentage | | | |
| | | | | | | | | | Total Vote | | Major Vote | |
CD	Year	Total Vote	Vote	Candidate	Vote	Candidate	Other Vote	Rep.-Dem. Plurality	Rep.	Dem.	Rep.	Dem.
14	2000	230,262	59,338	QURAISHI, BILL	161,720	ESHOO, ANNA G.	9,204	102,382 D	25.8%	70.2%	26.8%	73.2%
14	1998	188,910	53,719	HAUGEN, JOHN C.	129,663	ESHOO, ANNA G.	5,528	75,944 D	28.4%	68.6%	29.3%	70.7%
14	1996	230,175	71,573	BRINK, BEN	149,313	ESHOO, ANNA G.	9,289	77,740 D	31.1%	64.9%	32.4%	67.6%
14	1994	199,188	78,475	BRINK, BEN	120,713	ESHOO, ANNA G.		42,238 D	39.4%	60.6%	39.4%	60.6%
14	1992	259,222	101,202	HUENING, TOM	146,873	ESHOO, ANNA G.	11,147	45,671 D	39.0%	56.7%	40.8%	59.2%
15	2000	236,904	99,866	CUNNEEN, JIM	128,545	HONDA, MIKE	8,493	28,679 D	42.2%	54.3%	43.7%	56.3%
15	1998	184,786	111,876	CAMPBELL, TOM	70,059	LANE, DICK	2,851	41,817 R	60.5%	37.9%	61.5%	38.5%
15	1996	226,886	132,737	CAMPBELL, TOM	79,048	LANE, DICK	15,101	53,689 R	58.5%	34.8%	62.7%	37.3%
15	1994	200,204	80,266	WICK, ROBERT	119,921	MINETA, NORMAN Y.	17	39,655 D	40.1%	59.9%	40.1%	59.9%
15	1992	265,370	82,875	WICK, ROBERT	168,617	MINETA, NORMAN Y.	13,878	85,742 D	31.2%	63.5%	33.0%	67.0%
16	2000	159,746	37,213	THAYN, HORACE "GENE"	115,118	LOFGREN, ZOE	7,415	77,905 D	23.3%	72.1%	24.4%	75.6%
16	1998	117,414	27,494	THAYN, HORACE "GENE"	85,503	LOFGREN, ZOE	4,417	58,009 D	23.4%	72.8%	24.3%	75.7%
16	1996	143,207	43,197	WOJSLAW, CHUCK	94,020	LOFGREN, ZOE	5,990	50,823 D	30.2%	65.7%	31.5%	68.5%
16	1994	115,352	40,409	SMITH, LYLE J.	74,935	LOFGREN, ZOE	8	34,526 D	35.0%	65.0%	35.0%	65.0%
16	1992	155,883	49,843	BUNDESEN, TED	96,661	EDWARDS, DON	9,379	46,818 D	32.0%	62.0%	34.0%	66.0%
17	2000	208,760	51,557	ENGLER, CLINT	143,219	FARR, SAM	13,984	91,662 D	24.7%	68.6%	26.5%	73.5%
17	1998	160,690	52,470	MCCAMPBELL, BILL	103,719	FARR, SAM	4,501	51,249 D	32.7%	64.5%	33.6%	66.4%
17	1996	195,545	73,856	BROWN, JESS	115,116	FARR, SAM	6,573	41,260 D	37.8%	58.9%	39.1%	60.9%
17	1994	167,193	74,380	MCCAMPBELL, BILL	87,222	FARR, SAM	5,591	12,842 D	44.5%	52.2%	46.0%	54.0%
17	1992	210,367	49,947	MCCAMPBELL, BILL	151,565	PANETTA, LEON E.	8,855	101,618 D	23.7%	72.0%	24.8%	75.2%
18	2000	180,328	56,465	WILSON, STEVE R.	121,003	CONDIT, GARY A.	2,860	64,538 D	31.3%	67.1%	31.8%	68.2%
18	1998	136,931			118,842	CONDIT, GARY A.	18,089	118,842 D		86.8%		100.0%
18	1996	165,586	52,695	CONRAD, BILL	108,827	CONDIT, GARY A.	4,064	56,132 D	31.8%	65.7%	32.6%	67.4%
18	1994	139,052	44,046	CARTER, TOM	91,105	CONDIT, GARY A.	3,901	47,059 D	31.7%	65.5%	32.6%	67.4%
18	1992	165,011			139,704	CONDIT, GARY A.	25,307	139,704 D		84.7%		100.0%
19	2000	222,615	144,517	RADANOVICH, GEORGE P.	70,578	ROSENBERG, DAN	7,520	73,939 R	64.9%	31.7%	67.2%	32.8%
19	1998	165,149	131,105	RADANOVICH, GEORGE P.			34,044	131,105 R	79.4%		100.0%	
19	1996	206,379	137,402	RADANOVICH, GEORGE P.	58,452	BARILE, PAUL	10,525	78,950 R	66.6%	28.3%	70.2%	29.8%
19	1994	183,926	104,435	RADANOVICH, GEORGE P.	72,912	LEHMAN, RICHARD	6,579	31,523 R	56.8%	39.6%	58.9%	41.1%
19	1992	216,640	100,590	CLOUD, TAL L.	101,619	LEHMAN, RICHARD	14,431	1,029 D	46.4%	46.9%	49.7%	50.3%
20	2000	126,534	57,563	RODRIGUEZ, RICH	66,235	DOOLEY, CAL	2,736	8,672 D	45.5%	52.3%	46.5%	53.5%
20	1998	99,782	39,183	UNRUH, CLIFF	60,599	DOOLEY, CAL		21,416 D	39.3%	60.7%	39.3%	60.7%
20	1996	115,705	45,276	HARVEY, TRICE	65,381	DOOLEY, CAL	5,048	20,105 D	39.1%	56.5%	40.9%	59.1%
20	1994	101,230	43,836	YOUNG, PAUL	57,394	DOOLEY, CAL		13,558 D	43.3%	56.7%	43.3%	56.7%
20	1992	112,067	39,388	HUNT, ED	72,679	DOOLEY, CAL		33,291 D	35.1%	64.9%	35.1%	64.9%
21	2000	199,100	142,539	THOMAS, WILLIAM M.	49,318	MARTINEZ, PEDRO "PETE" JR.	7,243	93,221 R	71.6%	24.8%	74.3%	25.7%
21	1998	146,983	115,989	THOMAS, WILLIAM M.			30,994	115,989 R	78.9%		100.0%	
21	1996	191,324	125,916	THOMAS, WILLIAM M.	50,694	VOLLMER, DEBORAH A.	14,714	75,222 R	65.8%	26.5%	71.3%	28.7%
21	1994	171,629	116,874	THOMAS, WILLIAM M.	47,517	EVANS, JOHN L.	7,238	69,357 R	68.1%	27.7%	71.1%	28.9%
21	1992	195,965	127,758	THOMAS, WILLIAM M.	68,058	VOLLMER, DEBORAH	149	59,700 R	65.2%	34.7%	65.2%	34.8%
22	2000	255,070	113,094	STOKER, MIKE	135,538	CAPPS, LOIS	6,438	22,444 D	44.3%	53.1%	45.5%	54.5%
22	1998	202,190	86,921	BORDONARO, TOM J.	111,388	CAPPS, LOIS	3,881	24,467 D	43.0%	55.1%	43.8%	56.2%
22	1996	244,186	107,987	SEASTRAND, ANDREA	118,299	CAPPS, WALTER H.	17,900	10,312 D	44.2%	48.4%	47.7%	52.3%
22	1994	209,008	102,987	SEASTRAND, ANDREA	101,424	CAPPS, WALTER H.	4,597	1,563 R	49.3%	48.5%	50.4%	49.6%
22	1992	249,924	131,242	HUFFINGTON, MICHAEL	87,328	OCHOA, GLORIA	31,354	43,914 R	52.5%	34.9%	60.0%	40.0%
23	2000	221,034	119,479	GALLEGLY, ELTON	89,918	CASE, MICHAEL	11,637	29,561 R	54.1%	40.7%	57.1%	42.9%
23	1998	160,430	96,362	GALLEGLY, ELTON	64,068	GONZALEZ, DANIEL		32,294 R	60.1%	39.9%	60.1%	39.9%
23	1996	199,507	118,880	GALLEGLY, ELTON	70,035	UNRUHE, ROBERT R.	10,592	48,845 R	59.6%	35.1%	62.9%	37.1%
23	1994	172,340	114,043	GALLEGLY, ELTON	47,345	READY, KEVIN	10,952	66,698 R	66.2%	27.5%	70.7%	29.3%
23	1992	212,881	115,504	GALLEGLY, ELTON	88,225	FERGUSON, ANITA P.	9,152	27,279 R	54.3%	41.4%	56.7%	43.3%

CALIFORNIA

CONGRESS

CD	Year	Total Vote	Republican Vote	Republican Candidate	Democratic Vote	Democratic Candidate	Other Vote	Rep.-Dem. Plurality	Total Vote Rep.	Total Vote Dem.	Major Vote Rep.	Major Vote Dem.
24	2000	235,444	70,169	DOYLE, JERRY	155,398	SHERMAN, BRAD	9,877	85,229 D	29.8%	66.0%	31.1%	68.9%
24	1998	180,580	69,501	HOFFMAN, RANDY	103,491	SHERMAN, BRAD	7,588	33,990 D	38.5%	57.3%	40.2%	59.8%
24	1996	214,848	93,629	SYBERT, RICH	106,193	SHERMAN, BRAD	15,026	12,564 D	43.6%	49.4%	46.9%	53.1%
24	1994	193,179	91,806	SYBERT, RICH	95,342	BEILENSON, ANTHONY C.	6,031	3,536 D	47.5%	49.4%	49.1%	50.9%
24	1992	255,267	99,835	MCCLINTOCK, TOM	141,742	BEILENSON, ANTHONY C.	13,690	41,907 D	39.1%	55.5%	41.3%	58.7%
25	2000	222,778	138,628	MCKEON, HOWARD P.	73,921	GOLD, SID	10,229	64,707 R	62.2%	33.2%	65.2%	34.8%
25	1998	152,682	114,013	MCKEON, HOWARD P.			38,669	114,013 R	74.7%		100.0%	0.0%
25	1996	196,203	122,428	MCKEON, HOWARD P.	65,089	TRAUTMAN, DIANE	8,686	57,339 R	62.4%	33.2%	65.3%	34.7%
25	1994	169,971	110,301	MCKEON, HOWARD P.	53,445	GILMARTIN, JAMES H.	6,225	56,856 R	64.9%	31.4%	67.4%	32.6%
25	1992	218,715	113,611	MCKEON, HOWARD P.	72,233	GILMARTIN, JAMES H.	32,871	41,378 R	51.9%	33.0%	61.1%	38.9%
26	2000	114,786			96,500	BERMAN, HOWARD L.	18,286	96,500 D		84.1%		100.0%
26	1998	83,662			69,000	BERMAN, HOWARD L.	14,662	69,000 D		82.5%		100.0%
26	1996	102,515	29,332	GLASS, BILL	67,525	BERMAN, HOWARD L.	5,658	38,193 D	28.6%	65.9%	30.3%	69.7%
26	1994	88,138	28,423	FROSCH, GARY E.	55,145	BERMAN, HOWARD L.	4,570	26,722 D	32.2%	62.6%	34.0%	66.0%
26	1992	120,908	36,453	FROSCH, GARY E.	73,807	BERMAN, HOWARD L.	10,648	37,354 D	30.1%	61.0%	33.1%	66.9%
27	2000	215,774	94,518	ROGAN, JAMES E.	113,708	SCHIFF, ADAM	7,548	19,190 D	43.8%	52.7%	45.4%	54.6%
27	1998	159,066	80,702	ROGAN, JAMES E.	73,875	GORDON, BARRY A.	4,489	6,827 R	50.7%	46.4%	52.2%	47.8%
27	1996	189,930	95,310	ROGAN, JAMES E.	82,014	KAHN, DOUG	12,606	13,296 R	50.2%	43.2%	53.7%	46.3%
27	1994	166,774	88,341	MOORHEAD, CARLOS J.	70,267	KAHN, DOUG	8,166	18,074 R	53.0%	42.1%	55.7%	44.3%
27	1992	212,450	105,521	MOORHEAD, CARLOS J.	83,805	KAHN, DOUG	23,124	21,716 R	49.7%	39.4%	55.7%	44.3%
28	2000	205,199	116,557	DREIER, DAVID	81,804	NELSON, JANICE M.	6,838	34,753 R	56.8%	39.9%	58.8%	41.2%
28	1998	157,200	90,607	DREIER, DAVID	61,721	NELSON, JANICE M.	4,872	28,886 R	57.6%	39.3%	59.5%	40.5%
28	1996	186,885	113,389	DREIER, DAVID	69,037	LEVERING, DAVID	4,459	44,352 R	60.7%	36.9%	62.2%	37.8%
28	1994	164,277	110,179	DREIER, DAVID	50,022	RANDLE, TOMMY L.	4,076	60,157 R	67.1%	30.4%	68.8%	31.2%
28	1992	209,382	122,353	DREIER, DAVID	76,525	WACHTEL, AL	10,504	45,828 R	58.4%	36.5%	61.5%	38.5%
29	2000	238,201	45,784	SCILEPPI, JIM	180,295	WAXMAN, HENRY A.	12,122	134,511 D	19.2%	75.7%	20.3%	79.7%
29	1998	178,094	40,282	GOTTLIEB, MIKE	131,561	WAXMAN, HENRY A.	6,251	91,279 D	22.6%	73.9%	23.4%	76.6%
29	1996	214,817	52,857	STEPANEK, PAUL	145,278	WAXMAN, HENRY A.	16,682	92,421 D	24.6%	67.6%	26.7%	73.3%
29	1994	190,376	53,801	STEPANEK, PAUL	129,413	WAXMAN, HENRY A.	7,162	75,612 D	28.3%	68.0%	29.4%	70.6%
29	1992	261,486	67,141	ROBBINS, MARK A.	160,312	WAXMAN, HENRY A.	34,033	93,171 D	25.7%	61.3%	29.5%	70.5%
30	2000	99,920	11,788	GOSS, TONY	83,223	BECERRA, XAVIER	4,909	71,435 D	11.8%	83.3%	12.4%	87.6%
30	1998	71,671	13,441	PARKER, PATRICIA JEAN	58,230	BECERRA, XAVIER		44,789 D	18.8%	81.2%	18.8%	81.2%
30	1996	80,590	15,078	PARKER, PATRICIA JEAN	58,283	BECERRA, XAVIER	7,229	43,205 D	18.7%	72.3%	20.6%	79.4%
30	1994	66,425	18,741	RAMIREZ, DAVID A.	43,943	BECERRA, XAVIER	3,741	25,202 D	28.2%	66.2%	29.9%	70.1%
30	1992	83,543	20,034	WAKSBERG, MORRY	48,800	BECERRA, XAVIER	14,709	28,766 D	24.0%	58.4%	29.1%	70.9%
31	2000	112,914			89,600	SOLIS, HILDA L.	23,314	89,600 D		79.4%		100.0%
31	1998	87,360	19,786	MORENO, FRANK C.	61,173	MARTINEZ, MATTHEW G.	6,401	41,387 D	22.6%	70.0%	24.4%	75.6%
31	1996	102,690	28,705	FLORES, JOHN V.	69,285	MARTINEZ, MATTHEW G.	4,700	40,580 D	28.0%	67.5%	29.3%	70.7%
31	1994	85,467	34,926	FLORES, JOHN V.	50,541	MARTINEZ, MATTHEW G.		15,615 D	40.9%	59.1%	40.9%	59.1%
31	1992	109,197	40,873	FRANCO, REUBEN D.	68,324	MARTINEZ, MATTHEW G.		27,451 D	37.4%	62.6%	37.4%	62.6%
32	2000	164,527	19,924	WILLIAMSON, KATHY	137,447	DIXON, JULIAN C.	7,156	117,523 D	12.1%	83.5%	12.7%	87.3%
32	1998	129,492	14,622	ARDITO, LARRY	112,253	DIXON, JULIAN C.	2,617	97,631 D	11.3%	86.7%	11.5%	88.5%
32	1996	151,427	18,768	ARDITO, LARRY	124,712	DIXON, JULIAN C.	7,947	105,944 D	12.4%	82.4%	13.1%	86.9%
32	1994	126,306	22,190	FARHAT, ERNIE A.	98,017	DIXON, JULIAN C.	6,099	75,827 D	17.6%	77.6%	18.5%	81.5%
32	1992	172,812			150,644	DIXON, JULIAN C.	22,168	150,644 D		87.2%		100.0%
33	2000	71,571	8,260	MILLER, WAYNE	60,510	ROYBAL-ALLARD, LUCILLE	2,801	52,250 D	11.5%	84.5%	12.0%	88.0%
33	1998	49,674	6,364	MILLER, WAYNE	43,310	ROYBAL-ALLARD, LUCILLE		36,946 D	12.8%	87.2%	12.8%	87.2%
33	1996	57,828	8,147	LEONARD, JOHN P.	47,478	ROYBAL-ALLARD, LUCILLE	2,203	39,331 D	14.1%	82.1%	14.6%	85.4%
33	1994	41,508			33,814	ROYBAL-ALLARD, LUCILLE	7,694	33,814 D		81.5%		100.0%
33	1992	50,779	15,428	GUZMAN, ROBERT	32,010	ROYBAL-ALLARD, LUCILLE	3,341	16,582 D	30.4%	63.0%	32.5%	67.5%

CALIFORNIA

CONGRESS

CD	Year	Total Vote	Republican Vote	Republican Candidate	Democratic Vote	Democratic Candidate	Other Vote	Rep.-Dem. Plurality	Total Vote Rep.	Total Vote Dem.	Major Vote Rep.	Major Vote Dem.
34	2000	148,723	33,445	CANALES, ROBERT ARTHUR	105,980	NAPOLITANO, GRACE FLORES	9,298	72,535 D	22.5%	71.3%	24.0%	76.0%
34	1998	113,075	32,321	PEREZ, ED	76,471	NAPOLITANO, GRACE FLORES	4,283	44,150 D	28.6%	67.6%	29.7%	70.3%
34	1996	138,440	36,852	NUNEZ, DAVID G.	94,730	TORRES, ESTEBAN	6,858	57,878 D	26.6%	68.4%	28.0%	72.0%
34	1994	117,455	40,068	NUNEZ, ALBERT J.	72,439	TORRES, ESTEBAN	4,948	32,371 D	34.1%	61.7%	35.6%	64.4%
34	1992	149,718	50,907	HERNANDEZ, JAY	91,738	TORRES, ESTEBAN	7,073	40,831 D	34.0%	61.3%	35.7%	64.3%
35	2000	116,215	12,582	MCGILL, CARL	100,569	WATERS, MAXINE	3,064	87,987 D	10.8%	86.5%	11.1%	88.9%
35	1998	88,145			78,732	WATERS, MAXINE	9,413	78,732 D		89.3%		100.0%
35	1996	108,488	13,116	CARLSON, ERIC	92,762	WATERS, MAXINE	2,610	79,646 D	12.1%	85.5%	12.4%	87.6%
35	1994	84,081	18,390	TRUMAN, NATE	65,688	WATERS, MAXINE	3	47,298 D	21.9%	78.1%	21.9%	78.1%
35	1992	124,776	17,417	TRUMAN, NATE	102,941	WATERS, MAXINE	4,418	85,524 D	14.0%	82.5%	14.5%	85.5%
36	2000	239,131	111,199	KUYKENDALL, STEVEN	115,651	HARMAN, JANE	12,281	4,452 D	46.5%	48.4%	49.0%	51.0%
36	1998	181,706	88,843	KUYKENDALL, STEVEN	84,624	HAHN, JANICE	8,239	4,219 R	48.9%	46.6%	51.2%	48.8%
36	1996	224,459	98,538	BROOKS, SUSAN	117,752	HARMAN, JANE	8,169	19,214 D	43.9%	52.5%	45.6%	54.4%
36	1994	195,808	93,127	BROOKS, SUSAN M.	93,939	HARMAN, JANE	8,742	812 D	47.6%	48.0%	49.8%	50.2%
36	1992	259,757	109,684	FLORES, JOAN M.	125,751	HARMAN, JANE	24,322	16,067 D	42.2%	48.4%	46.6%	53.4%
37	2000	113,275	12,762	VAN, VERNON	93,269	MILLENDER-MCDONALD, JUANITA	7,244	80,507 D	11.3%	82.3%	12.0%	88.0%
37	1998	82,327	12,301	LANKSTER, SAUL E.	70,026	MILLENDER-MCDONALD, JUANITA		57,725 D	14.9%	85.1%	14.9%	85.1%
37	1996	102,646	15,399	VOETEE, MICHAEL E.	87,247	MILLENDER-MCDONALD, JUANITA		71,848 D	15.0%	85.0%	15.0%	85.0%
37	1994	82,931			64,166	TUCKER, WALTER R.	18,765	64,166 D		77.4%		100.0%
37	1992	113,337			97,159	TUCKER, WALTER R.	16,178	97,159 D		85.7%		100.0%
38	2000	180,122	87,266	HORN, STEVE	85,498	SCHIPSKE, GERRIE	7,358	1,768 R	48.4%	47.5%	50.5%	49.5%
38	1998	134,875	71,386	HORN, STEVE	59,767	MATHEWS, PETER	3,722	11,619 R	52.9%	44.3%	54.4%	45.6%
38	1996	167,645	88,136	HORN, STEVE	71,627	ZBUR, RICK	7,882	16,509 R	52.6%	42.7%	55.2%	44.8%
38	1994	145,769	85,225	HORN, STEVE	53,681	MATHEWS, PETER	6,863	31,544 R	58.5%	36.8%	61.4%	38.6%
38	1992	189,321	92,038	HORN, STEVE	82,108	BRAUDE, EVAN A.	15,175	9,930 R	48.6%	43.4%	52.9%	47.1%
39	2000	206,104	129,294	ROYCE, ED	64,938	KANEL, GILL G.	11,872	64,356 R	62.7%	31.5%	66.6%	33.4%
39	1998	155,465	97,366	ROYCE, ED	52,815	GROOM, A. "CECY" R.	5,284	44,551 R	62.6%	34.0%	64.8%	35.2%
39	1996	192,290	120,761	ROYCE, ED	61,392	DAVIS, R. O.	10,137	59,369 R	62.8%	31.9%	66.3%	33.7%
39	1994	171,244	113,641	ROYCE, ED	49,696	DAVIS, R. O.	7,907	63,945 R	66.4%	29.0%	69.6%	30.4%
39	1992	213,684	122,472	ROYCE, ED	81,728	MCCLANAHAN, MOLLY	9,484	40,744 R	57.3%	38.2%	60.0%	40.0%
40	2000	189,022	151,069	LEWIS, JERRY			37,953	151,069 R	79.9%		100.0%	
40	1998	150,125	97,406	LEWIS, JERRY	47,897	CONAWAY, ROBERT	4,822	49,509 R	64.9%	31.9%	67.0%	33.0%
40	1996	152,261	98,821	LEWIS, JERRY	44,102	CONAWAY, ROBERT	9,338	54,719 R	64.9%	29.0%	69.1%	30.9%
40	1994	163,731	115,728	LEWIS, JERRY	48,003	RUSK, DONALD M.		67,725 R	70.7%	29.3%	70.7%	29.3%
40	1992	205,283	129,563	LEWIS, JERRY	63,881	RUSK, DONALD M.	11,839	65,682 R	63.1%	31.1%	67.0%	33.0%
41	2000	177,616	104,695	MILLER, GARY	66,361	FAVILA, RODOLFO G.	6,560	38,334 R	58.9%	37.4%	61.2%	38.8%
41	1998	128,414	68,310	MILLER, GARY	52,264	ANSARI, EILEEN R.	7,840	16,046 R	53.2%	40.7%	56.7%	43.3%
41	1996	143,565	83,934	KIM, JAY C.	47,346	WALDRON, RICHARD L.	12,285	36,588 R	58.5%	33.0%	63.9%	36.1%
41	1994	132,143	82,100	KIM, JAY C.	50,043	TESSIER, ED		32,057 R	62.1%	37.9%	62.1%	37.9%
41	1992	170,666	101,753	KIM, JAY C.	58,777	BAKER, BOB	10,136	42,976 R	59.6%	34.4%	63.4%	36.6%
42	2000	151,577	53,239	PIROZZI, ELIA	90,585	BACA, JOE	7,753	37,346 D	35.1%	59.8%	37.0%	63.0%
42	1998	112,520	45,328	PIROZZI, ELIA	62,207	BROWN, GEORGE E.	4,985	16,879 D	40.3%	55.3%	42.2%	57.8%
42	1996	103,336	51,170	WILDE, LINDA M.	52,166	BROWN, GEORGE E.		996 D	49.5%	50.5%	49.5%	50.5%
42	1994	115,205	56,259	GUZMAN, ROB	58,888	BROWN, GEORGE E.	58	2,629 D	48.8%	51.1%	48.9%	51.1%
42	1992	157,455	69,251	RUTAN, RICHARD B.	79,780	BROWN, GEORGE E.	8,424	10,529 D	44.0%	50.7%	46.5%	53.5%
43	2000	190,332	140,201	CALVERT, KEN			50,131	140,201 R	73.7%		100.0%	
43	1998	149,071	83,012	CALVERT, KEN	56,373	RAYBURN, MIKE	9,686	26,639 R	55.7%	37.8%	59.6%	40.4%
43	1996	177,724	97,247	CALVERT, KEN	67,422	KIMBROUGH, GUY C.	13,055	29,825 R	54.7%	37.9%	59.1%	40.9%
43	1994	154,386	84,500	CALVERT, KEN	59,342	TAKANO, MARK A.	10,544	25,158 R	54.7%	38.4%	58.7%	41.3%
43	1992	190,639	88,987	CALVERT, KEN	88,468	TAKANO, MARK A.	13,184	519 R	46.7%	46.4%	50.1%	49.9%

CALIFORNIA

CONGRESS

CD	Year	Total Vote	Republican Vote	Republican Candidate	Democratic Vote	Democratic Candidate	Other Vote	Rep.-Dem. Plurality	Total Vote Rep.	Total Vote Dem.	Major Vote Rep.	Major Vote Dem.
44	2000	209,187	123,738	BONO, MARY	79,302	ODEN, RON	6,147	44,436 R	59.2%	37.9%	60.9%	39.1%
44	1998	161,528	97,013	BONO, MARY	57,697	WAITE, RALPH	6,818	39,316 R	60.1%	35.7%	62.7%	37.3%
44	1996	191,628	110,643	BONO, SONNY	73,844	RUFUS, ANITA	7,141	36,799 R	57.7%	38.5%	60.0%	40.0%
44	1994	171,776	95,521	BONO, SONNY	65,370	CLUTE, STEVE	10,885	30,151 R	55.6%	38.1%	59.4%	40.6%
44	1992	203,541	110,333	MCCANDLESS, AL	81,693	SMITH, GEORGIA	11,515	28,640 R	54.2%	40.1%	57.5%	42.5%
45	2000	219,385	136,275	ROHRABACHER, DANA	71,066	CRISELL, TED	12,044	65,209 R	62.1%	32.4%	65.7%	34.3%
45	1998	160,770	94,296	ROHRABACHER, DANA	60,022	NEAL, PATRICIA W.	6,452	34,274 R	58.7%	37.3%	61.1%	38.9%
45	1996	205,522	125,326	ROHRABACHER, DANA	68,312	ALEXANDER, SALLY J.	11,884	57,014 R	61.0%	33.2%	64.7%	35.3%
45	1994	180,724	124,875	ROHRABACHER, DANA	55,849	WILLIAMSON, BRETT		69,026 R	69.1%	30.9%	69.1%	30.9%
45	1992	227,016	123,731	ROHRABACHER, DANA	88,508	MCCABE, PATRICIA	14,777	35,223 R	54.5%	39.0%	58.3%	41.7%
46	2000	116,908	40,928	TUCHMAN, GLORIA MATTA	70,381	SANCHEZ, LORETTA	5,599	29,453 D	35.0%	60.2%	36.8%	63.2%
46	1998	85,002	33,388	DORNAN, ROBERT K.	47,964	SANCHEZ, LORETTA	3,650	14,576 D	39.3%	56.4%	41.0%	59.0%
46	1996	102,484	46,980	DORNAN, ROBERT K.	47,964	SANCHEZ, LORETTA	7,540	984 D	45.8%	46.8%	49.5%	50.5%
46	1994	88,697	50,616	DORNAN, ROBERT K.	33,004	FARBER, MICHAEL	5,077	17,612 R	57.1%	37.2%	60.5%	39.5%
46	1992	110,806	55,659	DORNAN, ROBERT K.	45,435	BANUELOS, ROBERT J.	9,712	10,224 R	50.2%	41.0%	55.1%	44.9%
47	2000	276,401	181,365	COX, CHRISTOPHER	83,186	GRAHAM, JOHN	11,850	98,179 R	65.6%	30.1%	68.6%	31.4%
47	1998	196,316	132,711	COX, CHRISTOPHER	57,938	AVALOS, CHRISTINA	5,667	74,773 R	67.6%	29.5%	69.6%	30.4%
47	1996	243,777	160,078	COX, CHRISTOPHER	70,362	LAINE, TINA LOUISE	13,337	89,716 R	65.7%	28.9%	69.5%	30.5%
47	1994	214,997	154,071	COX, CHRISTOPHER	53,669	KINGSBURY, GARY	7,257	100,402 R	71.7%	25.0%	74.2%	25.8%
47	1992	254,257	165,004	COX, CHRISTOPHER	76,924	ANWILER, JOHN F.	12,329	88,080 R	64.9%	30.3%	68.2%	31.8%
48	2000	261,478	160,627	ISSA, DARRELL	74,073	KOUVELIS, PETER	26,778	86,554 R	61.4%	28.3%	68.4%	31.6%
48	1998	180,719	138,948	PACKARD, RON			41,771	138,948 R	76.9%		100.0%	
48	1996	221,391	145,814	PACKARD, RON	59,558	FARRELL, DAN	16,019	86,256 R	65.9%	26.9%	71.0%	29.0%
48	1994	195,636	143,570	PACKARD, RON	43,523	LESCHICK, ANDREI	8,543	100,047 R	73.4%	22.2%	76.7%	23.3%
48	1992	230,495	140,935	PACKARD, RON	67,415	FARBER, MICHAEL	22,145	73,520 R	61.1%	29.2%	67.6%	32.4%
49	2000	228,489	105,515	BILBRAY, BRIAN P.	113,400	DAVIS, SUSAN A.	9,574	7,885 D	46.2%	49.6%	48.2%	51.8%
49	1998	185,519	90,516	BILBRAY, BRIAN P.	86,400	KEHOE, CHRISTINE T.	8,603	4,116 R	48.8%	46.6%	51.2%	48.8%
49	1996	206,768	108,806	BILBRAY, BRIAN P.	86,657	NAVARRO, PETER	11,305	22,149 R	52.6%	41.9%	55.7%	44.3%
49	1994	186,118	90,283	BILBRAY, BRIAN P.	85,597	SCHENK, LYNN	10,238	4,686 R	48.5%	46.0%	51.3%	48.7%
49	1992	248,898	106,170	JARVIS, JUDY	127,280	SCHENK, LYNN	15,448	21,110 D	42.7%	51.1%	45.5%	54.5%
50	2000	139,472	38,526	DIVINE, BOB	95,191	FILNER, BOB	5,755	56,665 D	27.6%	68.3%	28.8%	71.2%
50	1998	77,991			77,354	FILNER, BOB	637	77,354 D		99.2%		100.0%
50	1996	118,340	38,351	BAIZE, JIM	73,200	FILNER, BOB	6,789	34,849 D	32.4%	61.9%	34.4%	65.6%
50	1994	104,451	36,955	ACEVEDO, MARY ALICE	59,214	FILNER, BOB	8,282	22,259 D	35.4%	56.7%	38.4%	61.6%
50	1992	136,626	39,531	VALENCIA, TONY	77,293	FILNER, BOB	19,802	37,762 D	28.9%	56.6%	33.8%	66.2%
51	2000	267,799	172,291	CUNNINGHAM, RANDY	81,408	BARRAZA, GEORGE "JORGE"	14,100	90,883 R	64.3%	30.4%	67.9%	32.1%
51	1998	206,878	126,229	CUNNINGHAM, RANDY	71,706	KRIPKE, DAN	8,943	54,523 R	61.0%	34.7%	63.8%	36.2%
51	1996	229,024	149,032	CUNNINGHAM, RANDY	66,250	TAMERIUS, RITA	13,742	82,782 R	65.1%	28.9%	69.2%	30.8%
51	1994	206,988	138,547	CUNNINGHAM, RANDY	57,374	TAMERIUS, RITA	11,067	81,173 R	66.9%	27.7%	70.7%	29.3%
51	1992	252,995	141,890	CUNNINGHAM, RANDY	85,148	HERBERT, BEA	25,957	56,742 R	56.1%	33.7%	62.5%	37.5%
52	2000	202,994	131,345	HUNTER, DUNCAN L.	63,537	BARKACS, CRAIG	8,112	67,808 R	64.7%	31.3%	67.4%	32.6%
52	1998	153,568	116,251	HUNTER, DUNCAN L.			37,317	116,251 R	75.7%		100.0%	
52	1996	178,321	116,746	HUNTER, DUNCAN L.	53,104	WESLEY, DARITY	8,471	63,642 R	65.5%	29.8%	68.7%	31.3%
52	1994	170,686	109,201	HUNTER, DUNCAN L.	53,024	GASTIL, JANET M.	8,461	56,177 R	64.0%	31.1%	67.3%	32.7%
52	1992	213,784	112,995	HUNTER, DUNCAN L.	88,076	GASTIL, JANET M.	12,713	24,919 R	52.9%	41.2%	56.2%	43.8%

CALIFORNIA

GENERAL AND PRIMARY ELECTIONS

2000 GENERAL ELECTIONS

President Other vote was 45,520 Libertarian (Browne); 44,987 Reform (Buchanan); 17,042 American Independent (Phillips); 10,934 Natural Law (Hagelin); 28 write-in (McReynolds); 6 write-in (Kenyon).

Senator Other vote was 326,828 Green (Benjamin); 187,718 Libertarian (Lightfoot); 134,598 American Independent (Templin); 96,552 Reform (Camahort); 58,537 Natural Law (Rees); 6 write-in (Jones).

Congress Other vote was: CD 1: 7,173 Natural Law (Kreier), 6,376 Libertarian (Rossi), 3,161 Reform (Elizondo); CD 2: 8,910 Natural Law (McDermott), 6,699 Libertarian (Martin); CD 3: 5,227 Libertarian (Tuma), 2,634 Natural Law (Jones); CD 4: 9,494 Libertarian (Frey), 6,452 Natural Law (Ray); CD 5: 6,195 Green (Adams), 2,919 Libertarian (Lang), 1,975 Natural Law (Kersey); CD 6: 13,248 Green (Moscoso), 4,691 Libertarian (Barton); 2,894 Natural Law (Barreca); CD 7: 4,943 Natural Law (Sproul); CD 8: 5,645 Libertarian (Bauman), 2,638 Natural Law (Smithstein); CD 9: 7,051 Libertarian (Foldvary), 4,214 Natural Law (Jefferds); CD 10: 9,527 Natural Law (Janlois); CD 11: 5,036 Libertarian (Russow), 3,397 Natural Law (Kurey); CD 12: 6,431 Libertarian (Less), 3,559 Natural Law (Young); CD 13: 4,623 Libertarian (Mora), 2,647 Natural Law (Hoehner), 2,365 American Independent (Grundmann); CD 14: 4,715 Libertarian (Dehn), 4,489 Natural Law (Black); CD 15: 4,820 Libertarian (Wimmers), 3,591 Natural Law (Gorney), 82 write-in (Kronzer); CD 16: 4,742 Libertarian (Umphress), 2,673 Natural Law (Klein); CD 17: 8,215 Green (Coffin), 2,510 Libertarian (Garrett), 2,263 Reform (Fenton), 996 Natural Law (Hartley); CD 18: 2,860 Natural Law (Riskin); CD 19: 4,264 Libertarian (Taylor), 1,990 Natural Law (Miller), 1,266 American Independent (Kaiser); CD 20: 1,416 Natural Law (Ruehlig), 1,320 Libertarian (Kriegbaum); CD 21: 7,243 Libertarian (Manion); CD 22: 2,490 Reform (Porter), 2,060 Libertarian (Furcinite), 1,888 Natural Law (Aguirre); CD 23: 6,473 Reform (Savitch), 3,708 Libertarian (Peebles), 1,456 Natural Law (S. Hospodar); CD 24: 6,966 Libertarian (Ros), 2,911 Natural Law (Cuddehe); CD 25: 7,219 Libertarian (Acker), 3,010 Natural Law (Small); CD 26: 13,052 Libertarian (Farley), 5,229 Natural Law (Cossak), 5 write-in (Edwards); CD 27: 3,873 Natural Law (M. Hospodar), 3,675 Libertarian (Brown); CD 28: 2,823 Libertarian (Weissbuch), 2,083 Natural Law (Allison), 1,932 American Independent (Haytas); CD 29: 7,944 Libertarian (Anderson), 4,178 Natural Law (Currivan); CD 30: 2,858 Libertarian (Heath), 2,051 Natural Law (Hearne); CD 31: 10,294 Green (Lieberg-Wong), 7,138 Libertarian (McGuire), 5,882 Natural Law (Griffin); CD 32: 3,875 Libertarian (Weber), 3,281 Natural Law (Jibri); CD 33: 1,601 Libertarian (Craddock), 1,200 Natural Law (Harpur); CD 34: 9,262 Natural Law (Simon); 36 write-in (Brantuk); CD 35: 1,911 American Independent (Mego), 1,153 Natural Law (Dunstan); CD 36: 6,073 Libertarian (D. Sherman), 3,549 Reform (Konopka), 2,264 Natural Law (Ornati); 395 write-in (Davies); CD 37: 4,094 Natural Law (Glazer), 3,150 Libertarian (Peters); CD 38: 3,744 Natural Law (Blasdell-Wilkinson), 3,614 Libertarian (Neglia); CD 39: 6,597 Natural Law (Jevning), 5,275 Libertarian (Gann); CD 40: 19,029 Natural Law (Schmit), 18,924 Libertarian (Lindberg); CD 41: 6,560 Natural Law (Kramer); CD 42: 4,059 Libertarian (Ballard), 3,694 Natural Law (Hartley); CD 43: 29,755 Libertarian (Reed), 20,376 Natural Law (N. Adam); CD 44: 4,135 Reform (Smith), 2,012 Natural Law (Meuer); CD 45: 8,409 Libertarian (Hull), 3,635 Natural Law (Betton); CD 46: 3,159 Libertarian (Boddie), 2,440 Natural Law (Engwall); CD 47: 8,081 Libertarian (Nolan), 3,769 Natural Law (J. Adam); CD 48: 11,240 Reform (Rose), 8,269 Natural Law (Miles), 7,269 Libertarian (Cobb); CD 49: 6,526 Libertarian (Ball), 3,048 Natural Law (Bhatti); CD 50: 3,472 Libertarian (Willoughby), 2,283 Natural Law (Kendall); CD 51: 7,159 Libertarian (Muhe), 6,941 Natural Law (Bourdette); CD 52: 5,995 Libertarian (Benoit), 2,117 Natural Law (R. Sherman).

2000 PRIMARY ELECTIONS

Primary March 7, 2000

Registration
(as of Feb. 7, 2000)

Republican	5,140,951
Democratic	6,684,668
American Independent	295,387
Green	108,904
Libertarian	87,183
Reform	85,869
Natural Law	62,183
Miscellaneous	133,997
Non-Partisan	2,032,663
TOTAL	14,631,805

CALIFORNIA

GENERAL AND PRIMARY ELECTIONS

Primary Type Open—All candidates ran on a single, multi-party ballot and the primary was open to all registered voters. However, the delegate-selection portion of the Democratic and Republican presidential primaries was restricted to registered voters in each party.

Note: An asterisk (*) denotes incumbent. The party identification of candidates is indicated in parentheses. Results are listed according to the overall vote, as well as the vote within each party. The nominations went to the candidate with the highest vote in each party. (The results of the Democratic and Republican presidential primaries—which selected each party's delegates—are listed separately below, while the results for the open, all-party presidential primary are given for all candidates that received at least 10,000 votes.)

2000 PRIMARIES

President	Republican	George W. Bush	1,725,162	60.6%		
		John McCain	988,706	34.7%		
		Alan Keyes	112,747	4.0%		
		Steve Forbes	8,449	0.3%		
		Gary Bauer	6,860	0.2%		
		Orrin G. Hatch	5,997	0.2%		
		TOTAL	2,847,921			
	Democratic	Al Gore	2,155,321	81.2%		
		Bill Bradley	482,882	18.2%		
		Lyndon H. LaRouche Jr.	15,911	0.6%		
		TOTAL	2,654,114			
	All-Party Open Primary	Al Gore (D)	2,609,950	34.2%		
		George W. Bush (R)	2,168,466	28.4%		
		John McCain (R)	1,780,570	23.3%		
		Bill Bradley (D)	642,654	8.4%		
		Alan Keyes (R)	170,442	2.2%		
		Ralph Nader (Green)	112,345	1.5%		
		Harry Browne (Libertarian)	20,825	0.3%		
		Lyndon H. LaRouche Jr. (D)	19,419	0.3%		
		Donald J. Trump (Reform)	15,311	0.2%		
		Steve Forbes (R)	14,484	0.2%		
		Gary Bauer (R)	10,529	0.1%		
		Others	62,726	0.8%		
		GRAND TOTAL	7,627,721			

			Overall Percentage	Republican Percentage	Democratic Percentage
Senator	Dianne Feinstein (D)*	3,759,560	51.2%		95.4%
	Tom Campbell (R)	1,697,208	23.1%	56.2%	
	Ray Haynes (R)	679,034	9.2%	22.5%	
	Bill Horn (R)	453,630	6.2%	15.0%	
	Michael Schmier (D)	181,104	2.5%		4.6%
	Gail Katherine Lightfoot (Libertarian)	120,622	1.6%		
	Medea Susan Benjamin (Green)	99,716	1.4%		
	John M. Brown (R)	68,415	0.9%	2.3%	
	Linh Dao (R)	64,559	0.9%	2.1%	
	James Peter Gough (R)	58,853	0.8%	1.9%	
	Jose Luis Camahort (Reform)	46,278	0.6%		
	Diane Beall Templin (American Independent)	38,836	0.5%		
	Jan B. Tucker (Green)	35,124	0.5%		
	Brain M. Rees (Natural Law)	26,382	0.4%		
	Valli Sharpe-Geisler (Reform)	19,516	0.3%		
	GRAND TOTAL	7,348,837			
	Republican Total	3,021,699			
	Democratic Total	3,940,664			

CALIFORNIA

GENERAL AND PRIMARY ELECTIONS

2000 PRIMARIES

			Overall Percentage	Republican Percentage	Democratic Percentage
Congressional District 1	Mike Thompson (D)*	112,185	64.6%		100.0%
	Russel J. Chase (R)	21,456	12.4%	42.7%	
	Kenneth A. Hitt (R)	14,489	8.3%	28.8%	
	Lawrence R. Wiesner (R)	14,351	8.3%	28.5%	
	Emil P. Rossi (Libertarian)	4,394	2.5%		
	Cheryl Kreier (Natural Law)	4,375	2.5%		
	Pamela Elizondo (Reform)	2,327	1.3%		
	GRAND TOTAL	173,577			
	Republican Total	50,296			
	Democratic Total	112,185			
Congressional District 2	Wally Herger (R)*	120,375	64.9%	100.0%	
	Stan Morgan (D)	48,858	26.3%		100.0%
	John McDermott (Natural Law)	11,647	6.3%		
	Charles R. Martin (Libertarian)	4,634	2.5%		
	GRAND TOTAL	185,514			
	Republican Total	120,375			
	Democratic Total	48,858			
Congressional District 3	Doug Ose (R)*	101,571	61.2%	100.0%	
	Bob Kent (D)	58,250	35.1%		100.0%
	Douglas Arthur Tuma (Libertarian)	4,222	2.5%		
	Channing E. Jones (Natural Law)	2,048	1.2%		
	GRAND TOTAL	166,091			
	Republican Total	101,571			
	Democratic Total	58,250			
Congressional District 4	John T. Doolittle (R)*	149,735	66.2%	100.0%	
	Mark A. Norberg (D)	63,130	27.9%		100.0%
	William Fritz Frey (Libertarian)	7,020	3.1%		
	Robert E. Ray (Natural Law)	6,393	2.8%		
	GRAND TOTAL	226,278			
	Republican Total	149,735			
	Democratic Total	63,130			
Congressional District 5	Robert T. Matsui (D)*	112,132	70.8%		100.0%
	Ken Payne (R)	38,158	24.1%	100.0%	
	Ken Adams (Green)	3,428	2.2%		
	Cullene Lang (Libertarian)	2,815	1.8%		
	Charles Kersey (Natural Law)	1,838	1.2%		
	GRAND TOTAL	158,371			
	Republican Total	38,158			
	Democratic Total	112,132			
Congressional District 6	Lynn Woolsey (D)*	135,941	66.4%		100.0%
	Ken McAuliffe (R)	57,478	28.1%	100.0%	
	Justin "Justo" Moscoso (Green)	4,781	2.3%		
	Richard O. Barton (Libertarian)	4,043	2.0%		
	Alan Barreca (Natural Law)	2,591	1.3%		
	GRAND TOTAL	204,834			
	Republican Total	57,478			
	Democratic Total	135,941			
Congressional District 7	George Miller (D)*	98,451	75.3%		100.0%
	Christopher A. Hoffman (R)	18,926	14.5%	64.3%	
	Nicholas Mraovich (R)	10,503	8.0%	35.7%	
	Martin Sproul (Natural Law)	2,792	2.1%		
	GRAND TOTAL	130,672			
	Republican Total	29,429			
	Democratic Total	98,451			

CALIFORNIA

GENERAL AND PRIMARY ELECTIONS

2000 PRIMARIES

			Overall Percentage	Republican Percentage	Democratic Percentage
Congressional District 8	Nancy Pelosi (D)*	109,246	85.5%		100.0%
	Adam Sparks (R)	13,501	10.6%	100.0%	
	Erik Bauman (Libertarian)	3,575	2.8%		
	David Smithstein (Natural Law)	1,389	1.1%		
	GRAND TOTAL	127,711			
	Republican Total	13,501			
	Democratic Total	109,246			
Congressional District 9	Barbara Lee (D)*	117,173	85.1%		100.0%
	Arneze Washington (R)	13,563	9.9%	100.0%	
	Fred E. Foldvary (Libertarian)	4,565	3.3%		
	Ellen Jefferds (Natural Law)	2,333	1.7%		
	GRAND TOTAL	137,634			
	Republican Total	13,563			
	Democratic Total	117,173			
Congressional District 10	Ellen O. Tauscher (D)*	110,702	54.3%		100.0%
	Claude B. Hutchison Jr. (R)	36,257	17.8%	41.3%	
	Gordon Blake (R)	30,532	15.0%	34.8%	
	Dennis M. Kilian (R)	21,039	10.3%	24.0%	
	Valerie Janlois (Natural Law)	5,324	2.6%		
	GRAND TOTAL	203,854			
	Republican Total	87,828			
	Democratic Total	110,702			
Congressional District 11	Richard W. Pombo (R)*	87,160	61.0%	100.0%	
	Tom Y. Santos (D)	30,817	21.6%		61.7%
	Robert L. Figueroa (D)	19,152	13.4%		38.3%
	Kathryn A. Russow (Libertarian)	3,273	2.3%		
	Jon A. Kurey (Natural Law)	2,388	1.7%		
	GRAND TOTAL	142,790			
	Republican Total	87,160			
	Democratic Total	49,969			
Congressional District 12	Tom Lantos (D)*	103,807	74.2%		100.0%
	Mike Garza (R)	14,165	10.1%	47.0%	
	Bob Evans (R)	8,274	5.9%	27.5%	
	James D. Williams Jr. (R)	7,694	5.5%	25.5%	
	Barbara J. Less (Libertarian)	4,098	2.9%		
	Rifkin Young (Natural Law)	1,788	1.3%		
	GRAND TOTAL	139,826			
	Republican Total	30,133			
	Democratic Total	103,807			
Congressional District 13	Fortney Pete Stark (D)*	77,905	68.7%		100.0%
	James R. Goetz (R)	22,488	19.8%	74.4%	
	Saundra Duffy (R)	7,736	6.8%	25.6%	
	Howard Mora (Libertarian)	2,421	2.1%		
	Timothy R. Hoehner (Natural Law)	1,400	1.2%		
	Don J. Grundmann (American Independent)	1,373	1.2%		
	GRAND TOTAL	113,323			
	Republican Total	30,224			
	Democratic Total	77,905			
Congressional District 14	Anna G. Eshoo (D)*	111,136	70.6%		100.0%
	Bill Quraishi (R)	17,817	11.3%	43.5%	
	Craig L. DeLue (R)	11,662	7.4%	28.5%	
	Henry E. "Bud" Manzler (R)	11,453	7.3%	28.0%	
	Joseph W. Dehn III (Libertarian)	3,193	2.0%		
	John Black (Natural Law)	2,121	1.3%		
	GRAND TOTAL	157,382			
	Republican Total	40,932			
	Democratic Total	111,136			

CALIFORNIA

GENERAL AND PRIMARY ELECTIONS

2000 PRIMARIES

			Overall Percentage	Republican Percentage	Democratic Percentage
Congressional District 15	Mike Honda (D)	62,876	39.2%		66.6%
	Jim Cunneen (R)	53,282	33.2%	86.0%	
	Bill Peacock (D)	22,499	14.0%		23.8%
	Dale C. Mead (R)	8,638	5.4%	14.0%	
	Dick Lane (D)	3,968	2.5%		4.2%
	Robin Parker (D)	3,646	2.3%		3.9%
	Ed Wimmers (Libertarian)	2,566	1.6%		
	Connor Vlakancic (D)	1,449	0.9%		1.5%
	Douglas C. Gorney (Natural Law)	1,350	0.8%		
	GRAND TOTAL	160,274			
	Republican Total	61,920			
	Democratic Total	94,438			
Congressional District 16	Zoe Lofgren (D)*	72,515	71.9%		100.0%
	Horace "Gene" Thayn (R)	23,652	23.5%	100.0%	
	Dennis Michael Umphress (Libertarian)	2,914	2.9%		
	Edward J. Klein (Natural Law)	1,764	1.7%		
	GRAND TOTAL	100,845			
	Republican Total	23,652			
	Democratic Total	72,515			
Congressional District 17	Sam Farr (D)*	83,275	56.7%		82.2%
	Clint Engler (R)	21,258	14.5%	54.2%	
	Rob Roberts (R)	11,467	7.8%	29.2%	
	Joe Grossman (D)	8,104	5.5%		8.0%
	Debra Whitmore (D)	7,661	5.2%		7.6%
	Carole Dooley (R)	6,495	4.4%	16.6%	
	E. Craig Coffin (Green)	2,790	1.9%		
	Art Dunn (D)	2,271	1.5%		2.2%
	Rick S. Garrett (Libertarian)	1,696	1.2%		
	Larry Fenton (Reform)	1,152	0.8%		
	Scott R. Hartley (Natural Law)	662	0.5%		
	GRAND TOTAL	146,831			
	Republican Total	39,220			
	Democratic Total	101,311			
Congressional District 18	Gary A. Condit (D)*	80,543	65.3%		100.0%
	Steve R. Wilson (R)	35,335	28.7%	100.0%	
	Rodger McAfee (D)	6,142	5.0%		
	Page Roth Riskin (Natural Law)	1,262	1.0%		
	GRAND TOTAL	123,282			
	Republican Total	35,335			
	Democratic Total	80,543			
Congressional District 19	George P. Radanovich (R)*	109,723	66.5%	100.0%	
	Dan Rosenberg (D)	33,921	20.6%		68.4%
	John S. Hernandez (D)	15,647	9.5%		31.6%
	Elizabeth Taylor (Libertarian)	3,256	2.0%		
	Bob Miller (Natural Law)	1,220	0.7%		
	Edmon V. Kaiser (American Independent)	1,147	0.7%		
	GRAND TOTAL	164,914			
	Republican Total	109,723			
	Democratic Total	49,568			
Congressional District 20	Cal Dooley (D)*	43,608	51.7%		100.0%
	Rich Rodriguez (R)	38,661	45.8%	100.0%	
	Arnold Kriegbaum (Libertarian)	1,144	1.4%		
	Walter Kenneth Ruehlig (Natural Law)	999	1.2%		
	GRAND TOTAL	84,412			
	Republican Total	38,661			
	Democratic Total	43,608			

CALIFORNIA

GENERAL AND PRIMARY ELECTIONS

2000 PRIMARIES

			Overall Percentage	Republican Percentage	Democratic Percentage
Congressional District 21	William M. "Bill" Thomas (R)*	98,088	73.7%	100.0%	
	Pedro "Pete" Martinez Jr. (D)	29,511	22.2%		100.0%
	James RS Manion (Libertarian)	5,430	4.1%		
	GRAND TOTAL	133,029			
	Republican Total	98,088			
	Democratic Total	29,511			
Congressional District 22	Lois Capps (D)*	105,850	55.3%		100.0%
	Mike Stoker (R)	73,256	38.2%	89.7%	
	Allen Rowe (R)	8,385	4.4%	10.3%	
	Joe Furcinite (Libertarian)	1,462	0.8%		
	Richard D. Porter (Reform)	1,330	0.7%		
	J. Carlos Aguirre (Natural Law)	1,244	0.6%		
	GRAND TOTAL	191,527			
	Republican Total	81,641			
	Democratic Total	105,850			
Congressional District 23	Elton Gallegly (R)*	92,010	63.2%	100.0%	
	Michael Case (D)	36,221	24.9%		80.5%
	Albert Maxwell Goldberg (D)	8,786	6.0%		19.5%
	Cary Savitch (Reform)	4,306	3.0%		
	Roger Peebles (Libertarian)	2,994	2.1%		
	Stephen P. Hospodar (Natural Law)	1,247	0.9%		
	GRAND TOTAL	145,564			
	Republican Total	92,010			
	Democratic Total	45,007			
Congressional District 24	Brad Sherman (D)*	99,236	66.2%		100.0%
	Jerry Doyle (R)	43,762	29.2%	100.0%	
	Juan Carlos Ros (Libertarian)	4,981	3.3%		
	Michael Cuddehe (Natural Law)	1,884	1.3%		
	John M. Kennedy (D write-in)	2			
	GRAND TOTAL	149,865			
	Republican Total	43,762			
	Democratic Total	99,238			
Congressional District 25	Howard P. "Buck" McKeon (R)*	92,342	63.3%	92.2%	
	Sid Gold (D)	39,748	27.2%		100.00%
	Hal Brent Meyers (R)	7,842	5.4%	7.8%	
	Bruce R. Acker (Libertarian)	4,103	2.8%		
	Mews Small (Natural Law)	1,896	1.3%		
	GRAND TOTAL	145,931			
	Republican Total	100,184			
	Democratic Total	39,748			
Congressional District 26	Howard L. Berman (D)*	60,896	84.6%		100.0%
	Bill Farley (Libertarian)	8,190	11.4%		
	David L. Cossak (Natural Law)	2,887	4.0%		
	No Republican candidate was listed on the primary ballot.				
	GRAND TOTAL	71,973			
	Democratic Total	60,896			
Congressional District 27	Adam Schiff (D)	70,449	48.8%		100.0%
	James E. Rogan (R)*	68,179	47.2%	100.0%	
	Ted Brown (Libertarian)	2,938	2.0%		
	Miriam R. Hospodar (Natural Law)	2,799	1.9%		
	GRAND TOTAL	144,365			
	Republican Total	68,179			
	Democratic Total	70,449			

CALIFORNIA

GENERAL AND PRIMARY ELECTIONS

2000 PRIMARIES

			Overall Percentage	Republican Percentage	Democratic Percentage
Congressional District 28	David Dreier (R)*	88,837	62.5%	100.0%	
	Janice M. Nelson (D)	47,971	33.7%		100.0%
	Randall G. Weissbuch (Libertarian)	2,327	1.6%		
	Joe "Jay" Haytas (American Independent)	1,759	1.2%		
	Lawrence Allison (Natural Law)	1,358	1.0%		
	GRAND TOTAL	142,252			
	Republican Total	88,837			
	Democratic Total	47,971			
Congressional District 29	Henry A. Waxman (D)*	114,147	76.3%		100.0%
	Jim Scileppi (R)	27,870	18.6%	100.0%	
	Jack Anderson (Libertarian)	5,419	3.6%		
	Bruce Currivan (Natural Law)	2,135	1.4%		
	GRAND TOTAL	149,571			
	Republican Total	27,870			
	Democratic Total	114,147			
Congressional District 30	Xavier Becerra (D)*	53,145	83.4%		100.0%
	Tony Goss (R)	6,919	10.9%	100.0%	
	Jason E. Heath (Libertarian)	1,922	3.0%		
	Gary D. Hearne (Natural Law)	1,718	2.7%		
	GRAND TOTAL	63,704			
	Republican Total	6,919			
	Democratic Total	53,145			
Congressional District 31	Hilda L. Solis (D)	48,531	62.2%		68.6%
	Matthew G. Martinez (D)*	22,241	28.5%		31.4%
	Krista Lieberg-Wong (Green)	3,296	4.2%		
	Michael McGuire (Libertarian)	2,277	2.9%		
	Richard D. Griffin (Natural Law)	1,630	2.1%		
	Larry Munoz (R write-in)	88	0.1%	100.0%	
	No Republican candidate was listed on the primary ballot.				
	GRAND TOTAL	78,063			
	Republican Total	88			
	Democratic Total	70,772			
Congressional District 32	Julian C. Dixon (D)*	84,307	78.5%		93.0%
	Kathy Williamson (R)	13,040	12.1%	100.0%	
	Elisha Smitty Smith (D)	6,351	5.9%		7.0%
	Bob Weber (Libertarian)	2,038	1.9%		
	Rashied Jibri (Natural Law)	1,644	1.5%		
	GRAND TOTAL	107,380			
	Republican Total	13,040			
	Democratic Total	90,658			
Congressional District 33	Lucille Roybal-Allard (D)*	37,618	84.6%		100.0%
	Wayne Miller (R)	5,364	12.1%	100.0%	
	Nathan Thomas Craddock (Libertarian)	810	1.8%		
	William Harpur (Natural Law)	655	1.5%		
	GRAND TOTAL	44,447			
	Republican Total	5,364			
	Democratic Total	37,618			
Congressional District 34	Grace Flores Napolitano (D)*	68,631	69.4%		100.0%
	Robert Arthur Canales (R)	24,140	24.4%	100.0%	
	Julia F. Simon (Natural Law)	6,053	6.1%		
	GRAND TOTAL	98,824			
	Republican Total	24,140			
	Democratic Total	68,631			

CALIFORNIA

GENERAL AND PRIMARY ELECTIONS

2000 PRIMARIES

			Overall Percentage	Republican Percentage	Democratic Percentage
Congressional District 35	Maxine Waters (D)*	64,176	85.4%		100.0%
	Carl McGill (R)	8,898	11.8%	100.0%	
	Gordon Michael Mego (American Independent)	1,247	1.7%		
	Rick Dunstan (Natural Law)	861	1.1%		
	GRAND TOTAL	75,182			
	Republican Total	8,898			
	Democratic Total	64,176			
Congressional District 36	Steven T. Kuykendall (R)*	66,520	42.7%	84.0%	
	Jane Harman (D)	63,013	40.5%		87.6%
	Robert T. Pegram (R)	12,653	8.1%	16.0%	
	James C. Cavuoto (D)	6,423	4.1%		8.9%
	Daniel R. Sherman (Libertarian)	2,635	1.7%		
	Farshad Rastegar (D)	2,508	1.6%		3.5%
	John R. Konopka (Reform)	1,044	0.7%		
	Matt Ornati (Natural Law)	868	0.6%		
	GRAND TOTAL	155,664			
	Republican Total	79,173			
	Democratic Total	71,944			
Congressional District 37	Juanita Millender-McDonald (D)*	58,646	81.8%		100.0%
	Vernon Van (R)	8,048	11.2%	100.0%	
	Margaret Glazer (Natural Law)	2,751	3.8%		
	Herb Peters (Libertarian)	2,248	3.1%		
	GRAND TOTAL	71,693			
	Republican Total	8,048			
	Democratic Total	58,646			
Congressional District 38	Steve Horn (R)*	59,209	50.5%	100.0%	
	Gerrie Schipske (D)	17,676	15.1%		32.2%
	Erin Gruwell (D)	16,062	13.7%		29.2%
	Peter Mathews (D)	13,937	11.9%		25.4%
	Ken Graham (D)	7,248	6.2%		13.2%
	Jack Neglia (Libertarian)	1,765	1.5%		
	Karen Blasdell-Wilkinson (Natural Law)	1,396	1.2%		
	GRAND TOTAL	117,293			
	Republican Total	59,209			
	Democratic Total	54,923			
Congressional District 39	Ed Royce (R)*	91,626	67.9%	100.0%	
	Gill G. Kanel (D)	35,816	26.6%		100.0%
	Ron Jevning (Natural Law)	3,865	2.9%		
	Keith D. Gann (Libertarian)	3,576	2.7%		
	GRAND TOTAL	134,883			
	Republican Total	91,626			
	Democratic Total	35,816			
Congressional District 40	Jerry Lewis (R)*	86,315	83.6%	100.0%	
	Frank N. Schmit (Natural Law)	8,687	8.4%		
	Marion J. Lindberg (Libertarian)	8,155	7.9%		
	Ron Dwayne Martinez (D write-in)	92	0.1%		100.0%
	No Democratic candidate was listed on the primary ballot.				
	GRAND TOTAL	103,249			
	Republican Total	86,315			
	Democratic Total	92			
Congressional District 41	Gary G. Miller (R)*	60,953	58.5%	89.5%	
	Rodolfo G. Favila (D)	32,528	31.2%		100.0%
	Tony Ma (R)	7,140	6.9%	10.5%	
	David Kramer (Natural Law)	3,519	3.4%		
	GRAND TOTAL	104,140			
	Republican Total	68,093			
	Democratic Total	32,528			

CALIFORNIA

GENERAL AND PRIMARY ELECTIONS

2000 PRIMARIES

			Overall Percentage	Republican Percentage	Democratic Percentage
Congressional District 42	Joe Baca (D)*	49,234	55.8%		100.0%
	Elia Pirozzi (R)	27,947	31.7%	79.7%	
	Jay Kim (R)	7,119	8.1%	20.3%	
	John "Scott" Ballard (Libertarian)	2,066	2.3%		
	Gwyn Hartley (Natural Law)	1,855	2.1%		
	GRAND TOTAL	88,221			
	Republican Total	35,066			
	Democratic Total	49,234			
Congressional District 43	Ken Calvert (R)*	73,660	58.0%	67.0%	
	Martin Collen (R)	31,907	25.1%	29.0%	
	Bill Reed (Libertarian)	9,627	7.6%		
	Nat Adam (Natural Law)	6,956	5.5%		
	Khalid Jafri (R)	4,448	3.5%	4.0%	
	Louis John Vandenberg (D write-in)	290	0.2%		61.3%
	Cary James (D write-in)	148	0.1%		31.3%
	Herre Caudle (D write-in)	35			7.4%
	No Democratic candidate was listed on the primary ballot.				
	GRAND TOTAL	127,071			
	Republican Total	110,015			
	Democratic Total	473			
Congressional District 44	Mary Bono (R)*	79,365	56.4%	89.0%	
	Ron Oden (D)	20,079	14.3%		40.9%
	Tom Harney (D)	13,170	9.4%		26.8%
	Bud Mathewson (R)	9,800	7.0%	11.0%	
	Jon Gordon (D)	9,765	6.9%		19.9%
	Doug Wofford (D)	6,124	4.4%		12.5%
	Gene Smith (Reform)	1,628	1.2%		
	Jim Meuer (Natural Law)	764	0.5%		
	GRAND TOTAL	140,695			
	Republican Total	89,165			
	Democratic Total	49,138			
Congressional District 45	Dana Rohrabacher (R)*	89,174	61.5%	89.1%	
	Ted Crisell (D)	37,755	26.0%		100.0%
	Long K. Pham (R)	10,942	7.5%	10.9%	
	Don Hull (Libertarian)	4,901	3.4%		
	Constance Betton (Natural Law)	2,208	1.5%		
	GRAND TOTAL	144,980			
	Republican Total	100,116			
	Democratic Total	37,755			
Congressional District 46	Loretta Sanchez (D)*	40,031	57.7%		100.0%
	Gloria Matta Tuchman (R)	16,606	23.9%	63.6%	
	Howard Garber (R)	9,518	13.7%	36.4%	
	Richard B. Boddie (Libertarian)	1,769	2.6%		
	Larry Engwall (Natural Law)	1,431	2.1%		
	GRAND TOTAL	69,355			
	Republican Total	26,124			
	Democratic Total	40,031			
Congressional District 47	Christopher Cox (R)*	134,959	68.6%	100.0%	
	John Graham (D)	18,913	9.6%		34.8%
	Don Irvine (D)	16,510	8.4%		30.4%
	Jim Keysor (D)	10,010	5.1%		18.4%
	Maziar Mafi (D)	8,953	4.5%		16.5%
	David F. Nolan (Libertarian)	4,892	2.5%		
	Iris Adam (Natural Law)	2,619	1.3%		
	GRAND TOTAL	196,856			
	Republican Total	134,959			
	Democratic Total	54,386			

CALIFORNIA

GENERAL AND PRIMARY ELECTIONS

2000 PRIMARIES

			Overall Percentage	Republican Percentage	Democratic Percentage
Congressional District 48	Darrell Issa (R)	67,732	35.3%	45.4%	
	Bill Morrow (R)	45,223	23.6%	30.4%	
	Peter Kouvelis (D)	20,789	10.8%		60.3%
	Richard K. Maguire (D)	13,704	7.1%		39.7%
	Mark Dornan (R)	9,534	5.0%	6.4%	
	Joe Snyder (R)	8,480	4.4%	5.7%	
	William D. Griffith (R)	5,362	2.8%	3.6%	
	Don Udall (R)	5,258	2.7%	3.5%	
	Eddie Rose (Reform)	3,305	1.7%		
	James Luke (R)	3,043	1.6%	2.0%	
	Sharon K. Miles (Natural Law)	2,751	1.4%		
	Joe Michael Cobb (Libertarian)	2,511	1.3%		
	Kim DeBow (R)	1,998	1.0%	1.3%	
	Kevin M. Mahan (R)	1,584	0.8%	1.1%	
	Ed Mayerhofer (R)	753	0.4%	0.5%	
	GRAND TOTAL	192,027			
	Republican Total	148,967			
	Democratic Total	34,493			
Congressional District 49	Brian P. Bilbray (R)*	79,473	50.9%	100.0%	
	Susan A. Davis (D)	71,443	45.8%		100.0%
	Doris Ball (Libertarian)	3,505	2.2%		
	Tahir I. Bhatti (Natural Law)	1,738	1.1%		
	GRAND TOTAL	156,159			
	Republican Total	79,473			
	Democratic Total	71,443			
Congressional District 50	Bob Filner (D)*	61,742	67.4%		100.0%
	Bob Divine (R)	18,339	20.0%	68.4%	
	Alexander Sorongon (R)	5,420	5.9%	20.2%	
	James Allen Good (R)	3,044	3.3%	11.4%	
	David A. Willoughby (Libertarian)	1,934	2.1%		
	LeeAnn S. Kendall (Natural Law)	1,187	1.3%		
	GRAND TOTAL	91,666			
	Republican Total	26,803			
	Democratic Total	61,742			
Congressional District 51	Randy "Duke" Cunningham (R)*	126,038	67.7%	100.0%	
	George "Jorge" Barraza (D)	50,245	27.0%		100.0%
	Daniel L. Muhe (Libertarian)	5,103	2.7%		
	Eric Hunter Bourdette (Natural Law)	4,858	2.6%		
	GRAND TOTAL	186,244			
	Republican Total	126,038			
	Democratic Total	50,245			
Congressional District 52	Duncan Hunter (R)*	103,667	70.9%	100.0%	
	Craig Barkacs (D)	36,715	25.1%		100.0%
	Michael Benoit (Libertarian)	4,408	3.0%		
	Robert A. Sherman (Natural Law)	1,455	1.0%		
	GRAND TOTAL	146,245			
	Republican Total	103,667			
	Democratic Total	36,715			

COLORADO

GOVERNOR
Bill Owens (R). Elected 1998 to a four-year term.

SENATORS
Wayne Allard (R). Elected 1996 to a six-year term.

Ben N. Campbell (R). Re-elected 1998 to a six-year term. Previously elected 1992. Changed party affiliation from Democrat to Republican in March 1995.

REPRESENTATIVES
1. Diana DeGette (D)
2. Mark Udall (D)
3. Scott McInnis (R)
4. Bob Schaffer (R)
5. Joel Hefley (R)
6. Tom Tancredo (R)

POSTWAR VOTE FOR PRESIDENT

Year	Total Vote	Republican		Democratic		Other Vote	Plurality	Percentage			
		Vote	Candidate	Vote	Candidate			Total Vote		Major Vote	
								Rep.	Dem.	Rep.	Dem.
2000**	1,741,368	883,748	Bush, George W.	738,227	Gore, Al	119,393	145,521 R	50.8%	42.4%	54.5%	45.5%
1996**	1,510,704	691,848	Dole, Bob	671,152	Clinton, Bill	147,704	20,696 R	45.8%	44.4%	50.8%	49.2%
1992**	1,569,180	562,850	Bush, George	629,681	Clinton, Bill	376,649	66,831 D	35.9%	40.1%	47.2%	52.8%
1988	1,372,394	728,177	Bush, George	621,453	Dukakis, Michael S.	22,764	106,724 R	53.1%	45.3%	54.0%	46.0%
1984	1,295,380	821,817	Reagan, Ronald	454,975	Mondale, Walter F.	18,588	366,842 R	63.4%	35.1%	64.4%	35.6%
1980**	1,184,415	652,264	Reagan, Ronald	367,973	Carter, Jimmy	164,178	284,291 R	55.1%	31.1%	63.9%	36.1%
1976	1,081,554	584,367	Ford, Gerald R.	460,353	Carter, Jimmy	36,834	124,014 R	54.0%	42.6%	55.9%	44.1%
1972	953,884	597,189	Nixon, Richard M.	329,980	McGovern, George S.	26,715	267,209 R	62.6%	34.6%	64.4%	35.6%
1968	811,199	409,345	Nixon, Richard M.	335,174	Humphrey, Hubert H.	66,680	74,171 R	50.5%	41.3%	55.0%	45.0%
1964	776,986	296,767	Goldwater, Barry M.	476,024	Johnson, Lyndon B.	4,195	179,257 D	38.2%	61.3%	38.4%	61.6%
1960	736,236	402,242	Nixon, Richard M.	330,629	Kennedy, John F.	3,365	71,613 R	54.6%	44.9%	54.9%	45.1%
1956	657,074	394,479	Eisenhower, Dwight D.	257,997	Stevenson, Adlai E.	4,598	136,482 R	60.0%	39.3%	60.5%	39.5%
1952	630,103	379,782	Eisenhower, Dwight D.	245,504	Stevenson, Adlai E.	4,817	134,278 R	60.3%	39.0%	60.7%	39.3%
1948	515,237	239,714	Dewey, Thomas E.	267,288	Truman, Harry S.	8,235	27,574 D	46.5%	51.9%	47.3%	52.7%

In 2000 the other vote column includes 91,434 votes cast for Green (Nader). In 1996 the other vote column includes 99,629 votes cast for Perot. In 1992 the other vote column includes 366,010 votes cast for Perot. In 1980 the other column includes 130,633 votes for Independent (Anderson).

COLORADO

POSTWAR VOTE FOR GOVERNOR

Year	Total Vote	Republican Vote	Republican Candidate	Democratic Vote	Democratic Candidate	Other Vote	Rep.-Dem. Plurality	Total Vote Rep.	Total Vote Dem.	Major Vote Rep.	Major Vote Dem.
1998	1,321,307	648,202	Owens, Bill	639,905	Schoettler, Gail	33,200	8,297 R	49.1%	48.4%	50.3%	49.7%
1994	1,116,307	432,042	Benson, Bruce	619,205	Romer, Roy	65,060	187,163 D	38.7%	55.5%	41.1%	58.9%
1990	1,011,272	358,403	Andrews, John	626,032	Romer, Roy	26,837	267,629 D	35.4%	61.9%	36.4%	63.6%
1986	1,058,928	434,420	Strickland, Ted	616,325	Romer, Roy	8,183	181,905 D	41.0%	58.2%	41.3%	58.7%
1982	956,021	302,740	Fuhr, John D.	627,960	Lamm, Richard D.	25,321	325,220 D	31.7%	65.7%	32.5%	67.5%
1978	823,807	317,292	Strickland, Ted	483,985	Lamm, Richard D.	22,530	166,693 D	38.5%	58.7%	39.6%	60.4%
1974	828,968	378,698	Vanderhoof, John D.	441,408	Lamm, Richard D.	8,862	62,710 D	45.7%	53.2%	46.2%	53.8%
1970	668,496	350,690	Love, John A.	302,432	Hogan, Mark	15,374	48,258 R	52.5%	45.2%	53.7%	46.3%
1966	660,063	356,730	Love, John A.	287,132	Knous, Robert L.	16,201	69,598 R	54.0%	43.5%	55.4%	44.6%
1962	616,481	349,342	Love, John A.	262,890	McNichols, Stephen	4,249	86,452 R	56.7%	42.6%	57.1%	42.9%
1958**	549,808	228,643	Burch, Palmer L.	321,165	McNichols, Stephen		92,522 D	41.6%	58.4%	41.6%	58.4%
1956	645,233	313,950	Brotzman, Donald G.	331,283	McNichols, Stephen		17,333 D	48.7%	51.3%	48.7%	51.3%
1954	489,540	227,335	Brotzman, Donald G.	262,205	Johnson, Ed C.		34,870 D	46.4%	53.6%	46.4%	53.6%
1952	613,034	349,924	Thornton, Dan	260,044	Metzger, John W.	3,066	89,880 R	57.1%	42.4%	57.4%	42.6%
1950	450,994	236,472	Thornton, Dan	212,976	Johnson, Walter	1,546	23,496 R	52.4%	47.2%	52.6%	47.4%
1948	501,680	168,928	Hamil, David A.	332,752	Knous, William Lee		163,824 D	33.7%	66.3%	33.7%	66.3%
1946	335,087	160,483	Lavington, Leon E.	174,604	Knous, William Lee		14,121 D	47.9%	52.1%	47.9%	52.1%

The term of office of Colorado's Governor was increased from two to four years effective with the 1958 election.

POSTWAR VOTE FOR SENATOR

Year	Total Vote	Republican Vote	Republican Candidate	Democratic Vote	Democratic Candidate	Other Vote	Rep.-Dem. Plurality	Total Vote Rep.	Total Vote Dem.	Major Vote Rep.	Major Vote Dem.
1998	1,327,235	829,370	Campbell, Ben N.	464,754	Lamm, Dottie	33,111	364,616 R	62.5%	35.0%	64.1%	35.9%
1996	1,469,611	750,325	Allard, Wayne	677,600	Strickland, Tom	41,686	72,725 R	51.1%	46.1%	52.5%	47.5%
1992	1,552,289	662,893	Considine, Terry	803,725	Campbell, Ben N.	85,671	140,832 D	42.7%	51.8%	45.2%	54.8%
1990	1,022,027	569,048	Brown, Hank	425,746	Heath, Josie	27,233	143,302 R	55.7%	41.7%	57.2%	42.8%
1986	1,060,765	512,994	Kramer, Ken	529,449	Wirth, Timothy E.	18,322	16,455 D	48.4%	49.9%	49.2%	50.8%
1984	1,297,809	833,821	Armstrong, William L.	449,327	Dick, Nancy	14,661	384,494 R	64.2%	34.6%	65.0%	35.0%
1980	1,173,646	571,295	Buchanan, Mary E.	590,501	Hart, Gary W.	11,850	19,206 D	48.7%	50.3%	49.2%	50.8%
1978	819,150	480,596	Armstrong, William L.	330,247	Haskell, Floyd K.	8,307	150,349 R	58.7%	40.3%	59.3%	40.7%
1974	824,166	325,508	Dominick, Peter H.	471,691	Hart, Gary W.	26,967	146,183 D	39.5%	57.2%	40.8%	59.2%
1972	926,093	447,957	Allott, Gordon	457,545	Haskell, Floyd K.	20,591	9,588 D	48.4%	49.4%	49.5%	50.5%
1968	785,536	459,952	Dominick, Peter H.	325,584	McNichols, Stephen		134,368 R	58.6%	41.4%	58.6%	41.4%
1966	634,898	368,307	Allott, Gordon	266,259	Romer, Roy	332	102,048 R	58.0%	41.9%	58.0%	42.0%
1962	613,444	328,655	Dominick, Peter H.	279,586	Carroll, John A.	5,203	49,069 R	53.6%	45.6%	54.0%	46.0%
1960	727,633	389,428	Allott, Gordon	334,854	Knous, Robert L.	3,351	54,574 R	53.5%	46.0%	53.8%	46.2%
1956	636,974	317,102	Thornton, Dan	319,872	Carroll, John A.		2,770 D	49.8%	50.2%	49.8%	50.2%
1954	484,188	248,502	Allott, Gordon	235,686	Carroll, John A.		12,816 R	51.3%	48.7%	51.3%	48.7%
1950	450,176	239,734	Millikin, Eugene D.	210,442	Carroll, John A.		29,292 R	53.3%	46.7%	53.3%	46.7%
1948	510,121	165,069	Nicholson, W. F.	340,719	Johnson, Ed C.	4,333	175,650 D	32.4%	66.8%	32.6%	67.4%

COLORADO

Districts Established March 24, 1992

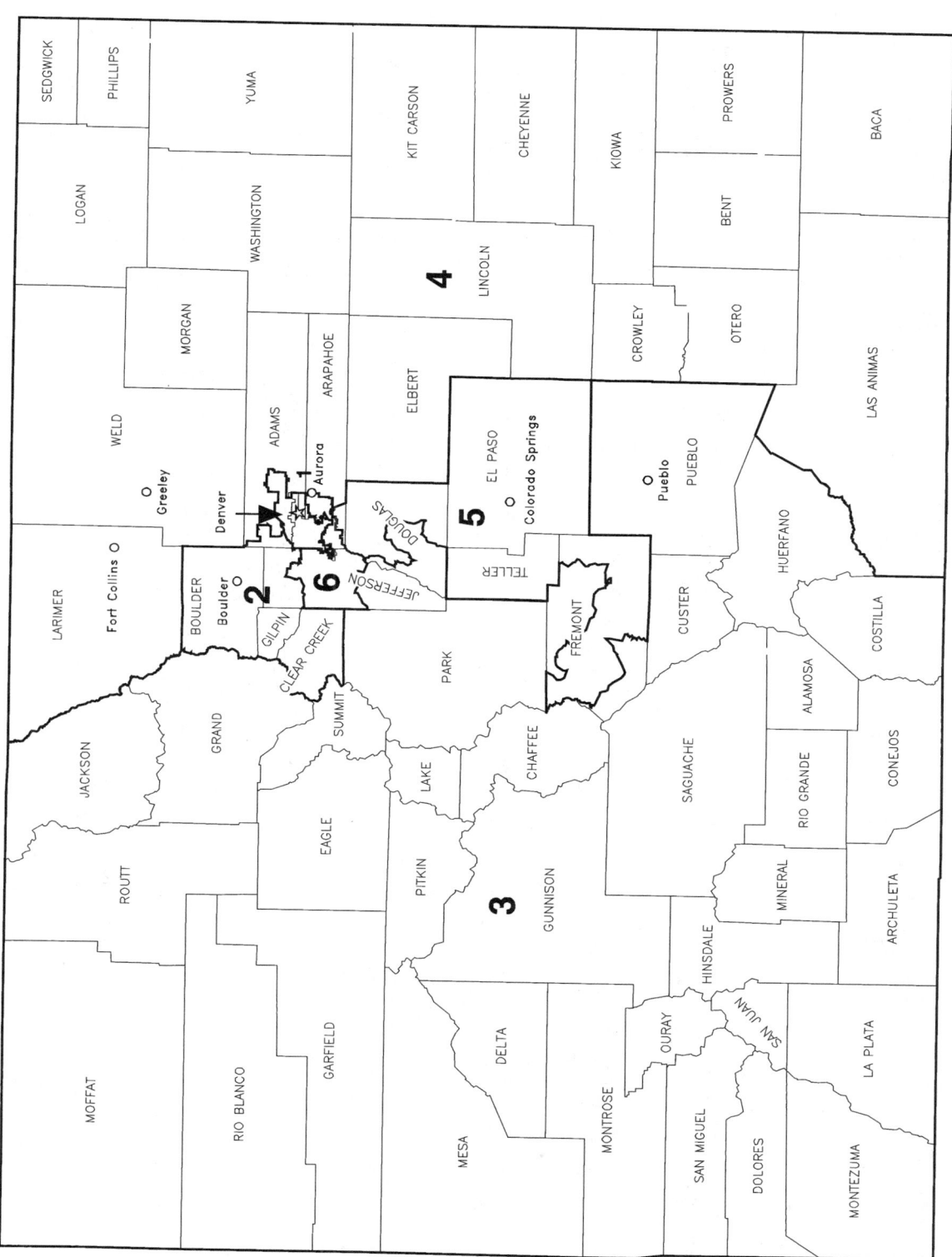

COLORADO

PRESIDENT 2000

2000 Census Population	County	Total Vote	Republican	Democratic	Green (Nader)	Other	Rep.-Dem. Plurality		Percentage of Total Vote Rep.	Dem.	Green
363,857	ADAMS	107,852	47,561	54,132	4,165	1,994	6,571	D	44.1%	50.2%	3.9%
14,966	ALAMOSA	5,659	2,857	2,455	265	82	402	R	50.5%	43.4%	4.7%
487,967	ARAPAHOE	189,942	97,768	82,614	6,952	2,608	15,154	R	51.5%	43.5%	3.7%
9,898	ARCHULETA	4,758	2,988	1,432	265	73	1,556	R	62.8%	30.1%	5.6%
4,517	BACA	2,278	1,663	531	47	37	1,132	R	73.0%	23.3%	2.1%
5,998	BENT	1,963	1,096	783	44	40	313	R	55.8%	39.9%	2.2%
291,288	BOULDER	139,626	50,873	69,983	16,498	2,272	19,110	D	36.4%	50.1%	11.8%
16,242	CHAFFEE	7,610	4,300	2,768	459	83	1,532	R	56.5%	36.4%	6.0%
2,231	CHEYENNE	1,212	957	209	22	24	748	R	79.0%	17.2%	1.8%
9,322	CLEAR CREEK	4,924	2,247	2,188	354	135	59	R	45.6%	44.4%	7.2%
8,400	CONEJOS	3,671	1,772	1,749	79	71	23	R	48.3%	47.6%	2.2%
3,663	COSTILLA	1,648	504	1,054	71	19	550	D	30.6%	64.0%	4.3%
5,518	CROWLEY	1,445	855	511	28	51	344	R	59.2%	35.4%	1.9%
3,503	CUSTER	2,111	1,451	507	100	53	944	R	68.7%	24.0%	4.7%
27,834	DELTA	12,686	8,372	3,264	852	198	5,108	R	66.0%	25.7%	6.7%
554,636	DENVER	198,347	61,224	122,693	11,624	2,806	61,469	D	30.9%	61.9%	5.9%
1,844	DOLORES	1,134	741	293	73	27	448	R	65.3%	25.8%	6.4%
175,766	DOUGLAS	86,225	56,007	27,076	2,230	912	28,931	R	65.0%	31.4%	2.6%
41,659	EAGLE	15,188	7,165	6,772	1,045	206	393	R	47.2%	44.6%	6.9%
19,872	ELBERT	8,965	6,151	2,326	292	196	3,825	R	68.6%	25.9%	3.3%
516,929	EL PASO	200,757	128,294	61,799	7,116	3,548	66,495	R	63.9%	30.8%	3.5%
46,145	FREMONT	16,056	9,914	5,293	516	333	4,621	R	61.7%	33.0%	3.2%
43,791	GARFIELD	17,104	9,103	6,087	1,608	306	3,016	R	53.2%	35.6%	9.4%
4,757	GILPIN	2,465	1,006	1,099	276	84	93	D	40.8%	44.6%	11.2%
12,442	GRAND	6,353	3,570	2,308	366	109	1,262	R	56.2%	36.3%	5.8%
13,956	GUNNISON	7,236	3,128	3,059	927	122	69	R	43.2%	42.3%	12.8%
790	HINSDALE	566	316	188	51	11	128	R	55.8%	33.2%	9.0%
7,862	HUERFANO	3,174	1,466	1,495	169	44	29	D	46.2%	47.1%	5.3%
1,577	JACKSON	925	682	173	40	30	509	R	73.7%	18.7%	4.3%
527,056	JEFFERSON	235,491	120,138	100,970	10,336	4,047	19,168	R	51.0%	42.9%	4.4%
1,622	KIOWA	968	728	211	13	16	517	R	75.2%	21.8%	1.3%
8,011	KIT CARSON	3,458	2,542	809	58	49	1,733	R	73.5%	23.4%	1.7%
7,812	LAKE	2,628	1,056	1,296	213	63	240	D	40.2%	49.3%	8.1%
43,941	LA PLATA	20,490	9,993	7,864	2,378	255	2,129	R	48.8%	38.4%	11.6%
251,494	LARIMER	118,537	62,429	46,055	8,194	1,859	16,374	R	52.7%	38.9%	6.9%
15,207	LAS ANIMAS	6,094	2,569	3,243	199	83	674	D	42.2%	53.2%	3.3%
6,087	LINCOLN	2,199	1,630	510	27	32	1,120	R	74.1%	23.2%	1.2%
20,504	LOGAN	8,096	5,531	2,296	140	129	3,235	R	68.3%	28.4%	1.7%
116,255	MESA	51,054	32,396	15,465	2,235	958	16,931	R	63.5%	30.3%	4.4%
831	MINERAL	486	294	168	19	5	126	R	60.5%	34.6%	3.9%
13,184	MOFFAT	5,337	3,840	1,223	169	105	2,617	R	72.0%	22.9%	3.2%
23,830	MONTEZUMA	9,384	6,158	2,556	530	140	3,602	R	65.6%	27.2%	5.6%
33,432	MONTROSE	14,215	9,266	4,041	656	252	5,225	R	65.2%	28.4%	4.6%
27,171	MORGAN	8,998	5,722	2,885	211	180	2,837	R	63.6%	32.1%	2.3%
20,311	OTERO	7,312	4,082	2,963	138	129	1,119	R	55.8%	40.5%	1.9%
3,742	OURAY	2,233	1,279	705	224	25	574	R	57.3%	31.6%	10.0%
14,523	PARK	6,665	3,677	2,393	404	191	1,284	R	55.2%	35.9%	6.1%
4,480	PHILLIPS	2,223	1,576	564	48	35	1,012	R	70.9%	25.4%	2.2%
14,872	PITKIN	7,800	2,565	4,137	1,013	85	1,572	D	32.9%	53.0%	13.0%
14,483	PROWERS	4,524	3,026	1,361	79	58	1,665	R	66.9%	30.1%	1.7%
141,472	PUEBLO	53,946	22,827	28,888	1,520	711	6,061	D	42.3%	53.5%	2.8%
5,986	RIO BLANCO	2,855	2,185	543	85	42	1,642	R	76.5%	19.0%	3.0%
12,413	RIO GRANDE	5,075	3,111	1,707	179	78	1,404	R	61.3%	33.6%	3.5%
19,690	ROUTT	9,638	4,472	4,208	820	138	264	R	46.4%	43.7%	8.5%
5,917	SAGUACHE	2,529	1,078	1,145	261	45	67	D	42.6%	45.3%	10.3%
558	SAN JUAN	436	210	149	58	19	61	R	48.2%	34.2%	13.3%
6,594	SAN MIGUEL	3,255	1,043	1,598	560	54	555	D	32.0%	49.1%	17.2%
2,747	SEDGWICK	1,303	877	384	25	17	493	R	67.3%	29.5%	1.9%
23,548	SUMMIT	11,068	4,497	5,304	1,131	136	807	D	40.6%	47.9%	10.2%
20,555	TELLER	9,847	6,477	2,750	429	191	3,727	R	65.8%	27.9%	4.4%

COLORADO

PRESIDENT 2000

2000 Census Population	County	Total Vote	Republican	Democratic	Green (Nader)	Other	Rep.-Dem. Plurality	Percentage of Total Vote		
								Rep.	Dem.	Green
4,926	WASHINGTON	2,445	1,878	477	50	40	1,401 R	76.8%	19.5%	2.0%
180,936	WELD	64,541	37,409	23,436	2,438	1,258	13,973 R	58.0%	36.3%	3.8%
9,841	YUMA	4,358	3,156	1,082	60	60	2,074 R	72.4%	24.8%	1.4%
4,301,261	TOTAL	1,741,368	883,748	738,227	91,434	27,959	145,521 R	50.8%	42.4%	5.3%

COLORADO

CONGRESS

CD	Year	Total Vote	Republican Vote	Republican Candidate	Democratic Vote	Democratic Candidate	Other Vote	Rep.-Dem. Plurality	Total Vote Rep.	Total Vote Dem.	Major Vote Rep.	Major Vote Dem.
1	2000	206,434	56,291	THOMAS, JESSE L.	141,831	DEGETTE, DIANA	8,312	85,540 D	27.3%	68.7%	28.4%	71.6%
1	1998	174,305	52,452	MCCLANAHAN, NANCY	116,628	DEGETTE, DIANA	5,225	64,176 D	30.1%	66.9%	31.0%	69.0%
1	1996	197,839	79,540	ROGERS, JOE	112,631	DEGETTE, DIANA	5,668	33,091 D	40.2%	56.9%	41.4%	58.6%
1	1994	155,255	61,978	EGGERT, WILLIAM F.	93,123	SCHROEDER, PATRICIA	154	31,145 D	39.9%	60.0%	40.0%	60.0%
1	1992	227,531	70,902	ARAGON, RAYMOND D.	156,629	SCHROEDER, PATRICIA		85,727 D	31.2%	68.8%	31.2%	68.8%
2	2000	283,116	109,338	COX, CAROLYN	155,725	UDALL, MARK	18,053	46,387 D	38.6%	55.0%	41.2%	58.8%
2	1998	228,442	108,385	GREENLEE, BOB	113,946	UDALL, MARK	6,111	5,561 D	47.4%	49.9%	48.7%	51.3%
2	1996	255,784	97,865	MILLER, PATRICIA	145,894	SKAGGS, DAVID	12,025	48,029 D	38.3%	57.0%	40.1%	59.9%
2	1994	186,661	80,723	MILLER, PATRICIA	105,938	SKAGGS, DAVID		25,215 D	43.2%	56.8%	43.2%	56.8%
2	1992	271,361	88,470	DAY, BRYAN	164,790	SKAGGS, DAVID	18,101	76,320 D	32.6%	60.7%	34.9%	65.1%
3	2000	302,540	199,204	MCINNIS, SCOTT	87,921	IMRIE, CURTIS	15,415	111,283 R	65.8%	29.1%	69.4%	30.6%
3	1998	236,653	156,501	MCINNIS, SCOTT	74,479	KELLEY, ROBERT REED	5,673	82,022 R	66.1%	31.5%	67.8%	32.2%
3	1996	266,476	183,523	MCINNIS, SCOTT	82,953	GURULE, ALBERT L.		100,570 R	68.9%	31.1%	68.9%	31.1%
3	1994	208,792	145,365	MCINNIS, SCOTT	63,427	POWERS, LINDA		81,938 R	69.6%	30.4%	69.6%	30.4%
3	1992	261,964	143,293	MCINNIS, SCOTT	114,480	CALLIHAN, MIKE	4,191	28,813 R	54.7%	43.7%	55.6%	44.4%
4	2000	263,006	209,078	SCHAFFER, BOB			53,928	209,078 R	79.5%		100.0%	
4	1998	221,291	131,318	SCHAFFER, BOB	89,973	KIRKPATRICK, SUSAN		41,345 R	59.3%	40.7%	59.3%	40.7%
4	1996	244,067	137,012	SCHAFFER, BOB	92,837	KELLEY, GUY	14,218	44,175 R	56.1%	38.0%	59.6%	40.4%
4	1994	188,453	136,251	ALLARD, WAYNE	52,202	KIPP, CATHY		84,049 R	72.3%	27.7%	72.3%	27.7%
4	1992	241,841	139,884	ALLARD, WAYNE	101,957	REDDER, TOM		37,927 R	57.8%	42.2%	57.8%	42.2%
5	2000	306,309	253,330	HEFLEY, JOEL			52,979	253,330 R	82.7%		100.0%	
5	1998	214,270	155,790	HEFLEY, JOEL	55,609	ALFORD, KEN	2,871	100,181 R	72.7%	26.0%	73.7%	26.3%
5	1996	262,465	188,805	HEFLEY, JOEL	73,660	ROBINSON, MIKE		115,145 R	71.9%	28.1%	71.9%	28.1%
5	1994	138,674	138,674	HEFLEY, JOEL				138,674 R	100.0%		100.0%	
5	1992	243,415	173,096	HEFLEY, JOEL	62,550	ORIEZ, CHARLES A.	7,769	110,546 R	71.1%	25.7%	73.5%	26.5%
6	2000	262,477	141,410	TANCREDO, TOM	110,568	TOLTZ, KENNETH A.	10,499	30,842 R	53.9%	42.1%	56.1%	43.9%
6	1998	199,188	111,374	TANCREDO, TOM	82,662	STRAUSS, HENRY L.	5,152	28,712 R	55.9%	41.5%	57.4%	42.6%
6	1996	234,618	146,018	SCHAEFER, DANIEL L.	88,600	FITZ-GERALD, JOAN		57,418 R	62.2%	37.8%	62.2%	37.8%
6	1994	177,709	124,079	SCHAEFER, DANIEL L.	49,701	HALLEN, JOHN	3,929	74,378 R	69.8%	28.0%	71.4%	28.6%
6	1992	233,097	142,021	SCHAEFER, DANIEL L.	91,073	KOLBE, TOM	3	50,948 R	60.9%	39.1%	60.9%	39.1%

COLORADO

GENERAL AND PRIMARY ELECTIONS

2000 GENERAL ELECTIONS

President Other vote was 12,799 Libertarian (Browne); 10,465 Unaffiliated/Freedom (Buchanan); 2,240 Natural Law (Hagelin); 1,319 American Constitution (Phillips); 712 Socialist (McReynolds); 216 Socialist Workers (Harris); 208 Prohibition (Dodge).

Congress Other vote was: CD 1: 5,852 Libertarian (Combs), 2,452 Reform (Nasser), 5 write-in (Swing), 3 write-in (P. Schaefer); CD 2: 12,398 Green (Forthofer), 5,655 Libertarian (D. Baker); CD 3: 9,982 Libertarian (Sakson), 5,433 Reform (Good); CD 4: 19,721 Natural Law (Ward), 19,713 Libertarian (K. Baker), 9,955 American Constitution (Hanks), 4,539 write-in (Swartz); CD 5: 37,719 Libertarian (Kantor), 15,260 Natural Law (MacKenzie); CD 6: 6,885 Libertarian (Katz), 3,614 Concerns of the People (Heckman).

2000 PRIMARY ELECTIONS

Primary March 10, 2000 (President)
August 8, 2000 (Congress)

Registration (as of July 18, 2000)

Republican	987,505
Democratic	832,754
Libertarian	3,976
Green	2,139
Natural Law	1,213
Unaffiliated	962,591
TOTAL	2,790,178

Primary Type Semi-open—Registered Democrats and Republicans could vote only in their party's primary. "Unaffiliated" voters could vote in either primary but became a member of that party.

Note: An asterisk (*) denotes incumbent.

	REPUBLICAN PRIMARIES			DEMOCRATIC PRIMARIES		
President	George W. Bush	116,897	64.7%	Al Gore	63,384	71.4%
	John McCain	48,996	27.1%	Bill Bradley	20,663	23.3%
	Alan Keyes	11,871	6.6%	Non-committed	3,867	4.4%
	Steve Forbes	1,197	0.7%	Lyndon H. LaRouche Jr.	821	0.9%
	Gary Bauer	1,190	0.7%			
	Orrin G. Hatch	504	0.3%			
	TOTAL	180,655		TOTAL	88,735	
Congressional District 1	Jesse L. Thomas	7,249	100.0%	Diana DeGette*	16,742	100.0%
	TOTAL	7,249		TOTAL	16,742	
Congressional District 2	Carolyn Cox	8,537	50.4%	Mark Udall*	17,388	100.0%
	Larry E. Johnson	7,390	43.6%			
	Sandy Hume (write-in)	987	5.8%			
	David L. Ryan (write-in)	40	0.2%			
	TOTAL	16,954		TOTAL	17,388	
Congressional District 3	Scott McInnis*	22,873	100.0%	Curtis Imrie	9,517	100.0%
	TOTAL	22,873		TOTAL	9,517	
Congressional District 4	Bob Schaffer*	20,938	100.0%	No Democratic candidate		
	TOTAL	20,938				
Congressional District 5	Joel Hefley*	33,121	100.0%	No Democratic candidate		
	TOTAL	33,121				
Congressional District 6	Tom Tancredo*	27,756	100.0%	Kenneth A. Toltz	12,254	100.0%
	TOTAL	27,756		TOTAL	12,254	

CONNECTICUT

GOVERNOR
John G. Rowland (R). Re-elected 1998 to a four-year term. Previously elected 1994.

SENATORS
Christopher J. Dodd (D). Re-elected 1998 to a six-year term. Previously elected 1992, 1986, 1980.

Joseph I. Lieberman (D). Re-elected 2000 to a six-year term. Previously elected 1994, 1988.

REPRESENTATIVES
1. John B. Larson (D)
2. Rob Simmons (R)
3. Rosa L. DeLauro (D)
4. Christopher Shays (R)
5. Jim Maloney (D)
6. Nancy L. Johnson (R)

POSTWAR VOTE FOR PRESIDENT

| Year | Total Vote | Republican | | Democratic | | Other Vote | Plurality | Percentage | | | |
| | | Vote | Candidate | Vote | Candidate | | | Total Vote | | Major Vote | |
								Rep.	Dem.	Rep.	Dem.
2000**	1,459,525	561,094	Bush, George W.	816,015	Gore, Al	82,416	254,921 D	38.4%	55.9%	40.7%	59.3%
1996**	1,392,614	483,109	Dole, Bob	735,740	Clinton, Bill	173,765	252,631 D	34.7%	52.8%	39.6%	60.4%
1992**	1,616,332	578,313	Bush, George	682,318	Clinton, Bill	355,701	104,005 D	35.8%	42.2%	45.9%	54.1%
1988	1,443,394	750,241	Bush, George	676,584	Dukakis, Michael S.	16,569	73,657 R	52.0%	46.9%	52.6%	47.4%
1984	1,466,900	890,877	Reagan, Ronald	569,597	Mondale, Walter F.	6,426	321,280 R	60.7%	38.8%	61.0%	39.0%
1980**	1,406,285	677,210	Reagan, Ronald	541,732	Carter, Jimmy	187,343	135,478 R	48.2%	38.5%	55.6%	44.4%
1976	1,381,526	719,261	Ford, Gerald R.	647,895	Carter, Jimmy	14,370	71,366 R	52.1%	46.9%	52.6%	47.4%
1972	1,384,277	810,763	Nixon, Richard M.	555,498	McGovern, George S.	18,016	255,265 R	58.6%	40.1%	59.3%	40.7%
1968	1,256,232	556,721	Nixon, Richard M.	621,561	Humphrey, Hubert H.	77,950	64,840 D	44.3%	49.5%	47.2%	52.8%
1964	1,218,578	390,996	Goldwater, Barry M.	826,269	Johnson, Lyndon B.	1,313	435,273 D	32.1%	67.8%	32.1%	67.9%
1960	1,222,883	565,813	Nixon, Richard M.	657,055	Kennedy, John F.	15	91,242 D	46.3%	53.7%	46.3%	53.7%
1956	1,117,121	711,837	Eisenhower, Dwight D.	405,079	Stevenson, Adlai E.	205	306,758 R	63.7%	36.3%	63.7%	36.3%
1952	1,096,911	611,012	Eisenhower, Dwight D.	481,649	Stevenson, Adlai E.	4,250	129,363 R	55.7%	43.9%	55.9%	44.1%
1948	883,518	437,754	Dewey, Thomas E.	423,297	Truman, Harry S.	22,467	14,457 R	49.5%	47.9%	50.8%	49.2%

In 2000 the other vote column includes 64,452 votes cast for Green (Nader). In 1996 the other vote column includes 139,523 votes cast for Perot. In 1992 the other vote column includes 348,771 votes cast for Perot. In 1980 the other column includes 171,807 votes for Independent (Anderson).

CONNECTICUT

POSTWAR VOTE FOR GOVERNOR

Year	Total Vote	Republican		Democratic		Other Vote	Rep.-Dem. Plurality	Percentage			
								Total Vote		Major Vote	
		Vote	Candidate	Vote	Candidate			Rep.	Dem.	Rep.	Dem.
1998	999,537	628,707	Rowland, John G.	354,187	Kennelly, Barbara B.	16,643	274,520 R	62.9%	35.4%	64.0%	36.0%
1994**	1,147,084	415,201	Rowland, John G.	375,133	Curry, Bill	356,750	40,068 R	36.2%	32.7%	52.5%	47.5%
1990**	1,141,122	427,840	Rowland, John G.	236,641	Morrison, Bruce A.	476,641	32,736 C	37.5%	20.7%	64.4%	35.6%
1986	993,692	408,489	Belaga, Julie D.	575,638	O'Neill, William A.	9,565	167,149 D	41.1%	57.9%	41.5%	58.5%
1982	1,084,156	497,773	Rome, Lewis B.	578,264	O'Neill, William A.	8,119	80,491 D	45.9%	53.3%	46.3%	53.7%
1978	1,036,608	422,316	Sarasin, Ronald A.	613,109	Grasso, Ella T.	1,183	190,793 D	40.7%	59.1%	40.8%	59.2%
1974	1,102,773	440,169	Steele, Robert H.	643,490	Grasso, Ella T.	19,114	203,321 D	39.9%	58.4%	40.6%	59.4%
1970	1,082,797	582,160	Meskill, Thomas J.	500,561	Daddario, Emilio	76	81,599 R	53.8%	46.2%	53.8%	46.2%
1966	1,008,557	446,536	Gengras, E. Clayton	561,599	Dempsey, John N.	422	115,063 D	44.3%	55.7%	44.3%	55.7%
1962	1,031,902	482,852	Alsop, John	549,027	Dempsey, John N.	23	66,175 D	46.8%	53.2%	46.8%	53.2%
1958	974,509	360,644	Zeller, Fred R.	607,012	Ribicoff, Abraham A.	6,853	246,368 D	37.0%	62.3%	37.3%	62.7%
1954	936,753	460,528	Lodge, John D.	463,643	Ribicoff, Abraham A.	12,582	3,115 D	49.2%	49.5%	49.8%	50.2%
1950**	878,735	436,418	Lodge, John D.	419,404	Bowles, Chester	22,913	17,014 R	49.7%	47.7%	51.0%	49.0%
1948	875,170	429,071	Shannon, James C.	431,296	Bowles, Chester	14,803	2,225 D	49.0%	49.3%	49.9%	50.1%
1946	683,831	371,852	McConaughy, J. L.	276,335	Snow, Wilbert	35,644	95,517 R	54.4%	40.4%	57.4%	42.6%

The term of office for Connecticut's Governor was increased from two to four years effective with the 1950 election. In 1990 Lowell P. Weicker, the Connecticut Party candidate, polled 460,576 votes (40.4% of the total vote) and won the election with a 32,736 plurality. In 1994 other vote was 216,585 Connecticut party (Groark); 130,128 Independence (Scott); 10,007 Concerned Citizens (Zdonczyk); 30 write-ins.

POSTWAR VOTE FOR SENATOR

Year	Total Vote	Republican		Democratic		Other Vote	Rep.-Dem. Plurality	Percentage			
								Total Vote		Major Vote	
		Vote	Candidate	Vote	Candidate			Rep.	Dem.	Rep.	Dem.
2000	1,311,261	448,077	Giordano, Philip A.	828,902	Lieberman, Joseph I.	34,282	380,825 D	34.2%	63.2%	35.1%	64.9%
1998	964,457	312,177	Franks, Gary A.	628,306	Dodd, Christopher J.	23,974	316,129 D	32.4%	65.1%	33.2%	66.8%
1994	1,079,767	334,833	Labriola, Jerry	723,842	Lieberman, Joseph I.	21,092	389,009 D	31.0%	67.0%	31.6%	68.4%
1992	1,500,709	572,036	Johnson, Brook	882,569	Dodd, Christopher J.	46,104	310,533 D	38.1%	58.8%	39.3%	60.7%
1988	1,383,526	678,454	Weicker, Lowell P.	688,499	Lieberman, Joseph I.	16,573	10,045 D	49.0%	49.8%	49.6%	50.4%
1986	976,933	340,438	Eddy, Roger W.	632,695	Dodd, Christopher J.	3,800	292,257 D	34.8%	64.8%	35.0%	65.0%
1982	1,083,613	545,987	Weicker, Lowell P.	499,146	Moffett, Anthony T.	38,480	46,841 R	50.4%	46.1%	52.2%	47.8%
1980	1,356,075	581,884	Buckley, James L.	763,969	Dodd, Christopher J.	10,222	182,085 D	42.9%	56.3%	43.2%	56.8%
1976	1,361,666	785,683	Weicker, Lowell P.	561,018	Schaffer, Gloria	14,965	224,665 R	57.7%	41.2%	58.3%	41.7%
1974	1,084,918	372,055	Brannen, James H.	690,820	Ribicoff, Abraham A.	22,043	318,765 D	34.3%	63.7%	35.0%	65.0%
1970	1,089,353	454,721	Weicker, Lowell P.	368,111	Duffey, Joseph D.	266,521	86,610 R	41.7%	33.8%	55.3%	44.7%
1968	1,206,537	551,455	May, Edwin H.	655,043	Ribicoff, Abraham A.	39	103,588 D	45.7%	54.3%	45.7%	54.3%
1964	1,208,163	426,939	Lodge, John D.	781,008	Dodd, Thomas J.	216	354,069 D	35.3%	64.6%	35.3%	64.7%
1962	1,029,301	501,694	Seely-Brown, Horace	527,522	Ribicoff, Abraham A.	85	25,828 D	48.7%	51.3%	48.7%	51.3%
1958	965,463	410,622	Purtell, William A.	554,841	Dodd, Thomas J.		144,219 D	42.5%	57.5%	42.5%	57.5%
1956	1,113,819	610,829	Bush, Prescott	479,460	Dodd, Thomas J.	23,530	131,369 R	54.8%	43.0%	56.0%	44.0%
1952	1,093,467	573,854	Purtell, William A.	485,066	Benton, William	34,547	88,788 R	52.5%	44.4%	54.2%	45.8%
1952S	1,093,268	559,465	Bush, Prescott	530,505	Ribicoff, Abraham A.	3,298	28,960 R	51.2%	48.5%	51.3%	48.7%
1950	877,827	409,053	Talbot, Joseph E.	453,646	McMahon, Brien	15,128	44,593 D	46.6%	51.7%	47.4%	52.6%
1950S	877,135	430,311	Bush, Prescott	431,413	Benton, William	15,411	1,102 D	49.1%	49.2%	49.9%	50.1%
1946	682,921	381,328	Baldwin, Raymond	276,424	Tone, Joseph M.	25,169	104,904 R	55.8%	40.5%	58.0%	42.0%

One each of the 1952 and 1950 elections was for a short term to fill a vacancy.

CONNECTICUT

Districts Established November 27, 1991

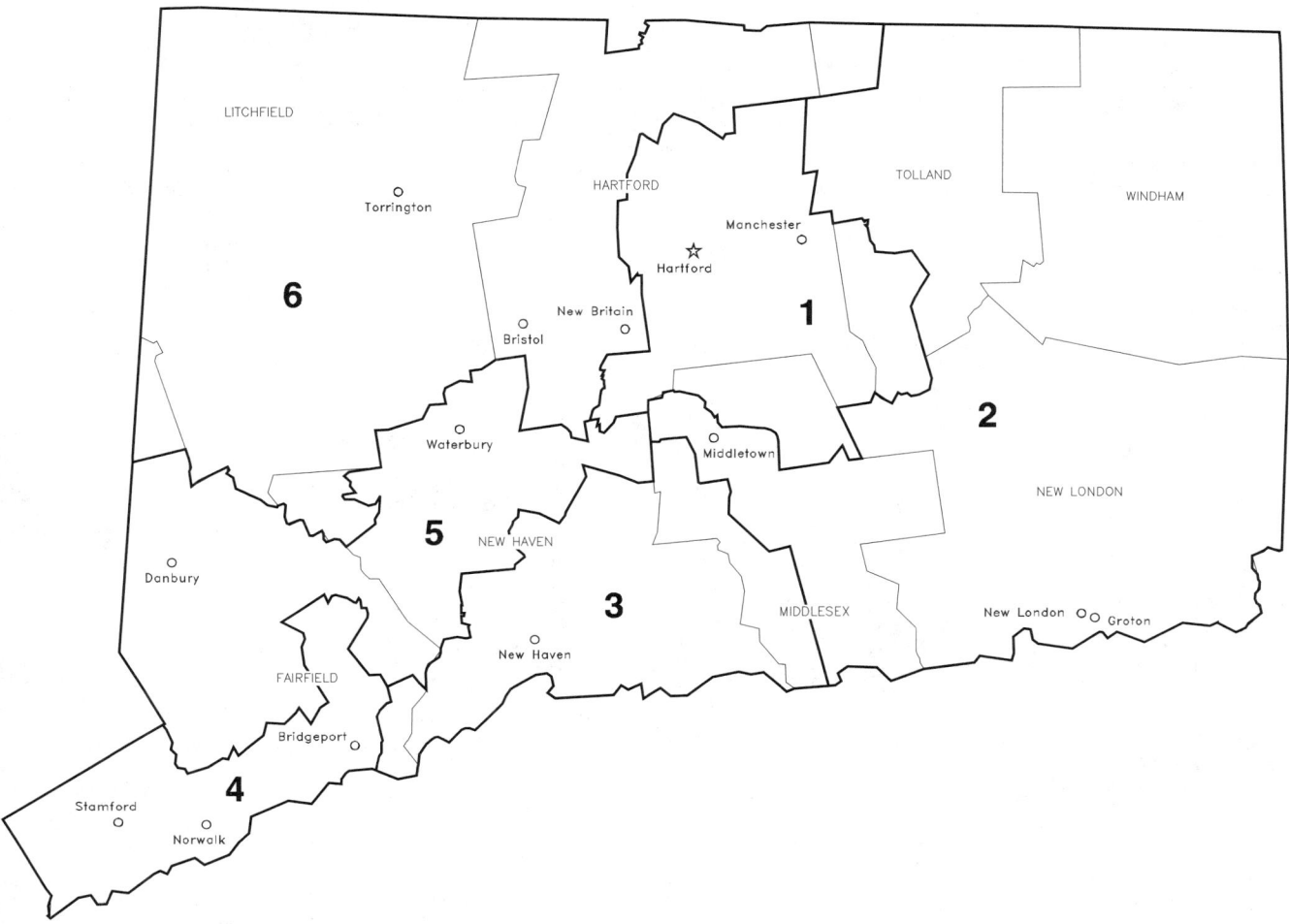

LITCHFIELD

HARTFORD

TOLLAND

WINDHAM

Torrington

Manchester

6

☆
Hartford

1

New Britain

Bristol

2

Waterbury

NEW LONDON

5

NEW HAVEN

Middletown

Danbury

3

MIDDLESEX

New London ○○ Groton

New Haven

FAIRFIELD

Bridgeport

4

Stamford

Norwalk

CONNECTICUT

PRESIDENT 2000

2000 Census Population	County	Total Vote	Republican	Democratic	Green (Nader)	Other	Rep.-Dem. Plurality	Percentage of Total Vote		
								Rep.	Dem.	Green
882,567	FAIRFIELD	370,289	159,659	193,769	12,664	4,197	34,110 D	43.1%	52.3%	3.4%
857,183	HARTFORD	367,556	127,468	221,167	14,214	4,707	93,699 D	34.7%	60.2%	3.9%
182,193	LITCHFIELD	87,338	39,172	41,806	5,413	947	2,634 D	44.9%	47.9%	6.2%
155,071	MIDDLESEX	77,433	29,295	43,319	4,039	780	14,024 D	37.8%	55.9%	5.2%
824,008	NEW HAVEN	341,099	122,919	197,928	15,567	4,685	75,009 D	36.0%	58.0%	4.6%
259,088	NEW LONDON	109,147	41,168	60,449	6,218	1,312	19,281 D	37.7%	55.4%	5.7%
136,364	TOLLAND	62,700	24,705	33,554	3,711	730	8,849 D	39.4%	53.5%	5.9%
109,091	WINDHAM	43,963	16,708	24,023	2,626	606	7,315 D	38.0%	54.6%	6.0%
3,405,565	TOTAL	1,459,525	561,094	816,015	64,452	17,964	254,921 D	38.4%	55.9%	4.4%
	City/Town									
18,554	ANSONIA	7,229	2,431	4,410	305	83	1,979 D	33.6%	61.0%	4.2%
19,587	BLOOMFIELD	10,111	1,849	7,907	236	119	6,058 D	18.3%	78.2%	2.3%
28,683	BRANFORD	14,366	5,133	8,302	809	122	3,169 D	35.7%	57.8%	5.6%
139,529	BRIDGEPORT	33,446	7,406	24,303	865	872	16,897 D	22.1%	72.7%	2.6%
60,062	BRISTOL	23,725	7,948	14,665	780	332	6,717 D	33.5%	61.8%	3.3%
28,543	CHESHIRE	14,204	6,507	6,977	597	123	470 D	45.8%	49.1%	4.2%
74,848	DANBURY	23,557	9,371	12,987	818	381	3,616 D	39.8%	55.1%	3.5%
19,607	DARIEN	10,217	6,446	3,496	214	61	2,950 R	63.1%	34.2%	2.1%
49,575	EAST HARTFORD	18,431	5,124	12,371	673	263	7,247 D	27.8%	67.1%	3.7%
28,189	EAST HAVEN	11,471	3,499	7,278	488	206	3,779 D	30.5%	63.4%	4.3%
45,212	ENFIELD	18,256	6,920	10,403	732	201	3,483 D	37.9%	57.0%	4.0%
57,340	FAIRFIELD	28,639	13,042	14,210	1,187	200	1,168 D	45.5%	49.6%	4.1%
23,641	FARMINGTON	12,382	5,443	6,374	481	84	931 D	44.0%	51.5%	3.9%
31,876	GLASTONBURY	17,956	7,928	9,134	760	134	1,206 D	44.2%	50.9%	4.2%
61,101	GREENWICH	28,940	14,905	12,780	802	453	2,125 R	51.5%	44.2%	2.8%
39,907	GROTON	13,680	5,486	7,242	800	152	1,756 D	40.1%	52.9%	5.8%
21,398	GUILFORD	11,843	4,721	6,377	666	79	1,656 D	39.9%	53.8%	5.6%
56,913	HAMDEN	25,921	7,833	16,638	1,187	263	8,805 D	30.2%	64.2%	4.6%
121,578	HARTFORD	26,734	3,095	21,445	818	1,376	18,350 D	11.6%	80.2%	3.1%
54,740	MANCHESTER	24,166	8,541	14,184	1,185	256	5,643 D	35.3%	58.7%	4.9%
20,720	MANSFIELD	6,629	1,617	4,183	745	84	2,566 D	24.4%	63.1%	11.2%
58,244	MERIDEN	21,383	6,614	13,668	770	331	7,054 D	30.9%	63.9%	3.6%
43,167	MIDDLETOWN	18,496	5,155	12,129	963	249	6,974 D	27.9%	65.6%	5.2%
52,305	MILFORD	23,977	9,514	12,949	1,158	356	3,435 D	39.7%	54.0%	4.8%
30,989	NAUGATUCK	11,561	4,930	5,980	501	150	1,050 D	42.6%	51.7%	4.3%
71,538	NEW BRITAIN	20,026	5,059	13,913	775	279	8,854 D	25.3%	69.5%	3.9%
123,626	NEW HAVEN	36,428	5,160	28,145	2,202	921	22,985 D	14.2%	77.3%	6.0%
25,671	NEW LONDON	7,261	1,738	4,924	496	103	3,186 D	23.9%	67.8%	6.8%
27,121	NEW MILFORD	11,728	5,546	5,498	576	108	48 R	47.3%	46.9%	4.9%
29,306	NEWINGTON	15,401	5,115	9,612	560	114	4,497 D	33.2%	62.4%	3.6%
25,031	NEWTOWN	12,394	6,059	5,606	633	96	453 R	48.9%	45.2%	5.1%
23,035	NORTH HAVEN	12,200	5,045	6,500	518	137	1,455 D	41.4%	53.3%	4.2%
82,951	NORWALK	32,211	11,519	19,293	1,038	361	7,774 D	35.8%	59.9%	3.2%
36,117	NORWICH	13,134	4,047	8,266	622	199	4,219 D	30.8%	62.9%	4.7%
23,643	RIDGEFIELD	13,241	6,902	5,760	509	70	1,142 R	52.1%	43.5%	3.8%
38,101	SHELTON	18,124	8,678	8,441	824	181	237 R	47.9%	46.6%	4.5%
23,234	SIMSBURY	13,308	6,492	6,156	570	90	336 R	48.8%	46.3%	4.3%
24,412	SOUTH WINDSOR	12,984	5,091	7,288	502	103	2,197 D	39.2%	56.1%	3.9%
39,728	SOUTHINGTON	19,430	7,614	10,977	680	159	3,363 D	39.2%	56.5%	3.5%
117,083	STAMFORD	44,223	15,159	27,430	1,148	486	12,271 D	34.3%	62.0%	2.6%
49,976	STRATFORD	22,646	9,152	12,310	934	250	3,158 D	40.4%	54.4%	4.1%
35,202	TORRINGTON	14,731	5,843	7,762	955	171	1,919 D	39.7%	52.7%	6.5%
34,243	TRUMBULL	18,495	9,142	8,659	555	139	483 R	49.4%	46.8%	3.0%
28,063	VERNON	12,558	4,831	7,014	609	104	2,183 D	38.5%	55.9%	4.8%
43,026	WALLINGFORD	20,741	7,699	11,916	928	198	4,217 D	37.1%	57.5%	4.5%

CONNECTICUT

PRESIDENT 2000

2000 Census Population	County	Total Vote	Republican	Democratic	Green (Nader)	Other	Rep.-Dem. Plurality		Percentage of Total Vote		
									Rep.	Dem.	Green
107,271	WATERBURY	32,227	12,415	18,069	1,057	686	5,654	D	38.5%	56.1%	3.3%
21,661	WATERTOWN	10,312	5,214	4,552	426	120	662	R	50.6%	44.1%	4.1%
63,589	WEST HARTFORD	33,148	10,447	21,069	1,389	243	10,622	D	31.5%	63.6%	4.2%
52,360	WEST HAVEN	19,807	5,344	13,350	832	281	8,006	D	27.0%	67.4%	4.2%
25,749	WESTPORT	14,485	5,590	8,304	500	91	2,714	D	38.6%	57.3%	3.5%
26,271	WETHERSFIELD	14,617	5,593	8,365	547	112	2,772	D	38.3%	57.2%	3.7%
22,857	WINDHAM	7,632	2,127	4,895	511	99	2,768	D	27.9%	64.1%	6.7%
28,237	WINDSOR	13,620	4,181	8,770	545	124	4,589	D	30.7%	64.4%	4.0%

CONNECTICUT

SENATOR 2000

2000 Census Population	County	Total Vote	Republican	Democratic	Other	Rep.-Dem. Plurality		Percentage			
								Total Vote		Major Vote	
								Rep.	Dem.	Rep.	Dem.
882,567	FAIRFIELD	333,876	126,961	199,960	6,955	72,999	D	38.0%	59.9%	38.8%	61.2%
857,183	HARTFORD	331,896	108,231	214,834	8,831	106,603	D	32.6%	64.7%	33.5%	66.5%
182,193	LITCHFIELD	78,268	30,678	44,841	2,749	14,163	D	39.2%	57.3%	40.6%	59.4%
155,071	MIDDLESEX	69,271	24,247	43,388	1,636	19,141	D	35.0%	62.6%	35.8%	64.2%
824,008	NEW HAVEN	307,057	91,226	207,670	8,161	116,444	D	29.7%	67.6%	30.5%	69.5%
259,088	NEW LONDON	97,081	32,754	61,351	2,976	28,597	D	33.7%	63.2%	34.8%	65.2%
136,364	TOLLAND	55,479	20,868	33,007	1,604	12,139	D	37.6%	59.5%	38.7%	61.3%
109,091	WINDHAM	38,333	13,112	23,851	1,370	10,739	D	34.2%	62.2%	35.5%	64.5%
3,405,565	TOTAL	1,311,261	448,077	828,902	34,282	380,825	D	34.2%	63.2%	35.1%	64.9%
	City/Town										
18,554	ANSONIA	6,548	1,881	4,519	148	2,638	D	28.7%	69.0%	29.4%	70.6%
19,587	BLOOMFIELD	9,002	1,734	7,081	187	5,347	D	19.3%	78.7%	19.7%	80.3%
28,683	BRANFORD	13,166	4,047	8,903	216	4,856	D	30.7%	67.6%	31.3%	68.7%
139,529	BRIDGEPORT	29,698	5,622	23,006	1,070	17,384	D	18.9%	77.5%	19.6%	80.4%
60,062	BRISTOL	21,469	6,738	14,081	650	7,343	D	31.4%	65.6%	32.4%	67.6%
28,543	CHESHIRE	13,187	4,687	8,181	319	3,494	D	35.5%	62.0%	36.4%	63.6%
74,848	DANBURY	20,678	7,311	12,868	499	5,557	D	35.4%	62.2%	36.2%	63.8%
19,607	DARIEN	9,260	5,202	3,948	110	1,254	R	56.2%	42.6%	56.9%	43.1%
49,575	EAST HARTFORD	16,315	4,645	11,285	385	6,640	D	28.5%	69.2%	29.2%	70.8%
28,189	EAST HAVEN	10,271	2,802	7,231	238	4,429	D	27.3%	70.4%	27.9%	72.1%
45,212	ENFIELD	16,584	5,853	10,265	466	4,412	D	35.3%	61.9%	36.3%	63.7%
57,340	FAIRFIELD	26,209	10,082	15,662	465	5,580	D	38.5%	59.8%	39.2%	60.8%
23,641	FARMINGTON	11,205	4,498	6,498	209	2,000	D	40.1%	58.0%	40.9%	59.1%
31,876	GLASTONBURY	16,558	6,840	9,447	271	2,607	D	41.3%	57.1%	42.0%	58.0%
61,101	GREENWICH	25,968	12,319	13,115	534	796	D	47.4%	50.5%	48.4%	51.6%
39,907	GROTON	12,117	4,416	7,324	377	2,908	D	36.4%	60.4%	37.6%	62.4%
21,398	GUILFORD	9,689	2,599	6,917	173	4,318	D	26.8%	71.4%	27.3%	72.7%
56,913	HAMDEN	23,247	6,134	16,668	445	10,534	D	26.4%	71.7%	26.9%	73.1%
121,578	HARTFORD	24,545	2,830	20,194	1,521	17,364	D	11.5%	82.3%	12.3%	87.7%
54,740	MANCHESTER	21,608	7,570	13,492	546	5,922	D	35.0%	62.4%	35.9%	64.1%
20,720	MANSFIELD	5,389	1,405	3,784	200	2,379	D	26.1%	70.2%	27.1%	72.9%
58,244	MERIDEN	19,366	5,711	13,065	590	7,354	D	29.5%	67.5%	30.4%	69.6%
43,167	MIDDLETOWN	16,329	4,772	11,082	475	6,310	D	29.2%	67.9%	30.1%	69.9%
52,305	MILFORD	21,704	7,173	13,998	533	6,825	D	33.0%	64.5%	33.9%	66.1%
30,989	NAUGATUCK	10,346	3,401	6,547	398	3,146	D	32.9%	63.3%	34.2%	65.8%

CONNECTICUT

SENATOR 2000

2000 Census Population	County	Total Vote	Republican	Democratic	Other	Rep.-Dem. Plurality		Percentage			
								Total Vote		Major Vote	
								Rep.	Dem.	Rep.	Dem.
71,538	NEW BRITAIN	17,019	4,346	12,070	603	7,724	D	25.5%	70.9%	26.5%	73.5%
123,626	NEW HAVEN	31,360	3,828	26,356	1,176	22,528	D	12.2%	84.0%	12.7%	87.3%
25,671	NEW LONDON	6,612	1,546	4,793	273	3,247	D	23.4%	72.5%	24.4%	75.6%
27,121	NEW MILFORD	10,466	4,451	5,730	285	1,279	D	42.5%	54.7%	43.7%	56.3%
29,306	NEWINGTON	13,868	4,385	9,186	297	4,801	D	31.6%	66.2%	32.3%	67.7%
25,031	NEWTOWN	11,071	4,565	6,245	261	1,680	D	41.2%	56.4%	42.2%	57.8%
23,035	NORTH HAVEN	11,184	4,115	6,887	182	2,772	D	36.8%	61.6%	37.4%	62.6%
82,951	NORWALK	28,846	9,554	18,727	565	9,173	D	33.1%	64.9%	33.8%	66.2%
36,117	NORWICH	11,703	3,142	8,106	455	4,964	D	26.8%	69.3%	27.9%	72.1%
23,643	RIDGEFIELD	12,374	5,875	6,337	162	462	D	47.5%	51.2%	48.1%	51.9%
38,101	SHELTON	16,297	6,618	9,278	401	2,660	D	40.6%	56.9%	41.6%	58.4%
23,234	SIMSBURY	12,498	5,326	6,916	256	1,590	D	42.6%	55.3%	43.5%	56.5%
24,412	SOUTH WINDSOR	11,850	4,333	7,292	225	2,959	D	36.6%	61.5%	37.3%	62.7%
39,728	SOUTHINGTON	17,768	6,212	11,126	430	4,914	D	35.0%	62.6%	35.8%	64.2%
117,083	STAMFORD	39,759	12,378	26,551	830	14,173	D	31.1%	66.8%	31.8%	68.2%
49,976	STRATFORD	20,356	6,829	13,087	440	6,258	D	33.5%	64.3%	34.3%	65.7%
35,202	TORRINGTON	13,301	5,039	7,746	516	2,707	D	37.9%	58.2%	39.4%	60.6%
34,243	TRUMBULL	17,028	7,019	9,745	264	2,726	D	41.2%	57.2%	41.9%	58.1%
28,063	VERNON	11,195	4,157	6,761	277	2,604	D	37.1%	60.4%	38.1%	61.9%
43,026	WALLINGFORD	18,920	6,160	12,393	367	6,233	D	32.6%	65.5%	33.2%	66.8%
107,271	WATERBURY	29,534	8,249	20,022	1,263	11,773	D	27.9%	67.8%	29.2%	70.8%
21,661	WATERTOWN	9,205	3,411	5,434	360	2,023	D	37.1%	59.0%	38.6%	61.4%
63,589	WEST HARTFORD	30,575	8,850	21,220	505	12,370	D	28.9%	69.4%	29.4%	70.6%
52,360	WEST HAVEN	17,807	4,172	13,301	334	9,129	D	23.4%	74.7%	23.9%	76.1%
25,749	WESTPORT	13,144	4,423	8,510	211	4,087	D	33.7%	64.7%	34.2%	65.8%
26,271	WETHERSFIELD	13,324	4,978	8,082	264	3,104	D	37.4%	60.7%	38.1%	61.9%
22,857	WINDHAM	6,496	1,726	4,562	208	2,836	D	26.6%	70.2%	27.4%	72.6%
28,237	WINDSOR	12,206	3,732	8,148	326	4,416	D	30.6%	66.8%	31.4%	68.6%

CONNECTICUT

CONGRESS

CD	Year	Total Vote	Republican		Democratic		Other Vote	Rep.-Dem. Plurality		Percentage			
			Vote	Candidate	Vote	Candidate				Total Vote		Major Vote	
										Rep.	Dem.	Rep.	Dem.
1	2000	211,263	59,331	BACKLUND, BOB	151,932	LARSON, JOHN B.		92,601	D	28.1%	71.9%	28.1%	71.9%
1	1998	168,264	69,668	O'CONNOR, KEVIN	97,681	LARSON, JOHN B.	915	28,013	D	41.4%	58.1%	41.6%	58.4%
1	1996	215,136	53,666	SLEATH, KENT	158,222	KENNELLY, BARBARA B.	3,248	104,556	D	24.9%	73.5%	25.3%	74.7%
1	1994	188,907	46,865	PUTNAM, DOUGLAS T.	138,637	*KENNELLY, BARBARA B.	3,405	91,772	D	24.8%	73.4%	25.3%	74.7%
1	1992	245,430	75,113	STEELE, PHILIP L.	164,735	*KENNELLY, BARBARA B.	5,582	89,622	D	30.6%	67.1%	31.3%	68.7%
2	2000	225,900	114,380	* SIMMONS, ROB	111,520	GEJDENSON, SAMUEL		2,860	R	50.6%	49.4%	50.6%	49.4%
2	1998	163,202	57,860	KOVAL, GARY M.	99,567	GEJDENSON, SAMUEL	5,775	41,707	D	35.5%	61.0%	36.8%	63.2%
2	1996	223,249	100,332	MUNSTER, EDWARD W.	115,175	GEJDENSON, SAMUEL	7,742	14,843	D	44.9%	51.6%	46.6%	53.4%
2	1994	186,073	79,167	MUNSTER, EDWARD W.	79,188	GEJDENSON, SAMUEL	27,718	21	D	42.5%	42.6%	50.0%	50.0%
2	1992	242,707	119,416	MUNSTER, EDWARD W.	123,291	*GEJDENSON, SAMUEL		3,875	D	49.2%	50.8%	49.2%	50.8%
3	2000	218,205	60,037	GOLD, JUNE M.	156,910	DELAURO, ROSA L.	1,258	96,873	D	27.5%	71.9%	27.7%	72.3%
3	1998	153,851	42,090	REUST, MARTIN T.	109,726	DELAURO, ROSA L.	2,035	67,636	D	27.4%	71.3%	27.7%	72.3%
3	1996	211,352	59,335	COPPOLA, JOHN	150,798	DELAURO, ROSA L.	1,219	91,463	D	28.1%	71.3%	28.2%	71.8%
3	1994	175,355	64,094	* JOHNSON, SUSAN E.	111,261	DELAURO, ROSA L.		47,167	D	36.6%	63.4%	36.6%	63.4%
3	1992	247,531	84,952	SCOTT, THOMAS	162,568	*DELAURO, ROSA L.	11	77,616	D	34.3%	65.7%	34.3%	65.7%

CONNECTICUT
CONGRESS

| CD | Year | Total Vote | Republican | | Democratic | | Other Vote | Rep.-Dem. Plurality | Percentage | | | |
| | | | Vote | Candidate | Vote | Candidate | | | Total Vote | | Major Vote | |
									Rep.	Dem.	Rep.	Dem.
4	2000	206,758	119,155	SHAYS, CHRISTOPHER	84,472	SANCHEZ, STEPHANIE	3,131	34,683 R	57.6%	40.9%	58.5%	41.5%
4	1998	137,204	94,767	SHAYS, CHRISTOPHER	40,988	KANTROWITZ, JOHATHAN D.	1,449	53,779 R	69.1%	29.9%	69.8%	30.2%
4	1996	201,712	121,949	SHAYS, CHRISTOPHER	75,902	FINCH, BILL	3,861	46,047 R	60.5%	37.6%	61.6%	38.4%
4	1994	147,062	109,436	SHAYS, CHRISTOPHER	34,962	KANTROWITZ, JOHATHAN D.	2,664	74,474 R	74.4%	23.8%	75.8%	24.2%
4	1992	219,615	147,816	SHAYS, CHRISTOPHER	58,666	SCHROPFER, DAVE	13,133	89,150 R	67.3%	26.7%	71.6%	28.4%
5	2000	221,821	98,229	NIELSEN, MARK	118,932	MALONEY, JAMES H.	4,660	20,703 D	44.3%	53.6%	45.2%	54.8%
5	1998	157,157	76,051	NIELSEN, MARK	78,394	MALONEY, JAMES H.	2,712	2,343 D	48.4%	49.9%	49.2%	50.8%
5	1996	215,130	98,782	FRANKS, GARY A.	111,974	MALONEY, JAMES H.	4,374	13,192 D	45.9%	52.0%	46.9%	53.1%
5	1994	179,053	93,471	FRANKS, GARY A.	81,523	*MALONEY, JAMES H.	4,059	11,948 R	52.2%	45.5%	53.4%	46.6%
5	1992	240,283	104,891	FRANKS, GARY A.	74,791	LAWLOR, JAMES J.	60,601	30,100 R	43.7%	31.1%	58.4%	41.6%
6	2000	229,543	143,698	JOHNSON, NANCY L.	75,471	VALENTI, PAUL	10,374	68,227 R	62.6%	32.9%	65.6%	34.4%
6	1998	174,781	101,630	JOHNSON, NANCY L.	69,201	KOSKOFF, CHARLOTTE	3,950	32,429 R	58.1%	39.6%	59.5%	40.5%
6	1996	227,756	113,020	JOHNSON, NANCY L.	111,433	KOSKOFF, CHARLOTTE	3,303	1,587 R	49.6%	48.9%	50.4%	49.6%
6	1994	192,717	123,101	JOHNSON, NANCY L.	60,701	KOSKOFF, CHARLOTTE	8,915	62,400 R	63.9%	31.5%	67.0%	33.0%
6	1992	239,597	166,967	JOHNSON, NANCY L.	60,373	SLASON, EUGENE F.	12,257	106,594 R	69.7%	25.2%	73.4%	26.6%

CONNECTICUT
GENERAL AND PRIMARY ELECTIONS

2000 GENERAL ELECTIONS

In addition to the county-by-county figures, data are presented for selected Connecticut communities. Since not all jurisdictions within the state are listed in this special tabulation, statewide totals are shown only with the county-by-county statistics. This same format is employed in other New England states except Rhode Island, where the votes for all towns and cities are listed.

President   Other vote was 9,695 Concerned Citizens (Phillips); 4,731 Reform (Buchanan); 3,484 Libertarian (Browne); 40 write-in (Hagelin); 4 write-in (Harris); 4 write-in (Reicher); 3 write-in (Huber); 2 write-in (Strickland); 1 write-in (Pettway).

Senator   Other vote was 25,509 Concerned Citizens (Kozak); 8,773 Libertarian (Moore).

Congress   Other vote was: CD 3: 1,258 Natural Law (Dalby); CD 4: 2,034 Libertarian (Gislao); 1,097 Independence (Don); CD 5: 4,653 Concerned Citizens (Zdonczyk); 7 write-in (Joy); CD 6: 7,303 Green (Cole); 3,071 Concerned Citizens (Knibbs).

2000 PRIMARY ELECTIONS

Primary   March 7, 2000 (President)
September 12, 2000 (Congress)

Registration (as of Oct. 19, 1999)

Republican	466,241
Democratic	685,656
Libertarian	493
Reform	446
Green	292
Other Parties	2,137
Unaffiliated	789,986
TOTAL	1,945,251

CONNECTICUT

GENERAL AND PRIMARY ELECTIONS

Primary Type   Closed—Only registered Democrats and Republicans could vote in their party's primary.

Note: An asterisk (*) denotes incumbent. A Senate or House candidate had to receive at least 15 percent of the vote in a pre-primary convention to force a primary.

	REPUBLICAN PRIMARIES			DEMOCRATIC PRIMARIES		
President	John McCain	87,176	48.7%	Al Gore	98,312	55.4%
	George W. Bush	82,881	46.3%	Bill Bradley	73,589	41.5%
	Alan Keyes	5,913	3.3%	Uncommitted	5,400	3.0%
	Steve Forbes	1,242	0.7%			
	Uncommitted	1,222	0.7%			
	Gary Bauer	373	0.2%			
	Orrin G. Hatch	178	0.1%			
	TOTAL	178,985		TOTAL	177,301	
Senator	Phil Giordano	Nominated by convention		Joseph I. Lieberman*	Nominated by convention	
Congressional District 1	Bob Backlund	Nominated by convention		John B. Larson*	Nominated by convention	
Congressional District 2	Rob Simmons	Nominated by convention		Sam Gejdenson*	Nominated by convention	
Congressional District 3	June M. Gold	Nominated by convention		Rosa L. DeLauro*	Nominated by convention	
Congressional District 4	Christopher Shays*	Nominated by convention		Stephanie Sanchez	Nominated by convention	
Congressional District 5	Mark Nielsen	Nominated by convention		James H. Maloney*	Nominated by convention	
Congressional District 6	Nancy L. Johnson*	Nominated by convention		Paul Valenti	Nominated by convention	

DELAWARE

GOVERNOR
Ruth Ann Minner (D). Elected 2000 to a four-year term.

SENATORS
Thomas R. Carper (D). Elected 2000 to a six-year term.

Joseph R. Biden (D). Re-elected 1996 to a six-year term. Previously elected 1990, 1984, 1978, 1972.

REPRESENTATIVE
At-Large. Michael N. Castle (R)

POSTWAR VOTE FOR PRESIDENT

| | | Republican | | Democratic | | | | Percentage | | | |
| | | | | | | Other | | Total Vote | | Major Vote | |
Year	Total Vote	Vote	Candidate	Vote	Candidate	Vote	Plurality	Rep.	Dem.	Rep.	Dem.
2000**	327,622	137,288	Bush, George W.	180,068	Gore, Al	10,266	42,780 D	41.9%	55.0%	43.3%	56.7%
1996**	271,084	99,062	Dole, Bob	140,355	Clinton, Bill	31,667	41,293 D	36.5%	51.8%	41.4%	58.6%
1992**	289,735	102,313	Bush, George	126,054	Clinton, Bill	61,368	23,741 D	35.3%	43.5%	44.8%	55.2%
1988	249,891	139,639	Bush, George	108,647	Dukakis, Michael S.	1,605	30,992 R	55.9%	43.5%	56.2%	43.8%
1984	254,572	152,190	Reagan, Ronald	101,656	Mondale, Walter F.	726	50,534 R	59.8%	39.9%	60.0%	40.0%
1980**	235,900	111,252	Reagan, Ronald	105,754	Carter, Jimmy	18,894	5,498 R	47.2%	44.8%	51.3%	48.7%
1976	235,834	109,831	Ford, Gerald R.	122,596	Carter, Jimmy	3,407	12,765 D	46.6%	52.0%	47.3%	52.7%
1972	235,516	140,357	Nixon, Richard M.	92,283	McGovern, George S.	2,876	48,074 R	59.6%	39.2%	60.3%	39.7%
1968	214,367	96,714	Nixon, Richard M.	89,194	Humphrey, Hubert H.	28,459	7,520 R	45.1%	41.6%	52.0%	48.0%
1964	201,320	78,078	Goldwater, Barry M.	122,704	Johnson, Lyndon B.	538	44,626 D	38.8%	60.9%	38.9%	61.1%
1960	196,683	96,373	Nixon, Richard M.	99,590	Kennedy, John F.	720	3,217 D	49.0%	50.6%	49.2%	50.8%
1956	177,988	98,057	Eisenhower, Dwight D.	79,421	Stevenson, Adlai E.	510	18,636 R	55.1%	44.6%	55.3%	44.7%
1952	174,025	90,059	Eisenhower, Dwight D.	83,315	Stevenson, Adlai E.	651	6,744 R	51.8%	47.9%	51.9%	48.1%
1948	139,073	69,588	Dewey, Thomas E.	67,813	Truman, Harry S.	1,672	1,775 R	50.0%	48.8%	50.6%	49.4%

In 2000 the other vote column includes 8,307 votes cast for Green (Nader). In 1996 the other vote column includes 28,719 votes cast for Perot. In 1992 the other vote column includes 59,213 votes cast for Perot. In 1980 the other column includes 16,288 votes for Independent (Anderson).

POSTWAR VOTE FOR GOVERNOR

| | | Republican | | Democratic | | | | Percentage | | | |
| | | | | | | Other | Rep.-Dem. | Total Vote | | Major Vote | |
Year	Total Vote	Vote	Candidate	Vote	Candidate	Vote	Plurality	Rep.	Dem.	Rep.	Dem.
2000	323,688	128,603	Burris, John M.	191,695	Minner, Ruth Ann	3,390	63,092 D	39.7%	59.2%	40.2%	59.8%
1996	271,122	82,654	Rzewnicki, Janet	188,300	Carper, Thomas R.	168	105,646 D	30.5%	69.5%	30.5%	69.5%
1992	277,058	90,725	Scott, B. Gary	179,365	Carper, Thomas R.	6,968	88,640 D	32.7%	64.7%	33.6%	66.4%
1988	239,969	169,733	Castle, Michael N.	70,236	Kreshtoll, Jacob		99,497 R	70.7%	29.3%	70.7%	29.3%
1984	243,565	135,250	Castle, Michael N.	108,315	Quillen, William T.		26,935 R	55.5%	44.5%	55.5%	44.5%
1980	225,081	159,004	duPont, Pierre	64,217	Gordy, William J.	1,860	94,787 R	70.6%	28.5%	71.2%	28.8%
1976	229,563	130,531	duPont, Pierre	97,480	Tribbitt, Sherman W.	1,552	33,051 R	56.9%	42.5%	57.2%	42.8%
1972	228,722	109,583	Peterson, Russell W.	117,274	Tribbitt, Sherman W.	1,865	7,691 D	47.9%	51.3%	48.3%	51.7%
1968	206,834	104,474	Peterson, Russell W.	102,360	Terry, Charles L.		2,114 R	50.5%	49.5%	50.5%	49.5%
1964	200,171	97,374	Buckson, David P.	102,797	Terry, Charles L.		5,423 D	48.6%	51.4%	48.6%	51.4%
1960	194,835	94,043	Rollins, John W.	100,792	Carvel, Elbert N.		6,749 D	48.3%	51.7%	48.3%	51.7%
1956	177,012	91,965	Boggs, J. Caleb	85,047	McConnell, J. H. T.		6,918 R	52.0%	48.0%	52.0%	48.0%
1952	170,749	88,977	Boggs, J. Caleb	81,772	Carvel, Elbert N.		7,205 R	52.1%	47.9%	52.1%	47.9%
1948	140,335	64,996	George, Hyland P.	75,339	Carvel, Elbert N.		10,343 D	46.3%	53.7%	46.3%	53.7%

DELAWARE

POSTWAR VOTE FOR SENATOR

Year	Total Vote	Republican		Democratic		Other Vote	Rep.-Dem. Plurality	Percentage			
								Total Vote		Major Vote	
		Vote	Candidate	Vote	Candidate			Rep.	Dem.	Rep.	Dem.
2000	327,017	142,891	Roth, William V.	181,566	Carper, Thomas R.	2,560	38,675 D	43.7%	55.5%	44.0%	56.0%
1996	275,605	105,088	Clatworthy, Raymond J.	165,465	Biden, Joseph R.	5,052	60,377 D	38.1%	60.0%	38.8%	61.2%
1994	199,029	111,088	Roth, William V.	84,554	Oberly, Charles M.	3,387	26,534 R	55.8%	42.5%	56.8%	43.2%
1990	180,152	64,554	Brady, M. Jane	112,918	Biden, Joseph R.	2,680	48,364 D	35.8%	62.7%	36.4%	63.6%
1988	243,493	151,115	Roth, William V.	92,378	Woo, S. B.		58,737 R	62.1%	37.9%	62.1%	37.9%
1984	245,932	98,101	Burris, John M.	147,831	Biden, Joseph R.		49,730 D	39.9%	60.1%	39.9%	60.1%
1982	190,960	105,357	Roth, William V.	84,413	Levinson, David N.	1,190	20,944 R	55.2%	44.2%	55.5%	44.5%
1978	162,072	66,479	Baxter, James H.	93,930	Biden, Joseph R.	1,663	27,451 D	41.0%	58.0%	41.4%	58.6%
1976	224,859	125,502	Roth, William V.	98,055	Maloney, Thomas C.	1,302	27,447 R	55.8%	43.6%	56.1%	43.9%
1972	229,828	112,844	Boggs, J. Caleb	116,006	Biden, Joseph R.	978	3,162 D	49.1%	50.5%	49.3%	50.7%
1970	161,439	94,979	Roth, William V.	64,740	Zimmerman, Jacob	1,720	30,239 R	58.8%	40.1%	59.5%	40.5%
1966	164,549	97,268	Boggs, J. Caleb	67,281	Tunnell, James M., Jr.		29,987 R	59.1%	40.9%	59.1%	40.9%
1964	200,703	103,782	Williams, John J.	96,850	Carvel, Elbert N.	71	6,932 R	51.7%	48.3%	51.7%	48.3%
1960	194,964	98,874	Boggs, J. Caleb	96,090	Frear, J. Allen		2,784 R	50.7%	49.3%	50.7%	49.3%
1958	154,432	82,280	Williams, John J.	72,152	Carvel, Elbert N.		10,128 R	53.3%	46.7%	53.3%	46.7%
1954	144,900	62,389	Warburton, H. B.	82,511	Frear, J. Allen		20,122 D	43.1%	56.9%	43.1%	56.9%
1952	170,705	93,020	Williams, John J.	77,685	Bayard, A. I. duP.		15,335 R	54.5%	45.5%	54.5%	45.5%
1948	141,362	68,246	Buck, C. Douglas	71,888	Frear, J. Allen	1,228	3,642 D	48.3%	50.9%	48.7%	51.3%
1946	113,513	62,603	Williams, John J.	50,910	Tunnell, James M.		11,693 R	55.2%	44.8%	55.2%	44.8%

DELAWARE

One At Large

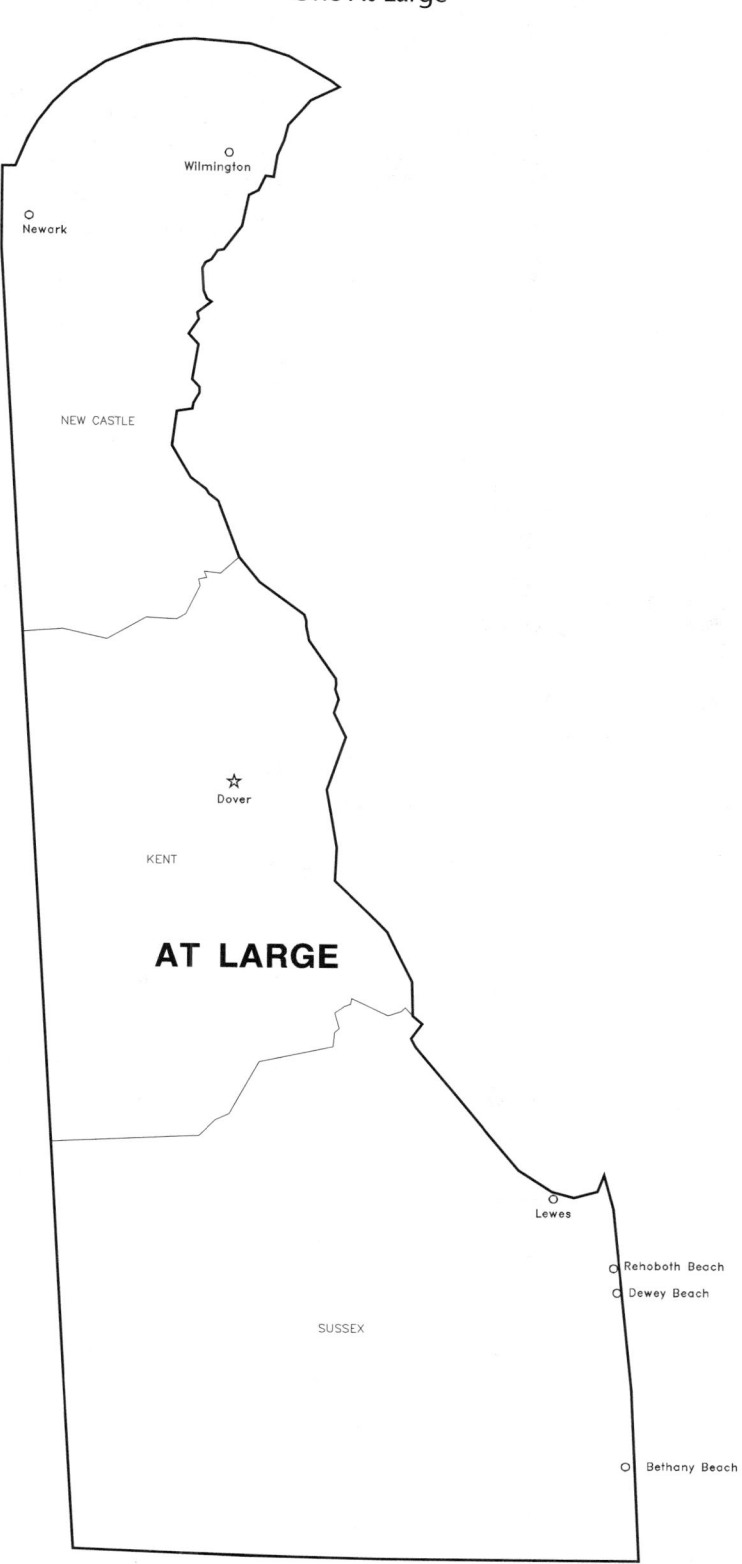

Wilmington

Newark

NEW CASTLE

☆
Dover

KENT

AT LARGE

Lewes

Rehoboth Beach

Dewey Beach

SUSSEX

Bethany Beach

DELAWARE

PRESIDENT 2000

2000 Census Population	County	Total Vote	Republican	Democratic	Green (Nader)	Other	Rep.-Dem. Plurality	Percentage of Total Vote		
								Rep.	Dem.	Green
126,697	KENT	48,264	24,081	22,790	1,082	311	1,291 R	49.9%	47.2%	2.2%
500,265	NEW CASTLE	213,059	78,587	127,539	5,767	1,166	48,952 D	36.9%	59.9%	2.7%
156,638	SUSSEX	66,299	34,620	29,739	1,458	482	4,881 R	52.2%	44.9%	2.2%
783,600	TOTAL	327,622	137,288	180,068	8,307	1,959	42,780 D	41.9%	55.0%	2.5%

DELAWARE

GOVERNOR 2000

2000 Census Population	County	Total Vote	Republican	Democratic	Other	Rep.-Dem. Plurality	Percentage			
							Total Vote		Major Vote	
							Rep.	Dem.	Rep.	Dem.
126,697	KENT	47,613	20,073	27,164	376	7,091 D	42.2%	57.1%	42.5%	57.5%
500,265	NEW CASTLE	210,946	81,311	127,112	2,523	45,801 D	38.6%	60.3%	39.0%	61.0%
156,638	SUSSEX	65,129	27,219	37,419	491	10,200 D	41.8%	57.5%	42.1%	57.9%
783,600	TOTAL	323,688	128,603	191,695	3,390	63,092 D	39.7%	59.2%	40.2%	59.8%

DELAWARE

SENATOR 2000

2000 Census Population	County	Total Vote	Republican	Democratic	Other	Rep.-Dem. Plurality	Percentage			
							Total Vote		Major Vote	
							Rep.	Dem.	Rep.	Dem.
126,697	KENT	47,732	25,387	21,998	347	3,389 R	53.2%	46.1%	53.6%	46.4%
500,265	NEW CASTLE	213,850	83,554	128,491	1,805	44,937 D	39.1%	60.1%	39.4%	60.6%
156,638	SUSSEX	65,435	33,950	31,077	408	2,873 R	51.9%	47.5%	52.2%	47.8%
783,600	TOTAL	327,017	142,891	181,566	2,560	38,675 D	43.7%	55.5%	44.0%	56.0%

DELAWARE

CONGRESS

CD	Year	Total Vote	Republican Vote	Republican Candidate	Democratic Vote	Democratic Candidate	Other Vote	Rep.-Dem. Plurality	Total Vote Rep.	Total Vote Dem.	Major Vote Rep.	Major Vote Dem.
AL	2000	313,171	211,797	CASTLE, MICHAEL N.	96,488	MILLER, MICHEAL C.	4,886	115,309 R	67.6%	30.8%	68.7%	31.3%
AL	1998	180,527	119,811	CASTLE, MICHAEL N.	57,446	WILLIAMS, DENNIS E.	3,270	62,365 R	66.4%	31.8%	67.6%	32.4%
AL	1996	266,836	185,576	CASTLE, MICHAEL N.	73,253	WILLIAMS, DENNIS E.	8,007	112,323 R	69.5%	27.5%	71.7%	28.3%
AL	1994	195,037	137,960	CASTLE, MICHAEL N.	51,803	DESANTIS, CAROL ANN	5,274	86,157 R	70.7%	26.6%	72.7%	27.3%
AL	1992	276,157	153,037	CASTLE, MICHAEL N.	117,426	WOO, S. B.	5,694	35,611 R	55.4%	42.5%	56.6%	43.4%
AL	1990	177,432	58,037	WILLIAMS, RALPH O.	116,274	CARPER, THOMAS R.	3,121	58,237 D	32.7%	65.5%	33.3%	66.7%
AL	1988	234,517	76,179	KRAPF, JAMES P.	158,338	CARPER, THOMAS R.		82,159 D	32.5%	67.5%	32.5%	67.5%
AL	1986	160,757	53,767	NEUBERGER, THOMAS S.	106,351	CARPER, THOMAS R.	639	52,584 D	33.4%	66.2%	33.6%	66.4%
AL	1984	243,014	100,650	DUPONT, ELISE	142,070	CARPER, THOMAS R.	294	41,420 D	41.4%	58.5%	41.5%	58.5%
AL	1982	188,064	87,153	EVANS, THOMAS B.	98,533	CARPER, THOMAS R.	2,378	11,380 D	46.3%	52.4%	46.9%	53.1%
AL	1980	216,629	133,842	EVANS, THOMAS B.	81,227	MAXWELL, ROBERT L.	1,560	52,615 R	61.8%	37.5%	62.2%	37.8%
AL	1978	157,566	91,689	EVANS, THOMAS B.	64,863	HINDES, GARY E.	1,014	26,826 R	58.2%	41.2%	58.6%	41.4%
AL	1976	214,799	110,677	EVANS, THOMAS B.	102,431	SHIPLEY, SAMUEL L.	1,691	8,246 R	51.5%	47.7%	51.9%	48.1%
AL	1974	160,328	93,826	DUPONT, PIERRE	63,490	SOLES, JAMES	3,012	30,336 R	58.5%	39.6%	59.6%	40.4%
AL	1972	225,851	141,237	DUPONT, PIERRE	83,230	HANDLOFF, NORMA	1,384	58,007 R	62.5%	36.9%	62.9%	37.1%
AL	1970	160,313	86,125	DUPONT, PIERRE	71,429	DANIELLO, JOHN D.	2,759	14,696 R	53.7%	44.6%	54.7%	45.3%
AL	1968	200,820	117,827	ROTH, WILLIAM V.	82,993	MCDOWELL, HARRIS B.		34,834 R	58.7%	41.3%	58.7%	41.3%
AL	1966	163,103	90,961	ROTH, WILLIAM V.	72,142	MCDOWELL, HARRIS B.		18,819 R	55.8%	44.2%	55.8%	44.2%
AL	1964	198,691	86,254	SNOWDEN, JAMES H.	112,361	MCDOWELL, HARRIS B.	76	26,107 D	43.4%	56.6%	43.4%	56.6%
AL	1962	153,356	71,934	WILLIAMS, WILMER F.	81,166	MCDOWELL, HARRIS B.	256	9,232 D	46.9%	52.9%	47.0%	53.0%
AL	1960	194,564	96,337	MCKINSTRY, JAMES T.	98,227	MCDOWELL, HARRIS B.		1,890 D	49.5%	50.5%	49.5%	50.5%
AL	1958	152,896	76,099	HASKELL, HARRY G.	76,797	MCDOWELL, HARRIS B.		698 D	49.8%	50.2%	49.8%	50.2%
AL	1956	176,182	91,538	HASKELL, HARRY G.	84,644	MCDOWELL, HARRIS B.		6,894 R	52.0%	48.0%	52.0%	48.0%
AL	1954	144,236	65,035	MARTIN, LILLIAN	79,201	MCDOWELL, HARRIS B.		14,166 D	45.1%	54.9%	45.1%	54.9%
AL	1952	170,015	88,285	WARBURTON, H. B.	81,730	SCANNELL, JOSEPH S.		6,555 R	51.9%	48.1%	51.9%	48.1%
AL	1950	129,404	73,313	BOGGS, J. CALEB	56,091	WINCHESTER, H. M.		17,222 R	56.7%	43.3%	56.7%	43.3%
AL	1948	140,535	71,127	BOGGS, J. CALEB	68,909	MCGUIGAN, J. CARL	499	2,218 R	50.6%	49.0%	50.8%	49.2%
AL	1946	112,621	63,516	BOGGS, J. CALEB	49,105	TRAYNOR, PHILIP A.		14,411 R	56.4%	43.6%	56.4%	43.6%

DELAWARE

GENERAL AND PRIMARY ELECTIONS

2000 GENERAL ELECTIONS

President   Other vote was 777 Reform (Buchanan); 774 Libertarian (Browne); 208 Constitution (Phillips); 107 Natural Law (Hagelin); 93 scattered write-in.

Governor   Other vote was 3,271 Independent Party of Delaware (McDowell); 119 scattered write-in.

Senator   Other vote was 1,103 Libertarian (Morrison); 1,044 Constitution (Dankof); 389 Natural Law (Mattson); 24 scattered write-in.

Congress   Other vote was 2,490 Constitution (Webster); 2,351 Libertarian (Thomas); 45 scattered write-in.

DELAWARE

GENERAL AND PRIMARY ELECTIONS

2000 PRIMARY ELECTIONS

Primary	February 5, 2000 (Democratic President) February 8, 2000 (Republican President) September 9, 2000 (Congress)	

Registration (as of Aug. 1, 2000)		
	Republican	167,981
	Democratic	208,412
	Other Parties	2,865
	Independent	111,926
	TOTAL	491,184

Note: The Republican presidential primary was conducted by the party. The others were conducted by the state.

Primary Type   Closed—Only registered Democrats and Republicans could vote in their party's primary.

Note: An asterisk (*) denotes incumbent. The names of unopposed candidates do not appear on the primary ballot; therefore, no votes are cast for these candidates.

	REPUBLICAN PRIMARIES			DEMOCRATIC PRIMARIES		
President	George W. Bush	15,250	50.7%	Al Gore	6,377	57.2%
	John McCain	7,638	25.4%	Bill Bradley	4,476	40.2%
	Steve Forbes	5,883	19.6%	Lyndon H. LaRouche Jr.	288	2.6%
	Alan Keyes	1,148	3.8%			
	Gary Bauer	120	0.4%			
	Orrin G. Hatch	21	0.1%			
	TOTAL	30,060		TOTAL	11,141	
Governor	John M. Burris	13,893	50.1%	Ruth Ann Minner	Unopposed	
	William Swain Lee	13,847	49.9%			
	TOTAL	27,740				
Senator	William V. Roth*	Unopposed		Thomas R. Carper	Unopposed	
Congressional At-large	Michael N. Castle*	Unopposed		Micheal C. Miller	Unopposed	

FLORIDA

GOVERNOR
Jeb Bush (R). Elected 1998 to a four-year term.

SENATORS
Bill Nelson (D). Elected 2000 to a six-year term.

Robert Graham (D). Re-elected 1998 to a six-year term. Previously elected 1992, 1986.

REPRESENTATIVES

1. Joe Scarborough (R)
2. Allen Boyd (D)
3. Corrine Brown (D)
4. Ander Crenshaw (R)
5. Karen L. Thurman (D)
6. Clifford B. Stearns (R)
7. John L. Mica (R)
8. Richard Keller (R)
9. Michael Bilirakis (R)
10. C. W. Young (R)
11. Jim Davis (D)
12. Adam Putnam (R)
13. Dan Miller (R)
14. Porter J. Goss (R)
15. Dave Weldon (R)
16. Mark Foley (R)
17. Carrie P. Meek (D)
18. Ileana Ros-Lehtinen (R)
19. Robert Wexler (D)
20. Peter Deutsch (D)
21. Lincoln Diaz-Balart (R)
22. Clay Shaw (R)
23. Alcee Hastings (D)

POSTWAR VOTE FOR PRESIDENT

		Republican		Democratic								
									Percentage			
									Total Vote		Major Vote	
Year	Total Vote	Vote	Candidate	Vote	Candidate	Other Vote	Plurality		Rep.	Dem.	Rep.	Dem.
2000**	5,963,110	2,912,790	Bush, George W.	2,912,253	Gore, Al	138,067	537 R		48.8%	48.8%	50.0%	50.0%
1996**	5,303,794	2,244,536	Dole, Bob	2,546,870	Clinton, Bill	512,388	302,334 D		42.3%	48.0%	46.8%	53.2%
1992**	5,314,392	2,173,310	Bush, George	2,072,698	Clinton, Bill	1,068,384	100,612 R		40.9%	39.0%	51.2%	48.8%
1988	4,302,313	2,618,885	Bush, George	1,656,701	Dukakis, Michael S.	26,727	962,184 R		60.9%	38.5%	61.3%	38.7%
1984	4,180,051	2,730,350	Reagan, Ronald	1,448,816	Mondale, Walter F.	885	1,281,534 R		65.3%	34.7%	65.3%	34.7%
1980**	3,686,930	2,046,951	Reagan, Ronald	1,419,475	Carter, Jimmy	220,504	627,476 R		55.5%	38.5%	59.1%	40.9%
1976	3,150,631	1,469,531	Ford, Gerald R.	1,636,000	Carter, Jimmy	45,100	166,469 D		46.6%	51.9%	47.3%	52.7%
1972	2,583,283	1,857,759	Nixon, Richard M.	718,117	McGovern, George S.	7,407	1,139,642 R		71.9%	27.8%	72.1%	27.9%
1968**	2,187,805	886,804	Nixon, Richard M.	676,794	Humphrey, Hubert H.	624,207	210,010 R		40.5%	30.9%	56.7%	43.3%
1964	1,854,481	905,941	Goldwater, Barry M.	948,540	Johnson, Lyndon B.		42,599 D		48.9%	51.1%	48.9%	51.1%
1960	1,544,176	795,476	Nixon, Richard M.	748,700	Kennedy, John F.		46,776 R		51.5%	48.5%	51.5%	48.5%
1956	1,125,762	643,849	Eisenhower, Dwight D.	480,371	Stevenson, Adlai E.	1,542	163,478 R		57.2%	42.7%	57.3%	42.7%
1952	989,337	544,036	Eisenhower, Dwight D.	444,950	Stevenson, Adlai E.	351	99,086 R		55.0%	45.0%	55.0%	45.0%
1948	577,643	194,280	Dewey, Thomas E.	281,988	Truman, Harry S.	101,375	87,708 D		33.6%	48.8%	40.8%	59.2%

In 2000 the other vote column includes 97,488 votes cast for Green (Nader). In 1996 the other vote column includes 483,870 votes cast for Perot. In 1992 the other vote column includes 1,053,067 votes cast for Perot. In 1980 the other column includes 189,692 votes for Independent (Anderson). In 1968 other vote was George Wallace party.

FLORIDA

POSTWAR VOTE FOR GOVERNOR

Year	Total Vote	Republican Vote	Candidate	Democratic Vote	Candidate	Other Vote	Rep.-Dem. Plurality	Total Vote Rep.	Dem.	Major Vote Rep.	Dem.
1998	3,964,441	2,191,105	Bush, Jeb	1,773,054	MacKay, Buddy	282	418,051 R	55.3%	44.7%	55.3%	44.7%
1994	4,206,659	2,071,068	Bush, Jeb	2,135,008	Chiles, Lawton	583	63,940 D	49.2%	50.8%	49.2%	50.8%
1990	3,530,871	1,535,068	Martinez, Bob	1,995,206	Chiles, Lawton	597	460,138 D	43.5%	56.5%	43.5%	56.5%
1986	3,386,171	1,847,525	Martinez, Bob	1,538,620	Pajcic, Steve	26	308,905 R	54.6%	45.4%	54.6%	45.4%
1982	2,688,566	949,013	Bafalis, L. A.	1,739,553	Graham, Robert		790,540 D	35.3%	64.7%	35.3%	64.7%
1978	2,530,468	1,123,888	Eckerd, Jack M.	1,406,580	Graham, Robert		282,692 D	44.4%	55.6%	44.4%	55.6%
1974	1,828,392	709,438	Thomas, Jerry	1,118,954	Askew, Reubin		409,516 D	38.8%	61.2%	38.8%	61.2%
1970	1,730,813	746,243	Kirk, Claude R.	984,305	Askew, Reubin	265	238,062 D	43.1%	56.9%	43.1%	56.9%
1966	1,489,661	821,190	Kirk, Claude R.	668,233	High, Robert King	238	152,957 R	55.1%	44.9%	55.1%	44.9%
1964S	1,663,481	686,297	Holley, Charles R.	933,554	Burns, Haydon	43,630	247,257 D	41.3%	56.1%	42.4%	57.6%
1960	1,419,343	569,936	Petersen, George C.	849,407	Bryant, Farris		279,471 D	40.2%	59.8%	40.2%	59.8%
1956	1,014,733	266,980	Washburne, W. A.	747,753	Collins, LeRoy		480,773 D	26.3%	73.7%	26.3%	73.7%
1954S	357,783	69,852	Watson, J. Tom	287,769	Collins, LeRoy	162	217,917 D	19.5%	80.4%	19.5%	80.5%
1952	834,518	210,009	Swan, Harry S.	624,463	McCarty, Dan	46	414,454 D	25.2%	74.8%	25.2%	74.8%
1948	457,638	76,153	Acker, Bert Lee	381,459	Warren, Fuller	26	305,306 D	16.6%	83.4%	16.6%	83.4%

The 1954 election was for a short term to fill a vacancy. The 1964 election was for a two-year term to permit shifting the vote for Governor to non-Presidential years.

POSTWAR VOTE FOR SENATOR

Year	Total Vote	Republican Vote	Candidate	Democratic Vote	Candidate	Other Vote	Rep.-Dem. Plurality	Total Vote Rep.	Dem.	Major Vote Rep.	Dem.
2000	5,856,731	2,705,348	McCollum, Bill	2,989,487	Nelson, Bill	161,896	284,139 D	46.2%	51.0%	47.5%	52.5%
1998	3,900,162	1,463,755	Crist, Charlie	2,436,407	Graham, Robert		972,652 D	37.5%	62.5%	37.5%	62.5%
1994	4,106,176	2,894,726	Mack, Connie	1,210,412	Rodham, Hugh E.	1,038	1,684,314 R	70.5%	29.5%	70.5%	29.5%
1992	4,962,290	1,716,505	Grant, Bill	3,245,565	Graham, Robert	220	1,529,060 D	34.6%	65.4%	34.6%	65.4%
1988	4,068,209	2,051,071	Mack, Connie	2,016,553	MacKay, Buddy	585	34,518 R	50.4%	49.6%	50.4%	49.6%
1986	3,429,996	1,552,376	Hawkins, Paula	1,877,543	Graham, Robert	77	325,167 D	45.3%	54.7%	45.3%	54.7%
1982	2,653,419	1,015,330	Poole, Van B.	1,637,667	Chiles, Lawton	422	622,337 D	38.3%	61.7%	38.3%	61.7%
1980	3,528,028	1,822,460	Hawkins, Paula	1,705,409	Gunter, Bill	159	117,051 R	51.7%	48.3%	51.7%	48.3%
1976	2,857,534	1,057,886	Grady, John	1,799,518	Chiles, Lawton	130	741,632 D	37.0%	63.0%	37.0%	63.0%
1974	1,800,539	736,674	Eckerd, Jack M.	781,031	Stone, Richard	282,834	44,357 D	40.9%	43.4%	48.5%	51.5%
1970	1,675,378	772,817	Cramer, William C.	902,438	Chiles, Lawton	123	129,621 D	46.1%	53.9%	46.1%	53.9%
1968	2,024,136	1,131,499	Gurney, Edward J.	892,637	Collins, LeRoy		238,862 R	55.9%	44.1%	55.9%	44.1%
1964	1,560,337	562,212	Kirk, Claude R.	997,585	Holland, Spessard L.	540	435,373 D	36.0%	63.9%	36.0%	64.0%
1962	939,207	281,381	Rupert, Emerson H.	657,633	Smathers, George A.	193	376,252 D	30.0%	70.0%	30.0%	70.0%
1958	542,069	155,956	Hyzer, Leland	386,113	Holland, Spessard L.		230,157 D	28.8%	71.2%	28.8%	71.2%
1956	655,418		—	655,418	Smathers, George A.		655,418 D		100.0%		100.0%
1952	617,800		—	616,665	Holland, Spessard L.	1,135	616,665 D		99.8%		100.0%
1950	313,487	74,228	Booth, John P.	238,987	Smathers, George A.	272	164,759 D	23.7%	76.2%	23.7%	76.3%
1946	198,640	42,408	Schad, J. Harry	156,232	Holland, Spessard L.		113,824 D	21.3%	78.7%	21.3%	78.7%

FLORIDA

Districts Established May 21, 1996

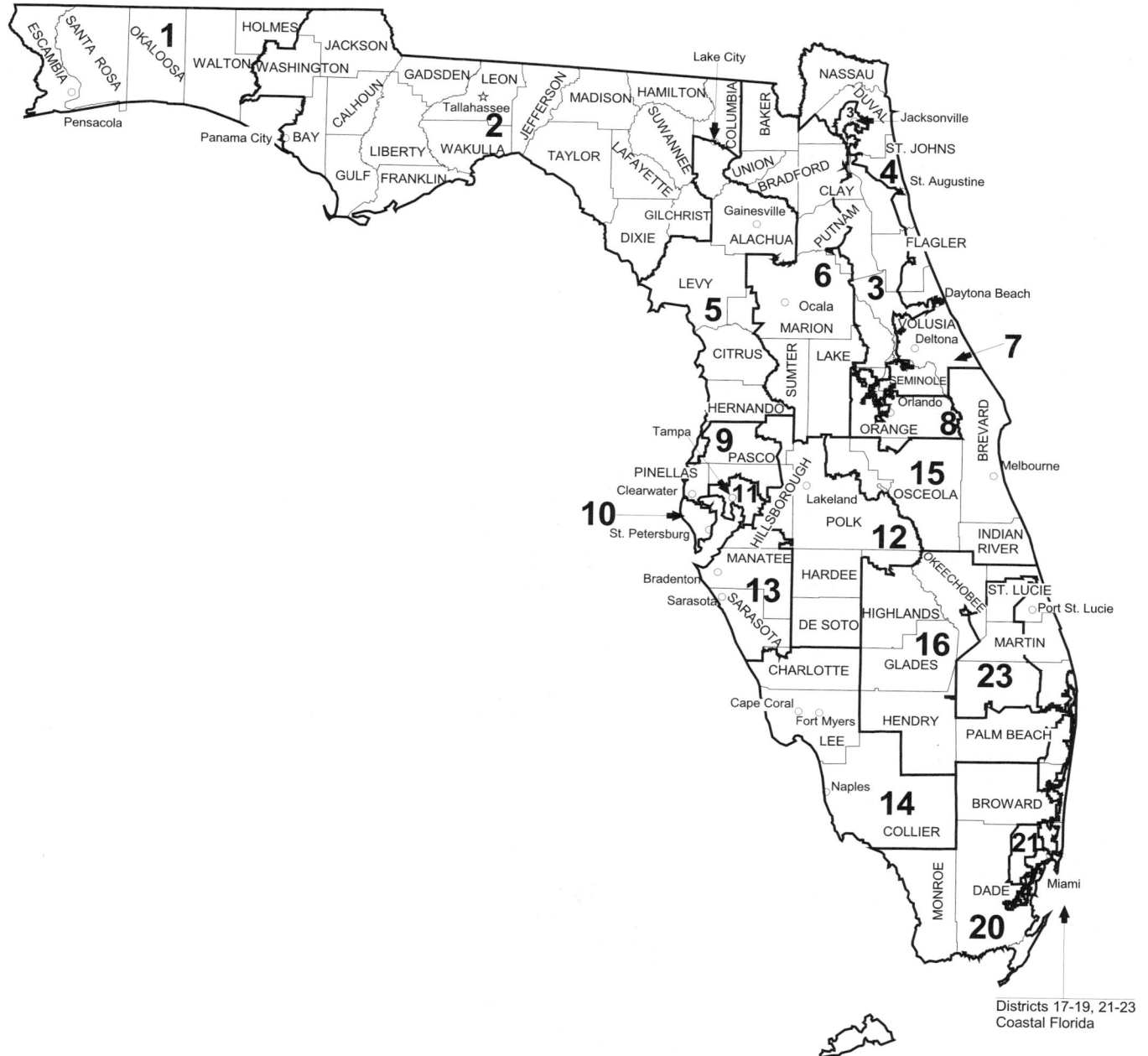

Districts 17-19, 21-23
Coastal Florida

MIAMI GOLD COAST

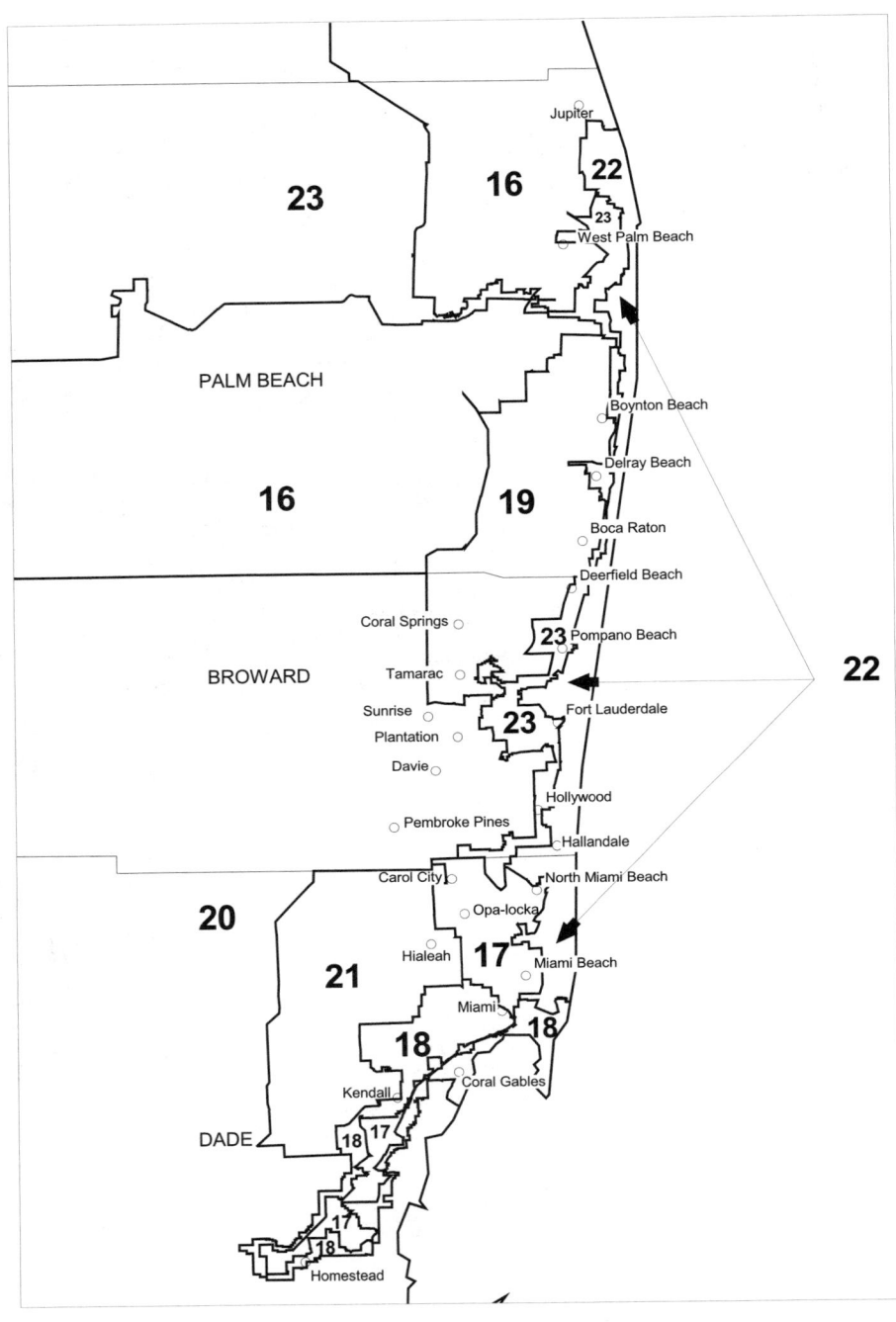

FLORIDA

PRESIDENT 2000

2000 Census Population	County	Total Vote	Republican	Democratic	Green (Nader)	Other	Rep.-Dem. Plurality		Percentage of Total Vote		
									Rep.	Dem.	Green
217,955	ALACHUA	85,729	34,124	47,365	3,226	1,014	13,241	D	39.8%	55.2%	3.8%
22,259	BAKER	8,154	5,610	2,392	53	99	3,218	R	68.8%	29.3%	0.6%
148,217	BAY	58,805	38,637	18,850	828	490	19,787	R	65.7%	32.1%	1.4%
26,088	BRADFORD	8,673	5,414	3,075	84	100	2,339	R	62.4%	35.5%	1.0%
476,230	BREVARD	218,395	115,185	97,318	4,470	1,422	17,867	R	52.7%	44.6%	2.0%
1,623,018	BROWARD	575,143	177,902	387,703	7,104	2,434	209,801	D	30.9%	67.4%	1.2%
13,017	CALHOUN	5,174	2,873	2,155	39	107	718	R	55.5%	41.7%	0.8%
141,627	CHARLOTTE	66,896	35,426	29,645	1,462	363	5,781	R	53.0%	44.3%	2.2%
118,085	CITRUS	57,204	29,767	25,525	1,379	533	4,242	R	52.0%	44.6%	2.4%
140,814	CLAY	57,353	41,736	14,632	562	423	27,104	R	72.8%	25.5%	1.0%
251,377	COLLIER	92,162	60,450	29,921	1,400	391	30,529	R	65.6%	32.5%	1.5%
56,513	COLUMBIA	18,508	10,964	7,047	258	239	3,917	R	59.2%	38.1%	1.4%
2,253,362	DADE	625,449	289,533	328,808	5,352	1,756	39,275	D	46.3%	52.6%	0.9%
32,209	DESOTO	7,811	4,256	3,320	157	78	936	R	54.5%	42.5%	2.0%
13,827	DIXIE	4,666	2,697	1,826	75	68	871	R	57.8%	39.1%	1.6%
778,879	DUVAL	264,636	152,098	107,864	2,757	1,917	44,234	R	57.5%	40.8%	1.0%
294,410	ESCAMBIA	116,648	73,017	40,943	1,727	961	32,074	R	62.6%	35.1%	1.5%
49,832	FLAGLER	27,111	12,613	13,897	435	166	1,284	D	46.5%	51.3%	1.6%
11,057	FRANKLIN	4,644	2,454	2,046	85	59	408	R	52.8%	44.1%	1.8%
45,087	GADSDEN	14,727	4,767	9,735	139	86	4,968	D	32.4%	66.1%	0.9%
14,437	GILCHRIST	5,395	3,300	1,910	97	88	1,390	R	61.2%	35.4%	1.8%
10,576	GLADES	3,365	1,841	1,442	56	26	399	R	54.7%	42.9%	1.7%
13,332	GULF	6,144	3,550	2,397	86	111	1,153	R	57.8%	39.0%	1.4%
13,327	HAMILTON	3,964	2,146	1,722	37	59	424	R	54.1%	43.4%	0.9%
26,938	HARDEE	6,233	3,765	2,339	75	54	1,426	R	60.4%	37.5%	1.2%
36,210	HENDRY	8,139	4,747	3,240	104	48	1,507	R	58.3%	39.8%	1.3%
130,802	HERNANDO	65,219	30,646	32,644	1,501	428	1,998	D	47.0%	50.1%	2.3%
87,366	HIGHLANDS	35,149	20,206	14,167	545	231	6,039	R	57.5%	40.3%	1.6%
998,948	HILLSBOROUGH	360,295	180,760	169,557	7,490	2,488	11,203	R	50.2%	47.1%	2.1%
18,564	HOLMES	7,395	5,011	2,177	94	113	2,834	R	67.8%	29.4%	1.3%
112,947	INDIAN RIVER	49,622	28,635	19,768	950	269	8,867	R	57.7%	39.8%	1.9%
46,755	JACKSON	16,300	9,138	6,868	138	156	2,270	R	56.1%	42.1%	0.8%
12,902	JEFFERSON	5,643	2,478	3,041	76	48	563	D	43.9%	53.9%	1.3%
7,022	LAFAYETTE	2,505	1,670	789	26	20	881	R	66.7%	31.5%	1.0%
210,528	LAKE	88,611	50,010	36,571	1,460	570	13,439	R	56.4%	41.3%	1.6%
440,888	LEE	184,377	106,141	73,560	3,587	1,089	32,581	R	57.6%	39.9%	1.9%
239,452	LEON	103,124	39,062	61,427	1,932	703	22,365	D	37.9%	59.6%	1.9%
34,450	LEVY	12,724	6,858	5,398	284	184	1,460	R	53.9%	42.4%	2.2%
7,021	LIBERTY	2,410	1,317	1,017	19	57	300	R	54.6%	42.2%	0.8%
18,733	MADISON	6,162	3,038	3,014	54	56	24	R	49.3%	48.9%	0.9%
264,002	MANATEE	110,221	57,952	49,177	2,491	601	8,775	R	52.6%	44.6%	2.3%
258,916	MARION	102,956	55,141	44,665	1,809	1,341	10,476	R	53.6%	43.4%	1.8%
126,731	MARTIN	62,013	33,970	26,620	1,118	305	7,350	R	54.8%	42.9%	1.8%
79,589	MONROE	33,887	16,059	16,483	1,090	255	424	D	47.4%	48.6%	3.2%
57,663	NASSAU	23,780	16,404	6,952	253	171	9,452	R	69.0%	29.2%	1.1%
170,498	OKALOOSA	70,680	52,093	16,948	985	654	35,145	R	73.7%	24.0%	1.4%
35,910	OKEECHOBEE	9,853	5,057	4,588	131	77	469	R	51.3%	46.6%	1.3%
896,344	ORANGE	280,125	134,517	140,220	3,879	1,509	5,703	D	48.0%	50.1%	1.4%
172,493	OSCEOLA	55,658	26,212	28,181	732	533	1,969	D	47.1%	50.6%	1.3%
1,131,184	PALM BEACH	433,186	152,951	269,732	5,565	4,938	116,781	D	35.3%	62.3%	1.3%
344,765	PASCO	142,731	68,582	69,564	3,393	1,192	982	D	48.0%	48.7%	2.4%
921,482	PINELLAS	398,472	184,825	200,630	10,022	2,995	15,805	D	46.4%	50.3%	2.5%
483,924	POLK	168,607	90,295	75,200	2,059	1,053	15,095	R	53.6%	44.6%	1.2%
70,423	PUTNAM	26,222	13,447	12,102	377	296	1,345	R	51.3%	46.2%	1.4%
123,135	ST. JOHNS	60,746	39,546	19,502	1,217	481	20,044	R	65.1%	32.1%	2.0%
192,695	ST. LUCIE	77,989	34,705	41,559	1,368	357	6,854	D	44.5%	53.3%	1.8%
117,743	SANTA ROSA	50,319	36,274	12,802	724	519	23,472	R	72.1%	25.4%	1.4%
325,957	SARASOTA	160,942	83,100	72,853	4,069	920	10,247	R	51.6%	45.3%	2.5%
365,196	SEMINOLE	137,634	75,677	59,174	1,946	837	16,503	R	55.0%	43.0%	1.4%
53,345	SUMTER	22,261	12,127	9,637	306	191	2,490	R	54.5%	43.3%	1.4%

FLORIDA

PRESIDENT 2000

2000 Census Population	County	Total Vote	Republican	Democratic	Green (Nader)	Other	Rep.-Dem. Plurality	Percentage of Total Vote		
								Rep.	Dem.	Green
34,844	SUWANNEE	12,457	8,006	4,075	180	196	3,931 R	64.3%	32.7%	1.4%
19,256	TAYLOR	6,808	4,056	2,649	59	44	1,407 R	59.6%	38.9%	0.9%
13,442	UNION	3,826	2,332	1,407	33	54	925 R	61.0%	36.8%	0.9%
443,343	VOLUSIA	183,653	82,357	97,304	2,910	1,082	14,947 D	44.8%	53.0%	1.6%
22,863	WAKULLA	8,587	4,512	3,838	149	88	674 R	52.5%	44.7%	1.7%
40,601	WALTON	18,318	12,182	5,642	265	229	6,540 R	66.5%	30.8%	1.4%
20,973	WASHINGTON	8,025	4,994	2,798	93	140	2,196 R	62.2%	34.9%	1.2%
	Federal Absentees	2,490	1,575	836	62	17	739 R	63.3%	33.6%	2.5%
15,982,378	TOTAL	5,963,110	2,912,790	2,912,253	97,488	40,579	537 R	48.8%	48.8%	1.6%

FLORIDA

SENATOR 2000

2000 Census Population	County	Total Vote	Republican	Democratic	Other	Rep.-Dem. Plurality	Percentage			
							Total Vote		Major Vote	
							Rep.	Dem.	Rep.	Dem.
217,955	ALACHUA	83,013	31,060	49,091	2,862	18,031 D	37.4%	59.1%	38.8%	61.2%
22,259	BAKER	7,840	4,578	3,104	158	1,474 R	58.4%	39.6%	59.6%	40.4%
148,217	BAY	57,886	33,901	22,914	1,071	10,987 R	58.6%	39.6%	59.7%	40.3%
26,088	BRADFORD	9,038	4,699	4,118	221	581 R	52.0%	45.6%	53.3%	46.7%
476,230	BREVARD	214,997	98,813	112,255	3,929	13,442 D	46.0%	52.2%	46.8%	53.2%
1,623,018	BROWARD	565,439	174,902	377,081	13,456	202,179 D	30.9%	66.7%	31.7%	68.3%
13,017	CALHOUN	4,989	2,055	2,809	125	754 D	41.2%	56.3%	42.2%	57.8%
141,627	CHARLOTTE	67,588	37,026	28,947	1,615	8,079 R	54.8%	42.8%	56.1%	43.9%
118,085	CITRUS	56,326	27,057	27,581	1,688	524 D	48.0%	49.0%	49.5%	50.5%
140,814	CLAY	56,406	39,055	16,098	1,253	22,957 R	69.2%	28.5%	70.8%	29.2%
251,377	COLLIER	90,550	60,526	28,211	1,813	32,315 R	66.8%	31.2%	68.2%	31.8%
56,513	COLUMBIA	18,516	9,031	8,942	543	89 R	48.8%	48.3%	50.2%	49.8%
2,253,362	DADE	594,074	264,820	304,893	24,361	40,073 D	44.6%	51.3%	46.5%	53.5%
32,209	DESOTO	7,556	3,736	3,594	226	142 R	49.4%	47.6%	51.0%	49.0%
13,827	DIXIE	4,585	2,007	2,450	128	443 D	43.8%	53.4%	45.0%	55.0%
778,879	DUVAL	274,098	145,930	121,850	6,318	24,080 R	53.2%	44.5%	54.5%	45.5%
294,410	ESCAMBIA	115,931	67,620	45,899	2,412	21,721 R	58.3%	39.6%	59.6%	40.4%
49,832	FLAGLER	26,572	11,988	13,980	604	1,992 D	45.1%	52.6%	46.2%	53.8%
11,057	FRANKLIN	4,641	2,019	2,499	123	480 D	43.5%	53.8%	44.7%	55.3%
45,087	GADSDEN	15,781	4,295	10,722	764	6,427 D	27.2%	67.9%	28.6%	71.4%
14,437	GILCHRIST	5,280	2,561	2,558	161	3 R	48.5%	48.4%	50.0%	50.0%
10,576	GLADES	3,403	1,620	1,649	134	29 D	47.6%	48.5%	49.6%	50.4%
13,332	GULF	6,256	2,739	3,393	124	654 D	43.8%	54.2%	44.7%	55.3%
13,327	HAMILTON	4,034	1,722	2,172	140	450 D	42.7%	53.8%	44.2%	55.8%
26,938	HARDEE	6,178	3,051	2,972	155	79 R	49.4%	48.1%	50.7%	49.3%
36,210	HENDRY	8,498	4,513	3,760	225	753 R	53.1%	44.2%	54.6%	45.4%
130,802	HERNANDO	64,170	29,099	32,916	2,155	3,817 D	45.3%	51.3%	46.9%	53.1%
87,366	HIGHLANDS	34,828	18,934	15,102	792	3,832 R	54.4%	43.4%	55.6%	44.4%
998,948	HILLSBOROUGH	353,517	162,435	179,629	11,453	17,194 D	45.9%	50.8%	47.5%	52.5%
18,564	HOLMES	7,006	3,552	3,201	253	351 R	50.7%	45.7%	52.6%	47.4%
112,947	INDIAN RIVER	49,343	27,223	21,050	1,070	6,173 R	55.2%	42.7%	56.4%	43.6%
46,755	JACKSON	16,556	7,529	8,648	379	1,119 D	45.5%	52.2%	46.5%	53.5%
12,902	JEFFERSON	5,822	2,101	3,513	208	1,412 D	36.1%	60.3%	37.4%	62.6%
7,022	LAFAYETTE	2,537	1,175	1,299	63	124 D	46.3%	51.2%	47.5%	52.5%
210,528	LAKE	89,579	47,361	40,741	1,477	6,620 R	52.9%	45.5%	53.8%	46.2%

FLORIDA

SENATOR 2000

2000 Census Population	County	Total Vote	Republican	Democratic	Other	Rep.-Dem. Plurality		Percentage			
								Total Vote		Major Vote	
								Rep.	Dem.	Rep.	Dem.
440,888	LEE	182,241	107,824	69,308	5,109	38,516	R	59.2%	38.0%	60.9%	39.1%
239,452	LEON	101,005	35,476	61,731	3,798	26,255	D	35.1%	61.1%	36.5%	63.5%
34,450	LEVY	12,854	5,797	6,652	405	855	D	45.1%	51.8%	46.6%	53.4%
7,021	LIBERTY	2,402	948	1,375	79	427	D	39.5%	57.2%	40.8%	59.2%
18,733	MADISON	6,172	2,492	3,528	152	1,036	D	40.4%	57.2%	41.4%	58.6%
264,002	MANATEE	108,361	54,110	51,396	2,855	2,714	R	49.9%	47.4%	51.3%	48.7%
258,916	MARION	101,993	50,896	48,947	2,150	1,949	R	49.9%	48.0%	51.0%	49.0%
126,731	MARTIN	53,169	29,291	22,709	1,169	6,582	R	55.1%	42.7%	56.3%	43.7%
79,589	MONROE	32,242	14,778	16,588	876	1,810	D	45.8%	51.4%	47.1%	52.9%
57,663	NASSAU	23,407	14,413	8,489	505	5,924	R	61.6%	36.3%	62.9%	37.1%
170,498	OKALOOSA	69,108	48,940	18,693	1,475	30,247	R	70.8%	27.0%	72.4%	27.6%
35,910	OKEECHOBEE	10,161	4,410	5,320	431	910	D	43.4%	52.4%	45.3%	54.7%
896,344	ORANGE	265,525	119,673	140,927	4,925	21,254	D	45.1%	53.1%	45.9%	54.1%
172,493	OSCEOLA	55,193	23,856	29,722	1,615	5,866	D	43.2%	53.9%	44.5%	55.5%
1,131,184	PALM BEACH	436,388	154,642	270,452	11,294	115,810	D	35.4%	62.0%	36.4%	63.6%
344,765	PASCO	141,339	63,083	73,344	4,912	10,261	D	44.6%	51.9%	46.2%	53.8%
921,482	PINELLAS	392,482	168,975	208,927	14,580	39,952	D	43.1%	53.2%	44.7%	55.3%
483,924	POLK	166,132	80,004	81,484	4,644	1,480	D	48.2%	49.0%	49.5%	50.5%
70,423	PUTNAM	25,604	11,876	13,124	604	1,248	D	46.4%	51.3%	47.5%	52.5%
123,135	ST. JOHNS	59,597	37,275	20,558	1,764	16,717	R	62.5%	34.5%	64.5%	35.5%
192,695	ST. LUCIE	76,230	33,050	41,082	2,098	8,032	D	43.4%	53.9%	44.6%	55.4%
117,743	SANTA ROSA	49,097	33,684	14,516	897	19,168	R	68.6%	29.6%	69.9%	30.1%
325,957	SARASOTA	156,492	80,641	71,434	4,417	9,207	R	51.5%	45.6%	53.0%	47.0%
365,196	SEMINOLE	135,311	69,865	63,037	2,409	6,828	R	51.6%	46.6%	52.6%	47.4%
53,345	SUMTER	22,129	11,384	10,271	474	1,113	R	51.4%	46.4%	52.6%	47.4%
34,844	SUWANNEE	12,649	6,789	5,528	332	1,261	R	53.7%	43.7%	55.1%	44.9%
19,256	TAYLOR	7,061	3,405	3,454	202	49	D	48.2%	48.9%	49.6%	50.4%
13,442	UNION	3,813	1,827	1,915	71	88	D	47.9%	50.2%	48.8%	51.2%
443,343	VOLUSIA	179,635	76,207	99,267	4,161	23,060	D	42.4%	55.3%	43.4%	56.6%
22,863	WAKULLA	8,536	3,778	4,496	262	718	D	44.3%	52.7%	45.7%	54.3%
40,601	WALTON	17,700	10,299	6,854	547	3,445	R	58.2%	38.7%	60.0%	40.0%
20,973	WASHINGTON	7,902	3,672	4,071	159	399	D	46.5%	51.5%	47.4%	52.6%
	Federal Absentees	1,968	1,255	647	66	608	R	63.8%	32.9%	66.0%	34.0%
15,982,378	TOTAL	5,856,731	2,705,348	2,989,487	161,896	284,139	D	46.2%	51.0%	47.5%	52.5%

FLORIDA

CONGRESS

CD	Year	Total Vote	Republican		Democratic		Other Vote	Rep.-Dem. Plurality		Percentage			
			Vote	Candidate	Vote	Candidate				Total Vote		Major Vote	
										Rep.	Dem.	Rep.	Dem.
1	2000	227,539	226,473	SCARBOROUGH, JOE			1,066	226,473	R	99.5%		100.0%	
1	1998	141,188	140,525	SCARBOROUGH, JOE			663	140,525	R	99.5%		100.0%	
1	1996	242,545	175,946	SCARBOROUGH, JOE	66,495	BECK, KEVIN	104	109,451	R	72.5%	27.4%	72.6%	27.4%
1	1994	183,420	112,901	SCARBOROUGH, JOE	70,389	WHIBBS, VINCE	130	42,512	R	61.6%	38.4%	61.6%	38.4%
1	1992	228,632	100,349	KETCHEL, TERRY	118,941	HUTTO, EARL D.	9,342	18,592	D	43.9%	52.0%	45.8%	54.2%
2	2000	257,403	71,754	DODD, DOUG	185,579	BOYD, ALLEN	70	113,825	D	27.9%	72.1%	27.9%	72.1%
2	1998	145,420			138,440	BOYD, ALLEN	6,980	138,440	D		95.2%		100.0%
2	1996	232,400	94,122	SUTTON, BILL	138,151	BOYD, ALLEN	127	44,029	D	40.5%	59.4%	40.5%	59.5%
3	2000	177,372	75,228	CARROLL, JENNIFER S.	102,143	BROWN, CORRINE	1	26,915	D	42.4%	57.6%	42.4%	57.6%
3	1998	120,151	53,530	RANDALL, BILL	66,621	BROWN, CORRINE		13,091	D	44.6%	55.4%	44.6%	55.4%
3	1996	160,281	62,196	FIELDS, PRESTON JAMES	98,085	BROWN, CORRINE		35,889	D	38.8%	61.2%	38.8%	61.2%

FLORIDA

CONGRESS

CD	Year	Total Vote	Republican		Democratic		Other Vote	Rep.-Dem. Plurality	Percentage			
									Total Vote		Major Vote	
			Vote	Candidate	Vote	Candidate			Rep.	Dem.	Rep.	Dem.
4	2000	303,286	203,090	CRENSHAW, ANDER	94,587	SULLIVAN, TOM	5,609	108,503 R	67.0%	31.2%	68.2%	31.8%
4	1998			FOWLER, TILLIE				R				
4	1996			FOWLER, TILLIE				R				
5	2000	280,598	100,244	ENWALL, PETE	180,338	THURMAN, KAREN L.	16	80,094 D	35.7%	64.3%	35.7%	64.3%
5	1998	199,152			132,005	THURMAN, KAREN L.	67,147	132,005 D		66.3%		100.0%
5	1996	261,101	100,051	GENTRY, DAVE	161,050	THURMAN, KAREN L.		60,999 D	38.3%	61.7%	38.3%	61.7%
6	2000	178,972	178,789	STEARNS, CLIFFORD B.			183	178,789 R	99.9%		100.0%	
6	1998			STEARNS, CLIFFORD B.				R				
6	1996	240,442	161,527	STEARNS, CLIFFORD B.	78,908	O'BRIEN, NEWELL	7	82,619 R	67.2%	32.8%	67.2%	32.8%
7	2000	270,560	171,018	MICA, JOHN L.	99,531	VAUGHEN, DAN	11	71,487 R	63.2%	36.8%	63.2%	36.8%
7	1998			MICA, JOHN L.				R				
7	1996	231,557	143,667	MICA, JOHN L.	87,832	STUART, GEORGE JR.	58	55,835 R	62.0%	37.9%	62.1%	37.9%
7	1994	179,458	131,711	MICA, JOHN L.	47,747	GODDARD, EDWARD D.		83,964 R	73.4%	26.6%	73.4%	26.6%
7	1992	223,023	125,823	MICA, JOHN L.	96,945	WEBSTER, DAN	255	28,878 R	56.4%	43.5%	56.5%	43.5%
8	2000	246,593	125,253	KELLER, RIC	121,295	CHAPIN, LINDA W.	45	3,958 R	50.8%	49.2%	50.8%	49.2%
8	1998	158,575	104,298	MCCOLLUM, BILL	54,245	KRULICK, AL	32	50,053 R	65.8%	34.2%	65.8%	34.2%
8	1996	202,326	136,515	MCCOLLUM, BILL	65,794	KRULICK, AL	17	70,721 R	67.5%	32.5%	67.5%	32.5%
8	1994	131,815	131,376	MCCOLLUM, BILL			439	131,376 R	99.7%		100.0%	
8	1992	207,122	141,977	MCCOLLUM, BILL	65,145	KOVALESKI, CHUCK		76,832 R	68.5%	31.5%	68.5%	31.5%
9	2000	256,794	210,318	BILIRAKIS, MICHAEL			46,476	210,318 R	81.9%		100.0%	
9	1998			BILIRAKIS, MICHAEL				R				
9	1996	235,517	161,708	BILIRAKIS, MICHAEL	73,809	PROVENZANO, JERRY		87,899 R	68.7%	31.3%	68.7%	31.3%
9	1994	177,405	177,253	BILIRAKIS, MICHAEL			152	177,253 R	99.9%		100.0%	
9	1992	268,163	158,028	BILIRAKIS, MICHAEL	110,135	KNAPP, CHERYL D.		47,893 R	58.9%	41.1%	58.9%	41.1%
10	2000	194,003	146,799	YOUNG, C. W.			47,204	146,799 R	75.7%		100.0%	
10	1998			YOUNG, C. W.				R				
10	1996	171,820	114,443	YOUNG, C. W.	57,375	GREEN, HENRY	2	57,068 R	66.6%	33.4%	66.6%	33.4%
10	1994			YOUNG, C. W.				R				
10	1992	264,415	149,606	YOUNG, C. W.	114,809	MOFFITT, KAREN		34,797 R	56.6%	43.4%	56.6%	43.4%
11	2000	176,683			149,465	DAVIS, JIM	27,218	149,465 D		84.6%		100.0%
11	1998	131,438	46,176	CHILLURA, JOE	85,262	DAVIS, JIM		39,086 D	35.1%	64.9%	35.1%	64.9%
11	1996	187,403	78,881	SHARPE, MARK	108,522	DAVIS, JIM		29,641 D	42.1%	57.9%	42.1%	57.9%
11	1994	148,942	72,119	SHARPE, MARK	76,814	GIBBONS, SAM M.	9	4,695 D	48.4%	51.6%	48.4%	51.6%
11	1992	191,354	77,640	SHARPE, MARK	100,984	GIBBONS, SAM M.	12,730	23,344 D	40.6%	52.8%	43.5%	56.5%
12	2000	219,625	125,224	PUTNAM, ADAM H.	94,395	STEDEM, MIKE	6	30,829 R	57.0%	43.0%	57.0%	43.0%
12	1998			CANADY, CHARLES T.				R				
12	1996	199,097	122,584	CANADY, CHARLES T.	76,513	CANADY, MIKE		46,071 R	61.6%	38.4%	61.6%	38.4%
12	1994	163,326	106,123	CANADY, CHARLES T.	57,203	CONNORS, ROBERT		48,920 R	65.0%	35.0%	65.0%	35.0%
12	1992	192,830	100,484	CANADY, CHARLES T.	92,346	MIMS, TOM		8,138 R	52.1%	47.9%	52.1%	47.9%
13	2000	275,587	175,918	MILLER, DAN	99,568	DUNN, DANIEL E.	101	76,350 R	63.8%	36.1%	63.9%	36.1%
13	1998			MILLER, DAN				R				
13	1996	269,904	173,671	MILLER, DAN	96,098	GORDON, SANFORD	135	77,573 R	64.3%	35.6%	64.4%	35.6%
13	1994			MILLER, DAN				R				
13	1992	274,648	158,881	MILLER, DAN	115,767	SNELL, RAND		43,114 R	57.8%	42.2%	57.8%	42.2%
14	2000	284,615	242,614	GOSS, PORTER J.			42,001	242,614 R	85.2%		100.0%	
14	1998			GOSS, PORTER J.				R				
14	1996	240,834	176,992	GOSS, PORTER J.	63,842	NOLAN, JIM		113,150 R	73.5%	26.5%	73.5%	26.5%
14	1994			GOSS, PORTER J.				R				
14	1992	268,511	220,351	GOSS, PORTER J.			48,160	220,351 R	82.1%		100.0%	

FLORIDA

CONGRESS

CD	Year	Total Vote	Republican Vote	Republican Candidate	Democratic Vote	Democratic Candidate	Other Vote	Rep.-Dem. Plurality	Total Vote Rep.	Total Vote Dem.	Major Vote Rep.	Major Vote Dem.
15	2000	299,445	176,189	WELDON, DAVE	117,511	KURTH, PATSY ANN	5,745	58,678 R	58.8%	39.2%	60.0%	40.0%
15	1998	204,932	129,278	WELDON, DAVE	75,654	GOLDING, DAVID R.		53,624 R	63.1%	36.9%	63.1%	36.9%
15	1996	270,350	139,014	WELDON, DAVE	115,981	BYRON, JOHN L.	15,355	23,033 R	51.4%	42.9%	54.5%	45.5%
15	1994	217,872	117,027	WELDON, DAVE	100,513	MUNSEY, SUE	332	16,514 R	53.7%	46.1%	53.8%	46.2%
15	1992	261,285	128,873	TOLLEY, BILL	132,412	BACCHUS, JIM		3,539 D	49.3%	50.7%	49.3%	50.7%
16	2000	292,500	176,153	FOLEY, MARK	108,782	BROWN, JEAN ELLIOTT	7,565	67,371 R	60.2%	37.2%	61.8%	38.2%
16	1998			FOLEY, MARK				R				
16	1996	274,541	175,714	FOLEY, MARK	98,827	STUBER, JIM		76,887 R	64.0%	36.0%	64.0%	36.0%
16	1994	211,380	122,734	FOLEY, MARK	88,646	COMERFORD, JOHN P.		34,088 R	58.1%	41.9%	58.1%	41.9%
16	1992	258,559	157,322	LEWIS, TOM	101,237	COMERFORD, JOHN P.		56,085 R	60.8%	39.2%	60.8%	39.2%
17	2000	100,718			100,715	MEEK, CARRIE P.	3	100,715 D		100.0%		100.0%
17	1998					MEEK, CARRIE P.		D				
17	1996	129,165	14,525	ROLLE, WELLINGTON	114,638	MEEK, CARRIE P.	2	100,113 D	11.2%	88.8%	11.2%	88.8%
17	1994	75,752			75,741	MEEK, CARRIE P.	11	75,741 D				
17	1992	102,799			102,784	MEEK, CARRIE P.	15	102,784 D				
18	2000	112,991	112,968	ROS-LEHTINEN, ILEANA			23	112,968 R	100.0%		100.0%	
18	1998			ROS-LEHTINEN, ILEANA				R				
18	1996	123,665	123,659	ROS-LEHTINEN, ILEANA			6	123,659 R	100.0%		100.0%	
18	1994			ROS-LEHTINEN, ILEANA				R				
18	1992	156,897	104,755	ROS-LEHTINEN, ILEANA	52,142	DAVIS, MAGDA M.		52,613 R	66.8%	33.2%	66.8%	33.2%
19	2000	238,869	67,789	THOMPSON, MORRIS KENT	171,080	WEXLER, ROBERT		103,291 D	28.4%	71.6%	28.4%	71.6%
19	1998					WEXLER, ROBERT		D				
19	1996	287,867	99,101	KENNEDY, BEVERLY	188,766	WEXLER, ROBERT		89,665 D	34.4%	65.6%	34.4%	65.6%
19	1994	223,370	75,779	TSAKANIKAS, PETER J.	147,591	JOHNSTON, HARRY		71,812 D	33.9%	66.1%	33.9%	66.1%
19	1992	281,294	103,867	METZ, LARRY	177,423	JOHNSTON, HARRY	4	73,556 D	36.9%	63.1%	36.9%	63.1%
20	2000	156,952			156,765	DEUTSCH, PETER	187	156,765 D		99.9%		100.0%
20	1998					DEUTSCH, PETER		D				
20	1996	245,033	85,777	JACOBS, JIM	159,256	DEUTSCH, PETER		73,479 D	35.0%	65.0%	35.0%	65.0%
20	1994	187,131	72,516	KENNEDY, BEVERLY	114,615	DEUTSCH, PETER		42,099 D	38.8%	61.2%	38.8%	61.2%
20	1992	237,889	91,589	KENNEDY, BEVERLY	130,959	DEUTSCH, PETER	15,341	39,370 D	38.5%	55.1%	41.2%	58.8%
21	2000	132,342	132,317	DIAZ-BALART, LINCOLN			25	132,317 R	100.0%		100.0%	
21	1998	112,396	84,018	DIAZ-BALART, LINCOLN	28,378	CUSACK, PATRICK		55,640 R	74.8%	25.2%	74.8%	25.2%
21	1996	125,473	125,469	DIAZ-BALART, LINCOLN			4	125,469 R	100.0%		100.0%	
21	1994	90,950	90,948	DIAZ-BALART, LINCOLN			2	90,948 R				
21	1992			DIAZ-BALART, LINCOLN				R				
22	2000	211,112	105,855	SHAW, CLAY	105,256	BLOOM, ELAINE	1	599 R	50.1%	49.9%	50.1%	49.9%
22	1998			SHAW, CLAY				R				
22	1996	221,618	137,098	SHAW, CLAY	84,517	COOPER, KENNETH D.	3	52,581 R	61.9%	38.1%	61.9%	38.1%
22	1994	188,905	119,690	SHAW, CLAY	69,215	WIENER, HERMINE L.		R	63.4%	36.6%	63.4%	36.6%
22	1992	247,088	128,400	SHAW, CLAY	91,625	MARGOLIS, GWEN	27,063	36,775 R	52.0%	37.1%	58.4%	41.6%
23	2000	116,813	27,630	LAMBERT, BILL	89,179	HASTINGS, ALCEE L.	4	61,549 D	23.7%	76.3%	23.7%	76.3%
23	1998					HASTINGS, ALCEE L.		D				
23	1996	139,089	36,907	BROWN, ROBERT PAUL	102,161	HASTINGS, ALCEE L.	21	65,254 D	26.5%	73.5%	26.5%	73.5%
23	1994					HASTINGS, ALCEE L.		D				
23	1992	143,935	44,807	FIELDING, ED	84,249	HASTINGS, ALCEE L.	14,879	39,442 D	31.1%	58.5%	34.7%	65.3%

NOTE: The lines for five Florida congressional districts were changed following legal challenges to the configurations used in 1992 and 1994. For those districts, election results for the earlier years are not included because the districts were not comparable. Results for those years may be found in *America Votes 21* (the edition for the 1994 elections).

FLORIDA
GENERAL AND PRIMARY ELECTIONS

2000 GENERAL ELECTIONS

President Other vote was 17,484 Reform (Buchanan); 16,415 Libertarian (Browne); 2,281 Natural Law (Hagelin); 1,804 Workers World (Moorehead); 1,371 Constitution (Phillips); 622 Socialist (McReynolds); 562 Socialist Workers (Harris); 34 write-in (Chote); 6 write-in (McCarthy).

Senator Other vote was 80,830 Independent (Logan); 26,087 Natural Law (Simonetta); 21,664 Independent (McCormick); 17,338 Reform (Deckard); 15,889 Independent (Martin); 36 write-in (Grayson); 29 write-in ("Nikki O."); 9 write-in (Malapanis); 8 write-in (Faulk); 6 write-in (Heady).

Congress Other vote was: CD 1: 376 write-in (Coutu), 311 write-in (Hoole), 192 write-in (Wiley), 187 write-in (Blue); CD 2: 70 write-in (Frederick); CD 3: 1 write-in (Sumner); CD 4: 5,609 Independent (Pueschel); CD 5: 16 write-in (Johnson); CD 6: 152 write-in (Clower), 31 write-in (Elliott); CD 7: 11 write-in (Nelson); CD 8: 39 write-in (Klein), 6 write-in (Hill); CD 9: 46,474 Reform (Duffey), 2 write-in (Ospina); CD 10: 26,908 Natural Law (Green), 20,296 Independent (Heine); CD 11: 27,197 Libertarian (Westlake), 21 write-in (Sauer); CD 12: 3 write-in (Harrison), 3 write-in (Kennedy); CD 13: 101 write-in (Vecchio); CD 14: 41,988 Natural Law (Farling), 13 write-in (Saylor); CD 15: 5,744 Independent (Newby), 1 write-in (Winsor); CD 16: 7,556 Reform (McGuire), 9 write-in (Bitowft); CD 17: 3 write-in (Barchers); CD 18: 23 write-in (Mullins); CD 20: 187 write-in (Kopanski); CD 21: 25 write-in (Maurer); CD 22: 1 write-in (Opperman); CD 23: 4 write-in (Faulk).

2000 PRIMARY ELECTIONS

Primary March 14, 2000 (President)
September 5, 2000 (Congress)

Primary Runoff October 3, 2000 (Congress)

Registration
(as of Aug. 7, 2000)

Republican	3,327,688
Democratic	3,673,844
Independent Party	139,235
Libertarian	8,603
Reform	4,577
Green	1,676
Other Parties	2,189
No Party Affiliation	1,258,064
TOTAL	8,415,876

Primary Type Closed—Only registered Democrats and Republicans could vote in their party's primary, with the exception of races where there were to be no other candidates (including write-ins) on the general election ballot. Then, the contested primary would be open to all voters. This exception, though, was not triggered in either the presidential or congressional primaries in 2000.

Note: An asterisk (*) denotes incumbent. The names of unopposed candidates do not appear on the primary ballot; therefore, no votes are cast for these candidates.

	REPUBLICAN PRIMARIES			DEMOCRATIC PRIMARIES		
President	George W. Bush	516,263	73.8%	Al Gore	451,718	81.8%
	John McCain	139,465	19.9%	Bill Bradley	100,277	18.2%
	Alan Keyes	32,354	4.6%			
	Steve Forbes	6,553	0.9%			
	Gary Bauer	3,496	0.5%			
	Orrin G. Hatch	1,372	0.2%			
	TOTAL	699,503		TOTAL	551,995	
Senator	Bill McCollum	660,592	81.1%	Bill Nelson	692,147	77.5%
	Hamilton A. S. Bartlett	153,613	18.9%	Newall Jerome Daughtrey	105,650	11.8%
				David B. Higginbottom	95,492	10.7%
	TOTAL	814,205		TOTAL	893,289	
Congressional District 1	Joe Scarborough*	54,032	77.4%	No Democratic candidate		
	Bob Condon	15,808	22.6%			
	TOTAL	69,840				

FLORIDA

GENERAL AND PRIMARY ELECTIONS

	REPUBLICAN PRIMARIES			DEMOCRATIC PRIMARIES		
Congressional District 2	Doug Dodd	Unopposed		Allen Boyd*	Unopposed	
Congressional District 3	Jennifer S. Carroll	Unopposed		Corrine Brown*	Unopposed	
Congressional District 4	Ander Crenshaw Dan Quiggle TOTAL	47,588 20,816 68,404	69.6% 30.4%	Tom Sullivan Kevin Schaun Sanders TOTAL	29,009 17,652 46,661	62.2% 37.8%
Congressional District 5	Pete Enwall Jim King TOTAL	19,405 18,375 37,780	51.4% 48.6%	Karen L. Thurman*	Unopposed	
Congressional District 6	Clifford B. Stearns*	Unopposed		No Democratic candidate		
Congressional District 7	John L. Mica*	Unopposed		Dan Vaughen	Unopposed	
Congressional District 8	Bill Sublette Ric Keller Bob Hering TOTAL **PRIMARY RUNOFF** Ric Keller Bill Sublette TOTAL	18,196 12,981 10,736 41,913 16,292 15,077 31,369	43.4% 31.0% 25.6% 51.9% 48.1%	Linda W. Chapin	Unopposed	
Congressional District 9	Michael Bilirakis*	Unopposed		No Democratic candidate		
Congressional District 10	C. W. Bill Young*	Unopposed		No Democratic candidate		
Congressional District 11	No Republican candidate			Jim Davis*	Unopposed	
Congressional District 12	Adam H. Putnam	Unopposed		Mike Stedem	Unopposed	
Congressional District 13	Dan Miller*	Unopposed		Daniel E. Dunn Robert Salzberg TOTAL	19,100 6,777 25,877	73.8% 26.2%
Congressional District 14	Porter J. Goss*	Unopposed		No Democratic candidate		
Congressional District 15	Dave Weldon*	Unopposed		Patsy Ann Kurth	Unopposed	
Congressional District 16	Mark Foley*	Unopposed		Jean Elliott Brown	Unopposed	
Congressional District 17	No Republican candidate			Carrie P. Meek*	Unopposed	
Congressional District 18	Ileana Ros-Lehtinen*	Unopposed		No Democratic candidate		
Congressional District 19	Morris Kent Thompson	Unopposed		Robert Wexler*	Unopposed	
Congressional District 20	No Republican candidate			Peter Deutsch*	Unopposed	
Congressional District 21	Lincoln Diaz-Balart*	Unopposed		No Democratic candidate		
Congressional District 22	Clay Shaw*	Unopposed		Elaine Bloom	Unopposed	
Congressional District 23	Bill Lambert	Unopposed		Alcee L. Hastings*	Unopposed	

GEORGIA

GOVERNOR

Roy Barnes (D). Elected 1998 to a four-year term.

SENATORS

Zell Miller (D). Elected 2000 to complete the term of Paul Coverdell (R), who died in July 2000. Miller previously elected governor.

Max Cleland (D). Elected 1996 to a six-year term.

REPRESENTATIVES

1. Jack Kingston (R)
2. Sanford Bishop (D)
3. Mac Collins (R)
4. Cynthia McKinney (D)
5. John Lewis (D)
6. Johnny Isakson (R)**
7. Bob Barr (R)
8. Saxby Chambliss (R)
9. Nathan Deal (R)
10. Charlie Norwood (R)
11. John Linder (R)

Johnny Isakson (R) was elected in a special election Feb. 23, 1999, to fill the two-year term vacated when Newt Gingrich (R) resigned.

POSTWAR VOTE FOR PRESIDENT

		Republican		Democratic		Other		Total Vote		Major Vote	
Year	Total Vote	Vote	Candidate	Vote	Candidate	Vote	Plurality	Rep.	Dem.	Rep.	Dem.
2000**	2,596,645	1,419,720	Bush, George W.	1,116,230	Gore, Al	60,695	303,490 R	54.7%	43.0%	56.0%	44.0%
1996**	2,299,071	1,080,843	Dole, Bob	1,053,849	Clinton, Bill	164,379	26,994 R	47.0%	45.8%	50.6%	49.4%
1992**	2,321,125	995,252	Bush, George	1,008,966	Clinton, Bill	316,907	13,714 D	42.9%	43.5%	49.7%	50.3%
1988	1,809,672	1,081,331	Bush, George	714,792	Dukakis, Michael S.	13,549	366,539 R	59.8%	39.5%	60.2%	39.8%
1984	1,776,120	1,068,722	Reagan, Ronald	706,628	Mondale, Walter F.	770	362,094 R	60.2%	39.8%	60.2%	39.8%
1980**	1,596,695	654,168	Reagan, Ronald	890,733	Carter, Jimmy	51,794	236,565 D	41.0%	55.8%	42.3%	57.7%
1976	1,467,458	483,743	Ford, Gerald R.	979,409	Carter, Jimmy	4,306	495,666 D	33.0%	66.7%	33.1%	66.9%
1972	1,174,772	881,496	Nixon, Richard M.	289,529	McGovern, George S.	3,747	591,967 R	75.0%	24.6%	75.3%	24.7%
1968**	1,250,266	380,111	Nixon, Richard M.	334,440	Humphrey, Hubert H.	535,715	155,439 A	30.4%	26.7%	53.2%	46.8%
1964	1,139,335	616,584	Goldwater, Barry M.	522,556	Johnson, Lyndon B.	195	94,028 R	54.1%	45.9%	54.1%	45.9%
1960	733,349	274,472	Nixon, Richard M.	458,638	Kennedy, John F.	239	184,166 D	37.4%	62.5%	37.4%	62.6%
1956	669,655	222,778	Eisenhower, Dwight D.	444,688	Stevenson, Adlai E.	2,189	221,910 D	33.3%	66.4%	33.4%	66.6%
1952	655,785	198,961	Eisenhower, Dwight D.	456,823	Stevenson, Adlai E.	1	257,862 D	30.3%	69.7%	30.3%	69.7%
1948**	418,844	76,691	Dewey, Thomas E.	254,646	Truman, Harry S.	87,507	169,511 D	18.3%	60.8%	23.1%	76.9%

In 2000 the other vote column includes 13,273 votes cast for Green (Nader). In 1996 the other vote column includes 146,337 votes cast for Perot. In 1992 the other vote column includes 309,657 votes cast for Perot. In 1980 the other column includes 36,055 votes for Independent (Anderson). In 1968 other vote was 535,550 American (Wallace) and 165 scattered. In 1948 other vote was 85,135 States Rights; 1,636 Progressive; 732 Prohibition; 3 Socialist and 1 scattered.

GEORGIA

POSTWAR VOTE FOR GOVERNOR

Year	Total Vote	Republican		Democratic		Other Vote	Rep.-Dem. Plurality	Percentage			
		Vote	Candidate	Vote	Candidate			Total Vote		Major Vote	
								Rep.	Dem.	Rep.	Dem.
1998	1,792,808	790,201	Millner, Guy	941,076	Barnes, Roy E.	61,531	150,875 D	44.1%	52.5%	45.6%	54.4%
1994	1,545,328	756,371	Millner, Guy	788,926	Miller, Zell	31	32,555 D	48.9%	51.1%	48.9%	51.1%
1990	1,449,682	645,625	Isakson, Johnny	766,662	Miller, Zell	37,395	121,037 D	44.5%	52.9%	45.7%	54.3%
1986	1,175,114	346,512	Davis, Guy	828,465	Harris, Joe Frank	137	481,953 D	29.5%	70.5%	29.5%	70.5%
1982	1,169,041	434,496	Bell, Robert H.	734,090	Harris, Joe Frank	455	299,594 D	37.2%	62.8%	37.2%	62.8%
1978	662,862	128,139	Cook, Rodney M.	534,572	Busbee, George	151	406,433 D	19.3%	80.6%	19.3%	80.7%
1974	936,438	289,113	Thompson, Ronnie	646,777	Busbee, George	548	357,664 D	30.9%	69.1%	30.9%	69.1%
1970	1,046,663	424,983	Suit, Hal	620,419	Carter, Jimmy	1,261	195,436 D	40.6%	59.3%	40.7%	59.3%
1966**	975,019	453,665	Callaway, Howard H.	450,626	Maddox, Lester	70,728	3,039 R	46.5%	46.2%	50.2%	49.8%
1962	311,691		—	311,524	Sanders, Carl E.	167	311,524 D		99.9%		100.0%
1958	168,497		—	168,414	Vandiver, Ernest	83	168,414 D		100.0%		100.0%
1954	331,966		—	331,899	Griffin, Marvin	67	331,899 D		100.0%		100.0%
1950	234,430		—	230,771	Talmadge, Herman	3,659	230,771 D		98.4%		100.0%
1948S	363,763		—	354,711	Talmadge, Herman	9,052	354,711 D		97.5%		100.0%
1946	145,403		—	143,279	Talmadge, Herman	2,124	143,279 D		98.5%		100.0%

In 1966 in the absence of a majority for any candidate, the State Legislature elected Lester Maddox to a four-year term. The 1948 election was for a short term to fill a vacancy.

POSTWAR VOTE FOR SENATOR

Year	Total Vote	Republican		Democratic		Other Vote	Rep.-Dem. Plurality	Percentage			
		Vote	Candidate	Vote	Candidate			Total Vote		Major Vote	
								Rep.	Dem.	Rep.	Dem.
2000S	2,428,510	920,478	Mattingly, Mack	1,413,224	Miller, Zell	94,808	492,746 D	37.9%	58.2%	39.4%	60.6%
1998	1,753,911	918,540	Coverdell, Paul	791,904	Coles, Michael	43,467	126,636 R	52.4%	45.2%	53.7%	46.3%
1996	2,259,232	1,073,969	Millner, Guy	1,103,993	Cleland, Max	81,270	30,024 D	47.5%	48.9%	49.3%	50.7%
1992**	1,253,991	635,114	Coverdell, Paul	618,877	Fowler, Wyche		16,237 R	50.6%	49.4%	50.6%	49.4%
1990	1,033,517		—	1,033,439	Nunn, Sam	78	1,033,439 D		100.0%		100.0%
1986	1,225,008	601,241	Mattingly, Mack	623,707	Fowler, Wyche	60	22,466 D	49.1%	50.9%	49.1%	50.9%
1984	1,681,344	337,196	Hicks, Jon Michael	1,344,104	Nunn, Sam	44	1,006,908 D	20.1%	79.9%	20.1%	79.9%
1980	1,580,340	803,686	Mattingly, Mack	776,143	Talmadge, Herman	511	27,543 R	50.9%	49.1%	50.9%	49.1%
1978	645,164	108,808	Stokes, John W.	536,320	Nunn, Sam	36	427,512 D	16.9%	83.1%	16.9%	83.1%
1974	874,555	246,866	Johnson, Jerry R.	627,376	Talmadge, Herman	313	380,510 D	28.2%	71.7%	28.2%	71.8%
1972	1,178,708	542,331	Thompson, Fletcher	635,970	Nunn, Sam	407	93,639 D	46.0%	54.0%	46.0%	54.0%
1968	1,141,889	256,796	Patton, E. Earl	885,093	Talmadge, Herman		628,297 D	22.5%	77.5%	22.5%	77.5%
1966	622,371		—	622,043	Russell, Richard B.	328	622,043 D		99.9%		100.0%
1962	306,250		—	306,250	Talmadge, Herman		306,250 D		100.0%		100.0%
1960	576,495		—	576,140	Russell, Richard B.	355	576,140 D		99.9%		100.0%
1956	541,267		—	541,094	Talmadge, Herman	173	541,094 D		100.0%		100.0%
1954	333,936		—	333,917	Russell, Richard B.	19	333,917 D		100.0%		100.0%
1950	261,293		—	261,290	George, Walter F.	3	261,290 D		100.0%		100.0%
1948	362,504		—	362,104	Russell, Richard B.	400	362,104 D		99.9%		100.0%

The 2000 election was for a short term to fill a vacancy. In 1992 the figures in the table are for the runoff election held November 24 as no candidate received a majority of the vote in the November 3 General Election. The vote in the November 3 election was 1,073,282 (47.7%) Republican (Coverdell); 1,108,416 (49.2%) Democratic (Fowler) and 69,889 (3.1%) other.

GEORGIA

Districts Established December 13, 1995

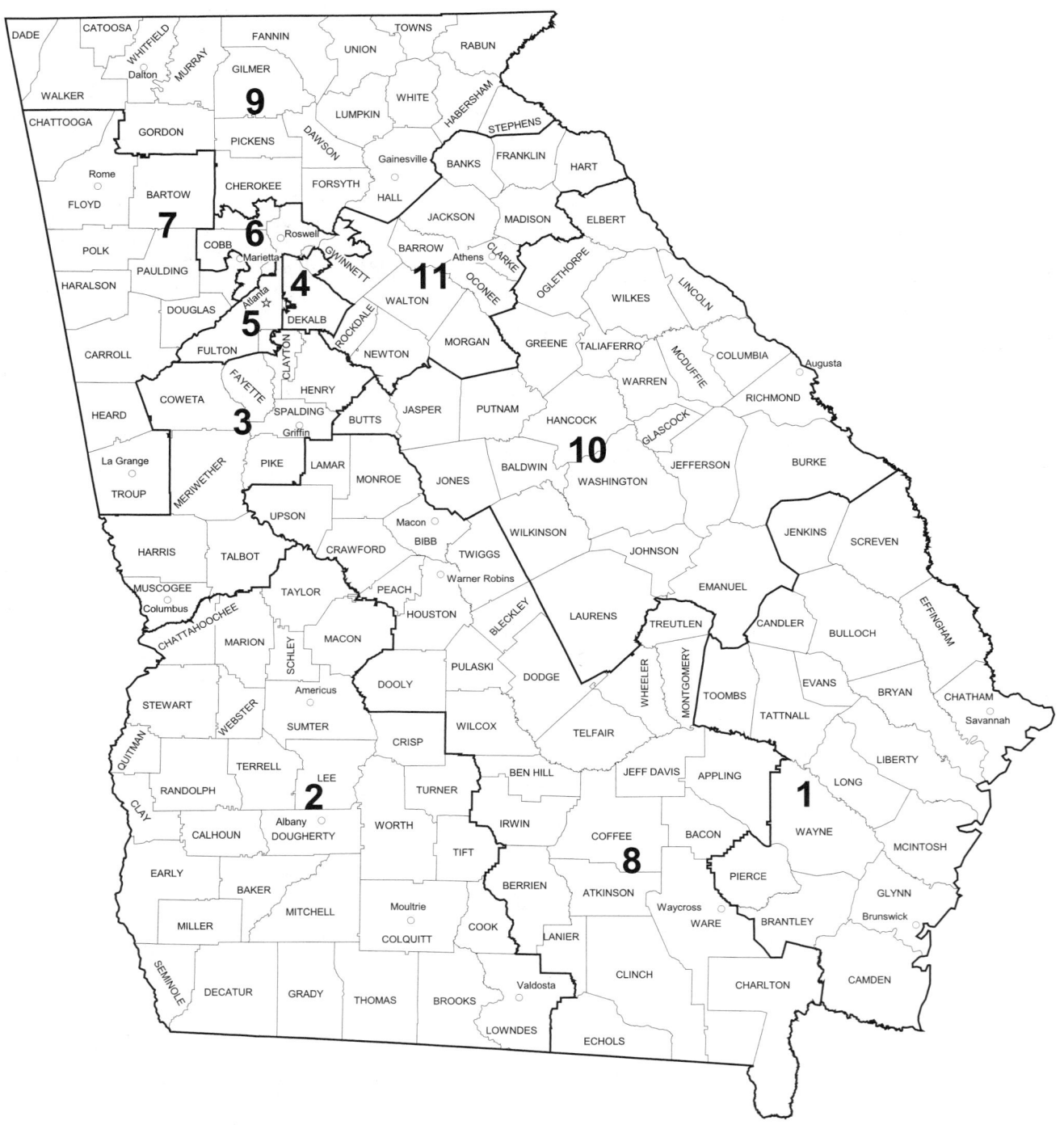

GEORGIA

PRESIDENT 2000

2000 Census Population	County	Total Vote	Republican	Democratic	Green (Nader)	Other	Rep.-Dem. Plurality	Percentage of Total Vote Rep.	Dem.	Green
17,419	APPLING	6,099	3,940	2,093	2	64	1,847 R	64.6%	34.3%	
7,609	ATKINSON	2,071	1,228	821	1	21	407 R	59.3%	39.6%	
10,103	BACON	2,995	2,010	956	2	27	1,054 R	67.1%	31.9%	0.1%
4,074	BAKER	1,519	615	893		11	278 D	40.5%	58.8%	
44,700	BALDWIN	12,126	6,041	5,893	22	170	148 R	49.8%	48.6%	0.2%
14,422	BANKS	4,533	3,202	1,220	14	97	1,982 R	70.6%	26.9%	0.3%
46,144	BARROW	12,102	7,925	3,657	61	459	4,268 R	65.5%	30.2%	0.5%
76,019	BARTOW	22,781	14,720	7,508	55	498	7,212 R	64.6%	33.0%	0.2%
17,484	BEN HILL	4,661	2,381	2,234		46	147 R	51.1%	47.9%	
16,235	BERRIEN	4,410	2,718	1,640		52	1,078 R	61.6%	37.2%	
153,887	BIBB	49,776	24,071	24,996	248	461	925 D	48.4%	50.2%	0.5%
11,666	BLECKLEY	3,749	2,436	1,273	1	39	1,163 R	65.0%	34.0%	
14,629	BRANTLEY	4,566	3,118	1,372	5	71	1,746 R	68.3%	30.0%	0.1%
16,450	BROOKS	4,551	2,406	2,096	12	37	310 R	52.9%	46.1%	0.3%
23,417	BRYAN	7,059	4,835	2,172		52	2,663 R	68.5%	30.8%	
55,983	BULLOCH	14,782	8,990	5,561	137	94	3,429 R	60.8%	37.6%	0.9%
22,243	BURKE	7,135	3,381	3,720	7	27	339 D	47.4%	52.1%	0.1%
19,522	BUTTS	5,635	3,198	2,281	8	148	917 R	56.8%	40.5%	0.1%
6,320	CALHOUN	1,887	768	1,107		12	339 D	40.7%	58.7%	
43,664	CAMDEN	10,119	6,371	3,636	10	102	2,735 R	63.0%	35.9%	0.1%
9,577	CANDLER	2,722	1,643	1,053		26	590 R	60.4%	38.7%	
87,268	CARROLL	25,741	16,326	8,752	157	506	7,574 R	63.4%	34.0%	0.6%
53,282	CATOOSA	17,721	12,033	5,470	66	152	6,563 R	67.9%	30.9%	0.4%
10,282	CHARLTON	2,816	1,770	1,015	5	26	755 R	62.9%	36.0%	0.2%
232,048	CHATHAM	76,475	37,847	37,590	596	442	257 R	49.5%	49.2%	0.8%
14,882	CHATTAHOOCHEE	1,207	590	600	4	13	10 D	48.9%	49.7%	0.3%
25,470	CHATTOOGA	6,477	3,640	2,729	5	103	911 R	56.2%	42.1%	0.1%
141,903	CHEROKEE	52,348	38,033	12,295	306	1,714	25,738 R	72.7%	23.5%	0.6%
101,489	CLARKE	28,904	11,850	15,167	1,247	640	3,317 D	41.0%	52.5%	4.3%
3,357	CLAY	1,277	448	821		8	373 D	35.1%	64.3%	
236,517	CLAYTON	61,402	19,966	40,042	176	1,218	20,076 D	32.5%	65.2%	0.3%
6,878	CLINCH	1,929	1,091	816		22	275 R	56.6%	42.3%	
607,751	COBB	235,027	140,494	86,676	2,134	5,723	53,818 R	59.8%	36.9%	0.9%
37,413	COFFEE	9,430	5,756	3,593	8	73	2,163 R	61.0%	38.1%	0.1%
42,053	COLQUITT	9,972	6,589	3,297	5	81	3,292 R	66.1%	33.1%	0.1%
89,288	COLUMBIA	36,008	26,660	8,969	122	257	17,691 R	74.0%	24.9%	0.3%
15,771	COOK	3,944	2,279	1,639	3	23	640 R	57.8%	41.6%	0.1%
89,215	COWETA	31,226	21,327	9,056	133	710	12,271 R	68.3%	29.0%	0.4%
12,495	CRAWFORD	3,567	1,987	1,513	5	62	474 R	55.7%	42.4%	0.1%
21,996	CRISP	5,609	3,285	2,268	1	55	1,017 R	58.6%	40.4%	
15,154	DADE	5,049	3,333	1,628	13	75	1,705 R	66.0%	32.2%	0.3%
15,999	DAWSON	5,898	4,210	1,458	28	202	2,752 R	71.4%	24.7%	0.5%
28,240	DECATUR	7,648	4,187	3,398	13	50	789 R	54.7%	44.4%	0.2%
665,865	DE KALB	219,980	58,807	154,509	1,930	4,734	95,702 D	26.7%	70.2%	0.9%
19,171	DODGE	5,877	3,472	2,326	1	78	1,146 R	59.1%	39.6%	
11,525	DOOLY	3,520	1,588	1,901		31	313 D	45.1%	54.0%	
96,065	DOUGHERTY	29,064	12,248	16,650	68	98	4,402 D	42.1%	57.3%	0.2%
92,174	DOUGLAS	30,964	18,893	11,162	162	747	7,731 R	61.0%	36.0%	0.5%
12,354	EARLY	3,585	1,938	1,622	4	21	316 R	54.1%	45.2%	0.1%
3,754	ECHOLS	898	614	272		12	342 R	68.4%	30.3%	
37,535	EFFINGHAM	10,650	7,326	3,232	13	79	4,094 R	68.8%	30.3%	0.1%
20,511	ELBERT	5,853	3,262	2,527	14	50	735 R	55.7%	43.2%	0.2%
21,837	EMANUEL	6,263	3,343	2,835	1	84	508 R	53.4%	45.3%	
10,495	EVANS	3,080	1,841	1,217	2	20	624 R	59.8%	39.5%	0.1%
19,798	FANNIN	8,390	5,463	2,736	33	158	2,727 R	65.1%	32.6%	0.4%
91,263	FAYETTE	42,449	29,338	11,912	259	940	17,426 R	69.1%	28.1%	0.6%
90,565	FLOYD	26,825	16,194	10,282		349	5,912 R	60.4%	38.3%	
98,407	FORSYTH	35,755	27,769	6,694	132	1,160	21,075 R	77.7%	18.7%	0.4%
20,285	FRANKLIN	5,762	3,659	2,040		63	1,619 R	63.5%	35.4%	
816,006	FULTON	263,212	104,870	152,039	1,264	5,039	47,169 D	39.8%	57.8%	0.5%

GEORGIA

PRESIDENT 2000

2000 Census Population	County	Total Vote	Republican	Democratic	Green (Nader)	Other	Rep.-Dem. Plurality	Percentage of Total Vote Rep.	Dem.	Green
23,456	GILMER	7,370	4,941	2,230	35	164	2,711 R	67.0%	30.3%	0.5%
2,556	GLASCOCK	1,020	763	249		8	514 R	74.8%	24.4%	0.6%
67,568	GLYNN	22,384	14,346	7,778	128	132	6,568 R	64.1%	34.7%	0.1%
44,104	GORDON	12,205	7,944	4,032	18	211	3,912 R	65.1%	33.0%	0.3%
23,659	GRADY	6,703	3,894	2,721	18	70	1,173 R	58.1%	40.6%	
14,406	GREENE	5,197	2,980	2,137	13	67	843 R	57.3%	41.1%	0.3%
588,448	GWINNETT	191,111	121,756	61,434	1,298	6,623	60,322 R	63.7%	32.1%	0.7%
35,902	HABERSHAM	9,691	6,964	2,530	36	161	4,434 R	71.9%	26.1%	0.4%
139,277	HALL	38,150	26,841	10,259	190	860	16,582 R	70.4%	26.9%	0.5%
10,076	HANCOCK	3,086	662	2,414	4	6	1,752 D	21.5%	78.2%	0.1%
25,690	HARALSON	8,167	5,153	2,869		145	2,284 R	63.1%	35.1%	
23,695	HARRIS	8,562	5,554	2,912	20	76	2,642 R	64.9%	34.0%	0.2%
22,997	HART	7,536	4,242	3,192	21	81	1,050 R	56.3%	42.4%	0.3%
11,012	HEARD	3,198	1,947	1,178	9	64	769 R	60.9%	36.8%	0.3%
119,341	HENRY	38,867	25,815	11,971	46	1,035	13,844 R	66.4%	30.8%	0.1%
110,765	HOUSTON	36,988	23,174	13,301	89	424	9,873 R	62.7%	36.0%	0.2%
9,931	IRWIN	2,852	1,720	1,105	3	24	615 R	60.3%	38.7%	0.1%
41,589	JACKSON	11,635	7,878	3,420	43	294	4,458 R	67.7%	29.4%	0.4%
11,426	JASPER	3,943	2,298	1,558	2	85	740 R	58.3%	39.5%	0.1%
12,684	JEFF DAVIS	4,221	2,797	1,379	2	43	1,418 R	66.3%	32.7%	
17,266	JEFFERSON	5,566	2,559	2,973	2	32	414 D	46.0%	53.4%	
8,575	JENKINS	2,593	1,317	1,250	5	21	67 R	50.8%	48.2%	0.2%
8,560	JOHNSON	2,883	1,797	1,065	1	20	732 R	62.3%	36.9%	
23,639	JONES	8,068	4,850	3,102	24	92	1,748 R	60.1%	38.4%	0.3%
15,912	LAMAR	5,230	2,912	2,194	15	109	718 R	55.7%	42.0%	0.3%
7,241	LANIER	1,904	1,048	832	3	21	216 R	55.0%	43.7%	0.2%
44,874	LAURENS	14,036	8,133	5,724		179	2,409 R	57.9%	40.8%	
24,757	LEE	7,884	5,872	1,936	9	67	3,936 R	74.5%	24.6%	0.1%
61,610	LIBERTY	9,972	4,455	5,347	26	144	892 D	44.7%	53.6%	0.3%
8,348	LINCOLN	3,103	1,807	1,275		21	532 R	58.2%	41.1%	
10,304	LONG	2,314	1,320	975	1	18	345 R	57.0%	42.1%	
92,115	LOWNDES	25,432	14,462	10,616	188	166	3,846 R	56.9%	41.7%	0.7%
21,016	LUMPKIN	6,750	4,427	2,121		202	2,306 R	65.6%	31.4%	
21,231	MCDUFFIE	6,550	3,926	2,580	6	38	1,346 R	59.9%	39.4%	0.1%
10,847	MCINTOSH	3,837	1,766	2,047	4	20	281 D	46.0%	53.3%	0.1%
14,074	MACON	4,355	1,566	2,757	3	29	1,191 D	36.0%	63.3%	0.1%
25,730	MADISON	7,993	5,529	2,285	44	135	3,244 R	69.2%	28.6%	0.6%
7,144	MARION	2,184	1,187	982		15	205 R	54.3%	45.0%	
22,534	MERIWETHER	6,709	3,162	3,441	13	93	279 D	47.1%	51.3%	0.2%
6,383	MILLER	2,150	1,349	783		18	566 R	62.7%	36.4%	
23,932	MITCHELL	5,799	2,790	2,971	5	33	181 D	48.1%	51.2%	0.1%
21,757	MONROE	7,541	4,561	2,839	18	123	1,722 R	60.5%	37.6%	0.2%
8,270	MONTGOMERY	2,509	1,465	1,013	8	23	452 R	58.4%	40.4%	0.3%
15,457	MORGAN	5,902	3,524	2,238	29	111	1,286 R	59.7%	37.9%	0.5%
36,506	MURRAY	8,372	5,539	2,684	10	139	2,855 R	66.2%	32.1%	0.1%
186,291	MUSCOGEE	52,163	23,479	28,193	243	248	4,714 D	45.0%	54.0%	0.5%
62,001	NEWTON	18,375	11,127	6,703	31	514	4,424 R	60.6%	36.5%	0.2%
26,225	OCONEE	11,168	7,611	3,184	148	225	4,427 R	68.2%	28.5%	1.3%
12,635	OGLETHORPE	4,385	2,706	1,519	69	91	1,187 R	61.7%	34.6%	1.6%
81,678	PAULDING	24,260	16,881	6,743	34	602	10,138 R	69.6%	27.8%	0.1%
23,668	PEACH	7,137	3,525	3,540	3	69	15 D	49.4%	49.6%	
22,983	PICKENS	8,201	5,488	2,489	9	215	2,999 R	66.9%	30.3%	0.1%
15,636	PIERCE	4,681	3,348	1,300	2	31	2,048 R	71.5%	27.8%	
13,688	PIKE	4,885	3,358	1,413	13	101	1,945 R	68.7%	28.9%	0.3%
38,127	POLK	10,116	5,841	4,112	26	137	1,729 R	57.7%	40.6%	0.3%
9,588	PULASKI	3,346	1,922	1,390	2	32	532 R	57.4%	41.5%	0.1%
18,812	PUTNAM	6,299	3,596	2,612	20	71	984 R	57.1%	41.5%	0.3%
2,598	QUITMAN	904	348	542		14	194 D	38.5%	60.0%	
15,050	RABUN	5,341	3,451	1,776	31	83	1,675 R	64.6%	33.3%	0.6%
7,791	RANDOLPH	2,569	1,174	1,381		14	207 D	45.7%	53.8%	

GEORGIA

PRESIDENT 2000

2000 Census Population	County	Total Vote	Republican	Democratic	Green (Nader)	Other	Rep.-Dem. Plurality		Percentage of Total Vote		
									Rep.	Dem.	Green
199,775	RICHMOND	57,538	25,485	31,413	175	465	5,928	D	44.3%	54.6%	0.3%
70,111	ROCKDALE	24,490	15,440	8,295		755	7,145	R	63.0%	33.9%	
3,766	SCHLEY	1,176	706	460	1	9	246	R	60.0%	39.1%	0.1%
15,374	SCREVEN	4,719	2,461	2,233	3	22	228	R	52.2%	47.3%	0.1%
9,369	SEMINOLE	2,877	1,537	1,313		27	224	R	53.4%	45.6%	
58,417	SPALDING	15,391	9,271	5,831	8	281	3,440	R	60.2%	37.9%	0.1%
25,435	STEPHENS	8,376	5,370	2,869	9	128	2,501	R	64.1%	34.3%	0.1%
5,252	STEWART	1,954	675	1,267		12	592	D	34.5%	64.8%	
33,200	SUMTER	9,697	4,847	4,748	40	62	99	R	50.0%	49.0%	0.4%
6,498	TALBOT	2,531	844	1,662	3	22	818	D	33.3%	65.7%	0.1%
2,077	TALIAFERRO	832	271	556	2	3	285	D	32.6%	66.8%	0.2%
22,305	TATTNALL	5,610	3,597	1,963	1	49	1,634	R	64.1%	35.0%	
8,815	TAYLOR	2,780	1,412	1,340	2	26	72	R	50.8%	48.2%	0.1%
11,794	TELFAIR	3,493	1,693	1,777	1	22	84	D	48.5%	50.9%	
10,970	TERRELL	3,113	1,504	1,584	2	23	80	D	48.3%	50.9%	0.1%
42,737	THOMAS	12,058	7,093	4,862	40	63	2,231	R	58.8%	40.3%	0.3%
38,407	TIFT	10,328	6,678	3,547	22	81	3,131	R	64.7%	34.3%	0.2%
26,067	TOOMBS	7,210	4,487	2,643	13	67	1,844	R	62.2%	36.7%	0.2%
9,319	TOWNS	4,497	2,902	1,495	34	66	1,407	R	64.5%	33.2%	0.8%
6,854	TREUTLEN	1,963	1,062	879	3	19	183	R	54.1%	44.8%	0.2%
58,779	TROUP	17,804	11,198	6,379	80	147	4,819	R	62.9%	35.8%	0.4%
9,504	TURNER	2,456	1,258	1,169	2	27	89	R	51.2%	47.6%	0.1%
10,590	TWIGGS	3,615	1,570	1,977	4	64	407	D	43.4%	54.7%	0.1%
17,289	UNION	6,956	4,567	2,230	54	105	2,337	R	65.7%	32.1%	0.8%
27,597	UPSON	8,282	5,019	3,158	12	93	1,861	R	60.6%	38.1%	0.1%
61,053	WALKER	18,895	12,326	6,341		228	5,985	R	65.2%	33.6%	
60,687	WALTON	19,083	12,966	5,484	38	595	7,482	R	67.9%	28.7%	0.2%
35,483	WARE	9,628	6,099	3,480		49	2,619	R	63.3%	36.1%	
6,336	WARREN	2,145	933	1,196	2	14	263	D	43.5%	55.8%	0.1%
21,176	WASHINGTON	6,691	3,162	3,476	7	46	314	D	47.3%	52.0%	0.1%
26,565	WAYNE	8,004	5,219	2,736		49	2,483	R	65.2%	34.2%	
2,390	WEBSTER	909	359	541	1	8	182	D	39.5%	59.5%	0.1%
6,179	WHEELER	1,575	813	752	2	8	61	R	51.6%	47.7%	0.1%
19,944	WHITE	7,043	4,857	2,014	47	125	2,843	R	69.0%	28.6%	0.7%
83,525	WHITFIELD	23,302	15,852	7,034	131	285	8,818	R	68.0%	30.2%	0.6%
8,577	WILCOX	2,365	1,381	962		22	419	R	58.4%	40.7%	
10,687	WILKES	4,026	2,044	1,940	8	34	104	R	50.8%	48.2%	0.2%
10,220	WILKINSON	3,740	1,800	1,884	3	53	84	D	48.1%	50.4%	0.1%
21,967	WORTH	6,061	3,792	2,214	8	47	1,578	R	62.6%	36.5%	0.1%
8,186,453	TOTAL	2,596,645	1,419,720	1,116,230	13,273	47,422	303,490	R	54.7%	43.0%	0.5%

Note: The votes cast for Nader were write-ins. A blank indicates that he received no votes in that particular county.

GEORGIA

SENATOR 2000

2000 Census Population	County	Total Vote	Republican	Democratic	Other	Rep.-Dem. Plurality		Percentage			
								Total Vote		Major Vote	
								Rep.	Dem.	Rep.	Dem.
17,419	APPLING	4,960	2,055	2,606	299	551	D	41.4%	52.5%	44.1%	55.9%
7,609	ATKINSON	1,474	538	846	90	308	D	36.5%	57.4%	38.9%	61.1%
10,103	BACON	2,284	901	1,265	118	364	D	39.4%	55.4%	41.6%	58.4%
4,074	BAKER	1,116	327	736	53	409	D	29.3%	65.9%	30.8%	69.2%
44,700	BALDWIN	9,231	3,663	4,969	599	1,306	D	39.7%	53.8%	42.4%	57.6%
14,422	BANKS	4,570	1,851	2,562	157	711	D	40.5%	56.1%	41.9%	58.1%
46,144	BARROW	13,450	6,650	6,334	466	316	R	49.4%	47.1%	51.2%	48.8%
76,019	BARTOW	22,181	8,978	12,455	748	3,477	D	40.5%	56.2%	41.9%	58.1%
17,484	BEN HILL	4,593	1,364	3,056	173	1,692	D	29.7%	66.5%	30.9%	69.1%
16,235	BERRIEN	4,428	1,510	2,757	161	1,247	D	34.1%	62.3%	35.4%	64.6%
153,887	BIBB	47,175	17,722	28,423	1,030	10,701	D	37.6%	60.3%	38.4%	61.6%
11,666	BLECKLEY	2,759	1,272	1,365	122	93	D	46.1%	49.5%	48.2%	51.8%
14,629	BRANTLEY	2,873	1,078	1,436	359	358	D	37.5%	50.0%	42.9%	57.1%
16,450	BROOKS	3,107	1,005	1,911	191	906	D	32.3%	61.5%	34.5%	65.5%
23,417	BRYAN	5,269	2,348	2,642	279	294	D	44.6%	50.1%	47.1%	52.9%
55,983	BULLOCH	14,338	5,436	8,510	392	3,074	D	37.9%	59.4%	39.0%	61.0%
22,243	BURKE	5,832	2,113	3,473	246	1,360	D	36.2%	59.6%	37.8%	62.2%
19,522	BUTTS	5,604	2,201	3,254	149	1,053	D	39.3%	58.1%	40.3%	59.7%
6,320	CALHOUN	1,878	447	1,379	52	932	D	23.8%	73.4%	24.5%	75.5%
43,664	CAMDEN	4,428	1,298	2,629	501	1,331	D	29.3%	59.4%	33.1%	66.9%
9,577	CANDLER	2,182	827	1,230	125	403	D	37.9%	56.4%	40.2%	59.8%
87,268	CARROLL	25,515	10,319	14,497	699	4,178	D	40.4%	56.8%	41.6%	58.4%
53,282	CATOOSA	16,886	5,758	10,164	964	4,406	D	34.1%	60.2%	36.2%	63.8%
10,282	CHARLTON	1,693	430	1,039	224	609	D	25.4%	61.4%	29.3%	70.7%
232,048	CHATHAM	72,124	27,100	43,198	1,826	16,098	D	37.6%	59.9%	38.6%	61.4%
14,882	CHATTAHOOCHEE	1,048	290	650	108	360	D	27.7%	62.0%	30.9%	69.1%
25,470	CHATTOOGA	6,238	1,477	3,863	898	2,386	D	23.7%	61.9%	27.7%	72.3%
141,903	CHEROKEE	50,823	25,905	23,218	1,700	2,687	R	51.0%	45.7%	52.7%	47.3%
101,489	CLARKE	22,713	6,835	14,211	1,667	7,376	D	30.1%	62.6%	32.5%	67.5%
3,357	CLAY	889	230	604	55	374	D	25.9%	67.9%	27.6%	72.4%
236,517	CLAYTON	60,113	13,845	43,440	2,828	29,595	D	23.0%	72.3%	24.2%	75.8%
6,878	CLINCH	1,138	299	746	93	447	D	26.3%	65.6%	28.6%	71.4%
607,751	COBB	222,795	99,303	116,132	7,360	16,829	D	44.6%	52.1%	46.1%	53.9%
37,413	COFFEE	6,296	2,340	3,622	334	1,282	D	37.2%	57.5%	39.2%	60.8%
42,053	COLQUITT	7,639	3,192	4,073	374	881	D	41.8%	53.3%	43.9%	56.1%
89,288	COLUMBIA	35,725	18,672	15,875	1,178	2,797	R	52.3%	44.4%	54.0%	46.0%
15,771	COOK	3,913	1,237	2,522	154	1,285	D	31.6%	64.5%	32.9%	67.1%
89,215	COWETA	30,575	15,286	14,413	876	873	R	50.0%	47.1%	51.5%	48.5%
12,495	CRAWFORD	2,441	970	1,321	150	351	D	39.7%	54.1%	42.3%	57.7%
21,996	CRISP	4,822	1,937	2,718	167	781	D	40.2%	56.4%	41.6%	58.4%
15,154	DADE	3,192	1,015	1,792	385	777	D	31.8%	56.1%	36.2%	63.8%
15,999	DAWSON	5,829	2,772	2,858	199	86	D	47.6%	49.0%	49.2%	50.8%
28,240	DECATUR	5,018	1,611	3,006	401	1,395	D	32.1%	59.9%	34.9%	65.1%
665,865	DE KALB	217,098	47,045	161,017	9,036	113,972	D	21.7%	74.2%	22.6%	77.4%
19,171	DODGE	4,041	1,692	2,085	264	393	D	41.9%	51.6%	44.8%	55.2%
11,525	DOOLY	2,841	989	1,756	96	767	D	34.8%	61.8%	36.0%	64.0%
96,065	DOUGHERTY	28,891	8,696	19,610	585	10,914	D	30.1%	67.9%	30.7%	69.3%
92,174	DOUGLAS	30,592	12,565	17,089	938	4,524	D	41.1%	55.9%	42.4%	57.6%
12,354	EARLY	3,389	885	2,359	145	1,474	D	26.1%	69.6%	27.3%	72.7%
3,754	ECHOLS	586	173	363	50	190	D	29.5%	61.9%	32.3%	67.7%
37,535	EFFINGHAM	9,388	4,431	4,606	351	175	D	47.2%	49.1%	49.0%	51.0%
20,511	ELBERT	5,960	1,732	3,928	300	2,196	D	29.1%	65.9%	30.6%	69.4%
21,837	EMANUEL	4,218	1,484	2,549	185	1,065	D	35.2%	60.4%	36.8%	63.2%
10,495	EVANS	2,502	979	1,419	104	440	D	39.1%	56.7%	40.8%	59.2%
19,798	FANNIN	7,853	2,818	4,679	356	1,861	D	35.9%	59.6%	37.6%	62.4%
91,263	FAYETTE	40,835	20,179	19,517	1,139	662	R	49.4%	47.8%	50.8%	49.2%
90,565	FLOYD	26,459	9,716	15,946	797	6,230	D	36.7%	60.3%	37.9%	62.1%
98,407	FORSYTH	35,518	19,780	14,326	1,412	5,454	R	55.7%	40.3%	58.0%	42.0%
20,285	FRANKLIN	5,535	1,916	3,311	308	1,395	D	34.6%	59.8%	36.7%	63.3%
816,006	FULTON	258,860	79,155	169,886	9,819	90,731	D	30.6%	65.6%	31.8%	68.2%

GEORGIA

SENATOR 2000

2000 Census Population	County	Total Vote	Republican	Democratic	Other	Rep.-Dem. Plurality		Percentage			
								Total Vote		Major Vote	
								Rep.	Dem.	Rep.	Dem.
23,456	GILMER	7,198	2,945	4,062	191	1,117	D	40.9%	56.4%	42.0%	58.0%
2,556	GLASCOCK	903	385	467	51	82	D	42.6%	51.7%	45.2%	54.8%
67,568	GLYNN	20,776	10,814	9,231	731	1,583	R	52.1%	44.4%	53.9%	46.1%
44,104	GORDON	10,455	3,703	6,256	496	2,553	D	35.4%	59.8%	37.2%	62.8%
23,659	GRADY	4,400	1,267	2,758	375	1,491	D	28.8%	62.7%	31.5%	68.5%
14,406	GREENE	5,229	1,996	3,111	122	1,115	D	38.2%	59.5%	39.1%	60.9%
588,448	GWINNETT	182,144	83,939	90,345	7,860	6,406	D	46.1%	49.6%	48.2%	51.8%
35,902	HABERSHAM	7,618	3,382	3,734	502	352	D	44.4%	49.0%	47.5%	52.5%
139,277	HALL	36,516	16,840	18,398	1,278	1,558	D	46.1%	50.4%	47.8%	52.2%
10,076	HANCOCK	1,896	373	1,400	123	1,027	D	19.7%	73.8%	21.0%	79.0%
25,690	HARALSON	8,208	3,144	4,841	223	1,697	D	38.3%	59.0%	39.4%	60.6%
23,695	HARRIS	6,396	2,713	3,232	451	519	D	42.4%	50.5%	45.6%	54.4%
22,997	HART	4,991	1,810	2,631	550	821	D	36.3%	52.7%	40.8%	59.2%
11,012	HEARD	3,215	1,055	2,025	135	970	D	32.8%	63.0%	34.3%	65.7%
119,341	HENRY	38,478	18,166	18,885	1,427	719	D	47.2%	49.1%	49.0%	51.0%
110,765	HOUSTON	36,448	15,189	20,197	1,062	5,008	D	41.7%	55.4%	42.9%	57.1%
9,931	IRWIN	2,435	944	1,408	83	464	D	38.8%	57.8%	40.1%	59.9%
41,589	JACKSON	11,319	4,922	6,067	330	1,145	D	43.5%	53.6%	44.8%	55.2%
11,426	JASPER	3,076	1,214	1,683	179	469	D	39.5%	54.7%	41.9%	58.1%
12,684	JEFF DAVIS	3,085	1,143	1,741	201	598	D	37.1%	56.4%	39.6%	60.4%
17,266	JEFFERSON	3,770	1,519	2,102	149	583	D	40.3%	55.8%	41.9%	58.1%
8,575	JENKINS	1,954	680	1,153	121	473	D	34.8%	59.0%	37.1%	62.9%
8,560	JOHNSON	1,884	853	908	123	55	D	45.3%	48.2%	48.4%	51.6%
23,639	JONES	7,771	3,285	4,255	231	970	D	42.3%	54.8%	43.6%	56.4%
15,912	LAMAR	5,215	1,947	3,143	125	1,196	D	37.3%	60.3%	38.3%	61.7%
7,241	LANIER	1,430	317	988	125	671	D	22.2%	69.1%	24.3%	75.7%
44,874	LAURENS	9,283	3,396	5,327	560	1,931	D	36.6%	57.4%	38.9%	61.1%
24,757	LEE	7,851	3,846	3,754	251	92	R	49.0%	47.8%	50.6%	49.4%
61,610	LIBERTY	5,727	1,754	3,758	215	2,004	D	30.6%	65.6%	31.8%	68.2%
8,348	LINCOLN	3,079	1,118	1,868	93	750	D	36.3%	60.7%	37.4%	62.6%
10,304	LONG	1,832	687	1,013	132	326	D	37.5%	55.3%	40.4%	59.6%
92,115	LOWNDES	24,474	8,138	15,344	992	7,206	D	33.3%	62.7%	34.7%	65.3%
21,016	LUMPKIN	6,675	2,476	4,012	187	1,536	D	37.1%	60.1%	38.2%	61.8%
21,231	MCDUFFIE	6,533	2,680	3,674	179	994	D	41.0%	56.2%	42.2%	57.8%
10,847	MCINTOSH	2,753	863	1,742	148	879	D	31.3%	63.3%	33.1%	66.9%
14,074	MACON	3,138	808	2,177	153	1,369	D	25.7%	69.4%	27.1%	72.9%
25,730	MADISON	6,047	2,611	2,981	455	370	D	43.2%	49.3%	46.7%	53.3%
7,144	MARION	2,180	614	1,449	117	835	D	28.2%	66.5%	29.8%	70.2%
22,534	MERIWETHER	6,721	2,077	4,483	161	2,406	D	30.9%	66.7%	31.7%	68.3%
6,383	MILLER	1,448	498	847	103	349	D	34.4%	58.5%	37.0%	63.0%
23,932	MITCHELL	5,969	1,692	4,142	135	2,450	D	28.3%	69.4%	29.0%	71.0%
21,757	MONROE	7,426	3,204	4,045	177	841	D	43.1%	54.5%	44.2%	55.8%
8,270	MONTGOMERY	2,225	947	1,221	57	274	D	42.6%	54.9%	43.7%	56.3%
15,457	MORGAN	5,838	2,411	3,282	145	871	D	41.3%	56.2%	42.4%	57.6%
36,506	MURRAY	8,064	2,805	4,821	438	2,016	D	34.8%	59.8%	36.8%	63.2%
186,291	MUSCOGEE	50,080	16,032	32,700	1,348	16,668	D	32.0%	65.3%	32.9%	67.1%
62,001	NEWTON	18,524	7,588	10,170	766	2,582	D	41.0%	54.9%	42.7%	57.3%
26,225	OCONEE	11,005	5,068	5,621	316	553	D	46.1%	51.1%	47.4%	52.6%
12,635	OGLETHORPE	4,303	1,565	2,544	194	979	D	36.4%	59.1%	38.1%	61.9%
81,678	PAULDING	24,045	11,116	12,038	891	922	D	46.2%	50.1%	48.0%	52.0%
23,668	PEACH	5,075	1,880	2,886	309	1,006	D	37.0%	56.9%	39.4%	60.6%
22,983	PICKENS	7,010	2,909	3,725	376	816	D	41.5%	53.1%	43.8%	56.2%
15,636	PIERCE	3,155	1,480	1,418	257	62	R	46.9%	44.9%	51.1%	48.9%
13,688	PIKE	4,803	2,288	2,406	109	118	D	47.6%	50.1%	48.7%	51.3%
38,127	POLK	10,209	3,551	6,396	262	2,845	D	34.8%	62.7%	35.7%	64.3%
9,588	PULASKI	2,597	962	1,518	117	556	D	37.0%	58.5%	38.8%	61.2%
18,812	PUTNAM	6,152	2,428	3,365	359	937	D	39.5%	54.7%	41.9%	58.1%
2,598	QUITMAN	523	140	334	49	194	D	26.8%	63.9%	29.5%	70.5%
15,050	RABUN	3,906	1,445	2,204	257	759	D	37.0%	56.4%	39.6%	60.4%
7,791	RANDOLPH	2,531	724	1,719	88	995	D	28.6%	67.9%	29.6%	70.4%

GEORGIA

SENATOR 2000

2000 Census Population	County	Total Vote	Republican	Democratic	Other	Rep.-Dem. Plurality		Percentage			
								Total Vote		Major Vote	
								Rep.	Dem.	Rep.	Dem.
199,775	RICHMOND	56,789	18,801	36,270	1,718	17,469	D	33.1%	63.9%	34.1%	65.9%
70,111	ROCKDALE	24,217	10,833	12,606	778	1,773	D	44.7%	52.1%	46.2%	53.8%
3,766	SCHLEY	915	341	516	58	175	D	37.3%	56.4%	39.8%	60.2%
15,374	SCREVEN	3,354	1,200	1,990	164	790	D	35.8%	59.3%	37.6%	62.4%
9,369	SEMINOLE	2,781	630	1,931	220	1,301	D	22.7%	69.4%	24.6%	75.4%
58,417	SPALDING	12,402	5,392	6,323	687	931	D	43.5%	51.0%	46.0%	54.0%
25,435	STEPHENS	5,894	2,007	3,322	565	1,315	D	34.1%	56.4%	37.7%	62.3%
5,252	STEWART	1,193	284	858	51	574	D	23.8%	71.9%	24.9%	75.1%
33,200	SUMTER	7,616	2,433	4,840	343	2,407	D	31.9%	63.6%	33.5%	66.5%
6,498	TALBOT	1,682	431	1,170	81	739	D	25.6%	69.6%	26.9%	73.1%
2,077	TALIAFERRO	685	170	505	10	335	D	24.8%	73.7%	25.2%	74.8%
22,305	TATTNALL	4,556	1,960	2,441	155	481	D	43.0%	53.6%	44.5%	55.5%
8,815	TAYLOR	2,826	865	1,876	85	1,011	D	30.6%	66.4%	31.6%	68.4%
11,794	TELFAIR	2,658	868	1,668	122	800	D	32.7%	62.8%	34.2%	65.8%
10,970	TERRELL	2,302	844	1,364	94	520	D	36.7%	59.3%	38.2%	61.8%
42,737	THOMAS	11,508	3,687	7,309	512	3,622	D	32.0%	63.5%	33.5%	66.5%
38,407	TIFT	8,129	3,552	4,139	438	587	D	43.7%	50.9%	46.2%	53.8%
26,067	TOOMBS	5,675	2,753	2,654	268	99	R	48.5%	46.8%	50.9%	49.1%
9,319	TOWNS	4,398	1,315	3,005	78	1,690	D	29.9%	68.3%	30.4%	69.6%
6,854	TREUTLEN	1,875	663	1,147	65	484	D	35.4%	61.2%	36.6%	63.4%
58,779	TROUP	17,220	6,519	10,183	518	3,664	D	37.9%	59.1%	39.0%	61.0%
9,504	TURNER	2,534	838	1,604	92	766	D	33.1%	63.3%	34.3%	65.7%
10,590	TWIGGS	3,576	1,097	2,333	146	1,236	D	30.7%	65.2%	32.0%	68.0%
17,289	UNION	6,617	1,995	4,449	173	2,454	D	30.1%	67.2%	31.0%	69.0%
27,597	UPSON	8,436	3,316	4,902	218	1,586	D	39.3%	58.1%	40.4%	59.6%
61,053	WALKER	18,471	6,335	10,940	1,196	4,605	D	34.3%	59.2%	36.7%	63.3%
60,687	WALTON	18,931	8,583	9,731	617	1,148	D	45.3%	51.4%	46.9%	53.1%
35,483	WARE	9,336	3,454	5,443	439	1,989	D	37.0%	58.3%	38.8%	61.2%
6,336	WARREN	1,494	542	870	82	328	D	36.3%	58.2%	38.4%	61.6%
21,176	WASHINGTON	4,624	1,617	2,791	216	1,174	D	35.0%	60.4%	36.7%	63.3%
26,565	WAYNE	7,679	3,325	4,071	283	746	D	43.3%	53.0%	45.0%	55.0%
2,390	WEBSTER	679	180	476	23	296	D	26.5%	70.1%	27.4%	72.6%
6,179	WHEELER	1,449	503	894	52	391	D	34.7%	61.7%	36.0%	64.0%
19,944	WHITE	7,003	2,805	3,961	237	1,156	D	40.1%	56.6%	41.5%	58.5%
83,525	WHITFIELD	21,840	10,175	10,645	1,020	470	D	46.6%	48.7%	48.9%	51.1%
8,577	WILCOX	1,997	906	1,040	51	134	D	45.4%	52.1%	46.6%	53.4%
10,687	WILKES	2,875	1,062	1,669	144	607	D	36.9%	58.1%	38.9%	61.1%
10,220	WILKINSON	2,493	810	1,531	152	721	D	32.5%	61.4%	34.6%	65.4%
21,967	WORTH	6,087	2,399	3,506	182	1,107	D	39.4%	57.6%	40.6%	59.4%
8,186,453	TOTAL	2,428,510	920,478	1,413,224	94,808	492,746	D	37.9%	58.2%	39.4%	60.6%

Note: The Georgia Senate race was a special election necessitated by the death in July 2000 of Republican Sen. Paul Coverdell. There was no primary and all candidates ran in November 2000 on a single ballot, including two other Republican candidates who together received 35,474 votes. Their votes are included in the total for "Other."

GEORGIA

CONGRESS

CD	Year	Total Vote	Republican		Democratic		Other Vote	Rep.-Dem. Plurality	Percentage			
			Vote	Candidate	Vote	Candidate			Total Vote		Major Vote	
									Rep.	Dem.	Rep.	Dem.
1	2000	190,460	131,684	KINGSTON, JACK	58,776	GRIGGS, JOYCE		72,908 R	69.1%	30.9%	69.1%	30.9%
1	1998	92,229	92,229	KINGSTON, JACK				92,229 R	100.0%		100.0%	
1	1996	159,238	108,616	KINGSTON, JACK	50,622	KASZANS, ROSEMARY D.		57,994 R	68.2%	31.8%	68.2%	31.8%
2	2000	180,300	83,870	GLENN, DYLAN	96,430	BISHOP, SANFORD		12,560 D	46.5%	53.5%	46.5%	53.5%
2	1998	137,258	59,305	MCCORMICK, JOE	77,953	BISHOP, SANFORD		18,648 D	43.2%	56.8%	43.2%	56.8%
2	1996	163,538	75,282	EALUM, DARREL	88,256	BISHOP, SANFORD		12,974 D	46.0%	54.0%	46.0%	54.0%
3	2000	236,706	150,200	COLLINS, MAC	86,309	NOTTI, GAIL	197	63,891 R	63.5%	36.5%	63.5%	36.5%
3	1998	123,064	123,064	COLLINS, MAC				123,064 R	100.0%		100.0%	
3	1996	196,789	120,251	COLLINS, MAC	76,538	CHAFIN, JIM		43,713 R	61.1%	38.9%	61.1%	38.9%
4	2000	229,856	90,277	WARREN, SUNNY	139,579	MCKINNEY, CYNTHIA		49,302 D	39.3%	60.7%	39.3%	60.7%
4	1998	164,768	64,146	WARREN, SUNNY	100,622	MCKINNEY, CYNTHIA		36,476 D	38.9%	61.1%	38.9%	61.1%
4	1996	220,142	92,985	MITNICK, JOHN	127,157	MCKINNEY, CYNTHIA		34,172 D	42.2%	57.8%	42.2%	57.8%
5	2000	177,942	40,606	SCHWAB, HANK	137,333	LEWIS, JOHN	3	96,727 D	22.8%	77.2%	22.8%	77.2%
5	1998	139,054	29,877	LEWIS, JOHN H. SR.	109,177	LEWIS, JOHN		79,300 D	21.5%	78.5%	21.5%	78.5%
5	1996	136,558			136,555	LEWIS, JOHN	3	136,555 D		100.0%		100.0%
6	2000	343,261	256,595	ISAKSON, JOHNNY	86,666	DEHART, BRETT		169,929 R	74.8%	25.2%	74.8%	25.2%
6	1998	233,332	164,966	GINGRICH, NEWT	68,366	PELPHREY, BATS		96,600 R	70.7%	29.3%	70.7%	29.3%
6	1996	301,290	174,155	GINGRICH, NEWT	127,135	COLES, MICHAEL		47,020 R	57.8%	42.2%	57.8%	42.2%
7	2000	228,584	126,312	BARR, BOB	102,272	KAHN, ROGER		24,040 R	55.3%	44.7%	55.3%	44.7%
7	1998	155,275	85,982	BARR, BOB	69,293	WILLIAMS, JIM		16,689 R	55.4%	44.6%	55.4%	44.6%
7	1996	193,774	112,009	BARR, BOB	81,765	WATTS, CHARLIE		30,244 R	57.8%	42.2%	57.8%	42.2%
8	2000	192,431	113,380	CHAMBLISS, SAXBY	79,051	MARSHALL, JIM		34,329 R	58.9%	41.1%	58.9%	41.1%
8	1998	141,072	87,993	CHAMBLISS, SAXBY	53,079	CAIN, RONALD		34,914 R	62.4%	37.6%	62.4%	37.6%
8	1996	178,125	93,619	CHAMBLISS, SAXBY	84,506	WIGGINS, JIM		9,113 R	52.6%	47.4%	52.6%	47.4%
9	2000	243,531	183,171	DEAL, NATHAN	60,360	HARRINGTON, JAMES		122,811 R	75.2%	24.8%	75.2%	24.8%
9	1998	122,713	122,713	DEAL, NATHAN				122,713 R	100.0%		100.0%	
9	1996	202,194	132,532	DEAL, NATHAN	69,662	POSTON, KEN		62,870 R	65.5%	34.5%	65.5%	34.5%
10	2000	193,899	122,590	NORWOOD, CHARLIE	71,309	FREEMAN, DENISE		51,281 R	63.2%	36.8%	63.2%	36.8%
10	1998	148,531	88,527	NORWOOD, CHARLIE	60,004	FREEMAN, DENISE		28,523 R	59.6%	40.4%	59.6%	40.4%
10	1996	184,777	96,723	NORWOOD, CHARLIE	88,054	BELL, DAVID		8,669 R	52.3%	47.7%	52.3%	47.7%
11	2000	199,652	199,652	LINDER, JOHN				199,652 R	100.0%		100.0%	
11	1998	174,419	120,909	LINDER, JOHN	53,510	LITTMAN, VINCE		67,399 R	69.3%	30.7%	69.3%	30.7%
11	1996	226,761	145,821	LINDER, JOHN	80,940	STEPHENSON, TOMMY		64,881 R	64.3%	35.7%	64.3%	35.7%

Note: The lines for Georgia's congressional districts were changed following legal challenges to the lines used in 1992 and 1994. Election results from the earlier years are not included because the districts were not comparable. Results for those years may be found in *America Votes 21*.

GEORGIA
GENERAL AND PRIMARY ELECTIONS

2000 GENERAL ELECTIONS

President   Other vote was 36,332 Libertarian (Browne); 10,926 Independent (Buchanan); 140 write-in (Phillips); 11 write-in (Harris); 8 write-in (Strickland); 5 write-in (Schriner).

Senator   Other vote was 25,942 Libertarian (MacGregor); 22,975 Republican (Ballenger); 21,249 Green (Gates); 12,499 Republican (Wood); 11,875 Independent (Walsh); 259 write-in (Dixon); 9 write-in (Averitt). The Senate election in Georgia was a non-partisan special election necessitated by the death in July 2000 of Republican Sen. Paul Coverdell. Candidates were not identified on the November ballot by party affiliation, although Mattingly and Miller ran with their party's backing.

Congress   Other vote was: CD 3: 197 write-in (Borcik); CD 5: 3 write-in (Fein).

2000 PRIMARY ELECTIONS

Primary   March 7, 2000   (President)
July 18, 2000   (Congress)
Primary Runoff   August 8, 2000   (Congress)

Registration   3,592,778   No Party Registration
(active registrants as of
June 19, 2000)

Primary Type   Open—Any registered voter could vote in either the Democratic or Republican primary, although if they voted in one party's primary they could not participate in a primary runoff of the other party.

Note: An asterisk (*) denotes incumbent.

	REPUBLICAN PRIMARIES			DEMOCRATIC PRIMARIES		
President	George W. Bush	430,480	66.9%	Al Gore	238,396	83.8%
	John McCain	179,046	27.8%	Bill Bradley	46,035	16.2%
	Alan Keyes	29,640	4.6%			
	Gary Bauer	1,962	0.3%			
	Steve Forbes	1,647	0.3%			
	Orrin G. Hatch	413	0.1%			
	TOTAL	643,188		TOTAL	284,431	
Senator	*A special election was held November 7, 2000, for the seat of Republican Sen. Paul Coverdell, who died in July 2000. No primaries were held and all candidates ran on a single ballot without party designation.*					
Congressional District 1	Jack Kingston*	25,270	100.0%	Joyce Griggs	20,622	50.5%
				Don Smart	20,214	49.5%
	TOTAL	25,270		TOTAL	40,836	
Congressional District 2	Dylan Green	7,197	100.0%	Sanford D. Bishop Jr.*	79,617	100.0%
	TOTAL	7,197		TOTAL	79,617	
Congressional District 3	Mac Collins*	39,153	89.2%	Gail Notti	17,574	67.3%
	Herbie Galloway	4,744	10.8%	J. P. Agrawal	8,526	32.7%
	TOTAL	43,897		TOTAL	26,100	
Congressional District 4	Sunny Warren	5,875	67.6%	Cynthia A. McKinney*	40,629	100.0%
	Dean Parkison	2,814	32.4%			
	TOTAL	8,689		TOTAL	40,629	
Congressional District 5	Hank Schwab	5,673	100.0%	John Lewis*	23,487	100.0%
	TOTAL	5,673		TOTAL	23,487	
Congressional District 6	Johnny Isakson*	43,378	100.0%	Brett DeHart	6,083	100.0%
	TOTAL	43,378		TOTAL	6,083	

GEORGIA

GENERAL AND PRIMARY ELECTIONS

	REPUBLICAN PRIMARIES			DEMOCRATIC PRIMARIES		
Congressional District 7	Bob Barr*	28,658	100.0%	Roger Kahn	17,421	47.4%
				Jim Williams	11,165	30.4%
				Chip Warren	8,180	22.2%
	TOTAL	28,658		TOTAL	36,766	
				PRIMARY RUNOFF		
				Roger Kahn	14,129	66.9%
				Jim Williams	6,975	33.1%
				TOTAL	21,104	
Congressional District 8	Saxby Chambliss*	9,310	100.0%	Jim Marshall	66,216	100.0%
	TOTAL	9,310		TOTAL	66,216	
Congressional District 9	Nathan Deal*	46,514	100.0%	James Harrington	32,460	100.0%
	TOTAL	46,514		TOTAL	32,460	
Congressional District 10	Charlie Norwood*	20,722	100.0%	Denise Freeman	44,859	100.0%
	TOTAL	20,722		TOTAL	44,859	
Congressional District 11	John Linder*	43,563	86.6%	No Democratic candidate		
	Vince Littman	6,717	13.4%			
	TOTAL	50,280				

HAWAII

GOVERNOR
Benjamin J. Cayetano (D). Re-elected 1998 to a four-year term. Previously elected 1994.

SENATORS
Daniel K. Akaka (D). Re-elected 2000 to a six-year term. Previously elected 1994 and 1990 to fill out the remaining four years of the term vacated by the death of Senator Spark M. Matsunaga (D); had previously been appointed May 1990 to fill this vacancy.

Daniel K. Inouye (D). Re-elected 1998 to a six-year term. Previously elected 1992, 1986, 1980, 1974, 1968, 1962.

REPRESENTATIVES
1. Neil Abercrombie (D)　　　　2. Patsy T. Mink (D)

POSTWAR VOTE FOR PRESIDENT

| | | Republican | | Democratic | | Other | | Percentage | | | |
| | Total | | | | | | | Total Vote | | Major Vote | |
Year	Vote	Vote	Candidate	Vote	Candidate	Vote	Plurality	Rep.	Dem.	Rep.	Dem.
2000**	367,951	137,845	Bush, George W.	205,286	Gore, Al	24,820	67,441 D	37.5%	55.8%	40.2%	59.8%
1996**	360,120	113,943	Dole, Bob	205,012	Clinton, Bill	41,165	91,069 D	31.6%	56.9%	35.7%	64.3%
1992**	372,842	136,822	Bush, George	179,310	Clinton, Bill	56,710	42,488 D	36.7%	48.1%	43.3%	56.7%
1988	354,461	158,625	Bush, George	192,364	Dukakis, Michael S.	3,472	33,739 D	44.8%	54.3%	45.2%	54.8%
1984	335,846	185,050	Reagan, Ronald	147,154	Mondale, Walter F.	3,642	37,896 R	55.1%	43.8%	55.7%	44.3%
1980**	303,287	130,112	Reagan, Ronald	135,879	Carter, Jimmy	37,296	5,767 D	42.9%	44.8%	48.9%	51.1%
1976	291,301	140,003	Ford, Gerald R.	147,375	Carter, Jimmy	3,923	7,372 D	48.1%	50.6%	48.7%	51.3%
1972	270,274	168,865	Nixon, Richard M.	101,409	McGovern, George S.		67,456 R	62.5%	37.5%	62.5%	37.5%
1968	236,218	91,425	Nixon, Richard M.	141,324	Humphrey, Hubert H.	3,469	49,899 D	38.7%	59.8%	39.3%	60.7%
1964	207,271	44,022	Goldwater, Barry M.	163,249	Johnson, Lyndon B.		119,227 D	21.2%	78.8%	21.2%	78.8%
1960	184,705	92,295	Nixon, Richard M.	92,410	Kennedy, John F.		115 D	50.0%	50.0%	50.0%	50.0%

In 2000 the other vote column includes 21,623 votes cast for Green (Nader). In 1996 the other vote column includes 27,358 votes cast for Perot. In 1992 the other vote column includes 53,003 votes cast for Perot. In 1980 the other column includes 32,021 votes for Independent (Anderson). Hawaii was formally admitted as a state in August 1959.

POSTWAR VOTE FOR GOVERNOR

| | | Republican | | Democratic | | Other | Rep.-Dem. | Percentage | | | |
| | Total | | | | | | | Total Vote | | Major Vote | |
Year	Vote	Vote	Candidate	Vote	Candidate	Vote	Plurality	Rep.	Dem.	Rep.	Dem.
1998	407,556	198,952	Lingle, Linda	204,206	Cayetano, Benjamin J.	4,398	5,254 D	48.8%	50.1%	49.3%	50.7%
1994**	369,013	107,908	Saiki, Patricia	134,978	Cayetano, Benjamin J.	126,127	27,070 D	29.2%	36.6%	44.4%	55.6%
1990	340,132	131,310	Hemmings, Fred	203,491	Waihee, John	5,331	72,181 D	38.6%	59.8%	39.2%	60.8%
1986	334,115	160,460	Anderson, D. G.	173,655	Waihee, John		13,195 D	48.0%	52.0%	48.0%	52.0%
1982**	311,853	81,507	Anderson, D. G.	141,043	Ariyoshi, George R.	89,303	59,536 D	26.1%	45.2%	36.6%	63.4%
1978	281,587	124,610	Leopold, John	153,394	Ariyoshi, George R.	3,583	28,784 D	44.3%	54.5%	44.8%	55.2%
1974	249,650	113,388	Crossley, Randolph	136,262	Ariyoshi, George R.		22,874 D	45.4%	54.6%	45.4%	54.6%
1970	239,061	101,249	King, Samuel P.	137,812	Burns, John A.		36,563 D	42.4%	57.6%	42.4%	57.6%
1966	213,164	104,324	Crossley, Randolph	108,840	Burns, John A.		4,516 D	48.9%	51.1%	48.9%	51.1%
1962	196,015	81,707	Quinn, William F.	114,308	Burns, John A.		32,601 D	41.7%	58.3%	41.7%	58.3%
1959S	168,662	86,213	Quinn, William F.	82,074	Burns, John A.	375	4,139 R	51.1%	48.7%	51.2%	48.8%

In 1994 the Best party candidate (Frank F. Fasi) ran second with 113,158 votes (30.7% of the total vote) and the plurality of the three-party vote was 21,820 (D). In 1982 other vote was for Independent Democrat (Frank F. Fasi) who ran second with 28.6% of the total vote and the plurality of the three-party vote was 51,740 (D). The 1959 election was for a short term pending the regular vote in 1962.

HAWAII

POSTWAR VOTE FOR SENATOR

Year	Total Vote	Republican Vote	Republican Candidate	Democratic Vote	Democratic Candidate	Other Vote	Rep.-Dem. Plurality	Percentage Total Vote Rep.	Percentage Total Vote Dem.	Percentage Major Vote Rep.	Percentage Major Vote Dem.
2000	345,623	84,701	Carroll, John S.	251,215	Akaka, Daniel K.	9,707	166,514 D	24.5%	72.7%	25.2%	74.8%
1998	398,124	70,964	Young, Crystal	315,252	Inouye, Daniel K.	11,908	244,288 D	17.8%	79.2%	18.4%	81.6%
1994	356,902	86,320	Hustace, Maria M.	256,189	Akaka, Daniel K.	14,393	169,869 D	24.2%	71.8%	25.2%	74.8%
1992	363,662	97,928	Reed, Rick	208,266	Inouye, Daniel K.	57,468	110,338 D	26.9%	57.3%	32.0%	68.0%
1990S	349,666	155,978	Saiki, Patricia	188,901	Akaka, Daniel K.	4,787	32,923 D	44.6%	54.0%	45.2%	54.8%
1988	323,876	66,987	Hustace, Maria M.	247,941	Matsunaga, Spark M.	8,948	180,954 D	20.7%	76.6%	21.3%	78.7%
1986	328,797	86,910	Hutchinson, Frank	241,887	Inouye, Daniel K.		154,977 D	26.4%	73.6%	26.4%	73.6%
1982	306,410	52,071	Brown, Clarence J.	245,386	Matsunaga, Spark M.	8,953	193,315 D	17.0%	80.1%	17.5%	82.5%
1980	288,006	53,068	Brown, Cooper	224,485	Inouye, Daniel K.	10,453	171,417 D	18.4%	77.9%	19.1%	80.9%
1976	302,092	122,724	Quinn, William F.	162,305	Matsunaga, Spark M.	17,063	39,581 D	40.6%	53.7%	43.1%	56.9%
1974	250,221		—	207,454	Inouye, Daniel K.	42,767	207,454 D		82.9%		100.0%
1970	240,760	124,163	Fong, Hiram L.	116,597	Heftel, Cecil		7,566 R	51.6%	48.4%	51.6%	48.4%
1968	226,927	34,008	Thiessen, Wayne C.	189,248	Inouye, Daniel K.	3,671	155,240 D	15.0%	83.4%	15.2%	84.8%
1964	208,814	110,747	Fong, Hiram L.	96,789	Gill, Thomas P.	1,278	13,958 R	53.0%	46.4%	53.4%	46.6%
1962	196,361	60,067	Dillingham, Ben F.	136,294	Inouye, Daniel K.		76,227 D	30.6%	69.4%	30.6%	69.4%
1959**	164,808	87,161	Fong, Hiram L.	77,647	Fasi, Frank F.		9,514 R	52.9%	47.1%	52.9%	47.1%
1959S	163,875	79,123	Tsukiyama, W. C.	83,700	Long, Oren E.	1,052	4,577 D	48.3%	51.1%	48.6%	51.4%

The two 1959 elections were held to indeterminate terms and the Senate later determined by lot that Senator Long would serve a short term, Senator Fong a long term. The 1990 election was for a short term to fill a vacancy.

HAWAII

Districts Established July 27, 1991

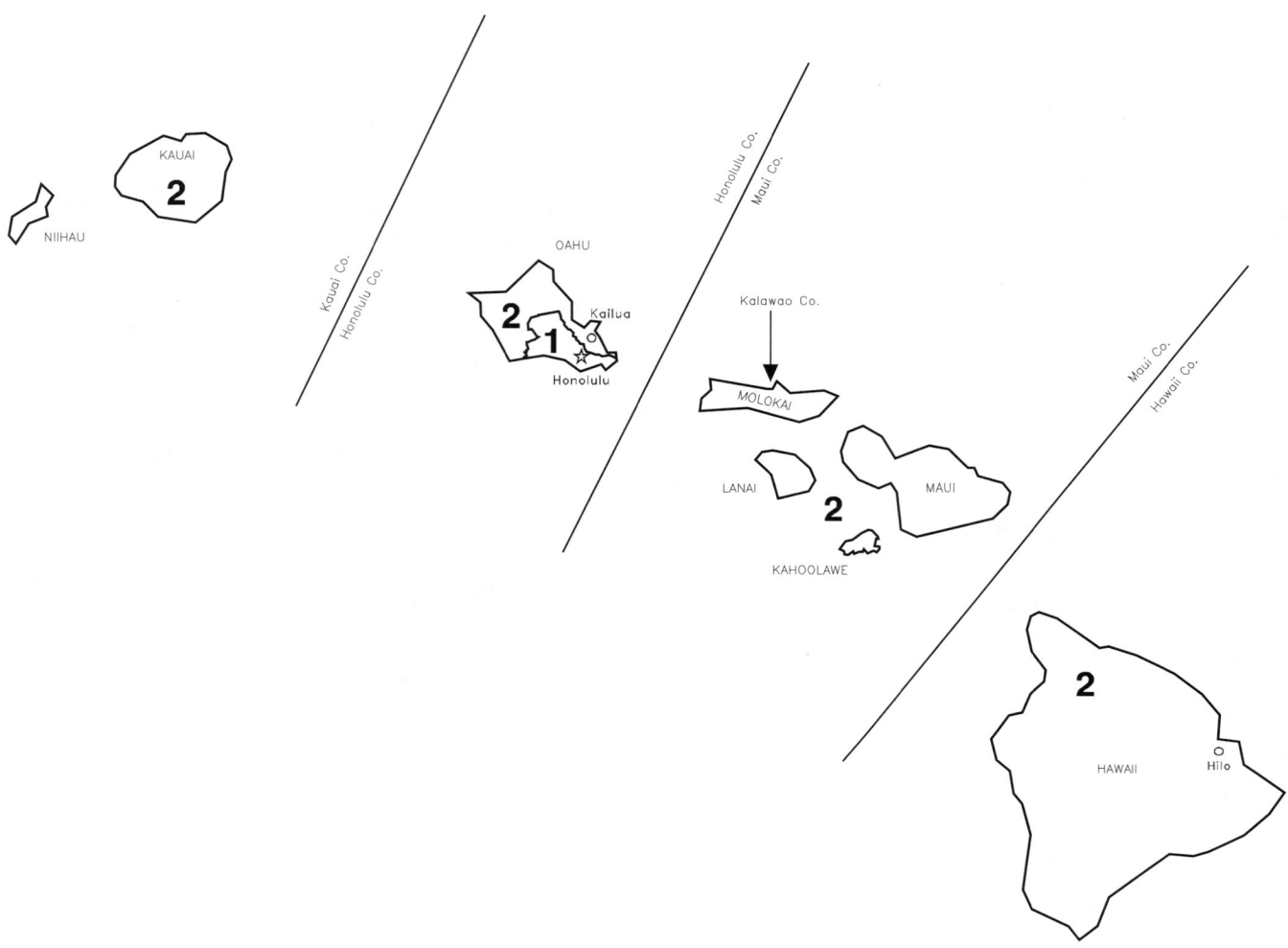

HAWAII

PRESIDENT 2000

2000 Census Population	County	Total Vote	Republican	Democratic	Green (Nader)	Other	Rep.-Dem. Plurality	Percentage of Total Vote		
								Rep.	Dem.	Green
148,677	HAWAII	50,860	17,050	28,670	4,604	536	11,620 D	33.5%	56.4%	9.1%
876,156	HONOLULU	255,990	101,310	139,618	13,037	2,025	38,308 D	39.6%	54.5%	5.1%
58,463	KAUAI	21,773	6,583	13,470	1,474	246	6,887 D	30.2%	61.9%	6.8%
128,094	MAUI	39,248	12,876	23,484	2,499	389	10,608 D	32.8%	59.8%	6.4%
	OVERSEAS BALLOTS	80	26	44	9	1	18 D	32.5%	55.0%	11.3%
1,211,537	TOTAL	367,951	137,845	205,286	21,623	3,197	67,441 D	37.5%	55.8%	5.9%

Note: The 2000 Census includes 147 people in Kalawao County; their votes are part of the Maui County results.

HAWAII

SENATOR 2000

2000 Census Population	County	Total Vote	Republican	Democratic	Other	Rep.-Dem. Plurality	Percentage			
							Total Vote		Major Vote	
							Rep.	Dem.	Rep.	Dem.
148,677	HAWAII	48,409	12,468	34,092	1,849	21,624 D	25.8%	70.4%	26.8%	73.2%
876,156	HONOLULU	239,339	59,943	173,345	6,051	113,402 D	25.0%	72.4%	25.7%	74.3%
58,463	KAUAI	20,273	3,462	16,039	772	12,577 D	17.1%	79.1%	17.8%	82.2%
128,094	MAUI	37,531	8,808	27,695	1,028	18,887 D	23.5%	73.8%	24.1%	75.9%
	OVERSEAS BALLOTS	71	20	44	7	24 D	28.2%	62.0%	31.3%	68.8%
1,211,537	TOTAL	345,623	84,701	251,215	9,707	166,514 D	24.5%	72.7%	25.2%	74.8%

Note: The 2000 Census includes 147 people in Kalawao County; their votes are part of the Maui County results.

HAWAII

CONGRESS

CD	Year	Total Vote	Republican		Democratic		Other Vote	Rep.-Dem. Plurality	Percentage			
			Vote	Candidate	Vote	Candidate			Total Vote		Major Vote	
									Rep.	Dem.	Rep.	Dem.
1	2000	157,194	44,989	MEYERS, PHIL	108,517	ABERCROMBIE, NEIL	3,688	63,528 D	28.6%	69.0%	29.3%	70.7%
1	1998	189,571	68,905	WARD, GENE	116,693	ABERCROMBIE, NEIL	3,973	47,788 D	36.3%	61.6%	37.1%	62.9%
1	1996	172,206	80,053	SWINDLE, ORSON	86,732	ABERCROMBIE, NEIL	5,421	6,679 D	46.5%	50.4%	48.0%	52.0%
1	1994	176,706	76,623	SWINDLE, ORSON	94,754	ABERCROMBIE, NEIL	5,329	18,131 D	43.4%	53.6%	44.7%	55.3%
1	1992	177,476	41,575	SUTTON, WARNER C. K.	129,332	ABERCROMBIE, NEIL	6,569	87,757 D	23.4%	72.9%	24.3%	75.7%
2	2000	183,230	65,906	FRANCIS, RUSS	112,856	MINK, PATSY T.	4,468	46,950 D	36.0%	61.6%	36.9%	63.1%
2	1998	207,871	50,423	DOUGLASS, CAROL J.	144,254	MINK, PATSY T.	13,194	93,831 D	24.3%	69.4%	25.9%	74.1%
2	1996	180,963	55,729	PICO, TOM JR.	109,178	MINK, PATSY T.	16,056	53,449 D	30.8%	60.3%	33.8%	66.2%
2	1994	177,396	42,891	GARNER, ROBERT H.	124,431	MINK, PATSY T.	10,074	81,540 D	24.2%	70.1%	25.6%	74.4%
2	1992	180,955	40,070	PRICE, KAMUELA	131,454	MINK, PATSY T.	9,431	91,384 D	22.1%	72.6%	23.4%	76.6%

HAWAII

GENERAL AND PRIMARY ELECTIONS

2000 GENERAL ELECTIONS

President   Other vote was 1,477 Libertarian (Browne); 1,071 Reform (Buchanan); 343 Constitution (Phillips); 306 Natural Law (Hagelin).

Senator   Other vote was 4,220 Natural Law (Clegg); 3,127 Libertarian (Mallan); 2,360 Constitution (Porter).

Congress   Other vote was: CD 1: 3,688 Libertarian (Murphy); CD 2: 4,468 Libertarian (Duquesne).

2000 PRIMARY ELECTIONS

Primary   September 23, 2000   **Registration**   629,162   No Party Registration
                                                       (as of Sept. 23, 2000)

Primary Type   Open—Any registered voter could vote in the primary of either party.

Note: An asterisk (*) denotes incumbent.

	REPUBLICAN PRIMARIES			DEMOCRATIC PRIMARIES		
Senator	John Carroll	33,349	71.5%	Daniel K. Akaka*	150,507	90.2%
	Eugene F. Douglass	6,117	13.1%	Art P. Reyes	16,312	9.8%
	James R. Deluze	3,910	8.4%			
	Harry J. Friel	3,277	7.0%			
	TOTAL	46,653		TOTAL	166,819	
Congressional District 1	Phil Meyers	9,408	54.7%	Neil Abercrombie*	72,289	84.6%
	Gladys Gerlich Hayes	7,783	45.3%	David L. Bourgoin	13,115	15.4%
	TOTAL	17,191		TOTAL	85,404	
Congressional District 2	Russ Francis	20,354	67.4%	Patsy T. Mink*	66,255	86.1%
	Carol J. Douglass	5,986	19.8%	Charles "Lucky" Collins	10,663	13.9%
	James M. "The Ump" Donovan	3,852	12.8%			
	TOTAL	30,192		TOTAL	76,918	

IDAHO

GOVERNOR

Dirk Kempthorne (R). Elected 1998 to a four-year term.

SENATORS

Larry Craig (R). Re-elected 1996 to a six-year term. Previously elected 1990.

Michael D. Crapo (R). Elected 1998 to a six-year term.

REPRESENTATIVES

1. C. L. Otter (R)   2. Mike Simpson (R)

POSTWAR VOTE FOR PRESIDENT

Year	Total Vote	Republican Vote	Candidate	Democratic Vote	Candidate	Other Vote	Plurality	Total Vote Rep.	Total Vote Dem.	Major Vote Rep.	Major Vote Dem.
2000**	501,621	336,937	Bush, George W.	138,637	Gore, Al	26,047	198,300 R	67.2%	27.6%	70.8%	29.2%
1996**	491,719	256,595	Dole, Bob	165,443	Clinton, Bill	69,681	91,152 R	52.2%	33.6%	60.8%	39.2%
1992**	482,142	202,645	Bush, George	137,013	Clinton, Bill	142,484	65,632 R	42.0%	28.4%	59.7%	40.3%
1988	408,968	253,881	Bush, George	147,272	Dukakis, Michael S.	7,815	106,609 R	62.1%	36.0%	63.3%	36.7%
1984	411,144	297,523	Reagan, Ronald	108,510	Mondale, Walter F.	5,111	189,013 R	72.4%	26.4%	73.3%	26.7%
1980**	437,431	290,699	Reagan, Ronald	110,192	Carter, Jimmy	36,540	180,507 R	66.5%	25.2%	72.5%	27.5%
1976	344,071	204,151	Ford, Gerald R.	126,549	Carter, Jimmy	13,371	77,602 R	59.3%	36.8%	61.7%	38.3%
1972	310,379	199,384	Nixon, Richard M.	80,826	McGovern, George S.	30,169	118,558 R	64.2%	26.0%	71.2%	28.8%
1968	291,183	165,369	Nixon, Richard M.	89,273	Humphrey, Hubert H.	36,541	76,096 R	56.8%	30.7%	64.9%	35.1%
1964	292,477	143,557	Goldwater, Barry M.	148,920	Johnson, Lyndon B.		5,363 D	49.1%	50.9%	49.1%	50.9%
1960	300,450	161,597	Nixon, Richard M.	138,853	Kennedy, John F.		22,744 R	53.8%	46.2%	53.8%	46.2%
1956	272,989	166,979	Eisenhower, Dwight D.	105,868	Stevenson, Adlai E.	142	61,111 R	61.2%	38.8%	61.2%	38.8%
1952	276,254	180,707	Eisenhower, Dwight D.	95,081	Stevenson, Adlai E.	466	85,626 R	65.4%	34.4%	65.5%	34.5%
1948	214,816	101,514	Dewey, Thomas E.	107,370	Truman, Harry S.	5,932	5,856 D	47.3%	50.0%	48.6%	51.4%

In 2000 the other vote column includes 12,292 votes cast for Green (Nader). In 1996 the other vote column includes 62,518 votes cast for Perot. In 1992 the other vote column includes 130,395 votes cast for Perot. In 1980 the other column includes 27,058 votes for Independent (Anderson).

POSTWAR VOTE FOR GOVERNOR

Year	Total Vote	Republican Vote	Candidate	Democratic Vote	Candidate	Other Vote	Rep.-Dem. Plurality	Total Vote Rep.	Total Vote Dem.	Major Vote Rep.	Major Vote Dem.
1998	381,248	258,095	Kempthorne, Dirk	110,815	Huntley, Robert C.	12,338	147,280 R	67.7%	29.1%	70.0%	30.0%
1994	413,346	216,123	Batt, Phil	181,363	EchoHawk, Larry	15,860	34,760 R	52.3%	43.9%	54.4%	45.6%
1990	320,610	101,937	Fairchild, Roger	218,673	Andrus, Cecil D.		116,736 D	31.8%	68.2%	31.8%	68.2%
1986	387,426	189,794	Leroy, David H.	193,429	Andrus, Cecil D.	4,203	3,635 D	49.0%	49.9%	49.5%	50.5%
1982	326,522	161,157	Batt, Philip	165,365	Evans, John V.		4,208 D	49.4%	50.6%	49.4%	50.6%
1978	288,566	114,149	Larsen, Allan	169,540	Evans, John V.	4,877	55,391 D	39.6%	58.8%	40.2%	59.8%
1974	259,632	68,731	Murphy, Jack M.	184,142	Andrus, Cecil D.	6,759	115,411 D	26.5%	70.9%	27.2%	72.8%
1970	245,112	117,108	Samuelson, Don	128,004	Andrus, Cecil D.		10,896 D	47.8%	52.2%	47.8%	52.2%
1966	252,593	104,586	Samuelson, Don	93,744	Andrus, Cecil D.	54,263	10,842 R	41.4%	37.1%	52.7%	47.3%
1962	255,454	139,578	Smylie, Robert E.	115,876	Smith, Vernon K.		23,702 R	54.6%	45.4%	54.6%	45.4%
1958	239,046	121,810	Smylie, Robert E.	117,236	Derr, A. M.		4,574 R	51.0%	49.0%	51.0%	49.0%
1954	228,685	124,038	Smylie, Robert E.	104,647	Hamilton, Clark		19,391 R	54.2%	45.8%	54.2%	45.8%
1950	204,792	107,642	Jordan, Len B.	97,150	Wright, Calvin E.		10,492 R	52.6%	47.4%	52.6%	47.4%
1946	181,364	102,233	Robins, C. A.	79,131	Williams, Arnold		23,102 R	56.4%	43.6%	56.4%	43.6%

IDAHO

POSTWAR VOTE FOR SENATOR

Year	Total Vote	Republican Vote	Republican Candidate	Democratic Vote	Democratic Candidate	Other Vote	Rep.-Dem. Plurality	Total Vote Rep.	Total Vote Dem.	Major Vote Rep.	Major Vote Dem.
1998	378,174	262,966	Crapo, Michael D.	107,375	Mauk, Bill	7,833	155,591 R	69.5%	28.4%	71.0%	29.0%
1996	497,233	283,532	Craig, Larry	198,422	Minnick, Walt	15,279	85,110 R	57.0%	39.9%	58.8%	41.2%
1992	478,522	270,468	Kempthorne, Dirk	208,036	Stallings, Richard	18	62,432 R	56.5%	43.5%	56.5%	43.5%
1990	315,936	193,641	Craig, Larry	122,295	Twilegar, Ron J.		71,346 R	61.3%	38.7%	61.3%	38.7%
1986	382,024	196,958	Symms, Steven D.	185,066	Evans, John V.		11,892 R	51.6%	48.4%	51.6%	48.4%
1984	406,168	293,193	McClure, James A.	105,591	Busch, Peter M.	7,384	187,602 R	72.2%	26.0%	73.5%	26.5%
1980	439,647	218,701	Symms, Steven D.	214,439	Church, Frank	6,507	4,262 R	49.7%	48.8%	50.5%	49.5%
1978	284,047	194,412	McClure, James A.	89,635	Jensen, Dwight		104,777 R	68.4%	31.6%	68.4%	31.6%
1974	258,847	109,072	Smith, Robert L.	145,140	Church, Frank	4,635	36,068 D	42.1%	56.1%	42.9%	57.1%
1972	309,602	161,804	McClure, James A.	140,913	Davis, William E.	6,885	20,891 R	52.3%	45.5%	53.5%	46.5%
1968	287,876	114,394	Hansen, George V.	173,482	Church, Frank		59,088 D	39.7%	60.3%	39.7%	60.3%
1966	252,456	139,819	Jordan, Len B.	112,637	Harding, Ralph R.		27,182 R	55.4%	44.6%	55.4%	44.6%
1962	258,786	117,129	Hawley, Jack	141,657	Church, Frank		24,528 D	45.3%	54.7%	45.3%	54.7%
1962S	257,677	131,279	Jordan, Len B.	126,398	Pfost, Gracie		4,881 R	50.9%	49.1%	50.9%	49.1%
1960	292,096	152,648	Dworshak, Henry C.	139,448	McLaughlin, Bob		13,200 R	52.3%	47.7%	52.3%	47.7%
1956	265,292	102,781	Welker, Herman	149,096	Church, Frank	13,415	46,315 D	38.7%	56.2%	40.8%	59.2%
1954	226,408	142,269	Dworshak, Henry C.	84,139	Taylor, Glen H.		58,130 R	62.8%	37.2%	62.8%	37.2%
1950	201,417	124,237	Welker, Herman	77,180	Clark, D. Worth		47,057 R	61.7%	38.3%	61.7%	38.3%
1950S	201,970	104,068	Dworshak, Henry C.	97,902	Burtenshaw, Claude		6,166 R	51.5%	48.5%	51.5%	48.5%
1948	214,188	103,868	Dworshak, Henry C.	107,000	Miller, Bert H.	3,320	3,132 D	48.5%	50.0%	49.3%	50.7%
1946S	180,152	105,523	Dworshak, Henry C.	74,629	Donart, George E.		30,894 R	58.6%	41.4%	58.6%	41.4%

The 1946 election and one each of the 1962 and 1950 elections were for short terms to fill vacancies.

IDAHO

Districts Established March 2, 1991

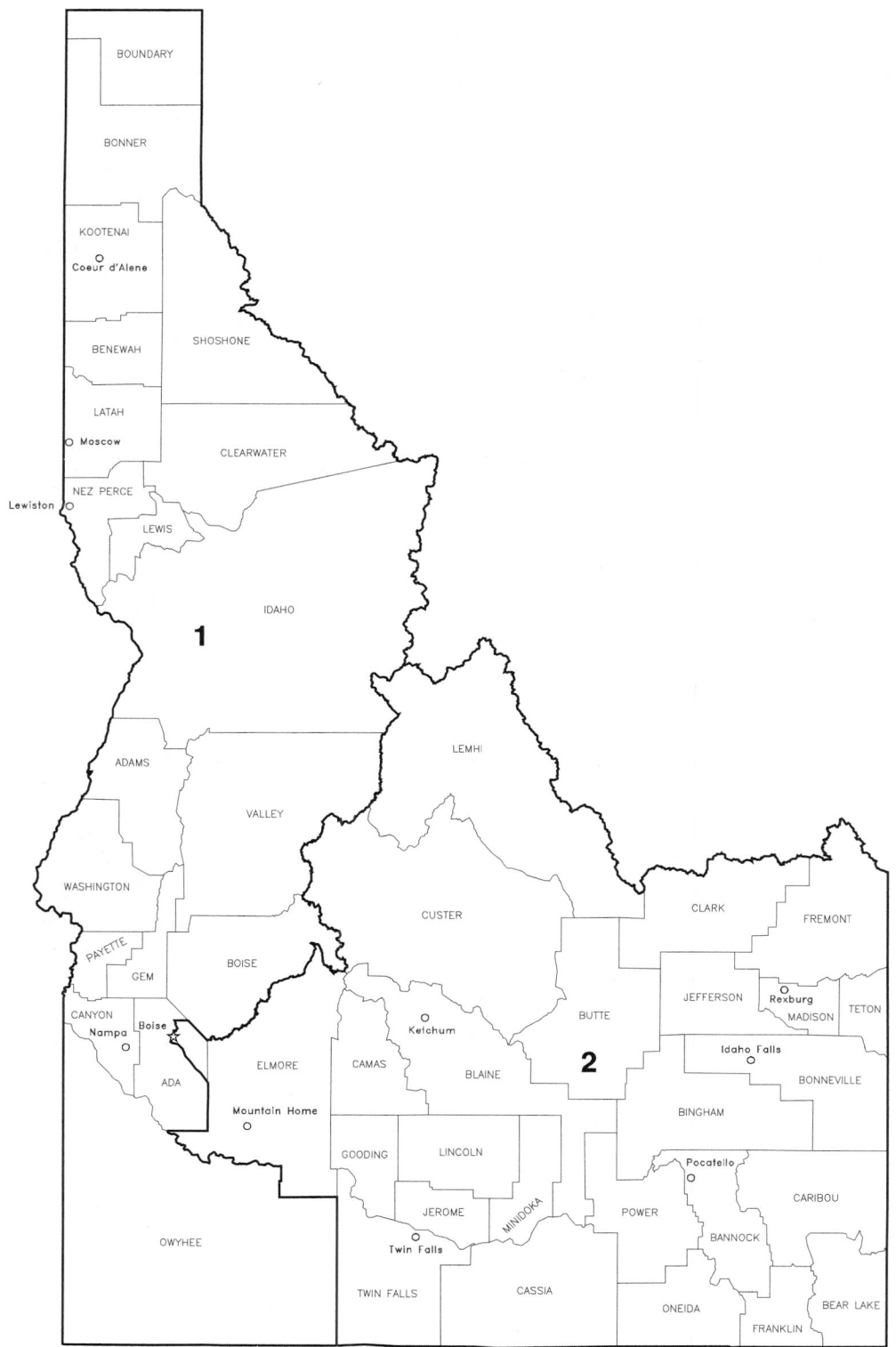

IDAHO

PRESIDENT 2000

2000 Census Population	County	Total Vote	Republican	Democratic	Green (Nader)	Other	Rep.-Dem. Plurality	Percentage of Total Vote		
								Rep.	Dem.	Green
300,904	ADA	123,485	75,050	40,650	4,846	2,939	34,400 R	60.8%	32.9%	3.9%
3,476	ADAMS	1,909	1,476	336	41	56	1,140 R	77.3%	17.6%	2.1%
75,565	BANNOCK	30,852	18,223	10,892	920	817	7,331 R	59.1%	35.3%	3.0%
6,411	BEAR LAKE	2,899	2,296	517	15	71	1,779 R	79.2%	17.8%	0.5%
9,171	BENEWAH	3,687	2,606	895	56	130	1,711 R	70.7%	24.3%	1.5%
41,735	BINGHAM	14,465	10,628	3,310	74	453	7,318 R	73.5%	22.9%	0.5%
18,991	BLAINE	7,938	3,528	3,748	428	234	220 D	44.4%	47.2%	5.4%
6,670	BOISE	3,055	2,019	745	123	168	1,274 R	66.1%	24.4%	4.0%
36,835	BONNER	14,537	8,945	4,318	893	381	4,627 R	61.5%	29.7%	6.1%
82,522	BONNEVILLE	33,556	24,988	7,235	363	970	17,753 R	74.5%	21.6%	1.1%
9,871	BOUNDARY	3,884	2,797	832	132	123	1,965 R	72.0%	21.4%	3.4%
2,899	BUTTE	1,460	1,054	354	5	47	700 R	72.2%	24.2%	0.3%
991	CAMAS	507	359	113	7	28	246 R	70.8%	22.3%	1.4%
131,441	CANYON	43,000	30,560	10,588	588	1,264	19,972 R	71.1%	24.6%	1.4%
7,304	CARIBOU	3,177	2,601	475	28	73	2,126 R	81.9%	15.0%	0.9%
21,416	CASSIA	7,279	5,983	1,087	20	189	4,896 R	82.2%	14.9%	0.3%
1,022	CLARK	382	311	63	1	7	248 R	81.4%	16.5%	0.3%
8,930	CLEARWATER	3,896	2,885	841	34	136	2,044 R	74.1%	21.6%	0.9%
4,342	CUSTER	2,330	1,794	416	44	76	1,378 R	77.0%	17.9%	1.9%
29,130	ELMORE	6,966	4,891	1,840	97	138	3,051 R	70.2%	26.4%	1.4%
11,329	FRANKLIN	4,243	3,594	513	19	117	3,081 R	84.7%	12.1%	0.4%
11,819	FREMONT	5,088	4,242	699	33	114	3,543 R	83.4%	13.7%	0.6%
15,181	GEM	5,983	4,376	1,346	45	216	3,030 R	73.1%	22.5%	0.8%
14,155	GOODING	5,026	3,502	1,282	55	187	2,220 R	69.7%	25.5%	1.1%
15,511	IDAHO	7,452	5,806	1,187	106	353	4,619 R	77.9%	15.9%	1.4%
19,155	JEFFERSON	7,836	6,480	1,100	25	231	5,380 R	82.7%	14.0%	0.3%
18,342	JEROME	6,007	4,418	1,360	24	205	3,058 R	73.5%	22.6%	0.4%
108,685	KOOTENAI	43,812	28,162	13,488	1,083	1,079	14,674 R	64.3%	30.8%	2.5%
34,935	LATAH	15,311	8,161	5,661	999	490	2,500 R	53.3%	37.0%	6.5%
7,806	LEMHI	3,641	2,859	660	12	110	2,199 R	78.5%	18.1%	0.3%
3,747	LEWIS	1,688	1,295	335	13	45	960 R	76.7%	19.8%	0.8%
4,044	LINCOLN	1,574	1,049	437	18	70	612 R	66.6%	27.8%	1.1%
27,467	MADISON	8,970	7,941	816	37	176	7,125 R	88.5%	9.1%	0.4%
20,174	MINIDOKA	6,518	4,907	1,344	30	237	3,563 R	75.3%	20.6%	0.5%
37,410	NEZ PERCE	16,021	10,577	4,995	141	308	5,582 R	66.0%	31.2%	0.9%
4,125	ONEIDA	1,798	1,426	307	8	57	1,119 R	79.3%	17.1%	0.4%
10,644	OWYHEE	3,188	2,450	623	22	93	1,827 R	76.9%	19.5%	0.7%
20,578	PAYETTE	6,858	4,961	1,643	80	174	3,318 R	72.3%	24.0%	1.2%
7,538	POWER	2,709	1,872	755	9	73	1,117 R	69.1%	27.9%	0.3%
13,771	SHOSHONE	5,385	2,879	2,225	92	189	654 R	53.5%	41.3%	1.7%
5,999	TETON	2,671	1,745	720	151	55	1,025 R	65.3%	27.0%	5.7%
64,284	TWIN FALLS	22,530	15,794	5,777	310	649	10,017 R	70.1%	25.6%	1.4%
7,651	VALLEY	3,978	2,548	1,129	201	100	1,419 R	64.1%	28.4%	5.1%
9,977	WASHINGTON	4,070	2,899	980	64	127	1,919 R	71.2%	24.1%	1.6%
1,293,953	TOTAL	501,621	336,937	138,637	12,292	13,755	198,300 R	67.2%	27.6%	2.5%

Note: The votes cast for Nader were write-ins.

IDAHO

CONGRESS

CD	Year	Total Vote	Republican Vote	Republican Candidate	Democratic Vote	Democratic Candidate	Other Vote	Rep.-Dem. Plurality	Total Vote Rep.	Total Vote Dem.	Major Vote Rep.	Major Vote Dem.
1	2000	268,116	173,743	OTTER, C.L. "BUTCH"	84,080	PALL, LINDA	10,293	89,663 R	64.8%	31.4%	67.4%	32.6%
1	1998	204,884	113,231	CHENOWETH, HELEN	91,653	WILLIAMS, DAN		21,578 R	55.3%	44.7%	55.3%	44.7%
1	1996	264,778	132,344	CHENOWETH, HELEN	125,899	WILLIAMS, DAN	6,535	6,445 R	50.0%	47.5%	51.2%	48.8%
1	1994	201,554	111,728	CHENOWETH, HELEN	89,826	LAROCCO, LARRY		21,902 R	55.4%	44.6%	55.4%	44.6%
1	1992	242,790	90,983	GILBERT, RACHEL S.	140,985	LAROCCO, LARRY	10,822	50,002 D	37.5%	58.1%	39.2%	60.8%
2	2000	224,719	158,912	SIMPSON, MIKE	58,265	WILLIAMS, CRAIG	7,542	100,647 R	70.7%	25.9%	73.2%	26.8%
2	1998	173,945	91,337	SIMPSON, MIKE	77,736	STALLINGS, RICHARD H.	4,872	13,601 R	52.5%	44.7%	54.0%	46.0%
2	1996	229,248	157,646	CRAPO, MICHAEL D.	67,625	SEIDL, JOHN D.	3,977	90,021 R	68.8%	29.5%	70.0%	30.0%
2	1994	191,529	143,593	CRAPO, MICHAEL D.	47,936	FLETCHER, PENNY		95,657 R	75.0%	25.0%	75.0%	25.0%
2	1992	229,957	139,783	CRAPO, MICHAEL D.	81,450	WILLIAMS, J. D.	8,724	58,333 R	60.8%	35.4%	63.2%	36.8%

IDAHO

GENERAL AND PRIMARY ELECTIONS

2000 GENERAL ELECTIONS

President   Other vote was 7,615 Reform (Buchanan); 3,488 Libertarian (Browne); 1,469 Constitution (Phillips); 1,177 Natural Law (Hagelin); 4 write-in (Schriner); 1 write-in (Daigneau); 1 write-in (Msmere).

Congress   Other vote was: CD 1: 6,093 Libertarian (Wittig); 4,200 Reform (Hambsch); CD 2: 7,542 Libertarian (Bramwell).

2000 PRIMARY ELECTIONS

Primary   May 23, 2000

Registration (as of May 23, 2000)   630,341   No Party Registration

Primary Type   Open—Any registered voter could vote in the primary of either party.

Note: An asterisk (*) denotes incumbent.

	REPUBLICAN PRIMARIES			DEMOCRATIC PRIMARIES		
President	George W. Bush	116,385	73.5%	Al Gore	27,025	75.7%
	Alan Keyes	30,263	19.1%	None of the Names Shown	5,722	16.0%
	None of the Names Shown	11,798	7.4%	Lyndon H. LaRouche Jr.	2,941	8.2%
	TOTAL	158,446		TOTAL	35,688	
Congressional District 1	C. L. "Butch" Otter	41,516	47.6%	Linda Pall	16,657	100.0%
	Dennis Mansfield	23,559	27.0%			
	Ron McMurray	14,434	16.6%			
	Craig S. Benjamin	2,966	3.4%			
	A. "Big Jim" Pratt	1,281	1.5%			
	Gene Summa	1,240	1.4%			
	David Shepherd	1,181	1.4%			
	Harley D. Brown	983	1.1%			
	TOTAL	87,160		TOTAL	16,657	
Congressional District 2	Mike Simpson*	60,984	100.0%	Craig Williams	10,771	77.3%
				Jack Wayne Chappell	3,169	22.7%
	TOTAL	60,984		TOTAL	13,940	

ILLINOIS

GOVERNOR
George H. Ryan (R). Elected 1998 to a four-year term.

SENATORS
Peter Fitzgerald (R). Elected 1998 to a six-year term.

Richard J. Durbin (D). Elected 1996 to a six-year term.

REPRESENTATIVES
1. Bobby L. Rush (D)
2. Jesse L. Jackson Jr. (D)
3. William O. Lipinski (D)
4. Luis V. Gutierrez (D)
5. Rod R. Blagojevich (D)
6. Henry J. Hyde (R)
7. Danny K. Davis (D)
8. Philip M. Crane (R)
9. Jan Schakowsky (D)
10. Mark Steven Kirk (R)
11. Gerald C. Weller (R)
12. Jerry F. Costello (D)
13. Judy Biggert (R)
14. J. Dennis Hastert (R)
15. Timothy V. Johnson (R)
16. Donald Manzullo (R)
17. Lane Evans (D)
18. Ray LaHood (R)
19. David D. Phelps (D)
20. John M. Shimkus (R)

POSTWAR VOTE FOR PRESIDENT

| | | Republican | | Democratic | | Other | | Percentage | | | |
| | | | | | | | | Total Vote | | Major Vote | |
Year	Total Vote	Vote	Candidate	Vote	Candidate	Vote	Plurality	Rep.	Dem.	Rep.	Dem.
2000**	4,742,123	2,019,421	Bush, George W.	2,589,026	Gore, Al	133,676	569,605 D	42.6%	54.6%	43.8%	56.2%
1996**	4,311,391	1,587,021	Dole, Bob	2,341,744	Clinton, Bill	382,626	754,723 D	36.8%	54.3%	40.4%	59.6%
1992**	5,050,157	1,734,096	Bush, George	2,453,350	Clinton, Bill	862,711	719,254 D	34.3%	48.6%	41.4%	58.6%
1988	4,559,120	2,310,939	Bush, George	2,215,940	Dukakis, Michael S.	32,241	94,999 R	50.7%	48.6%	51.0%	49.0%
1984	4,819,088	2,707,103	Reagan, Ronald	2,086,499	Mondale, Walter F.	25,486	620,604 R	56.2%	43.3%	56.5%	43.5%
1980**	4,749,721	2,358,049	Reagan, Ronald	1,981,413	Carter, Jimmy	410,259	376,636 R	49.6%	41.7%	54.3%	45.7%
1976	4,718,914	2,364,269	Ford, Gerald R.	2,271,295	Carter, Jimmy	83,350	92,974 R	50.1%	48.1%	51.0%	49.0%
1972	4,723,236	2,788,179	Nixon, Richard M.	1,913,472	McGovern, George S.	21,585	874,707 R	59.0%	40.5%	59.3%	40.7%
1968	4,619,749	2,174,774	Nixon, Richard M.	2,039,814	Humphrey, Hubert H.	405,161	134,960 R	47.1%	44.2%	51.6%	48.4%
1964	4,702,841	1,905,946	Goldwater, Barry M.	2,796,833	Johnson, Lyndon B.	62	890,887 D	40.5%	59.5%	40.5%	59.5%
1960	4,757,409	2,368,988	Nixon, Richard M.	2,377,846	Kennedy, John F.	10,575	8,858 D	49.8%	50.0%	49.9%	50.1%
1956	4,407,407	2,623,327	Eisenhower, Dwight D.	1,775,682	Stevenson, Adlai E.	8,398	847,645 R	59.5%	40.3%	59.6%	40.4%
1952	4,481,058	2,457,327	Eisenhower, Dwight D.	2,013,920	Stevenson, Adlai E.	9,811	443,407 R	54.8%	44.9%	55.0%	45.0%
1948	3,984,046	1,961,103	Dewey, Thomas E.	1,994,715	Truman, Harry S.	28,228	33,612 D	49.2%	50.1%	49.6%	50.4%

In 2000 the other vote column includes 103,759 votes cast for Green (Nader). In 1996 the other vote column includes 346,408 votes cast for Perot. In 1992 the other vote column includes 840,515 votes cast for Perot. In 1980 the other column includes 346,754 votes for Independent (Anderson).

ILLINOIS

POSTWAR VOTE FOR GOVERNOR

Year	Total Vote	Republican Vote	Republican Candidate	Democratic Vote	Democratic Candidate	Other Vote	Rep.-Dem. Plurality	Total Vote Rep.	Total Vote Dem.	Major Vote Rep.	Major Vote Dem.
1998	3,358,705	1,714,094	Ryan, George H.	1,594,191	Poshard, Glenn	50,420	119,903 R	51.0%	47.5%	51.8%	48.2%
1994	3,106,566	1,984,318	Edgar, Jim	1,069,850	Netsch, Dawn C.	52,398	914,468 R	63.9%	34.4%	65.0%	35.0%
1990	3,257,410	1,653,126	Edgar, Jim	1,569,217	Hartigan, Neil F.	35,067	83,909 R	50.7%	48.2%	51.3%	48.7%
1986**	3,143,978	1,655,849	Thompson, James R.	208,830	[See note below]	1,279,299	1,447,019 R	52.7%	6.6%	88.8%	11.2%
1982	3,673,681	1,816,101	Thompson, James R.	1,811,027	Stevenson, Adlai E., III	46,553	5,074 R	49.4%	49.3%	50.1%	49.9%
1978	3,150,095	1,859,684	Thompson, James R.	1,263,134	Bakalis, Michael	27,277	596,550 R	59.0%	40.1%	59.6%	40.4%
1976S	4,638,997	3,000,395	Thompson, James R.	1,610,258	Howlett, Michael J.	28,344	1,390,137 R	64.7%	34.7%	65.1%	34.9%
1972	4,678,804	2,293,809	Ogilvie, Richard B.	2,371,303	Walker, Daniel	13,692	77,494 D	49.0%	50.7%	49.2%	50.8%
1968	4,506,000	2,307,295	Ogilvie, Richard B.	2,179,501	Shapiro, Samuel H.	19,204	127,794 R	51.2%	48.4%	51.4%	48.6%
1964	4,657,500	2,239,095	Percy, Charles H.	2,418,394	Kerner, Otto	11	179,299 D	48.1%	51.9%	48.1%	51.9%
1960	4,674,187	2,070,479	Stratton, William G.	2,594,731	Kerner, Otto	8,977	524,252 D	44.3%	55.5%	44.4%	55.6%
1956	4,314,611	2,171,786	Stratton, William G.	2,134,909	Austin, Richard B.	7,916	36,877 R	50.3%	49.5%	50.4%	49.6%
1952	4,415,864	2,317,363	Stratton, William G.	2,089,721	Dixon, Sherwood	8,780	227,642 R	52.5%	47.3%	52.6%	47.4%
1948	3,940,257	1,678,007	Green, Dwight H.	2,250,074	Stevenson, Adlai E.	12,176	572,067 D	42.6%	57.1%	42.7%	57.3%

In 1986 there was no Democratic candidate for Governor on the ballot, Mark Fairchild being the "paired" Democrat for Lt. Governor and the Democratic vote above was cast for this ticket of "no name" and Fairchild. Other vote in this election was 1,256,626 Adlai E. Stevenson III (Solidarity) who received 40.0% of the total vote and came in second; 15,646 Gary L. Shilts (Libertarian); 6,843 Diane Roling (Socialist Workers) and 184 scattered. The 1976 vote was for a two-year term to permit shifting the vote for Governor to non-Presidential years.

POSTWAR VOTE FOR SENATOR

Year	Total Vote	Republican Vote	Republican Candidate	Democratic Vote	Democratic Candidate	Other Vote	Rep.-Dem. Plurality	Total Vote Rep.	Total Vote Dem.	Major Vote Rep.	Major Vote Dem.
1998	3,394,521	1,709,041	Fitzgerald, Peter G.	1,610,496	Moseley-Braun, Carol	74,984	98,545 R	50.3%	47.4%	51.5%	48.5%
1996	4,250,722	1,728,824	Salvi, Al	2,384,028	Durbin, Richard J.	137,870	655,204 D	40.7%	56.1%	42.0%	58.0%
1992	4,939,558	2,126,833	Williamson, Richard S.	2,631,229	Moseley-Braun, Carol	181,496	504,396 D	43.1%	53.3%	44.7%	55.3%
1990	3,251,005	1,135,628	Martin, Lynn	2,115,377	Simon, Paul		979,749 D	34.9%	65.1%	34.9%	65.1%
1986	3,122,883	1,053,734	Koehler, Judy	2,033,783	Dixon, Alan J.	35,366	980,049 D	33.7%	65.1%	34.1%	65.9%
1984	4,787,473	2,308,039	Percy, Charles H.	2,397,303	Simon, Paul	82,131	89,264 D	48.2%	50.1%	49.1%	50.9%
1980	4,580,029	1,946,296	O'Neal, David C.	2,565,302	Dixon, Alan J.	68,431	619,006 D	42.5%	56.0%	43.1%	56.9%
1978	3,184,764	1,698,711	Percy, Charles H.	1,448,187	Seith, Alex	37,866	250,524 R	53.3%	45.5%	54.0%	46.0%
1974	2,914,666	1,084,884	Burditt, George M.	1,811,496	Stevenson, Adlai E., III	18,286	726,612 D	37.2%	62.2%	37.5%	62.5%
1972	4,608,380	2,867,078	Percy, Charles H.	1,721,031	Pucinski, Roman C.	20,271	1,146,047 R	62.2%	37.3%	62.5%	37.5%
1970S	3,599,272	1,519,718	Smith, Ralph T.	2,065,054	Stevenson, Adlai E., III	14,500	545,336 D	42.2%	57.4%	42.4%	57.6%
1968	4,449,757	2,358,947	Dirksen, Everett M.	2,073,242	Clark, William G.	17,568	285,705 R	53.0%	46.6%	53.2%	46.8%
1966	3,822,725	2,100,449	Percy, Charles H.	1,678,147	Douglas, Paul H.	44,129	422,302 R	54.9%	43.9%	55.6%	44.4%
1962	3,709,216	1,961,202	Dirksen, Everett M.	1,748,007	Yates, Sidney R.	7	213,195 R	52.9%	47.1%	52.9%	47.1%
1960	4,632,796	2,093,846	Witwer, Samuel W.	2,530,943	Douglas, Paul H.	8,007	437,097 D	45.2%	54.6%	45.3%	54.7%
1956	4,264,830	2,307,352	Dirksen, Everett M.	1,949,883	Stengel, Richard	7,595	357,469 R	54.1%	45.7%	54.2%	45.8%
1954	3,368,025	1,563,683	Meek, Joseph T.	1,804,338	Douglas, Paul H.	4	240,655 D	46.4%	53.6%	46.4%	53.6%
1950	3,622,673	1,951,984	Dirksen, Everett M.	1,657,630	Lucas, Scott W.	13,059	294,354 R	53.9%	45.8%	54.1%	45.9%
1948	3,900,285	1,740,026	Brooks, C. Wayland	2,147,754	Douglas, Paul H.	12,505	407,728 D	44.6%	55.1%	44.8%	55.2%

The 1970 election was for a short term to fill a vacancy.

150

ILLINOIS

Districts Established November 6, 1991

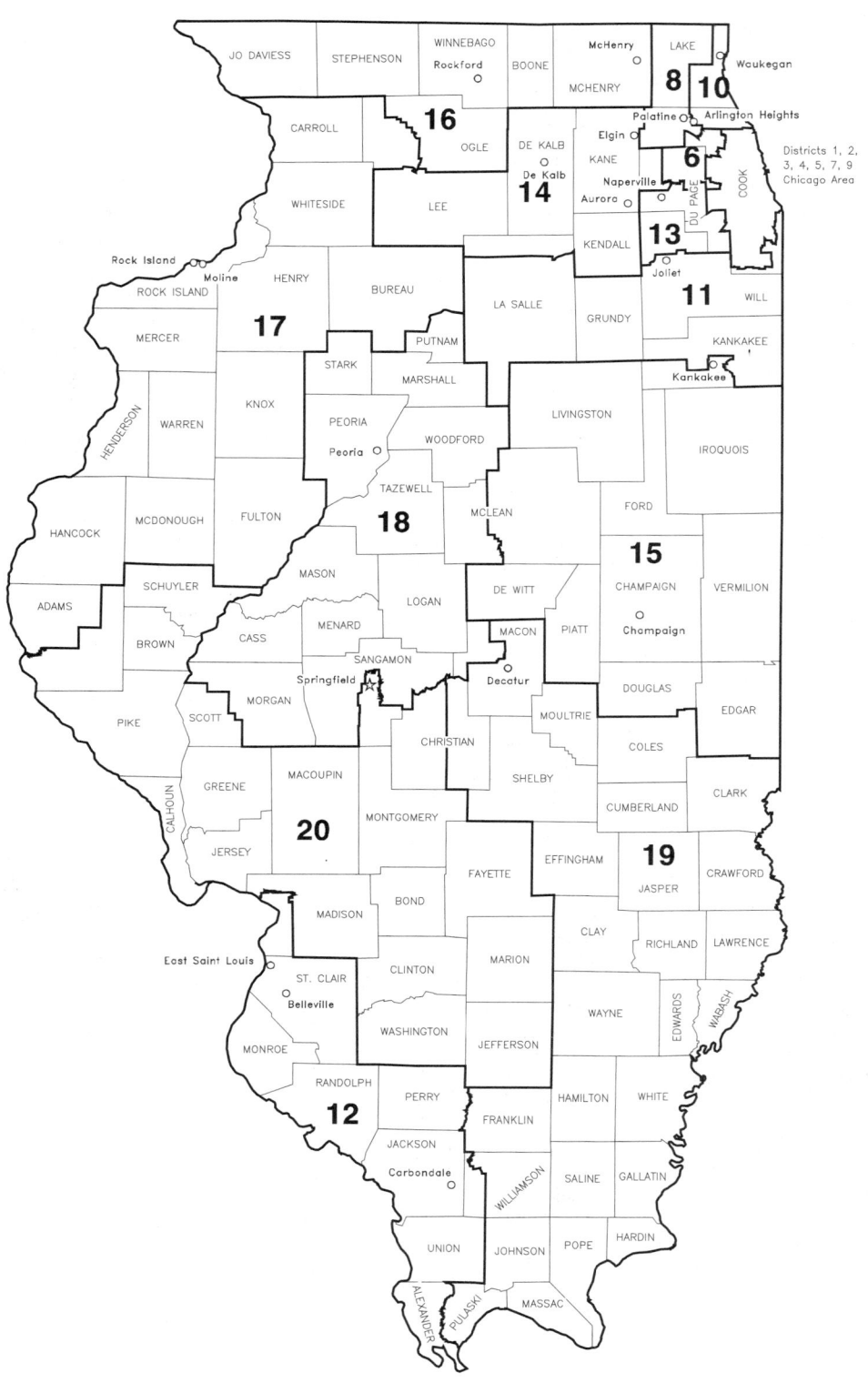

Districts 1, 2, 3, 4, 5, 7, 9 Chicago Area

COOK/DU PAGE COUNTY
CONGRESSIONAL DISTRICTS

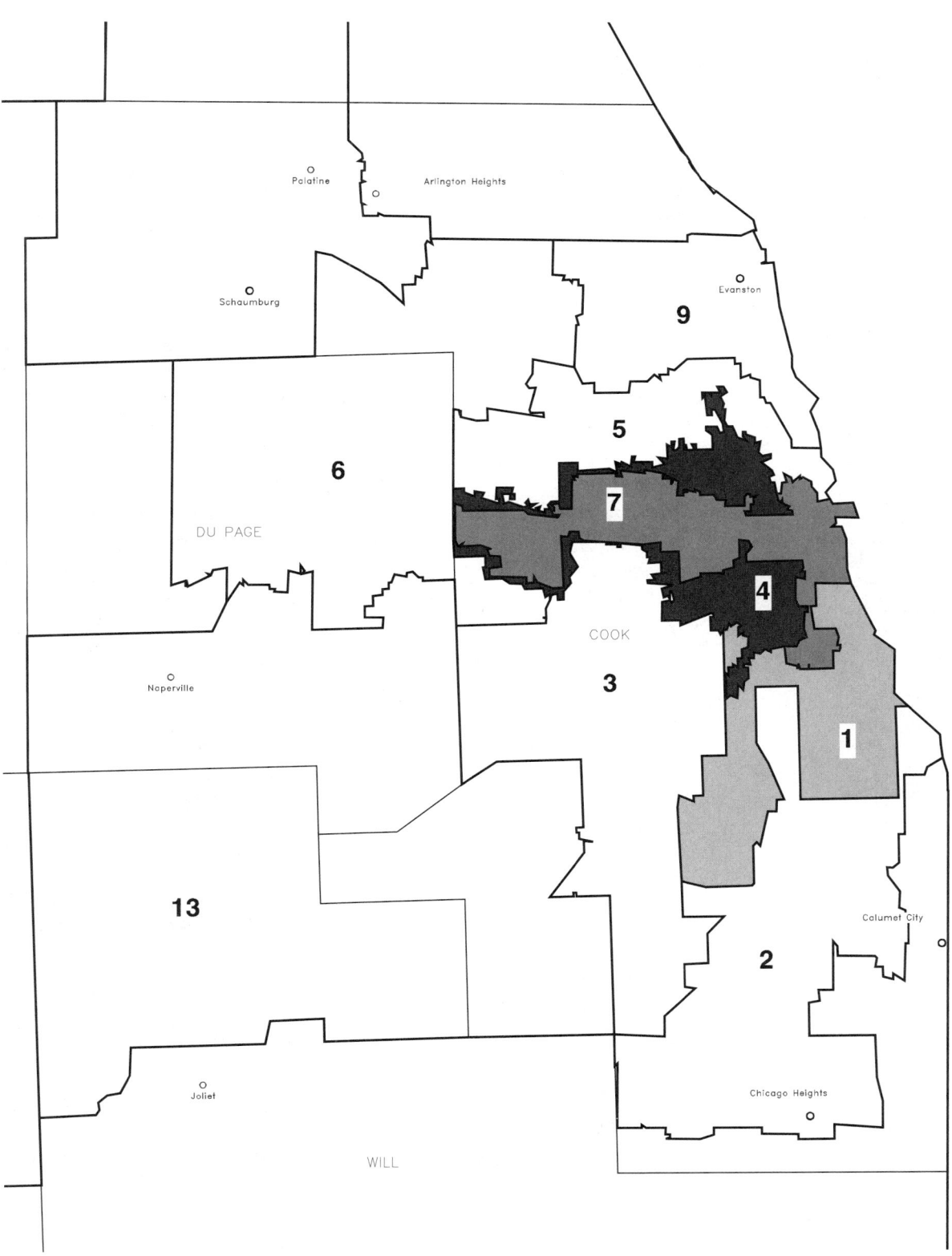

ILLINOIS

PRESIDENT 2000

2000 Census Population	County	Total Vote	Republican	Democratic	Green (Nader)	Other	Rep.-Dem. Plurality	Percentage of Total Vote		
								Rep.	Dem.	Green
68,277	ADAMS	30,109	17,331	12,197	371	210	5,134 R	57.6%	40.5%	1.2%
9,590	ALEXANDER	4,022	1,588	2,357	28	49	769 D	39.5%	58.6%	0.7%
17,633	BOND	7,032	3,804	3,060	113	55	744 R	54.1%	43.5%	1.6%
41,786	BOONE	15,523	8,617	6,481	325	100	2,136 R	55.5%	41.8%	2.1%
6,950	BROWN	2,660	1,529	1,077	29	25	452 R	57.5%	40.5%	1.1%
35,503	BUREAU	16,823	8,526	7,754	363	180	772 R	50.7%	46.1%	2.2%
5,084	CALHOUN	2,602	1,229	1,310	42	21	81 D	47.2%	50.3%	1.6%
16,674	CARROLL	7,177	3,835	3,113	154	75	722 R	53.4%	43.4%	2.1%
13,695	CASS	5,899	2,968	2,789	94	48	179 R	50.3%	47.3%	1.6%
179,669	CHAMPAIGN	74,285	34,645	35,515	3,543	582	870 D	46.6%	47.8%	4.8%
35,372	CHRISTIAN	14,771	7,537	6,799	269	166	738 R	51.0%	46.0%	1.8%
17,008	CLARK	7,512	4,398	2,932	126	56	1,466 R	58.5%	39.0%	1.7%
14,560	CLAY	6,135	3,789	2,212	78	56	1,577 R	61.8%	36.1%	1.3%
35,535	CLINTON	15,427	8,588	6,436	295	108	2,152 R	55.7%	41.7%	1.9%
53,196	COLES	20,093	10,495	8,904	507	187	1,591 R	52.2%	44.3%	2.5%
5,376,741	COOK	1,865,907	534,542	1,280,547	42,068	8,750	746,005 D	28.6%	68.6%	2.3%
20,452	CRAWFORD	8,500	4,974	3,333	118	75	1,641 R	58.5%	39.2%	1.4%
11,253	CUMBERLAND	4,975	2,964	1,870	72	69	1,094 R	59.6%	37.6%	1.4%
88,969	DE KALB	33,233	17,139	14,798	1,032	264	2,341 R	51.6%	44.5%	3.1%
16,798	DE WITT	7,051	3,968	2,870	133	80	1,098 R	56.3%	40.7%	1.9%
19,922	DOUGLAS	8,152	4,734	3,215	132	71	1,519 R	58.1%	39.4%	1.6%
904,161	DU PAGE	364,362	201,037	152,550	8,711	2,064	48,487 R	55.2%	41.9%	2.4%
19,704	EDGAR	8,232	4,833	3,216	113	70	1,617 R	58.7%	39.1%	1.4%
6,971	EDWARDS	3,260	2,212	978	42	28	1,234 R	67.9%	30.0%	1.3%
34,264	EFFINGHAM	14,485	9,855	4,225	213	192	5,630 R	68.0%	29.2%	1.5%
21,802	FAYETTE	9,338	5,200	3,886	122	130	1,314 R	55.7%	41.6%	1.3%
14,241	FORD	6,153	3,889	2,090	116	58	1,799 R	63.2%	34.0%	1.9%
39,018	FRANKLIN	19,212	8,490	10,201	347	174	1,711 D	44.2%	53.1%	1.8%
38,250	FULTON	16,277	6,936	8,940	276	125	2,004 D	42.6%	54.9%	1.7%
6,445	GALLATIN	3,558	1,591	1,878	40	49	287 D	44.7%	52.8%	1.1%
14,761	GREENE	5,767	3,129	2,490	93	55	639 R	54.3%	43.2%	1.6%
37,535	GRUNDY	16,584	8,709	7,516	257	102	1,193 R	52.5%	45.3%	1.5%
8,621	HAMILTON	4,587	2,519	1,943	75	50	576 R	54.9%	42.4%	1.6%
20,121	HANCOCK	9,691	5,134	4,256	161	140	878 R	53.0%	43.9%	1.7%
4,800	HARDIN	2,637	1,366	1,184	41	46	182 R	51.8%	44.9%	1.6%
8,213	HENDERSON	3,866	1,708	2,030	74	54	322 D	44.2%	52.5%	1.9%
51,020	HENRY	23,470	10,896	11,921	428	225	1,025 D	46.4%	50.8%	1.8%
31,334	IROQUOIS	13,424	8,685	4,397	229	113	4,288 R	64.7%	32.8%	1.7%
59,612	JACKSON	23,090	9,823	11,773	1,228	266	1,950 D	42.5%	51.0%	5.3%
10,117	JASPER	5,021	3,119	1,815	50	37	1,304 R	62.1%	36.1%	1.0%
40,045	JEFFERSON	15,360	8,362	6,685	211	102	1,677 R	54.4%	43.5%	1.4%
21,668	JERSEY	9,413	4,699	4,355	231	128	344 R	49.9%	46.3%	2.5%
22,289	JO DAVIESS	10,322	5,304	4,585	314	119	719 R	51.4%	44.4%	3.0%
12,878	JOHNSON	5,362	3,285	1,928	83	66	1,357 R	61.3%	36.0%	1.5%
404,119	KANE	141,405	76,996	60,127	3,274	1,008	16,869 R	54.5%	42.5%	2.3%
103,833	KANKAKEE	40,183	20,049	19,180	713	241	869 R	49.9%	47.7%	1.8%
54,544	KENDALL	22,769	13,688	8,444	481	156	5,244 R	60.1%	37.1%	2.1%
55,836	KNOX	23,174	9,912	12,572	455	235	2,660 D	42.8%	54.3%	2.0%
644,356	LAKE	242,164	120,988	115,058	4,843	1,275	5,930 R	50.0%	47.5%	2.0%
111,509	LA SALLE	46,007	21,276	23,355	992	384	2,079 D	46.2%	50.8%	2.2%
15,452	LAWRENCE	6,578	3,594	2,822	101	61	772 R	54.6%	42.9%	1.5%
36,062	LEE	14,620	8,069	6,111	320	120	1,958 R	55.2%	41.8%	2.2%
39,678	LIVINGSTON	15,421	9,187	5,829	285	120	3,358 R	59.6%	37.8%	1.8%
31,183	LOGAN	13,065	8,141	4,600	208	116	3,541 R	62.3%	35.2%	1.6%
32,913	MCDONOUGH	13,012	6,465	6,080	364	103	385 R	49.7%	46.7%	2.8%
260,077	MCHENRY	106,185	62,112	40,698	2,751	624	21,414 R	58.5%	38.3%	2.6%
150,433	MCLEAN	60,898	34,008	24,936	1,546	408	9,072 R	55.8%	40.9%	2.5%
114,706	MACON	49,499	23,830	24,262	982	425	432 D	48.1%	49.0%	2.0%
49,019	MACOUPIN	21,389	9,749	11,015	426	199	1,266 D	45.6%	51.5%	2.0%
258,941	MADISON	111,104	48,821	59,077	2,359	847	10,256 D	43.9%	53.2%	2.1%

ILLINOIS

PRESIDENT 2000

2000 Census Population	County	Total Vote	Republican	Democratic	Green (Nader)	Other	Rep.-Dem. Plurality	Percentage of Total Vote		
								Rep.	Dem.	Green
41,691	MARION	16,663	8,240	8,068	238	117	172 R	49.5%	48.4%	1.4%
13,180	MARSHALL	5,907	3,145	2,570	134	58	575 R	53.2%	43.5%	2.3%
16,038	MASON	6,772	3,411	3,192	117	52	219 R	50.4%	47.1%	1.7%
15,161	MASSAC	6,744	3,676	2,912	83	73	764 R	54.5%	43.2%	1.2%
12,486	MENARD	6,202	3,862	2,164	135	41	1,698 R	62.3%	34.9%	2.2%
16,957	MERCER	8,318	3,688	4,400	156	74	712 D	44.3%	52.9%	1.9%
27,619	MONROE	13,796	7,632	5,797	262	105	1,835 R	55.3%	42.0%	1.9%
30,652	MONTGOMERY	13,093	6,226	6,542	191	134	316 D	47.6%	50.0%	1.5%
36,616	MORGAN	14,334	8,058	5,899	253	124	2,159 R	56.2%	41.2%	1.8%
14,287	MOULTRIE	5,725	3,058	2,529	78	60	529 R	53.4%	44.2%	1.4%
51,032	OGLE	20,601	12,325	7,673	467	136	4,652 R	59.8%	37.2%	2.3%
183,433	PEORIA	76,812	36,398	38,604	1,332	478	2,206 D	47.4%	50.3%	1.7%
23,094	PERRY	9,942	4,802	4,862	173	105	60 D	48.3%	48.9%	1.7%
16,365	PIATT	8,385	4,619	3,488	217	61	1,131 R	55.1%	41.6%	2.6%
17,384	PIKE	8,112	4,706	3,198	115	93	1,508 R	58.0%	39.4%	1.4%
4,413	POPE	2,330	1,346	927	31	26	419 R	57.8%	39.8%	1.3%
7,348	PULASKI	3,016	1,430	1,518	31	37	88 D	47.4%	50.3%	1.0%
6,086	PUTNAM	3,179	1,437	1,657	58	27	220 D	45.2%	52.1%	1.8%
33,893	RANDOLPH	14,287	7,127	6,794	229	137	333 R	49.9%	47.6%	1.6%
16,149	RICHLAND	7,428	4,718	2,491	134	85	2,227 R	63.5%	33.5%	1.8%
149,374	ROCK ISLAND	65,095	25,194	37,957	1,364	580	12,763 D	38.7%	58.3%	2.1%
256,082	ST. CLAIR	100,393	42,299	55,961	1,569	564	13,662 D	42.1%	55.7%	1.6%
26,733	SALINE	11,650	5,933	5,427	181	109	506 R	50.9%	46.6%	1.6%
188,951	SANGAMON	91,485	50,374	38,414	2,001	696	11,960 R	55.1%	42.0%	2.2%
7,189	SCHUYLER	3,772	2,077	1,587	72	36	490 R	55.1%	42.1%	1.9%
5,537	SCOTT	2,469	1,458	954	31	26	504 R	59.1%	38.6%	1.3%
22,893	SHELBY	10,163	5,851	4,018	162	132	1,833 R	57.6%	39.5%	1.6%
6,332	STARK	2,989	1,694	1,211	55	29	483 R	56.7%	40.5%	1.8%
48,979	STEPHENSON	19,378	10,715	8,062	476	125	2,653 R	55.3%	41.6%	2.5%
128,485	TAZEWELL	58,348	31,537	25,379	1,022	410	6,158 R	54.0%	43.5%	1.8%
18,293	UNION	8,660	4,397	3,982	189	92	415 R	50.8%	46.0%	2.2%
83,919	VERMILION	32,100	15,783	15,406	605	306	377 R	49.2%	48.0%	1.9%
12,937	WABASH	5,508	3,406	1,987	75	40	1,419 R	61.8%	36.1%	1.4%
18,735	WARREN	7,631	3,899	3,524	130	78	375 R	51.1%	46.2%	1.7%
15,148	WASHINGTON	7,138	4,353	2,638	96	51	1,715 R	61.0%	37.0%	1.3%
17,151	WAYNE	7,693	5,347	2,209	77	60	3,138 R	69.5%	28.7%	1.0%
15,371	WHITE	7,637	4,521	2,958	113	45	1,563 R	59.2%	38.7%	1.5%
60,653	WHITESIDE	24,837	11,252	12,886	515	184	1,634 D	45.3%	51.9%	2.1%
502,266	WILL	191,670	95,828	90,902	3,769	1,171	4,926 R	50.0%	47.4%	2.0%
61,296	WILLIAMSON	26,939	14,012	12,192	476	259	1,820 R	52.0%	45.3%	1.8%
278,418	WINNEBAGO	109,297	53,816	51,981	2,637	863	1,835 R	49.2%	47.6%	2.4%
35,469	WOODFORD	16,793	10,905	5,529	263	96	5,376 R	64.9%	32.9%	1.6%
12,419,293	TOTAL	4,742,123	2,019,421	2,589,026	103,759	29,917	569,605 D	42.6%	54.6%	2.2%

CHICAGO

PRESIDENT 2000

2000 Census Population	Ward	Total Vote	Republican	Democratic	Green (Nader)	Other	Rep.-Dem. Plurality	Percentage of Total Vote		
								Rep.	Dem.	Green
	Ward 1	14,391	2,303	10,986	1,009	93	8,683 D	16.0%	76.3%	7.0%
	Ward 2	19,106	1,724	16,954	346	82	15,230 D	9.0%	88.7%	1.8%
	Ward 3	12,943	258	12,572	55	58	12,314 D	2.0%	97.1%	0.4%
	Ward 4	20,864	986	19,351	464	63	18,365 D	4.7%	92.7%	2.2%
	Ward 5	21,691	947	20,265	415	64	19,318 D	4.4%	93.4%	1.9%
	Ward 6	24,647	433	24,071	100	43	23,638 D	1.8%	97.7%	0.4%
	Ward 7	20,457	559	19,724	123	51	19,165 D	2.7%	96.4%	0.6%
	Ward 8	26,270	445	25,665	107	53	25,220 D	1.7%	97.7%	0.4%
	Ward 9	20,360	407	19,824	76	53	19,417 D	2.0%	97.4%	0.4%
	Ward 10	16,849	3,559	12,830	329	131	9,271 D	21.1%	76.1%	2.0%
	Ward 11	17,433	3,567	13,376	391	99	9,809 D	20.5%	76.7%	2.2%
	Ward 12	6,230	1,162	4,932	109	27	3,770 D	18.7%	79.2%	1.7%
	Ward 13	21,651	6,639	14,347	526	139	7,708 D	30.7%	66.3%	2.4%
	Ward 14	13,827	2,674	10,866	229	58	8,192 D	19.3%	78.6%	1.7%
	Ward 15	18,358	834	17,378	97	49	16,544 D	4.5%	94.7%	0.5%
	Ward 16	12,431	487	11,850	53	41	11,363 D	3.9%	95.3%	0.4%
	Ward 17	19,455	259	19,083	65	48	18,824 D	1.3%	98.1%	0.3%
	Ward 18	24,319	1,461	22,607	176	75	21,146 D	6.0%	93.0%	0.7%
	Ward 19	27,967	9,485	17,577	739	166	8,092 D	33.9%	62.8%	2.6%
	Ward 20	17,078	337	16,592	100	49	16,255 D	2.0%	97.2%	0.6%
	Ward 21	25,483	414	24,906	98	65	24,492 D	1.6%	97.7%	0.4%
	Ward 22	9,323	830	8,393	76	24	7,563 D	8.9%	90.0%	0.8%
	Ward 23	23,333	8,270	14,396	543	124	6,126 D	35.4%	61.7%	2.3%
	Ward 24	17,711	286	17,331	43	51	17,045 D	1.6%	97.9%	0.2%
	Ward 25	9,964	1,522	8,064	336	42	6,542 D	15.3%	80.9%	3.4%
	Ward 26	13,791	2,050	11,101	561	79	9,051 D	14.9%	80.5%	4.1%
	Ward 27	20,607	3,145	16,989	383	90	13,844 D	15.3%	82.4%	1.9%
	Ward 28	17,236	276	16,863	53	44	16,587 D	1.6%	97.8%	0.3%
	Ward 29	19,292	927	18,205	93	67	17,278 D	4.8%	94.4%	0.5%
	Ward 30	14,422	3,768	10,141	425	88	6,373 D	26.1%	70.3%	2.9%
	Ward 31	11,657	1,926	9,509	176	46	7,583 D	16.5%	81.6%	1.5%
	Ward 32	23,643	6,760	15,489	1,255	139	8,729 D	28.6%	65.5%	5.3%
	Ward 33	15,191	3,035	11,493	577	86	8,458 D	20.0%	75.7%	3.8%
	Ward 34	23,277	360	22,792	75	50	22,432 D	1.5%	97.9%	0.3%
	Ward 35	12,850	2,181	9,785	791	93	7,604 D	17.0%	76.1%	6.2%
	Ward 36	20,945	6,668	13,770	398	109	7,102 D	31.8%	65.7%	1.9%
	Ward 37	18,195	409	17,673	66	47	17,264 D	2.2%	97.1%	0.4%
	Ward 38	19,585	6,703	12,229	538	115	5,526 D	34.2%	62.4%	2.7%
	Ward 39	16,658	5,409	10,635	526	88	5,226 D	32.5%	63.8%	3.2%
	Ward 40	16,352	3,512	11,927	788	125	8,415 D	21.5%	72.9%	4.8%
	Ward 41	25,046	11,292	12,951	661	142	1,659 D	45.1%	51.7%	2.6%
	Ward 42	31,027	10,972	19,127	795	133	8,155 D	35.4%	61.6%	2.6%
	Ward 43	27,929	10,470	16,550	793	116	6,080 D	37.5%	59.3%	2.8%
	Ward 44	28,945	8,394	19,276	1,111	164	10,882 D	29.0%	66.6%	3.8%
	Ward 45	22,678	8,420	13,370	755	133	4,950 D	37.1%	59.0%	3.3%
	Ward 46	21,038	3,886	16,077	928	147	12,191 D	18.5%	76.4%	4.4%
	Ward 47	21,695	4,673	15,563	1,317	142	10,890 D	21.5%	71.7%	6.1%
	Ward 48	19,571	3,221	15,412	833	105	12,191 D	16.5%	78.7%	4.3%
	Ward 49	14,737	1,940	11,831	859	107	9,891 D	13.2%	80.3%	5.8%
	Ward 50	16,753	3,365	12,843	467	78	9,478 D	20.1%	76.7%	2.8%
	Absentees	5,798	1,320	4,318	139	21	2,998 D	22.8%	74.5%	2.4%
2,896,016	TOTAL	961,061	164,930	769,859	21,968	4,304	604,929 D	17.2%	80.1%	2.3%

Note: There were two write-in votes included in the "Other" column that were not assigned to any particular ward.

ILLINOIS

CONGRESS

CD	Year	Total Vote	Republican Vote	Republican Candidate	Democratic Vote	Democratic Candidate	Other Vote	Rep.-Dem. Plurality	Total Vote Rep.	Total Vote Dem.	Major Vote Rep.	Major Vote Dem.
1	2000	196,186	23,915	WARDINGLEY, RAYMOND G.	172,271	RUSH, BOBBY L.		148,356 D	12.2%	87.8%	12.2%	87.8%
1	1998	174,365	18,429	AHIMAZ, MARLENE	151,890	RUSH, BOBBY L.		133,461 D	10.6%	87.1%	10.8%	89.2%
1	1996	203,113	25,659	NAUGHTON, NOEL	174,005	RUSH, BOBBY L.	4,046	148,346 D	12.6%	85.7%	12.9%	87.1%
1	1994	148,512	36,038	KELLY, WILLIAM J.	112,474	RUSH, BOBBY L.	3,449	76,436 D	24.3%	75.7%	24.3%	75.7%
1	1992	252,711	43,453	WALKER, JAY	209,258	RUSH, BOBBY L.		165,805 D	17.2%	82.8%	17.2%	82.8%
2	2000	195,901	19,906	GORDON, ROBERT III	175,995	JACKSON, JESSE L. JR.		156,089 D	10.2%	89.8%	10.2%	89.8%
2	1998	166,668	16,075	GORDON, ROBERT III	148,985	JACKSON, JESSE L. JR.	1,608	132,910 D	9.6%	89.4%	9.7%	90.3%
2	1996	183,543			172,648	JACKSON, JESSE L. JR.	10,895	172,648 D		94.1%		100.0%
2	1994	95,855			93,998	REYNOLDS, MELVIN J.	1,857	93,998 D		98.1%		100.0%
2	1992	233,864	31,957	BLACKSTONE, RON	182,614	REYNOLDS, MELVIN J.	19,293	150,657 D	13.7%	78.1%	14.9%	85.1%
3	2000	192,503	47,005	GROTH, KARL	145,498	LIPINSKI, WILLIAM O.		98,493 D	24.4%	75.6%	24.4%	75.6%
3	1998	159,899	44,012	MARSHALL, ROBERT	115,887	LIPINSKI, WILLIAM O.		71,875 D	27.5%	72.5%	27.5%	72.5%
3	1996	209,916	67,214	NALEPA, JIM	137,153	LIPINSKI, WILLIAM O.	5,549	69,939 D	32.0%	65.3%	32.9%	67.1%
3	1994	170,516	78,163	NALEPA, JIM	92,353	LIPINSKI, WILLIAM O.		14,190 D	45.8%	54.2%	45.8%	54.2%
3	1992	255,293	93,128	LEPINSKE, HARRY C.	162,165	LIPINSKI, WILLIAM O.		69,037 D	36.5%	63.5%	36.5%	63.5%
4	2000	100,963			89,487	GUTIERREZ, LUIS V.	11,476	89,487 D		88.6%		100.0%
4	1998	66,356	10,529	BIRCH, JOHN	54,244	GUTIERREZ, LUIS V.	1,583	43,715 D	15.9%	81.7%	16.3%	83.7%
4	1996	91,135			85,278	GUTIERREZ, LUIS V.	5,857	85,278 D		93.6%		100.0%
4	1994	62,079	15,384	VALTIERRA, STEVEN	46,695	GUTIERREZ, LUIS V.		31,311 D	24.8%	75.2%	24.8%	75.2%
4	1992	116,606	26,154	RODRIGUEZ-SCHEIMAN, H.	90,452	GUTIERREZ, LUIS V.		64,298 D	22.4%	77.6%	22.4%	77.6%
5	2000	162,889			142,161	BLAGOJEVICH, ROD R.	20,728	142,161 D		87.3%		100.0%
5	1998	129,425	33,687	SPITZ, ALAN	95,738	BLAGOJEVICH, ROD R.		62,051 D	26.0%	74.0%	26.0%	74.0%
5	1996	183,326	65,768	FLANAGAN, MICHAEL P.	117,544	BLAGOJEVICH, ROD R.	14	51,776 D	35.9%	64.1%	35.9%	64.1%
5	1994	138,393	75,328	FLANAGAN, MICHAEL P.	63,065	ROSTENKOWSKI, DANIEL		12,263 R	54.4%	45.6%	54.4%	45.6%
5	1992	232,083	90,738	ZENKICH, ELIAS R.	132,889	ROSTENKOWSKI, DANIEL	8,456	42,151 D	39.1%	57.3%	40.6%	59.4%
6	2000	226,207	133,327	HYDE, HENRY J.	92,880	CHRISTENSEN, BRENT		40,447 R	58.9%	41.1%	58.9%	41.1%
6	1998	165,708	111,603	HYDE, HENRY J.	49,906	CRAMER, THOMAS A.	4,199	61,697 R	67.3%	30.1%	69.1%	30.9%
6	1996	205,954	132,401	HYDE, HENRY J.	68,807	DE LA ROSA, STEPHEN	4,746	63,594 R	64.3%	33.4%	65.8%	34.2%
6	1994	157,378	115,664	HYDE, HENRY J.	37,163	BERRY, TOM	4,551	78,501 R	73.5%	23.6%	75.7%	24.3%
6	1992	251,904	165,009	HYDE, HENRY J.	86,891	WATKINS, BARRY W.	4	78,118 R	65.5%	34.5%	65.5%	34.5%
7	2000	191,027	26,872	DALLAS, ROBERT	164,155	DAVIS, DANNY K.		137,283 D	14.1%	85.9%	14.1%	85.9%
7	1998	140,968			130,984	DAVIS, DANNY K.	9,984	130,984 D		92.9%		100.0%
7	1996	181,095	27,241	BOROW, RANDY	149,568	DAVIS, DANNY K.	4,286	122,327 D	15.0%	82.6%	15.4%	84.6%
7	1994	117,468	24,011	MOBLEY, CHARLES	93,457	COLLINS, CARDISS		69,446 D	20.4%	79.6%	20.4%	79.6%
7	1992	225,281	35,346	BOCCIO, NORMAN G.	182,811	COLLINS, CARDISS	7,124	147,465 D	15.7%	81.1%	16.2%	83.8%
8	2000	232,695	141,918	CRANE, PHILIP M.	90,777	PRESSL, LANCE		51,141 R	61.0%	39.0%	61.0%	39.0%
8	1998	151,856	104,242	CRANE, PHILIP M.	47,614	ROTHMAN, MIKE		56,628 R	68.6%	31.4%	68.6%	31.4%
8	1996	205,305	127,763	CRANE, PHILIP M.	74,068	HULL, ELIZABETH A.	3,474	53,695 R	62.2%	36.1%	63.3%	36.7%
8	1994	135,879	88,225	CRANE, PHILIP M.	47,654	WALBERG, ROBERT C.		40,571 R	64.9%	35.1%	64.9%	35.1%
8	1992	238,633	132,887	CRANE, PHILIP M.	96,419	SMITH, SHEILA A.	9,327	36,468 R	55.7%	40.4%	58.0%	42.0%
9	2000	192,346	45,344	DRISCOLL, DENNIS J.	147,002	SCHAKOWSKY, JANICE D. "JAN"		101,658 D	23.6%	76.4%	23.6%	76.4%
9	1998	144,610	33,448	SOHN, HERBERT	107,878	SCHAKOWSKY, JANICE D. "JAN"	3,284	74,430 D	23.1%	74.6%	23.7%	76.3%
9	1996	196,082	71,763	WALSH, JOSEPH	124,319	YATES, SIDNEY R.		52,556 D	36.6%	63.4%	36.6%	63.4%
9	1994	142,823	48,419	LARNEY, GEORGE E.	94,404	YATES, SIDNEY R.		45,985 D	33.9%	66.1%	33.9%	66.1%
9	1992	239,703	64,760	SOHN, HERBERT	162,942	YATES, SIDNEY R.	12,001	98,182 D	27.0%	68.0%	28.4%	71.6%
10	2000	237,506	121,582	KIRK, MARK STEVEN	115,924	GASH, LAUREN BETH		5,658 R	51.2%	48.8%	51.2%	48.8%
10	1998	138,429	138,429	PORTER, JOHN E.				138,429 R	100.0%		100.0%	
10	1996	210,773	145,626	PORTER, JOHN E.	65,144	TORF, PHILIP R.	3	80,482 R	69.1%	30.9%	69.1%	30.9%
10	1994	153,075	114,884	PORTER, JOHN E.	38,191	KRUPP, ANDREW M.		76,693 R	75.1%	24.9%	75.1%	24.9%
10	1992	240,630	155,230	PORTER, JOHN E.	85,400	KENNEDY, MICHAEL J.		69,830 R	64.5%	35.5%	64.5%	35.5%

ILLINOIS

CONGRESS

CD	Year	Total Vote	Republican Vote	Republican Candidate	Democratic Vote	Democratic Candidate	Other Vote	Rep.-Dem. Plurality		Total Vote Rep.	Total Vote Dem.	Major Vote Rep.	Major Vote Dem.
11	2000	234,869	132,384	WELLER, GERALD C.	102,485	STEVENSON, JAMES P.		29,899	R	56.4%	43.6%	56.4%	43.6%
11	1998	171,055	100,597	WELLER, GERALD C.	70,458	MUELLER, GARY S.		30,139	R	58.8%	41.2%	58.8%	41.2%
11	1996	212,284	109,896	WELLER, GERALD C.	102,388	BALANOFF, CLEM		7,508	R	51.8%	48.2%	51.8%	48.2%
11	1994	160,395	97,241	WELLER, GERALD C.	63,150	GIGLIO, FRANK	4	34,091	R	60.6%	39.4%	60.6%	39.4%
11	1992	243,247	107,860	HERBOLSHEIMER, ROBERT T.	135,387	SANGMEISTER, GEORGE E.		27,527	D	44.3%	55.7%	44.3%	55.7%
12	2000	183,257			183,208	COSTELLO, JERRY F.	49	183,208	D		100.0%		100.0%
12	1998	165,014	65,409	PRICE, WILLIAM MELVIN	99,605	COSTELLO, JERRY F.		34,196	D	39.6%	60.4%	39.6%	60.4%
12	1996	209,519	55,690	HUNTER, SHAPLEY R.	150,005	COSTELLO, JERRY F.	3,824	94,315	D	26.6%	71.6%	27.1%	72.9%
12	1994	153,810	52,419	MORRIS, JAN	101,391	COSTELLO, JERRY F.		48,972	D	34.1%	65.9%	34.1%	65.9%
12	1992	236,877	68,115	STARR, MIKE	168,762	COSTELLO, JERRY F.		100,647	D	28.8%	71.2%	28.8%	71.2%
13	2000	292,018	193,250	BIGGERT, JUDY	98,768	MASON, THOMAS		94,482	R	66.2%	33.8%	66.2%	33.8%
13	1998	199,767	121,889	BIGGERT, JUDY	77,878	HYNES, SUSAN W.		44,011	R	61.0%	39.0%	61.0%	39.0%
13	1996	236,344	141,651	FAWELL, HARRIS W.	94,693	HYNES, SUSAN W.		46,958	R	59.9%	40.1%	59.9%	40.1%
13	1994	170,021	124,312	FAWELL, HARRIS W.	45,709	RILEY, WILLIAM A.		78,603	R	73.1%	26.9%	73.1%	26.9%
13	1992	262,255	179,257	FAWELL, HARRIS W.	82,985	TEMPLE, DENNIS M.	13	96,272	R	68.4%	31.6%	68.4%	31.6%
14	2000	254,909	188,597	HASTERT, J. DENNIS	66,309	DELJONSON, VERN	3	122,288	R	74.0%	26.0%	74.0%	26.0%
14	1998	168,148	117,304	HASTERT, J. DENNIS	50,844	COZZI, ROBERT A. JR.		66,460	R	69.8%	30.2%	69.8%	30.2%
14	1996	208,764	134,432	HASTERT, J. DENNIS	74,332	MAINS, DOUG		60,100	R	64.4%	35.6%	64.4%	35.6%
14	1994	144,095	110,204	HASTERT, J. DENNIS	33,891	DENARI, STEVE		76,313	R	76.5%	23.5%	76.5%	23.5%
14	1992	230,624	155,271	HASTERT, J. DENNIS	75,294	REICH, JONATHAN A.	59	79,977	R	67.3%	32.6%	67.3%	32.7%
15	2000	236,622	125,943	JOHNSON, TIM	110,679	KELLEHER, F. MICHAEL JR.		15,264	R	53.2%	46.8%	53.2%	46.8%
15	1998	169,309	104,255	EWING, THOMAS	65,054	PRUSSING, LAUREL L.		39,201	R	61.6%	38.4%	61.6%	38.4%
15	1996	211,084	121,019	EWING, THOMAS	90,065	PRUSSING, LAUREL L.		30,954	R	57.3%	42.7%	57.3%	42.7%
15	1994	159,731	108,857	EWING, THOMAS	50,874	ALEXANDER, PAUL		57,983	R	68.2%	31.8%	68.2%	31.8%
15	1992	239,586	142,167	EWING, THOMAS	97,190	MATTIS, CHARLES D.	229	44,977	R	59.3%	40.6%	59.4%	40.6%
16	2000	267,071	178,174	MANZULLO, DONALD	88,781	HENDRICKSON, CHARLES W.	116	89,393	R	66.7%	33.2%	66.7%	33.3%
16	1998	143,686	143,686	MANZULLO, DONALD				143,686	R	100.0%		100.0%	
16	1996	228,100	137,523	MANZULLO, DONALD	90,575	LEE, CATHERINE M.	2	46,948	R	60.3%	39.7%	60.3%	39.7%
16	1994	165,974	117,238	MANZULLO, DONALD	48,736	SULLIVAN, PETE		68,502	R	70.6%	29.4%	70.6%	29.4%
16	1992	255,943	142,388	MANZULLO, DONALD	113,555	COX, JOHN W.		28,833	R	55.6%	44.4%	55.6%	44.4%
17	2000	241,347	108,853	BAKER, MARK	132,494	EVANS, LANE		23,641	D	45.1%	54.9%	45.1%	54.9%
17	1998	194,200	94,072	BAKER, MARK	100,128	EVANS, LANE		6,056	D	48.4%	51.6%	48.4%	51.6%
17	1996	231,173	109,240	BAKER, MARK	120,008	EVANS, LANE	1,925	10,768	D	47.3%	51.9%	47.7%	52.3%
17	1994	174,783	79,471	ANDERSON, JIM	95,312	EVANS, LANE		15,841	D	45.5%	54.5%	45.5%	54.5%
17	1992	259,952	103,719	SCHLOEMER, KEN	156,233	EVANS, LANE		52,514	D	39.9%	60.1%	39.9%	60.1%
18	2000	259,023	173,706	LAHOOD, RAY	85,317	HARANT, JOYCE		88,389	R	67.1%	32.9%	67.1%	32.9%
18	1998	158,177	158,175	LAHOOD, RAY			2	158,175	R	100.0%		100.0%	
18	1996	241,523	143,110	LAHOOD, RAY	98,413	CURRAN, MIKE		44,697	R	59.3%	40.7%	59.3%	40.7%
18	1994	199,125	119,838	LAHOOD, RAY	78,332	STEPHENS, G. DOUGLAS	955	41,506	R	60.2%	39.3%	60.5%	39.5%
18	1992	270,976	156,533	MICHEL, ROBERT H.	114,413	HAWKINS, RONALD C.	30	42,120	R	57.8%	42.2%	57.8%	42.2%
19	2000	240,238	85,137	EATHERLY, JAMES	155,101	PHELPS, DAVID D.		69,964	D	35.4%	64.6%	35.4%	64.6%
19	1998	210,044	87,614	WINTERS, BRENT	122,430	PHELPS, DAVID D.		34,816	D	41.7%	58.3%	41.7%	58.3%
19	1996	237,955	75,751	WINTERS, BRENT	158,668	POSHARD, GLENN	3,536	82,917	D	31.8%	66.7%	32.3%	67.7%
19	1994	197,040	81,995	WINTERS, BRENT	115,045	POSHARD, GLENN		33,050	D	41.6%	58.4%	41.6%	58.4%
19	1992	270,685	83,526	LEE, DOUGLAS E.	187,156	POSHARD, GLENN	3	103,630	D	30.9%	69.1%	30.9%	69.1%
20	2000	255,775	161,393	SHIMKUS, JOHN M.	94,382	COOPER, JEFFREY S.		67,011	R	63.1%	36.9%	63.1%	36.9%
20	1998	197,578	121,103	SHIMKUS, JOHN M.	76,475	VERTICCHIO, RICK		44,628	R	61.3%	38.7%	61.3%	38.7%
20	1996	240,618	120,926	SHIMKUS, JOHN M.	119,688	HOFFMAN, JAY C.	4	1,238	R	50.3%	49.7%	50.3%	49.7%
20	1994	196,998	88,964	OWENS, BILL	108,034	DURBIN, RICHARD J.		19,070	D	45.2%	54.8%	45.2%	54.8%
20	1992	274,088	119,219	SHIMKUS, JOHN M.	154,869	DURBIN, RICHARD J.		35,650	D	43.5%	56.5%	43.5%	56.5%

ILLINOIS
GENERAL AND PRIMARY ELECTIONS

2000 GENERAL ELECTIONS

President Other vote was 16,106 Independent (Buchanan); 11,623 Libertarian (Browne); 2,127 Reform (Hagelin); 57 write-in (Phillips); 4 write-in (McReynolds).

Congress Other vote was: CD 4: 11,476 Libertarian (Sailor); CD 5: 20,728 Libertarian (Beauchamp); CD 12: 47 write-in (Sigler), 2 write-in (Wallace); CD 14: 3 write-in (Rosengarten); CD 16: 104 write-in (Hippie), 12 write-in (Brown).

2000 PRIMARY ELECTIONS

Primary March 21, 2000

Registration (as of March 21, 2000) 6,745,655 No Party Registration

Primary Type Open—Any registered voter could vote in the primary of either party.

Note: An asterisk (*) denotes incumbent.

REPUBLICAN PRIMARIES			DEMOCRATIC PRIMARIES		
President					
George W. Bush	496,685	67.4%	Al Gore	682,932	84.3%
John McCain	158,768	21.5%	Bill Bradley	115,320	14.2%
Alan Keyes	66,066	9.0%	Lyndon H. LaRouche Jr.	11,415	1.4%
Steve Forbes	10,334	1.4%			
Gary Bauer	5,068	0.7%			
TOTAL	736,921		TOTAL	809,667	
Congressional District 1					
Raymond G. Wardingley	2,721	100.0%	Bobby L. Rush*	59,599	61.0%
			Barack Obama	29,649	30.4%
			Donne E. Trotter	6,915	7.1%
			George C. Roby	1,501	1.5%
TOTAL	2,721		TOTAL	97,664	
Congressional District 2					
No Republican candidate filed for the primary. Robert Gordon III was subsequently named to fill the vacancy on the general election ballot.			Jesse L. Jackson Jr.*	67,784	100.0%
			Robert Gordon III (write-in)	4	
			TOTAL	67,788	
Congressional District 3					
Karl Groth	13,527	72.3%	William O. Lipinski*	46,459	90.3%
Ramiro Gonzalez	5,176	27.7%	R. Benedict Mayers	5,009	9.7%
TOTAL	18,703		TOTAL	51,468	
Congressional District 4					
John Birch	2,184	100.0%	Luis V. Gutierrez*	35,593	82.3%
			Joseph L. Pagan	7,663	17.7%
TOTAL	2,184		TOTAL	43,256	
Birch subsequently withdrew from the race. No Republican candidate appeared on the general election ballot.					
Congressional District 5					
No Republican candidate			Rod R. Blagojevich*	40,701	100.0%
			TOTAL	40,701	
Congressional District 6					
Henry J. Hyde*	33,056	100.0%	Brent Christensen	10,546	62.0%
			Thomas A. Cramer	6,464	38.0%
TOTAL	33,056		TOTAL	17,010	
Congressional District 7					
Robert Dallas	2,787	52.0%	Danny K. Davis*	59,100	100.0%
Steve Denari	2,569	48.0%			
TOTAL	5,356		TOTAL	59,100	
Congressional District 8					
Philip M. Crane*	31,060	100.0%	Lance Pressl	10,929	100.0%
TOTAL	31,060		TOTAL	10,929	
Congressional District 9					
Dennis J. Driscoll	8,064	76.8%	Janice D. "Jan" Schakowsky*	49,429	100.0%
Leonard R. Reinebach	2,441	23.2%			
TOTAL	10,505		TOTAL	49,429	

ILLINOIS

GENERAL AND PRIMARY ELECTIONS

REPUBLICAN PRIMARIES				DEMOCRATIC PRIMARIES		
Congressional District 10	Mark Steven Kirk	19,717	31.4%	Lauren Beth Gash	19,696	100.0%
	Shawn Margaret Donnelley	9,585	15.3%			
	Mark William Damisch	9,016	14.4%			
	Andrew Hochberg	7,480	11.9%			
	John H. Cox	6,339	10.1%			
	Scott Phelps	3,712	5.9%			
	Thomas Fredric Lachner	2,555	4.1%			
	Terry Gladman	2,172	3.5%			
	James E. Goulka	1,469	2.3%			
	John F. Guy	397	0.6%			
	Jon Stewart	363	0.6%			
	TOTAL	62,805		TOTAL	19,696	
Congressional District 11	Gerald C. "Jerry" Weller*	30,194	100.0%	James P. Stevenson	25,080	100.0%
	TOTAL	30,194		TOTAL	25,080	
Congressional District 12	*No Republican candidate filed for the primary and none appeared on the general election ballot. Arno Sponeman received 8 write-in votes in the primary.*			Jerry F. Costello*	37,234	89.9%
				Kenneth Charles "Bud" Wiezer	4,189	10.1%
				TOTAL	41,423	
Congressional District 13	Judy Biggert*	39,121	100.0%	*No Democratic candidate filed for the primary. Thomas Mason was subsequently named to fill the vacancy on the general election ballot.*		
	TOTAL	39,121				
Congressional District 14	J. Dennis Hastert*	50,055	100.0%	Vern Deljonson	10,809	100.0%
	TOTAL	50,055		TOTAL	10,809	
Congressional District 15	Tim Johnson	31,485	43.6%	F. Michael Kelleher Jr.	15,147	52.6%
	Bill Brady	26,004	36.0%	Laurel Lunt Prussing	13,636	47.4%
	Samuel Y. Ewing	12,526	17.4%			
	Jeffrey Jones	2,155	3.0%			
	TOTAL	72,170		TOTAL	28,783	
Congressional District 16	Donald Manzullo*	58,703	100.0%	Charles W. Hendrickson	13,107	100.0%
	TOTAL	58,703		TOTAL	13,107	
Congressional District 17	Mark Baker	27,994	65.4%	Lane Evans*	26,138	100.0%
	Hal Bayne	12,104	28.3%			
	Michael Curtiss	2,697	6.3%			
	TOTAL	42,795		TOTAL	26,138	
Congressional District 18	Ray LaHood*	40,746	100.0%	Joyce Harant	15,163	73.3%
				Al Probyn	5,535	26.7%
	TOTAL	40,746		TOTAL	20,698	
Congressional District 19	James Eatherly	21,939	100.0%	David D. Phelps*	39,500	100.0%
	TOTAL	21,939		TOTAL	39,500	
Congressional District 20	John M. Shimkus*	23,943	100.0%	Jeffrey S. Cooper	24,876	100.0%
	TOTAL	23,943		TOTAL	24,876	

INDIANA

GOVERNOR

Frank L. O'Bannon (D). Re-elected 2000 to a four-year term. Previously elected 1996.

SENATORS

Evan Bayh (D). Elected 1998 to a six-year term.

Richard G. Lugar (R). Re-elected 2000 to a six-year term. Previously elected 1994, 1988, 1982, 1976.

REPRESENTATIVES

1. Peter J. Visclosky (D)
2. Mike Pence (R)
3. Timothy J. Roemer (D)
4. Mark E. Souder (R)
5. Steve Buyer (R)
6. Dan Burton (R)
7. Brian Kerns (R)
8. John Hostettler (R)
9. Baron Hill (D)
10. Julia Carson (D)

POSTWAR VOTE FOR PRESIDENT

Year	Total Vote	Republican Vote	Candidate	Democratic Vote	Candidate	Other Vote	Plurality	Rep.	Dem.	Rep.	Dem.
2000**	2,199,302	1,245,836	Bush, George W.	901,980	Gore, Al	51,486	343,856 R	56.6%	41.0%	58.0%	42.0%
1996**	2,135,842	1,006,693	Dole, Bob	887,424	Clinton, Bill	241,725	119,269 R	47.1%	41.5%	53.1%	46.9%
1992**	2,305,871	989,375	Bush, George	848,420	Clinton, Bill	468,076	140,955 R	42.9%	36.8%	53.8%	46.2%
1988	2,168,621	1,297,763	Bush, George	860,643	Dukakis, Michael S.	10,215	437,120 R	59.8%	39.7%	60.1%	39.9%
1984	2,233,069	1,377,230	Reagan, Ronald	841,481	Mondale, Walter F.	14,358	535,749 R	61.7%	37.7%	62.1%	37.9%
1980**	2,242,033	1,255,656	Reagan, Ronald	844,197	Carter, Jimmy	142,180	411,459 R	56.0%	37.7%	59.8%	40.2%
1976	2,220,362	1,183,958	Ford, Gerald R.	1,014,714	Carter, Jimmy	21,690	169,244 R	53.3%	45.7%	53.8%	46.2%
1972	2,125,529	1,405,154	Nixon, Richard M.	708,568	McGovern, George S.	11,807	696,586 R	66.1%	33.3%	66.5%	33.5%
1968	2,123,597	1,067,885	Nixon, Richard M.	806,659	Humphrey, Hubert H.	249,053	261,226 R	50.3%	38.0%	57.0%	43.0%
1964	2,091,606	911,118	Goldwater, Barry M.	1,170,848	Johnson, Lyndon B.	9,640	259,730 D	43.6%	56.0%	43.8%	56.2%
1960	2,135,360	1,175,120	Nixon, Richard M.	952,358	Kennedy, John F.	7,882	222,762 R	55.0%	44.6%	55.2%	44.8%
1956	1,974,607	1,182,811	Eisenhower, Dwight D.	783,908	Stevenson, Adlai E.	7,888	398,903 R	59.9%	39.7%	60.1%	39.9%
1952	1,955,049	1,136,259	Eisenhower, Dwight D.	801,530	Stevenson, Adlai E.	17,260	334,729 R	58.1%	41.0%	58.6%	41.4%
1948	1,656,212	821,079	Dewey, Thomas E.	807,831	Truman, Harry S.	27,302	13,248 R	49.6%	48.8%	50.4%	49.6%

In 2000 the other vote column includes 18,531 votes cast for Green (Nader). In 1996 the other vote column includes 224,299 votes cast for Perot. In 1992 the other vote column includes 455,934 votes cast for Perot. In 1980 the other column includes 111,639 votes for Independent (Anderson).

INDIANA

POSTWAR VOTE FOR GOVERNOR

Year	Total Vote	Republican Vote	Republican Candidate	Democratic Vote	Democratic Candidate	Other Vote	Rep.-Dem. Plurality	Percentage Total Vote Rep.	Percentage Total Vote Dem.	Percentage Major Vote Rep.	Percentage Major Vote Dem.
2000	2,179,413	908,285	McIntosh, David M.	1,232,525	O'Bannon, Frank L.	38,603	324,240 D	41.7%	56.6%	42.4%	57.6%
1996	2,110,047	986,982	Goldsmith, Stephen	1,087,128	O'Bannon, Frank	35,937	100,146 D	46.8%	51.5%	47.6%	52.4%
1992	2,229,116	822,533	Pearson, Linley E.	1,382,151	Bayh, Evan	24,432	559,618 D	36.9%	62.0%	37.3%	62.7%
1988	2,140,781	1,002,207	Mutz, John M.	1,138,574	Bayh, Evan		136,367 D	46.8%	53.2%	46.8%	53.2%
1984	2,197,988	1,146,497	Orr, Robert D.	1,036,922	Townsend, W. Wayne	14,569	109,575 R	52.2%	47.2%	52.5%	47.5%
1980	2,178,403	1,257,383	Orr, Robert D.	913,116	Hillenbrand, John A.	7,904	344,267 R	57.7%	41.9%	57.9%	42.1%
1976	2,175,324	1,236,555	Bowen, Otis R.	927,243	Conrad, Larry A.	11,526	309,312 R	56.8%	42.6%	57.1%	42.9%
1972	2,120,847	1,203,903	Bowen, Otis R.	900,489	Welsh, Matthew E.	16,455	303,414 R	56.8%	42.5%	57.2%	42.8%
1968	2,049,072	1,080,271	Whitcomb, Edgar D.	965,816	Rock, Robert L.	2,985	114,455 R	52.7%	47.1%	52.8%	47.2%
1964	2,072,915	901,342	Ristine, Richard O.	1,164,620	Branigin, Roger D.	6,953	263,278 D	43.5%	56.2%	43.6%	56.4%
1960	2,128,965	1,049,540	Parker, Crawford F.	1,072,717	Welsh, Matthew E.	6,708	23,177 D	49.3%	50.4%	49.5%	50.5%
1956	1,954,290	1,086,868	Handley, Harold W.	859,393	Tucker, Ralph	8,029	227,475 R	55.6%	44.0%	55.8%	44.2%
1952	1,931,869	1,075,685	Craig, George N.	841,984	Watkins, John A.	14,200	233,701 R	55.7%	43.6%	56.1%	43.9%
1948	1,652,321	745,892	Creighton, Hobart	884,995	Schricker, Henry F.	21,434	139,103 D	45.1%	53.6%	45.7%	54.3%

POSTWAR VOTE FOR SENATOR

Year	Total Vote	Republican Vote	Republican Candidate	Democratic Vote	Democratic Candidate	Other Vote	Rep.-Dem. Plurality	Percentage Total Vote Rep.	Percentage Total Vote Dem.	Percentage Major Vote Rep.	Percentage Major Vote Dem.
2000	2,145,209	1,427,944	Lugar, Richard G.	683,273	Johnson, David L.	33,992	744,671 R	66.6%	31.9%	67.6%	32.4%
1998	1,588,617	552,732	Helmke, Paul	1,012,244	Bayh, Evan	23,641	459,512 D	34.8%	63.7%	35.3%	64.7%
1994	1,543,568	1,039,625	Lugar, Richard G.	470,799	Jontz, Jim	33,144	568,826 R	67.4%	30.5%	68.8%	31.2%
1992	2,211,426	1,267,972	Coats, Daniel R.	900,148	Hogsett, Joseph H.	43,306	367,824 R	57.3%	40.7%	58.5%	41.5%
1990S	1,504,302	806,048	Coats, Daniel R.	696,639	Hill, Baron P.	1,615	109,409 R	53.6%	46.3%	53.6%	46.4%
1988	2,099,303	1,430,525	Lugar, Richard G.	668,778	Wickes, Jack		761,747 R	68.1%	31.9%	68.1%	31.9%
1986	1,545,563	936,143	Quayle, J. Danforth	595,192	Long, Jill L.	14,228	340,951 R	60.6%	38.5%	61.1%	38.9%
1982	1,817,287	978,301	Lugar, Richard G.	828,400	Fithian, Floyd	10,586	149,901 R	53.8%	45.6%	54.1%	45.9%
1980	2,198,376	1,182,414	Quayle, J. Danforth	1,015,962	Bayh, Birch		166,452 R	53.8%	46.2%	53.8%	46.2%
1976	2,171,187	1,275,833	Lugar, Richard G.	878,522	Hartke, R. Vance	16,832	397,311 R	58.8%	40.5%	59.2%	40.8%
1974	1,752,978	814,117	Lugar, Richard G.	889,269	Bayh, Birch	49,592	75,152 D	46.4%	50.7%	47.8%	52.2%
1970	1,737,697	866,707	Roudebush, Richard	870,990	Hartke, R. Vance		4,283 D	49.9%	50.1%	49.9%	50.1%
1968	2,053,118	988,571	Ruckelshaus, William	1,060,456	Bayh, Birch	4,091	71,885 D	48.1%	51.7%	48.2%	51.8%
1964	2,076,963	941,519	Bontrager, D. Russell	1,128,505	Hartke, R. Vance	6,939	186,986 D	45.3%	54.3%	45.5%	54.5%
1962	1,800,038	894,547	Capehart, Homer E.	905,491	Bayh, Birch		10,944 D	49.7%	50.3%	49.7%	50.3%
1958	1,724,598	731,635	Handley, Harold W.	973,636	Hartke, R. Vance	19,327	242,001 D	42.4%	56.5%	42.9%	57.1%
1956	1,963,986	1,084,262	Capehart, Homer E.	871,781	Wickard, Claude	7,943	212,481 R	55.2%	44.4%	55.4%	44.6%
1952	1,946,118	1,020,605	Jenner, William E.	911,169	Schricker, Henry F.	14,344	109,436 R	52.4%	46.8%	52.8%	47.2%
1950	1,598,724	844,303	Capehart, Homer E.	741,025	Campbell, Alex M.	13,396	103,278 R	52.8%	46.4%	53.3%	46.7%
1946	1,347,434	739,809	Jenner, William E.	584,288	Townsend, M. Clifford	23,337	155,521 R	54.9%	43.4%	55.9%	44.1%

The 1990 election was for a short term to fill a vacancy.

INDIANA

Districts Established June 13, 1991

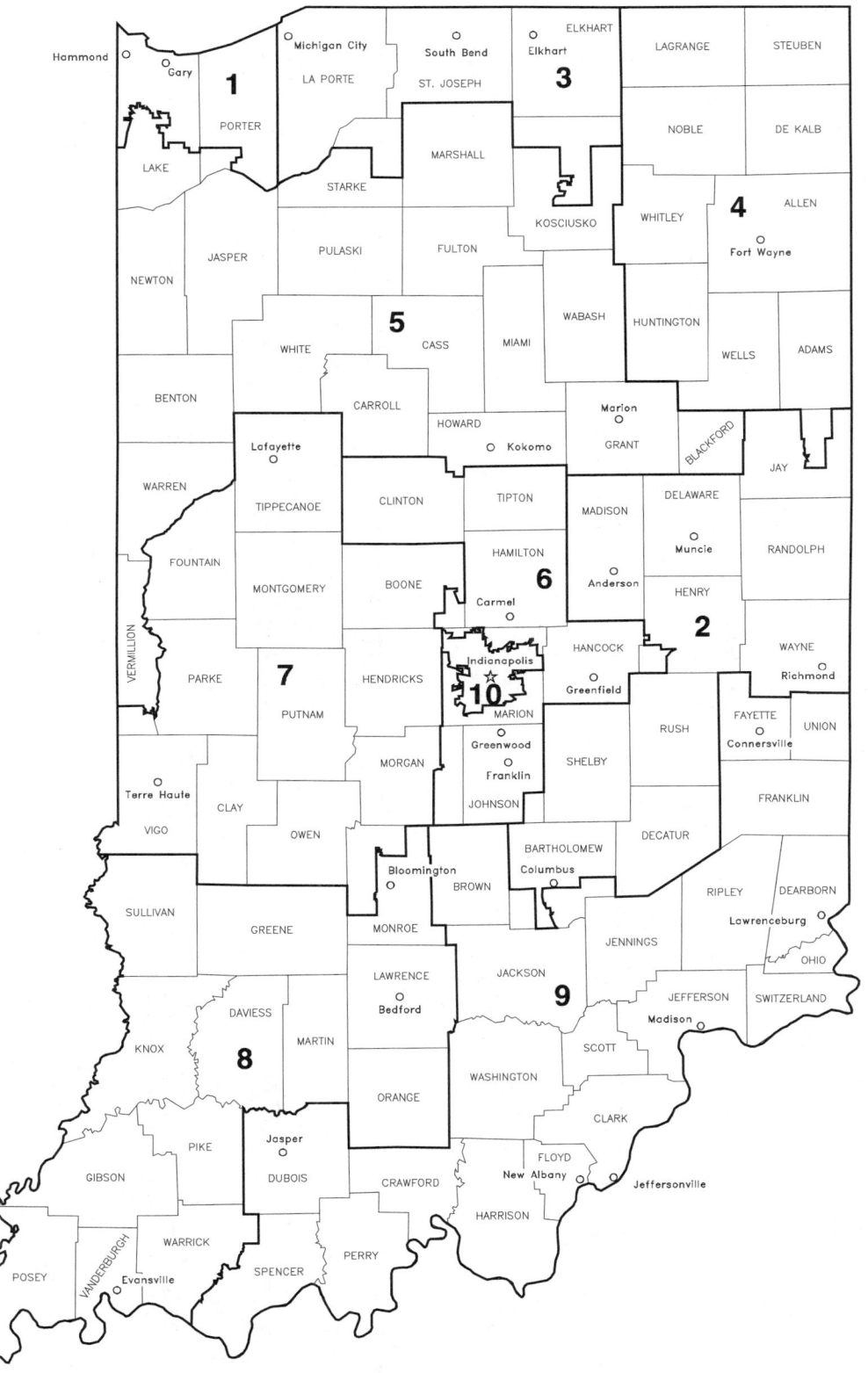

INDIANA

PRESIDENT 2000

2000 Census Population	County	Total Vote	Republican	Democratic	Green (Nader)	Other	Rep.-Dem. Plurality	Percentage of Total Vote Rep.	Dem.	Green
33,625	ADAMS	12,590	8,555	3,775	45	215	4,780 R	68.0%	30.0%	0.4%
331,849	ALLEN	114,320	70,426	41,636	556	1,702	28,790 R	61.6%	36.4%	0.5%
71,435	BARTHOLOMEW	25,769	16,200	9,015	181	373	7,185 R	62.9%	35.0%	0.7%
9,421	BENTON	3,874	2,441	1,328	20	85	1,113 R	63.0%	34.3%	0.5%
14,048	BLACKFORD	4,893	2,699	2,103	18	73	596 R	55.2%	43.0%	0.4%
46,107	BOONE	18,396	13,161	4,763	196	276	8,398 R	71.5%	25.9%	1.1%
14,957	BROWN	6,817	3,871	2,608	210	128	1,263 R	56.8%	38.3%	3.1%
20,165	CARROLL	8,268	5,102	2,965	87	114	2,137 R	61.7%	35.9%	1.1%
40,930	CASS	15,106	9,305	5,412		389	3,893 R	61.6%	35.8%	
96,472	CLARK	37,336	19,417	17,360	212	347	2,057 R	52.0%	46.5%	0.6%
26,556	CLAY	10,158	6,393	3,605	19	141	2,788 R	62.9%	35.5%	0.2%
33,866	CLINTON	10,991	7,141	3,643	40	167	3,498 R	65.0%	33.1%	0.4%
10,743	CRAWFORD	4,209	2,327	1,817	17	48	510 R	55.3%	43.2%	0.4%
29,820	DAVIESS	9,761	6,872	2,697	49	143	4,175 R	70.4%	27.6%	0.5%
46,109	DEARBORN	17,650	11,452	6,020		178	5,432 R	64.9%	34.1%	
24,555	DECATUR	9,171	6,115	2,889	11	156	3,226 R	66.7%	31.5%	0.1%
40,285	DE KALB	13,785	8,701	4,776	71	237	3,925 R	63.1%	34.6%	0.5%
118,769	DELAWARE	44,147	22,105	20,876	386	780	1,229 R	50.1%	47.3%	0.9%
39,674	DUBOIS	15,504	10,134	5,090	42	238	5,044 R	65.4%	32.8%	0.3%
182,791	ELKHART	54,482	36,756	16,402	642	682	20,354 R	67.5%	30.1%	1.2%
25,588	FAYETTE	8,647	5,060	3,415	31	141	1,645 R	58.5%	39.5%	0.4%
70,823	FLOYD	30,030	16,486	13,209	52	283	3,277 R	54.9%	44.0%	0.2%
17,954	FOUNTAIN	7,281	4,408	2,717	18	138	1,691 R	60.5%	37.3%	0.2%
22,151	FRANKLIN	8,339	5,587	2,591	25	136	2,996 R	67.0%	31.1%	0.3%
20,511	FULTON	8,327	5,218	2,960	37	112	2,258 R	62.7%	35.5%	0.4%
32,500	GIBSON	13,772	7,734	5,802	77	159	1,932 R	56.2%	42.1%	0.6%
73,403	GRANT	26,386	16,153	9,712	84	437	6,441 R	61.2%	36.8%	0.3%
33,157	GREENE	12,619	7,452	4,898	57	212	2,554 R	59.1%	38.8%	0.5%
182,740	HAMILTON	75,926	56,372	18,002	669	883	38,370 R	74.2%	23.7%	0.9%
55,391	HANCOCK	22,950	15,943	6,503	126	378	9,440 R	69.5%	28.3%	0.5%
34,325	HARRISON	14,896	8,711	5,870	101	214	2,841 R	58.5%	39.4%	0.7%
104,093	HENDRICKS	40,221	28,651	10,786	164	620	17,865 R	71.2%	26.8%	0.4%
48,508	HENRY	18,315	10,321	7,647	9	338	2,674 R	56.4%	41.8%	
84,964	HOWARD	34,095	20,331	12,899	343	522	7,432 R	59.6%	37.8%	1.0%
38,075	HUNTINGTON	14,620	10,113	4,119	162	226	5,994 R	69.2%	28.2%	1.1%
41,335	JACKSON	14,602	9,054	5,330	27	191	3,724 R	62.0%	36.5%	0.2%
30,043	JASPER	11,167	7,212	3,744	71	140	3,468 R	64.6%	33.5%	0.6%
21,806	JAY	8,030	4,687	3,167	15	161	1,520 R	58.4%	39.4%	0.2%
31,705	JEFFERSON	11,931	6,582	5,117	84	148	1,465 R	55.2%	42.9%	0.7%
27,554	JENNINGS	9,494	5,732	3,549	47	166	2,183 R	60.4%	37.4%	0.5%
115,209	JOHNSON	42,284	29,404	11,952	178	750	17,452 R	69.5%	28.3%	0.4%
39,256	KNOX	15,054	8,485	6,300	76	193	2,185 R	56.4%	41.8%	0.5%
74,057	KOSCIUSKO	25,284	19,040	5,785	92	367	13,255 R	75.3%	22.9%	0.4%
34,909	LAGRANGE	8,333	5,437	2,733	51	112	2,704 R	65.2%	32.8%	0.6%
484,564	LAKE	175,994	63,389	109,078	1,659	1,868	45,689 D	36.0%	62.0%	0.9%
110,106	LA PORTE	39,747	18,994	19,736	413	604	742 D	47.8%	49.7%	1.0%
45,922	LAWRENCE	16,142	10,677	5,071	101	293	5,606 R	66.1%	31.4%	0.6%
133,358	MADISON	52,216	27,956	23,403		857	4,553 R	53.5%	44.8%	
860,454	MARION	279,903	137,810	134,189	2,967	4,937	3,621 R	49.2%	47.9%	1.1%
45,128	MARSHALL	16,150	10,266	5,541	109	234	4,725 R	63.6%	34.3%	0.7%
10,369	MARTIN	4,609	3,008	1,518	14	69	1,490 R	65.3%	32.9%	0.3%
36,082	MIAMI	12,928	8,401	4,155	44	328	4,246 R	65.0%	32.1%	0.3%
120,563	MONROE	40,220	19,147	17,523	2,991	559	1,624 R	47.6%	43.6%	7.4%
37,629	MONTGOMERY	13,101	8,891	3,899	132	179	4,992 R	67.9%	29.8%	1.0%
66,689	MORGAN	22,036	15,286	6,228	151	371	9,058 R	69.4%	28.3%	0.7%
14,566	NEWTON	5,510	3,250	2,101	28	131	1,149 R	59.0%	38.1%	0.5%
46,275	NOBLE	14,216	9,103	4,822	66	225	4,281 R	64.0%	33.9%	0.5%
5,623	OHIO	2,492	1,515	951	6	20	564 R	60.8%	38.2%	0.2%
19,306	ORANGE	7,458	4,687	2,601	46	124	2,086 R	62.8%	34.9%	0.6%
21,786	OWEN	6,503	4,019	2,253	85	146	1,766 R	61.8%	34.6%	1.3%

INDIANA

PRESIDENT 2000

2000 Census Population	County	Total Vote	Republican	Democratic	Green (Nader)	Other	Rep.-Dem. Plurality	Percentage of Total Vote		
								Rep.	Dem.	Green
17,241	PARKE	6,447	3,841	2,481	20	105	1,360 R	59.6%	38.5%	0.3%
18,899	PERRY	7,387	3,461	3,823	26	77	362 D	46.9%	51.8%	0.4%
12,837	PIKE	6,302	3,566	2,605	3	128	961 R	56.6%	41.3%	
146,798	PORTER	59,378	31,157	26,790	592	839	4,367 R	52.5%	45.1%	1.0%
27,061	POSEY	11,110	6,498	4,430	52	130	2,068 R	58.5%	39.9%	0.5%
13,755	PULASKI	5,518	3,497	1,919	17	85	1,578 R	63.4%	34.8%	0.3%
36,019	PUTNAM	11,871	7,352	4,123	144	252	3,229 R	61.9%	34.7%	1.2%
27,401	RANDOLPH	10,132	6,020	3,906	20	186	2,114 R	59.4%	38.6%	0.2%
26,523	RIPLEY	10,675	6,988	3,498	23	166	3,490 R	65.5%	32.8%	0.2%
18,261	RUSH	7,284	4,749	2,370	21	144	2,379 R	65.2%	32.5%	0.3%
265,559	ST. JOSEPH	97,474	47,581	47,703	905	1,285	122 D	48.8%	48.9%	0.9%
22,960	SCOTT	7,846	3,761	3,915	40	130	154 D	47.9%	49.9%	0.5%
43,445	SHELBY	15,310	9,590	5,374	71	275	4,216 R	62.6%	35.1%	0.5%
20,391	SPENCER	8,987	5,096	3,752	42	97	1,344 R	56.7%	41.7%	0.5%
23,556	STARKE	8,701	4,349	4,136	27	189	213 R	50.0%	47.5%	0.3%
33,214	STEUBEN	11,277	6,953	4,103	40	181	2,850 R	61.7%	36.4%	0.4%
21,751	SULLIVAN	8,262	4,319	3,833	4	106	486 R	52.3%	46.4%	
9,065	SWITZERLAND	3,239	1,831	1,336	15	57	495 R	56.5%	41.2%	0.5%
148,955	TIPPECANOE	46,295	26,106	18,220	1,054	915	7,886 R	56.4%	39.4%	2.3%
16,577	TIPTON	7,316	4,784	2,392	6	134	2,392 R	65.4%	32.7%	0.1%
7,349	UNION	2,828	1,838	927	11	52	911 R	65.0%	32.8%	0.4%
171,922	VANDERBURGH	66,221	35,846	29,222	381	772	6,624 R	54.1%	44.1%	0.6%
16,788	VERMILLION	6,633	3,130	3,370	13	120	240 D	47.2%	50.8%	0.2%
105,848	VIGO	36,228	18,021	17,570	158	479	451 R	49.7%	48.5%	0.4%
34,960	WABASH	12,883	8,321	4,277	125	160	4,044 R	64.6%	33.2%	1.0%
8,419	WARREN	3,768	2,218	1,471	21	58	747 R	58.9%	39.0%	0.6%
52,383	WARRICK	22,309	13,205	8,749	105	250	4,456 R	59.2%	39.2%	0.5%
27,223	WASHINGTON	9,801	5,868	3,675	52	206	2,193 R	59.9%	37.5%	0.5%
71,097	WAYNE	25,151	14,273	10,273	209	396	4,000 R	56.7%	40.8%	0.8%
27,600	WELLS	11,281	7,755	3,319	30	177	4,436 R	68.7%	29.4%	0.3%
25,267	WHITE	9,904	6,037	3,655	39	173	2,382 R	61.0%	36.9%	0.4%
30,707	WHITLEY	12,432	8,080	4,107	30	215	3,973 R	65.0%	33.0%	0.2%
6,080,485	TOTAL	2,199,302	1,245,836	901,980	18,531	32,955	343,856 R	56.6%	41.0%	0.8%

Note: The votes cast for Nader were write-ins. A blank indicates that he received no votes in that particular county. The vote totals for each candidate listed above are as certified, although the county totals for Nader add to 18,506 and the county totals for the "Other" vote adds to 32,983.

INDIANA

GOVERNOR 2000

2000 Census Population	County	Total Vote	Republican	Democratic	Other	Rep.-Dem. Plurality	Percentage			
							Total Vote		Major Vote	
							Rep.	Dem.	Rep.	Dem.
33,625	ADAMS	12,551	5,864	6,471	216	607 D	46.7%	51.6%	47.5%	52.5%
331,849	ALLEN	113,915	53,401	58,139	2,375	4,738 D	46.9%	51.0%	47.9%	52.1%
71,435	BARTHOLOMEW	25,863	11,857	13,526	480	1,669 D	45.8%	52.3%	46.7%	53.3%
9,421	BENTON	3,886	1,797	2,019	70	222 D	46.2%	52.0%	47.1%	52.9%
14,048	BLACKFORD	4,866	1,891	2,885	90	994 D	38.9%	59.3%	39.6%	60.4%
46,107	BOONE	18,244	9,776	7,927	541	1,849 R	53.6%	43.4%	55.2%	44.8%
14,957	BROWN	6,818	2,780	3,818	220	1,038 D	40.8%	56.0%	42.1%	57.9%
20,165	CARROLL	8,259	3,771	4,356	132	585 D	45.7%	52.7%	46.4%	53.6%
40,930	CASS	14,975	6,998	7,711	266	713 D	46.7%	51.5%	47.6%	52.4%
96,472	CLARK	37,076	12,258	24,455	363	12,197 D	33.1%	66.0%	33.4%	66.6%

INDIANA

GOVERNOR 2000

2000 Census Population	County	Total Vote	Republican	Democratic	Other	Rep.-Dem. Plurality		Percentage			
								Total Vote		Major Vote	
								Rep.	Dem.	Rep.	Dem.
26,556	CLAY	10,110	3,807	6,173	130	2,366	D	37.7%	61.1%	38.1%	61.9%
33,866	CLINTON	10,917	5,411	5,289	217	122	R	49.6%	48.4%	50.6%	49.4%
10,743	CRAWFORD	4,182	1,426	2,714	42	1,288	D	34.1%	64.9%	34.4%	65.6%
29,820	DAVIESS	9,655	5,242	4,319	94	923	R	54.3%	44.7%	54.8%	45.2%
46,109	DEARBORN	17,310	8,250	8,737	323	487	D	47.7%	50.5%	48.6%	51.4%
24,555	DECATUR	9,149	4,333	4,638	178	305	D	47.4%	50.7%	48.3%	51.7%
40,285	DE KALB	13,646	6,599	6,819	228	220	D	48.4%	50.0%	49.2%	50.8%
118,769	DELAWARE	43,891	16,200	26,896	795	10,696	D	36.9%	61.3%	37.6%	62.4%
39,674	DUBOIS	14,994	6,790	8,093	111	1,303	D	45.3%	54.0%	45.6%	54.4%
182,791	ELKHART	54,181	28,829	24,803	549	4,026	R	53.2%	45.8%	53.8%	46.2%
25,588	FAYETTE	8,548	3,783	4,639	126	856	D	44.3%	54.3%	44.9%	55.1%
70,823	FLOYD	30,039	10,140	19,660	239	9,520	D	33.8%	65.4%	34.0%	66.0%
17,954	FOUNTAIN	7,258	3,295	3,845	118	550	D	45.4%	53.0%	46.1%	53.9%
22,151	FRANKLIN	8,171	3,876	4,177	118	301	D	47.4%	51.1%	48.1%	51.9%
20,511	FULTON	8,376	3,745	4,533	98	788	D	44.7%	54.1%	45.2%	54.8%
32,500	GIBSON	13,746	5,429	8,176	141	2,747	D	39.5%	59.5%	39.9%	60.1%
73,403	GRANT	26,161	12,132	13,674	355	1,542	D	46.4%	52.3%	47.0%	53.0%
33,157	GREENE	12,336	4,885	7,304	147	2,419	D	39.6%	59.2%	40.1%	59.9%
182,740	HAMILTON	75,404	43,415	30,093	1,896	13,322	R	57.6%	39.9%	59.1%	40.9%
55,391	HANCOCK	22,839	11,066	11,096	677	30	D	48.5%	48.6%	49.9%	50.1%
34,325	HARRISON	14,969	4,655	10,168	146	5,513	D	31.1%	67.9%	31.4%	68.6%
104,093	HENDRICKS	40,117	21,828	17,303	986	4,525	R	54.4%	43.1%	55.8%	44.2%
48,508	HENRY	18,303	7,830	10,165	308	2,335	D	42.8%	55.5%	43.5%	56.5%
84,964	HOWARD	34,125	14,862	18,672	591	3,810	D	43.6%	54.7%	44.3%	55.7%
38,075	HUNTINGTON	14,390	7,544	6,610	236	934	R	52.4%	45.9%	53.3%	46.7%
41,335	JACKSON	14,647	6,250	8,221	176	1,971	D	42.7%	56.1%	43.2%	56.8%
30,043	JASPER	11,005	5,364	5,520	121	156	D	48.7%	50.2%	49.3%	50.7%
21,806	JAY	8,004	3,473	4,391	140	918	D	43.4%	54.9%	44.2%	55.8%
31,705	JEFFERSON	11,727	4,301	7,293	133	2,992	D	36.7%	62.2%	37.1%	62.9%
27,554	JENNINGS	9,472	4,086	5,249	137	1,163	D	43.1%	55.4%	43.8%	56.2%
115,209	JOHNSON	42,044	21,385	19,636	1,023	1,749	R	50.9%	46.7%	52.1%	47.9%
39,256	KNOX	14,838	5,063	9,619	156	4,556	D	34.1%	64.8%	34.5%	65.5%
74,057	KOSCIUSKO	25,173	14,748	10,035	390	4,713	R	58.6%	39.9%	59.5%	40.5%
34,909	LAGRANGE	8,310	4,012	4,195	103	183	D	48.3%	50.5%	48.9%	51.1%
484,564	LAKE	172,294	47,859	122,784	1,651	74,925	D	27.8%	71.3%	28.0%	72.0%
110,106	LA PORTE	39,405	13,026	25,816	563	12,790	D	33.1%	65.5%	33.5%	66.5%
45,922	LAWRENCE	15,991	8,336	7,436	219	900	R	52.1%	46.5%	52.9%	47.1%
133,358	MADISON	52,251	21,189	30,210	852	9,021	D	40.6%	57.8%	41.2%	58.8%
860,454	MARION	276,898	105,281	163,077	8,540	57,796	D	38.0%	58.9%	39.2%	60.8%
45,128	MARSHALL	16,089	7,412	8,555	122	1,143	D	46.1%	53.2%	46.4%	53.6%
10,369	MARTIN	4,573	2,040	2,465	68	425	D	44.6%	53.9%	45.3%	54.7%
36,082	MIAMI	12,656	6,255	6,209	192	46	R	49.4%	49.1%	50.2%	49.8%
120,563	MONROE	39,572	14,299	24,033	1,240	9,734	D	36.1%	60.7%	37.3%	62.7%
37,629	MONTGOMERY	13,113	6,263	6,570	280	307	D	47.8%	50.1%	48.8%	51.2%
66,689	MORGAN	21,912	11,335	10,018	559	1,317	R	51.7%	45.7%	53.1%	46.9%
14,566	NEWTON	5,442	2,311	3,035	96	724	D	42.5%	55.8%	43.2%	56.8%
46,275	NOBLE	14,162	6,866	7,081	215	215	D	48.5%	50.0%	49.2%	50.8%
5,623	OHIO	2,452	1,026	1,399	27	373	D	41.8%	57.1%	42.3%	57.7%
19,306	ORANGE	7,363	3,281	4,004	78	723	D	44.6%	54.4%	45.0%	55.0%
21,786	OWEN	6,451	2,805	3,474	172	669	D	43.5%	53.9%	44.7%	55.3%
17,241	PARKE	6,414	2,556	3,762	96	1,206	D	39.9%	58.7%	40.5%	59.5%
18,899	PERRY	7,345	2,382	4,902	61	2,520	D	32.4%	66.7%	32.7%	67.3%
12,837	PIKE	6,218	2,504	3,630	84	1,126	D	40.3%	58.4%	40.8%	59.2%
146,798	PORTER	58,776	21,575	36,444	757	14,869	D	36.7%	62.0%	37.2%	62.8%
27,061	POSEY	11,023	4,284	6,614	125	2,330	D	38.9%	60.0%	39.3%	60.7%
13,755	PULASKI	5,311	2,510	2,748	53	238	D	47.3%	51.7%	47.7%	52.3%
36,019	PUTNAM	11,803	5,275	6,273	255	998	D	44.7%	53.1%	45.7%	54.3%
27,401	RANDOLPH	10,071	4,583	5,346	142	763	D	45.5%	53.1%	46.2%	53.8%
26,523	RIPLEY	10,583	4,839	5,587	157	748	D	45.7%	52.8%	46.4%	53.6%
18,261	RUSH	7,270	3,339	3,744	187	405	D	45.9%	51.5%	47.1%	52.9%

INDIANA

GOVERNOR 2000

2000 Census Population	County	Total Vote	Republican	Democratic	Other	Rep.-Dem. Plurality		Percentage			
								Total Vote		Major Vote	
								Rep.	Dem.	Rep.	Dem.
265,559	ST. JOSEPH	95,988	34,699	60,608	681	25,909	D	36.1%	63.1%	36.4%	63.6%
22,960	SCOTT	7,792	2,267	5,445	80	3,178	D	29.1%	69.9%	29.4%	70.6%
43,445	SHELBY	15,215	6,774	8,106	335	1,332	D	44.5%	53.3%	45.5%	54.5%
20,391	SPENCER	8,963	3,660	5,233	70	1,573	D	40.8%	58.4%	41.2%	58.8%
23,556	STARKE	8,366	3,108	5,171	87	2,063	D	37.2%	61.8%	37.5%	62.5%
33,214	STEUBEN	11,240	5,069	5,972	199	903	D	45.1%	53.1%	45.9%	54.1%
21,751	SULLIVAN	7,912	2,626	5,215	71	2,589	D	33.2%	65.9%	33.5%	66.5%
9,065	SWITZERLAND	3,195	1,174	1,965	56	791	D	36.7%	61.5%	37.4%	62.6%
148,955	TIPPECANOE	45,738	18,896	25,798	1,044	6,902	D	41.3%	56.4%	42.3%	57.7%
16,577	TIPTON	7,196	3,466	3,602	128	136	D	48.2%	50.1%	49.0%	51.0%
7,349	UNION	2,779	1,423	1,322	34	101	R	51.2%	47.6%	51.8%	48.2%
171,922	VANDERBURGH	65,555	25,267	39,533	755	14,266	D	38.5%	60.3%	39.0%	61.0%
16,788	VERMILLION	6,589	1,912	4,566	111	2,654	D	29.0%	69.3%	29.5%	70.5%
105,848	VIGO	36,067	11,452	24,017	598	12,565	D	31.8%	66.6%	32.3%	67.7%
34,960	WABASH	12,752	6,365	6,215	172	150	R	49.9%	48.7%	50.6%	49.4%
8,419	WARREN	3,754	1,646	2,065	43	419	D	43.8%	55.0%	44.4%	55.6%
52,383	WARRICK	22,091	9,193	12,647	251	3,454	D	41.6%	57.2%	42.1%	57.9%
27,223	WASHINGTON	9,766	3,859	5,751	156	1,892	D	39.5%	58.9%	40.2%	59.8%
71,097	WAYNE	24,975	11,617	13,061	297	1,444	D	46.5%	52.3%	47.1%	52.9%
27,600	WELLS	11,277	5,825	5,244	208	581	R	51.7%	46.5%	52.6%	47.4%
25,267	WHITE	9,867	4,328	5,385	154	1,057	D	43.9%	54.6%	44.6%	55.4%
30,707	WHITLEY	12,408	5,781	6,326	301	545	D	46.6%	51.0%	47.7%	52.3%
6,080,485	TOTAL	2,179,413	908,285	1,232,525	38,603	324,240	D	41.7%	56.6%	42.4%	57.6%

INDIANA

SENATOR 2000

2000 Census Population	County	Total Vote	Republican	Democratic	Other	Rep.-Dem. Plurality		Percentage			
								Total Vote		Major Vote	
								Rep.	Dem.	Rep.	Dem.
33,625	ADAMS	12,207	9,384	2,635	188	6,749	R	76.9%	21.6%	78.1%	21.9%
331,849	ALLEN	113,479	83,279	28,477	1,723	54,802	R	73.4%	25.1%	74.5%	25.5%
71,435	BARTHOLOMEW	25,480	18,585	6,512	383	12,073	R	72.9%	25.6%	74.1%	25.9%
9,421	BENTON	3,863	2,804	965	94	1,839	R	72.6%	25.0%	74.4%	25.6%
14,048	BLACKFORD	4,853	3,245	1,539	69	1,706	R	66.9%	31.7%	67.8%	32.2%
46,107	BOONE	18,191	14,527	3,311	353	11,216	R	79.9%	18.2%	81.4%	18.6%
14,957	BROWN	6,795	4,609	1,982	204	2,627	R	67.8%	29.2%	69.9%	30.1%
20,165	CARROLL	8,250	5,888	2,245	117	3,643	R	71.4%	27.2%	72.4%	27.6%
40,930	CASS	14,689	10,191	4,275	223	5,916	R	69.4%	29.1%	70.4%	29.6%
96,472	CLARK	36,754	23,087	13,230	437	9,857	R	62.8%	36.0%	63.6%	36.4%
26,556	CLAY	9,808	7,091	2,575	142	4,516	R	72.3%	26.3%	73.4%	26.6%
33,866	CLINTON	10,862	7,899	2,790	173	5,109	R	72.7%	25.7%	73.9%	26.1%
10,743	CRAWFORD	4,078	2,541	1,472	65	1,069	R	62.3%	36.1%	63.3%	36.7%
29,820	DAVIESS	9,655	7,434	2,117	104	5,317	R	77.0%	21.9%	77.8%	22.2%
46,109	DEARBORN	17,309	11,878	5,103	328	6,775	R	68.6%	29.5%	69.9%	30.1%
24,555	DECATUR	8,744	6,544	2,068	132	4,476	R	74.8%	23.7%	76.0%	24.0%
40,285	DE KALB	13,544	10,116	3,244	184	6,872	R	74.7%	24.0%	75.7%	24.3%
118,769	DELAWARE	42,459	27,066	14,650	743	12,416	R	63.7%	34.5%	64.9%	35.1%
39,674	DUBOIS	14,677	10,648	3,908	121	6,740	R	72.5%	26.6%	73.2%	26.8%
182,791	ELKHART	54,031	42,285	11,081	665	31,204	R	78.3%	20.5%	79.2%	20.8%

INDIANA

SENATOR 2000

2000 Census Population	County	Total Vote	Republican	Democratic	Other	Rep.-Dem. Plurality		Percentage			
								Total Vote		Major Vote	
								Rep.	Dem.	Rep.	Dem.
25,588	FAYETTE	8,509	5,714	2,658	137	3,056	R	67.2%	31.2%	68.3%	31.7%
70,823	FLOYD	29,782	19,759	9,719	304	10,040	R	66.3%	32.6%	67.0%	33.0%
17,954	FOUNTAIN	7,020	4,934	1,974	112	2,960	R	70.3%	28.1%	71.4%	28.6%
22,151	FRANKLIN	8,157	5,902	2,127	128	3,775	R	72.4%	26.1%	73.5%	26.5%
20,511	FULTON	8,334	6,141	2,082	111	4,059	R	73.7%	25.0%	74.7%	25.3%
32,500	GIBSON	13,726	8,936	4,616	174	4,320	R	65.1%	33.6%	65.9%	34.1%
73,403	GRANT	26,044	17,704	7,999	341	9,705	R	68.0%	30.7%	68.9%	31.1%
33,157	GREENE	12,088	7,797	4,132	159	3,665	R	64.5%	34.2%	65.4%	34.6%
182,740	HAMILTON	75,244	63,216	10,834	1,194	52,382	R	84.0%	14.4%	85.4%	14.6%
55,391	HANCOCK	22,231	17,376	4,404	451	12,972	R	78.2%	19.8%	79.8%	20.2%
34,325	HARRISON	14,748	10,112	4,379	257	5,733	R	68.6%	29.7%	69.8%	30.2%
104,093	HENDRICKS	40,007	31,800	7,525	682	24,275	R	79.5%	18.8%	80.9%	19.1%
48,508	HENRY	17,640	11,765	5,611	264	6,154	R	66.7%	31.8%	67.7%	32.3%
84,964	HOWARD	34,051	22,827	10,616	608	12,211	R	67.0%	31.2%	68.3%	31.7%
38,075	HUNTINGTON	14,298	11,171	2,941	186	8,230	R	78.1%	20.6%	79.2%	20.8%
41,335	JACKSON	14,598	10,389	4,027	182	6,362	R	71.2%	27.6%	72.1%	27.9%
30,043	JASPER	10,979	7,775	3,047	157	4,728	R	70.8%	27.8%	71.8%	28.2%
21,806	JAY	7,935	5,442	2,349	144	3,093	R	68.6%	29.6%	69.8%	30.2%
31,705	JEFFERSON	11,611	7,641	3,830	140	3,811	R	65.8%	33.0%	66.6%	33.4%
27,554	JENNINGS	9,433	6,673	2,620	140	4,053	R	70.7%	27.8%	71.8%	28.2%
115,209	JOHNSON	40,888	32,295	7,761	832	24,534	R	79.0%	19.0%	80.6%	19.4%
39,256	KNOX	14,726	9,940	4,549	237	5,391	R	67.5%	30.9%	68.6%	31.4%
74,057	KOSCIUSKO	24,594	20,282	3,871	441	16,411	R	82.5%	15.7%	84.0%	16.0%
34,909	LAGRANGE	8,284	6,464	1,712	108	4,752	R	78.0%	20.7%	79.1%	20.9%
484,564	LAKE	171,466	71,574	97,809	2,083	26,235	D	41.7%	57.0%	42.3%	57.7%
110,106	LA PORTE	37,408	22,589	13,864	955	8,725	R	60.4%	37.1%	62.0%	38.0%
45,922	LAWRENCE	15,901	11,733	3,913	255	7,820	R	73.8%	24.6%	75.0%	25.0%
133,358	MADISON	50,599	31,664	18,154	781	13,510	R	62.6%	35.9%	63.6%	36.4%
860,454	MARION	272,888	158,620	109,736	4,532	48,884	R	58.1%	40.2%	59.1%	40.9%
45,128	MARSHALL	16,025	12,208	3,654	163	8,554	R	76.2%	22.8%	77.0%	23.0%
10,369	MARTIN	4,545	3,214	1,268	63	1,946	R	70.7%	27.9%	71.7%	28.3%
36,082	MIAMI	12,511	8,712	3,623	176	5,089	R	69.6%	29.0%	70.6%	29.4%
120,563	MONROE	39,409	25,168	12,837	1,404	12,331	R	63.9%	32.6%	66.2%	33.8%
37,629	MONTGOMERY	13,090	10,280	2,571	239	7,709	R	78.5%	19.6%	80.0%	20.0%
66,689	MORGAN	21,823	16,731	4,640	452	12,091	R	76.7%	21.3%	78.3%	21.7%
14,566	NEWTON	5,410	3,463	1,814	133	1,649	R	64.0%	33.5%	65.6%	34.4%
46,275	NOBLE	14,113	10,661	3,245	207	7,416	R	75.5%	23.0%	76.7%	23.3%
5,623	OHIO	2,435	1,614	777	44	837	R	66.3%	31.9%	67.5%	32.5%
19,306	ORANGE	7,084	5,143	1,832	109	3,311	R	72.6%	25.9%	73.7%	26.3%
21,786	OWEN	6,434	4,502	1,756	176	2,746	R	70.0%	27.3%	71.9%	28.1%
17,241	PARKE	6,198	4,303	1,801	94	2,502	R	69.4%	29.1%	70.5%	29.5%
18,899	PERRY	6,863	3,754	3,041	68	713	R	54.7%	44.3%	55.2%	44.8%
12,837	PIKE	5,937	3,821	2,007	109	1,814	R	64.4%	33.8%	65.6%	34.4%
146,798	PORTER	56,188	34,785	20,430	973	14,355	R	61.9%	36.4%	63.0%	37.0%
27,061	POSEY	10,682	7,487	3,074	121	4,413	R	70.1%	28.8%	70.9%	29.1%
13,755	PULASKI	5,341	3,719	1,566	56	2,153	R	69.6%	29.3%	70.4%	29.6%
36,019	PUTNAM	11,411	8,359	2,792	260	5,567	R	73.3%	24.5%	75.0%	25.0%
27,401	RANDOLPH	9,720	6,776	2,808	136	3,968	R	69.7%	28.9%	70.7%	29.3%
26,523	RIPLEY	10,557	7,657	2,704	196	4,953	R	72.5%	25.6%	73.9%	26.1%
18,261	RUSH	7,047	5,334	1,552	161	3,782	R	75.7%	22.0%	77.5%	22.5%
265,559	ST. JOSEPH	94,123	59,818	33,378	927	26,440	R	63.6%	35.5%	64.2%	35.8%
22,960	SCOTT	7,723	4,798	2,810	115	1,988	R	62.1%	36.4%	63.1%	36.9%
43,445	SHELBY	15,161	10,925	3,986	250	6,939	R	72.1%	26.3%	73.3%	26.7%
20,391	SPENCER	8,969	5,747	3,147	75	2,600	R	64.1%	35.1%	64.6%	35.4%
23,556	STARKE	8,147	4,866	3,168	113	1,698	R	59.7%	38.9%	60.6%	39.4%
33,214	STEUBEN	11,257	8,549	2,479	229	6,070	R	75.9%	22.0%	77.5%	22.5%
21,751	SULLIVAN	7,451	4,645	2,720	86	1,925	R	62.3%	36.5%	63.1%	36.9%
9,065	SWITZERLAND	3,168	1,885	1,216	67	669	R	59.5%	38.4%	60.8%	39.2%
148,955	TIPPECANOE	44,492	32,101	11,357	1,034	20,744	R	72.2%	25.5%	73.9%	26.1%
16,577	TIPTON	7,165	5,111	1,958	96	3,153	R	71.3%	27.3%	72.3%	27.7%

INDIANA

SENATOR 2000

2000 Census Population	County	Total Vote	Republican	Democratic	Other	Rep.-Dem. Plurality		Total Vote		Major Vote	
								Rep.	Dem.	Rep.	Dem.
7,349	UNION	2,780	2,068	673	39	1,395	R	74.4%	24.2%	75.4%	24.6%
171,922	VANDERBURGH	62,866	41,482	20,552	832	20,930	R	66.0%	32.7%	66.9%	33.1%
16,788	VERMILLION	6,265	3,585	2,577	103	1,008	R	57.2%	41.1%	58.2%	41.8%
105,848	VIGO	35,651	22,886	12,176	589	10,710	R	64.2%	34.2%	65.3%	34.7%
34,960	WABASH	12,696	9,404	3,167	125	6,237	R	74.1%	24.9%	74.8%	25.2%
8,419	WARREN	3,623	2,454	1,106	63	1,348	R	67.7%	30.5%	68.9%	31.1%
52,383	WARRICK	21,190	14,538	6,402	250	8,136	R	68.6%	30.2%	69.4%	30.6%
27,223	WASHINGTON	9,696	6,828	2,629	239	4,199	R	70.4%	27.1%	72.2%	27.8%
71,097	WAYNE	23,872	15,926	7,590	356	8,336	R	66.7%	31.8%	67.7%	32.3%
27,600	WELLS	10,958	8,565	2,235	158	6,330	R	78.2%	20.4%	79.3%	20.7%
25,267	WHITE	9,839	7,310	2,360	169	4,950	R	74.3%	24.0%	75.6%	24.4%
30,707	WHITLEY	12,377	9,426	2,757	194	6,669	R	76.2%	22.3%	77.4%	22.6%
6,080,485	TOTAL	2,145,209	1,427,944	683,273	33,992	744,671	R	66.6%	31.9%	67.6%	32.4%

INDIANA

CONGRESS

CD	Year	Total Vote	Republican		Democratic		Other Vote	Rep.-Dem. Plurality		Total Vote		Major Vote	
			Vote	Candidate	Vote	Candidate				Rep.	Dem.	Rep.	Dem.
1	2000	207,790	56,200	REYNOLDS, JACK	148,683	VISCLOSKY, PETER J.	2,907	92,483	D	27.0%	71.6%	27.4%	72.6%
1	1998	127,754	33,503	PETYO, MICHAEL	92,634	VISCLOSKY, PETER J.	1,617	59,131	D	26.2%	72.5%	26.6%	73.4%
1	1996	193,113	56,418	PETYO, MICHAEL	133,553	VISCLOSKY, PETER J.	3,142	77,135	D	29.2%	69.2%	29.7%	70.3%
1	1994	121,532	52,920	LARSON, JOHN	68,612	VISCLOSKY, PETER J.		15,692	D	43.5%	56.5%	43.5%	56.5%
1	1992	211,824	64,770	VUCICH, DAVID J.	147,054	VISCLOSKY, PETER J.		82,284	D	30.6%	69.4%	30.6%	69.4%
2	2000	208,407	106,023	PENCE, MIKE	80,885	ROCK, ROBERT W.	21,499	25,138	R	50.9%	38.8%	56.7%	43.3%
2	1998	164,296	99,608	MCINTOSH, DAVID M.	62,452	BOLES, SHERMAN A.	2,236	37,156	R	60.6%	38.0%	61.5%	38.5%
2	1996	212,883	123,113	MCINTOSH, DAVID M.	85,105	CARMICHAEL, R. MARC	4,665	38,008	R	57.8%	40.0%	59.1%	40.9%
2	1994	171,833	93,592	MCINTOSH, DAVID M.	78,241	HOGSETT, JOSEPH H.		15,351	R	54.5%	45.5%	54.5%	45.5%
2	1992	229,295	90,593	FRAZIER, WILLIAM G.	130,881	SHARP, PHILIP R.	7,821	40,288	D	39.5%	57.1%	40.9%	59.1%
3	2000	208,315	98,822	CHOCOLA, CHRIS	107,438	ROEMER, TIMOTHY J.	2,055	8,616	D	47.4%	51.6%	47.9%	52.1%
3	1998	145,666	61,041	HOLTZ, DANIEL A.	84,625	ROEMER, TIMOTHY J.		23,584	D	41.9%	58.1%	41.9%	58.1%
3	1996	197,312	80,699	ZAKAS, JOE	114,288	ROEMER, TIMOTHY J.	2,325	33,589	D	40.9%	57.9%	41.4%	58.6%
3	1994	131,375	58,878	BURKETT, RICHARD	72,497	ROEMER, TIMOTHY J.		13,619	D	44.8%	55.2%	44.8%	55.2%
3	1992	211,103	89,834	BAXMEYER, CARL H.	121,269	ROEMER, TIMOTHY J.		31,435	D	42.6%	57.4%	42.6%	57.4%
4	2000	210,430	131,051	SOUDER, MARK E.	74,492	FOSTER, MICHAEL DEWAYNE	4,887	56,559	R	62.3%	35.4%	63.8%	36.2%
4	1998	147,957	93,671	SOUDER, MARK E.	54,286	WEHRLE, MARK J.		39,385	R	63.3%	36.7%	63.3%	36.7%
4	1996	207,880	121,344	SOUDER, MARK E.	81,740	HOUSEMAN, GERALD L.	4,796	39,604	R	58.4%	39.3%	59.8%	40.2%
4	1994	159,819	88,584	SOUDER, MARK E.	71,235	LONG, JILL L.		17,349	R	55.4%	44.6%	55.4%	44.6%
4	1992	217,375	82,468	PIERSON, CHARLES W.	134,907	LONG, JILL L.		52,439	D	37.9%	62.1%	37.9%	62.1%
5	2000	216,985	132,051	BUYER, STEVE	81,427	GOODNIGHT, GREG	3,507	50,624	R	60.9%	37.5%	61.9%	38.1%
5	1998	162,388	101,567	BUYER, STEVE	58,504	STEELE, DAVID	2,317	43,063	R	62.5%	36.0%	63.5%	36.5%
5	1996	216,008	133,627	BUYER, STEVE	77,128	CLARK, DOUGLAS L.	5,253	56,499	R	61.9%	35.7%	63.4%	36.6%
5	1994	159,658	111,031	BUYER, STEVE	45,224	BEATTY, J. D.	3,403	65,807	R	69.5%	28.3%	71.1%	28.9%
5	1992	220,465	112,492	BUYER, STEVE	107,973	JONTZ, JIM		4,519	R	51.0%	49.0%	51.0%	49.0%

INDIANA

CONGRESS

			Republican		Democratic				Percentage			
									Total Vote		Major Vote	
CD	Year	Total Vote	Vote	Candidate	Vote	Candidate	Other Vote	Rep.-Dem. Plurality	Rep.	Dem.	Rep.	Dem.
6	2000	283,175	199,207	BURTON, DAN	74,881	GRIESEY, DARIN PATRICK	9,087	124,326 R	70.3%	26.4%	72.7%	27.3%
6	1998	187,827	135,250	BURTON, DAN	31,472	KERN, BOB	21,105	103,778 R	72.0%	16.8%	81.1%	18.9%
6	1996	258,888	194,224	BURTON, DAN	59,661	DILLARD-TRAMMELL, CARRIE J.	5,003	134,563 R	75.0%	23.0%	76.5%	23.5%
6	1994	177,691	136,876	BURTON, DAN	40,815	BRUNER, NATALIE M.		96,061 R	77.0%	23.0%	77.0%	23.0%
6	1992	258,455	186,499	BURTON, DAN	71,952	BRUNER, NATALIE M.	4	114,547 R	72.2%	27.8%	72.2%	27.8%
7	2000	209,665	135,869	KERNS, BRIAN D.	66,764	GRAF, MICHAEL DOUGLAS	7,032	69,105 R	64.8%	31.8%	67.1%	32.9%
7	1998	159,314	109,712	PEASE, EDWARD A.	44,823	HILLENBERG, SAMUEL "DUTCH"	4,779	64,889 R	68.9%	28.1%	71.0%	29.0%
7	1996	209,840	130,010	PEASE, EDWARD A.	72,705	HELLMANN, ROBERT F.	7,125	57,305 R	62.0%	34.6%	64.1%	35.9%
7	1994	160,300	104,359	MYERS, JOHN T.	55,941	HARMLESS, MICHAEL M.		48,418 R	65.1%	34.9%	65.1%	34.9%
7	1992	217,194	129,189	MYERS, JOHN T.	88,005	WEDUM, ELLEN E.		41,184 R	59.5%	40.5%	59.5%	40.5%
8	2000	221,992	116,879	HOSTETTLER, JOHN	100,488	PERRY, PAUL E.	4,625	16,391 R	52.7%	45.3%	53.8%	46.2%
8	1998	178,057	92,785	HOSTETTLER, JOHN	81,871	RIECKEN, GAIL	3,401	10,914 R	52.1%	46.0%	53.1%	46.9%
8	1996	219,864	109,860	HOSTETTLER, JOHN	106,201	WEINZAPFEL, JONATHAN	3,803	3,659 R	50.0%	48.3%	50.8%	49.2%
8	1994	178,386	93,529	HOSTETTLER, JOHN	84,857	MCCLOSKEY, FRANCIS		8,672 R	52.4%	47.6%	52.4%	47.6%
8	1992	238,397	108,054	MOURDOCK, RICHARD	125,244	MCCLOSKEY, FRANCIS	5,099	17,190 D	45.3%	52.5%	46.3%	53.7%
9	2000	233,283	102,219	BAILEY, MICHAEL E.	126,420	HILL, BARON	4,644	24,201 D	43.8%	54.2%	44.7%	55.3%
9	1998	183,176	87,797	LEISING, JEAN	92,973	HILL, BARON	2,406	5,176 D	47.9%	50.8%	48.6%	51.4%
9	1996	226,872	96,442	LEISING, JEAN	128,123	HAMILTON, LEE H.	2,307	31,681 D	42.5%	56.5%	42.9%	57.1%
9	1994	175,774	84,315	LEISING, JEAN	91,459	HAMILTON, LEE H.		7,144 D	48.0%	52.0%	48.0%	52.0%
9	1992	231,037	70,057	BAILEY, MICHAEL E.	160,980	HAMILTON, LEE H.		90,923 D	30.3%	69.7%	30.3%	69.7%
10	2000	156,702	62,233	SCOTT, MARVIN B.	91,689	CARSON, JULIA M.	2,780	29,456 D	39.7%	58.5%	40.4%	59.6%
10	1998	119,436	47,017	HOFMEISTER, GARY A.	69,682	CARSON, JULIA M.	2,737	22,665 D	39.4%	58.3%	40.3%	59.7%
10	1996	162,373	72,796	BLANKENBAKER, VIRGINIA	85,965	CARSON, JULIA M.	3,612	13,169 D	44.8%	52.9%	45.9%	54.1%
10	1994	109,571	50,998	SCOTT, MARVIN B.	58,573	JACOBS, ANDREW, JR.		7,575 D	46.5%	53.5%	46.5%	53.5%
10	1992	183,831	64,378	HORVATH, JANOS	117,604	JACOBS, ANDREW, JR.	1,849	53,226 D	35.0%	64.0%	35.4%	64.6%

INDIANA

GENERAL AND PRIMARY ELECTIONS

2000 GENERAL ELECTIONS

President Other vote was 16,959 Independent (Buchanan); 15,530 Libertarian (Browne); 167 Natural Law write-in (Hagelin); 200 Constitution write-in (Phillips); 43 Independent write-in (McReynolds); 24 Independent write-in (Schriner); 15 Independent write-in (Judd); 8 Republican write-in (Birchler); 5 Veterans Industrial Party write-in (Easton); 4 Independent write-in (Strickland). In Indiana, write-in candidates can be designated by party or as Independent. Nader was a Green Party write-in.

Governor Other vote was 38,458 Libertarian (Schreiber); 145 Reform write-in (Wilson).

Senator Other vote was 33,992 Libertarian (Hager).

Congress Other vote was: CD 1: 2,907 Libertarian (Nelson); CD 2: 19,077 Independent (Frazier), 2,422 Libertarian (Anderson); CD 3: 2,050 Libertarian (Baker), 5 Independent write-in (Blatt); CD 4: 4,887 Libertarian (Donlan); CD 5: 3,507 Libertarian (Benson); CD 6: 9,087 Libertarian (Hauptmann); CD 7: 7,032 Libertarian (Thayer); CD 8: 4,342 Libertarian (Tindle), 283 Green write-in (Haggerty); CD 9: 4,644 Libertarian (Chambers); CD 10: 2,780 Libertarian (Ali).

INDIANA

GENERAL AND PRIMARY ELECTIONS

2000 PRIMARY ELECTIONS

Primary	May 2, 2000
Primary Type	Open—Any registered voter could vote in the primary of either party.

Registration (as of May 2, 2000)   3,910,116   No Party Registration

Note: An asterisk (*) denotes incumbent.

	REPUBLICAN PRIMARIES			DEMOCRATIC PRIMARIES		
President	George W. Bush	330,095	81.2%	Al Gore	219,604	74.9%
	John McCain	76,569	18.8%	Bill Bradley	64,339	21.9%
				Lyndon H. LaRouche Jr.	9,229	3.1%
	TOTAL	406,664		TOTAL	293,172	
Governor	Frank O'Bannon*	272,213	100.0%	David McIntosh	279,920	71.0%
				John Price	114,580	29.0%
	TOTAL	272,213		TOTAL	394,500	
Senator	Richard G. Lugar*	356,888	100.0%	David L. Johnson	192,531	100.0%
	TOTAL	356,888		TOTAL	192,531	
Congressional District 1	Jack Reynolds	6,618	65.6%	Peter J. Visclosky*	31,507	81.1%
	Mark J. Leyva	3,478	34.4%	Sandra K. Smith	6,098	15.7%
				Cyril B. "Cy" Huerter	1,229	3.2%
	TOTAL	10,096		TOTAL	38,834	
Congressional District 2	Mike Pence	21,582	44.5%	Robert W. Rock	9,545	30.3%
	Jeffrey M. Linder	11,615	23.9%	Ronald A. Gyure	7,232	23.0%
	Luke Messer	10,075	20.8%	Troy Liggett	6,805	21.6%
	Brad D. Steele	2,819	5.8%	Angela "Angie" Burks	5,513	17.5%
	David M. "Mike" Campbell	1,913	3.9%	Sean David Harding	2,375	7.5%
	Cliff Federle	513	1.1%			
	TOTAL	48,517		TOTAL	31,470	
Congressional District 3	Chris Chocola	25,697	100.0%	Timothy J. Roemer*	22,823	88.4%
				Steven W. Osborn	3,008	11.6%
	TOTAL	25,697		TOTAL	25,831	
Congressional District 4	Mark E. Souder*	28,710	61.8%	Michael Dewayne Foster	10,410	71.4%
	Mike Loomis	17,768	38.2%	David Christopher Roach	4,176	28.6%
	TOTAL	46,478		TOTAL	14,586	
Congressional District 5	Steve Buyer*	43,293	100.0%	Greg Goodnight	12,765	59.0%
				R. McAlister Ellis Jr.	3,509	16.2%
				John Arnold	3,359	15.5%
				Hugh Salisbury	2,012	9.3%
	TOTAL	43,293		TOTAL	21,645	
Congressional District 6	Dan Burton*	54,399	79.4%	Darin Patrick Griesey	4,719	39.0%
	George Thomas Holland	14,106	20.6%	Nick Arena	4,181	34.5%
				R. Nag Nagarajan	3,214	26.5%
	TOTAL	68,505		TOTAL	12,114	
Congressional District 7	Brian D. Kerns	22,766	39.1%	Michael Douglas Graf	7,891	32.5%
	Bob Griffiths	18,792	32.2%	Jeffrey L. Clapper	7,131	29.4%
	Alex Gatzimos	7,233	12.4%	Samuel W. "Dutch" Hillenberg	5,266	21.7%
	Bryan L. Donaldson	2,869	4.9%	Daniel Scott Grinestaff	3,998	16.5%
	Matt Branam	2,156	3.7%			
	Tony W. Duncan	2,079	3.6%			
	Douglas Edwin Hess	1,458	2.5%			
	John W. Timm	933	1.6%			
	TOTAL	58,286		TOTAL	24,286	
Congressional District 8	John Hostettler*	29,806	100.0%	Paul E. Perry	25,930	57.3%
				John Hamilton	17,231	38.1%
				John W. Taylor	2,068	4.6%
	TOTAL	29,806		TOTAL	45,229	
Congressional District 9	Michael E. Bailey	14,314	51.3%	Baron Hill*	42,235	85.5%
	Kevin Kellems	13,590	48.7%	James R. McClure Jr.	5,264	10.7%
				Lendall B. Terry	1,921	3.9%
	TOTAL	27,904		TOTAL	49,420	
Congressional District 10	Marvin B. Scott	11,041	58.4%	Julia M. Carson*	22,891	89.8%
	Anthony A. Samuel	7,877	41.6%	Ralph Spelbring	1,639	6.4%
				Bobby "Kern" Hidalgo	956	3.8%
	TOTAL	18,918		TOTAL	25,486	

IOWA

GOVERNOR
Tom Vilsack (D). Elected 1998 to a four-year term.

SENATORS
Charles E. Grassley (R). Re-elected 1998 to a six-year term. Previously elected 1992, 1986, 1980.

Tom Harkin (D). Re-elected 1996 to a six-year term. Previously elected 1990, 1984.

REPRESENTATIVES
1. James A. Leach (R)
2. Jim Nussle (R)
3. Leonard L. Boswell (D)
4. Greg Ganske (R)
5. Tom Latham (R)

POSTWAR VOTE FOR PRESIDENT

Year	Total Vote	Republican Vote	Candidate	Democratic Vote	Candidate	Other Vote	Plurality	Total Vote Rep.	Total Vote Dem.	Major Vote Rep.	Major Vote Dem.
2000**	1,315,563	634,373	Bush, George W.	638,517	Gore, Al	42,673	4,144 D	48.2%	48.5%	49.8%	50.2%
1996**	1,234,075	492,644	Dole, Bob	620,258	Clinton, Bill	121,173	127,614 D	39.9%	50.3%	44.3%	55.7%
1992**	1,354,607	504,891	Bush, George	586,353	Clinton, Bill	263,363	81,462 D	37.3%	43.3%	46.3%	53.7%
1988	1,225,614	545,355	Bush, George	670,557	Dukakis, Michael S.	9,702	125,202 D	44.5%	54.7%	44.9%	55.1%
1984	1,319,805	703,088	Reagan, Ronald	605,620	Mondale, Walter F.	11,097	97,468 R	53.3%	45.9%	53.7%	46.3%
1980**	1,317,661	676,026	Reagan, Ronald	508,672	Carter, Jimmy	132,963	167,354 R	51.3%	38.6%	57.1%	42.9%
1976	1,279,306	632,863	Ford, Gerald R.	619,931	Carter, Jimmy	26,512	12,932 R	49.5%	48.5%	50.5%	49.5%
1972	1,225,944	706,207	Nixon, Richard M.	496,206	McGovern, George S.	23,531	210,001 R	57.6%	40.5%	58.7%	41.3%
1968	1,167,931	619,106	Nixon, Richard M.	476,699	Humphrey, Hubert H.	72,126	142,407 R	53.0%	40.8%	56.5%	43.5%
1964	1,184,539	449,148	Goldwater, Barry M.	733,030	Johnson, Lyndon B.	2,361	283,882 D	37.9%	61.9%	38.0%	62.0%
1960	1,273,810	722,381	Nixon, Richard M.	550,565	Kennedy, John F.	864	171,816 R	56.7%	43.2%	56.7%	43.3%
1956	1,234,564	729,187	Eisenhower, Dwight D.	501,858	Stevenson, Adlai E.	3,519	227,329 R	59.1%	40.7%	59.2%	40.8%
1952	1,268,773	808,906	Eisenhower, Dwight D.	451,513	Stevenson, Adlai E.	8,354	357,393 R	63.8%	35.6%	64.2%	35.8%
1948	1,038,264	494,018	Dewey, Thomas E.	522,380	Truman, Harry S.	21,866	28,362 D	47.6%	50.3%	48.6%	51.4%

In 2000 the other vote column includes 29,374 votes cast for Green (Nader). In 1996 the other vote column includes 105,159 votes cast for Perot. In 1992 the other vote column includes 253,468 votes cast for Perot. In 1980 the other column includes 115,633 votes for Independent (Anderson).

IOWA

POSTWAR VOTE FOR GOVERNOR

Year	Total Vote	Republican Vote	Candidate	Democratic Vote	Candidate	Other Vote	Rep.-Dem. Plurality	Percentage Total Vote Rep.	Dem.	Major Vote Rep.	Dem.
1998	956,418	444,787	Lightfoot, Jim Ross	500,231	Vilsack, Tom	11,400	55,444 D	46.5%	52.3%	47.1%	52.9%
1994	997,248	566,395	Branstad, Terry E.	414,453	Campbell, Bonnie J.	16,400	151,942 R	56.8%	41.6%	57.7%	42.3%
1990	976,483	591,852	Branstad, Terry E.	379,372	Avenson, Donald D.	5,259	212,480 R	60.6%	38.9%	60.9%	39.1%
1986	910,623	472,712	Branstad, Terry E.	436,987	Junkins, Lowell L.	924	35,725 R	51.9%	48.0%	52.0%	48.0%
1982	1,038,229	548,313	Branstad, Terry E.	483,291	Conlin, Roxanne	6,625	65,022 R	52.8%	46.5%	53.2%	46.8%
1978	843,190	491,713	Ray, Robert	345,519	Fitzgerald, Jerome D.	5,958	146,194 R	58.3%	41.0%	58.7%	41.3%
1974**	920,458	534,518	Ray, Robert	377,553	Schaben, James, F.	8,387	156,965 R	58.1%	41.0%	58.6%	41.4%
1972	1,210,222	707,177	Ray, Robert	487,282	Franzenburg, Paul	15,763	219,895 R	58.4%	40.3%	59.2%	40.8%
1970	791,241	403,394	Ray, Robert	368,911	Fulton, Robert	18,936	34,483 R	51.0%	46.6%	52.2%	47.8%
1968	1,136,489	614,328	Ray, Robert	521,216	Franzenburg, Paul	945	93,112 R	54.1%	45.9%	54.1%	45.9%
1966	893,175	394,518	Murray, William G.	494,259	Hughes, Harold E.	4,398	99,741 D	44.2%	55.3%	44.4%	55.6%
1964	1,167,734	365,131	Hultman, Evan	794,610	Hughes, Harold E.	7,993	429,479 D	31.3%	68.0%	31.5%	68.5%
1962	819,854	388,955	Erbe, Norman A.	430,899	Hughes, Harold E.		41,944 D	47.4%	52.6%	47.4%	52.6%
1960	1,237,089	645,026	Erbe, Norman A.	592,063	McManus, E. J.		52,963 R	52.1%	47.9%	52.1%	47.9%
1958	859,095	394,071	Murray, William G.	465,024	Loveless, Herschel C.		70,953 D	45.9%	54.1%	45.9%	54.1%
1956	1,204,235	587,383	Hoegh, Leo A.	616,852	Loveless, Herschel C.		29,469 D	48.8%	51.2%	48.8%	51.2%
1954	848,592	435,944	Hoegh, Leo A.	410,255	Herring, Clyde E.	2,393	25,689 R	51.4%	48.3%	51.5%	48.5%
1952	1,230,045	638,388	Beardsley, William	587,671	Loveless, Herschel C.	3,986	50,717 R	51.9%	47.8%	52.1%	47.9%
1950	857,213	506,642	Beardsley, William	347,176	Gillette, Lester S.	3,395	159,466 R	59.1%	40.5%	59.3%	40.7%
1948	994,833	553,900	Beardsley, William	434,432	Switzer, Carroll O.	6,501	119,468 R	55.7%	43.7%	56.0%	44.0%
1946	631,681	362,592	Blue, Robert D.	266,190	Miles, Frank	2,899	96,402 R	57.4%	42.1%	57.7%	42.3%

The term of office of Iowa's Governor was increased from two to four years effective with the 1974 election.

POSTWAR VOTE FOR SENATOR

Year	Total Vote	Republican Vote	Candidate	Democratic Vote	Candidate	Other Vote	Rep.-Dem. Plurality	Percentage Total Vote Rep.	Dem.	Major Vote Rep.	Dem.
1998	947,907	648,480	Grassley, Charles E.	289,049	Osterberg, David	10,378	359,431 R	68.4%	30.5%	69.2%	30.8%
1996	1,224,054	571,807	Lightfoot, Jim Ross	634,166	Harkin, Tom	18,081	62,359 D	46.7%	51.8%	47.4%	52.6%
1992	1,292,494	899,761	Grassley, Charles E.	351,561	Lloyd-Jones, Jean	41,172	548,200 R	69.6%	27.2%	71.9%	28.1%
1990	983,933	446,869	Tauke, Tom	535,975	Harkin, Tom	1,089	89,106 D	45.4%	54.5%	45.5%	54.5%
1986	891,762	588,880	Grassley, Charles E.	299,406	Roehrick, John P.	3,476	289,474 R	66.0%	33.6%	66.3%	33.7%
1984	1,292,700	564,381	Jepsen, Roger W.	716,883	Harkin, Tom	11,436	152,502 D	43.7%	55.5%	44.0%	56.0%
1980	1,277,034	683,014	Grassley, Charles E.	581,545	Culver, John C.	12,475	101,469 R	53.5%	45.5%	54.0%	46.0%
1978	824,654	421,598	Jepsen, Roger W.	395,066	Clark, Richard	7,990	26,532 R	51.1%	47.9%	51.6%	48.4%
1974	889,561	420,546	Stanley, David M.	462,947	Culver, John C.	6,068	42,401 D	47.3%	52.0%	47.6%	52.4%
1972	1,203,333	530,525	Miller, Jack	662,637	Clark, Richard	10,171	132,112 D	44.1%	55.1%	44.5%	55.5%
1968	1,144,086	568,469	Stanley, David M.	574,884	Hughes, Harold E.	733	6,415 D	49.7%	50.2%	49.7%	50.3%
1966	857,496	522,339	Miller, Jack	324,114	Smith, E. B.	11,043	198,225 R	60.9%	37.8%	61.7%	38.3%
1962	807,972	431,364	Hickenlooper, Bourke B.	376,602	Smith, E. B.	6	54,762 R	53.4%	46.6%	53.4%	46.6%
1960	1,237,582	642,463	Miller, Jack	595,119	Loveless, Herschel C.		47,344 R	51.9%	48.1%	51.9%	48.1%
1956	1,178,655	635,499	Hickenlooper, Bourke B.	543,156	Evans, R. M.		92,343 R	53.9%	46.1%	53.9%	46.1%
1954	847,355	442,409	Martin, Thomas E.	402,712	Gillette, Guy	2,234	39,697 R	52.2%	47.5%	52.3%	47.7%
1950	858,523	470,613	Hickenlooper, Bourke B.	383,766	Loveland, A. J.	4,144	86,847 R	54.8%	44.7%	55.1%	44.9%
1948	1,000,412	415,778	Wilson, George A.	578,226	Gillette, Guy	6,408	162,448 D	41.6%	57.8%	41.8%	58.2%

IOWA

Districts Established May 30, 1991

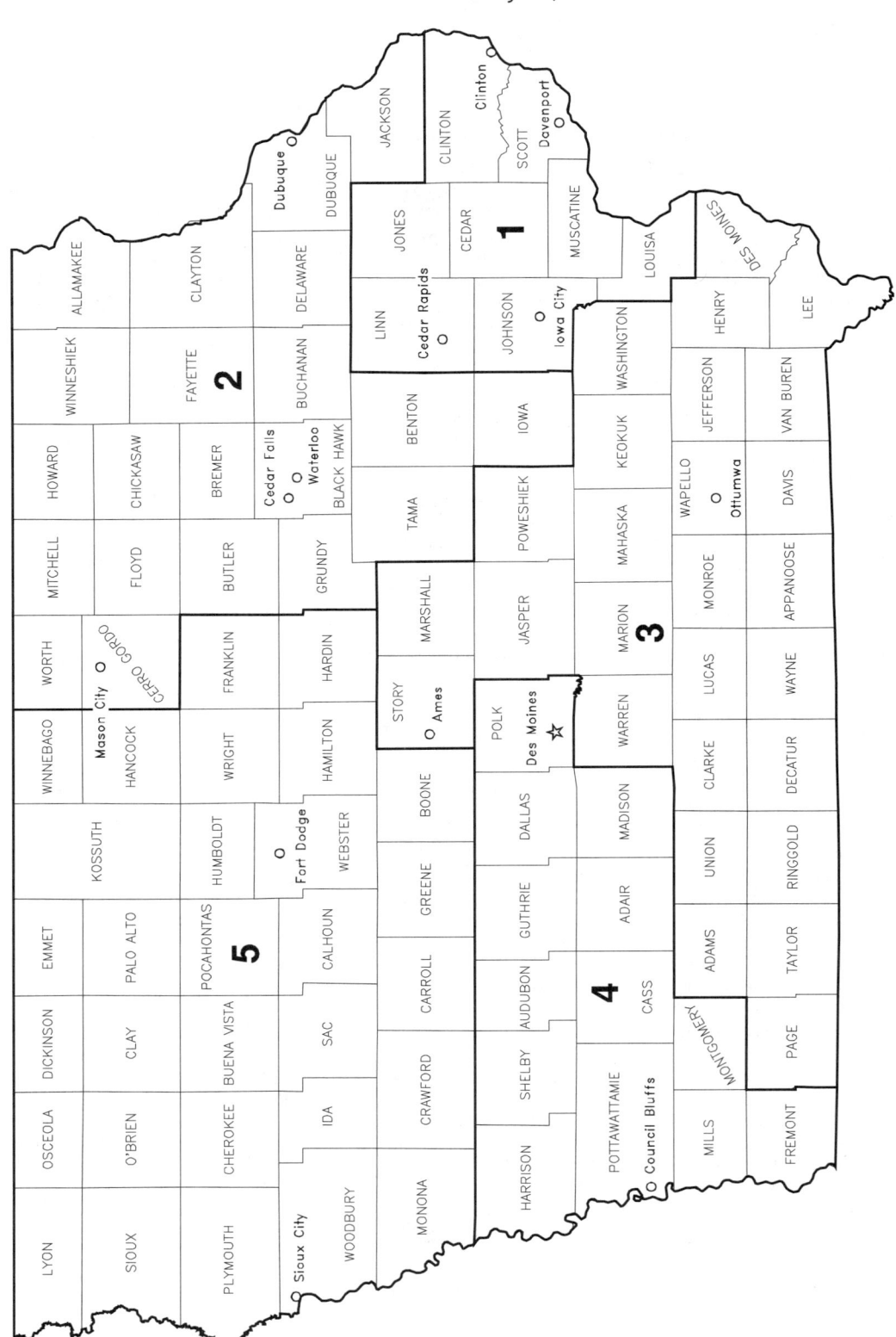

IOWA

PRESIDENT 2000

2000 Census Population	County	Total Vote	Republican	Democratic	Green (Nader)	Other	Rep.-Dem. Plurality	Percentage of Total Vote		
								Rep.	Dem.	Green
8,243	ADAIR	4,123	2,275	1,753	66	29	522 R	55.2%	42.5%	1.6%
4,482	ADAMS	2,145	1,170	897	51	27	273 R	54.5%	41.8%	2.4%
14,675	ALLAMAKEE	6,462	3,277	2,883	199	103	394 R	50.7%	44.6%	3.1%
13,721	APPANOOSE	5,704	2,992	2,560	105	47	432 R	52.5%	44.9%	1.8%
6,830	AUDUBON	3,784	1,909	1,780	56	39	129 R	50.4%	47.0%	1.5%
25,308	BENTON	11,766	5,468	5,915	231	152	447 D	46.5%	50.3%	2.0%
128,012	BLACK HAWK	55,085	23,468	30,112	1,132	373	6,644 D	42.6%	54.7%	2.1%
26,224	BOONE	12,249	5,625	6,270	252	102	645 D	45.9%	51.2%	2.1%
23,325	BREMER	11,175	5,675	5,169	260	71	506 R	50.8%	46.3%	2.3%
21,093	BUCHANAN	9,410	4,092	5,045	171	102	953 D	43.5%	53.6%	1.8%
20,411	BUENA VISTA	7,977	4,354	3,297	227	99	1,057 R	54.6%	41.3%	2.8%
15,305	BUTLER	6,724	3,837	2,735	113	39	1,102 R	57.1%	40.7%	1.7%
11,115	CALHOUN	5,041	2,776	2,132	93	40	644 R	55.1%	42.3%	1.8%
21,421	CARROLL	9,568	4,879	4,463	146	80	416 R	51.0%	46.6%	1.5%
14,684	CASS	6,880	4,206	2,481	147	46	1,725 R	61.1%	36.1%	2.1%
18,187	CEDAR	8,344	4,031	4,033	212	68	2 D	48.3%	48.3%	2.5%
46,447	CERRO GORDO	22,162	9,397	12,185	408	172	2,788 D	42.4%	55.0%	1.8%
13,035	CHEROKEE	6,592	3,463	2,845	160	124	618 R	52.5%	43.2%	2.4%
13,095	CHICKASAW	6,584	2,936	3,435	145	68	499 D	44.6%	52.2%	2.2%
9,133	CLARKE	4,176	1,984	2,081	75	36	97 D	47.5%	49.8%	1.8%
17,372	CLAY	7,578	3,992	3,294	166	126	698 R	52.7%	43.5%	2.2%
18,678	CLAYTON	8,571	4,034	4,238	206	93	204 D	47.1%	49.4%	2.4%
50,149	CLINTON	22,180	9,229	12,276	471	204	3,047 D	41.6%	55.3%	2.1%
16,942	CRAWFORD	6,555	3,482	2,838	146	89	644 R	53.1%	43.3%	2.2%
40,750	DALLAS	19,330	10,306	8,561	320	143	1,745 R	53.3%	44.3%	1.7%
8,541	DAVIS	3,758	1,956	1,691	67	44	265 R	52.0%	45.0%	1.8%
8,689	DECATUR	3,709	1,903	1,674	94	38	229 R	51.3%	45.1%	2.5%
18,404	DELAWARE	8,349	4,273	3,808	161	107	465 R	51.2%	45.6%	1.9%
42,351	DES MOINES	19,365	7,385	11,351	409	220	3,966 D	38.1%	58.6%	2.1%
16,424	DICKINSON	8,121	4,225	3,660	169	67	565 R	52.0%	45.1%	2.1%
89,143	DUBUQUE	40,323	16,462	22,341	987	533	5,879 D	40.8%	55.4%	2.4%
11,027	EMMET	4,630	2,331	2,165	98	36	166 R	50.3%	46.8%	2.1%
22,008	FAYETTE	9,621	4,747	4,640	174	60	107 R	49.3%	48.2%	1.8%
16,900	FLOYD	7,238	3,191	3,830	154	63	639 D	44.1%	52.9%	2.1%
10,704	FRANKLIN	4,938	2,657	2,122	110	49	535 R	53.8%	43.0%	2.2%
8,010	FREMONT	3,616	2,069	1,459	63	25	610 R	57.2%	40.3%	1.7%
10,366	GREENE	4,719	2,282	2,301	106	30	19 D	48.4%	48.8%	2.2%
12,369	GRUNDY	6,111	3,851	2,139	70	51	1,712 R	63.0%	35.0%	1.1%
11,353	GUTHRIE	5,469	2,840	2,493	86	50	347 R	51.9%	45.6%	1.6%
16,438	HAMILTON	7,574	3,968	3,407	141	58	561 R	52.4%	45.0%	1.9%
12,100	HANCOCK	5,438	2,988	2,281	123	46	707 R	54.9%	41.9%	2.3%
18,812	HARDIN	8,435	4,486	3,734	141	74	752 R	53.2%	44.3%	1.7%
15,666	HARRISON	6,543	3,802	2,551	126	64	1,251 R	58.1%	39.0%	1.9%
20,336	HENRY	8,671	4,476	3,907	183	105	569 R	51.6%	45.1%	2.1%
9,932	HOWARD	4,491	1,922	2,426	100	43	504 D	42.8%	54.0%	2.2%
10,381	HUMBOLDT	4,940	2,846	1,949	100	45	897 R	57.6%	39.5%	2.0%
7,837	IDA	3,491	1,968	1,411	58	54	557 R	56.4%	40.4%	1.7%
15,671	IOWA	7,413	3,894	3,230	188	101	664 R	52.5%	43.6%	2.5%
20,296	JACKSON	9,032	3,769	4,945	227	91	1,176 D	41.7%	54.7%	2.5%
37,213	JASPER	17,835	8,729	8,699	267	140	30 R	48.9%	48.8%	1.5%
16,181	JEFFERSON	7,548	3,248	2,863	206	1,231	385 R	43.0%	37.9%	2.7%
111,006	JOHNSON	52,769	17,899	31,174	3,248	448	13,275 D	33.9%	59.1%	6.2%
20,221	JONES	9,143	4,201	4,690	195	57	489 D	45.9%	51.3%	2.1%
11,400	KEOKUK	4,947	2,571	2,181	99	96	390 R	52.0%	44.1%	2.0%
17,163	KOSSUTH	8,878	4,612	3,960	206	100	652 R	51.9%	44.6%	2.3%
38,052	LEE	16,572	6,339	9,632	325	276	3,293 D	38.3%	58.1%	2.0%
191,701	LINN	92,064	40,417	48,897	2,106	644	8,480 D	43.9%	53.1%	2.3%
12,183	LOUISA	4,637	2,207	2,294	85	51	87 D	47.6%	49.5%	1.8%
9,422	LUCAS	4,303	2,262	1,934	65	42	328 R	52.6%	44.9%	1.5%
11,763	LYON	5,342	3,918	1,313	68	43	2,605 R	73.3%	24.6%	1.3%

IOWA

PRESIDENT 2000

2000 Census Population	County	Total Vote	Republican	Democratic	Green (Nader)	Other	Rep.-Dem. Plurality	Percentage of Total Vote		
								Rep.	Dem.	Green
14,019	MADISON	6,969	3,662	3,093	128	86	569 R	52.5%	44.4%	1.8%
22,335	MAHASKA	9,543	5,971	3,370	143	59	2,601 R	62.6%	35.3%	1.5%
32,052	MARION	14,408	8,358	5,741	208	101	2,617 R	58.0%	39.8%	1.4%
39,311	MARSHALL	17,624	8,785	8,322	340	177	463 R	49.8%	47.2%	1.9%
14,547	MILLS	5,915	3,684	2,039	126	66	1,645 R	62.3%	34.5%	2.1%
10,874	MITCHELL	5,162	2,388	2,650	87	37	262 D	46.3%	51.3%	1.7%
10,020	MONONA	4,560	2,304	2,086	93	77	218 R	50.5%	45.7%	2.0%
8,016	MONROE	3,647	1,858	1,699	54	36	159 R	50.9%	46.6%	1.5%
11,771	MONTGOMERY	5,394	3,417	1,838	85	54	1,579 R	63.3%	34.1%	1.6%
41,722	MUSCATINE	16,076	7,483	8,058	371	164	575 D	46.5%	50.1%	2.3%
15,102	O'BRIEN	7,044	4,674	2,170	108	92	2,504 R	66.4%	30.8%	1.5%
7,003	OSCEOLA	3,063	2,064	913	56	30	1,151 R	67.4%	29.8%	1.8%
16,976	PAGE	7,059	4,588	2,293	125	53	2,295 R	65.0%	32.5%	1.8%
10,147	PALO ALTO	4,823	2,341	2,326	81	75	15 R	48.5%	48.2%	1.7%
24,849	PLYMOUTH	10,118	6,189	3,499	198	232	2,690 R	61.2%	34.6%	2.0%
8,662	POCAHONTAS	4,141	2,242	1,736	78	85	506 R	54.1%	41.9%	1.9%
374,601	POLK	174,167	79,927	89,715	3,366	1,159	9,788 D	45.9%	51.5%	1.9%
87,704	POTTAWATTAMIE	34,467	18,783	14,726	690	268	4,057 R	54.5%	42.7%	2.0%
18,815	POWESHIEK	8,980	4,396	4,222	287	75	174 R	49.0%	47.0%	3.2%
5,469	RINGGOLD	2,692	1,369	1,246	47	30	123 R	50.9%	46.3%	1.7%
11,529	SAC	5,033	2,776	2,099	97	61	677 R	55.2%	41.7%	1.9%
158,668	SCOTT	70,568	32,801	35,857	1,386	524	3,056 D	46.5%	50.8%	2.0%
13,173	SHELBY	6,009	3,655	2,179	113	62	1,476 R	60.8%	36.3%	1.9%
31,589	SIOUX	14,692	12,241	2,148	156	147	10,093 R	83.3%	14.6%	1.1%
79,981	STORY	35,364	16,228	17,478	1,317	341	1,250 D	45.9%	49.4%	3.7%
18,103	TAMA	8,315	4,034	4,045	160	76	11 D	48.5%	48.6%	1.9%
6,958	TAYLOR	3,096	1,770	1,247	46	33	523 R	57.2%	40.3%	1.5%
12,309	UNION	5,740	3,003	2,540	108	89	463 R	52.3%	44.3%	1.9%
7,809	VAN BUREN	3,561	2,016	1,440	51	54	576 R	56.6%	40.4%	1.4%
36,051	WAPELLO	15,139	6,313	8,355	317	154	2,042 D	41.7%	55.2%	2.1%
40,671	WARREN	19,653	9,621	9,521	371	140	100 R	49.0%	48.4%	1.9%
20,670	WASHINGTON	9,094	4,827	3,932	245	90	895 R	53.1%	43.2%	2.7%
6,730	WAYNE	3,021	1,666	1,300	31	24	366 R	55.1%	43.0%	1.0%
40,235	WEBSTER	17,048	8,172	8,479	282	115	307 D	47.9%	49.7%	1.7%
11,723	WINNEBAGO	5,527	2,662	2,691	115	59	29 D	48.2%	48.7%	2.1%
21,310	WINNESHIEK	9,417	4,647	4,339	343	88	308 R	49.3%	46.1%	3.6%
103,877	WOODBURY	37,896	18,864	17,691	804	537	1,173 R	49.8%	46.7%	2.1%
7,909	WORTH	4,004	1,659	2,208	91	46	549 D	41.4%	55.1%	2.3%
14,334	WRIGHT	6,336	3,384	2,796	107	49	588 R	53.4%	44.1%	1.7%
2,926,324	TOTAL	1,315,563	634,373	638,517	29,374	13,299	4,144 D	48.2%	48.5%	2.2%

IOWA

CONGRESS

CD	Year	Total Vote	Republican		Democratic		Other Vote	Rep.-Dem. Plurality	Percentage			
			Vote	Candidate	Vote	Candidate			Total Vote		Major Vote	
									Rep.	Dem.	Rep.	Dem.
1	2000	266,990	164,972	LEACH, JAMES A.	96,283	SIMPSON, BOB	5,735	68,689 R	61.8%	36.1%	63.1%	36.9%
1	1998	188,208	106,419	LEACH, JAMES A.	79,529	RUSH, BOB	2,260	26,890 R	56.5%	42.3%	57.2%	42.8%
1	1996	244,596	129,242	LEACH, JAMES A.	111,595	RUSH, BOB	3,759	17,647 R	52.8%	45.6%	53.7%	46.3%
1	1994	183,461	110,448	LEACH, JAMES A.	69,461	WINEKAUF, GLEN	3,552	40,987 R	60.2%	37.9%	61.4%	38.6%
1	1992	261,309	178,042	LEACH, JAMES A.	81,600	ZONNEVELD, JAN J.	1,667	96,442 R	68.1%	31.2%	68.6%	31.4%
2	2000	252,567	139,906	NUSSLE, JIM	110,327	SMITH, DONNA L.	2,334	29,579 R	55.4%	43.7%	55.9%	44.1%
2	1998	189,574	104,613	NUSSLE, JIM	83,405	TULLY, ROB	1,556	21,208 R	55.2%	44.0%	55.6%	44.4%
2	1996	239,299	127,827	NUSSLE, JIM	109,731	SMITH, DONNA L.	1,741	18,096 R	53.4%	45.9%	53.8%	46.2%
2	1994	198,487	111,076	NUSSLE, JIM	86,087	NAGLE, DAVID R.	1,324	24,989 R	56.0%	43.4%	56.3%	43.7%
2	1992	267,892	134,536	NUSSLE, JIM	131,570	NAGLE, DAVID R.	1,786	2,966 R	50.2%	49.1%	50.6%	49.4%
3	2000	248,926	83,810	MARCUS, JAY	156,327	BOSWELL, LEONARD L.	8,789	72,517 D	33.7%	62.8%	34.9%	65.1%
3	1998	189,752	78,063	MCKIBBEN, LARRY	107,947	BOSWELL, LEONARD L.	3,742	29,884 D	41.1%	56.9%	42.0%	58.0%
3	1996	234,875	111,895	MAHAFFEY, MIKE	115,914	BOSWELL, LEONARD L.	7,066	4,019 D	47.6%	49.4%	49.1%	50.9%
3	1994	193,531	111,862	LIGHTFOOT, JIM R.	79,310	BAXTER, ELAINE	2,359	32,552 R	57.8%	41.0%	58.5%	41.5%
3	1992	257,276	125,931	LIGHTFOOT, JIM R.	121,063	BAXTER, ELAINE	10,282	4,868 R	48.9%	47.1%	51.0%	49.0%
4	2000	275,645	169,267	GANSKE, GREG	101,112	HUSTON, MICHAEL L.	5,266	68,155 R	61.4%	36.7%	62.6%	37.4%
4	1998	199,396	129,942	GANSKE, GREG	67,550	DVORAK, JON	1,904	62,392 R	65.2%	33.9%	65.8%	34.2%
4	1996	256,509	133,419	GANSKE, GREG	119,790	MCBURNEY, CONNIE	3,300	13,629 R	52.0%	46.7%	52.7%	47.3%
4	1994	213,206	111,935	GANSKE, GREG	98,824	SMITH, NEAL	2,447	13,111 R	52.5%	46.4%	53.1%	46.9%
4	1992	257,593	94,045	LUNDE, PAUL	158,610	SMITH, NEAL	4,938	64,565 D	36.5%	61.6%	37.2%	62.8%
5	2000	231,806	159,367	LATHAM, TOM	67,593	PALECEK, MIKE	4,846	91,774 R	68.8%	29.2%	70.2%	29.8%
5	1998	133,771	132,730	LATHAM, TOM			1,041	132,730 R	99.2%		100.0%	
5	1996	225,479	147,576	LATHAM, TOM	75,785	SMITH, MACDONALD	2,118	71,791 R	65.4%	33.6%	66.1%	33.9%
5	1994	188,721	114,796	LATHAM, TOM	73,627	MCGUIRE, SHELIA	298	41,169 R	60.8%	39.0%	60.9%	39.1%
5	1992	198,366	196,942	GRANDY, FRED			1,424	196,942 R	99.3%		100.0%	

IOWA

GENERAL, CAUCUS, AND PRIMARY ELECTIONS

2000 GENERAL ELECTIONS

President   Other vote was 5,731 Reform (Buchanan); 3,209 Libertarian (Browne); 2,281 Nominated by Petition (Hagelin); 613 Constitution (Phillips); 190 Socialist Workers (Harris); 107 Socialist (McReynolds); 1,168 scattered write-in.

Congress   Other vote was: CD 1: 5,564 Libertarian (Madden), 171 scattered write-in; CD 2: 2,288 Libertarian (Schoeman), 46 scattered write-in; CD 3: 5,563 Independence Party (Atkinson), 2,263 Libertarian (Seehusen), 851 Earth Federation (Hennager), 112 scattered write-in; CD 4: 4,552 Libertarian (Zimmerman), 612 Socialist Workers (Fruit), 102 scattered write-in; CD 5: 2,875 Libertarian (Olson), 1,917 Nominated by Petition (Holtorf), 54 scattered write-in.

2000 CAUCUS AND PRIMARY ELECTIONS

Precinct Caucuses	January 24, 2000 (President)	**Registration**	Republican	588,687
Primary	June 6, 2000 (Congress)	(active registrants	Democratic	566,477
		as of May 30, 2000)	No Party	673,844
			TOTAL	1,829,008

Primary Type   Modified-Registered Democrats and Republicans could only vote in their party's primary, although any registered voter could vote in another party's primary by changing their registration to that party on primary day.

Note: An asterisk (*) denotes incumbent. Because of the importance of the Iowa precinct caucuses in the presidential nominating process, the Democratic and Republican results are included in this table. Republican results reflect the outcome of a straw vote held in conjunction with the precinct caucuses. Democratic results reflect a measurement devised by the state party and not an actual vote total.

REPUBLICAN CAUCUSES			DEMOCRATIC CAUCUSES		
President	George W. Bush	35,787	41.0%	Al Gore	63.4%
(Precinct Caucuses)	Steve Forbes	26,595	30.5%	Bill Bradley	34.9%
	Alan Keyes	12,430	14.2%	Uncommitted	1.6%
	Gary Bauer	7,444	8.5%	Other	0.1%
	John McCain	4,084	4.7%		
	Orrin G. Hatch	893	1.0%		
	TOTAL	87,233			

REPUBLICAN PRIMARIES				DEMOCRATIC PRIMARIES		
Congressional	Jim Leach*	12,010	99.2%	Bob Simpson	5,865	64.4%
District 1	Write-in	91	0.8%	Gregory T. Guy	3,153	34.6%
				Write-in	86	0.9%
	TOTAL	12,101		TOTAL	9,104	
Congressional	Jim Nussle*	20,282	99.4%	Donna L. Smith	11,556	99.5%
District 2	Write-in	121	0.6%	Write-in	54	0.5%
	TOTAL	20,403		TOTAL	11,610	
Congressional	Jay Marcus	11,103	51.1%	Leonard L. Boswell*	20,204	99.5%
District 3	Philip K. Ferren	10,551	48.6%	Write-in	106	0.5%
	Write-in	78	0.4%			
	TOTAL	21,732		TOTAL	20,310	
Congressional	Greg Ganske*	17,301	99.4%	Michael L. Huston	17,324	99.0%
District 4	Write-in	105	0.6%	Write-in	169	1.0%
	TOTAL	17,406		TOTAL	17,493	
Congressional	Tom Latham*	22,516	90.1%	Mike Palecek	5,790	54.6%
District 5	Thomas D. Hall	2,458	9.8%	Conrad Lawlor	4,787	45.1%
	Write-in	18	0.1%	Write-in	31	0.3%
	TOTAL	24,992		TOTAL	10,608	

KANSAS

GOVERNOR
Bill Graves (R). Re-elected 1998 to a four-year term. Previously elected 1994.

SENATORS
Pat Roberts (R). Elected 1996 to a six-year term.

Sam Brownback (R). Re-elected 1998 to a six-year term. Had been elected 1996 to fill out the remaining two years of the term vacated when Senator Robert Dole (R) resigned to run for president.

REPRESENTATIVES
1. Jerry Moran (R)
2. Jim Ryun (R)
3. Dennis Moore (D)
4. Todd Tiahrt (R)

POSTWAR VOTE FOR PRESIDENT

| | | Republican | | Democratic | | Other | | Percentage | | | |
| | | | | | | | | Total Vote | | Major Vote | |
Year	Total Vote	Vote	Candidate	Vote	Candidate	Vote	Plurality	Rep.	Dem.	Rep.	Dem.
2000**	1,072,218	622,332	Bush, George W.	399,276	Gore, Al	50,610	223,056 R	58.0%	37.2%	60.9%	39.1%
1996**	1,074,300	583,245	Dole, Bob	387,659	Clinton, Bill	103,396	195,586 R	54.3%	36.1%	60.1%	39.9%
1992**	1,157,335	449,951	Bush, George	390,434	Clinton, Bill	316,950	59,517 R	38.9%	33.7%	53.5%	46.5%
1988	993,044	554,049	Bush, George	422,636	Dukakis, Michael S.	16,359	131,413 R	55.8%	42.6%	56.7%	43.3%
1984	1,021,991	677,296	Reagan, Ronald	333,149	Mondale, Walter F.	11,546	344,147 R	66.3%	32.6%	67.0%	33.0%
1980**	979,795	566,812	Reagan, Ronald	326,150	Carter, Jimmy	86,833	240,662 R	57.9%	33.3%	63.5%	36.5%
1976	957,845	502,752	Ford, Gerald R.	430,421	Carter, Jimmy	24,672	72,331 R	52.5%	44.9%	53.9%	46.1%
1972	916,095	619,812	Nixon, Richard M.	270,287	McGovern, George S.	25,996	349,525 R	67.7%	29.5%	69.6%	30.4%
1968	872,783	478,674	Nixon, Richard M.	302,996	Humphrey, Hubert H.	91,113	175,678 R	54.8%	34.7%	61.2%	38.8%
1964	857,901	386,579	Goldwater, Barry M.	464,028	Johnson, Lyndon B.	7,294	77,449 D	45.1%	54.1%	45.4%	54.6%
1960	928,825	561,474	Nixon, Richard M.	363,213	Kennedy, John F.	4,138	198,261 R	60.4%	39.1%	60.7%	39.3%
1956	866,243	566,878	Eisenhower, Dwight D.	296,317	Stevenson, Adlai E.	3,048	270,561 R	65.4%	34.2%	65.7%	34.3%
1952	896,166	616,302	Eisenhower, Dwight D.	273,296	Stevenson, Adlai E.	6,568	343,006 R	68.8%	30.5%	69.3%	30.7%
1948	788,819	423,039	Dewey, Thomas E.	351,902	Truman, Harry S.	13,878	71,137 R	53.6%	44.6%	54.6%	45.4%

In 2000 the other vote column includes 36,086 votes cast for Green (Nader). In 1996 the other vote column includes 92,639 votes cast for Perot. In 1992 the other vote column includes 312,358 votes cast for Perot. In 1980 the other column includes 68,231 votes for Independent (Anderson).

KANSAS

POSTWAR VOTE FOR GOVERNOR

Year	Total Vote	Republican Vote	Republican Candidate	Democratic Vote	Democratic Candidate	Other Vote	Rep.-Dem. Plurality	Total Vote Rep.	Total Vote Dem.	Major Vote Rep.	Major Vote Dem.
1998	742,665	544,882	Graves, Bill	168,243	Sawyer, Tom	29,540	376,639 R	73.4%	22.7%	76.4%	23.6%
1994	821,030	526,113	Graves, Bill	294,733	Slattery, Jim	184	231,380 R	64.1%	35.9%	64.1%	35.9%
1990	783,325	333,589	Hayden, Mike	380,609	Finney, Joan	69,127	47,020 D	42.6%	48.6%	46.7%	53.3%
1986	840,605	436,267	Hayden, Mike	404,338	Docking, Thomas R.		31,929 R	51.9%	48.1%	51.9%	48.1%
1982	763,263	339,356	Hardage, Sam	405,772	Carlin, John	18,135	66,416 D	44.5%	53.2%	45.5%	54.5%
1978	736,246	348,015	Bennett, Robert F.	363,835	Carlin, John	24,396	15,820 D	47.3%	49.4%	48.9%	51.1%
1974**	783,875	387,792	Bennett, Robert F.	384,115	Miller, Vern	11,968	3,677 R	49.5%	49.0%	50.2%	49.8%
1972	921,552	341,440	Kay, Morris	571,256	Docking, Robert	8,856	229,816 D	37.1%	62.0%	37.4%	62.6%
1970	745,196	333,227	Frizzell, Kent	404,611	Docking, Robert	7,358	71,384 D	44.7%	54.3%	45.2%	54.8%
1968	862,473	410,673	Harman, Rick	447,269	Docking, Robert	4,531	36,596 D	47.6%	51.9%	47.9%	52.1%
1966	692,955	304,325	Avery, William H.	380,030	Docking, Robert	8,600	75,705 D	43.9%	54.8%	44.5%	55.5%
1964	850,414	432,667	Avery, William H.	400,264	Wiles, Harry G.	17,483	32,403 R	50.9%	47.1%	51.9%	48.1%
1962	638,798	341,257	Anderson, John	291,285	Saffels, Dale E.	6,256	49,972 R	53.4%	45.6%	54.0%	46.0%
1960	922,522	511,534	Anderson, John	402,261	Docking, George	8,727	109,273 R	55.4%	43.6%	56.0%	44.0%
1958	735,939	313,036	Reed, Clyde M.	415,506	Docking, George	7,397	102,470 D	42.5%	56.5%	43.0%	57.0%
1956	864,935	364,340	Shaw, Warren W.	479,701	Docking, George	20,894	115,361 D	42.1%	55.5%	43.2%	56.8%
1954	622,633	329,868	Hall, Fred	286,218	Docking, George	6,547	43,650 R	53.0%	46.0%	53.5%	46.5%
1952	872,139	491,338	Arn, Edward F.	363,482	Rooney, Charles	17,319	127,856 R	56.3%	41.7%	57.5%	42.5%
1950	619,310	333,001	Arn, Edward F.	275,494	Anderson, Kenneth	10,815	57,507 R	53.8%	44.5%	54.7%	45.3%
1948	760,407	433,396	Carlson, Frank	307,485	Carpenter, Randolph	19,526	125,911 R	57.0%	40.4%	58.5%	41.5%
1946	577,694	309,064	Carlson, Frank	254,283	Woodring, Harry H.	14,347	54,781 R	53.5%	44.0%	54.9%	45.1%

The term of office of Kansas' Governor was increased from two to four years effective with the 1974 election.

POSTWAR VOTE FOR SENATOR

Year	Total Vote	Republican Vote	Republican Candidate	Democratic Vote	Democratic Candidate	Other Vote	Rep.-Dem. Plurality	Total Vote Rep.	Total Vote Dem.	Major Vote Rep.	Major Vote Dem.
1998	727,236	474,639	Brownback, Sam	229,718	Feleciano, Paul, Jr.	22,879	244,921 R	65.3%	31.6%	67.4%	32.6%
1996	1,052,300	652,677	Roberts, Pat	362,380	Thompson, Sally	37,243	290,297 R	62.0%	34.4%	64.3%	35.7%
1996S	1,064,716	574,021	Brownback, Sam	461,344	Docking, Jill	29,351	112,677 R	53.9%	43.3%	55.4%	44.6%
1992	1,126,447	706,246	Dole, Robert	349,525	O'Dell, Gloria	70,676	356,721 R	62.7%	31.0%	66.9%	33.1%
1990	786,235	578,605	Kassebaum, Nancy Landon	207,491	Williams, Dick	139	371,114 R	73.6%	26.4%	73.6%	26.4%
1986	823,566	576,902	Dole, Robert	246,664	MacDonald, Guy		330,238 R	70.0%	30.0%	70.0%	30.0%
1984	996,729	757,402	Kassebaum, Nancy Landon	211,664	Maher, James	27,663	545,738 R	76.0%	21.2%	78.2%	21.8%
1980	938,957	598,686	Dole, Robert	340,271	Simpson, John		258,415 R	63.8%	36.2%	63.8%	36.2%
1978	748,839	403,354	Kassebaum, Nancy Landon	317,602	Roy, William R.	27,883	85,752 R	53.9%	42.4%	55.9%	44.1%
1974	794,437	403,983	Dole, Robert	390,451	Roy, William R.	3	13,532 R	50.9%	49.1%	50.9%	49.1%
1972	871,722	622,591	Pearson, James B.	200,764	Tetzlaff, Arch O.	48,367	421,827 R	71.4%	23.0%	75.6%	24.4%
1968	817,096	490,911	Dole, Robert	315,911	Robinson, William I.	10,274	175,000 R	60.1%	38.7%	60.8%	39.2%
1966	671,345	350,077	Pearson, James B.	303,223	Breeding, J. Floyd	18,045	46,854 R	52.1%	45.2%	53.6%	46.4%
1962	622,232	388,500	Carlson, Frank	223,630	Smith, K. L.	10,102	164,870 R	62.4%	35.9%	63.5%	36.5%
1962S	613,250	344,689	Pearson, James B.	260,756	Aylward, Paul L.	7,805	83,933 R	56.2%	42.5%	56.9%	43.1%
1960	888,592	485,499	Schoeppel, Andrew F.	388,895	Theis, Frank	14,198	96,604 R	54.6%	43.8%	55.5%	44.5%
1956	825,280	477,822	Carlson, Frank	333,939	Hart, George	13,519	143,883 R	57.9%	40.5%	58.9%	41.1%
1954	618,063	348,144	Schoeppel, Andrew F.	258,575	McGill, George	11,344	89,569 R	56.3%	41.8%	57.4%	42.6%
1950	619,104	335,880	Carlson, Frank	271,365	Aiken, Paul	11,859	64,515 R	54.3%	43.8%	55.3%	44.7%
1948	716,342	393,412	Schoeppel, Andrew F.	305,987	McGill, George	16,943	87,425 R	54.9%	42.7%	56.3%	43.7%

One of the 1996 and 1962 elections was for a short term to fill a vacancy.

KANSAS

Districts Established June 3, 1991

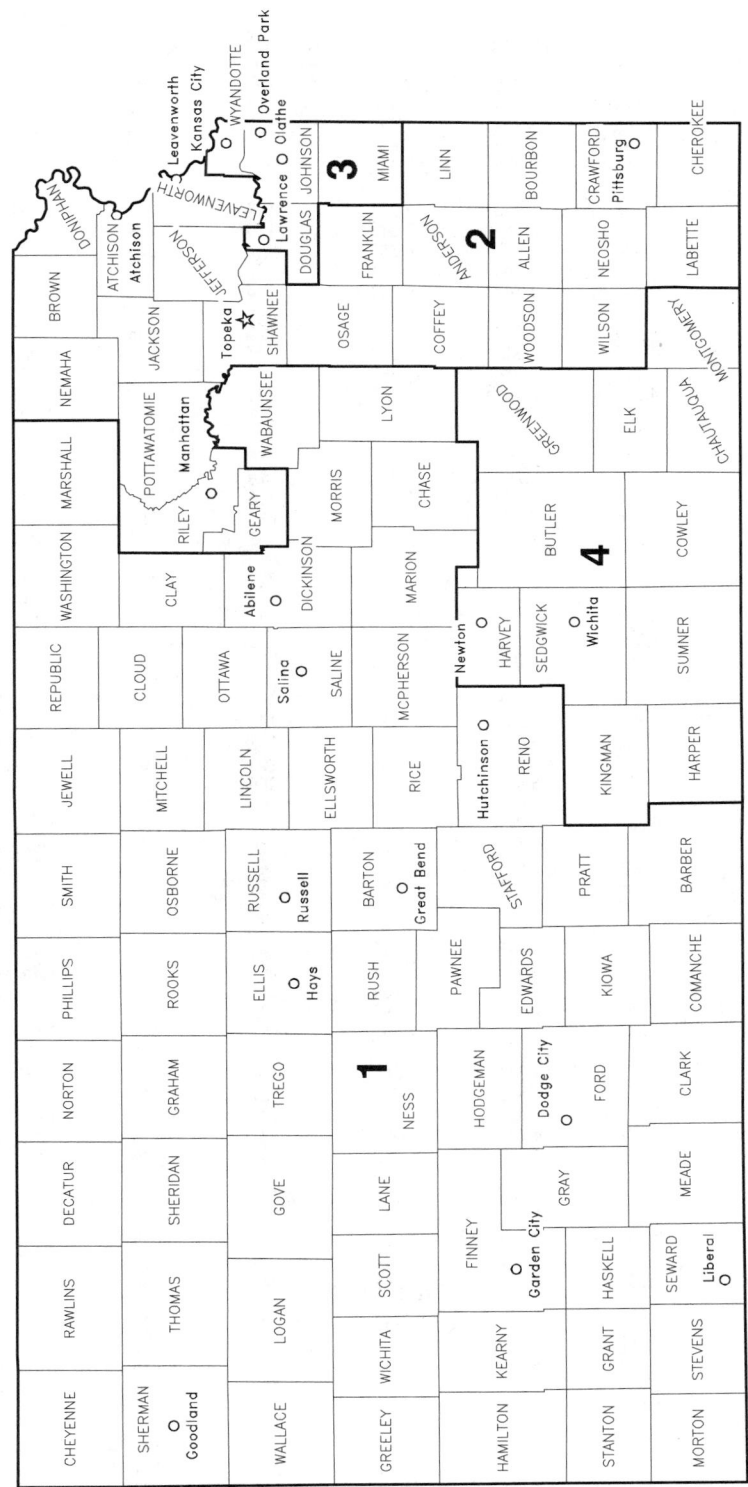

KANSAS

PRESIDENT 2000

2000 Census Population	County	Total Vote	Republican	Democratic	Green (Nader)	Other	Rep.-Dem. Plurality	Percentage of Total Vote		
								Rep.	Dem.	Green
14,385	ALLEN	5,766	3,379	2,132	164	91	1,247 R	58.6%	37.0%	2.8%
8,110	ANDERSON	3,478	1,984	1,327	94	73	657 R	57.0%	38.2%	2.7%
16,774	ATCHISON	6,900	3,378	3,171	233	118	207 R	49.0%	46.0%	3.4%
5,307	BARBER	2,498	1,755	637	73	33	1,118 R	70.3%	25.5%	2.9%
28,205	BARTON	10,955	7,302	3,238	251	164	4,064 R	66.7%	29.6%	2.3%
15,379	BOURBON	6,308	3,852	2,211	159	86	1,641 R	61.1%	35.1%	2.5%
10,724	BROWN	4,691	2,985	1,512	120	74	1,473 R	63.6%	32.2%	2.6%
59,482	BUTLER	21,002	13,377	6,755	497	373	6,622 R	63.7%	32.2%	2.4%
3,030	CHASE	1,317	848	391	56	22	457 R	64.4%	29.7%	4.3%
4,359	CHAUTAUQUA	1,880	1,347	443	36	54	904 R	71.6%	23.6%	1.9%
22,605	CHEROKEE	9,130	5,014	3,783	225	108	1,231 R	54.9%	41.4%	2.5%
3,165	CHEYENNE	1,727	1,312	350	47	18	962 R	76.0%	20.3%	2.7%
2,390	CLARK	1,261	926	292	34	9	634 R	73.4%	23.2%	2.7%
8,822	CLAY	4,088	2,998	951	93	46	2,047 R	73.3%	23.3%	2.3%
10,268	CLOUD	4,503	2,918	1,314	210	61	1,604 R	64.8%	29.2%	4.7%
8,865	COFFEY	4,040	2,700	1,196	96	48	1,504 R	66.8%	29.6%	2.4%
1,967	COMANCHE	1,006	760	211	18	17	549 R	75.5%	21.0%	1.8%
36,291	COWLEY	14,210	8,080	5,535	416	179	2,545 R	56.9%	39.0%	2.9%
38,242	CRAWFORD	15,034	7,160	7,076	630	168	84 R	47.6%	47.1%	4.2%
3,472	DECATUR	1,759	1,255	424	51	29	831 R	71.3%	24.1%	2.9%
19,344	DICKINSON	8,092	5,243	2,413	322	114	2,830 R	64.8%	29.8%	4.0%
8,249	DONIPHAN	3,649	2,350	1,134	90	75	1,216 R	64.4%	31.1%	2.5%
99,962	DOUGLAS	39,838	17,062	18,249	4,031	496	1,187 D	42.8%	45.8%	10.1%
3,449	EDWARDS	1,563	1,062	447	33	21	615 R	67.9%	28.6%	2.1%
3,261	ELK	1,550	1,080	402	34	34	678 R	69.7%	25.9%	2.2%
27,507	ELLIS	11,160	6,516	3,926	543	175	2,590 R	58.4%	35.2%	4.9%
6,525	ELLSWORTH	2,839	1,845	825	130	39	1,020 R	65.0%	29.1%	4.6%
40,523	FINNEY	9,150	6,442	2,431	182	95	4,011 R	70.4%	26.6%	2.0%
32,458	FORD	8,917	6,050	2,566	200	101	3,484 R	67.8%	28.8%	2.2%
24,784	FRANKLIN	9,658	5,925	3,321	306	106	2,604 R	61.3%	34.4%	3.2%
27,947	GEARY	6,866	3,977	2,660	158	71	1,317 R	57.9%	38.7%	2.3%
3,068	GOVE	1,495	1,122	296	44	33	826 R	75.1%	19.8%	2.9%
2,946	GRAHAM	1,474	1,058	346	47	23	712 R	71.8%	23.5%	3.2%
7,909	GRANT	2,856	2,126	683	39	8	1,443 R	74.4%	23.9%	1.4%
5,904	GRAY	2,160	1,631	482	27	20	1,149 R	75.5%	22.3%	1.3%
1,534	GREELEY	803	628	143	24	8	485 R	78.2%	17.8%	3.0%
7,673	GREENWOOD	3,561	2,392	1,027	81	61	1,365 R	67.2%	28.8%	2.3%
2,670	HAMILTON	1,192	901	264	15	12	637 R	75.6%	22.1%	1.3%
6,536	HARPER	3,055	2,076	869	75	35	1,207 R	68.0%	28.4%	2.5%
32,869	HARVEY	13,684	8,271	4,591	651	171	3,680 R	60.4%	33.6%	4.8%
4,307	HASKELL	1,616	1,323	263	16	14	1,060 R	81.9%	16.3%	1.0%
2,085	HODGEMAN	1,088	835	217	21	15	618 R	76.7%	19.9%	1.9%
12,657	JACKSON	5,250	3,001	1,990	123	136	1,011 R	57.2%	37.9%	2.3%
18,426	JEFFERSON	7,877	4,423	3,000	321	133	1,423 R	56.2%	38.1%	4.1%
3,791	JEWELL	1,877	1,400	380	57	40	1,020 R	74.6%	20.2%	3.0%
451,086	JOHNSON	217,536	129,965	79,118	6,493	1,960	50,847 R	59.7%	36.4%	3.0%
4,531	KEARNY	1,437	1,084	320	16	17	764 R	75.4%	22.3%	1.1%
8,673	KINGMAN	3,808	2,672	991	86	59	1,681 R	70.2%	26.0%	2.3%
3,278	KIOWA	1,608	1,262	294	34	18	968 R	78.5%	18.3%	2.1%
22,835	LABETTE	8,538	4,475	3,745	230	88	730 R	52.4%	43.9%	2.7%
2,155	LANE	1,133	846	252	23	12	594 R	74.7%	22.2%	2.0%
68,691	LEAVENWORTH	23,271	12,583	9,733	679	276	2,850 R	54.1%	41.8%	2.9%
3,578	LINCOLN	1,890	1,295	469	98	28	826 R	68.5%	24.8%	5.2%
9,570	LINN	4,259	2,513	1,587	91	68	926 R	59.0%	37.3%	2.1%
3,046	LOGAN	1,397	1,088	231	49	29	857 R	77.9%	16.5%	3.5%
35,935	LYON	12,455	6,652	5,190	417	196	1,462 R	53.4%	41.7%	3.3%
29,554	MCPHERSON	12,461	8,501	3,272	534	154	5,229 R	68.2%	26.3%	4.3%
13,361	MARION	5,903	4,156	1,475	189	83	2,681 R	70.4%	25.0%	3.2%
10,965	MARSHALL	5,115	3,066	1,831	134	84	1,235 R	59.9%	35.8%	2.6%
4,631	MEADE	2,053	1,604	400	33	16	1,204 R	78.1%	19.5%	1.6%

KANSAS

PRESIDENT 2000

2000 Census Population	County	Total Vote	Republican	Democratic	Green (Nader)	Other	Rep.-Dem. Plurality	Percentage of Total Vote Rep.	Dem.	Green
28,351	MIAMI	11,607	6,611	4,554	294	148	2,057 R	57.0%	39.2%	2.5%
6,932	MITCHELL	3,266	2,350	751	115	50	1,599 R	72.0%	23.0%	3.5%
36,252	MONTGOMERY	13,745	8,496	4,770	269	210	3,726 R	61.8%	34.7%	2.0%
6,104	MORRIS	2,641	1,599	882	104	56	717 R	60.5%	33.4%	3.9%
3,496	MORTON	1,557	1,203	321	19	14	882 R	77.3%	20.6%	1.2%
10,717	NEMAHA	5,290	3,578	1,494	102	116	2,084 R	67.6%	28.2%	1.9%
16,997	NEOSHO	6,886	4,014	2,588	194	90	1,426 R	58.3%	37.6%	2.8%
3,454	NESS	1,876	1,420	383	49	24	1,037 R	75.7%	20.4%	2.6%
5,953	NORTON	2,451	1,744	598	65	44	1,146 R	71.2%	24.4%	2.7%
16,712	OSAGE	6,613	3,770	2,530	171	142	1,240 R	57.0%	38.3%	2.6%
4,452	OSBORNE	2,030	1,432	484	74	40	948 R	70.5%	23.8%	3.6%
6,163	OTTAWA	2,791	1,977	631	145	38	1,346 R	70.8%	22.6%	5.2%
7,233	PAWNEE	2,940	1,850	968	93	29	882 R	62.9%	32.9%	3.2%
6,001	PHILLIPS	2,792	2,057	611	85	39	1,446 R	73.7%	21.9%	3.0%
18,209	POTTAWATOMIE	7,731	4,985	2,037	252	457	2,948 R	64.5%	26.3%	3.3%
9,647	PRATT	4,416	2,885	1,314	149	68	1,571 R	65.3%	29.8%	3.4%
2,966	RAWLINS	1,740	1,349	306	49	36	1,043 R	77.5%	17.6%	2.8%
64,790	RENO	25,430	15,179	9,025	877	349	6,154 R	59.7%	35.5%	3.4%
5,835	REPUBLIC	2,985	2,239	604	103	39	1,635 R	75.0%	20.2%	3.5%
10,761	RICE	4,520	2,903	1,422	128	67	1,481 R	64.2%	31.5%	2.8%
62,843	RILEY	18,253	10,672	6,188	1,171	222	4,484 R	58.5%	33.9%	6.4%
5,685	ROOKS	2,775	2,016	597	105	57	1,419 R	72.6%	21.5%	3.8%
3,551	RUSH	1,854	1,235	505	82	32	730 R	66.6%	27.2%	4.4%
7,370	RUSSELL	3,482	2,434	886	121	41	1,548 R	69.9%	25.4%	3.5%
53,597	SALINE	21,527	12,412	7,487	1,367	261	4,925 R	57.7%	34.8%	6.4%
5,120	SCOTT	2,303	1,811	418	52	22	1,393 R	78.6%	18.2%	2.3%
452,869	SEDGWICK	163,417	93,724	62,561	4,669	2,463	31,163 R	57.4%	38.3%	2.9%
22,510	SEWARD	5,096	3,869	1,126	60	41	2,743 R	75.9%	22.1%	1.2%
169,871	SHAWNEE	74,373	35,894	34,818	2,529	1,132	1,076 R	48.3%	46.8%	3.4%
2,813	SHERIDAN	1,489	1,132	281	55	21	851 R	76.0%	18.9%	3.7%
6,760	SHERMAN	2,682	1,894	681	60	47	1,213 R	70.6%	25.4%	2.2%
4,536	SMITH	2,184	1,534	534	79	37	1,000 R	70.2%	24.5%	3.6%
4,789	STAFFORD	2,200	1,546	567	54	33	979 R	70.3%	25.8%	2.5%
2,406	STANTON	1,029	785	215	16	13	570 R	76.3%	20.9%	1.6%
5,463	STEVENS	2,111	1,714	345	34	18	1,369 R	81.2%	16.3%	1.6%
25,946	SUMNER	10,232	6,176	3,549	306	201	2,627 R	60.4%	34.7%	3.0%
8,180	THOMAS	3,780	2,822	807	93	58	2,015 R	74.7%	21.3%	2.5%
3,319	TREGO	1,837	1,220	516	69	32	704 R	66.4%	28.1%	3.8%
6,885	WABAUNSEE	3,420	2,182	1,025	96	117	1,157 R	63.8%	30.0%	2.8%
1,749	WALLACE	861	737	103	14	7	634 R	85.6%	12.0%	1.6%
6,483	WASHINGTON	3,267	2,446	687	77	57	1,759 R	74.9%	21.0%	2.4%
2,531	WICHITA	1,090	859	207	15	9	652 R	78.8%	19.0%	1.4%
10,332	WILSON	4,095	2,748	1,186	100	61	1,562 R	67.1%	29.0%	2.4%
3,788	WOODSON	1,595	974	521	59	41	453 R	61.1%	32.7%	3.7%
157,882	WYANDOTTE	48,272	14,024	32,411	1,287	550	18,387 D	29.1%	67.1%	2.7%
2,688,418	TOTAL	1,072,218	622,332	399,276	36,086	14,524	223,056 R	58.0%	37.2%	3.4%

KANSAS

CONGRESS

CD	Year	Total Vote	Republican		Democratic		Other Vote	Rep.-Dem. Plurality	Percentage			
									Total Vote		Major Vote	
			Vote	Candidate	Vote	Candidate			Rep.	Dem.	Rep.	Dem.
1	2000	242,327	216,484	MORAN, JERRY			25,843	216,484 R	89.3%		100.0%	
1	1998	189,393	152,775	MORAN, JERRY	36,618	PHILLIPS, JIM		116,157 R	80.7%	19.3%	80.7%	19.3%
1	1996	261,145	191,899	MORAN, JERRY	63,948	DIVINE, JOHN	5,298	127,951 R	73.5%	24.5%	75.0%	25.0%
1	1994	219,008	169,531	ROBERTS, PAT	49,477	NICHOLS, TERRY L.		120,054 R	77.4%	22.6%	77.4%	22.6%
1	1992	285,297	194,912	ROBERTS, PAT	83,620	WEST, DUANE	6,765	111,292 R	68.3%	29.3%	70.0%	30.0%
2	2000	244,759	164,951	RYUN, JIM	71,709	WILES, STANLEY	8,099	93,242 R	67.4%	29.3%	69.7%	30.3%
2	1998	178,048	108,527	RYUN, JIM	69,521	CLARK, JIM		39,006 R	61.0%	39.0%	61.0%	39.0%
2	1996	252,078	131,592	RYUN, JIM	114,644	FRIEDEN, JOHN	5,842	16,948 R	52.2%	45.5%	53.4%	46.6%
2	1994	206,750	135,725	BROWNBACK, SAM	71,025	CARLIN, JOHN		64,700 R	65.6%	34.4%	65.6%	34.4%
2	1992	268,806	109,801	VAN SLYKE, JIM	151,019	SLATTERY, JIM	7,986	41,218 D	40.8%	56.2%	42.1%	57.9%
3	2000	308,710	144,672	KLINE, PHILL	154,505	MOORE, DENNIS	9,533	9,833 D	46.9%	50.0%	48.4%	51.6%
3	1998	197,314	93,938	SNOWBARGER, VINCE	103,376	MOORE, DENNIS		9,438 D	47.6%	52.4%	47.6%	52.4%
3	1996	279,264	139,169	SNOWBARGER, VINCE	126,848	HANCOCK, JUDY	13,247	12,321 R	49.8%	45.4%	52.3%	47.7%
3	1994	180,619	102,218	MEYERS, JAN	78,401	HANCOCK, JUDY		23,817 R	56.6%	43.4%	56.6%	43.4%
3	1992	292,796	169,929	MEYERS, JAN	110,076	LOVE, TOM	12,791	59,853 R	58.0%	37.6%	60.7%	39.3%
4	2000	242,583	131,871	TIAHRT, TODD	101,980	NOLLA, CARLOS	8,732	29,891 R	54.4%	42.0%	56.4%	43.6%
4	1998	162,693	94,785	TIAHRT, TODD	62,737	LAWING, JIM	5,171	32,048 R	58.3%	38.6%	60.2%	39.8%
4	1996	256,391	128,486	TIAHRT, TODD	119,544	RATHBUN, RANDY	8,361	8,942 R	50.1%	46.6%	51.8%	48.2%
4	1994	211,019	111,653	TIAHRT, TODD	99,366	GLICKMAN, DAN		12,287 R	52.9%	47.1%	52.9%	47.1%
4	1992	278,016	117,070	YOST, ERIC R.	143,671	GLICKMAN, DAN	17,275	26,601 D	42.1%	51.7%	44.9%	55.1%

KANSAS

GENERAL AND PRIMARY ELECTIONS

2000 GENERAL ELECTIONS

President Other vote was 7,370 Reform (Buchanan); 4,525 Libertarian (Browne); 1,375 Independent (Hagelin); 1,254 Constitution (Phillips). Nader was listed on the ballot as an Independent.

Congress Other vote was: CD 1: 25,843 Libertarian (Warner); CD 2: 8,099 Libertarian (Hawver); CD 3: 9,533 Libertarian (Mina); CD 4: 8,732 Libertarian (Rosile).

2000 PRIMARY ELECTIONS

Primary August 1, 2000

Registration
(as of July 17, 2000)

Republican	696,480
Democratic	430,410
Libertarian	9,369
Taxpayer	2,256
Reform	2,194
Unaffiliated	416,971
TOTAL	1,557,680

KANSAS

GENERAL AND PRIMARY ELECTIONS

Primary Type   Modified—Registered Democrats and Republicans could only vote in their party's primary. "Unaffiliated" voters could vote in either primary if they changed their registration to that party on primary day.

Note: An asterisk (*) denotes incumbent.

	REPUBLICAN PRIMARIES			DEMOCRATIC PRIMARIES		
Congressional District 1	Jerry Moran*	88,943	100.0%	No Democratic candidate		
	TOTAL	88,943				
Congressional District 2	Jim Ryun*	57,740	100.0%	Stanley Wiles	22,897	100.0%
	TOTAL	57,740		TOTAL	22,897	
Congressional District 3	Phill Kline	36,042	49.9%	Dennis Moore*	22,311	100.0%
	Greg Musil	27,068	37.5%			
	Gary Morsch	9,121	12.6%			
	TOTAL	72,231		TOTAL	22,311	
Congressional District 4	Todd Tiahrt*	49,441	100.0%	Carlos Nolla	17,519	100.0%
	TOTAL	49,441		TOTAL	17,519	

KENTUCKY

GOVERNOR
Paul Patton (D). Re-elected 1999 to a four-year term. Previously elected 1995.

SENATORS
Jim Bunning (R). Elected 1998 to a six-year term.

Mitch McConnell (R). Re-elected 1996 to a six-year term. Previously elected 1990, 1984.

REPRESENTATIVES

1. Edward Whitfield (R)	3. Anne M. Northup (R)	5. Harold Rogers (R)
2. Ron Lewis (R)	4. Ken Lucas (D)	6. Ernie Fletcher (R)

POSTWAR VOTE FOR PRESIDENT

		Republican		Democratic		Other		Percentage			
								Total Vote		Major Vote	
Year	Total Vote	Vote	Candidate	Vote	Candidate	Vote	Plurality	Rep.	Dem.	Rep.	Dem.
2000**	1,544,187	872,492	Bush, George W.	638,898	Gore, Al	32,797	233,594 R	56.5%	41.4%	57.7%	42.3%
1996**	1,388,708	623,283	Dole, Bob	636,614	Clinton, Bill	128,811	13,331 D	44.9%	45.8%	49.5%	50.5%
1992**	1,492,900	617,178	Bush, George	665,104	Clinton, Bill	210,618	47,926 D	41.3%	44.6%	48.1%	51.9%
1988	1,322,517	734,281	Bush, George	580,368	Dukakis, Michael S.	7,868	153,913 R	55.5%	43.9%	55.9%	44.1%
1984	1,369,345	821,702	Reagan, Ronald	539,539	Mondale, Walter F.	8,104	282,163 R	60.0%	39.4%	60.4%	39.6%
1980**	1,294,627	635,274	Reagan, Ronald	616,417	Carter, Jimmy	42,936	18,857 R	49.1%	47.6%	50.8%	49.2%
1976	1,167,142	531,852	Ford, Gerald R.	615,717	Carter, Jimmy	19,573	83,865 D	45.6%	52.8%	46.3%	53.7%
1972	1,067,499	676,446	Nixon, Richard M.	371,159	McGovern, George S.	19,894	305,287 R	63.4%	34.8%	64.6%	35.4%
1968	1,055,893	462,411	Nixon, Richard M.	397,541	Humphrey, Hubert H.	195,941	64,870 R	43.8%	37.6%	53.8%	46.2%
1964	1,046,105	372,977	Goldwater, Barry M.	669,659	Johnson, Lyndon B.	3,469	296,682 D	35.7%	64.0%	35.8%	64.2%
1960	1,124,462	602,607	Nixon, Richard M.	521,855	Kennedy, John F.		80,752 R	53.6%	46.4%	53.6%	46.4%
1956	1,053,805	572,192	Eisenhower, Dwight D.	476,453	Stevenson, Adlai E.	5,160	95,739 R	54.3%	45.2%	54.6%	45.4%
1952	993,148	495,029	Eisenhower, Dwight D.	495,729	Stevenson, Adlai E.	2,390	700 D	49.8%	49.9%	50.0%	50.0%
1948	822,658	341,210	Dewey, Thomas E.	466,756	Truman, Harry S.	14,692	125,546 D	41.5%	56.7%	42.2%	57.8%

In 2000 the other vote column includes 23,192 votes cast for Green (Nader). In 1996 the other vote column includes 120,396 votes cast for Perot. In 1992 the other vote column includes 203,944 votes cast for Perot. In 1980 the other column includes 31,127 votes for Independent (Anderson).

KENTUCKY

POSTWAR VOTE FOR GOVERNOR

Year	Total Vote	Republican		Democratic		Other Vote	Rep.-Dem. Plurality	Percentage			
								Total Vote		Major Vote	
		Vote	Candidate	Vote	Candidate			Rep.	Dem.	Rep.	Dem.
1999	580,074	128,788	Martin, Peppy	352,099	Patton, Paul E.	99,187	223,311 D	22.2%	60.7%	26.8%	73.2%
1995	983,979	479,227	Forgy, Larry	500,787	Patton, Paul E.	3,965	21,560 D	48.7%	50.9%	48.9%	51.1%
1991	834,920	294,452	Hopkins, Larry J.	540,468	Jones, Brereton C.		246,016 D	35.3%	64.7%	35.3%	64.7%
1987	777,815	273,141	Harper, John	504,674	Wilkinson, Wallace G.		231,533 D	35.1%	64.9%	35.1%	64.9%
1983	1,030,671	454,650	Bunning, Jim	561,674	Collins, Martha Layne	14,347	107,024 D	44.1%	54.5%	44.7%	55.3%
1979	939,366	381,278	Nunn, Louie B.	558,088	Brown, J. Y., Jr.		176,810 D	40.6%	59.4%	40.6%	59.4%
1975	748,157	277,998	Gable, Robert E.	470,159	Carroll, Julian		192,161 D	37.2%	62.8%	37.2%	62.8%
1971	930,790	412,653	Emberton, Thomas	470,720	Ford, Wendell H.	47,417	58,067 D	44.3%	50.6%	46.7%	53.3%
1967	886,946	454,123	Nunn, Louie B.	425,674	Ward, Henry	7,149	28,449 R	51.2%	48.0%	51.6%	48.4%
1963	886,047	436,496	Nunn, Louie B.	449,551	Breathitt, Edward T.		13,055 D	49.3%	50.7%	49.3%	50.7%
1959	853,005	336,456	Robsion, John M.	516,549	Combs, Bert T.		180,093 D	39.4%	60.6%	39.4%	60.6%
1955	778,488	322,671	Denney, Edwin R.	451,647	Chandler, Albert B.	4,170	128,976 D	41.4%	58.0%	41.7%	58.3%
1951	634,359	288,014	Siler, Eugene	346,345	Wetherby, Lawrence		58,331 D	45.4%	54.6%	45.4%	54.6%
1947	672,372	287,130	Dummit, Eldon S.	385,242	Clements, Earle C.		98,112 D	42.7%	57.3%	42.7%	57.3%

In 1999 the other vote column includes 88,930 votes cast for Reform (Galbraith).

POSTWAR VOTE FOR SENATOR

Year	Total Vote	Republican		Democratic		Other Vote	Rep.-Dem. Plurality	Percentage			
								Total Vote		Major Vote	
		Vote	Candidate	Vote	Candidate			Rep.	Dem.	Rep.	Dem.
1998	1,145,414	569,817	Bunning, Jim	563,051	Baesler, Scotty	12,546	6,766 R	49.7%	49.2%	50.3%	49.7%
1996	1,307,046	724,794	McConnell, Mitch	560,012	Beshear, Steven L.	22,240	164,782 R	55.5%	42.8%	56.4%	43.6%
1992	1,330,858	476,604	Williams, David L.	836,888	Ford, Wendell H.	17,366	360,284 D	35.8%	62.9%	36.3%	63.7%
1990	916,010	478,034	McConnell, Mitch	437,976	Sloane, Harvey		40,058 R	52.2%	47.8%	52.2%	47.8%
1986	677,280	173,330	Andrews, Jackson M.	503,775	Ford, Wendell H.	175	330,445 D	25.6%	74.4%	25.6%	74.4%
1984	1,292,407	644,990	McConnell, Mitch	639,721	Huddleston, Walter	7,696	5,269 R	49.9%	49.5%	50.2%	49.8%
1980	1,106,890	386,029	Foust, Mary Louise	720,861	Ford, Wendell H.		334,832 D	34.9%	65.1%	34.9%	65.1%
1978	476,783	175,766	Guenthner, Louie	290,730	Huddleston, Walter	10,287	114,964 D	36.9%	61.0%	37.7%	62.3%
1974	745,994	328,982	Cook, Marlow W.	399,406	Ford, Wendell H.	17,606	70,424 D	44.1%	53.5%	45.2%	54.8%
1972	1,037,861	494,337	Nunn, Louie B.	528,550	Huddleston, Walter	14,974	34,213 D	47.6%	50.9%	48.3%	51.7%
1968	942,865	484,260	Cook, Marlow W.	448,960	Peden, Katherine	9,645	35,300 R	51.4%	47.6%	51.9%	48.1%
1966	749,884	483,805	Cooper, John Sherman	266,079	Brown, J. Y.		217,726 R	64.5%	35.5%	64.5%	35.5%
1962	820,088	432,648	Morton, Thruston B.	387,440	Wyatt, Wilson W.		45,208 R	52.8%	47.2%	52.8%	47.2%
1960	1,088,377	644,087	Cooper, John Sherman	444,290	Johnson, Keen		199,797 R	59.2%	40.8%	59.2%	40.8%
1956	1,006,825	506,903	Morton, Thruston B.	499,922	Clements, Earle C.	6,981	6,981 R	50.3%	49.7%	50.3%	49.7%
1956S	1,011,645	538,505	Cooper, John Sherman	473,140	Wetherby, Lawrence		65,365 R	53.2%	46.8%	53.2%	46.8%
1954	797,057	362,948	Cooper, John Sherman	434,109	Barkley, Alben W.		71,161 D	45.5%	54.5%	45.5%	54.5%
1952S	960,228	494,576	Cooper, John Sherman	465,652	Underwood, Thomas R.		28,924 R	51.5%	48.5%	51.5%	48.5%
1950	612,617	278,368	Dawson, Charles L.	334,249	Clements, Earle C.		55,881 D	45.4%	54.6%	45.4%	54.6%
1948	794,469	383,776	Cooper, John Sherman	408,256	Chapman, Virgil	2,437	24,480 D	48.3%	51.4%	48.5%	51.5%
1946S	615,119	327,652	Cooper, John Sherman	285,829	Brown, J. Y.	1,638	41,823 R	53.3%	46.5%	53.4%	46.6%

One of the 1956 elections and those in 1952 and 1946 were for short terms to fill vacancies.

KENTUCKY

Districts Established April 13, 1994

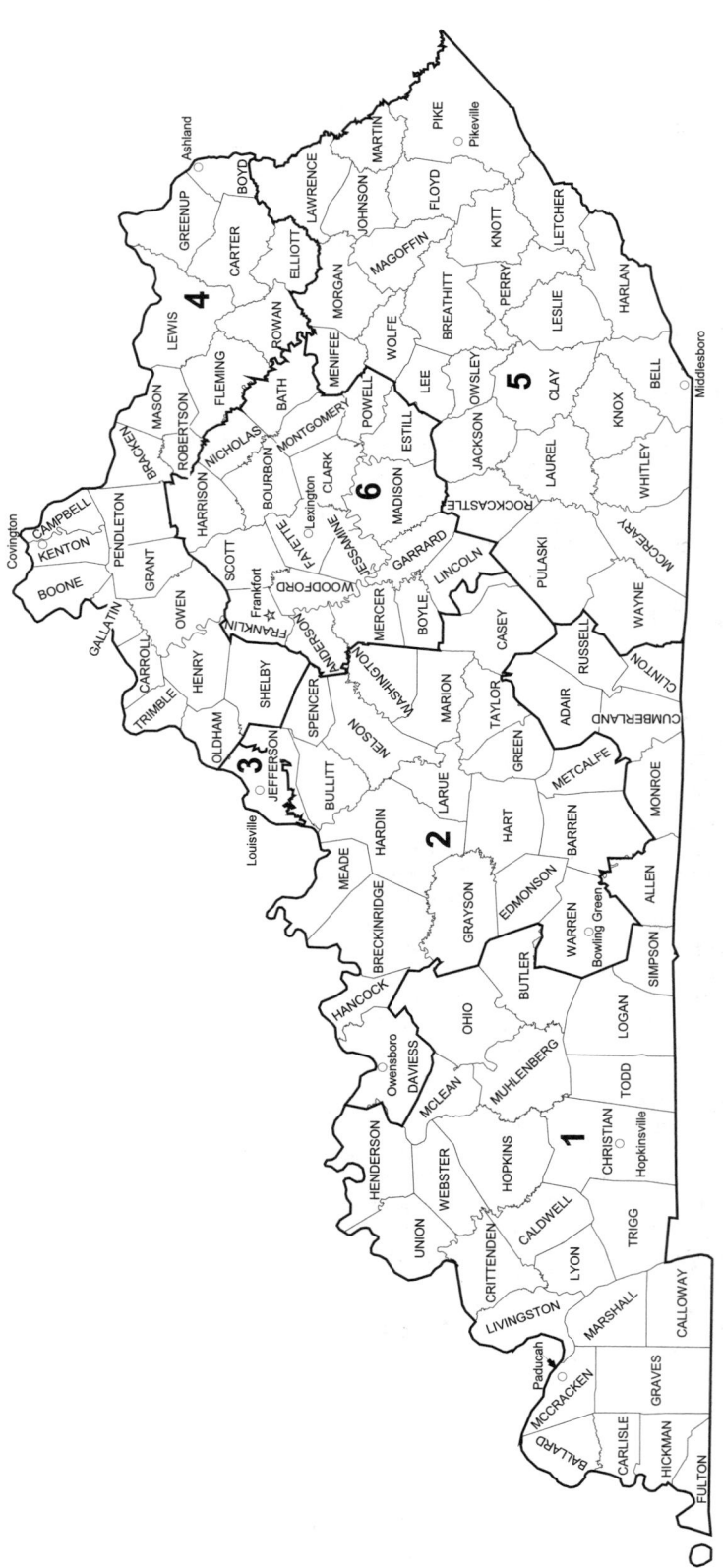

KENTUCKY

PRESIDENT 2000

2000 Census Population	County	Total Vote	Republican	Democratic	Green (Nader)	Other	Rep.-Dem. Plurality	Percentage of Total Vote		
								Rep.	Dem.	Green
17,244	ADAIR	7,328	5,460	1,779	48	41	3,681 R	74.5%	24.3%	0.7%
17,800	ALLEN	6,429	4,415	1,950	31	33	2,465 R	68.7%	30.3%	0.5%
19,111	ANDERSON	7,967	4,909	2,902	120	36	2,007 R	61.6%	36.4%	1.5%
8,286	BALLARD	3,770	1,824	1,880	23	43	56 D	48.4%	49.9%	0.6%
38,033	BARREN	13,844	8,741	4,930	108	65	3,811 R	63.1%	35.6%	0.8%
11,085	BATH	4,473	2,303	2,087	49	34	216 R	51.5%	46.7%	1.1%
30,060	BELL	10,611	5,585	4,787	102	137	798 R	52.6%	45.1%	1.0%
85,991	BOONE	31,984	22,016	9,248	485	235	12,768 R	68.8%	28.9%	1.5%
19,360	BOURBON	7,102	3,881	3,048	126	47	833 R	54.6%	42.9%	1.8%
49,752	BOYD	19,182	9,247	9,541	274	120	294 D	48.2%	49.7%	1.4%
27,697	BOYLE	10,326	6,126	3,963	177	60	2,163 R	59.3%	38.4%	1.7%
8,279	BRACKEN	3,019	2,065	888	37	29	1,177 R	68.4%	29.4%	1.2%
16,100	BREATHITT	5,073	2,084	2,902	57	30	818 D	41.1%	57.2%	1.1%
18,648	BRECKINRIDGE	7,453	4,763	2,595	48	47	2,168 R	63.9%	34.8%	0.6%
61,236	BULLITT	22,701	14,054	8,195	270	182	5,859 R	61.9%	36.1%	1.2%
13,010	BUTLER	5,010	3,654	1,299	27	30	2,355 R	72.9%	25.9%	0.5%
13,060	CALDWELL	5,482	3,161	2,223	54	44	938 R	57.7%	40.6%	1.0%
34,177	CALLOWAY	13,673	7,705	5,635	236	97	2,070 R	56.4%	41.2%	1.7%
88,616	CAMPBELL	33,829	20,789	12,040	720	280	8,749 R	61.5%	35.6%	2.1%
5,351	CARLISLE	2,593	1,405	1,149	14	25	256 R	54.2%	44.3%	0.5%
10,155	CARROLL	3,499	1,818	1,601	57	23	217 R	52.0%	45.8%	1.6%
26,889	CARTER	8,959	4,617	4,182	97	63	435 R	51.5%	46.7%	1.1%
15,447	CASEY	5,469	4,284	1,122	36	27	3,162 R	78.3%	20.5%	0.7%
72,265	CHRISTIAN	17,773	10,787	6,778	137	71	4,009 R	60.7%	38.1%	0.8%
33,144	CLARK	12,473	7,297	4,918	191	67	2,379 R	58.5%	39.4%	1.5%
24,556	CLAY	6,719	4,926	1,723	28	42	3,203 R	73.3%	25.6%	0.4%
9,634	CLINTON	4,305	3,224	1,032	24	25	2,192 R	74.9%	24.0%	0.6%
9,384	CRITTENDEN	4,154	2,469	1,610	41	34	859 R	59.4%	38.8%	1.0%
7,147	CUMBERLAND	3,006	2,220	736	22	28	1,484 R	73.9%	24.5%	0.7%
91,545	DAVIESS	36,240	21,361	14,126	506	247	7,235 R	58.9%	39.0%	1.4%
11,644	EDMONSON	4,995	3,250	1,710	17	18	1,540 R	65.1%	34.2%	0.3%
6,748	ELLIOTT	2,381	827	1,525	19	10	698 D	34.7%	64.0%	0.8%
15,307	ESTILL	4,710	3,033	1,591	51	35	1,442 R	64.4%	33.8%	1.1%
260,512	FAYETTE	105,477	54,495	47,277	3,052	653	7,218 R	51.7%	44.8%	2.9%
13,792	FLEMING	5,179	3,282	1,813	43	41	1,469 R	63.4%	35.0%	0.8%
42,441	FLOYD	15,394	5,068	10,088	129	109	5,020 D	32.9%	65.5%	0.8%
47,687	FRANKLIN	21,654	10,209	10,853	449	143	644 D	47.1%	50.1%	2.1%
7,752	FULTON	2,788	1,293	1,452	20	23	159 D	46.4%	52.1%	0.7%
7,870	GALLATIN	2,459	1,345	1,049	38	27	296 R	54.7%	42.7%	1.5%
14,792	GARRARD	5,823	4,043	1,713	43	24	2,330 R	69.4%	29.4%	0.7%
22,384	GRANT	7,103	4,405	2,568	90	40	1,837 R	62.0%	36.2%	1.3%
37,028	GRAVES	14,235	7,849	6,097	131	158	1,752 R	55.1%	42.8%	0.9%
24,053	GRAYSON	8,554	5,843	2,604	58	49	3,239 R	68.3%	30.4%	0.7%
11,518	GREEN	4,756	3,615	1,085	31	25	2,530 R	76.0%	22.8%	0.7%
36,891	GREENUP	14,663	7,233	7,164	178	88	69 R	49.3%	48.9%	1.2%
8,392	HANCOCK	3,610	2,032	1,508	49	21	524 R	56.3%	41.8%	1.4%
94,174	HARDIN	30,690	18,964	11,095	437	194	7,869 R	61.8%	36.2%	1.4%
33,202	HARLAN	10,535	4,980	5,365	110	80	385 D	47.3%	50.9%	1.0%
17,983	HARRISON	6,611	3,793	2,658	114	46	1,135 R	57.4%	40.2%	1.7%
17,445	HART	6,019	3,725	2,201	53	40	1,524 R	61.9%	36.6%	0.9%
44,829	HENDERSON	16,039	7,698	8,054	217	70	356 D	48.0%	50.2%	1.4%
15,060	HENRY	5,473	3,244	2,117	73	39	1,127 R	59.3%	38.7%	1.3%
5,262	HICKMAN	2,124	1,151	940	18	15	211 R	54.2%	44.3%	0.8%
46,519	HOPKINS	16,489	9,490	6,734	160	105	2,756 R	57.6%	40.8%	1.0%
13,495	JACKSON	4,855	4,079	701	45	30	3,378 R	84.0%	14.4%	0.9%
693,604	JEFFERSON	302,362	145,052	149,901	5,935	1,474	4,849 D	48.0%	49.6%	2.0%
39,041	JESSAMINE	15,061	10,074	4,633	266	88	5,441 R	66.9%	30.8%	1.8%
23,445	JOHNSON	8,180	4,783	3,251	85	61	1,532 R	58.5%	39.7%	1.0%
151,464	KENTON	56,249	35,363	19,100	1,293	493	16,263 R	62.9%	34.0%	2.3%
17,649	KNOTT	6,458	2,029	4,349	42	38	2,320 D	31.4%	67.3%	0.7%

KENTUCKY

PRESIDENT 2000

2000 Census Population	County	Total Vote	Republican	Democratic	Green (Nader)	Other	Rep.-Dem. Plurality	Percentage of Total Vote		
								Rep.	Dem.	Green
31,795	KNOX	9,910	6,058	3,690	83	79	2,368 R	61.1%	37.2%	0.8%
13,373	LARUE	5,179	3,384	1,727	41	27	1,657 R	65.3%	33.3%	0.8%
52,715	LAUREL	18,120	13,029	4,856	138	97	8,173 R	71.9%	26.8%	0.8%
15,569	LAWRENCE	5,307	2,969	2,258	47	33	711 R	55.9%	42.5%	0.9%
7,916	LEE	2,764	1,893	836	17	18	1,057 R	68.5%	30.2%	0.6%
12,401	LESLIE	4,434	3,159	1,210	28	37	1,949 R	71.2%	27.3%	0.6%
25,277	LETCHER	8,985	4,092	4,698	127	68	606 D	45.5%	52.3%	1.4%
14,092	LEWIS	4,568	3,217	1,293	39	19	1,924 R	70.4%	28.3%	0.9%
23,361	LINCOLN	7,597	4,795	2,678	71	53	2,117 R	63.1%	35.3%	0.9%
9,804	LIVINGSTON	4,230	2,118	2,022	43	47	96 R	50.1%	47.8%	1.0%
26,573	LOGAN	9,332	5,344	3,885	61	42	1,459 R	57.3%	41.6%	0.7%
8,080	LYON	3,420	1,688	1,680	30	22	8 R	49.4%	49.1%	0.9%
65,514	MCCRACKEN	26,689	14,745	11,412	302	230	3,333 R	55.2%	42.8%	1.1%
17,080	MCCREARY	4,799	3,321	1,418	38	22	1,903 R	69.2%	29.5%	0.8%
9,938	MCLEAN	4,022	2,219	1,747	44	12	472 R	55.2%	43.4%	1.1%
70,872	MADISON	23,666	13,682	9,309	525	150	4,373 R	57.8%	39.3%	2.2%
13,332	MAGOFFIN	5,453	2,785	2,603	23	42	182 R	51.1%	47.7%	0.4%
18,212	MARION	6,176	3,259	2,778	93	46	481 R	52.8%	45.0%	1.5%
30,125	MARSHALL	13,761	7,294	6,203	140	124	1,091 R	53.0%	45.1%	1.0%
12,578	MARTIN	4,456	2,667	1,714	36	39	953 R	59.9%	38.5%	0.8%
16,800	MASON	5,873	3,572	2,178	88	35	1,394 R	60.8%	37.1%	1.5%
26,349	MEADE	9,071	5,319	3,596	104	52	1,723 R	58.6%	39.6%	1.1%
6,556	MENIFEE	2,249	1,170	1,038	19	22	132 R	52.0%	46.2%	0.8%
20,817	MERCER	8,632	5,362	3,092	129	49	2,270 R	62.1%	35.8%	1.5%
10,037	METCALFE	3,849	2,476	1,318	41	14	1,158 R	64.3%	34.2%	1.1%
11,756	MONROE	5,569	4,377	1,158	15	19	3,219 R	78.6%	20.8%	0.3%
22,554	MONTGOMERY	8,519	4,534	3,833	87	65	701 R	53.2%	45.0%	1.0%
13,948	MORGAN	4,240	2,295	1,875	44	26	420 R	54.1%	44.2%	1.0%
31,839	MUHLENBERG	11,956	5,518	6,295	87	56	777 D	46.2%	52.7%	0.7%
37,477	NELSON	13,488	7,714	5,481	212	81	2,233 R	57.2%	40.6%	1.6%
6,813	NICHOLAS	2,673	1,613	994	42	24	619 R	60.3%	37.2%	1.6%
22,916	OHIO	8,882	5,413	3,303	103	63	2,110 R	60.9%	37.2%	1.2%
46,178	OLDHAM	20,268	13,580	6,236	349	103	7,344 R	67.0%	30.8%	1.7%
10,547	OWEN	4,070	2,582	1,394	68	26	1,188 R	63.4%	34.3%	1.7%
4,858	OWSLEY	1,826	1,466	339	10	11	1,127 R	80.3%	18.6%	0.5%
14,390	PENDLETON	4,803	3,044	1,670	57	32	1,374 R	63.4%	34.8%	1.2%
29,390	PERRY	11,000	5,300	5,514	103	83	214 D	48.2%	50.1%	0.9%
68,736	PIKE	24,935	11,005	13,611	169	150	2,606 D	44.1%	54.6%	0.7%
13,237	POWELL	4,362	2,258	2,008	63	33	250 R	51.8%	46.0%	1.4%
56,217	PULASKI	21,541	15,845	5,415	178	103	10,430 R	73.6%	25.1%	0.8%
2,266	ROBERTSON	998	630	341	24	3	289 R	63.1%	34.2%	2.4%
16,582	ROCKCASTLE	5,247	3,992	1,174	45	36	2,818 R	76.1%	22.4%	0.9%
22,094	ROWAN	7,226	3,546	3,505	136	39	41 R	49.1%	48.5%	1.9%
16,315	RUSSELL	7,074	5,268	1,710	54	42	3,558 R	74.5%	24.2%	0.8%
33,061	SCOTT	13,786	7,952	5,472	272	90	2,480 R	57.7%	39.7%	2.0%
33,337	SHELBY	12,738	8,068	4,435	179	56	3,633 R	63.3%	34.8%	1.4%
16,405	SIMPSON	5,824	3,169	2,583	38	34	586 R	54.4%	44.4%	0.7%
11,766	SPENCER	4,772	3,150	1,554	35	33	1,596 R	66.0%	32.6%	0.7%
22,927	TAYLOR	9,051	6,151	2,790	70	40	3,361 R	68.0%	30.8%	0.8%
11,971	TODD	4,187	2,646	1,496	14	31	1,150 R	63.2%	35.7%	0.3%
12,597	TRIGG	5,344	3,130	2,110	69	35	1,020 R	58.6%	39.5%	1.3%
8,125	TRIMBLE	3,081	1,837	1,181	37	26	656 R	59.6%	38.3%	1.2%
15,637	UNION	5,368	2,749	2,547	54	18	202 R	51.2%	47.4%	1.0%
92,522	WARREN	32,975	20,235	12,180	407	153	8,055 R	61.4%	36.9%	1.2%
10,916	WASHINGTON	4,588	3,044	1,458	59	27	1,586 R	66.3%	31.8%	1.3%
19,923	WAYNE	6,474	4,069	2,312	45	48	1,757 R	62.9%	35.7%	0.7%
14,120	WEBSTER	5,072	2,599	2,388	52	33	211 R	51.2%	47.1%	1.0%
35,865	WHITLEY	11,774	7,502	4,101	107	64	3,401 R	63.7%	34.8%	0.9%
7,065	WOLFE	2,425	1,267	1,136	11	11	131 R	52.2%	46.8%	0.5%
23,208	WOODFORD	10,137	5,890	3,995	199	53	1,895 R	58.1%	39.4%	2.0%
4,041,769	TOTAL	1,544,187	872,492	638,898	23,192	9,605	233,594 R	56.5%	41.4%	1.5%

KENTUCKY

GOVERNOR 1999

2000 Census Population	County	Total Vote	Republican	Democratic	Reform (Galbraith)	Other	Rep.-Dem. Plurality	Percentage of Total Vote		
								Rep.	Dem.	Reform
17,244	ADAIR	2,301	663	1,441	194	3	778 D	28.8%	62.6%	8.4%
17,800	ALLEN	1,182	339	741	97	5	402 D	28.7%	62.7%	8.2%
19,111	ANDERSON	3,322	496	1,961	826	39	1,465 D	14.9%	59.0%	24.9%
8,286	BALLARD	1,480	99	1,230	138	13	1,131 D	6.7%	83.1%	9.3%
38,033	BARREN	3,454	598	2,616	204	36	2,018 D	17.3%	75.7%	5.9%
11,085	BATH	1,244	197	682	356	9	485 D	15.8%	54.8%	28.6%
30,060	BELL	4,872	2,059	2,208	540	65	149 D	42.3%	45.3%	11.1%
85,991	BOONE	8,547	2,495	5,149	813	90	2,654 D	29.2%	60.2%	9.5%
19,360	BOURBON	2,581	370	1,311	866	34	941 D	14.3%	50.8%	33.6%
49,752	BOYD	6,939	1,287	4,665	798	189	3,378 D	18.5%	67.2%	11.5%
27,697	BOYLE	5,028	693	3,334	937	64	2,641 D	13.8%	66.3%	18.6%
8,279	BRACKEN	885	221	539	118	7	318 D	25.0%	60.9%	13.3%
16,100	BREATHITT	1,586	388	836	359	3	448 D	24.5%	52.7%	22.6%
18,648	BRECKINRIDGE	2,717	679	1,748	267	23	1,069 D	25.0%	64.3%	9.8%
61,236	BULLITT	7,376	1,573	4,554	1,141	108	2,981 D	21.3%	61.7%	15.5%
13,010	BUTLER	1,001	346	566	81	8	220 D	34.6%	56.5%	8.1%
13,060	CALDWELL	1,883	279	1,419	167	18	1,140 D	14.8%	75.4%	8.9%
34,177	CALLOWAY	3,890	366	3,074	414	36	2,708 D	9.4%	79.0%	10.6%
88,616	CAMPBELL	10,905	2,783	7,114	916	92	4,331 D	25.5%	65.2%	8.4%
5,351	CARLISLE	923	75	768	79	1	693 D	8.1%	83.2%	8.6%
10,155	CARROLL	1,533	249	1,134	136	14	885 D	16.2%	74.0%	8.9%
26,889	CARTER	3,378	634	2,301	388	55	1,667 D	18.8%	68.1%	11.5%
15,447	CASEY	2,577	935	1,179	439	24	244 D	36.3%	45.8%	17.0%
72,265	CHRISTIAN	7,062	1,064	5,517	410	71	4,453 D	15.1%	78.1%	5.8%
33,144	CLARK	4,944	777	2,836	1,246	85	2,059 D	15.7%	57.4%	25.2%
24,556	CLAY	1,962	858	738	351	15	120 R	43.7%	37.6%	17.9%
9,634	CLINTON	691	244	344	96	7	100 D	35.3%	49.8%	13.9%
9,384	CRITTENDEN	964	188	651	98	27	463 D	19.5%	67.5%	10.2%
7,147	CUMBERLAND	987	279	620	80	8	341 D	28.3%	62.8%	8.1%
91,545	DAVIESS	18,530	3,645	13,646	1,123	116	10,001 D	19.7%	73.6%	6.1%
11,644	EDMONSON	994	318	617	53	6	299 D	32.0%	62.1%	5.3%
6,748	ELLIOTT	1,191	87	1,013	77	14	926 D	7.3%	85.1%	6.5%
15,307	ESTILL	1,414	371	686	340	17	315 D	26.2%	48.5%	24.0%
260,512	FAYETTE	42,619	6,669	21,166	13,729	1,055	14,497 D	15.6%	49.7%	32.2%
13,792	FLEMING	1,870	458	1,021	371	20	563 D	24.5%	54.6%	19.8%
42,441	FLOYD	10,404	2,857	4,193	3,198	156	1,336 D	27.5%	40.3%	30.7%
47,687	FRANKLIN	12,978	1,090	8,873	2,869	146	7,783 D	8.4%	68.4%	22.1%
7,752	FULTON	869	75	732	51	11	657 D	8.6%	84.2%	5.9%
7,870	GALLATIN	894	164	603	117	10	439 D	18.3%	67.4%	13.1%
14,792	GARRARD	1,661	439	783	427	12	344 D	26.4%	47.1%	25.7%
22,384	GRANT	3,074	702	2,005	337	30	1,303 D	22.8%	65.2%	11.0%
37,028	GRAVES	4,286	327	3,480	454	25	3,153 D	7.6%	81.2%	10.6%
24,053	GRAYSON	2,915	907	1,747	228	33	840 D	31.1%	59.9%	7.8%
11,518	GREEN	1,811	581	1,054	163	13	473 D	32.1%	58.2%	9.0%
36,891	GREENUP	5,537	988	3,372	502	675	2,384 D	17.8%	60.9%	9.1%
8,392	HANCOCK	1,202	216	903	73	10	687 D	18.0%	75.1%	6.1%
94,174	HARDIN	12,881	2,593	8,808	1,277	203	6,215 D	20.1%	68.4%	9.9%
33,202	HARLAN	4,495	2,194	1,448	800	53	746 R	48.8%	32.2%	17.8%
17,983	HARRISON	2,510	418	1,471	599	22	1,053 D	16.7%	58.6%	23.9%
17,445	HART	1,756	493	1,114	140	9	621 D	28.1%	63.4%	8.0%
44,829	HENDERSON	4,437	465	3,521	394	57	3,056 D	10.5%	79.4%	8.9%
15,060	HENRY	2,140	364	1,372	375	29	1,008 D	17.0%	64.1%	17.5%
5,262	HICKMAN	785	70	637	72	6	567 D	8.9%	81.1%	9.2%
46,519	HOPKINS	7,259	1,422	5,107	644	86	3,685 D	19.6%	70.4%	8.9%
13,495	JACKSON	874	363	362	141	8	1 R	41.5%	41.4%	16.1%
693,604	JEFFERSON	126,707	27,844	80,442	14,850	3,571	52,598 D	22.0%	63.5%	11.7%
39,041	JESSAMINE	4,469	987	1,949	1,436	97	962 D	22.1%	43.6%	32.1%
23,445	JOHNSON	3,189	1,062	1,564	531	32	502 D	33.3%	49.0%	16.7%
151,464	KENTON	13,683	3,518	8,609	1,352	204	5,091 D	25.7%	62.9%	9.9%
17,649	KNOTT	4,652	1,616	2,006	982	48	390 D	34.7%	43.1%	21.1%

KENTUCKY

GOVERNOR 1999

2000 Census Population	County	Total Vote	Republican	Democratic	Reform (Galbraith)	Other	Rep.-Dem. Plurality	Percentage of Total Vote		
								Rep.	Dem.	Reform
31,795	KNOX	2,398	1,002	1,079	285	32	77 D	41.8%	45.0%	11.9%
13,373	LARUE	1,581	362	1,058	145	16	696 D	22.9%	66.9%	9.2%
52,715	LAUREL	3,951	1,622	1,716	545	68	94 D	41.1%	43.4%	13.8%
15,569	LAWRENCE	1,941	448	1,341	128	24	893 D	23.1%	69.1%	6.6%
7,916	LEE	1,065	320	447	289	9	127 D	30.0%	42.0%	27.1%
12,401	LESLIE	1,941	1,356	282	284	19	1,074 R	69.9%	14.5%	14.6%
25,277	LETCHER	5,541	2,237	1,900	1,324	80	337 R	40.4%	34.3%	23.9%
14,092	LEWIS	1,093	401	591	92	9	190 D	36.7%	54.1%	8.4%
23,361	LINCOLN	2,058	427	1,197	409	25	770 D	20.7%	58.2%	19.9%
9,804	LIVINGSTON	1,230	139	936	146	9	797 D	11.3%	76.1%	11.9%
26,573	LOGAN	2,116	299	1,703	97	17	1,404 D	14.1%	80.5%	4.6%
8,080	LYON	1,336	182	1,013	131	10	831 D	13.6%	75.8%	9.8%
65,514	MCCRACKEN	7,481	712	5,705	1,010	54	4,993 D	9.5%	76.3%	13.5%
17,080	MCCREARY	981	420	454	80	27	34 D	42.8%	46.3%	8.2%
9,938	MCLEAN	1,355	293	933	110	19	640 D	21.6%	68.9%	8.1%
70,872	MADISON	9,459	2,042	5,306	1,964	147	3,264 D	21.6%	56.1%	20.8%
13,332	MAGOFFIN	3,208	959	1,824	385	40	865 D	29.9%	56.9%	12.0%
18,212	MARION	3,134	348	2,288	467	31	1,940 D	11.1%	73.0%	14.9%
30,125	MARSHALL	4,545	450	3,507	535	53	3,057 D	9.9%	77.2%	11.8%
12,578	MARTIN	1,465	874	402	173	16	472 R	59.7%	27.4%	11.8%
16,800	MASON	1,718	358	1,073	271	16	715 D	20.8%	62.5%	15.8%
26,349	MEADE	3,638	659	2,513	424	42	1,854 D	18.1%	69.1%	11.7%
6,556	MENIFEE	1,245	245	720	265	15	475 D	19.7%	57.8%	21.3%
20,817	MERCER	4,158	788	2,361	935	74	1,573 D	19.0%	56.8%	22.5%
10,037	METCALFE	1,064	220	773	67	4	553 D	20.7%	72.7%	6.3%
11,756	MONROE	1,879	659	1,094	99	27	435 D	35.1%	58.2%	5.3%
22,554	MONTGOMERY	2,726	411	1,626	660	29	1,215 D	15.1%	59.6%	24.2%
13,948	MORGAN	1,993	458	1,196	308	31	738 D	23.0%	60.0%	15.5%
31,839	MUHLENBERG	2,973	562	2,134	247	30	1,572 D	18.9%	71.8%	8.3%
37,477	NELSON	5,586	902	3,763	832	89	2,861 D	16.1%	67.4%	14.9%
6,813	NICHOLAS	1,107	87	625	392	3	538 D	7.9%	56.5%	35.4%
22,916	OHIO	4,952	1,687	2,926	308	31	1,239 D	34.1%	59.1%	6.2%
46,178	OLDHAM	6,003	1,530	3,209	1,098	166	1,679 D	25.5%	53.5%	18.3%
10,547	OWEN	3,017	434	1,916	615	52	1,482 D	14.4%	63.5%	20.4%
4,858	OWSLEY	575	161	304	107	3	143 D	28.0%	52.9%	18.6%
14,390	PENDLETON	1,337	273	907	143	14	634 D	20.4%	67.8%	10.7%
29,390	PERRY	4,599	1,965	1,668	920	46	297 R	42.7%	36.3%	20.0%
68,736	PIKE	13,469	4,129	6,183	3,027	130	2,054 D	30.7%	45.9%	22.5%
13,237	POWELL	1,490	280	865	334	11	585 D	18.8%	58.1%	22.4%
56,217	PULASKI	6,067	2,502	2,611	873	81	109 D	41.2%	43.0%	14.4%
2,266	ROBERTSON	383	89	193	101		104 D	23.2%	50.4%	26.4%
16,582	ROCKCASTLE	1,438	546	565	312	15	19 D	38.0%	39.3%	21.7%
22,094	ROWAN	2,463	361	1,575	492	35	1,214 D	14.7%	63.9%	20.0%
16,315	RUSSELL	1,568	562	808	189	9	246 D	35.8%	51.5%	12.1%
33,061	SCOTT	4,759	764	2,618	1,303	74	1,854 D	16.1%	55.0%	27.4%
33,337	SHELBY	4,202	673	2,728	713	88	2,055 D	16.0%	64.9%	17.0%
16,405	SIMPSON	1,131	176	858	79	18	682 D	15.6%	75.9%	7.0%
11,766	SPENCER	1,533	258	1,013	236	26	755 D	16.8%	66.1%	15.4%
22,927	TAYLOR	4,023	932	2,723	322	46	1,791 D	23.2%	67.7%	8.0%
11,971	TODD	1,000	161	757	69	13	596 D	16.1%	75.7%	6.9%
12,597	TRIGG	1,557	265	1,159	107	26	894 D	17.0%	74.4%	6.9%
8,125	TRIMBLE	1,016	145	700	165	6	555 D	14.3%	68.9%	16.2%
15,637	UNION	1,529	209	1,179	119	22	970 D	13.7%	77.1%	7.8%
92,522	WARREN	12,757	2,347	9,101	1,165	144	6,754 D	18.4%	71.3%	9.1%
10,916	WASHINGTON	1,887	357	1,212	302	16	855 D	18.9%	64.2%	16.0%
19,923	WAYNE	2,876	935	1,590	327	24	655 D	32.5%	55.3%	11.4%
14,120	WEBSTER	1,546	259	1,106	169	12	847 D	16.8%	71.5%	10.9%
35,865	WHITLEY	2,919	1,052	1,475	321	71	423 D	36.0%	50.5%	11.0%
7,065	WOLFE	883	180	544	151	8	364 D	20.4%	61.6%	17.1%
23,208	WOODFORD	4,829	777	2,466	1,504	82	1,689 D	16.1%	51.1%	31.1%
4,041,769	TOTAL	580,074	128,788	352,099	88,930	10,257	223,311 D	22.2%	60.7%	15.3%

KENTUCKY

CONGRESS

CD	Year	Total Vote	Republican Vote	Republican Candidate	Democratic Vote	Democratic Candidate	Other Vote	Rep.-Dem. Plurality	Total Vote Rep.	Total Vote Dem.	Major Vote Rep.	Major Vote Dem.
1	2000	227,921	132,115	WHITFIELD, EDWARD	95,806	ROY, BRIAN S.		36,309 R	58.0%	42.0%	58.0%	42.0%
1	1998	172,710	95,308	WHITFIELD, EDWARD	77,402	BARLOW, TOM		17,906 R	55.2%	44.8%	55.2%	44.8%
1	1996	208,157	111,473	WHITFIELD, EDWARD	96,684	NULL, DENNIS L.		14,789 R	53.6%	46.4%	53.6%	46.4%
1	1994	127,236	64,849	WHITFIELD, EDWARD	62,387	BARLOW, TOM		2,462 R	51.0%	49.0%	51.0%	49.0%
1	1992	212,574	83,088	HAMRICK, STEVE	128,524	BARLOW, TOM	962	45,436 D	39.1%	60.5%	39.3%	60.7%
2	2000	237,462	160,800	LEWIS, RON	74,537	PEDIGO, BRIAN	2,125	86,263 R	67.7%	31.4%	68.3%	31.7%
2	1998	177,966	113,285	LEWIS, RON	62,848	EVANS, BOB	1,833	50,437 R	63.7%	35.3%	64.3%	35.7%
2	1996	215,916	125,433	LEWIS, RON	90,483	WRIGHT, JOE		34,950 R	58.1%	41.9%	58.1%	41.9%
2	1994	151,402	90,535	LEWIS, RON	60,867	ADKISSON, DAVID		29,668 R	59.8%	40.2%	59.8%	40.2%
2	1992	206,578	79,684	BARTLEY, BRUCE R.	126,894	NATCHER, WILLIAM H.		47,210 D	38.6%	61.4%	38.6%	61.4%
3	2000	268,785	142,106	NORTHUP, ANNE M.	118,875	JORDAN, ELEANOR	7,804	23,231 R	52.9%	44.2%	54.5%	45.5%
3	1998	195,436	100,690	NORTHUP, ANNE M.	92,865	GORMAN, CHRIS	1,881	7,825 R	51.5%	47.5%	52.0%	48.0%
3	1996	251,951	126,625	NORTHUP, ANNE M.	125,326	WARD, MIKE		1,299 R	50.3%	49.7%	50.3%	49.7%
3	1994	152,523	67,238	STOKES, SUSAN B.	67,663	WARD, MIKE	17,622	425 D	44.1%	44.4%	49.8%	50.2%
3	1992	280,770	132,689	STOKES, SUSAN B.	148,066	MAZZOLI, RAMANO L.	15	15,377 D	47.3%	52.7%	47.3%	52.7%
4	2000	231,963	100,943	BELL, DON	125,872	LUCAS, KEN	5,148	24,929 D	43.5%	54.3%	44.5%	55.5%
4	1998	175,032	81,547	WILLIAMS, GEX "JAY"	93,485	LUCAS, KEN		11,938 D	46.6%	53.4%	46.6%	53.4%
4	1996	218,074	149,135	BUNNING, JIM	68,939	BOWMAN, DENNY		80,196 R	68.4%	31.6%	68.4%	31.6%
4	1994	130,412	96,695	BUNNING, JIM	33,717	SKAGGS, SALLY H.		62,978 R	74.1%	25.9%	74.1%	25.9%
4	1992	226,524	139,634	BUNNING, JIM	86,890	POORE, FLOYD G.		52,744 R	61.6%	38.4%	61.6%	38.4%
5	2000	198,475	145,980	ROGERS, HAROLD	52,495	BAILEY, SIDNEY JANE		93,485 R	73.6%	26.4%	73.6%	26.4%
5	1998	181,800	142,215	ROGERS, HAROLD	39,585	BAILEY-BAMER, SIDNEY		102,630 R	78.2%	21.8%	78.2%	21.8%
5	1996	117,853	117,842	ROGERS, HAROLD			11	117,842 R	100.0%		100.0%	
5	1994	103,609	82,291	ROGERS, HAROLD	21,318	BLEVINS, WALTER		60,973 R	79.4%	20.6%	79.4%	20.6%
5	1992	211,015	115,255	ROGERS, HAROLD	95,760	HAYS, JOHN D.		19,495 R	54.6%	45.4%	54.6%	45.4%
6	2000	270,803	142,971	FLETCHER, ERNEST	94,167	BAESLER, SCOTT	33,665	48,804 R	52.8%	34.8%	60.3%	39.7%
6	1998	195,918	104,046	FLETCHER, ERNEST	90,033	SCORSONE, ERNESTO	1,839	14,013 R	53.1%	46.0%	53.6%	46.4%
6	1996	226,230	100,231	FLETCHER, ERNEST	125,999	BAESLER, SCOTT		25,768 D	44.3%	55.7%	44.3%	55.7%
6	1994	119,117	49,032	WILLS, MATTHEW E.	70,085	BAESLER, SCOTT		21,053 D	41.2%	58.8%	41.2%	58.8%
6	1992	223,450	87,816	ELLINGER, CHARLES W.	135,613	BAESLER, SCOTT	21	47,797 D	39.3%	60.7%	39.3%	60.7%

KENTUCKY

GENERAL AND PRIMARY ELECTIONS

1999–2000 GENERAL ELECTIONS

President   Other vote was 4,173 Reform (Buchanan); 2,896 Libertarian (Browne); 1,533 Natural Law (Hagelin); 923 Constitution (Phillips); 80 write-in (Strickland).

Governor (1999) Other vote was 6,934 Natural Law (Jumoke-Yarbrough);   3,323 write-in (Anderson).

Congress   Other vote was: CD 2: 2,125 Libertarian (Kirkman); CD 3: 7,804 Libertarian (Mancini); CD 4: 3,662 Green (Sain); 1,486 Libertarian (Handleman); CD 6: 32,436 Reform (Galbraith), 1,229 Libertarian (Novak).

1999–2000 PRIMARY ELECTIONS

Primary	May 25, 1999 (Governor) May 23, 2000		**Registration** (as of May, 23, 2000)	Republican Democratic Other	819,992 1,517,831 166,620
				TOTAL	2,504,443

Primary Type   Closed—Only registered Democrats and Republicans could vote in their party's primary.

Note: An asterisk (*) denotes incumbent. The names of unopposed candidates do not appear on the primary ballot; therefore, no votes are cast for these candidates.

	REPUBLICAN PRIMARIES			DEMOCRATIC PRIMARIES		
President	George W. Bush	75,783	83.0%	Al Gore	156,966	71.3%
	John McCain	5,780	6.3%	Bill Bradley	32,340	14.7%
	Alan Keyes	4,337	4.7%	Uncommitted	26,046	11.8%
	Gary Bauer	2,408	2.6%	Lyndon H. LaRouche Jr.	4,927	2.2%
	Uncommitted	1,829	2.0%			
	Steve Forbes	1,186	1.3%			
	TOTAL	91,323		TOTAL	220,279	
Governor **(1999)**	Peppy Martin	19,248	51.3%	Paul E. Patton*	Unopposed	
	David L. Williams	18,295	48.7%			
	TOTAL	37,543				
Congressional **District 1**	Edward Whitfield*	12,013	83.8%	Brian S. Roy	Unopposed	
	David Lynn Williams	2,317	16.2%			
	TOTAL	14,330				
Congressional **District 2**	Ron Lewis*	Unopposed		Brian Pedigo	Unopposed	
Congressional **District 3**	Anne M. Northup*	Unopposed		Eleanor Jordan	24,236	69.3%
				Ray Abbott	5,583	16.0%
				Burrel Charles Farnsley	5,138	14.7%
				TOTAL	34,957	
Congressional **District 4**	Don Bell	6,427	57.0%	Ken Lucas*	Unopposed	
	Scott Tooley	2,700	24.0%			
	Roger Thoney	2,140	19.0%			
	TOTAL	11,267				
Congressional **District 5**	Harold Rogers*	Unopposed		Sidney Jane Bailey	20,726	66.2%
				Michael Vincent Vacca Jr.	10,594	33.8%
				TOTAL	31,320	
Congressional **District 6**	Ernie Fletcher*	Unopposed		Scotty Baesler	38,463	76.1%
				Will L. McGinnis III	12,090	23.9%
				TOTAL	50,553	

LOUISIANA

GOVERNOR
Mike Foster (R). Re-elected 1999 to a four-year term. Previously elected 1995.

SENATORS
John B. Breaux (D). Re-elected 1998 to a six-year term. Previously elected 1992, 1986.

Mary L. Landrieu (D). Elected 1996 to a six-year term.

REPRESENTATIVES
1. David Vitter (R)
2. William J. Jefferson (D)
3. W. J. Tauzin (R)
4. Jim McCrery (R)
5. John Cooksey (R)
6. Richard H. Baker (R)
7. Chris John (D)

David Vitter (R) was elected in a special election May 29, 1999, to fill the remainder of the two-year term vacated when Bob Livingston (R) resigned.

POSTWAR VOTE FOR PRESIDENT

		Republican		Democratic		Other		Percentage Total Vote		Major Vote	
Year	Total Vote	Vote	Candidate	Vote	Candidate	Vote	Plurality	Rep.	Dem.	Rep.	Dem.
2000**	1,765,656	927,871	Bush, George W.	792,344	Gore, Al	45,441	135,527 R	52.6%	44.9%	53.9%	46.1%
1996**	1,783,959	712,586	Dole, Bob	927,837	Clinton, Bill	143,536	215,251 D	39.9%	52.0%	43.4%	56.6%
1992**	1,790,017	733,386	Bush, George	815,971	Clinton, Bill	240,660	82,585 D	41.0%	45.6%	47.3%	52.7%
1988	1,628,202	883,702	Bush, George	717,460	Dukakis, Michael S.	27,040	166,242 R	54.3%	44.1%	55.2%	44.8%
1984	1,706,822	1,037,299	Reagan, Ronald	651,586	Mondale, Walter F.	17,937	385,713 R	60.8%	38.2%	61.4%	38.6%
1980**	1,548,591	792,853	Reagan, Ronald	708,453	Carter, Jimmy	47,285	84,400 R	51.2%	45.7%	52.8%	47.2%
1976	1,278,439	587,446	Ford, Gerald R.	661,365	Carter, Jimmy	29,628	73,919 D	46.0%	51.7%	47.0%	53.0%
1972	1,051,491	686,852	Nixon, Richard M.	298,142	McGovern, George S.	66,497	388,710 R	65.3%	28.4%	69.7%	30.3%
1968**	1,097,450	257,535	Nixon, Richard M.	309,615	Humphrey, Hubert H.	530,300	220,685 A	23.5%	28.2%	45.4%	54.6%
1964	896,293	509,225	Goldwater, Barry M.	387,068	Johnson, Lyndon B.		122,157 R	56.8%	43.2%	56.8%	43.2%
1960	807,891	230,980	Nixon, Richard M.	407,339	Kennedy, John F.	169,572	176,359 D	28.6%	50.4%	36.2%	63.8%
1956	617,544	329,047	Eisenhower, Dwight D.	243,977	Stevenson, Adlai E.	44,520	85,070 R	53.3%	39.5%	57.4%	42.6%
1952	651,952	306,925	Eisenhower, Dwight D.	345,027	Stevenson, Adlai E.		38,102 D	47.1%	52.9%	47.1%	52.9%
1948**	416,336	72,657	Dewey, Thomas E.	136,344	Truman, Harry S.	207,335	67,946 SR	17.5%	32.7%	34.8%	65.2%

In 2000 the other vote column includes 20,473 votes cast for Green (Nader). In 1996 the other vote column includes 123,293 votes cast for Perot. In 1992 the other vote column includes 211,478 votes cast for Perot. In 1980 the other column includes 26,345 votes for Independent (Anderson). In 1968 other vote was American (Wallace). In 1948 other vote was 204,290 States Rights; 3,035 Progressive and 10 scattered.

LOUISIANA

POSTWAR VOTE FOR GOVERNOR

Year	Total Vote	Republican		Democratic		Other Vote	Rep.-Dem. Plurality	Percentage			
								Total Vote		Major Vote	
		Vote	Candidate	Vote	Candidate			Rep.	Dem.	Rep.	Dem.
1999	1,295,205	805,203	Foster, Mike	382,445	Jefferson, William J.	107,557	422,758 R	62.2%	29.5%	67.8%	32.2%
1995	1,550,360	984,499	Foster, Mike	565,861	Fields, Cleo		418,638 R	63.5%	36.5%	63.5%	36.5%
1991	1,728,040	671,009	Duke, David E.	1,057,031	Edwards, Edwin W.		386,022 D	38.8%	61.2%	38.8%	61.2%
1987**		—			Roemer, Charles		D				
1983**		—			Edwards, Edwin W.		D				
1979	1,371,825	690,691	Treen, David C.	681,134	Lambert, Louis		9,557 R	50.3%	49.7%	50.3%	49.7%
1975	430,095		—	430,095	Edwards, Edwin W.		430,095 D		100.0%		100.0%
1972	1,121,570	480,424	Treen, David C.	641,146	Edwards, Edwin W.		160,722 D	42.8%	57.2%	42.8%	57.2%
1968	372,762		—	372,762	McKeithen, John J.		372,762 D		100.0%		100.0%
1964	773,390	297,753	Lyons, C. H.	469,589	McKeithen, John J.	6,048	171,836 D	38.5%	60.7%	38.8%	61.2%
1960	506,562	86,135	Grevemberg, F. C.	407,907	Davis, Jimmie H.	12,520	321,772 D	17.0%	80.5%	17.4%	82.6%
1956	172,291		—	172,291	Long, Earl K.		172,291 D		100.0%		100.0%
1952	123,681	4,958	Bagwell, Harrison G.	118,723	Kennon, Robert F.		113,765 D	4.0%	96.0%	4.0%	96.0%
1948	76,566		—	76,566	Long, Earl K.		76,566 D		100.0%		100.0%

For the 1987 and 1983 elections, no general election runoff was required (see note section in *America Votes* editions for those years).

POSTWAR VOTE FOR SENATOR

Year	Total Vote	Republican		Democratic		Other Vote	Rep.-Dem. Plurality	Percentage			
								Total Vote		Major Vote	
		Vote	Candidate	Vote	Candidate			Rep.	Dem.	Rep.	Dem.
1998**	969,165	306,616	Donelon, Jim	620,502	Breaux, John B.	42,047	313,886 D	31.6%	64.0%	33.1%	66.9%
1996	1,700,102	847,157	Jenkins, Louis	852,945	Landrieu, Mary L.		5,788 D	49.8%	50.2%	49.8%	50.2%
1992**		—			Breaux, John B.		D				
1990**		—			Johnston, J. Bennett		D				
1986	1,369,897	646,311	Moore, W. Henson	723,586	Breaux, John B.		77,275 D	47.2%	52.8%	47.2%	52.8%
1984**		—			Johnston, J. Bennett		D				
1980**		—			Long, Russell B.		D				
1978**		—			Johnston, J. Bennett		D				
1974	434,643		—	434,643	Long, Russell B.		434,643 D		100.0%		100.0%
1972	1,084,904	206,846	Toledano, Ben C.	598,987	Johnston, J. Bennett	279,071	392,141 D	19.1%	55.2%	25.7%	74.3%
1968	518,586		—	518,586	Long, Russell B.		518,586 D		100.0%		100.0%
1966	437,695		—	437,695	Ellender, Allen J.		437,695 D		100.0%		100.0%
1962	421,904	103,066	O'Hearn, Taylor W.	318,838	Long, Russell B.		215,772 D	24.4%	75.6%	24.4%	75.6%
1960	541,928	109,698	Reese, George W.	432,228	Ellender, Allen J.	2	322,530 D	20.2%	79.8%	20.2%	79.8%
1956	335,564		—	335,564	Long, Russell B.		335,564 D		100.0%		100.0%
1954	207,115		—	207,115	Ellender, Allen J.		207,115 D		100.0%		100.0%
1950	251,838	30,931	Gerth, Charles S.	220,907	Long, Russell B.		189,976 D	12.3%	87.7%	12.3%	87.7%
1948	330,124		—	330,115	Ellender, Allen J.	9	330,115 D		100.0%		100.0%
1948S	408,667	102,331	Clarke, Clem S.	306,336	Long, Russell B.		204,005 D	25.0%	75.0%	25.0%	75.0%

In November 1998, all candidates ran on a single ballot, including another Democratic candidate who received 9,893 votes, and another Republican candidate who received 7,964 votes. Their votes are included in the total for "Other." For the 1992, 1990, 1984, 1980 and 1978 elections, no runoff election was required (see note section in *America Votes* editions for those years). One of the 1948 elections was for a short term to fill a vacancy.

LOUISIANA

Districts Established January 5, 1996

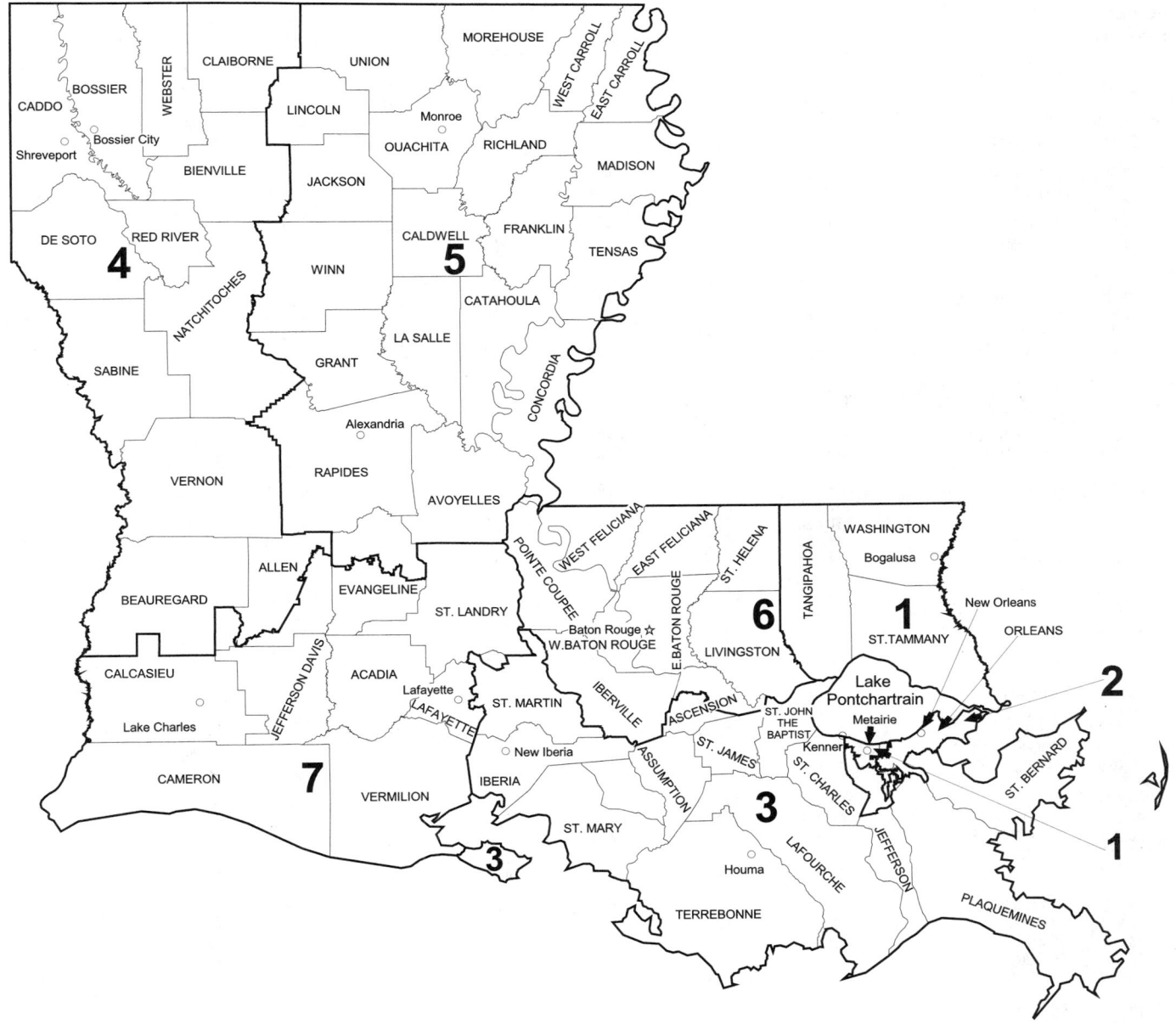

LOUISIANA

PRESIDENT 2000

2000 Census Population	Parish	Total Vote	Republican	Democratic	Green (Nader)	Other	Rep.-Dem. Plurality	Percentage of Total Vote		
								Rep.	Dem.	Green
58,861	ACADIA	23,238	13,814	8,892	227	305	4,922 R	59.4%	38.3%	1.0%
25,440	ALLEN	8,292	4,035	3,914	115	228	121 R	48.7%	47.2%	1.4%
76,627	ASCENSION	30,844	16,818	13,385	340	301	3,433 R	54.5%	43.4%	1.1%
23,388	ASSUMPTION	10,053	4,388	5,222	119	324	834 D	43.6%	51.9%	1.2%
41,481	AVOYELLES	14,653	7,329	6,701	170	453	628 R	50.0%	45.7%	1.2%
32,986	BEAUREGARD	12,205	7,862	3,958	155	230	3,904 R	64.4%	32.4%	1.3%
15,752	BIENVILLE	7,006	3,269	3,413	50	274	144 D	46.7%	48.7%	0.7%
98,310	BOSSIER	35,915	23,224	11,933	295	463	11,291 R	64.7%	33.2%	0.8%
252,161	CADDO	95,639	46,807	47,530	734	568	723 D	48.9%	49.7%	0.8%
183,577	CALCASIEU	73,636	38,086	33,919	895	736	4,167 R	51.7%	46.1%	1.2%
10,560	CALDWELL	4,328	2,817	1,359	37	115	1,458 R	65.1%	31.4%	0.9%
9,991	CAMERON	4,183	2,593	1,435	46	109	1,158 R	62.0%	34.3%	1.1%
10,920	CATAHOULA	4,765	2,912	1,718	28	107	1,194 R	61.1%	36.1%	0.6%
16,851	CLAIBORNE	6,281	3,384	2,721	35	141	663 R	53.9%	43.3%	0.6%
20,247	CONCORDIA	8,499	4,627	3,569	54	249	1,058 R	54.4%	42.0%	0.6%
25,494	DE SOTO	10,596	5,260	5,036	67	233	224 R	49.6%	47.5%	0.6%
412,852	EAST BATON ROUGE	168,989	89,128	76,516	2,105	1,240	12,612 R	52.7%	45.3%	1.2%
9,421	EAST CARROLL	3,245	1,280	1,876	16	73	596 D	39.4%	57.8%	0.5%
21,360	EAST FELICIANA	8,099	4,051	3,870	60	118	181 R	50.0%	47.8%	0.7%
35,434	EVANGELINE	13,612	7,290	5,763	140	419	1,527 R	53.6%	42.3%	1.0%
21,263	FRANKLIN	8,356	5,363	2,792	51	150	2,571 R	64.2%	33.4%	0.6%
18,698	GRANT	7,055	4,784	2,099	57	115	2,685 R	67.8%	29.8%	0.8%
73,266	IBERIA	30,020	17,236	11,762	365	657	5,474 R	57.4%	39.2%	1.2%
33,320	IBERVILLE	14,503	5,573	8,355	175	400	2,782 D	38.4%	57.6%	1.2%
15,397	JACKSON	7,106	4,347	2,582	53	124	1,765 R	61.2%	36.3%	0.7%
455,466	JEFFERSON	179,151	105,003	70,411	2,293	1,444	34,592 R	58.6%	39.3%	1.3%
31,435	JEFFERSON DAVIS	12,546	6,945	5,162	143	296	1,783 R	55.4%	41.1%	1.1%
190,503	LAFAYETTE	78,293	48,491	27,190	1,510	1,102	21,301 R	61.9%	34.7%	1.9%
89,974	LAFOURCHE	34,449	18,575	14,627	424	823	3,948 R	53.9%	42.5%	1.2%
14,282	LA SALLE	6,108	4,564	1,397	57	90	3,167 R	74.7%	22.9%	0.9%
42,509	LINCOLN	16,551	9,246	6,851	124	330	2,395 R	55.9%	41.4%	0.7%
91,814	LIVINGSTON	36,865	24,889	11,008	384	584	13,881 R	67.5%	29.9%	1.0%
13,728	MADISON	4,743	2,127	2,489	37	90	362 D	44.8%	52.5%	0.8%
31,021	MOREHOUSE	12,321	6,641	5,289	103	288	1,352 R	53.9%	42.9%	0.8%
39,080	NATCHITOCHES	14,857	7,332	6,924	109	492	408 R	49.4%	46.6%	0.7%
484,674	ORLEANS	181,221	39,404	137,630	3,025	1,162	98,226 D	21.7%	75.9%	1.7%
147,250	OUACHITA	58,211	35,107	21,457	529	1,118	13,650 R	60.3%	36.9%	0.9%
26,757	PLAQUEMINES	10,931	6,302	4,425	104	100	1,877 R	57.7%	40.5%	1.0%
22,763	POINTE COUPEE	10,832	4,710	5,813	108	201	1,103 D	43.5%	53.7%	1.0%
126,337	RAPIDES	49,024	28,831	18,898	446	849	9,933 R	58.8%	38.5%	0.9%
9,622	RED RIVER	4,522	2,200	2,177	35	110	23 R	48.7%	48.1%	0.8%
20,981	RICHLAND	8,485	4,895	3,282	51	257	1,613 R	57.7%	38.7%	0.6%
23,459	SABINE	8,862	5,754	2,846	81	181	2,908 R	64.9%	32.1%	0.9%
67,229	ST. BERNARD	28,621	16,255	11,682	397	287	4,573 R	56.8%	40.8%	1.4%
48,072	ST. CHARLES	21,510	11,981	8,918	215	396	3,063 R	55.7%	41.5%	1.0%
10,525	ST. HELENA	5,254	1,965	3,059	65	165	1,094 D	37.4%	58.2%	1.2%
21,216	ST. JAMES	10,705	3,813	6,523	61	308	2,710 D	35.6%	60.9%	0.6%
43,044	ST. JOHN THE BAPTIST	17,713	7,423	9,745	164	381	2,322 D	41.9%	55.0%	0.9%
87,700	ST. LANDRY	34,151	15,449	18,067	225	410	2,618 D	45.2%	52.9%	0.7%
48,583	ST. MARTIN	20,778	9,961	9,853	268	696	108 R	47.9%	47.4%	1.3%
53,500	ST. MARY	21,810	11,325	9,851	214	420	1,474 R	51.9%	45.2%	1.0%
191,268	ST. TAMMANY	83,737	59,193	22,722	1,199	623	36,471 R	70.7%	27.1%	1.4%
100,588	TANGIPAHOA	37,155	20,421	15,843	405	486	4,578 R	55.0%	42.6%	1.1%
6,618	TENSAS	3,010	1,330	1,580	20	80	250 D	44.2%	52.5%	0.7%
104,503	TERREBONNE	36,675	21,314	14,414	310	637	6,900 R	58.1%	39.3%	0.8%
22,803	UNION	9,343	5,772	3,205	66	300	2,567 R	61.8%	34.3%	0.7%
53,807	VERMILION	22,235	12,495	8,704	307	729	3,791 R	56.2%	39.1%	1.4%
52,531	VERNON	13,827	8,794	4,655	151	227	4,139 R	63.6%	33.7%	1.1%
43,926	WASHINGTON	16,887	8,983	7,399	126	379	1,584 R	53.2%	43.8%	0.7%
41,831	WEBSTER	17,090	9,420	7,197	120	353	2,223 R	55.1%	42.1%	0.7%

LOUISIANA

PRESIDENT 2000

2000 Census Population	Parish	Total Vote	Republican	Democratic	Green (Nader)	Other	Rep.-Dem. Plurality		Percentage of Total Vote		
									Rep.	Dem.	Green
21,601	WEST BATON ROUGE	10,169	4,924	5,058	69	118	134	D	48.4%	49.7%	0.7%
12,314	WEST CARROLL	4,675	3,220	1,319	25	111	1,901	R	68.9%	28.2%	0.5%
15,111	WEST FELICIANA	4,860	2,512	2,187	62	99	325	R	51.7%	45.0%	1.3%
16,894	WINN	6,361	4,028	2,167	52	114	1,861	R	63.3%	34.1%	0.8%
4,468,976	TOTAL	1,765,656	927,871	792,344	20,473	24,968	135,527	R	52.6%	44.9%	1.2%

LOUISIANA

GOVERNOR 1999

2000 Census Population	Parish	Total Vote	Republican (Foster)	Democratic (Jefferson)	Other	Rep.-Dem. Plurality		Percentage			
								Total Vote		Major Vote	
								Rep.	Dem.	Rep.	Dem.
58,861	ACADIA	18,137	13,161	3,764	1,212	9,397	R	72.6%	20.8%	77.8%	22.2%
25,440	ALLEN	6,249	3,965	1,518	766	2,447	R	63.5%	24.3%	72.3%	27.7%
76,627	ASCENSION	24,826	16,406	5,973	2,447	10,433	R	66.1%	24.1%	73.3%	26.7%
23,388	ASSUMPTION	10,050	5,842	2,827	1,381	3,015	R	58.1%	28.1%	67.4%	32.6%
41,481	AVOYELLES	13,987	8,828	3,141	2,018	5,687	R	63.1%	22.5%	73.8%	26.2%
32,986	BEAUREGARD	8,737	6,502	1,300	935	5,202	R	74.4%	14.9%	83.3%	16.7%
15,752	BIENVILLE	6,224	3,381	2,123	720	1,258	R	54.3%	34.1%	61.4%	38.6%
98,310	BOSSIER	17,966	12,238	4,482	1,246	7,756	R	68.1%	24.9%	73.2%	26.8%
252,161	CADDO	56,298	30,391	23,508	2,399	6,883	R	54.0%	41.8%	56.4%	43.6%
183,577	CALCASIEU	53,658	34,761	14,992	3,905	19,769	R	64.8%	27.9%	69.9%	30.1%
10,560	CALDWELL	4,935	3,717	697	521	3,020	R	75.3%	14.1%	84.2%	15.8%
9,991	CAMERON	4,287	3,220	600	467	2,620	R	75.1%	14.0%	84.3%	15.7%
10,920	CATAHOULA	4,526	3,173	836	517	2,337	R	70.1%	18.5%	79.1%	20.9%
16,851	CLAIBORNE	5,139	3,185	1,484	470	1,701	R	62.0%	28.9%	68.2%	31.8%
20,247	CONCORDIA	7,486	4,779	1,989	718	2,790	R	63.8%	26.6%	70.6%	29.4%
25,494	DE SOTO	8,223	4,830	2,617	776	2,213	R	58.7%	31.8%	64.9%	35.1%
412,852	EAST BATON ROUGE	109,103	60,494	37,539	11,070	22,955	R	55.4%	34.4%	61.7%	38.3%
9,421	EAST CARROLL	3,486	1,543	1,592	351	49	D	44.3%	45.7%	49.2%	50.8%
21,360	EAST FELICIANA	7,145	4,015	2,528	602	1,487	R	56.2%	35.4%	61.4%	38.6%
35,434	EVANGELINE	12,720	8,224	3,094	1,402	5,130	R	64.7%	24.3%	72.7%	27.3%
21,263	FRANKLIN	8,002	5,755	1,569	678	4,186	R	71.9%	19.6%	78.6%	21.4%
18,698	GRANT	5,764	4,379	803	582	3,576	R	76.0%	13.9%	84.5%	15.5%
73,266	IBERIA	23,859	16,323	5,811	1,725	10,512	R	68.4%	24.4%	73.7%	26.3%
33,320	IBERVILLE	13,491	5,954	5,504	2,033	450	R	44.1%	40.8%	52.0%	48.0%
15,397	JACKSON	6,417	4,338	1,543	536	2,795	R	67.6%	24.0%	73.8%	26.2%
455,466	JEFFERSON	113,870	82,073	25,475	6,322	56,598	R	72.1%	22.4%	76.3%	23.7%
31,435	JEFFERSON DAVIS	10,574	7,315	2,247	1,012	5,068	R	69.2%	21.3%	76.5%	23.5%
190,503	LAFAYETTE	58,026	40,674	12,579	4,773	28,095	R	70.1%	21.7%	76.4%	23.6%
89,974	LAFOURCHE	29,218	18,687	6,031	4,500	12,656	R	64.0%	20.6%	75.6%	24.4%
14,282	LA SALLE	6,306	5,178	558	570	4,620	R	82.1%	8.8%	90.3%	9.7%
42,509	LINCOLN	10,211	6,076	3,133	1,002	2,943	R	59.5%	30.7%	66.0%	34.0%
91,814	LIVINGSTON	29,118	23,240	2,627	3,251	20,613	R	79.8%	9.0%	89.8%	10.2%
13,728	MADISON	3,819	2,115	1,270	434	845	R	55.4%	33.3%	62.5%	37.5%
31,021	MOREHOUSE	10,393	6,674	2,818	901	3,856	R	64.2%	27.1%	70.3%	29.7%
39,080	NATCHITOCHES	13,134	7,610	4,201	1,323	3,409	R	57.9%	32.0%	64.4%	35.6%
484,674	ORLEANS	117,057	32,087	80,295	4,675	48,208	D	27.4%	68.6%	28.6%	71.4%
147,250	OUACHITA	40,054	28,681	8,677	2,696	20,004	R	71.6%	21.7%	76.8%	23.2%
26,757	PLAQUEMINES	9,289	6,267	2,499	523	3,768	R	67.5%	26.9%	71.5%	28.5%
22,763	POINTE COUPEE	10,869	5,149	3,300	2,420	1,849	R	47.4%	30.4%	60.9%	39.1%
126,337	RAPIDES	34,078	22,066	8,997	3,015	13,069	R	64.8%	26.4%	71.0%	29.0%

LOUISIANA

GOVERNOR 1999

2000 Census Population	Parish	Total Vote	Republican (Foster)	Democratic (Jefferson)	Other	Rep.-Dem. Plurality		Percentage			
								Total Vote		Major Vote	
								Rep.	Dem.	Rep.	Dem.
9,622	RED RIVER	4,351	2,443	1,280	628	1,163	R	56.1%	29.4%	65.6%	34.4%
20,981	RICHLAND	8,102	5,353	2,161	588	3,192	R	66.1%	26.7%	71.2%	28.8%
23,459	SABINE	7,845	5,098	1,316	1,431	3,782	R	65.0%	16.8%	79.5%	20.5%
67,229	ST. BERNARD	22,738	18,646	2,635	1,457	16,011	R	82.0%	11.6%	87.6%	12.4%
48,072	ST. CHARLES	17,726	11,918	4,564	1,244	7,354	R	67.2%	25.7%	72.3%	27.7%
10,525	ST. HELENA	5,605	2,652	2,225	728	427	R	47.3%	39.7%	54.4%	45.6%
21,216	ST. JAMES	10,158	5,060	4,271	827	789	R	49.8%	42.0%	54.2%	45.8%
43,044	ST. JOHN THE BAPTIST	15,118	8,241	5,693	1,184	2,548	R	54.5%	37.7%	59.1%	40.9%
87,700	ST. LANDRY	29,411	16,345	11,044	2,022	5,301	R	55.6%	37.6%	59.7%	40.3%
48,583	ST. MARTIN	16,515	10,493	4,416	1,606	6,077	R	63.5%	26.7%	70.4%	29.6%
53,500	ST. MARY	17,681	11,331	4,839	1,511	6,492	R	64.1%	27.4%	70.1%	29.9%
191,268	ST. TAMMANY	53,487	42,442	7,412	3,633	35,030	R	79.4%	13.9%	85.1%	14.9%
100,588	TANGIPAHOA	27,265	18,929	6,777	1,559	12,152	R	69.4%	24.9%	73.6%	26.4%
6,618	TENSAS	3,412	1,622	1,399	391	223	R	47.5%	41.0%	53.7%	46.3%
104,503	TERREBONNE	28,739	19,431	6,300	3,008	13,131	R	67.6%	21.9%	75.5%	24.5%
22,803	UNION	7,170	4,819	1,428	923	3,391	R	67.2%	19.9%	77.1%	22.9%
53,807	VERMILION	19,957	15,051	3,170	1,736	11,881	R	75.4%	15.9%	82.6%	17.4%
52,531	VERNON	13,446	9,976	2,032	1,438	7,944	R	74.2%	15.1%	83.1%	16.9%
43,926	WASHINGTON	13,102	8,921	2,948	1,233	5,973	R	68.1%	22.5%	75.2%	24.8%
41,831	WEBSTER	13,833	8,701	3,888	1,244	4,813	R	62.9%	28.1%	69.1%	30.9%
21,601	WEST BATON ROUGE	8,278	4,657	2,690	931	1,967	R	56.3%	32.5%	63.4%	36.6%
12,314	WEST CARROLL	4,296	3,397	550	349	2,847	R	79.1%	12.8%	86.1%	13.9%
15,111	WEST FELICIANA	4,240	2,260	1,510	470	750	R	53.3%	35.6%	59.9%	40.1%
16,894	WINN	5,999	4,121	1,356	522	2,765	R	68.7%	22.6%	75.2%	24.8%
4,468,976	TOTAL	1,295,205	805,203	382,445	107,557	422,758	R	62.2%	29.5%	67.8%	32.2%

LOUISIANA

CONGRESS

CD	Year	Total Vote	Republican		Democratic		Other Vote	Rep.-Dem. Plurality		Percentage			
			Vote	Candidate	Vote	Candidate				Total Vote		Major Vote	
										Rep.	Dem.	Rep.	Dem.
1	2000	237,810	191,379	VITTER, DAVID	40,917	ARMATO/DEATON	5,514	161,444	R	80.5%	17.2%	82.4%	17.6%
1	1998			LIVINGSTON, BOB					R				
1	1996			LIVINGSTON, BOB					R				
2	2000					JEFFERSON, WILLIAM J.			D				
2	1998	118,949			118,949	JEFFERSON/REED/VEAL		118,949	D		100.0%		100.0%
2	1996					JEFFERSON, WILLIAM J.			D				
3	2000	183,960	143,446	TAUZIN, W.J. "BILLY"			40,514	143,446	R	78.0%		100.0%	
3	1998			TAUZIN, W.J. "BILLY"					R				
3	1996			TAUZIN, W.J. "BILLY"					R				
4	2000	173,967	122,678	MCCRERY, JIM	43,600	GREEN, PHILLIP R.	7,689	79,078	R	70.5%	25.1%	73.8%	26.2%
4	1998			MCCRERY, JIM					R				
4	1996			MCCRERY, JIM					R				
5	2000	179,473	123,975	COOKSEY, JOHN C.	50,163	BEALL/MELTON	5,335	80,998	R	69.1%	28.0%	71.2%	28.8%
5	1998			COOKSEY, JOHN C.					R				
5	1996	233,353	135,990	COOKSEY, JOHN C.	97,363	THOMPSON, FRANCIS		38,627	R	58.3%	41.7%	58.3%	41.7%

LOUISIANA

CONGRESS

CD	Year	Total Vote	Republican Vote	Republican Candidate	Democratic Vote	Democratic Candidate	Other Vote	Rep.-Dem. Plurality	Percentage Total Vote Rep.	Percentage Total Vote Dem.	Percentage Major Vote Rep.	Percentage Major Vote Dem.
6	2000	243,478	165,637	BAKER, RICHARD H.	72,192	ROGILLIO, KATHY J.	5,649	93,445 R	68.0%	29.7%	69.6%	30.4%
6	1998	191,245	97,044	BAKER, RICHARD H.	94,201	MCKEITHEN, MARJORIE		2,843 R	50.7%	49.3%	50.7%	49.3%
6	1996			BAKER, RICHARD H.				R				
7	2000	183,483			152,796	JOHN, CHRIS	30,687	152,796 D		83.3%		100.0%
7	1998					JOHN, CHRIS		D				
7	1996	241,800			241,800	JOHN/LUNDY		D				

Note: The lines for Louisiana's congressional districts were changed after both the 1992 and 1994 elections. Results from these earlier years can be found in *America Votes 21*. Because there were two Democratic candidates in both the 1st and 5th Districts in 2000, the Democratic vote and vote percentage represent the aggregate for both candidates. The plurality in those districts, though, is based on the difference between the vote for the Republican winner and the Democrat with the highest vote.

LOUISIANA

GENERAL AND PRIMARY ELECTIONS

1999–2000 GENERAL ELECTIONS

President   Other vote was 14,356 Reform (Buchanan); 5,483 Constitution (Phillips); 2,951 Libertarian (Browne); 1,103 Socialist Workers (Harris); 1,075 Natural Law (Hagelin).

Governor (1999)   Other vote was 35,434 Republican (Greene); 23,445 Democrat (Preis); 12,497 Democrat (Bush); 8,978 Reform (Alexandrenko); 7,645 Democrat (Ward); 7,511 Democrat (McElroy); 5,432 Democrat (Bellone); 3,669 Other (Baron); 2,946 Other (Johnson). Democrats, Republicans and Reform were the only designated parties in Louisiana at the time. Candidates not affiliated with one of these three parties was designated as "Other." While there were six Democratic candidates on the ballot receiving an aggregate total of 438,975 votes and two Republican candidates winning a combined total of 840,637 votes, Republican Foster and Democrat Jefferson were considered their party's leading candidates and their votes were listed in the gubernatorial vote table.

Congress   In CD 1, the Democratic vote was 29,935 Armato, 10,982 Deaton; the Other vote was 3,129 M. Rosenthal, 2,385 Simanonok; In CD 3, the Other vote was 16,908 Albares, 13,488 A. Rosenthal, 10,118 Bourque. In CD 4, the Other vote was 4,059 Taylor, 3,630 Skains. In CD 5, the Democratic vote was 42,977 Beall, 7,186 Melton; the Other vote was 5,335 Dumas. In CD 6, the Other vote was 5,649 Wolf. In CD 7, the Other vote was 30,687 Harris.

1999–2000 PRIMARY ELECTIONS

Open Election Primary   October 23, 1999   (Governor)
March 14, 2000   (President)
Open Election   November 7, 2000   (Congress)

Registration
(as of October 9, 2000)

Republican	616,982
Democratic	1,674,643
Other	504,926
TOTAL	2,796,551

Primary Type   Only registered Democrats and Republicans could vote in their party's presidential primary. For governor and Congress, Louisiana holds a two-tier system of elections open to all voters, with a first round of voting featuring candidates from all parties running on the same ballot. A candidate that wins a majority of the vote in the first round is elected. Otherwise, there is a runoff held several weeks later. No runoffs for governor or Congress were necessary in the 1999-2000 election cycle.

LOUISIANA

GENERAL AND PRIMARY ELECTIONS

Note: An asterisk (*) denotes incumbent. The names of unopposed candidates do not appear on the ballot; therefore, no votes are cast for these candidates. Since the races for governor (in October 1999) and Congress (in November 2000) were all decided in the first round of voting, their results can be found in the general election tables. The only primary as such was for president.

	REPUBLICAN PRIMARY			DEMOCRATIC PRIMARY		
President	George W. Bush	86,038	83.6%	Al Gore	114,942	73.0%
	John McCain	9,165	8.9%	Bill Bradley	31,385	19.9%
	Alan Keyes	5,900	5.7%	Lyndon H. LaRouche Jr.	6,127	3.9%
	Steve Forbes	1,041	1.0%	Randy Crow	5,097	3.2%
	Gary Bauer	768	0.7%			
Total	TOTAL	102,912		TOTAL	157,551	

MAINE

GOVERNOR
Angus King (Independent). Re-elected 1998 to a four-year term. Previously elected 1994.

SENATORS
Susan Collins (R). Elected 1996 to a six-year term.

Olympia J. Snowe (R). Re-elected 2000 to a six-year term. Previously elected 1994.

REPRESENTATIVES
1. Tom Allen (D)   2. John Baldacci (D)

POSTWAR VOTE FOR PRESIDENT

Year	Total Vote	Republican Vote	Republican Candidate	Democratic Vote	Democratic Candidate	Other Vote	Plurality	Percentage Total Vote Rep.	Percentage Total Vote Dem.	Percentage Major Vote Rep.	Percentage Major Vote Dem.
2000**	651,817	286,616	Bush, George W.	319,951	Gore, Al	45,250	33,335 D	44.0%	49.1%	47.3%	52.7%
1996**	605,897	186,378	Dole, Bob	312,788	Clinton, Bill	106,731	126,410 D	30.8%	51.6%	37.3%	62.7%
1992**	679,499	206,504	Bush, George	263,420	Clinton, Bill	209,575	56,600 D	30.4%	38.8%	43.9%	56.1%
1988	555,035	307,131	Bush, George	243,569	Dukakis, Michael S.	4,335	63,562 R	55.3%	43.9%	55.8%	44.2%
1984	553,144	336,500	Reagan, Ronald	214,515	Mondale, Walter F.	2,129	121,985 R	60.8%	38.8%	61.1%	38.9%
1980**	523,011	238,522	Reagan, Ronald	220,974	Carter, Jimmy	63,515	17,548 R	45.6%	42.3%	51.9%	48.1%
1976	483,216	236,320	Ford, Gerald R.	232,279	Carter, Jimmy	14,617	4,041 R	48.9%	48.1%	50.4%	49.6%
1972	417,042	256,458	Nixon, Richard M.	160,584	McGovern, George S.		95,874 R	61.5%	38.5%	61.5%	38.5%
1968	392,936	169,254	Nixon, Richard M.	217,312	Humphrey, Hubert H.	6,370	48,058 D	43.1%	55.3%	43.8%	56.2%
1964	380,965	118,701	Goldwater, Barry M.	262,264	Johnson, Lyndon B.		143,563 D	31.2%	68.8%	31.2%	68.8%
1960	421,767	240,608	Nixon, Richard M.	181,159	Kennedy, John F.		59,449 R	57.0%	43.0%	57.0%	43.0%
1956	351,706	249,238	Eisenhower, Dwight D.	102,468	Stevenson, Adlai E.		146,770 R	70.9%	29.1%	70.9%	29.1%
1952	351,786	232,353	Eisenhower, Dwight D.	118,806	Stevenson, Adlai E.	627	113,547 R	66.0%	33.8%	66.2%	33.8%
1948	264,787	150,234	Dewey, Thomas E.	111,916	Truman, Harry S.	2,637	38,318 R	56.7%	42.3%	57.3%	42.7%

In 2000 the other vote column includes 37,127 votes cast for Green (Nader). In 1996 the other vote column includes 85,970 votes cast for Perot. In 1992 the other vote column includes 206,820 votes cast for Perot who came in second statewide. In 1980 the other column includes 53,327 votes for Independent (Anderson).

MAINE

POSTWAR VOTE FOR GOVERNOR

Year	Total Vote	Republican		Democratic		Other Vote	Rep.-Dem. Plurality	Percentage			
								Total Vote		Major Vote	
		Vote	Candidate	Vote	Candidate			Rep.	Dem.	Rep.	Dem.
1998**	421,009	79,716	Longley, James B., Jr.	50,506	Connolly, Thomas J.	290,787	167,056 I	18.9%	12.0%	61.2%	38.8%
1994**	511,308	117,990	Collins, Susan M.	172,951	Brennan, Joseph E.	220,367	7,878 I	23.1%	33.8%	40.6%	59.4%
1990	522,492	243,766	McKernan, John R.	230,038	Brennan, Joseph E.	48,688	13,728 R	46.7%	44.0%	51.4%	48.6%
1986**	426,861	170,312	McKernan, John R.	128,744	Tierney, James	127,805	41,568 R	39.9%	30.2%	56.9%	43.1%
1982	460,295	172,949	Cragin, Charles L.	281,066	Brennan, Joseph E.	6,280	108,117 D	37.6%	61.1%	38.1%	61.9%
1978	370,258	126,862	Palmer, Linwood E.	176,493	Brennan, Joseph E.	66,903	49,631 D	34.3%	47.7%	41.8%	58.2%
1974**	363,945	84,176	Erwin, James S.	132,219	Mitchell, George J.	147,550	10,245 I	23.1%	36.3%	38.9%	61.1%
1970	325,386	162,248	Erwin, James S.	163,138	Curtis, Kenneth M.		890 D	49.9%	50.1%	49.9%	50.1%
1966	323,838	151,802	Reed, John H.	172,036	Curtis, Kenneth M.		20,234 D	46.9%	53.1%	46.9%	53.1%
1962	292,725	146,604	Reed, John H.	146,121	Dolloff, Maynard C.		483 R	50.1%	49.9%	50.1%	49.9%
1960S	417,315	219,768	Reed, John H.	197,547	Coffin, Frank M.		22,221 R	52.7%	47.3%	52.7%	47.3%
1958**	280,295	134,572	Hildreth, Horace A.	145,723	Clauson, Clinton A.		11,151 D	48.0%	52.0%	48.0%	52.0%
1956	304,649	124,395	Trafton, Willis A.	180,254	Muskie, Edmund S.		55,859 D	40.8%	59.2%	40.8%	59.2%
1954	248,971	113,298	Cross, Burton M.	135,673	Muskie, Edmund S.		22,375 D	45.5%	54.5%	45.5%	54.5%
1952	248,441	128,532	Cross, Burton M.	82,538	Oliver, James C.	37,371	45,994 R	51.7%	33.2%	60.9%	39.1%
1950	241,177	145,823	Payne, Frederick G.	94,304	Grant, Earl S.	1,050	51,519 R	60.5%	39.1%	60.7%	39.3%
1948	222,500	145,956	Payne, Frederick G.	76,544	Lausier, Louis B.		69,412 R	65.6%	34.4%	65.6%	34.4%
1946	179,951	110,327	Hildreth, Horace A.	69,624	Clark, F. Davis		40,703 R	61.3%	38.7%	61.3%	38.7%

In 1998 Angus King received 246,772 votes (58.6% of the total vote) as an Independent and won by a plurality of 167,056 votes. In 1994 Angus King, as an Independent candidate, polled 180,829 votes (35.4% of the total vote) and won the election with a 7,878-vote plurality. In 1986 other vote was 64,317 Sherry F. Huber (Independent); 63,474 John E. Menario (Independent) and 14 scattered. In 1974 James B. Longley, an Independent candidate, polled 142,464 votes (39.1% of the total vote) and won the election with a 10,245-vote plurality. The 1960 election was for a short term to fill a vacancy. The term of office of Maine's Governor was increased from two to four years effective with the 1958 election.

POSTWAR VOTE FOR SENATOR

Year	Total Vote	Republican		Democratic		Other Vote	Rep.-Dem. Plurality	Percentage			
								Total Vote		Major Vote	
		Vote	Candidate	Vote	Candidate			Rep.	Dem.	Rep.	Dem.
2000	634,872	437,689	Snowe, Olympia J.	197,183	Lawrence, Mark		240,506 R	68.9%	31.1%	68.9%	31.1%
1996	606,777	298,422	Collins, Susan M.	266,226	Brennan, Joseph E.	42,129	32,196 R	49.2%	43.9%	52.9%	47.1%
1994	511,733	308,244	Snowe, Olympia J.	186,042	Andrews, Thomas H.	17,447	122,202 R	60.2%	36.4%	62.4%	37.6%
1990	520,320	319,167	Cohen, William S.	201,053	Rolde, Neil	100	118,114 R	61.3%	38.6%	61.4%	38.6%
1988	557,375	104,758	Wyman, Jasper S.	452,590	Mitchell, George J.	27	347,832 D	18.8%	81.2%	18.8%	81.2%
1984	551,406	404,414	Cohen, William S.	142,626	Mitchell, Elizabeth H.	4,366	261,788 R	73.3%	25.9%	73.9%	26.1%
1982	459,715	179,882	Emery, David F.	279,819	Mitchell, George J.	14	99,937 D	39.1%	60.9%	39.1%	60.9%
1978	375,172	212,294	Cohen, William S.	127,327	Hathaway, William D.	35,551	84,967 R	56.6%	33.9%	62.5%	37.5%
1976	486,254	193,489	Monks, Robert A. G.	292,704	Muskie, Edmund S.	61	99,215 D	39.8%	60.2%	39.8%	60.2%
1972	421,310	197,040	Smith, Margaret Chase	224,270	Hathaway, William D.		27,230 D	46.8%	53.2%	46.8%	53.2%
1970	323,860	123,906	Bishop, Neil S.	199,954	Muskie, Edmund S.		76,048 D	38.3%	61.7%	38.3%	61.7%
1966	319,535	188,291	Smith, Margaret Chase	131,136	Violette, Elmer H.	108	57,155 R	58.9%	41.0%	58.9%	41.1%
1964	380,551	127,040	McIntire, Clifford	253,511	Muskie, Edmund S.		126,471 D	33.4%	66.6%	33.4%	66.6%
1960	416,699	256,890	Smith, Margaret Chase	159,809	Cormier, Lucia M.		97,081 R	61.6%	38.4%	61.6%	38.4%
1958	284,226	111,522	Payne, Frederick G.	172,704	Muskie, Edmund S.		61,182 D	39.2%	60.8%	39.2%	60.8%
1954	246,605	144,530	Smith, Margaret Chase	102,075	Fullam, Paul A.		42,455 R	58.6%	41.4%	58.6%	41.4%
1952	237,164	139,205	Payne, Frederick G.	82,665	Dube, Roger P.	15,294	56,540 R	58.7%	34.9%	62.7%	37.3%
1948	223,256	159,182	Smith, Margaret Chase	64,074	Scolten, Adrian H.		95,108 R	71.3%	28.7%	71.3%	28.7%
1946	175,014	111,215	Brewster, Owen	63,799	MacDonald, Peter		47,416 R	63.5%	36.5%	63.5%	36.5%

MAINE

Districts Established April 7, 1994

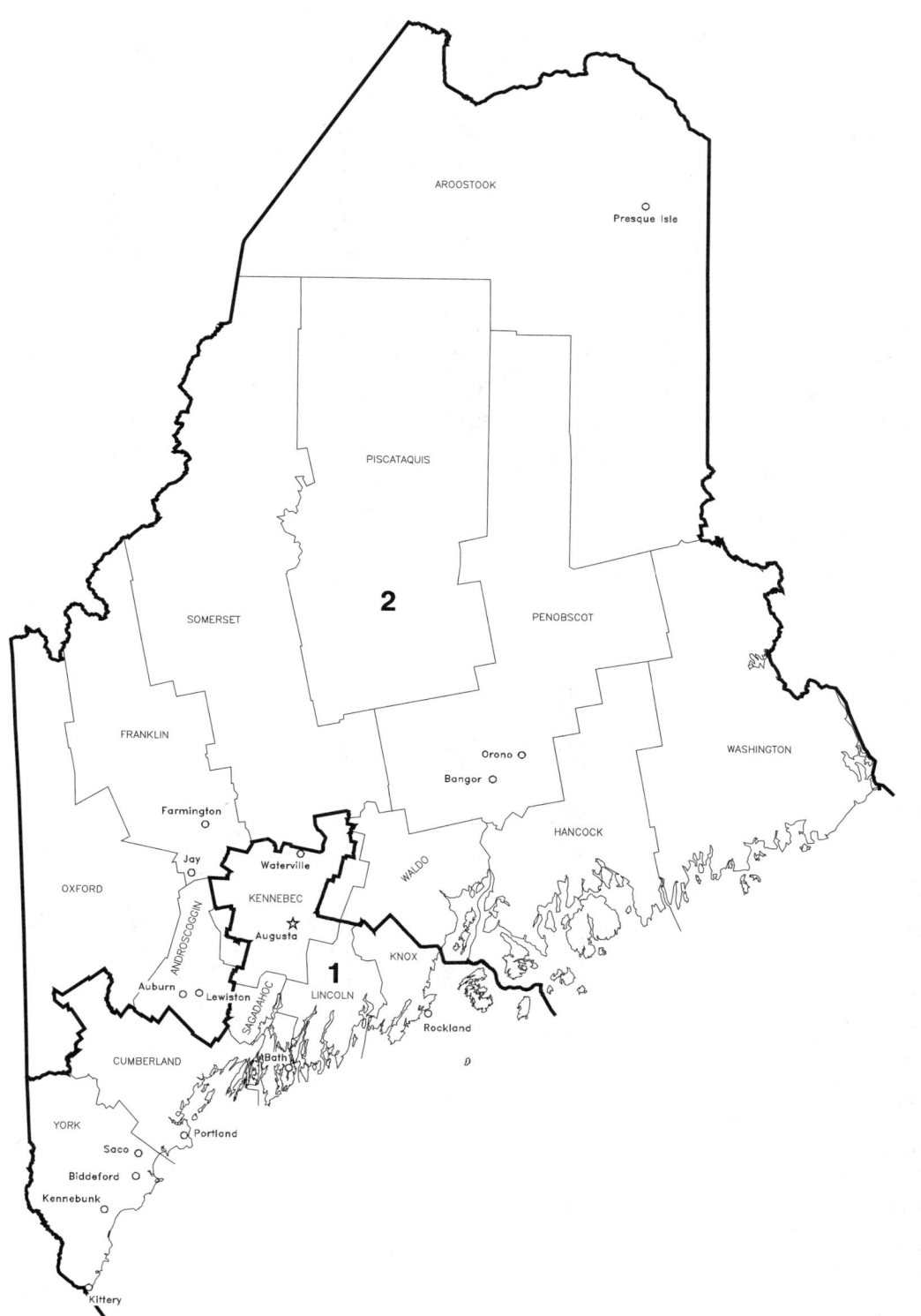

MAINE

PRESIDENT 2000

2000 Census Population	County	Total Vote	Republican	Democratic	Green (Nader)	Other	Rep.-Dem. Plurality	Percentage of Total Vote Rep.	Dem.	Green
103,793	ANDROSCOGGIN	49,245	19,948	26,251	2,388	658	6,303 D	40.5%	53.3%	4.8%
73,938	AROOSTOOK	35,143	16,555	17,196	1,055	337	641 D	47.1%	48.9%	3.0%
265,612	CUMBERLAND	142,620	58,543	74,203	8,576	1,298	15,660 D	41.0%	52.0%	6.0%
29,467	FRANKLIN	15,448	6,459	7,593	1,115	281	1,134 D	41.8%	49.2%	7.2%
51,791	HANCOCK	28,574	12,732	12,983	2,513	346	251 D	44.6%	45.4%	8.8%
117,114	KENNEBEC	58,907	23,967	31,198	2,955	787	7,231 D	40.7%	53.0%	5.0%
39,618	KNOX	20,501	8,968	9,453	1,810	270	485 D	43.7%	46.1%	8.8%
33,616	LINCOLN	19,671	9,457	8,634	1,323	257	823 R	48.1%	43.9%	6.7%
54,755	OXFORD	27,493	11,835	13,649	1,509	500	1,814 D	43.0%	49.6%	5.5%
144,919	PENOBSCOT	73,206	35,620	32,868	3,772	946	2,752 R	48.7%	44.9%	5.2%
17,235	PISCATAQUIS	9,256	4,845	3,745	471	195	1,100 R	52.3%	40.5%	5.1%
35,214	SAGADAHOC	18,406	8,052	8,844	1,278	232	792 D	43.7%	48.0%	6.9%
50,888	SOMERSET	23,951	10,684	11,538	1,239	490	854 D	44.6%	48.2%	5.2%
36,280	WALDO	19,138	8,689	8,477	1,690	282	212 R	45.4%	44.3%	8.8%
33,941	WASHINGTON	15,708	7,958	6,701	802	247	1,257 R	50.7%	42.7%	5.1%
186,742	YORK	94,550	42,304	46,618	4,631	997	4,314 D	44.7%	49.3%	4.9%
1,274,923	TOTAL	651,817	286,616	319,951	37,127	8,123	33,335 D	44.0%	49.1%	5.7%
	City/Town									
23,203	AUBURN	11,333	4,568	6,014	586	165	1,446 D	40.3%	53.1%	5.2%
18,560	AUGUSTA	8,986	3,344	5,116	391	135	1,772 D	37.2%	56.9%	4.4%
31,473	BANGOR	14,320	6,131	7,311	746	132	1,180 D	42.8%	51.1%	5.2%
9,266	BATH	4,512	1,803	2,330	323	56	527 D	40.0%	51.6%	7.2%
6,381	BELFAST	3,347	1,390	1,597	307	53	207 D	41.5%	47.7%	9.2%
6,353	BERWICK	2,774	1,387	1,264	99	24	123 R	50.0%	45.6%	3.6%
20,942	BIDDEFORD	9,045	3,126	5,383	415	121	2,257 D	34.6%	59.5%	4.6%
8,987	BREWER	5,029	2,603	2,201	183	42	402 R	51.8%	43.8%	3.6%
21,172	BRUNSWICK	10,034	3,767	5,547	634	86	1,780 D	37.5%	55.3%	6.3%
7,452	BUXTON	3,847	1,833	1,780	173	61	53 R	47.6%	46.3%	4.5%
5,254	CAMDEN	3,139	1,125	1,664	335	15	539 D	35.8%	53.0%	10.7%
9,068	CAPE ELIZABETH	6,014	2,709	2,962	310	33	253 D	45.0%	49.3%	5.2%
8,312	CARIBOU	3,574	1,574	1,855	101	44	281 D	44.0%	51.9%	2.8%
7,159	CUMBERLAND	4,505	2,327	1,921	227	30	406 R	51.7%	42.6%	5.0%
5,954	ELIOT	3,423	1,592	1,662	155	14	70 D	46.5%	48.6%	4.5%
6,456	ELLSWORTH	3,408	1,729	1,406	229	44	323 R	50.7%	41.3%	6.7%
6,573	FAIRFIELD	2,997	1,122	1,646	173	56	524 D	37.4%	54.9%	5.8%
10,310	FALMOUTH	6,443	3,261	2,858	288	36	403 R	50.6%	44.4%	4.5%
7,410	FARMINGTON	3,599	1,340	1,888	313	58	548 D	37.2%	52.5%	8.7%
7,800	FREEPORT	4,471	1,766	2,346	318	41	580 D	39.5%	52.5%	7.1%
6,198	GARDINER	2,942	1,159	1,587	150	46	428 D	39.4%	53.9%	5.1%
14,141	GORHAM	7,191	3,353	3,394	396	48	41 D	46.6%	47.2%	5.5%
6,820	GRAY	3,830	1,948	1,608	219	55	340 R	50.9%	42.0%	5.7%
6,327	HAMPDEN	3,681	1,962	1,508	180	31	454 R	53.3%	41.0%	4.9%
5,239	HARPSWELL	3,346	1,479	1,606	224	37	127 D	44.2%	48.0%	6.7%
6,476	HOULTON	2,706	1,595	998	93	20	597 R	58.9%	36.9%	3.4%
4,985	JAY	2,563	828	1,568	124	43	740 D	32.3%	61.2%	4.8%
10,476	KENNEBUNK	6,405	3,258	2,749	344	54	509 R	50.9%	42.9%	5.4%
9,543	KITTERY	4,678	1,787	2,591	254	46	804 D	38.2%	55.4%	5.4%
35,690	LEWISTON	15,823	5,255	9,663	690	215	4,408 D	33.2%	61.1%	4.4%
2,361	LIMESTONE	941	376	512	46	7	136 D	40.0%	54.4%	4.9%
5,221	LINCOLN TOWN	2,477	1,410	916	92	59	494 R	56.9%	37.0%	3.7%
9,077	LISBON	4,275	1,943	2,039	230	63	96 D	45.5%	47.7%	5.4%
5,203	MILLINOCKET	2,976	1,320	1,495	92	69	175 D	44.4%	50.2%	3.1%
5,959	OAKLAND	2,763	1,196	1,414	119	34	218 D	43.3%	51.2%	4.3%

MAINE

PRESIDENT 2000

2000 Census Population	County	Total Vote	Republican	Democratic	Green (Nader)	Other	Rep.-Dem. Plurality		Percentage of Total Vote		
									Rep.	Dem.	Green
8,856	OLD ORCHARD BEACH	4,890	1,855	2,708	269	58	853	D	37.9%	55.4%	5.5%
8,130	OLD TOWN	4,024	1,504	2,213	264	43	709	D	37.4%	55.0%	6.6%
9,112	ORONO	4,855	1,506	2,701	599	49	1,195	D	31.0%	55.6%	12.3%
62,249	PORTLAND	32,341	8,838	20,506	2,707	290	11,668	D	27.3%	63.4%	8.4%
9,511	PRESQUE ISLE	4,415	2,231	2,004	136	44	227	R	50.5%	45.4%	3.1%
7,609	ROCKLAND	3,320	1,430	1,549	291	50	119	D	43.1%	46.7%	8.8%
6,472	RUMFORD	3,172	1,023	1,945	135	69	922	D	32.3%	61.3%	4.3%
16,822	SACO	8,653	3,402	4,783	399	69	1,381	D	39.3%	55.3%	4.6%
20,806	SANFORD	9,053	3,871	4,653	423	106	782	D	42.8%	51.4%	4.7%
16,970	SCARBOROUGH	9,725	4,964	4,278	413	70	686	R	51.0%	44.0%	4.2%
8,824	SKOWHEGAN	3,883	1,513	2,158	155	57	645	D	39.0%	55.6%	4.0%
6,671	SOUTH BERWICK	3,254	1,552	1,532	140	30	20	R	47.7%	47.1%	4.3%
23,324	SOUTH PORTLAND	12,389	4,390	7,267	631	101	2,877	D	35.4%	58.7%	5.1%
9,285	STANDISH	4,464	2,186	2,017	204	57	169	R	49.0%	45.2%	4.6%
9,100	TOPSHAM	4,588	2,042	2,240	254	52	198	D	44.5%	48.8%	5.5%
15,605	WATERVILLE	6,893	2,115	4,279	407	92	2,164	D	30.7%	62.1%	5.9%
9,400	WELLS	5,207	2,540	2,377	253	37	163	R	48.8%	45.7%	4.9%
16,142	WESTBROOK	8,049	3,258	4,316	385	90	1,058	D	40.5%	53.6%	4.8%
14,904	WINDHAM	7,766	3,754	3,550	377	85	204	R	48.3%	45.7%	4.9%
7,743	WINSLOW	3,971	1,466	2,280	171	54	814	D	36.9%	57.4%	4.3%
6,232	WINTHROP	3,317	1,468	1,644	174	31	176	D	44.3%	49.6%	5.2%
8,360	YARMOUTH	5,241	2,447	2,459	304	31	12	D	46.7%	46.9%	5.8%
12,854	YORK TOWN	7,626	3,462	3,708	410	46	246	D	45.4%	48.6%	5.4%

MAINE

SENATOR 2000

2000 Census Population	County	Total Vote	Republican	Democratic	Other	Rep.-Dem. Plurality		Percentage			
								Total Vote		Major Vote	
								Rep.	Dem.	Rep.	Dem.
103,793	ANDROSCOGGIN	48,611	32,483	16,128		16,355	R	66.8%	33.2%	66.8%	33.2%
73,938	AROOSTOOK	34,373	25,035	9,338		15,697	R	72.8%	27.2%	72.8%	27.2%
265,612	CUMBERLAND	138,787	95,680	43,107		52,573	R	68.9%	31.1%	68.9%	31.1%
29,467	FRANKLIN	14,992	10,485	4,507		5,978	R	69.9%	30.1%	69.9%	30.1%
51,791	HANCOCK	27,522	19,096	8,426		10,670	R	69.4%	30.6%	69.4%	30.6%
117,114	KENNEBEC	57,855	38,245	19,610		18,635	R	66.1%	33.9%	66.1%	33.9%
39,618	KNOX	19,714	14,329	5,385		8,944	R	72.7%	27.3%	72.7%	27.3%
33,616	LINCOLN	19,126	14,150	4,976		9,174	R	74.0%	26.0%	74.0%	26.0%
54,755	OXFORD	26,964	19,486	7,478		12,008	R	72.3%	27.7%	72.3%	27.7%
144,919	PENOBSCOT	71,389	49,428	21,961		27,467	R	69.2%	30.8%	69.2%	30.8%
17,235	PISCATAQUIS	8,938	6,428	2,510		3,918	R	71.9%	28.1%	71.9%	28.1%
35,214	SAGADAHOC	17,839	12,785	5,054		7,731	R	71.7%	28.3%	71.7%	28.3%
50,888	SOMERSET	23,392	15,581	7,811		7,770	R	66.6%	33.4%	66.6%	33.4%
36,280	WALDO	18,422	12,580	5,842		6,738	R	68.3%	31.7%	68.3%	31.7%
33,941	WASHINGTON	15,183	11,073	4,110		6,963	R	72.9%	27.1%	72.9%	27.1%
186,742	YORK	91,765	60,825	30,940		29,885	R	66.3%	33.7%	66.3%	33.7%
1,274,923	TOTAL	634,872	437,689	197,183		240,506	R	68.9%	31.1%	68.9%	31.1%

MAINE

SENATOR 2000

2000 Census Population	City/Town	Total Vote	Republican	Democratic	Other	Rep.-Dem. Plurality		Percentage			
								Total Vote		Major Vote	
								Rep.	Dem.	Rep.	Dem.
23,203	AUBURN	11,089	7,572	3,517		4,055	R	68.3%	31.7%	68.3%	31.7%
18,560	AUGUSTA	8,896	5,771	3,125		2,646	R	64.9%	35.1%	64.9%	35.1%
31,473	BANGOR	13,999	9,313	4,686		4,627	R	66.5%	33.5%	66.5%	33.5%
9,266	BATH	4,383	3,081	1,302		1,779	R	70.3%	29.7%	70.3%	29.7%
6,381	BELFAST	3,244	2,161	1,083		1,078	R	66.6%	33.4%	66.6%	33.4%
6,353	BERWICK	2,618	1,664	954		710	R	63.6%	36.4%	63.6%	36.4%
20,942	BIDDEFORD	8,947	5,551	3,396		2,155	R	62.0%	38.0%	62.0%	38.0%
8,987	BREWER	4,915	3,540	1,375		2,165	R	72.0%	28.0%	72.0%	28.0%
21,172	BRUNSWICK	9,835	6,387	3,448		2,939	R	64.9%	35.1%	64.9%	35.1%
7,452	BUXTON	3,732	2,801	931		1,870	R	75.1%	24.9%	75.1%	24.9%
5,254	CAMDEN	3,030	2,067	963		1,104	R	68.2%	31.8%	68.2%	31.8%
9,068	CAPE ELIZABETH	5,888	4,192	1,696		2,496	R	71.2%	28.8%	71.2%	28.8%
8,312	CARIBOU	3,496	2,651	845		1,806	R	75.8%	24.2%	75.8%	24.2%
7,158	CUMBERLAND TOWN	4,364	3,421	943		2,478	R	78.4%	21.6%	78.4%	21.6%
5,954	ELIOT	3,308	1,785	1,523		262	R	54.0%	46.0%	54.0%	46.0%
6,456	ELLSWORTH	3,332	2,377	955		1,422	R	71.3%	28.7%	71.3%	28.7%
6,573	FAIRFIELD	2,953	1,812	1,141		671	R	61.4%	38.6%	61.4%	38.6%
10,310	FALMOUTH	6,284	4,805	1,479		3,326	R	76.5%	23.5%	76.5%	23.5%
7,410	FARMINGTON	3,498	2,400	1,098		1,302	R	68.6%	31.4%	68.6%	31.4%
7,800	FREEPORT	4,372	3,066	1,306		1,760	R	70.1%	29.9%	70.1%	29.9%
6,198	GARDINER	2,893	1,981	912		1,069	R	68.5%	31.5%	68.5%	31.5%
14,141	GORHAM	6,930	5,084	1,846		3,238	R	73.4%	26.6%	73.4%	26.6%
6,820	GRAY	3,745	2,881	864		2,017	R	76.9%	23.1%	76.9%	23.1%
6,327	HAMPDEN	3,580	2,593	987		1,606	R	72.4%	27.6%	72.4%	27.6%
5,239	HARPSWELL	3,293	2,445	848		1,597	R	74.2%	25.8%	74.2%	25.8%
6,476	HOULTON	2,670	2,118	552		1,566	R	79.3%	20.7%	79.3%	20.7%
4,985	JAY	2,583	1,533	1,050		483	R	59.3%	40.7%	59.3%	40.7%
10,476	KENNEBUNK	6,184	4,519	1,665		2,854	R	73.1%	26.9%	73.1%	26.9%
9,543	KITTERY	4,530	2,058	2,472		414	D	45.4%	54.6%	45.4%	54.6%
35,690	LEWISTON	15,800	9,595	6,205		3,390	R	60.7%	39.3%	60.7%	39.3%
2,361	LIMESTONE	939	708	231		477	R	75.4%	24.6%	75.4%	24.6%
5,221	LINCOLN TOWN	2,425	1,740	685		1,055	R	71.8%	28.2%	71.8%	28.2%
9,077	LISBON	4,196	3,004	1,192		1,812	R	71.6%	28.4%	71.6%	28.4%
5,203	MILLINOCKET	2,934	1,876	1,058		818	R	63.9%	36.1%	63.9%	36.1%
5,959	OAKLAND	2,711	1,810	901		909	R	66.8%	33.2%	66.8%	33.2%
2%,856	OLD ORCHARD BEACH	4,712	3,152	1,560		1,592	R	66.9%	33.1%	66.9%	33.1%
8,130	OLD TOWN	3,889	2,466	1,423		1,043	R	63.4%	36.6%	63.4%	36.6%
9,112	ORONO	4,665	2,913	1,752		1,161	R	62.4%	37.6%	62.4%	37.6%
62,249	PORTLAND	31,260	17,959	13,301		4,658	R	57.5%	42.5%	57.5%	42.5%
9,511	PRESQUE ISLE	4,333	3,353	980		2,373	R	77.4%	22.6%	77.4%	22.6%
7,609	ROCKLAND	3,215	2,328	887		1,441	R	72.4%	27.6%	72.4%	27.6%
6,472	RUMFORD	3,238	1,931	1,307		624	R	59.6%	40.4%	59.6%	40.4%
16,822	SACO	8,412	5,730	2,682		3,048	R	68.1%	31.9%	68.1%	31.9%
20,806	SANFORD	8,783	6,040	2,743		3,297	R	68.8%	31.2%	68.8%	31.2%
16,970	SCARBOROUGH	9,346	7,047	2,299		4,748	R	75.4%	24.6%	75.4%	24.6%
8,824	SKOWHEGAN	3,868	2,552	1,316		1,236	R	66.0%	34.0%	66.0%	34.0%
6,671	SOUTH BERWICK	3,188	1,676	1,512		164	R	52.6%	47.4%	52.6%	47.4%
23,324	SOUTH PORTLAND	12,064	7,899	4,165		3,734	R	65.5%	34.5%	65.5%	34.5%
9,285	STANDISH	4,349	3,261	1,088		2,173	R	75.0%	25.0%	75.0%	25.0%
9,100	TOPSHAM	4,427	3,239	1,188		2,051	R	73.2%	26.8%	73.2%	26.8%
15,605	WATERVILLE	6,729	3,787	2,942		845	R	56.3%	43.7%	56.3%	43.7%
9,400	WELLS	5,032	3,648	1,384		2,264	R	72.5%	27.5%	72.5%	27.5%
16,142	WESTBROOK	7,914	5,518	2,396		3,122	R	69.7%	30.3%	69.7%	30.3%
14,904	WINDHAM	7,535	5,604	1,931		3,673	R	74.4%	25.6%	74.4%	25.6%
7,743	WINSLOW	3,939	2,438	1,501		937	R	61.9%	38.1%	61.9%	38.1%
6,232	WINTHROP	3,283	2,361	922		1,439	R	71.9%	28.1%	71.9%	28.1%
8,360	YARMOUTH	5,138	3,891	1,247		2,644	R	75.7%	24.3%	75.7%	24.3%
12,854	YORK TOWN	7,403	4,304	3,099		1,205	R	58.1%	41.9%	58.1%	41.9%

MAINE
CONGRESS

CD	Year	Total Vote	Republican		Democratic		Other Vote	Rep.-Dem. Plurality	Percentage			
									Total Vote		Major Vote	
			Vote	Candidate	Vote	Candidate			Rep.	Dem.	Rep.	Dem.
1	2000	339,094	123,915	AMERO, JANE A.	202,823	ALLEN, THOMAS H.	12,356	78,908 D	36.5%	59.8%	37.9%	62.1%
1	1998	222,677	79,160	CONNELLY, ROSS J.	134,335	ALLEN, THOMAS H.	9,182	55,175 D	35.5%	60.3%	37.1%	62.9%
1	1996	314,164	140,354	LONGLEY, JAMES B.,JR.	173,745	ALLEN, THOMAS H.	65	33,391 D	44.7%	55.3%	44.7%	55.3%
1	1994	262,769	136,316	LONGLEY, JAMES B.,JR.	126,373	DUTREMBLE, DENNIS L.	80	9,943 R	51.9%	48.1%	51.9%	48.1%
2	2000	299,305	79,522	CAMPBELL, RICHARD H.	219,783	BALDACCI, JOHN		140,261 D	26.6%	73.4%	26.6%	73.4%
2	1998	191,876	45,674	REISMAN, JONATHAN	146,202	BALDACCI, JOHN		100,528 D	23.8%	76.2%	23.8%	76.2%
2	1996	285,636	70,856	YOUNG, PAUL R.	205,439	BALDACCI, JOHN	9,341	134,583 D	24.8%	71.9%	25.6%	74.4%
2	1994	239,894	97,754	BENNETT, RICHARD A.	109,615	BALDACCI, JOHN	32,525	11,861 D	40.7%	45.7%	47.1%	52.9%

MAINE
GENERAL AND PRIMARY ELECTIONS

2000 GENERAL ELECTIONS

President Other vote was 4,443 Reform (Buchanan); 3,074 Libertarian (Browne); 579 Constitution (Phillips); 27 write-in (Hagelin). The official returns listed the Hagelin vote as "Other."

Congress Other vote was: CD 1: 12,356 Libertarian (Staples).

2000 PRIMARY ELECTIONS

Primary March 7, 2000 (President)
June 13, 2000 (Congress)

Registration (as of June 13, 2000)

Republican	265,889
Democratic	280,987
Reform	2,879
Green Independent	2,152
Unenrolled	330,430
TOTAL	882,337

Primary Type Modified—Registered Democrats and Republicans can only vote in their party's primary. "Unenrolled" and new voters can vote in either party's primary by enrolling in that party on primary day.

Note: An asterisk (*) denotes incumbent.

	REPUBLICAN PRIMARIES			DEMOCRATIC PRIMARIES		
President	George W. Bush	49,308	51.0%	Al Gore	34,725	54.0%
	John McCain	42,510	44.0%	Bill Bradley	26,520	41.3%
	Alan Keyes	2,989	3.1%	Uncommitted	2,634	4.1%
	Uncommitted	1,038	1.1%	Lyndon H. LaRouche Jr.	208	0.3%
	Steve Forbes	455	0.5%	Richard Jan Epstein	192	0.3%
	Gary Bauer	324	0.3%			
	TOTAL	96,624		TOTAL	64,279	
Senator	Olympia J. Snowe*	34,757	100.0%	Mark W. Lawrence	26,543	100.0%
	TOTAL	34,757		TOTAL	26,543	
Congressional District 1	Jane A. Amero	17,362	100.0%	Thomas H. Allen*	15,115	100.0%
	TOTAL	17,362		TOTAL	15,115	
Congressional District 2	Richard H. Campbell	9,491	62.8%	John E. Baldacci*	16,729	100.0%
	Lynwood C. Winslow	5,612	37.2%			
	TOTAL	15,103		TOTAL	16,729	

MARYLAND

GOVERNOR
Parris N. Glendening (D). Re-elected 1998 to a four-year term. Previously elected 1994.

SENATORS
Barbara A. Mikulski (D). Re-elected 1998 to a six-year term. Previously elected 1992, 1986.

Paul S. Sarbanes (D). Re-elected 2000 to a six-year term. Previously elected 1994, 1988, 1982, 1976.

REPRESENTATIVES
1. Wayne T. Gilchrest (R)
2. Robert L. Ehrlich (R)
3. Benjamin L. Cardin (D)
4. Albert R. Wynn (D)
5. Steny H. Hoyer (D)
6. Roscoe Bartlett (R)
7. Elijah E. Cummings (D)
8. Constance A. Morella (R)

POSTWAR VOTE FOR PRESIDENT

Year	Total Vote	Republican Vote	Republican Candidate	Democratic Vote	Democratic Candidate	Other Vote	Plurality	Percentage Total Vote Rep.	Percentage Total Vote Dem.	Percentage Major Vote Rep.	Percentage Major Vote Dem.
2000**	2,020,480	813,797	Bush, George W.	1,140,782	Gore, Al	65,901	326,985 D	40.3%	56.5%	41.6%	58.4%
1996**	1,780,870	681,530	Dole, Bob	966,207	Clinton, Bill	133,133	284,677 D	38.3%	54.3%	41.4%	58.6%
1992**	1,985,046	707,094	Bush, George	988,571	Clinton, Bill	289,381	281,477 D	35.6%	49.8%	41.7%	58.3%
1988	1,714,358	876,167	Bush, George	826,304	Dukakis, Michael S.	11,887	49,863 R	51.1%	48.2%	51.5%	48.5%
1984	1,675,873	879,918	Reagan, Ronald	787,935	Mondale, Walter F.	8,020	91,983 R	52.5%	47.0%	52.8%	47.2%
1980**	1,540,496	680,606	Reagan, Ronald	726,161	Carter, Jimmy	133,729	45,555 D	44.2%	47.1%	48.4%	51.6%
1976	1,439,897	672,661	Ford, Gerald R.	759,612	Carter, Jimmy	7,624	86,951 D	46.7%	52.8%	47.0%	53.0%
1972	1,353,812	829,305	Nixon, Richard M.	505,781	McGovern, George S.	18,726	323,524 R	61.3%	37.4%	62.1%	37.9%
1968	1,235,039	517,995	Nixon, Richard M.	538,310	Humphrey, Hubert H.	178,734	20,315 D	41.9%	43.6%	49.0%	51.0%
1964	1,116,457	385,495	Goldwater, Barry M.	730,912	Johnson, Lyndon B.	50	345,417 D	34.5%	65.5%	34.5%	65.5%
1960	1,055,349	489,538	Nixon, Richard M.	565,808	Kennedy, John F.	3	76,270 D	46.4%	53.6%	46.4%	53.6%
1956	932,827	559,738	Eisenhower, Dwight D.	372,613	Stevenson, Adlai E.	476	187,125 R	60.0%	39.9%	60.0%	40.0%
1952	902,074	499,424	Eisenhower, Dwight D.	395,337	Stevenson, Adlai E.	7,313	104,087 R	55.4%	43.8%	55.8%	44.2%
1948	596,748	294,814	Dewey, Thomas E.	286,521	Truman, Harry S.	15,413	8,293 R	49.4%	48.0%	50.7%	49.3%

In 2000 the other vote column includes 53,768 votes cast for Green (Nader). In 1996 the other vote column includes 115,812 votes cast for Perot. In 1992 the other vote column includes 281,414 votes cast for Perot. In 1980 the other column includes 119,537 votes for Independent (Anderson).

MARYLAND

POSTWAR VOTE FOR GOVERNOR

Year	Total Vote	Republican		Democratic		Other Vote	Rep.-Dem. Plurality	Percentage			
		Vote	Candidate	Vote	Candidate			Total Vote		Major Vote	
								Rep.	Dem.	Rep.	Dem.
1998	1,535,978	688,357	Sauerbrey, Ellen R.	846,972	Glendening, Parris N.	649	158,615 D	44.8%	55.1%	44.8%	55.2%
1994	1,410,300	702,101	Sauerbrey, Ellen R.	708,094	Glendening, Parris N.	105	5,993 D	49.8%	50.2%	49.8%	50.2%
1990	1,111,088	446,980	Shepard, William S.	664,015	Schaefer, William D.	93	217,035 D	40.2%	59.8%	40.2%	59.8%
1986	1,101,476	194,185	Mooney, Thomas J.	907,291	Schaefer, William D.		713,106 D	17.6%	82.4%	17.6%	82.4%
1982	1,139,149	432,826	Pascal, Robert A.	705,910	Hughes, Harry	413	273,084 D	38.0%	62.0%	38.0%	62.0%
1978	1,011,963	293,635	Beall, J. Glenn, Jr.	718,328	Hughes, Harry		424,693 D	29.0%	71.0%	29.0%	71.0%
1974	949,097	346,449	Gore, Louise	602,648	Mandel, Marvin		256,199 D	36.5%	63.5%	36.5%	63.5%
1970	973,099	314,336	Blain, C. Stanley	639,579	Mandel, Marvin	19,184	325,243 D	32.3%	65.7%	33.0%	67.0%
1966	918,761	455,318	Agnew, Spiro T.	373,543	Mahoney, George P.	89,900	81,775 R	49.6%	40.7%	54.9%	45.1%
1962	775,101	343,051	Small, Frank	432,045	Tawes, J. Millard	5	88,994 D	44.3%	55.7%	44.3%	55.7%
1958	763,234	278,173	Devereux, James	485,061	Tawes, J. Millard		206,888 D	36.4%	63.6%	36.4%	63.6%
1954	700,484	381,451	McKeldin, Theodore	319,033	Byrd, Harry C.		62,418 R	54.5%	45.5%	54.5%	45.5%
1950	645,631	369,807	McKeldin, Theodore	275,824	Lane, William P.		93,983 R	57.3%	42.7%	57.3%	42.7%
1946	489,836	221,752	McKeldin, Theodore	268,084	Lane, William P.		46,332 D	45.3%	54.7%	45.3%	54.7%

POSTWAR VOTE FOR SENATOR

Year	Total Vote	Republican		Democratic		Other Vote	Rep.-Dem. Plurality	Percentage			
		Vote	Candidate	Vote	Candidate			Total Vote		Major Vote	
								Rep.	Dem.	Rep.	Dem.
2000	1,946,898	715,178	Rappaport, Paul	1,230,013	Sarbanes, Paul S.	1,707	514,835 D	36.7%	63.2%	36.8%	63.2%
1998	1,507,447	444,637	Pierpont, Ross Z.	1,062,810	Mikulski, Barbara A.		618,173 D	29.5%	70.5%	29.5%	70.5%
1994	1,369,104	559,908	Brock, William E.	809,125	Sarbanes, Paul S.	71	249,217 D	40.9%	59.1%	40.9%	59.1%
1992	1,841,735	533,688	Keyes, Alan L.	1,307,610	Mikulski, Barbara A.	437	773,922 D	29.0%	71.0%	29.0%	71.0%
1988	1,617,065	617,537	Keyes, Alan L.	999,166	Sarbanes, Paul S.	362	381,629 D	38.2%	61.8%	38.2%	61.8%
1986	1,112,637	437,411	Chavez, Linda	675,225	Mikulski, Barbara A.	1	237,814 D	39.3%	60.7%	39.3%	60.7%
1982	1,114,690	407,334	Hogan, Lawrence J.	707,356	Sarbanes, Paul S.		300,022 D	36.5%	63.5%	36.5%	63.5%
1980	1,286,088	850,970	Mathias, Charles	435,118	Conroy, Edward T.		415,852 R	66.2%	33.8%	66.2%	33.8%
1976	1,365,568	530,439	Beall, J. Glenn, Jr.	772,101	Sarbanes, Paul S.	63,028	241,662 D	38.8%	56.5%	40.7%	59.3%
1974	877,786	503,223	Mathias, Charles	374,563	Mikulski, Barbara A.		128,660 R	57.3%	42.7%	57.3%	42.7%
1970	956,370	484,960	Beall, J. Glenn, Jr.	460,422	Tydings, Joseph D.	10,988	24,538 R	50.7%	48.1%	51.3%	48.7%
1968	1,133,727	541,893	Mathias, Charles	443,367	Brewster, Daniel B.	148,467	98,526 R	47.8%	39.1%	55.0%	45.0%
1964	1,081,049	402,393	Beall, J. Glenn	678,649	Tydings, Joseph D.	7	276,256 D	37.2%	62.8%	37.2%	62.8%
1962	714,248	270,312	Miller, Edward T.	443,935	Brewster, Daniel B.	1	173,623 D	37.8%	62.2%	37.8%	62.2%
1958	749,291	382,021	Beall, J. Glenn	367,270	D'Alesandro, Thomas		14,751 R	51.0%	49.0%	51.0%	49.0%
1956	892,167	473,059	Butler, John Marshall	419,108	Mahoney, George P.		53,951 R	53.0%	47.0%	53.0%	47.0%
1952	856,193	449,823	Beall, J. Glenn	406,370	Mahoney, George P.		43,453 R	52.5%	47.5%	52.5%	47.5%
1950	615,614	326,291	Butler, John Marshall	283,180	Tydings, Millard E.	6,143	43,111 R	53.0%	46.0%	53.5%	46.5%
1946	472,232	235,000	Markey, David John	237,232	O'Conor, Herbert R.		2,232 D	49.8%	50.2%	49.8%	50.2%

MARYLAND

Districts Established October 23, 1991

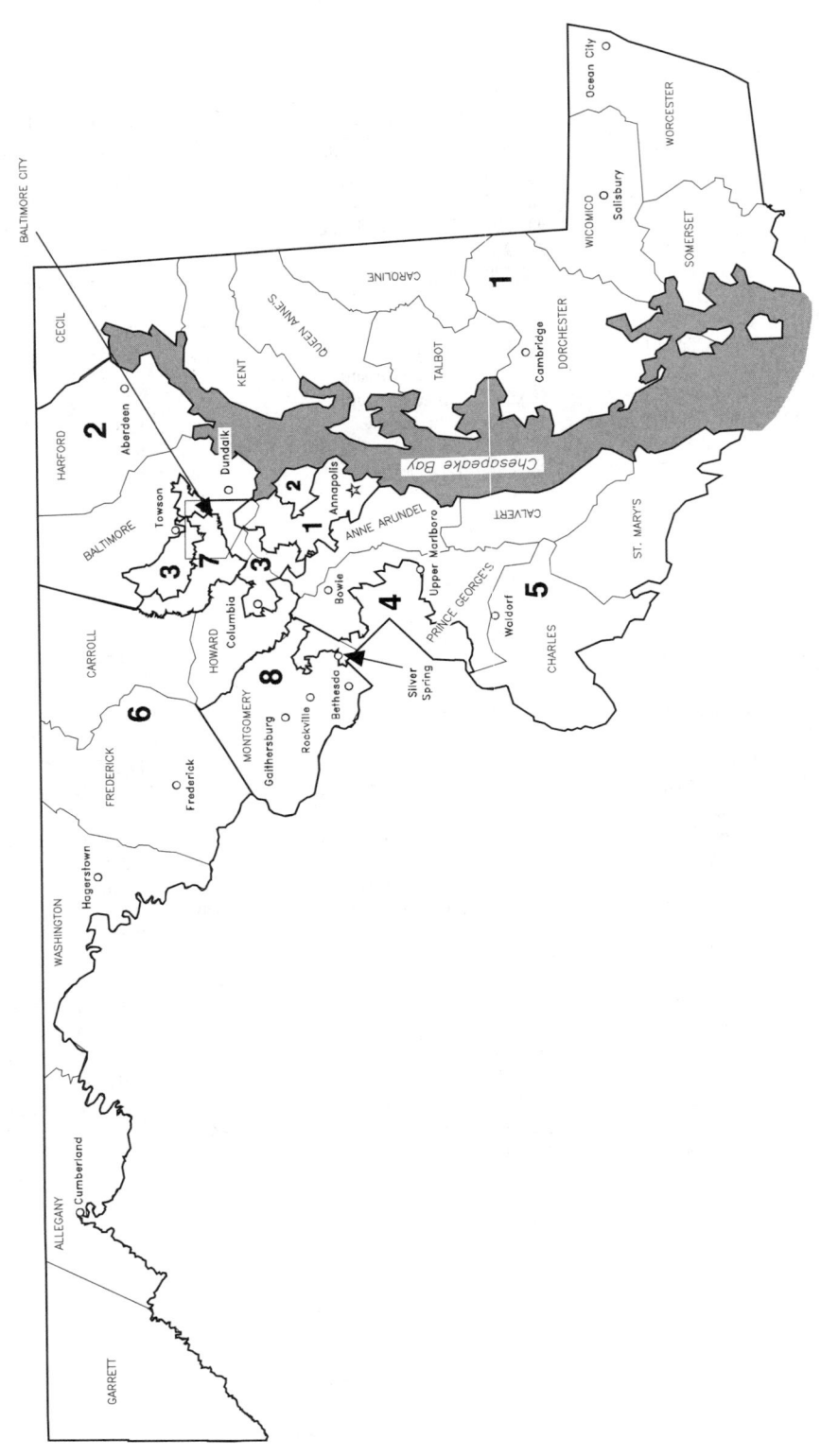

MARYLAND

PRESIDENT 2000

2000 Census Population	County	Total Vote	Republican	Democratic	Green (Nader)	Other	Rep.-Dem. Plurality	Percentage of Total Vote		
								Rep.	Dem.	Green
74,930	ALLEGANY	26,371	14,656	10,894	610	211	3,762 R	55.6%	41.3%	2.3%
489,656	ANNE ARUNDEL	200,657	104,209	89,624	5,493	1,331	14,585 R	51.9%	44.7%	2.7%
651,154	BALTIMORE CITY	192,404	27,150	158,765	5,512	977	131,615 D	14.1%	82.5%	2.9%
754,292	BALTIMORE COUNTY	304,084	133,033	160,635	8,544	1,872	27,602 D	43.7%	52.8%	2.8%
74,563	CALVERT	29,806	16,004	12,986	660	156	3,018 R	53.7%	43.6%	2.2%
29,772	CAROLINE	8,952	5,300	3,396	198	58	1,904 R	59.2%	37.9%	2.2%
150,897	CARROLL	64,027	41,742	20,146	1,681	458	21,596 R	65.2%	31.5%	2.6%
85,951	CECIL	28,876	15,494	12,327	794	261	3,167 R	53.7%	42.7%	2.7%
120,546	CHARLES	44,592	21,768	21,873	755	196	105 D	48.8%	49.1%	1.7%
30,674	DORCHESTER	11,392	5,847	5,232	222	91	615 R	51.3%	45.9%	1.9%
195,277	FREDERICK	78,661	45,350	30,725	2,052	534	14,625 R	57.7%	39.1%	2.6%
29,846	GARRETT	10,655	7,514	2,872	203	66	4,642 R	70.5%	27.0%	1.9%
218,590	HARFORD	91,424	52,862	35,665	2,298	599	17,197 R	57.8%	39.0%	2.5%
247,842	HOWARD	112,779	49,809	58,556	3,643	771	8,747 D	44.2%	51.9%	3.2%
19,197	KENT	8,085	4,155	3,627	270	33	528 R	51.4%	44.9%	3.3%
873,341	MONTGOMERY	371,688	124,580	232,453	12,485	2,170	107,873 D	33.5%	62.5%	3.4%
801,515	PRINCE GEORGES	266,909	49,987	211,119	4,497	1,306	161,132 D	18.7%	79.1%	1.7%
40,563	QUEEN ANNES	16,761	9,970	6,257	446	88	3,713 R	59.5%	37.3%	2.7%
86,211	ST. MARYS	29,501	16,856	11,912	568	165	4,944 R	57.1%	40.4%	1.9%
24,747	SOMERSET	7,604	3,609	3,785	142	68	176 D	47.5%	49.8%	1.9%
33,812	TALBOT	15,234	8,874	5,854	424	82	3,020 R	58.3%	38.4%	2.8%
131,923	WASHINGTON	47,470	27,948	18,221	1,027	274	9,727 R	58.9%	38.4%	2.2%
84,644	WICOMICO	31,795	16,338	14,469	762	226	1,869 R	51.4%	45.5%	2.4%
46,543	WORCESTER	20,753	10,742	9,389	482	140	1,353 R	51.8%	45.2%	2.3%
5,296,486	TOTAL	2,020,480	813,797	1,140,782	53,768	12,133	326,985 D	40.3%	56.5%	2.7%

MARYLAND

SENATOR 2000

2000 Census Population	County	Total Vote	Republican	Democratic	Other	Rep.-Dem. Plurality	Percentage			
							Total Vote		Major Vote	
							Rep.	Dem.	Rep.	Dem.
74,930	ALLEGANY	21,408	8,768	12,638	2	3,870 D	41.0%	59.0%	41.0%	59.0%
489,656	ANNE ARUNDEL	197,558	95,737	101,627	194	5,890 D	48.5%	51.4%	48.5%	51.5%
651,154	BALTIMORE CITY	182,441	24,019	158,260	162	134,241 D	13.2%	86.7%	13.2%	86.8%
754,292	BALTIMORE COUNTY	298,454	122,601	175,551	302	52,950 D	41.1%	58.8%	41.1%	58.9%
74,563	CALVERT	28,951	13,618	15,305	28	1,687 D	47.0%	52.9%	47.1%	52.9%
29,772	CAROLINE	8,719	4,472	4,239	8	233 R	51.3%	48.6%	51.3%	48.7%
150,897	CARROLL	62,630	38,790	23,781	59	15,009 R	61.9%	38.0%	62.0%	38.0%
85,951	CECIL	28,148	13,955	14,168	25	213 D	49.6%	50.3%	49.6%	50.4%
120,546	CHARLES	43,624	18,321	25,278	25	6,957 D	42.0%	57.9%	42.0%	58.0%
30,674	DORCHESTER	10,000	4,276	5,724		1,448 D	42.8%	57.2%	42.8%	57.2%
195,277	FREDERICK	76,425	39,031	37,315	79	1,716 R	51.1%	48.8%	51.1%	48.9%
29,846	GARRETT	10,177	5,858	4,319		1,539 R	57.6%	42.4%	57.6%	42.4%
218,590	HARFORD	90,077	48,322	41,679	76	6,643 R	53.6%	46.3%	53.7%	46.3%
247,842	HOWARD	110,541	47,786	62,636	119	14,850 D	43.2%	56.7%	43.3%	56.7%
19,197	KENT	7,831	3,481	4,346	4	865 D	44.5%	55.5%	44.5%	55.5%
873,341	MONTGOMERY	361,063	109,911	250,664	488	140,753 D	30.4%	69.4%	30.5%	69.5%
801,515	PRINCE GEORGES	244,673	40,033	204,622	18	164,589 D	16.4%	83.6%	16.4%	83.6%
40,563	QUEEN ANNES	16,323	8,775	7,539	9	1,236 R	53.8%	46.2%	53.8%	46.2%
86,211	ST. MARYS	28,651	13,357	15,273	21	1,916 D	46.6%	53.3%	46.7%	53.3%
24,747	SOMERSET	7,219	2,536	4,681	2	2,145 D	35.1%	64.8%	35.1%	64.9%
33,812	TALBOT	14,840	7,820	6,996	24	824 R	52.7%	47.1%	52.8%	47.2%
131,923	WASHINGTON	45,690	23,291	22,362	37	929 R	51.0%	48.9%	51.0%	49.0%
84,644	WICOMICO	31,194	12,234	18,946	14	6,712 D	39.2%	60.7%	39.2%	60.8%
46,543	WORCESTER	20,261	8,186	12,064	11	3,878 D	40.4%	59.5%	40.4%	59.6%
5,296,486	TOTAL	1,946,898	715,178	1,230,013	1,707	514,835 D	36.7%	63.2%	36.8%	63.2%

MARYLAND

CONGRESS

CD	Year	Total Vote	Republican Vote	Republican Candidate	Democratic Vote	Democratic Candidate	Other Vote	Rep.-Dem. Plurality	Total Vote Rep.	Total Vote Dem.	Major Vote Rep.	Major Vote Dem.
1	2000	256,682	165,293	GILCHREST, WAYNE T.	91,022	BOZMAN, BENNETT	367	74,271 R	64.4%	35.5%	64.5%	35.5%
1	1998	196,221	135,771	GILCHREST, WAYNE T.	60,450	PINDER, IRVING		75,321 R	69.2%	30.8%	69.2%	30.8%
1	1996	212,876	131,033	GILCHREST, WAYNE T.	81,825	EASTAUGH, STEVEN R.	18	49,208 R	61.6%	38.4%	61.6%	38.4%
1	1994	178,814	120,975	GILCHREST, WAYNE T.	57,712	GIES, RALPH T.	127	63,263 R	67.7%	32.3%	67.7%	32.3%
1	1992	234,203	120,084	GILCHREST, WAYNE T.	112,771	MCMILLEN, THOMAS	1,348	7,313 R	51.3%	48.2%	51.6%	48.4%
2	2000	260,432	178,556	EHRLICH, ROBERT L.	81,591	BOSLEY, KENNETH T.	285	96,965 R	68.6%	31.3%	68.6%	31.4%
2	1998	210,206	145,711	EHRLICH, ROBERT L.	64,474	BOSLEY, KENNETH T.	21	81,237 R	69.3%	30.7%	69.3%	30.7%
2	1996	231,419	143,075	EHRLICH, ROBERT L.	88,344	DEJULIIS, CONNIE G.		54,731 R	61.8%	38.2%	61.8%	38.2%
2	1994	199,480	125,162	EHRLICH, ROBERT L.	74,275	BREWSTER, GERRY L.	43	50,887 R	62.7%	37.2%	62.8%	37.2%
2	1992	254,106	165,443	BENTLEY, HELEN D.	88,658	HICKEY, MICHAEL C.	5	76,785 R	65.1%	34.9%	65.1%	34.9%
3	2000	223,818	53,827	HARBY, COLIN	169,347	CARDIN, BENJAMIN L.	644	115,520 D	24.0%	75.7%	24.1%	75.9%
3	1998	177,168	39,667	HARBY, COLIN	137,501	CARDIN, BENJAMIN L.		97,834 D	22.4%	77.6%	22.4%	77.6%
3	1996	193,433	63,229	MCDONOUGH, PATRICK L.	130,204	CARDIN, BENJAMIN L.		66,975 D	32.7%	67.3%	32.7%	67.3%
3	1994	165,235	47,966	TOUSEY, ROBERT R.	117,269	CARDIN, BENJAMIN L.		69,303 D	29.0%	71.0%	29.0%	71.0%
3	1992	222,255	58,869	BRICKER, WILLIAM T. S.	163,354	CARDIN, BENJAMIN L.	32	104,485 D	26.5%	73.5%	26.5%	73.5%
4	2000	197,969	24,973	KIMBLE, JOHN B.	172,624	WYNN, ALBERT R.	372	147,651 D	12.6%	87.2%	12.6%	87.4%
4	1998	150,657	21,518	KIMBLE, JOHN B.	129,139	WYNN, ALBERT R.		107,621 D	14.3%	85.7%	14.3%	85.7%
4	1996	166,794	24,700	KIMBLE, JOHN B.	142,094	WYNN, ALBERT R.		117,394 D	14.8%	85.2%	14.8%	85.2%
4	1994	124,147	30,999	DYSON, MICHELE	93,148	WYNN, ALBERT R.		62,149 D	25.0%	75.0%	25.0%	75.0%
4	1992	182,185	45,166	DYSON, MICHELE	136,902	WYNN, ALBERT R.	117	91,736 D	24.8%	75.1%	24.8%	75.2%
5	2000	255,375	89,019	HUTCHINS, THOMAS E. "TIM"	166,231	HOYER, STENY H.	125	77,212 D	34.9%	65.1%	34.9%	65.1%
5	1998	193,968	67,176	OSTROM, ROBERT B.	126,792	HOYER, STENY H.		59,616 D	34.6%	65.4%	34.6%	65.4%
5	1996	213,094	91,806	MORGAN, JOHN S.	121,288	HOYER, STENY H.		29,482 D	43.1%	56.9%	43.1%	56.9%
5	1994	168,045	69,211	DEVINE, DONALD	98,821	HOYER, STENY H.	13	29,610 D	41.2%	58.8%	41.2%	58.8%
5	1992	223,326	97,982	HOGAN, LAWRENCE J., JR.	118,312	HOYER, STENY H.	7,032	20,330 D	43.9%	53.0%	45.3%	54.7%
6	2000	278,045	168,624	BARTLETT, ROSCOE	109,136	DEARMON, DONALD M.	285	59,488 R	60.6%	39.3%	60.7%	39.3%
6	1998	201,530	127,802	BARTLETT, ROSCOE	73,728	MCCOWN, TIMOTHY D.		54,074 R	63.4%	36.6%	63.4%	36.6%
6	1996	233,788	132,853	BARTLETT, ROSCOE	100,910	CRAWFORD, STEPHEN	25	31,943 R	56.8%	43.2%	56.8%	43.2%
6	1994	186,220	122,809	BARTLETT, ROSCOE	63,411	MULDOWNEY, PAUL		59,398 R	65.9%	34.1%	65.9%	34.1%
6	1992	231,959	125,564	BARTLETT, ROSCOE	106,224	HATTERY, THOMAS H.	171	19,340 R	54.1%	45.8%	54.2%	45.8%
7	2000	153,974	19,773	KONDNER, KENNETH	134,066	CUMMINGS, ELIJAH E.	135	114,293 D	12.8%	87.1%	12.9%	87.1%
7	1998	131,447	18,742	KONDNER, KENNETH	112,699	CUMMINGS, ELIJAH E.	6	93,957 D	14.3%	85.7%	14.3%	85.7%
7	1996	138,695	22,929	KONDNER, KENNETH	115,764	CUMMINGS, ELIJAH E.	2	92,835 D	16.5%	83.5%	16.5%	83.5%
7	1994	119,023	22,007	KONDNER, KENNETH	97,016	MFUME, KWEISI		75,009 D	18.5%	81.5%	18.5%	81.5%
7	1992	178,998	26,304	KONDNER, KENNETH	152,689	MFUME, KWEISI	5	126,385 D	14.7%	85.3%	14.7%	85.3%
8	2000	300,469	156,241	MORELLA, CONSTANCE A.	136,840	LIERMAN, TERRY	7,388	19,401 R	52.0%	45.5%	53.3%	46.7%
8	1998	220,748	133,145	MORELLA, CONSTANCE A.	87,497	NEAS, RALPH G.	106	45,648 R	60.3%	39.6%	60.3%	39.7%
8	1996	249,146	152,538	MORELLA, CONSTANCE A.	96,229	MOOERS, DONALD	379	56,309 R	61.2%	38.6%	61.3%	38.7%
8	1994	204,109	143,449	MORELLA, CONSTANCE A.	60,660	VANGRACK, STEVEN		82,789 R	70.3%	29.7%	70.3%	29.7%
8	1992	280,475	203,377	MORELLA, CONSTANCE A.	77,042	HEFFERNAN, EDWARD J.	56	126,335 R	72.5%	27.5%	72.5%	27.5%

MARYLAND

GENERAL AND PRIMARY ELECTIONS

2000 GENERAL ELECTIONS

President Other vote was 5,310 Libertarian (Browne); 4,248 Reform (Buchanan); 919 Constitution (Phillips); 176 write-in (Hagelin); 3 write-in (Miller); 3 write-in (Officewala); 3 write-in (Schriner); 2 write-in (Crawford); 2 write-in (Peters); 1 write-in/Democratic (Brown); 1 write-in (Easton); 1 write-in (LaBelle); 1 write-in (Pearlman); 1 write-in (Strickland); 1,462 scattered write-in. Write-in candidates could indicate a party affiliation.

Senator Other vote was 113 write-in/Republican (Vaughn); 1,594 scattered write-in.

Congress Other vote was: CD 1: 73 write-in/Green (Gross), 294 scattered write-in; CD 2: 285 scattered write-in; CD 3: 238 write-in/Libertarian (Pomykala), 406 scattered write-in; CD 4: 13 write-in (Mooney), 359 scattered write-in; CD 5: 125 scattered write-in; CD 6: 82 write-in/Green (McCown), 203 scattered write-in; CD 7: 135 scattered write-in; CD 8: 7,017 Constitution (Saunders), 77 write-in/Democratic (Young), 19 write-in (Walker), 275 scattered write-in.

2000 PRIMARY ELECTIONS

Primary March 7, 2000

Registration
(as of Feb. 29, 2000)

Republican	769,329
Democratic	1,482,530
Libertarian	2,227
Declined and Others	323,024
TOTAL	2,577,110

Primary Type Only registered Democrats could vote in their party's primary. The Republican primary was open to registered Republicans and voters not registered with a recognized political party.

Note: An asterisk (*) denotes incumbent.

	REPUBLICAN PRIMARIES			DEMOCRATIC PRIMARIES		
President	George W. Bush	211,439	56.2%	Al Gore	341,630	67.3%
	John McCain	135,981	36.2%	Bill Bradley	144,387	28.5%
	Alan Keyes	25,020	6.7%	Uncommitted	16,935	3.3%
	Steve Forbes	1,678	0.4%	Lyndon H. LaRouche Jr.	4,510	0.9%
	Gary Bauer	1,328	0.4%			
	Orrin G. Hatch	588	0.2%			
	TOTAL	376,034		TOTAL	507,462	
Senator	Paul H. Rappaport	70,231	22.7%	Paul S. Sarbanes*	384,748	83.2%
	Ron Sobhani	53,084	17.1%	George English	45,984	9.9%
	Ross Z. Pierpont	52,052	16.8%	Sidney Altman	31,502	6.8%
	Robin Ficker	46,995	15.2%			
	Kenneth R. Timmerman	30,146	9.7%			
	Ken Wayman	28,461	9.2%			
	John Stafford	18,656	6.0%			
	Howard David Greyber	10,252	3.3%			
	TOTAL	309,877		TOTAL	462,234	
Congressional District 1	Wayne T. Gilchrest*	49,232	100.0%	Bennett Bozman	14,842	32.0%
				Michael J. Serabian	13,640	29.4%
				John Rea	10,253	22.1%
				Donald David Long	7,636	16.5%
	TOTAL	49,232		TOTAL	46,371	
Congressional District 2	Robert L. Ehrlich Jr.*	43,804	100.0%	Kenneth T. Bosley	21,845	48.0%
				Jake Mohorovic	16,626	36.5%
				Walter Thomas Kuebler	3,833	8.4%
				Edward J. Hornzell	3,186	7.0%
	TOTAL	43,804		TOTAL	45,490	

MARYLAND

GENERAL AND PRIMARY ELECTIONS

	REPUBLICAN PRIMARIES			DEMOCRATIC PRIMARIES		
Congressional District 3	Colin Harby	18,150	100.0%	Benjamin L. Cardin*	56,484	100.0%
	TOTAL	18,150		TOTAL	56,484	
Congressional District 4	John B. Kimble	7,412	100.0%	Albert R. Wynn*	60,873	88.1%
				E. Richard Rosenthal	8,217	11.9%
	TOTAL	7,412		TOTAL	69,090	
Congressional District 5	Thomas E. "Tim" Hutchins	32,344	100.0%	Steny H. Hoyer*	46,599	80.7%
				Bruce M. Ross	11,163	19.3%
	TOTAL	32,344		TOTAL	57,762	
Congressional District 6	Roscoe G. Bartlett*	57,977	77.8%	Donald M. DeArmon	23,089	54.0%
	Timothy R. Mayberry	16,539	22.2%	John Ewald	10,138	23.7%
				Anthony J. McGuffin	5,686	13.3%
				Walter E. Carson	3,868	9.0%
	TOTAL	74,516		TOTAL	42,781	
Congressional District 7	Kenneth Kondner	5,614	76.0%	Elijah E. Cummings*	49,068	100.0%
	Charles U. Smith	1,774	24.0%			
	TOTAL	7,388		TOTAL	49,068	
Congressional District 8	Constance A. Morella*	35,472	100.0%	Terry Lierman	39,904	61.4%
				Deborah A. Vollmer	9,025	13.9%
				K. Joyce Kimble	8,156	12.5%
				Cyrus Homayounpour	4,080	6.3%
				Lih Young	3,847	5.9%
	TOTAL	35,472		TOTAL	65,012	

MASSACHUSETTS

GOVERNOR

Jane Swift (R). Became Acting Governor in April 2001 upon the resignation of Governor Paul Cellucci (R) to become Ambassador to Canada. Cellucci and Swift had been elected to four-year terms in November 1998, Swift as lieutenant governor.

SENATORS

Edward M. Kennedy (D). Re-elected 2000 to a six-year term. Previously elected 1994, 1988, 1982, 1976, 1970, 1964 and in 1962 to fill out term vacated by the December 1960 resignation of Senator John F. Kennedy who was elected President November 1960.

John F. Kerry (D). Re-elected 1996 to a six-year term. Previously elected 1990, 1984.

REPRESENTATIVES

1. John Olver (D)
2. Richard E. Neal (D)
3. Jim McGovern (D)
4. Barney Frank (D)
5. Martin T. Meehan (D)
6. John F. Tierney (D)
7. Edward J. Markey (D)
8. Michael E. Capuano (D)
9. John J. Moakley (D)
10. Bill Delahunt (D)

POSTWAR VOTE FOR PRESIDENT

Year	Total Vote	Republican		Democratic		Other Vote	Plurality	Percentage			
								Total Vote		Major Vote	
		Vote	Candidate	Vote	Candidate			Rep.	Dem.	Rep.	Dem.
2000**	2,702,984	878,502	Bush, George W.	1,616,487	Gore, Al	207,995	737,985 D	32.5%	59.8%	35.2%	64.8%
1996**	2,556,785	718,107	Dole, Bob	1,571,763	Clinton, Bill	266,915	853,656 D	28.1%	61.5%	31.4%	68.6%
1992**	2,773,700	805,049	Bush, George	1,318,662	Clinton, Bill	649,989	513,613 D	29.0%	47.5%	37.9%	62.1%
1988	2,632,805	1,194,635	Bush, George	1,401,415	Dukakis, Michael S.	36,755	206,780 D	45.4%	53.2%	46.0%	54.0%
1984	2,559,453	1,310,936	Reagan, Ronald	1,239,606	Mondale, Walter F.	8,911	71,330 R	51.2%	48.4%	51.4%	48.6%
1980**	2,524,298	1,057,631	Reagan, Ronald	1,053,802	Carter, Jimmy	412,865	3,829 R	41.9%	41.7%	50.1%	49.9%
1976	2,547,558	1,030,276	Ford, Gerald R.	1,429,475	Carter, Jimmy	87,807	399,199 D	40.4%	56.1%	41.9%	58.1%
1972	2,458,756	1,112,078	Nixon, Richard M.	1,332,540	McGovern, George S.	14,138	220,462 D	45.2%	54.2%	45.5%	54.5%
1968	2,331,752	766,844	Nixon, Richard M.	1,469,218	Humphrey, Hubert H.	95,690	702,374 D	32.9%	63.0%	34.3%	65.7%
1964	2,344,798	549,727	Goldwater, Barry M.	1,786,422	Johnson, Lyndon B.	8,649	1,236,695 D	23.4%	76.2%	23.5%	76.5%
1960	2,469,480	976,750	Nixon, Richard M.	1,487,174	Kennedy, John F.	5,556	510,424 D	39.6%	60.2%	39.6%	60.4%
1956	2,348,506	1,393,197	Eisenhower, Dwight D.	948,190	Stevenson, Adlai E.	7,119	445,007 R	59.3%	40.4%	59.5%	40.5%
1952	2,383,398	1,292,325	Eisenhower, Dwight D.	1,083,525	Stevenson, Adlai E.	7,548	208,800 R	54.2%	45.5%	54.4%	45.6%
1948	2,107,146	909,370	Dewey, Thomas E.	1,151,788	Truman, Harry S.	45,988	242,418 D	43.2%	54.7%	44.1%	55.9%

In 2000 the other vote column includes 173,564 votes cast for Green (Nader). In 1996 the other vote column includes 227,217 votes cast for Perot. In 1992 the other vote column includes 630,731 votes cast for Perot. In 1980 the other column includes 382,539 votes for Independent (Anderson).

MASSACHUSETTS

POSTWAR VOTE FOR GOVERNOR

Year	Total Vote	Republican Vote	Republican Candidate	Democratic Vote	Democratic Candidate	Other Vote	Rep.-Dem. Plurality	Total Vote Rep.	Total Vote Dem.	Major Vote Rep.	Major Vote Dem.
1998	1,903,336	967,160	Cellucci, Paul	901,843	Harshbarger, Scott	34,333	65,317 R	50.8%	47.4%	51.7%	48.3%
1994	2,164,318	1,533,430	Weld, William F.	611,650	Roosevelt, Mark	19,238	921,780 R	70.9%	28.3%	71.5%	28.5%
1990	2,342,927	1,175,817	Weld, William F.	1,099,878	Silber, John	67,232	75,939 R	50.2%	46.9%	51.7%	48.3%
1986	1,684,079	525,364	Kariotis, George	1,157,786	Dukakis, Michael S.	929	632,422 D	31.2%	68.7%	31.2%	68.8%
1982	2,050,254	749,679	Sears, John W.	1,219,109	Dukakis, Michael S.	81,466	469,430 D	36.6%	59.5%	38.1%	61.9%
1978	1,962,251	926,072	Hatch, Francis W.	1,030,294	King, Edward J.	5,885	104,222 D	47.2%	52.5%	47.3%	52.7%
1974	1,854,798	784,353	Sargent, Francis W.	992,284	Dukakis, Michael S.	78,161	207,931 D	42.3%	53.5%	44.1%	55.9%
1970	1,867,906	1,058,623	Sargent, Francis W.	799,269	White, Kevin H.	10,014	259,354 R	56.7%	42.8%	57.0%	43.0%
1966**	2,041,177	1,277,358	Volpe, John A.	752,720	McCormack, Edward J.	11,099	524,638 R	62.6%	36.9%	62.9%	37.1%
1964	2,340,130	1,176,462	Volpe, John A.	1,153,416	Bellotti, Francis X.	10,252	23,046 R	50.3%	49.3%	50.5%	49.5%
1962	2,109,089	1,047,891	Volpe, John A.	1,053,322	Peabody, Endicott	7,876	5,431 D	49.7%	49.9%	49.9%	50.1%
1960	2,417,133	1,269,295	Volpe, John A.	1,130,810	Ward, Joseph D.	17,028	138,485 R	52.5%	46.8%	52.9%	47.1%
1958	1,899,117	818,463	Gibbons, Charles	1,067,020	Furcolo, Foster	13,634	248,557 D	43.1%	56.2%	43.4%	56.6%
1956	2,339,884	1,096,759	Whittier, Sumner G.	1,234,618	Furcolo, Foster	8,507	137,859 D	46.9%	52.8%	47.0%	53.0%
1954	1,903,774	985,339	Herter, Christian A.	910,087	Murphy, Robert F.	8,348	75,252 R	51.8%	47.8%	52.0%	48.0%
1952	2,356,298	1,175,955	Herter, Christian A.	1,161,499	Dever, Paul A.	18,844	14,456 R	49.9%	49.3%	50.3%	49.7%
1950	1,910,180	824,069	Coolidge, Arthur W.	1,074,570	Dever, Paul A.	11,541	250,501 D	43.1%	56.3%	43.4%	56.6%
1948	2,099,250	849,895	Bradford, Robert F.	1,239,247	Dever, Paul A.	10,108	389,352 D	40.5%	59.0%	40.7%	59.3%
1946	1,683,452	911,152	Bradford, Robert F.	762,743	Tobin, Maurice	9,557	148,409 R	54.1%	45.3%	54.4%	45.6%

The term of office of Massachusetts' Governor was increased from two to four years effective with the 1966 election.

POSTWAR VOTE FOR SENATOR

Year	Total Vote	Republican Vote	Republican Candidate	Democratic Vote	Democratic Candidate	Other Vote	Rep.-Dem. Plurality	Total Vote Rep.	Total Vote Dem.	Major Vote Rep.	Major Vote Dem.
2000	2,599,420	334,341	Robinson, Jack E.	1,889,494	Kennedy, Edward M.	375,585	1,555,153 D	12.9%	72.7%	15.0%	85.0%
1996	2,555,886	1,142,837	Weld, William F.	1,334,345	Kerry, John F.	78,704	191,508 D	44.7%	52.2%	46.1%	53.9%
1994	2,179,964	894,005	Romney, W. Mitt	1,266,011	Kennedy, Edward M.	19,948	372,006 D	41.0%	58.1%	41.4%	58.6%
1990	2,316,212	992,917	Rappaport, Jim	1,321,712	Kerry, John F.	1,583	328,795 D	42.9%	57.1%	42.9%	57.1%
1988	2,606,225	884,267	Malone, Joseph	1,693,344	Kennedy, Edward M.	28,614	809,077 D	33.9%	65.0%	34.3%	65.7%
1984	2,530,195	1,136,806	Shamie, Raymond	1,392,981	Kerry, John F.	408	256,175 D	44.9%	55.1%	44.9%	55.1%
1982	2,050,769	784,602	Shamie, Raymond	1,247,084	Kennedy, Edward M.	19,083	462,482 D	38.3%	60.8%	38.6%	61.4%
1978	1,985,700	890,584	Brooke, Edward W.	1,093,283	Tsongas, Paul E.	1,833	202,699 D	44.8%	55.1%	44.9%	55.1%
1976	2,491,255	722,641	Robertson, Michael	1,726,657	Kennedy, Edward M.	41,957	1,004,016 D	29.0%	69.3%	29.5%	70.5%
1972	2,370,676	1,505,932	Brooke, Edward W.	823,278	Droney, John J.	41,466	682,654 R	63.5%	34.7%	64.7%	35.3%
1970	1,935,607	715,978	Spaulding, Josiah A.	1,202,856	Kennedy, Edward M.	16,773	486,878 D	37.0%	62.1%	37.3%	62.7%
1966	1,999,949	1,213,473	Brooke, Edward W.	774,761	Peabody, Endicott	11,715	438,712 R	60.7%	38.7%	61.0%	39.0%
1964	2,312,028	587,663	Whitmore, Howard	1,716,907	Kennedy, Edward M.	7,458	1,129,244 D	25.4%	74.3%	25.5%	74.5%
1962S	2,097,085	877,669	Lodge, George C.	1,162,611	Kennedy, Edward M.	56,805	284,942 D	41.9%	55.4%	43.0%	57.0%
1960	2,417,813	1,358,556	Saltonstall, Leverett	1,050,725	O'Connor, Thomas J.	8,532	307,831 R	56.2%	43.5%	56.4%	43.6%
1958	1,862,041	488,318	Celeste, Vincent J.	1,362,926	Kennedy, John F.	10,797	874,608 D	26.2%	73.2%	26.4%	73.6%
1954	1,892,710	956,605	Saltonstall, Leverett	927,899	Furcolo, Foster	8,206	28,706 R	50.5%	49.0%	50.8%	49.2%
1952	2,360,425	1,141,247	Lodge, Henry Cabot	1,211,984	Kennedy, John F.	7,194	70,737 D	48.3%	51.3%	48.5%	51.5%
1948	2,055,798	1,088,475	Saltonstall, Leverett	954,398	Fitzgerald, John I.	12,925	134,077 R	52.9%	46.4%	53.3%	46.7%
1946	1,662,063	989,736	Lodge, Henry Cabot	660,200	Walsh, David I.	12,127	329,536 R	59.5%	39.7%	60.0%	40.0%

The 1962 election was for a short term to fill a vacancy.

MASSACHUSETTS

Districts Established July 9, 1992

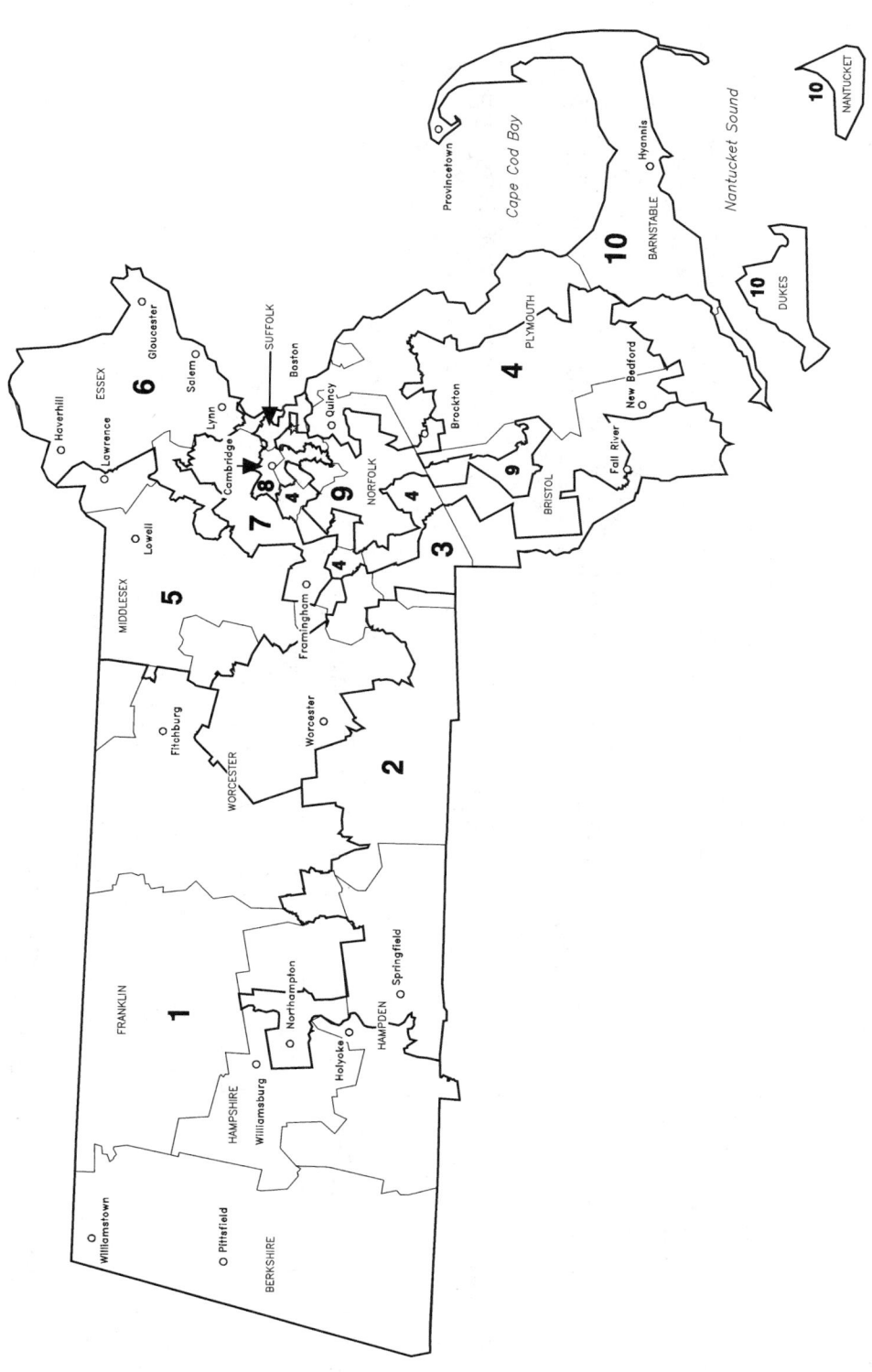

MASSACHUSETTS

PRESIDENT 2000

2000 Census Population	County	Total Vote	Republican	Democratic	Green (Nader)	Other	Rep.-Dem. Plurality	Percentage of Total Vote		
								Rep.	Dem.	Green
222,230	BARNSTABLE	121,086	49,686	62,363	7,976	1,061	12,677 D	41.0%	51.5%	6.6%
134,953	BERKSHIRE	59,411	15,805	37,934	4,472	1,200	22,129 D	26.6%	63.9%	7.5%
534,678	BRISTOL	211,337	62,848	136,325	9,554	2,610	73,477 D	29.7%	64.5%	4.5%
14,987	DUKES	8,856	2,315	5,474	983	84	3,159 D	26.1%	61.8%	11.1%
723,419	ESSEX	310,333	110,010	178,400	17,955	3,968	68,390 D	35.4%	57.5%	5.8%
71,535	FRANKLIN	33,366	10,176	17,945	4,627	618	7,769 D	30.5%	53.8%	13.9%
456,228	HAMPDEN	172,093	59,558	100,103	10,326	2,106	40,545 D	34.6%	58.2%	6.0%
152,251	HAMPSHIRE	68,626	19,202	38,543	10,010	871	19,341 D	28.0%	56.2%	14.6%
1,465,396	MIDDLESEX	657,048	198,914	404,043	45,529	8,562	205,129 D	30.3%	61.5%	6.9%
9,520	NANTUCKET	4,926	1,624	2,874	378	50	1,250 D	33.0%	58.3%	7.7%
650,308	NORFOLK	317,177	107,033	188,450	17,505	4,189	81,417 D	33.7%	59.4%	5.5%
472,822	PLYMOUTH	211,577	82,751	115,376	11,021	2,429	32,625 D	39.1%	54.5%	5.2%
689,807	SUFFOLK	217,000	44,441	154,888	15,051	2,620	110,447 D	20.5%	71.4%	6.9%
750,963	WORCESTER	310,148	114,139	173,769	18,177	4,063	59,630 D	36.8%	56.0%	5.9%
6,349,097	TOTAL	2,702,984	878,502	1,616,487	173,564	34,431	737,985 D	32.5%	59.8%	6.4%

	City/Town									
20,331	ACTON	10,382	3,457	5,993	814	118	2,536 D	33.3%	57.7%	7.8%
28,144	AGAWAM	12,792	4,859	7,017	749	167	2,158 D	38.0%	54.9%	5.9%
34,874	AMHERST	11,779	1,593	7,061	2,950	175	5,468 D	13.5%	59.9%	25.0%
31,247	ANDOVER	16,429	7,323	7,899	1,042	165	576 D	44.6%	48.1%	6.3%
42,389	ARLINGTON	24,117	6,026	15,550	2,203	338	9,524 D	25.0%	64.5%	9.1%
42,068	ATTLEBORO	15,670	5,679	8,924	791	276	3,245 D	36.2%	56.9%	5.0%
47,821	BARNSTABLE	24,008	10,237	12,080	1,467	224	1,843 D	42.6%	50.3%	6.1%
24,194	BELMONT	13,594	4,412	7,997	1,038	147	3,585 D	32.5%	58.8%	7.6%
39,862	BEVERLY	18,762	6,540	10,803	1,187	232	4,263 D	34.9%	57.6%	6.3%
38,981	BILLERICA	16,762	6,079	9,536	893	254	3,457 D	36.3%	56.9%	5.3%
589,141	BOSTON	184,603	36,389	132,393	13,588	2,233	96,004 D	19.7%	71.7%	7.4%
33,828	BRAINTREE	17,434	6,335	10,038	857	204	3,703 D	36.3%	57.6%	4.9%
94,304	BROCKTON	28,287	8,288	18,563	1,096	340	10,275 D	29.3%	65.6%	3.9%
57,107	BROOKLINE	26,082	4,350	19,384	2,137	211	15,034 D	16.7%	74.3%	8.2%
22,876	BURLINGTON	11,467	4,254	6,507	562	144	2,253 D	37.1%	56.7%	4.9%
101,355	CAMBRIDGE	39,985	5,166	28,846	5,469	504	23,680 D	12.9%	72.1%	13.7%
20,775	CANTON	10,924	3,948	6,320	543	113	2,372 D	36.1%	57.9%	5.0%
33,858	CHELMSFORD	17,221	6,997	8,978	991	255	1,981 D	40.6%	52.1%	5.8%
54,653	CHICOPEE	21,276	6,512	13,236	1,179	349	6,724 D	30.6%	62.2%	5.5%
16,993	CONCORD	9,702	3,178	5,534	861	129	2,356 D	32.8%	57.0%	8.9%
25,212	DANVERS	12,644	5,008	6,855	659	122	1,847 D	39.6%	54.2%	5.2%
30,666	DARTMOUTH	13,526	3,916	8,800	661	149	4,884 D	29.0%	65.1%	4.9%
23,464	DEDHAM	11,955	4,110	7,028	645	172	2,918 D	34.4%	58.8%	5.4%
28,562	DRACUT	12,845	4,810	7,270	598	167	2,460 D	37.4%	56.6%	4.7%
22,299	EASTON	10,675	4,379	5,675	500	121	1,296 D	41.0%	53.2%	4.7%
38,037	EVERETT	13,306	3,239	9,342	559	166	6,103 D	24.3%	70.2%	4.2%
91,938	FALL RIVER	29,015	5,621	22,051	1,002	341	16,430 D	19.4%	76.0%	3.5%
32,660	FALMOUTH	17,631	6,414	9,835	1,226	156	3,421 D	36.4%	55.8%	7.0%
39,102	FITCHBURG	12,476	3,839	7,773	657	207	3,934 D	30.8%	62.3%	5.3%
66,910	FRAMINGHAM	26,417	7,347	17,308	1,429	333	9,961 D	27.8%	65.5%	5.4%
29,560	FRANKLIN	13,914	5,213	7,882	674	145	2,669 D	37.5%	56.6%	4.8%
30,273	GLOUCESTER	13,667	4,156	8,352	987	172	4,196 D	30.4%	61.1%	7.2%
58,969	HAVERHILL	22,239	7,761	12,926	1,250	302	5,165 D	34.9%	58.1%	5.6%
19,882	HINGHAM	11,507	5,116	5,681	610	100	565 D	44.5%	49.4%	5.3%
39,838	HOLYOKE	13,771	3,989	8,703	855	224	4,714 D	29.0%	63.2%	6.2%
72,043	LAWRENCE	14,519	3,700	10,048	569	202	6,348 D	25.5%	69.2%	3.9%
41,303	LEOMINSTER	15,995	5,597	9,399	736	263	3,802 D	35.0%	58.8%	4.6%
30,355	LEXINGTON	16,751	4,741	10,623	1,215	172	5,882 D	28.3%	63.4%	7.3%
105,167	LOWELL	27,147	7,790	17,554	1,341	462	9,764 D	28.7%	64.7%	4.9%
89,050	LYNN	27,350	6,776	18,836	1,356	382	12,060 D	24.8%	68.9%	5.0%

MASSACHUSETTS

PRESIDENT 2000

2000 Census Population	City/Town	Total Vote	Republican	Democratic	Green (Nader)	Other	Rep.-Dem. Plurality	Percentage of Total Vote		
								Rep.	Dem.	Green
56,340	MALDEN	19,657	4,627	13,737	999	294	9,110 D	23.5%	69.9%	5.1%
20,377	MARBLEHEAD	11,814	4,442	6,486	759	127	2,044 D	37.6%	54.9%	6.4%
36,255	MARLBOROUGH	14,474	5,218	8,194	849	213	2,976 D	36.1%	56.6%	5.9%
24,324	MARSHFIELD	12,255	4,893	6,478	788	96	1,585 D	39.9%	52.9%	6.4%
55,765	MEDFORD	24,976	6,353	16,776	1,505	342	10,423 D	25.4%	67.2%	6.0%
27,134	MELROSE	14,405	4,705	8,647	879	174	3,942 D	32.7%	60.0%	6.1%
43,789	METHUEN	17,369	6,751	9,465	940	213	2,714 D	38.9%	54.5%	5.4%
26,799	MILFORD	11,308	3,646	7,007	539	116	3,361 D	32.2%	62.0%	4.8%
26,062	MILTON	14,304	5,068	8,292	800	144	3,224 D	35.4%	58.0%	5.6%
32,170	NATICK	17,106	5,309	10,469	1,072	256	5,160 D	31.0%	61.2%	6.3%
28,911	NEEDHAM	16,157	5,480	9,686	833	158	4,206 D	33.9%	59.9%	5.2%
93,768	NEW BEDFORD	30,888	5,473	23,880	1,068	467	18,407 D	17.7%	77.3%	3.5%
83,829	NEWTON	41,004	8,132	29,918	2,579	375	21,786 D	19.8%	73.0%	6.3%
27,202	NORTH ANDOVER	13,060	5,927	6,292	719	122	365 D	45.4%	48.2%	5.5%
27,143	NORTH ATTLEBOROUGH	12,116	4,980	6,351	622	163	1,371 D	41.1%	52.4%	5.1%
28,978	NORTHAMPTON	14,216	2,648	8,716	2,680	172	6,068 D	18.6%	61.3%	18.9%
28,587	NORWOOD	13,785	4,783	8,056	763	183	3,273 D	34.7%	58.4%	5.5%
48,129	PEABODY	23,131	6,789	15,078	925	339	8,289 D	29.4%	65.2%	4.0%
45,793	PITTSFIELD	18,567	4,402	12,572	1,092	501	8,170 D	23.7%	67.7%	5.9%
51,701	PLYMOUTH	23,352	8,964	12,865	1,269	254	3,901 D	38.4%	55.1%	5.4%
88,025	QUINCY	37,552	11,282	23,117	2,064	1,089	11,835 D	30.0%	61.6%	5.5%
30,963	RANDOLPH	12,763	3,040	9,140	468	115	6,100 D	23.8%	71.6%	3.7%
23,708	READING	12,559	4,690	6,995	725	149	2,305 D	37.3%	55.7%	5.8%
47,283	REVERE	17,261	4,232	12,151	683	195	7,919 D	24.5%	70.4%	4.0%
40,407	SALEM	16,855	4,380	11,173	1,059	243	6,793 D	26.0%	66.3%	6.3%
26,078	SAUGUS	12,867	4,198	7,941	591	137	3,743 D	32.6%	61.7%	4.6%
17,863	SCITUATE	10,481	4,384	5,300	659	138	916 D	41.8%	50.6%	6.3%
31,640	SHREWSBURY	15,182	6,044	8,168	829	141	2,124 D	39.8%	53.8%	5.5%
77,478	SOMERVILLE	28,844	4,468	19,984	3,968	424	15,516 D	15.5%	69.3%	13.8%
152,082	SPRINGFIELD	42,656	10,288	29,728	2,205	435	19,440 D	24.1%	69.7%	5.2%
22,219	STONEHAM	11,199	3,681	6,878	520	120	3,197 D	32.9%	61.4%	4.6%
27,149	STOUGHTON	12,515	3,668	8,191	534	122	4,523 D	29.3%	65.4%	4.3%
55,976	TAUNTON	19,793	5,816	12,886	894	197	7,070 D	29.4%	65.1%	4.5%
28,851	TEWKSBURY	13,740	5,252	7,685	628	175	2,433 D	38.2%	55.9%	4.6%
24,804	WAKEFIELD	13,153	4,534	7,742	722	155	3,208 D	34.5%	58.9%	5.5%
22,824	WALPOLE	11,954	4,974	6,164	659	157	1,190 D	41.6%	51.6%	5.5%
59,226	WALTHAM	22,108	6,700	13,736	1,408	264	7,036 D	30.3%	62.1%	6.4%
32,986	WATERTOWN	15,329	3,846	10,050	1,249	184	6,204 D	25.1%	65.6%	8.1%
26,613	WELLESLEY	13,697	5,439	7,266	850	142	1,827 D	39.7%	53.0%	6.2%
27,899	WEST SPRINGFIELD	11,725	4,577	6,163	817	168	1,586 D	39.0%	52.6%	7.0%
40,072	WESTFIELD	15,429	6,457	7,714	1,063	195	1,257 D	41.8%	50.0%	6.9%
53,988	WEYMOUTH	26,140	8,884	15,570	1,408	278	6,686 D	34.0%	59.6%	5.4%
20,810	WINCHESTER	11,768	4,596	6,258	809	105	1,662 D	39.1%	53.2%	6.9%
37,258	WOBURN	16,870	5,806	10,071	764	229	4,265 D	34.4%	59.7%	4.5%
172,648	WORCESTER	53,702	14,402	35,231	3,474	595	20,829 D	26.8%	65.6%	6.5%
24,807	YARMOUTH	13,505	5,799	6,881	714	111	1,082 D	42.9%	51.0%	5.3%

MASSACHUSETTS

SENATOR 2000

2000 Census Population	County	Total Vote	Republican	Democratic	Libertarian (Howell)	Other	Rep.-Dem. Plurality	Percentage of Total Vote		
								Rep.	Dem.	Lib.
222,230	BARNSTABLE	117,017	19,460	79,222	14,326	4,009	59,762 D	16.6%	67.7%	12.2%
134,953	BERKSHIRE	57,313	7,859	45,259	2,917	1,278	37,400 D	13.7%	79.0%	5.1%
534,678	BRISTOL	204,376	28,053	153,422	19,017	3,884	125,369 D	13.7%	75.1%	9.3%
14,987	DUKES	8,571	991	6,641	753	186	5,650 D	11.6%	77.5%	8.8%
723,419	ESSEX	298,836	41,174	213,609	37,740	6,313	172,435 D	13.8%	71.5%	12.6%
71,535	FRANKLIN	32,590	4,865	22,505	4,156	1,064	17,640 D	14.9%	69.1%	12.8%
456,228	HAMPDEN	165,112	30,523	116,894	11,079	6,616	86,371 D	18.5%	70.8%	6.7%
152,251	HAMPSHIRE	65,904	9,695	47,896	6,530	1,783	38,201 D	14.7%	72.7%	9.9%
1,465,396	MIDDLESEX	632,854	68,517	470,257	80,365	13,715	401,740 D	10.8%	74.3%	12.7%
9,520	NANTUCKET	4,761	841	3,441	396	83	2,600 D	17.7%	72.3%	8.3%
650,308	NORFOLK	305,262	36,374	221,390	39,323	8,175	185,016 D	11.9%	72.5%	12.9%
472,822	PLYMOUTH	204,614	29,443	139,443	31,005	4,723	110,000 D	14.4%	68.1%	15.2%
689,807	SUFFOLK	202,266	18,684	162,406	16,798	4,378	143,722 D	9.2%	80.3%	8.3%
750,963	WORCESTER	299,944	37,862	207,109	44,455	10,518	169,247 D	12.6%	69.0%	14.8%
6,349,097	TOTAL	2,599,420	334,341	1,889,494	308,860	66,725	1,555,153 D	12.9%	72.7%	11.9%
	City/Town									
20,331	ACTON	10,003	1,277	7,034	1,503	189	5,757 D	12.8%	70.3%	15.0%
28,144	AGAWAM	11,888	2,197	8,154	914	623	5,957 D	18.5%	68.6%	7.7%
34,874	AMHERST	10,767	842	8,316	1,393	216	7,474 D	7.8%	77.2%	12.9%
31,247	ANDOVER	15,641	2,771	10,125	2,395	350	7,354 D	17.7%	64.7%	15.3%
42,389	ARLINGTON	23,351	2,116	18,176	2,486	573	16,060 D	9.1%	77.8%	10.6%
42,068	ATTLEBORO	15,135	2,729	10,355	1,649	402	7,626 D	18.0%	68.4%	10.9%
47,821	BARNSTABLE	23,245	3,824	15,928	2,623	870	12,104 D	16.5%	68.5%	11.3%
24,194	BELMONT	13,009	1,459	9,720	1,495	335	8,261 D	11.2%	74.7%	11.5%
39,862	BEVERLY	18,118	2,423	13,098	2,176	421	10,675 D	13.4%	72.3%	12.0%
38,981	BILLERICA	16,259	2,191	11,287	2,431	350	9,096 D	13.5%	69.4%	15.0%
589,141	BOSTON	171,196	15,942	137,782	13,742	3,730	121,840 D	9.3%	80.5%	8.0%
33,828	BRAINTREE	16,765	2,094	12,068	2,071	532	9,974 D	12.5%	72.0%	12.4%
94,304	BROCKTON	27,473	3,058	20,546	3,364	505	17,488 D	11.1%	74.8%	12.2%
57,107	BROOKLINE	24,886	1,941	20,809	1,851	285	18,868 D	7.8%	83.6%	7.4%
22,876	BURLINGTON	11,117	1,354	7,875	1,631	257	6,521 D	12.2%	70.8%	14.7%
101,355	CAMBRIDGE	38,599	2,610	32,759	2,676	554	30,149 D	6.8%	84.9%	6.9%
20,775	CANTON	10,549	1,252	7,640	1,411	246	6,388 D	11.9%	72.4%	13.4%
33,858	CHELMSFORD	16,514	2,262	11,147	2,702	403	8,885 D	13.7%	67.5%	16.4%
54,653	CHICOPEE	20,665	3,322	15,126	1,317	900	11,804 D	16.1%	73.2%	6.4%
16,993	CONCORD	9,239	1,174	6,613	1,268	184	5,439 D	12.7%	71.6%	13.7%
25,212	DANVERS	12,210	1,813	8,480	1,666	251	6,667 D	14.8%	69.5%	13.6%
30,666	DARTMOUTH	13,049	1,784	9,900	1,195	170	8,116 D	13.7%	75.9%	9.2%
23,464	DEDHAM	11,517	1,295	8,277	1,457	488	6,982 D	11.2%	71.9%	12.7%
28,562	DRACUT	12,461	1,585	8,925	1,661	290	7,340 D	12.7%	71.6%	13.3%
22,299	EASTON	10,276	1,482	6,749	1,844	201	5,267 D	14.4%	65.7%	17.9%
38,037	EVERETT	12,700	1,124	10,055	1,243	278	8,931 D	8.9%	79.2%	9.8%
91,938	FALL RIVER	27,964	2,565	23,592	1,342	465	21,027 D	9.2%	84.4%	4.8%
32,660	FALMOUTH	17,012	2,536	12,064	1,849	563	9,528 D	14.9%	70.9%	10.9%
39,102	FITCHBURG	12,216	1,308	8,976	1,554	378	7,668 D	10.7%	73.5%	12.7%
66,910	FRAMINGHAM	25,603	2,453	19,231	3,351	568	16,778 D	9.6%	75.1%	13.1%
29,560	FRANKLIN	13,442	1,751	9,426	1,989	276	7,675 D	13.0%	70.1%	14.8%
30,273	GLOUCESTER	13,208	1,564	9,919	1,516	209	8,355 D	11.8%	75.1%	11.5%
58,969	HAVERHILL	21,389	3,144	15,138	2,658	449	11,994 D	14.7%	70.8%	12.4%
19,882	HINGHAM	10,920	1,776	7,351	1,515	278	5,575 D	16.3%	67.3%	13.9%
39,838	HOLYOKE	13,290	1,957	10,081	727	525	8,124 D	14.7%	75.9%	5.5%
72,043	LAWRENCE	13,809	1,480	10,851	1,174	304	9,371 D	10.7%	78.6%	8.5%
41,303	LEOMINSTER	15,644	1,898	11,029	2,229	488	9,131 D	12.1%	70.5%	14.2%
30,355	LEXINGTON	16,094	1,685	12,327	1,813	269	10,642 D	10.5%	76.6%	11.3%
105,167	LOWELL	26,344	2,734	20,347	2,797	466	17,613 D	10.4%	77.2%	10.6%
89,050	LYNN	26,601	2,445	21,031	2,521	604	18,586 D	9.2%	79.1%	9.5%

MASSACHUSETTS

SENATOR 2000

2000 Census Population	City/Town	Total Vote	Republican	Democratic	Libertarian (Howell)	Other	Rep.-Dem. Plurality	Percentage of Total Vote		
								Rep.	Dem.	Lib.
56,340	MALDEN	18,996	1,733	15,180	1,658	425	13,447 D	9.1%	79.9%	8.7%
20,377	MARBLEHEAD	11,297	1,591	7,895	1,655	156	6,304 D	14.1%	69.9%	14.6%
36,255	MARLBOROUGH	14,085	1,601	9,892	2,235	357	8,291 D	11.4%	70.2%	15.9%
24,324	MARSHFIELD	11,920	1,658	8,223	1,751	288	6,565 D	13.9%	69.0%	14.7%
55,765	MEDFORD	24,193	2,138	18,931	2,487	637	16,793 D	8.8%	78.2%	10.3%
27,134	MELROSE	13,883	1,569	10,373	1,634	307	8,804 D	11.3%	74.7%	11.8%
43,789	METHUEN	16,673	2,568	11,455	2,228	422	8,887 D	15.4%	68.7%	13.4%
26,799	MILFORD	10,983	1,199	8,204	1,383	197	7,005 D	10.9%	74.7%	12.6%
26,062	MILTON	13,625	1,463	10,203	1,540	419	8,740 D	10.7%	74.9%	11.3%
32,170	NATICK	16,577	1,757	12,120	2,321	379	10,363 D	10.6%	73.1%	14.0%
28,911	NEEDHAM	15,523	1,898	11,422	1,801	402	9,524 D	12.2%	73.6%	11.6%
93,768	NEW BEDFORD	30,020	2,520	25,367	1,660	473	22,847 D	8.4%	84.5%	5.5%
83,829	NEWTON	39,406	3,087	32,328	3,468	523	29,241 D	7.8%	82.0%	8.8%
27,202	NORTH ANDOVER	12,459	2,310	8,089	1,786	274	5,779 D	18.5%	64.9%	14.3%
27,143	NORTH ATTLEBOROUGH	11,710	2,120	7,746	1,569	275	5,626 D	18.1%	66.1%	13.4%
28,978	NORTHAMPTON	13,796	1,239	11,126	1,190	241	9,887 D	9.0%	80.6%	8.6%
28,587	NORWOOD	13,274	1,489	9,639	1,724	422	8,150 D	11.2%	72.6%	13.0%
48,129	PEABODY	22,490	2,354	17,259	2,439	438	14,905 D	10.5%	76.7%	10.8%
45,793	PITTSFIELD	17,660	1,921	14,473	846	420	12,552 D	10.9%	82.0%	4.8%
51,701	PLYMOUTH	22,671	3,166	15,529	3,377	599	12,363 D	14.0%	68.5%	14.9%
88,025	QUINCY	36,134	3,922	26,648	3,977	1,587	22,726 D	10.9%	73.7%	11.0%
30,963	RANDOLPH	12,445	1,150	9,880	1,191	224	8,730 D	9.2%	79.4%	9.6%
23,708	READING	12,091	1,678	8,511	1,578	324	6,833 D	13.9%	70.4%	13.1%
47,283	REVERE	16,540	1,444	13,102	1,639	355	11,658 D	8.7%	79.2%	9.9%
40,407	SALEM	16,406	1,559	12,794	1,743	310	11,235 D	9.5%	78.0%	10.6%
26,078	SAUGUS	12,387	1,492	9,280	1,370	245	7,788 D	12.0%	74.9%	11.1%
17,863	SCITUATE	10,071	1,383	6,815	1,566	307	5,432 D	13.7%	67.7%	15.5%
31,640	SHREWSBURY	14,582	1,974	10,192	1,912	504	8,218 D	13.5%	69.9%	13.1%
77,478	SOMERVILLE	27,925	1,771	23,004	2,278	872	21,233 D	6.3%	82.4%	8.2%
152,082	SPRINGFIELD	41,174	5,060	32,825	1,927	1,362	27,765 D	12.3%	79.7%	4.7%
22,219	STONEHAM	10,831	1,245	8,168	1,212	206	6,923 D	11.5%	75.4%	11.2%
27,149	STOUGHTON	12,204	1,310	8,985	1,692	217	7,675 D	10.7%	73.6%	13.9%
55,976	TAUNTON	19,086	2,205	14,563	1,946	372	12,358 D	11.6%	76.3%	10.2%
28,851	TEWKSBURY	13,273	1,684	9,398	1,911	280	7,714 D	12.7%	70.8%	14.4%
24,804	WAKEFIELD	12,699	1,548	9,354	1,530	267	7,806 D	12.2%	73.7%	12.0%
22,824	WALPOLE	11,439	1,501	7,991	1,616	331	6,490 D	13.1%	69.9%	14.1%
59,226	WALTHAM	20,730	2,038	15,431	2,802	459	13,393 D	9.8%	74.4%	13.5%
32,986	WATERTOWN	14,884	1,398	11,731	1,471	284	10,333 D	9.4%	78.8%	9.9%
26,613	WELLESLEY	12,998	1,983	8,911	1,805	299	6,928 D	15.3%	68.6%	13.9%
27,899	WEST SPRINGFIELD	10,901	2,050	7,373	861	617	5,323 D	18.8%	67.6%	7.9%
40,072	WESTFIELD	14,939	3,669	9,633	1,099	538	5,964 D	24.6%	64.5%	7.4%
53,988	WEYMOUTH	25,269	2,968	18,371	3,180	750	15,403 D	11.7%	72.7%	12.6%
20,810	WINCHESTER	11,251	1,514	7,918	1,532	287	6,404 D	13.5%	70.4%	13.6%
37,258	WOBURN	16,085	1,770	11,654	2,167	494	9,884 D	11.0%	72.5%	13.5%
172,648	WORCESTER	51,911	5,029	39,898	5,118	1,866	34,869 D	9.7%	76.9%	9.9%
24,807	YARMOUTH	13,015	2,262	8,798	1,486	469	6,536 D	17.4%	67.6%	11.4%

MASSACHUSETTS

CONGRESS

CD	Year	Total Vote	Republican Vote	Republican Candidate	Democratic Vote	Democratic Candidate	Other Vote	Rep.-Dem. Plurality	Total Vote Rep.	Total Vote Dem.	Major Vote Rep.	Major Vote Dem.
1	2000	248,201	73,580	ABAIR, PETER J.	169,375	OLVER, JOHN	5,246	95,795 D	29.6%	68.2%	30.3%	69.7%
1	1998	169,976	48,055	MORGAN, GREGORY L.	121,863	OLVER, JOHN	58	73,808 D	28.3%	71.7%	28.3%	71.7%
1	1996	245,144	115,805	SWIFT, JANE MARIA	129,261	OLVER, JOHN	78	13,456 D	47.2%	52.7%	47.3%	52.7%
1	1994	151,018			150,047	OLVER, JOHN	971	150,047 D		99.4%		100.0%
1	1992	262,120	113,828	LARKIN, PATRICK	135,049	OLVER, JOHN	13,243	21,221 D	43.4%	51.5%	45.7%	54.3%
2	2000	198,846			196,670	NEAL, RICHARD E.	2,176	196,670 D		98.9%		100.0%
2	1998	131,933			130,550	NEAL, RICHARD E.	1,383	130,550 D		99.0%		100.0%
2	1996	227,430	49,887	STEELE, MARK	163,010	NEAL, RICHARD E.	14,533	113,123 D	21.9%	71.7%	23.4%	76.6%
2	1994	200,077	72,732	BRIARE, JOHN M.	117,178	NEAL, RICHARD E.	10,167	44,446 D	36.4%	58.6%	38.3%	61.7%
2	1992	247,151	76,795	RAVOSA, ANTHONY W.	131,215	NEAL, RICHARD E.	39,141	54,420 D	31.1%	53.1%	36.9%	63.1%
3	2000	215,561			213,065	MCGOVERN, JAMES	2,496	213,065 D		98.8%		100.0%
3	1998	190,878	79,174	AMORELLO, MATTHEW J.	108,613	MCGOVERN, JAMES	3,091	29,439 D	41.5%	56.9%	42.2%	57.8%
3	1996	255,102	115,695	BLUTE, PETER	135,047	MCGOVERN, JAMES	4,360	19,352 D	45.4%	52.9%	46.1%	53.9%
3	1994	212,035	115,810	BLUTE, PETER	93,689	O'SULLIVAN, KEVIN	2,536	4,360 R	54.6%	44.2%	55.3%	44.7%
3	1992	260,941	131,476	BLUTE, PETER	115,592	EARLY, JOSEPH D.	13,873	15,884 R	50.4%	44.3%	53.2%	46.8%
4	2000	267,880	56,553	TRAVIS, MARTIN D.	200,638	FRANK, BARNEY	10,689	144,085 D	21.1%	74.9%	22.0%	78.0%
4	1998	150,720			148,340	FRANK, BARNEY	2,380	148,340 D		98.4%		100.0%
4	1996	256,648	72,702	RAYMOND, JONATHAN P.	183,854	FRANK, BARNEY	92	111,152 D	28.3%	71.6%	28.3%	71.7%
4	1994	169,795			168,942	FRANK, BARNEY	853	168,942 D		99.5%		100.0%
4	1992	269,814	70,666	MCCORMICK, EDWARD J., III	182,633	FRANK, BARNEY	16,515	111,967 D	26.2%	67.7%	27.9%	72.1%
5	2000	203,641			199,601	MEEHAN, MARTIN T.	4,040	199,601 D		98.0%		100.0%
5	1998	180,230	52,725	COLEMAN, DAVID E.	127,418	MEEHAN, MARTIN T.	87	74,693 D	29.3%	70.7%	29.3%	70.7%
5	1996	185,165			183,457	MEEHAN, MARTIN T.	1,708	183,457 D		99.1%		100.0%
5	1994	201,459	60,734	COLEMAN, DAVID E.	140,725	MEEHAN, MARTIN T.		79,991 D	30.1%	69.9%	30.1%	69.9%
5	1992	256,564	96,206	CRONIN, PAUL W.	133,844	MEEHAN, MARTIN T.	26,514	37,638 D	37.5%	52.2%	41.8%	58.2%
6	2000	289,043	83,501	MCCARTHY, PAUL	205,324	TIERNEY, JOHN F.	218	121,823 D	28.9%	71.0%	28.9%	71.1%
6	1998	214,706	90,986	TORKILDSEN, PETER	117,132	TIERNEY, JOHN F.	6,588	26,146 D	42.4%	54.6%	43.7%	56.3%
6	1996	277,451	133,315	TORKILDSEN, PETER	133,687	TIERNEY, JOHN F.	10,449	372 D	48.0%	48.2%	49.9%	50.1%
6	1994	239,393	120,952	TORKILDSEN, PETER	113,481	TIERNEY, JOHN F.	4,960	7,471 R	50.5%	47.4%	51.6%	48.4%
6	1992	290,312	159,165	TORKILDSEN, PETER	130,248	MAVROULES, NICHOLAS	899	28,917 R	54.8%	44.9%	55.0%	45.0%
7	2000	213,811			211,543	MARKEY, EDWARD J.	2,268	211,543 D		98.9%		100.0%
7	1998	194,305	56,977	LONG, PATRICIA	137,178	MARKEY, EDWARD J.	150	80,201 D	29.3%	70.6%	29.3%	70.7%
7	1996	253,570	76,407	LONG, PATRICIA	177,053	MARKEY, EDWARD J.	110	100,646 D	30.1%	69.8%	30.1%	69.9%
7	1994	226,920	80,674	BAILEY, BRAD	146,246	MARKEY, EDWARD J.		65,572 D	35.6%	64.4%	35.6%	64.4%
7	1992	281,558	78,262	SOHN, STEPHEN A.	174,837	MARKEY, EDWARD J.	28,459	96,575 D	27.8%	62.1%	30.9%	69.1%
8	2000	145,072			144,031	CAPUANO, MICHAEL E.	1,041	144,031 D		99.3%		100.0%
8	1998	121,887	14,125	HYDE, PHILIP	99,603	CAPUANO, MICHAEL E.	8,159	85,478 D	11.6%	81.7%	12.4%	87.6%
8	1996	174,752	27,315	HYDE, PHILIP	147,246	KENNEDY, JOSEPH P.	191	119,931 D	15.6%	84.3%	15.6%	84.4%
8	1994	114,423			113,224	KENNEDY, JOSEPH P.	1,199	113,224 D		99.0%		100.0%
8	1992	180,492			149,907	KENNEDY, JOSEPH P.	30,585	149,907 D		83.1%		100.0%
9	2000	248,756	48,672	JEGHELIAN, JANET E.	193,020	MOAKLEY, JOHN J.	7,064	144,348 D	19.6%	77.6%	20.1%	79.9%
9	1998	151,555			150,667	MOAKLEY, JOHN J.	888	150,667 D		99.4%		100.0%
9	1996	238,158	66,080	GRYSKA, PAUL	172,012	MOAKLEY, JOHN J.	66	105,932 D	27.7%	72.2%	27.8%	72.2%
9	1994	209,656	63,369	MURPHY, MICHAEL M.	146,287	MOAKLEY, JOHN J.		82,918 D	30.2%	69.8%	30.2%	69.8%
9	1992	253,634	54,291	CONBOY, MARTIN D.	175,550	MOAKLEY, JOHN J.	23,793	121,259 D	21.4%	69.2%	23.6%	76.4%
10	2000	316,564	81,192	BLEICKEN, ERIC V.	234,675	DELAHUNT, BILL	697	153,483 D	25.6%	74.1%	25.7%	74.3%
10	1998	235,563	70,466	BLEICKEN, ERIC V.	164,917	DELAHUNT, BILL	180	94,451 D	29.9%	70.0%	29.9%	70.1%
10	1996	295,932	123,523	TEAGUE, EDWARD	160,747	DELAHUNT, BILL	11,662	37,224 D	41.7%	54.3%	43.5%	56.5%
10	1994	251,240	78,487	HEMEON, KEITH J.	172,753	STUDDS, GERRY E.		94,266 D	31.2%	68.8%	31.2%	68.8%
10	1992	311,651	75,887	DALY, DANIEL W.	189,343	STUDDS, GERRY E.	46,421	113,456 D	24.3%	60.8%	28.6%	71.4%

MASSACHUSETTS

GENERAL AND PRIMARY ELECTIONS

2000 GENERAL ELECTIONS

President Other vote was 16,366 Libertarian (Browne); 11,149 Reform (Buchanan); 2,884 Independent (Hagelin); 42 write-in (McReynolds); 3,990 scattered write-in.

Senator Other vote was 42,113 Constitution (Lawler); 13,687 Independent (Friedgen); 8,452 Timesizing Not Downsizing (Hyde); 2,473 scattered write-in.

Congress Other vote was: CD 1: 5,157 Independent (Potvin), 89 scattered write-in; CD 2: 2,176 scattered write-in; CD 3: 2,496 scattered write-in; CD 4: 10,553 Libertarian (Euchner), 136 scattered write-in; CD 5: 4,040 scattered write-in; CD 6: 218 scattered write-in; CD 7: 2,268 scattered write-in; CD 8: 1,041 scattered write-in; CD 9: 6,998 Independent (Rosa), 66 scattered write-in; CD 10: 697 scattered write-in.

2000 PRIMARY ELECTIONS

Primary March 7, 2000 (President)
September 19, 2000 (Congress)

Registration
(as of Aug. 30, 2000)

Republican	535,706
Democratic	1,406,377
Libertarian	13,979
Other Parties	6,957
Unenrolled	1,874,351
TOTAL	3,837,370

Primary Type Modified—Registered Democrats and Republicans could vote only in their party's primary. "Unenrolled" voters could vote in either party's primary.

Note: An asterisk (*) denotes incumbent.

	REPUBLICAN PRIMARIES			DEMOCRATIC PRIMARIES		
President	John McCain	324,708	64.7%	Al Gore	341,586	59.9%
	George W. Bush	159,534	31.8%	Bill Bradley	212,452	37.3%
	Alan Keyes	12,630	2.5%	No Preference	11,281	2.0%
	Gary Bauer	1,744	0.3%	Lyndon H. LaRouche Jr.	2,135	0.4%
	Steve Forbes	1,407	0.3%	Write-in	2,620	0.5%
	No Preference	1,292	0.3%			
	Orrin G. Hatch	262	0.1%			
	Write-in	374	0.1%			
	TOTAL	501,951		TOTAL	570,074	
Senator	Jack E. Robinson III	42,263	96.6%	Edward M. Kennedy*	236,883	99.0%
	Write-in	1,492	3.4%	Write-in	2,467	1.0%
	TOTAL	43,755		TOTAL	239,350	
Congressional District 1	Peter J. Abair	3,223	99.4%	John W. Olver*	10,715	99.5%
	Write-in	18	0.6%	Write-in	57	0.5%
	TOTAL	3,241		TOTAL	10,772	
Congressional District 2	*No Republican candidate filed for the primary. There were 211 scattered write-in votes.*			Richard E. Neal*	20,253	86.4%
				Joseph R. Fountain	3,149	13.4%
				Write-in	26	0.1%
				TOTAL	23,428	
Congressional District 3	*No Republican candidate filed for the primary. There were 401 scattered write-in votes.*			James P. McGovern*	36,705	99.2%
				Write-in	290	0.8%
				TOTAL	36,995	

MASSACHUSETTS

GENERAL AND PRIMARY ELECTIONS

REPUBLICAN PRIMARIES				DEMOCRATIC PRIMARIES		
Congressional District 4	Martin D. Travis	5,850	98.5%	Barney Frank*	27,728	99.6%
	Write-in	91	1.5%	Write-in	118	0.4%
	TOTAL	5,941		TOTAL	27,846	
Congressional District 5	*No Republican candidate filed for the primary. There were 1,905 scattered write-in votes.*			Martin T. Meehan*	16,394	73.0%
				Thomas P. Tierney	4,253	18.9%
				Joseph F. Osbaldeston	1,687	7.5%
				Write-in	128	0.6%
				TOTAL	22,462	
Congressional District 6	Paul McCarthy	5,417	67.3%	John F. Tierney*	24,873	99.6%
	Frederick T. Golder	2,574	32.0%	Write-in	109	0.4%
	Write-in	57	0.7%			
	TOTAL	8,048		TOTAL	24,982	
Congressional District 7	*No Republican candidate filed for the primary. There were 425 scattered write-in votes.*			Edward J. Markey*	26,785	99.2%
				Write-in	222	0.8%
				TOTAL	27,007	
Congressional District 8	*No Republican candidate filed for the primary. There were 122 scattered write-in votes.*			Michael E. Capuano*	14,950	99.3%
				Write-in	106	0.7%
				TOTAL	15,056	
Congressional District 9	Janet E. Jeghelian	3,705	99.0%	John Joseph Moakley*	19,334	99.6%
	Write-in	36	1.0%	Write-in	70	0.4%
	TOTAL	3,741		TOTAL	19,404	
Congressional District 10	Eric V. Bleicken	9,808	99.1%	Bill Delahunt*	29,886	99.6%
	Write-in	93	0.9%	Write-in	132	0.4%
	TOTAL	9,901		TOTAL	30,018	

MICHIGAN

GOVERNOR
John Engler (R). Re-elected 1998 to a four-year term. Previously elected 1994, 1990.

SENATORS
Debbie Stabenow (D). Elected 2000 to a six-year term.

Carl Levin (D). Re-elected 1996 to a six-year term. Previously elected 1990, 1984, 1978.

REPRESENTATIVES
1. Bart Stupak (D)
2. Peter Hoekstra (R)
3. Vernon J. Ehlers (R)
4. Dave Camp (R)
5. James A. Barcia (D)
6. Frederick Upton (R)
7. Nick Smith (R)
8. Mike Rogers (R)
9. Dale E. Kildee (D)
10. David E. Bonior (D)
11. Joseph K. Knollenberg (R)
12. Sander Levin (D)
13. Lynn Rivers (D)
14. John Conyers Jr. (D)
15. Carolyn Kilpatrick (D)
16. John D. Dingell, Jr. (D)

POSTWAR VOTE FOR PRESIDENT

		Republican		Democratic							Major Vote	
Year	Total Vote	Vote	Candidate	Vote	Candidate	Other Vote	Plurality	Rep.	Dem.	Rep.	Dem.
2000**	4,232,711	1,953,139	Bush, George W.	2,170,418	Gore, Al	109,154	217,279 D	46.1%	51.3%	47.4%	52.6%
1996**	3,848,844	1,481,212	Dole, Bob	1,989,653	Clinton, Bill	377,979	508,441 D	38.5%	51.7%	42.7%	57.3%
1992**	4,274,673	1,554,940	Bush, George	1,871,182	Clinton, Bill	848,551	316,242 D	36.4%	43.8%	45.4%	54.6%
1988	3,669,163	1,965,486	Bush, George	1,675,783	Dukakis, Michael S.	27,894	289,703 R	53.6%	45.7%	54.0%	46.0%
1984	3,801,658	2,251,571	Reagan, Ronald	1,529,638	Mondale, Walter F.	20,449	721,933 R	59.2%	40.2%	59.5%	40.5%
1980**	3,909,725	1,915,225	Reagan, Ronald	1,661,532	Carter, Jimmy	332,968	253,693 R	49.0%	42.5%	53.5%	46.5%
1976	3,653,749	1,893,742	Ford, Gerald R.	1,696,714	Carter, Jimmy	63,293	197,028 R	51.8%	46.4%	52.7%	47.3%
1972	3,489,727	1,961,721	Nixon, Richard M.	1,459,435	McGovern, George S.	68,571	502,286 R	56.2%	41.8%	57.3%	42.7%
1968	3,306,250	1,370,665	Nixon, Richard M.	1,593,082	Humphrey, Hubert H.	342,503	222,417 D	41.5%	48.2%	46.2%	53.8%
1964	3,203,102	1,060,152	Goldwater, Barry M.	2,136,615	Johnson, Lyndon B.	6,335	1,076,463 D	33.1%	66.7%	33.2%	66.8%
1960	3,318,097	1,620,428	Nixon, Richard M.	1,687,269	Kennedy, John F.	10,400	66,841 D	48.8%	50.9%	49.0%	51.0%
1956	3,080,468	1,713,647	Eisenhower, Dwight D.	1,359,898	Stevenson, Adlai E.	6,923	353,749 R	55.6%	44.1%	55.8%	44.2%
1952	2,798,592	1,551,529	Eisenhower, Dwight D.	1,230,657	Stevenson, Adlai E.	16,406	320,872 R	55.4%	44.0%	55.8%	44.2%
1948	2,109,609	1,038,595	Dewey, Thomas E.	1,003,448	Truman, Harry S.	67,566	35,147 R	49.2%	47.6%	50.9%	49.1%

In 2000 the other vote column includes 84,165 votes cast for Green (Nader). In 1996 the other vote column includes 336,670 votes cast for Perot. In 1992 the other vote column includes 824,813 votes cast for Perot. In 1980 the other column includes 275,223 votes for Independent (Anderson).

MICHIGAN

POSTWAR VOTE FOR GOVERNOR

Year	Total Vote	Republican		Democratic		Other Vote	Rep.-Dem. Plurality	Percentage			
								Total Vote		Major Vote	
		Vote	Candidate	Vote	Candidate			Rep.	Dem.	Rep.	Dem.
1998	3,027,104	1,883,005	Engler, John	1,143,574	Fieger, Geoffrey	525	739,431 R	62.2%	37.8%	62.2%	37.8%
1994	3,089,077	1,899,101	Engler, John	1,188,438	Wolpe, Howard	1,538	710,663 R	61.5%	38.5%	61.5%	38.5%
1990	2,564,563	1,276,134	Engler, John	1,258,539	Blanchard, James J.	29,890	17,595 R	49.8%	49.1%	50.3%	49.7%
1986	2,396,564	753,647	Lucas, William	1,632,138	Blanchard, James J.	10,779	878,491 D	31.4%	68.1%	31.6%	68.4%
1982	3,040,008	1,369,582	Headlee, Richard H.	1,561,291	Blanchard, James J.	109,135	191,709 D	45.1%	51.4%	46.7%	53.3%
1978	2,867,212	1,628,485	Milliken, William G.	1,237,256	Fitzgerald, William	1,471	391,229 R	56.8%	43.2%	56.8%	43.2%
1974	2,657,017	1,356,865	Milliken, William G.	1,242,247	Levin, Sander	57,905	114,618 R	51.1%	46.8%	52.2%	47.8%
1970	2,656,162	1,339,047	Milliken, William G.	1,294,638	Levin, Sander	22,477	44,409 R	50.4%	48.7%	50.8%	49.2%
1966**	2,461,909	1,490,430	Romney, George W.	963,383	Ferency, Zolton A.	8,096	527,047 R	60.5%	39.1%	60.7%	39.3%
1964	3,158,102	1,764,355	Romney, George W.	1,381,442	Staebler, Neil	12,305	382,913 R	55.9%	43.7%	56.1%	43.9%
1962	2,764,839	1,420,086	Romney, George W.	1,339,513	Swainson, John B.	5,240	80,573 R	51.4%	48.4%	51.5%	48.5%
1960	3,255,991	1,602,022	Bagwell, Paul D.	1,643,634	Swainson, John B.	10,335	41,612 D	49.2%	50.5%	49.4%	50.6%
1958	2,312,184	1,078,089	Bagwell, Paul D.	1,225,533	Williams, G. Mennen	8,562	147,444 D	46.6%	53.0%	46.8%	53.2%
1956	3,049,651	1,376,376	Cobo, Albert E.	1,666,689	Williams, G. Mennen	6,586	290,313 D	45.1%	54.7%	45.2%	54.8%
1954	2,187,027	963,300	Leonard, Donald S.	1,216,308	Williams, G. Mennen	7,419	253,008 D	44.0%	55.6%	44.2%	55.8%
1952	2,865,980	1,423,275	Alger, Fred M.	1,431,893	Williams, G. Mennen	10,812	8,618 D	49.7%	50.0%	49.8%	50.2%
1950	1,879,382	933,998	Kelly, Harry F.	935,152	Williams, G. Mennen	10,232	1,154 D	49.7%	49.8%	50.0%	50.0%
1948	2,113,122	964,810	Sigler, Kim	1,128,664	Williams, G. Mennen	19,648	163,854 D	45.7%	53.4%	46.1%	53.9%
1946	1,665,475	1,003,878	Sigler, Kim	644,540	Van Wagoner, Murray	17,057	359,338 R	60.3%	38.7%	60.9%	39.1%

The term of office of Michigan's Governor was increased from two to four years effective with the 1966 election.

POSTWAR VOTE FOR SENATOR

Year	Total Vote	Republican		Democratic		Other Vote	Rep.-Dem. Plurality	Percentage			
								Total Vote		Major Vote	
		Vote	Candidate	Vote	Candidate			Rep.	Dem.	Rep.	Dem.
2000	4,167,685	1,994,693	Abraham, Spencer	2,061,952	Stabenow, Debbie	111,040	67,259 D	47.9%	49.5%	49.2%	50.8%
1996	3,762,575	1,500,106	Romney, Ronna	2,195,738	Levin, Carl	66,731	695,632 D	39.9%	58.4%	40.6%	59.4%
1994	3,043,385	1,578,770	Abraham, Spencer	1,300,960	Carr, M. Robert	163,655	277,810 R	51.9%	42.7%	54.8%	45.2%
1990	2,560,494	1,055,695	Schuette, Bill	1,471,753	Levin, Carl	33,046	416,058 D	41.2%	57.5%	41.8%	58.2%
1988	3,505,985	1,348,219	Dunn, Jim	2,116,865	Riegle, Donald W.	40,901	768,646 D	38.5%	60.4%	38.9%	61.1%
1984	3,700,938	1,745,302	Lousma, Jack	1,915,831	Levin, Carl	39,805	170,529 D	47.2%	51.8%	47.7%	52.3%
1982	2,994,334	1,223,288	Ruppe, Philip E.	1,728,793	Riegle, Donald W.	42,253	505,505 D	40.9%	57.7%	41.4%	58.6%
1978	2,846,630	1,362,165	Griffin, Robert P.	1,484,193	Levin, Carl	272	122,028 D	47.9%	52.1%	47.9%	52.1%
1976	3,490,664	1,635,087	Esch, Marvin L.	1,831,031	Riegle, Donald W.	24,546	195,944 D	46.8%	52.5%	47.2%	52.8%
1972	3,406,906	1,781,065	Griffin, Robert P.	1,577,178	Kelley, Frank J.	48,663	203,887 R	52.3%	46.3%	53.0%	47.0%
1970	2,610,839	858,470	Romney, Lenore	1,744,716	Hart, Philip A.	7,653	886,246 D	32.9%	66.8%	33.0%	67.0%
1966	2,439,365	1,363,530	Griffin, Robert P.	1,069,484	Williams, G. Mennen	6,351	294,046 R	55.9%	43.8%	56.0%	44.0%
1964	3,101,667	1,096,272	Peterson, Elly M.	1,996,912	Hart, Philip A.	8,483	900,640 D	35.3%	64.4%	35.4%	64.6%
1960	3,226,647	1,548,873	Bentley, Alvin M.	1,669,179	McNamara, Patrick V.	8,595	120,306 D	48.0%	51.7%	48.1%	51.9%
1958	2,271,644	1,046,963	Potter, Charles E.	1,216,966	Hart, Philip A.	7,715	170,003 D	46.1%	53.6%	46.2%	53.8%
1954	2,144,840	1,049,420	Ferguson, Homer	1,088,550	McNamara, Patrick V.	6,870	39,130 D	48.9%	50.8%	49.1%	50.9%
1952	2,821,133	1,428,352	Potter, Charles E.	1,383,416	Moody, Blair	9,365	44,936 R	50.6%	49.0%	50.8%	49.2%
1948	2,062,097	1,045,156	Ferguson, Homer	1,000,329	Hook, Frank E.	16,612	44,827 R	50.7%	48.5%	51.1%	48.9%
1946	1,618,720	1,085,570	Vandenberg, Arthur	517,923	Lee, James H.	15,227	567,647 R	67.1%	32.0%	67.7%	32.3%

MICHIGAN

Districts Established April 6, 1992

Isle Royale

KEWEENAW

Lake Superior

KEWEENAW

HOUGHTON

Lake Superior

Marquette

ONTONAGON

BARAGA

GOGEBIC

IRON

MARQUETTE

1

ALGER

LUCE

CHIPPEWA

SCHOOLCRAFT

DICKINSON

MACKINAC

DELTA

MENOMINEE

Lake Huron

EMMET

CHEBOYGAN

1

PRESQUE ISLE

Lake Michigan

CHARLEVOIX

OTSEGO

MONTMORENCY

ALPENA

LEELANAU

ANTRIM

Traverse City

BENZIE

GRAND TRAVERSE

KALKASKA

CRAWFORD

OSCODA

ALCONA

MANISTEE

WEXFORD

MISSAUKEE

ROSCOMMON

OGEMAW

IOSCO

MASON

LAKE

OSCEOLA

CLARE

GLADWIN

ARENAC

Saginaw Bay

HURON

2

4

OCEANA

NEWAYGO

MECOSTA

ISABELLA

MIDLAND

Midland

BAY

Bay City

5

MUSKEGON

MONTCALM

GRATIOT

SAGINAW

Saginaw

TUSCOLA

SANILAC

Muskegon

KENT

IONIA

CLINTON

SHIAWASSEE

GENESEE

Flint

LAPEER

ST. CLAIR

Port Huron

OTTAWA

Grand Rapids

3

9

OAKLAND

Pontiac

MACOMB

10

Holland

BARRY

EATON

Lansing

8

11

12

ALLEGAN

INGHAM

LIVINGSTON

WAYNE

7

WASHTENAW

Kalamazoo

Battle Creek

Jackson

13

VAN BUREN

KALAMAZOO

CALHOUN

JACKSON

Ypsilanti

Benton Harbor

6

St. Joseph

BERRIEN

CASS

ST. JOSEPH

BRANCH

HILLSDALE

LENAWEE

MONROE

16

Ann Arbor

Districts 13, 14, 15 and 16 Wayne County, including city of Detroit

228

DETROIT AREA

CONGRESSIONAL DISTRICTS

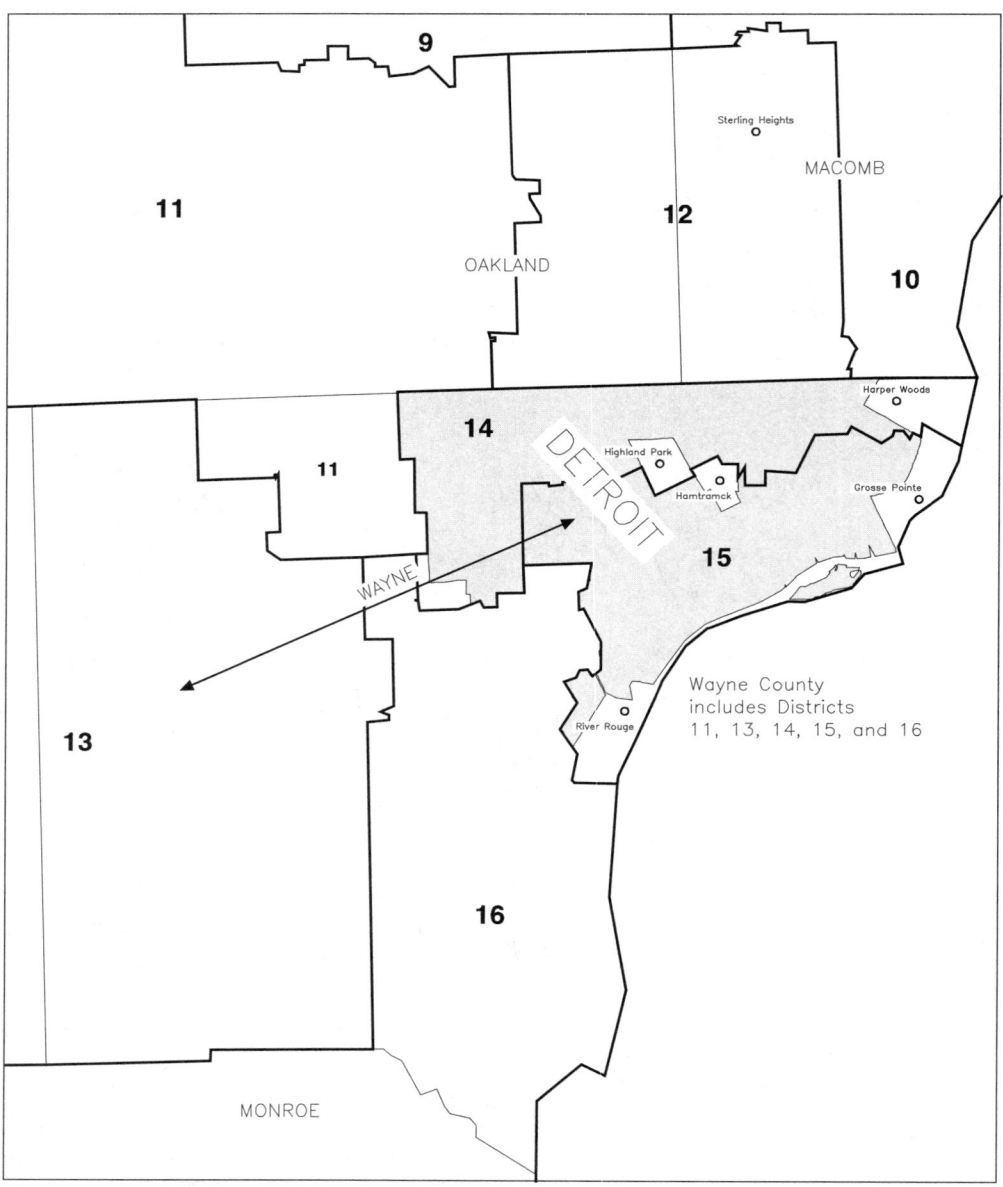

Wayne County
includes Districts
11, 13, 14, 15, and 16

MICHIGAN

PRESIDENT 2000

2000 Census Population	County	Total Vote	Republican	Democratic	Green (Nader)	Other	Rep.-Dem. Plurality	Percentage of Total Vote Rep.	Dem.	Green
11,719	ALCONA	5,997	3,152	2,696	124	25	456 R	52.6%	45.0%	2.1%
9,862	ALGER	4,366	2,142	2,071	126	27	71 R	49.1%	47.4%	2.9%
105,665	ALLEGAN	44,891	28,197	15,495	930	269	12,702 R	62.8%	34.5%	2.1%
31,314	ALPENA	14,132	6,769	7,053	262	48	284 D	47.9%	49.9%	1.9%
23,110	ANTRIM	11,507	6,780	4,329	312	86	2,451 R	58.9%	37.6%	2.7%
17,269	ARENAC	7,267	3,421	3,685	117	44	264 D	47.1%	50.7%	1.6%
8,746	BARAGA	3,393	1,836	1,400	141	16	436 R	54.1%	41.3%	4.2%
56,755	BARRY	26,244	15,716	9,769	612	147	5,947 R	59.9%	37.2%	2.3%
110,157	BAY	51,636	22,150	28,251	972	263	6,101 D	42.9%	54.7%	1.9%
15,998	BENZIE	8,072	4,172	3,546	312	42	626 R	51.7%	43.9%	3.9%
162,453	BERRIEN	65,241	35,689	28,152	1,154	246	7,537 R	54.7%	43.2%	1.8%
45,787	BRANCH	15,783	8,743	6,691	279	70	2,052 R	55.4%	42.4%	1.8%
137,985	CALHOUN	55,080	26,291	27,312	1,176	301	1,021 D	47.7%	49.6%	2.1%
51,104	CASS	19,825	10,545	8,808	371	101	1,737 R	53.2%	44.4%	1.9%
26,090	CHARLEVOIX	12,487	7,018	4,958	424	87	2,060 R	56.2%	39.7%	3.4%
26,448	CHEBOYGAN	12,617	6,815	5,484	257	61	1,331 R	54.0%	43.5%	2.0%
38,543	CHIPPEWA	14,354	7,526	6,370	361	97	1,156 R	52.4%	44.4%	2.5%
31,252	CLARE	12,607	5,937	6,287	262	121	350 D	47.1%	49.9%	2.1%
64,753	CLINTON	32,199	18,054	13,394	602	149	4,660 R	56.1%	41.6%	1.9%
14,273	CRAWFORD	6,364	3,345	2,790	176	53	555 R	52.6%	43.8%	2.8%
38,520	DELTA	17,316	8,871	7,970	390	85	901 R	51.2%	46.0%	2.3%
27,472	DICKINSON	12,832	6,932	5,533	301	66	1,399 R	54.0%	43.1%	2.3%
103,655	EATON	49,272	24,803	23,211	989	269	1,592 R	50.3%	47.1%	2.0%
31,437	EMMET	14,711	8,602	5,451	534	124	3,151 R	58.5%	37.1%	3.6%
436,141	GENESEE	190,865	66,641	119,833	3,623	768	53,192 D	34.9%	62.8%	1.9%
26,023	GLADWIN	11,629	5,743	5,573	227	86	170 R	49.4%	47.9%	2.0%
17,370	GOGEBIC	8,339	3,929	4,066	285	59	137 D	47.1%	48.8%	3.4%
77,654	GRAND TRAVERSE	38,229	22,358	14,371	1,263	237	7,987 R	58.5%	37.6%	3.3%
42,285	GRATIOT	15,179	8,312	6,538	265	64	1,774 R	54.8%	43.1%	1.7%
46,527	HILLSDALE	17,473	10,483	6,495	363	132	3,988 R	60.0%	37.2%	2.1%
36,016	HOUGHTON	14,216	7,895	5,688	518	115	2,207 R	55.5%	40.0%	3.6%
36,079	HURON	16,095	8,911	6,899	230	55	2,012 R	55.4%	42.9%	1.4%
279,320	INGHAM	120,595	47,314	69,231	3,290	760	21,917 D	39.2%	57.4%	2.7%
61,518	IONIA	23,970	13,915	9,481	423	151	4,434 R	58.1%	39.6%	1.8%
27,339	IOSCO	13,222	6,345	6,505	308	64	160 D	48.0%	49.2%	2.3%
13,138	IRON	6,188	2,967	3,014	160	47	47 D	47.9%	48.7%	2.6%
63,351	ISABELLA	21,069	10,053	10,228	666	122	175 D	47.7%	48.5%	3.2%
158,422	JACKSON	61,946	32,066	28,160	1,329	391	3,906 R	51.8%	45.5%	2.1%
238,603	KALAMAZOO	100,656	48,254	48,807	3,086	509	553 D	47.9%	48.5%	3.1%
16,571	KALKASKA	6,849	3,842	2,774	173	60	1,068 R	56.1%	40.5%	2.5%
574,335	KENT	250,318	148,602	95,442	5,019	1,255	53,160 R	59.4%	38.1%	2.0%
2,301	KEWEENAW	1,343	740	540	53	10	200 R	55.1%	40.2%	3.9%
11,333	LAKE	4,693	1,961	2,584	110	38	623 D	41.8%	55.1%	2.3%
87,904	LAPEER	37,234	20,351	15,749	794	340	4,602 R	54.7%	42.3%	2.1%
21,119	LEELANAU	12,009	6,840	4,635	456	78	2,205 R	57.0%	38.6%	3.8%
98,890	LENAWEE	40,093	20,681	18,365	760	287	2,316 R	51.6%	45.8%	1.9%
156,951	LIVINGSTON	75,475	44,637	28,780	1,498	560	15,857 R	59.1%	38.1%	2.0%
7,024	LUCE	2,536	1,480	956	74	26	524 R	58.4%	37.7%	2.9%
11,943	MACKINAC	5,970	3,272	2,533	136	29	739 R	54.8%	42.4%	2.3%
788,149	MACOMB	345,559	164,265	172,625	6,145	2,524	8,360 D	47.5%	50.0%	1.8%
24,527	MANISTEE	11,428	5,401	5,639	320	68	238 D	47.3%	49.3%	2.8%
64,634	MARQUETTE	29,179	12,577	15,503	936	163	2,926 D	43.1%	53.1%	3.2%
28,274	MASON	13,016	7,066	5,579	301	70	1,487 R	54.3%	42.9%	2.3%
40,553	MECOSTA	14,754	8,072	6,300	325	57	1,772 R	54.7%	42.7%	2.2%
25,326	MENOMINEE	10,434	5,529	4,597	269	39	932 R	53.0%	44.1%	2.6%
82,874	MIDLAND	38,888	21,887	15,959	794	248	5,928 R	56.3%	41.0%	2.0%
14,478	MISSAUKEE	6,496	4,274	2,062	123	37	2,212 R	65.8%	31.7%	1.9%
145,945	MONROE	61,795	28,940	31,555	996	304	2,615 D	46.8%	51.1%	1.6%
61,266	MONTCALM	22,904	12,696	9,627	483	98	3,069 R	55.4%	42.0%	2.1%
10,315	MONTMORENCY	5,009	2,750	2,139	92	28	611 R	54.9%	42.7%	1.8%

MICHIGAN

PRESIDENT 2000

2000 Census Population	County	Total Vote	Republican	Democratic	Green (Nader)	Other	Rep.-Dem. Plurality	Percentage of Total Vote		
								Rep.	Dem.	Green
170,200	MUSKEGON	69,270	30,028	37,865	1,131	246	7,837 D	43.3%	54.7%	1.6%
47,874	NEWAYGO	19,557	11,399	7,677	361	120	3,722 R	58.3%	39.3%	1.8%
1,194,156	OAKLAND	570,265	274,319	281,201	10,382	4,363	6,882 D	48.1%	49.3%	1.8%
26,873	OCEANA	10,772	5,913	4,597	211	51	1,316 R	54.9%	42.7%	2.0%
21,645	OGEMAW	9,855	4,706	4,896	191	62	190 D	47.8%	49.7%	1.9%
7,818	ONTONAGON	4,151	2,472	1,514	135	30	958 R	59.6%	36.5%	3.3%
23,197	OSCEOLA	9,930	5,680	4,006	186	58	1,674 R	57.2%	40.3%	1.9%
9,418	OSCODA	3,992	2,207	1,677	88	20	530 R	55.3%	42.0%	2.2%
23,301	OTSEGO	10,505	6,108	4,034	315	48	2,074 R	58.1%	38.4%	3.0%
238,314	OTTAWA	110,599	78,703	29,600	1,866	430	49,103 R	71.2%	26.8%	1.7%
14,411	PRESQUE ISLE	7,080	3,660	3,242	136	42	418 R	51.7%	45.8%	1.9%
25,469	ROSCOMMON	12,928	6,190	6,433	256	49	243 D	47.9%	49.8%	2.0%
210,039	SAGINAW	93,756	41,152	50,825	1,418	361	9,673 D	43.9%	54.2%	1.5%
164,235	ST. CLAIR	68,516	33,571	33,002	1,341	602	569 R	49.0%	48.2%	2.0%
62,422	ST. JOSEPH	22,024	12,906	8,574	434	110	4,332 R	58.6%	38.9%	2.0%
44,547	SANILAC	18,566	10,966	7,153	320	127	3,813 R	59.1%	38.5%	1.7%
8,903	SCHOOLCRAFT	4,198	2,088	2,036	56	18	52 R	49.7%	48.5%	1.3%
71,687	SHIAWASSEE	32,218	15,816	15,520	639	243	296 R	49.1%	48.2%	2.0%
58,266	TUSCOLA	24,652	13,213	10,845	454	140	2,368 R	53.6%	44.0%	1.8%
76,263	VAN BUREN	29,482	14,792	13,796	686	208	996 R	50.2%	46.8%	2.3%
322,895	WASHTENAW	144,940	52,459	86,647	4,843	991	34,188 D	36.2%	59.8%	3.3%
2,061,162	WAYNE	768,627	223,021	530,414	11,287	3,905	307,393 D	29.0%	69.0%	1.5%
30,484	WEXFORD	12,982	7,215	5,326	352	89	1,889 R	55.6%	41.0%	2.7%
9,938,444	TOTAL	4,232,711	1,953,139	2,170,418	84,165	24,989	217,279 D	46.1%	51.3%	2.0%

DETROIT

PRESIDENT 2000

2000 Census Population	District	Total Vote	Republican	Democratic	Green (Nader)	Other	Rep.-Dem. Plurality	Percentage of Total Vote		
								Rep.	Dem.	Green
	District 3	4,801	162	4,590	26	23	4,428 D	3.4%	95.6%	0.5%
	District 4	12,872	1,204	11,482	140	46	10,278 D	9.4%	89.2%	1.1%
	District 5	13,321	557	12,657	64	43	12,100 D	4.2%	95.0%	0.5%
	District 6	14,192	788	13,288	75	41	12,500 D	5.6%	93.6%	0.5%
	District 7	7,394	367	6,960	46	21	6,593 D	5.0%	94.1%	0.6%
	District 8	6,263	90	6,153	10	10	6,063 D	1.4%	98.2%	0.2%
	District 9	7,863	376	7,378	81	28	7,002 D	4.8%	93.8%	1.0%
	District 10	2,549	75	2,441	30	3	2,366 D	2.9%	95.8%	1.2%
	District 11	5,122	390	4,583	125	24	4,193 D	7.6%	89.5%	2.4%
	District 12	5,901	217	5,619	46	19	5,402 D	3.7%	95.2%	0.8%
	District 13	12,932	321	12,516	57	38	12,195 D	2.5%	96.8%	0.4%
	District 14	11,480	406	10,960	94	20	10,554 D	3.5%	95.5%	0.8%
	District 15	21,686	452	21,146	60	28	20,694 D	2.1%	97.5%	0.3%
	District 16	19,579	733	18,732	70	44	17,999 D	3.7%	95.7%	0.4%
	District 17	18,781	1,031	17,595	113	42	16,564 D	5.5%	93.7%	0.6%
	District 18	14,261	1,785	12,293	138	45	10,508 D	12.5%	86.2%	1.0%
	District 19	14,000	607	13,296	68	29	12,689 D	4.3%	95.0%	0.5%
	District 20	13,658	224	13,372	40	22	13,148 D	1.6%	97.9%	0.3%
	District 21	11,826	411	11,310	60	45	10,899 D	3.5%	95.6%	0.5%
	District 22	8,006	138	7,829	28	11	7,691 D	1.7%	97.8%	0.3%
	District 23	6,319	125	6,152	32	10	6,027 D	2.0%	97.4%	0.5%
	District 24	3,448	238	3,126	70	14	2,888 D	6.9%	90.7%	2.0%
	District 25	4,633	816	3,730	70	17	2,914 D	17.6%	80.5%	1.5%
	District 26	4,231	227	3,968	22	14	2 D	5.4%	93.8%	0.5%
	Absentees	55,382	3,948	50,935	386	113	46,987 D	7.1%	92.0%	0.7%
951,270	TOTAL	300,500	15,688	282,111	1,951	750	266,423 D	5.2%	93.9%	0.6%

MICHIGAN

SENATOR 2000

2000 Census Population	County	Total Vote	Republican	Democratic	Other	Rep.-Dem. Plurality		Percentage			
								Total Vote		Major Vote	
								Rep.	Dem.	Rep.	Dem.
11,719	ALCONA	5,775	3,356	2,305	114	1,051	R	58.1%	39.9%	59.3%	40.7%
9,862	ALGER	4,211	2,113	1,978	120	135	R	50.2%	47.0%	51.6%	48.4%
105,665	ALLEGAN	44,536	28,847	14,520	1,169	14,327	R	64.8%	32.6%	66.5%	33.5%
31,314	ALPENA	13,519	7,316	5,902	301	1,414	R	54.1%	43.7%	55.3%	44.7%
23,110	ANTRIM	11,355	6,984	4,018	353	2,966	R	61.5%	35.4%	63.5%	36.5%
17,269	ARENAC	7,024	3,560	3,317	147	243	R	50.7%	47.2%	51.8%	48.2%
8,746	BARAGA	3,240	1,734	1,423	83	311	R	53.5%	43.9%	54.9%	45.1%
56,755	BARRY	26,053	15,897	9,429	727	6,468	R	61.0%	36.2%	62.8%	37.2%
110,157	BAY	50,912	23,986	25,503	1,423	1,517	D	47.1%	50.1%	48.5%	51.5%
15,998	BENZIE	7,655	4,290	3,133	232	1,157	R	56.0%	40.9%	57.8%	42.2%
162,453	BERRIEN	63,833	37,721	24,727	1,385	12,994	R	59.1%	38.7%	60.4%	39.6%
45,787	BRANCH	15,483	9,057	6,043	383	3,014	R	58.5%	39.0%	60.0%	40.0%
137,985	CALHOUN	54,549	28,068	25,116	1,365	2,952	R	51.5%	46.0%	52.8%	47.2%
51,104	CASS	19,296	11,102	7,744	450	3,358	R	57.5%	40.1%	58.9%	41.1%
26,090	CHARLEVOIX	12,297	7,274	4,588	435	2,686	R	59.2%	37.3%	61.3%	38.7%
26,448	CHEBOYGAN	12,340	7,094	4,933	313	2,161	R	57.5%	40.0%	59.0%	41.0%
38,543	CHIPPEWA	14,087	7,849	5,899	339	1,950	R	55.7%	41.9%	57.1%	42.9%
31,252	CLARE	12,453	6,211	5,855	387	356	R	49.9%	47.0%	51.5%	48.5%
64,753	CLINTON	31,846	17,991	13,141	714	4,850	R	56.5%	41.3%	57.8%	42.2%
14,273	CRAWFORD	6,255	3,605	2,412	238	1,193	R	57.6%	38.6%	59.9%	40.1%
38,520	DELTA	17,016	9,151	7,566	299	1,585	R	53.8%	44.5%	54.7%	45.3%
27,472	DICKINSON	12,614	7,023	5,319	272	1,704	R	55.7%	42.2%	56.9%	43.1%
103,655	EATON	48,716	24,990	22,657	1,069	2,333	R	51.3%	46.5%	52.4%	47.6%
31,437	EMMET	14,536	8,957	5,061	518	3,896	R	61.6%	34.8%	63.9%	36.1%
436,141	GENESEE	186,510	66,910	115,373	4,227	48,463	D	35.9%	61.9%	36.7%	63.3%
26,023	GLADWIN	11,472	5,948	5,211	313	737	R	51.8%	45.4%	53.3%	46.7%
17,370	GOGEBIC	7,973	3,304	4,460	209	1,156	D	41.4%	55.9%	42.6%	57.4%
77,654	GRAND TRAVERSE	37,720	23,371	13,055	1,294	10,316	R	62.0%	34.6%	64.2%	35.8%
42,285	GRATIOT	14,890	8,687	5,845	358	2,842	R	58.3%	39.3%	59.8%	40.2%
46,527	HILLSDALE	16,768	10,366	5,931	471	4,435	R	61.8%	35.4%	63.6%	36.4%
36,016	HOUGHTON	13,702	7,437	5,857	408	1,580	R	54.3%	42.7%	55.9%	44.1%
36,079	HURON	15,671	9,720	5,672	279	4,048	R	62.0%	36.2%	63.1%	36.9%
279,320	INGHAM	119,843	47,171	69,582	3,090	22,411	D	39.4%	58.1%	40.4%	59.6%
61,518	IONIA	23,254	13,971	8,772	511	5,199	R	60.1%	37.7%	61.4%	38.6%
27,339	IOSCO	12,970	6,822	5,815	333	1,007	R	52.6%	44.8%	54.0%	46.0%
13,138	IRON	6,023	2,921	2,944	158	23	D	48.5%	48.9%	49.8%	50.2%
63,351	ISABELLA	20,774	10,742	9,314	718	1,428	R	51.7%	44.8%	53.6%	46.4%
158,422	JACKSON	61,257	32,958	26,616	1,683	6,342	R	53.8%	43.4%	55.3%	44.7%
238,603	KALAMAZOO	99,479	51,478	45,295	2,706	6,183	R	51.7%	45.5%	53.2%	46.8%
16,571	KALKASKA	6,492	3,853	2,457	182	1,396	R	59.3%	37.8%	61.1%	38.9%
574,335	KENT	248,083	151,844	90,732	5,507	61,112	R	61.2%	36.6%	62.6%	37.4%
2,301	KEWEENAW	1,309	704	568	37	136	R	53.8%	43.4%	55.3%	44.7%
11,333	LAKE	4,607	2,127	2,309	171	182	D	46.2%	50.1%	47.9%	52.1%
87,904	LAPEER	36,803	20,486	14,934	1,383	5,552	R	55.7%	40.6%	57.8%	42.2%
21,119	LEELANAU	11,782	7,046	4,376	360	2,670	R	59.8%	37.1%	61.7%	38.3%
98,890	LENAWEE	38,481	20,483	16,994	1,004	3,489	R	53.2%	44.2%	54.7%	45.3%
156,951	LIVINGSTON	74,974	43,471	29,319	2,184	14,152	R	58.0%	39.1%	59.7%	40.3%
7,024	LUCE	2,495	1,497	935	63	562	R	60.0%	37.5%	61.6%	38.4%
11,943	MACKINAC	5,833	3,390	2,298	145	1,092	R	58.1%	39.4%	59.6%	40.4%
788,149	MACOMB	338,811	163,150	164,596	11,065	1,446	D	48.2%	48.6%	49.8%	50.2%
24,527	MANISTEE	11,078	5,831	4,961	286	870	R	52.6%	44.8%	54.0%	46.0%
64,634	MARQUETTE	28,662	13,575	14,238	849	663	D	47.4%	49.7%	48.8%	51.2%
28,274	MASON	12,844	7,190	5,275	379	1,915	R	56.0%	41.1%	57.7%	42.3%
40,553	MECOSTA	14,431	8,388	5,695	348	2,693	R	58.1%	39.5%	59.6%	40.4%
25,326	MENOMINEE	9,929	5,368	4,277	284	1,091	R	54.1%	43.1%	55.7%	44.3%
82,874	MIDLAND	38,428	22,885	14,438	1,105	8,447	R	59.6%	37.6%	61.3%	38.7%
14,478	MISSAUKEE	6,449	4,359	1,905	185	2,454	R	67.6%	29.5%	69.6%	30.4%
145,945	MONROE	59,999	29,049	29,227	1,723	178	D	48.4%	48.7%	49.8%	50.2%
61,266	MONTCALM	22,124	12,880	8,801	443	4,079	R	58.2%	39.8%	59.4%	40.6%
10,315	MONTMORENCY	4,838	2,799	1,900	139	899	R	57.9%	39.3%	59.6%	40.4%

MICHIGAN

SENATOR 2000

2000 Census Population	County	Total Vote	Republican	Democratic	Other	Rep.-Dem. Plurality		Total Vote Rep.	Dem.	Major Vote Rep.	Dem.
170,200	MUSKEGON	67,948	32,510	34,142	1,296	1,632	D	47.8%	50.2%	48.8%	51.2%
47,874	NEWAYGO	19,238	11,641	7,139	458	4,502	R	60.5%	37.1%	62.0%	38.0%
1,194,156	OAKLAND	563,098	277,180	268,853	17,065	8,327	R	49.2%	47.7%	50.8%	49.2%
26,873	OCEANA	10,344	5,931	4,212	201	1,719	R	57.3%	40.7%	58.5%	41.5%
21,645	OGEMAW	9,646	5,028	4,345	273	683	R	52.1%	45.0%	53.6%	46.4%
7,818	ONTONAGON	3,985	2,095	1,777	113	318	R	52.6%	44.6%	54.1%	45.9%
23,197	OSCEOLA	9,537	5,714	3,556	267	2,158	R	59.9%	37.3%	61.6%	38.4%
9,418	OSCODA	3,918	2,336	1,478	104	858	R	59.6%	37.7%	61.2%	38.8%
23,301	OTSEGO	10,374	6,364	3,682	328	2,682	R	61.3%	35.5%	63.3%	36.7%
238,314	OTTAWA	109,645	79,601	27,974	2,070	51,627	R	72.6%	25.5%	74.0%	26.0%
14,411	PRESQUE ISLE	7,006	3,854	3,007	145	847	R	55.0%	42.9%	56.2%	43.8%
25,469	ROSCOMMON	12,702	6,756	5,603	343	1,153	R	53.2%	44.1%	54.7%	45.3%
210,039	SAGINAW	92,675	43,277	47,564	1,834	4,287	D	46.7%	51.3%	47.6%	52.4%
164,235	ST. CLAIR	67,408	34,364	30,659	2,385	3,705	R	51.0%	45.5%	52.8%	47.2%
62,422	ST. JOSEPH	21,515	13,366	7,569	580	5,797	R	62.1%	35.2%	63.8%	36.2%
44,547	SANILAC	18,316	11,095	6,643	578	4,452	R	60.6%	36.3%	62.5%	37.5%
8,903	SCHOOLCRAFT	4,096	2,124	1,909	63	215	R	51.9%	46.6%	52.7%	47.3%
71,687	SHIAWASSEE	31,804	16,693	14,253	858	2,440	R	52.5%	44.8%	53.9%	46.1%
58,266	TUSCOLA	24,271	13,863	9,762	646	4,101	R	57.1%	40.2%	58.7%	41.3%
76,263	VAN BUREN	28,472	15,443	12,399	630	3,044	R	54.2%	43.5%	55.5%	44.5%
322,895	WASHTENAW	143,017	52,990	85,305	4,722	32,315	D	37.1%	59.6%	38.3%	61.7%
2,061,162	WAYNE	759,508	228,547	512,759	18,202	284,212	D	30.1%	67.5%	30.8%	69.2%
30,484	WEXFORD	12,803	7,564	4,796	443	2,768	R	59.1%	37.5%	61.2%	38.8%
9,938,444	TOTAL	4,167,685	1,994,693	2,061,952	111,040	67,259	D	47.9%	49.5%	49.2%	50.8%

DETROIT

SENATOR 2000

2000 Census Population	County		Total Vote	Republican	Democratic	Other	Rep.-Dem. Plurality		Total Vote Rep.	Dem.	Major Vote Rep.	Dem.
	District	3	4,780	209	4,479	92	4,270	D	4.4%	93.7%	4.5%	95.5%
	District	4	12,795	1,266	11,266	263	10,000	D	9.9%	88.1%	10.1%	89.9%
	District	5	13,260	645	12,454	161	11,809	D	4.9%	93.9%	4.9%	95.1%
	District	6	14,116	951	13,003	162	12,052	D	6.7%	92.1%	6.8%	93.2%
	District	7	7,351	471	6,765	115	6,294	D	6.4%	92.0%	6.5%	93.5%
	District	8	6,229	164	5,987	78	5,823	D	2.6%	96.1%	2.7%	97.3%
	District	9	7,817	451	7,229	137	6,778	D	5.8%	92.5%	5.9%	94.1%
	District	10	2,524	101	2,380	43	2,279	D	4.0%	94.3%	4.1%	95.9%
	District	11	5,076	443	4,496	137	4,053	D	8.7%	88.6%	9.0%	91.0%
	District	12	5,885	252	5,537	96	5,285	D	4.3%	94.1%	4.4%	95.6%
	District	13	12,875	427	12,262	186	11,835	D	3.3%	95.2%	3.4%	96.6%
	District	14	11,420	498	10,783	139	10,285	D	4.4%	94.4%	4.4%	95.6%
	District	15	21,583	566	20,827	190	20,261	D	2.6%	96.5%	2.6%	97.4%
	District	16	19,461	893	18,336	232	17,443	D	4.6%	94.2%	4.6%	95.4%
	District	17	18,714	1,190	17,290	234	16,100	D	6.4%	92.4%	6.4%	93.6%
	District	18	14,153	1,918	11,958	277	10,040	D	13.6%	84.5%	13.8%	86.2%
	District	19	13,939	712	13,050	177	12,338	D	5.1%	93.6%	5.2%	94.8%
	District	20	13,602	371	13,095	136	12,724	D	2.7%	96.3%	2.8%	97.2%
	District	21	11,752	492	11,075	185	10,583	D	4.2%	94.2%	4.3%	95.7%
	District	22	7,959	211	7,649	99	7,438	D	2.7%	96.1%	2.7%	97.3%
	District	23	6,280	203	5,995	82	5,792	D	3.2%	95.5%	3.3%	96.7%
	District	24	3,436	288	3,066	82	2,778	D	8.4%	89.2%	8.6%	91.4%
	District	25	4,579	879	3,547	153	2,668	D	19.2%	77.5%	19.9%	80.1%
	District	26	4,197	283	3,828	86	3,545	D	6.7%	91.2%	6.9%	93.1%
	Absentees		54,877	4,761	49,431	685	44,670	D	8.7%	90.1%	8.8%	91.2%
951,270	TOTAL		298,660	18,645	275,788	4,227	257,143	D	6.2%	92.3%	6.3%	93.7%

MICHIGAN

CONGRESS

CD	Year	Total Vote	Republican Vote	Republican Candidate	Democratic Vote	Democratic Candidate	Other Vote	Rep.-Dem. Plurality	Total Vote Rep.	Total Vote Dem.	Major Vote Rep.	Major Vote Dem.
1	2000	290,569	117,300	YOB, CHUCK	169,649	STUPAK, BART	3,620	52,349 D	40.4%	58.4%	40.9%	59.1%
1	1998	221,796	87,630	MCMANUS, MICHELLE	130,129	STUPAK, BART	4,037	42,499 D	39.5%	58.7%	40.2%	59.8%
1	1996	256,791	69,957	CARR, BOB	181,486	STUPAK, BART	5,348	111,529 D	27.2%	70.7%	27.8%	72.2%
1	1994	213,492	89,660	ZIEGLER, GIL	121,433	STUPAK, BART	2,399	31,773 D	42.0%	56.9%	42.5%	57.5%
1	1992	268,619	117,056	RUPPE, PHILIP E.	144,857	STUPAK, BART	6,706	27,801 D	43.6%	53.9%	44.7%	55.3%
2	2000	289,925	186,762	HOEKSTRA, PETER	96,370	SHRAUGER, BOB	6,793	90,392 R	64.4%	33.2%	66.0%	34.0%
2	1998	213,622	146,854	HOEKSTRA, PETER	63,573	SHRAUGER, BOB	3,195	83,281 R	68.7%	29.8%	69.8%	30.2%
2	1996	253,699	165,608	HOEKSTRA, PETER	83,603	KRUSZYNSKI, DAN	4,488	82,005 R	65.3%	33.0%	66.5%	33.5%
2	1994	194,153	146,164	HOEKSTRA, PETER	46,097	HOOVER, MARCUS P.	1,892	100,067 R	75.3%	23.7%	76.0%	24.0%
2	1992	246,761	155,577	HOEKSTRA, PETER	86,265	MILTNER, JOHN H.	4,919	69,312 R	63.0%	35.0%	64.3%	35.7%
3	2000	276,263	179,539	EHLERS, VERNON J.	91,309	STEELE, TIMOTHY	5,415	88,230 R	65.0%	33.1%	66.3%	33.7%
3	1998	200,251	146,364	EHLERS, VERNON J.	49,489	FERGUSON, JOHN JR.	4,398	96,875 R	73.1%	24.7%	74.7%	25.3%
3	1996	247,043	169,466	EHLERS, VERNON J.	72,791	FLORY, BETSY J.	4,786	96,675 R	68.6%	29.5%	70.0%	30.0%
3	1994	185,066	136,711	EHLERS, VERNON J.	43,580	FLORY, BETSY J.	4,775	93,131 R	73.9%	23.5%	75.8%	24.2%
3	1992	264,948	162,451	HENRY, PAUL	95,927	KOOISTRA, CAROL S.	6,570	66,524 R	61.3%	36.2%	62.9%	37.1%
4	2000	267,819	182,128	CAMP, DAVE	78,019	HOLLENBECK, LAWRENCE	7,672	104,109 R	68.0%	29.1%	70.0%	30.0%
4	1998	170,109	155,343	CAMP, DAVE			14,766	155,343 R	91.3%		100.0%	
4	1996	243,645	159,561	CAMP, DAVE	79,691	DONALDSON, LISA	4,393	79,870 R	65.5%	32.7%	66.7%	33.3%
4	1994	198,517	145,176	CAMP, DAVE	50,544	FRASIER, DAMION	2,797	94,632 R	73.1%	25.5%	74.2%	25.8%
4	1992	251,539	157,337	CAMP, DAVE	87,573	DONALDSON, LISA	6,629	69,764 R	62.5%	34.8%	64.2%	35.8%
5	2000	247,737	59,274	ACTIS, RONALD	184,048	BARCIA, JAMES A.	4,415	124,774 D	23.9%	74.3%	24.4%	75.6%
5	1998	189,971	51,442	BREWSTER, DONALD	135,254	BARCIA, JAMES A.	3,275	83,812 D	27.1%	71.2%	27.6%	72.4%
5	1996	232,451	65,542	SIMS, LAWRENCE	162,675	BARCIA, JAMES A.	4,234	97,133 D	28.2%	70.0%	28.7%	71.3%
5	1994	193,143	61,342	ANDERSON, WILLIAM T.	126,456	BARCIA, JAMES A.	5,345	65,114 D	31.8%	65.5%	32.7%	67.3%
5	1992	244,992	93,098	MUXLOW, KEITH	147,618	BARCIA, JAMES A.	4,276	54,520 D	38.0%	60.3%	38.7%	61.3%
6	2000	234,640	159,373	UPTON, FRED	68,532	BUPP, JAMES	6,735	90,841 R	67.9%	29.2%	69.9%	30.1%
6	1998	161,627	113,292	UPTON, FRED	45,358	ANNEN, CLARENCE	2,977	67,934 R	70.1%	28.1%	71.4%	28.6%
6	1996	215,834	146,170	UPTON, FRED	66,243	ANNEN, CLARENCE	3,421	79,927 R	67.7%	30.7%	68.8%	31.2%
6	1994	165,938	121,923	UPTON, FRED	42,348	TAYLOR, DAVID	1,667	79,575 R	73.5%	25.5%	74.2%	25.8%
6	1992	233,112	144,083	UPTON, FRED	89,020	DAVIS, ANDY	9	55,063 R	61.8%	38.2%	61.8%	38.2%
7	2000	241,010	147,369	SMITH, NICK	86,080	CRITTENDON, JENNIE	7,561	61,289 R	61.1%	35.7%	63.1%	36.9%
7	1998	182,127	104,656	SMITH, NICK	72,998	BERRYMAN, JIM	4,473	31,658 R	57.5%	40.1%	58.9%	41.1%
7	1996	218,544	120,227	SMITH, NICK	93,725	TUNNICLIFF, KIM	4,592	26,502 R	55.0%	42.9%	56.2%	43.8%
7	1994	177,481	115,621	SMITH, NICK	57,326	MCCAUGHTRY, KIM	4,534	58,295 R	65.1%	32.3%	66.9%	33.1%
7	1992	152,868	133,972	SMITH, NICK			18,896	133,972 R	87.6%		100.0%	
8	2000	297,609	145,190	ROGERS, MIKE	145,079	BYRUM, DIANNE	7,340	111 R	48.8%	48.7%	50.0%	50.0%
8	1998	218,040	84,254	MUNSELL, SUSAN	125,169	STABENOW, DEBBIE	8,617	40,915 D	38.6%	57.4%	40.2%	59.8%
8	1996	262,421	115,836	CHRYSLER, DICK	141,086	STABENOW, DEBBIE	5,499	25,250 D	44.1%	53.8%	45.1%	54.9%
8	1994	212,470	109,663	CHRYSLER, DICK	95,383	MITCHELL, BOB	7,424	14,280 R	51.6%	44.9%	53.5%	46.5%
8	1992	284,707	131,906	CHRYSLER, DICK	135,517	CARR, M. ROBERT	17,284	3,611 D	46.3%	47.6%	49.3%	50.7%
9	2000	258,928	92,926	GARRETT, GRANT	158,184	KILDEE, DALE E.	7,818	65,258 D	35.9%	61.1%	37.0%	63.0%
9	1998	188,525	79,062	MCMILLIN, TOM	105,457	KILDEE, DALE E.	4,006	26,395 D	41.9%	55.9%	42.8%	57.2%
9	1996	231,200	89,733	NOWAK, PATRICK	136,856	KILDEE, DALE E.	4,611	47,123 D	38.8%	59.2%	39.6%	60.4%
9	1994	189,484	89,148	O'NEILL, MEGAN	97,096	KILDEE, DALE E.	3,240	7,948 D	47.0%	51.2%	47.9%	52.1%
9	1992	249,530	111,798	O'NEILL, MEGAN	133,956	KILDEE, DALE E.	3,776	22,158 D	44.8%	53.7%	45.5%	54.5%

MICHIGAN

CONGRESS

CD	Year	Total Vote	Republican Vote	Republican Candidate	Democratic Vote	Democratic Candidate	Other Vote	Rep.-Dem. Plurality	Total Vote Rep.	Total Vote Dem.	Major Vote Rep.	Major Vote Dem.
10	2000	282,269	93,713	TURNER, TOM	181,818	BONIOR, DAVID E.	6,738	88,105 D	33.2%	64.4%	34.0%	66.0%
10	1998	207,524	94,027	PALMER, BRIAN	108,770	BONIOR, DAVID E.	4,727	14,743 D	45.3%	52.4%	46.4%	53.6%
10	1996	244,281	106,444	HEINTZ, SUSY	132,829	BONIOR, DAVID E.	5,008	26,385 D	43.6%	54.4%	44.5%	55.5%
10	1994	195,738	73,862	LOBSINGER, DONALD J.	121,876	BONIOR, DAVID E.		48,014 D	37.7%	62.3%	37.7%	62.3%
10	1992	260,213	114,918	CARL, DOUGLAS	138,193	BONIOR, DAVID E.	7,102	23,275 D	44.2%	53.1%	45.4%	54.6%
11	2000	306,302	170,790	KNOLLENBERG, JOE	124,053	FRUMIN, MATTHEW	11,459	46,737 R	55.8%	40.5%	57.9%	42.1%
11	1998	225,804	144,264	KNOLLENBERG, JOE	76,107	REEDS, TRAVIS	5,433	68,157 R	63.9%	33.7%	65.5%	34.5%
11	1996	276,618	169,165	KNOLLENBERG, JOE	99,303	FRUMIN, MORRIS	8,150	69,862 R	61.2%	35.9%	63.0%	37.0%
11	1994	226,792	154,696	KNOLLENBERG, JOE	69,168	BRESHGOLD, MIKE	2,928	85,528 R	68.2%	30.5%	69.1%	30.9%
11	1992	293,098	168,940	KNOLLENBERG, JOE	117,725	BRIGGS, WALTER	6,433	51,215 R	57.6%	40.2%	58.9%	41.1%
12	2000	245,169	78,795	BARON, BART	157,720	LEVIN, SANDER	8,654	78,925 D	32.1%	64.3%	33.3%	66.7%
12	1998	189,428	79,619	TOUMA, LESLIE	105,824	LEVIN, SANDER	3,985	26,205 D	42.0%	55.9%	42.9%	57.1%
12	1996	232,475	94,235	PAPPAGEORGE, JOHN	133,436	LEVIN, SANDER	4,804	39,201 D	40.5%	57.4%	41.4%	58.6%
12	1994	198,996	92,762	PAPPAGEORGE, JOHN	103,508	LEVIN, SANDER	2,726	10,746 D	46.6%	52.0%	47.3%	52.7%
12	1992	261,349	119,357	PAPPAGEORGE, JOHN	137,514	LEVIN, SANDER	4,478	18,157 D	45.7%	52.6%	46.5%	53.5%
13	2000	247,521	79,445	BERRY, CARL	160,084	RIVERS, LYNN	7,992	80,639 D	32.1%	64.7%	33.2%	66.8%
13	1998	171,887	68,328	HICKEY, TOM	99,935	RIVERS, LYNN	3,624	31,607 D	39.8%	58.1%	40.6%	59.4%
13	1996	217,658	89,907	FITZSIMMONS, JOE	123,133	RIVERS, LYNN	4,618	33,226 D	41.3%	56.6%	42.2%	57.8%
13	1994	172,661	77,908	SCHALL, JOHN A.	89,573	RIVERS, LYNN	5,180	11,665 D	45.1%	51.9%	46.5%	53.5%
13	1992	245,888	105,169	GEAKE, R. ROBERT	127,642	FORD, WILLIAM D.	13,077	22,473 D	42.8%	51.9%	45.2%	54.8%
14	2000	189,707	17,582	ASHE, WILLIAM	168,982	CONYERS, JOHN, JR.	3,143	151,400 D	9.3%	89.1%	9.4%	90.6%
14	1998	145,305	16,140	COLLINS, VENDELLA	126,321	CONYERS, JOHN, JR.	2,844	110,181 D	11.1%	86.9%	11.3%	88.7%
14	1996	183,695	22,152	ASHE, WILLIAM	157,722	CONYERS, JOHN, JR.	3,821	135,570 D	12.1%	85.9%	12.3%	87.7%
14	1994	157,631	26,215	FOURNIER, RICHARD C.	128,463	CONYERS, JOHN, JR.	2,953	102,248 D	16.6%	81.5%	16.9%	83.1%
14	1992	200,879	32,036	GORDON, JOHN W.	165,496	CONYERS, JOHN, JR.	3,347	133,460 D	15.9%	82.4%	16.2%	83.8%
15	2000	158,751	14,336	BOYD-FIELDS, CHRYSANTHEA	140,609	KILPATRICK, CAROLYN	3,806	126,273 D	9.0%	88.6%	9.3%	90.7%
15	1998	124,860	12,887	BOYD-FIELDS, CHRYSANTHEA	108,582	KILPATRICK, CAROLYN	3,391	95,695 D	10.3%	87.0%	10.6%	89.4%
15	1996	162,600	16,009	HUME, STEPHEN	143,683	KILPATRICK, CAROLYN	2,908	127,674 D	9.8%	88.4%	10.0%	90.0%
15	1994	142,005	20,074	SAVAGE, JOHN	119,442	COLLINS, BARBARA-ROSE	2,489	99,368 D	14.1%	84.1%	14.4%	85.6%
15	1992	184,964	31,849	VINCENT, CHARLES C.	148,908	COLLINS, BARBARA-ROSE	4,207	117,059 D	17.2%	80.5%	17.6%	82.4%
16	2000	235,517	62,469	MORSE, WILLIAM	167,142	DINGELL, JOHN D., JR.	5,906	104,673 D	26.5%	71.0%	27.2%	72.8%
16	1998	174,357	54,121	MORSE, WILLIAM	116,145	DINGELL, JOHN D., JR.	4,091	62,024 D	31.0%	66.6%	31.8%	68.2%
16	1996	220,612	78,723	DESANA, JAMES	136,854	DINGELL, JOHN D., JR.	5,035	58,131 D	35.7%	62.0%	36.5%	63.5%
16	1994	178,976	71,159	LARKIN, KEN	105,849	DINGELL, JOHN D., JR.	1,968	34,690 D	39.8%	59.1%	40.2%	59.8%
16	1992	240,936	75,694	BEAUMONT, FRANK	156,964	DINGELL, JOHN D., JR.	8,278	81,270 D	31.4%	65.1%	32.5%	67.5%

MICHIGAN
GENERAL AND PRIMARY ELECTIONS

2000 GENERAL ELECTIONS

President   Other vote was 16,711 Libertarian (Browne); 3,791 U.S. Taxpayers (Phillips); 2,426 Natural Law (Hagelin); 2,061 write-in (Buchanan). Official state returns listed Buchanan with 1,851 votes, but later totals from Wayne County increased his vote there from 14 to 224, an increase of 210 votes.

Senator   Other vote was 37,542 Green (Abel); 29,966 Libertarian (Corliss); 26,274 Reform (Forton); 11,628 U.S. Taxpayers (Mangopoulos); 5,630 Natural Law (Quarton).

Congress   Other vote was: CD 1: 1,839 Natural Law (Conway), 1,757 Libertarian (Loosemore), 24 write-in (Johnson); CD 2: 2,705 Natural Law (Susan Goldberg), 2,639 Libertarian (Smith), 1,449 U.S. Taxpayers (Graeser); CD 3: 2,403 Libertarian (Haas), 1,093 U.S. Taxpayers (Grego), 1,053 Reform (Lowndes), 866 Natural Law (Berta); CD 4: 3,790 Green (Gamble), 2,112 Libertarian (Whitelock), 978 U.S. Taxpayers (Emerick), 792 Natural Law (Stuart Goldberg); CD 5: 3,070 Libertarian (Foster), 1,345 Natural Law (Ellison); CD 6: 3,573 Libertarian (Bradley), 1,872 Reform (Overton), 1,290 U.S. Taxpayers (James); CD 7: 2,359 Reform (Spencer), 2,158 Libertarian (Broda), 1,878 U.S. Taxpayers (Cousino), 1,159 Natural Law (Petrosoff), 7 write-in (Wunsch); CD 8: 3,467 Green (Bucqueroux), 2,467 Libertarian (Eyster), 715 Natural Law (Allen), 691 U.S. Taxpayers (Gualdoni); CD 9: 5,337 Libertarian (Martin), 1,657 U.S. Taxpayers (Haines), 824 Natural Law (Bouche'); CD 10: 4,412 Libertarian (Friend), 2,322 U.S. Taxpayers (Pilchak), 4 write-in (America); CD 11: 4,191 Green (MacDermaid), 3,371 Libertarian (Gach), 1,425 Reform (Ditzhazy), 1,244 U.S. Taxpayers (Malone), 1,228 Natural Law (Hixson); CD 12: 4,137 Green (Ness), 3,630 Libertarian (Le Cureaux), 887 Natural Law (Rosenberg); CD 13: 4,578 Libertarian (Corliss), 2,110 U.S. Taxpayers (Dunn), 1,304 Natural Law (Arndt); CD 14: 2,113 Libertarian (Catalfio), 1,030 Natural Law (Miller); CD 15: 1,690 Libertarian (Warner), 1,402 U.S. Taxpayers (Thomas), 714 Natural Law (Smith); CD 16: 2,814 Libertarian (Hlavac), 2,154 U.S. Taxpayers (Larkin), 938 Natural Law (Hamze).

2000 PRIMARY ELECTIONS

Primary   February 22, 2000   (President)   **Registration**   6,745,138   No Party Registration
August 8, 2000   (Congress)   (as of July 10, 2000)

Primary Type   Open—Any registered voter could vote in the primary of either party.

Note: An asterisk (*) denotes incumbent.

	REPUBLICAN PRIMARIES			DEMOCRATIC PRIMARIES		
President	John McCain	650,805	51.0%	Uncommitted	31,655	70.6%
	George W. Bush	549,665	43.1%	Lyndon H. LaRouche Jr.	13,195	29.4%
	Alan Keyes	59,032	4.6%			
	Uncommitted	8,714	0.7%			
	Steve Forbes	4,894	0.4%			
	Gary Bauer	2,733	0.2%			
	Orrin G. Hatch	905	0.1%			
	Joe Schriner	22				
	TOTAL	1,276,770		TOTAL	44,850	
Senator	Spencer Abraham*	527,278	100.0%	Debbie Stabenow	417,503	100.0%
	TOTAL	527,278		TOTAL	417,503	
Congressional District 1	Chuck Yob	40,491	100.0%	Bart Stupak*	40,601	88.9%
				Sven Johnson	5,051	11.1%
	TOTAL	40,491		TOTAL	45,652	
Congressional District 2	Peter Hoekstra*	57,170	100.0%	Bob Shrauger	12,786	100.0%
	TOTAL	57,170		TOTAL	12,786	

MICHIGAN

GENERAL AND PRIMARY ELECTIONS

REPUBLICAN PRIMARIES			DEMOCRATIC PRIMARIES		
Congressional District 3	Vernon J. Ehlers*	59,202	100.0%	Timothy Steele	10,743	73.5%
				Gregory Frushour	3,877	26.5%
	TOTAL	59,202		TOTAL	14,620	
Congressional District 4	Dave Camp*	51,264	100.0%	Lawrence Hollenbeck	15,785	100.0%
	TOTAL	51,264		TOTAL	15,785	
Congressional District 5	Ronald Actis	26,562	100.0%	James A. Barcia*	43,120	100.0%
	TOTAL	26,562		TOTAL	43,120	
Congressional District 6	Fred Upton*	45,192	100.0%	James Bupp	6,386	100.0%
	TOTAL	45,192		TOTAL	6,386	
Congressional District 7	Nick Smith*	37,729	100.0%	Jennie Crittendon	8,406	100.0%
	TOTAL	37,729		TOTAL	8,406	
Congressional District 8	Mike Rogers	30,441	100.0%	Dianne Byrum	24,195	100.0%
	TOTAL	30,441		TOTAL	24,195	
Congressional District 9	Grant Garrett	11,541	43.1%	Dale E. Kildee*	27,034	100.0%
	John Geisler	10,965	40.9%			
	Carlo Iovannitti	4,297	16.0%			
	TOTAL	26,803		TOTAL	27,034	
Congressional District 10	Tom Turner	24,259	100.0%	David E. Bonior*	31,835	89.2%
				Mario Fundaro	2,137	6.0%
				Anthony America	1,708	4.8%
	TOTAL	24,259		TOTAL	35,680	
Congressional District 11	Joe Knollenberg*	39,798	100.0%	Matthew Frumin	21,121	100.0%
	TOTAL	39,798		TOTAL	21,121	
Congressional District 12	Bart Baron	18,154	100.0%	Sander Levin*	25,549	100.0%
	TOTAL	18,154		TOTAL	25,549	
Congressional District 13	Carl Berry	13,363	100.0%	Lynn Rivers*	24,469	100.0%
	TOTAL	13,363		TOTAL	24,469	
Congressional District 14	William Ashe	3,538	100.0%	John Conyers Jr.*	48,014	100.0%
	TOTAL	3,538		TOTAL	48,014	
Congressional District 15	Chrysanthea Boyd-Fields	2,336	100.0%	Carolyn Kilpatrick*	40,993	100.0%
	TOTAL	2,336			40,993	
Congressional District 16	William Morse	11,908	100.0%	John D. Dingell*	35,574	100.0%
	TOTAL	11,908		TOTAL	35,574	

MINNESOTA

GOVERNOR

Jesse Ventura (Independence Party of Minnesota). Elected 1998 to a four-year term.

SENATORS

Mark Dayton (D). Elected 2000 to a six-year term.

Paul D. Wellstone (D). Re-elected 1996 to a six-year term. Previously elected 1990.

REPRESENTATIVES

1. Gil Gutknecht (R)
2. Mark Kennedy (R)
3. Jim Ramstad (R)
4. Betty McCollum (D)
5. Martin O. Sabo (D)
6. William P. Luther (D)
7. Collin C. Peterson (D)
8. James L. Oberstar (D)

POSTWAR VOTE FOR PRESIDENT

Year	Total Vote	Republican		Democratic		Other Vote	Plurality	Percentage			
								Total Vote		Major Vote	
		Vote	Candidate	Vote	Candidate			Rep.	Dem.	Rep.	Dem.
2000**	2,438,685	1,109,659	Bush, George W.	1,168,266	Gore, Al	160,760	58,607 D	45.5%	47.9%	48.7%	51.3%
1996**	2,192,640	766,476	Dole, Bob	1,120,438	Clinton, Bill	305,726	353,962 D	35.0%	51.1%	40.6%	59.4%
1992**	2,347,948	747,841	Bush, George	1,020,997	Clinton, Bill	579,110	273,156 D	31.9%	43.5%	42.3%	57.7%
1988	2,096,790	962,337	Bush, George	1,109,471	Dukakis, Michael S.	24,982	147,134 D	45.9%	52.9%	46.4%	53.6%
1984	2,084,449	1,032,603	Reagan, Ronald	1,036,364	Mondale, Walter F.	15,482	3,761 D	49.5%	49.7%	49.9%	50.1%
1980**	2,051,980	873,268	Reagan, Ronald	954,174	Carter, Jimmy	224,538	80,906 D	42.6%	46.5%	47.8%	52.2%
1976	1,949,931	819,395	Ford, Gerald R.	1,070,440	Carter, Jimmy	60,096	251,045 D	42.0%	54.9%	43.4%	56.6%
1972	1,741,652	898,269	Nixon, Richard M.	802,346	McGovern, George S.	41,037	95,923 R	51.6%	46.1%	52.8%	47.2%
1968	1,588,506	658,643	Nixon, Richard M.	857,738	Humphrey, Hubert H.	72,125	199,095 D	41.5%	54.0%	43.4%	56.6%
1964	1,554,462	559,624	Goldwater, Barry M.	991,117	Johnson, Lyndon B.	3,721	431,493 D	36.0%	63.8%	36.1%	63.9%
1960	1,541,887	757,915	Nixon, Richard M.	779,933	Kennedy, John F.	4,039	22,018 D	49.2%	50.6%	49.3%	50.7%
1956	1,340,005	719,302	Eisenhower, Dwight D.	617,525	Stevenson, Adlai E.	3,178	101,777 R	53.7%	46.1%	53.8%	46.2%
1952	1,379,483	763,211	Eisenhower, Dwight D.	608,458	Stevenson, Adlai E.	7,814	154,753 R	55.3%	44.1%	55.6%	44.4%
1948	1,212,226	483,617	Dewey, Thomas E.	692,966	Truman, Harry S.	35,643	209,349 D	39.9%	57.2%	41.1%	58.9%

In 2000 the other vote column includes 126,696 votes cast for Green (Nader). In 1996 the other vote column includes 257,704 votes cast for Perot. In 1992 the other vote column includes 562,506 votes cast for Perot. In 1980 the other column includes 174,990 votes for Independent (Anderson).

MINNESOTA

POSTWAR VOTE FOR GOVERNOR

Year	Total Vote	Republican		Democratic		Other Vote	Rep.-Dem. Plurality	Percentage			
								Total Vote		Major Vote	
		Vote	Candidate	Vote	Candidate			Rep.	Dem.	Rep.	Dem.
1998**	2,090,518	716,880	Coleman, Norm	587,060	Humphrey, Hubert H., III	786,578	56,523 V	34.3%	28.1%	55.0%	45.0%
1994	1,765,590	1,094,165	Carlson, Arne	589,344	Marty, John	82,081	504,821 R	62.0%	33.4%	65.0%	35.0%
1990	1,806,777	895,988	Carlson, Arne	836,218	Perpich, Rudy	74,571	59,770 R	49.6%	46.3%	51.7%	48.3%
1986	1,415,989	606,755	Ludeman, Cal R.	790,138	Perpich, Rudy	19,096	183,383 D	42.9%	55.8%	43.4%	56.6%
1982	1,789,539	715,796	Whitney, Wheelock	1,049,104	Perpich, Rudy	24,639	333,308 D	40.0%	58.6%	40.6%	59.4%
1978	1,585,702	830,019	Quie, Albert H.	718,244	Perpich, Rudy	37,439	111,775 R	52.3%	45.3%	53.6%	46.4%
1974	1,252,898	367,722	Johnson, John W.	786,787	Anderson, Wendell R.	98,389	419,065 D	29.3%	62.8%	31.9%	68.1%
1970	1,365,443	621,780	Head, Douglas M.	737,921	Anderson, Wendell R.	5,742	116,141 D	45.5%	54.0%	45.7%	54.3%
1966	1,295,058	680,593	LeVander, Harold	607,943	Rolvaag, Karl F.	6,522	72,650 R	52.6%	46.9%	52.8%	47.2%
1962**	1,246,904	619,751	Andersen, Elmer L.	619,842	Rolvaag, Karl F.	7,311	91 D	49.7%	49.7%	50.0%	50.0%
1960	1,550,265	783,813	Andersen, Elmer L.	760,934	Freeman, Orville L.	5,518	22,879 R	50.6%	49.1%	50.7%	49.3%
1958	1,159,915	490,731	MacKinnon, George	658,326	Freeman, Orville L.	10,858	167,595 D	42.3%	56.8%	42.7%	57.3%
1956	1,422,161	685,196	Nelsen, Ancher	731,180	Freeman, Orville L.	5,785	45,984 D	48.2%	51.4%	48.4%	51.6%
1954	1,151,417	538,865	Anderson, C. Elmer	607,099	Freeman, Orville L.	5,453	68,234 D	46.8%	52.7%	47.0%	53.0%
1952	1,418,869	785,125	Anderson, C. Elmer	624,480	Freeman, Orville L.	9,264	160,645 R	55.3%	44.0%	55.7%	44.3%
1950	1,046,632	635,800	Youngdahl, Luther	400,637	Peterson, Harry H.	10,195	235,163 R	60.7%	38.3%	61.3%	38.7%
1948	1,210,894	643,572	Youngdahl, Luther	545,766	Halsted, Charles L.	21,556	97,806 R	53.1%	45.1%	54.1%	45.9%
1946	880,348	519,067	Youngdahl, Luther	349,565	Barker, Harold H.	11,716	169,502 R	59.0%	39.7%	59.8%	40.2%

In 1998 Jesse Ventura, the Reform Party candidate, received 773,403 votes (37.0 percent of the total vote) and was elected with a plurality of 56,523 votes. The term of office of Minnesota's Governor was increased from two to four years effective with the 1962 election.

POSTWAR VOTE FOR SENATOR

Year	Total Vote	Republican		Democratic		Other Vote	Rep.-Dem. Plurality	Percentage			
								Total Vote		Major Vote	
		Vote	Candidate	Vote	Candidate			Rep.	Dem.	Rep.	Dem.
2000	2,419,520	1,047,474	Gams, Rod	1,181,553	Dayton, Mark	190,493	134,079 D	43.3%	48.8%	47.0%	53.0%
1996	2,183,062	901,282	Boschwitz, Rudy	1,098,493	Wellstone, Paul	183,287	197,211 D	41.3%	50.3%	45.1%	54.9%
1994	1,772,929	869,653	Grams, Rod	781,860	Wynia, Ann	121,416	87,793 R	49.1%	44.1%	52.7%	47.3%
1990	1,808,045	864,375	Boschwitz, Rudy	911,999	Wellstone, Paul D.	31,671	47,624 D	47.8%	50.4%	48.7%	51.3%
1988	2,093,953	1,176,210	Durenberger, David	856,694	Humphrey, Hubert H.,III	61,049	319,516 R	56.2%	40.9%	57.9%	42.1%
1984	2,066,143	1,199,926	Boschwitz, Rudy	852,844	Growe, Joan Anderson	13,373	347,082 R	58.1%	41.3%	58.5%	41.5%
1982	1,804,675	949,207	Durenberger, David	840,401	Dayton, Mark	15,067	108,806 R	52.6%	46.6%	53.0%	47.0%
1978	1,580,778	894,092	Boschwitz, Rudy	638,375	Anderson, Wendell R.	48,311	255,717 R	56.6%	40.4%	58.3%	41.7%
1978S	1,560,724	957,908	Durenberger, David	538,675	Short, Robert E.	64,141	419,233 R	61.4%	34.5%	64.0%	36.0%
1976	1,912,068	478,611	Brekke, Gerald W.	1,290,736	Humphrey, Hubert H.	142,721	812,125 D	25.0%	67.5%	27.1%	72.9%
1972	1,731,653	742,121	Hansen, Philip	981,340	Mondale, Walter F.	8,192	239,219 D	42.9%	56.7%	43.1%	56.9%
1970	1,364,887	568,025	MacGregor, Clark	788,256	Humphrey, Hubert H.	8,606	220,231 D	41.6%	57.8%	41.9%	58.1%
1966	1,271,426	574,868	Forsythe, Robert A.	685,840	Mondale, Walter F.	10,718	110,972 D	45.2%	53.9%	45.6%	54.4%
1964	1,543,590	605,933	Whitney, Wheelock	931,353	McCarthy, Eugene J.	6,304	325,420 D	39.3%	60.3%	39.4%	60.6%
1960	1,536,839	648,586	Peterson, P. K.	884,168	Humphrey, Hubert H.	4,085	235,582 D	42.2%	57.5%	42.3%	57.7%
1958	1,150,883	536,629	Thye, Edward J.	608,847	McCarthy, Eugene J.	5,407	72,218 D	46.6%	52.9%	46.8%	53.2%
1954	1,138,952	479,619	Bjornson, Val	642,193	Humphrey, Hubert H.	17,140	162,574 D	42.1%	56.4%	42.8%	57.2%
1952	1,387,419	785,649	Thye, Edward J.	590,011	Carlson, William E.	11,759	195,638 R	56.6%	42.5%	57.1%	42.9%
1948	1,220,250	485,801	Ball, Joseph H.	729,494	Humphrey, Hubert H.	4,955	243,693 D	39.8%	59.8%	40.0%	60.0%
1946	878,731	517,775	Thye, Edward J.	349,520	Jorgenson, Theodore	11,436	168,255 R	58.9%	39.8%	59.7%	40.3%

One of the 1978 elections was for a short term to fill a vacancy.

MINNESOTA

Districts Established April 11, 1994

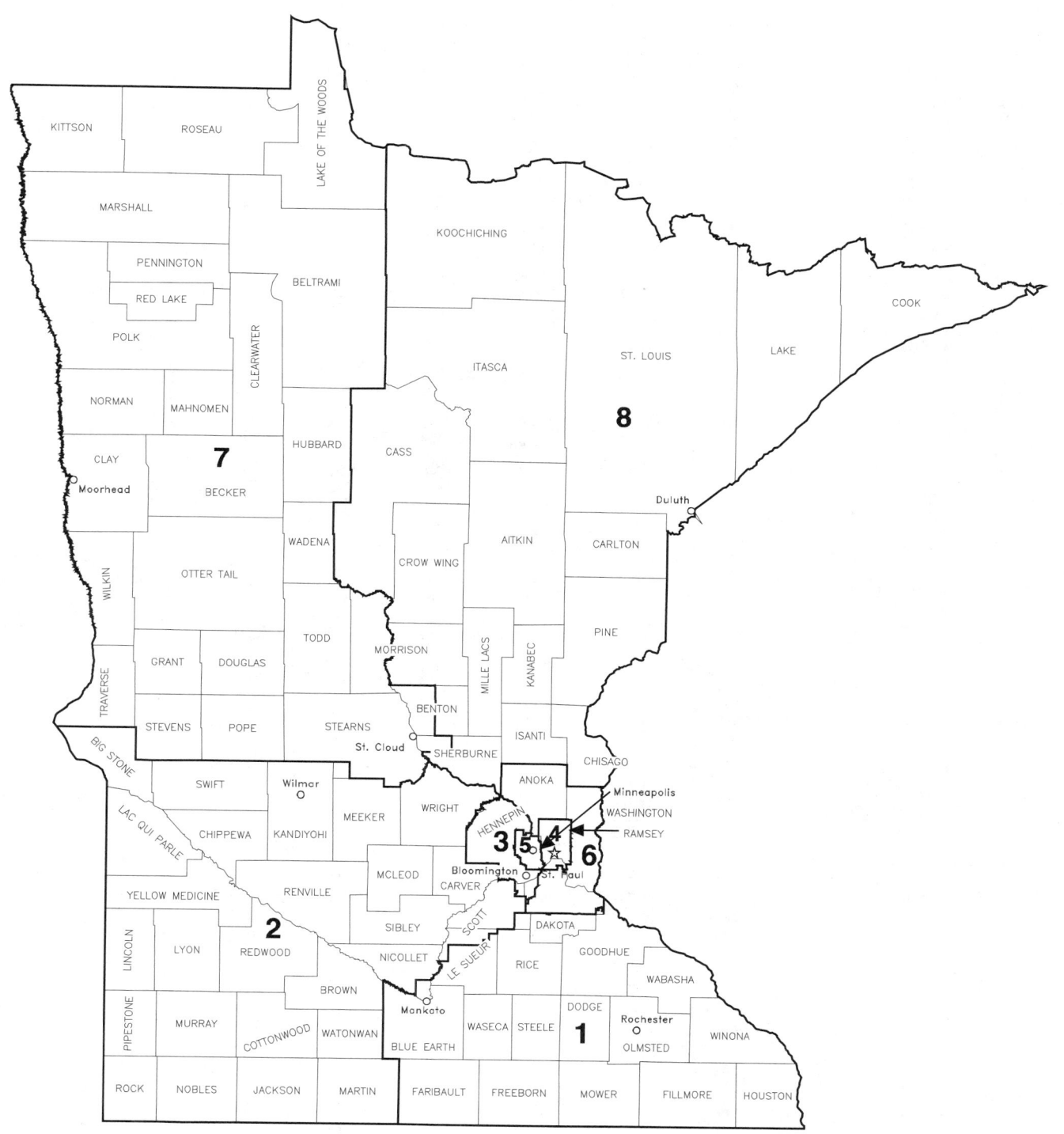

MINNESOTA

PRESIDENT 2000

2000 Census Population	County	Total Vote	Republican	Democratic	Green (Nader)	Other	Rep.-Dem. Plurality	Percentage of Total Vote Rep.	Dem.	Green
15,301	AITKIN	8,260	3,755	3,830	403	272	75 D	45.5%	46.4%	4.9%
298,084	ANOKA	145,619	69,256	68,008	6,616	1,739	1,248 R	47.6%	46.7%	4.5%
30,000	BECKER	14,333	8,152	5,253	591	337	2,899 R	56.9%	36.6%	4.1%
39,650	BELTRAMI	17,217	8,346	7,301	1,269	301	1,045 R	48.5%	42.4%	7.4%
34,226	BENTON	14,908	7,663	6,009	862	374	1,654 R	51.4%	40.3%	5.8%
5,820	BIG STONE	2,980	1,370	1,430	109	71	60 D	46.0%	48.0%	3.7%
55,941	BLUE EARTH	27,402	12,942	12,329	1,761	370	613 R	47.2%	45.0%	6.4%
26,911	BROWN	12,834	7,370	4,650	561	253	2,720 R	57.4%	36.2%	4.4%
31,671	CARLTON	15,081	5,578	8,620	634	249	3,042 D	37.0%	57.2%	4.2%
70,205	CARVER	35,021	20,790	12,462	1,381	388	8,328 R	59.4%	35.6%	3.9%
27,150	CASS	13,593	7,134	5,534	663	262	1,600 R	52.5%	40.7%	4.9%
13,088	CHIPPEWA	6,352	2,977	2,952	268	155	25 R	46.9%	46.5%	4.2%
41,101	CHISAGO	21,987	10,937	9,593	1,116	341	1,344 R	49.7%	43.6%	5.1%
51,229	CLAY	23,358	11,712	10,128	963	555	1,584 R	50.1%	43.4%	4.1%
8,423	CLEARWATER	3,824	2,137	1,466	134	87	671 R	55.9%	38.3%	3.5%
5,168	COOK	2,820	1,295	1,171	290	64	124 R	45.9%	41.5%	10.3%
12,167	COTTONWOOD	6,181	3,369	2,503	208	101	866 R	54.5%	40.5%	3.4%
55,099	CROW WING	28,128	15,035	11,255	1,314	524	3,780 R	53.5%	40.0%	4.7%
355,904	DAKOTA	182,249	87,250	85,446	7,799	1,754	1,804 R	47.9%	46.9%	4.3%
17,731	DODGE	8,050	4,213	3,370	327	140	843 R	52.3%	41.9%	4.1%
32,821	DOUGLAS	17,205	9,811	6,352	746	296	3,459 R	57.0%	36.9%	4.3%
16,181	FARIBAULT	8,424	4,336	3,624	309	155	712 R	51.5%	43.0%	3.7%
21,122	FILLMORE	10,223	4,646	5,020	409	148	374 D	45.4%	49.1%	4.0%
32,584	FREEBORN	16,139	6,843	8,514	555	227	1,671 D	42.4%	52.8%	3.4%
44,127	GOODHUE	22,257	10,852	9,981	1,093	331	871 R	48.8%	44.8%	4.9%
6,289	GRANT	3,624	1,804	1,507	214	99	297 R	49.8%	41.6%	5.9%
1,116,200	HENNEPIN	573,846	225,657	307,599	35,584	5,006	81,942 D	39.3%	53.6%	6.2%
19,718	HOUSTON	10,167	5,077	4,502	421	167	575 R	49.9%	44.3%	4.1%
18,376	HUBBARD	9,613	5,307	3,632	484	190	1,675 R	55.2%	37.8%	5.0%
31,287	ISANTI	14,929	7,668	6,247	753	261	1,421 R	51.4%	41.8%	5.0%
43,992	ITASCA	21,714	9,545	10,583	1,137	449	1,038 D	44.0%	48.7%	5.2%
11,268	JACKSON	5,438	2,773	2,364	194	107	409 R	51.0%	43.5%	3.6%
14,996	KANABEC	6,811	3,480	2,831	344	156	649 R	51.1%	41.6%	5.1%
41,203	KANDIYOHI	19,285	10,026	8,220	734	305	1,806 R	52.0%	42.6%	3.8%
5,285	KITTSON	2,637	1,353	1,107	68	109	246 R	51.3%	42.0%	2.6%
14,355	KOOCHICHING	6,879	3,523	2,903	302	151	620 R	51.2%	42.2%	4.4%
8,067	LAC QUI PARLE	4,453	1,941	2,244	160	108	303 D	43.6%	50.4%	3.6%
11,058	LAKE	6,563	2,465	3,579	426	93	1,114 D	37.6%	54.5%	6.5%
4,522	LAKE OF THE WOODS	2,187	1,216	848	74	49	368 R	55.6%	38.8%	3.4%
25,426	LE SUEUR	12,331	6,138	5,361	603	229	777 R	49.8%	43.5%	4.9%
6,429	LINCOLN	3,284	1,513	1,590	105	76	77 D	46.1%	48.4%	3.2%
25,425	LYON	11,489	6,087	4,737	460	205	1,350 R	53.0%	41.2%	4.0%
34,898	MCLEOD	15,394	8,782	5,609	681	322	3,173 R	57.0%	36.4%	4.4%
5,190	MAHNOMEN	2,224	1,122	921	96	85	201 R	50.4%	41.4%	4.3%
10,155	MARSHALL	5,199	2,912	1,910	160	217	1,002 R	56.0%	36.7%	3.1%
21,802	MARTIN	10,371	5,686	4,166	376	143	1,520 R	54.8%	40.2%	3.6%
22,644	MEEKER	10,672	5,520	4,402	517	233	1,118 R	51.7%	41.2%	4.8%
22,330	MILLE LACS	10,253	5,223	4,376	448	206	847 R	50.9%	42.7%	4.4%
31,712	MORRISON	14,677	8,197	5,274	633	573	2,923 R	55.8%	35.9%	4.3%
38,603	MOWER	18,480	6,873	10,693	678	236	3,820 D	37.2%	57.9%	3.7%
9,165	MURRAY	4,753	2,407	2,093	149	104	314 R	50.6%	44.0%	3.1%
29,771	NICOLLET	15,327	7,221	7,041	842	223	180 R	47.1%	45.9%	5.5%
20,832	NOBLES	8,872	4,766	3,760	238	108	1,006 R	53.7%	42.4%	2.7%
7,442	NORMAN	3,641	1,808	1,575	123	135	233 R	49.7%	43.3%	3.4%
124,277	OLMSTED	59,392	30,641	25,822	2,198	731	4,819 R	51.6%	43.5%	3.7%
57,159	OTTER TAIL	28,511	16,963	9,844	1,120	584	7,119 R	59.5%	34.5%	3.9%
13,584	PENNINGTON	6,320	3,380	2,458	255	227	922 R	53.5%	38.9%	4.0%
26,530	PINE	13,068	5,854	6,148	734	332	294 D	44.8%	47.0%	5.6%
9,895	PIPESTONE	4,894	2,693	1,970	140	91	723 R	55.0%	40.3%	2.9%
31,369	POLK	14,140	7,609	5,764	369	398	1,845 R	53.8%	40.8%	2.6%

MINNESOTA

PRESIDENT 2000

2000 Census Population	County	Total Vote	Republican	Democratic	Green (Nader)	Other	Rep.-Dem. Plurality		Percentage of Total Vote		
									Rep.	Dem.	Green
11,236	POPE	5,987	2,808	2,771	264	144	37	R	46.9%	46.3%	4.4%
511,035	RAMSEY	244,278	87,669	138,470	15,522	2,617	50,801	D	35.9%	56.7%	6.4%
4,299	RED LAKE	2,090	1,090	830	68	102	260	R	52.2%	39.7%	3.3%
16,815	REDWOOD	7,748	4,589	2,681	314	164	1,908	R	59.2%	34.6%	4.1%
17,154	RENVILLE	8,122	4,036	3,533	355	198	503	R	49.7%	43.5%	4.4%
56,665	RICE	26,021	10,876	13,140	1,639	366	2,264	D	41.8%	50.5%	6.3%
9,721	ROCK	5,010	2,772	2,081	116	41	691	R	55.3%	41.5%	2.3%
16,338	ROSEAU	7,166	4,695	2,128	176	167	2,567	R	65.5%	29.7%	2.5%
200,528	ST. LOUIS	107,464	35,420	64,237	6,290	1,517	28,817	D	33.0%	59.8%	5.9%
89,498	SCOTT	43,793	23,954	17,503	1,829	507	6,451	R	54.7%	40.0%	4.2%
64,417	SHERBURNE	30,835	16,813	12,109	1,501	412	4,704	R	54.5%	39.3%	4.9%
15,356	SIBLEY	7,335	4,087	2,687	361	200	1,400	R	55.7%	36.6%	4.9%
133,166	STEARNS	62,476	32,402	24,800	3,820	1,454	7,602	R	51.9%	39.7%	6.1%
33,680	STEELE	16,066	8,223	6,900	697	246	1,323	R	51.2%	42.9%	4.3%
10,053	STEVENS	5,752	2,831	2,434	393	94	397	R	49.2%	42.3%	6.8%
11,956	SWIFT	5,437	2,376	2,698	218	145	322	D	43.7%	49.6%	4.0%
24,426	TODD	11,092	6,031	4,132	485	444	1,899	R	54.4%	37.3%	4.4%
4,134	TRAVERSE	2,106	1,074	884	86	62	190	R	51.0%	42.0%	4.1%
21,610	WABASHA	10,531	5,245	4,522	571	193	723	R	49.8%	42.9%	5.4%
13,713	WADENA	6,382	3,733	2,251	253	145	1,482	R	58.5%	35.3%	4.0%
19,526	WASECA	8,864	4,608	3,694	398	164	914	R	52.0%	41.7%	4.5%
201,130	WASHINGTON	107,009	51,502	49,637	4,891	979	1,865	R	48.1%	46.4%	4.6%
11,876	WATONWAN	5,134	2,562	2,258	212	102	304	R	49.9%	44.0%	4.1%
7,138	WILKIN	3,305	2,032	1,046	77	150	986	R	61.5%	31.6%	2.3%
49,985	WINONA	23,918	10,773	11,069	1,750	326	296	D	45.0%	46.3%	7.3%
89,986	WRIGHT	43,366	23,861	16,762	1,977	766	7,099	R	55.0%	38.7%	4.6%
11,080	YELLOW MEDICINE	5,515	2,598	2,528	232	157	70	R	47.1%	45.8%	4.2%
4,919,479	TOTAL	2,438,685	1,109,659	1,168,266	126,696	34,064	58,607	D	45.5%	47.9%	5.2%

MINNESOTA

SENATOR 2000

2000 Census Population	County	Total Vote	Republican	Democratic	Other	Rep.-Dem. Plurality		Percentage			
								Total Vote		Major Vote	
								Rep.	Dem.	Rep.	Dem.
15,301	AITKIN	8,229	3,357	4,306	566	949	D	40.8%	52.3%	43.8%	56.2%
298,084	ANOKA	144,571	68,018	64,681	11,872	3,337	R	47.0%	44.7%	51.3%	48.7%
30,000	BECKER	14,180	7,543	6,022	615	1,521	R	53.2%	42.5%	55.6%	44.4%
39,650	BELTRAMI	17,083	7,902	8,123	1,058	221	D	46.3%	47.6%	49.3%	50.7%
34,226	BENTON	14,839	7,157	6,396	1,286	761	R	48.2%	43.1%	52.8%	47.2%
5,820	BIG STONE	2,966	1,177	1,621	168	444	D	39.7%	54.7%	42.1%	57.9%
55,941	BLUE EARTH	27,148	12,110	12,657	2,381	547	D	44.6%	46.6%	48.9%	51.1%
26,911	BROWN	12,762	6,731	5,295	736	1,436	R	52.7%	41.5%	56.0%	44.0%
31,671	CARLTON	15,059	5,261	9,148	650	3,887	D	34.9%	60.7%	36.5%	63.5%
70,205	CARVER	34,854	19,959	12,219	2,676	7,740	R	57.3%	35.1%	62.0%	38.0%
27,150	CASS	13,541	6,422	6,289	830	133	R	47.4%	46.4%	50.5%	49.5%
13,088	CHIPPEWA	6,345	2,668	3,294	383	626	D	42.0%	51.9%	44.8%	55.2%
41,101	CHISAGO	21,845	10,663	9,289	1,893	1,374	R	48.8%	42.5%	53.4%	46.6%
51,229	CLAY	23,010	10,293	11,647	1,070	1,354	D	44.7%	50.6%	46.9%	53.1%
8,423	CLEARWATER	3,785	2,069	1,575	141	494	R	54.7%	41.6%	56.8%	43.2%
5,168	COOK	2,793	1,224	1,377	192	153	D	43.8%	49.3%	47.1%	52.9%
12,167	COTTONWOOD	6,176	3,049	2,807	320	242	R	49.4%	45.5%	52.1%	47.9%
55,099	CROW WING	28,029	13,199	13,122	1,708	77	R	47.1%	46.8%	50.1%	49.9%
355,904	DAKOTA	180,856	83,356	82,412	15,088	944	R	46.1%	45.6%	50.3%	49.7%
17,731	DODGE	8,033	4,098	3,491	444	607	R	51.0%	43.5%	54.0%	46.0%

MINNESOTA

SENATOR 2000

2000 Census Population	County	Total Vote	Republican	Democratic	Other	Rep.-Dem. Plurality		Percentage			
								Total Vote		Major Vote	
								Rep.	Dem.	Rep.	Dem.
32,821	DOUGLAS	17,074	8,783	7,257	1,034	1,526	R	51.4%	42.5%	54.8%	45.2%
16,181	FARIBAULT	8,400	3,967	3,949	484	18	R	47.2%	47.0%	50.1%	49.9%
21,122	FILLMORE	10,157	4,747	4,976	434	229	D	46.7%	49.0%	48.8%	51.2%
32,584	FREEBORN	16,119	6,660	8,642	817	1,982	D	41.3%	53.6%	43.5%	56.5%
44,127	GOODHUE	22,201	10,679	9,939	1,583	740	R	48.1%	44.8%	51.8%	48.2%
6,289	GRANT	3,615	1,572	1,787	256	215	D	43.5%	49.4%	46.8%	53.2%
1,116,200	HENNEPIN	568,111	212,718	298,660	56,733	85,942	D	37.4%	52.6%	41.6%	58.4%
19,718	HOUSTON	9,928	5,106	4,316	506	790	R	51.4%	43.5%	54.2%	45.8%
18,376	HUBBARD	9,530	4,825	4,119	586	706	R	50.6%	43.2%	53.9%	46.1%
31,287	ISANTI	14,901	7,666	5,983	1,252	1,683	R	51.4%	40.2%	56.2%	43.8%
43,992	ITASCA	21,654	8,710	11,855	1,089	3,145	D	40.2%	54.7%	42.4%	57.6%
11,268	JACKSON	5,416	2,532	2,614	270	82	D	46.8%	48.3%	49.2%	50.8%
14,996	KANABEC	6,761	3,289	2,948	524	341	R	48.6%	43.6%	52.7%	47.3%
41,203	KANDIYOHI	19,281	8,947	9,120	1,214	173	D	46.4%	47.3%	49.5%	50.5%
5,285	KITTSON	2,622	1,119	1,415	88	296	D	42.7%	54.0%	44.2%	55.8%
14,355	KOOCHICHING	6,818	3,211	3,323	284	112	D	47.1%	48.7%	49.1%	50.9%
8,067	LAC QUI PARLE	4,458	1,774	2,431	253	657	D	39.8%	54.5%	42.2%	57.8%
11,058	LAKE	6,522	2,491	3,731	300	1,240	D	38.2%	57.2%	40.0%	60.0%
4,522	LAKE OF THE WOODS	2,182	1,085	1,001	96	84	R	49.7%	45.9%	52.0%	48.0%
25,426	LE SUEUR	12,300	5,964	5,479	857	485	R	48.5%	44.5%	52.1%	47.9%
6,429	LINCOLN	3,292	1,496	1,629	167	133	D	45.4%	49.5%	47.9%	52.1%
25,425	LYON	11,414	5,525	5,221	668	304	R	48.4%	45.7%	51.4%	48.6%
34,898	MCLEOD	15,371	8,228	5,921	1,222	2,307	R	53.5%	38.5%	58.2%	41.8%
5,190	MAHNOMEN	2,205	948	1,161	96	213	D	43.0%	52.7%	45.0%	55.0%
10,155	MARSHALL	5,155	2,482	2,510	163	28	D	48.1%	48.7%	49.7%	50.3%
21,802	MARTIN	10,380	5,173	4,631	576	542	R	49.8%	44.6%	52.8%	47.2%
22,644	MEEKER	10,661	5,284	4,595	782	689	R	49.6%	43.1%	53.5%	46.5%
22,330	MILLE LACS	10,241	4,976	4,457	808	519	R	48.6%	43.5%	52.8%	47.2%
31,712	MORRISON	14,646	7,489	6,185	972	1,304	R	51.1%	42.2%	54.8%	45.2%
38,603	MOWER	18,389	6,624	10,997	768	4,373	D	36.0%	59.8%	37.6%	62.4%
9,165	MURRAY	4,729	2,233	2,220	276	13	R	47.2%	46.9%	50.1%	49.9%
29,771	NICOLLET	15,218	6,866	7,154	1,198	288	D	45.1%	47.0%	49.0%	51.0%
20,832	NOBLES	8,757	4,384	3,889	484	495	R	50.1%	44.4%	53.0%	47.0%
7,442	NORMAN	3,622	1,543	1,948	131	405	D	42.6%	53.8%	44.2%	55.8%
124,277	OLMSTED	58,621	28,300	27,073	3,248	1,227	R	48.3%	46.2%	51.1%	48.9%
57,159	OTTER TAIL	28,322	15,235	11,587	1,500	3,648	R	53.8%	40.9%	56.8%	43.2%
13,584	PENNINGTON	6,286	2,807	3,187	292	380	D	44.7%	50.7%	46.8%	53.2%
26,530	PINE	12,990	5,494	6,460	1,036	966	D	42.3%	49.7%	46.0%	54.0%
9,895	PIPESTONE	4,812	2,456	2,076	280	380	R	51.0%	43.1%	54.2%	45.8%
31,369	POLK	14,065	6,602	6,954	509	352	D	46.9%	49.4%	48.7%	51.3%
11,236	POPE	5,988	2,653	2,942	393	289	D	44.3%	49.1%	47.4%	52.6%
511,035	RAMSEY	241,709	82,698	135,852	23,159	53,154	D	34.2%	56.2%	37.8%	62.2%
4,299	RED LAKE	2,086	896	1,115	75	219	D	43.0%	53.5%	44.6%	55.4%
16,815	REDWOOD	7,740	4,252	3,005	483	1,247	R	54.9%	38.8%	58.6%	41.4%
17,154	RENVILLE	8,102	3,737	3,801	564	64	D	46.1%	46.9%	49.6%	50.4%
56,665	RICE	25,709	10,953	12,649	2,107	1,696	D	42.6%	49.2%	46.4%	53.6%
9,721	ROCK	4,921	2,488	2,146	287	342	R	50.6%	43.6%	53.7%	46.3%
16,338	ROSEAU	7,120	4,113	2,783	224	1,330	R	57.8%	39.1%	59.6%	40.4%
200,528	ST. LOUIS	106,654	33,773	67,519	5,362	33,746	D	31.7%	63.3%	33.3%	66.7%
89,498	SCOTT	43,593	23,271	16,939	3,383	6,332	R	53.4%	38.9%	57.9%	42.1%
64,417	SHERBURNE	30,675	16,476	11,742	2,457	4,734	R	53.7%	38.3%	58.4%	41.6%
15,356	SIBLEY	7,322	3,773	3,004	545	769	R	51.5%	41.0%	55.7%	44.3%
133,166	STEARNS	61,688	30,348	26,343	4,997	4,005	R	49.2%	42.7%	53.5%	46.5%
33,680	STEELE	16,020	7,932	6,946	1,142	986	R	49.5%	43.4%	53.3%	46.7%
10,053	STEVENS	5,691	2,640	2,635	416	5	R	46.4%	46.3%	50.0%	50.0%
11,956	SWIFT	5,416	2,167	2,925	324	758	D	40.0%	54.0%	42.6%	57.4%
24,426	TODD	11,086	5,699	4,781	606	918	R	51.4%	43.1%	54.4%	45.6%
4,134	TRAVERSE	2,099	954	1,033	112	79	D	45.5%	49.2%	48.0%	52.0%
21,610	WABASHA	10,546	5,088	4,800	658	288	R	48.2%	45.5%	51.5%	48.5%
13,713	WADENA	6,361	3,388	2,599	374	789	R	53.3%	40.9%	56.6%	43.4%

MINNESOTA

SENATOR 2000

2000 Census Population	County	Total Vote	Republican	Democratic	Other	Rep.-Dem. Plurality		Percentage			
								Total Vote		Major Vote	
								Rep.	Dem.	Rep.	Dem.
19,526	WASECA	8,835	4,468	3,740	627	728	R	50.6%	42.3%	54.4%	45.6%
201,130	WASHINGTON	106,339	49,193	48,597	8,549	596	R	46.3%	45.7%	50.3%	49.7%
11,876	WATONWAN	5,099	2,390	2,372	337	18	R	46.9%	46.5%	50.2%	49.8%
7,138	WILKIN	3,279	1,758	1,389	132	369	R	53.6%	42.4%	55.9%	44.1%
49,985	WINONA	23,437	10,596	11,261	1,580	665	D	45.2%	48.0%	48.5%	51.5%
89,986	WRIGHT	43,148	23,123	16,663	3,362	6,460	R	53.6%	38.6%	58.1%	41.9%
11,080	YELLOW MEDICINE	5,527	2,401	2,801	325	400	D	43.4%	50.7%	46.2%	53.8%
4,919,479	TOTAL	2,419,520	1,047,474	1,181,553	190,493	134,079	D	43.3%	48.8%	47.0%	53.0%

MINNESOTA

CONGRESS

CD	Year	Total Vote	Republican		Democratic		Other Vote	Rep.-Dem. Plurality		Percentage			
			Vote	Candidate	Vote	Candidate				Total Vote		Major Vote	
										Rep.	Dem.	Rep.	Dem.
1	2000	283,221	159,835	GUTKNECHT, GIL	117,946	RIEDER, MARY	5,440	41,889	R	56.4%	41.6%	57.5%	42.5%
1	1998	239,903	131,233	GUTKNECHT, GIL	108,420	BECKMAN, TRACY L.	250	22,813	R	54.7%	45.2%	54.8%	45.2%
1	1996	261,162	137,545	GUTKNECHT, GIL	123,188	RIEDER, MARY	429	14,357	R	52.7%	47.2%	52.8%	47.2%
1	1994	213,218	117,613	GUTKNECHT, GIL	95,328	HOTTINGER, JOHN C.	277	22,285	R	55.2%	44.7%	55.2%	44.8%
1	1992	279,430	72,367	DROOGSMA, TIMOTHY R.	206,369	PENNY, TIMOTHY J.	694	134,002	D	25.9%	73.9%	26.0%	74.0%
2	2000	288,900	138,957	KENNEDY, MARK	138,802	MINGE, DAVID	11,141	155	R	48.1%	48.0%	50.0%	50.0%
2	1998	261,127	99,490	DUEHRING, CRAIG	148,933	MINGE, DAVID	12,704	49,443	D	38.1%	57.0%	40.0%	60.0%
2	1996	262,353	107,807	REVIER, GARY B.	144,083	MINGE, DAVID	10,463	36,276	D	41.1%	54.9%	42.8%	57.2%
2	1994	219,785	98,881	REVIER, GARY B.	114,289	MINGE, DAVID	6,615	15,408	D	45.0%	52.0%	46.4%	53.6%
2	1992	276,303	131,587	LUDEMAN, CAL R.	132,156	MINGE, DAVID	12,560	569	D	47.6%	47.8%	49.9%	50.1%
3	2000	329,062	222,571	RAMSTAD, JIM	98,219	SHUFF, SUE	8,272	124,352	R	67.6%	29.8%	69.4%	30.6%
3	1998	283,309	203,731	RAMSTAD, JIM	66,505	LEINO, STANLEY J.	13,073	137,226	R	71.9%	23.5%	75.4%	24.6%
3	1996	293,621	205,845	RAMSTAD, JIM	87,359	LEINO, STANLEY J.	417	118,486	R	70.1%	29.8%	70.2%	29.8%
3	1994	236,531	173,223	RAMSTAD, JIM	62,211	OLSON, BOB	1,097	111,012	R	73.2%	26.3%	73.6%	26.4%
3	1992	314,731	200,240	RAMSTAD, JIM	104,606	MANDELL, PAUL	9,885	95,634	R	63.6%	33.2%	65.7%	34.3%
4	2000	271,439	83,852	RUNBECK, LINDA	130,403	MCCOLLUM, BETTY	57,184	46,551	D	30.9%	48.0%	39.1%	60.9%
4	1998	238,560	94,923	NEWINSKI, DENNIS	128,005	VENTO, BRUCE F.	15,632	33,082	D	39.8%	53.7%	42.6%	57.4%
4	1996	255,759	94,110	NEWINSKI, DENNIS	145,831	VENTO, BRUCE F.	15,818	51,721	D	36.8%	57.0%	39.2%	60.8%
4	1994	210,630	88,344	NEWINSKI, DENNIS	115,638	VENTO, BRUCE F.	6,648	27,294	D	41.9%	54.9%	43.3%	56.7%
4	1992	277,956	101,744	MAITLAND, IAN	159,796	VENTO, BRUCE F.	16,416	58,052	D	36.6%	57.5%	38.9%	61.1%
5	2000	255,145	58,191	TAYLOR, FRANK	176,629	SABO, MARTIN O.	20,325	118,438	D	22.8%	69.2%	24.8%	75.2%
5	1998	217,612	60,035	TAYLOR, FRANK	145,535	SABO, MARTIN O.	12,042	85,500	D	27.6%	66.9%	29.2%	70.8%
5	1996	246,061	70,115	ULDRICH, JACK	158,275	SABO, MARTIN O.	17,671	88,160	D	28.5%	64.3%	30.7%	69.3%
5	1994	196,172	73,258	LEGRAND, DOROTHY	121,515	SABO, MARTIN O.	1,399	48,257	D	37.3%	61.9%	37.6%	62.4%
5	1992	277,094	77,093	MORIARTY, STEPHEN A.	174,139	SABO, MARTIN O.	25,862	97,046	D	27.8%	62.8%	30.7%	69.3%
6	2000	355,824	170,900	KLINE, JOHN	176,340	LUTHER, WILLIAM P.	8,584	5,440	D	48.0%	49.6%	49.2%	50.8%
6	1998	297,701	136,866	KLINE, JOHN	148,728	LUTHER, WILLIAM P.	12,107	11,862	D	46.0%	50.0%	47.9%	52.1%
6	1996	295,482	129,989	JUDE, TAD	164,921	LUTHER, WILLIAM P.	572	34,932	D	44.0%	55.8%	44.1%	55.9%
6	1994	227,775	113,190	JUDE, TAD	113,740	LUTHER, WILLIAM P.	845	550	D	49.7%	49.9%	49.9%	50.1%
6	1992	301,023	133,564	GRAMS, ROD	100,016	SIKORSKI, GERRY	67,443	33,548	R	44.4%	33.2%	57.2%	42.8%

MINNESOTA

CONGRESS

CD	Year	Total Vote	Republican		Democratic		Other Vote	Rep.-Dem. Plurality	Percentage			
									Total Vote		Major Vote	
			Vote	Candidate	Vote	Candidate			Rep.	Dem.	Rep.	Dem.
7	2000	270,496	79,175	MENZE, GLEN	185,771	PETERSON, COLLIN C.	5,550	106,596 D	29.3%	68.7%	29.9%	70.1%
7	1998	236,942	66,562	EDIN, ALETA	169,907	PETERSON, COLLIN C.	473	103,345 D	28.1%	71.7%	28.1%	71.9%
7	1996	251,599	80,132	MCKIGNEY, DARRELL	170,936	PETERSON, COLLIN C.	531	90,804 D	31.8%	67.9%	31.9%	68.1%
7	1994	211,003	102,623	OMANN, BERNIE	108,023	PETERSON, COLLIN C.	357	5,400 D	48.6%	51.2%	48.7%	51.3%
7	1992	265,524	130,396	OMANN, BERNIE	133,886	PETERSON, COLLIN C.	1,242	3,490 D	49.1%	50.4%	49.3%	50.7%
8	2000	309,651	79,890	LEMEN, BOB	210,094	OBERSTAR, JAMES L.	19,667	130,204 D	25.8%	67.8%	27.5%	72.5%
8	1998	263,263	69,667	SHUSTER, JERRY	173,734	OBERSTAR, JAMES L.	19,862	104,067 D	26.5%	66.0%	28.6%	71.4%
8	1996	275,338	69,460	LARSON, ANDY	185,333	OBERSTAR, JAMES L.	20,545	115,873 D	25.2%	67.3%	27.3%	72.7%
8	1994	233,271	79,818	HERWIG, PHIL	153,161	OBERSTAR, JAMES L.	292	73,343 D	34.2%	65.7%	34.3%	65.7%
8	1992	283,031	83,823	HERWIG, PHIL	167,104	OBERSTAR, JAMES L.	32,104	83,281 D	29.6%	59.0%	33.4%	66.6%

MINNESOTA

GENERAL AND PRIMARY ELECTIONS

2000 GENERAL ELECTIONS

President Other vote was 22,166 Reform Party Minnesota (Buchanan); 5,282 Libertarian (Browne); 3,272 Constitution (Phillips); 2,294 Reform (Hagelin); 1,022 Socialist Workers (Harris); 17 write-in (Marcus); 7 write-in (Mooney); 4 write-in (Strickland).

Senator Other vote was 140,583 Independence Party (Gibson); 21,447 Grassroots (Daniels); 12,956 Socialist Workers (Ellis); 8,915 Constitution (Swan); 6,588 Libertarian (Pakieser); 4 write-in (Savior).

Congress Other vote was: CD 1: 5,440 Libertarian (Osness); CD 2: 7,875 Independence Party (Brekke), 1,929 Libertarian (Helwig), 1,337 Constitution (Burda); CD 3: 5,302 Libertarian (Odden), 2,970 Constitution (Niska); CD 4: 55,899 Independence Party (Foley), 1,285 Constitution (Skrivanek); CD 5: 11,323 Independence Party (Tomich), 4,522 Constitution (Lavoi), 4,480 Libertarian (Charnstrom); CD 6: 8,584 Constitution (Hubbard); CD 7: 5,550 Constitution (Sivertson); CD 8: 19,667 Independent (Darling).

2000 PRIMARY ELECTIONS

Primary September 12, 2000 **Registration** 2,790,322 No Party Registration
(as of Sept. 12, 2000)

Primary Type Open—Any registered voter could vote in the primary of either party.

Note: An asterisk (*) denotes incumbent.

MINNESOTA

GENERAL AND PRIMARY ELECTIONS

	REPUBLICAN PRIMARIES			DEMOCRATIC PRIMARIES		
Senator	Rod Grams*	112,335	89.1%	Mark Dayton	178,972	41.3%
	Bill Dahn	13,728	10.9%	Mike Ciresi	96,874	22.4%
				Jerry R. Janezich	90,074	20.8%
				Rebecca Yanisch	63,289	14.6%
				"Dick" Franson	1,336	0.3%
				Ole Savior	1,206	0.3%
				Gregg A. Iverson	1,038	0.2%
				Hal Dorland	610	0.1%
	TOTAL	126,063		TOTAL	433,399	
Congressional District 1	Gil Gutknecht*	17,824	100.0%	Mary Rieder	31,244	100.0%
	TOTAL	17,824		TOTAL	31,244	
Congressional District 2	Mark Kennedy	13,779	79.3%	David Minge*	30,089	100.0%
	Joe Wagner	3,598	20.7%			
	TOTAL	17,377		TOTAL	30,089	
Congressional District 3	Jim Ramstad*	13,995	100.0%	Sue Shuff	29,841	74.5%
				Darryl Tyree Stanton	10,197	25.5%
	TOTAL	13,995		TOTAL	40,038	
Congressional District 4	Linda Runbeck	10,722	86.2%	Betty McCollum	35,911	50.4%
	Patricia Reagan	1,713	13.8%	Steven G. Novak	16,332	22.9%
				Chris Coleman	13,555	19.0%
				Cathie Hartnett	5,454	7.7%
	TOTAL	12,435		TOTAL	71,252	
Congressional District 5	Frank Taylor	4,837	63.2%	Martin Olav Sabo*	55,879	100.0%
	Chris Flynn	2,815	36.8%			
	TOTAL	7,652		TOTAL	55,879	
Congressional District 6	John Kline	19,029	100.0%	William P. "Bill" Luther*	45,378	100.0%
	TOTAL	19,029		TOTAL	45,378	
Congressional District 7	Glen Menze	10,258	65.4%	Collin C. Peterson*	33,948	100.0%
	Aleta Edin	5,433	34.6%			
	TOTAL	15,691		TOTAL	33,948	
Congressional District 8	Bob Lemen	7,197	50.1%	James L. Oberstar*	64,189	100.0%
	Warren L. Nelson	7,179	49.9%			
	TOTAL	14,376		TOTAL	64,189	

MISSISSIPPI

GOVERNOR

Ronnie Musgrove (D). Elected 2000 to a four-year term by the Mississippi House after neither Republican nor Democratic candidate won a majority in November 1999 election.

SENATORS

Thad Cochran (R). Re-elected 1996 to a six-year term. Previously elected 1990, 1984, 1978.

Trent Lott (R). Re-elected 2000 to a six-year term. Previously elected 1994, 1988.

REPRESENTATIVES

1. Roger F. Wicker (R)
2. Bennie Thompson (D)
3. Charles W. Pickering (R)
4. Ronnie Shows (D)
5. Gene Taylor (D)

POSTWAR VOTE FOR PRESIDENT

Year	Total Vote	Republican Vote	Republican Candidate	Democratic Vote	Democratic Candidate	Other Vote	Plurality	Total Vote Rep.	Total Vote Dem.	Major Vote Rep.	Major Vote Dem.
2000**	994,184	572,844	Bush, George W.	404,614	Gore, Al	16,726	168,230 R	57.6%	40.7%	58.6%	41.4%
1996**	893,857	439,838	Dole, Bob	394,022	Clinton, Bill	59,997	45,816 R	49.2%	44.1%	52.7%	47.3%
1992**	981,793	487,793	Bush, George	400,258	Clinton, Bill	93,742	87,535 R	49.7%	40.8%	54.9%	45.1%
1988	931,527	557,890	Bush, George	363,921	Dukakis, Michael S.	9,716	193,969 R	59.9%	39.1%	60.5%	39.5%
1984	941,104	582,377	Reagan, Ronald	352,192	Mondale, Walter F.	6,535	230,185 R	61.9%	37.4%	62.3%	37.7%
1980**	892,620	441,089	Reagan, Ronald	429,281	Carter, Jimmy	22,250	11,808 R	49.4%	48.1%	50.7%	49.3%
1976	769,361	366,846	Ford, Gerald R.	381,309	Carter, Jimmy	21,206	14,463 D	47.7%	49.6%	49.0%	51.0%
1972	645,963	505,125	Nixon, Richard M.	126,782	McGovern, George S.	14,056	378,343 R	78.2%	19.6%	79.9%	20.1%
1968**	654,509	88,516	Nixon, Richard M.	150,644	Humphrey, Hubert H.	415,349	264,705 A	13.5%	23.0%	37.0%	63.0%
1964	409,146	356,528	Goldwater, Barry M.	52,618	Johnson, Lyndon B.		303,910 R	87.1%	12.9%	87.1%	12.9%
1960**	298,171	73,561	Nixon, Richard M.	108,362	Kennedy, John F.	116,248	7,886 U	24.7%	36.3%	40.4%	59.6%
1956	248,104	60,685	Eisenhower, Dwight D.	144,453	Stevenson, Adlai E.	42,966	83,768 D	24.5%	58.2%	29.6%	70.4%
1952	285,532	112,966	Eisenhower, Dwight D.	172,566	Stevenson, Adlai E.		59,600 D	39.6%	60.4%	39.6%	60.4%
1948**	192,190	5,043	Dewey, Thomas E.	19,384	Truman, Harry S.	167,763	148,154 SR	2.6%	10.1%	20.6%	79.4%

In 2000 the other vote column includes 8,122 votes cast for Green (Nader). In 1996 the other vote column includes 52,222 votes cast for Perot. In 1992 the other vote column includes 85,626 votes cast for Perot. In 1980 the other column includes 12,036 votes for Independent (Anderson). In 1968 other vote was Independent (Wallace). In 1960 other vote was Unpledged Independent Democratic. In 1948 other vote was 167,538 States Rights and 225 Progressive.

MISSISSIPPI

POSTWAR VOTE FOR GOVERNOR

Year	Total Vote	Republican		Democratic		Other Vote	Rep.-Dem. Plurality	Percentage			
		Vote	Candidate	Vote	Candidate			Total Vote		Major Vote	
								Rep.	Dem.	Rep.	Dem.
1999**	763,938	370,691	Parker, Mike	379,034	Musgrove, Ronnie	14,213	8,343 D	48.5%	49.6%	49.4%	50.6%
1995	819,471	455,261	Fordice, Kirk	364,210	Molpus, Dick		91,051 R	55.6%	44.4%	55.6%	44.4%
1991	711,188	361,500	Fordice, Kirk	338,435	Mabus, Ray	11,253	23,065 R	50.8%	47.6%	51.6%	48.4%
1987	721,695	336,006	Reed, Jack	385,689	Mabus, Ray		49,683 D	46.6%	53.4%	46.6%	53.4%
1983	742,737	288,764	Bramlett, Leon	409,209	Allain, William A.	44,764	120,445 D	38.9%	55.1%	41.4%	58.6%
1979	677,322	263,702	Carmichael, Gil	413,620	Winter, William F.		149,918 D	38.9%	61.1%	38.9%	61.1%
1975	708,033	319,632	Carmichael, Gil	369,568	Finch, Cliff	18,833	49,936 D	45.1%	52.2%	46.4%	53.6%
1971	780,537		—	601,122	Waller, William L.	179,415	601,122 D		77.0%		100.0%
1967	448,697	133,379	Phillips, Rubel L.	315,318	Williams, John Bell		181,939 D	29.7%	70.3%	29.7%	70.3%
1963	363,971	138,515	Phillips, Rubel L.	225,456	Johnson, Paul B.		86,941 D	38.1%	61.9%	38.1%	61.9%
1959	57,671		—	57,671	Barnett, Ross R.		57,671 D		100.0%		100.0%
1955	40,707		—	40,707	Coleman, James P.		40,707 D		100.0%		100.0%
1951	43,422		—	43,422	White, Hugh		43,422 D		100.0%		100.0%
1947	166,095		—	161,993	Wright, Fielding L.	4,102	161,993 D		97.5%		100.0%

In 1999 no candidate received a majority of the vote. Democrat Musgrove was elected in January 2000 by the Mississippi House of Representatives.

POSTWAR VOTE FOR SENATOR

Year	Total Vote	Republican		Democratic		Other Vote	Rep.-Dem. Plurality	Percentage			
		Vote	Candidate	Vote	Candidate			Total Vote		Major Vote	
								Rep.	Dem.	Rep.	Dem.
2000	994,144	654,941	Lott, Trent	314,090	Brown, Troy	25,113	340,851 R	65.9%	31.6%	67.6%	32.4%
1996	878,662	624,154	Cochran, Thad	240,647	Hunt, James W.	13,861	383,507 R	71.0%	27.4%	72.2%	27.8%
1994	608,085	418,333	Lott, Trent	189,752	Harper, Ken		228,581 R	68.8%	31.2%	68.8%	31.2%
1990	274,244	274,244	Cochran, Thad		—		274,244 R	100.0%		100.0%	
1988	946,719	510,380	Lott, Trent	436,339	Dowdy, Wayne		74,041 R	53.9%	46.1%	53.9%	46.1%
1984	952,240	580,314	Cochran, Thad	371,926	Winter, William F.		208,388 R	60.9%	39.1%	60.9%	39.1%
1982	645,026	230,927	Barbour, Haley	414,099	Stennis, John		183,172 D	35.8%	64.2%	35.8%	64.2%
1978	583,936	263,089	Cochran, Thad	185,454	Dantin, Maurice	135,393	77,635 R	45.1%	31.8%	58.7%	41.3%
1976	554,433		—	554,433	Stennis, John		554,433 D		100.0%		100.0%
1972	645,746	249,779	Carmichael, Gil	375,102	Eastland, James O.	20,865	125,323 D	38.7%	58.1%	40.0%	60.0%
1970	324,215		—	286,622	Stennis, John	37,593	286,622 D		88.4%		100.0%
1966	393,900	105,150	Walker, Prentiss	258,248	Eastland, James O.	30,502	153,098 D	26.7%	65.6%	28.9%	71.1%
1964	343,364		—	343,364	Stennis, John		343,364 D		100.0%		100.0%
1960	266,148	21,807	Moore, Joe A.	244,341	Eastland, James O.		222,534 D	8.2%	91.8%	8.2%	91.8%
1958	61,039		—	61,039	Stennis, John		61,039 D		100.0%		100.0%
1954	105,526	4,678	White, James A.	100,848	Eastland, James O.		96,170 D	4.4%	95.6%	4.4%	95.6%
1952	233,919		—	233,919	Stennis, John		233,919 D		100.0%		100.0%
1948	151,478		—	151,478	Eastland, James O.		151,478 D		100.0%		100.0%
1947S	193,709		[See note below]				D				
1946	46,747		—	46,747	Bilbo, Theodore		46,747 D		100.0%		100.0%

The 1947 election was for a short term to fill a vacancy and was held without party designation or nomination; John Stennis polled 52,068 votes (26.9% of the total vote) and won the election with a 6,343-vote plurality. Other candidate votes in this election were 45,725 W. M. Colmer; 43,642 Forrest B. Jackson; 27,159 Paul B. Johnson; 24,492 John E. Rankin and 623 R. L. Collins.

MISSISSIPPI

Districts Established February 21, 1992

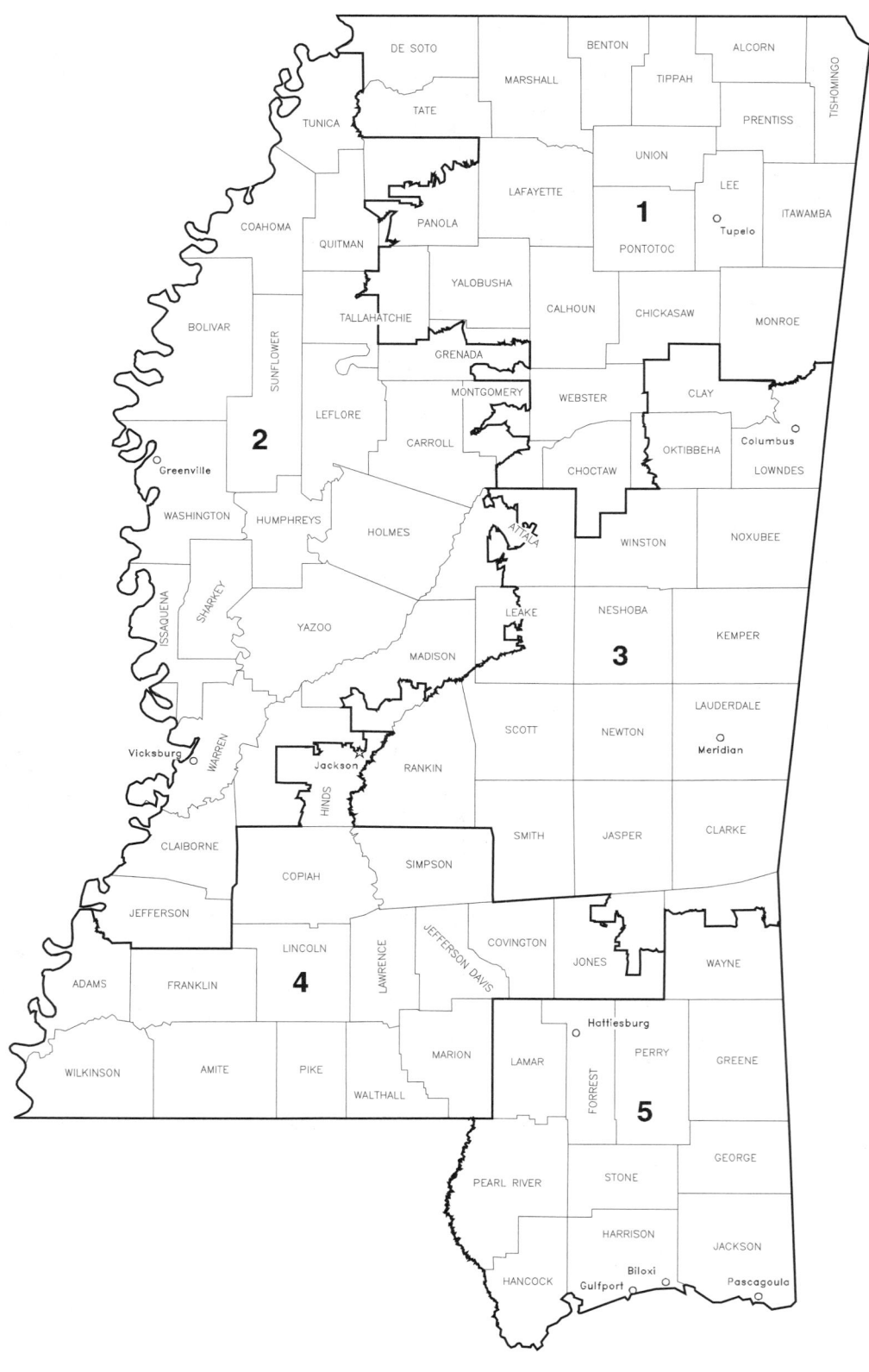

MISSISSIPPI

PRESIDENT 2000

2000 Census Population	County	Total Vote	Republican	Democratic	Green (Nader)	Other	Rep.-Dem. Plurality	Percentage of Total Vote		
								Rep.	Dem.	Green
34,340	ADAMS	14,879	6,691	8,065	89	34	1,374 D	45.0%	54.2%	0.6%
34,558	ALCORN	12,638	7,254	5,059	101	224	2,195 R	57.4%	40.0%	0.8%
13,599	AMITE	6,408	3,677	2,673	28	30	1,004 R	57.4%	41.7%	0.4%
19,661	ATTALA	7,173	4,206	2,922	22	23	1,284 R	58.6%	40.7%	0.3%
8,026	BENTON	3,481	1,561	1,886	17	17	325 D	44.8%	54.2%	0.5%
40,633	BOLIVAR	13,538	4,847	8,436	64	191	3,589 D	35.8%	62.3%	0.5%
15,069	CALHOUN	5,758	3,448	2,251	31	28	1,197 R	59.9%	39.1%	0.5%
10,769	CARROLL	4,924	3,165	1,726	18	15	1,439 R	64.3%	35.1%	0.4%
19,440	CHICKASAW	7,175	3,549	3,519	36	71	30 R	49.5%	49.0%	0.5%
9,758	CHOCTAW	3,719	2,398	1,278	27	16	1,120 R	64.5%	34.4%	0.7%
11,831	CLAIBORNE	4,615	883	3,670	12	50	2,787 D	19.1%	79.5%	0.3%
17,955	CLARKE	6,919	4,503	2,368	17	31	2,135 R	65.1%	34.2%	0.2%
21,979	CLAY	8,165	3,570	4,515	41	39	945 D	43.7%	55.3%	0.5%
30,622	COAHOMA	9,553	3,695	5,662	48	148	1,967 D	38.7%	59.3%	0.5%
28,757	COPIAH	10,587	5,643	4,845	52	47	798 R	53.3%	45.8%	0.5%
19,407	COVINGTON	6,881	4,180	2,623	30	48	1,557 R	60.7%	38.1%	0.4%
107,199	DE SOTO	34,936	24,879	9,586	302	169	15,293 R	71.2%	27.4%	0.9%
72,604	FORREST	22,251	13,281	8,500	353	117	4,781 R	59.7%	38.2%	1.6%
8,448	FRANKLIN	3,953	2,427	1,486	20	20	941 R	61.4%	37.6%	0.5%
19,144	GEORGE	7,284	5,143	1,977	69	95	3,166 R	70.6%	27.1%	0.9%
13,299	GREENE	4,436	3,082	1,317	14	23	1,765 R	69.5%	29.7%	0.3%
23,263	GRENADA	8,643	4,743	3,813	38	49	930 R	54.9%	44.1%	0.4%
42,967	HANCOCK	14,548	9,326	4,801	285	136	4,525 R	64.1%	33.0%	2.0%
189,601	HARRISON	52,616	32,256	19,142	923	295	13,114 R	61.3%	36.4%	1.8%
250,800	HINDS	87,770	37,753	46,789	711	2,517	9,036 D	43.0%	53.3%	0.8%
21,609	HOLMES	7,422	1,937	5,447	15	23	3,510 D	26.1%	73.4%	0.2%
11,206	HUMPHREYS	3,944	1,628	2,288	17	11	660 D	41.3%	58.0%	0.4%
2,274	ISSAQUENA	941	366	555	4	16	189 D	38.9%	59.0%	0.4%
22,770	ITAWAMBA	8,564	5,424	2,994	70	76	2,430 R	63.3%	35.0%	0.8%
131,420	JACKSON	45,107	30,068	14,193	567	279	15,875 R	66.7%	31.5%	1.3%
18,149	JASPER	6,447	3,294	3,104	23	26	190 R	51.1%	48.1%	0.4%
9,740	JEFFERSON	3,408	600	2,786	6	16	2,186 D	17.6%	81.7%	0.2%
13,962	JEFFERSON DAVIS	5,317	2,437	2,835	11	34	398 D	45.8%	53.3%	0.2%
64,958	JONES	24,340	16,341	7,713	150	136	8,628 R	67.1%	31.7%	0.6%
10,453	KEMPER	4,261	1,915	2,311	18	17	396 D	44.9%	54.2%	0.4%
38,744	LAFAYETTE	12,678	7,081	5,139	385	73	1,942 R	55.9%	40.5%	3.0%
39,070	LAMAR	16,602	12,795	3,478	212	117	9,317 R	77.1%	20.9%	1.3%
78,161	LAUDERDALE	25,970	17,315	8,412	160	83	8,903 R	66.7%	32.4%	0.6%
13,258	LAWRENCE	6,587	3,674	2,841	32	40	833 R	55.8%	43.1%	0.5%
20,940	LEAKE	6,952	4,114	2,793	20	25	1,321 R	59.2%	40.2%	0.3%
75,755	LEE	25,094	15,551	9,142	240	161	6,409 R	62.0%	36.4%	1.0%
37,947	LEFLORE	11,276	4,626	6,401	43	206	1,775 D	41.0%	56.8%	0.4%
33,166	LINCOLN	13,000	8,540	4,358	60	42	4,182 R	65.7%	33.5%	0.5%
61,586	LOWNDES	19,230	11,404	7,537	172	117	3,867 R	59.3%	39.2%	0.9%
74,674	MADISON	29,859	19,109	10,416	219	115	8,693 R	64.0%	34.9%	0.7%
25,595	MARION	10,998	6,796	4,114	58	30	2,682 R	61.8%	37.4%	0.5%
34,993	MARSHALL	12,592	4,723	7,735	73	61	3,012 D	37.5%	61.4%	0.6%
38,014	MONROE	13,360	7,397	5,783	113	67	1,614 R	55.4%	43.3%	0.8%
12,189	MONTGOMERY	4,849	2,630	2,187	15	17	443 R	54.2%	45.1%	0.3%
28,684	NESHOBA	9,066	6,409	2,563	53	41	3,846 R	70.7%	28.3%	0.6%
21,838	NEWTON	7,738	5,540	2,147	28	23	3,393 R	71.6%	27.7%	0.4%
12,548	NOXUBEE	4,954	1,530	3,383	15	26	1,853 D	30.9%	68.3%	0.3%
42,902	OKTIBBEHA	14,804	7,959	6,443	255	147	1,516 R	53.8%	43.5%	1.7%
34,274	PANOLA	11,389	5,424	5,880	41	44	456 D	47.6%	51.6%	0.4%
48,621	PEARL RIVER	16,477	11,575	4,611	173	118	6,964 R	70.2%	28.0%	1.0%
12,138	PERRY	4,359	3,026	1,285	22	26	1,741 R	69.4%	29.5%	0.5%
38,940	PIKE	14,166	7,464	6,544	114	44	920 R	52.7%	46.2%	0.8%
26,726	PONTOTOC	9,510	6,601	2,771	84	54	3,830 R	69.4%	29.1%	0.9%
25,556	PRENTISS	8,482	5,101	3,287	54	40	1,814 R	60.1%	38.8%	0.6%
10,117	QUITMAN	3,413	1,280	2,103	8	22	823 D	37.5%	61.6%	0.2%

MISSISSIPPI

PRESIDENT 2000

2000 Census Population	County	Total Vote	Republican	Democratic	Green (Nader)	Other	Rep.-Dem. Plurality	Percentage of Total Vote		
								Rep.	Dem.	Green
115,327	RANKIN	41,435	32,983	8,050	261	141	24,933 R	79.6%	19.4%	0.6%
28,423	SCOTT	9,206	5,601	3,548	27	30	2,053 R	60.8%	38.5%	0.3%
6,580	SHARKEY	2,903	1,074	1,706	16	107	632 D	37.0%	58.8%	0.6%
27,639	SIMPSON	9,574	6,254	3,227	39	54	3,027 R	65.3%	33.7%	0.4%
16,182	SMITH	6,528	4,838	1,620	26	44	3,218 R	74.1%	24.8%	0.4%
13,622	STONE	5,523	3,702	1,677	65	79	2,025 R	67.0%	30.4%	1.2%
34,369	SUNFLOWER	8,415	3,369	4,981	30	35	1,612 D	40.0%	59.2%	0.4%
14,903	TALLAHATCHIE	5,523	2,428	3,041	20	34	613 D	44.0%	55.1%	0.4%
25,370	TATE	8,693	5,148	3,441	66	38	1,707 R	59.2%	39.6%	0.8%
20,826	TIPPAH	8,403	5,381	2,908	60	54	2,473 R	64.0%	34.6%	0.7%
19,163	TISHOMINGO	6,992	4,122	2,747	64	59	1,375 R	59.0%	39.3%	0.9%
9,227	TUNICA	2,366	792	1,539	9	26	747 D	33.5%	65.0%	0.4%
25,362	UNION	9,311	6,087	3,094	69	61	2,993 R	65.4%	33.2%	0.7%
15,156	WALTHALL	5,895	3,476	2,356	30	33	1,120 R	59.0%	40.0%	0.5%
49,644	WARREN	18,623	10,892	7,485	173	73	3,407 R	58.5%	40.2%	0.9%
62,977	WASHINGTON	18,328	7,367	10,405	70	486	3,038 D	40.2%	56.8%	0.4%
21,216	WAYNE	7,705	4,635	2,981	42	47	1,654 R	60.2%	38.7%	0.5%
10,294	WEBSTER	4,545	3,069	1,426	24	26	1,643 R	67.5%	31.4%	0.5%
10,312	WILKINSON	4,098	1,423	2,551	32	92	1,128 D	34.7%	62.2%	0.8%
20,160	WINSTON	8,368	4,645	3,672	20	31	973 R	55.5%	43.9%	0.2%
13,051	YALOBUSHA	5,228	2,470	2,674	51	33	204 D	47.2%	51.1%	1.0%
28,149	YAZOO	10,516	5,254	4,997	50	215	257 R	50.0%	47.5%	0.5%
2,844,658	TOTAL	994,184	572,844	404,614	8,122	8,604	168,230 R	57.6%	40.7%	0.8%

MISSISSIPPI

GOVERNOR 1999

2000 Census Population	County	Total Vote	Republican	Democratic	Other	Rep.-Dem. Plurality	Percentage			
							Total Vote		Major Vote	
							Rep.	Dem.	Rep.	Dem.
34,340	ADAMS	11,845	4,906	6,815	124	1,909 D	41.4%	57.5%	41.9%	58.1%
34,558	ALCORN	7,267	2,885	4,198	184	1,313 D	39.7%	57.8%	40.7%	59.3%
13,599	AMITE	5,839	3,110	2,593	136	517 R	53.3%	44.4%	54.5%	45.5%
19,661	ATTALA	5,537	2,790	2,680	67	110 R	50.4%	48.4%	51.0%	49.0%
8,026	BENTON	2,386	636	1,653	97	1,017 D	26.7%	69.3%	27.8%	72.2%
40,633	BOLIVAR	10,834	3,806	6,765	263	2,959 D	35.1%	62.4%	36.0%	64.0%
15,069	CALHOUN	4,780	2,449	2,249	82	200 R	51.2%	47.1%	52.1%	47.9%
10,769	CARROLL	4,976	2,734	2,166	76	568 R	54.9%	43.5%	55.8%	44.2%
19,440	CHICKASAW	6,652	2,812	3,397	443	585 D	42.3%	51.1%	45.3%	54.7%
9,758	CHOCTAW	3,103	1,644	1,393	66	251 R	53.0%	44.9%	54.1%	45.9%
11,831	CLAIBORNE	4,154	954	3,114	86	2,160 D	23.0%	75.0%	23.5%	76.5%
17,955	CLARKE	6,480	3,457	2,869	154	588 R	53.3%	44.3%	54.6%	45.4%
21,979	CLAY	5,738	2,247	3,402	89	1,155 D	39.2%	59.3%	39.8%	60.2%
30,622	COAHOMA	6,108	1,822	4,208	78	2,386 D	29.8%	68.9%	30.2%	69.8%
28,757	COPIAH	8,247	4,250	3,910	87	340 R	51.5%	47.4%	52.1%	47.9%
19,407	COVINGTON	5,441	2,834	2,504	103	330 R	52.1%	46.0%	53.1%	46.9%
107,199	DE SOTO	18,710	9,301	9,144	265	157 R	49.7%	48.9%	50.4%	49.6%
72,604	FORREST	16,127	8,105	7,832	190	273 R	50.3%	48.6%	50.9%	49.1%
8,448	FRANKLIN	3,292	2,051	1,205	36	846 R	62.3%	36.6%	63.0%	37.0%
19,144	GEORGE	5,601	2,755	2,742	104	13 R	49.2%	49.0%	50.1%	49.9%
13,299	GREENE	2,992	1,407	1,549	36	142 D	47.0%	51.8%	47.6%	52.4%
23,263	GRENADA	6,535	2,975	3,502	58	527 D	45.5%	53.6%	45.9%	54.1%
42,967	HANCOCK	12,585	6,026	5,595	964	431 R	47.9%	44.5%	51.9%	48.1%
189,601	HARRISON	36,145	19,246	16,120	779	3,126 R	53.2%	44.6%	54.4%	45.6%
250,800	HINDS	66,562	28,389	36,788	1,385	8,399 D	42.7%	55.3%	43.6%	56.4%

MISSISSIPPI

GOVERNOR 1999

2000 Census Population	County	Total Vote	Republican	Democratic	Other	Rep.-Dem. Plurality		Total Vote		Major Vote	
								Rep.	Dem.	Rep.	Dem.
21,609	HOLMES	6,144	1,587	4,465	92	2,878	D	25.8%	72.7%	26.2%	73.8%
11,206	HUMPHREYS	4,882	1,874	2,844	164	970	D	38.4%	58.3%	39.7%	60.3%
2,274	ISSAQUENA	811	284	494	33	210	D	35.0%	60.9%	36.5%	63.5%
22,770	ITAWAMBA	5,813	2,619	3,121	73	502	D	45.1%	53.7%	45.6%	54.4%
131,420	JACKSON	31,488	17,736	13,076	676	4,660	R	56.3%	41.5%	57.6%	42.4%
18,149	JASPER	5,471	2,272	3,104	95	832	D	41.5%	56.7%	42.3%	57.7%
9,740	JEFFERSON	2,739	647	2,053	39	1,406	D	23.6%	75.0%	24.0%	76.0%
13,962	JEFFERSON DAVIS	4,851	1,912	2,890	49	978	D	39.4%	59.6%	39.8%	60.2%
64,958	JONES	19,437	10,501	8,664	272	1,837	R	54.0%	44.6%	54.8%	45.2%
10,453	KEMPER	4,613	1,851	2,682	80	831	D	40.1%	58.1%	40.8%	59.2%
38,744	LAFAYETTE	9,421	3,910	5,390	121	1,480	D	41.5%	57.2%	42.0%	58.0%
39,070	LAMAR	12,997	7,844	4,948	205	2,896	R	60.4%	38.1%	61.3%	38.7%
78,161	LAUDERDALE	19,345	11,341	7,684	320	3,657	R	58.6%	39.7%	59.6%	40.4%
13,258	LAWRENCE	5,828	3,121	2,627	80	494	R	53.6%	45.1%	54.3%	45.7%
20,940	LEAKE	5,575	2,922	2,589	64	333	R	52.4%	46.4%	53.0%	47.0%
75,755	LEE	17,012	8,341	8,501	170	160	D	49.0%	50.0%	49.5%	50.5%
37,947	LEFLORE	9,036	3,824	4,855	357	1,031	D	42.3%	53.7%	44.1%	55.9%
33,166	LINCOLN	11,293	7,408	3,788	97	3,620	R	65.6%	33.5%	66.2%	33.8%
61,586	LOWNDES	16,094	8,131	7,732	231	399	R	50.5%	48.0%	51.3%	48.7%
74,674	MADISON	22,165	13,228	8,683	254	4,545	R	59.7%	39.2%	60.4%	39.6%
25,595	MARION	8,635	4,694	3,854	87	840	R	54.4%	44.6%	54.9%	45.1%
34,993	MARSHALL	7,167	2,234	4,845	88	2,611	D	31.2%	67.6%	31.6%	68.4%
38,014	MONROE	9,201	3,687	5,409	105	1,722	D	40.1%	58.8%	40.5%	59.5%
12,189	MONTGOMERY	4,465	1,991	2,404	70	413	D	44.6%	53.8%	45.3%	54.7%
28,684	NESHOBA	7,168	3,849	3,201	118	648	R	53.7%	44.7%	54.6%	45.4%
21,838	NEWTON	6,170	3,723	2,357	90	1,366	R	60.3%	38.2%	61.2%	38.8%
12,548	NOXUBEE	4,792	1,487	3,179	126	1,692	D	31.0%	66.3%	31.9%	68.1%
42,902	OKTIBBEHA	10,628	5,014	5,460	154	446	D	47.2%	51.4%	47.9%	52.1%
34,274	PANOLA	9,317	2,095	7,140	82	5,045	D	22.5%	76.6%	22.7%	77.3%
48,621	PEARL RIVER	13,506	7,213	5,895	398	1,318	R	53.4%	43.6%	55.0%	45.0%
12,138	PERRY	3,517	1,892	1,571	54	321	R	53.8%	44.7%	54.6%	45.4%
38,940	PIKE	12,637	6,025	6,463	149	438	D	47.7%	51.1%	48.2%	51.8%
26,726	PONTOTOC	7,362	4,080	3,175	107	905	R	55.4%	43.1%	56.2%	43.8%
25,556	PRENTISS	7,324	2,922	4,271	131	1,349	D	39.9%	58.3%	40.6%	59.4%
10,117	QUITMAN	3,482	852	2,486	144	1,634	D	24.5%	71.4%	25.5%	74.5%
115,327	RANKIN	30,661	21,587	8,751	323	12,836	R	70.4%	28.5%	71.2%	28.8%
28,423	SCOTT	6,912	3,683	3,148	81	535	R	53.3%	45.5%	53.9%	46.1%
6,580	SHARKEY	2,432	999	1,376	57	377	D	41.1%	56.6%	42.1%	57.9%
27,639	SIMPSON	9,395	5,272	3,972	151	1,300	R	56.1%	42.3%	57.0%	43.0%
16,182	SMITH	5,514	3,092	2,337	85	755	R	56.1%	42.4%	57.0%	43.0%
13,622	STONE	4,737	2,349	2,203	185	146	R	49.6%	46.5%	51.6%	48.4%
34,369	SUNFLOWER	7,054	2,685	4,270	99	1,585	D	38.1%	60.5%	38.6%	61.4%
14,903	TALLAHATCHIE	5,312	1,819	3,361	132	1,542	D	34.2%	63.3%	35.1%	64.9%
25,370	TATE	5,888	1,935	3,861	92	1,926	D	32.9%	65.6%	33.4%	66.6%
20,826	TIPPAH	7,130	2,938	3,999	193	1,061	D	41.2%	56.1%	42.4%	57.6%
19,163	TISHOMINGO	4,992	2,083	2,786	123	703	D	41.7%	55.8%	42.8%	57.2%
9,227	TUNICA	2,598	658	1,829	111	1,171	D	25.3%	70.4%	26.5%	73.5%
25,362	UNION	7,053	3,145	3,823	85	678	D	44.6%	54.2%	45.1%	54.9%
15,156	WALTHALL	4,238	2,330	1,813	95	517	R	55.0%	42.8%	56.2%	43.8%
49,644	WARREN	15,091	8,345	6,564	182	1,781	R	55.3%	43.5%	56.0%	44.0%
62,977	WASHINGTON	12,794	5,370	7,123	301	1,753	D	42.0%	55.7%	43.0%	57.0%
21,216	WAYNE	7,117	3,111	3,860	146	749	D	43.7%	54.2%	44.6%	55.4%
10,294	WEBSTER	4,509	2,491	1,949	69	542	R	55.2%	43.2%	56.1%	43.9%
10,312	WILKINSON	2,428	1,008	1,356	64	348	D	41.5%	55.8%	42.6%	57.4%
20,160	WINSTON	6,491	3,187	3,224	80	37	D	49.1%	49.7%	49.7%	50.3%
13,051	YALOBUSHA	4,218	1,588	2,550	80	962	D	37.6%	60.5%	38.4%	61.6%
28,149	YAZOO	9,052	4,314	4,586	152	272	D	47.7%	50.7%	48.5%	51.5%
2,844,658	TOTAL	763,938	370,691	379,034	14,213	8,343	D	48.5%	49.6%	49.4%	50.6%

MISSISSIPPI

SENATOR 2000

2000 Census Population	County	Total Vote	Republican	Democratic	Other	Rep.-Dem. Plurality		Percentage			
								Total Vote		Major Vote	
								Rep.	Dem.	Rep.	Dem.
34,340	ADAMS	14,396	7,183	7,062	151	121	R	49.9%	49.1%	50.4%	49.6%
34,558	ALCORN	10,868	7,895	2,581	392	5,314	R	72.6%	23.7%	75.4%	24.6%
13,599	AMITE	6,700	4,114	2,405	181	1,709	R	61.4%	35.9%	63.1%	36.9%
19,661	ATTALA	7,484	4,931	2,428	125	2,503	R	65.9%	32.4%	67.0%	33.0%
8,026	BENTON	3,447	2,139	1,178	130	961	R	62.1%	34.2%	64.5%	35.5%
40,633	BOLIVAR	12,533	5,781	6,391	361	610	D	46.1%	51.0%	47.5%	52.5%
15,069	CALHOUN	5,782	4,356	1,313	113	3,043	R	75.3%	22.7%	76.8%	23.2%
10,769	CARROLL	5,128	3,600	1,443	85	2,157	R	70.2%	28.1%	71.4%	28.6%
19,440	CHICKASAW	7,208	4,508	2,400	300	2,108	R	62.5%	33.3%	65.3%	34.7%
9,758	CHOCTAW	3,773	2,739	960	74	1,779	R	72.6%	25.4%	74.0%	26.0%
11,831	CLAIBORNE	4,590	1,452	3,075	63	1,623	D	31.6%	67.0%	32.1%	67.9%
17,955	CLARKE	7,243	4,993	2,100	150	2,893	R	68.9%	29.0%	70.4%	29.6%
21,979	CLAY	8,609	4,700	3,737	172	963	R	54.6%	43.4%	55.7%	44.3%
30,622	COAHOMA	8,076	4,163	3,719	194	444	R	51.5%	46.1%	52.8%	47.2%
28,757	COPIAH	11,021	6,381	4,431	209	1,950	R	57.9%	40.2%	59.0%	41.0%
19,407	COVINGTON	7,133	5,178	1,653	302	3,525	R	72.6%	23.2%	75.8%	24.2%
107,199	DE SOTO	34,716	27,103	6,692	921	20,411	R	78.1%	19.3%	80.2%	19.8%
72,604	FORREST	22,599	15,571	6,371	657	9,200	R	68.9%	28.2%	71.0%	29.0%
8,448	FRANKLIN	4,001	2,799	1,125	77	1,674	R	70.0%	28.1%	71.3%	28.7%
19,144	GEORGE	7,318	5,759	1,386	173	4,373	R	78.7%	18.9%	80.6%	19.4%
13,299	GREENE	4,620	3,649	893	78	2,756	R	79.0%	19.3%	80.3%	19.7%
23,263	GRENADA	9,175	5,666	3,319	190	2,347	R	61.8%	36.2%	63.1%	36.9%
42,967	HANCOCK	14,641	10,978	3,151	512	7,827	R	75.0%	21.5%	77.7%	22.3%
189,601	HARRISON	52,056	37,221	13,160	1,675	24,061	R	71.5%	25.3%	73.9%	26.1%
250,800	HINDS	83,595	42,960	37,112	3,523	5,848	R	51.4%	44.4%	53.7%	46.3%
21,609	HOLMES	7,654	2,611	4,908	135	2,297	D	34.1%	64.1%	34.7%	65.3%
11,206	HUMPHREYS	4,327	1,978	2,254	95	276	D	45.7%	52.1%	46.7%	53.3%
2,274	ISSAQUENA	887	432	435	20	3	D	48.7%	49.0%	49.8%	50.2%
22,770	ITAWAMBA	8,570	6,688	1,645	237	5,043	R	78.0%	19.2%	80.3%	19.7%
131,420	JACKSON	44,304	32,638	10,144	1,522	22,494	R	73.7%	22.9%	76.3%	23.7%
18,149	JASPER	7,044	4,170	2,696	178	1,474	R	59.2%	38.3%	60.7%	39.3%
9,740	JEFFERSON	3,463	1,270	2,087	106	817	D	36.7%	60.3%	37.8%	62.2%
13,962	JEFFERSON DAVIS	5,422	3,059	2,218	145	841	R	56.4%	40.9%	58.0%	42.0%
64,958	JONES	24,464	17,922	6,098	444	11,824	R	73.3%	24.9%	74.6%	25.4%
10,453	KEMPER	4,556	2,235	2,222	99	13	R	49.1%	48.8%	50.1%	49.9%
38,744	LAFAYETTE	12,608	8,417	3,873	318	4,544	R	66.8%	30.7%	68.5%	31.5%
39,070	LAMAR	16,623	13,734	2,118	771	11,616	R	82.6%	12.7%	86.6%	13.4%
78,161	LAUDERDALE	25,494	18,271	6,736	487	11,535	R	71.7%	26.4%	73.1%	26.9%
13,258	LAWRENCE	6,315	4,298	1,830	187	2,468	R	68.1%	29.0%	70.1%	29.9%
20,940	LEAKE	7,276	4,858	2,246	172	2,612	R	66.8%	30.9%	68.4%	31.6%
75,755	LEE	24,728	17,834	6,499	395	11,335	R	72.1%	26.3%	73.3%	26.7%
37,947	LEFLORE	10,884	5,068	5,582	234	514	D	46.6%	51.3%	47.6%	52.4%
33,166	LINCOLN	13,615	9,775	3,614	226	6,161	R	71.8%	26.5%	73.0%	27.0%
61,586	LOWNDES	19,846	12,855	6,534	457	6,321	R	64.8%	32.9%	66.3%	33.7%
74,674	MADISON	30,319	20,884	8,717	718	12,167	R	68.9%	28.8%	70.6%	29.4%
25,595	MARION	11,347	7,796	3,308	243	4,488	R	68.7%	29.2%	70.2%	29.8%
34,993	MARSHALL	11,467	5,439	5,858	170	419	D	47.4%	51.1%	48.1%	51.9%
38,014	MONROE	13,837	8,905	4,689	243	4,216	R	64.4%	33.9%	65.5%	34.5%
12,189	MONTGOMERY	5,093	3,213	1,785	95	1,428	R	63.1%	35.0%	64.3%	35.7%
28,684	NESHOBA	9,306	7,360	1,715	231	5,645	R	79.1%	18.4%	81.1%	18.9%
21,838	NEWTON	7,865	5,846	1,890	129	3,956	R	74.3%	24.0%	75.6%	24.4%
12,548	NOXUBEE	5,276	2,156	2,986	134	830	D	40.9%	56.6%	41.9%	58.1%
42,902	OKTIBBEHA	14,901	9,190	5,429	282	3,761	R	61.7%	36.4%	62.9%	37.1%
34,274	PANOLA	12,016	6,884	4,900	232	1,984	R	57.3%	40.8%	58.4%	41.6%
48,621	PEARL RIVER	16,603	12,603	3,599	401	9,004	R	75.9%	21.7%	77.8%	22.2%
12,138	PERRY	4,614	3,618	867	129	2,751	R	78.4%	18.8%	80.7%	19.3%
38,940	PIKE	15,474	8,755	6,339	380	2,416	R	56.6%	41.0%	58.0%	42.0%
26,726	PONTOTOC	9,472	7,474	1,881	117	5,593	R	78.9%	19.9%	79.9%	20.1%
25,556	PRENTISS	8,639	6,288	2,183	168	4,105	R	72.8%	25.3%	74.2%	25.8%
10,117	QUITMAN	3,748	1,773	1,849	126	76	D	47.3%	49.3%	49.0%	51.0%

MISSISSIPPI

SENATOR 2000

2000 Census Population	County	Total Vote	Republican	Democratic	Other	Rep.-Dem. Plurality		Percentage			
								Total Vote		Major Vote	
								Rep.	Dem.	Rep.	Dem.
115,327	RANKIN	42,525	35,141	6,621	763	28,520	R	82.6%	15.6%	84.1%	15.9%
28,423	SCOTT	9,178	6,153	2,929	96	3,224	R	67.0%	31.9%	67.7%	32.3%
6,580	SHARKEY	2,644	1,283	1,303	58	20	D	48.5%	49.3%	49.6%	50.4%
27,639	SIMPSON	9,763	6,870	2,719	174	4,151	R	70.4%	27.9%	71.6%	28.4%
16,182	SMITH	6,731	5,464	1,124	143	4,340	R	81.2%	16.7%	82.9%	17.1%
13,622	STONE	5,547	4,144	1,180	223	2,964	R	74.7%	21.3%	77.8%	22.2%
34,369	SUNFLOWER	9,035	4,313	4,539	183	226	D	47.7%	50.2%	48.7%	51.3%
14,903	TALLAHATCHIE	5,865	3,225	2,479	161	746	R	55.0%	42.3%	56.5%	43.5%
25,370	TATE	9,035	5,982	2,895	158	3,087	R	66.2%	32.0%	67.4%	32.6%
20,826	TIPPAH	8,543	6,516	1,844	183	4,672	R	76.3%	21.6%	77.9%	22.1%
19,163	TISHOMINGO	7,038	4,800	2,098	140	2,702	R	68.2%	29.8%	69.6%	30.4%
9,227	TUNICA	2,493	1,137	1,232	124	95	D	45.6%	49.4%	48.0%	52.0%
25,362	UNION	9,240	6,979	2,172	89	4,807	R	75.5%	23.5%	76.3%	23.7%
15,156	WALTHALL	6,087	4,136	1,712	239	2,424	R	67.9%	28.1%	70.7%	29.3%
49,644	WARREN	18,239	12,253	5,672	314	6,581	R	67.2%	31.1%	68.4%	31.6%
62,977	WASHINGTON	16,720	8,915	7,465	340	1,450	R	53.3%	44.6%	54.4%	45.6%
21,216	WAYNE	8,159	5,677	2,326	156	3,351	R	69.6%	28.5%	70.9%	29.1%
10,294	WEBSTER	4,733	3,754	881	98	2,873	R	79.3%	18.6%	81.0%	19.0%
10,312	WILKINSON	4,231	1,773	2,299	159	526	D	41.9%	54.3%	43.5%	56.5%
20,160	WINSTON	8,748	5,381	3,232	135	2,149	R	61.5%	36.9%	62.5%	37.5%
13,051	YALOBUSHA	5,388	3,194	2,067	127	1,127	R	59.3%	38.4%	60.7%	39.3%
28,149	YAZOO	9,433	5,735	3,482	216	2,253	R	60.8%	36.9%	62.2%	37.8%
2,844,658	TOTAL	994,144	654,941	314,090	25,113	340,851	R	65.9%	31.6%	67.6%	32.4%

MISSISSIPPI

CONGRESS

CD	Year	Total Vote	Republican Vote	Republican Candidate	Democratic Vote	Democratic Candidate	Other Vote	Rep.-Dem. Plurality		Percentage			
										Total Vote		Major Vote	
										Rep.	Dem.	Rep.	Dem.
1	2000	209,040	145,967	WICKER, ROGER F.	59,763	GRIST, JOE T., JR.	3,310	86,204	R	69.8%	28.6%	71.0%	29.0%
1	1998	99,333	66,738	WICKER, ROGER F.	30,438	WEATHERS, REX N.	2,157	36,300	R	67.2%	30.6%	68.7%	31.3%
1	1996	182,966	123,724	WICKER, ROGER F.	55,998	BOYD, HENRY JR.	3,244	67,726	R	67.6%	30.6%	68.8%	31.2%
1	1994	127,745	80,553	WICKER, ROGER F.	47,192	WHEELER, BILL		33,361	R	63.1%	36.9%	63.1%	36.9%
1	1992	204,616	82,952	WHITAKER, CLYDE E.	121,664	WHITTEN, JAMIE L.		38,712	D	40.5%	59.5%	40.5%	59.5%
2	2000	173,307	54,090	CARAWAY, HARDY	112,777	THOMPSON, BENNIE	6,440	58,687	D	31.2%	65.1%	32.4%	67.6%
2	1998	113,040			80,507	THOMPSON, BENNIE	32,533	80,507	D		71.2%		100.0%
2	1996	171,933	65,263	COVINGTON, DANNY	102,503	THOMPSON, BENNIE	4,167	37,240	D	38.0%	59.6%	38.9%	61.1%
2	1994	126,692	49,270	JORDAN, BILL	68,014	THOMPSON, BENNIE	9,408	18,744	D	38.9%	53.7%	42.0%	58.0%
2	1992	174,609	41,248	BENFORD, DOROTHY	133,361	EPSY, MIKE		92,113	D	23.6%	76.4%	23.6%	76.4%
3	2000	210,363	153,899	PICKERING, CHARLES W.	54,151	THRASH, WILLIAM	2,313	99,748	R	73.2%	25.7%	74.0%	26.0%
3	1998	100,250	84,785	PICKERING, CHARLES W.			15,465	84,785	R	84.6%		100.0%	
3	1996	188,144	115,443	PICKERING, CHARLES W.	68,658	EAVES, JOHN ARTHUR	4,043	46,785	R	61.4%	36.5%	62.7%	37.3%
3	1994	122,989	39,826	DABBS, DUTCH	83,163	MONTGOMERY, G. V.		43,337	D	32.4%	67.6%	32.4%	67.6%
3	1992	200,574	37,710	WILLIAMS, MICHAEL E.	162,864	MONTGOMERY, G. V.		125,154	D	18.8%	81.2%	18.8%	81.2%
4	2000	199,034	79,218	LAMPTON, DUNN	115,732	SHOWS, RONNIE	4,084	36,514	D	39.8%	58.1%	40.6%	59.4%
4	1998	137,199	61,551	HOSEMANN, DELBERT	73,252	SHOWS, RONNIE	2,396	11,701	D	44.9%	53.4%	45.7%	54.3%
4	1996	183,663	112,444	PARKER, MIKE	66,836	ANTOINE, KEVIN	4,383	45,608	R	61.2%	36.4%	62.7%	37.3%
4	1994	121,139	38,200	WOOD, MIKE	82,939	PARKER, MIKE		44,739	D	31.5%	68.5%	31.5%	68.5%
4	1992	194,544	43,705	MCMILLAN, JACK L.	130,927	PARKER, MIKE	19,912	87,222	D	22.5%	67.3%	25.0%	75.0%
5	2000	194,395	35,309	MCCONNELL, RANDY	153,264	TAYLOR, GENE	5,822	117,955	D	18.2%	78.8%	18.7%	81.3%
5	1998	101,095	19,341	MCCONNELL, RANDY	78,661	TAYLOR, GENE	3,093	59,320	D	19.1%	77.8%	19.7%	80.3%
5	1996	177,445	71,114	DOLLAR, DENNIS	103,415	TAYLOR, GENE	2,916	32,301	D	40.1%	58.3%	40.7%	59.3%
5	1994	121,754	48,575	BARLOS, GEORGE	73,179	TAYLOR, GENE		24,604	D	39.9%	60.1%	39.9%	60.1%
5	1992	191,058	67,619	HARVEY, PAUL A.	120,766	TAYLOR, GENE	2,673	53,147	D	35.4%	63.2%	35.9%	64.1%

MISSISSIPPI

GENERAL AND PRIMARY ELECTIONS

1999–2000 GENERAL ELECTIONS

President Other vote was 3,267 Constitution (Phillips); 2,265 Reform (Buchanan); 2,009 Libertarian (Browne); 613 Independent (Harris); 450 Natural Law (Hagelin). Nader was listed on the Mississippi ballot as an independent.

Governor (1999) Other vote was 8,208 Reform (Ladner); 6,005 Independent (Perkins).

Senator Other vote was 9,344 Independent (Giles); 8,454 Libertarian (Napper); 7,315 Reform (O'Hara).

Congress Other vote was: CD 1: 3,310 Libertarian (Lawrence); CD 2: 4,305 Libertarian (Chipman), 2,135 Reform (Dilworth); CD 3: 2,313 Libertarian (Golden); CD 4: 2,580 Libertarian (Hopkins), 1,504 Reform (Pharr); CD 5: 3,002 Libertarian (Parker), 2,820 Reform (Perrone).

1999–2000 PRIMARY ELECTIONS

Primary August 3, 1999 (Governor)
March 14, 2000

Primary Runoff April 4, 2000

Registration (as of December 1996) 1,732,529 No Party Registration

Note: Mississippi does not regularly compile statewide voter registration totals.

Primary Type Open—Any registered voter could vote in the primary of either party.

Note: An asterisk (*) denotes incumbent.

	REPUBLICAN PRIMARIES			DEMOCRATIC PRIMARIES		
President	George W. Bush	101,042	87.9%	Al Gore	79,408	89.6%
	Alan Keyes	6,478	5.6%	Bill Bradley	7,621	8.6%
	John McCain	6,263	5.4%	Lyndon H. LaRouche Jr.	1,573	1.8%
	Steve Forbes	588	0.5%			
	Gary Bauer	475	0.4%			
	Orrin G. Hatch	133	0.1%			
	TOTAL	114,979		TOTAL	88,602	
Governor (1999)	Mike Parker	77,674	50.7%	Ronnie Musgrove	309,519	56.7%
	Eddie Briggs	42,763	27.9%	James Roberts Jr.	142,617	26.1%
	Charlie Williams	17,176	11.2%	Richard Barrett	32,383	5.9%
	Dan Gibson	11,348	7.4%	Katie Perrone	16,476	3.0%
	George "Wagon Wheel" Blair	2,453	1.6%	Charles Bell	13,159	2.4%
	Shawn O'Hara	1,728	1.1%	Carrie Harris	11,645	2.1%
				James "Bootie" Hunt	11,572	2.1%
				Elton Davis Wall	8,184	1.5%
	TOTAL	153,142		TOTAL	545,555	
Senator	Trent Lott*	107,127	100.0%	Troy Brown	27,457	36.6%
				Rickey L. Cole	15,449	20.6%
				Clinton Allison	14,671	19.6%
				Robert R. Richmond Jr.	8,809	11.7%
				James "Bootie" Hunt	8,616	11.5%
	TOTAL	107,127		TOTAL	75,002	
				PRIMARY RUNOFF		
				Troy Brown	20,358	66.9%
				Rickey L. Cole	10,080	33.1%
				TOTAL	30,438	

MISSISSIPPI

GENERAL AND PRIMARY ELECTIONS

	REPUBLICAN PRIMARIES			DEMOCRATIC PRIMARIES		
Congressional District 1	Roger F. Wicker*	16,224	100.0%	Joe T. Grist Jr.	10,662	100.0%
	TOTAL	16,224		TOTAL	10,662	
Congressional District 2	Hardy Caraway	5,135	52.6%	Bennie Thompson*	21,177	100.0%
	Robert C. Brown	4,632	47.4%			
	TOTAL	9,767		TOTAL	21,177	
Congressional District 3	Charles W. "Chip" Pickering Jr.*	28,753	100.0%	William Thrash	10,213	100.0%
	TOTAL	28,753		TOTAL	10,213	
Congressional District 4	Dunn Lampton	16,929	61.3%	Ronnie Shows*	21,665	100.0%
	Geoffrey Yoste	10,690	38.7%			
	TOTAL	27,619		TOTAL	21,665	
Congressional District 5	Randy McDonnell	9,429	45.2%	Gene Taylor*	11,496	100.0%
	Nicholas N. Owens	5,858	28.1%			
	Karl Cleveland Mertz	5,574	26.7%			
	TOTAL	20,861		TOTAL	11,496	
	PRIMARY RUNOFF					
	Randy McDonnell	2,668	52.9%			
	Nicholas N. Owens	2,379	47.1%			
	TOTAL	5,047				

MISSOURI

GOVERNOR
Bob Holden (D). Elected 2000 to a four-year term.

SENATORS
Jean Carnahan (D). Appointed December 2000 effective January 2001 for a two-year term to the Senate seat her husband won in November 2000 after he had died in an airplane crash during the campaign.

Christopher Bond (R). Re-elected 1998 to a six-year term. Previously elected 1992, 1986.

REPRESENTATIVES
1. William Lacy Clay (D)
2. Todd Akin (R)
3. Richard A. Gephardt (D)
4. Ike Skelton (D)
5. Karen McCarthy (D)
6. Samuel B. Graves, Jr. (R)
7. Roy Blunt (R)
8. Jo Ann Emerson (R)
9. Kenny Hulshof (R)

POSTWAR VOTE FOR PRESIDENT

Year	Total Vote	Republican Vote	Republican Candidate	Democratic Vote	Democratic Candidate	Other Vote	Plurality	Total Vote Rep.	Total Vote Dem.	Major Vote Rep.	Major Vote Dem.
2000**	2,359,892	1,189,924	Bush, George W.	1,111,138	Gore, Al	58,830	78,786 R	50.4%	47.1%	51.7%	48.3%
1996**	2,158,065	890,016	Dole, Bob	1,025,935	Clinton, Bill	242,114	135,919 D	41.2%	47.5%	46.5%	53.5%
1992**	2,391,565	811,159	Bush, George	1,053,873	Clinton, Bill	526,533	242,714 D	33.9%	44.1%	43.5%	56.5%
1988	2,093,713	1,084,953	Bush, George	1,001,619	Dukakis, Michael S.	7,141	83,334 R	51.8%	47.8%	52.0%	48.0%
1984	2,122,783	1,274,188	Reagan, Ronald	848,583	Mondale, Walter F.	12	425,605 R	60.0%	40.0%	60.0%	40.0%
1980**	2,099,824	1,074,181	Reagan, Ronald	931,182	Carter, Jimmy	94,461	142,999 R	51.2%	44.3%	53.6%	46.4%
1976	1,953,600	927,443	Ford, Gerald R.	998,387	Carter, Jimmy	27,770	70,944 D	47.5%	51.1%	48.2%	51.8%
1972	1,855,803	1,153,852	Nixon, Richard M.	697,147	McGovern, George S.	4,804	456,705 R	62.2%	37.6%	62.3%	37.7%
1968	1,809,502	811,932	Nixon, Richard M.	791,444	Humphrey, Hubert H.	206,126	20,488 R	44.9%	43.7%	50.6%	49.4%
1964	1,817,879	653,535	Goldwater, Barry M.	1,164,344	Johnson, Lyndon B.		510,809 D	36.0%	64.0%	36.0%	64.0%
1960	1,934,422	962,221	Nixon, Richard M.	972,201	Kennedy, John F.		9,980 D	49.7%	50.3%	49.7%	50.3%
1956	1,832,562	914,289	Eisenhower, Dwight D.	918,273	Stevenson, Adlai E.		3,984 D	49.9%	50.1%	49.9%	50.1%
1952	1,892,062	959,429	Eisenhower, Dwight D.	929,830	Stevenson, Adlai E.	2,803	29,599 R	50.7%	49.1%	50.8%	49.2%
1948	1,578,628	655,039	Dewey, Thomas E.	917,315	Truman, Harry S.	6,274	262,276 D	41.5%	58.1%	41.7%	58.3%

In 2000 the other vote column includes 38,515 votes cast for Green (Nader). In 1996 the other vote column includes 217,188 votes cast for Perot. In 1992 the other vote column includes 518,741 votes cast for Perot. In 1980 the other column includes 77,920 votes for Independent (Anderson).

MISSOURI

POSTWAR VOTE FOR GOVERNOR

Year	Total Vote	Republican Vote	Republican Candidate	Democratic Vote	Democratic Candidate	Other Vote	Rep.-Dem. Plurality	Total Vote Rep.	Total Vote Dem.	Major Vote Rep.	Major Vote Dem.
2000	2,346,830	1,131,307	Talent, James M.	1,152,752	Holden, Bob	62,771	21,445 D	48.2%	49.1%	49.5%	50.5%
1996	2,142,518	866,268	Kelly, Margaret	1,224,801	Carnahan, Mel	51,449	358,533 D	40.4%	57.2%	41.4%	58.6%
1992	2,344,121	968,574	Webster, William L.	1,375,425	Carnahan, Mel	122	406,851 D	41.3%	58.7%	41.3%	58.7%
1988	2,085,928	1,339,531	Ashcroft, John	724,919	Hearnes, Betty C.	21,478	614,612 R	64.2%	34.8%	64.9%	35.1%
1984	2,108,210	1,194,506	Ashcroft, John	913,700	Rothman, Kenneth J.	4	280,806 R	56.7%	43.3%	56.7%	43.3%
1980	2,088,028	1,098,950	Bond, Christopher	981,884	Teasdale, Joseph P.	7,194	117,066 R	52.6%	47.0%	52.8%	47.2%
1976	1,933,575	958,110	Bond, Christopher	971,184	Teasdale, Joseph P.	4,281	13,074 D	49.6%	50.2%	49.7%	50.3%
1972	1,865,683	1,029,451	Bond, Christopher	832,751	Dowd, Edward L.	3,481	196,700 R	55.2%	44.6%	55.3%	44.7%
1968	1,764,602	691,797	Roos, Lawrence K.	1,072,805	Hearnes, Warren E.		381,008 D	39.2%	60.8%	39.2%	60.8%
1964	1,789,600	678,949	Shepley, Ethan	1,110,651	Hearnes, Warren E.		431,702 D	37.9%	62.1%	37.9%	62.1%
1960	1,887,331	792,131	Farmer, Edward G.	1,095,200	Dalton, John M.		303,069 D	42.0%	58.0%	42.0%	58.0%
1956	1,808,338	866,810	Hocker, Lon	941,528	Blair, James T.		74,718 D	47.9%	52.1%	47.9%	52.1%
1952	1,871,095	886,370	Elliott, Howard	983,166	Donnelly, Phil M.	1,559	96,796 D	47.4%	52.5%	47.4%	52.6%
1948	1,567,338	670,064	Thompson, Murray	893,092	Smith, Forrest	4,182	223,028 D	42.8%	57.0%	42.9%	57.1%

POSTWAR VOTE FOR SENATOR

Year	Total Vote	Republican Vote	Republican Candidate	Democratic Vote	Democratic Candidate	Other Vote	Rep.-Dem. Plurality	Total Vote Rep.	Total Vote Dem.	Major Vote Rep.	Major Vote Dem.
2000**	2,361,586	1,142,852	Ashcroft, John	1,191,812	Carnahan, Mel	26,922	48,960 D	48.4%	50.5%	49.0%	51.0%
1998	1,576,857	830,625	Bond, Christopher	690,208	Nixon, Jeremiah W.	56,024	140,417 R	52.7%	43.8%	54.6%	45.4%
1994	1,775,116	1,060,149	Ashcroft, John	633,697	Wheat, Alan	81,270	426,452 R	59.7%	35.7%	62.6%	37.4%
1992	2,354,925	1,221,901	Bond, Christopher	1,057,967	Rothman-Serot, Geri	75,057	163,934 R	51.9%	44.9%	53.6%	46.4%
1988	2,078,875	1,407,416	Danforth, John C.	660,045	Nixon, Jeremiah W.	11,414	747,371 R	67.7%	31.8%	68.1%	31.9%
1986	1,477,327	777,612	Bond, Christopher	699,624	Woods, Harriett	91	77,988 R	52.6%	47.4%	52.6%	47.4%
1982	1,543,521	784,876	Danforth, John C.	758,629	Woods, Harriett	16	26,247 R	50.8%	49.1%	50.9%	49.1%
1980	2,066,965	985,399	McNary, Gene	1,074,859	Eagleton, Thomas F.	6,707	89,460 D	47.7%	52.0%	47.8%	52.2%
1976	1,914,777	1,090,067	Danforth, John C.	813,571	Hearnes, Warren E.	11,139	276,496 R	56.9%	42.5%	57.3%	42.7%
1974	1,224,303	480,900	Curtis, Thomas B.	735,433	Eagleton, Thomas F.	7,970	254,533 D	39.3%	60.1%	39.5%	60.5%
1970	1,283,912	617,903	Danforth, John C.	655,431	Symington, Stuart	10,578	37,528 D	48.1%	51.0%	48.5%	51.5%
1968	1,737,958	850,544	Curtis, Thomas B.	887,414	Eagleton, Thomas F.		36,870 D	48.9%	51.1%	48.9%	51.1%
1964	1,783,043	596,377	Bradshaw, Jean P.	1,186,666	Symington, Stuart		590,289 D	33.4%	66.6%	33.4%	66.6%
1962	1,222,259	555,330	Kemper, Crosby	666,929	Long, Edward V.		111,599 D	45.4%	54.6%	45.4%	54.6%
1960S	1,880,232	880,576	Hocker, Lon	999,656	Long, Edward V.		119,080 D	46.8%	53.2%	46.8%	53.2%
1958	1,173,903	393,847	Palmer, Hazel	780,056	Symington, Stuart		386,209 D	33.6%	66.4%	33.6%	66.4%
1956	1,800,984	785,048	Douglas, Herbert	1,015,936	Hennings, Thomas C.		230,888 D	43.6%	56.4%	43.6%	56.4%
1952	1,868,083	858,170	Kem, James P.	1,008,523	Symington, Stuart	1,390	150,353 D	45.9%	54.0%	46.0%	54.0%
1950	1,279,414	592,922	Donnell, Forrest C.	685,732	Hennings, Thomas C.	760	92,810 D	46.3%	53.6%	46.4%	53.6%
1946	1,084,100	572,556	Kem, James P.	511,544	Briggs, Frank P.		61,012 R	52.8%	47.2%	52.8%	47.2%

In the 2000 election, the Democratic candidate was killed in an airplane crash in October but his name remained on the ballot. The 1960 election was for a short term to fill a vacancy.

MISSOURI

Districts Established July 8, 1991

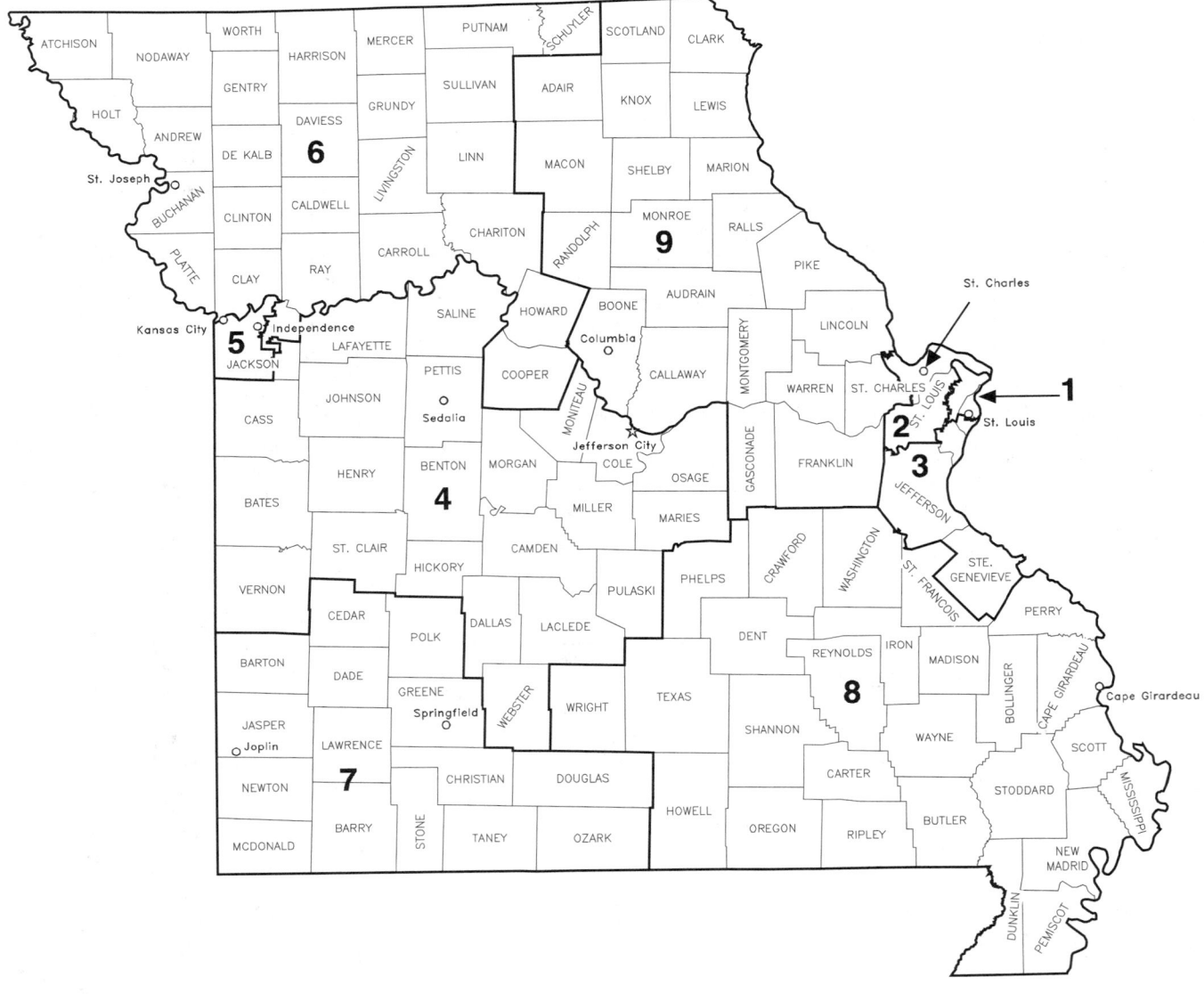

MISSOURI

PRESIDENT 2000

2000 Census Population	County	Total Vote	Republican	Democratic	Green (Nader)	Other	Rep.-Dem. Plurality	Percentage of Total Vote Rep.	Dem.	Green
24,977	ADAIR	10,552	6,050	4,101	301	100	1,949 R	57.3%	38.9%	2.9%
16,492	ANDREW	7,274	4,257	2,795	128	94	1,462 R	58.5%	38.4%	1.8%
6,430	ATCHISON	2,871	1,798	1,013	35	25	785 R	62.6%	35.3%	1.2%
25,853	AUDRAIN	9,985	5,256	4,551	113	65	705 R	52.6%	45.6%	1.1%
34,010	BARRY	12,368	7,885	4,135	193	155	3,750 R	63.8%	33.4%	1.6%
12,541	BARTON	5,366	3,836	1,424	75	31	2,412 R	71.5%	26.5%	1.4%
16,653	BATES	7,792	4,245	3,386	84	77	859 R	54.5%	43.5%	1.1%
17,180	BENTON	7,534	4,218	3,150	97	69	1,068 R	56.0%	41.8%	1.3%
12,029	BOLLINGER	5,294	3,487	1,692	41	74	1,795 R	65.9%	32.0%	0.8%
135,454	BOONE	59,609	28,426	28,811	1,894	478	385 D	47.7%	48.3%	3.2%
85,998	BUCHANAN	34,751	16,423	17,085	776	467	662 D	47.3%	49.2%	2.2%
40,867	BUTLER	14,397	9,111	4,996	149	141	4,115 R	63.3%	34.7%	1.0%
8,969	CALDWELL	3,850	2,220	1,488	76	66	732 R	57.7%	38.6%	2.0%
40,766	CALLAWAY	15,308	8,238	6,708	220	142	1,530 R	53.8%	43.8%	1.4%
37,051	CAMDEN	17,099	10,358	6,323	258	160	4,035 R	60.6%	37.0%	1.5%
68,693	CAPE GIRARDEAU	29,859	19,832	9,334	376	317	10,498 R	66.4%	31.3%	1.3%
10,285	CARROLL	4,581	2,880	1,620	54	27	1,260 R	62.9%	35.4%	1.2%
5,941	CARTER	2,808	1,730	997	40	41	733 R	61.6%	35.5%	1.4%
82,092	CASS	35,869	20,113	14,921	511	324	5,192 R	56.1%	41.6%	1.4%
13,733	CEDAR	5,663	3,530	1,979	81	73	1,551 R	62.3%	34.9%	1.4%
8,438	CHARITON	4,154	2,300	1,792	30	32	508 R	55.4%	43.1%	0.7%
54,285	CHRISTIAN	23,228	14,824	7,896	279	229	6,928 R	63.8%	34.0%	1.2%
7,416	CLARK	3,802	1,899	1,812	53	38	87 R	49.9%	47.7%	1.4%
184,006	CLAY	80,173	39,083	39,084	1,427	579	1 D	48.7%	48.7%	1.8%
18,979	CLINTON	8,531	4,323	3,994	124	90	329 R	50.7%	46.8%	1.5%
71,397	COLE	32,775	20,167	12,056	370	182	8,111 R	61.5%	36.8%	1.1%
16,670	COOPER	6,790	4,072	2,567	78	73	1,505 R	60.0%	37.8%	1.1%
22,804	CRAWFORD	8,302	4,754	3,350	100	98	1,404 R	57.3%	40.4%	1.2%
7,923	DADE	3,752	2,468	1,193	42	49	1,275 R	65.8%	31.8%	1.1%
15,661	DALLAS	6,219	3,723	2,311	76	109	1,412 R	59.9%	37.2%	1.2%
8,016	DAVIESS	3,494	2,011	1,367	58	58	644 R	57.6%	39.1%	1.7%
11,597	DE KALB	4,049	2,363	1,562	63	61	801 R	58.4%	38.6%	1.6%
14,927	DENT	5,988	3,996	1,839	66	87	2,157 R	66.7%	30.7%	1.1%
13,084	DOUGLAS	5,281	3,599	1,546	54	82	2,053 R	68.1%	29.3%	1.0%
33,155	DUNKLIN	10,525	5,426	4,947	78	74	479 R	51.6%	47.0%	0.7%
93,807	FRANKLIN	39,194	21,863	16,172	670	489	5,691 R	55.8%	41.3%	1.7%
15,342	GASCONADE	6,629	4,190	2,257	110	72	1,933 R	63.2%	34.0%	1.7%
6,861	GENTRY	3,105	1,771	1,271	39	24	500 R	57.0%	40.9%	1.3%
240,391	GREENE	102,926	59,178	41,091	1,760	897	18,087 R	57.5%	39.9%	1.7%
10,432	GRUNDY	4,708	2,976	1,563	102	67	1,413 R	63.2%	33.2%	2.2%
8,850	HARRISON	3,991	2,552	1,328	62	49	1,224 R	63.9%	33.3%	1.6%
21,997	HENRY	9,778	5,120	4,459	125	74	661 R	52.4%	45.6%	1.3%
8,940	HICKORY	4,238	2,172	1,961	54	51	211 R	51.3%	46.3%	1.3%
5,351	HOLT	2,662	1,738	871	23	30	867 R	65.3%	32.7%	0.9%
10,212	HOWARD	4,512	2,414	1,944	83	71	470 R	53.5%	43.1%	1.8%
37,238	HOWELL	14,075	9,018	4,641	197	219	4,377 R	64.1%	33.0%	1.4%
10,697	IRON	4,414	2,237	2,044	64	69	193 R	50.7%	46.3%	1.4%
654,880	JACKSON	272,062	104,418	160,419	5,041	2,184	56,001 D	38.4%	59.0%	1.9%
104,686	JASPER	37,481	24,899	11,737	574	271	13,162 R	66.4%	31.3%	1.5%
198,099	JEFFERSON	77,204	36,766	38,616	1,182	640	1,850 D	47.6%	50.0%	1.5%
48,258	JOHNSON	16,787	9,339	6,926	321	201	2,413 R	55.6%	41.3%	1.9%
4,361	KNOX	2,055	1,226	787	24	18	439 R	59.7%	38.3%	1.2%
32,513	LACLEDE	13,046	8,556	4,183	142	165	4,373 R	65.6%	32.1%	1.1%
32,960	LAFAYETTE	14,520	7,849	6,343	205	123	1,506 R	54.1%	43.7%	1.4%
35,204	LAWRENCE	12,903	8,305	4,235	177	186	4,070 R	64.4%	32.8%	1.4%
10,494	LEWIS	4,484	2,388	2,023	34	39	365 R	53.3%	45.1%	0.8%
38,944	LINCOLN	15,913	8,549	6,961	224	179	1,588 R	53.7%	43.7%	1.4%
13,754	LINN	6,010	3,246	2,646	66	52	600 R	54.0%	44.0%	1.1%
14,558	LIVINGSTON	6,276	3,709	2,425	98	44	1,284 R	59.1%	38.6%	1.6%
21,681	MCDONALD	6,529	4,460	1,866	107	96	2,594 R	68.3%	28.6%	1.6%

MISSOURI

PRESIDENT 2000

2000 Census Population	County	Total Vote	Republican	Democratic	Green (Nader)	Other	Rep.-Dem. Plurality		Percentage of Total Vote		
									Rep.	Dem.	Green
15,762	MACON	7,175	4,232	2,817	75	51	1,415	R	59.0%	39.3%	1.0%
11,800	MADISON	4,373	2,460	1,828	42	43	632	R	56.3%	41.8%	1.0%
8,903	MARIES	3,854	2,216	1,554	32	52	662	R	57.5%	40.3%	0.8%
28,289	MARION	11,712	6,550	4,993	87	82	1,557	R	55.9%	42.6%	0.7%
3,757	MERCER	1,842	1,250	555	20	17	695	R	67.9%	30.1%	1.1%
23,564	MILLER	9,356	5,945	3,217	133	61	2,728	R	63.5%	34.4%	1.4%
13,427	MISSISSIPPI	5,215	2,395	2,756	29	35	361	D	45.9%	52.8%	0.6%
14,827	MONITEAU	6,065	3,764	2,176	60	65	1,588	R	62.1%	35.9%	1.0%
9,311	MONROE	4,094	2,175	1,860	20	39	315	R	53.1%	45.4%	0.5%
12,136	MONTGOMERY	5,303	3,106	2,092	70	35	1,014	R	58.6%	39.4%	1.3%
19,309	MORGAN	7,881	4,460	3,235	87	99	1,225	R	56.6%	41.0%	1.1%
19,760	NEW MADRID	7,266	3,416	3,738	45	67	322	D	47.0%	51.4%	0.6%
52,636	NEWTON	21,162	14,232	6,447	326	157	7,785	R	67.3%	30.5%	1.5%
21,912	NODAWAY	9,049	5,161	3,553	215	120	1,608	R	57.0%	39.3%	2.4%
10,344	OREGON	4,233	2,521	1,568	60	84	953	R	59.6%	37.0%	1.4%
13,062	OSAGE	6,178	4,154	1,938	50	36	2,216	R	67.2%	31.4%	0.8%
9,542	OZARK	4,292	2,663	1,432	118	79	1,231	R	62.0%	33.4%	2.7%
20,047	PEMISCOT	6,060	2,750	3,245	37	28	495	D	45.4%	53.5%	0.6%
18,132	PERRY	6,903	4,667	2,085	70	81	2,582	R	67.6%	30.2%	1.0%
39,403	PETTIS	15,755	9,533	5,855	223	144	3,678	R	60.5%	37.2%	1.4%
39,825	PHELPS	16,146	9,444	6,262	253	187	3,182	R	58.5%	38.8%	1.6%
18,351	PIKE	7,351	3,648	3,557	79	67	91	R	49.6%	48.4%	1.1%
73,781	PLATTE	34,054	17,785	15,325	648	296	2,460	R	52.2%	45.0%	1.9%
26,992	POLK	10,294	6,430	3,606	119	139	2,824	R	62.5%	35.0%	1.2%
41,165	PULASKI	10,531	6,531	3,800	120	80	2,731	R	62.0%	36.1%	1.1%
5,223	PUTNAM	2,334	1,593	708	19	14	885	R	68.3%	30.3%	0.8%
9,626	RALLS	4,542	2,446	2,033	36	27	413	R	53.9%	44.8%	0.8%
24,663	RANDOLPH	9,186	4,844	4,116	114	112	728	R	52.7%	44.8%	1.2%
23,354	RAY	9,747	4,517	4,970	145	115	453	D	46.3%	51.0%	1.5%
6,689	REYNOLDS	3,131	1,762	1,298	42	29	464	R	56.3%	41.5%	1.3%
13,509	RIPLEY	5,065	3,121	1,820	58	66	1,301	R	61.6%	35.9%	1.1%
283,883	ST. CHARLES	128,686	72,114	53,806	1,900	866	18,308	R	56.0%	41.8%	1.5%
9,652	ST. CLAIR	4,739	2,731	1,866	80	62	865	R	57.6%	39.4%	1.7%
55,641	ST. FRANCOIS	18,841	9,327	9,075	265	174	252	R	49.5%	48.2%	1.4%
1,016,315	ST. LOUIS COUNTY	486,884	224,689	250,631	8,474	3,090	25,942	D	46.1%	51.5%	1.7%
348,189	ST. LOUIS CITY	124,752	24,799	96,557	2,592	804	71,758	D	19.9%	77.4%	2.1%
17,842	STE. GENEVIEVE	7,311	3,505	3,600	127	79	95	D	47.9%	49.2%	1.7%
23,756	SALINE	9,355	4,572	4,585	131	67	13	D	48.9%	49.0%	1.4%
4,170	SCHUYLER	2,006	1,159	808	16	23	351	R	57.8%	40.3%	0.8%
4,983	SCOTLAND	2,179	1,335	790	37	17	545	R	61.3%	36.3%	1.7%
40,422	SCOTT	15,704	8,999	6,452	113	140	2,547	R	57.3%	41.1%	0.7%
8,324	SHANNON	3,781	2,245	1,430	48	58	815	R	59.4%	37.8%	1.3%
6,799	SHELBY	3,257	1,936	1,262	37	22	674	R	59.4%	38.7%	1.1%
29,705	STODDARD	12,454	7,727	4,476	114	137	3,251	R	62.0%	35.9%	0.9%
28,658	STONE	12,151	7,793	4,055	179	124	3,738	R	64.1%	33.4%	1.5%
7,219	SULLIVAN	3,064	1,877	1,127	27	33	750	R	61.3%	36.8%	0.9%
39,703	TANEY	15,112	9,647	5,092	204	169	4,555	R	63.8%	33.7%	1.3%
23,003	TEXAS	9,932	6,136	3,486	137	173	2,650	R	61.8%	35.1%	1.4%
20,454	VERNON	8,408	4,985	3,156	156	111	1,829	R	59.3%	37.5%	1.9%
24,525	WARREN	10,740	5,979	4,524	150	87	1,455	R	55.7%	42.1%	1.4%
23,344	WASHINGTON	8,265	4,020	4,047	95	103	27	D	48.6%	49.0%	1.1%
13,259	WAYNE	5,848	3,346	2,387	55	60	959	R	57.2%	40.8%	0.9%
31,045	WEBSTER	11,880	7,350	4,174	161	195	3,176	R	61.9%	35.1%	1.4%
2,382	WORTH	1,158	651	469	15	23	182	R	56.2%	40.5%	1.3%
17,955	WRIGHT	7,841	5,391	2,250	86	114	3,141	R	68.8%	28.7%	1.1%
5,595,211	TOTAL	2,359,892	1,189,924	1,111,138	38,515	20,315	78,786	R	50.4%	47.1%	1.6%

MISSOURI

GOVERNOR 2000

2000 Census Population	County	Total Vote	Republican	Democratic	Other	Rep.-Dem. Plurality		Percentage			
								Total Vote		Major Vote	
								Rep.	Dem.	Rep.	Dem.
24,977	ADAIR	10,231	5,518	4,473	240	1,045	R	53.9%	43.7%	55.2%	44.8%
16,492	ANDREW	7,228	3,943	3,142	143	801	R	54.6%	43.5%	55.7%	44.3%
6,430	ATCHISON	2,822	1,610	1,169	43	441	R	57.1%	41.4%	57.9%	42.1%
25,853	AUDRAIN	9,885	4,576	5,086	223	510	D	46.3%	51.5%	47.4%	52.6%
34,010	BARRY	12,272	7,352	4,681	239	2,671	R	59.9%	38.1%	61.1%	38.9%
12,541	BARTON	5,366	3,764	1,535	67	2,229	R	70.1%	28.6%	71.0%	29.0%
16,653	BATES	7,739	3,783	3,794	162	11	D	48.9%	49.0%	49.9%	50.1%
17,180	BENTON	7,475	3,944	3,407	124	537	R	52.8%	45.6%	53.7%	46.3%
12,029	BOLLINGER	5,165	3,190	1,910	65	1,280	R	61.8%	37.0%	62.5%	37.5%
135,454	BOONE	59,383	25,609	31,007	2,767	5,398	D	43.1%	52.2%	45.2%	54.8%
85,998	BUCHANAN	34,530	15,602	17,998	930	2,396	D	45.2%	52.1%	46.4%	53.6%
40,867	BUTLER	14,215	8,301	5,657	257	2,644	R	58.4%	39.8%	59.5%	40.5%
8,969	CALDWELL	3,857	2,006	1,701	150	305	R	52.0%	44.1%	54.1%	45.9%
40,766	CALLAWAY	15,223	6,641	8,129	453	1,488	D	43.6%	53.4%	45.0%	55.0%
37,051	CAMDEN	16,990	9,555	7,059	376	2,496	R	56.2%	41.5%	57.5%	42.5%
68,693	CAPE GIRARDEAU	29,669	18,543	10,491	635	8,052	R	62.5%	35.4%	63.9%	36.1%
10,285	CARROLL	4,580	2,643	1,872	65	771	R	57.7%	40.9%	58.5%	41.5%
5,941	CARTER	2,735	1,441	1,153	141	288	R	52.7%	42.2%	55.6%	44.4%
82,092	CASS	35,603	18,777	16,084	742	2,693	R	52.7%	45.2%	53.9%	46.1%
13,733	CEDAR	5,644	3,297	2,240	107	1,057	R	58.4%	39.7%	59.5%	40.5%
8,438	CHARITON	4,122	1,998	2,077	47	79	D	48.5%	50.4%	49.0%	51.0%
54,285	CHRISTIAN	23,167	13,646	9,148	373	4,498	R	58.9%	39.5%	59.9%	40.1%
7,416	CLARK	3,768	1,751	1,928	89	177	D	46.5%	51.2%	47.6%	52.4%
184,006	CLAY	79,419	36,983	40,747	1,689	3,764	D	46.6%	51.3%	47.6%	52.4%
18,979	CLINTON	8,441	3,943	4,313	185	370	D	46.7%	51.1%	47.8%	52.2%
71,397	COLE	32,602	16,673	15,397	532	1,276	R	51.1%	47.2%	52.0%	48.0%
16,670	COOPER	6,820	3,641	3,013	166	628	R	53.4%	44.2%	54.7%	45.3%
22,804	CRAWFORD	8,285	4,352	3,624	309	728	R	52.5%	43.7%	54.6%	45.4%
7,923	DADE	3,694	2,306	1,337	51	969	R	62.4%	36.2%	63.3%	36.7%
15,661	DALLAS	6,216	3,429	2,672	115	757	R	55.2%	43.0%	56.2%	43.8%
8,016	DAVIESS	3,473	1,768	1,604	101	164	R	50.9%	46.2%	52.4%	47.6%
11,597	DE KALB	4,022	2,129	1,798	95	331	R	52.9%	44.7%	54.2%	45.8%
14,927	DENT	5,930	3,403	2,401	126	1,002	R	57.4%	40.5%	58.6%	41.4%
13,084	DOUGLAS	5,221	3,317	1,813	91	1,504	R	63.5%	34.7%	64.7%	35.3%
33,155	DUNKLIN	10,471	4,471	5,875	125	1,404	D	42.7%	56.1%	43.2%	56.8%
93,807	FRANKLIN	38,970	21,336	16,216	1,418	5,120	R	54.7%	41.6%	56.8%	43.2%
15,342	GASCONADE	6,616	4,091	2,336	189	1,755	R	61.8%	35.3%	63.7%	36.3%
6,861	GENTRY	3,091	1,522	1,523	46	1	D	49.2%	49.3%	50.0%	50.0%
240,391	GREENE	102,243	54,770	45,612	1,861	9,158	R	53.6%	44.6%	54.6%	45.4%
10,432	GRUNDY	4,696	3,029	1,520	147	1,509	R	64.5%	32.4%	66.6%	33.4%
8,850	HARRISON	3,835	2,307	1,430	98	877	R	60.2%	37.3%	61.7%	38.3%
21,997	HENRY	9,686	4,420	5,072	194	652	D	45.6%	52.4%	46.6%	53.4%
8,940	HICKORY	4,225	2,017	2,132	76	115	D	47.7%	50.5%	48.6%	51.4%
5,351	HOLT	2,643	1,563	1,031	49	532	R	59.1%	39.0%	60.3%	39.7%
10,212	HOWARD	4,513	2,029	2,352	132	323	D	45.0%	52.1%	46.3%	53.7%
37,238	HOWELL	14,085	7,537	6,306	242	1,231	R	53.5%	44.8%	54.4%	45.6%
10,697	IRON	4,408	2,002	2,258	148	256	D	45.4%	51.2%	47.0%	53.0%
654,880	JACKSON	270,834	99,064	165,490	6,280	66,426	D	36.6%	61.1%	37.4%	62.6%
104,686	JASPER	37,259	24,335	12,203	721	12,132	R	65.3%	32.8%	66.6%	33.4%
198,099	JEFFERSON	76,643	36,060	37,808	2,775	1,748	D	47.0%	49.3%	48.8%	51.2%
48,258	JOHNSON	16,680	8,219	7,964	497	255	R	49.3%	47.7%	50.8%	49.2%
4,361	KNOX	2,026	1,124	878	24	246	R	55.5%	43.3%	56.1%	43.9%
32,513	LACLEDE	13,021	7,595	5,115	311	2,480	R	58.3%	39.3%	59.8%	40.2%
32,960	LAFAYETTE	14,459	7,276	6,932	251	344	R	50.3%	47.9%	51.2%	48.8%
35,204	LAWRENCE	12,786	7,447	5,106	233	2,341	R	58.2%	39.9%	59.3%	40.7%
10,494	LEWIS	4,445	2,224	2,154	67	70	R	50.0%	48.5%	50.8%	49.2%
38,944	LINCOLN	15,891	8,282	7,034	575	1,248	R	52.1%	44.3%	54.1%	45.9%
13,754	LINN	5,975	2,869	3,003	103	134	D	48.0%	50.3%	48.9%	51.1%
14,558	LIVINGSTON	6,224	3,236	2,873	115	363	R	52.0%	46.2%	53.0%	47.0%
21,681	MCDONALD	6,494	4,216	2,087	191	2,129	R	64.9%	32.1%	66.9%	33.1%

MISSOURI

GOVERNOR 2000

2000 Census Population	County	Total Vote	Republican	Democratic	Other	Rep.-Dem. Plurality		Percentage			
								Total Vote		Major Vote	
								Rep.	Dem.	Rep.	Dem.
15,762	MACON	7,110	3,633	3,355	122	278	R	51.1%	47.2%	52.0%	48.0%
11,800	MADISON	4,376	2,210	2,050	116	160	R	50.5%	46.8%	51.9%	48.1%
8,903	MARIES	3,863	1,897	1,836	130	61	R	49.1%	47.5%	50.8%	49.2%
28,289	MARION	11,653	5,832	5,696	125	136	R	50.0%	48.9%	50.6%	49.4%
3,757	MERCER	1,782	1,144	606	32	538	R	64.2%	34.0%	65.4%	34.6%
23,564	MILLER	9,354	5,343	3,684	327	1,659	R	57.1%	39.4%	59.2%	40.8%
13,427	MISSISSIPPI	5,170	2,170	2,936	64	766	D	42.0%	56.8%	42.5%	57.5%
14,827	MONITEAU	6,059	3,217	2,689	153	528	R	53.1%	44.4%	54.5%	45.5%
9,311	MONROE	4,086	1,801	2,214	71	413	D	44.1%	54.2%	44.9%	55.1%
12,136	MONTGOMERY	5,277	2,857	2,198	222	659	R	54.1%	41.7%	56.5%	43.5%
19,309	MORGAN	7,854	4,207	3,424	223	783	R	53.6%	43.6%	55.1%	44.9%
19,760	NEW MADRID	7,214	2,978	4,148	88	1,170	D	41.3%	57.5%	41.8%	58.2%
52,636	NEWTON	21,070	13,917	6,780	373	7,137	R	66.1%	32.2%	67.2%	32.8%
21,912	NODAWAY	8,939	4,294	4,425	220	131	D	48.0%	49.5%	49.2%	50.8%
10,344	OREGON	4,230	1,938	2,187	105	249	D	45.8%	51.7%	47.0%	53.0%
13,062	OSAGE	6,185	3,450	2,646	89	804	R	55.8%	42.8%	56.6%	43.4%
9,542	OZARK	4,266	2,502	1,644	120	858	R	58.6%	38.5%	60.3%	39.7%
20,047	PEMISCOT	5,931	2,053	3,784	94	1,731	D	34.6%	63.8%	35.2%	64.8%
18,132	PERRY	7,248	4,735	2,419	94	2,316	R	65.3%	33.4%	66.2%	33.8%
39,403	PETTIS	15,618	8,536	6,692	390	1,844	R	54.7%	42.8%	56.1%	43.9%
39,825	PHELPS	16,049	8,280	7,345	424	935	R	51.6%	45.8%	53.0%	47.0%
18,351	PIKE	7,332	3,427	3,717	188	290	D	46.7%	50.7%	48.0%	52.0%
73,781	PLATTE	33,789	16,971	16,115	703	856	R	50.2%	47.7%	51.3%	48.7%
26,992	POLK	10,223	5,996	4,068	159	1,928	R	58.7%	39.8%	59.6%	40.4%
41,165	PULASKI	10,484	5,533	4,738	213	795	R	52.8%	45.2%	53.9%	46.1%
5,223	PUTNAM	2,305	1,531	752	22	779	R	66.4%	32.6%	67.1%	32.9%
9,626	RALLS	4,544	2,145	2,347	52	202	D	47.2%	51.7%	47.8%	52.2%
24,663	RANDOLPH	9,137	4,066	4,897	174	831	D	44.5%	53.6%	45.4%	54.6%
23,354	RAY	9,689	4,045	5,407	237	1,362	D	41.7%	55.8%	42.8%	57.2%
6,689	REYNOLDS	3,059	1,416	1,480	163	64	D	46.3%	48.4%	48.9%	51.1%
13,509	RIPLEY	4,984	2,651	2,211	122	440	R	53.2%	44.4%	54.5%	45.5%
283,883	ST. CHARLES	127,679	74,357	50,415	2,907	23,942	R	58.2%	39.5%	59.6%	40.4%
9,652	ST. CLAIR	4,741	2,405	2,245	91	160	R	50.7%	47.4%	51.7%	48.3%
55,641	ST. FRANCOIS	18,769	8,712	9,425	632	713	D	46.4%	50.2%	48.0%	52.0%
1,016,315	ST. LOUIS COUNTY	485,369	233,031	239,341	12,997	6,310	D	48.0%	49.3%	49.3%	50.7%
348,189	ST. LOUIS CITY	123,841	25,710	89,680	8,451	63,970	D	20.8%	72.4%	22.3%	77.7%
17,842	STE. GENEVIEVE	7,289	3,525	3,554	210	29	D	48.4%	48.8%	49.8%	50.2%
23,756	SALINE	9,342	3,945	5,245	152	1,300	D	42.2%	56.1%	42.9%	57.1%
4,170	SCHUYLER	1,985	1,006	946	33	60	R	50.7%	47.7%	51.5%	48.5%
4,983	SCOTLAND	2,130	1,129	962	39	167	R	53.0%	45.2%	54.0%	46.0%
40,422	SCOTT	15,654	8,159	7,293	202	866	R	52.1%	46.6%	52.8%	47.2%
8,324	SHANNON	3,726	1,623	2,031	72	408	D	43.6%	54.5%	44.4%	55.6%
6,799	SHELBY	3,239	1,668	1,547	24	121	R	51.5%	47.8%	51.9%	48.1%
29,705	STODDARD	12,373	6,537	5,689	147	848	R	52.8%	46.0%	53.5%	46.5%
28,658	STONE	12,047	7,338	4,484	225	2,854	R	60.9%	37.2%	62.1%	37.9%
7,219	SULLIVAN	3,020	1,755	1,218	47	537	R	58.1%	40.3%	59.0%	41.0%
39,703	TANEY	14,997	9,003	5,594	400	3,409	R	60.0%	37.3%	61.7%	38.3%
23,003	TEXAS	9,915	5,030	4,709	176	321	R	50.7%	47.5%	51.6%	48.4%
20,454	VERNON	8,325	4,370	3,763	192	607	R	52.5%	45.2%	53.7%	46.3%
24,525	WARREN	10,676	6,060	4,318	298	1,742	R	56.8%	40.4%	58.4%	41.6%
23,344	WASHINGTON	8,237	3,536	4,110	591	574	D	42.9%	49.9%	46.2%	53.8%
13,259	WAYNE	5,803	3,008	2,684	111	324	R	51.8%	46.3%	52.8%	47.2%
31,045	WEBSTER	11,861	6,721	4,904	236	1,817	R	56.7%	41.3%	57.8%	42.2%
2,382	WORTH	1,133	557	552	24	5	R	49.2%	48.7%	50.2%	49.8%
17,955	WRIGHT	7,788	4,872	2,783	133	2,089	R	62.6%	35.7%	63.6%	36.4%
5,595,211	TOTAL	2,346,830	1,131,307	1,152,752	62,771	21,445	D	48.2%	49.1%	49.5%	50.5%

MISSOURI

SENATOR 2000

2000 Census Population	County	Total Vote	Republican	Democratic	Other	Rep.-Dem. Plurality		Total Vote Rep.	Dem.	Major Vote Rep.	Dem.
24,977	ADAIR	10,345	5,439	4,762	144	677	R	52.6%	46.0%	53.3%	46.7%
16,492	ANDREW	7,267	4,094	3,078	95	1,016	R	56.3%	42.4%	57.1%	42.9%
6,430	ATCHISON	2,853	1,634	1,192	27	442	R	57.3%	41.8%	57.8%	42.2%
25,853	AUDRAIN	10,014	5,058	4,882	74	176	R	50.5%	48.8%	50.9%	49.1%
34,010	BARRY	12,366	7,878	4,330	158	3,548	R	63.7%	35.0%	64.5%	35.5%
12,541	BARTON	5,396	3,979	1,376	41	2,603	R	73.7%	25.5%	74.3%	25.7%
16,653	BATES	7,804	3,900	3,837	67	63	R	50.0%	49.2%	50.4%	49.6%
17,180	BENTON	7,567	4,061	3,422	84	639	R	53.7%	45.2%	54.3%	45.7%
12,029	BOLLINGER	5,018	3,142	1,833	43	1,309	R	62.6%	36.5%	63.2%	36.8%
135,454	BOONE	59,661	26,280	32,501	880	6,221	D	44.0%	54.5%	44.7%	55.3%
85,998	BUCHANAN	34,712	16,364	17,757	591	1,393	D	47.1%	51.2%	48.0%	52.0%
40,867	BUTLER	14,434	8,472	5,803	159	2,669	R	58.7%	40.2%	59.3%	40.7%
8,969	CALDWELL	3,914	2,005	1,821	88	184	R	51.2%	46.5%	52.4%	47.6%
40,766	CALLAWAY	15,385	7,098	8,120	167	1,022	D	46.1%	52.8%	46.6%	53.4%
37,051	CAMDEN	17,131	9,761	7,159	211	2,602	R	57.0%	41.8%	57.7%	42.3%
68,693	CAPE GIRARDEAU	29,964	18,997	10,486	481	8,511	R	63.4%	35.0%	64.4%	35.6%
10,285	CARROLL	4,618	2,526	2,052	40	474	R	54.7%	44.4%	55.2%	44.8%
5,941	CARTER	2,799	1,490	1,271	38	219	R	53.2%	45.4%	54.0%	46.0%
82,092	CASS	35,871	18,742	16,752	377	1,990	R	52.2%	46.7%	52.8%	47.2%
13,733	CEDAR	5,701	3,499	2,121	81	1,378	R	61.4%	37.2%	62.3%	37.7%
8,438	CHARITON	4,159	2,107	2,021	31	86	R	50.7%	48.6%	51.0%	49.0%
54,285	CHRISTIAN	23,243	15,040	7,979	224	7,061	R	64.7%	34.3%	65.3%	34.7%
7,416	CLARK	3,809	1,808	1,947	54	139	D	47.5%	51.1%	48.1%	51.9%
184,006	CLAY	79,824	37,376	41,599	849	4,223	D	46.8%	52.1%	47.3%	52.7%
18,979	CLINTON	8,507	3,909	4,501	97	592	D	46.0%	52.9%	46.5%	53.5%
71,397	COLE	32,867	16,780	15,863	224	917	R	51.1%	48.3%	51.4%	48.6%
16,670	COOPER	6,828	3,716	3,052	60	664	R	54.4%	44.7%	54.9%	45.1%
22,804	CRAWFORD	8,359	4,408	3,859	92	549	R	52.7%	46.2%	53.3%	46.7%
7,923	DADE	3,726	2,485	1,213	28	1,272	R	66.7%	32.6%	67.2%	32.8%
15,661	DALLAS	6,244	3,732	2,442	70	1,290	R	59.8%	39.1%	60.4%	39.6%
8,016	DAVIESS	3,514	1,824	1,646	44	178	R	51.9%	46.8%	52.6%	47.4%
11,597	DE KALB	4,048	2,146	1,839	63	307	R	53.0%	45.4%	53.9%	46.1%
14,927	DENT	6,041	3,619	2,335	87	1,284	R	59.9%	38.7%	60.8%	39.2%
13,084	DOUGLAS	5,264	3,512	1,699	53	1,813	R	66.7%	32.3%	67.4%	32.6%
33,155	DUNKLIN	10,564	5,043	5,441	80	398	D	47.7%	51.5%	48.1%	51.9%
93,807	FRANKLIN	39,264	20,899	17,806	559	3,093	R	53.2%	45.3%	54.0%	46.0%
15,342	GASCONADE	6,661	3,974	2,626	61	1,348	R	59.7%	39.4%	60.2%	39.8%
6,861	GENTRY	3,113	1,632	1,450	31	182	R	52.4%	46.6%	53.0%	47.0%
240,391	GREENE	102,940	61,600	40,150	1,190	21,450	R	59.8%	39.0%	60.5%	39.5%
10,432	GRUNDY	4,695	2,877	1,754	64	1,123	R	61.3%	37.4%	62.1%	37.9%
8,850	HARRISON	3,935	2,373	1,500	62	873	R	60.3%	38.1%	61.3%	38.7%
21,997	HENRY	9,798	4,634	5,069	95	435	D	47.3%	51.7%	47.8%	52.2%
8,940	HICKORY	4,232	2,259	1,929	44	330	R	53.4%	45.6%	53.9%	46.1%
5,351	HOLT	2,668	1,609	1,029	30	580	R	60.3%	38.6%	61.0%	39.0%
10,212	HOWARD	4,522	2,205	2,269	48	64	D	48.8%	50.2%	49.3%	50.7%
37,238	HOWELL	14,144	8,676	5,291	177	3,385	R	61.3%	37.4%	62.1%	37.9%
10,697	IRON	4,428	1,993	2,372	63	379	D	45.0%	53.6%	45.7%	54.3%
654,880	JACKSON	272,192	100,196	168,564	3,432	68,368	D	36.8%	61.9%	37.3%	62.7%
104,686	JASPER	37,554	25,481	11,612	461	13,869	R	67.9%	30.9%	68.7%	31.3%
198,099	JEFFERSON	77,252	34,980	41,321	951	6,341	D	45.3%	53.5%	45.8%	54.2%
48,258	JOHNSON	16,771	8,351	8,184	236	167	R	49.8%	48.8%	50.5%	49.5%
4,361	KNOX	2,069	1,125	933	11	192	R	54.4%	45.1%	54.7%	45.3%
32,513	LACLEDE	13,048	8,308	4,612	128	3,696	R	63.7%	35.3%	64.3%	35.7%
32,960	LAFAYETTE	14,518	7,107	7,292	119	185	D	49.0%	50.2%	49.4%	50.6%
35,204	LAWRENCE	12,990	8,272	4,564	154	3,708	R	63.7%	35.1%	64.4%	35.6%
10,494	LEWIS	4,478	2,300	2,142	36	158	R	51.4%	47.8%	51.8%	48.2%
38,944	LINCOLN	15,916	8,087	7,652	177	435	R	50.8%	48.1%	51.4%	48.6%
13,754	LINN	6,038	2,810	3,157	71	347	D	46.5%	52.3%	47.1%	52.9%
14,558	LIVINGSTON	6,294	3,281	2,953	60	328	R	52.1%	46.9%	52.6%	47.4%
21,681	MCDONALD	6,589	4,441	2,009	139	2,432	R	67.4%	30.5%	68.9%	31.1%

MISSOURI

SENATOR 2000

2000 Census Population	County	Total Vote	Republican	Democratic	Other	Rep.-Dem. Plurality		Total Vote Rep.	Total Vote Dem.	Major Vote Rep.	Major Vote Dem.
15,762	MACON	7,171	3,741	3,366	64	375	R	52.2%	46.9%	52.6%	47.4%
11,800	MADISON	4,382	2,239	2,102	41	137	R	51.1%	48.0%	51.6%	48.4%
8,903	MARIES	3,872	2,075	1,764	33	311	R	53.6%	45.6%	54.1%	45.9%
28,289	MARION	11,785	6,435	5,250	100	1,185	R	54.6%	44.5%	55.1%	44.9%
3,757	MERCER	1,814	1,140	653	21	487	R	62.8%	36.0%	63.6%	36.4%
23,564	MILLER	9,384	5,482	3,808	94	1,674	R	58.4%	40.6%	59.0%	41.0%
13,427	MISSISSIPPI	5,225	2,208	2,981	36	773	D	42.3%	57.1%	42.6%	57.4%
14,827	MONITEAU	6,087	3,320	2,710	57	610	R	54.5%	44.5%	55.1%	44.9%
9,311	MONROE	4,110	2,054	2,023	33	31	R	50.0%	49.2%	50.4%	49.6%
12,136	MONTGOMERY	5,290	2,934	2,310	46	624	R	55.5%	43.7%	55.9%	44.1%
19,309	MORGAN	7,886	4,285	3,517	84	768	R	54.3%	44.6%	54.9%	45.1%
19,760	NEW MADRID	7,262	3,109	4,100	53	991	D	42.8%	56.5%	43.1%	56.9%
52,636	NEWTON	21,147	14,562	6,366	219	8,196	R	68.9%	30.1%	69.6%	30.4%
21,912	NODAWAY	9,045	4,647	4,276	122	371	R	51.4%	47.3%	52.1%	47.9%
10,344	OREGON	4,268	2,268	1,940	60	328	R	53.1%	45.5%	53.9%	46.1%
13,062	OSAGE	6,192	3,543	2,612	37	931	R	57.2%	42.2%	57.6%	42.4%
9,542	OZARK	4,289	2,691	1,516	82	1,175	R	62.7%	35.3%	64.0%	36.0%
20,047	PEMISCOT	6,042	2,322	3,664	56	1,342	D	38.4%	60.6%	38.8%	61.2%
18,132	PERRY	7,222	4,611	2,540	71	2,071	R	63.8%	35.2%	64.5%	35.5%
39,403	PETTIS	15,815	8,985	6,665	165	2,320	R	56.8%	42.1%	57.4%	42.6%
39,825	PHELPS	16,231	8,426	7,604	201	822	R	51.9%	46.8%	52.6%	47.4%
18,351	PIKE	7,364	3,536	3,757	71	221	D	48.0%	51.0%	48.5%	51.5%
73,781	PLATTE	34,003	17,024	16,578	401	446	R	50.1%	48.8%	50.7%	49.3%
26,992	POLK	10,319	6,397	3,822	100	2,575	R	62.0%	37.0%	62.6%	37.4%
41,165	PULASKI	10,524	6,009	4,385	130	1,624	R	57.1%	41.7%	57.8%	42.2%
5,223	PUTNAM	2,325	1,529	785	11	744	R	65.8%	33.8%	66.1%	33.9%
9,626	RALLS	4,558	2,374	2,141	43	233	R	52.1%	47.0%	52.6%	47.4%
24,663	RANDOLPH	9,228	4,450	4,695	83	245	D	48.2%	50.9%	48.7%	51.3%
23,354	RAY	9,798	3,977	5,697	124	1,720	D	40.6%	58.1%	41.1%	58.9%
6,689	REYNOLDS	3,106	1,512	1,565	29	53	D	48.7%	50.4%	49.1%	50.9%
13,509	RIPLEY	5,045	2,806	2,163	76	643	R	55.6%	42.9%	56.5%	43.5%
283,883	ST. CHARLES	128,096	70,396	56,226	1,474	14,170	R	55.0%	43.9%	55.6%	44.4%
9,652	ST. CLAIR	4,758	2,592	2,115	51	477	R	54.5%	44.5%	55.1%	44.9%
55,641	ST. FRANCOIS	18,886	8,712	9,980	194	1,268	D	46.1%	52.8%	46.6%	53.4%
1,016,315	ST. LOUIS COUNTY	488,400	220,200	263,291	4,909	43,091	D	45.1%	53.9%	45.5%	54.5%
348,189	ST. LOUIS CITY	124,528	24,851	98,048	1,629	73,197	D	20.0%	78.7%	20.2%	79.8%
17,842	STE. GENEVIEVE	7,441	3,427	3,883	131	456	D	46.1%	52.2%	46.9%	53.1%
23,756	SALINE	9,386	4,083	5,239	64	1,156	D	43.5%	55.8%	43.8%	56.2%
4,170	SCHUYLER	2,023	1,023	974	26	49	R	50.6%	48.1%	51.2%	48.8%
4,983	SCOTLAND	2,153	1,128	1,004	21	124	R	52.4%	46.6%	52.9%	47.1%
40,422	SCOTT	15,695	8,385	7,183	127	1,202	R	53.4%	45.8%	53.9%	46.1%
8,324	SHANNON	3,741	1,916	1,779	46	137	R	51.2%	47.6%	51.9%	48.1%
6,799	SHELBY	3,264	1,753	1,493	18	260	R	53.7%	45.7%	54.0%	46.0%
29,705	STODDARD	12,416	6,899	5,427	90	1,472	R	55.6%	43.7%	56.0%	44.0%
28,658	STONE	12,170	7,843	4,184	143	3,659	R	64.4%	34.4%	65.2%	34.8%
7,219	SULLIVAN	2,753	1,562	1,160	31	402	R	56.7%	42.1%	57.4%	42.6%
39,703	TANEY	15,155	9,786	5,180	189	4,606	R	64.6%	34.2%	65.4%	34.6%
23,003	TEXAS	9,946	5,819	3,992	135	1,827	R	58.5%	40.1%	59.3%	40.7%
20,454	VERNON	8,384	4,797	3,484	103	1,313	R	57.2%	41.6%	57.9%	42.1%
24,525	WARREN	10,732	5,732	4,885	115	847	R	53.4%	45.5%	54.0%	46.0%
23,344	WASHINGTON	8,231	3,667	4,469	95	802	D	44.6%	54.3%	45.1%	54.9%
13,259	WAYNE	5,846	3,039	2,761	46	278	R	52.0%	47.2%	52.4%	47.6%
31,045	WEBSTER	11,874	7,296	4,455	123	2,841	R	61.4%	37.5%	62.1%	37.9%
2,382	WORTH	1,163	638	506	19	132	R	54.9%	43.5%	55.8%	44.2%
17,955	WRIGHT	7,830	5,223	2,508	99	2,715	R	66.7%	32.0%	67.6%	32.4%
5,595,211	TOTAL	2,361,586	1,142,852	1,191,812	26,922	48,960	D	48.4%	50.5%	49.0%	51.0%

Note: Jean Carnahan (D) was appointed December 2000 effective January 2001 to the Senate seat her husband, Mel Carnahan, won in November 2000 after he had died in an airplane crash during the campaign. The appointment was for a two-year period with an election in 2002 to fill the remaining four years of the term.

MISSOURI

CONGRESS

CD	Year	Total Vote	Republican		Democratic		Other Vote	Rep.-Dem. Plurality	Percentage			
									Total Vote		Major Vote	
			Vote	Candidate	Vote	Candidate			Rep.	Dem.	Rep.	Dem.
1	2000	198,347	42,730	BILLINGSLY, Z. DWIGHT	149,173	CLAY, WILLIAM LACY	6,444	106,443 D	21.5%	75.2%	22.3%	77.7%
1	1998	125,051	30,635	SOLUADE, RICHMOND A.	90,840	CLAY, WILLIAM	3,576	60,205 D	24.5%	72.6%	25.2%	74.8%
1	1996	187,653	51,857	O'SULLIVAN, DANIEL F. JR.	131,659	CLAY, WILLIAM	4,137	79,802 D	27.6%	70.2%	28.3%	71.7%
1	1994	153,018	50,303	COUNTS, DONALD R.	97,061	CLAY, WILLIAM	5,654	46,758 D	32.9%	63.4%	34.1%	65.9%
1	1992	233,175	74,482	MONTGOMERY, ARTHUR S.	158,693	CLAY, WILLIAM		84,211 D	31.9%	68.1%	31.9%	68.1%
2	2000	298,062	164,926	AKIN, TODD	126,441	HOUSE, TED	6,695	38,485 R	55.3%	42.4%	56.6%	43.4%
2	1998	203,259	142,313	TALENT, JAMES M.	57,565	ROSS, JOHN	3,381	84,748 R	70.0%	28.3%	71.2%	28.8%
2	1996	270,726	165,999	TALENT, JAMES M.	100,372	HORN, JOAN KELLY	4,355	65,627 R	61.3%	37.1%	62.3%	37.7%
2	1994	230,287	154,882	TALENT, JAMES M.	70,480	KELLY, PAT	4,925	84,402 R	67.3%	30.6%	68.7%	31.3%
2	1992	312,445	157,594	TALENT, JAMES M.	148,729	HORN, JOAN KELLY	6,122	8,865 R	50.4%	47.6%	51.4%	48.6%
3	2000	254,539	100,967	FEDERER, BILL	147,222	GEPHARDT, RICHARD A.	6,350	46,255 D	39.7%	57.8%	40.7%	59.3%
3	1998	176,099	74,005	FEDERER, BILL	98,287	GEPHARDT, RICHARD A.	3,807	24,282 D	42.0%	55.8%	43.0%	57.0%
3	1996	232,755	90,202	WHEELEHAN, DEBORAH	137,300	GEPHARDT, RICHARD A.	5,253	47,098 D	38.8%	59.0%	39.6%	60.4%
3	1994	203,940	80,977	GILL, GARY	117,601	GEPHARDT, RICHARD A.	5,362	36,624 D	39.7%	57.7%	40.8%	59.2%
3	1992	271,834	90,006	HOLEKAMP, MALCOLM L.	174,000	GEPHARDT, RICHARD A.	7,828	83,994 D	33.1%	64.0%	34.1%	65.9%
4	2000	269,889	84,406	NOLAND, JIM	180,634	SKELTON, IKE	4,849	96,228 D	31.3%	66.9%	31.8%	68.2%
4	1998	187,616	51,005	NOLAND, CECILIA D.	133,173	SKELTON, IKE	3,438	82,168 D	27.2%	71.0%	27.7%	72.3%
4	1996	240,789	81,650	PHELPS, BILL	153,566	SKELTON, IKE	5,573	71,916 D	33.9%	63.8%	34.7%	65.3%
4	1994	203,492	65,616	NOLAND, JAMES A.	137,876	SKELTON, IKE		72,260 D	32.2%	67.8%	32.2%	67.8%
4	1992	251,452	74,475	CARLEY, JOHN	176,977	SKELTON, IKE		102,502 D	29.6%	70.4%	29.6%	70.4%
5	2000	232,137	66,439	GORDON, STEVE	159,826	MCCARTHY, KAREN	5,872	93,387 D	28.6%	68.8%	29.4%	70.6%
5	1998	153,685	47,582	BENNETT, PENNY	101,313	MCCARTHY, KAREN	4,790	53,731 D	31.0%	65.9%	32.0%	68.0%
5	1996	213,971	61,803	BENNETT, PENNY	144,223	MCCARTHY, KAREN	7,945	82,420 D	28.9%	67.4%	30.0%	70.0%
5	1994	177,511	77,120	FREEMAN, RON	100,391	MCCARTHY, KAREN		23,271 D	43.4%	56.6%	43.4%	56.6%
5	1992	255,312	93,562	MOODY, EDWARD	151,014	WHEAT, ALAN	10,736	57,452 D	36.6%	59.1%	38.3%	61.7%
6	2000	273,201	138,925	GRAVES, SAMUEL B., JR.	127,792	DANNER, STEVE	6,484	11,133 R	50.9%	46.8%	52.1%	47.9%
6	1998	192,777	51,679	BAILEY, JEFF	136,774	DANNER, PAT	4,324	85,095 D	26.8%	70.9%	27.4%	72.6%
6	1996	246,282	72,064	BAILEY, JEFF	169,006	DANNER, PAT	5,212	96,942 D	29.3%	68.6%	29.9%	70.1%
6	1994	211,817	71,709	TUCKER, TINA	140,108	DANNER, PAT		68,399 D	33.9%	66.1%	33.9%	66.1%
6	1992	268,524	119,637	COLEMAN, E. THOMAS	148,887	DANNER, PAT		29,250 D	44.6%	55.4%	44.6%	55.4%
7	2000	273,937	202,305	BLUNT, ROY	65,510	CHRISTRUP, CHARLES	6,122	136,795 R	73.9%	23.9%	75.5%	24.5%
7	1998	178,801	129,746	BLUNT, ROY	43,416	PERKEL, MARC	5,639	86,330 R	72.6%	24.3%	74.9%	25.1%
7	1996	250,584	162,558	BLUNT, ROY	79,306	BAMBERGER, RUTH	8,720	83,252 R	64.9%	31.6%	67.2%	32.8%
7	1994	195,916	112,228	HANCOCK, MELTON D.	77,836	FOSSARD, JAMES R.	5,852	34,392 R	57.3%	39.7%	59.0%	41.0%
7	1992	260,065	160,303	HANCOCK, MELTON D.	99,762	DEATON, THOMAS P.		60,541 R	61.6%	38.4%	61.6%	38.4%
8	2000	234,066	162,239	EMERSON, JO ANN	67,760	CAMP, BOB	4,067	94,479 R	69.3%	28.9%	70.5%	29.5%
8	1998	166,524	104,271	EMERSON, JO ANN	59,426	HECKEMEYER, ANTHONY J.	2,827	44,845 R	62.6%	35.7%	63.7%	36.3%
8	1996	222,854	23,477	KLINE, RICHARD	83,084	FIREBAUGH, EMILY	116,293	29,388 I	10.5%	37.3%	22.0%	78.0%
8	1994	184,586	129,320	EMERSON, BILL	48,987	THOMPSON, JAMES L.	6,279	80,333 R	70.1%	26.5%	72.5%	27.5%
8	1992	234,418	147,398	EMERSON, BILL	86,730	BULLOCK, THAD	290	60,668 R	62.9%	37.0%	63.0%	37.0%
9	2000	291,610	172,787	HULSHOF, KENNY	111,662	CARROLL, STEVEN R.	7,161	61,125 R	59.3%	38.3%	60.7%	39.3%
9	1998	188,305	117,196	HULSHOF, KENNY	66,861	VOGT, LINDA	4,248	50,335 R	62.2%	35.5%	63.7%	36.3%
9	1996	250,230	123,580	HULSHOF, KENNY	117,685	VOLKMER, HAROLD	8,965	5,895 R	49.4%	47.0%	51.2%	48.8%
9	1994	204,942	92,301	HULSHOF, KENNY	103,443	VOLKMER, HAROLD	9,198	11,142 D	45.0%	50.5%	47.2%	52.8%
9	1992	261,335	118,811	HARDY, RICK	124,694	VOLKMER, HAROLD	17,830	5,883 D	45.5%	47.7%	48.8%	51.2%

Note: Missouri 8th was won in 1996 by Jo Ann Emerson, who ran simultaneously as an independent in voting for a seat in the 105th Congress and as a Republican in a November 1996 special election to fill a vacancy in the 104th Congress. She won both races.

MISSOURI

GENERAL AND PRIMARY ELECTIONS

2000 GENERAL ELECTIONS

President Other vote was 9,818 Reform (Buchanan); 7,436 Libertarian (Browne); 1,957 Constitution (Phillips); 1,104 Natural Law (Hagelin).

Governor Other vote was 34,431 Independent (Rice); 11,274 Libertarian (Swenson); 9,008 Green (Reed); 4,916 Reform (Kline); 3,142 Constitution (Smith).

Senator Other vote was 10,612 Green (Taylor); 10,198 Libertarian (Stauffer); 4,166 Reform (Foley); 1,933 Natural Law (Dockins); 8 write-in (Kennedy); 5 write-in (Day).

Congress Other vote was: CD 1: 3,099 Green (Reddick), 2,253 Libertarian (Millay), 1,092 Reform (Penningroth); CD 2: 2,907 Green (Odell), 2,524 Libertarian (Higgins), 1,264 Reform (Gimpelson); CD 3: 3,266 Green (Maroney), 2,245 Libertarian (Crist), 839 Reform (Windisch); CD 4: 2,878 Libertarian (Knapp), 1,971 Reform (Rinehart); CD 5: 2,548 Green (Reitz), 2,350 Libertarian (Newberry), 974 Reform (Carriger); CD 6: 3,696 Libertarian (Dykes), 2,788 Natural Law (Richey); CD 7: 2,965 Libertarian (Burlison), 2,169 Natural Law (Harris), 988 Reform (Lapham); CD 8: 2,328 Libertarian (Hendricks), 1,739 Green (Sager); CD 9: 3,608 Libertarian (Hoffman), 2,388 Green (Scherubel), 1,165 Reform (Dotson).

2000 PRIMARY ELECTIONS

Primary March 7, 2000 (President) **Registration** 3,492,023 No Party Registration
August 8, 2000 (Congress) (as of Aug. 8, 2000)

Primary Type Open—Any registered voter could vote in the primary of either party.

Note: An asterisk (*) denotes incumbent.

	REPUBLICAN PRIMARIES			DEMOCRATIC PRIMARIES		
President	George W. Bush	275,366	57.9%	Al Gore	171,562	64.6%
	John McCain	167,831	35.3%	Bill Bradley	89,092	33.6%
	Alan Keyes	27,282	5.7%	Uncommitted	3,364	1.3%
	Steve Forbes	2,044	0.4%	Lyndon H. LaRouche Jr.	906	0.3%
	Uncommitted	1,345	0.3%	Pat Price	565	0.2%
	Gary Bauer	1,038	0.2%			
	Orrin G. Hatch	363	0.1%			
	Lawrence L. Hornung	94				
	TOTAL	475,363		TOTAL	265,489	
Governor	Jim Talent	296,159	84.5%	Bob Holden	362,457	100.0%
	Jennie Lee Sievers	33,674	9.6%			
	Elgar Macy	20,681	5.9%			
	TOTAL	350,514		TOTAL	362,457	
Senator	John Ashcroft*	327,442	89.6%	Mel Carnahan	323,841	78.2%
	Marc Perkel	38,103	10.4%	Ronald William Wagganer	90,251	21.8%
	TOTAL	365,545		TOTAL	414,092	
Congressional District 1	Z. Dwight Billingsly	5,399	70.1%	William Lacy Clay	34,398	60.6%
	Richmond A. Soluade	2,308	29.9%	Charlie Dooley	15,612	27.5%
				Eric Erfan Vickers	3,543	6.2%
				Bill Haas	1,602	2.8%
				Steven G. Bailey	1,144	2.0%
				Joe Mondrak	504	0.9%
	TOTAL	7,707		TOTAL	56,803	

MISSOURI

GENERAL AND PRIMARY ELECTIONS

REPUBLICAN PRIMARIES				DEMOCRATIC PRIMARIES		
Congressional District 2	Todd Akin	14,911	25.9%	Ted House	20,964	100.0%
	Gene McNary	14,855	25.8%			
	Francis E. Flotron Jr.	12,362	21.5%			
	Barbara Cooper	10,538	18.3%			
	Jack Jackson	4,955	8.6%			
	TOTAL	57,621		TOTAL	20,964	
Congressional District 3	Bill Federer	24,387	88.9%	Richard A. Gephardt*	40,111	100.0%
	George Simpson	3,052	11.1%			
	TOTAL	27,439		TOTAL	40,111	
Congressional District 4	Jim Noland	29,172	62.5%	Ike Skelton*	48,531	100.0%
	Bob Brown	17,516	37.5%			
	TOTAL	46,688		TOTAL	48,531	
Congressional District 5	Steve Gordon	7,906	45.8%	Karen MCarthy*	35,071	85.4%
	Walter Wright	5,677	32.9%	Charles Lindsey	6,013	14.6%
	Chet Southworth	3,694	21.4%			
	TOTAL	17,277		TOTAL	41,084	
Congressional District 6	Samuel B. Graves Jr.	30,014	68.1%	Steve Danner	32,037	55.9%
	Teresa Anne Loar	7,493	17.0%	Tom Mann	10,056	17.5%
	Jeff Bailey	4,575	10.4%	Sandra Lee Reeves	9,084	15.8%
	John Dady	1,122	2.5%	Ida Cox	6,151	10.7%
	Jack C. DeSelms	901	2.0%			
	TOTAL	44,105		TOTAL	57,328	
Congressional District 7	Roy Blunt*	62,711	86.4%	Charles Christrup	14,196	100.0%
	Mike Harman	9,856	13.6%			
	TOTAL	72,567		TOTAL	14,196	
Congressional District 8	Jo Ann Emerson*	36,957	100.0%	Bob Camp	29,990	57.1%
				Earl Durnell	22,531	42.9%
	TOTAL	36,957		TOTAL	52,521	
Congressional District 9	Kenny Hulshof*	34,649	100.0%	Steven R. Carroll	37,465	69.0%
				Michael Charles Glawson	10,231	18.8%
				Joe Cefius Terry	6,618	12.2%
	TOTAL	34,649		TOTAL	54,314	

MONTANA

GOVERNOR
Judy Martz (R). Elected 2000 to a four-year term.

SENATORS
Max S. Baucus (D). Re-elected 1996 to a six-year term. Previously elected 1990, 1984, 1978.

Conrad Burns (R). Re-elected 2000 to a six-year term. Previously elected 1994, 1988.

REPRESENTATIVE
At-Large. Dennis Rehberg (R)

POSTWAR VOTE FOR PRESIDENT

| | | Republican | | Democratic | | Other | | Percentage | | | |
| | | | | | | | | Total Vote | | Major Vote | |
Year	Total Vote	Vote	Candidate	Vote	Candidate	Vote	Plurality	Rep.	Dem.	Rep.	Dem.
2000**	410,997	240,178	Bush, George W.	137,126	Gore, Al	33,693	103,052 R	58.4%	33.4%	63.7%	36.3%
1996**	407,261	179,652	Dole, Bob	167,922	Clinton, Bill	59,687	11,730 R	44.1%	41.2%	51.7%	48.3%
1992**	410,611	144,207	Bush, George	154,507	Clinton, Bill	111,897	10,300 D	35.1%	37.6%	48.3%	51.7%
1988	365,674	190,412	Bush, George	168,936	Dukakis, Michael S.	6,326	21,476 R	52.1%	46.2%	53.0%	47.0%
1984	384,377	232,450	Reagan, Ronald	146,742	Mondale, Walter F.	5,185	85,708 R	60.5%	38.2%	61.3%	38.7%
1980**	363,952	206,814	Reagan, Ronald	118,032	Carter, Jimmy	39,106	88,782 R	56.8%	32.4%	63.7%	36.3%
1976	328,734	173,703	Ford, Gerald R.	149,259	Carter, Jimmy	5,772	24,444 R	52.8%	45.4%	53.8%	46.2%
1972	317,603	183,976	Nixon, Richard M.	120,197	McGovern, George S.	13,430	63,779 R	57.9%	37.8%	60.5%	39.5%
1968	274,404	138,835	Nixon, Richard M.	114,117	Humphrey, Hubert H.	21,452	24,718 R	50.6%	41.6%	54.9%	45.1%
1964	278,628	113,032	Goldwater, Barry M.	164,246	Johnson, Lyndon B.	1,350	51,214 D	40.6%	58.9%	40.8%	59.2%
1960	277,579	141,841	Nixon, Richard M.	134,891	Kennedy, John F.	847	6,950 R	51.1%	48.6%	51.3%	48.7%
1956	271,171	154,933	Eisenhower, Dwight D.	116,238	Stevenson, Adlai E.		38,695 R	57.1%	42.9%	57.1%	42.9%
1952	265,037	157,394	Eisenhower, Dwight D.	106,213	Stevenson, Adlai E.	1,430	51,181 R	59.4%	40.1%	59.7%	40.3%
1948	224,278	96,770	Dewey, Thomas E.	119,071	Truman, Harry S.	8,437	22,301 D	43.1%	53.1%	44.8%	55.2%

In 2000 the other vote column includes 24,437 votes cast for Green (Nader). In 1996 the other vote column includes 55,229 votes cast for Perot. In 1992 the other vote column includes 107,225 votes cast for Perot. In 1980 the other column includes 29,281 votes for Independent (Anderson).

MONTANA

POSTWAR VOTE FOR GOVERNOR

Year	Total Vote	Republican		Democratic		Other Vote	Rep.-Dem. Plurality	Percentage			
								Total Vote		Major Vote	
		Vote	Candidate	Vote	Candidate			Rep.	Dem.	Rep.	Dem.
2000	410,192	209,135	Martz, Judy	193,131	O'Keefe, Mark	7,926	16,004 R	51.0%	47.1%	52.0%	48.0%
1996**	405,175	320,768	Racicot, Marc	84,407	Jacobson, Judy		236,361 R	79.2%	20.8%	79.2%	20.8%
1992	407,842	209,401	Racicot, Marc	198,421	Bradley, Dorothy	20	10,980 R	51.3%	48.7%	51.3%	48.7%
1988	367,021	190,604	Stephens, Stan	169,313	Judge, Thomas L.	7,104	21,291 R	51.9%	46.1%	53.0%	47.0%
1984	378,970	100,070	Goodover, Pat M.	266,578	Schwinden, Ted	12,322	166,508 D	26.4%	70.3%	27.3%	72.7%
1980	360,466	160,892	Ramirez, Jack	199,574	Schwinden, Ted		38,682 D	44.6%	55.4%	44.6%	55.4%
1976	316,720	115,848	Woodahl, Robert	195,420	Judge, Thomas L.	5,452	79,572 D	36.6%	61.7%	37.2%	62.8%
1972	318,754	146,231	Smith, Ed	172,523	Judge, Thomas L.		26,292 D	45.9%	54.1%	45.9%	54.1%
1968	278,112	116,432	Babcock, Tim M.	150,481	Anderson, Forrest H.	11,199	34,049 D	41.9%	54.1%	43.6%	56.4%
1964	280,975	144,113	Babcock, Tim M.	136,862	Renne, Roland		7,251 R	51.3%	48.7%	51.3%	48.7%
1960	279,881	154,230	Nutter, Donald G.	125,651	Cannon, Paul		28,579 R	55.1%	44.9%	55.1%	44.9%
1956	270,366	138,878	Aronson, J. Hugo	131,488	Olsen, Arnold H.		7,390 R	51.4%	48.6%	51.4%	48.6%
1952	263,792	134,423	Aronson, J. Hugo	129,369	Bonner, John W.		5,054 R	51.0%	49.0%	51.0%	49.0%
1948	222,964	97,792	Ford, Sam C.	124,267	Bonner, John W.	905	26,475 D	43.9%	55.7%	44.0%	56.0%

Note: In 1996, the Democratic vote total includes 7,936 absentee ballots cast for the party's initial gubernatorial candidate, Chet Blaylock, who died in October 1996.

POSTWAR VOTE FOR SENATOR

Year	Total Vote	Republican		Democratic		Other Vote	Rep.-Dem. Plurality	Percentage			
								Total Vote		Major Vote	
		Vote	Candidate	Vote	Candidate			Rep.	Dem.	Rep.	Dem.
2000	411,601	208,082	Burns, Conrad	194,430	Schweitzer, Brian	9,089	13,652 R	50.6%	47.2%	51.7%	48.3%
1996	407,490	182,111	Rehberg, Dennis	201,935	Baucus, Max S.	23,444	19,824 D	44.7%	49.6%	47.4%	52.6%
1994	350,409	218,542	Burns, Conrad	131,845	Mudd, Jack	22	86,697 R	62.4%	37.6%	62.4%	37.6%
1990	319,336	93,836	Kolstad, Allen C.	217,563	Baucus, Max S.	7,937	123,727 D	29.4%	68.1%	30.1%	69.9%
1988	365,254	189,445	Burns, Conrad	175,809	Melcher, John		13,636 R	51.9%	48.1%	51.9%	48.1%
1984	379,155	154,308	Cozzens, Chuck	215,704	Baucus, Max S.	9,143	61,396 D	40.7%	56.9%	41.7%	58.3%
1982	321,062	133,789	Williams, Larry	174,861	Melcher, John	12,412	41,072 D	41.7%	54.5%	43.3%	56.7%
1978	287,942	127,589	Williams, Larry	160,353	Baucus, Max S.		32,764 D	44.3%	55.7%	44.3%	55.7%
1976	321,445	115,213	Burger, Stanley C.	206,232	Melcher, John		91,019 D	35.8%	64.2%	35.8%	64.2%
1972	314,925	151,316	Hibbard, Henry S.	163,609	Metcalf, Lee		12,293 D	48.0%	52.0%	48.0%	52.0%
1970	247,869	97,809	Wallace, Harold E.	150,060	Mansfield, Mike		52,251 D	39.5%	60.5%	39.5%	60.5%
1966	259,863	121,697	Babcock, Tim M.	138,166	Metcalf, Lee		16,469 D	46.8%	53.2%	46.8%	53.2%
1964	280,010	99,367	Blewett, Alex	180,643	Mansfield, Mike		81,276 D	35.5%	64.5%	35.5%	64.5%
1960	276,612	136,281	Fjare, Orvin B.	140,331	Metcalf, Lee		4,050 D	49.3%	50.7%	49.3%	50.7%
1958	229,483	54,573	Welch. Lou W.	174,910	Mansfield, Mike		120,337 D	23.8%	76.2%	23.8%	76.2%
1954	227,454	112,863	D'Ewart, Wesley A.	114,591	Murray, James E.		1,728 D	49.6%	50.4%	49.6%	50.4%
1952	262,297	127,360	Ecton, Zales N.	133,109	Mansfield, Mike	1,828	5,749 D	48.6%	50.7%	48.9%	51.1%
1948	221,003	94,458	David, Tom J.	125,193	Murray, James E.	1,352	30,735 D	42.7%	56.6%	43.0%	57.0%
1946	190,566	101,901	Ecton, Zales N.	86,476	Erickson, Leif	2,189	15,425 R	53.5%	45.4%	54.1%	45.9%

270

MONTANA

One At Large

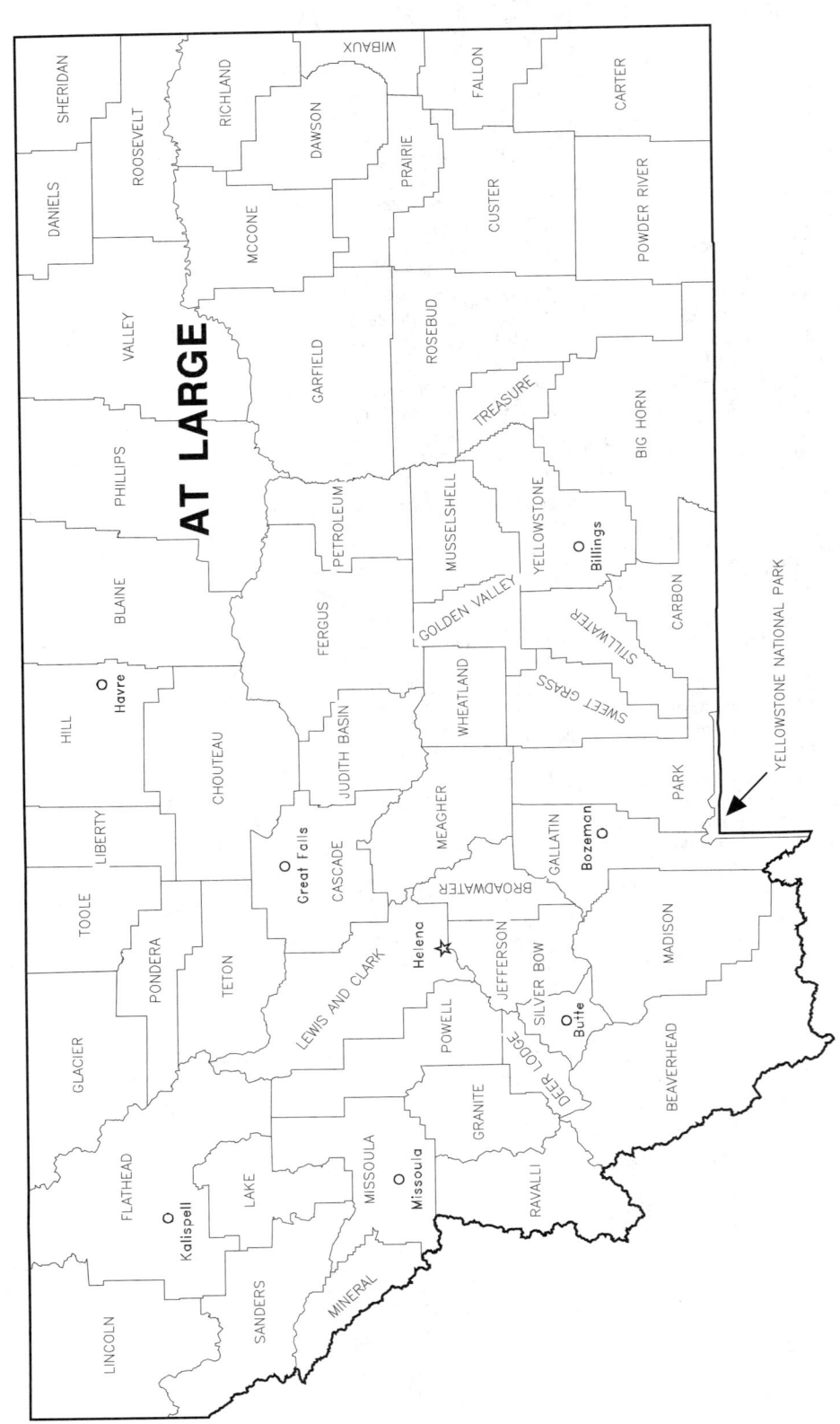

MONTANA

PRESIDENT 2000

2000 Census Population	County	Total Vote	Republican	Democratic	Green (Nader)	Other	Rep.-Dem. Plurality	Percentage of Total Vote		
								Rep.	Dem.	Green
9,202	BEAVERHEAD	4,196	3,113	799	218	66	2,314 R	74.2%	19.0%	5.2%
12,671	BIG HORN	4,161	1,651	2,345	101	64	694 D	39.7%	56.4%	2.4%
7,009	BLAINE	2,759	1,410	1,246	58	45	164 R	51.1%	45.2%	2.1%
4,385	BROADWATER	2,074	1,488	462	63	61	1,026 R	71.7%	22.3%	3.0%
9,552	CARBON	4,789	3,008	1,434	237	110	1,574 R	62.8%	29.9%	4.9%
1,360	CARTER	645	573	53	10	9	520 R	88.8%	8.2%	1.6%
80,357	CASCADE	33,328	18,164	13,137	1,202	825	5,027 R	54.5%	39.4%	3.6%
5,970	CHOUTEAU	2,885	2,039	686	86	74	1,353 R	70.7%	23.8%	3.0%
11,696	CUSTER	4,905	3,156	1,501	154	94	1,655 R	64.3%	30.6%	3.1%
2,017	DANIELS	1,110	750	303	39	18	447 R	67.6%	27.3%	3.5%
9,059	DAWSON	4,271	2,723	1,364	115	69	1,359 R	63.8%	31.9%	2.7%
9,417	DEER LODGE	4,534	1,493	2,672	232	137	1,179 D	32.9%	58.9%	5.1%
2,837	FALLON	1,369	1,061	256	31	21	805 R	77.5%	18.7%	2.3%
11,893	FERGUS	5,994	4,353	1,352	165	124	3,001 R	72.6%	22.6%	2.8%
74,471	FLATHEAD	33,839	22,519	8,329	2,037	954	14,190 R	66.5%	24.6%	6.0%
67,831	GALLATIN	32,040	18,833	10,009	2,545	653	8,824 R	58.8%	31.2%	7.9%
1,279	GARFIELD	744	651	61	12	20	590 R	87.5%	8.2%	1.6%
13,247	GLACIER	4,124	1,709	2,211	139	65	502 D	41.4%	53.6%	3.4%
1,042	GOLDEN VALLEY	531	405	88	17	21	317 R	76.3%	16.6%	3.2%
2,830	GRANITE	1,590	1,181	295	75	39	886 R	74.3%	18.6%	4.7%
16,673	HILL	6,558	3,392	2,760	278	128	632 R	51.7%	42.1%	4.2%
10,049	JEFFERSON	5,163	3,308	1,513	189	153	1,795 R	64.1%	29.3%	3.7%
2,329	JUDITH BASIN	1,394	1,057	278	31	28	779 R	75.8%	19.9%	2.2%
26,507	LAKE	11,448	6,441	3,884	762	361	2,557 R	56.3%	33.9%	6.7%
55,716	LEWIS AND CLARK	27,269	15,091	9,982	1,645	551	5,109 R	55.3%	36.6%	6.0%
2,158	LIBERTY	1,044	752	243	24	25	509 R	72.0%	23.3%	2.3%
18,837	LINCOLN	7,846	5,578	1,629	402	237	3,949 R	71.1%	20.8%	5.1%
1,977	MCCONE	1,142	827	267	34	14	560 R	72.4%	23.4%	3.0%
6,851	MADISON	3,656	2,656	758	161	81	1,898 R	72.6%	20.7%	4.4%
1,932	MEAGHER	935	698	176	27	34	522 R	74.7%	18.8%	2.9%
3,884	MINERAL	1,639	1,078	382	127	52	696 R	65.8%	23.3%	7.7%
95,802	MISSOULA	46,576	21,474	17,241	6,999	862	4,233 R	46.1%	37.0%	15.0%
4,497	MUSSELSHELL	2,207	1,582	512	53	60	1,070 R	71.7%	23.2%	2.4%
15,694	PARK	7,406	4,523	2,154	498	231	2,369 R	61.1%	29.1%	6.7%
493	PETROLEUM	306	254	36	6	10	218 R	83.0%	11.8%	2.0%
4,601	PHILLIPS	2,228	1,727	423	44	34	1,304 R	77.5%	19.0%	2.0%
6,424	PONDERA	2,896	1,948	792	96	60	1,156 R	67.3%	27.3%	3.3%
1,858	POWDER RIVER	1,008	860	115	21	12	745 R	85.3%	11.4%	2.1%
7,180	POWELL	2,832	1,971	638	129	94	1,333 R	69.6%	22.5%	4.6%
1,199	PRAIRIE	746	541	164	24	17	377 R	72.5%	22.0%	3.2%
36,070	RAVALLI	17,238	11,241	4,451	1,128	418	6,790 R	65.2%	25.8%	6.5%
9,667	RICHLAND	4,033	2,858	1,018	79	78	1,840 R	70.9%	25.2%	2.0%
10,620	ROOSEVELT	3,813	1,605	2,059	95	54	454 D	42.1%	54.0%	2.5%
9,383	ROSEBUD	3,423	1,826	1,394	130	73	432 R	53.3%	40.7%	3.8%
10,227	SANDERS	4,721	3,144	1,165	305	107	1,979 R	66.6%	24.7%	6.5%
4,105	SHERIDAN	1,965	1,176	702	62	25	474 R	59.8%	35.7%	3.2%
34,606	SILVER BOW	16,703	6,299	8,967	876	561	2,668 D	37.7%	53.7%	5.2%
8,195	STILLWATER	3,918	2,765	925	141	87	1,840 R	70.6%	23.6%	3.6%
3,609	SWEET GRASS	1,846	1,450	305	59	32	1,145 R	78.5%	16.5%	3.2%
6,445	TETON	3,314	2,294	847	102	71	1,447 R	69.2%	25.6%	3.1%
5,267	TOOLE	2,378	1,639	630	77	32	1,009 R	68.9%	26.5%	3.2%
861	TREASURE	479	344	106	12	17	238 R	71.8%	22.1%	2.5%
7,675	VALLEY	3,963	2,500	1,273	103	87	1,227 R	63.1%	32.1%	2.6%
2,259	WHEATLAND	999	708	243	21	27	465 R	70.9%	24.3%	2.1%
1,068	WIBAUX	518	369	121	16	12	248 R	71.2%	23.4%	3.1%
129,352	YELLOWSTONE	57,499	33,922	20,370	2,145	1,062	13,552 R	59.0%	35.4%	3.7%
902,195	TOTAL	410,997	240,178	137,126	24,437	9,256	103,052 R	58.4%	33.4%	5.9%

MONTANA

GOVERNOR 2000

2000 Census Population	County	Total Vote	Republican	Democratic	Other	Rep.-Dem. Plurality		Percentage			
								Total Vote		Major Vote	
								Rep.	Dem.	Rep.	Dem.
9,202	BEAVERHEAD	4,197	2,889	1,246	62	1,643	R	68.8%	29.7%	69.9%	30.1%
12,671	BIG HORN	4,167	1,402	2,699	66	1,297	D	33.6%	64.8%	34.2%	65.8%
7,009	BLAINE	2,752	1,102	1,610	40	508	D	40.0%	58.5%	40.6%	59.4%
4,385	BROADWATER	2,061	1,316	707	38	609	R	63.9%	34.3%	65.1%	34.9%
9,552	CARBON	4,859	2,739	2,019	101	720	R	56.4%	41.6%	57.6%	42.4%
1,360	CARTER	630	515	106	9	409	R	81.7%	16.8%	82.9%	17.1%
80,357	CASCADE	33,225	14,479	18,096	650	3,617	D	43.6%	54.5%	44.4%	55.6%
5,970	CHOUTEAU	2,885	1,722	1,112	51	610	R	59.7%	38.5%	60.8%	39.2%
11,696	CUSTER	4,973	2,582	2,333	58	249	R	51.9%	46.9%	52.5%	47.5%
2,017	DANIELS	1,082	691	377	14	314	R	63.9%	34.8%	64.7%	35.3%
9,059	DAWSON	4,264	2,433	1,760	71	673	R	57.1%	41.3%	58.0%	42.0%
9,417	DEER LODGE	4,576	1,218	3,297	61	2,079	D	26.6%	72.0%	27.0%	73.0%
2,837	FALLON	1,325	870	426	29	444	R	65.7%	32.2%	67.1%	32.9%
11,893	FERGUS	6,012	3,829	2,061	122	1,768	R	63.7%	34.3%	65.0%	35.0%
74,471	FLATHEAD	33,640	20,593	12,298	749	8,295	R	61.2%	36.6%	62.6%	37.4%
67,831	GALLATIN	31,981	16,909	14,438	634	2,471	R	52.9%	45.1%	53.9%	46.1%
1,279	GARFIELD	729	597	125	7	472	R	81.9%	17.1%	82.7%	17.3%
13,247	GLACIER	4,192	1,410	2,700	82	1,290	D	33.6%	64.4%	34.3%	65.7%
1,042	GOLDEN VALLEY	531	382	137	12	245	R	71.9%	25.8%	73.6%	26.4%
2,830	GRANITE	1,586	1,010	528	48	482	R	63.7%	33.3%	65.7%	34.3%
16,673	HILL	6,547	2,544	3,858	145	1,314	D	38.9%	58.9%	39.7%	60.3%
10,049	JEFFERSON	5,147	2,967	2,086	94	881	R	57.6%	40.5%	58.7%	41.3%
2,329	JUDITH BASIN	1,387	905	459	23	446	R	65.2%	33.1%	66.3%	33.7%
26,507	LAKE	11,430	5,983	5,179	268	804	R	52.3%	45.3%	53.6%	46.4%
55,716	LEWIS AND CLARK	27,313	13,185	13,704	424	519	D	48.3%	50.2%	49.0%	51.0%
2,158	LIBERTY	1,047	652	374	21	278	R	62.3%	35.7%	63.5%	36.5%
18,837	LINCOLN	7,809	4,735	2,833	241	1,902	R	60.6%	36.3%	62.6%	37.4%
1,977	MCCONE	1,140	699	429	12	270	R	61.3%	37.6%	62.0%	38.0%
6,851	MADISON	3,658	2,468	1,115	75	1,353	R	67.5%	30.5%	68.9%	31.1%
1,932	MEAGHER	935	656	258	21	398	R	70.2%	27.6%	71.8%	28.2%
3,884	MINERAL	1,629	836	744	49	92	R	51.3%	45.7%	52.9%	47.1%
95,802	MISSOULA	46,301	18,215	27,034	1,052	8,819	D	39.3%	58.4%	40.3%	59.7%
4,497	MUSSELSHELL	2,193	1,371	766	56	605	R	62.5%	34.9%	64.2%	35.8%
15,694	PARK	7,404	4,004	3,243	157	761	R	54.1%	43.8%	55.3%	44.7%
493	PETROLEUM	310	235	70	5	165	R	75.8%	22.6%	77.0%	23.0%
4,601	PHILLIPS	2,217	1,598	589	30	1,009	R	72.1%	26.6%	73.1%	26.9%
6,424	PONDERA	2,912	1,569	1,300	43	269	R	53.9%	44.6%	54.7%	45.3%
1,858	POWDER RIVER	983	745	229	9	516	R	75.8%	23.3%	76.5%	23.5%
7,180	POWELL	2,839	1,688	1,077	74	611	R	59.5%	37.9%	61.0%	39.0%
1,199	PRAIRIE	741	498	231	12	267	R	67.2%	31.2%	68.3%	31.7%
36,070	RAVALLI	17,129	9,772	6,982	375	2,790	R	57.0%	40.8%	58.3%	41.7%
9,667	RICHLAND	4,022	2,658	1,293	71	1,365	R	66.1%	32.1%	67.3%	32.7%
10,620	ROOSEVELT	3,832	1,369	2,417	46	1,048	D	35.7%	63.1%	36.2%	63.8%
9,383	ROSEBUD	3,492	1,466	1,955	71	489	D	42.0%	56.0%	42.9%	57.1%
10,227	SANDERS	4,676	2,633	1,911	132	722	R	56.3%	40.9%	57.9%	42.1%
4,105	SHERIDAN	1,943	1,052	868	23	184	R	54.1%	44.7%	54.8%	45.2%
34,606	SILVER BOW	16,800	5,750	10,837	213	5,087	D	34.2%	64.5%	34.7%	65.3%
8,195	STILLWATER	3,892	2,417	1,392	83	1,025	R	62.1%	35.8%	63.5%	36.5%
3,609	SWEET GRASS	1,834	1,382	422	30	960	R	75.4%	23.0%	76.6%	23.4%
6,445	TETON	3,301	1,892	1,360	49	532	R	57.3%	41.2%	58.2%	41.8%
5,267	TOOLE	2,396	1,283	1,071	42	212	R	53.5%	44.7%	54.5%	45.5%
861	TREASURE	475	306	163	6	143	R	64.4%	34.3%	65.2%	34.8%
7,675	VALLEY	3,973	2,137	1,750	86	387	R	53.8%	44.0%	55.0%	45.0%
2,259	WHEATLAND	998	688	298	12	390	R	68.9%	29.9%	69.8%	30.2%
1,068	WIBAUX	505	302	187	16	115	R	59.8%	37.0%	61.8%	38.2%
129,352	YELLOWSTONE	57,315	29,787	26,572	956	3,215	R	52.0%	46.4%	52.9%	47.1%
902,195	TOTAL	410,192	209,135	193,131	7,926	16,004	R	51.0%	47.1%	52.0%	48.0%

MONTANA
SENATOR 2000

2000 Census Population	County	Total Vote	Republican	Democratic	Other	Rep.-Dem. Plurality		Total Vote Rep.	Total Vote Dem.	Major Vote Rep.	Major Vote Dem.
9,202	BEAVERHEAD	4,175	2,862	1,240	73	1,622	R	68.6%	29.7%	69.8%	30.2%
12,671	BIG HORN	4,038	1,437	2,534	67	1,097	D	35.6%	62.8%	36.2%	63.8%
7,009	BLAINE	2,762	1,238	1,482	42	244	D	44.8%	53.7%	45.5%	54.5%
4,385	BROADWATER	2,072	1,294	724	54	570	R	62.5%	34.9%	64.1%	35.9%
9,552	CARBON	4,908	2,636	2,151	121	485	R	53.7%	43.8%	55.1%	44.9%
1,360	CARTER	636	571	62	3	509	R	89.8%	9.7%	90.2%	9.8%
80,357	CASCADE	33,363	15,298	17,288	777	1,990	D	45.9%	51.8%	46.9%	53.1%
5,970	CHOUTEAU	2,889	1,840	998	51	842	R	63.7%	34.5%	64.8%	35.2%
11,696	CUSTER	5,025	2,751	2,158	116	593	R	54.7%	42.9%	56.0%	44.0%
2,017	DANIELS	1,103	709	370	24	339	R	64.3%	33.5%	65.7%	34.3%
9,059	DAWSON	4,332	2,525	1,724	83	801	R	58.3%	39.8%	59.4%	40.6%
9,417	DEER LODGE	4,528	1,154	3,297	77	2,143	D	25.5%	72.8%	25.9%	74.1%
2,837	FALLON	1,288	914	346	28	568	R	71.0%	26.9%	72.5%	27.5%
11,893	FERGUS	6,042	3,850	2,067	125	1,783	R	63.7%	34.2%	65.1%	34.9%
74,471	FLATHEAD	34,025	19,684	13,495	846	6,189	R	57.9%	39.7%	59.3%	40.7%
67,831	GALLATIN	32,102	16,879	14,612	611	2,267	R	52.6%	45.5%	53.6%	46.4%
1,279	GARFIELD	738	589	135	14	454	R	79.8%	18.3%	81.4%	18.6%
13,247	GLACIER	4,204	1,415	2,682	107	1,267	D	33.7%	63.8%	34.5%	65.5%
1,042	GOLDEN VALLEY	517	343	157	17	186	R	66.3%	30.4%	68.6%	31.4%
2,830	GRANITE	1,592	1,006	552	34	454	R	63.2%	34.7%	64.6%	35.4%
16,673	HILL	6,568	2,757	3,686	125	929	D	42.0%	56.1%	42.8%	57.2%
10,049	JEFFERSON	5,171	2,762	2,288	121	474	R	53.4%	44.2%	54.7%	45.3%
2,329	JUDITH BASIN	1,388	893	472	23	421	R	64.3%	34.0%	65.4%	34.6%
26,507	LAKE	11,444	5,632	5,471	341	161	R	49.2%	47.8%	50.7%	49.3%
55,716	LEWIS AND CLARK	27,443	12,373	14,564	506	2,191	D	45.1%	53.1%	45.9%	54.1%
2,158	LIBERTY	1,057	648	393	16	255	R	61.3%	37.2%	62.2%	37.8%
18,837	LINCOLN	7,877	5,010	2,629	238	2,381	R	63.6%	33.4%	65.6%	34.4%
1,977	MCCONE	1,146	777	358	11	419	R	67.8%	31.2%	68.5%	31.5%
6,851	MADISON	3,653	2,379	1,207	67	1,172	R	65.1%	33.0%	66.3%	33.7%
1,932	MEAGHER	929	625	267	37	358	R	67.3%	28.7%	70.1%	29.9%
3,884	MINERAL	1,656	926	673	57	253	R	55.9%	40.6%	57.9%	42.1%
95,802	MISSOULA	46,429	17,876	27,494	1,059	9,618	D	38.5%	59.2%	39.4%	60.6%
4,497	MUSSELSHELL	2,206	1,414	732	60	682	R	64.1%	33.2%	65.9%	34.1%
15,694	PARK	7,428	3,970	3,229	229	741	R	53.4%	43.5%	55.1%	44.9%
493	PETROLEUM	311	240	63	8	177	R	77.2%	20.3%	79.2%	20.8%
4,601	PHILLIPS	2,224	1,567	630	27	937	R	70.5%	28.3%	71.3%	28.7%
6,424	PONDERA	2,861	1,563	1,234	64	329	R	54.6%	43.1%	55.9%	44.1%
1,858	POWDER RIVER	999	806	178	15	628	R	80.7%	17.8%	81.9%	18.1%
7,180	POWELL	2,869	1,749	1,057	63	692	R	61.0%	36.8%	62.3%	37.7%
1,199	PRAIRIE	740	500	227	13	273	R	67.6%	30.7%	68.8%	31.2%
36,070	RAVALLI	17,193	9,790	6,966	437	2,824	R	56.9%	40.5%	58.4%	41.6%
9,667	RICHLAND	4,048	2,733	1,220	95	1,513	R	67.5%	30.1%	69.1%	30.9%
10,620	ROOSEVELT	3,857	1,629	2,142	86	513	D	42.2%	55.5%	43.2%	56.8%
9,383	ROSEBUD	3,523	1,582	1,847	94	265	D	44.9%	52.4%	46.1%	53.9%
10,227	SANDERS	4,731	2,795	1,819	117	976	R	59.1%	38.4%	60.6%	39.4%
4,105	SHERIDAN	1,955	1,080	854	21	226	R	55.2%	43.7%	55.8%	44.2%
34,606	SILVER BOW	16,866	5,221	11,298	347	6,077	D	31.0%	67.0%	31.6%	68.4%
8,195	STILLWATER	3,926	2,342	1,487	97	855	R	59.7%	37.9%	61.2%	38.8%
3,609	SWEET GRASS	1,807	1,346	424	37	922	R	74.5%	23.5%	76.0%	24.0%
6,445	TETON	3,219	1,947	1,215	57	732	R	60.5%	37.7%	61.6%	38.4%
5,267	TOOLE	2,358	1,302	992	64	310	R	55.2%	42.1%	56.8%	43.2%
861	TREASURE	472	276	182	14	94	R	58.5%	38.6%	60.3%	39.7%
7,675	VALLEY	4,009	2,182	1,746	81	436	R	54.4%	43.6%	55.5%	44.5%
2,259	WHEATLAND	996	642	335	19	307	R	64.5%	33.6%	65.7%	34.3%
1,068	WIBAUX	516	319	187	10	132	R	61.8%	36.2%	63.0%	37.0%
129,352	YELLOWSTONE	57,387	29,434	26,790	1,163	2,644	R	51.3%	46.7%	52.4%	47.6%
902,195	TOTAL	411,601	208,082	194,430	9,089	13,652	R	50.6%	47.2%	51.7%	48.3%

MONTANA

CONGRESS

CD	Year	Total Vote	Republican Vote	Republican Candidate	Democratic Vote	Democratic Candidate	Other Vote	Rep.-Dem. Plurality	Total Vote Rep.	Total Vote Dem.	Major Vote Rep.	Major Vote Dem.
AL	2000	410,523	211,418	REHBERG, DENNIS	189,971	KEENAN, NANCY	9,134	21,447 R	51.5%	46.3%	52.7%	47.3%
AL	1998	331,551	175,748	HILL, RICK	147,073	DESCHAMPS, DUSTY	8,730	28,675 R	53.0%	44.4%	54.4%	45.6%
AL	1996	404,426	211,975	HILL, RICK	174,516	YELLOWTAIL, BILL	17,935	37,459 R	52.4%	43.2%	54.8%	45.2%
AL	1994	352,133	148,715	JAMISON, CY	171,372	WILLIAMS, PAT	32,046	22,657 D	42.2%	48.7%	46.5%	53.5%
AL	1992	403,735	189,570	MARLENEE, RON	203,711	WILLIAMS, PAT	10,454	14,141 D	47.0%	50.5%	48.2%	51.8%

MONTANA

GENERAL AND PRIMARY ELECTIONS

2000 GENERAL ELECTIONS

President Other vote was 5,697 Reform (Buchanan); 1,718 Libertarian (Browne); 1,155 Constitution (Phillips); 675 Natural Law (Hagelin); 11 write-in (Laible).

Governor Other vote was 7,926 Libertarian (Jones).

Senator Other vote was 9,089 Reform (Lee).

Congress Other vote was 9,132 Libertarian (Tikalsky); 2 write-in (Ferren).

2000 PRIMARY ELECTIONS

Primary June 6, 2000

Registration (as of June 6, 2000) 671,325 No Party Registration

Primary Type Open—Any registered voter could vote in the primary of either party.

Note: An asterisk (*) denotes incumbent.

	REPUBLICAN PRIMARIES			DEMOCRATIC PRIMARIES		
President	George W. Bush	88,194	77.6%	Al Gore	68,420	77.9%
	Alan Keyes	20,822	18.3%	No Preference	19,447	22.1%
	No Preference	4,655	4.1%			
	John McCain (write-in)	2				
	TOTAL	113,673		TOTAL	87,867	
Governor	Judy Martz	64,278	56.9%	Mark O'Keefe	46,294	48.0%
	Rob Natelson	48,738	43.1%	Joseph Mazurek	34,385	35.7%
	Write-in	2		Mike Cooney	15,677	16.3%
	TOTAL	113,018		TOTAL	96,356	
Senator	Conrad Burns*	102,125	100.0%	Brian Schweitzer	59,189	66.2%
				John Driscoll	30,242	33.8%
	TOTAL	102,125		TOTAL	89,431	
Congressional At-Large	Dennis Rehberg	98,646	100.0%	Nancy Keenan	86,114	100.0%
	TOTAL	98,646		TOTAL	86,114	

NEBRASKA

GOVERNOR
Mike Johanns (R). Elected 1998 to a four-year term.

SENATORS
Chuck Hagel (R). Elected 1996 to a six-year term.

Ben Nelson (D). Elected 2000 to a six-year term.

REPRESENTATIVES
1. Douglas K. Bereuter (R)   2. Lee Terry (R)   3. Tom Osborne (R)

POSTWAR VOTE FOR PRESIDENT

Year	Total Vote	Republican Vote	Republican Candidate	Democratic Vote	Democratic Candidate	Other Vote	Plurality	Total Vote Rep.	Total Vote Dem.	Major Vote Rep.	Major Vote Dem.
2000**	697,019	433,862	Bush, George W.	231,780	Gore, Al	31,377	202,082 R	62.2%	33.3%	65.2%	34.8%
1996**	677,415	363,467	Dole, Bob	236,761	Clinton, Bill	77,187	126,706 R	53.7%	35.0%	60.6%	39.4%
1992**	737,546	343,678	Bush, George	216,864	Clinton, Bill	177,004	126,814 R	46.6%	29.4%	61.3%	38.7%
1988	661,465	397,956	Bush, George	259,235	Dukakis, Michael S.	4,274	138,721 R	60.2%	39.2%	60.6%	39.4%
1984	652,090	460,054	Reagan, Ronald	187,866	Mondale, Walter F.	4,170	272,188 R	70.6%	28.8%	71.0%	29.0%
1980**	640,854	419,937	Reagan, Ronald	166,851	Carter, Jimmy	54,066	253,086 R	65.5%	26.0%	71.6%	28.4%
1976	607,668	359,705	Ford, Gerald R.	233,692	Carter, Jimmy	14,271	126,013 R	59.2%	38.5%	60.6%	39.4%
1972	576,289	406,298	Nixon, Richard M.	169,991	McGovern, George S.		236,307 R	70.5%	29.5%	70.5%	29.5%
1968	536,851	321,163	Nixon, Richard M.	170,784	Humphrey, Hubert H.	44,904	150,379 R	59.8%	31.8%	65.3%	34.7%
1964	584,154	276,847	Goldwater, Barry M.	307,307	Johnson, Lyndon B.		30,460 D	47.4%	52.6%	47.4%	52.6%
1960	613,095	380,553	Nixon, Richard M.	232,542	Kennedy, John F.		148,011 R	62.1%	37.9%	62.1%	37.9%
1956	577,137	378,108	Eisenhower, Dwight D.	199,029	Stevenson, Adlai E.		179,079 R	65.5%	34.5%	65.5%	34.5%
1952	609,660	421,603	Eisenhower, Dwight D.	188,057	Stevenson, Adlai E.		233,546 R	69.2%	30.8%	69.2%	30.8%
1948	488,940	264,774	Dewey, Thomas E.	224,165	Truman, Harry S.	1	40,609 R	54.2%	45.8%	54.2%	45.8%

In 2000 the other vote column includes 24,540 votes cast for Green (Nader). In 1996 the other vote column includes 71,278 votes cast for Perot. In 1992 the other vote column includes 174,104 votes cast for Perot. In 1980 the other column includes 44,993 votes for Independent (Anderson).

NEBRASKA

POSTWAR VOTE FOR GOVERNOR

Year	Total Vote	Republican Vote	Republican Candidate	Democratic Vote	Democratic Candidate	Other Vote	Rep.-Dem. Plurality	Total Vote Rep.	Total Vote Dem.	Major Vote Rep.	Major Vote Dem.
1998	545,238	293,910	Johanns, Mike	250,678	Hoppner, Bill	650	43,232 R	53.9%	46.0%	54.0%	46.0%
1994	579,561	148,230	Spence, Gene	423,270	Nelson, Ben	8,061	275,040 D	25.6%	73.0%	25.9%	74.1%
1990	586,542	288,741	Orr, Kay	292,771	Nelson, Ben	5,030	4,030 D	49.2%	49.9%	49.7%	50.3%
1986	564,422	298,325	Orr, Kay	265,156	Boosalis, Helen	941	33,169 R	52.9%	47.0%	52.9%	47.1%
1982	547,902	270,203	Thone, Charles	277,436	Kerrey, Bob	263	7,233 D	49.3%	50.6%	49.3%	50.7%
1978	492,423	275,473	Thone, Charles	216,754	Whelan, Gerald T.	196	58,719 R	55.9%	44.0%	56.0%	44.0%
1974	451,306	159,780	Marvel, Richard D.	267,012	Exon, J. J.	24,514	107,232 D	35.4%	59.2%	37.4%	62.6%
1970	461,619	201,994	Tiemann, Norbert T.	248,552	Exon, J. J.	11,073	46,558 D	43.8%	53.8%	44.8%	55.2%
1966**	486,396	299,245	Tiemann, Norbert T.	186,985	Sorensen, Philip C.	166	112,260 R	61.5%	38.4%	61.5%	38.5%
1964	578,090	231,029	Burney, Dwight W.	347,026	Morrison, Frank B.	35	115,997 D	40.0%	60.0%	40.0%	60.0%
1962	464,585	221,885	Seaton, Fred A.	242,669	Morrison, Frank B.	31	20,784 D	47.8%	52.2%	47.8%	52.2%
1960	598,971	287,302	Cooper, John R.	311,344	Morrison, Frank B.	325	24,042 D	48.0%	52.0%	48.0%	52.0%
1958	421,067	209,705	Anderson, Victor E.	211,345	Brooks, Ralph G.	17	1,640 D	49.8%	50.2%	49.8%	50.2%
1956	567,933	308,293	Anderson, Victor E.	228,048	Sorrell, Frank	31,592	80,245 R	54.3%	40.2%	57.5%	42.5%
1954	414,841	250,080	Anderson, Victor E.	164,753	Ritchie, William	8	85,327 R	60.3%	39.7%	60.3%	39.7%
1952	595,714	366,009	Crosby, Robert B.	229,700	Raecke, Walter R.	5	136,309 R	61.4%	38.6%	61.4%	38.6%
1950	449,720	247,081	Peterson, Val	202,638	Raecke, Walter R.	1	44,443 R	54.9%	45.1%	54.9%	45.1%
1948	476,352	286,119	Peterson, Val	190,214	Sorrell, Frank	19	95,905 R	60.1%	39.9%	60.1%	39.9%
1946	380,835	249,468	Peterson, Val	131,367	Sorrell, Frank		118,101 R	65.5%	34.5%	65.5%	34.5%

The term of office of Nebraska's Governor was increased from two to four years effective with the 1966 election.

POSTWAR VOTE FOR SENATOR

Year	Total Vote	Republican Vote	Republican Candidate	Democratic Vote	Democratic Candidate	Other Vote	Rep.-Dem. Plurality	Total Vote Rep.	Total Vote Dem.	Major Vote Rep.	Major Vote Dem.
2000	692,344	337,967	Stenberg, Don	353,097	Nelson, Ben	1,280	15,130 D	48.8%	51.0%	48.9%	51.1%
1996	676,789	379,933	Hagel, Chuck	281,904	Nelson, Ben	14,952	98,029 R	56.1%	41.7%	57.4%	42.6%
1994	579,205	260,668	Stoney, Jan	317,297	Kerrey, Bob	1,240	56,629 D	45.0%	54.8%	45.1%	54.9%
1990	593,828	243,013	Daub, Harold J.	349,779	Exon, J. J.	1,036	106,766 D	40.9%	58.9%	41.0%	59.0%
1988	667,860	278,250	Karnes, David	378,717	Kerrey, Bob	10,893	100,467 D	41.7%	56.7%	42.4%	57.6%
1984	639,668	307,147	Hoch, Nancy	332,217	Exon, J. J.	304	25,070 D	48.0%	51.9%	48.0%	52.0%
1982	545,647	155,760	Keck, Jim	363,350	Zorinsky, Edward	26,537	207,590 D	28.5%	66.6%	30.0%	70.0%
1978	494,368	159,806	Shasteen, Donald	334,276	Exon, J. J.	286	174,470 D	32.3%	67.6%	32.3%	67.7%
1976	598,314	284,284	McCollister, John Y.	313,809	Zorinsky, Edward	221	29,525 D	47.5%	52.4%	47.5%	52.5%
1972	568,580	301,841	Curtis, Carl T.	265,922	Carpenter, Terry	817	35,919 R	53.1%	46.8%	53.2%	46.8%
1970	458,966	240,894	Hruska, Roman L.	217,681	Morrison, Frank B.	391	23,213 R	52.5%	47.4%	52.5%	47.5%
1966	485,101	296,116	Curtis, Carl T.	187,950	Morrison, Frank B.	1,035	108,166 R	61.0%	38.7%	61.2%	38.8%
1964	563,401	345,772	Hruska, Roman L.	217,605	Arndt, Raymond W.	24	128,167 R	61.4%	38.6%	61.4%	38.6%
1960	598,743	352,748	Curtis, Carl T.	245,837	Conrad, Robert	158	106,911 R	58.9%	41.1%	58.9%	41.1%
1958	417,385	232,227	Hruska, Roman L.	185,152	Morrison, Frank B.	6	47,075 R	55.6%	44.4%	55.6%	44.4%
1954	418,691	255,695	Curtis, Carl T.	162,990	Neville, Keith	6	92,705 R	61.1%	38.9%	61.1%	38.9%
1954S	411,225	250,341	Hruska, Roman L.	160,881	Green, James F.	3	89,460 R	60.9%	39.1%	60.9%	39.1%
1952	591,749	408,971	Butler, Hugh	164,660	Long, Stanley D.	18,118	244,311 R	69.1%	27.8%	71.3%	28.7%
1952S	581,750	369,841	Griswold, Dwight	211,898	Ritchie, William	11	157,943 R	63.6%	36.4%	63.6%	36.4%
1948	471,895	267,575	Wherry, Kenneth S.	204,320	Carpenter, Terry		63,255 R	56.7%	43.3%	56.7%	43.3%
1946	382,958	271,208	Butler, Hugh	111,750	Mekota, John E.		159,458 R	70.8%	29.2%	70.8%	29.2%

One each of the 1954 and 1952 elections was for a short term to fill a vacancy.

NEBRASKA

Districts Established June 10, 1991

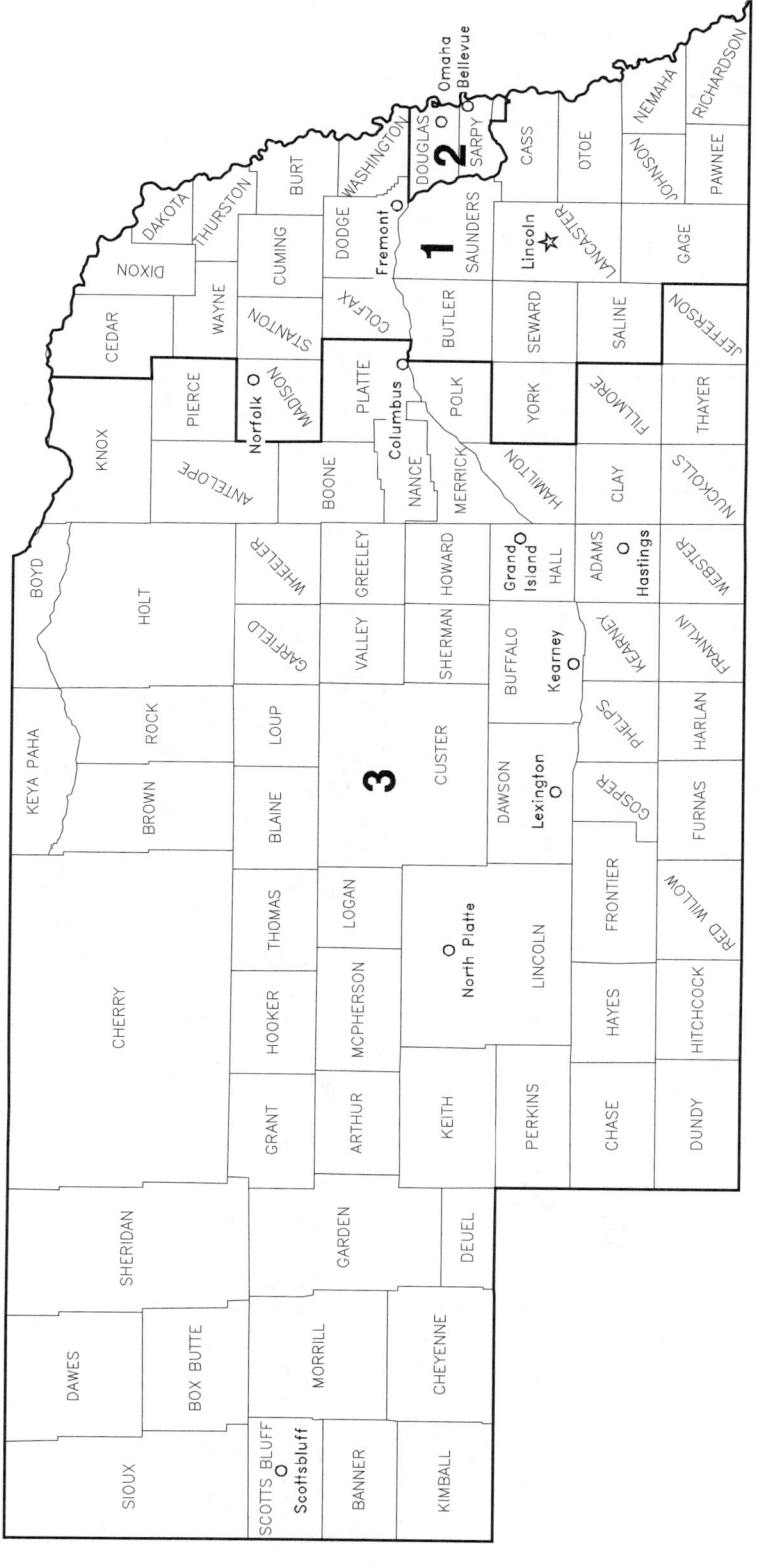

NEBRASKA

PRESIDENT 2000

2000 Census Population	County	Total Vote	Republican	Democratic	Green (Nader)	Other	Rep.-Dem. Plurality	Percentage of Total Vote		
								Rep.	Dem.	Green
31,151	ADAMS	12,438	8,162	3,686	472	118	4,476 R	65.6%	29.6%	3.8%
7,452	ANTELOPE	3,368	2,562	678	84	44	1,884 R	76.1%	20.1%	2.5%
444	ARTHUR	272	235	26	6	5	209 R	86.4%	9.6%	2.2%
819	BANNER	462	390	65	2	5	325 R	84.4%	14.1%	0.4%
583	BLAINE	349	299	43	5	2	256 R	85.7%	12.3%	1.4%
6,259	BOONE	2,862	2,196	575	65	26	1,621 R	76.7%	20.1%	2.3%
12,158	BOX BUTTE	5,089	3,208	1,614	203	64	1,594 R	63.0%	31.7%	4.0%
2,438	BOYD	1,242	931	265	25	21	666 R	75.0%	21.3%	2.0%
3,525	BROWN	1,684	1,375	250	36	23	1,125 R	81.7%	14.8%	2.1%
42,259	BUFFALO	16,461	11,931	3,927	483	120	8,004 R	72.5%	23.9%	2.9%
7,791	BURT	3,392	2,056	1,223	73	40	833 R	60.6%	36.1%	2.2%
8,767	BUTLER	3,828	2,638	1,028	108	54	1,610 R	68.9%	26.9%	2.8%
24,334	CASS	10,280	6,144	3,656	369	111	2,488 R	59.8%	35.6%	3.6%
9,615	CEDAR	4,269	2,989	1,062	140	78	1,927 R	70.0%	24.9%	3.3%
4,068	CHASE	1,875	1,505	306	38	26	1,199 R	80.3%	16.3%	2.0%
6,148	CHERRY	2,847	2,322	446	50	29	1,876 R	81.6%	15.7%	1.8%
9,830	CHEYENNE	4,186	3,207	844	76	59	2,363 R	76.6%	20.2%	1.8%
7,039	CLAY	3,215	2,326	774	86	29	1,552 R	72.3%	24.1%	2.7%
10,441	COLFAX	3,315	2,338	863	72	42	1,475 R	70.5%	26.0%	2.2%
10,203	CUMING	4,215	3,232	857	91	35	2,375 R	76.7%	20.3%	2.2%
11,793	CUSTER	5,414	4,245	976	140	53	3,269 R	78.4%	18.0%	2.6%
20,253	DAKOTA	6,061	3,119	2,695	141	106	424 R	51.5%	44.5%	2.3%
9,060	DAWES	3,621	2,549	823	212	37	1,726 R	70.4%	22.7%	5.9%
24,365	DAWSON	7,507	5,511	1,740	143	113	3,771 R	73.4%	23.2%	1.9%
2,098	DEUEL	1,033	783	213	27	10	570 R	75.8%	20.6%	2.6%
6,339	DIXON	2,792	1,834	820	60	78	1,014 R	65.7%	29.4%	2.1%
36,160	DODGE	14,472	8,871	5,021	443	137	3,850 R	61.3%	34.7%	3.1%
463,585	DOUGLAS	183,156	101,025	73,347	7,109	1,675	27,678 R	55.2%	40.0%	3.9%
2,292	DUNDY	1,011	801	179	19	12	622 R	79.2%	17.7%	1.9%
6,634	FILLMORE	2,998	2,024	848	103	23	1,176 R	67.5%	28.3%	3.4%
3,574	FRANKLIN	1,668	1,196	420	36	16	776 R	71.7%	25.2%	2.2%
3,099	FRONTIER	1,393	1,102	244	27	20	858 R	79.1%	17.5%	1.9%
5,324	FURNAS	2,431	1,849	534	29	19	1,315 R	76.1%	22.0%	1.2%
22,993	GAGE	9,506	5,538	3,516	355	97	2,022 R	58.3%	37.0%	3.7%
2,292	GARDEN	1,219	963	203	38	15	760 R	79.0%	16.7%	3.1%
1,902	GARFIELD	963	718	202	33	10	516 R	74.6%	21.0%	3.4%
2,143	GOSPER	1,014	757	228	19	10	529 R	74.7%	22.5%	1.9%
747	GRANT	385	324	49	10	2	275 R	84.2%	12.7%	2.6%
2,714	GREELEY	1,310	839	416	37	18	423 R	64.0%	31.8%	2.8%
53,534	HALL	18,546	11,803	5,952	595	196	5,851 R	63.6%	32.1%	3.2%
9,403	HAMILTON	4,491	3,251	1,066	141	33	2,185 R	72.4%	23.7%	3.1%
3,786	HARLAN	1,852	1,358	438	37	19	920 R	73.3%	23.7%	2.0%
1,068	HAYES	571	486	66	8	11	420 R	85.1%	11.6%	1.4%
3,111	HITCHCOCK	1,480	1,126	312	21	21	814 R	76.1%	21.1%	1.4%
11,551	HOLT	4,959	3,954	846	93	66	3,108 R	79.7%	17.1%	1.9%
783	HOOKER	409	317	74	13	5	243 R	77.5%	18.1%	3.2%
6,567	HOWARD	2,827	1,760	955	71	41	805 R	62.3%	33.8%	2.5%
8,333	JEFFERSON	3,847	2,351	1,361	102	33	990 R	61.1%	35.4%	2.7%
4,488	JOHNSON	2,112	1,210	794	74	34	416 R	57.3%	37.6%	3.5%
6,882	KEARNEY	3,122	2,333	680	75	34	1,653 R	74.7%	21.8%	2.4%
8,875	KEITH	3,849	2,953	778	75	43	2,175 R	76.7%	20.2%	1.9%
983	KEYA PAHA	513	422	78	6	7	344 R	82.3%	15.2%	1.2%
4,089	KIMBALL	1,820	1,379	379	41	21	1,000 R	75.8%	20.8%	2.3%
9,374	KNOX	3,978	2,784	1,037	110	47	1,747 R	70.0%	26.1%	2.8%
250,291	LANCASTER	107,132	55,514	44,650	6,182	786	10,864 R	51.8%	41.7%	5.8%
34,632	LINCOLN	15,114	9,220	5,205	502	187	4,015 R	61.0%	34.4%	3.3%
774	LOGAN	412	336	60	11	5	276 R	81.6%	14.6%	2.7%
712	LOUP	378	284	84	7	3	200 R	75.1%	22.2%	1.9%
533	MCPHERSON	301	244	48	1	8	196 R	81.1%	15.9%	0.3%
35,226	MADISON	12,853	9,636	2,772	290	155	6,864 R	75.0%	21.6%	2.3%

NEBRASKA

PRESIDENT 2000

2000 Census Population	County	Total Vote	Republican	Democratic	Green (Nader)	Other	Rep.-Dem. Plurality	Percentage of Total Vote		
								Rep.	Dem.	Green
8,204	MERRICK	3,340	2,380	848	84	28	1,532 R	71.3%	25.4%	2.5%
5,440	MORRILL	2,138	1,597	460	46	35	1,137 R	74.7%	21.5%	2.2%
4,038	NANCE	1,665	1,105	497	46	17	608 R	66.4%	29.8%	2.8%
7,576	NEMAHA	3,369	2,177	1,063	94	35	1,114 R	64.6%	31.6%	2.8%
5,057	NUCKOLLS	2,443	1,701	644	66	32	1,057 R	69.6%	26.4%	2.7%
15,396	OTOE	6,662	4,178	2,208	218	58	1,970 R	62.7%	33.1%	3.3%
3,087	PAWNEE	1,519	937	522	38	22	415 R	61.7%	34.4%	2.5%
3,200	PERKINS	1,452	1,170	243	31	8	927 R	80.6%	16.7%	2.1%
9,747	PHELPS	4,627	3,575	934	86	32	2,641 R	77.3%	20.2%	1.9%
7,857	PIERCE	3,208	2,534	570	52	52	1,964 R	79.0%	17.8%	1.6%
31,662	PLATTE	12,859	9,861	2,612	266	120	7,249 R	76.7%	20.3%	2.1%
5,639	POLK	2,613	1,925	610	52	26	1,315 R	73.7%	23.3%	2.0%
11,448	RED WILLOW	5,025	3,680	1,188	103	54	2,492 R	73.2%	23.6%	2.0%
9,531	RICHARDSON	4,150	2,623	1,382	83	62	1,241 R	63.2%	33.3%	2.0%
1,756	ROCK	894	725	141	17	11	584 R	81.1%	15.8%	1.9%
13,843	SALINE	5,145	2,581	2,321	187	56	260 R	50.2%	45.1%	3.6%
122,595	SARPY	45,278	28,979	14,637	1,308	354	14,342 R	64.0%	32.3%	2.9%
19,830	SAUNDERS	8,919	5,688	2,852	277	102	2,836 R	63.8%	32.0%	3.1%
36,951	SCOTTS BLUFF	13,839	9,397	3,937	400	105	5,460 R	67.9%	28.4%	2.9%
16,496	SEWARD	7,016	4,457	2,250	245	64	2,207 R	63.5%	32.1%	3.5%
6,198	SHERIDAN	2,576	2,105	392	54	25	1,713 R	81.7%	15.2%	2.1%
3,318	SHERMAN	1,705	1,072	564	48	21	508 R	62.9%	33.1%	2.8%
1,475	SIOUX	752	629	98	18	7	531 R	83.6%	13.0%	2.4%
6,455	STANTON	2,486	1,895	500	53	38	1,395 R	76.2%	20.1%	2.1%
6,055	THAYER	3,006	2,096	821	65	24	1,275 R	69.7%	27.3%	2.2%
729	THOMAS	395	329	55	9	2	274 R	83.3%	13.9%	2.3%
7,171	THURSTON	2,082	1,040	924	56	62	116 R	50.0%	44.4%	2.7%
4,647	VALLEY	2,263	1,610	583	45	25	1,027 R	71.1%	25.8%	2.0%
18,780	WASHINGTON	8,626	5,758	2,550	234	84	3,208 R	66.8%	29.6%	2.7%
9,851	WAYNE	3,940	2,774	1,001	119	46	1,773 R	70.4%	25.4%	3.0%
4,061	WEBSTER	1,945	1,302	584	48	11	718 R	66.9%	30.0%	2.5%
886	WHEELER	453	351	85	11	6	266 R	77.5%	18.8%	2.4%
14,598	YORK	6,460	4,816	1,407	161	76	3,409 R	74.6%	21.8%	2.5%
1,711,263	TOTAL	697,019	433,862	231,780	24,540	6,837	202,082 R	62.2%	33.3%	3.5%

NEBRASKA

SENATOR 2000

2000 Census Population	County	Total Vote	Republican	Democratic	Other	Rep.-Dem. Plurality	Percentage			
							Total Vote		Major Vote	
							Rep.	Dem.	Rep.	Dem.
31,151	ADAMS	12,486	6,166	6,301	19	135 D	49.4%	50.5%	49.5%	50.5%
7,452	ANTELOPE	3,313	2,016	1,297		719 R	60.9%	39.1%	60.9%	39.1%
444	ARTHUR	268	212	56		156 R	79.1%	20.9%	79.1%	20.9%
819	BANNER	454	315	139		176 R	69.4%	30.6%	69.4%	30.6%
583	BLAINE	350	251	99		152 R	71.7%	28.3%	71.7%	28.3%
6,259	BOONE	2,870	1,685	1,185		500 R	58.7%	41.3%	58.7%	41.3%
12,158	BOX BUTTE	5,061	2,721	2,340		381 R	53.8%	46.2%	53.8%	46.2%
2,438	BOYD	1,224	667	557		110 R	54.5%	45.5%	54.5%	45.5%
3,525	BROWN	1,672	1,137	535		602 R	68.0%	32.0%	68.0%	32.0%
42,259	BUFFALO	16,278	8,650	7,612	16	1,038 R	53.1%	46.8%	53.2%	46.8%

NEBRASKA

SENATOR 2000

2000 Census Population	County	Total Vote	Republican	Democratic	Other	Rep.-Dem. Plurality		Percentage			
								Total Vote		Major Vote	
								Rep.	Dem.	Rep.	Dem.
7,791	BURT	3,420	1,793	1,624	3	169	R	52.4%	47.5%	52.5%	47.5%
8,767	BUTLER	3,800	1,949	1,851		98	R	51.3%	48.7%	51.3%	48.7%
24,334	CASS	10,254	4,893	5,345	16	452	D	47.7%	52.1%	47.8%	52.2%
9,615	CEDAR	4,265	1,935	2,326	4	391	D	45.4%	54.5%	45.4%	54.6%
4,068	CHASE	1,787	1,123	663	1	460	R	62.8%	37.1%	62.9%	37.1%
6,148	CHERRY	2,789	1,899	890		1,009	R	68.1%	31.9%	68.1%	31.9%
9,830	CHEYENNE	4,160	2,810	1,350		1,460	R	67.5%	32.5%	67.5%	32.5%
7,039	CLAY	3,200	1,819	1,377	4	442	R	56.8%	43.0%	56.9%	43.1%
10,441	COLFAX	3,351	1,811	1,538	2	273	R	54.0%	45.9%	54.1%	45.9%
10,203	CUMING	4,250	2,566	1,680	4	886	R	60.4%	39.5%	60.4%	39.6%
11,793	CUSTER	5,405	3,378	2,027		1,351	R	62.5%	37.5%	62.5%	37.5%
20,253	DAKOTA	6,039	2,106	3,930	3	1,824	D	34.9%	65.1%	34.9%	65.1%
9,060	DAWES	3,590	2,222	1,368		854	R	61.9%	38.1%	61.9%	38.1%
24,365	DAWSON	7,490	4,229	3,261		968	R	56.5%	43.5%	56.5%	43.5%
2,098	DEUEL	1,022	689	333		356	R	67.4%	32.6%	67.4%	32.6%
6,339	DIXON	2,821	1,250	1,570	1	320	D	44.3%	55.7%	44.3%	55.7%
36,160	DODGE	14,342	6,882	7,460		578	D	48.0%	52.0%	48.0%	52.0%
463,585	DOUGLAS	181,668	80,957	100,146	565	19,189	D	44.6%	55.1%	44.7%	55.3%
2,292	DUNDY	1,010	623	387		236	R	61.7%	38.3%	61.7%	38.3%
6,634	FILLMORE	3,004	1,394	1,606	4	212	D	46.4%	53.5%	46.5%	53.5%
3,574	FRANKLIN	1,674	884	790		94	R	52.8%	47.2%	52.8%	47.2%
3,099	FRONTIER	1,370	834	536		298	R	60.9%	39.1%	60.9%	39.1%
5,324	FURNAS	2,460	1,274	1,186		88	R	51.8%	48.2%	51.8%	48.2%
22,993	GAGE	9,515	4,070	5,428	17	1,358	D	42.8%	57.0%	42.9%	57.1%
2,292	GARDEN	1,132	791	341		450	R	69.9%	30.1%	69.9%	30.1%
1,902	GARFIELD	967	607	360		247	R	62.8%	37.2%	62.8%	37.2%
2,143	GOSPER	1,017	576	441		135	R	56.6%	43.4%	56.6%	43.4%
747	GRANT	382	296	86		210	R	77.5%	22.5%	77.5%	22.5%
2,714	GREELEY	1,288	624	664		40	D	48.4%	51.6%	48.4%	51.6%
53,534	HALL	18,550	8,701	9,818	31	1,117	D	46.9%	52.9%	47.0%	53.0%
9,403	HAMILTON	4,458	2,535	1,923		612	R	56.9%	43.1%	56.9%	43.1%
3,786	HARLAN	1,832	940	892		48	R	51.3%	48.7%	51.3%	48.7%
1,068	HAYES	562	376	186		190	R	66.9%	33.1%	66.9%	33.1%
3,111	HITCHCOCK	1,453	813	640		173	R	56.0%	44.0%	56.0%	44.0%
11,551	HOLT	4,932	3,332	1,600		1,732	R	67.6%	32.4%	67.6%	32.4%
783	HOOKER	424	279	145		134	R	65.8%	34.2%	65.8%	34.2%
6,567	HOWARD	2,801	1,277	1,524		247	D	45.6%	54.4%	45.6%	54.4%
8,333	JEFFERSON	3,824	1,785	2,038	1	253	D	46.7%	53.3%	46.7%	53.3%
4,488	JOHNSON	2,081	935	1,145	1	210	D	44.9%	55.0%	45.0%	55.0%
6,882	KEARNEY	3,089	1,734	1,355		379	R	56.1%	43.9%	56.1%	43.9%
8,875	KEITH	3,823	2,512	1,311		1,201	R	65.7%	34.3%	65.7%	34.3%
983	KEYA PAHA	504	360	144		216	R	71.4%	28.6%	71.4%	28.6%
4,089	KIMBALL	1,816	1,206	609	1	597	R	66.4%	33.5%	66.4%	33.6%
9,374	KNOX	3,986	2,157	1,821	8	336	R	54.1%	45.7%	54.2%	45.8%
250,291	LANCASTER	106,173	41,701	64,102	370	22,401	D	39.3%	60.4%	39.4%	60.6%
34,632	LINCOLN	15,089	7,501	7,568	20	67	D	49.7%	50.2%	49.8%	50.2%
774	LOGAN	403	282	121		161	R	70.0%	30.0%	70.0%	30.0%
712	LOUP	372	226	146		80	R	60.8%	39.2%	60.8%	39.2%
533	MCPHERSON	295	210	85		125	R	71.2%	28.8%	71.2%	28.8%
35,226	MADISON	12,882	7,705	5,166	11	2,539	R	59.8%	40.1%	59.9%	40.1%
8,204	MERRICK	3,327	1,854	1,469	4	385	R	55.7%	44.2%	55.8%	44.2%
5,440	MORRILL	2,134	1,332	802		530	R	62.4%	37.6%	62.4%	37.6%
4,038	NANCE	1,650	831	819		12	R	50.4%	49.6%	50.4%	49.6%
7,576	NEMAHA	3,403	1,877	1,523	3	354	R	55.2%	44.8%	55.2%	44.8%
5,057	NUCKOLLS	2,416	1,172	1,242	2	70	D	48.5%	51.4%	48.6%	51.4%
15,396	OTOE	6,673	3,321	3,345	7	24	D	49.8%	50.1%	49.8%	50.2%
3,087	PAWNEE	1,499	732	767		35	D	48.8%	51.2%	48.8%	51.2%
3,200	PERKINS	1,404	885	519		366	R	63.0%	37.0%	63.0%	37.0%
9,747	PHELPS	4,642	2,588	2,050	4	538	R	55.8%	44.2%	55.8%	44.2%
7,857	PIERCE	3,201	1,926	1,275		651	R	60.2%	39.8%	60.2%	39.8%

NEBRASKA

SENATOR 2000

2000 Census Population	County	Total Vote	Republican	Democratic	Other	Rep.-Dem. Plurality		Percentage			
								Total Vote		Major Vote	
								Rep.	Dem.	Rep.	Dem.
31,662	PLATTE	12,709	7,694	4,998	17	2,696	R	60.5%	39.3%	60.6%	39.4%
5,639	POLK	2,583	1,468	1,115		353	R	56.8%	43.2%	56.8%	43.2%
11,448	RED WILLOW	5,013	2,330	2,683		353	D	46.5%	53.5%	46.5%	53.5%
9,531	RICHARDSON	4,082	2,087	1,994	1	93	R	51.1%	48.8%	51.1%	48.9%
1,756	ROCK	873	604	269		335	R	69.2%	30.8%	69.2%	30.8%
13,843	SALINE	5,134	1,843	3,291		1,448	D	35.9%	64.1%	35.9%	64.1%
122,595	SARPY	44,897	22,862	21,946	89	916	R	50.9%	48.9%	51.0%	49.0%
19,830	SAUNDERS	8,893	4,432	4,448	13	16	D	49.8%	50.0%	49.9%	50.1%
36,951	SCOTTS BLUFF	13,794	7,969	5,814	11	2,155	R	57.8%	42.1%	57.8%	42.2%
16,496	SEWARD	7,008	3,291	3,708	9	417	D	47.0%	52.9%	47.0%	53.0%
6,198	SHERIDAN	2,541	1,876	665		1,211	R	73.8%	26.2%	73.8%	26.2%
3,318	SHERMAN	1,682	801	881		80	D	47.6%	52.4%	47.6%	52.4%
1,475	SIOUX	743	542	201		341	R	72.9%	27.1%	72.9%	27.1%
6,455	STANTON	2,462	1,538	920	4	618	R	62.5%	37.4%	62.6%	37.4%
6,055	THAYER	2,956	1,530	1,426		104	R	51.8%	48.2%	51.8%	48.2%
729	THOMAS	390	282	108		174	R	72.3%	27.7%	72.3%	27.7%
7,171	THURSTON	2,084	733	1,349	2	616	D	35.2%	64.7%	35.2%	64.8%
4,647	VALLEY	2,137	1,219	917	1	302	R	57.0%	42.9%	57.1%	42.9%
18,780	WASHINGTON	8,550	4,707	3,843		864	R	55.1%	44.9%	55.1%	44.9%
9,851	WAYNE	3,921	2,037	1,880	4	157	R	52.0%	47.9%	52.0%	48.0%
4,061	WEBSTER	1,914	909	1,005		96	D	47.5%	52.5%	47.5%	52.5%
886	WHEELER	451	268	183		85	R	59.4%	40.6%	59.4%	40.6%
14,598	YORK	6,381	3,756	2,618	7	1,138	R	58.9%	41.0%	58.9%	41.1%
1,711,263	TOTAL	692,344	337,967	353,097	1,280	15,130	D	48.8%	51.0%	48.9%	51.1%

Note: Results from Nebraska election officials gave the vote as follows: Democrat Ben Nelson, 353,093; Republican Don Stenberg, 337,977. But the county totals add to the results above.

NEBRASKA

CONGRESS

CD	Year	Total Vote	Republican		Democratic		Other Vote	Rep.-Dem. Plurality		Percentage			
			Vote	Candidate	Vote	Candidate				Total Vote		Major Vote	
										Rep.	Dem.	Rep.	Dem.
1	2000	234,698	155,485	BEREUTER, DOUGLAS K.	72,859	JACOBSEN, ALAN	6,354	82,626	R	66.2%	31.0%	68.1%	31.9%
1	1998	185,227	136,058	BEREUTER, DOUGLAS K.	48,826	ERET, DON	343	87,232	R	73.5%	26.4%	73.6%	26.4%
1	1996	224,563	157,108	BEREUTER, DOUGLAS K.	67,152	COMBS, PATRICK	303	89,956	R	70.0%	29.9%	70.1%	29.9%
1	1994	188,550	117,967	BEREUTER, DOUGLAS K.	70,369	COMBS, PATRICK	214	47,598	R	62.6%	37.3%	62.6%	37.4%
1	1992	239,108	142,713	BEREUTER, DOUGLAS K.	96,309	FINNEGAN, GERRY	86	46,404	R	59.7%	40.3%	59.7%	40.3%
2	2000	226,280	148,911	TERRY, LEE	70,268	KIEL, SHELLEY	7,101	78,643	R	65.8%	31.1%	67.9%	32.1%
2	1998	163,003	106,782	TERRY, LEE	55,722	SCOTT, MICHAEL	499	51,060	R	65.5%	34.2%	65.7%	34.3%
2	1996	220,324	125,201	CHRISTENSEN, JON	88,447	DAVIS, JAMES M.	6,676	36,754	R	56.8%	40.1%	58.6%	41.4%
2	1994	185,310	92,516	CHRISTENSEN, JON	90,750	HOAGLAND, PETER	2,044	1,766	R	49.9%	49.0%	50.5%	49.5%
2	1992	233,372	113,828	STASKIEWICZ, RONALD L.	119,512	HOAGLAND, PETER	32	5,684	D	48.8%	51.2%	48.8%	51.2%
3	2000	222,093	182,117	OSBORNE, TOM	34,944	REYNOLDS, ROLAND E.	5,032	147,173	R	82.0%	15.7%	83.9%	16.1%
3	1998	177,729	149,896	BARRETT, BILL			27,833	149,896	R	84.3%		100.0%	
3	1996	216,757	167,758	BARRETT, BILL	48,833	WEBSTER, JOHN	166	118,925	R	77.4%	22.5%	77.5%	22.5%
3	1994	196,862	154,919	BARRETT, BILL	41,943	CHAPIN, GIL		112,976	R	78.7%	21.3%	78.7%	21.3%
3	1992	238,355	170,857	BARRETT, BILL	67,457	FISHER, LOWELL	41	103,400	R	71.7%	28.3%	71.7%	28.3%

NEBRASKA

GENERAL AND PRIMARY ELECTIONS

2000 GENERAL ELECTIONS

President	Other vote was 3,646 By Petition (Buchanan); 2,245 Libertarian (Browne); 478 Natural Law (Hagelin); 468 By Petition (Phillips).
Senator	Other vote was 1,280 scattered write-in.
Congress	Other vote was: CD 1: 6,147 Libertarian (Oenbring), 207 scattered write-in; CD 2: 6,856 Libertarian (Graziano), 245 scattered write-in; CD 3: 4,909 Libertarian (Hickman), 123 scattered write-in.

2000 PRIMARY ELECTIONS

Primary	May 9, 2000	**Registration** (as of May 1, 2000)	Republican	517,347
			Democratic	381,155
			Libertarian	1,197
			Other Parties	85
			Nonpartisan	144,564
			TOTAL	1,044,348

Primary Type   Modified—Registered Democrats and Republicans could only vote in their party's primary. Voters registered as nonpartisan could vote in either party's primary for the Senate and House (but not president).

Note: An asterisk (*) denotes incumbent. Ballots cast by nonpartisan voters in primaries for the House and Senate were tallied separately but are included in the overall totals.

	REPUBLICAN PRIMARIES			DEMOCRATIC PRIMARIES		
President	George W. Bush	145,176	78.2%	Al Gore	73,639	70.0%
	John McCain	28,065	15.1%	Bill Bradley	27,884	26.5%
	Alan Keyes	12,073	6.5%	Lyndon H. LaRouche Jr.	3,191	3.0%
	Write-in	444	0.2%	Write-in	557	0.5%
	TOTAL	185,758		TOTAL	105,271	
Senator	Don Stenberg	94,394	49.9%	Ben Nelson	105,661	92.1%
	Scott Moore	41,120	21.7%	Al Hamburg	8,482	7.4%
	David Hergert	32,228	17.0%	Write-in	558	0.5%
	George Grogan	8,293	4.4%			
	John DeCamp	7,469	4.0%			
	Elliott Rustad	5,317	2.8%			
	Write-in	237	0.1%			
	TOTAL	189,058		TOTAL	114,701	
Congressional District 1	Doug Bereuter*	50,365	99.0%	Alan Jacobsen	25,940	99.0%
	Write-in	516	1.0%	Write-in	256	1.0%
	TOTAL	50,881		TOTAL	26,196	
Congressional District 2	Lee Terry*	55,696	98.7%	Shelley Kiel	30,578	68.6%
	Write-in	758	1.3%	Allen C. Johnson	13,724	30.8%
				Write-in	259	0.6%
	TOTAL	56,454		TOTAL	44,561	
Congressional District 3	Tom Osborne	52,438	70.7%	Roland E. Reynolds	23,364	99.1%
	John A. Gale	12,553	16.9%	Write-in	218	0.9%
	Kathy Wilmot	9,127	12.3%			
	Write-in	26				
	TOTAL	74,144		TOTAL	23,582	

NEVADA

GOVERNOR
Kenny Guinn (R). Elected 1998 to a four-year term.

SENATORS
John Ensign (R). Elected 2000 to a six-year term.

Harry Reid (D). Re-elected 1998 to a six-year term. Previously elected 1992, 1986.

REPRESENTATIVES
1. Shelley Berkley (D)   2. Jim Gibbons (R)

POSTWAR VOTE FOR PRESIDENT

| | | Republican | | Democratic | | Other | | Percentage | | | |
| | | | | | | | | Total Vote | | Major Vote | |
Year	Total Vote	Vote	Candidate	Vote	Candidate	Vote	Plurality	Rep.	Dem.	Rep.	Dem.
2000**	608,970	301,575	Bush, George W.	279,978	Gore, Al	27,417	21,597 R	49.5%	46.0%	51.9%	48.1%
1996**	464,279	199,244	Dole, Bob	203,974	Clinton, Bill	61,061	4,730 D	42.9%	43.9%	49.4%	50.6%
1992**	506,318	175,828	Bush, George	189,148	Clinton, Bill	141,342	13,320 D	34.7%	37.4%	48.2%	51.8%
1988	350,067	206,040	Bush, George	132,738	Dukakis, Michael S.	11,289	73,302 R	58.9%	37.9%	60.8%	39.2%
1984	286,667	188,770	Reagan, Ronald	91,655	Mondale, Walter F.	6,242	97,115 R	65.8%	32.0%	67.3%	32.7%
1980**	247,885	155,017	Reagan, Ronald	66,666	Carter, Jimmy	26,202	88,351 R	62.5%	26.9%	69.9%	30.1%
1976	201,876	101,273	Ford, Gerald R.	92,479	Carter, Jimmy	8,124	8,794 R	50.2%	45.8%	52.3%	47.7%
1972	181,766	115,750	Nixon, Richard M.	66,016	McGovern, George S.		49,734 R	63.7%	36.3%	63.7%	36.3%
1968	154,218	73,188	Nixon, Richard M.	60,598	Humphrey, Hubert H.	20,432	12,590 R	47.5%	39.3%	54.7%	45.3%
1964	135,433	56,094	Goldwater, Barry M.	79,339	Johnson, Lyndon B.		23,245 D	41.4%	58.6%	41.4%	58.6%
1960	107,267	52,387	Nixon, Richard M.	54,880	Kennedy, John F.		2,493 D	48.8%	51.2%	48.8%	51.2%
1956	96,689	56,049	Eisenhower, Dwight D.	40,640	Stevenson, Adlai E.		15,409 R	58.0%	42.0%	58.0%	42.0%
1952	82,190	50,502	Eisenhower, Dwight D.	31,688	Stevenson, Adlai E.		18,814 R	61.4%	38.6%	61.4%	38.6%
1948	62,117	29,357	Dewey, Thomas E.	31,291	Truman, Harry S.	1,469	1,934 D	47.3%	50.4%	48.4%	51.6%

In 2000 the other vote column includes 15,008 votes cast for Green (Nader). In 1996, the other vote column includes 43,986 votes cast for Perot. In 1992 the other vote column includes 132,580 votes cast for Perot. In 1980 the other column includes 17,651 votes for Independent (Anderson).

POSTWAR VOTE FOR GOVERNOR

| | | Republican | | Democratic | | Other | Rep.-Dem. | Percentage | | | |
| | | | | | | | | Total Vote | | Major Vote | |
Year	Total Vote	Vote	Candidate	Vote	Candidate	Vote	Plurality	Rep.	Dem.	Rep.	Dem.
1998	433,630	223,892	Guinn, Kenny	182,281	Jones, Jan Laverty	27,457	41,611 R	51.6%	42.0%	55.1%	44.9%
1994	379,676	156,875	Gibbons, Jim	200,026	Miller, Robert J.	22,775	43,151 D	41.3%	52.7%	44.0%	56.0%
1990	320,743	95,789	Gallaway, Jim	207,878	Miller, Robert J.	17,076	112,089 D	29.9%	64.8%	31.5%	68.5%
1986	260,375	65,081	Cafferata, Patty	187,268	Bryan, Richard H.	8,026	122,187 D	25.0%	71.9%	25.8%	74.2%
1982	239,751	100,104	List, Robert F.	128,132	Bryan, Richard H.	11,515	28,028 D	41.8%	53.4%	43.9%	56.1%
1978	192,445	108,097	List, Robert F.	76,361	Rose, Robert E.	7,987	31,736 R	56.2%	39.7%	58.6%	41.4%
1974	169,358	28,959	Crumpler, Shirley	114,114	O'Callaghan, Mike	26,285	85,155 D	17.1%	67.4%	20.2%	79.8%
1970	146,991	64,400	Fike, Ed	70,697	O'Callaghan, Mike	11,894	6,297 D	43.8%	48.1%	47.7%	52.3%
1966	137,677	71,807	Laxalt, Paul	65,870	Sawyer, Grant		5,937 R	52.2%	47.8%	52.2%	47.8%
1962	96,929	32,145	Gragson, Oran K.	64,784	Sawyer, Grant		32,639 D	33.2%	66.8%	33.2%	66.8%
1958	84,889	34,025	Russell, Charles H.	50,864	Sawyer, Grant		16,839 D	40.1%	59.9%	40.1%	59.9%
1954	78,462	41,665	Russell, Charles H.	36,797	Pittman, Vail		4,868 R	53.1%	46.9%	53.1%	46.9%
1950	61,773	35,609	Russell, Charles H.	26,164	Pittman, Vail		9,445 R	57.6%	42.4%	57.6%	42.4%
1946	49,902	21,247	Jepson, Melvin E.	28,655	Pittman, Vail		7,408 D	42.6%	57.4%	42.6%	57.4%

NEVADA

POSTWAR VOTE FOR SENATOR

Year	Total Vote	Republican Vote	Republican Candidate	Democratic Vote	Democratic Candidate	Other Vote	Rep.-Dem. Plurality	Percentage Total Vote Rep.	Percentage Total Vote Dem.	Percentage Major Vote Rep.	Percentage Major Vote Dem.
2000	600,250	330,687	Ensign, John	238,260	Bernstein, Ed	31,303	92,427 R	55.1%	39.7%	58.1%	41.9%
1998	435,790	208,222	Ensign, John	208,650	Reid, Harry	18,918	428 D	47.8%	47.9%	49.9%	50.1%
1994	380,530	156,020	Furman, Hal	193,804	Bryan, Richard H.	30,706	37,784 D	41.0%	50.9%	44.6%	55.4%
1992	495,887	199,413	Dahl, Demar	253,150	Reid, Harry	43,324	53,737 D	40.2%	51.0%	44.1%	55.9%
1988	349,649	161,336	Hecht, Chic	175,548	Bryan, Richard H.	12,765	14,212 D	46.1%	50.2%	47.9%	52.1%
1986	261,932	116,606	Santini, James	130,955	Reid, Harry	14,371	14,349 D	44.5%	50.0%	47.1%	52.9%
1982	240,394	120,377	Hecht, Chic	114,720	Cannon, Howard W.	5,297	5,657 R	50.1%	47.7%	51.2%	48.8%
1980	246,436	144,224	Laxalt, Paul	92,129	Gojack, Mary	10,083	52,095 R	58.5%	37.4%	61.0%	39.0%
1976	201,980	63,471	Towell, David	127,295	Cannon, Howard W.	11,214	63,824 D	31.4%	63.0%	33.3%	66.7%
1974	169,473	79,605	Laxalt, Paul	78,981	Reid, Harry	10,887	624 R	47.0%	46.6%	50.2%	49.8%
1970	147,768	60,838	Raggio, William J.	85,187	Cannon, Howard W.	1,743	24,349 D	41.2%	57.6%	41.7%	58.3%
1968	152,690	69,068	Fike, Ed	83,622	Bible, Alan		14,554 D	45.2%	54.8%	45.2%	54.8%
1964	134,624	67,288	Laxalt, Paul	67,336	Cannon, Howard W.		48 D	50.0%	50.0%	50.0%	50.0%
1962	97,192	33,749	Wright, William B.	63,443	Bible, Alan		29,694 D	34.7%	65.3%	34.7%	65.3%
1958	84,492	35,760	Malone, George W.	48,732	Cannon, Howard W.		12,972 D	42.3%	57.7%	42.3%	57.7%
1956	96,389	45,712	Young, Clifton	50,677	Bible, Alan		4,965 D	47.4%	52.6%	47.4%	52.6%
1954S	77,513	32,470	Brown, Ernest S.	45,043	Bible, Alan		12,573 D	41.9%	58.1%	41.9%	58.1%
1952	81,090	41,906	Malone, George W.	39,184	Mechling, Thomas B.		2,722 R	51.7%	48.3%	51.7%	48.3%
1950	61,762	25,933	Marshall, George E.	35,829	McCarran, Pat		9,896 D	42.0%	58.0%	42.0%	58.0%
1946	50,354	27,801	Malone, George W.	22,553	Bunker, Berkeley		5,248 R	55.2%	44.8%	55.2%	44.8%

The 1954 election was for a short term to fill a vacancy.

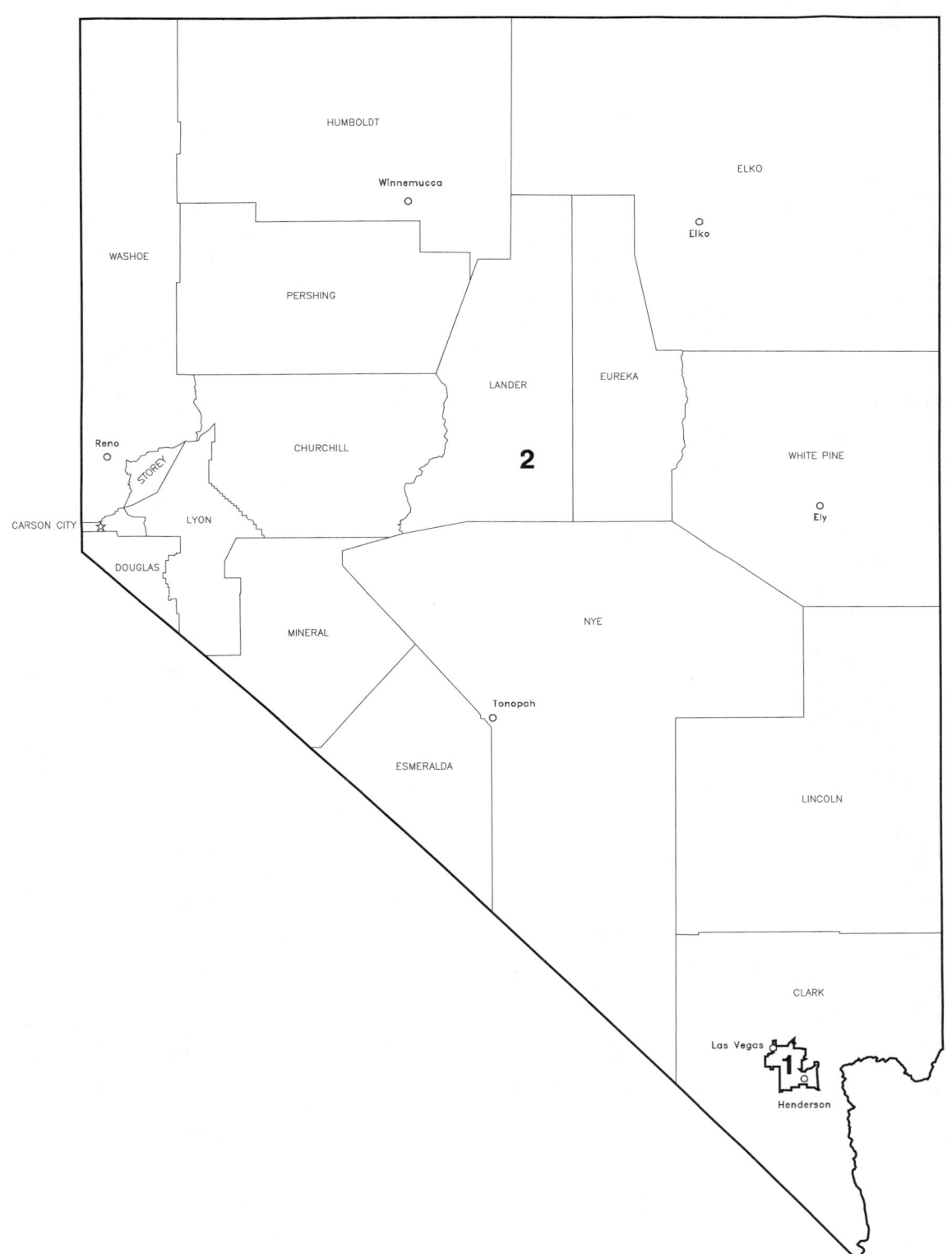

NEVADA

Districts Established June 20, 1991

HUMBOLDT

Winnemucca ○

ELKO

Elko ○

WASHOE

PERSHING

LANDER

EUREKA

2

WHITE PINE

Reno ○

STOREY

CHURCHILL

CARSON CITY ☆

LYON

DOUGLAS

Ely ○

MINERAL

NYE

Tonopah ○

ESMERALDA

LINCOLN

CLARK

Las Vegas

1

Henderson

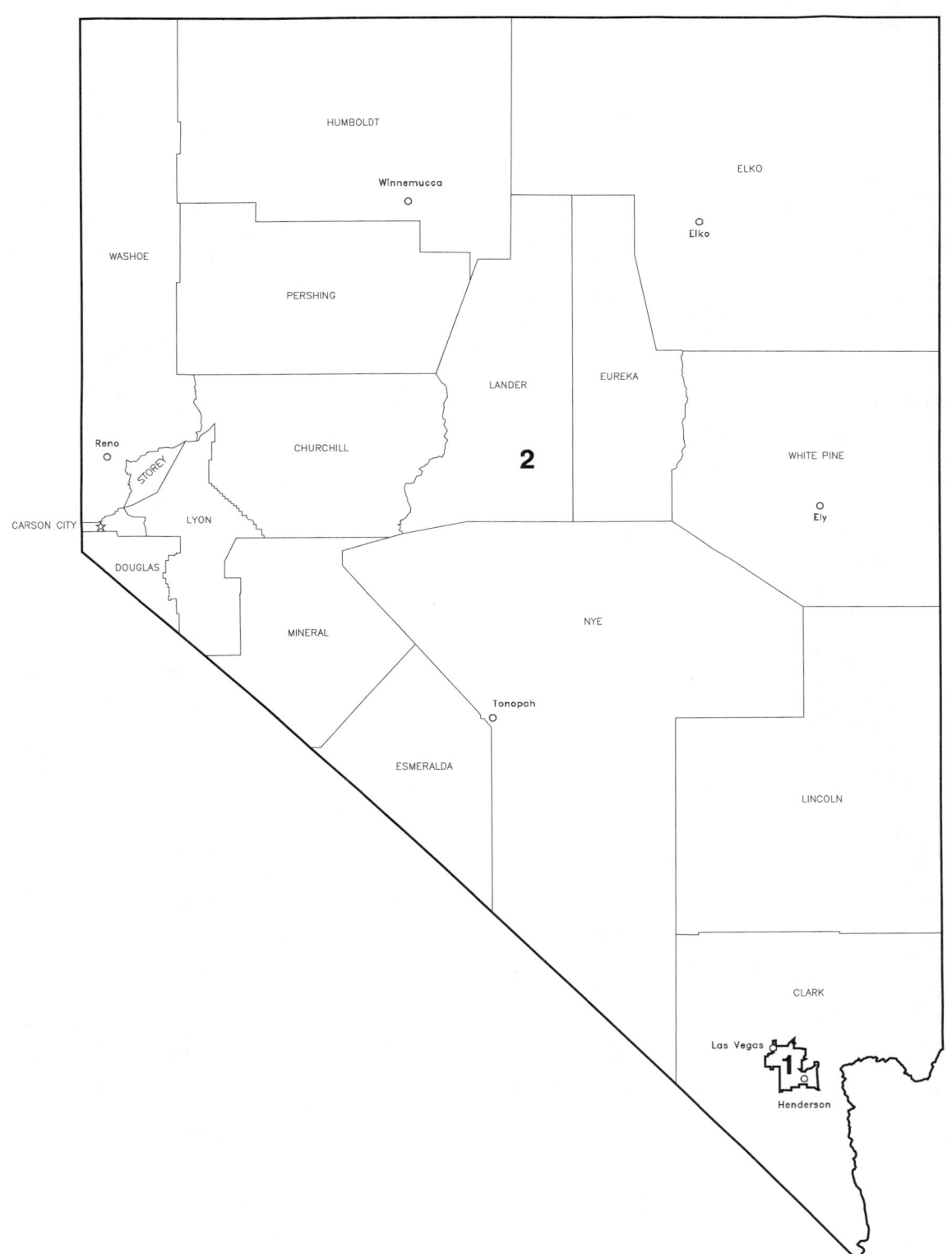

NEVADA

PRESIDENT 2000

2000 Census Population	County	Total Vote	Republican	Democratic	Green (Nader)	Other	Rep.-Dem. Plurality	Percentage of Total Vote		
								Rep.	Dem.	Green
52,457	CARSON CITY	19,452	11,084	7,354	605	409	3,730 R	57.0%	37.8%	3.1%
23,982	CHURCHILL	8,823	6,237	2,191	189	206	4,046 R	70.7%	24.8%	2.1%
1,375,765	CLARK	382,198	170,932	196,100	7,942	7,224	25,168 D	44.7%	51.3%	2.1%
41,259	DOUGLAS	17,974	11,193	5,837	593	351	5,356 R	62.3%	32.5%	3.3%
45,291	ELKO	14,180	11,025	2,542	221	392	8,483 R	77.8%	17.9%	1.6%
971	ESMERALDA	491	333	116	14	28	217 R	67.8%	23.6%	2.9%
1,651	EUREKA	837	632	150	15	40	482 R	75.5%	17.9%	1.8%
16,106	HUMBOLDT	5,030	3,638	1,128	137	127	2,510 R	72.3%	22.4%	2.7%
5,794	LANDER	2,119	1,619	395	37	68	1,224 R	76.4%	18.6%	1.7%
4,165	LINCOLN	1,956	1,372	461	40	83	911 R	70.1%	23.6%	2.0%
34,501	LYON	11,992	7,270	3,955	382	385	3,315 R	60.6%	33.0%	3.2%
5,071	MINERAL	2,293	1,227	916	81	69	311 R	53.5%	39.9%	3.5%
32,485	NYE	12,181	6,904	4,525	332	420	2,379 R	56.7%	37.1%	2.7%
6,693	PERSHING	1,802	1,221	476	46	59	745 R	67.8%	26.4%	2.6%
3,399	STOREY	1,798	1,014	666	79	39	348 R	56.4%	37.0%	4.4%
339,486	WASHOE	122,301	63,640	52,097	4,209	2,355	11,543 R	52.0%	42.6%	3.4%
9,181	WHITE PINE	3,543	2,234	1,069	86	154	1,165 R	63.1%	30.2%	2.4%
1,998,257	TOTAL	608,970	301,575	279,978	15,008	12,409	21,597 R	49.5%	46.0%	2.5%

NEVADA

SENATOR 2000

2000 Census Population	County	Total Vote	Republican	Democratic	Other	Rep.-Dem. Plurality	Percentage			
							Total Vote		Major Vote	
							Rep.	Dem.	Rep.	Dem.
52,457	CARSON CITY	19,356	11,793	6,369	1,194	5,424 R	60.9%	32.9%	64.9%	35.1%
23,982	CHURCHILL	8,793	6,453	1,941	399	4,512 R	73.4%	22.1%	76.9%	23.1%
1,375,765	CLARK	374,785	190,071	168,039	16,675	22,032 R	50.7%	44.8%	53.1%	46.9%
41,259	DOUGLAS	17,928	12,027	4,795	1,106	7,232 R	67.1%	26.7%	71.5%	28.5%
45,291	ELKO	14,097	11,303	2,120	674	9,183 R	80.2%	15.0%	84.2%	15.8%
971	ESMERALDA	489	334	109	46	225 R	68.3%	22.3%	75.4%	24.6%
1,651	EUREKA	838	630	154	54	476 R	75.2%	18.4%	80.4%	19.6%
16,106	HUMBOLDT	5,032	3,723	1,006	303	2,717 R	74.0%	20.0%	78.7%	21.3%
5,794	LANDER	2,104	1,609	364	131	1,245 R	76.5%	17.3%	81.6%	18.4%
4,165	LINCOLN	1,922	1,402	418	102	984 R	72.9%	21.7%	77.0%	23.0%
34,501	LYON	11,894	7,789	3,343	762	4,446 R	65.5%	28.1%	70.0%	30.0%
5,071	MINERAL	2,277	1,272	854	151	418 R	55.9%	37.5%	59.8%	40.2%
32,485	NYE	12,153	7,362	4,150	641	3,212 R	60.6%	34.1%	64.0%	36.0%
6,693	PERSHING	1,792	1,262	410	120	852 R	70.4%	22.9%	75.5%	24.5%
3,399	STOREY	1,775	1,108	543	124	565 R	62.4%	30.6%	67.1%	32.9%
339,486	WASHOE	121,479	70,161	42,672	8,646	27,489 R	57.8%	35.1%	62.2%	37.8%
9,181	WHITE PINE	3,536	2,388	973	175	1,415 R	67.5%	27.5%	71.1%	28.9%
1,998,257	TOTAL	600,250	330,687	238,260	31,303	92,427 R	55.1%	39.7%	58.1%	41.9%

NEVADA

CONGRESS

CD	Year	Total Vote	Republican Vote	Republican Candidate	Democratic Vote	Democratic Candidate	Other Vote	Rep.-Dem. Plurality	Total Vote Rep.	Total Vote Dem.	Major Vote Rep.	Major Vote Dem.
1	2000	229,235	101,276	PORTER, JON	118,469	BERKLEY, SHELLEY	9,490	17,193 D	44.2%	51.7%	46.1%	53.9%
1	1998	161,082	73,540	CHAIREZ, DON	79,315	BERKLEY, SHELLEY	8,227	5,775 D	45.7%	49.2%	48.1%	51.9%
1	1996	172,593	86,472	ENSIGN, JOHN	75,081	COFFIN, BOB	11,040	11,391 R	50.1%	43.5%	53.5%	46.5%
1	1994	152,167	73,769	ENSIGN, JOHN	72,333	BILBRAY, JAMES	6,065	1,436 R	48.5%	47.5%	50.5%	49.5%
1	1992	221,488	84,217	PETTYJOHN, J. COY	128,278	BILBRAY, JAMES	8,993	44,061 D	38.0%	57.9%	39.6%	60.4%
2	2000	355,969	229,608	GIBBONS, JIM	106,379	CAHILL, TIERNEY	19,982	123,229 R	64.5%	29.9%	68.3%	31.7%
2	1998	248,763	201,623	GIBBONS, JIM			47,140	201,623 R	81.1%		100.0%	
2	1996	277,192	162,310	GIBBONS, JIM	97,742	WILSON, THOMAS	17,140	64,568 R	58.6%	35.3%	62.4%	37.6%
2	1994	223,932	142,202	VUCANOVICH, BARBARA	65,390	GREESON, JANET	16,340	76,812 R	63.5%	29.2%	68.5%	31.5%
2	1992	270,461	129,575	VUCANOVICH, BARBARA	117,199	SFERRAZZA, PETE	23,687	12,376 R	47.9%	43.3%	52.5%	47.5%

NEVADA

GENERAL AND PRIMARY ELECTIONS

2000 GENERAL ELECTIONS

President   Other vote was 4,747 Citizens First (Buchanan); 3,315 "None of These Candidates"; 3,311 Libertarian (Browne); 621 Independent American (Phillips); 415 Natural Law (Hagelin).

Senator   Other vote was 11,503 "None of These Candidates"; 10,286 Green (Rusco); 5,395 Libertarian (Johnson); 2,540 Independent American (Berghof); 1,579 Citizens First (Grutzmacher).

Congress   Other vote was: CD 1: 4,011 Libertarian (Schneider), 3,933 Independent American (C. Hansen), 1,546 Citizens First (Swenson); CD 2: 5,582 Independent American (D. Hansen), 5,547 Green (Laws), 5,343 Libertarian (Savage), 2,367 Citizens First (Brenneman), 1,143 Natural Law (Winquist).

2000 PRIMARY ELECTIONS

Primary   September 5, 2000

Registration
(as of Sept. 5, 2000)

Republican	358,582
Democratic	350,547
Independent American	15,284
Libertarian	4,676
Green	1,089
Reform	724
Natural Law	593
Other	1,736
Nonpartisan	118,927
TOTAL	852,158

Primary Type   Closed—Only registered Democrats and Republicans could vote in their party's primary.

Note: An asterisk (*) denotes incumbent. The names of unopposed candidates do not appear on the primary ballot; therefore, no votes are cast for these candidates.

NEVADA

GENERAL AND PRIMARY ELECTIONS

	REPUBLICAN PRIMARIES			DEMOCRATIC PRIMARIES	
Senator	John Ensign	95,904	88.0%	Ed Bernstein	Unopposed
	Richard Hamzik	6,202	5.7%		
	None of These Candidates	5,290	4.9%		
	Fernando Platin Jr.	1,543	1.4%		
	TOTAL	108,939			
Congressional District 1	Jon Porter	18,683	65.1%	Shelley Berkley*	Unopposed
	Nancy Price	5,313	18.5%		
	Jim Blockey	4,698	16.4%		
	TOTAL	28,694			
Congressional District 2	Jim Gibbons*	68,917	89.6%	Tierney Cahill	Unopposed
	Mitchell T. Tracy	7,986	10.4%		
	None of These Candidates	18			
	TOTAL	76,921			

NEW HAMPSHIRE

GOVERNOR
Jeanne Shaheen (D). Re-elected 2000 to a two-year term. Previously elected 1998, 1996.

SENATORS
Judd Gregg (R). Re-elected 1998 to a six-year term. Previously elected 1992.

Robert C. Smith (R). Re-elected 1996 to a six-year term. Previously elected 1990; was appointed December 1990 to fill the last few weeks of the term vacated when Senator Gordon J. Humphrey resigned to be sworn in as a state senator in New Hampshire.

REPRESENTATIVES
1. John E. Sununu (R)   2. Charles Bass (R)

POSTWAR VOTE FOR PRESIDENT

| | | Republican | | Democratic | | Other | | Percentage | | | |
| | | | | | | | | Total Vote | | Major Vote | |
Year	Total Vote	Vote	Candidate	Vote	Candidate	Vote	Plurality	Rep.	Dem.	Rep.	Dem.
2000**	569,081	273,559	Bush, George W.	266,348	Gore, Al	29,174	7,211 R	48.1%	46.8%	50.7%	49.3%
1996**	499,175	196,532	Dole, Bob	246,214	Clinton, Bill	56,429	49,682 D	39.4%	49.3%	44.4%	55.6%
1992**	537,943	202,484	Bush, George	209,040	Clinton, Bill	126,419	6,556 D	37.6%	38.9%	49.2%	50.8%
1988	451,074	281,537	Bush, George	163,696	Dukakis, Michael S.	5,841	117,841 R	62.4%	36.3%	63.2%	36.8%
1984	389,066	267,051	Reagan, Ronald	120,395	Mondale, Walter F.	1,620	146,656 R	68.6%	30.9%	68.9%	31.1%
1980**	383,990	221,705	Reagan, Ronald	108,864	Carter, Jimmy	53,421	112,841 R	57.7%	28.4%	67.1%	32.9%
1976	339,618	185,935	Ford, Gerald R.	147,635	Carter, Jimmy	6,048	38,300 R	54.7%	43.5%	55.7%	44.3%
1972	334,055	213,724	Nixon, Richard M.	116,435	McGovern, George S.	3,896	97,289 R	64.0%	34.9%	64.7%	35.3%
1968	297,298	154,903	Nixon, Richard M.	130,589	Humphrey, Hubert H.	11,806	24,314 R	52.1%	43.9%	54.3%	45.7%
1964	288,093	104,029	Goldwater, Barry M.	184,064	Johnson, Lyndon B.		80,035 D	36.1%	63.9%	36.1%	63.9%
1960	295,761	157,989	Nixon, Richard M.	137,772	Kennedy, John F.		20,217 R	53.4%	46.6%	53.4%	46.6%
1956	266,994	176,519	Eisenhower, Dwight D.	90,364	Stevenson, Adlai E.	111	86,155 R	66.1%	33.8%	66.1%	33.9%
1952	272,950	166,287	Eisenhower, Dwight D.	106,663	Stevenson, Adlai E.		59,624 R	60.9%	39.1%	60.9%	39.1%
1948	231,440	121,299	Dewey, Thomas E.	107,995	Truman, Harry S.	2,146	13,304 R	52.4%	46.7%	52.9%	47.1%

In 2000 the other vote column includes 22,198 votes cast for Green (Nader). In 1996 the other vote column includes 48,390 votes cast for Perot. In 1992 the other vote column includes 121,337 votes cast for Perot. In 1980 the other column includes 49,693 votes for Independent (Anderson).

NEW HAMPSHIRE

POSTWAR VOTE FOR GOVERNOR

Year	Total Vote	Republican Vote	Candidate	Democratic Vote	Candidate	Other Vote	Rep.-Dem. Plurality	Total Vote Rep.	Total Vote Dem.	Major Vote Rep.	Major Vote Dem.
2000	564,953	246,952	Humphrey, Gordon	275,038	Shaheen, Jeanne	42,963	28,086 D	43.7%	48.7%	47.3%	52.7%
1998	318,940	98,473	Lucas, Jay	210,769	Shaheen, Jeanne	9,698	112,296 D	30.9%	66.1%	31.8%	68.2%
1996	497,040	196,321	Lamontagne, Ovide	284,175	Shaheen, Jeanne	16,544	87,854 D	39.5%	57.2%	40.9%	59.1%
1994	311,882	218,134	Merrill, Steve	79,686	King, Wayne D.	14,062	138,448 R	69.9%	25.6%	73.2%	26.8%
1992	516,170	289,170	Merrill, Steve	206,232	Arnesen, Deborah A.	20,768	82,938 R	56.0%	40.0%	58.4%	41.6%
1990	295,018	177,773	Gregg, Judd	101,923	Grandmaison, J. Joseph	15,322	75,850 R	60.3%	34.5%	63.6%	36.4%
1988	441,923	267,064	Gregg, Judd	172,543	McEachern, Paul	2,316	94,521 R	60.4%	39.0%	60.8%	39.2%
1986	251,107	134,824	Sununu, John H.	116,142	McEachern, Paul	141	18,682 R	53.7%	46.3%	53.7%	46.3%
1984	383,910	256,574	Sununu, John H.	127,156	Spirou, Chris	180	129,418 R	66.8%	33.1%	66.9%	33.1%
1982	282,588	145,389	Sununu, John H.	132,317	Gallen, Hugh J.	4,882	13,072 R	51.4%	46.8%	52.4%	47.6%
1980	384,031	156,178	Thomson, Meldrim	226,436	Gallen, Hugh J.	1,417	70,258 D	40.7%	59.0%	40.8%	59.2%
1978	269,587	122,464	Thomson, Meldrim	133,133	Gallen, Hugh J.	13,990	10,669 D	45.4%	49.4%	47.9%	52.1%
1976	342,669	197,589	Thomson, Meldrim	145,015	Spanos, Harry V.	65	52,574 R	57.7%	42.3%	57.7%	42.3%
1974	226,665	115,933	Thomson, Meldrim	110,591	Leonard, Richard W.	141	5,342 R	51.1%	48.8%	51.2%	48.8%
1972	323,102	133,702	Thomson, Meldrim	126,107	Crowley, Roger J.	63,293	7,595 R	41.4%	39.0%	51.5%	48.5%
1970	222,441	102,298	Peterson, Walter R.	98,098	Crowley, Roger J.	22,045	4,200 R	46.0%	44.1%	51.0%	49.0%
1968	285,342	149,902	Peterson, Walter R.	135,378	Bussiere, Emile R.	62	14,524 R	52.5%	47.4%	52.5%	47.5%
1966	233,642	107,259	Gregg, Hugh	125,882	King, John W.	501	18,623 D	45.9%	53.9%	46.0%	54.0%
1964	285,863	94,824	Pillsbury, John	190,863	King, John W.	176	96,039 D	33.2%	66.8%	33.2%	66.8%
1962	230,048	94,567	Pillsbury, John	135,481	King, John W.		40,914 D	41.1%	58.9%	41.1%	58.9%
1960	290,527	161,123	Powell, Wesley	129,404	Boutin, Bernard L.		31,719 R	55.5%	44.5%	55.5%	44.5%
1958	206,745	106,790	Powell, Wesley	99,955	Boutin, Bernard L.		6,835 R	51.7%	48.3%	51.7%	48.3%
1956	258,695	141,578	Dwinell, Lane	117,117	Shaw, John		24,461 R	54.7%	45.3%	54.7%	45.3%
1954	194,631	107,287	Dwinell, Lane	87,344	Shaw, John		19,943 R	55.1%	44.9%	55.1%	44.9%
1952	265,715	167,791	Gregg, Hugh	97,924	Craig, William H.		69,867 R	63.1%	36.9%	63.1%	36.9%
1950	191,239	108,907	Adams, Sherman	82,258	Bingham, Robert P.	74	26,649 R	56.9%	43.0%	57.0%	43.0%
1948	222,571	116,212	Adams, Sherman	105,207	Hill, Herbert W.	1,152	11,005 R	52.2%	47.3%	52.5%	47.5%
1946	163,451	103,204	Dale, Charles M.	60,247	Keefe, F. Clyde		42,957 R	63.1%	36.9%	63.1%	36.9%

POSTWAR VOTE FOR SENATOR

Year	Total Vote	Republican Vote	Candidate	Democratic Vote	Candidate	Other Vote	Rep.-Dem. Plurality	Total Vote Rep.	Total Vote Dem.	Major Vote Rep.	Major Vote Dem.
1998	314,956	213,477	Gregg, Judd	88,883	Condodemetraky, George	12,596	124,594 R	67.8%	28.2%	70.6%	29.4%
1996	492,598	242,304	Smith, Robert C.	227,397	Swett, Dick	22,897	14,907 R	49.2%	46.2%	51.6%	48.4%
1992	518,416	249,591	Gregg, Judd	234,982	Rauh, John	33,843	14,609 R	48.1%	45.3%	51.5%	48.5%
1990	291,393	189,792	Smith, Robert C.	91,299	Durkin, John A.	10,302	98,493 R	65.1%	31.3%	67.5%	32.5%
1986	244,797	154,090	Rudman, Warren	79,225	Peabody, Endicott	11,482	74,865 R	62.9%	32.4%	66.0%	34.0%
1984	384,406	225,828	Humphrey, Gordon J.	157,447	D'Amours, Norman E.	1,131	68,381 R	58.7%	41.0%	58.9%	41.1%
1980	375,064	195,563	Rudman, Warren	179,455	Durkin, John A.	46	16,108 R	52.1%	47.8%	52.1%	47.9%
1978	263,779	133,745	Humphrey, Gordon J.	127,945	McIntyre, Thomas J.	2,089	5,800 R	50.7%	48.5%	51.1%	48.9%
1975S	262,682	113,007	Wyman, Louis C.	140,778	Durkin, John A.	8,897	27,771 D	43.0%	53.6%	44.5%	55.5%
1974**	223,363	110,926	Wyman, Louis C.	110,924	Durkin, John A.	1,513	2 R	49.7%	49.7%	50.0%	50.0%
1972	324,354	139,852	Powell, Wesley	184,495	McIntyre, Thomas J.	7	44,643 D	43.1%	56.9%	43.1%	56.9%
1968	286,989	170,163	Cotton, Norris	116,816	King, John W.	10	53,347 R	59.3%	40.7%	59.3%	40.7%
1966	229,305	105,241	Thyng, Harrison R.	123,888	McIntyre, Thomas J.	176	18,647 D	45.9%	54.0%	45.9%	54.1%
1962	224,479	134,035	Cotton, Norris	90,444	Catalfo, Alfred		43,591 R	59.7%	40.3%	59.7%	40.3%
1962S	224,811	107,199	Bass, Perkins	117,612	McIntyre, Thomas J.		10,413 D	47.7%	52.3%	47.7%	52.3%
1960	287,545	173,521	Bridges, Styles	114,024	Hill, Herbert W.		59,497 R	60.3%	39.7%	60.3%	39.7%
1956	251,943	161,424	Cotton, Norris	90,519	Pickett, Laurence M.		70,905 R	64.1%	35.9%	64.1%	35.9%
1954	194,536	117,150	Bridges, Styles	77,386	Morin, Gerard L.		39,764 R	60.2%	39.8%	60.2%	39.8%
1954S	189,558	114,068	Cotton, Norris	75,490	Bentley, Stanley J.		38,578 R	60.2%	39.8%	60.2%	39.8%
1950	190,573	106,142	Tobey, Charles W.	72,473	Kelley, Emmet J.	11,958	33,669 R	55.7%	38.0%	59.4%	40.6%
1948	222,898	129,600	Bridges, Styles	91,760	Fortin, Alfred E.	1,538	37,840 R	58.1%	41.2%	58.5%	41.5%

One each of the 1962 and 1954 elections were for short terms to fill vacancies. Following the 1974 election, neither candidate was seated and the 1975 special election was held for the remaining years of this term.

NEW HAMPSHIRE

Districts Established March 27, 1992

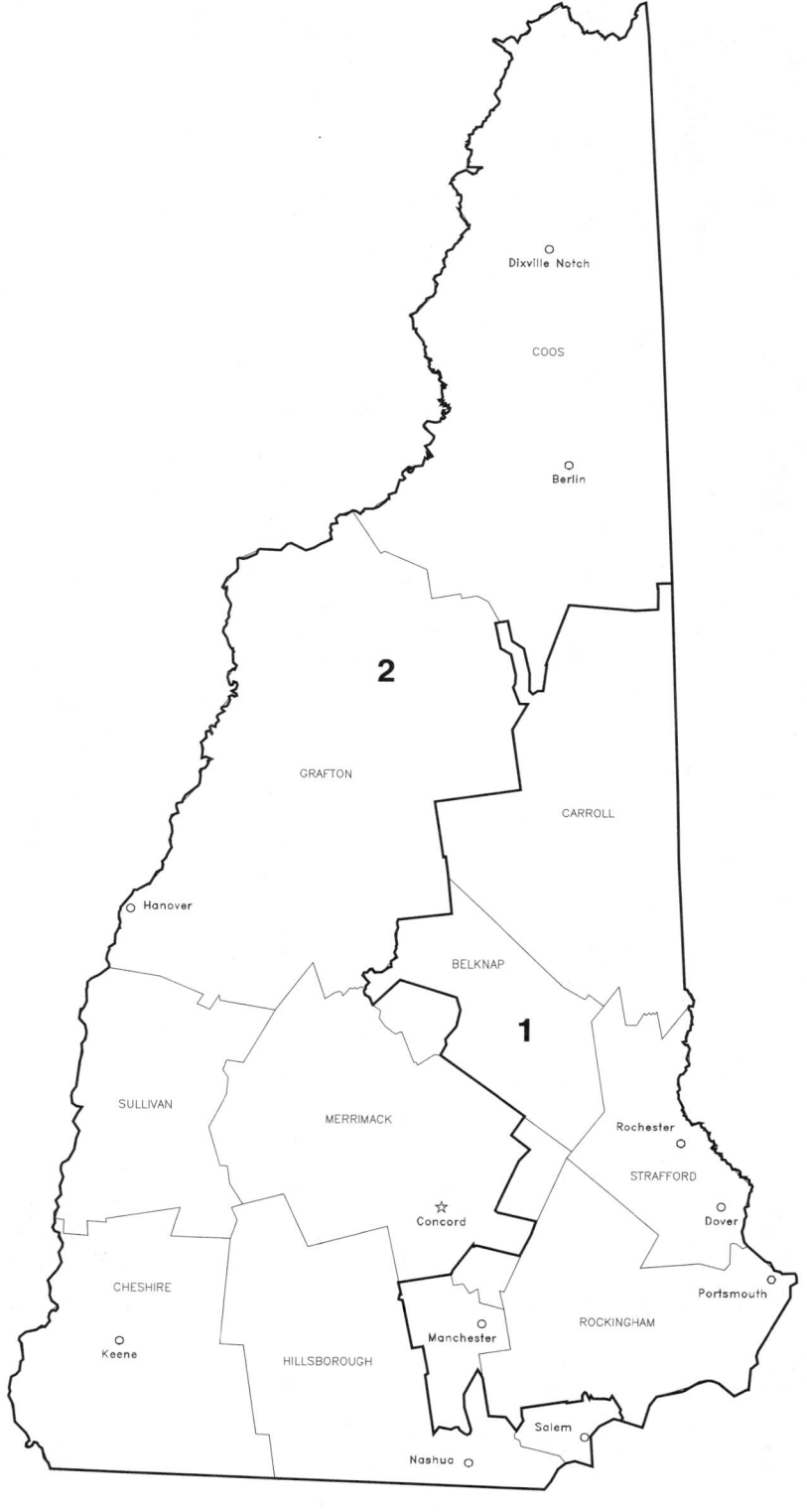

COOS

Dixville Notch

Berlin

2

GRAFTON

CARROLL

Hanover

BELKNAP

1

SULLIVAN

MERRIMACK

Rochester

STRAFFORD

☆
Concord

Dover

CHESHIRE

Keene

HILLSBOROUGH

Manchester

ROCKINGHAM

Portsmouth

Salem

Nashua

NEW HAMPSHIRE

PRESIDENT 2000

2000 Census Population	County	Total Vote	Republican	Democratic	Green (Nader)	Other	Rep.-Dem. Plurality	Percentage of Total Vote		
								Rep.	Dem.	Green
56,325	BELKNAP	26,795	14,799	10,719	977	300	4,080 R	55.2%	40.0%	3.6%
43,666	CARROLL	23,879	12,597	9,852	1,086	344	2,745 R	52.8%	41.3%	4.5%
73,825	CHESHIRE	33,395	13,793	17,382	1,750	470	3,589 D	41.3%	52.0%	5.2%
33,111	COOS	14,600	7,329	6,570	463	238	759 R	50.2%	45.0%	3.2%
81,743	GRAFTON	38,733	18,092	18,326	1,783	532	234 D	46.7%	47.3%	4.6%
380,841	HILLSBOROUGH	165,761	80,649	77,625	5,465	2,022	3,024 R	48.7%	46.8%	3.3%
136,225	MERRIMACK	63,684	30,028	30,622	2,343	691	594 D	47.2%	48.1%	3.7%
277,359	ROCKINGHAM	134,173	65,860	61,628	5,213	1,472	4,232 R	49.1%	45.9%	3.9%
112,233	STRAFFORD	49,393	21,108	25,400	2,273	612	4,292 D	42.7%	51.4%	4.6%
40,458	SULLIVAN	18,668	9,304	8,224	845	295	1,080 R	49.8%	44.1%	4.5%
1,235,786	TOTAL	569,081	273,559	266,348	22,198	6,976	7,211 R	48.1%	46.8%	3.9%
	City/Town									
10,769	AMHERST	6,081	3,219	2,615	202	45	604 R	52.9%	43.0%	3.3%
6,178	ATKINSON	4,616	2,616	1,826	136	38	790 R	56.7%	39.6%	2.9%
7,475	BARRINGTON	3,514	1,627	1,668	163	56	41 D	46.3%	47.5%	4.6%
18,274	BEDFORD	10,276	6,381	3,624	200	71	2,757 R	62.1%	35.3%	1.9%
6,716	BELMONT	2,611	1,424	1,082	81	24	342 R	54.5%	41.4%	3.1%
10,331	BERLIN	4,283	1,625	2,504	91	63	879 D	37.9%	58.5%	2.1%
7,138	BOW	3,951	2,079	1,758	91	23	321 R	52.6%	44.5%	2.3%
13,151	CLAREMONT	5,198	2,382	2,532	176	108	150 D	45.8%	48.7%	3.4%
40,687	CONCORD	17,876	6,981	10,025	688	182	3,044 D	39.1%	56.1%	3.8%
8,604	CONWAY	4,265	1,872	2,116	226	51	244 D	43.9%	49.6%	5.3%
34,021	DERRY	12,158	6,093	5,530	415	120	563 R	50.1%	45.5%	3.4%
26,884	DOVER	12,540	5,008	6,812	617	103	1,804 D	39.9%	54.3%	4.9%
12,664	DURHAM	5,422	1,585	3,362	437	38	1,777 D	29.2%	62.0%	8.1%
5,476	EPPING	2,523	1,220	1,172	96	35	48 R	48.4%	46.5%	3.8%
14,058	EXETER	7,109	3,169	3,591	290	59	422 D	44.6%	50.5%	4.1%
5,774	FARMINGTON	2,198	1,078	990	94	36	88 R	49.0%	45.0%	4.3%
8,405	FRANKLIN	3,012	1,484	1,380	101	47	104 R	49.3%	45.8%	3.4%
6,803	GILFORD	3,929	2,248	1,514	130	37	734 R	57.2%	38.5%	3.3%
16,929	GOFFSTOWN	7,568	4,069	3,186	244	69	883 R	53.8%	42.1%	3.2%
8,297	HAMPSTEAD	4,173	2,226	1,746	172	29	480 R	53.3%	41.8%	4.1%
14,937	HAMPTON	8,249	3,907	3,956	316	70	49 D	47.4%	48.0%	3.8%
10,850	HANOVER	5,224	1,541	3,391	250	42	1,850 D	29.5%	64.9%	4.8%
7,015	HOLLIS	4,008	2,050	1,739	166	53	311 R	51.1%	43.4%	4.1%
11,721	HOOKSETT	5,295	2,973	2,152	134	36	821 R	56.1%	40.6%	2.5%
22,928	HUDSON	9,510	4,527	4,573	290	120	46 D	47.6%	48.1%	3.0%
5,476	JAFFREY	2,363	1,082	1,156	99	26	74 D	45.8%	48.9%	4.2%
22,563	KEENE	10,234	3,704	5,856	580	94	2,152 D	36.2%	57.2%	5.7%
5,862	KINGSTON	2,826	1,435	1,251	110	30	184 R	50.8%	44.3%	3.9%
16,411	LACONIA	7,115	3,814	3,015	217	69	799 R	53.6%	42.4%	3.0%
12,568	LEBANON	5,535	2,226	3,044	215	50	818 D	40.2%	55.0%	3.9%
7,360	LITCHFIELD	3,386	1,742	1,480	116	48	262 R	51.4%	43.7%	3.4%
5,845	LITTLETON	2,518	1,418	989	83	28	429 R	56.3%	39.3%	3.3%
23,236	LONDONDERRY	10,240	5,463	4,348	323	106	1,115 R	53.3%	42.5%	3.2%
107,006	MANCHESTER	40,766	19,152	19,991	1,138	485	839 D	47.0%	49.0%	2.8%
25,119	MERRIMACK TOWN	12,287	6,239	5,571	351	126	668 R	50.8%	45.3%	2.9%
13,535	MILFORD	6,010	2,989	2,683	258	80	306 R	49.7%	44.6%	4.3%
86,605	NASHUA	34,625	14,803	18,398	1,001	423	3,595 D	42.8%	53.1%	2.9%
8,027	NEWMARKET	3,983	1,477	2,202	247	57	725 D	37.1%	55.3%	6.2%
6,269	NEWPORT	2,381	1,271	988	89	33	283 R	53.4%	41.5%	3.7%
10,914	PELHAM	5,158	2,641	2,295	170	52	346 R	51.2%	44.5%	3.3%
6,897	PEMBROKE	3,083	1,450	1,480	109	44	30 D	47.0%	48.0%	3.5%
5,883	PETERBOROUGH	3,270	1,375	1,683	174	38	308 D	42.0%	51.5%	5.3%
7,747	PLAISTOW	3,471	1,738	1,551	135	47	187 R	50.1%	44.7%	3.9%
5,892	PLYMOUTH	2,602	939	1,407	222	34	468 D	36.1%	54.1%	8.5%
20,784	PORTSMOUTH	11,478	3,896	6,862	611	109	2,966 D	33.9%	59.8%	5.3%

NEW HAMPSHIRE

PRESIDENT 2000

2000 Census Population	City/Town	Total Vote	Republican	Democratic	Green (Nader)	Other	Rep.-Dem. Plurality		Percentage of Total Vote		
									Rep.	Dem.	Green
9,674	RAYMOND	3,854	2,020	1,644	125	65	376	R	52.4%	42.7%	3.2%
28,461	ROCHESTER	11,509	5,522	5,401	388	198	121	R	48.0%	46.9%	3.4%
28,112	SALEM	11,985	5,713	5,711	442	119	2	R	47.7%	47.7%	3.7%
7,934	SEABROOK	3,521	1,677	1,670	127	47	7	R	47.6%	47.4%	3.6%
11,477	SOMERSWORTH	4,656	1,924	2,532	143	57	608	D	41.3%	54.4%	3.1%
6,800	SWANZEY	2,795	1,255	1,404	104	32	149	D	44.9%	50.2%	3.7%
7,776	WEARE	3,434	1,826	1,398	154	56	428	R	53.2%	40.7%	4.5%
10,709	WINDHAM	5,542	3,135	2,174	178	55	961	R	56.6%	39.2%	3.2%

NEW HAMPSHIRE

GOVERNOR 2000

2000 Census Population	County	Total Vote	Republican	Democratic	Other	Rep.-Dem. Plurality		Percentage			
								Total Vote		Major Vote	
								Rep.	Dem.	Rep.	Dem.
56,325	BELKNAP	26,867	12,980	11,994	1,893	986	R	48.3%	44.6%	52.0%	48.0%
43,666	CARROLL	23,618	11,691	10,363	1,564	1,328	R	49.5%	43.9%	53.0%	47.0%
73,825	CHESHIRE	33,053	12,554	17,734	2,765	5,180	D	38.0%	53.7%	41.4%	58.6%
33,111	COOS	14,537	6,470	7,011	1,056	541	D	44.5%	48.2%	48.0%	52.0%
81,743	GRAFTON	38,178	17,030	18,425	2,723	1,395	D	44.6%	48.3%	48.0%	52.0%
380,841	HILLSBOROUGH	165,047	75,067	78,522	11,458	3,455	D	45.5%	47.6%	48.9%	51.1%
136,225	MERRIMACK	63,602	24,479	33,571	5,552	9,092	D	38.5%	52.8%	42.2%	57.8%
277,359	ROCKINGHAM	132,351	60,837	61,247	10,267	410	D	46.0%	46.3%	49.8%	50.2%
112,233	STRAFFORD	49,262	17,234	28,044	3,984	10,810	D	35.0%	56.9%	38.1%	61.9%
40,458	SULLIVAN	18,438	8,610	8,127	1,701	483	R	46.7%	44.1%	51.4%	48.6%
1,235,786	TOTAL	564,953	246,952	275,038	42,963	28,086	D	43.7%	48.7%	47.3%	52.7%
	City/Town										
10,769	AMHERST	6,059	2,889	2,777	393	112	R	47.7%	45.8%	51.0%	49.0%
6,178	ATKINSON	4,572	2,481	1,831	260	650	R	54.3%	40.0%	57.5%	42.5%
7,475	BARRINGTON	3,497	1,314	1,869	314	555	D	37.6%	53.4%	41.3%	58.7%
18,274	BEDFORD	10,193	5,985	3,829	379	2,156	R	58.7%	37.6%	61.0%	39.0%
6,716	BELMONT	2,624	1,149	1,295	180	146	D	43.8%	49.4%	47.0%	53.0%
10,331	BERLIN	4,365	1,510	2,462	393	952	D	34.6%	56.4%	38.0%	62.0%
7,138	BOW	3,980	1,695	2,017	268	322	D	42.6%	50.7%	45.7%	54.3%
13,151	CLAREMONT	5,120	2,167	2,434	519	267	D	42.3%	47.5%	47.1%	52.9%
40,687	CONCORD	17,980	5,518	10,906	1,556	5,388	D	30.7%	60.7%	33.6%	66.4%
8,604	CONWAY	4,245	1,726	2,249	270	523	D	40.7%	53.0%	43.4%	56.6%
34,021	DERRY	12,088	5,230	6,043	815	813	D	43.3%	50.0%	46.4%	53.6%
26,884	DOVER	12,573	4,230	7,359	984	3,129	D	33.6%	58.5%	36.5%	63.5%
12,664	DURHAM	5,242	1,271	3,503	468	2,232	D	24.2%	66.8%	26.6%	73.4%
5,476	EPPING	2,518	1,093	1,229	196	136	D	43.4%	48.8%	47.1%	52.9%
14,058	EXETER	7,068	2,666	3,764	638	1,098	D	37.7%	53.3%	41.5%	58.5%
5,774	FARMINGTON	2,206	883	1,115	208	232	D	40.0%	50.5%	44.2%	55.8%
8,405	FRANKLIN	3,010	1,198	1,583	229	385	D	39.8%	52.6%	43.1%	56.9%
6,803	GILFORD	3,938	1,959	1,740	239	219	R	49.7%	44.2%	53.0%	47.0%
16,929	GOFFSTOWN	7,567	3,742	3,347	478	395	R	49.5%	44.2%	52.8%	47.2%
8,297	HAMPSTEAD	4,138	1,925	1,907	306	18	R	46.5%	46.1%	50.2%	49.8%
14,937	HAMPTON	8,190	3,596	3,868	726	272	D	43.9%	47.2%	48.2%	51.8%
10,850	HANOVER	4,979	1,547	3,148	284	1,601	D	31.1%	63.2%	32.9%	67.1%
7,015	HOLLIS	3,962	1,824	1,761	377	63	R	46.0%	44.4%	50.9%	49.1%
11,721	HOOKSETT	5,302	2,655	2,342	305	313	R	50.1%	44.2%	53.1%	46.9%
22,928	HUDSON	9,517	4,245	4,604	668	359	D	44.6%	48.4%	48.0%	52.0%

NEW HAMPSHIRE

GOVERNOR 2000

2000 Census Population	City/Town	Total Vote	Republican	Democratic	Other	Rep.-Dem. Plurality		Percentage			
								Total Vote		Major Vote	
								Rep.	Dem.	Rep.	Dem.
5,476	JAFFREY	2,357	994	1,149	214	155	D	42.2%	48.7%	46.4%	53.6%
22,563	KEENE	10,176	3,313	6,016	847	2,703	D	32.6%	59.1%	35.5%	64.5%
5,862	KINGSTON	2,809	1,352	1,251	206	101	R	48.1%	44.5%	51.9%	48.1%
16,411	LACONIA	7,312	3,543	3,341	428	202	R	48.5%	45.7%	51.5%	48.5%
12,568	LEBANON	5,500	2,181	2,936	383	755	D	39.7%	53.4%	42.6%	57.4%
7,360	LITCHFIELD	3,366	1,562	1,569	235	7	D	46.4%	46.6%	49.9%	50.1%
5,845	LITTLETON	2,527	1,254	1,150	123	104	R	49.6%	45.5%	52.2%	47.8%
23,236	LONDONDERRY	10,181	5,160	4,484	537	676	R	50.7%	44.0%	53.5%	46.5%
107,006	MANCHESTER	40,870	18,869	19,468	2,533	599	D	46.2%	47.6%	49.2%	50.8%
25,119	MERRIMACK TOWN	12,222	5,802	5,687	733	115	R	47.5%	46.5%	50.5%	49.5%
13,535	MILFORD	5,969	2,659	2,805	505	146	D	44.5%	47.0%	48.7%	51.3%
86,605	NASHUA	34,370	13,748	18,397	2,225	4,649	D	40.0%	53.5%	42.8%	57.2%
8,027	NEWMARKET	3,926	1,219	2,326	381	1,107	D	31.0%	59.2%	34.4%	65.6%
6,269	NEWPORT	2,374	1,116	1,029	229	87	R	47.0%	43.3%	52.0%	48.0%
10,914	PELHAM	5,094	2,352	2,307	435	45	R	46.2%	45.3%	50.5%	49.5%
6,897	PEMBROKE	3,084	1,164	1,643	277	479	D	37.7%	53.3%	41.5%	58.5%
5,883	PETERBOROUGH	3,210	1,182	1,730	298	548	D	36.8%	53.9%	40.6%	59.4%
7,747	PLAISTOW	3,458	1,562	1,619	277	57	D	45.2%	46.8%	49.1%	50.9%
5,892	PLYMOUTH	2,506	812	1,439	255	627	D	32.4%	57.4%	36.1%	63.9%
20,784	PORTSMOUTH	11,317	3,590	6,599	1,128	3,009	D	31.7%	58.3%	35.2%	64.8%
9,674	RAYMOND	3,496	1,771	1,687	38	84	R	50.7%	48.3%	51.2%	48.8%
28,461	ROCHESTER	11,469	4,578	6,082	809	1,504	D	39.9%	53.0%	42.9%	57.1%
28,112	SALEM	11,381	6,682	4,308	391	2,374	R	58.7%	37.9%	60.8%	39.2%
7,934	SEABROOK	3,512	1,821	1,266	425	555	R	51.9%	36.0%	59.0%	41.0%
11,477	SOMERSWORTH	4,686	1,543	2,798	345	1,255	D	32.9%	59.7%	35.5%	64.5%
6,800	SWANZEY	2,800	1,125	1,471	204	346	D	40.2%	52.5%	43.3%	56.7%
7,776	WEARE	3,411	1,538	1,559	314	21	D	45.1%	45.7%	49.7%	50.3%
10,709	WINDHAM	5,484	2,938	2,266	280	672	R	53.6%	41.3%	56.5%	43.5%

NEW HAMPSHIRE

CONGRESS

CD	Year	Total Vote	Republican		Democratic		Other Vote	Rep.-Dem. Plurality		Percentage			
			Vote	Candidate	Vote	Candidate				Total Vote		Major Vote	
										Rep.	Dem.	Rep.	Dem.
1	2000	284,862	150,609	SUNUNU, JOHN E.	128,387	CLARK, MARTHA FULLER	5,866	22,222	R	52.9%	45.1%	54.0%	46.0%
1	1998	156,369	104,430	SUNUNU, JOHN E.	51,783	FLOOD, PETER	156	52,647	R	66.8%	33.1%	66.9%	33.1%
1	1996	247,736	123,939	SUNUNU, JOHN E.	115,462	KEEFE, JOE	8,335	8,477	R	50.0%	46.6%	51.8%	48.2%
1	1994	147,822	97,017	ZELIFF, BILL	42,481	VERGE, BILL	8,324	54,536	R	65.6%	28.7%	69.5%	30.5%
1	1992	255,853	135,936	ZELIFF, BILL	108,578	PRESTON, ROBERT T.	11,339	27,358	R	53.1%	42.4%	55.6%	44.4%
2	2000	271,555	152,581	BASS, CHARLES	110,367	BRANNEN, BARNEY	8,607	42,214	R	56.2%	40.6%	58.0%	42.0%
2	1998	161,376	85,740	BASS, CHARLES	72,217	RAUH, MARY	3,419	13,523	R	53.1%	44.8%	54.3%	45.7%
2	1996	243,587	123,001	BASS, CHARLES	105,867	ARNESEN, DEBORAH	14,719	17,134	R	50.5%	43.5%	53.7%	46.3%
2	1994	161,573	83,121	BASS, CHARLES	74,243	SWETT, DICK	4,209	8,878	R	51.4%	46.0%	52.8%	47.2%
2	1992	255,185	91,126	HATCH, BILL	157,328	SWETT, DICK	6,731	66,202	D	35.7%	61.7%	36.7%	63.3%

NEW HAMPSHIRE
GENERAL AND PRIMARY ELECTIONS

2000 GENERAL ELECTIONS

President Other vote was 2,757 Libertarian (Browne); 2,615 Independence Party (Buchanan); 328 Constitution (Phillips); 55 write-in (Hagelin); 1,221 scattered write-in.

Governor Other vote was 35,904 Independent (Brown); 6,446 Libertarian (Babiarz); 613 scattered write-in.

Congress Other vote was: CD 1: 5,713 Libertarian (Belforti), 153 scattered write-in; CD 2: 6,188 Libertarian (Christeson), 2,204 Constitutional American (Kendel), 215 scattered write-in.

2000 PRIMARY ELECTIONS

Primary February 1, 2000 (President)   **Registration**   Republican   305,377
September 12, 2000 (Congress)   (as of Sept. 12, 2000)   Democratic   214,046
Undeclared   282,975

TOTAL   802,398

Primary Type Modified—Registered Democrats and Republicans could vote only in their party's primary. "Undeclared" voters could vote in either party's primary.

Note: An asterisk (*) denotes incumbent.

	REPUBLICAN PRIMARIES			DEMOCRATIC PRIMARIES		
President	John McCain	115,606	48.5%	Al Gore	76,897	49.7%
	George W. Bush	72,330	30.4%	Bill Bradley	70,502	45.6%
	Steve Forbes	30,166	12.7%	Charles Buckley	322	0.2%
	Alan Keyes	15,179	6.4%	Heather Harder	192	0.1%
	Gary Bauer	1,640	0.7%	Jeffrey B. Peters	156	0.1%
	Orrin G. Hatch	163	0.1%	John B. Eaton	134	0.1%
	Dorian Yeager	98		Lyndon H. LaRouche Jr.	124	0.1%
	Andy Martin	81		Jim Taylor	87	0.1%
	Samuel H. Berry Jr.	61		Mark Greenstein	75	
	Kenneth A. Capalbo	51		Nathaniel Thomas Mullins	35	
	Timothy Lee Mosby	41		Edward T. O'Donnell Jr.	35	
	Mark "Dick" Harnes	34		Willie F. Carter	30	
	Richard C. Peet	23		Randolph "Randy" W. Crow	29	
	Tom Oyler	14		Vincent S. Hamm	22	
	Write-in	2,719	1.1%	Thomas Koos	19	
				Michael Skok	18	
				Write-in	5,962	3.9%
	TOTAL	238,206		TOTAL	154,639	
	Among the Republican write-ins were 1,155 for Al Gore, 1,025 for Bill Bradley and 231 for Elizabeth Dole.			*Among the Democratic write-ins were 3,320 for John McCain, 998 for Steve Forbes and 827 for George W. Bush.*		
Governor	Gordon Humphrey	54,134	51.9%	Jeanne Shaheen*	45,249	60.4%
	James Squires	23,582	22.6%	Mark D. Fernald	28,488	38.0%
	Jeffrey Howard	21,734	20.8%	Write-in	1,164	1.6%
	Fred Bramante	2,500	2.4%			
	Jim Marron	584	0.6%			
	Write-in	1,851	1.8%			
	TOTAL	104,385		TOTAL	74,901	
Congressional District 1	John E. Sununu*	45,798	99.4%	Martha Fuller Clark	29,164	99.1%
	Write-in	279	0.6%	Write-in	252	0.9%
	TOTAL	46,077		TOTAL	29,416	
Congressional District 2	Charles Bass*	44,928	99.0%	Barney Brannen	20,496	68.2%
	Write-in	452	1.0%	Norman H. Jackman	9,291	30.9%
				Write-in	248	0.8%
	TOTAL	45,380		TOTAL	30,035	

NEW JERSEY

GOVERNOR

Donald T. DiFrancesco (R). Became Acting Governor Feb. 1, 2001, on resignation of Christine T. Whitman (R) to accept appointment by President Bush as director of the U.S. Environmental Protection Agency. Whitman was re-elected in 1997 to a four-year term. Previously elected 1993.

SENATORS

Robert G. Torricelli (D). Elected 1996 to a six-year term.

Jon Corzine (D). Elected 2000 to a six-year term.

REPRESENTATIVES

1. Robert E. Andrews (D)
2. Frank A. LoBiondo (R)
3. H. James Saxton (R)
4. Christopher H. Smith (R)
5. Margaret S. Roukema (R)
6. Frank Pallone (D)
7. Mike Ferguson (R)
8. Bill Pascrell Jr. (D)
9. Steven R. Rothman (D)
10. Donald M. Payne (D)
11. Rodney Frelinghuysen (R)
12. Rush Holt (D)
13. Robert Menendez (D)

POSTWAR VOTE FOR PRESIDENT

| | | Republican | | Democratic | | Other | | Percentage | | | |
| | | | | | | | | Total Vote | | Major Vote | |
Year	Total Vote	Vote	Candidate	Vote	Candidate	Vote	Plurality	Rep.	Dem.	Rep.	Dem.
2000**	3,187,226	1,284,173	Bush, George W.	1,788,850	Gore, Al	114,203	504,677 D	40.3%	56.1%	41.8%	58.2%
1996**	3,075,807	1,103,078	Dole, Bob	1,652,329	Clinton, Bill	320,400	549,251 D	35.9%	53.7%	40.0%	60.0%
1992**	3,343,594	1,356,865	Bush, George	1,436,206	Clinton, Bill	550,523	79,341 D	40.6%	43.0%	48.6%	51.4%
1988	3,099,553	1,743,192	Bush, George	1,320,352	Dukakis, Michael S.	36,009	422,840 R	56.2%	42.6%	56.9%	43.1%
1984	3,217,862	1,933,630	Reagan, Ronald	1,261,323	Mondale, Walter F.	22,909	672,307 R	60.1%	39.2%	60.5%	39.5%
1980**	2,975,684	1,546,557	Reagan, Ronald	1,147,364	Carter, Jimmy	281,763	399,193 R	52.0%	38.6%	57.4%	42.6%
1976	3,014,472	1,509,688	Ford, Gerald R.	1,444,653	Carter, Jimmy	60,131	65,035 R	50.1%	47.9%	51.1%	48.9%
1972	2,997,229	1,845,502	Nixon, Richard M.	1,102,211	McGovern, George S.	49,516	743,291 R	61.6%	36.8%	62.6%	37.4%
1968	2,875,395	1,325,467	Nixon, Richard M.	1,264,206	Humphrey, Hubert H.	285,722	61,261 R	46.1%	44.0%	51.2%	48.8%
1964	2,847,663	964,174	Goldwater, Barry M.	1,868,231	Johnson, Lyndon B.	15,258	904,057 D	33.9%	65.6%	34.0%	66.0%
1960	2,773,111	1,363,324	Nixon, Richard M.	1,385,415	Kennedy, John F.	24,372	22,091 D	49.2%	50.0%	49.6%	50.4%
1956	2,484,312	1,606,942	Eisenhower, Dwight D.	850,337	Stevenson, Adlai E.	27,033	756,605 R	64.7%	34.2%	65.4%	34.6%
1952	2,418,554	1,373,613	Eisenhower, Dwight D.	1,015,902	Stevenson, Adlai E.	29,039	357,711 R	56.8%	42.0%	57.5%	42.5%
1948	1,949,555	981,124	Dewey, Thomas E.	895,455	Truman, Harry S.	72,976	85,669 R	50.3%	45.9%	52.3%	47.7%

In 2000 the other vote column includes 94,554 votes cast for Green (Nader). In 1996 the other vote column includes 262,134 votes cast for Perot. In 1992 the other vote column includes 521,829 votes cast for Perot. In 1980 the other column includes 234,632 votes for Independent (Anderson).

NEW JERSEY

POSTWAR VOTE FOR GOVERNOR

Year	Total Vote	Republican Vote	Republican Candidate	Democratic Vote	Democratic Candidate	Other Vote	Rep.-Dem. Plurality	Percentage Total Vote Rep.	Percentage Total Vote Dem.	Percentage Major Vote Rep.	Percentage Major Vote Dem.
1997	2,418,344	1,133,394	Whitman, Christine T.	1,107,968	McGreevey, James	176,982	25,426 R	46.9%	45.8%	50.6%	49.4%
1993	2,505,964	1,236,124	Whitman, Christine T.	1,210,031	Florio, James J.	59,809	26,093 R	49.3%	48.3%	50.5%	49.5%
1989	2,253,764	838,553	Courter, James A.	1,379,937	Florio, James J.	35,274	541,384 D	37.2%	61.2%	37.8%	62.2%
1985	1,972,624	1,372,631	Kean, Thomas H.	578,402	Shapiro, Peter	21,591	794,229 R	69.6%	29.3%	70.4%	29.6%
1981	2,317,239	1,145,999	Kean, Thomas H.	1,144,202	Florio, James J.	27,038	1,797 R	49.5%	49.4%	50.0%	50.0%
1977	2,126,264	888,880	Bateman, Raymond H.	1,184,564	Byrne, Brendan T.	52,820	295,684 D	41.8%	55.7%	42.9%	57.1%
1973	2,122,009	676,235	Sandman, Charles W.	1,414,613	Byrne, Brendan T.	31,161	738,378 D	31.9%	66.7%	32.3%	67.7%
1969	2,366,606	1,411,905	Cahill, William T.	911,003	Meyner, Robert B.	43,698	500,902 R	59.7%	38.5%	60.8%	39.2%
1965	2,229,583	915,996	Dumont, Wayne	1,279,568	Hughes, Richard J.	34,019	363,572 D	41.1%	57.4%	41.7%	58.3%
1961	2,152,662	1,049,274	Mitchell, James P.	1,084,194	Hughes, Richard J.	19,194	34,920 D	48.7%	50.4%	49.2%	50.8%
1957	2,018,488	897,321	Forbes, Malcolm S.	1,101,130	Meyner, Robert B.	20,037	203,809 D	44.5%	54.6%	44.9%	55.1%
1953	1,810,812	809,068	Troast, Paul L.	962,710	Meyner, Robert B.	39,034	153,642 D	44.7%	53.2%	45.7%	54.3%
1949**	1,718,788	885,882	Driscoll, Alfred	810,022	Wene, Elmer H.	22,884	75,860 R	51.5%	47.1%	52.2%	47.8%
1946	1,414,527	807,378	Driscoll, Alfred	585,960	Hansen, Lewis G.	21,189	221,418 R	57.1%	41.4%	57.9%	42.1%

The term of office of New Jersey's Governor was increased from three to four years effective with the 1949 election.

POSTWAR VOTE FOR SENATOR

Year	Total Vote	Republican Vote	Republican Candidate	Democratic Vote	Democratic Candidate	Other Vote	Rep.-Dem. Plurality	Percentage Total Vote Rep.	Percentage Total Vote Dem.	Percentage Major Vote Rep.	Percentage Major Vote Dem.
2000	3,015,662	1,420,267	Franks, Bob	1,511,237	Corzine, Jon	84,158	90,970 D	47.1%	50.1%	48.4%	51.6%
1996	2,884,106	1,227,817	Zimmer, Dick	1,519,328	Torricelli, Robert G.	136,961	291,511 D	42.6%	52.7%	44.7%	55.3%
1994	2,054,887	966,244	Haytaian, Garabed	1,033,487	Lautenberg, Frank R.	55,156	67,243 D	47.0%	50.3%	48.3%	51.7%
1990	1,938,454	918,874	Whitman, Christine T.	977,810	Bradley, Bill	41,770	58,936 D	47.4%	50.4%	48.4%	51.6%
1988	2,987,634	1,349,937	Dawkins, Peter M.	1,599,905	Lautenberg, Frank R.	37,792	249,968 D	45.2%	53.6%	45.8%	54.2%
1984	3,096,456	1,080,100	Mochary, Mary V.	1,986,644	Bradley, Bill	29,712	906,544 D	34.9%	64.2%	35.2%	64.8%
1982	2,193,945	1,047,626	Fenwick, Millicent	1,117,549	Lautenberg, Frank R.	28,770	69,923 D	47.8%	50.9%	48.4%	51.6%
1978	1,957,515	844,200	Bell, Jeffrey	1,082,960	Bradley, Bill	30,355	238,760 D	43.1%	55.3%	43.8%	56.2%
1976	2,771,390	1,054,508	Norcross, David F.	1,681,140	Williams, Harrison	35,742	626,632 D	38.0%	60.7%	38.5%	61.5%
1972	2,791,907	1,743,854	Case, Clifford P.	963,573	Krebs, Paul J.	84,480	780,281 R	62.5%	34.5%	64.4%	35.6%
1970	2,142,105	903,026	Gross, Nelson G.	1,157,074	Williams, Harrison	82,005	254,048 D	42.2%	54.0%	43.8%	56.2%
1966	2,131,188	1,279,343	Case, Clifford P.	788,021	Wilentz, Warren W.	63,824	491,322 R	60.0%	37.0%	61.9%	38.1%
1964	2,710,441	1,011,610	Shanley, Bernard M.	1,678,051	Williams, Harrison	20,780	666,441 D	37.3%	61.9%	37.6%	62.4%
1960	2,664,556	1,483,832	Case, Clifford P.	1,151,385	Lord, Thorn	29,339	332,447 R	55.7%	43.2%	56.3%	43.7%
1958	1,881,329	882,287	Kean, Robert W.	966,832	Williams, Harrison	32,210	84,545 D	46.9%	51.4%	47.7%	52.3%
1954	1,770,557	861,528	Case, Clifford P.	858,158	Howell, Charles R.	50,871	3,370 R	48.7%	48.5%	50.1%	49.9%
1952	2,318,232	1,286,782	Smith, H. Alexander	1,011,187	Alexander, Archibald	20,263	275,595 R	55.5%	43.6%	56.0%	44.0%
1948	1,869,882	934,720	Hendrickson, Robert	884,414	Alexander, Archibald	50,748	50,306 R	50.0%	47.3%	51.4%	48.6%
1946	1,367,155	799,808	Smith, H. Alexander	548,458	Brunner, George E.	18,889	251,350 R	58.5%	40.1%	59.3%	40.7%

NEW JERSEY

Districts Established March 20, 1992

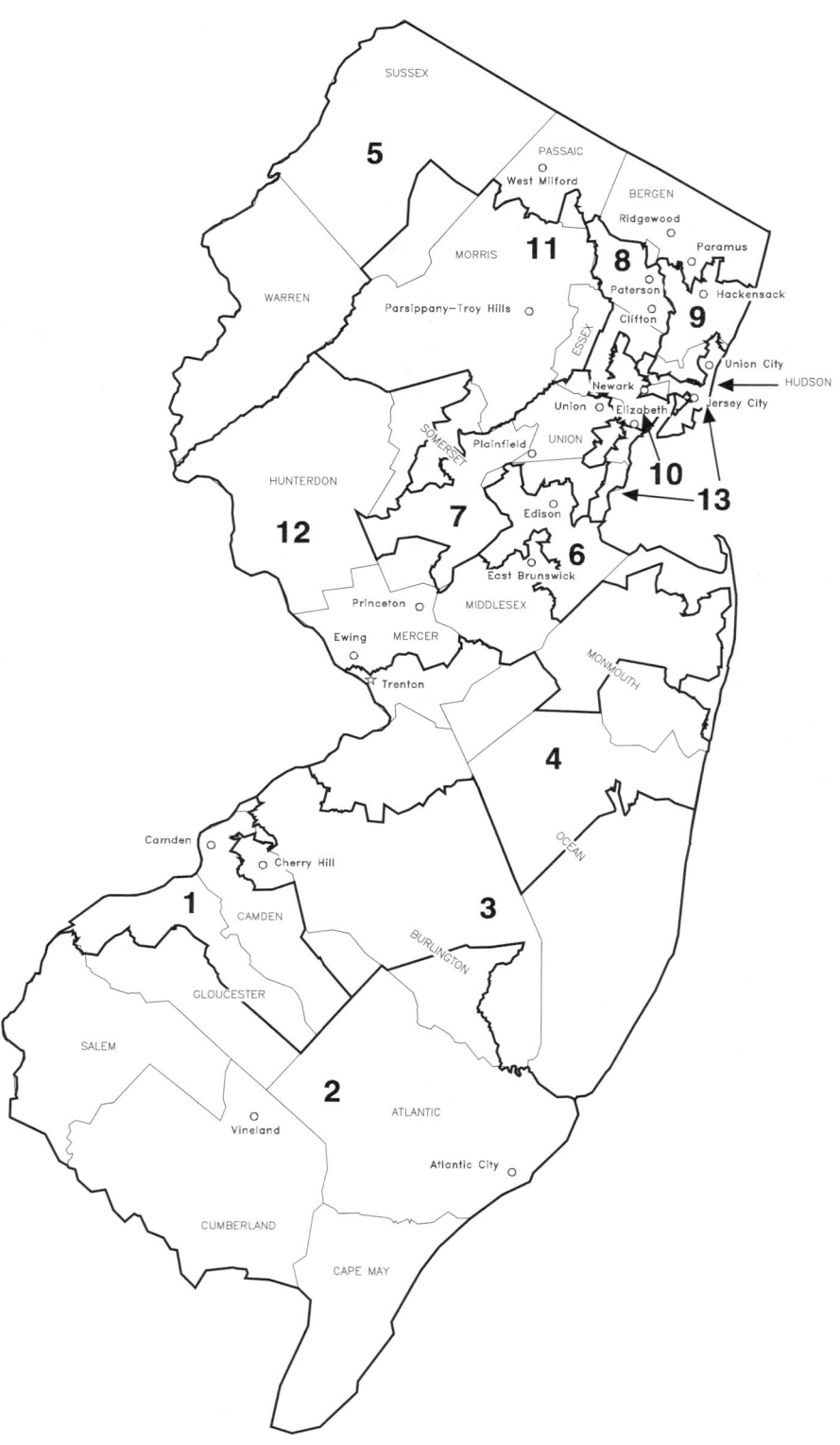

NEW JERSEY

PRESIDENT 2000

2000 Census Population	County	Total Vote	Republican	Democratic	Green (Nader)	Other	Rep.-Dem. Plurality		Percentage of Total Vote		
									Rep.	Dem.	Green
252,552	ATLANTIC	91,102	35,593	52,880	2,188	441	17,287	D	39.1%	58.0%	2.4%
884,118	BERGEN	366,721	152,731	202,682	9,688	1,620	49,951	D	41.6%	55.3%	2.6%
423,394	BURLINGTON	177,541	72,254	99,506	4,894	887	27,252	D	40.7%	56.0%	2.8%
508,932	CAMDEN	196,861	62,464	127,166	6,124	1,107	64,702	D	31.7%	64.6%	3.1%
102,326	CAPE MAY	47,594	23,794	22,189	1,291	320	1,605	R	50.0%	46.6%	2.7%
146,438	CUMBERLAND	48,684	18,882	28,188	1,004	610	9,306	D	38.8%	57.9%	2.1%
793,633	ESSEX	259,573	66,842	185,505	5,641	1,585	118,663	D	25.8%	71.5%	2.2%
254,673	GLOUCESTER	107,298	42,315	61,095	3,196	692	18,780	D	39.4%	56.9%	3.0%
608,975	HUDSON	167,361	43,804	118,206	4,436	915	74,402	D	26.2%	70.6%	2.7%
121,989	HUNTERDON	56,455	32,210	21,387	2,459	399	10,823	R	57.1%	37.9%	4.4%
350,761	MERCER	135,559	46,670	83,256	4,561	1,072	36,586	D	34.4%	61.4%	3.4%
750,162	MIDDLESEX	258,849	93,545	154,998	8,934	1,372	61,453	D	36.1%	59.9%	3.5%
615,301	MONMOUTH	262,141	119,291	131,476	9,059	2,315	12,185	D	45.5%	50.2%	3.5%
470,212	MORRIS	206,508	111,066	88,039	6,333	1,070	23,027	R	53.8%	42.6%	3.1%
510,916	OCEAN	216,393	105,684	102,104	7,354	1,251	3,580	R	48.8%	47.2%	3.4%
489,049	PASSAIC	156,573	61,043	90,324	3,752	1,454	29,281	D	39.0%	57.7%	2.4%
64,285	SALEM	26,972	12,257	13,718	714	283	1,461	D	45.4%	50.9%	2.6%
297,490	SOMERSET	120,377	59,725	56,232	3,776	644	3,493	R	49.6%	46.7%	3.1%
144,166	SUSSEX	57,490	33,277	21,353	2,399	461	11,924	R	57.9%	37.1%	4.2%
522,541	UNION	186,373	68,554	112,003	4,945	871	43,449	D	36.8%	60.1%	2.7%
102,437	WARREN	40,801	22,172	16,543	1,806	280	5,629	R	54.3%	40.5%	4.4%
8,414,350	TOTAL	3,187,226	1,284,173	1,788,850	94,554	19,649	504,677	D	40.3%	56.1%	3.0%

NEW JERSEY

SENATOR 2000

2000 Census Population	County	Total Vote	Republican	Democratic	Other	Rep.-Dem. Plurality		Percentage			
								Total Vote		Major Vote	
								Rep.	Dem.	Rep.	Dem.
252,552	ATLANTIC	83,675	39,738	42,146	1,791	2,408	D	47.5%	50.4%	48.5%	51.5%
884,118	BERGEN	351,624	174,949	171,017	5,658	3,932	R	49.8%	48.6%	50.6%	49.4%
423,394	BURLINGTON	167,505	83,840	80,119	3,546	3,721	R	50.1%	47.8%	51.1%	48.9%
508,932	CAMDEN	182,137	74,620	103,179	4,338	28,559	D	41.0%	56.6%	42.0%	58.0%
102,326	CAPE MAY	44,352	26,665	16,781	906	9,884	R	60.1%	37.8%	61.4%	38.6%
146,438	CUMBERLAND	42,936	19,698	21,581	1,657	1,883	D	45.9%	50.3%	47.7%	52.3%
793,633	ESSEX	249,776	73,757	170,756	5,263	96,999	D	29.5%	68.4%	30.2%	69.8%
254,673	GLOUCESTER	103,577	49,660	49,802	4,115	142	D	47.9%	48.1%	49.9%	50.1%
608,975	HUDSON	160,384	43,820	112,502	4,062	68,682	D	27.3%	70.1%	28.0%	72.0%
121,989	HUNTERDON	54,355	34,468	17,796	2,091	16,672	R	63.4%	32.7%	65.9%	34.1%
350,761	MERCER	129,028	53,542	72,250	3,236	18,708	D	41.5%	56.0%	42.6%	57.4%
750,162	MIDDLESEX	245,046	104,652	132,476	7,918	27,824	D	42.7%	54.1%	44.1%	55.9%
615,301	MONMOUTH	242,353	123,447	109,282	9,624	14,165	R	50.9%	45.1%	53.0%	47.0%
470,212	MORRIS	193,989	118,283	69,889	5,817	48,394	R	61.0%	36.0%	62.9%	37.1%
510,916	OCEAN	205,295	115,686	82,596	7,013	33,090	R	56.4%	40.2%	58.3%	41.7%
489,049	PASSAIC	143,484	63,460	75,378	4,646	11,918	D	44.2%	52.5%	45.7%	54.3%
64,285	SALEM	26,567	13,900	11,566	1,101	2,334	R	52.3%	43.5%	54.6%	45.4%
297,490	SOMERSET	117,804	69,045	45,948	2,811	23,097	R	58.6%	39.0%	60.0%	40.0%
144,166	SUSSEX	56,887	35,740	18,453	2,694	17,287	R	62.8%	32.4%	65.9%	34.1%
522,541	UNION	174,929	77,111	93,879	3,939	16,768	D	44.1%	53.7%	45.1%	54.9%
102,437	WARREN	39,959	24,186	13,841	1,932	10,345	R	60.5%	34.6%	63.6%	36.4%
8,414,350	TOTAL	3,015,662	1,420,267	1,511,237	84,158	90,970	D	47.1%	50.1%	48.4%	51.6%

NEW JERSEY

CONGRESS

CD	Year	Total Vote	Republican Vote	Republican Candidate	Democratic Vote	Democratic Candidate	Other Vote	Rep.-Dem. Plurality	Total Vote Rep.	Total Vote Dem.	Major Vote Rep.	Major Vote Dem.
1	2000	219,612	46,455	CATHCART, CHARLENE	167,327	ANDREWS, ROBERT E.	5,830	120,872 D	21.2%	76.2%	21.7%	78.3%
1	1998	123,342	27,855	RICHARDS, RONALD L.	90,279	ANDREWS, ROBERT E.	5,208	62,424 D	22.6%	73.2%	23.6%	76.4%
1	1996	210,735	44,286	SUPLEE, MEL	160,415	ANDREWS, ROBERT E.	6,034	116,129 D	21.0%	76.1%	21.6%	78.4%
1	1994	149,660	41,505	HOGAN, JAMES N.	108,155	ANDREWS, ROBERT E.		66,650 D	27.7%	72.3%	27.7%	72.3%
1	1992	228,072	65,123	SOLOMON, LEE A.	153,525	ANDREWS, ROBERT E.	9,424	88,402 D	28.6%	67.3%	29.8%	70.2%
2	2000	233,859	155,187	LOBIONDO, FRANK A.	74,632	JANOSIK, EDWARD G.	4,040	80,555 R	66.4%	31.9%	67.5%	32.5%
2	1998	141,514	93,248	LOBIONDO, FRANK A.	43,563	HUNSBERGER, DEREK	4,703	49,685 R	65.9%	30.8%	68.2%	31.8%
2	1996	220,739	133,130	LOBIONDO, FRANK A.	83,912	KATZ, RUTH	3,697	49,218 R	60.3%	38.0%	61.3%	38.7%
2	1994	158,717	102,566	LOBIONDO, FRANK A.	56,151	MAGAZZU, LOUIS N.		46,415 R	64.6%	35.4%	64.6%	35.4%
2	1992	237,027	98,315	LOBIONDO, FRANK A.	132,465	HUGHES, WILLIAM J.	6,247	34,150 D	41.5%	55.9%	42.6%	57.4%
3	2000	274,083	157,053	SAXTON, H. JAMES	112,848	LEVIN, SUSAN BASS	4,182	44,205 R	57.3%	41.2%	58.2%	41.8%
3	1998	157,239	97,508	SAXTON, H. JAMES	55,248	POLANSKY, STEVEN J.	4,483	42,260 R	62.0%	35.1%	63.8%	36.2%
3	1996	245,278	157,503	SAXTON, H. JAMES	81,590	LEONARDI, JOHN	6,185	75,913 R	64.2%	33.3%	65.9%	34.1%
3	1994	174,328	115,750	SAXTON, H. JAMES	54,441	SMITH, JAMES B.	4,137	61,309 R	66.4%	31.2%	68.0%	32.0%
3	1992	255,798	151,368	SAXTON, H. JAMES	94,012	RYAN, TIMOTHY E.	10,418	57,356 R	59.2%	36.8%	61.7%	38.3%
4	2000	250,810	158,515	SMITH, CHRISTOPHER H.	87,956	GUSCIORA, REED	4,339	70,559 R	63.2%	35.1%	64.3%	35.7%
4	1998	149,577	92,991	SMITH, CHRISTOPHER H.	52,281	SCHNEIDER, LARRY	4,305	40,710 R	62.2%	35.0%	64.0%	36.0%
4	1996	230,114	146,404	SMITH, CHRISTOPHER H.	77,565	MEARA, KEVIN J.	6,145	68,839 R	63.6%	33.7%	65.4%	34.6%
4	1994	161,767	109,818	SMITH, CHRISTOPHER H.	49,537	WALSH, RALPH	2,412	60,281 R	67.9%	30.6%	68.9%	31.1%
4	1992	241,225	149,095	SMITH, CHRISTOPHER H.	84,514	HUGHES, BRIAN M.	7,616	64,581 R	61.8%	35.0%	63.8%	36.2%
5	2000	268,524	175,546	ROUKEMA, MARGARET S.	81,715	MERCURIO, LINDA A.	11,263	93,831 R	65.4%	30.4%	68.2%	31.8%
5	1998	166,818	106,304	ROUKEMA, MARGARET S.	55,487	SCHNEIDER, MIKE	5,027	50,817 R	63.7%	33.3%	65.7%	34.3%
5	1996	254,333	181,323	ROUKEMA, MARGARET S.	62,956	AUER, BILL	10,054	118,367 R	71.3%	24.8%	74.2%	25.8%
5	1994	188,505	139,964	ROUKEMA, MARGARET S.	41,275	AUER, BILL	7,266	98,689 R	74.2%	21.9%	77.2%	22.8%
5	1992	274,371	196,198	ROUKEMA, MARGARET S.	67,579	LUCAS, FRANK R.	10,594	128,619 R	71.5%	24.6%	74.4%	25.6%
6	2000	209,852	62,454	KENNEDY, BRIAN T.	141,698	PALLONE, FRANK	5,700	79,244 D	29.8%	67.5%	30.6%	69.4%
6	1998	137,012	55,180	FERGUSON, MICHAEL	78,102	PALLONE, FRANK	3,730	22,922 D	40.3%	57.0%	41.4%	58.6%
6	1996	203,478	73,402	CORODEMUS, STEVEN J.	124,635	PALLONE, FRANK	5,441	51,233 D	36.1%	61.3%	37.1%	62.9%
6	1994	147,331	55,287	HERSON, MIKE	88,922	PALLONE, FRANK	3,122	33,635 D	37.5%	60.4%	38.3%	61.7%
6	1992	226,093	100,949	KYRILLOS, JOSEPH M.	118,266	PALLONE, FRANK	6,878	17,317 D	44.6%	52.3%	46.1%	53.9%
7	2000	248,999	128,434	FERGUSON, MIKE	113,479	CONNELLY, MARYANNE	7,086	14,955 R	51.6%	45.6%	53.1%	46.9%
7	1998	148,042	77,751	FRANKS, BOB	65,776	CONNELLY, MARYANNE	4,515	11,975 R	52.5%	44.4%	54.2%	45.8%
7	1996	232,565	128,817	FRANKS, BOB	97,283	LERNER, LARRY	6,465	31,534 R	55.4%	41.8%	57.0%	43.0%
7	1994	165,857	98,814	FRANKS, BOB	64,231	CARROLL, KAREN	2,812	34,583 R	59.6%	38.7%	60.6%	39.4%
7	1992	248,082	132,174	FRANKS, BOB	105,761	SENDELSKY, LEONARD R.	10,147	26,413 R	53.3%	42.6%	55.6%	44.4%
8	2000	200,132	60,606	FUSCO, ANTHONY, JR.	134,074	PASCRELL, BILL, JR.	5,452	73,468 D	30.3%	67.0%	31.1%	68.9%
8	1998	130,588	46,289	KIRNAN, MATTHEW J.	81,068	PASCRELL, BILL, JR.	3,231	34,779 D	35.4%	62.1%	36.3%	63.7%
8	1996	193,078	92,604	MARTINI, BILL	98,853	PASCRELL, BILL, JR.	1,621	6,249 D	48.0%	51.2%	48.4%	51.6%
8	1994	141,368	70,494	MARTINI, BILL	68,661	KLEIN, HERBERT C.	2,213	1,833 R	49.9%	48.6%	50.7%	49.3%
8	1992	205,828	84,674	BUBBA, JOSEPH L.	96,742	KLEIN, HERBERT C.	24,412	12,068 D	41.1%	47.0%	46.7%	53.3%
9	2000	206,771	61,984	TEDESCHI, JOSEPH	140,462	ROTHMAN, STEVEN R.	4,325	78,478 D	30.0%	67.9%	30.6%	69.4%
9	1998	141,459	47,817	LONEGAN, STEVE	91,330	ROTHMAN, STEVEN R.	2,312	43,513 D	33.8%	64.6%	34.4%	65.6%
9	1996	210,930	89,005	DONOVAN, KATHLEEN A.	117,646	ROTHMAN, STEVEN R.	4,279	28,641 D	42.2%	55.8%	43.1%	56.9%
9	1994	159,888	57,651	RUSSO, PETER J.	99,984	TORRICELLI, ROBERT G.	2,253	42,333 D	36.1%	62.5%	36.6%	63.4%
9	1992	238,704	88,179	ROMA, PATRICK J.	139,188	TORRICELLI, ROBERT G.	11,337	51,009 D	36.9%	58.3%	38.8%	61.2%

NEW JERSEY
CONGRESS

CD	Year	Total Vote	Republican		Democratic		Other Vote	Rep.-Dem. Plurality	Percentage			
			Vote	Candidate	Vote	Candidate			Total Vote		Major Vote	
									Rep.	Dem.	Rep.	Dem.
10	2000	152,045	18,436	WEBER, DIRK B.	133,073	PAYNE, DONALD M.	536	114,637 D	12.1%	87.5%	12.2%	87.8%
10	1998	98,494	10,678	WNUCK, WILLIAM STANLEY	82,244	PAYNE, DONALD M.	5,572	71,566 D	10.8%	83.5%	11.5%	88.5%
10	1996	151,060	22,086	WILLIAMS, VANESSA	127,126	PAYNE, DONALD M.	1,848	105,040 D	14.6%	84.2%	14.8%	85.2%
10	1994	98,368	21,524	FORD, JIM	74,622	PAYNE, DONALD M.	2,222	53,098 D	21.9%	75.9%	22.4%	77.6%
10	1992	149,632	30,160	PALERMO, ALFRED D.	117,287	PAYNE, DONALD M.	2,185	87,127 D	20.2%	78.4%	20.5%	79.5%
11	2000	273,838	186,140	FRELINGHUYSEN, RODNEY	80,958	SCOLLO, JOHN P.	6,740	105,182 R	68.0%	29.6%	69.7%	30.3%
11	1998	148,971	100,910	FRELINGHUYSEN, RODNEY	44,160	SCOLLO, JOHN P.	3,901	56,750 R	67.7%	29.6%	69.6%	30.4%
11	1996	255,158	169,091	FRELINGHUYSEN, RODNEY	78,742	EVANGEL, CHRIS	7,325	90,349 R	66.3%	30.9%	68.2%	31.8%
11	1994	179,580	127,868	FRELINGHUYSEN, RODNEY	50,211	HERBERT, FRANK	1,501	77,657 R	71.2%	28.0%	71.8%	28.2%
11	1992	268,436	188,165	GALLO, DEAN A.	68,871	SPIRIDELLIS, ONA	11,400	119,294 R	70.1%	25.7%	73.2%	26.8%
12	2000	299,942	145,511	ZIMMER, DICK	146,162	HOLT, RUSH	8,269	651 D	48.5%	48.7%	49.9%	50.1%
12	1998	184,610	87,221	PAPPAS, MICHAEL	92,528	HOLT, RUSH	4,861	5,307 D	47.2%	50.1%	48.5%	51.5%
12	1996	269,221	135,811	PAPPAS, MICHAEL	125,594	DEL VECCHIO, DAVID M.	7,816	10,217 R	50.4%	46.7%	52.0%	48.0%
12	1994	184,280	125,939	ZIMMER, DICK	55,977	YOUSSOUF, JOSEPH D.	2,364	69,962 R	68.3%	30.4%	69.2%	30.8%
12	1992	272,757	174,216	ZIMMER, DICK	83,035	ABATE, FRANK G.	15,506	91,181 R	63.9%	30.4%	67.7%	32.3%
13	2000	149,766	27,849	DE LEON, THERESA	117,856	MENENDEZ, ROBERT	4,061	90,007 D	18.6%	78.7%	19.1%	80.9%
13	1998	87,823	14,615	DE LEON, THERESA	70,308	MENENDEZ, ROBERT	2,900	55,693 D	16.6%	80.1%	17.2%	82.8%
13	1996	146,470	25,426	MUNOZ, CARLOS E.	115,457	MENENDEZ, ROBERT	5,587	90,031 D	17.4%	78.8%	18.0%	82.0%
13	1994	95,467	24,071	ALONSO, FERNANDO A.	67,688	MENENDEZ, ROBERT	3,708	43,617 D	25.2%	70.9%	26.2%	73.8%
13	1992	145,714	44,529	THEEMLING, FRED J.	93,670	MENENDEZ, ROBERT	7,515	49,141 D	30.6%	64.3%	32.2%	67.8%

NEW JERSEY
GENERAL AND PRIMARY ELECTIONS

2000 GENERAL ELECTIONS

President   Other vote was 6,989 Reform (Buchanan); 6,312 Libertarian (Browne); 2,215 Independent (Hagelin); 1,880 Socialist (McReynolds); 1,409 Constitution (Phillips); 844 Socialist Workers (Harris). All of these candidates, including Nader, were listed on the ballot as Independent, with their partisan designation indicated as a "Slogan."

Senator   Other vote was 32,841 Green (Afran); 19,312 Reform (DiNizio); 7,241 Libertarian (Ellett); 6,061 Independent (Breen); 5,657 Trust In God (Carter); 3,836 NJ Conservative (LaNeve); 3,365 Socialist (Pason); 3,309 Socialist Workers (Rosenstock); 2,536 God Bless Jersey (Gostigian). All of these candidates were listed on the ballot as Independent, with their partisan designation indicated as a "Slogan."

Congress   Other vote was: CD 1: 3,090 Green (Parrish), 1,959 Legalize Marijuana (Forchion), 781 NJ Conservative (Patalivo); CD 2: 3,252 Green (Gabrielsky), 788 Socialist (Rozzo); CD 3: 2,515 Green (Kromash), 948 Reform (Feduniewicz), 719 NJ Conservative (Wahner); CD 4: 3,627 Green (Chaifetz), 712 Unthinkable Courage (Teel); CD 5: 5,329 Green (King), 4,095 New Jersey Independents (McCafferty), 1,358 Reform (Goodman), 481 Natural Law (Hamilton); CD 6: 4,252 Green (Gray), 1,120 Reform (Zaletel), 328 NJ Conservative (Kuzmak); CD 7: 5,444 Green (Coleman), 973 Libertarian (Young), 386 NJ Conservative (Gianella), 283 Natural Law (Johnson); CD 8: 4,469 Green (Fortunato), 983 New Jersey Independents (Sargis); CD 9: 2,273 Green (Pell),

NEW JERSEY

GENERAL AND PRIMARY ELECTIONS

Congress *(cont.)* 1,072 Independent/Progressive (Perrone), 980 NJ Conservative (Corriston); CD 10: 536 Socialist Workers (Williams); CD 11: 5,199 Green (Pickarski), 1,541 NJ Conservative (Spinosa); CD 12: 5,811 Green (Mayer), 1,233 NJ Conservative (Desmond), 1,225 Libertarian (Winslow); CD 13: 2,741 Green (Meliere), 562 Constitution (Hester), 357 Politicians Are Crooks (Shaw), 233 In Common Effort (Fonteboa), 168 Socialist Workers (Sachs). All of these candidates were listed on the ballot as Independent, with their partisan designation indicated as a "Slogan."

2000 PRIMARY ELECTIONS

Primary	June 6, 2000	**Registration** (as of June 5, 2000)	Republican	833,801
			Democratic	1,095,744
			Independent	11,855
			Unaffiliated	2,589,419
			TOTAL	4,530,819

Primary Type   Modified—Registered Democrats and Republicans could vote only in their party's primary. "Unaffiliated" voters could vote in either party's primary if they were willing to become a member of that party.

Note: An asterisk (*) denotes incumbent.

	REPUBLICAN PRIMARIES			DEMOCRATIC PRIMARIES		
President	George W. Bush	201,209	83.6%	Al Gore	358,951	94.9%
	Alan Keyes	39,601	16.4%	Lyndon H. LaRouche Jr.	19,321	5.1%
	TOTAL	240,810		TOTAL	378,272	
Senator	Bob Franks	98,370	35.7%	Jon S. Corzine	251,216	58.0%
	William L. Gormley	94,010	34.1%	Jim Florio	182,212	42.0%
	James W. Treffinger	48,674	17.7%			
	Murray Sabrin	34,629	12.6%			
	TOTAL	275,683		TOTAL	433,428	
Congressional District 1	Charlene Cathcart	9,877	100.0%	Robert E. Andrews*	38,737	100.0%
	TOTAL	9,877		TOTAL	38,737	
Congressional District 2	Frank A. LoBiondo*	28,834	100.0%	Edward G. Janosik	14,148	81.7%
				Steven A. Farkas	3,168	18.3%
	TOTAL	28,834		TOTAL	17,316	
Congressional District 3	Jim Saxton*	25,280	100.0%	Susan Bass Levin	24,241	100.0%
	TOTAL	25,280		TOTAL	24,241	
Congressional District 4	Christopher H. Smith*	20,062	100.0%	Reed Gusciora	18,952	100.0%
	TOTAL	20,062		TOTAL	18,952	
Congressional District 5	Marge Roukema*	23,043	52.3%	Linda A. Mercurio	14,743	100.0%
	E. Scott Garrett	21,051	47.7%			
	TOTAL	44,094		TOTAL	14,743	
Congressional District 6	Brian T. Kennedy	5,683	66.0%	Frank Pallone Jr.*	24,475	100.0%
	Charles T. Hutchins	2,930	34.0%			
	TOTAL	8,613		TOTAL	24,475	
Congressional District 7	Mike Ferguson	10,748	40.6%	Maryanne Connelly	14,931	45.5%
	Tom Kean Jr.	7,358	27.8%	Mike Lapolla	14,637	44.6%
	Joel M. Weingarten	6,089	23.0%	Jeffrey Golkin	2,698	8.2%
	Patrick Morrisey	2,284	8.6%	Joel Farley	585	1.8%
	TOTAL	26,479		TOTAL	32,851	
Congressional District 8	Anthony Fusco Jr.	8,690	78.9%	Bill Pascrell Jr.*	23,701	100.0%
	Bernard Anthony George	2,325	21.1%			
	TOTAL	11,015		TOTAL	23,701	

NEW JERSEY

GENERAL AND PRIMARY ELECTIONS

	REPUBLICAN PRIMARIES			DEMOCRATIC PRIMARIES		
Congressional District 9	Joseph Tedeschi	7,091	100.0%	Steven R. Rothman*	25,686	100.0%
	TOTAL	7,091		TOTAL	25,686	
Congressional District 10	Dirk B. Weber	1,492	100.0%	Donald M. Payne*	45,880	100.0%
	TOTAL	1,492		TOTAL	45,880	
Congressional District 11	Rodney Frelinghuysen*	35,820	100.0%	John P. Scollo	15,419	100.0%
	TOTAL	35,820		TOTAL	15,419	
Congressional District 12	Dick Zimmer	19,084	62.0%	Rush Holt*	27,104	100.0%
	Mike Pappas	11,692	38.0%			
	TOTAL	30,776		TOTAL	27,104	
Congressional District 13	Theresa de Leon	2,045	57.5%	Robert Menendez*	38,651	100.0%
	Carlos E. Munoz	849	23.9%			
	Harold Turner	661	18.6%			
	TOTAL	3,555		TOTAL	38,651	

NEW MEXICO

GOVERNOR
Gary E. Johnson (R). Re-elected 1998 to a four-year term. Previously elected 1994.

SENATORS
Jeff Bingaman (D). Re-elected 2000 to a six-year term. Previously elected 1994, 1988, 1982.

Peter V. Domenici (R). Re-elected 1996 to a six-year term. Previously elected 1990, 1984, 1978, 1972.

REPRESENTATIVES
1. Heather A. Wilson (R)   2. Joseph R. Skeen (R)   3. Tom Udall (D)

POSTWAR VOTE FOR PRESIDENT

| | | Republican | | Democratic | | Other | | Percentage | | | |
| | | | | | | | | Total Vote | | Major Vote | |
Year	Total Vote	Vote	Candidate	Vote	Candidate	Vote	Plurality	Rep.	Dem.	Rep.	Dem.
2000**	598,605	286,417	Bush, George W.	286,783	Gore, Al	25,405	366 D	47.8%	47.9%	50.0%	50.0%
1996**	556,074	232,751	Dole, Bob	273,495	Clinton, Bill	49,828	40,744 D	41.9%	49.2%	46.0%	54.0%
1992**	569,986	212,824	Bush, George	261,617	Clinton, Bill	95,545	48,793 D	37.3%	45.9%	44.9%	55.1%
1988	521,287	270,341	Bush, George	244,497	Dukakis, Michael S.	6,449	25,844 R	51.9%	46.9%	52.5%	47.5%
1984	514,370	307,101	Reagan, Ronald	201,769	Mondale, Walter F.	5,500	105,332 R	59.7%	39.2%	60.3%	39.7%
1980**	456,971	250,779	Reagan, Ronald	167,826	Carter, Jimmy	38,366	82,953 R	54.9%	36.7%	59.9%	40.1%
1976	418,409	211,419	Ford, Gerald R.	201,148	Carter, Jimmy	5,842	10,271 R	50.5%	48.1%	51.2%	48.8%
1972	386,241	235,606	Nixon, Richard M.	141,084	McGovern, George S.	9,551	94,522 R	61.0%	36.5%	62.5%	37.5%
1968	327,350	169,692	Nixon, Richard M.	130,081	Humphrey, Hubert H.	27,577	39,611 R	51.8%	39.7%	56.6%	43.4%
1964	328,645	132,838	Goldwater, Barry M.	194,015	Johnson, Lyndon B.	1,792	61,177 D	40.4%	59.0%	40.6%	59.4%
1960	311,107	153,733	Nixon, Richard M.	156,027	Kennedy, John F.	1,347	2,294 D	49.4%	50.2%	49.6%	50.4%
1956	253,926	146,788	Eisenhower, Dwight D.	106,098	Stevenson, Adlai E.	1,040	40,690 R	57.8%	41.8%	58.0%	42.0%
1952	238,608	132,170	Eisenhower, Dwight D.	105,661	Stevenson, Adlai E.	777	26,509 R	55.4%	44.3%	55.6%	44.4%
1948	187,063	80,303	Dewey, Thomas E.	105,464	Truman, Harry S.	1,296	25,161 D	42.9%	56.4%	43.2%	56.8%

In 2000 the other vote column includes 21,251 votes cast for Green (Nader). In 1996 the other vote column includes 32,257 votes cast for Perot. In 1992 the other vote column includes 91,895 votes cast for Perot. In 1980 the other column includes 29,459 votes for Independent (Anderson).

NEW MEXICO

POSTWAR VOTE FOR GOVERNOR

Year	Total Vote	Republican Vote	Republican Candidate	Democratic Vote	Democratic Candidate	Other Vote	Rep.-Dem. Plurality	Total Vote Rep.	Total Vote Dem.	Major Vote Rep.	Major Vote Dem.
1998	498,703	271,948	Johnson, Gary E.	226,755	Chavez, Martin J.		45,193 R	54.5%	45.5%	54.5%	45.5%
1994	467,621	232,945	Johnson, Gary E.	186,686	King, Bruce	47,990	46,259 R	49.8%	39.9%	55.5%	44.5%
1990	411,236	185,692	Bond, Frank M.	224,564	King, Bruce	980	38,872 D	45.2%	54.6%	45.3%	54.7%
1986	394,833	209,455	Carruthers, Garrey E.	185,378	Powell. Ray B.		24,077 R	53.0%	47.0%	53.0%	47.0%
1982	407,466	191,626	Irick, John B.	215,840	Anaya, Toney		24,214 D	47.0%	53.0%	47.0%	53.0%
1978	345,577	170,848	Skeen, Joseph R.	174,631	King, Bruce	98	3,783 D	49.4%	50.5%	49.5%	50.5%
1974	328,742	160,430	Skeen, Joseph R.	164,172	Apodaca, Jerry	4,140	3,742 D	48.8%	49.9%	49.4%	50.6%
1970**	290,375	134,640	Domenici, Peter V.	148,835	King, Bruce	6,900	14,195 D	46.4%	51.3%	47.5%	52.5%
1968	318,975	160,140	Cargo, David F.	157,230	Chavez, Fabian	1,605	2,910 R	50.2%	49.3%	50.5%	49.5%
1966	260,232	134,625	Cargo, David F.	125,587	Lusk, Thomas E.	20	9,038 R	51.7%	48.3%	51.7%	48.3%
1964	318,042	126,540	Tucker, Merle H.	191,497	Campbell, Jack M.	5	64,957 D	39.8%	60.2%	39.8%	60.2%
1962	247,135	116,184	Mechem, Edwin L.	130,933	Campbell, Jack M.	18	14,749 D	47.0%	53.0%	47.0%	53.0%
1960	305,542	153,765	Mechem, Edwin L.	151,777	Burroughs, John		1,988 R	50.3%	49.7%	50.3%	49.7%
1958	205,048	101,567	Mechem, Edwin L.	103,481	Burroughs, John		1,914 D	49.5%	50.5%	49.5%	50.5%
1956	251,751	131,488	Mechem, Edwin L.	120,263	Simms, John F.		11,225 R	52.2%	47.8%	52.2%	47.8%
1954	193,956	83,373	Stockton, Alvin	110,583	Simms, John F.		27,210 D	43.0%	57.0%	43.0%	57.0%
1952	240,150	129,116	Mechem, Edwin L.	111,034	Grantham, Everett		18,082 R	53.8%	46.2%	53.8%	46.2%
1950	180,205	96,846	Mechem, Edwin L.	83,359	Miles, John E.		13,487 R	53.7%	46.3%	53.7%	46.3%
1948	189,992	86,023	Lujan, Manuel	103,969	Mabry, Thomas J.		17,946 D	45.3%	54.7%	45.3%	54.7%
1946	132,930	62,875	Safford, Edward L.	70,055	Mabry, Thomas J.		7,180 D	47.3%	52.7%	47.3%	52.7%

The term of New Mexico's Governor was increased from two to four years effective with the 1970 election.

POSTWAR VOTE FOR SENATOR

Year	Total Vote	Republican Vote	Republican Candidate	Democratic Vote	Democratic Candidate	Other Vote	Rep.-Dem. Plurality	Total Vote Rep.	Total Vote Dem.	Major Vote Rep.	Major Vote Dem.
2000	589,526	225,517	Redmond, Bill	363,744	Bingaman, Jeff	265	138,227 D	38.3%	61.7%	38.3%	61.7%
1996	551,821	357,171	Domenici, Peter V.	164,356	Trujillo, Art	30,294	192,815 R	64.7%	29.8%	68.5%	31.5%
1994	463,196	213,025	McMillan, Colin R.	249,989	Bingaman, Jeff	182	36,964 D	46.0%	54.0%	46.0%	54.0%
1990	406,938	296,712	Domenici, Peter V.	110,033	Benavides, Tom R.	193	186,679 R	72.9%	27.0%	72.9%	27.1%
1988	508,598	186,579	Valentine, William	321,983	Bingaman, Jeff	36	135,404 D	36.7%	63.3%	36.7%	63.3%
1984	502,634	361,371	Domenici, Peter V.	141,253	Pratt, Judith A.	10	220,118 R	71.9%	28.1%	71.9%	28.1%
1982	404,810	187,128	Schmitt, Harrison	217,682	Bingaman, Jeff		30,554 D	46.2%	53.8%	46.2%	53.8%
1978	343,554	183,442	Domenici, Peter V.	160,045	Anaya, Toney	67	23,397 R	53.4%	46.6%	53.4%	46.6%
1976	413,141	234,681	Schmitt, Harrison	176,382	Montoya, Joseph M.	2,078	58,299 R	56.8%	42.7%	57.1%	42.9%
1972	378,330	204,253	Domenici, Peter V.	173,815	Daniels, Jack	262	30,438 R	54.0%	45.9%	54.0%	46.0%
1970	289,906	135,004	Carter, Anderson	151,486	Montoya, Joseph M.	3,416	16,482 D	46.6%	52.3%	47.1%	52.9%
1966	258,203	120,988	Carter, Anderson	137,205	Anderson, Clinton P.	10	16,217 D	46.9%	53.1%	46.9%	53.1%
1964	325,774	147,562	Mechem, Edwin L.	178,209	Montoya, Joseph M.	3	30,647 D	45.3%	54.7%	45.3%	54.7%
1960	300,551	109,897	Colwes, William F.	190,654	Anderson, Clinton P.		80,757 D	36.6%	63.4%	36.6%	63.4%
1958	203,323	75,827	Atchley, Forrest S.	127,496	Chavez, Dennis		51,669 D	37.3%	62.7%	37.3%	62.7%
1954	194,422	83,071	Mechem, Edwin L.	111,351	Anderson, Clinton P.		28,280 D	42.7%	57.3%	42.7%	57.3%
1952	239,711	117,168	Hurley, Patrick J.	122,543	Chavez, Dennis		5,375 D	48.9%	51.1%	48.9%	51.1%
1948	188,495	80,226	Hurley, Patrick J.	108,269	Anderson, Clinton P.		28,043 D	42.6%	57.4%	42.6%	57.4%
1946	133,282	64,632	Hurley, Patrick J.	68,650	Chavez, Dennis		4,018 D	48.5%	51.5%	48.5%	51.5%

NEW MEXICO

Districts Established December 18, 1991

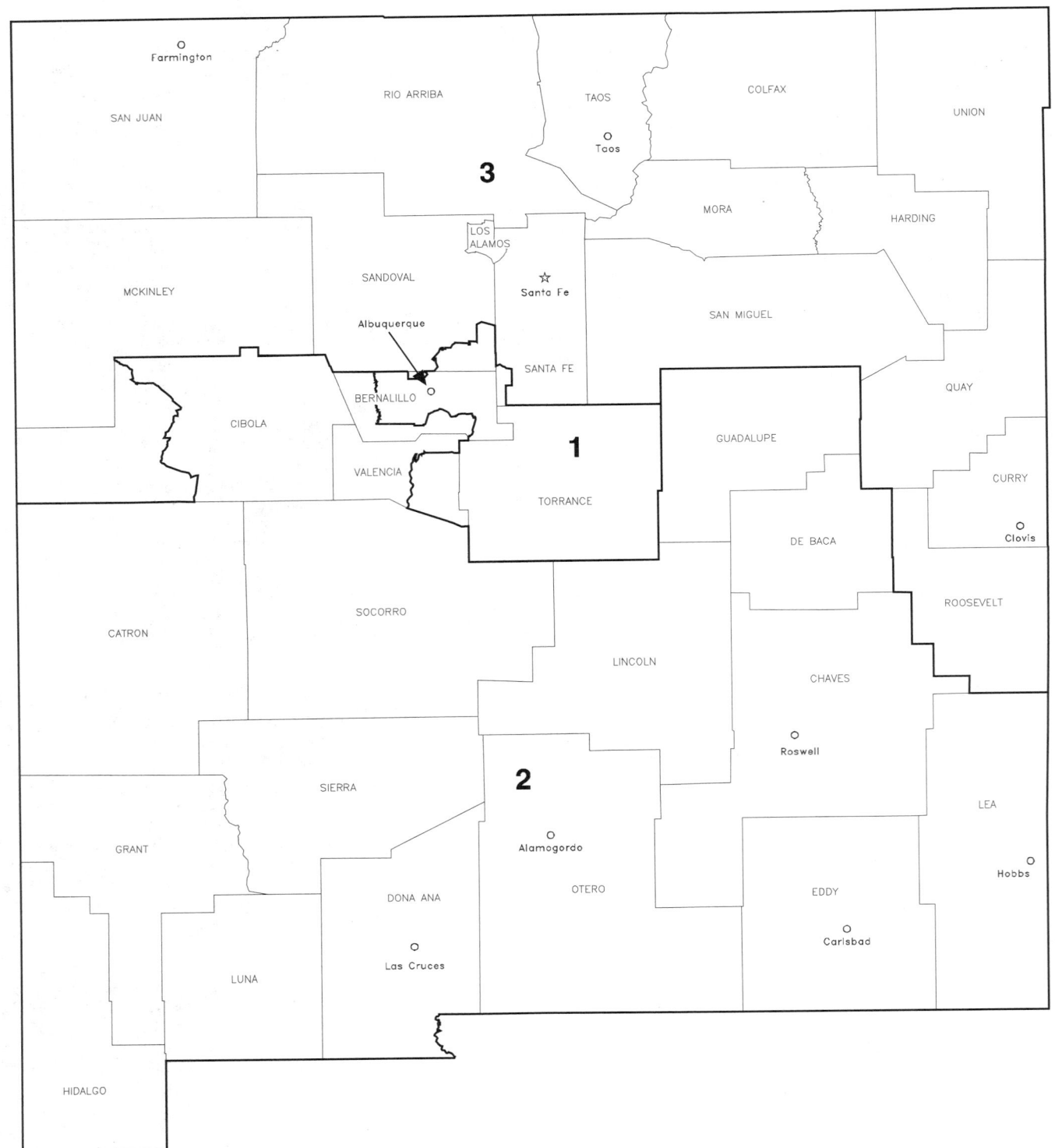

NEW MEXICO

PRESIDENT 2000

2000 Census Population	County	Total Vote	Republican	Democratic	Green (Nader)	Other	Rep.-Dem. Plurality	Percentage of Total Vote		
								Rep.	Dem.	Green
556,678	BERNALILLO	204,319	95,249	99,461	8,274	1,335	4,212 D	46.6%	48.7%	4.0%
3,543	CATRON	1,711	1,273	353	57	28	920 R	74.4%	20.6%	3.3%
61,382	CHAVES	18,149	11,378	6,340	307	124	5,038 R	62.7%	34.9%	1.7%
25,595	CIBOLA	7,088	2,752	4,127	164	45	1,375 D	38.8%	58.2%	2.3%
14,189	COLFAX	5,461	2,600	2,653	163	45	53 D	47.6%	48.6%	3.0%
45,044	CURRY	11,969	8,301	3,471	147	50	4,830 R	69.4%	29.0%	1.2%
2,240	DE BACA	982	612	349	12	9	263 R	62.3%	35.5%	1.2%
174,682	DONA ANA	46,653	21,263	23,912	1,158	320	2,649 D	45.6%	51.3%	2.5%
51,658	EDDY	17,787	10,335	7,108	256	88	3,227 R	58.1%	40.0%	1.4%
31,002	GRANT	11,241	4,961	5,673	530	77	712 D	44.1%	50.5%	4.7%
4,680	GUADALUPE	1,651	548	1,076	24	3	528 D	33.2%	65.2%	1.5%
810	HARDING	593	366	214	9	4	152 R	61.7%	36.1%	1.5%
5,932	HIDALGO	1,834	954	839	28	13	115 R	52.0%	45.7%	1.5%
55,511	LEA	14,256	10,157	3,855	169	75	6,302 R	71.2%	27.0%	1.2%
19,411	LINCOLN	6,772	4,458	2,027	168	119	2,431 R	65.8%	29.9%	2.5%
18,343	LOS ALAMOS	10,218	5,623	4,149	329	117	1,474 R	55.0%	40.6%	3.2%
25,016	LUNA	6,612	3,395	2,975	186	56	420 R	51.3%	45.0%	2.8%
74,798	MCKINLEY	15,879	5,070	10,281	392	136	5,211 D	31.9%	64.7%	2.5%
5,180	MORA	2,191	668	1,456	49	18	788 D	30.5%	66.5%	2.2%
62,298	OTERO	16,204	10,258	5,465	338	143	4,793 R	63.3%	33.7%	2.1%
10,155	QUAY	3,844	2,292	1,471	51	30	821 R	59.6%	38.3%	1.3%
41,190	RIO ARRIBA	12,097	3,495	8,169	377	56	4,674 D	28.9%	67.5%	3.1%
18,018	ROOSEVELT	5,651	3,762	1,762	98	29	2,000 R	66.6%	31.2%	1.7%
89,908	SANDOVAL	31,755	15,423	14,899	1,211	222	524 R	48.6%	46.9%	3.8%
113,801	SAN JUAN	34,657	21,434	11,980	923	320	9,454 R	61.8%	34.6%	2.7%
30,126	SAN MIGUEL	9,161	2,215	6,540	344	62	4,325 D	24.2%	71.4%	3.8%
129,292	SANTA FE	49,471	13,974	32,017	3,215	265	18,043 D	28.2%	64.7%	6.5%
13,270	SIERRA	4,586	2,721	1,689	132	44	1,032 R	59.3%	36.8%	2.9%
18,078	SOCORRO	6,826	3,173	3,294	279	80	121 D	46.5%	48.3%	4.1%
29,979	TAOS	10,895	2,744	7,039	1,064	48	4,295 D	25.2%	64.6%	9.8%
16,911	TORRANCE	4,960	2,891	1,868	163	38	1,023 R	58.3%	37.7%	3.3%
4,174	UNION	1,755	1,269	452	19	15	817 R	72.3%	25.8%	1.1%
66,152	VALENCIA	21,377	10,803	9,819	615	140	984 R	50.5%	45.9%	2.9%
1,819,046	TOTAL	598,605	286,417	286,783	21,251	4,154	366 D	47.8%	47.9%	3.6%

NEW MEXICO

SENATOR 2000

2000 Census Population	County	Total Vote	Republican	Democratic	Other	Rep.-Dem. Plurality	Percentage			
							Total Vote		Major Vote	
							Rep.	Dem.	Rep.	Dem.
556,678	BERNALILLO	201,527	77,425	123,994	108	46,569 D	38.4%	61.5%	38.4%	61.6%
3,543	CATRON	1,677	993	678	6	315 R	59.2%	40.4%	59.4%	40.6%
61,382	CHAVES	17,889	8,650	9,239		589 D	48.4%	51.6%	48.4%	51.6%
25,595	CIBOLA	6,985	1,952	5,031	2	3,079 D	27.9%	72.0%	28.0%	72.0%
14,189	COLFAX	5,363	2,041	3,322		1,281 D	38.1%	61.9%	38.1%	61.9%
45,044	CURRY	11,825	6,482	5,336	7	1,146 R	54.8%	45.1%	54.8%	45.2%
2,240	DE BACA	965	353	610	2	257 D	36.6%	63.2%	36.7%	63.3%
174,682	DONA ANA	45,864	16,745	29,111	8	12,366 D	36.5%	63.5%	36.5%	63.5%
51,658	EDDY	17,540	7,320	10,219	1	2,899 D	41.7%	58.3%	41.7%	58.3%
31,002	GRANT	11,053	3,525	7,521	7	3,996 D	31.9%	68.0%	31.9%	68.1%

NEW MEXICO

SENATOR 2000

2000 Census Population	County	Total Vote	Republican	Democratic	Other	Rep.-Dem. Plurality		Percentage			
								Total Vote		Major Vote	
								Rep.	Dem.	Rep.	Dem.
4,680	GUADALUPE	1,634	375	1,259		884	D	22.9%	77.1%	22.9%	77.1%
810	HARDING	587	279	308		29	D	47.5%	52.5%	47.5%	52.5%
5,932	HIDALGO	1,823	569	1,250	4	681	D	31.2%	68.6%	31.3%	68.7%
55,511	LEA	14,005	6,989	7,014	2	25	D	49.9%	50.1%	49.9%	50.1%
19,411	LINCOLN	6,642	3,338	3,299	5	39	R	50.3%	49.7%	50.3%	49.7%
18,343	LOS ALAMOS	10,091	4,233	5,858		1,625	D	41.9%	58.1%	41.9%	58.1%
25,016	LUNA	6,518	2,525	3,984	9	1,459	D	38.7%	61.1%	38.8%	61.2%
74,798	MCKINLEY	15,589	4,005	11,578	6	7,573	D	25.7%	74.3%	25.7%	74.3%
5,180	MORA	2,128	535	1,592	1	1,057	D	25.1%	74.8%	25.2%	74.8%
62,298	OTERO	15,953	7,353	8,597	3	1,244	D	46.1%	53.9%	46.1%	53.9%
10,155	QUAY	3,811	1,640	2,167	4	527	D	43.0%	56.9%	43.1%	56.9%
41,190	RIO ARRIBA	11,924	2,733	9,191		6,458	D	22.9%	77.1%	22.9%	77.1%
18,018	ROOSEVELT	5,584	2,924	2,649	11	275	R	52.4%	47.4%	52.5%	47.5%
89,908	SANDOVAL	31,308	13,349	17,940	19	4,591	D	42.6%	57.3%	42.7%	57.3%
113,801	SAN JUAN	34,120	17,995	16,119	6	1,876	R	52.7%	47.2%	52.7%	47.3%
30,126	SAN MIGUEL	9,002	1,821	7,180	1	5,359	D	20.2%	79.8%	20.2%	79.8%
129,292	SANTA FE	48,581	11,507	37,045	29	25,538	D	23.7%	76.3%	23.7%	76.3%
13,270	SIERRA	4,519	2,078	2,432	9	354	D	46.0%	53.8%	46.1%	53.9%
18,078	SOCORRO	6,719	2,231	4,483	5	2,252	D	33.2%	66.7%	33.2%	66.8%
29,979	TAOS	10,585	2,109	8,473	3	6,364	D	19.9%	80.0%	19.9%	80.1%
16,911	TORRANCE	4,866	2,245	2,620	1	375	D	46.1%	53.8%	46.1%	53.9%
4,174	UNION	1,718	957	761		196	R	55.7%	44.3%	55.7%	44.3%
66,152	VALENCIA	21,131	8,241	12,884	6	4,643	D	39.0%	61.0%	39.0%	61.0%
1,819,046	TOTAL	589,526	225,517	363,744	265	138,227	D	38.3%	61.7%	38.3%	61.7%

NEW MEXICO

CONGRESS

CD	Year	Total Vote	Republican		Democratic		Other Vote	Rep.-Dem. Plurality		Percentage			
			Vote	Candidate	Vote	Candidate				Total Vote		Major Vote	
										Rep.	Dem.	Rep.	Dem.
1	2000	213,139	107,296	WILSON, HEATHER A.	92,187	KELLY, JOHN J.	13,656	15,109	R	50.3%	43.3%	53.8%	46.2%
1	1998	179,168	86,784	WILSON, HEATHER A.	75,040	MALOOF, PHILLIP J.	17,344	11,744	R	48.4%	41.9%	53.6%	46.4%
1	1996	193,078	109,290	SCHIFF, STEVEN H.	71,635	WERTHEIM, JOHN	12,153	37,655	R	56.6%	37.1%	60.4%	39.6%
1	1994	162,312	119,996	SCHIFF, STEVEN H.	42,316	ZOLLINGER, PETER L.		77,680	R	73.9%	26.1%	73.9%	26.1%
1	1992	205,214	128,426	SCHIFF, STEVEN H.	76,600	ARAGON, ROBERT J.	188	51,826	R	62.6%	37.3%	62.6%	37.4%
2	2000	173,356	100,742	SKEEN, JOSEPH R.	72,614	MONTOYA, MICHAEL A.		28,128	R	58.1%	41.9%	58.1%	41.9%
2	1998	146,873	85,077	SKEEN, JOSEPH R.	61,796	BACA, E. SHIRLEY		23,281	R	57.9%	42.1%	57.9%	42.1%
2	1996	170,006	95,091	SKEEN, JOSEPH R.	74,915	BACA, E. SHIRLEY		20,176	R	55.9%	44.1%	55.9%	44.1%
2	1994	142,180	89,966	SKEEN, JOSEPH R.	45,316	CHAVEZ, BENJAMIN A.	6,898	44,650	R	63.3%	31.9%	66.5%	33.5%
2	1992	168,170	94,838	SKEEN, JOSEPH R.	73,157	SOSA, DAN	175	21,681	R	56.4%	43.5%	56.5%	43.5%
3	2000	201,019	65,979	LUTZ, LISA L.	135,040	UDALL, TOM		69,061	D	32.8%	67.2%	32.8%	67.2%
3	1998	171,649	74,266	REDMOND, BILL	91,248	UDALL, TOM	6,135	16,982	D	43.3%	53.2%	44.9%	55.1%
3	1996	185,271	56,580	REDMOND, BILL	124,594	RICHARDSON, BILL	4,097	68,014	D	30.5%	67.2%	31.2%	68.8%
3	1994	157,112	53,515	BEMIS, F. GREGG	99,900	RICHARDSON, BILL	3,697	46,385	D	34.1%	63.6%	34.9%	65.1%
3	1992	182,217	54,569	BEMIS, F. GREGG	122,850	RICHARDSON, BILL	4,798	68,281	D	29.9%	67.4%	30.8%	69.2%

NEW MEXICO

GENERAL AND PRIMARY ELECTIONS

2000 GENERAL ELECTIONS

President   Other vote was 2,058 Libertarian (Browne); 1,392 Reform (Buchanan); 361 Natural Law (Hagelin); 343 Constitution (Phillips).

Senator   Other vote was 265 write-in (Cole).

Congress   Other vote was: CD 1: 13,656 Green (Kerlinsky).

2000 PRIMARY ELECTIONS

Primary   June 6, 2000

Registration (as of June 6, 2000)		
Republican	296,285
Democratic	485,966
Green	9,332
Other Parties	17,835
No Party	100,932
TOTAL	910,350

Primary Type   Closed—Only registered Democrats and Republicans could vote in their party's primary.

Note: An asterisk (*) denotes incumbent.

	REPUBLICAN PRIMARIES			DEMOCRATIC PRIMARIES		
President	George W. Bush	62,161	82.6%	Al Gore	98,715	74.6%
	John McCain	7,619	10.1%	Bill Bradley	27,204	20.6%
	Alan Keyes	4,850	6.4%	Uncommitted Delegates	3,298	2.5%
	Uncommitted Delegates	600	0.8%	Lyndon H. LaRouche Jr.	3,063	2.3%
	TOTAL	75,230		TOTAL	132,280	
Senator	Bill Redmond	43,780	60.4%	Jeff Bingaman*	124,887	100.0%
	Steve Pearce	15,628	21.6%			
	William F. Davis	13,083	18.0%			
	TOTAL	72,491		TOTAL	124,887	
Congressional District 1	Heather A. Wilson*	25,063	100.0%	John J. Kelly	16,212	42.4%
				Sam Bregman	12,824	33.5%
				John V. Wertheim	9,209	24.1%
	TOTAL	25,063		TOTAL	38,245	
Congressional District 2	Joe R. Skeen*	23,112	100.0%	Michael A. Montoya	19,388	51.6%
				Mike Runnels	18,185	48.4%
	TOTAL	23,112		TOTAL	37,573	
Congressional District 3	Lisa L. Lutz	19,030	100.0%	Tom Udall*	49,585	82.6%
				Francesca Lobato	10,441	17.4%
	TOTAL	19,030		TOTAL	60,026	

NEW YORK

GOVERNOR

George E. Pataki (R). Re-elected 1998 to a four-year term. Previously elected 1994.

SENATORS

Hillary Rodham Clinton (D). Elected 2000 to a six-year term.

Charles E. Schumer (D). Elected 1998 to a six-year term.

REPRESENTATIVES

1. Felix J. Grucci, Jr. (R)
2. Steven Israel (D)
3. Peter T. King (R)
4. Carolyn McCarthy (D)
5. Gary L. Ackerman (D)
6. Gregory W. Meeks (D)
7. Joseph Crowley (D)
8. Jerrold Nadler (D)
9. Anthony Weiner (D)
10. Edolphus Towns (D)
11. Major R. Owens (D)
12. Nydia M. Velázquez (D)
13. Vito J. Fossella (R)
14. Carolyn B. Maloney (D)
15. Charles B. Rangel (D)
16. Jose E. Serrano (D)
17. Eliot L. Engel (D)
18. Nita M. Lowey (D)
19. Sue W. Kelly (R)
20. Benjamin A. Gilman (R)
21. Michael R. McNulty (D)
22. John E. Sweeney (R)
23. Sherwood L. Boehlert (R)
24. John M. McHugh (R)
25. James T. Walsh (R)
26. Maurice D. Hinchey (D)
27. Thomas M. Reynolds (R)
28. Louise M. Slaughter (D)
29. John J. LaFalce (D)
30. Jack Quinn (R)
31. Amory Houghton (R)

POSTWAR VOTE FOR PRESIDENT

| | | Republican | | Democratic | | Other | | Total Vote | | Major Vote | |
| | Total | | | | | | | Percentage | | | |
Year	Vote	Vote	Candidate	Vote	Candidate	Vote	Plurality	Rep.	Dem.	Rep.	Dem.
2000**	6,821,999	2,403,374	Bush, George W.	4,107,697	Gore, Al	310,928	1,704,323 R	35.2%	60.2%	36.9%	63.1%
1996**	6,316,129	1,933,492	Dole, Bob	3,756,177	Clinton, Bill	626,460	1,822,685 D	30.6%	59.5%	34.0%	66.0%
1992**	6,926,925	2,346,649	Bush, George	3,444,450	Clinton, Bill	1,135,826	1,097,801 D	33.9%	49.7%	40.5%	59.5%
1988	6,485,683	3,081,871	Bush, George	3,347,882	Dukakis, Michael S.	55,930	266,011 D	47.5%	51.6%	47.9%	52.1%
1984	6,806,810	3,664,763	Reagan, Ronald	3,119,609	Mondale, Walter F.	22,438	545,154 R	53.8%	45.8%	54.0%	46.0%
1980**	6,201,959	2,893,831	Reagan, Ronald	2,728,372	Carter, Jimmy	579,756	165,459 R	46.7%	44.0%	51.5%	48.5%
1976	6,534,170	3,100,791	Ford, Gerald R.	3,389,558	Carter, Jimmy	43,821	288,767 D	47.5%	51.9%	47.8%	52.2%
1972	7,165,919	4,192,778	Nixon, Richard M.	2,951,084	McGovern, George S.	22,057	1,241,694 R	58.5%	41.2%	58.7%	41.3%
1968	6,791,688	3,007,932	Nixon, Richard M.	3,378,470	Humphrey, Hubert H.	405,286	370,538 D	44.3%	49.7%	47.1%	52.9%
1964	7,166,275	2,243,559	Goldwater, Barry M.	4,913,102	Johnson, Lyndon B.	9,614	2,669,543 D	31.3%	68.6%	31.3%	68.7%
1960	7,291,079	3,446,419	Nixon, Richard M.	3,830,085	Kennedy, John F.	14,575	383,666 D	47.3%	52.5%	47.4%	52.6%
1956	7,095,971	4,345,506	Eisenhower, Dwight D.	2,747,944	Stevenson, Adlai E.	2,521	1,597,562 R	61.2%	38.7%	61.3%	38.7%
1952	7,128,239	3,952,813	Eisenhower, Dwight D.	3,104,601	Stevenson, Adlai E.	70,825	848,212 R	55.5%	43.6%	56.0%	44.0%
1948	6,177,337	2,841,163	Dewey, Thomas E.	2,780,204	Truman, Harry S.	555,970	60,959 R	46.0%	45.0%	50.5%	49.5%

In 2000 the other vote column includes 244,030 votes cast for Green (Nader). In 1996 the other vote column includes 503,458 votes cast for Perot. In 1992 the other vote column includes 1,090,721 votes cast for Perot. In 1980 the other column includes 467,801 votes for Independent (Anderson).

NEW YORK

POSTWAR VOTE FOR GOVERNOR

Year	Total Vote	Republican		Democratic		Other Vote	Rep.-Dem. Plurality	Percentage			
								Total Vote		Major Vote	
		Vote	Candidate	Vote	Candidate			Rep.	Dem.	Rep.	Dem.
1998	4,735,236	2,571,991	Pataki, George E.	1,570,317	Vallone, Peter F.	592,928	1,001,674 R	54.3%	33.2%	62.1%	37.9%
1994	5,208,762	2,538,702	Pataki, George E.	2,364,904	Cuomo, Mario M.	305,156	173,798 R	48.7%	45.4%	51.8%	48.2%
1990**	4,056,896	865,948	Rinfret, Pierre A.	2,157,087	Cuomo, Mario M.	1,033,861	1,291,139 D	21.3%	53.2%	28.6%	71.4%
1986	4,294,124	1,363,810	O'Rourke, Andrew P.	2,775,229	Cuomo, Mario M.	155,085	1,411,419 D	31.8%	64.6%	32.9%	67.1%
1982	5,254,891	2,494,827	Lehrman, Lew	2,675,213	Cuomo, Mario M.	84,851	180,386 D	47.5%	50.9%	48.3%	51.7%
1978	4,768,820	2,156,404	Duryea, Perry B.	2,429,272	Carey, Hugh L.	183,144	272,868 D	45.2%	50.9%	47.0%	53.0%
1974	5,293,176	2,219,667	Wilson, Malcolm	3,028,503	Carey, Hugh L.	45,006	808,836 D	41.9%	57.2%	42.3%	57.7%
1970	6,013,064	3,151,432	Rockefeller, Nelson A.	2,421,426	Goldberg, Arthur	440,206	730,006 R	52.4%	40.3%	56.5%	43.5%
1966**	6,031,585	2,690,626	Rockefeller, Nelson A.	2,298,363	O'Connor, Frank D.	1,042,596	392,263 R	44.6%	38.1%	53.9%	46.1%
1962	5,805,631	3,081,587	Rockefeller, Nelson A.	2,552,418	Morgenthau, Robert M.	171,626	529,169 R	53.1%	44.0%	54.7%	45.3%
1958	5,712,665	3,126,929	Rockefeller, Nelson A.	2,553,895	Harriman, Averell	31,841	573,034 R	54.7%	44.7%	55.0%	45.0%
1954	5,161,942	2,549,613	Ives, Irving M.	2,560,738	Harriman, Averell	51,591	11,125 D	49.4%	49.6%	49.9%	50.1%
1950	5,308,889	2,819,523	Dewey, Thomas E.	2,246,855	Lynch, Walter A.	242,511	572,668 R	53.1%	42.3%	55.7%	44.3%
1946	4,964,552	2,825,633	Dewey, Thomas E.	2,138,482	Mead, James M.	437	687,151 R	56.9%	43.1%	56.9%	43.1%

In 1990 other vote was 827,614 Conservative (London); 137,804 Right to Life (Wein); 31,089 New Alliance (Fulani); 24,611 Libertarian (Johnson) and 12,743 Socialist Workers (Gannon). In 1966 other vote was 510,023 Conservative (Adams); 507,234 Liberal (F. D. Roosevelt, Jr.); 12,730 Socialist Labor (Herder); 12,506 Socialist Workers (White) and 103 scattered.

POSTWAR VOTE FOR SENATOR

Year	Total Vote	Republican		Democratic		Other Vote	Rep.-Dem. Plurality	Percentage			
								Total Vote		Major Vote	
		Vote	Candidate	Vote	Candidate			Rep.	Dem.	Rep.	Dem.
2000	6,779,839	2,915,730	Lazio, Rick A.	3,747,310	Clinton, Hillary Rodham	116,799	831,580 D	43.0%	55.3%	43.8%	56.2%
1998	4,670,805	2,058,988	D'Amato, Alfonse M.	2,551,065	Schumer, Charles E.	60,752	492,077 D	44.1%	54.6%	44.7%	55.3%
1994	4,794,601	1,988,308	Castro, Bernadette	2,646,541	Moynihan, Daniel P.	159,752	658,233 D	41.5%	55.2%	42.9%	57.1%
1992	6,458,826	3,166,994	D'Amato, Alfonse M.	3,086,200	Abrams, Robert	205,632	80,794 R	49.0%	47.8%	50.6%	49.4%
1988	6,040,980	1,875,784	McMillan, Robert	4,048,649	Moynihan, Daniel P.	116,547	2,172,865 D	31.1%	67.0%	31.7%	68.3%
1986	4,179,447	2,378,197	D'Amato, Alfonse M.	1,723,216	Green, Mark	78,034	654,981 R	56.9%	41.2%	58.0%	42.0%
1982	4,967,729	1,696,766	Sullivan, Florence M.	3,232,146	Moynihan, Daniel P.	38,817	1,535,380 D	34.2%	65.1%	34.4%	65.6%
1980	6,014,914	2,699,652	D'Amato, Alfonse M.	2,618,661	Holtzman, Elizabeth	696,601	80,991 R	44.9%	43.5%	50.8%	49.2%
1976	6,319,755	2,836,633	Buckley, James L.	3,422,594	Moynihan, Daniel P.	60,528	585,961 D	44.9%	54.2%	45.3%	54.7%
1974	5,163,600	2,340,188	Javits, Jacob K.	1,973,781	Clark, Ramsey	849,631	366,407 R	45.3%	38.2%	54.2%	45.8%
1970**	5,904,782	1,434,472	Goodell, Charles	2,171,232	Ottinger, Richard L.	2,299,078	116,958 C	24.3%	36.8%	39.8%	60.2%
1968**	6,581,587	3,269,772	Javits, Jacob K.	2,150,695	O'Dwyer, Paul	1,161,120	1,119,077 R	49.7%	32.7%	60.3%	39.7%
1964	7,151,686	3,104,056	Keating, Kenneth B.	3,823,749	Kennedy, Robert F.	223,881	719,693 D	43.4%	53.5%	44.8%	55.2%
1962	5,700,186	3,269,417	Javits, Jacob K.	2,289,341	Donovan, James B.	141,428	980,076 R	57.4%	40.2%	58.8%	41.2%
1958	5,602,088	2,842,942	Keating, Kenneth B.	2,709,950	Hogan, Frank S.	49,196	132,992 R	50.7%	48.4%	51.2%	48.8%
1956	6,991,136	3,723,933	Javits, Jacob K.	3,265,159	Wagner, Robert F.	2,044	458,774 R	53.3%	46.7%	53.3%	46.7%
1952	6,980,259	3,853,934	Ives, Irving M.	2,521,736	Cashmore, John	604,589	1,332,198 R	55.2%	36.1%	60.4%	39.6%
1950	5,228,403	2,367,353	Hanley, Joe R.	2,632,313	Lehman, Herbert H.	228,737	264,960 D	45.3%	50.3%	47.4%	52.6%
1949S	4,966,878	2,384,381	Dulles, John Foster	2,582,438	Lehman, Herbert H.	59	198,057 D	48.0%	52.0%	48.0%	52.0%
1946	4,867,564	2,559,365	Ives, Irving M.	2,308,112	Lehman, Herbert H.	87	251,253 R	52.6%	47.4%	52.6%	47.4%

In 1970 James L. Buckley, the Conservative candidate, polled 2,288,190 votes (38.8% of the total vote) and won the election with a 116,958-vote plurality. In 1968 other vote was 1,139,402 Conservative (Buckley); 8,775 Freedom and Peace (Ferguson); 7,964 Socialist Labor (Emanuel); 4,979 Socialist Workers (Garza). The 1949 election was for a short term to fill a vacancy.

NEW YORK

Districts Established June 9, 1992

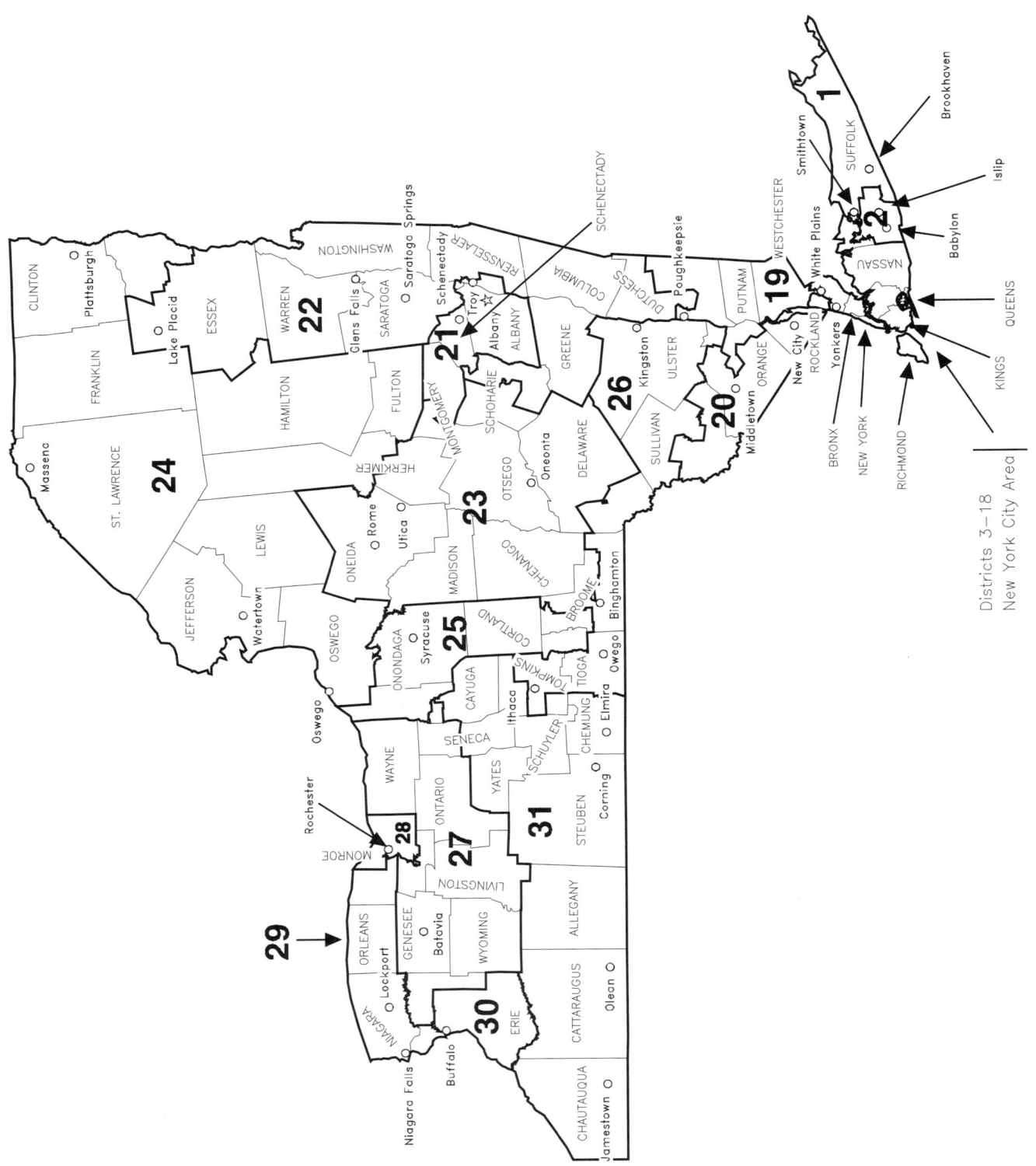

Districts 3–18
New York City Area

NEW YORK CITY AREA

CONGRESSIONAL DISTRICTS

Districts Established October 1997

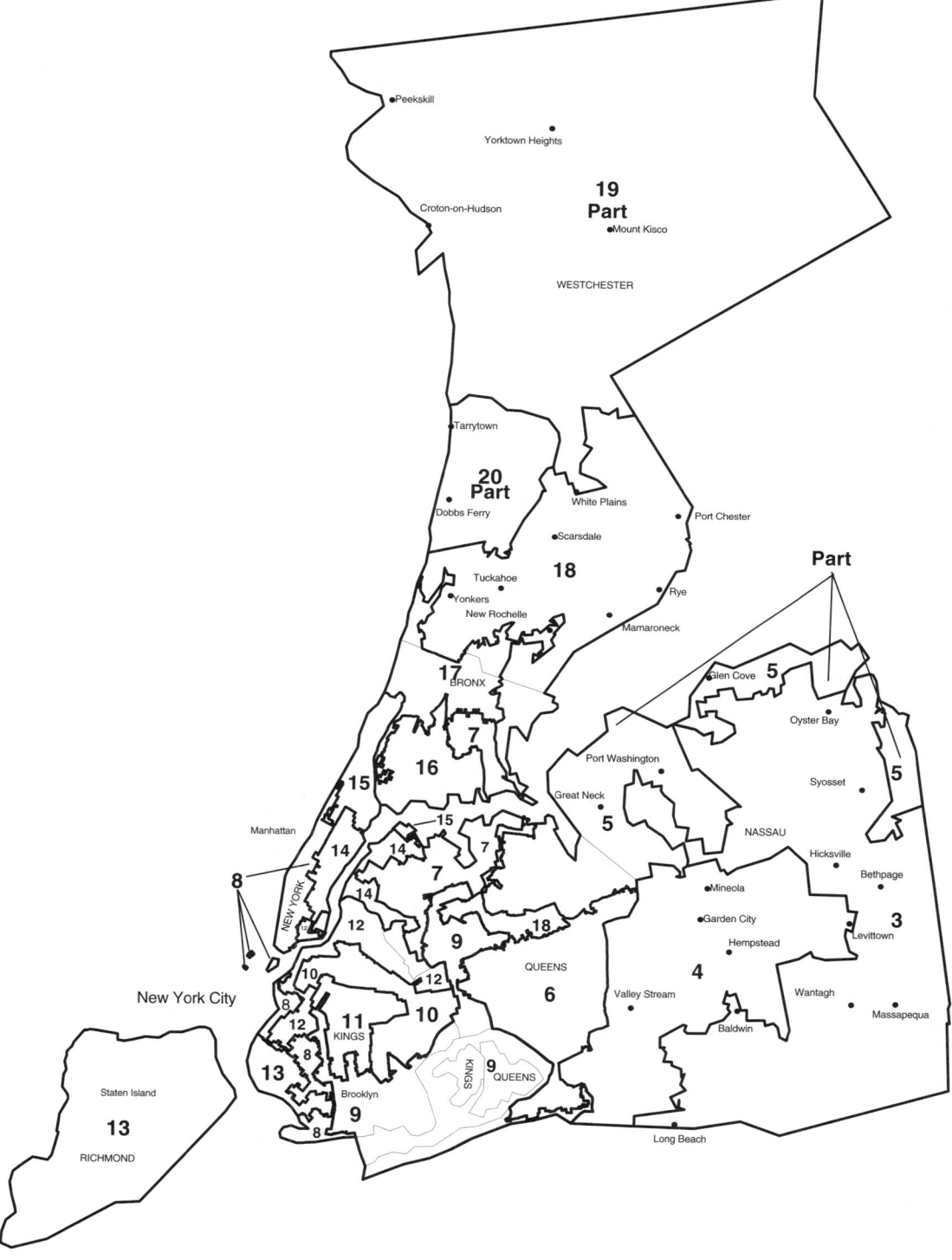

NEW YORK

PRESIDENT 2000

2000 Census Population	County	Total Vote	Republican	Democratic	Green (Nader)	Other	Rep.-Dem. Plurality	Percentage of Total Vote		
								Rep.	Dem.	Green
294,565	ALBANY	141,969	47,624	85,617	7,182	1,546	37,993 D	33.5%	60.3%	5.1%
49,927	ALLEGANY	18,689	11,436	6,336	657	260	5,100 R	61.2%	33.9%	3.5%
1,332,650	BRONX	308,048	36,245	265,801	4,265	1,737	229,556 D	11.8%	86.3%	1.4%
200,536	BROOME	87,063	36,946	45,381	3,826	910	8,435 D	42.4%	52.1%	4.4%
83,955	CATTARAUGUS	33,733	18,382	13,697	1,094	560	4,685 R	54.5%	40.6%	3.2%
81,963	CAYUGA	33,978	14,988	17,031	1,448	511	2,043 D	44.1%	50.1%	4.3%
139,750	CHAUTAUQUA	58,720	29,064	27,016	1,888	752	2,048 R	49.5%	46.0%	3.2%
91,070	CHEMUNG	37,710	18,779	17,424	1,195	312	1,355 R	49.8%	46.2%	3.2%
51,401	CHENANGO	20,250	10,033	9,112	869	236	921 R	49.5%	45.0%	4.3%
79,894	CLINTON	30,555	13,274	15,542	1,205	534	2,268 D	43.4%	50.9%	3.9%
63,094	COLUMBIA	28,691	13,153	13,489	1,707	342	336 D	45.8%	47.0%	5.9%
48,599	CORTLAND	20,723	9,857	9,691	943	232	166 R	47.6%	46.8%	4.6%
48,055	DELAWARE	20,175	10,662	8,450	833	230	2,212 R	52.8%	41.9%	4.1%
280,150	DUTCHESS	111,762	52,669	52,390	5,553	1,150	279 R	47.1%	46.9%	5.0%
950,265	ERIE	424,654	160,176	240,176	18,166	6,136	80,000 D	37.7%	56.6%	4.3%
38,851	ESSEX	17,932	8,822	7,927	848	335	895 R	49.2%	44.2%	4.7%
51,134	FRANKLIN	17,447	7,643	8,870	658	276	1,227 D	43.8%	50.8%	3.8%
55,073	FULTON	21,671	11,434	9,314	668	255	2,120 R	52.8%	43.0%	3.1%
60,370	GENESEE	26,069	14,459	10,191	924	495	4,268 R	55.5%	39.1%	3.5%
48,195	GREENE	21,094	11,332	8,480	924	358	2,852 R	53.7%	40.2%	4.4%
5,379	HAMILTON	3,682	2,388	1,114	133	47	1,274 R	64.9%	30.3%	3.6%
64,427	HERKIMER	27,705	14,147	12,224	969	365	1,923 R	51.1%	44.1%	3.5%
111,738	JEFFERSON	36,418	18,192	16,799	1,029	398	1,393 R	50.0%	46.1%	2.8%
2,465,326	KINGS	617,105	96,605	497,468	19,977	3,055	400,863 D	15.7%	80.6%	3.2%
26,944	LEWIS	10,923	6,103	4,333	324	163	1,770 R	55.9%	39.7%	3.0%
64,328	LIVINGSTON	27,223	15,244	10,476	1,053	450	4,768 R	56.0%	38.5%	3.9%
69,441	MADISON	28,366	14,879	12,017	1,092	378	2,862 R	52.5%	42.4%	3.8%
735,343	MONROE	317,762	141,266	161,743	11,520	3,233	20,477 D	44.5%	50.9%	3.6%
49,708	MONTGOMERY	20,809	9,765	10,249	487	308	484 D	46.9%	49.3%	2.3%
1,334,544	NASSAU	589,707	226,954	341,610	14,780	6,363	114,656 D	38.5%	57.9%	2.5%
1,537,195	NEW YORK	563,232	79,921	449,300	30,923	3,088	369,379 D	14.2%	79.8%	5.5%
219,846	NIAGARA	93,257	40,952	47,781	3,257	1,267	6,829 D	43.9%	51.2%	3.5%
235,469	ONEIDA	95,996	47,603	43,933	3,160	1,300	3,670 R	49.6%	45.8%	3.3%
458,336	ONONDAGA	203,629	83,678	109,896	7,670	2,385	26,218 D	41.1%	54.0%	3.8%
100,224	ONTARIO	45,948	23,885	19,761	1,793	509	4,124 R	52.0%	43.0%	3.9%
341,367	ORANGE	126,549	62,852	58,170	4,192	1,335	4,682 R	49.7%	46.0%	3.3%
44,171	ORLEANS	15,843	9,202	5,991	474	176	3,211 R	58.1%	37.8%	3.0%
122,377	OSWEGO	48,473	23,249	22,857	1,699	668	392 R	48.0%	47.2%	3.5%
61,676	OTSEGO	25,358	12,219	11,460	1,419	260	759 R	48.2%	45.2%	5.6%
95,745	PUTNAM	42,547	21,853	18,525	1,730	439	3,328 R	51.4%	43.5%	4.1%
2,229,379	QUEENS	555,930	122,052	416,967	13,720	3,191	294,915 D	22.0%	75.0%	2.5%
152,538	RENSSELAER	68,436	29,562	34,808	3,291	775	5,246 D	43.2%	50.9%	4.8%
443,728	RICHMOND	142,121	63,903	73,828	3,550	840	9,925 D	45.0%	51.9%	2.5%
286,753	ROCKLAND	122,580	48,441	69,530	3,502	1,107	21,089 D	39.5%	56.7%	2.9%
111,931	ST. LAWRENCE	39,779	16,449	21,386	1,488	456	4,937 D	41.4%	53.8%	3.7%
200,635	SARATOGA	95,057	46,623	43,359	4,149	926	3,264 R	49.0%	45.6%	4.4%
146,555	SCHENECTADY	66,946	27,961	35,534	2,750	701	7,573 D	41.8%	53.1%	4.1%
31,582	SCHOHARIE	13,548	7,459	5,390	551	148	2,069 R	55.1%	39.8%	4.1%
19,224	SCHUYLER	8,153	4,381	3,301	369	102	1,080 R	53.7%	40.5%	4.5%
33,342	SENECA	14,333	6,734	6,841	560	198	107 D	47.0%	47.7%	3.9%
98,726	STEUBEN	40,563	24,200	14,600	1,248	515	9,600 R	59.7%	36.0%	3.1%
1,419,369	SUFFOLK	573,866	240,992	306,306	18,130	8,438	65,314 D	42.0%	53.4%	3.2%
73,966	SULLIVAN	28,524	12,703	14,348	1,156	317	1,645 D	44.5%	50.3%	4.1%
51,784	TIOGA	22,454	12,239	9,170	846	199	3,069 R	54.5%	40.8%	3.8%
96,501	TOMPKINS	40,060	13,351	21,807	4,548	354	8,456 D	33.3%	54.4%	11.4%

NEW YORK

PRESIDENT 2000

2000 Census Population	County	Total Vote	Republican	Democratic	Green (Nader)	Other	Rep.-Dem. Plurality	Percentage of Total Vote		
								Rep.	Dem.	Green
177,749	ULSTER	78,225	33,447	38,162	5,732	884	4,715 D	42.8%	48.8%	7.3%
63,303	WARREN	28,621	14,993	12,193	1,177	258	2,800 R	52.4%	42.6%	4.1%
61,042	WASHINGTON	23,555	12,596	9,641	997	321	2,955 R	53.5%	40.9%	4.2%
93,765	WAYNE	38,329	21,701	14,977	1,202	449	6,724 R	56.6%	39.1%	3.1%
923,459	WESTCHESTER	371,775	139,278	218,010	11,596	2,891	78,732 D	37.5%	58.6%	3.1%
43,424	WYOMING	17,627	10,809	5,935	548	335	4,874 R	61.3%	33.7%	3.1%
24,621	YATES	10,052	5,565	3,962	386	139	1,603 R	55.4%	39.4%	3.8%
18,976,457	TOTAL	6,821,999	2,403,374	4,107,697	244,030	66,898	1,704,323 D	35.2%	60.2%	3.6%

NEW YORK CITY

BRONX COUNTY
PRESIDENT 2000

2000 Census Population	Assembly District	Total Vote	Republican	Democratic	Green (Nader)	Other	Rep.-Dem. Plurality	Percentage of Total Vote		
								Rep.	Dem.	Green
	DISTRICT 74	27,707	1,431	25,932	163	181	24,501 D	5.2%	93.6%	0.6%
	DISTRICT 75	26,998	1,615	25,075	177	131	23,460 D	6.0%	92.9%	0.7%
	DISTRICT 76	29,855	2,674	26,766	275	140	24,092 D	9.0%	89.7%	0.9%
	DISTRICT 77	27,021	1,044	25,727	150	100	24,683 D	3.9%	95.2%	0.6%
	DISTRICT 78	22,296	1,429	20,588	179	100	19,159 D	6.4%	92.3%	0.8%
	DISTRICT 79	28,679	1,573	26,764	209	133	25,191 D	5.5%	93.3%	0.7%
	DISTRICT 80	31,712	6,780	23,981	679	272	17,201 D	21.4%	75.6%	2.1%
	DISTRICT 81	38,475	7,373	29,542	1,253	307	22,169 D	19.2%	76.8%	3.3%
	DISTRICT 82	41,164	10,059	30,014	829	262	19,955 D	24.4%	72.9%	2.0%
	DISTRICT 83	34,156	2,267	31,412	351	126	29,145 D	6.6%	92.0%	1.0%
1,332,650	TOTAL	308,063	36,245	265,801	4,265	1,752	229,556 D	11.8%	86.3%	1.4%

NEW YORK CITY

KINGS COUNTY
PRESIDENT 2000

2000 Census Population	Assembly District	Total Vote	Republican	Democratic	Green (Nader)	Other	Rep.-Dem. Plurality	Percentage of Total Vote		
								Rep.	Dem.	Green
	DISTRICT 39	38,784	8,469	29,569	583	163	21,100 D	21.8%	76.2%	1.5%
	DISTRICT 40	29,587	857	28,404	187	139	27,547 D	2.9%	96.0%	0.6%
	DISTRICT 41	38,445	6,091	31,653	553	148	25,562 D	15.8%	82.3%	1.4%
	DISTRICT 42	26,309	1,585	24,318	314	92	22,733 D	6.0%	92.4%	1.2%
	DISTRICT 43	29,189	2,307	26,473	341	68	24,166 D	7.9%	90.7%	1.2%
	DISTRICT 44	39,717	6,329	29,880	3,273	235	23,551 D	15.9%	75.2%	8.2%
	DISTRICT 45	31,630	8,615	22,256	605	154	13,641 D	27.2%	70.4%	1.9%
	DISTRICT 46	30,208	6,845	22,489	664	210	15,644 D	22.7%	74.4%	2.2%
	DISTRICT 47	26,795	8,019	18,187	454	135	10,168 D	29.9%	67.9%	1.7%
	DISTRICT 48	26,459	9,998	15,871	449	141	5,873 D	37.8%	60.0%	1.7%

NEW YORK CITY

KINGS COUNTY
PRESIDENT 2000

2000 Census Population	Assembly District	Total Vote	Republican	Democratic	Green (Nader)	Other	Rep.-Dem. Plurality	Percentage of Total Vote		
								Rep.	Dem.	Green
	DISTRICT 49	25,873	9,970	15,228	516	159	5,258 D	38.5%	58.9%	2.0%
	DISTRICT 50	27,114	5,622	19,219	2,116	157	13,597 D	20.7%	70.9%	7.8%
	DISTRICT 51	26,014	3,288	21,036	1,534	156	17,748 D	12.6%	80.9%	5.9%
	DISTRICT 52	46,387	11,342	30,967	3,755	323	19,625 D	24.5%	66.8%	8.1%
	DISTRICT 53	23,358	2,047	19,770	1,406	135	17,723 D	8.8%	84.6%	6.0%
	DISTRICT 54	22,866	1,607	20,926	227	106	19,319 D	7.0%	91.5%	1.0%
	DISTRICT 55	28,427	652	27,516	142	117	26,864 D	2.3%	96.8%	0.5%
	DISTRICT 56	31,197	668	30,045	322	162	29,377 D	2.1%	96.3%	1.0%
	DISTRICT 57	37,289	1,217	33,514	2,419	139	32,297 D	3.3%	89.9%	6.5%
	DISTRICT 58	31,589	1,081	30,192	198	118	29,111 D	3.4%	95.6%	0.6%
2,465,326	TOTAL	617,237	96,609	497,513	20,058	3,057	400,904 D	15.7%	80.6%	3.2%

NEW YORK CITY

NEW YORK COUNTY
PRESIDENT 2000

2000 Census Population	Assembly District	Total Vote	Republican	Democratic	Green (Nader)	Other	Rep.-Dem. Plurality	Percentage of Total Vote		
								Rep.	Dem.	Green
	DISTRICT 62	33,570	5,331	25,741	2,267	231	20,410 D	15.9%	76.7%	6.8%
	DISTRICT 63	51,427	8,211	39,188	3,693	335	30,977 D	16.0%	76.2%	7.2%
	DISTRICT 64	54,786	8,783	42,163	3,465	375	33,380 D	16.0%	77.0%	6.3%
	DISTRICT 65	56,720	13,563	40,422	2,483	252	26,859 D	23.9%	71.3%	4.4%
	DISTRICT 66	60,849	6,842	47,356	6,245	406	40,514 D	11.2%	77.8%	10.3%
	DISTRICT 67	62,777	9,248	49,980	3,224	325	40,732 D	14.7%	79.6%	5.1%
	DISTRICT 68	37,144	2,429	33,680	835	200	31,251 D	6.5%	90.7%	2.2%
	DISTRICT 69	52,899	4,550	43,978	4,063	308	39,428 D	8.6%	83.1%	7.7%
	DISTRICT 70	37,964	1,062	35,971	749	182	34,909 D	2.8%	94.8%	2.0%
	DISTRICT 71	37,986	2,907	33,308	1,574	197	30,401 D	7.7%	87.7%	4.1%
	DISTRICT 72	26,883	2,157	23,973	608	145	21,816 D	8.0%	89.2%	2.3%
	DISTRICT 73	58,001	17,030	38,763	1,966	242	21,733 D	29.4%	66.8%	3.4%
1,537,195	TOTAL	571,006	82,113	454,523	31,172	3,198	372,410 D	14.4%	79.6%	5.5%

NEW YORK CITY

QUEENS COUNTY
PRESIDENT 2000

2000 Census Population	Assembly District	Total Vote	Republican	Democratic	Green (Nader)	Other	Rep.-Dem. Plurality	Percentage of Total Vote		
								Rep.	Dem.	Green
	DISTRICT 23	38,659	12,770	24,712	923	254	11,942 D	33.0%	63.9%	2.4%
	DISTRICT 24	45,601	12,671	31,509	1,173	248	18,838 D	27.8%	69.1%	2.6%
	DISTRICT 25	26,363	7,324	18,259	639	141	10,935 D	27.8%	69.3%	2.4%
	DISTRICT 26	45,675	15,320	28,861	1,208	286	13,541 D	33.5%	63.2%	2.6%
	DISTRICT 27	37,773	8,613	28,010	918	232	19,397 D	22.8%	74.2%	2.4%
	DISTRICT 28	41,968	10,945	29,505	1,301	217	18,560 D	26.1%	70.3%	3.1%
	DISTRICT 29	38,454	2,512	35,445	387	110	32,933 D	6.5%	92.2%	1.0%
	DISTRICT 30	32,986	10,109	21,416	1,198	263	11,307 D	30.6%	64.9%	3.6%
	DISTRICT 31	31,830	2,325	29,023	315	167	26,698 D	7.3%	91.2%	1.0%
	DISTRICT 32	34,007	2,413	31,063	376	155	28,650 D	7.1%	91.3%	1.1%

NEW YORK CITY

QUEENS COUNTY
PRESIDENT 2000

2000 Census Population	Assembly District	Total Vote	Republican	Democratic	Green (Nader)	Other	Rep.-Dem. Plurality	Percentage of Total Vote		
								Rep.	Dem.	Green
	DISTRICT 33	42,490	4,448	37,312	544	186	32,864 D	10.5%	87.8%	1.3%
	DISTRICT 34	23,492	4,193	18,750	426	123	14,557 D	17.8%	79.8%	1.8%
	DISTRICT 35	24,504	3,425	20,595	389	95	17,170 D	14.0%	84.0%	1.6%
	DISTRICT 36	33,879	8,763	22,728	2,080	308	13,965 D	25.9%	67.1%	6.1%
	DISTRICT 37	26,456	5,160	20,121	949	226	14,961 D	19.5%	76.1%	3.6%
	DISTRICT 38	31,854	11,061	19,658	894	241	8,597 D	34.7%	61.7%	2.8%
2,229,379	TOTAL	555,991	122,052	416,967	13,720	3,252	294,915 D	22.0%	75.0%	2.5%

NEW YORK CITY

RICHMOND COUNTY
PRESIDENT 2000

2000 Census Population	Assembly District	Total Vote	Republican	Democratic	Green (Nader)	Other	Rep.-Dem. Plurality	Percentage of Total Vote		
								Rep.	Dem.	Green
	DISTRICT 59	43,134	14,553	26,972	1,317	292	12,419 D	33.7%	62.5%	3.1%
	DISTRICT 60	46,009	20,211	24,467	1,072	259	4,256 D	43.9%	53.2%	2.3%
	DISTRICT 61	52,986	29,139	22,389	1,161	297	6,750 R	55.0%	42.3%	2.2%
443,728	TOTAL	142,129	63,903	73,828	3,550	848	9,925 D	45.0%	51.9%	2.5%

Note: Assembly district results for New York city boroughs did not add to the total vote certified by the state, which were: Bronx 308,048; Kings 617,105; New York 563,232; Queens 555,930; Richmond 142,121.

NEW YORK CITY

PRESIDENT 2000

2000 Census Population	County	Total Vote	Republican	Democratic	Green (Nader)	Other	Rep.-Dem. Plurality	Percentage of Total Vote		
								Rep.	Dem.	Green
1,332,650	BRONX	308,048	36,245	265,801	4,265	1,737	229,556 D	11.8%	86.3%	1.4%
2,465,326	KINGS	617,105	96,605	497,468	19,977	3,055	400,863 D	15.7%	80.6%	3.2%
1,537,195	NEW YORK	563,232	79,921	449,300	30,923	3,088	369,379 D	14.2%	79.8%	5.5%
2,229,379	QUEENS	555,930	122,052	416,967	13,720	3,191	294,915 D	22.0%	75.0%	2.5%
443,728	RICHMOND	142,121	63,903	73,828	3,550	840	9,925 D	45.0%	51.9%	2.5%
8,008,278	TOTAL	2,186,436	398,726	1,703,364	72,435	11,911	1,304,638 D	18.2%	77.9%	3.3%

Note: The New York city totals are based on state certified returns, which differ slightly from returns certified by city election officials that are used in the Assembly district tables.

NEW YORK

SENATOR 2000

2000 Census Population	County	Total Vote	Republican	Democratic	Other	Rep.-Dem. Plurality		Percentage			
								Total Vote		Major Vote	
								Rep.	Dem.	Rep.	Dem.
294,565	ALBANY	141,391	56,485	81,867	3,039	25,382	D	39.9%	57.9%	40.8%	59.2%
49,927	ALLEGANY	18,034	11,255	6,364	415	4,891	R	62.4%	35.3%	63.9%	36.1%
1,332,650	BRONX	307,875	44,078	261,378	2,419	217,300	D	14.3%	84.9%	14.4%	85.6%
200,536	BROOME	86,625	42,760	41,819	2,046	941	R	49.4%	48.3%	50.6%	49.4%
83,955	CATTARAUGUS	33,375	18,539	13,955	881	4,584	R	55.5%	41.8%	57.1%	42.9%
81,963	CAYUGA	33,856	16,203	16,931	722	728	D	47.9%	50.0%	48.9%	51.1%
139,750	CHAUTAUQUA	58,084	31,184	25,787	1,113	5,397	R	53.7%	44.4%	54.7%	45.3%
91,070	CHEMUNG	37,372	20,381	16,419	572	3,962	R	54.5%	43.9%	55.4%	44.6%
51,401	CHENANGO	20,158	11,110	8,546	502	2,564	R	55.1%	42.4%	56.5%	43.5%
79,894	CLINTON	30,231	15,185	14,343	703	842	R	50.2%	47.4%	51.4%	48.6%
63,094	COLUMBIA	28,333	14,859	12,685	789	2,174	R	52.4%	44.8%	53.9%	46.1%
48,599	CORTLAND	20,635	10,736	9,472	427	1,264	R	52.0%	45.9%	53.1%	46.9%
48,055	DELAWARE	19,952	11,523	7,918	511	3,605	R	57.8%	39.7%	59.3%	40.7%
280,150	DUTCHESS	110,501	62,393	45,658	2,450	16,735	R	56.5%	41.3%	57.7%	42.3%
950,265	ERIE	423,481	177,168	237,770	8,543	60,602	D	41.8%	56.1%	42.7%	57.3%
38,851	ESSEX	17,708	10,012	7,222	474	2,790	R	56.5%	40.8%	58.1%	41.9%
51,134	FRANKLIN	17,235	8,229	8,665	341	436	D	47.7%	50.3%	48.7%	51.3%
55,073	FULTON	21,460	12,322	8,739	399	3,583	R	57.4%	40.7%	58.5%	41.5%
60,370	GENESEE	25,765	15,198	9,947	620	5,251	R	59.0%	38.6%	60.4%	39.6%
48,195	GREENE	20,964	12,621	7,821	522	4,800	R	60.2%	37.3%	61.7%	38.3%
5,379	HAMILTON	3,653	2,474	1,119	60	1,355	R	67.7%	30.6%	68.9%	31.1%
64,427	HERKIMER	27,503	14,880	12,007	616	2,873	R	54.1%	43.7%	55.3%	44.7%
111,738	JEFFERSON	36,137	17,121	16,044	2,972	1,077	R	47.4%	44.4%	51.6%	48.4%
2,465,326	KINGS	615,267	140,788	467,699	6,780	326,911	D	22.9%	76.0%	23.1%	76.9%
26,944	LEWIS	10,805	6,058	4,040	707	2,018	R	56.1%	37.4%	60.0%	40.0%
64,328	LIVINGSTON	26,737	15,925	10,186	626	5,739	R	59.6%	38.1%	61.0%	39.0%
69,441	MADISON	28,165	15,837	11,689	639	4,148	R	56.2%	41.5%	57.5%	42.5%
735,343	MONROE	315,972	157,820	152,603	5,549	5,217	R	49.9%	48.3%	50.8%	49.2%
49,708	MONTGOMERY	20,488	10,357	9,742	389	615	R	50.6%	47.5%	51.5%	48.5%
1,334,544	NASSAU	584,671	312,252	263,962	8,457	48,290	R	53.4%	45.1%	54.2%	45.8%
1,537,195	NEW YORK	561,832	119,263	433,599	8,970	314,336	D	21.2%	77.2%	21.6%	78.4%
219,846	NIAGARA	92,577	43,432	47,356	1,789	3,924	D	46.9%	51.2%	47.8%	52.2%
235,469	ONEIDA	95,624	52,431	41,138	2,055	11,293	R	54.8%	43.0%	56.0%	44.0%
458,336	ONONDAGA	202,843	92,132	106,796	3,915	14,664	D	45.4%	52.6%	46.3%	53.7%
100,224	ONTARIO	45,588	25,905	18,753	930	7,152	R	56.8%	41.1%	58.0%	42.0%
341,367	ORANGE	125,276	74,328	48,515	2,433	25,813	R	59.3%	38.7%	60.5%	39.5%
44,171	ORLEANS	15,739	9,285	6,194	260	3,091	R	59.0%	39.4%	60.0%	40.0%
122,377	OSWEGO	48,063	23,921	23,080	1,062	841	R	49.8%	48.0%	50.9%	49.1%
61,676	OTSEGO	25,080	13,309	11,079	692	2,230	R	53.1%	44.2%	54.6%	45.4%
95,745	PUTNAM	42,215	26,384	15,024	807	11,360	R	62.5%	35.6%	63.7%	36.3%
2,229,379	QUEENS	552,717	162,747	384,457	5,513	221,710	D	29.4%	69.6%	29.7%	70.3%
152,538	RENSSELAER	67,945	33,056	33,287	1,602	231	D	48.7%	49.0%	49.8%	50.2%
443,728	RICHMOND	140,979	81,584	57,816	1,579	23,768	R	57.9%	41.0%	58.5%	41.5%
286,753	ROCKLAND	122,016	63,983	56,340	1,693	7,643	R	52.4%	46.2%	53.2%	46.8%
111,931	ST. LAWRENCE	39,648	16,887	20,864	1,897	3,977	D	42.6%	52.6%	44.7%	55.3%
200,635	SARATOGA	94,106	51,106	41,165	1,835	9,941	R	54.3%	43.7%	55.4%	44.6%
146,555	SCHENECTADY	66,331	32,271	32,800	1,260	529	D	48.7%	49.4%	49.6%	50.4%
31,582	SCHOHARIE	13,421	7,825	5,303	293	2,522	R	58.3%	39.5%	59.6%	40.4%
19,224	SCHUYLER	8,081	4,644	3,247	190	1,397	R	57.5%	40.2%	58.9%	41.1%
33,342	SENECA	14,287	7,297	6,693	297	604	R	51.1%	46.8%	52.2%	47.8%
98,726	STEUBEN	39,832	24,896	14,124	812	10,772	R	62.5%	35.5%	63.8%	36.2%
1,419,369	SUFFOLK	570,387	326,230	234,418	9,739	91,812	R	57.2%	41.1%	58.2%	41.8%
73,966	SULLIVAN	28,207	14,723	12,813	671	1,910	R	52.2%	45.4%	53.5%	46.5%
51,784	TIOGA	22,286	13,282	8,579	425	4,703	R	59.6%	38.5%	60.8%	39.2%
96,501	TOMPKINS	39,635	15,699	22,672	1,264	6,973	D	39.6%	57.2%	40.9%	59.1%

NEW YORK

SENATOR 2000

2000 Census Population	County	Total Vote	Republican	Democratic	Other	Rep.-Dem. Plurality		Percentage			
								Total Vote		Major Vote	
								Rep.	Dem.	Rep.	Dem.
177,749	ULSTER	77,406	39,249	35,862	2,295	3,387	R	50.7%	46.3%	52.3%	47.7%
63,303	WARREN	28,180	16,530	11,105	545	5,425	R	58.7%	39.4%	59.8%	40.2%
61,042	WASHINGTON	23,459	13,483	9,183	793	4,300	R	57.5%	39.1%	59.5%	40.5%
93,765	WAYNE	38,033	22,717	14,527	789	8,190	R	59.7%	38.2%	61.0%	39.0%
923,459	WESTCHESTER	368,032	174,533	188,038	5,461	13,505	D	47.4%	51.1%	48.1%	51.9%
43,424	WYOMING	17,515	10,914	6,134	467	4,780	R	62.3%	35.0%	64.0%	36.0%
24,621	YATES	10,066	5,931	3,952	183	1,979	R	58.9%	39.3%	60.0%	40.0%
18,976,457	TOTAL	6,779,839	2,915,730	3,747,310	116,799	831,580	D	43.0%	55.3%	43.8%	56.2%

NEW YORK

BRONX COUNTY SENATOR 2000

2000 Census Population	Assembly District	Total Vote	Republican	Democratic	Other	Rep.-Dem. Plurality		Percentage			
								Total Vote		Major Vote	
								Rep.	Dem.	Rep.	Dem.
	DISTRICT 74	27,944	1,154	26,617	173	25,463	D	4.1%	95.3%	4.2%	95.8%
	DISTRICT 75	27,210	1,396	25,657	157	24,261	D	5.1%	94.3%	5.2%	94.8%
	DISTRICT 76	29,929	2,659	27,069	201	24,410	D	8.9%	90.4%	8.9%	91.1%
	DISTRICT 77	27,172	840	26,182	150	25,342	D	3.1%	96.4%	3.1%	96.9%
	DISTRICT 78	22,384	1,280	20,986	118	19,706	D	5.7%	93.8%	5.7%	94.3%
	DISTRICT 79	28,874	1,412	27,301	161	25,889	D	4.9%	94.6%	4.9%	95.1%
	DISTRICT 80	31,362	8,875	22,162	325	13,287	D	28.3%	70.7%	28.6%	71.4%
	DISTRICT 81	38,149	10,844	26,780	525	15,936	D	28.4%	70.2%	28.8%	71.2%
	DISTRICT 82	40,526	13,140	26,985	401	13,845	D	32.4%	66.6%	32.7%	67.3%
	DISTRICT 83	34,328	2,478	31,639	211	29,161	D	7.2%	92.2%	7.3%	92.7%
1,332,650	TOTAL	307,878	44,078	261,378	2,422	217,300	D	14.3%	84.9%	14.4%	85.6%

NEW YORK

KINGS COUNTY SENATOR 2000

2000 Census Population	Assembly District	Total Vote	Republican	Democratic	Other	Rep.-Dem. Plurality		Percentage			
								Total Vote		Major Vote	
								Rep.	Dem.	Rep.	Dem.
	DISTRICT 39	38,476	12,579	25,643	254	13,064	D	32.7%	66.6%	32.9%	67.1%
	DISTRICT 40	29,650	695	28,809	146	28,114	D	2.3%	97.2%	2.4%	97.6%
	DISTRICT 41	38,527	10,553	27,704	270	17,151	D	27.4%	71.9%	27.6%	72.4%
	DISTRICT 42	26,141	2,238	23,745	158	21,507	D	8.6%	90.8%	8.6%	91.4%
	DISTRICT 43	29,297	2,935	26,230	132	23,295	D	10.0%	89.5%	10.1%	89.9%
	DISTRICT 44	39,438	9,421	29,142	875	19,721	D	23.9%	73.9%	24.4%	75.6%
	DISTRICT 45	31,116	15,794	15,034	288	760	R	50.8%	48.3%	51.2%	48.8%
	DISTRICT 46	29,720	9,992	19,369	359	9,377	D	33.6%	65.2%	34.0%	66.0%
	DISTRICT 47	26,549	12,582	13,753	214	1,171	D	47.4%	51.8%	47.8%	52.2%
	DISTRICT 48	26,268	16,440	9,617	211	6,823	R	62.6%	36.6%	63.1%	36.9%

NEW YORK

KINGS COUNTY
SENATOR 2000

2000 Census Population	Assembly District	Total Vote	Republican	Democratic	Other	Rep.-Dem. Plurality		Percentage			
---	---	---	---	---	---	---	---	Total Vote		Major Vote	
								Rep.	Dem.	Rep.	Dem.
	DISTRICT 49	25,543	14,607	10,710	226	3,897	R	57.2%	41.9%	57.7%	42.3%
	DISTRICT 50	27,041	7,003	19,470	568	12,467	D	25.9%	72.0%	26.5%	73.5%
	DISTRICT 51	26,030	3,634	21,967	429	18,333	D	14.0%	84.4%	14.2%	85.8%
	DISTRICT 52	46,028	14,967	29,995	1,066	15,028	D	32.5%	65.2%	33.3%	66.7%
	DISTRICT 53	23,518	2,305	20,770	443	18,465	D	9.8%	88.3%	10.0%	90.0%
	DISTRICT 54	22,895	1,420	21,299	176	19,879	D	6.2%	93.0%	6.3%	93.7%
	DISTRICT 55	28,742	495	28,109	138	27,614	D	1.7%	97.8%	1.7%	98.3%
	DISTRICT 56	31,362	574	30,625	163	30,051	D	1.8%	97.7%	1.8%	98.2%
	DISTRICT 57	37,293	1,516	35,223	554	33,707	D	4.1%	94.4%	4.1%	95.9%
	DISTRICT 58	31,665	1,038	30,485	142	29,447	D	3.3%	96.3%	3.3%	96.7%
2,465,326	TOTAL	615,299	140,788	467,699	6,812	326,911	D	22.9%	76.0%	23.1%	76.9%

NEW YORK

NEW YORK COUNTY
SENATOR 2000

2000 Census Population	Assembly District	Total Vote	Republican	Democratic	Other	Rep.-Dem. Plurality		Percentage			
---	---	---	---	---	---	---	---	Total Vote		Major Vote	
								Rep.	Dem.	Rep.	Dem.
	DISTRICT 62	33,707	7,639	25,356	712	17,717	D	22.7%	75.2%	23.2%	76.8%
	DISTRICT 63	51,138	12,112	37,967	1,059	25,855	D	23.7%	74.2%	24.2%	75.8%
	DISTRICT 64	54,751	13,338	40,388	1,025	27,050	D	24.4%	73.8%	24.8%	75.2%
	DISTRICT 65	56,254	20,895	34,577	782	13,682	D	37.1%	61.5%	37.7%	62.3%
	DISTRICT 66	60,308	11,097	47,707	1,504	36,610	D	18.4%	79.1%	18.9%	81.1%
	DISTRICT 67	62,132	15,270	45,881	981	30,611	D	24.6%	73.8%	25.0%	75.0%
	DISTRICT 68	37,396	2,804	34,255	337	31,451	D	7.5%	91.6%	7.6%	92.4%
	DISTRICT 69	52,458	7,267	44,187	1,004	36,920	D	13.9%	84.2%	14.1%	85.9%
	DISTRICT 70	38,223	973	36,932	318	35,959	D	2.5%	96.6%	2.6%	97.4%
	DISTRICT 71	37,767	3,958	33,297	512	29,339	D	10.5%	88.2%	10.6%	89.4%
	DISTRICT 72	27,400	2,300	24,842	258	22,542	D	8.4%	90.7%	8.5%	91.5%
	DISTRICT 73	57,945	24,721	32,616	608	7,895	D	42.7%	56.3%	43.1%	56.9%
1,537,195	TOTAL	569,479	122,374	438,005	9,100	315,631	D	21.5%	76.9%	21.8%	78.2%

NEW YORK

QUEENS COUNTY
SENATOR 2000

2000 Census Population	Assembly District	Total Vote	Republican	Democratic	Other	Rep.-Dem. Plurality		Percentage			
---	---	---	---	---	---	---	---	Total Vote		Major Vote	
								Rep.	Dem.	Rep.	Dem.
	DISTRICT 23	38,572	18,353	19,824	395	1,471	D	47.6%	51.4%	48.1%	51.9%
	DISTRICT 24	45,361	17,958	26,956	447	8,998	D	39.6%	59.4%	40.0%	60.0%
	DISTRICT 25	26,183	8,511	17,421	251	8,910	D	32.5%	66.5%	32.8%	67.2%
	DISTRICT 26	45,385	21,189	23,748	448	2,559	D	46.7%	52.3%	47.2%	52.8%
	DISTRICT 27	37,369	13,888	23,085	396	9,197	D	37.2%	61.8%	37.6%	62.4%
	DISTRICT 28	41,724	16,559	24,666	499	8,107	D	39.7%	59.1%	40.2%	59.8%
	DISTRICT 29	38,458	2,603	35,674	181	33,071	D	6.8%	92.8%	6.8%	93.2%
	DISTRICT 30	32,708	12,839	19,380	489	6,541	D	39.3%	59.3%	39.8%	60.2%
	DISTRICT 31	32,066	2,568	29,319	179	26,751	D	8.0%	91.4%	8.1%	91.9%
	DISTRICT 32	34,051	2,752	31,106	193	28,354	D	8.1%	91.4%	8.1%	91.9%

NEW YORK

QUEENS COUNTY
SENATOR 2000

2000 Census Population	Assembly District	Total Vote	Republican	Democratic	Other	Rep.-Dem. Plurality		Percentage			
								Total Vote		Major Vote	
								Rep.	Dem.	Rep.	Dem.
	DISTRICT 33	42,394	5,445	36,694	255	31,249	D	12.8%	86.6%	12.9%	87.1%
	DISTRICT 34	23,375	4,689	18,488	198	13,799	D	20.1%	79.1%	20.2%	79.8%
	DISTRICT 35	24,403	3,732	20,508	163	16,776	D	15.3%	84.0%	15.4%	84.6%
	DISTRICT 36	32,824	11,131	21,013	680	9,882	D	33.9%	64.0%	34.6%	65.4%
	DISTRICT 37	26,251	6,139	19,730	382	13,591	D	23.4%	75.2%	23.7%	76.3%
	DISTRICT 38	31,622	14,391	16,845	386	2,454	D	45.5%	53.3%	46.1%	53.9%
2,229,379	TOTAL	552,746	162,747	384,457	5,542	221,710	D	29.4%	69.6%	29.7%	70.3%

NEW YORK

RICHMOND COUNTY
SENATOR 2000

2000 Census Population	Assembly District	Total Vote	Republican	Democratic	Other	Rep.-Dem. Plurality		Percentage			
								Total Vote		Major Vote	
								Rep.	Dem.	Rep.	Dem.
	DISTRICT 59	42,927	18,402	23,904	621	5,502	D	42.9%	55.7%	43.5%	56.5%
	DISTRICT 60	45,572	26,824	18,285	463	8,539	R	58.9%	40.1%	59.5%	40.5%
	DISTRICT 61	52,482	36,358	15,627	497	20,731	R	69.3%	29.8%	69.9%	30.1%
443,728	TOTAL	140,981	81,584	57,816	1,581	23,768	R	57.9%	41.0%	58.5%	41.5%

Note: Assembly district results for New York city boroughs did not add to the total vote certified by the state, which were: Bronx 307,875; Kings 615,267; New York 561,832; Queens 552,717; Richmond 140,979.

NEW YORK CITY

SENATOR 2000

2000 Census Population	County	Total Vote	Republican	Democratic	Other	Rep.-Dem. Plurality		Percentage			
								Total Vote		Major Vote	
								Rep.	Dem.	Rep.	Dem.
1,332,650	BRONX	307,875	44,078	261,378	2,419	217,300	D	14.3%	84.9%	14.4%	85.6%
2,465,326	KINGS	615,267	140,788	467,699	6,780	326,911	D	22.9%	76.0%	23.1%	76.9%
1,537,195	NEW YORK	561,832	119,263	433,599	8,970	314,336	D	21.2%	77.2%	21.6%	78.4%
2,229,379	QUEENS	552,717	162,747	384,457	5,513	221,710	D	29.4%	69.6%	29.7%	70.3%
443,728	RICHMOND	140,979	81,584	57,816	1,579	23,768	R	57.9%	41.0%	58.5%	41.5%
8,008,278	TOTAL	2,178,670	548,460	1,604,949	25,261	1,056,489	D	25.2%	73.7%	25.5%	74.5%

Note: The New York city totals are based on state certified returns, which differ slightly from returns certified by city election officials that are used in the Assembly district tables.

NEW YORK

CONGRESS

CD	Year	Total Vote	Republican Vote	Republican Candidate	Democratic Vote	Democratic Candidate	Other Vote	Rep.-Dem. Plurality	Total Vote Rep.	Total Vote Dem.	Major Vote Rep.	Major Vote Dem.
1	2000	239,604	133,020	*GRUCCI, FELIX J., JR.	97,299	SELTZER, REGINA	9,285	35,721 R	55.5%	40.6%	57.8%	42.2%
1	1998	155,090	99,460	*FORBES, MICHAEL P.	55,630	*HOLST, WILLIAM G.		43,830 R	64.1%	35.9%	64.1%	35.9%
1	1996	213,116	116,620	*FORBES, MICHAEL P.	96,496	*BREDES, NORA L.		20,124 R	54.7%	45.3%	54.7%	45.3%
1	1994	172,240	90,491	*FORBES, MICHAEL P.	80,146	*HOCHBRUECKNER, GEORGE J.	1,603	10,345 R	52.5%	46.5%	53.0%	47.0%
1	1992	227,983	110,043	*ROMAINE, EDWARD P.	117,940	*HOCHBRUECKNER, GEORGE J.		7,897 D	48.3%	51.7%	48.3%	51.7%
2	2000	188,632	65,880	JOHNSON, JOAN B.	90,438	ISRAEL, STEVE J.	32,314	24,558 D	34.9%	47.9%	42.1%	57.9%
2	1998	128,438	85,089	*LAZIO, RICK A.	37,949	BACE, JOHN C.	5,400	47,140 R	66.2%	29.5%	69.2%	30.8%
2	1996	174,594	112,135	*LAZIO, RICK A.	57,953	*HERMAN, KENNETH J.	4,506	54,182 R	64.2%	33.2%	65.9%	34.1%
2	1994	146,776	100,107	*LAZIO, RICK A.	41,102	*MANFRE, JAMES L.	5,567	59,005 R	68.2%	28.0%	70.9%	29.1%
2	1992	205,714	109,386	*LAZIO, RICK A.	96,328	*DOWNEY, THOMAS J.		13,058 R	53.2%	46.8%	53.2%	46.8%
3	2000	240,428	143,126	*KING, PETER T.	95,787	*LAMAGNA, DAL	1,515	47,339 R	59.5%	39.8%	59.9%	40.1%
3	1998	182,383	117,258	*KING, PETER T.	63,628	LANGBERG, KEVIN N.	1,497	53,630 R	64.3%	34.9%	64.8%	35.2%
3	1996	231,426	127,972	*KING, PETER T.	97,518	*LAMAGNA, DAL A.	5,936	30,454 R	55.3%	42.1%	56.8%	43.2%
3	1994	194,532	115,236	*KING, PETER T.	77,774	GRILL, NORMA	1,522	37,462 R	59.2%	40.0%	59.7%	40.3%
3	1992	251,622	124,727	*KING, PETER T.	116,915	ORLINS, STEVE A.	9,980	7,812 R	49.6%	46.5%	51.6%	48.4%
4	2000	225,755	87,830	*BECKER, GREGORY R.	136,703	*MCCARTHY, CAROLYN	1,222	48,873 D	38.9%	60.6%	39.1%	60.9%
4	1998	171,583	79,984	*BECKER, GREGORY R.	90,256	*MCCARTHY, CAROLYN	1,343	10,272 D	46.6%	52.6%	47.0%	53.0%
4	1996	221,016	89,542	*FRISA, DANIEL	127,060	*MCCARTHY, CAROLYN	4,414	37,518 D	40.5%	57.5%	41.3%	58.7%
4	1994	174,963	87,815	FRISA, DANIEL	65,286	SCHILIRO, PHILIP	21,862	22,529 R	50.2%	37.3%	57.4%	42.6%
4	1992	220,644	110,710	*LEVY, DAVID A.	100,386	*SCHILIRO, PHILIP	9,548	10,324 R	50.2%	45.5%	52.4%	47.6%
5	2000	202,614	61,084	*ELKOWITZ, EDWARD	137,684	*ACKERMAN, GARY L.	3,846	76,600 D	30.1%	68.0%	30.7%	69.3%
5	1998	149,862	49,586	*PINZON, DAVID C.	97,404	*ACKERMAN, GARY L.	2,872	47,818 D	33.1%	65.0%	33.7%	66.3%
5	1996	197,785	69,244	*LALLY, GRANT M.	125,918	*ACKERMAN, GARY L.	2,623	56,674 D	35.0%	63.7%	35.5%	64.5%
5	1994	170,642	73,884	*LALLY, GRANT M.	93,896	*ACKERMAN, GARY L.	2,862	20,012 D	43.3%	55.0%	44.0%	56.0%
5	1992	210,831	94,907	*BINDER, ALLAN E.	110,476	*ACKERMAN, GARY L.	5,448	15,569 D	45.0%	52.4%	46.2%	53.8%
6	2000	120,818			120,818	*MEEKS, GREGORY W.		120,818 D		100.0%		100.0%
6	1998	76,122			76,122	*MEEKS, GREGORY W.		76,122 D		100.0%		100.0%
6	1996	121,147	18,348	*MISIR, JORAWAR	102,799	FLAKE, FLOYD H.		84,451 D	15.1%	84.9%	15.1%	84.9%
6	1994	85,271	16,675	*BHAGWANDIN, DIANAND D.	68,596	FLAKE, FLOYD H.		51,921 D	19.6%	80.4%	19.6%	80.4%
6	1992	119,659	22,687	*BHAGWANDIN, DIANAND D.	96,972	FLAKE, FLOYD H.		74,285 D	19.0%	81.0%	19.0%	81.0%
7	2000	109,101	24,592	BIRTLEY, ROSE	78,207	CROWLEY, JOSEPH	6,302	53,615 D	22.5%	71.7%	23.9%	76.1%
7	1998	73,780	18,896	DILLON, JAMES J.	50,924	CROWLEY, JOSEPH	3,960	32,028 D	25.6%	69.0%	27.1%	72.9%
7	1996	110,940	32,092	*BIRTLEY, ROSE	78,848	MANTON, THOMAS J.		46,756 D	28.9%	71.1%	28.9%	71.1%
7	1994	67,633			58,935	MANTON, THOMAS J.	8,698	58,935 D		87.1%		100.0%
7	1992	126,919	54,639	*SHEA, DENNIS C.	72,280	MANTON, THOMAS J.		17,641 D	43.1%	56.9%	43.1%	56.9%
8	2000	184,969	27,057	HENRY, MARIAN S.	150,273	*NADLER, JERROLD	7,639	123,216 D	14.6%	81.2%	15.3%	84.7%
8	1998	131,331	18,383	HOWARD, THEODORE	112,948	*NADLER, JERROLD		94,565 D	14.0%	86.0%	14.0%	86.0%
8	1996	160,352	26,028	*BENJAMIN, MICHAEL	131,943	*NADLER, JERROLD	2,381	105,915 D	16.2%	82.3%	16.5%	83.5%
8	1994	134,086	21,132	ASKREN, DAVID L.	109,946	*NADLER, JERROLD	3,008	88,814 D	15.8%	82.0%	16.1%	83.9%
8	1992	170,248	25,548	ASKREN, DAVID L.	138,296	*NADLER, JERROLD	6,404	112,748 D	15.0%	81.2%	15.6%	84.4%
9	2000	144,632	45,649	*DEAR, NOACH	98,983	*WEINER, ANTHONY		53,334 D	31.6%	68.4%	31.6%	68.4%
9	1998	104,522	24,486	TELANO, LOUIS	69,439	*WEINER, ANTHONY	10,597	44,953 D	23.4%	66.4%	26.1%	73.9%
9	1996	143,213	30,488	*VERGA, ROBERT J.	107,107	*SCHUMER, CHARLES E.	5,618	76,619 D	21.3%	74.8%	22.2%	77.8%
9	1994	131,019	35,880	*MCCALL, JAMES P.	95,139	*SCHUMER, CHARLES E.		59,259 D	27.4%	72.6%	27.4%	72.6%
9	1992	131,530			116,545	*SCHUMER, CHARLES E.	14,985	116,545 D		88.6%		100.0%
10	2000	133,884	6,852	BROWN, ERNESTINE M.	120,700	*TOWNS, EDOLPHUS	6,332	113,848 D	5.1%	90.2%	5.4%	94.6%
10	1998	90,501	5,577	BROWN, ERNESTINE M.	83,528	*TOWNS, EDOLPHUS	1,396	77,951 D	6.2%	92.3%	6.3%	93.7%
10	1996	109,442	8,660	*SMITH-PARKER, AMELIA	99,889	*TOWNS, EDOLPHUS	893	91,229 D	7.9%	91.3%	8.0%	92.0%

NEW YORK

CONGRESS

CD	Year	Total Vote	Republican		Democratic		Other Vote	Rep.-Dem. Plurality	Percentage			
									Total Vote		Major Vote	
			Vote	Candidate	Vote	Candidate			Rep.	Dem.	Rep.	Dem.
10	1994	86,510	7,995	PARKER, AMELIA S.	77,026	*TOWNS, EDOLPHUS	1,489	69,031 D	9.2%	89.0%	9.4%	90.6%
10	1992	101,824			97,509	*TOWNS, EDOLPHUS	4,315	97,509 D		95.8%		100.0%
11	2000	128,784	8,406	*CLEARY, SUSAN	112,050	*OWENS, MAJOR R.	8,328	103,644 D	6.5%	87.0%		
11	1998	84,201	7,284	*GREENE, DAVID	75,773	*OWENS, MAJOR R.	1,144	68,489 D	8.7%	90.0%	8.8%	91.2%
11	1996	97,771	7,866	*HAYLE, CLAUDETTE	89,905	*OWENS, MAJOR R.		82,039 D	8.0%	92.0%	8.0%	92.0%
11	1994	69,700	6,605	*POPKIN, GARY S.	61,945	*OWENS, MAJOR R.	1,150	55,340 D	9.5%	88.9%	9.6%	90.4%
11	1992	85,494			80,028	*OWENS, MAJOR R.	5,466	80,028 D		93.6%		100.0%
12	2000	99,080	10,052	MARKGRAF, ROSEMARY	86,288	*VELAZQUEZ, NYDIA M.	2,740	76,236 D	10.1%	87.1%	10.4%	89.6%
12	1998	63,706	7,405	MARKGRAF, ROSEMARIE	53,269	VELAZQUEZ, NYDIA M.	3,032	45,864 D	11.6%	83.6%	12.2%	87.8%
12	1996	73,174	9,978	*PRADO, MIGUEL I.	61,913	*VELAZQUEZ, NYDIA M.	1,283	51,935 D	13.6%	84.6%	13.9%	86.1%
12	1994	43,265			39,929	*VELAZQUEZ, NYDIA M.	3,336	39,929 D		92.3%		100.0%
12	1992	73,067	14,976	*DIAZ, ANGEL	55,926	VELAZQUEZ, NYDIA M.	2,165	40,950 D	20.5%	76.5%	21.1%	78.9%
13	2000	170,062	109,806	*FOSSELLA, VITO J.	57,603	*JOHNSTONE, KATINA M.	2,653	52,203 R	64.6%	33.9%	65.6%	34.4%
13	1998	117,550	76,138	*FOSSELLA, VITO J.	40,167	*PRISCO, EUGENE V.	1,245	35,971 R	64.8%	34.2%	65.5%	34.5%
13	1996	153,769	94,660	*MOLINARI, SUSAN	53,376	*BUTLER, TYRONE G.	5,733	41,284 R	61.6%	34.7%	63.9%	36.1%
13	1994	135,083	96,491	*MOLINARI, SUSAN	33,937	*BUTLER, TYRONE G.	4,655	62,554 R	71.4%	25.1%	74.0%	26.0%
13	1992	192,248	107,903	*MOLINARI, SUSAN	73,520	*ALBANESE, SAL F.	10,825	34,383 R	56.1%	38.2%	59.5%	40.5%
14	2000	200,348	45,453	RHODES, C. ADRIENNE	148,080	*MALONEY, CAROLYN B.	6,815	102,627 D	22.7%	73.9%	23.5%	76.5%
14	1998	143,530	32,458	KUPFERMAN, STEPHANIE E.	111,072	*MALONEY, CAROLYN B.		78,614 D	22.6%	77.4%	22.6%	77.4%
14	1996	179,737	42,641	LIVINGSTON, JEFFREY E.	130,175	*MALONEY, CAROLYN B.	6,921	87,534 D	23.7%	72.4%	24.7%	75.3%
14	1994	153,322	54,277	*MILLARD, CHARLES	98,479	*MALONEY, CAROLYN B.	566	44,202 D	35.4%	64.2%	35.5%	64.5%
14	1992	201,837	97,215	*GREEN, S. WILLIAM	101,652	*MALONEY, CAROLYN B.	2,970	4,437 D	48.2%	50.4%	48.9%	51.1%
15	2000	141,664	7,346	*SUERO, JOSE AGUSTIN	130,161	*RANGEL, CHARLES B.	4,157	122,815 D	5.2%	91.9%	5.3%	94.7%
15	1998	97,139	5,633	CUNNINGHAM, DAVID E.	90,424	*RANGEL, CHARLES B.	1,082	84,791 D	5.8%	93.1%	5.9%	94.1%
15	1996	124,734	5,951	ADAMS, EDWARD R.	113,898	*RANGEL, CHARLES B.	4,885	107,947 D	4.8%	91.3%	5.0%	95.0%
15	1994	80,642			77,830	*RANGEL, CHARLES B.	2,812	77,830 D		96.5%		100.0%
15	1992	110,693			105,011	*RANGEL, CHARLES B.	5,682	105,011 D		94.9%		100.0%
16	2000	107,546	3,934	JUSTICE, AARON	103,041	*SERRANO, JOSE E.	571	99,107 D	3.7%	95.8%	3.7%	96.3%
16	1998	70,580	2,457	BAYLEY, THOMAS W. JR.	67,367	*SERRANO, JOSE E.	756	64,910 D	3.5%	95.4%	3.5%	96.5%
16	1996	99,233	2,878	TORRES, RODNEY	95,568	*SERRANO, JOSE E.	787	92,690 D	2.9%	96.3%	2.9%	97.1%
16	1994	60,829			58,572	*SERRANO, JOSE E.	2,257	58,572 D		96.3%		100.0%
16	1992	93,197	7,975	*WALTERS, MICHAEL	85,222	*SERRANO, JOSE E.		77,247 D	8.6%	91.4%	8.6%	91.4%
17	2000	128,294	13,201	*MCMANUS, PATRICK	115,093	*ENGEL, ELIOT L.		101,892 D	10.3%	89.7%	10.3%	89.7%
17	1998	91,984	11,037	*FLUMEFREDDO, PETER	80,947	*ENGEL, ELIOT L.		69,910 D	12.0%	88.0%	12.0%	88.0%
17	1996	119,187	15,892	*MCCARTHY, DENIS	101,287	*ENGEL, ELIOT L.	2,008	85,395 D	13.3%	85.0%	13.6%	86.4%
17	1994	94,479	16,896	MARSHALL, EDWARD T.	73,321	*ENGEL, ELIOT L.	4,262	56,425 D	17.9%	77.6%	18.7%	81.3%
17	1992	122,381	16,511	RICHMAN, MARTIN	98,068	*ENGEL, ELIOT L.	7,802	81,557 D	13.5%	80.1%	14.4%	85.6%
18	2000	188,647	58,022	*VONGLIS, JOHN G.	126,878	LOWEY, NITA M.	3,747	68,856 D	30.8%	67.3%	31.4%	68.6%
18	1998	110,702			91,623	LOWEY, NITA M.	19,079	91,623 D		82.8%		100.0%
18	1996	185,722	59,487	*KATSORHIS, KERRY J.	118,194	LOWEY, NITA M.	8,041	58,707 D	32.0%	63.6%	33.5%	66.5%
18	1994	160,053	65,517	*HARTZELL, ANDREW C.	91,663	LOWEY, NITA M.	2,873	26,146 D	40.9%	57.3%	41.7%	58.3%
18	1992	208,528	92,687	*DIOGUARDI, JOSEPH J.	115,841	LOWEY, NITA M.		23,154 D	44.4%	55.6%	44.4%	55.6%
19	2000	239,151	145,532	*KELLY, SUE W.	85,871	*GRAHAM, LARRY OTIS	7,748	59,661 R	60.9%	35.9%	62.9%	37.1%
19	1998	167,832	104,467	*KELLY, SUE W.	56,378	COLLINS, DICK	6,987	48,089 R	62.2%	33.6%	64.9%	35.1%
19	1996	220,596	102,142	*KELLY, SUE W.	86,926	*KLEIN, RICHARD S.	31,528	15,216 R	46.3%	39.4%	54.0%	46.0%
19	1994	192,309	100,173	KELLY, SUE W.	70,696	FISH, HAMILTON, JR.	21,440	29,477 R	52.1%	36.8%	58.6%	41.4%
19	1992	232,464	139,610	*FISH, HAMILTON	92,854	MCCARTHY, CORNELIUS P.		46,756 R	60.1%	39.9%	60.1%	39.9%

NEW YORK

CONGRESS

CD	Year	Total Vote	Republican Vote	Republican Candidate	Democratic Vote	Democratic Candidate	Other Vote	Rep.-Dem. Plurality	Total Vote Rep.	Total Vote Dem.	Major Vote Rep.	Major Vote Dem.
20	2000	236,033	136,016	GILMAN, BENJAMIN A.	94,646	*FEINER, PAUL J.	5,371	41,370 R	57.6%	40.1%	59.0%	41.0%
20	1998	168,904	98,546	GILMAN, BENJAMIN A.	65,589	*FEINER, PAUL J.	4,769	32,957 R	58.3%	38.8%	60.0%	40.0%
20	1996	214,612	122,479	GILMAN, BENJAMIN A.	80,761	*AGGARWAL, YASH P.	11,372	41,718 R	57.1%	37.6%	60.3%	39.7%
20	1994	178,291	120,334	GILMAN, BENJAMIN A.	52,345	JULIAN, GREGORY B.	5,612	67,989 R	67.5%	29.4%	69.7%	30.3%
20	1992	227,331	150,301	GILMAN, BENJAMIN A.	66,826	LEVINE, JOHATHAN L.	10,204	83,475 R	66.1%	29.4%	69.2%	30.8%
21	2000	235,672	60,333	PILLSWORTH, THOMAS G.	175,339	*MCNULTY, MICHAEL R.		115,006 D	25.6%	74.4%	25.6%	74.4%
21	1998	197,570	50,931	AYERS, LAUREN	146,639	*MCNULTY, MICHAEL R.		95,708 D	25.8%	74.2%	25.8%	74.2%
21	1996	239,756	64,471	*NORMAN, NANCY	158,491	*MCNULTY, MICHAEL R.	16,794	94,020 D	26.9%	66.1%	28.9%	71.1%
21	1994	220,674	68,745	GOMEZ, JOSEPH A.	147,804	*MCNULTY, MICHAEL R.	4,125	79,059 D	31.2%	67.0%	31.7%	68.3%
21	1992	265,278	91,184	*NORMAN, NANCY	166,371	*MCNULTY, MICHAEL R.	7,723	75,187 D	34.4%	62.7%	35.4%	64.6%
22	2000	246,479	167,368	*SWEENEY, JOHN E.	79,111	*MCCALLION, KENNETH F.		88,257 R	67.9%	32.1%	67.9%	32.1%
22	1998	193,266	106,919	*SWEENEY, JOHN E.	81,296	BORDEWICH, JEAN P.	5,051	25,623 R	55.3%	42.1%	56.8%	43.2%
22	1996	238,317	144,125	*SOLOMON, GERALD B.	94,192	JAMES, STEVE		49,933 R	60.5%	39.5%	60.5%	39.5%
22	1994	214,781	157,717	*SOLOMON, GERALD B.	57,064	LAWRENCE, L. ROBERT		100,653 R	73.4%	26.6%	73.4%	26.6%
22	1992	251,332	164,436	*SOLOMON, GERALD B.	86,896	ROBERTS, DAVID		77,540 R	65.4%	34.6%	65.4%	34.6%
23	2000	205,035	124,132	*BOEHLERT, SHERWOOD L.	38,049	ENGLEBRECHT, RICHARD W.	42,854	86,083 R	60.5%	18.6%	76.5%	23.5%
23	1998	137,735	111,242	BOEHLERT, SHERWOOD L.			26,493	111,242 R	80.8%		100.0%	
23	1996	193,687	124,626	*BOEHLERT, SHERWOOD L.	50,436	HAPANOWICZ, BRUCE W.	18,625	74,190 R	64.3%	26.0%	71.2%	28.8%
23	1994	176,488	124,486	BOEHLERT, SHERWOOD L.	40,786	SKEELE, CHARLES W.	11,216	83,700 R	70.5%	23.1%	75.3%	24.7%
23	1992	219,662	139,774	BOEHLERT, SHERWOOD L.	61,835	DIPERNA, PAULA	18,053	77,939 R	63.6%	28.2%	69.3%	30.7%
24	2000	186,187	138,322	*MCHUGH, JOHN M.	42,698	*TALLON, NEIL P.	5,167	95,624 R	74.3%	22.9%	76.4%	23.6%
24	1998	147,693	116,682	*MCHUGH, JOHN M.	31,011	TALLON, NEIL P.		85,671 R	79.0%	21.0%	79.0%	21.0%
24	1996	174,682	124,240	*MCHUGH, JOHN M.	43,692	RAVENSCROFT, DONALD	6,750	80,548 R	71.1%	25.0%	74.0%	26.0%
24	1994	158,677	124,645	*MCHUGH, JOHN M.	34,032	FRANCIS, DANNY M.		90,613 R	78.6%	21.4%	78.6%	21.4%
24	1992	201,069	122,257	*MCHUGH, JOHN M.	47,675	RAVENSCROFT, MARGARET M.	31,137	74,582 R	60.8%	23.7%	71.9%	28.1%
25	2000	220,243	151,880	*WALSH, JAMES T.	64,533	GAVIN, FRANCIS J.	3,830	87,347 R	69.0%	29.3%	70.2%	29.8%
25	1998	174,665	121,204	*WALSH, JAMES T.	53,461	*ROTHENBERG, YVONNE		67,743 R	69.4%	30.6%	69.4%	30.6%
25	1996	229,890	126,691	*WALSH, JAMES T.	103,199	MACK, MARTY		23,492 R	55.1%	44.9%	55.1%	44.9%
25	1994	197,802	113,949	*WALSH, JAMES T.	83,853	*JEZER, RHEA		30,096 R	57.6%	42.4%	57.6%	42.4%
25	1992	242,386	135,076	*WALSH, JAMES T.	107,310	*JEZER, RHEA		27,766 R	55.7%	44.3%	55.7%	44.3%
26	2000	226,579	83,856	*MOPPERT, BOB	140,395	*HINCHEY, MAURICE D.	2,328	56,539 D	37.0%	62.0%	37.4%	62.6%
26	1998	175,140	54,776	*WALKER, WILLIAM H.	108,204	*HINCHEY, MAURICE D.	12,160	53,428 D	31.3%	61.8%	33.6%	66.4%
26	1996	222,506	94,125	*WITTIG, SUE	122,850	*HINCHEY, MAURICE D.	5,531	28,725 D	42.3%	55.2%	43.4%	56.6%
26	1994	194,508	94,244	*MOPPERT, BOB	95,492	*HINCHEY, MAURICE D.	4,772	1,248 D	48.5%	49.1%	49.7%	50.3%
26	1992	237,116	110,738	*MOPPERT, BOB	119,557	*HINCHEY, MAURICE D.	6,821	8,819 D	46.7%	50.4%	48.1%	51.9%
27	2000	227,564	157,694	*REYNOLDS, THOMAS M.	69,870	PECORARO, THOMAS W.		87,824 R	69.3%	30.7%	69.3%	30.7%
27	1998	178,020	102,042	*REYNOLDS, THOMAS M.	75,978	*COOK, BILL		26,064 R	57.3%	42.7%	57.3%	42.7%
27	1996	238,071	142,568	*PAXON, L. WILLIAM	95,503	*FRICANO, THOMAS M.		47,065 R	59.9%	40.1%	59.9%	40.1%
27	1994	204,770	152,610	*PAXON, L. WILLIAM	52,160	LONG, WILLIAM A.		100,450 R	74.5%	25.5%	74.5%	25.5%
27	1992	246,502	156,596	*PAXON, L. WILLIAM	89,906	CALL, W. DOUGLAS		66,690 R	63.5%	36.5%	63.5%	36.5%
28	2000	230,856	75,348	*JOHNS, MARK C.	151,688	SLAUGHTER, LOUISE M.	3,820	76,340 D	32.6%	65.7%	33.2%	66.8%
28	1998	183,458	56,443	*KAPLAN, RICHARD A.	118,856	SLAUGHTER, LOUISE M.	8,159	62,413 D	30.8%	64.8%	32.2%	67.8%
28	1996	232,450	99,366	*ROSENBERGER, GEOFF H.	133,084	SLAUGHTER, LOUISE M.		33,718 D	42.7%	57.3%	42.7%	57.3%
28	1994	195,967	78,516	*DAVISON, RENEE F.	110,987	SLAUGHTER, LOUISE M.	6,464	32,471 D	40.1%	56.6%	41.4%	58.6%
28	1992	255,078	112,273	*POLITO, WILLIAM P.	140,908	SLAUGHTER, LOUISE M.	1,897	28,635 D	44.0%	55.2%	44.3%	55.7%
29	2000	209,487	81,159	*SOMMER, BRETT M.	128,328	*LAFALCE, JOHN J.		47,169 D	38.7%	61.3%	38.7%	61.3%
29	1998	170,529	69,481	*COLLINS, CHRIS	97,235	*LAFALCE, JOHN J.	3,813	27,754 D	40.7%	57.0%	41.7%	58.3%
29	1996	213,452	81,135	*CALLARD, DAVID B.	132,317	*LAFALCE, JOHN J.		51,182 D	38.0%	62.0%	38.0%	62.0%

NEW YORK

CONGRESS

CD	Year	Total Vote	Republican Vote	Republican Candidate	Democratic Vote	Democratic Candidate	Other Vote	Rep.-Dem. Plurality	Total Vote Rep.	Total Vote Dem.	Major Vote Rep.	Major Vote Dem.
29	1994	186,704	80,355	*MILLER, WILLIAM E., JR.	103,053	*LAFALCE, JOHN J.	3,296	22,698 D	43.0%	55.2%	43.8%	56.2%
29	1992	235,458	98,031	*MILLER, WILLIAM E., JR.	128,230	*LAFALCE, JOHN J.	9,197	30,199 D	41.6%	54.5%	43.3%	56.7%
30	2000	206,271	138,452	*QUINN, JACK	67,819	*FEE, JOHN		70,633 R	67.1%	32.9%	67.1%	32.9%
30	1998	171,292	116,093	*QUINN, JACK	55,199	PEOPLES, CRYSTAL D.		60,894 R	67.8%	32.2%	67.8%	32.2%
30	1996	221,409	121,369	*QUINN, JACK	100,040	*PORDUM, FRANCIS J.		21,329 R	54.8%	45.2%	54.8%	45.2%
30	1994	186,130	124,738	*QUINN, JACK	61,392	*FRANCZYK, DAVID A.		63,346 R	67.0%	33.0%	67.0%	33.0%
30	1992	243,204	125,734	*QUINN, JACK	111,445	*GORSKI, DENNIS T.	6,025	14,289 R	51.7%	45.8%	53.0%	47.0%
31	2000	199,431	154,238	*HOUGHTON, AMORY	45,193	PETERS, KISUN J.		109,045 R	77.3%	22.7%	77.3%	22.7%
31	1998	158,252	107,615	*HOUGHTON, AMORY	40,091	ROSSITER, CALEB	10,546	67,524 R	68.0%	25.3%	72.9%	27.1%
31	1996	195,267	139,734	*HOUGHTON, AMORY	49,502	MACBAIN, BRUCE D.	6,031	90,232 R	71.6%	25.4%	73.8%	26.2%
31	1994	142,925	121,178	*HOUGHTON, AMORY			21,747	121,178 R	84.8%		100.0%	
31	1992	213,554	150,696	*HOUGHTON, AMORY	52,010	LEAHEY, JOSEPH P.	10,848	98,686 R	70.6%	24.4%	74.3%	25.7%

Note: An asterisk (*) in the congressional vote table indicates that a candidate received votes on the ballot line of another party or parties.

NEW YORK

GENERAL AND PRIMARY ELECTIONS

2000 GENERAL ELECTIONS

President Other vote was 31,599 Right to Life (Buchanan)/Reform (Buchanan); 24,361 Independence Party (Hagelin); 7,649 Libertarian (Browne); 1,789 Socialist Workers (Harris); 1,498 Constitution (Phillips); 2 write-in (McReynolds).

Senator Other vote was 43,181 Independence Party (Graham); 40,991 Green (Dunau); 21,439 Right to Life (Adefope); 4,734 Libertarian (Clifton); 3,414 Constitution (Wein); 3,040 Socialist Workers (Perasso).

Congress Other vote was: CD 1: 6,318 Working Families (Forbes), 2,967 Green (Holst); CD 2: 11,224 Right to Life (Walsh), 10,824 Conservative (Thompson), 10,266 Independence Party/Green/Working Families (Bishop); CD 3: 1,515 Liberal (Olchin); CD 4: 1,222 Liberal (Vitanza); CD 5: 3,846 Right to Life (Robinson); CD 7: 3,131 Conservative (Hurley), 1,999 Green (Gilman), 1,172 Right to Life (Christea); CD 8: 4,765 Green (Wentzel), 1,849 Conservative (LaBella), 1,025 Independence Party (Kresky); CD 10: 5,530 Working Families (Ford), 802 Conservative (Johnson); CD 11: 7,366 Liberal (Clarke), 962 Conservative (Gore); CD 12: 1,025 Socialist Workers (Pederson), 865 Right to Life (Rosario), 850 Conservative (Estevez); CD 13: 2,653 Independence Party/Green (Lerman); CD 14: 4,869 Green (Stevens), 1,946 Independence Party (Newman); CD 15: 2,134 Green (Loren), 1,051 Independence Party (Fields), 492 Conservative (Valle), 480 Libertarian (Jeffery); CD 16; 571 Conservative (Retcho); CD 18: 3,747 Right to Life (O'Grady); CD 19: 4,086 Right to Life (Lloyd), 3,662 Green (Jacobs); CD 20: 5,371 Right to Life (Tighe); CD 23: 42,854 Conservative/Right to Life (Vickers); CD 24: 5,167 Independence Party/Green (Smith); CD 25: 3,830 Green (Hawkins); CD 26: 2,328 Right to Life (Laux); CD 28: 2,292 Green (Hawkins), 1,528 Libertarian (Healey).

NEW YORK

GENERAL AND PRIMARY ELECTIONS

2000 PRIMARY ELECTIONS

Primary	March 7, 2000 (President) September 12, 2000 (Congress)	**Registration** (as of March 1, 2000)	Republican 3,089,345 Democratic 4,960,666 Independence Party 172,471 Conservative 171,496 Liberal 92,074 Right to Life 51,392 Green 3,611 Working Families 4,611 Other 2,150,806 TOTAL 10,696,472

Primary Type   Closed-Only registered Democrats and Republicans could vote in their party's primary.

Note: An asterisk (*) denotes incumbent. Names of unopposed candidates do not appear on the primary ballot; therefore, no votes are cast for these candidates.

	REPUBLICAN PRIMARIES			DEMOCRATIC PRIMARIES		
President	George W. Bush	1,102,850	51.0%	Al Gore	639,417	65.6%
	John McCain	937,655	43.4%	Bill Bradley	326,038	33.5%
	Alan Keyes	71,196	3.3%	Lyndon H. LaRouche Jr.	9,008	0.9%
	Steve Forbes	49,817	2.3%			
	TOTAL	2,161,518		TOTAL	974,463	
	The Republican vote was for delegates only, with three elected per congressional district. Totals reflect the aggregate vote for delegates, with each voter allowed to cast three votes. There was no direct vote for candidates.					
Senator	Rick Lazio	Unopposed		Hillary Rodham Clinton	565,353	82.0%
				Mark S. McMahon	124,315	18.0%
				Write-in	43	
				TOTAL	689,711	
Congressional District 1	Felix J. Grucci Jr.	Unopposed		Regina Seltzer	6,077	50.1%
				Michael P. Forbes*	6,042	49.9%
				TOTAL	12,119	
Congressional District 2	Joan B. Johnson	6,823	61.6%	Steve J. Israel	6,004	45.4%
	Robert T. Walsh	4,255	38.4%	David A. Bishop	5,449	41.2%
				Ghenya B. Grant	1,785	13.5%
				Write-in	1	
	TOTAL	11,078		TOTAL	13,239	
Congressional District 3	Peter T. King*	8,651	77.6%	Dal LaMagna	Unopposed	
	Robert Previdi	2,495	22.4%			
	TOTAL	11,146				
Congressional District 4	Gregory R. Becker	Unopposed		Carolyn McCarthy*	Unopposed	
Congressional District 5	Edward Elkowitz	Unopposed		Gary L. Ackerman*	Unopposed	
Congressional District 6	No Republican candidate			Gregory W. Meeks*	Unopposed	
Congressional District 7	Rose Birtley	Unopposed		Joseph Crowley*	Unopposed	
Congressional District 8	Marian S. Henry	Unopposed		Jerrold Nadler*	Unopposed	
Congressional District 9	Noach Dear	Unopposed		Anthony D. Weiner*	24,895	73.8%
				Noach Dear	8,847	26.2%
				TOTAL	33,742	

NEW YORK

GENERAL AND PRIMARY ELECTIONS

	REPUBLICAN PRIMARIES			DEMOCRATIC PRIMARIES		
Congressional District 10	Ernestine M. Brown	Unopposed		Edolphus Towns* Barry D. Ford TOTAL	25,735 19,040 44,775	57.5% 42.5%
Congressional District 11	Susan Cleary	Unopposed		Major R. Owens* Una S. T. Clarke TOTAL	25,962 21,769 47,731	54.4% 45.6%
Congressional District 12	Rosemary Markgraf	Unopposed		Nydia M. Velazquez* Mildred Rosario TOTAL	15,894 4,713 20,607	77.1% 22.9%
Congressional District 13	Vito J. Fossella*	Unopposed		Katina M. Johnstone	Unopposed	
Congressional District 14	C. Adrienne Rhodes	Unopposed		Carolyn B. Maloney*	Unopposed	
Congressional District 15	Jose Agustin Suero	Unopposed		Charles B. Rangel* Ruben D. Vargas TOTAL	33,526 7,136 40,662	82.5% 17.5%
Congressional District 16	Aaron Justice	Unopposed		Jose E. Serrano*	Unopposed	
Congressional District 17	Patrick McManus	Unopposed		Eliot L. Engel* Larry B. Seabrook Sonny A. Zayas Write-in TOTAL	24,159 19,629 4,115 1 47,904	50.4% 41.0% 8.6%
Congressional District 18	John G. Vonglis	Unopposed		Nita M. Lowey*	Unopposed	
Congressional District 19	Sue W. Kelly*	Unopposed		Larry Otis Graham	Unopposed	
Congressional District 20	Benjamin A. Gilman*	Unopposed		Paul J. Feiner	Unopposed	
Congressional District 21	Thomas G. Pillsworth	Unopposed		Michael R. McNulty*	Unopposed	
Congressional District 22	John E. Sweeney*	Unopposed		Kenneth F. McCallion	Unopposed	
Congressional District 23	Sherwood L. Boehlert* David B. Vickers Write-in TOTAL	15,269 11,382 3 26,654	57.3% 42.7%	Richard W. Englebrecht	Unopposed	
Congressional District 24	John M. McHugh*	Unopposed		Neil P. Tallon	Unopposed	
Congressional District 25	James T. Walsh*	Unopposed		Francis J. Gavin	Unopposed	
Congressional District 26	Bob Moppert	Unopposed		Maurice D. Hinchey*	Unopposed	
Congressional District 27	Thomas M. Reynolds*	Unopposed		Thomas W. Pecoraro	Unopposed	
Congressional District 28	Mark C. Johns	Unopposed		Louise M. Slaughter*	Unopposed	
Congressional District 29	Brett M. Sommer	Unopposed		John J. LaFalce*	Unopposed	
Congressional District 30	Jack Quinn*	Unopposed		John Fee	Unopposed	
Congressional District 31	Amo Houghton*	Unopposed		Kisun J. Peters	Unopposed	

NORTH CAROLINA

GOVERNOR
Mike Easley (D). Elected 2000 to a four-year term.

SENATORS
John Edwards (D). Elected 1998 to a six-year term.

Jesse Helms (R). Re-elected 1996 to a six-year term. Previously elected 1990, 1984, 1978, 1972.

REPRESENTATIVES

1. Eva Clayton (D)
2. Bob Etheridge (D)
3. Walter B. Jones, Jr. (R)
4. David E. Price (D)
5. Richard M. Burr (R)
6. Howard Coble (R)
7. Mike McIntyre (D)
8. Robin Hayes (R)
9. Sue Myrick (R)
10. Cass Ballenger (R)
11. Charles H. Taylor (R)
12. Melvin Watt (D)

POSTWAR VOTE FOR PRESIDENT

Year	Total Vote	Republican Vote	Republican Candidate	Democratic Vote	Democratic Candidate	Other Vote	Plurality	Total Vote Rep.	Total Vote Dem.	Major Vote Rep.	Major Vote Dem.
2000	2,911,262	1,631,163	Bush, George W.	1,257,692	Gore, Al	22,407	373,471 R	56.0%	43.2%	56.5%	43.5%
1996**	2,515,807	1,225,938	Dole, Bob	1,107,849	Clinton, Bill	182,020	118,089 R	48.7%	44.0%	52.5%	47.5%
1992**	2,611,850	1,134,661	Bush, George	1,114,042	Clinton, Bill	363,147	20,619 R	43.4%	42.7%	50.5%	49.5%
1988	2,134,370	1,237,258	Bush, George	890,167	Dukakis, Michael S.	6,945	347,091 R	58.0%	41.7%	58.2%	41.8%
1984	2,175,361	1,346,481	Reagan, Ronald	824,287	Mondale, Walter F.	4,593	522,194 R	61.9%	37.9%	62.0%	38.0%
1980**	1,855,833	915,018	Reagan, Ronald	875,635	Carter, Jimmy	65,180	39,383 R	49.3%	47.2%	51.1%	48.9%
1976	1,678,914	741,960	Ford, Gerald R.	927,365	Carter, Jimmy	9,589	185,405 D	44.2%	55.2%	44.4%	55.6%
1972	1,518,612	1,054,889	Nixon, Richard M.	438,705	McGovern, George S.	25,018	616,184 R	69.5%	28.9%	70.6%	29.4%
1968**	1,587,493	627,192	Nixon, Richard M.	464,113	Humphrey, Hubert H.	496,188	131,004 R	39.5%	29.2%	57.5%	42.5%
1964	1,424,983	624,844	Goldwater, Barry M.	800,139	Johnson, Lyndon B.		175,295 D	43.8%	56.2%	43.8%	56.2%
1960	1,368,556	655,420	Nixon, Richard M.	713,136	Kennedy, John F.		57,716 D	47.9%	52.1%	47.9%	52.1%
1956	1,165,592	575,062	Eisenhower, Dwight D.	590,530	Stevenson, Adlai E.		15,468 D	49.3%	50.7%	49.3%	50.7%
1952	1,210,910	558,107	Eisenhower, Dwight D.	652,803	Stevenson, Adlai E.		94,696 D	46.1%	53.9%	46.1%	53.9%
1948	791,209	258,572	Dewey, Thomas E.	459,070	Truman, Harry S.	73,567	200,498 D	32.7%	58.0%	36.0%	64.0%

In 1996 the other vote column includes 168,059 votes cast for Perot. In 1992 the other vote column includes 357,864 votes cast for Perot. In 1980 the other column includes 52,800 votes for Independent (Anderson). In 1968 other vote was American (Wallace).

NORTH CAROLINA

POSTWAR VOTE FOR GOVERNOR

Year	Total Vote	Republican		Democratic		Other Vote	Rep.-Dem. Plurality	Percentage			
		Vote	Candidate	Vote	Candidate			Total Vote		Major Vote	
								Rep.	Dem.	Rep.	Dem.
2000	2,942,062	1,360,960	Vinroot, Richard	1,530,324	Easley, Mike	50,778	169,364 D	46.3%	52.0%	47.1%	52.9%
1996	2,566,185	1,097,053	Hayes, Robin	1,436,638	Hunt, James B.	32,494	339,585 D	42.8%	56.0%	43.3%	56.7%
1992	2,595,184	1,121,955	Gardner, James C.	1,368,246	Hunt, James B.	104,983	246,291 D	43.2%	52.7%	45.1%	54.9%
1988	2,180,025	1,222,338	Martin, James G.	957,687	Jordan, Robert B.		264,651 R	56.1%	43.9%	56.1%	43.9%
1984	2,226,727	1,208,167	Martin, James G.	1,011,209	Edmisten, Rufus	7,351	196,958 R	54.3%	45.4%	54.4%	45.6%
1980	1,847,432	691,449	Lake, Beverly	1,143,145	Hunt, James B.	12,838	451,696 D	37.4%	61.9%	37.7%	62.3%
1976	1,663,824	564,102	Flaherty, David T.	1,081,293	Hunt, James B.	18,429	517,191 D	33.9%	65.0%	34.3%	65.7%
1972	1,504,785	767,470	Holshouser, James E.	729,104	Bowles, Hargrove	8,211	38,366 R	51.0%	48.5%	51.3%	48.7%
1968	1,558,308	737,075	Gardner, James C.	821,233	Scott, Robert W.		84,158 D	47.3%	52.7%	47.3%	52.7%
1964	1,396,508	606,165	Gavin, Robert L.	790,343	Moore, Dan K.		184,178 D	43.4%	56.6%	43.4%	56.6%
1960	1,350,360	613,975	Gavin, Robert L.	735,248	Sanford, Terry	1,137	121,273 D	45.5%	54.4%	45.5%	54.5%
1956	1,135,859	375,379	Hayes, Kyle	760,480	Hodges, Luther H.		385,101 D	33.0%	67.0%	33.0%	67.0%
1952	1,179,635	383,329	Seawell, H. F.	796,306	Umstead, William B.		412,977 D	32.5%	67.5%	32.5%	67.5%
1948	780,525	206,166	Pritchard, George	570,995	Scott, William Kerr	3,364	364,829 D	26.4%	73.2%	26.5%	73.5%

POSTWAR VOTE FOR SENATOR

Year	Total Vote	Republican		Democratic		Other Vote	Rep.-Dem. Plurality	Percentage			
		Vote	Candidate	Vote	Candidate			Total Vote		Major Vote	
								Rep.	Dem.	Rep.	Dem.
1998	2,012,143	945,943	Faircloth, Lauch	1,029,237	Edwards, John	36,963	83,294 D	47.0%	51.2%	47.9%	52.1%
1996	2,556,456	1,345,833	Helms, Jesse	1,173,875	Gantt, Harvey B.	36,748	171,958 R	52.6%	45.9%	53.4%	46.6%
1992	2,577,891	1,297,892	Faircloth, Lauch	1,194,015	Sanford, Terry	85,984	103,877 R	50.3%	46.3%	52.1%	47.9%
1990	2,069,585	1,087,331	Helms, Jesse	981,573	Gantt, Harvy B.	681	105,758 R	52.5%	47.4%	52.6%	47.4%
1986	1,591,330	767,668	Broyhill, James T.	823,662	Sanford, Terry		55,994 D	48.2%	51.8%	48.2%	51.8%
1984	2,239,051	1,156,768	Helms, Jesse	1,070,488	Hunt, James B.	11,795	86,280 R	51.7%	47.8%	51.9%	48.1%
1980	1,797,665	898,064	East, John P.	887,653	Morgan, Robert	11,948	10,411 R	50.0%	49.4%	50.3%	49.7%
1978	1,135,814	619,151	Helms, Jesse	516,663	Ingram, John		102,488 R	54.5%	45.5%	54.5%	45.5%
1974	1,020,367	377,618	Stevens, William E.	633,775	Morgan, Robert	8,974	256,157 D	37.0%	62.1%	37.3%	62.7%
1972	1,472,541	795,248	Helms, Jesse	677,293	Galifianakis, Nick		117,955 R	54.0%	46.0%	54.0%	46.0%
1968	1,437,340	566,934	Somers, Robert V.	870,406	Ervin, Sam J.		303,472 D	39.4%	60.6%	39.4%	60.6%
1966	901,978	400,502	Shallcross, John S.	501,440	Jordan, B. Everett	36	100,938 D	44.4%	55.6%	44.4%	55.6%
1962	813,155	321,635	Greene, Claude L.	491,520	Ervin, Sam J.		169,885 D	39.6%	60.4%	39.6%	60.4%
1960	1,291,485	497,964	Hayes, Kyle	793,521	Jordan, B. Everett		295,557 D	38.6%	61.4%	38.6%	61.4%
1958S	616,469	184,977	Clarke, Richard C.	431,492	Jordan, B. Everett		246,515 D	30.0%	70.0%	30.0%	70.0%
1956	1,098,828	367,475	Johnson, Joel A.	731,353	Ervin, Sam J.		363,878 D	33.4%	66.6%	33.4%	66.6%
1954	619,634	211,322	West, Paul C.	408,312	Scott, William Kerr		196,990 D	34.1%	65.9%	34.1%	65.9%
1954S	410,574		—	410,574	Ervin, Sam J.		410,574 D		100.0%		100.0%
1950	548,276	171,804	Leavitt, Halsey B.	376,472	Hoey, Clyde R.		204,668 D	31.3%	68.7%	31.3%	68.7%
1950S	544,924	177,753	Gavin, E. L.	364,912	Smith, Willis	2,259	187,159 D	32.6%	67.0%	32.8%	67.2%
1948	764,559	220,307	Wilkinson, John A.	540,762	Broughton, J. M.	3,490	320,455 D	28.8%	70.7%	28.9%	71.1%

The 1958 election and one each of the 1954 and 1950 elections were for short terms to fill vacancies.

NORTH CAROLINA

Districts Established May 17, 1999

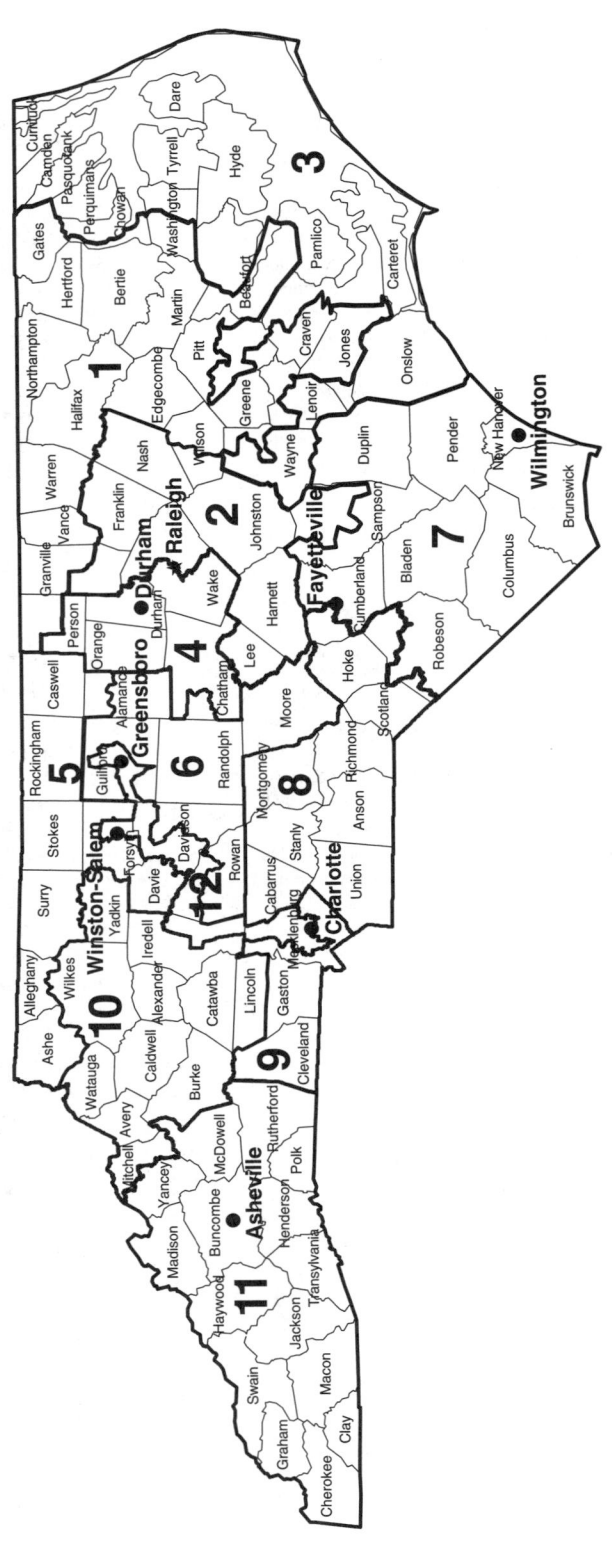

NORTH CAROLINA

PRESIDENT 2000

2000 Census Population	County	Total Vote	Republican	Democratic	Green (Nader)	Other	Rep.-Dem. Plurality	Percentage of Total Vote Rep.	Dem.	Green
130,800	ALAMANCE	47,091	29,305	17,459		327	11,846 R	62.2%	37.1%	
33,603	ALEXANDER	13,492	9,242	4,166		84	5,076 R	68.5%	30.9%	
10,677	ALLEGHANY	4,313	2,531	1,715		67	816 R	58.7%	39.8%	
25,275	ANSON	7,985	3,161	4,792		32	1,631 D	39.6%	60.0%	
24,384	ASHE	10,316	6,226	4,011		79	2,215 R	60.4%	38.9%	
17,167	AVERY	6,694	4,956	1,686		52	3,270 R	74.0%	25.2%	
44,958	BEAUFORT	17,313	10,531	6,634		148	3,897 R	60.8%	38.3%	
19,773	BERTIE	7,176	2,488	4,660		28	2,172 D	34.7%	64.9%	
32,278	BLADEN	10,908	4,977	5,889		42	912 D	45.6%	54.0%	
73,143	BRUNSWICK	28,839	15,427	13,118		294	2,309 R	53.5%	45.5%	
206,330	BUNCOMBE	85,476	46,101	38,545		830	7,556 R	53.9%	45.1%	
89,148	BURKE	30,658	18,466	11,924		268	6,542 R	60.2%	38.9%	
131,063	CABARRUS	49,381	32,704	16,284		343	16,420 R	66.2%	33.0%	
77,415	CALDWELL	26,115	17,337	8,588		190	8,749 R	66.4%	32.9%	
6,885	CAMDEN	2,831	1,628	1,187		16	441 R	57.5%	41.9%	
59,383	CARTERET	26,461	17,381	8,839		241	8,542 R	65.7%	33.4%	
23,501	CASWELL	8,422	4,270	4,091		61	179 R	50.7%	48.6%	
141,685	CATAWBA	50,841	34,244	16,246		351	17,998 R	67.4%	32.0%	
49,329	CHATHAM	20,931	10,248	10,461		222	213 D	49.0%	50.0%	
24,298	CHEROKEE	9,674	6,305	3,239		130	3,066 R	65.2%	33.5%	
14,526	CHOWAN	4,890	2,415	2,430		45	15 D	49.4%	49.7%	
8,775	CLAY	3,852	2,416	1,361		75	1,055 R	62.7%	35.3%	
96,287	CLEVELAND	32,746	19,064	13,455		227	5,609 R	58.2%	41.1%	
54,749	COLUMBUS	18,425	8,342	9,986		97	1,644 D	45.3%	54.2%	
91,436	CRAVEN	31,985	19,494	12,213		278	7,281 R	60.9%	38.2%	
302,963	CUMBERLAND	77,151	38,129	38,626		396	497 D	49.4%	50.1%	
18,190	CURRITUCK	6,739	4,095	2,595		49	1,500 R	60.8%	38.5%	
29,967	DARE	13,002	7,301	5,589		112	1,712 R	56.2%	43.0%	
147,246	DAVIDSON	52,047	35,387	16,199		461	19,188 R	68.0%	31.1%	
34,835	DAVIE	13,998	10,184	3,651		163	6,533 R	72.8%	26.1%	
49,063	DUPLIN	14,390	7,840	6,475		75	1,365 R	54.5%	45.0%	
223,314	DURHAM	84,604	30,150	53,907		547	23,757 D	35.6%	63.7%	
55,606	EDGECOMBE	18,202	6,836	11,315		51	4,479 D	37.6%	62.2%	
306,067	FORSYTH	120,942	67,700	52,457		785	15,243 R	56.0%	43.4%	
47,260	FRANKLIN	16,051	8,501	7,454		96	1,047 R	53.0%	46.4%	
190,365	GASTON	59,179	39,453	19,281		445	20,172 R	66.7%	32.6%	
10,516	GATES	3,446	1,480	1,944		22	464 D	42.9%	56.4%	
7,993	GRAHAM	3,361	2,304	1,006		51	1,298 R	68.6%	29.9%	
48,498	GRANVILLE	15,194	7,364	7,733		97	369 D	48.5%	50.9%	
18,974	GREENE	5,870	3,353	2,478		39	875 R	57.1%	42.2%	
421,048	GUILFORD	166,264	84,394	80,787		1,083	3,607 R	50.8%	48.6%	
57,370	HALIFAX	16,970	6,698	10,222		50	3,524 D	39.5%	60.2%	
91,025	HARNETT	24,167	14,762	9,155		250	5,607 R	61.1%	37.9%	
54,033	HAYWOOD	22,273	12,118	9,793		362	2,325 R	54.4%	44.0%	
89,173	HENDERSON	38,607	25,688	12,562		357	13,126 R	66.5%	32.5%	
22,601	HERTFORD	7,897	2,382	5,484		31	3,102 D	30.2%	69.4%	
33,646	HOKE	8,582	3,439	5,017		126	1,578 D	40.1%	58.5%	
5,826	HYDE	2,237	1,132	1,088		17	44 R	50.6%	48.6%	
122,660	IREDELL	45,586	29,853	15,434		299	14,419 R	65.5%	33.9%	
33,121	JACKSON	12,121	6,237	5,722		162	515 R	51.5%	47.2%	
121,965	JOHNSTON	41,155	27,212	13,704		239	13,508 R	66.1%	33.3%	
10,381	JONES	3,964	2,114	1,822		28	292 R	53.3%	46.0%	
49,040	LEE	16,283	9,406	6,785		92	2,621 R	57.8%	41.7%	
59,648	LENOIR	21,163	11,512	9,527		124	1,985 R	54.4%	45.0%	
63,780	LINCOLN	24,529	15,951	8,412		166	7,539 R	65.0%	34.3%	
42,151	MCDOWELL	14,011	9,109	4,747		155	4,362 R	65.0%	33.9%	
29,811	MACON	13,234	8,406	4,683		145	3,723 R	63.5%	35.4%	
19,635	MADISON	8,325	4,676	3,505		144	1,171 R	56.2%	42.1%	
25,593	MARTIN	9,366	4,420	4,929		17	509 D	47.2%	52.6%	
695,454	MECKLENBURG	263,036	134,068	126,911		2,057	7,157 R	51.0%	48.2%	

NORTH CAROLINA

PRESIDENT 2000

2000 Census Population	County	Total Vote	Republican	Democratic	Green (Nader)	Other	Rep.-Dem. Plurality	Percentage of Total Vote		
								Rep.	Dem.	Green
15,687	MITCHELL	6,600	4,984	1,535		81	3,449 R	75.5%	23.3%	
26,822	MONTGOMERY	8,974	4,946	3,979		49	967 R	55.1%	44.3%	
74,769	MOORE	31,301	19,882	11,232		187	8,650 R	63.5%	35.9%	
87,420	NASH	30,513	17,995	12,376		142	5,619 R	59.0%	40.6%	
160,307	NEW HANOVER	66,319	36,503	29,292		524	7,211 R	55.0%	44.2%	
22,086	NORTHAMPTON	8,200	2,667	5,513		20	2,846 D	32.5%	67.2%	
150,355	ONSLOW	30,215	19,657	10,269		289	9,388 R	65.1%	34.0%	
118,227	ORANGE	49,344	17,930	30,921		493	12,991 D	36.3%	62.7%	
12,934	PAMLICO	5,242	2,999	2,188		55	811 R	57.2%	41.7%	
34,897	PASQUOTANK	10,903	4,943	5,874		86	931 D	45.3%	53.9%	
41,082	PENDER	14,154	7,661	6,415		78	1,246 R	54.1%	45.3%	
11,368	PERQUIMANS	4,306	2,230	2,033		43	197 R	51.8%	47.2%	
35,623	PERSON	11,833	6,722	5,042		69	1,680 R	56.8%	42.6%	
133,798	PITT	43,075	23,192	19,685		198	3,507 R	53.8%	45.7%	
18,324	POLK	8,303	5,074	3,114		115	1,960 R	61.1%	37.5%	
130,454	RANDOLPH	42,696	30,959	11,366		371	19,593 R	72.5%	26.6%	
46,564	RICHMOND	14,269	6,263	7,935		71	1,672 D	43.9%	55.6%	
123,339	ROBESON	29,747	11,721	17,834		192	6,113 D	39.4%	60.0%	
91,928	ROCKINGHAM	32,528	18,979	13,260		289	5,719 R	58.3%	40.8%	
130,340	ROWAN	44,133	28,922	14,891		320	14,031 R	65.5%	33.7%	
62,899	RUTHERFORD	21,716	13,755	7,697		264	6,058 R	63.3%	35.4%	
60,161	SAMPSON	19,239	10,410	8,768		61	1,642 R	54.1%	45.6%	
35,998	SCOTLAND	9,403	3,740	5,627		36	1,887 D	39.8%	59.8%	
58,100	STANLY	22,818	15,548	7,066		204	8,482 R	68.1%	31.0%	
44,711	STOKES	17,182	12,028	5,030		124	6,998 R	70.0%	29.3%	
71,219	SURRY	23,358	15,401	7,757		200	7,644 R	65.9%	33.2%	
12,968	SWAIN	4,370	2,224	2,097		49	127 R	50.9%	48.0%	
29,334	TRANSYLVANIA	14,225	9,011	5,044		170	3,967 R	63.3%	35.5%	
4,149	TYRRELL	1,566	706	849		11	143 D	45.1%	54.2%	
123,677	UNION	47,161	31,876	14,890		395	16,986 R	67.6%	31.6%	
42,954	VANCE	12,701	5,564	7,092		45	1,528 D	43.8%	55.8%	
627,846	WAKE	268,220	142,494	123,466		2,260	19,028 R	53.1%	46.0%	
19,972	WARREN	6,795	2,202	4,576		17	2,374 D	32.4%	67.3%	
13,723	WASHINGTON	4,890	2,169	2,704		17	535 D	44.4%	55.3%	
42,695	WATAUGA	18,723	10,438	7,959		326	2,479 R	55.7%	42.5%	
113,329	WAYNE	33,884	20,758	13,005		121	7,753 R	61.3%	38.4%	
65,632	WILKES	24,323	16,826	7,226		271	9,600 R	69.2%	29.7%	
73,814	WILSON	24,826	13,466	11,266		94	2,200 R	54.2%	45.4%	
36,348	YADKIN	13,682	10,435	3,127		120	7,308 R	76.3%	22.9%	
17,774	YANCEY	8,764	4,970	3,714		80	1,256 R	56.7%	42.4%	
8,049,313	TOTAL	2,911,262	1,631,163	1,257,692		22,407	373,471 R	56.0%	43.2%	

Note: No votes were tallied for Nader in North Carolina. He qualified neither for the ballot nor as a write-in candidate.

NORTH CAROLINA

GOVERNOR 2000

2000 Census Population	County	Total Vote	Republican	Democratic	Other	Rep.-Dem. Plurality	Percentage			
							Total Vote		Major Vote	
							Rep.	Dem.	Rep.	Dem.
130,800	ALAMANCE	47,334	24,447	22,180	707	2,267 R	51.6%	46.9%	52.4%	47.6%
33,603	ALEXANDER	13,792	8,218	5,381	193	2,837 R	59.6%	39.0%	60.4%	39.6%
10,677	ALLEGHANY	4,312	1,938	2,293	81	355 D	44.9%	53.2%	45.8%	54.2%
25,275	ANSON	8,064	2,481	5,473	110	2,992 D	30.8%	67.9%	31.2%	68.8%
24,384	ASHE	10,512	5,494	4,831	187	663 R	52.3%	46.0%	53.2%	46.8%

NORTH CAROLINA

GOVERNOR 2000

2000 Census Population	County	Total Vote	Republican	Democratic	Other	Rep.-Dem. Plurality		Percentage			
								Total Vote		Major Vote	
								Rep.	Dem.	Rep.	Dem.
17,167	AVERY	6,716	4,343	2,187	186	2,156	R	64.7%	32.6%	66.5%	33.5%
44,958	BEAUFORT	17,737	8,438	9,108	191	670	D	47.6%	51.4%	48.1%	51.9%
19,773	BERTIE	7,301	1,679	5,568	54	3,889	D	23.0%	76.3%	23.2%	76.8%
32,278	BLADEN	10,926	3,112	7,689	125	4,577	D	28.5%	70.4%	28.8%	71.2%
73,143	BRUNSWICK	28,921	11,682	16,685	554	5,003	D	40.4%	57.7%	41.2%	58.8%
206,330	BUNCOMBE	85,961	39,802	43,436	2,723	3,634	D	46.3%	50.5%	47.8%	52.2%
89,148	BURKE	28,958	15,068	13,408	482	1,660	R	52.0%	46.3%	52.9%	47.1%
131,063	CABARRUS	50,124	29,641	19,540	943	10,101	R	59.1%	39.0%	60.3%	39.7%
77,415	CALDWELL	26,595	14,958	10,963	674	3,995	R	56.2%	41.2%	57.7%	42.3%
6,885	CAMDEN	2,807	1,121	1,621	65	500	D	39.9%	57.7%	40.9%	59.1%
59,383	CARTERET	25,755	13,536	11,786	433	1,750	R	52.6%	45.8%	53.5%	46.5%
23,501	CASWELL	8,411	3,349	4,968	94	1,619	D	39.8%	59.1%	40.3%	59.7%
141,685	CATAWBA	51,500	30,595	20,001	904	10,594	R	59.4%	38.8%	60.5%	39.5%
49,329	CHATHAM	21,535	8,746	12,371	418	3,625	D	40.6%	57.4%	41.4%	58.6%
24,298	CHEROKEE	9,697	5,492	4,050	155	1,442	R	56.6%	41.8%	57.6%	42.4%
14,526	CHOWAN	4,817	1,636	3,057	124	1,421	D	34.0%	63.5%	34.9%	65.1%
8,775	CLAY	3,936	2,238	1,597	101	641	R	56.9%	40.6%	58.4%	41.6%
96,287	CLEVELAND	33,245	15,586	17,218	441	1,632	D	46.9%	51.8%	47.5%	52.5%
54,749	COLUMBUS	18,875	4,964	13,689	222	8,725	D	26.3%	72.5%	26.6%	73.4%
91,436	CRAVEN	31,938	15,531	15,970	437	439	D	48.6%	50.0%	49.3%	50.7%
302,963	CUMBERLAND	78,479	30,952	46,386	1,141	15,434	D	39.4%	59.1%	40.0%	60.0%
18,190	CURRITUCK	6,683	3,074	3,389	220	315	D	46.0%	50.7%	47.6%	52.4%
29,967	DARE	13,107	5,195	7,589	323	2,394	D	39.6%	57.9%	40.6%	59.4%
147,246	DAVIDSON	51,938	28,583	22,505	850	6,078	R	55.0%	43.3%	55.9%	44.1%
34,835	DAVIE	13,915	8,377	5,214	324	3,163	R	60.2%	37.5%	61.6%	38.4%
49,063	DUPLIN	14,563	6,148	8,291	124	2,143	D	42.2%	56.9%	42.6%	57.4%
223,314	DURHAM	86,236	25,250	59,667	1,319	34,417	D	29.3%	69.2%	29.7%	70.3%
55,606	EDGECOMBE	18,717	4,864	13,753	100	8,889	D	26.0%	73.5%	26.1%	73.9%
306,067	FORSYTH	121,276	56,369	62,677	2,230	6,308	D	46.5%	51.7%	47.4%	52.6%
47,260	FRANKLIN	16,253	6,515	9,528	210	3,013	D	40.1%	58.6%	40.6%	59.4%
190,365	GASTON	59,702	35,101	23,572	1,029	11,529	R	58.8%	39.5%	59.8%	40.2%
10,516	GATES	3,516	974	2,473	69	1,499	D	27.7%	70.3%	28.3%	71.7%
7,993	GRAHAM	3,407	1,874	1,471	62	403	R	55.0%	43.2%	56.0%	44.0%
48,498	GRANVILLE	15,336	5,461	9,706	169	4,245	D	35.6%	63.3%	36.0%	64.0%
18,974	GREENE	5,803	2,329	3,435	39	1,106	D	40.1%	59.2%	40.4%	59.6%
421,048	GUILFORD	168,258	70,922	94,523	2,813	23,601	D	42.2%	56.2%	42.9%	57.1%
57,370	HALIFAX	17,782	4,927	12,691	164	7,764	D	27.7%	71.4%	28.0%	72.0%
91,025	HARNETT	24,654	11,277	13,037	340	1,760	D	45.7%	52.9%	46.4%	53.6%
54,033	HAYWOOD	23,048	9,853	12,698	497	2,845	D	42.7%	55.1%	43.7%	56.3%
89,173	HENDERSON	38,902	23,043	15,138	721	7,905	R	59.2%	38.9%	60.4%	39.6%
22,601	HERTFORD	7,841	1,587	6,193	61	4,606	D	20.2%	79.0%	20.4%	79.6%
33,646	HOKE	8,390	2,469	5,797	124	3,328	D	29.4%	69.1%	29.9%	70.1%
5,826	HYDE	2,195	774	1,396	25	622	D	35.3%	63.6%	35.7%	64.3%
122,660	IREDELL	45,893	26,496	18,620	777	7,876	R	57.7%	40.6%	58.7%	41.3%
33,121	JACKSON	12,251	5,258	6,695	298	1,437	D	42.9%	54.6%	44.0%	56.0%
121,965	JOHNSTON	42,209	20,214	21,369	626	1,155	D	47.9%	50.6%	48.6%	51.4%
10,381	JONES	4,001	1,658	2,309	34	651	D	41.4%	57.7%	41.8%	58.2%
49,040	LEE	16,303	7,230	8,856	217	1,626	D	44.3%	54.3%	44.9%	55.1%
59,648	LENOIR	21,422	8,499	12,802	121	4,303	D	39.7%	59.8%	39.9%	60.1%
63,780	LINCOLN	24,911	14,003	10,465	443	3,538	R	56.2%	42.0%	57.2%	42.8%
42,151	MCDOWELL	14,076	7,336	6,458	282	878	R	52.1%	45.9%	53.2%	46.8%
29,811	MACON	13,443	7,231	5,930	282	1,301	R	53.8%	44.1%	54.9%	45.1%
19,635	MADISON	8,291	3,748	4,352	191	604	D	45.2%	52.5%	46.3%	53.7%
25,593	MARTIN	9,627	3,005	6,563	59	3,558	D	31.2%	68.2%	31.4%	68.6%
695,454	MECKLENBURG	264,173	133,728	126,480	3,965	7,248	R	50.6%	47.9%	51.4%	48.6%
15,687	MITCHELL	6,647	4,540	1,971	136	2,569	R	68.3%	29.7%	69.7%	30.3%
26,822	MONTGOMERY	9,184	3,861	5,194	129	1,333	D	42.0%	56.6%	42.6%	57.4%
74,769	MOORE	32,044	17,738	14,032	274	3,706	R	55.4%	43.8%	55.8%	44.2%
87,420	NASH	31,439	12,953	18,261	225	5,308	D	41.2%	58.1%	41.5%	58.5%
160,307	NEW HANOVER	66,507	27,992	36,971	1,544	8,979	D	42.1%	55.6%	43.1%	56.9%

NORTH CAROLINA

GOVERNOR 2000

2000 Census Population	County	Total Vote	Republican	Democratic	Other	Rep.-Dem. Plurality		Percentage			
								Total Vote		Major Vote	
								Rep.	Dem.	Rep.	Dem.
22,086	NORTHAMPTON	8,571	1,850	6,636	85	4,786	D	21.6%	77.4%	21.8%	78.2%
150,355	ONSLOW	30,304	15,804	13,622	878	2,182	R	52.2%	45.0%	53.7%	46.3%
118,227	ORANGE	50,507	15,528	33,837	1,142	18,309	D	30.7%	67.0%	31.5%	68.5%
12,934	PAMLICO	5,251	2,325	2,852	74	527	D	44.3%	54.3%	44.9%	55.1%
34,897	PASQUOTANK	10,766	3,576	6,995	195	3,419	D	33.2%	65.0%	33.8%	66.2%
41,082	PENDER	14,259	6,052	7,993	214	1,941	D	42.4%	56.1%	43.1%	56.9%
11,368	PERQUIMANS	4,237	1,548	2,604	85	1,056	D	36.5%	61.5%	37.3%	62.7%
35,623	PERSON	12,017	5,071	6,800	146	1,729	D	42.2%	56.6%	42.7%	57.3%
133,798	PITT	43,110	16,969	25,738	403	8,769	D	39.4%	59.7%	39.7%	60.3%
18,324	POLK	8,204	4,395	3,559	250	836	R	53.6%	43.4%	55.3%	44.7%
130,454	RANDOLPH	43,303	26,235	16,410	658	9,825	R	60.6%	37.9%	61.5%	38.5%
46,564	RICHMOND	15,725	4,567	9,658	1,500	5,091	D	29.0%	61.4%	32.1%	67.9%
123,339	ROBESON	31,073	7,517	23,118	438	15,601	D	24.2%	74.4%	24.5%	75.5%
91,928	ROCKINGHAM	32,785	14,681	17,525	579	2,844	D	44.8%	53.5%	45.6%	54.4%
130,340	ROWAN	44,504	24,978	18,643	883	6,335	R	56.1%	41.9%	57.3%	42.7%
62,899	RUTHERFORD	21,394	10,736	10,190	468	546	R	50.2%	47.6%	51.3%	48.7%
60,161	SAMPSON	19,553	8,455	10,943	155	2,488	D	43.2%	56.0%	43.6%	56.4%
35,998	SCOTLAND	9,639	2,759	6,777	103	4,018	D	28.6%	70.3%	28.9%	71.1%
58,100	STANLY	22,575	13,015	9,197	363	3,818	R	57.7%	40.7%	58.6%	41.4%
44,711	STOKES	17,611	9,841	7,488	282	2,353	R	55.9%	42.5%	56.8%	43.2%
71,219	SURRY	23,343	12,602	10,454	287	2,148	R	54.0%	44.8%	54.7%	45.3%
12,968	SWAIN	4,375	1,855	2,437	83	582	D	42.4%	55.7%	43.2%	56.8%
29,334	TRANSYLVANIA	14,200	8,219	5,557	424	2,662	R	57.9%	39.1%	59.7%	40.3%
4,149	TYRRELL	1,531	402	1,118	11	716	D	26.3%	73.0%	26.4%	73.6%
123,677	UNION	46,708	28,892	16,986	830	11,906	R	61.9%	36.4%	63.0%	37.0%
42,954	VANCE	13,100	4,147	8,875	78	4,728	D	31.7%	67.7%	31.8%	68.2%
627,846	WAKE	272,125	117,283	150,014	4,828	32,731	D	43.1%	55.1%	43.9%	56.1%
19,972	WARREN	6,997	1,804	5,138	55	3,334	D	25.8%	73.4%	26.0%	74.0%
13,723	WASHINGTON	5,165	1,581	3,526	58	1,945	D	30.6%	68.3%	31.0%	69.0%
42,695	WATAUGA	18,945	9,015	9,177	753	162	D	47.6%	48.4%	49.6%	50.4%
113,329	WAYNE	34,480	16,608	17,526	346	918	D	48.2%	50.8%	48.7%	51.3%
65,632	WILKES	25,284	14,463	10,448	373	4,015	R	57.2%	41.3%	58.1%	41.9%
73,814	WILSON	25,370	9,706	15,463	201	5,757	D	38.3%	60.9%	38.6%	61.4%
36,348	YADKIN	13,937	8,719	4,980	238	3,739	R	62.6%	35.7%	63.6%	36.4%
17,774	YANCEY	8,923	4,259	4,513	151	254	D	47.7%	50.6%	48.6%	51.4%
8,049,313	TOTAL	2,942,062	1,360,960	1,530,324	50,778	169,364	D	46.3%	52.0%	47.1%	52.9%

NORTH CAROLINA

CONGRESS

CD	Year	Total Vote	Republican		Democratic		Other Vote	Rep.-Dem. Plurality		Percentage			
			Vote	Candidate	Vote	Candidate				Total Vote		Major Vote	
										Rep.	Dem.	Rep.	Dem.
1	2000	189,168	62,198	KRATZER, DUANE E., JR.	124,171	CLAYTON, EVA	2,799	61,973	D	32.9%	65.6%	33.4%	66.6%
1	1998	136,747	50,578	TYLER, TED	85,125	CLAYTON, EVA	1,044	34,547	D	37.0%	62.2%	37.3%	62.7%
2	2000	251,838	103,011	HAYNES, DOUG	146,733	ETHERIDGE, BOB	2,094	43,722	D	40.9%	58.3%	41.2%	58.8%
2	1998	175,194	72,997	PAGE, DAN	100,550	ETHERIDGE, BOB	1,647	27,553	D	41.7%	57.4%	42.1%	57.9%
3	2000	198,455	121,940	JONES, WALTER B., JR.	74,058	MCNAIRY, LEIGH HARVEY	2,457	47,882	R	61.4%	37.3%	62.2%	37.8%
3	1998	134,912	83,529	JONES, WALTER B., JR.	50,041	WILLIAMS, JON	1,342	33,488	R	61.9%	37.1%	62.5%	37.5%
4	2000	325,870	119,412	WARD, JESS	200,885	PRICE, DAVID E.	5,573	81,473	D	36.6%	61.6%	37.3%	62.7%
4	1998	224,910	93,469	ROBERG, TOM	129,157	PRICE, DAVID E.	2,284	35,688	D	41.6%	57.4%	42.0%	58.0%

NORTH CAROLINA

CONGRESS

| CD | Year | Total Vote | Republican | | Democratic | | Other Vote | Rep.-Dem. Plurality | Percentage | | | |
| | | | Vote | Candidate | Vote | Candidate | | | Total Vote | | Major Vote | |
									Rep.	Dem.	Rep.	Dem.
5	2000	185,855	172,489	BURR, RICHARD M.			13,366	172,489 R	92.8%		100.0%	
6	2000	215,085	195,727	COBLE, HOWARD			19,358	195,727 R	91.0%		100.0%	
7	2000	229,666	66,463	ADAMS, JAMES R.	160,185	MCINTYRE, MIKE	3,018	93,722 D	28.9%	69.7%	29.3%	70.7%
7	1998	136,290			124,366	MCINTYRE, MIKE	11,924	124,366 D		91.3%		100.0%
8	2000	203,464	111,950	HAYES, ROBIN	89,505	TAYLOR, MIKE	2,009	22,445 R	55.0%	44.0%	55.6%	44.4%
8	1998	133,124	67,505	HAYES, ROBIN	64,127	TAYLOR, MIKE	1,492	3,378 R	50.7%	48.2%	51.3%	48.7%
9	2000	264,220	181,161	MYRICK, SUE	79,382	MCGUIRE, ED	3,677	101,779 R	68.6%	30.0%	69.5%	30.5%
10	2000	240,658	164,182	BALLENGER, CASS	70,877	PARKER, DELMAS	5,599	93,305 R	68.2%	29.5%	69.8%	30.2%
11	2000	266,377	146,677	TAYLOR, CHARLES H.	112,234	NEILL, SAM	7,466	34,443 R	55.1%	42.1%	56.7%	43.3%
11	1998	199,423	112,908	TAYLOR, CHARLES H.	84,256	YOUNG, DAVID	2,259	28,652 R	56.6%	42.2%	57.3%	42.7%
12	2000	209,144	69,596	MITCHELL, CHAD	135,570	WATT, MELVIN	3,978	65,974 D	33.3%	64.8%	33.9%	66.1%

Note: Following legal challenges, the lines for North Carolina's congressional districts were changed prior to both the 1998 and 2000 elections. Results for the elections of 1992, 1994 and 1996 can be found in *America Votes 22*.

NORTH CAROLINA

GENERAL AND PRIMARY ELECTIONS

2000 GENERAL ELECTIONS

President   Other vote was 12,307 Libertarian (Browne); 8,874 Reform (Buchanan); 1,226 write-in (McReynolds).

Governor   Other vote was 42,674 Libertarian (Howe); 8,104 Reform (Schell).

Congress   Other vote was: CD 1: 2,799 Libertarian (Delaney); CD 2: 2,094 Libertarian (Jackson); CD 3: 2,457 Libertarian (Russell); CD 4: 5,573 Libertarian (Towey); CD 5: 13,366 Libertarian (LeBoeuf); CD 6: 18,726 Libertarian (Bentley), 632 write-in (Gay); CD 7: 3,018 Libertarian (Burns); CD 8: 2,009 Libertarian (Schwartz); CD 9: 2,459 Libertarian (Cole), 1,218 Reform (Cahaney); CD 10: 5,599 Libertarian (Eddins); CD 11: 7,466 Libertarian (Williams); CD 12: 3,978 Libertarian (Lyon).

2000 PRIMARY ELECTIONS

Primary   May 2, 2000

Registration (as of April 7, 2000)		
	Republican	1,671,571
	Democratic	2,495,399
	Libertarian	5,627
	Unaffiliated	757,722
	TOTAL	4,930,319

NORTH CAROLINA

GENERAL AND PRIMARY ELECTIONS

Primary Type   Modified—Registered Democrats and Republicans could vote only in their party's primary. "Unaffiliated" voters could vote in the primary of either party.

Note: An asterisk (*) denotes incumbent. The names of unopposed candidates do not appear on the primary ballot; therefore, no votes are cast for these candidates. The threshold to avoid a primary runoff is 40 percent of the vote.

	REPUBLICAN PRIMARIES			DEMOCRATIC PRIMARIES		
President	George W. Bush	253,485	78.6%	Al Gore	383,696	70.4%
	John McCain	35,018	10.9%	Bill Bradley	99,796	18.3%
	Alan Keyes	25,320	7.9%	No Preference	49,905	9.2%
	No Preference	5,383	1.7%	Lyndon H. LaRouche Jr.	11,525	2.1%
	Gary Bauer	3,311	1.0%			
	TOTAL	322,517		TOTAL	544,922	
Governor	Richard Vinroot	142,820	45.5%	Mike Easley	330,764	58.9%
	Leo Daughtry	116,115	37.0%	Dennis A. Wicker	203,723	36.3%
	Charles B. Neely	48,101	15.3%	Bob Ayers	9,224	1.6%
	Art Manning	7,019	2.2%	Ken Rogers	7,998	1.4%
				Kenneth R. Gottfried	3,792	0.7%
				Bryan Ipock	3,335	0.6%
				Roger Maines	3,104	0.6%
	TOTAL	314,055		TOTAL	561,940	
Congressional District 1	Duane Kratzer	3,371	52.1%	Eva Clayton*	Unopposed	
	Albert Wiley	3,096	47.9%			
	TOTAL	6,467				
Congressional District 2	Doug Haynes	14,124	62.2%	Bob Etheridge*	Unopposed	
	Dan Heimbach	8,591	37.8%			
	TOTAL	22,715				
Congressional District 3	Walter B. Jones Jr.*	Unopposed		Leigh Harvey McNairy	Unopposed	
Congressional District 4	Jess Ward	Unopposed		David E. Price*	56,886	89.2%
				John Winters	6,919	10.8%
				TOTAL	63,805	
Congressional District 5	Richard M. Burr*	Unopposed		No Democratic candidate		
Congressional District 6	Howard Coble*	Unopposed		No Democratic candidate		
Congressional District 7	James R. Adams	12,554	68.4%	Mike McIntyre*	63,520	93.5%
	Howard T. Knupp	5,794	31.6%	Randy Crow	4,440	6.5%
	TOTAL	18,348		TOTAL	67,960	
Congressional District 8	Robin Hayes*	Unopposed		Mike Taylor	Unopposed	
Congressional District 9	Sue Myrick*	Unopposed		Ed McGuire	10,443	48.0%
				Jeri Clement	5,661	26.0%
				Gene Gay	5,632	25.9%
				TOTAL	21,736	
Congressional District 10	T. Cass Ballenger*	Unopposed		Delmas Parker	Unopposed	
Congressional District 11	Charles H. Taylor*	Unopposed		Sam Neill	Unopposed	
Congressional District 12	Chad Mitchell	4,734	41.0%	Melvin Watt*	Unopposed	
	John Cosgrove	4,629	40.1%			
	Leonard Plyler	2,195	19.0%			
	TOTAL	11,558				

NORTH DAKOTA

GOVERNOR
John Hoeven (R). Elected 2000 to a four-year term.

SENATORS
Kent Conrad (D). Re-elected 2000 to a six-year term. Previously elected in a special election December 1992 to fill out the remaining two years of the term vacated by the death of Senator Quentin N. Burdick (D) who died in September 1992; elected 1986 to a six-year term.

Byron L. Dorgan (D). Re-elected 1998 to a six year term. Previously elected 1992.

REPRESENTATIVE
At-Large. Earl Pomeroy (D)

POSTWAR VOTE FOR PRESIDENT

| | | Republican | | Democratic | | | | Percentage | | | |
| | | | | | | Other | | Total Vote | | Major Vote | |
Year	Total Vote	Vote	Candidate	Vote	Candidate	Vote	Plurality	Rep.	Dem.	Rep.	Dem.
2000**	288,256	174,852	Bush, George W.	95,284	Gore, Al	18,120	79,568 R	60.7%	33.1%	64.7%	35.3%
1996**	266,411	125,050	Dole, Bob	106,905	Clinton, Bill	34,456	18,145 R	46.9%	40.1%	53.9%	46.1%
1992**	308,133	136,244	Bush, George	99,168	Clinton, Bill	72,721	37,076 R	44.2%	32.2%	57.9%	42.1%
1988	297,261	166,559	Bush, George	127,739	Dukakis, Michael S.	2,963	38,820 R	56.0%	43.0%	56.6%	43.4%
1984	308,971	200,336	Reagan, Ronald	104,429	Mondale, Walter F.	4,206	95,907 R	64.8%	33.8%	65.7%	34.3%
1980**	301,545	193,695	Reagan, Ronald	79,189	Carter, Jimmy	28,661	114,506 R	64.2%	26.3%	71.0%	29.0%
1976	297,188	153,470	Ford, Gerald R.	136,078	Carter, Jimmy	7,640	17,392 R	51.6%	45.8%	53.0%	47.0%
1972	280,514	174,109	Nixon, Richard M.	100,384	McGovern, George S.	6,021	73,725 R	62.1%	35.8%	63.4%	36.6%
1968	247,882	138,669	Nixon, Richard M.	94,769	Humphrey, Hubert H.	14,444	43,900 R	55.9%	38.2%	59.4%	40.6%
1964	258,389	108,207	Goldwater, Barry M.	149,784	Johnson, Lyndon B.	398	41,577 D	41.9%	58.0%	41.9%	58.1%
1960	278,431	154,310	Nixon, Richard M.	123,963	Kennedy, John F.	158	30,347 R	55.4%	44.5%	55.5%	44.5%
1956	253,991	156,766	Eisenhower, Dwight D.	96,742	Stevenson, Adlai E.	483	60,024 R	61.7%	38.1%	61.8%	38.2%
1952	270,127	191,712	Eisenhower, Dwight D.	76,694	Stevenson, Adlai E.	1,721	115,018 R	71.0%	28.4%	71.4%	28.6%
1948	220,716	115,139	Dewey, Thomas E.	95,812	Truman, Harry S.	9,765	19,327 R	52.2%	43.4%	54.6%	45.4%

In 2000 the other vote column includes 9,486 votes cast for Green (Nader). In 1996 the other vote column includes 32,515 votes cast for Perot. In 1992 the other vote column includes 71,084 votes cast for Perot. In 1980 the other column includes 23,640 votes for Independent (Anderson).

NORTH DAKOTA

POSTWAR VOTE FOR GOVERNOR

Year	Total Vote	Republican		Democratic		Other Vote	Rep.-Dem. Plurality	Percentage			
		Vote	Candidate	Vote	Candidate			Total Vote		Major Vote	
								Rep.	Dem.	Rep.	Dem.
2000	289,412	159,255	Hoeven, John	130,144	Heitkamp, Heidi	13	29,111 R	55.0%	45.0%	55.0%	45.0%
1996	264,298	174,937	Schafer, Edward T.	89,349	Kaldor, Lee	12	85,588 R	66.2%	33.8%	66.2%	33.8%
1992	304,861	176,398	Schafer, Edward T.	123,845	Spaeth, Nicholas	4,618	52,553 R	57.9%	40.6%	58.8%	41.2%
1988	299,080	119,986	Mallberg, Leon L.	179,094	Sinner, George		59,108 D	40.1%	59.9%	40.1%	59.9%
1984	314,382	140,460	Olson, Allen I.	173,922	Sinner, George		33,462 D	44.7%	55.3%	44.7%	55.3%
1980	302,621	162,230	Olson, Allen I.	140,391	Link, Arthur A.		21,839 R	53.6%	46.4%	53.6%	46.4%
1976	297,249	138,321	Elkin, Richard	153,309	Link, Arthur A.	5,619	14,988 D	46.5%	51.6%	47.4%	52.6%
1972	281,931	138,032	Larsen, Richard	143,899	Link, Arthur A.		5,867 D	49.0%	51.0%	49.0%	51.0%
1968	248,000	108,382	McCarney, Robert P.	135,955	Guy, William L.	3,663	27,573 D	43.7%	54.8%	44.4%	55.6%
1964**	262,661	116,247	Halcrow, Donald M.	146,414	Guy, William L.		30,167 D	44.3%	55.7%	44.3%	55.7%
1962	228,509	113,251	Andrews, Mark	115,258	Guy, William L.		2,007 D	49.6%	50.4%	49.6%	50.4%
1960	275,375	122,486	Dahl, C. P.	136,148	Guy, William L.	16,741	13,662 D	44.5%	49.4%	47.4%	52.6%
1958	210,599	111,836	Davis, John E.	98,763	Lord, John F.		13,073 R	53.1%	46.9%	53.1%	46.9%
1956	252,435	147,566	Davis, John E.	104,869	Warner, Wallace E.		42,697 R	58.5%	41.5%	58.5%	41.5%
1954	193,501	124,253	Brunsdale, C. Norman	69,248	Bymers, Cornelius		55,005 R	64.2%	35.8%	64.2%	35.8%
1952	253,934	199,944	Brunsdale, C. Norman	53,990	Johnson, Ole C.		145,954 R	78.7%	21.3%	78.7%	21.3%
1950	183,772	121,822	Brunsdale, C. Norman	61,950	Byerly, Clyde G.		59,872 R	66.3%	33.7%	66.3%	33.7%
1948	214,858	131,764	Aandahl, Fred G.	80,555	Henry, Howard	2,539	51,209 R	61.3%	37.5%	62.1%	37.9%
1946	169,391	116,672	Aandahl, Fred G.	52,719	Burdick, Quentin N.		63,953 R	68.9%	31.1%	68.9%	31.1%

The term of office of North Dakota's Governor was increased from two to four years effective with the 1964 election.

POSTWAR VOTE FOR SENATOR

Year	Total Vote	Republican		Democratic		Other Vote	Rep.-Dem. Plurality	Percentage			
		Vote	Candidate	Vote	Candidate			Total Vote		Major Vote	
								Rep.	Dem.	Rep.	Dem.
2000	287,539	111,069	Sand, Duane	176,470	Conrad, Kent		65,401 D	38.6%	61.4%	38.6%	61.4%
1998	213,358	75,013	Nalewaja, Donna	134,747	Dorgan, Byron L.	3,598	59,734 D	35.2%	63.2%	35.8%	64.2%
1994	236,547	99,390	Clayburg, Ben	137,157	Conrad, Kent		37,767 D	42.0%	58.0%	42.0%	58.0%
1992	303,957	118,162	Sydness, Steve	179,347	Dorgan, Byron L.	6,448	61,185 D	38.9%	59.0%	39.7%	60.3%
1992S	163,311	55,194	Dalrymple, Jack	103,246	Conrad, Kent	4,871	48,052 D	33.8%	63.2%	34.8%	65.2%
1988	289,170	112,937	Striden, Earl	171,899	Burdick, Quentin N.	4,334	58,962 D	39.1%	59.4%	39.6%	60.4%
1986	288,998	141,797	Andrews, Mark	143,932	Conrad, Kent	3,269	2,135 D	49.1%	49.8%	49.6%	50.4%
1982	262,465	89,304	Knorr, Gene	164,873	Burdick, Quentin N.	8,288	75,569 D	34.0%	62.8%	35.1%	64.9%
1980	299,272	210,347	Andrews, Mark	86,658	Johanneson, Kent	2,267	123,689 R	70.3%	29.0%	70.8%	29.2%
1976	283,062	103,466	Stroup, Richard	175,772	Burdick, Quentin N.	3,824	72,306 D	36.6%	62.1%	37.1%	62.9%
1974	235,661	114,117	Young, Milton R.	113,931	Guy, William L.	7,613	186 R	48.4%	48.3%	50.0%	50.0%
1970	219,560	82,996	Kleppe, Tom	134,519	Burdick, Quentin N.	2,045	51,523 D	37.8%	61.3%	38.2%	61.8%
1968	239,776	154,968	Young, Milton R.	80,815	Lashkowitz, Herschel	3,993	74,153 R	64.6%	33.7%	65.7%	34.3%
1964	258,945	109,681	Kleppe, Tom	149,264	Burdick, Quentin N.		39,583 D	42.4%	57.6%	42.4%	57.6%
1962	223,737	135,705	Young, Milton R.	88,032	Lanier, William		47,673 R	60.7%	39.3%	60.7%	39.3%
1960S	210,349	103,475	Davis, John E.	104,593	Burdick, Quentin N.	2,281	1,118 D	49.2%	49.7%	49.7%	50.3%
1958	204,635	117,070	Langer, William	84,892	Vendsel, Raymond	2,673	32,178 R	57.2%	41.5%	58.0%	42.0%
1956	244,161	155,305	Young, Milton R.	87,919	Burdick, Quentin N.	937	67,386 R	63.6%	36.0%	63.9%	36.1%
1952	237,995	157,907	Langer, William	55,347	Morrison, Harold A.	24,741	102,560 R	66.3%	23.3%	74.0%	26.0%
1950	186,716	126,209	Young, Milton R.	60,507	O'Brien, Harry		65,702 R	67.6%	32.4%	67.6%	32.4%
1946**	165,382	88,210	Langer, William	38,368	Larson, Abner B.	38,804	49,842 R	53.3%	23.2%	69.7%	30.3%
1946S	136,852	75,998	Young, Milton R.	37,507	Lanier, William	23,347	38,491 R	55.5%	27.4%	67.0%	33.0%

One of the 1992 elections was for a short term to fill a vacancy and the special election was held in December. The 1960 and 1946 special elections were held in June for short terms to fill vacancies. In 1946 other vote was Arthur Thompson (Independent) who received 23.5% of the total vote and ran second.

NORTH DAKOTA

One At Large

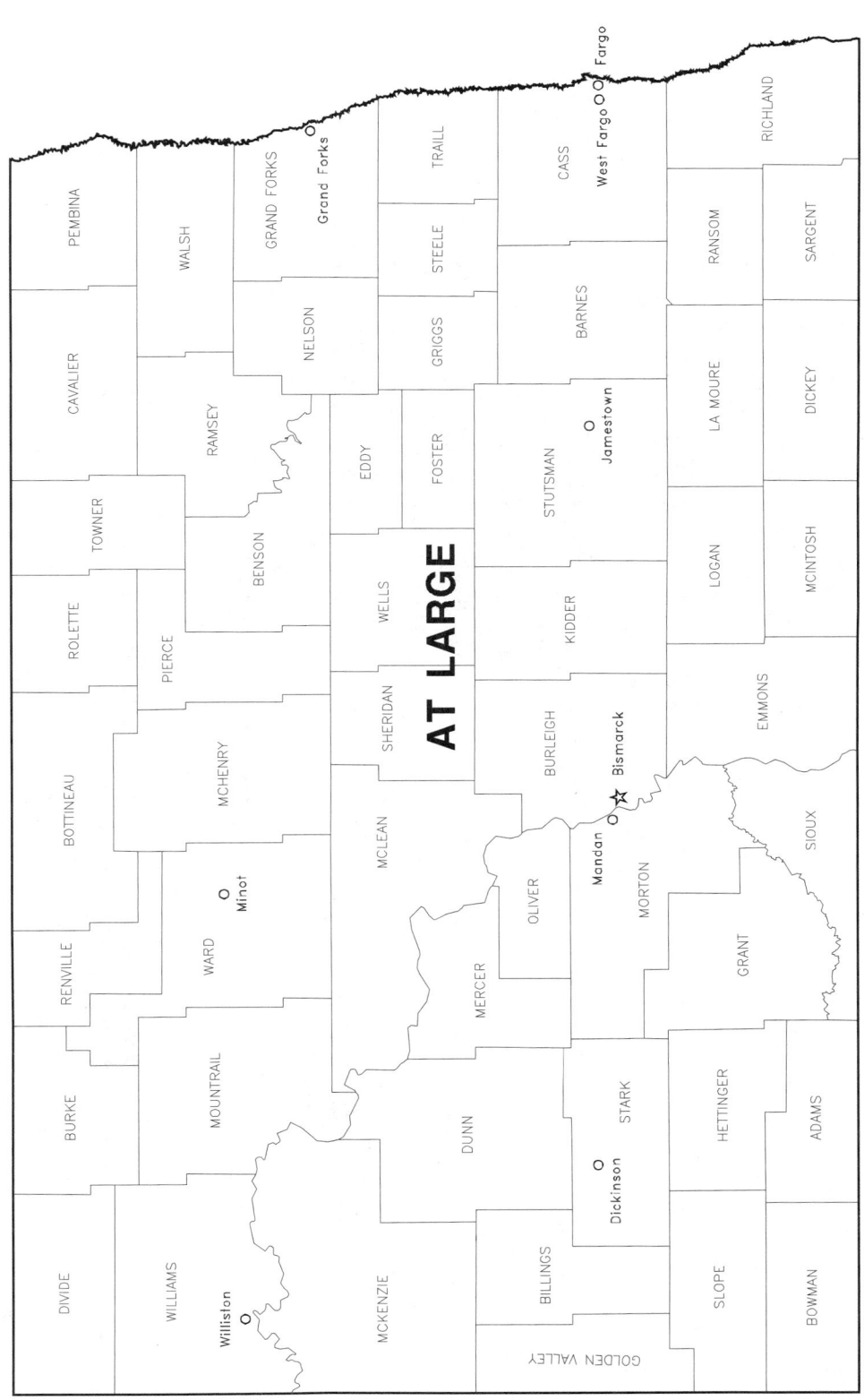

NORTH DAKOTA

PRESIDENT 2000

2000 Census Population	County	Total Vote	Republican	Democratic	Green (Nader)	Other	Rep.-Dem. Plurality	Percentage of Total Vote		
								Rep.	Dem.	Green
2,593	ADAMS	1,160	826	286	23	25	540 R	71.2%	24.7%	2.0%
11,775	BARNES	5,748	3,452	1,933	160	203	1,519 R	60.1%	33.6%	2.8%
6,964	BENSON	2,154	1,055	952	50	97	103 R	49.0%	44.2%	2.3%
888	BILLINGS	525	394	82	15	34	312 R	75.0%	15.6%	2.9%
7,149	BOTTINEAU	3,690	2,349	1,173	95	73	1,176 R	63.7%	31.8%	2.6%
3,242	BOWMAN	1,471	1,080	330	40	21	750 R	73.4%	22.4%	2.7%
2,242	BURKE	1,039	698	296	20	25	402 R	67.2%	28.5%	1.9%
69,416	BURLEIGH	34,482	22,467	9,842	1,142	1,031	12,625 R	65.2%	28.5%	3.3%
123,138	CASS	58,995	33,536	21,451	2,560	1,448	12,085 R	56.8%	36.4%	4.3%
4,831	CAVALIER	2,371	1,513	618	73	167	895 R	63.8%	26.1%	3.1%
5,757	DICKEY	2,786	1,853	806	52	75	1,047 R	66.5%	28.9%	1.9%
2,283	DIVIDE	794	443	306	24	21	137 R	55.8%	38.5%	3.0%
3,600	DUNN	1,728	1,124	474	54	76	650 R	65.0%	27.4%	3.1%
2,757	EDDY	1,268	703	458	36	71	245 R	55.4%	36.1%	2.8%
4,331	EMMONS	1,992	1,430	405	42	115	1,025 R	71.8%	20.3%	2.1%
3,759	FOSTER	1,743	1,172	474	46	51	698 R	67.2%	27.2%	2.6%
1,924	GOLDEN VALLEY	812	611	156	26	19	455 R	75.2%	19.2%	3.2%
66,109	GRAND FORKS	28,385	15,875	10,593	1,367	550	5,282 R	55.9%	37.3%	4.8%
2,841	GRANT	1,427	1,077	235	27	88	842 R	75.5%	16.5%	1.9%
2,754	GRIGGS	1,469	920	484	19	46	436 R	62.6%	32.9%	1.3%
2,715	HETTINGER	1,519	1,057	353	44	65	704 R	69.6%	23.2%	2.9%
2,753	KIDDER	1,276	837	283	29	127	554 R	65.6%	22.2%	2.3%
4,701	LA MOURE	2,468	1,590	689	50	139	901 R	64.4%	27.9%	2.0%
2,308	LOGAN	1,145	812	223	14	96	589 R	70.9%	19.5%	1.2%
5,987	MCHENRY	2,737	1,682	888	79	88	794 R	61.5%	32.4%	2.9%
3,390	MCINTOSH	1,626	1,178	350	25	73	828 R	72.4%	21.5%	1.5%
5,737	MCKENZIE	2,364	1,634	653	45	32	981 R	69.1%	27.6%	1.9%
9,311	MCLEAN	4,646	2,891	1,465	117	173	1,426 R	62.2%	31.5%	2.5%
8,644	MERCER	4,353	2,984	1,011	157	201	1,973 R	68.6%	23.2%	3.6%
25,303	MORTON	11,223	6,993	3,439	341	450	3,554 R	62.3%	30.6%	3.0%
6,631	MOUNTRAIL	2,896	1,466	1,256	105	69	210 R	50.6%	43.4%	3.6%
3,715	NELSON	1,840	1,031	687	49	73	344 R	56.0%	37.3%	2.7%
2,065	OLIVER	1,051	709	244	36	62	465 R	67.5%	23.2%	3.4%
8,585	PEMBINA	3,779	2,430	1,093	110	146	1,337 R	64.3%	28.9%	2.9%
4,675	PIERCE	1,971	1,348	500	54	69	848 R	68.4%	25.4%	2.7%
12,066	RAMSEY	4,977	3,005	1,658	161	153	1,347 R	60.4%	33.3%	3.2%
5,890	RANSOM	2,719	1,488	1,080	67	84	408 R	54.7%	39.7%	2.5%
2,610	RENVILLE	1,332	820	443	37	32	377 R	61.6%	33.3%	2.8%
17,998	RICHLAND	8,015	4,999	2,490	240	286	2,509 R	62.4%	31.1%	3.0%
13,674	ROLETTE	4,398	1,416	2,681	137	164	1,265 D	32.2%	61.0%	3.1%
4,366	SARGENT	2,184	1,103	959	48	74	144 R	50.5%	43.9%	2.2%
1,710	SHERIDAN	928	707	161	13	47	546 R	76.2%	17.3%	1.4%
4,044	SIOUX	1,041	269	724	16	32	455 D	25.8%	69.5%	1.5%
767	SLOPE	442	316	85	17	24	231 R	71.5%	19.2%	3.8%
22,636	STARK	9,777	6,387	2,784	301	305	3,603 R	65.3%	28.5%	3.1%
2,258	STEELE	1,210	655	475	28	52	180 R	54.1%	39.3%	2.3%
21,908	STUTSMAN	9,118	5,488	3,067	256	307	2,421 R	60.2%	33.6%	2.8%
2,876	TOWNER	1,189	694	410	31	54	284 R	58.4%	34.5%	2.6%
8,477	TRAILL	4,112	2,392	1,512	95	113	880 R	58.2%	36.8%	2.3%
12,389	WALSH	5,182	3,099	1,743	107	233	1,356 R	59.8%	33.6%	2.1%
58,795	WARD	22,482	13,997	7,533	598	354	6,464 R	62.3%	33.5%	2.7%
5,102	WELLS	2,410	1,610	661	51	88	949 R	66.8%	27.4%	2.1%
19,761	WILLIAMS	7,807	5,187	2,330	157	133	2,857 R	66.4%	29.8%	2.0%
642,200	TOTAL	288,256	174,852	95,284	9,486	8,634	79,568 R	60.7%	33.1%	3.3%

NORTH DAKOTA

GOVERNOR 2000

2000 Census Population	County	Total Vote	Republican	Democratic	Other	Rep.-Dem. Plurality		Percentage			
								Total Vote		Major Vote	
								Rep.	Dem.	Rep.	Dem.
2,593	ADAMS	1,186	601	585		16	R	50.7%	49.3%	50.7%	49.3%
11,775	BARNES	5,762	3,060	2,702		358	R	53.1%	46.9%	53.1%	46.9%
6,964	BENSON	2,181	849	1,332		483	D	38.9%	61.1%	38.9%	61.1%
888	BILLINGS	530	345	183	2	162	R	65.1%	34.5%	65.3%	34.7%
7,149	BOTTINEAU	3,687	2,137	1,550		570	R	58.0%	42.0%	58.0%	42.0%
3,242	BOWMAN	1,485	915	570		345	R	61.6%	38.4%	61.6%	38.4%
2,242	BURKE	1,045	601	443	1	158	R	57.5%	42.4%	57.6%	42.4%
69,416	BURLEIGH	34,555	21,781	12,771	3	9,010	R	63.0%	37.0%	63.0%	37.0%
123,138	CASS	59,010	31,930	27,078	2	4,852	R	54.1%	45.9%	54.1%	45.9%
4,831	CAVALIER	2,398	1,350	1,045	3	305	R	56.3%	43.6%	56.4%	43.6%
5,757	DICKEY	2,790	1,631	1,159		472	R	58.5%	41.5%	58.5%	41.5%
2,283	DIVIDE	807	387	420		33	D	48.0%	52.0%	48.0%	52.0%
3,600	DUNN	1,739	960	779		181	R	55.2%	44.8%	55.2%	44.8%
2,757	EDDY	1,280	650	630		20	R	50.8%	49.2%	50.8%	49.2%
4,331	EMMONS	2,009	1,355	654		701	R	67.4%	32.6%	67.4%	32.6%
3,759	FOSTER	1,742	991	751		240	R	56.9%	43.1%	56.9%	43.1%
1,924	GOLDEN VALLEY	813	539	274		265	R	66.3%	33.7%	66.3%	33.7%
66,109	GRAND FORKS	28,287	14,405	13,882		523	R	50.9%	49.1%	50.9%	49.1%
2,841	GRANT	1,438	952	486		466	R	66.2%	33.8%	66.2%	33.8%
2,754	GRIGGS	1,489	814	675		139	R	54.7%	45.3%	54.7%	45.3%
2,715	HETTINGER	1,530	888	642		246	R	58.0%	42.0%	58.0%	42.0%
2,753	KIDDER	1,285	814	469	2	345	R	63.3%	36.5%	63.4%	36.6%
4,701	LA MOURE	2,495	1,430	1,065		365	R	57.3%	42.7%	57.3%	42.7%
2,308	LOGAN	1,161	795	366		429	R	68.5%	31.5%	68.5%	31.5%
5,987	MCHENRY	2,762	1,499	1,263		236	R	54.3%	45.7%	54.3%	45.7%
3,390	MCINTOSH	1,675	1,163	512		651	R	69.4%	30.6%	69.4%	30.6%
5,737	MCKENZIE	2,355	1,281	1,074		207	R	54.4%	45.6%	54.4%	45.6%
9,311	MCLEAN	4,684	2,700	1,984		716	R	57.6%	42.4%	57.6%	42.4%
8,644	MERCER	4,389	2,605	1,784		821	R	59.4%	40.6%	59.4%	40.6%
25,303	MORTON	11,256	6,303	4,953		1,350	R	56.0%	44.0%	56.0%	44.0%
6,631	MOUNTRAIL	2,917	1,233	1,684		451	D	42.3%	57.7%	42.3%	57.7%
3,715	NELSON	1,868	860	1,008		148	D	46.0%	54.0%	46.0%	54.0%
2,065	OLIVER	1,057	639	418		221	R	60.5%	39.5%	60.5%	39.5%
8,585	PEMBINA	3,793	2,005	1,788		217	R	52.9%	47.1%	52.9%	47.1%
4,675	PIERCE	2,002	1,192	810		382	R	59.5%	40.5%	59.5%	40.5%
12,066	RAMSEY	5,023	2,649	2,374		275	R	52.7%	47.3%	52.7%	47.3%
5,890	RANSOM	2,733	1,049	1,684		635	D	38.4%	61.6%	38.4%	61.6%
2,610	RENVILLE	1,342	765	577		188	R	57.0%	43.0%	57.0%	43.0%
17,998	RICHLAND	8,086	3,884	4,202		318	D	48.0%	52.0%	48.0%	52.0%
13,674	ROLETTE	4,390	1,201	3,189		1,988	D	27.4%	72.6%	27.4%	72.6%
4,366	SARGENT	2,210	910	1,300		390	D	41.2%	58.8%	41.2%	58.8%
1,710	SHERIDAN	932	635	297		338	R	68.1%	31.9%	68.1%	31.9%
4,044	SIOUX	1,065	204	861		657	D	19.2%	80.8%	19.2%	80.8%
767	SLOPE	448	250	198		52	R	55.8%	44.2%	55.8%	44.2%
22,636	STARK	9,804	5,791	4,013		1,778	R	59.1%	40.9%	59.1%	40.9%
2,258	STEELE	1,209	548	661		113	D	45.3%	54.7%	45.3%	54.7%
21,908	STUTSMAN	9,175	4,810	4,365		445	R	52.4%	47.6%	52.4%	47.6%
2,876	TOWNER	1,204	573	631		58	D	47.6%	52.4%	47.6%	52.4%
8,477	TRAILL	4,152	1,948	2,204		256	D	46.9%	53.1%	46.9%	53.1%
12,389	WALSH	5,383	2,748	2,635		113	R	51.0%	49.0%	51.0%	49.0%
58,795	WARD	22,521	13,589	8,932		4,657	R	60.3%	39.7%	60.3%	39.7%
5,102	WELLS	2,417	1,448	969		479	R	59.9%	40.1%	59.9%	40.1%
19,761	WILLIAMS	7,856	4,593	3,263		1,330	R	58.5%	41.5%	58.5%	41.5%
642,200	TOTAL	289,412	159,255	130,144	13	29,111	R	55.0%	45.0%	55.0%	45.0%

NORTH DAKOTA

SENATOR 2000

2000 Census Population	County	Total Vote	Republican	Democratic	Other	Rep.-Dem. Plurality		Percentage			
								Total Vote		Major Vote	
								Rep.	Dem.	Rep.	Dem.
2,593	ADAMS	1,177	475	702		227	D	40.4%	59.6%	40.4%	59.6%
11,775	BARNES	5,741	2,047	3,694		1,647	D	35.7%	64.3%	35.7%	64.3%
6,964	BENSON	2,181	609	1,572		963	D	27.9%	72.1%	27.9%	72.1%
888	BILLINGS	522	280	242		38	R	53.6%	46.4%	53.6%	46.4%
7,149	BOTTINEAU	3,670	1,306	2,364		1,058	D	35.6%	64.4%	35.6%	64.4%
3,242	BOWMAN	1,492	707	785		78	D	47.4%	52.6%	47.4%	52.6%
2,242	BURKE	1,035	386	649		263	D	37.3%	62.7%	37.3%	62.7%
69,416	BURLEIGH	34,343	15,615	18,728		3,113	D	45.5%	54.5%	45.5%	54.5%
123,138	CASS	58,633	22,683	35,950		13,267	D	38.7%	61.3%	38.7%	61.3%
4,831	CAVALIER	2,368	859	1,509		650	D	36.3%	63.7%	36.3%	63.7%
5,757	DICKEY	2,789	1,351	1,438		87	D	48.4%	51.6%	48.4%	51.6%
2,283	DIVIDE	800	233	567		334	D	29.1%	70.9%	29.1%	70.9%
3,600	DUNN	1,740	685	1,055		370	D	39.4%	60.6%	39.4%	60.6%
2,757	EDDY	1,278	435	843		408	D	34.0%	66.0%	34.0%	66.0%
4,331	EMMONS	1,974	956	1,018		62	D	48.4%	51.6%	48.4%	51.6%
3,759	FOSTER	1,738	689	1,049		360	D	39.6%	60.4%	39.6%	60.4%
1,924	GOLDEN VALLEY	811	390	421		31	D	48.1%	51.9%	48.1%	51.9%
66,109	GRAND FORKS	28,109	9,215	18,894		9,679	D	32.8%	67.2%	32.8%	67.2%
2,841	GRANT	1,429	679	750		71	D	47.5%	52.5%	47.5%	52.5%
2,754	GRIGGS	1,454	588	866		278	D	40.4%	59.6%	40.4%	59.6%
2,715	HETTINGER	1,534	635	899		264	D	41.4%	58.6%	41.4%	58.6%
2,753	KIDDER	1,269	600	669		69	D	47.3%	52.7%	47.3%	52.7%
4,701	LA MOURE	2,485	1,018	1,467		449	D	41.0%	59.0%	41.0%	59.0%
2,308	LOGAN	1,156	520	636		116	D	45.0%	55.0%	45.0%	55.0%
5,987	MCHENRY	2,774	1,027	1,747		720	D	37.0%	63.0%	37.0%	63.0%
3,390	MCINTOSH	1,676	846	830		16	R	50.5%	49.5%	50.5%	49.5%
5,737	MCKENZIE	2,343	980	1,363		383	D	41.8%	58.2%	41.8%	58.2%
9,311	MCLEAN	4,642	1,962	2,680		718	D	42.3%	57.7%	42.3%	57.7%
8,644	MERCER	4,356	1,984	2,372		388	D	45.5%	54.5%	45.5%	54.5%
25,303	MORTON	11,239	4,721	6,518		1,797	D	42.0%	58.0%	42.0%	58.0%
6,631	MOUNTRAIL	2,905	774	2,131		1,357	D	26.6%	73.4%	26.6%	73.4%
3,715	NELSON	1,852	584	1,268		684	D	31.5%	68.5%	31.5%	68.5%
2,065	OLIVER	1,056	514	542		28	D	48.7%	51.3%	48.7%	51.3%
8,585	PEMBINA	3,780	1,481	2,299		818	D	39.2%	60.8%	39.2%	60.8%
4,675	PIERCE	1,985	809	1,176		367	D	40.8%	59.2%	40.8%	59.2%
12,066	RAMSEY	4,991	1,614	3,377		1,763	D	32.3%	67.7%	32.3%	67.7%
5,890	RANSOM	2,726	865	1,861		996	D	31.7%	68.3%	31.7%	68.3%
2,610	RENVILLE	1,339	417	922		505	D	31.1%	68.9%	31.1%	68.9%
17,998	RICHLAND	8,019	3,103	4,916		1,813	D	38.7%	61.3%	38.7%	61.3%
13,674	ROLETTE	4,369	789	3,580		2,791	D	18.1%	81.9%	18.1%	81.9%
4,366	SARGENT	2,207	694	1,513		819	D	31.4%	68.6%	31.4%	68.6%
1,710	SHERIDAN	934	532	402		130	R	57.0%	43.0%	57.0%	43.0%
4,044	SIOUX	1,050	152	898		746	D	14.5%	85.5%	14.5%	85.5%
767	SLOPE	447	209	238		29	D	46.8%	53.2%	46.8%	53.2%
22,636	STARK	9,748	3,695	6,053		2,358	D	37.9%	62.1%	37.9%	62.1%
2,258	STEELE	1,220	408	812		404	D	33.4%	66.6%	33.4%	66.6%
21,908	STUTSMAN	9,122	3,514	5,608		2,094	D	38.5%	61.5%	38.5%	61.5%
2,876	TOWNER	1,205	372	833		461	D	30.9%	69.1%	30.9%	69.1%
8,477	TRAILL	4,142	1,488	2,654		1,166	D	35.9%	64.1%	35.9%	64.1%
12,389	WALSH	5,161	1,941	3,220		1,279	D	37.6%	62.4%	37.6%	62.4%
58,795	WARD	22,364	8,462	13,902		5,440	D	37.8%	62.2%	37.8%	62.2%
5,102	WELLS	2,407	1,066	1,341		275	D	44.3%	55.7%	44.3%	55.7%
19,761	WILLIAMS	7,752	3,105	4,647		1,542	D	40.1%	59.9%	40.1%	59.9%
642,200	TOTAL	287,539	111,069	176,470		65,401	D	38.6%	61.4%	38.6%	61.4%

NORTH DAKOTA

CONGRESS

CD	Year	Total Vote	Republican Vote	Republican Candidate	Democratic Vote	Democratic Candidate	Other Vote	Rep.-Dem. Plurality	Total Vote Rep.	Total Vote Dem.	Major Vote Rep.	Major Vote Dem.
AL	2000	285,658	127,251	DORSO, JOHN	151,173	POMEROY, EARL	7,234	23,922 D	44.5%	52.9%	45.7%	54.3%
AL	1998	215,469	75,013	CRAMER, KEVIN	134,747	POMEROY, EARL	5,709	59,734 D	34.8%	62.5%	35.8%	64.2%
AL	1996	263,010	113,684	CRAMER, KEVIN	144,833	POMEROY, EARL	4,493	31,149 D	43.2%	55.1%	44.0%	56.0%
AL	1994	235,389	105,988	PORTER, GARY	123,134	POMEROY, EARL	6,267	17,146 D	45.0%	52.3%	46.3%	53.7%
AL	1992	297,898	117,442	KORSMO, JOHN T.	169,273	POMEROY, EARL	11,183	51,831 D	39.4%	56.8%	41.0%	59.0%
AL	1990	233,979	81,443	SCHAFER, EDWARD T.	152,530	DORGAN, BYRON L.	6	71,087 D	34.8%	65.2%	34.8%	65.2%
AL	1988	299,982	84,475	SYDNESS, STEVE	212,583	DORGAN, BYRON L.	2,924	128,108 D	28.2%	70.9%	28.4%	71.6%
AL	1986	286,361	66,989	VINJE, SYVER	216,258	DORGAN, BYRON L.	3,114	149,269 D	23.4%	75.5%	23.7%	76.3%
AL	1984	308,729	65,761	ALTENBURG, LOIS I.	242,968	DORGAN, BYRON L.		177,207 D	21.3%	78.7%	21.3%	78.7%
AL	1982	260,499	72,241	JONES, KENT	186,534	DORGAN, BYRON L.	1,724	114,293 D	27.7%	71.6%	27.9%	72.1%
AL	1980	293,076	124,707	SMYKOWSKI, JIM	166,437	DORGAN, BYRON L.	1,932	41,730 D	42.6%	56.8%	42.8%	57.2%
AL	1978	220,348	147,746	ANDREWS, MARK	68,016	HAGEN, BRUCE	4,586	79,730 R	67.1%	30.9%	68.5%	31.5%
AL	1976	289,881	181,018	ANDREWS, MARK	104,263	OMDAHL, LLOYD B.	4,600	76,755 R	62.4%	36.0%	63.5%	36.5%
AL	1974	233,688	130,184	ANDREWS, MARK	103,504	DORGAN, BYRON L.		26,680 R	55.7%	44.3%	55.7%	44.3%
AL	1972	268,721	195,360	ANDREWS, MARK	72,850	ISTA, RICHARD	511	122,510 R	72.7%	27.1%	72.8%	27.2%

NORTH DAKOTA

GENERAL AND PRIMARY ELECTIONS

2000 GENERAL ELECTIONS

President — Other vote was 7,288 Reform (Buchanan); 660 Independent Nomination (Browne); 373 Constitution (Phillips); 313 Independent Nomination (Hagelin). Nader was listed on the ballot as an Independent Nomination.

Governor — Other vote was 8 write-in (Anderson); 5 write-in (Roszkowski).

Senator

Congress — Other vote was 4,731 Independent (Shelver); 2,481 Independent (Loughead); 22 write-in (Brandenburg).

2000 PRIMARY ELECTIONS

Primary — June 13, 2000

Registration — No Formal Registration

Primary Type — Open—Any person of voting age could vote in the primary.

Note: An asterisk (*) denotes incumbent.

	REPUBLICAN PRIMARIES			DEMOCRATIC PRIMARIES		
Governor	John Hoeven	40,308	100.0%	Heidi Heitkamp	34,851	100.0%
	TOTAL	40,308		TOTAL	34,851	
Senator	Duane Sand	37,878	100.0%	Kent Conrad*	36,585	100.0%
	TOTAL	37,878		TOTAL	36,585	
Congressional At-Large	John Dorso	36,381	100.0%	Earl Pomeroy*	35,701	100.0%
	TOTAL	36,381		TOTAL	35,701	

OHIO

GOVERNOR
Robert A. Taft II (R). Elected 1998 to a four-year term.

SENATORS
Mike DeWine (R). Re-elected 2000 to a six-year term. Previously elected 1994.

George V. Voinovich (R). Elected 1998 to a six-year term.

REPRESENTATIVES
1. Steve Chabot (R)
2. Rob Portman (R)
3. Tony P. Hall (D)
4. Michael G. Oxley (R)
5. Paul E. Gillmor (R)
6. Ted Strickland (D)
7. David L. Hobson (R)
8. John A. Boehner (R)
9. Marcy Kaptur (D)
10. Dennis J. Kucinich (D)
11. Stephanie Tubbs Jones (D)
12. Pat Tiberi (R)
13. Sherrod Brown (D)
14. Thomas C. Sawyer (D)
15. Deborah Pryce (R)
16. Ralph S. Regula (R)
17. James A. Traficant (D)
18. Bob Ney (R)
19. Steven C. LaTourette (R)

POSTWAR VOTE FOR PRESIDENT

		Republican		Democratic		Other		Total Vote		Major Vote	
Year	Total Vote	Vote	Candidate	Vote	Candidate	Vote	Plurality	Rep.	Dem.	Rep.	Dem.
2000**	4,701,998	2,350,363	Bush, George W.	2,183,628	Gore, Al	168,007	166,735 R	50.0%	46.4%	51.8%	48.2%
1996**	4,534,434	1,859,883	Dole, Bob	2,148,222	Clinton, Bill	526,329	288,339 D	41.0%	47.4%	46.4%	53.6%
1992**	4,939,967	1,894,310	Bush, George	1,984,942	Clinton, Bill	1,060,715	90,632 D	38.3%	40.2%	48.8%	51.2%
1988	4,393,699	2,416,549	Bush, George	1,939,629	Dukakis, Michael S.	37,521	476,920 R	55.0%	44.1%	55.5%	44.5%
1984	4,547,619	2,678,560	Reagan, Ronald	1,825,440	Mondale, Walter F.	43,619	853,120 R	58.9%	40.1%	59.5%	40.5%
1980**	4,283,603	2,206,545	Reagan, Ronald	1,752,414	Carter, Jimmy	324,644	454,131 R	51.5%	40.9%	55.7%	44.3%
1976	4,111,873	2,000,505	Ford, Gerald R.	2,011,621	Carter, Jimmy	99,747	11,116 D	48.7%	48.9%	49.9%	50.1%
1972	4,094,787	2,441,827	Nixon, Richard M.	1,558,889	McGovern, George S.	94,071	882,938 R	59.6%	38.1%	61.0%	39.0%
1968	3,959,698	1,791,014	Nixon, Richard M.	1,700,586	Humphrey, Hubert H.	468,098	90,428 R	45.2%	42.9%	51.3%	48.7%
1964	3,969,196	1,470,865	Goldwater, Barry M.	2,498,331	Johnson, Lyndon B.		1,027,466 D	37.1%	62.9%	37.1%	62.9%
1960	4,161,859	2,217,611	Nixon, Richard M.	1,944,248	Kennedy, John F.		273,363 R	53.3%	46.7%	53.3%	46.7%
1956	3,702,265	2,262,610	Eisenhower, Dwight D.	1,439,655	Stevenson, Adlai E.		822,955 R	61.1%	38.9%	61.1%	38.9%
1952	3,700,758	2,100,391	Eisenhower, Dwight D.	1,600,367	Stevenson, Adlai E.		500,024 R	56.8%	43.2%	56.8%	43.2%
1948	2,936,071	1,445,684	Dewey, Thomas E.	1,452,791	Truman, Harry S.	37,596	7,107 D	49.2%	49.5%	49.9%	50.1%

In 2000 the other vote column includes 117,799 votes cast for Green (Nader). In 1996 the other vote column includes 483,207 votes cast for Perot. In 1992 the other vote column includes 1,036,426 votes cast for Perot. In 1980 the other column includes 254,472 votes for Independent (Anderson).

OHIO

POSTWAR VOTE FOR GOVERNOR

Year	Total Vote	Republican		Democratic		Other Vote	Rep.-Dem. Plurality	Percentage			
		Vote	Candidate	Vote	Candidate			Total Vote		Major Vote	
								Rep.	Dem.	Rep.	Dem.
1998	3,354,213	1,678,721	Taft, Robert A., II	1,498,956	Fisher, Lee	176,536	179,765 R	50.0%	44.7%	52.8%	47.2%
1994	3,346,238	2,401,572	Voinovich, George	835,849	Burch, Robert L.	108,817	1,565,723 R	71.8%	25.0%	74.2%	25.8%
1990	3,477,650	1,938,103	Voinovich, George	1,539,416	Celebrezze, Anthony J.	131	398,687 R	55.7%	44.3%	55.7%	44.3%
1986	3,066,611	1,207,264	Rhodes, James A.	1,858,372	Celeste, Richard F.	975	651,108 D	39.4%	60.6%	39.4%	60.6%
1982	3,356,721	1,303,962	Brown, Clarence, Jr.	1,981,882	Celeste, Richard F.	70,877	677,920 D	38.8%	59.0%	39.7%	60.3%
1978	2,843,351	1,402,167	Rhodes, James A.	1,354,631	Celeste, Richard F.	86,553	47,536 R	49.3%	47.6%	50.9%	49.1%
1974	3,072,010	1,493,679	Rhodes, James A.	1,482,191	Gilligan, John J.	96,140	11,488 R	48.6%	48.2%	50.2%	49.8%
1970	3,184,133	1,382,659	Cloud, Roger	1,725,560	Gilligan, John J.	75,914	342,901 D	43.4%	54.2%	44.5%	55.5%
1966	2,887,331	1,795,277	Rhodes, James A.	1,092,054	Reams, Frazier, Jr.		703,223 R	62.2%	37.8%	62.2%	37.8%
1962	3,116,711	1,836,190	Rhodes, James A.	1,280,521	DiSalle, Michael V.		555,669 R	58.9%	41.1%	58.9%	41.1%
1958**	3,284,134	1,414,874	O'Neill, C. William	1,869,260	DiSalle, Michael V.		454,386 D	43.1%	56.9%	43.1%	56.9%
1956	3,542,091	1,984,988	O'Neill, C. William	1,557,103	DiSalle, Michael V.		427,885 R	56.0%	44.0%	56.0%	44.0%
1954	2,597,790	1,192,528	Rhodes, James A.	1,405,262	Lausche, Frank J.		212,734 D	45.9%	54.1%	45.9%	54.1%
1952	3,605,168	1,590,058	Taft, Charles P.	2,015,110	Lausche, Frank J.		425,052 D	44.1%	55.9%	44.1%	55.9%
1950	2,892,819	1,370,570	Ebright, Don H.	1,522,249	Lausche, Frank J.		151,679 D	47.4%	52.6%	47.4%	52.6%
1948	3,018,289	1,398,514	Herbert, Thomas J.	1,619,775	Lausche, Frank J.		221,261 D	46.3%	53.7%	46.3%	53.7%
1946	2,303,750	1,166,550	Herbert, Thomas J.	1,125,997	Lausche, Frank J.	11,203	40,553 R	50.6%	48.9%	50.9%	49.1%

The term of office of Ohio's Governor was increased from two to four years effective with the 1958 election.

POSTWAR VOTE FOR SENATOR

Year	Total Vote	Republican		Democratic		Other Vote	Rep.-Dem. Plurality	Percentage			
		Vote	Candidate	Vote	Candidate			Total Vote		Major Vote	
								Rep.	Dem.	Rep.	Dem.
2000	4,448,801	2,665,512	DeWine, Mike	1,595,066	Celeste, Ted	188,223	1,070,446 R	59.9%	35.9%	62.6%	37.4%
1998	3,404,351	1,922,087	Voinovich, George	1,482,054	Boyle, Mary O.	210	440,033 R	56.5%	43.5%	56.5%	43.5%
1994	3,436,884	1,836,556	DeWine, Mike	1,348,213	Hyatt, Joel	252,115	488,343 R	53.4%	39.2%	57.7%	42.3%
1992	4,793,953	2,028,300	DeWine, Mike	2,444,419	Glenn, John H.	321,234	416,119 D	42.3%	51.0%	45.3%	54.7%
1988	4,352,905	1,872,716	Voinovich, George	2,480,038	Metzenbaum, Howard	151	607,322 D	43.0%	57.0%	43.0%	57.0%
1986	3,121,189	1,171,893	Kindness, Thomas N.	1,949,208	Glenn, John H.	88	777,315 D	37.5%	62.5%	37.5%	62.5%
1982	3,395,463	1,396,790	Pfeifer, Paul E.	1,923,767	Metzenbaum, Howard	74,906	526,977 D	41.1%	56.7%	42.1%	57.9%
1980	4,027,303	1,137,695	Betts, James E.	2,770,786	Glenn, John H.	118,822	1,633,091 D	28.2%	68.8%	29.1%	70.9%
1976	3,920,613	1,823,774	Taft, Robert A.,Jr.	1,941,113	Metzenbaum, Howard	155,726	117,339 D	46.5%	49.5%	48.4%	51.6%
1974	2,987,951	918,133	Perk, Ralph J.	1,930,670	Glenn, John H.	139,148	1,012,537 D	30.7%	64.6%	32.2%	67.8%
1970	3,151,274	1,565,682	Taft, Robert A.,Jr.	1,495,262	Metzenbaum, Howard	90,330	70,420 R	49.7%	47.4%	51.2%	48.8%
1968	3,743,121	1,928,964	Saxbe, William B.	1,814,152	Gilligan, John J.	5	114,812 R	51.5%	48.5%	51.5%	48.5%
1964	3,830,389	1,906,781	Taft, Robert A.,Jr.	1,923,608	Young, Stephen M.		16,827 D	49.8%	50.2%	49.8%	50.2%
1962	2,994,986	1,151,173	Briley, John M.	1,843,813	Lausche, Frank J.		692,640 D	38.4%	61.6%	38.4%	61.6%
1958	3,149,410	1,497,199	Bricker, John W.	1,652,211	Young, Stephen M.		155,012 D	47.5%	52.5%	47.5%	52.5%
1956	3,525,499	1,660,910	Bender, George H.	1,864,589	Lausche, Frank J.		203,679 D	47.1%	52.9%	47.1%	52.9%
1954S	2,512,778	1,257,874	Bender, George H.	1,254,904	Burke, Thomas A.		2,970 R	50.1%	49.9%	50.1%	49.9%
1952	3,442,291	1,878,961	Bricker, John W.	1,563,330	DiSalle, Michael V.		315,631 R	54.6%	45.4%	54.6%	45.4%
1950	2,860,102	1,645,643	Taft, Robert A.	1,214,459	Ferguson, Joseph T.		431,184 R	57.5%	42.5%	57.5%	42.5%
1946	2,237,269	1,275,774	Bricker, John W.	947,610	Huffman, James W.	13,885	328,164 R	57.0%	42.4%	57.4%	42.6%

The 1954 election was for a short term to fill a vacancy.

OHIO

Districts Established March 27, 1992

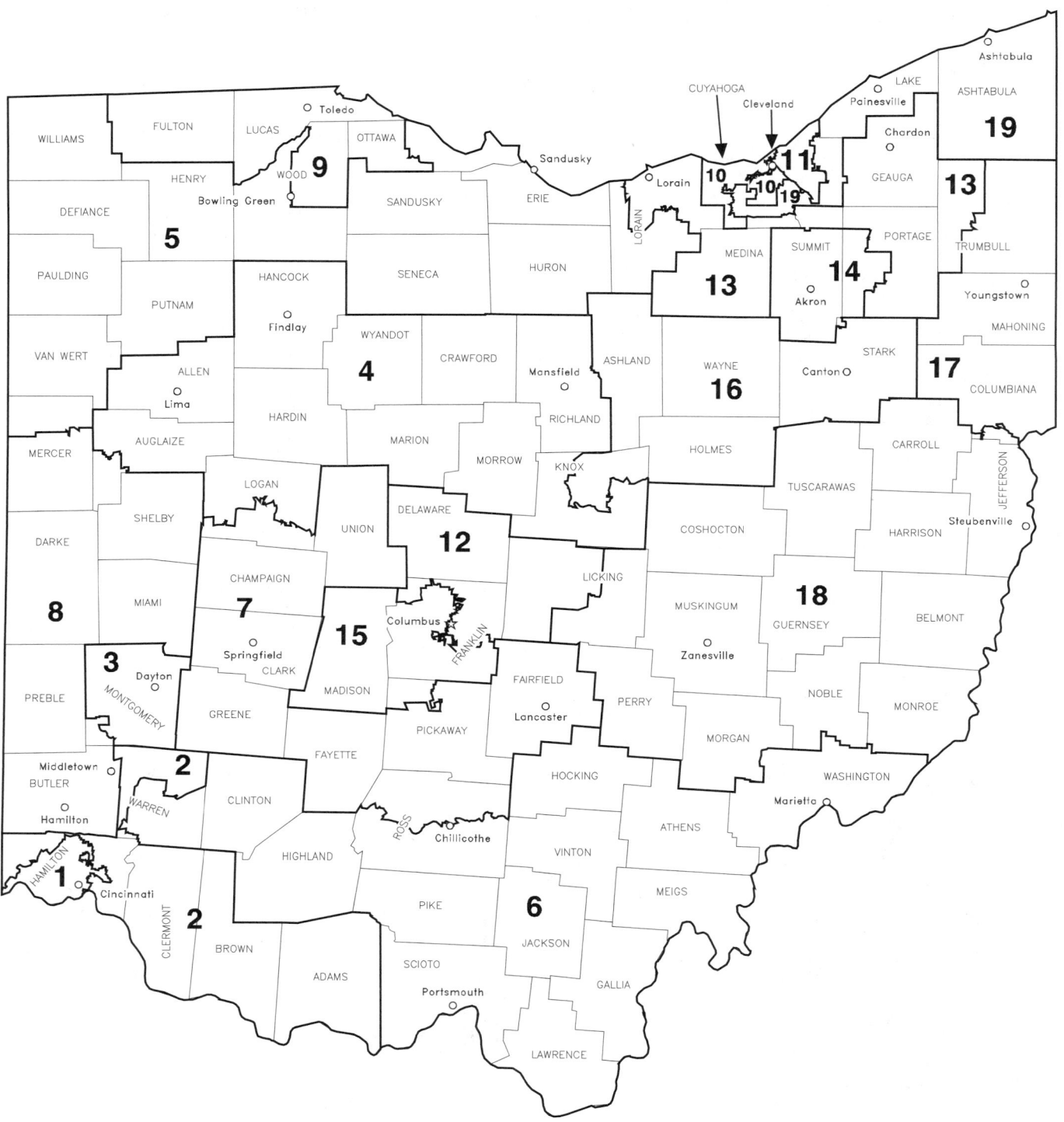

OHIO

PRESIDENT 2000

2000 Census Population	County	Total Vote	Republican	Democratic	Green (Nader)	Other	Rep.-Dem. Plurality	Percentage of Total Vote		
								Rep.	Dem.	Green
27,330	ADAMS	10,235	6,380	3,581	162	112	2,799 R	62.3%	35.0%	1.6%
108,473	ALLEN	43,795	28,647	13,996	760	392	14,651 R	65.4%	32.0%	1.7%
52,523	ASHLAND	21,258	13,533	6,685	563	477	6,848 R	63.7%	31.4%	2.6%
102,728	ASHTABULA	39,472	17,940	19,831	1,109	592	1,891 D	45.4%	50.2%	2.8%
62,223	ATHENS	25,447	9,703	13,158	1,663	923	3,455 D	38.1%	51.7%	6.5%
46,611	AUGLAIZE	19,892	13,770	5,564	372	186	8,206 R	69.2%	28.0%	1.9%
70,226	BELMONT	30,141	12,625	15,980	723	813	3,355 D	41.9%	53.0%	2.4%
42,285	BROWN	16,429	10,027	5,972	269	161	4,055 R	61.0%	36.4%	1.6%
332,807	BUTLER	136,737	86,587	46,390	2,708	1,052	40,197 R	63.3%	33.9%	2.0%
28,836	CARROLL	12,261	6,732	4,960	271	298	1,772 R	54.9%	40.5%	2.2%
38,890	CHAMPAIGN	15,680	9,220	5,955	346	159	3,265 R	58.8%	38.0%	2.2%
144,742	CLARK	57,559	27,660	27,984	1,347	568	324 D	48.1%	48.6%	2.3%
177,977	CLERMONT	69,877	47,129	20,927	1,303	518	26,202 R	67.4%	29.9%	1.9%
40,543	CLINTON	15,070	9,824	4,791	325	130	5,033 R	65.2%	31.8%	2.2%
112,075	COLUMBIANA	44,427	21,804	20,657	1,217	749	1,147 R	49.1%	46.5%	2.7%
36,655	COSHOCTON	14,268	8,243	5,594	295	136	2,649 R	57.8%	39.2%	2.1%
46,966	CRAWFORD	19,176	11,666	6,721	536	253	4,945 R	60.8%	35.0%	2.8%
1,393,978	CUYAHOGA	571,323	191,253	357,351	16,898	5,821	166,098 D	33.5%	62.5%	3.0%
53,309	DARKE	23,267	14,817	7,741	452	257	7,076 R	63.7%	33.3%	1.9%
39,500	DEFIANCE	16,242	9,540	6,175	365	162	3,365 R	58.7%	38.0%	2.2%
109,989	DELAWARE	55,403	36,639	17,134	1,212	418	19,505 R	66.1%	30.9%	2.2%
79,551	ERIE	35,015	16,105	17,732	872	306	1,627 D	46.0%	50.6%	2.5%
122,759	FAIRFIELD	54,094	33,523	19,065	1,115	391	14,458 R	62.0%	35.2%	2.1%
28,433	FAYETTE	9,278	5,685	3,363	165	65	2,322 R	61.3%	36.2%	1.8%
1,068,978	FRANKLIN	414,074	197,862	202,018	10,702	3,492	4,156 D	47.8%	48.8%	2.6%
42,084	FULTON	18,896	11,546	6,805	376	169	4,741 R	61.1%	36.0%	2.0%
31,069	GALLIA	12,776	7,511	4,872	215	178	2,639 R	58.8%	38.1%	1.7%
90,895	GEAUGA	42,600	25,417	15,327	1,405	451	10,090 R	59.7%	36.0%	3.3%
147,886	GREENE	65,204	37,946	25,059	1,592	607	12,887 R	58.2%	38.4%	2.4%
40,792	GUERNSEY	15,430	8,181	6,643	405	201	1,538 R	53.0%	43.1%	2.6%
845,303	HAMILTON	377,899	204,175	161,578	9,222	2,924	42,597 R	54.0%	42.8%	2.4%
71,295	HANCOCK	30,617	20,985	8,798	592	242	12,187 R	68.5%	28.7%	1.9%
31,945	HARDIN	12,068	7,124	4,557	243	144	2,567 R	59.0%	37.8%	2.0%
15,856	HARRISON	7,161	3,417	3,351	192	201	66 R	47.7%	46.8%	2.7%
29,210	HENRY	13,252	8,530	4,367	258	97	4,163 R	64.4%	33.0%	1.9%
40,875	HIGHLAND	15,447	9,728	5,328	245	146	4,400 R	63.0%	34.5%	1.6%
28,241	HOCKING	10,756	5,702	4,474	291	289	1,228 R	53.0%	41.6%	2.7%
38,943	HOLMES	9,145	6,754	2,066	172	153	4,688 R	73.9%	22.6%	1.9%
59,487	HURON	21,360	12,286	8,183	560	331	4,103 R	57.5%	38.3%	2.6%
32,641	JACKSON	12,490	6,958	5,131	222	179	1,827 R	55.7%	41.1%	1.8%
73,894	JEFFERSON	34,636	15,038	17,488	897	1,213	2,450 D	43.4%	50.5%	2.6%
54,500	KNOX	21,260	13,393	7,133	452	282	6,260 R	63.0%	33.6%	2.1%
227,511	LAKE	102,564	51,747	46,497	3,166	1,154	5,250 R	50.5%	45.3%	3.1%
62,319	LAWRENCE	24,452	12,531	11,307	402	212	1,224 R	51.2%	46.2%	1.6%
145,491	LICKING	62,466	37,180	23,196	1,498	592	13,984 R	59.5%	37.1%	2.4%
46,005	LOGAN	18,455	11,849	5,945	449	212	5,904 R	64.2%	32.2%	2.4%
284,664	LORAIN	112,130	47,957	59,809	3,183	1,231	11,852 D	42.8%	53.3%	2.8%
455,054	LUCAS	187,350	73,342	108,344	4,227	1,437	35,002 D	39.1%	57.8%	2.3%
40,213	MADISON	14,667	8,892	5,287	299	189	3,605 R	60.6%	36.0%	2.0%
257,555	MAHONING	114,119	40,460	69,212	3,322	1,125	28,752 D	35.5%	60.6%	2.9%
66,217	MARION	24,815	13,617	10,370	588	240	3,247 R	54.9%	41.8%	2.4%
151,095	MEDINA	66,883	37,349	26,635	1,960	939	10,714 R	55.8%	39.8%	2.9%
23,072	MEIGS	9,795	5,750	3,674	226	145	2,076 R	58.7%	37.5%	2.3%
40,924	MERCER	18,294	12,485	5,212	392	205	7,273 R	68.2%	28.5%	2.1%
98,868	MIAMI	42,841	26,037	15,584	879	341	10,453 R	60.8%	36.4%	2.1%
15,180	MONROE	7,115	3,145	3,605	149	216	460 D	44.2%	50.7%	2.1%
559,062	MONTGOMERY	230,987	109,792	114,597	4,690	1,908	4,805 D	47.5%	49.6%	2.0%
14,897	MORGAN	5,993	3,451	2,261	177	104	1,190 R	57.6%	37.7%	3.0%
31,628	MORROW	12,839	7,842	4,529	305	163	3,313 R	61.1%	35.3%	2.4%
84,585	MUSKINGUM	32,624	17,995	13,415	882	332	4,580 R	55.2%	41.1%	2.7%

OHIO

PRESIDENT 2000

2000 Census Population	County	Total Vote	Republican	Democratic	Green (Nader)	Other	Rep.-Dem. Plurality		Percentage of Total Vote		
									Rep.	Dem.	Green
14,058	NOBLE	5,988	3,435	2,296	154	103	1,139	R	57.4%	38.3%	2.6%
40,985	OTTAWA	19,968	9,917	9,485	432	134	432	R	49.7%	47.5%	2.2%
20,293	PAULDING	8,946	5,210	3,384	242	110	1,826	R	58.2%	37.8%	2.7%
34,078	PERRY	12,828	6,440	5,895	334	159	545	R	50.2%	46.0%	2.6%
52,727	PICKAWAY	17,740	10,717	6,598	276	149	4,119	R	60.4%	37.2%	1.6%
27,695	PIKE	10,560	5,333	4,923	176	128	410	R	50.5%	46.6%	1.7%
152,061	PORTAGE	62,899	28,271	31,446	2,340	842	3,175	D	44.9%	50.0%	3.7%
42,337	PREBLE	18,166	11,176	6,375	404	211	4,801	R	61.5%	35.1%	2.2%
34,726	PUTNAM	17,344	12,837	4,063	254	190	8,774	R	74.0%	23.4%	1.5%
128,852	RICHLAND	52,779	30,138	20,572	1,306	763	9,566	R	57.1%	39.0%	2.5%
73,345	ROSS	26,016	13,706	11,662	421	227	2,044	R	52.7%	44.8%	1.6%
61,792	SANDUSKY	25,744	13,699	11,146	587	312	2,553	R	53.2%	43.3%	2.3%
79,195	SCIOTO	29,945	15,022	13,997	590	336	1,025	R	50.2%	46.7%	2.0%
58,683	SENECA	24,351	13,863	9,512	666	310	4,351	R	56.9%	39.1%	2.7%
47,910	SHELBY	19,670	12,476	6,593	392	209	5,883	R	63.4%	33.5%	2.0%
378,098	STARK	159,844	78,153	75,308	4,032	2,351	2,845	R	48.9%	47.1%	2.5%
542,899	SUMMIT	224,839	96,721	119,759	5,955	2,404	23,038	D	43.0%	53.3%	2.6%
225,116	TRUMBULL	96,239	34,654	57,643	2,749	1,193	22,989	D	36.0%	59.9%	2.9%
90,914	TUSCARAWAS	37,118	19,549	15,879	1,061	629	3,670	R	52.7%	42.8%	2.9%
40,909	UNION	17,024	11,502	5,040	336	146	6,462	R	67.6%	29.6%	2.0%
29,659	VAN WERT	13,219	8,679	4,209	216	115	4,470	R	65.7%	31.8%	1.6%
12,806	VINTON	4,946	2,720	2,037	110	79	683	R	55.0%	41.2%	2.2%
158,383	WARREN	69,078	48,318	19,142	1,067	551	29,176	R	69.9%	27.7%	1.5%
63,251	WASHINGTON	26,515	15,342	10,383	571	219	4,959	R	57.9%	39.2%	2.2%
111,564	WAYNE	42,436	25,901	14,779	1,171	585	11,122	R	61.0%	34.8%	2.8%
39,188	WILLIAMS	15,919	9,941	5,454	347	177	4,487	R	62.4%	34.3%	2.2%
121,065	WOOD	52,194	27,504	22,687	1,536	467	4,817	R	52.7%	43.5%	2.9%
22,908	WYANDOT	9,827	6,113	3,397	191	126	2,716	R	62.2%	34.6%	1.9%
11,353,140	TOTAL	4,701,998	2,350,363	2,183,628	117,799	50,208	166,735	R	50.0%	46.4%	2.5%

OHIO

SENATOR 2000

2000 Census Population	County	Total Vote	Republican	Democratic	Other	Rep.-Dem. Plurality		Percentage			
								Total Vote		Major Vote	
								Rep.	Dem.	Rep.	Dem.
27,330	ADAMS	9,882	6,508	2,949	425	3,559	R	65.9%	29.8%	68.8%	31.2%
108,473	ALLEN	40,559	27,926	11,134	1,499	16,792	R	68.9%	27.5%	71.5%	28.5%
52,523	ASHLAND	20,564	14,992	4,708	864	10,284	R	72.9%	22.9%	76.1%	23.9%
102,728	ASHTABULA	38,164	21,628	14,764	1,772	6,864	R	56.7%	38.7%	59.4%	40.6%
62,223	ATHENS	24,168	11,466	11,069	1,633	397	R	47.4%	45.8%	50.9%	49.1%
46,611	AUGLAIZE	19,486	14,578	4,194	714	10,384	R	74.8%	21.5%	77.7%	22.3%
70,226	BELMONT	28,798	13,467	14,176	1,155	709	D	46.8%	49.2%	48.7%	51.3%
42,285	BROWN	15,864	10,467	4,755	642	5,712	R	66.0%	30.0%	68.8%	31.2%
332,807	BUTLER	131,964	91,886	34,748	5,330	57,138	R	69.6%	26.3%	72.6%	27.4%
28,836	CARROLL	11,917	7,525	3,833	559	3,692	R	63.1%	32.2%	66.3%	33.7%
38,890	CHAMPAIGN	15,205	8,497	5,299	1,409	3,198	R	55.9%	34.9%	61.6%	38.4%
144,742	CLARK	56,569	34,297	19,508	2,764	14,789	R	60.6%	34.5%	63.7%	36.3%
177,977	CLERMONT	68,508	49,325	16,167	3,016	33,158	R	72.0%	23.6%	75.3%	24.7%
40,543	CLINTON	14,666	10,688	3,293	685	7,395	R	72.9%	22.5%	76.4%	23.6%
112,075	COLUMBIANA	43,360	24,145	17,111	2,104	7,034	R	55.7%	39.5%	58.5%	41.5%

OHIO

SENATOR 2000

2000 Census Population	County	Total Vote	Republican	Democratic	Other	Rep.-Dem. Plurality		Percentage			
								Total Vote		Major Vote	
								Rep.	Dem.	Rep.	Dem.
36,655	COSHOCTON	13,790	8,910	4,375	505	4,535	R	64.6%	31.7%	67.1%	32.9%
46,966	CRAWFORD	18,945	12,845	5,221	879	7,624	R	67.8%	27.6%	71.1%	28.9%
1,393,978	CUYAHOGA	492,209	241,330	234,421	16,458	6,909	R	49.0%	47.6%	50.7%	49.3%
53,309	DARKE	22,759	16,905	4,999	855	11,906	R	74.3%	22.0%	77.2%	22.8%
39,500	DEFIANCE	15,797	10,133	5,070	594	5,063	R	64.1%	32.1%	66.7%	33.3%
109,989	DELAWARE	53,603	38,290	12,794	2,519	25,496	R	71.4%	23.9%	75.0%	25.0%
79,551	ERIE	33,991	18,987	13,878	1,126	5,109	R	55.9%	40.8%	57.8%	42.2%
122,759	FAIRFIELD	52,604	36,304	13,971	2,329	22,333	R	69.0%	26.6%	72.2%	27.8%
28,433	FAYETTE	9,099	6,468	2,267	364	4,201	R	71.1%	24.9%	74.0%	26.0%
1,068,978	FRANKLIN	392,741	218,164	155,855	18,722	62,309	R	55.5%	39.7%	58.3%	41.7%
42,084	FULTON	18,408	13,007	4,799	602	8,208	R	70.7%	26.1%	73.0%	27.0%
31,069	GALLIA	12,183	7,580	4,049	554	3,531	R	62.2%	33.2%	65.2%	34.8%
90,895	GEAUGA	40,947	29,528	10,007	1,412	19,521	R	72.1%	24.4%	74.7%	25.3%
147,886	GREENE	64,134	46,293	14,832	3,009	31,461	R	72.2%	23.1%	75.7%	24.3%
40,792	GUERNSEY	14,934	9,254	5,046	634	4,208	R	62.0%	33.8%	64.7%	35.3%
845,303	HAMILTON	369,290	223,984	130,106	15,200	93,878	R	60.7%	35.2%	63.3%	36.7%
71,295	HANCOCK	29,669	22,337	6,384	948	15,953	R	75.3%	21.5%	77.8%	22.2%
31,945	HARDIN	11,307	6,891	3,304	1,112	3,587	R	60.9%	29.2%	67.6%	32.4%
15,856	HARRISON	6,913	3,628	2,971	314	657	R	52.5%	43.0%	55.0%	45.0%
29,210	HENRY	12,951	9,361	3,124	466	6,237	R	72.3%	24.1%	75.0%	25.0%
40,875	HIGHLAND	15,081	10,237	4,196	648	6,041	R	67.9%	27.8%	70.9%	29.1%
28,241	HOCKING	10,484	6,047	3,916	521	2,131	R	57.7%	37.4%	60.7%	39.3%
38,943	HOLMES	8,822	6,745	1,770	307	4,975	R	76.5%	20.1%	79.2%	20.8%
59,487	HURON	20,727	13,710	6,117	900	7,593	R	66.1%	29.5%	69.1%	30.9%
32,641	JACKSON	11,863	7,517	3,827	519	3,690	R	63.4%	32.3%	66.3%	33.7%
73,894	JEFFERSON	33,253	16,316	15,222	1,715	1,094	R	49.1%	45.8%	51.7%	48.3%
54,500	KNOX	20,391	13,659	5,699	1,033	7,960	R	67.0%	27.9%	70.6%	29.4%
227,511	LAKE	95,248	62,519	29,568	3,161	32,951	R	65.6%	31.0%	67.9%	32.1%
62,319	LAWRENCE	23,271	13,032	9,323	916	3,709	R	56.0%	40.1%	58.3%	41.7%
145,491	LICKING	61,401	40,006	18,373	3,022	21,633	R	65.2%	29.9%	68.5%	31.5%
46,005	LOGAN	18,148	12,410	4,614	1,124	7,796	R	68.4%	25.4%	72.9%	27.1%
284,664	LORAIN	108,605	60,490	44,097	4,018	16,393	R	55.7%	40.6%	57.8%	42.2%
455,054	LUCAS	173,677	89,753	74,682	9,242	15,071	R	51.7%	43.0%	54.6%	45.4%
40,213	MADISON	13,820	5,534	6,070	2,216	536	D	40.0%	43.9%	47.7%	52.3%
257,555	MAHONING	109,532	50,568	55,064	3,900	4,496	D	46.2%	50.3%	47.9%	52.1%
66,217	MARION	24,439	15,554	7,675	1,210	7,879	R	63.6%	31.4%	67.0%	33.0%
151,095	MEDINA	64,360	44,629	17,145	2,586	27,484	R	69.3%	26.6%	72.2%	27.8%
23,072	MEIGS	9,253	5,881	2,860	512	3,021	R	63.6%	30.9%	67.3%	32.7%
40,924	MERCER	17,998	13,239	4,259	500	8,980	R	73.6%	23.7%	75.7%	24.3%
98,868	MIAMI	41,785	30,394	9,494	1,897	20,900	R	72.7%	22.7%	76.2%	23.8%
15,180	MONROE	6,721	3,217	3,241	263	24	D	47.9%	48.2%	49.8%	50.2%
559,062	MONTGOMERY	204,137	126,983	69,676	7,478	57,307	R	62.2%	34.1%	64.6%	35.4%
14,897	MORGAN	5,787	3,786	1,730	271	2,056	R	65.4%	29.9%	68.6%	31.4%
31,628	MORROW	12,510	8,065	3,646	799	4,419	R	64.5%	29.1%	68.9%	31.1%
84,585	MUSKINGUM	31,736	19,930	10,441	1,365	9,489	R	62.8%	32.9%	65.6%	34.4%
14,058	NOBLE	5,704	3,604	1,857	243	1,747	R	63.2%	32.6%	66.0%	34.0%
40,985	OTTAWA	19,577	11,641	7,336	600	4,305	R	59.5%	37.5%	61.3%	38.7%
20,293	PAULDING	8,632	5,175	2,973	484	2,202	R	60.0%	34.4%	63.5%	36.5%
34,078	PERRY	12,441	7,177	4,676	588	2,501	R	57.7%	37.6%	60.6%	39.4%
52,727	PICKAWAY	17,040	11,694	4,589	757	7,105	R	68.6%	26.9%	71.8%	28.2%
27,695	PIKE	10,238	5,353	4,513	372	840	R	52.3%	44.1%	54.3%	45.7%
152,061	PORTAGE	60,603	34,078	23,218	3,307	10,860	R	56.2%	38.3%	59.5%	40.5%
42,337	PREBLE	17,682	12,378	4,424	880	7,954	R	70.0%	25.0%	73.7%	26.3%
34,726	PUTNAM	16,870	12,714	3,616	540	9,098	R	75.4%	21.4%	77.9%	22.1%
128,852	RICHLAND	51,467	33,237	16,334	1,896	16,903	R	64.6%	31.7%	67.0%	33.0%
73,345	ROSS	25,049	15,062	9,140	847	5,922	R	60.1%	36.5%	62.2%	37.8%
61,792	SANDUSKY	25,121	16,053	8,084	984	7,969	R	63.9%	32.2%	66.5%	33.5%
79,195	SCIOTO	28,854	15,814	11,906	1,134	3,908	R	54.8%	41.3%	57.0%	43.0%
58,683	SENECA	23,809	16,045	6,732	1,032	9,313	R	67.4%	28.3%	70.4%	29.6%
47,910	SHELBY	19,106	13,630	4,586	890	9,044	R	71.3%	24.0%	74.8%	25.2%

OHIO

SENATOR 2000

2000 Census Population	County	Total Vote	Republican	Democratic	Other	Rep.-Dem. Plurality		Percentage			
								Total Vote		Major Vote	
								Rep.	Dem.	Rep.	Dem.
378,098	STARK	156,084	95,570	54,351	6,163	41,219	R	61.2%	34.8%	63.7%	36.3%
542,899	SUMMIT	218,487	122,148	87,933	8,406	34,215	R	55.9%	40.2%	58.1%	41.9%
225,116	TRUMBULL	84,107	39,137	41,444	3,526	2,307	D	46.5%	49.3%	48.6%	51.4%
90,914	TUSCARAWAS	35,618	21,076	13,124	1,418	7,952	R	59.2%	36.8%	61.6%	38.4%
40,909	UNION	16,428	9,453	5,127	1,848	4,326	R	57.5%	31.2%	64.8%	35.2%
29,659	VAN WERT	12,889	8,954	3,416	519	5,538	R	69.5%	26.5%	72.4%	27.6%
12,806	VINTON	4,713	2,764	1,737	212	1,027	R	58.6%	36.9%	61.4%	38.6%
158,383	WARREN	67,278	51,135	13,546	2,597	37,589	R	76.0%	20.1%	79.1%	20.9%
63,251	WASHINGTON	25,408	15,574	8,858	976	6,716	R	61.3%	34.9%	63.7%	36.3%
111,564	WAYNE	41,126	28,511	11,000	1,615	17,511	R	69.3%	26.7%	72.2%	27.8%
39,188	WILLIAMS	15,439	10,820	3,980	639	6,840	R	70.1%	25.8%	73.1%	26.9%
121,065	WOOD	50,427	32,097	16,333	1,997	15,764	R	63.7%	32.4%	66.3%	33.7%
22,908	WYANDOT	9,607	6,803	2,347	457	4,456	R	70.8%	24.4%	74.3%	25.7%
11,353,140	TOTAL	4,448,801	2,665,512	1,595,066	188,223	1,070,446	R	59.9%	35.9%	62.6%	37.4%

OHIO

CONGRESS

CD	Year	Total Vote	Republican		Democratic		Other Vote	Rep.-Dem. Plurality		Percentage			
			Vote	Candidate	Vote	Candidate				Total Vote		Major Vote	
										Rep.	Dem.	Rep.	Dem.
1	2000	220,428	116,768	CHABOT, STEVE	98,328	CRANLEY, JOHN	5,332	18,440	R	53.0%	44.6%	54.3%	45.7%
1	1998	174,424	92,421	CHABOT, STEVE	82,003	QUALLS, ROXANNE		10,418	R	53.0%	47.0%	53.0%	47.0%
1	1996	218,424	118,324	CHABOT, STEVE	94,719	LONGABAUGH, MARK P.	5,381	23,605	R	54.2%	43.4%	55.5%	44.5%
1	1994	165,819	92,997	CHABOT, STEVE	72,822	MANN, DAVID		20,175	R	56.1%	43.9%	56.1%	43.9%
1	1992	234,433			120,190	MANN, DAVID	114,243	120,190	D		51.3%		100.0%
2	2000	277,541	204,184	PORTMAN, ROB	64,091	SANDERS, CHARLES W.	9,266	140,093	R	73.6%	23.1%	76.1%	23.9%
2	1998	203,637	154,344	PORTMAN, ROB	49,293	SANDERS, CHARLES W.		105,051	R	75.8%	24.2%	75.8%	24.2%
2	1996	259,473	186,853	PORTMAN, ROB	58,715	CHANDLER, THOMAS R.	13,905	128,138	R	72.0%	22.6%	76.1%	23.9%
2	1994	193,858	150,128	PORTMAN, ROB	43,730	MANN, LES		106,398	R	77.4%	22.6%	77.4%	22.6%
2	1992	253,651	177,720	GRADISON, WILLIS D.	75,924	CHANDLER, THOMAS R.	7	101,796	R	70.1%	29.9%	70.1%	29.9%
3	2000	214,247			177,731	HALL, TONY P.	36,516	177,731	D		83.0%		100.0%
3	1998	164,742	50,544	SHONDEL, JOHN S.	114,198	HALL, TONY P.		63,654	D	30.7%	69.3%	30.7%	69.3%
3	1996	227,203	75,732	WESTBROCK, DAVID A.	144,583	HALL, TONY P.	6,888	68,851	D	33.3%	63.6%	34.4%	65.6%
3	1994	177,656	72,314	WESTBROCK, DAVID A.	105,342	HALL, TONY P.		33,028	D	40.7%	59.3%	40.7%	59.3%
3	1992	244,811	98,733	DAVIS, PETER W.	146,072	HALL, TONY P.	6	47,339	D	40.3%	59.7%	40.3%	59.7%
4	2000	232,118	156,510	OXLEY, MICHAEL G.	67,330	DICKMAN, DANIEL	8,278	89,180	R	67.4%	29.0%	69.9%	30.1%
4	1998	175,540	112,011	OXLEY, MICHAEL G.	63,529	MCCLAIN, PAUL		48,482	R	63.8%	36.2%	63.8%	36.2%
4	1996	227,761	147,608	OXLEY, MICHAEL G.	69,096	MCCLAIN, PAUL	11,057	78,512	R	64.8%	30.3%	68.1%	31.9%
4	1994	139,841	139,841	OXLEY, MICHAEL G.				139,841	R	100.0%		100.0%	
4	1992	240,440	147,346	OXLEY, MICHAEL G.	92,608	BALL, RAYMOND M.	486	54,738	R	61.3%	38.5%	61.4%	38.6%
5	2000	243,340	169,857	GILLMOR, PAUL E.	62,138	EDMON, DANNIE	11,345	107,719	R	69.8%	25.5%	73.2%	26.8%
5	1998	185,905	123,979	GILLMOR, PAUL E.	61,926	DARROW, SUSAN D.		62,053	R	66.7%	33.3%	66.7%	33.3%
5	1996	238,323	145,692	GILLMOR, PAUL E.	81,170	SAUNDERS, ANNIE	11,461	64,522	R	61.1%	34.1%	64.2%	35.8%
5	1994	185,214	135,879	GILLMOR, PAUL E.	49,335	TUDOR, JARROD		86,544	R	73.4%	26.6%	73.4%	26.6%
5	1992	187,860	187,860	GILLMOR, PAUL E.				187,860	R	100.0%		100.0%	

OHIO

CONGRESS

CD	Year	Total Vote	Republican Vote	Republican Candidate	Democratic Vote	Democratic Candidate	Other Vote	Rep.-Dem. Plurality	Total Vote Rep.	Total Vote Dem.	Major Vote Rep.	Major Vote Dem.
6	2000	240,574	96,966	AZINGER, MIKE	138,849	STRICKLAND, TED	4,759	41,883 D	40.3%	57.7%	41.1%	58.9%
6	1998	180,563	77,711	HOLLISTER, NANCY P.	102,852	STRICKLAND, TED		25,141 D	43.0%	57.0%	43.0%	57.0%
6	1996	229,926	111,907	CREMEANS, FRANK A.	118,003	STRICKLAND, TED	16	6,096 D	48.7%	51.3%	48.7%	51.3%
6	1994	179,124	91,263	CREMEANS, FRANK A.	87,861	STRICKLAND, TED		3,402 R	50.9%	49.1%	50.9%	49.1%
6	1992	241,972	119,252	MCEWEN, BOB	122,720	STRICKLAND, TED		3,468 D	49.3%	50.7%	49.3%	50.7%
7	2000	242,186	163,646	HOBSON, DAVID L.	60,755	MINOR, DONALD E.	17,785	102,891 R	67.6%	25.1%	72.9%	27.1%
7	1998	179,697	120,765	HOBSON, DAVID L.	49,780	MINOR, DONALD E.	9,152	70,985 R	67.2%	27.7%	70.8%	29.2%
7	1996	233,001	158,087	HOBSON, DAVID L.	61,419	BLAIN, RICHARD K.	13,495	96,668 R	67.8%	26.4%	72.0%	28.0%
7	1994	140,124	140,124	HOBSON, DAVID L.				140,124 R	100.0%		100.0%	
7	1992	230,432	164,195	HOBSON, DAVID L.	66,237	HESKETT, CLIFFORD S.		97,958 R	71.3%	28.7%	71.3%	28.7%
8	2000	253,303	179,756	BOEHNER, JOHN A.	66,293	PARKS, JOHN	7,254	113,463 R	71.0%	26.2%	73.1%	26.9%
8	1998	180,891	127,979	BOEHNER, JOHN A.	52,912	GRIFFIN, JOHN W.		75,067 R	70.7%	29.3%	70.7%	29.3%
8	1996	235,943	165,815	BOEHNER, JOHN A.	61,515	KITCHEN, JEFFREY D.	8,613	104,300 R	70.3%	26.1%	72.9%	27.1%
8	1994	148,425	148,338	BOEHNER, JOHN A.			87	148,338 R	99.9%		100.0%	
8	1992	238,395	176,362	BOEHNER, JOHN A.	62,033	STENNET, FRED		114,329 R	74.0%	26.0%	74.0%	26.0%
9	2000	225,328	49,446	BRYAN, DWIGHT	168,547	KAPTUR, MARCY	7,335	119,101 D	21.9%	74.8%	22.7%	77.3%
9	1998	161,105	30,312	EMERY, EDWARD S.	130,793	KAPTUR, MARCY		100,481 D	18.8%	81.2%	18.8%	81.2%
9	1996	221,334	46,040	WHITMAN, RANDY	170,617	KAPTUR, MARCY	4,677	124,577 D	20.8%	77.1%	21.3%	78.7%
9	1994	156,785	38,665	WHITMAN, RANDY	118,120	KAPTUR, MARCY		79,455 D	24.7%	75.3%	24.7%	75.3%
9	1992	243,102	53,011	BROWN, KEN D.	178,879	KAPTUR, MARCY	11,212	125,868 D	21.8%	73.6%	22.9%	77.1%
10	2000	222,755	48,930	SMITH, BILL	167,063	KUCINICH, DENNIS J.	6,762	118,133 D	22.0%	75.0%	22.7%	77.3%
10	1998	165,567	55,015	SLOVENIC, JOE	110,552	KUCINICH, DENNIS J.		55,537 D	33.2%	66.8%	33.2%	66.8%
10	1996	225,696	104,546	HOKE, MARTIN R.	110,723	KUCINICH, DENNIS J.	10,427	6,177 D	46.3%	49.1%	48.6%	51.4%
10	1994	183,639	95,226	HOKE, MARTIN R.	70,918	GAUL, FRANCIS E.	17,495	24,308 R	51.9%	38.6%	57.3%	42.7%
10	1992	240,239	136,433	HOKE, MARTIN R.	103,788	OAKAR, MARY ROSE	18	32,645 R	56.8%	43.2%	56.8%	43.2%
11	2000	193,519	21,630	SYKORA, JAMES J.	164,134	JONES, STEPHANIE TUBBS	7,755	142,504 D	11.2%	84.8%	11.6%	88.4%
11	1998	143,295	18,592	HEREFORD, JAMES D.	115,226	JONES, STEPHANIE TUBBS	9,477	96,634 D	13.0%	80.4%	13.9%	86.1%
11	1996	189,039	28,821	SYKORA, JAMES J.	153,546	STOKES, LOUIS	6,672	124,725 D	15.2%	81.2%	15.8%	84.2%
11	1994	147,928	33,705	SYKORA, JAMES J.	114,220	STOKES, LOUIS	3	80,515 D	22.8%	77.2%	22.8%	77.2%
11	1992	223,624	43,866	ROTHSCHILD, BERYL E.	154,718	STOKES, LOUIS	25,040	110,852 D	19.6%	69.2%	22.1%	77.9%
12	2000	263,386	139,242	TIBERI, PAT	115,432	O'SHAUGHNESSY, MARYELLEN	8,712	23,810 R	52.9%	43.8%	54.7%	45.3%
12	1998	184,891	124,197	KASICH, JOHN R.	60,694	BROWN, EDWARD S.		63,503 R	67.2%	32.8%	67.2%	32.8%
12	1996	237,434	151,667	KASICH, JOHN R.	78,762	RUCCIA, CYNTHIA L.	7,005	72,905 R	63.9%	33.2%	65.8%	34.2%
12	1994	172,345	114,608	KASICH, JOHN R.	57,294	RUCCIA, CYNTHIA L.	443	57,314 R	66.5%	33.2%	66.7%	33.3%
12	1992	239,058	170,297	KASICH, JOHN R.	68,761	FITRAKIS, BOB		101,536 R	71.2%	28.8%	71.2%	28.8%
13	2000	263,298	84,295	JERIC, RICK	170,058	BROWN, SHERROD	8,945	85,763 D	32.0%	64.6%	33.1%	66.9%
13	1998	188,975	72,666	DRAKE, GRACE L.	116,309	BROWN, SHERROD		43,643 D	38.5%	61.5%	38.5%	61.5%
13	1996	242,505	87,108	BLAIR, KENNETH C.	146,690	BROWN, SHERROD	8,707	59,582 D	35.9%	60.5%	37.3%	62.7%
13	1994	189,776	86,422	WHITE, GREGORY A.	93,147	BROWN, SHERROD	10,207	6,725 D	45.5%	49.1%	48.1%	51.9%
13	1992	252,258	88,889	MUELLER, MARGARET R.	134,486	BROWN, SHERROD	28,883	45,597 D	35.2%	53.3%	39.8%	60.2%
14	2000	230,088	71,432	WOOD, RICK	149,184	SAWYER, THOMAS C.	9,472	77,752 D	31.0%	64.8%	32.4%	67.6%
14	1998	169,073	63,027	WATKINS, TOM	106,046	SAWYER, THOMAS C.		43,019 D	37.3%	62.7%	37.3%	62.7%
14	1996	228,435	95,307	GEORGE, JOYCE	124,136	SAWYER, THOMAS C.	8,992	28,829 D	41.7%	54.3%	43.4%	56.6%
14	1994	185,404	89,106	SLABY, LYNN	96,274	SAWYER, THOMAS C.	24	7,168 D	48.1%	51.9%	48.1%	51.9%
14	1992	243,994	78,659	MORGAN, ROBERT	165,335	SAWYER, THOMAS C.		86,676 D	32.2%	67.8%	32.2%	67.8%
15	2000	232,297	156,792	PRYCE, DEBORAH	64,805	BUCKEL, BILL	10,700	91,987 R	67.5%	27.9%	70.8%	29.2%
15	1998	173,176	113,846	PRYCE, DEBORAH	49,334	MILLER, ADAM CLAY	9,996	64,512 R	65.7%	28.5%	69.8%	30.2%

OHIO

CONGRESS

CD	Year	Total Vote	Republican Vote	Republican Candidate	Democratic Vote	Democratic Candidate	Other Vote	Rep.-Dem. Plurality	Total Vote Rep.	Total Vote Dem.	Major Vote Rep.	Major Vote Dem.
15	1996	221,441	156,776	PRYCE, DEBORAH	64,665	ARNEBECK, CLIFF		92,111 R	70.8%	29.2%	70.8%	29.2%
15	1994	159,696	112,912	PRYCE, DEBORAH	46,480	BUCKEL, BILL	304	66,432 R	70.7%	29.1%	70.8%	29.2%
15	1992	250,205	110,390	PRYCE, DEBORAH	94,907	CORDRAY, RICHARD	44,908	15,483 R	44.1%	37.9%	53.8%	46.2%
16	2000	234,400	162,294	REGULA, RALPH S.	62,709	SMITH, WILLIAM	9,397	99,585 R	69.2%	26.8%	72.1%	27.9%
16	1998	183,473	117,426	REGULA, RALPH S.	66,047	FERGUSON, PETER D.		51,379 R	64.0%	36.0%	64.0%	36.0%
16	1996	231,827	159,314	REGULA, RALPH S.	64,902	BURKHART, THOMAS E.	7,611	94,412 R	68.7%	28.0%	71.1%	28.9%
16	1994	183,103	137,322	REGULA, RALPH S.	45,781	FINN, J. MICHAEL		91,541 R	75.0%	25.0%	75.0%	25.0%
16	1992	248,713	158,489	REGULA, RALPH S.	90,224	MENDENHALL, WARNER D.		68,265 R	63.7%	36.3%	63.7%	36.3%
17	2000	240,877	54,751	ALBERTY, PAUL H.	120,333	TRAFICANT, JAMES A.	65,793	65,582 D	22.7%	50.0%	31.3%	68.7%
17	1998	181,421	57,703	ALBERTY, PAUL H.	123,718	TRAFICANT, JAMES A.		66,015 D	31.8%	68.2%	31.8%	68.2%
17	1996	239,968			218,283	TRAFICANT, JAMES A.	21,685	218,283 D		91.0%		100.0%
17	1994	192,494	43,490	MEISTER, MIKE G.	149,004	TRAFICANT, JAMES A.		105,514 D	22.6%	77.4%	22.6%	77.4%
17	1992	257,246	40,743	PANSINO, SALVATORE	216,503	TRAFICANT, JAMES A.		175,760 D	15.8%	84.2%	15.8%	84.2%
18	2000	236,505	152,325	NEY, BOB	79,232	GUTHRIE, MARC	4,948	73,093 R	64.4%	33.5%	65.8%	34.2%
18	1998	187,690	113,119	NEY, BOB	74,571	BURCH, ROBERT L.		38,548 R	60.3%	39.7%	60.3%	39.7%
18	1996	233,843	117,365	NEY, BOB	108,332	BURCH, ROBERT L.	8,146	9,033 R	50.2%	46.3%	52.0%	48.0%
18	1994	191,041	103,115	NEY, BOB	87,926	DIDONATO, GREG L.		15,189 R	54.0%	46.0%	54.0%	46.0%
18	1992	243,418	77,229	RESS, BILL	166,189	APPLEGATE, DOUGLAS		88,960 D	31.7%	68.3%	31.7%	68.3%
19	2000	251,648	174,262	LATOURETTE, STEVEN C.	70,429	BLANCHARD, DALE	6,957	103,833 R	69.2%	28.0%	71.2%	28.8%
19	1998	190,876	126,786	LATOURETTE, STEVEN C.	64,090	KELLEY, ELIZABETH		62,696 R	66.4%	33.6%	66.4%	33.6%
19	1996	246,819	135,012	LATOURETTE, STEVEN C.	101,152	COYNE, THOMAS J.	10,655	33,860 R	54.7%	41.0%	57.2%	42.8%
19	1994	206,242	99,997	LATOURETTE, STEVEN C.	89,701	FINGERHUT, ERIC D.	16,544	10,296 R	48.5%	43.5%	52.7%	47.3%
19	1992	263,083	124,606	GARDNER, ROBERT A.	138,465	FINGERHUT, ERIC D.	12	13,859 D	47.4%	52.6%	47.4%	52.6%

OHIO

GENERAL AND PRIMARY ELECTIONS

2000 GENERAL ELECTIONS

President Other vote was 26,721 no designation (Buchanan); 13,473 Libertarian (Browne); 6,181 Natural Law (Hagelin); 3,823 no designation (Phillips); 10 write-in (Harris). Nader was listed on the ballot with no designation.

Senator Other vote was 117,436 Libertarian (McAlister); 70,713 Natural Law (Eastman); 45 write-in (Fitzsimmons); 29 write-in (Flower). Certified returns were 116,724 McAlister and 757 Fitzsimmons, but their votes were transposed in two counties.

Congress Other vote was: CD 1: 3,399 Libertarian (Groshoff), 1,933 Natural Law (Stevenson); CD 2: 9,266 Libertarian (Bidwell); CD 3: 36,516 Natural Law (Burch); CD 4: 8,278 Libertarian (Mullinger); CD 5: 5,881 Natural Law (Schaffer), 5,464 Libertarian (Green); CD 6: 4,759 Libertarian (MacCutcheon); CD 7: 13,983 Independent (Mitchel), 3,802 Libertarian (Null); CD 8: 7,254 Libertarian (Shock); CD 9: 4,239 Libertarian (Fries), 3,096 Natural Law (Slotnick); CD 10: 6,762 Libertarian (Petrie); CD 11: 4,230 Libertarian (Turner), 3,525 Natural Law (Glavina); CD 12: 4,546 Libertarian (Hogan), 2,600 Natural Law (Richey), 1,566 no designation (Jordan); CD 13: 5,837 Libertarian (Chmura), 3,108 Natural Law (Kluter); CD 14: 5,603 Libertarian (McDaniel), 3,869 Natural Law (Keith); CD 15: 10,700 Libertarian (Smith); CD 16: 6,166 Libertarian (Shetler), 3,231 Natural Law (Graef); CD 17: 51,793 no designation (Walter), 9,568 no designation (D'Apolito), 3,154 Natural Law (McCoy), 1,278 Libertarian (Norris); CD 18: 4,948 Libertarian (Bargar); CD 19: 6,957 Libertarian (Stone).

OHIO

GENERAL AND PRIMARY ELECTIONS

2000 PRIMARY ELECTIONS

Primary   March 7, 2000

Registration   7,229,511   No Formal System of
(as of March 7, 2000)   Party Registration

Primary Type   Open—Any registered voter could vote in the primary of either party.

Note: An asterisk (*) denotes incumbent. The Democratic presidential primary results reflect the vote for congressional district delegate slates. The district votes were aggregated into a statewide total. Republican presidential primary results reflect the vote for statewide at-large slates.

	REPUBLICAN PRIMARIES			DEMOCRATIC PRIMARIES		
President	George W. Bush	810,369	58.0%	Al Gore	720,311	73.6%
	John McCain	516,790	37.0%	Bill Bradley	241,688	24.7%
	Alan Keyes	55,266	4.0%	Lyndon H. LaRouche Jr.	16,513	1.7%
	Steve Forbes	8,934	0.6%			
	Gary Bauer	6,169	0.4%			
	TOTAL	1,397,528		TOTAL	978,512	
Senator	Mike DeWine*	1,029,860	79.5%	Theodore S. Celeste	375,205	43.9%
	Ronald Dickson	161,185	12.4%	Marvin A. McMickle	208,291	24.3%
	Frank Cremeans	104,219	8.0%	Richard Cordray	202,345	23.7%
				Daniel I. Radakovich	69,620	8.1%
	TOTAL	1,295,264		TOTAL	855,461	
Congressional District 1	Steve Chabot*	47,509	100.0%	John Cranley	24,181	100.0%
	TOTAL	47,509		TOTAL	24,181	
Congressional District 2	Rob Portman*	92,084	100.0%	Charles Sanders	20,986	100.0%
	TOTAL	92,084		TOTAL	20,986	
Congressional District 3	*No Republican candidate filed for the primary and none appeared on the general election ballot. Ronald V. Williamitis received 34 write-in votes in the primary.*			Tony P. Hall*	43,675	100.0%
				TOTAL	43,675	
Congressional District 4	Michael G. Oxley*	79,022	100.0%	Daniel Dickman	27,054	100.0%
	TOTAL	79,022		TOTAL	27,054	
Congressional District 5	Paul E. Gillmor*	75,057	100.0%	Dannie Edmon	30,865	100.0%
	TOTAL	75,057		TOTAL	30,865	
Congressional District 6	Mike Azinger	36,234	51.2%	Ted Strickland*	42,289	100.0%
	Jimmy Stewart	34,515	48.8%			
	TOTAL	70,749		TOTAL	42,289	
Congressional District 7	David L. Hobson*	85,654	100.0%	Donald Minor	27,518	100.0%
	TOTAL	85,654		TOTAL	27,518	
Congressional District 8	John A. Boehner*	84,245	100.0%	John Parks	15,924	53.0%
				John Griffin	14,126	47.0%
	TOTAL	84,245		TOTAL	30,050	
Congressional District 9	Dwight E. Bryan	32,903	100.0%	Marcy Kaptur*	42,403	100.0%
	TOTAL	32,903		TOTAL	42,403	
Congressional District 10	Bill Smith	36,445	100.0%	Dennis J. Kucinich*	56,781	93.2%
	Chris Blondin (write-in)	14		C. River Smith	4,145	6.8%
				Robert Reed III (write-in)	2	
	TOTAL	36,459		TOTAL	60,928	
Congressional District 11	*No Republican candidate filed for the primary. James J. Sykora received 50 write-in votes and was the party's candidate in the general election.*			Stephanie Tubbs Jones*	67,680	91.5%
				Gerald Henley	6,286	8.5%
				TOTAL	73,966	

354

OHIO

GENERAL AND PRIMARY ELECTIONS

	REPUBLICAN PRIMARIES			DEMOCRATIC PRIMARIES		
Congressional District 12	Pat Tiberi	57,548	73.0%	Maryellen O'Shaughnessy	27,032	78.5%
	Eugene Watts	16,331	20.7%	Edward Brown	4,906	14.2%
	Ramona Whisler	3,481	4.4%	Ralph Applegate	2,513	7.3%
	Andrew G. Zukowski	1,469	1.9%			
	TOTAL	78,829			34,451	
Congressional District 13	Rick Jeric	51,278	100.0%	Sherrod Brown*	50,765	100.0%
	TOTAL	51,278		TOTAL	50,765	
Congressional District 14	Rick Wood	25,386	57.8%	Thomas C. Sawyer*	48,418	100.0%
	James C. Hrubik	18,536	42.2%			
	TOTAL	43,922		TOTAL	48,418	
Congressional District 15	Deborah Pryce*	61,931	88.1%	Bill Buckel	20,241	100.0%
	Craig Lortz	8,400	11.9%			
	TOTAL	70,331		TOTAL	20,241	
Congressional District 16	Ralph Regula*	77,101	100.0%	William Smith	42,714	100.0%
				Earl Rodd (write-in)	4	
	TOTAL	77,101		TOTAL	42,718	
Congressional District 17	Paul H. Alberty	21,630	52.4%	James A. Traficant*	59,415	50.5%
	Lyle Williams	19,684	47.6%	Robert Hagan	40,079	34.1%
				George Tablack	16,203	13.8%
				Christopher Doutt	1,988	1.7%
	TOTAL	41,314		TOTAL	117,685	
Congressional District 18	Bob Ney*	59,911	100.0%	Marc D. Guthrie	54,232	100.0%
	TOTAL	59,911		TOTAL	54,232	
Congressional District 19	Steven C. LaTourette*	61,133	100.0%	Dale Blanchard	38,741	100.0%
	TOTAL	61,133		TOTAL	38,741	

OKLAHOMA

GOVERNOR
Frank Keating (R). Re-elected 1998 to a four-year term. Previously elected 1994.

SENATORS
James M. Inhofe (R). Re-elected 1996 to a six-year term. Previously elected 1994 to fill out the remaining two years of the term vacated when David L. Boren (D) resigned to become president of the University of Oklahoma.

Don Nickles (R). Re-elected 1998 to a six-year term. Previously elected 1992, 1986, 1980.

REPRESENTATIVES
1. Steve Largent (R)
2. Brad Carson (D)
3. Wes Watkins (R)
4. J. C. Watts (R)
5. Ernest J. Istook (R)
6. Frank D. Lucas (R)

POSTWAR VOTE FOR PRESIDENT

Year	Total Vote	Republican Vote	Republican Candidate	Democratic Vote	Democratic Candidate	Other Vote	Plurality	Total Vote Rep.	Total Vote Dem.	Major Vote Rep.	Major Vote Dem.
2000	1,234,229	744,337	Bush, George W.	474,276	Gore, Al	15,616	270,061 R	60.3%	38.4%	61.1%	38.9%
1996**	1,206,713	582,315	Dole, Bob	488,105	Clinton, Bill	136,293	94,210 R	48.3%	40.4%	54.4%	45.6%
1992**	1,390,359	592,929	Bush, George	473,066	Clinton, Bill	324,364	119,863 R	42.6%	34.0%	55.6%	44.4%
1988	1,171,036	678,367	Bush, George	483,423	Dukakis, Michael S.	9,246	194,944 R	57.9%	41.3%	58.4%	41.6%
1984	1,255,676	861,530	Reagan, Ronald	385,080	Mondale, Walter F.	9,066	476,450 R	68.6%	30.7%	69.1%	30.9%
1980**	1,149,708	695,570	Reagan, Ronald	402,026	Carter, Jimmy	52,112	293,544 R	60.5%	35.0%	63.4%	36.6%
1976	1,092,251	545,708	Ford, Gerald R.	532,442	Carter, Jimmy	14,101	13,266 R	50.0%	48.7%	50.6%	49.4%
1972	1,029,900	759,025	Nixon, Richard M.	247,147	McGovern, George S.	23,728	511,878 R	73.7%	24.0%	75.4%	24.6%
1968	943,086	449,697	Nixon, Richard M.	301,658	Humphrey, Hubert H.	191,731	148,039 R	47.7%	32.0%	59.9%	40.1%
1964	932,499	412,665	Goldwater, Barry M.	519,834	Johnson, Lyndon B.		107,169 D	44.3%	55.7%	44.3%	55.7%
1960	903,150	533,039	Nixon, Richard M.	370,111	Kennedy, John F.		162,928 R	59.0%	41.0%	59.0%	41.0%
1956	859,350	473,769	Eisenhower, Dwight D.	385,581	Stevenson, Adlai E.		88,188 R	55.1%	44.9%	55.1%	44.9%
1952	948,984	518,045	Eisenhower, Dwight D.	430,939	Stevenson, Adlai E.		87,106 R	54.6%	45.4%	54.6%	45.4%
1948	721,599	268,817	Dewey, Thomas E.	452,782	Truman, Harry S.		183,965 D	37.3%	62.7%	37.3%	62.7%

In 1996 the other vote column includes 130,788 votes cast for Perot. In 1992 the other vote column includes 319,878 votes cast for Perot. In 1980 the other column includes 38,284 votes for Independent (Anderson).

OKLAHOMA

POSTWAR VOTE FOR GOVERNOR

Year	Total Vote	Republican		Democratic		Other Vote	Rep.-Dem. Plurality	Percentage			
								Total Vote		Major Vote	
		Vote	Candidate	Vote	Candidate			Rep.	Dem.	Rep.	Dem.
1998	873,585	505,498	Keating, Frank	357,552	Boyd, Laura	10,535	147,946 R	57.9%	40.9%	58.6%	41.4%
1994**	995,012	466,740	Keating, Frank	294,936	Mildren, Jack	233,336	171,804 R	46.9%	29.6%	61.3%	38.7%
1990	911,314	297,584	Price, Bill	523,196	Walters, David	90,534	225,612 D	32.7%	57.4%	36.3%	63.7%
1986	909,925	431,762	Bellmon, Henry	405,295	Walters, David	72,868	26,467 R	47.5%	44.5%	51.6%	48.4%
1982	883,130	332,207	Daxon, Tom	548,159	Nigh, George	2,764	215,952 D	37.6%	62.1%	37.7%	62.3%
1978	777,414	367,055	Shotts, Ron	402,240	Nigh, George	8,119	35,185 D	47.2%	51.7%	47.7%	52.3%
1974	804,848	290,459	Inhofe, James M.	514,389	Boren, David L.		223,930 D	36.1%	63.9%	36.1%	63.9%
1970	698,790	336,157	Bartlett, Dewey F.	338,338	Hall, David	24,295	2,181 D	48.1%	48.4%	49.8%	50.2%
1966	677,258	377,078	Bartlett, Dewey F.	296,328	Moore, Preston J.	3,852	80,750 R	55.7%	43.8%	56.0%	44.0%
1962	709,763	392,316	Bellmon, Henry	315,357	Atkinson, W. P.	2,090	76,959 R	55.3%	44.4%	55.4%	44.6%
1958	538,839	107,495	Ferguson, Phil	399,504	Edmondson, J. Howard	31,840	292,009 D	19.9%	74.1%	21.2%	78.8%
1954	609,194	251,808	Sparks, Reuben K.	357,386	Gary, Raymond		105,578 D	41.3%	58.7%	41.3%	58.7%
1950	644,276	313,205	Ferguson, Jo O.	329,308	Murray, Johnston	1,763	16,103 D	48.6%	51.1%	48.7%	51.3%
1946	494,599	227,426	Flynn, Olney F.	259,491	Turner, Roy J.	7,682	32,065 D	46.0%	52.5%	46.7%	53.3%

In 1994 other vote was Independent (Watkins).

POSTWAR VOTE FOR SENATOR

Year	Total Vote	Republican		Democratic		Other Vote	Rep.-Dem. Plurality	Percentage			
								Total Vote		Major Vote	
		Vote	Candidate	Vote	Candidate			Rep.	Dem.	Rep.	Dem.
1998	859,713	570,682	Nickles, Don	268,898	Carroll, Don E.	20,133	301,784 R	66.4%	31.3%	68.0%	32.0%
1996	1,183,150	670,610	Inhofe, James M.	474,162	Boren, Jim	38,378	196,448 R	56.7%	40.1%	58.6%	41.4%
1994S	982,430	542,390	Inhofe, James M.	392,488	McCurdy, Dave	47,552	149,902 R	55.2%	40.0%	58.0%	42.0%
1992	1,294,423	757,876	Nickles, Don	494,350	Lewis, Steve	42,197	263,526 R	58.5%	38.2%	60.5%	39.5%
1990	884,498	148,814	Jones, Stephen	735,684	Boren, David L.		586,870 D	16.8%	83.2%	16.8%	83.2%
1986	893,666	493,436	Nickles, Don	400,230	Jones, James R.		93,206 R	55.2%	44.8%	55.2%	44.8%
1984	1,197,937	280,638	Crozier, Will E.	906,131	Boren, David L.	11,168	625,493 D	23.4%	75.6%	23.6%	76.4%
1980	1,098,294	587,252	Nickles, Don	478,283	Coats, Andrew	32,759	108,969 R	53.5%	43.5%	55.1%	44.9%
1978	754,264	247,857	Kamm, Robert B.	493,953	Boren, David L.	12,454	246,096 D	32.9%	65.5%	33.4%	66.6%
1974	791,809	390,997	Bellmon, Henry	387,162	Edmondson, Ed	13,650	3,835 R	49.4%	48.9%	50.2%	49.8%
1972	1,005,148	516,934	Bartlett, Dewey F.	478,212	Edmondson, Ed	10,002	38,722 R	51.4%	47.6%	51.9%	48.1%
1968	909,119	470,120	Bellmon, Henry	419,658	Monroney, A. S. Mike	19,341	50,462 R	51.7%	46.2%	52.8%	47.2%
1966	638,742	295,585	Patterson, Pat J.	343,157	Harris, Fred R.		47,572 D	46.3%	53.7%	46.3%	53.7%
1964S	912,174	445,392	Wilkinson, Bud	466,782	Harris, Fred R.		21,390 D	48.8%	51.2%	48.8%	51.2%
1962	664,712	307,966	Crawford, B. Hayden	353,890	Monroney, A. S. Mike	2,856	45,924 D	46.3%	53.2%	46.5%	53.5%
1960	864,475	385,646	Crawford, B. Hayden	474,116	Kerr, Robert S.	4,713	88,470 D	44.6%	54.8%	44.9%	55.1%
1956	831,142	371,146	McKeever, Douglas	459,996	Monroney, A. S. Mike		88,850 D	44.7%	55.3%	44.7%	55.3%
1954	600,120	262,013	Mock, Fred M.	335,127	Kerr, Robert S.	2,980	73,114 D	43.7%	55.8%	43.9%	56.1%
1950	631,177	285,224	Alexander, W. H.	345,953	Monroney, A. S. Mike		60,729 D	45.2%	54.8%	45.2%	54.8%
1948	708,931	265,169	Rizley, Ross	441,654	Kerr, Robert S.	2,108	176,485 D	37.4%	62.3%	37.5%	62.5%

The 1994 and 1964 elections were for short terms to fill a vacancy.

OKLAHOMA

Districts Established May 27, 1991

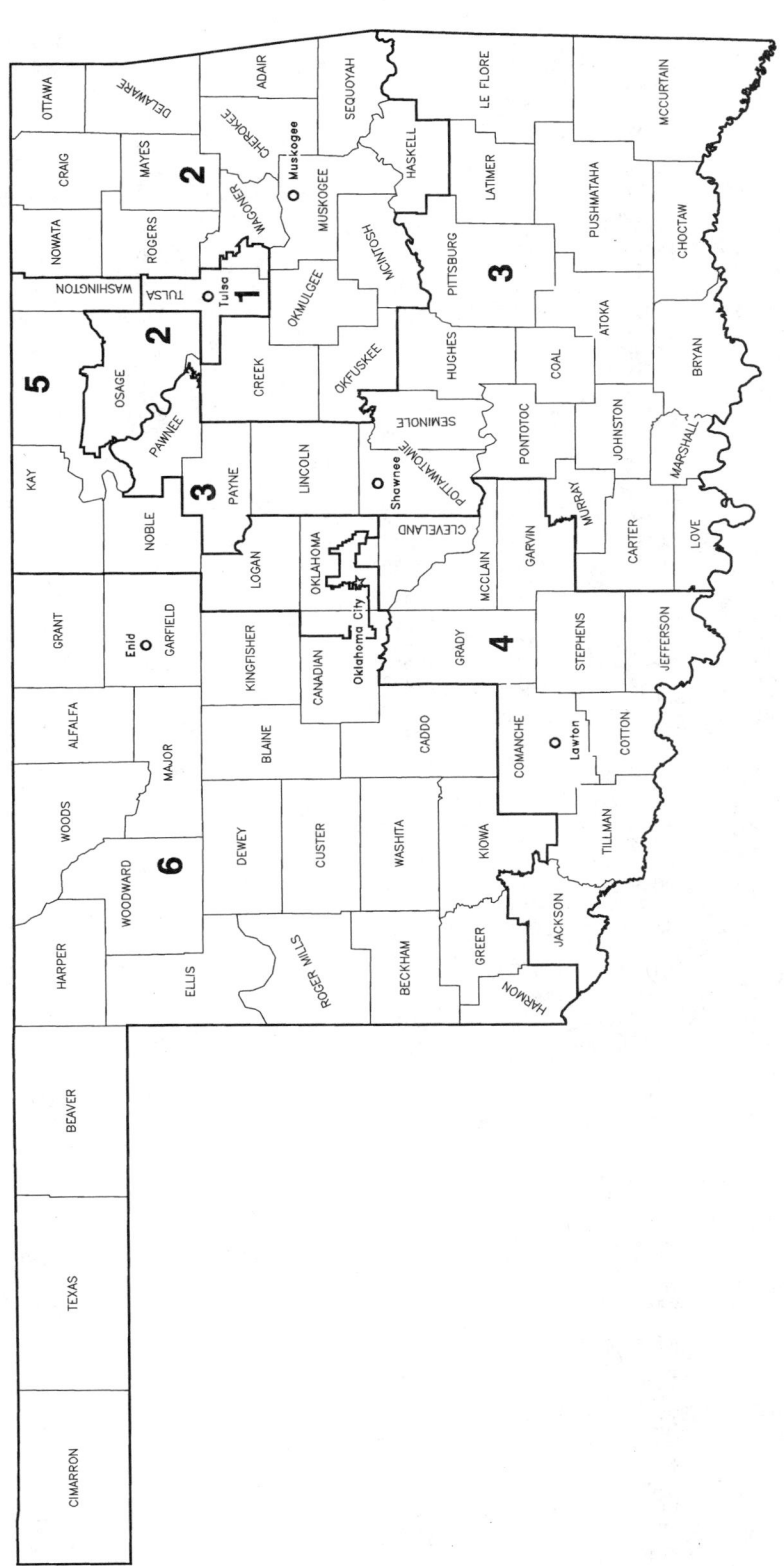

OKLAHOMA

PRESIDENT 2000

2000 Census Population	County	Total Vote	Republican	Democratic	Green (Nader)	Other	Rep.-Dem. Plurality	Percentage of Total Vote		
								Rep.	Dem.	Green
21,038	ADAIR	5,977	3,503	2,361		113	1,142 R	58.6%	39.5%	
6,105	ALFALFA	2,507	1,886	583		38	1,303 R	75.2%	23.3%	
13,879	ATOKA	4,324	2,375	1,906		43	469 R	54.9%	44.1%	
5,857	BEAVER	2,456	2,092	339		25	1,753 R	85.2%	13.8%	
19,799	BECKHAM	6,532	4,067	2,408		57	1,659 R	62.3%	36.9%	
11,976	BLAINE	4,094	2,633	1,402		59	1,231 R	64.3%	34.2%	
36,534	BRYAN	11,746	6,084	5,554		108	530 R	51.8%	47.3%	
30,150	CADDO	9,210	4,835	4,272		103	563 R	52.5%	46.4%	
87,697	CANADIAN	31,360	22,679	8,367		314	14,312 R	72.3%	26.7%	
45,621	CARTER	16,458	9,667	6,659		132	3,008 R	58.7%	40.5%	
42,521	CHEROKEE	14,468	6,918	7,256		294	338 D	47.8%	50.2%	
15,342	CHOCTAW	5,315	2,461	2,799		55	338 D	46.3%	52.7%	
3,148	CIMARRON	1,484	1,230	227		27	1,003 R	82.9%	15.3%	
208,016	CLEVELAND	76,171	47,393	27,792		986	19,601 R	62.2%	36.5%	
6,031	COAL	2,362	1,196	1,148		18	48 R	50.6%	48.6%	
114,996	COMANCHE	29,333	17,103	11,971		259	5,132 R	58.3%	40.8%	
6,614	COTTON	2,482	1,388	1,068		26	320 R	55.9%	43.0%	
14,950	CRAIG	5,484	2,815	2,568		101	247 R	51.3%	46.8%	
67,367	CREEK	23,741	13,580	9,753		408	3,827 R	57.2%	41.1%	
26,142	CUSTER	9,743	6,527	3,115		101	3,412 R	67.0%	32.0%	
37,077	DELAWARE	13,353	7,618	5,514		221	2,104 R	57.1%	41.3%	
4,743	DEWEY	2,220	1,607	599		14	1,008 R	72.4%	27.0%	
4,075	ELLIS	2,013	1,513	468		32	1,045 R	75.2%	23.2%	
57,813	GARFIELD	21,683	14,902	6,543		238	8,359 R	68.7%	30.2%	
27,210	GARVIN	9,843	5,536	4,189		118	1,347 R	56.2%	42.6%	
45,516	GRADY	16,276	10,040	6,037		199	4,003 R	61.7%	37.1%	
5,144	GRANT	2,503	1,762	709		32	1,053 R	70.4%	28.3%	
6,061	GREER	2,152	1,287	839		26	448 R	59.8%	39.0%	
3,283	HARMON	1,205	692	507		6	185 R	57.4%	42.1%	
3,562	HARPER	1,683	1,296	374		13	922 R	77.0%	22.2%	
11,792	HASKELL	4,628	2,039	2,510		79	471 D	44.1%	54.2%	
14,154	HUGHES	4,585	2,196	2,334		55	138 D	47.9%	50.9%	
28,439	JACKSON	8,159	5,591	2,515		53	3,076 R	68.5%	30.8%	
6,818	JEFFERSON	2,593	1,320	1,245		28	75 R	50.9%	48.0%	
10,513	JOHNSTON	3,930	2,072	1,809		49	263 R	52.7%	46.0%	
48,080	KAY	18,162	11,768	6,122		272	5,646 R	64.8%	33.7%	
13,926	KINGFISHER	6,056	4,693	1,304		59	3,389 R	77.5%	21.5%	
10,227	KIOWA	3,750	2,173	1,544		33	629 R	57.9%	41.2%	
10,692	LATIMER	3,669	1,739	1,865		65	126 D	47.4%	50.8%	
48,109	LE FLORE	14,985	8,215	6,536		234	1,679 R	54.8%	43.6%	
32,080	LINCOLN	11,701	7,387	4,140		174	3,247 R	63.1%	35.4%	
33,924	LOGAN	12,870	8,187	4,510		173	3,677 R	63.6%	35.0%	
8,831	LOVE	3,372	1,807	1,530		35	277 R	53.6%	45.4%	
27,740	MCCLAIN	10,539	6,750	3,679		110	3,071 R	64.0%	34.9%	
34,402	MCCURTAIN	10,482	6,601	3,752		129	2,849 R	63.0%	35.8%	
19,456	MCINTOSH	7,781	3,444	4,206		131	762 D	44.3%	54.1%	
7,545	MAJOR	3,352	2,672	635		45	2,037 R	79.7%	18.9%	
13,184	MARSHALL	4,900	2,641	2,210		49	431 R	53.9%	45.1%	
38,369	MAYES	14,001	7,132	6,618		251	514 R	50.9%	47.3%	
12,623	MURRAY	4,922	2,609	2,263		50	346 R	53.0%	46.0%	
69,451	MUSKOGEE	24,693	11,820	12,520		353	700 D	47.9%	50.7%	
11,411	NOBLE	4,697	3,230	1,416		51	1,814 R	68.8%	30.1%	
10,569	NOWATA	3,849	2,069	1,703		77	366 R	53.8%	44.2%	
11,814	OKFUSKEE	3,788	1,910	1,814		64	96 R	50.4%	47.9%	
660,448	OKLAHOMA	223,111	139,078	81,590		2,443	57,488 R	62.3%	36.6%	
39,685	OKMULGEE	13,178	5,797	7,186		195	1,389 D	44.0%	54.5%	
44,437	OSAGE	15,909	8,138	7,540		231	598 R	51.2%	47.4%	
33,194	OTTAWA	11,411	5,625	5,647		139	22 D	49.3%	49.5%	
16,612	PAWNEE	5,925	3,386	2,435		104	951 R	57.1%	41.1%	
68,190	PAYNE	24,947	15,256	9,319		372	5,937 R	61.2%	37.4%	

OKLAHOMA

PRESIDENT 2000

2000 Census Population	County	Total Vote	Republican	Democratic	Green (Nader)	Other	Rep.-Dem. Plurality	Percentage of Total Vote Rep.	Dem.	Green
43,953	PITTSBURG	16,357	8,514	7,627		216	887 R	52.1%	46.6%	
35,143	PONTOTOC	12,836	7,299	5,387		150	1,912 R	56.9%	42.0%	
65,521	POTTAWATOMIE	22,316	13,235	8,763		318	4,472 R	59.3%	39.3%	
11,667	PUSHMATAHA	4,348	2,331	1,969		48	362 R	53.6%	45.3%	
3,436	ROGER MILLS	1,687	1,234	441		12	793 R	73.1%	26.1%	
70,641	ROGERS	28,951	17,713	10,813		425	6,900 R	61.2%	37.3%	
24,894	SEMINOLE	7,866	4,011	3,783		72	228 R	51.0%	48.1%	
38,972	SEQUOYAH	12,254	6,614	5,425		215	1,189 R	54.0%	44.3%	
43,182	STEPHENS	17,488	10,860	6,467		161	4,393 R	62.1%	37.0%	
20,107	TEXAS	6,088	4,964	1,084		40	3,880 R	81.5%	17.8%	
9,287	TILLMAN	3,349	1,920	1,400		29	520 R	57.3%	41.8%	
563,299	TULSA	218,691	134,152	81,656		2,883	52,496 R	61.3%	37.3%	
57,491	WAGONER	21,517	12,981	8,244		292	4,737 R	60.3%	38.3%	
48,996	WASHINGTON	20,744	13,788	6,644		312	7,144 R	66.5%	32.0%	
11,508	WASHITA	4,468	2,850	1,564		54	1,286 R	63.8%	35.0%	
9,089	WOODS	4,046	2,774	1,235		37	1,539 R	68.6%	30.5%	
18,486	WOODWARD	7,100	5,067	1,950		83	3,117 R	71.4%	27.5%	
3,450,654	TOTAL	1,234,229	744,337	474,276		15,616	270,061 R	60.3%	38.4%	

Note: No votes for Nader were tallied in Oklahoma. He did not qualify for the ballot and write-in votes were not allowed.

OKLAHOMA

CONGRESS

CD	Year	Total Vote	Republican Vote	Candidate	Democratic Vote	Candidate	Other Vote	Rep.-Dem. Plurality	Total Vote Rep.	Dem.	Major Vote Rep.	Dem.
1	2000	200,005	138,528	LARGENT, STEVE	58,493	LOWE, DAN	2,984	80,035 R	69.3%	29.2%	70.3%	29.7%
1	1998	147,340	91,031	LARGENT, STEVE	56,309	PLOWMAN, HOWARD		34,722 R	61.8%	38.2%	61.8%	38.2%
1	1996	210,407	143,415	LARGENT, STEVE	57,996	AMEN, JOHN R.	8,996	85,419 R	68.2%	27.6%	71.2%	28.8%
1	1994	170,838	107,085	LARGENT, STEVE	63,753	PRICE, STUART		43,332 R	62.7%	37.3%	62.7%	37.3%
1	1992	225,830	119,211	INHOFE, JAMES M.	106,619	SELPH, JOHN		12,592 R	52.8%	47.2%	52.8%	47.2%
2	2000	195,412	81,672	EWING, ANDY	107,273	CARSON, BRAD	6,467	25,601 D	41.8%	54.9%	43.2%	56.8%
2	1998	148,264	85,581	COBURN, TOM	59,042	PHARAOH, KENT	3,641	26,539 R	57.7%	39.8%	59.2%	40.8%
2	1996	202,393	112,273	COBURN, TOM	90,120	JOHNSON, GLEN D.		22,153 R	55.5%	44.5%	55.5%	44.5%
2	1994	158,422	82,479	COBURN, TOM	75,943	COOPER, VIRGIL R.		6,536 R	52.1%	47.9%	52.1%	47.9%
2	1992	213,513	87,657	HILL, JERRY	118,542	SYNAR, MIKE	7,314	30,885 D	41.1%	55.5%	42.5%	57.5%
3	2000	159,216	137,826	WATKINS, WES			21,390	137,826 R	86.6%		100.0%	
3	1998	144,995	89,832	WATKINS, WES	55,163	ROBERTS, WALT		34,669 R	62.0%	38.0%	62.0%	38.0%
3	1996	191,508	98,526	WATKINS, WES	86,647	ROBERTS, DARRYL	6,335	11,879 R	51.4%	45.2%	53.2%	46.8%
3	1994	156,878	41,147	TALLANT, DARREL D.	115,731	BREWSTER, BILL		74,584 D	26.2%	73.8%	26.2%	73.8%
3	1992	207,659	51,725	STOKES, ROBERT W.	155,934	BREWSTER, BILL		104,209 D	24.9%	75.1%	24.9%	75.1%
4	2000	175,684	114,000	WATTS, J. C.	54,808	WEATHERFORD, LARRY	6,876	59,192 R	64.9%	31.2%	67.5%	32.5%
4	1998	135,379	83,272	WATTS, J. C.	52,107	ODOM, BEN		31,165 R	61.5%	38.5%	61.5%	38.5%
4	1996	185,373	106,923	WATTS, J. C.	73,950	CROCKER, ED	4,500	32,973 R	57.7%	39.9%	59.1%	40.9%
4	1994	155,401	80,251	WATTS, J. C.	67,237	PERRYMAN, DAVID	7,913	13,014 R	51.6%	43.3%	54.4%	45.6%
4	1992	199,076	58,235	BELL, HOWARD	140,841	MCCURDY, DAVE		82,606 D	29.3%	70.7%	29.3%	70.7%

OKLAHOMA

CONGRESS

CD	Year	Total Vote	Republican		Democratic		Other Vote	Rep.-Dem. Plurality	Percentage			
			Vote	Candidate	Vote	Candidate			Total Vote		Major Vote	
									Rep.	Dem.	Rep.	Dem.
5	2000	196,022	134,159	ISTOOK, ERNEST J.	53,275	MCWATTERS, GARLAND	8,588	80,884 R	68.4%	27.2%	71.6%	28.4%
5	1998	151,399	103,217	ISTOOK, ERNEST J.	48,182	SMOTHERMON, M.C.		55,035 R	68.2%	31.8%	68.2%	31.8%
5	1996	212,791	148,362	ISTOOK, ERNEST J.	57,594	FORSYTHE, JAMES L.	6,835	90,768 R	69.7%	27.1%	72.0%	28.0%
5	1994	175,147	136,877	ISTOOK, ERNEST J.			38,270	136,877 R	78.1%		100.0%	
5	1992	230,816	123,237	ISTOOK, ERNEST J.	107,579	WILLIAMS, LAURIE		15,658 R	53.4%	46.6%	53.4%	46.6%
6	2000	161,176	95,635	LUCAS, FRANK D.	63,106	BEUTLER, RANDY	2,435	32,529 R	59.3%	39.2%	60.2%	39.8%
6	1998	131,271	85,261	LUCAS, FRANK D.	43,555	BARBY, PAUL M.	2,455	41,706 R	65.0%	33.2%	66.2%	33.8%
6	1996	177,672	113,499	LUCAS, FRANK D.	64,173	BARBY, PAUL M.		49,326 R	63.9%	36.1%	63.9%	36.1%
6	1994	152,360	106,961	LUCAS, FRANK D.	45,399	TOLLETT, JEFFREY S.		61,562 R	70.2%	29.8%	70.2%	29.8%
6	1992	198,802	64,068	ANTHONY, BOB	134,734	ENGLISH, GLENN		70,666 D	32.2%	67.8%	32.2%	67.8%

OKLAHOMA

GENERAL AND PRIMARY ELECTIONS

2000 GENERAL ELECTIONS

President   Other vote was 9,014 Reform (Buchanan); 6,602 Libertarian (Browne).

Congress   Other vote was: CD 1: 2,984 Libertarian (Clem); CD 2: 6,467 Libertarian (Mavis); CD 3: 14,660 Independent (Yandell), 6,730 Libertarian (White); CD 4: 4,897 Reform (Ducey), 1,979 Libertarian (Johnson); CD 5: 5,930 Independent (Maguire), 2,658 Libertarian (Murphy); CD 6: 2,435 Libertarian (Cristiano).

2000 PRIMARY ELECTIONS

Primary	March 14, 2000	(President)	**Registration**	Republican	759,791
	August 22, 2000	(Congress)	(as of July, 31, 2000)	Democratic	1,203,434
Primary Runoff	September 19, 2000	(Congress)		Libertarian	430
				Reform	216
				Independent	187,785
				TOTAL	2,151,656

Primary Type   Closed—Only registered Democrats and Republicans could vote in their party's primary.

Note: An asterisk (*) denotes incumbent. The names of unopposed candidates do not appear on the primary ballot; therefore, no votes are cast for these candidates.

	REPUBLICAN PRIMARIES			DEMOCRATIC PRIMARIES		
President	George W. Bush	98,781	79.1%	Al Gore	92,654	68.7%
	John McCain	12,973	10.4%	Bill Bradley	34,311	25.4%
	Alan Keyes	11,595	9.3%	Lyndon H. LaRouche Jr.	7,885	5.8%
	Steve Forbes	1,066	0.9%			
	Gary Bauer	394	0.3%			
	TOTAL	124,809		TOTAL	134,850	
Congressional District 1	Steve Largent*	38,206	87.7%	Dan Lowe	25,985	79.7%
	Evelyn L. Rogers	5,355	12.3%	John Krymski	6,629	20.3%
	TOTAL	43,561		TOTAL	32,614	

OKLAHOMA

GENERAL AND PRIMARY ELECTIONS

	REPUBLICAN PRIMARIES			DEMOCRATIC PRIMARIES		
Congressional District 2	Andy Ewing	16,639	59.9%	Brad Carson	39,837	44.9%
	Jack Ross	7,758	27.9%	Bill Settle	34,964	39.4%
	Steve Money	1,639	5.9%	James R. Wilson	13,949	15.7%
	Eric Troutt	815	2.9%			
	Terry Gorham	468	1.7%			
	Tennie Rogers	266	1.0%			
	Mark Detro	197	0.7%			
	TOTAL	27,782		TOTAL	88,750	
				PRIMARY RUNOFF		
				Brad Carson	35,410	56.8%
				Bill Settle	26,981	43.2%
				TOTAL	62,391	
Congressional District 3	Wes Watkins*	Unopposed		No Democratic candidate		
Congressional District 4	J. C. Watts*	21,960	81.0%	Larry Weatherford	Unopposed	
	James Odom	5,163	19.0%			
	TOTAL	27,123				
Congressional District 5	Ernest Istook*	39,976	84.8%	Garland McWatters	Unopposed	
	Phillip A. Hillian	7,179	15.2%			
	TOTAL	47,155				
Congressional District 6	Frank D. Lucas*	Unopposed		Randy Beutler	33,771	69.0%
				Bob Mooneyham	15,173	31.0%
				TOTAL	48,944	

OREGON

GOVERNOR
John Kitzhaber (D). Re-elected 1998 to a four-year term. Previously elected 1994.

SENATORS
Ron Wyden (D). Re-elected 1998 to a six-year term. Had been elected in a special election January 30, 1996, to fill out the remaining three years of the term vacated when Senator Robert W. Packwood (R) resigned.

Gordon H. Smith (R). Elected 1996 to a six-year term.

REPRESENTATIVES
1. David Wu (D)
2. Greg Walden (R)
3. Earl Blumenauer (D)
4. Peter A. DeFazio (D)
5. Darlene Hooley (D)

POSTWAR VOTE FOR PRESIDENT

| | | Republican | | Democratic | | Other | | Percentage | | | |
| | | | | | | | | Total Vote | | Major Vote | |
Year	Total Vote	Vote	Candidate	Vote	Candidate	Vote	Plurality	Rep.	Dem.	Rep.	Dem.
2000**	1,533,968	713,577	Bush, George W.	720,342	Gore, Al	100,049	6,765 D	46.5%	47.0%	49.8%	50.2%
1996**	1,377,760	538,152	Dole, Bob	649,641	Clinton, Bill	189,967	111,489 D	39.1%	47.2%	45.3%	54.7%
1992**	1,462,643	475,757	Bush, George	621,314	Clinton, Bill	365,572	145,557 D	32.5%	42.5%	43.4%	56.6%
1988	1,201,694	560,126	Bush, George	616,206	Dukakis, Michael S.	25,362	56,080 D	46.6%	51.3%	47.6%	52.4%
1984	1,226,527	685,700	Reagan, Ronald	536,479	Mondale, Walter F.	4,348	149,221 R	55.9%	43.7%	56.1%	43.9%
1980**	1,181,516	571,044	Reagan, Ronald	456,890	Carter, Jimmy	153,582	114,154 R	48.3%	38.7%	55.6%	44.4%
1976	1,029,876	492,120	Ford, Gerald R.	490,407	Carter, Jimmy	47,349	1,713 R	47.8%	47.6%	50.1%	49.9%
1972	927,946	486,686	Nixon, Richard M.	392,760	McGovern, George S.	48,500	93,926 R	52.4%	42.3%	55.3%	44.7%
1968	819,622	408,433	Nixon, Richard M.	358,866	Humphrey, Hubert H.	52,323	49,567 R	49.8%	43.8%	53.2%	46.8%
1964	786,305	282,779	Goldwater, Barry M.	501,017	Johnson, Lyndon B.	2,509	218,238 D	36.0%	63.7%	36.1%	63.9%
1960	776,421	408,060	Nixon, Richard M.	367,402	Kennedy, John F.	959	40,658 R	52.6%	47.3%	52.6%	47.4%
1956	736,132	406,393	Eisenhower, Dwight D.	329,204	Stevenson, Adlai E.	535	77,189 R	55.2%	44.7%	55.2%	44.8%
1952	695,059	420,815	Eisenhower, Dwight D.	270,579	Stevenson, Adlai E.	3,665	150,236 R	60.5%	38.9%	60.9%	39.1%
1948	524,080	260,904	Dewey, Thomas E.	243,147	Truman, Harry S.	20,029	17,757 R	49.8%	46.4%	51.8%	48.2%

In 2000 the other vote column includes 77,357 votes cast for Green (Nader). In 1996 the other vote column includes 121,221 votes cast for Perot. In 1992 the other vote column includes 354,091 votes cast for Perot. In 1980 the other column includes 112,389 votes for Independent (Anderson).

OREGON

POSTWAR VOTE FOR GOVERNOR

Year	Total Vote	Republican Vote	Republican Candidate	Democratic Vote	Democratic Candidate	Other Vote	Rep.-Dem. Plurality	Percentage Total Vote Rep.	Total Vote Dem.	Major Vote Rep.	Major Vote Dem.
1998	1,113,098	334,001	Sizemore, Bill	717,061	Kitzhaber, John	62,036	383,060 D	30.0%	64.4%	31.8%	68.2%
1994	1,221,010	517,874	Smith, Denny	622,083	Kitzhaber, John	81,053	104,209 D	42.4%	50.9%	45.4%	54.6%
1990	1,112,847	444,646	Frohnmayer, Dave	508,749	Roberts, Barbara	159,452	64,103 D	40.0%	45.7%	46.6%	53.4%
1986	1,059,630	506,986	Paulus, Norma	549,456	Goldschmidt, Neil	3,188	42,470 D	47.8%	51.9%	48.0%	52.0%
1982	1,042,009	639,841	Atiyeh, Victor	374,316	Kulongoski, Ted	27,852	265,525 R	61.4%	35.9%	63.1%	36.9%
1978	911,143	498,452	Atiyeh, Victor	409,411	Straub, Robert W.	3,280	89,041 R	54.7%	44.9%	54.9%	45.1%
1974	770,574	324,751	Atiyeh, Victor	444,812	Straub, Robert W.	1,011	120,061 D	42.1%	57.7%	42.2%	57.8%
1970	666,394	369,964	McCall, Tom	293,892	Straub, Robert W.	2,538	76,072 R	55.5%	44.1%	55.7%	44.3%
1966	682,862	377,346	McCall, Tom	305,008	Straub, Robert W.	508	72,338 R	55.3%	44.7%	55.3%	44.7%
1962	637,407	345,497	Hatfield, Mark	265,359	Thornton, Robert Y.	26,551	80,138 R	54.2%	41.6%	56.6%	43.4%
1958	599,994	331,900	Hatfield, Mark	267,934	Holmes, Robert D.	160	63,966 R	55.3%	44.7%	55.3%	44.7%
1956S	731,279	361,840	Smith, Elmo E.	369,439	Holmes, Robert D.		7,599 D	49.5%	50.5%	49.5%	50.5%
1954	566,701	322,522	Patterson, Paul	244,179	Carson, Joseph K.		78,343 R	56.9%	43.1%	56.9%	43.1%
1950	505,910	334,160	McKay, Douglas	171,750	Flegel, Austin F.		162,410 R	66.1%	33.9%	66.1%	33.9%
1948S	509,633	271,295	McKay, Douglas	226,958	Wallace, Lew	11,380	44,337 R	53.2%	44.5%	54.4%	45.6%
1946	344,155	237,681	Snell, Earl	106,474	Donaugh, Carl C.		131,207 R	69.1%	30.9%	69.1%	30.9%

The 1956 and 1948 elections were for short terms to fill vacancies.

POSTWAR VOTE FOR SENATOR

Year	Total Vote	Republican Vote	Republican Candidate	Democratic Vote	Democratic Candidate	Other Vote	Rep.-Dem. Plurality	Percentage Total Vote Rep.	Total Vote Dem.	Major Vote Rep.	Major Vote Dem.
1998	1,117,747	377,739	Lim, John	682,425	Wyden, Ron	57,583	304,686 D	33.8%	61.1%	35.6%	64.4%
1996	1,360,230	677,336	Smith, Gordon H.	624,370	Bruggere, Tom	58,524	52,966 R	49.8%	45.9%	52.0%	48.0%
1996S	1,196,608	553,519	Smith, Gordon H.	571,739	Wyden, Ron	71,350	18,220 D	46.3%	47.8%	49.2%	50.8%
1992	1,376,033	717,455	Packwood, Robert W.	639,851	AuCoin, Les	18,727	77,604 R	52.1%	46.5%	52.9%	47.1%
1990	1,099,255	590,095	Hatfield, Mark	507,743	Lonsdale, Harry	1,417	82,352 R	53.7%	46.2%	53.8%	46.2%
1986	1,042,555	656,317	Packwood, Robert W.	375,735	Bauman, Rick	10,503	280,582 R	63.0%	36.0%	63.6%	36.4%
1984	1,214,735	808,152	Hatfield, Mark	406,122	Hendriksen, Margie	461	402,030 R	66.5%	33.4%	66.6%	33.4%
1980	1,140,494	594,290	Packwood, Robert W.	501,963	Kulongoski, Ted	44,241	92,327 R	52.1%	44.0%	54.2%	45.8%
1978	892,518	550,165	Hatfield, Mark	341,616	Cook, Vernon	737	208,549 R	61.6%	38.3%	61.7%	38.3%
1974	766,414	420,984	Packwood, Robert W.	338,591	Roberts, Betty	6,839	82,393 R	54.9%	44.2%	55.4%	44.6%
1972	920,833	494,671	Hatfield, Mark	425,036	Morse, Wayne L.	1,126	69,635 R	53.7%	46.2%	53.8%	46.2%
1968	814,176	408,646	Packwood, Robert W.	405,353	Morse, Wayne L.	177	3,293 R	50.2%	49.8%	50.2%	49.8%
1966	685,067	354,391	Hatfield, Mark	330,374	Duncan, Robert B.	302	24,017 R	51.7%	48.2%	51.8%	48.2%
1962	636,558	291,587	Unander, Sig	344,716	Morse, Wayne L.	255	53,129 D	45.8%	54.2%	45.8%	54.2%
1960	755,875	343,009	Smith, Elmo E.	412,757	Neuberger, Maurine	109	69,748 D	45.4%	54.6%	45.4%	54.6%
1956	732,254	335,405	McKay, Douglas	396,849	Morse, Wayne L.		61,444 D	45.8%	54.2%	45.8%	54.2%
1954	569,088	283,313	Cordon, Guy	285,775	Neuberger, Richard L.		2,462 D	49.8%	50.2%	49.8%	50.2%
1950	503,455	376,510	Morse, Wayne L.	116,780	Latourette, Howard	10,165	259,730 R	74.8%	23.2%	76.3%	23.7%
1948	498,570	299,295	Cordon, Guy	199,275	Wilson, Manley J.		100,020 R	60.0%	40.0%	60.0%	40.0%

Note: The January 1996 election was for a short term to fill a vacancy.

OREGON

Districts Established December 18, 1991

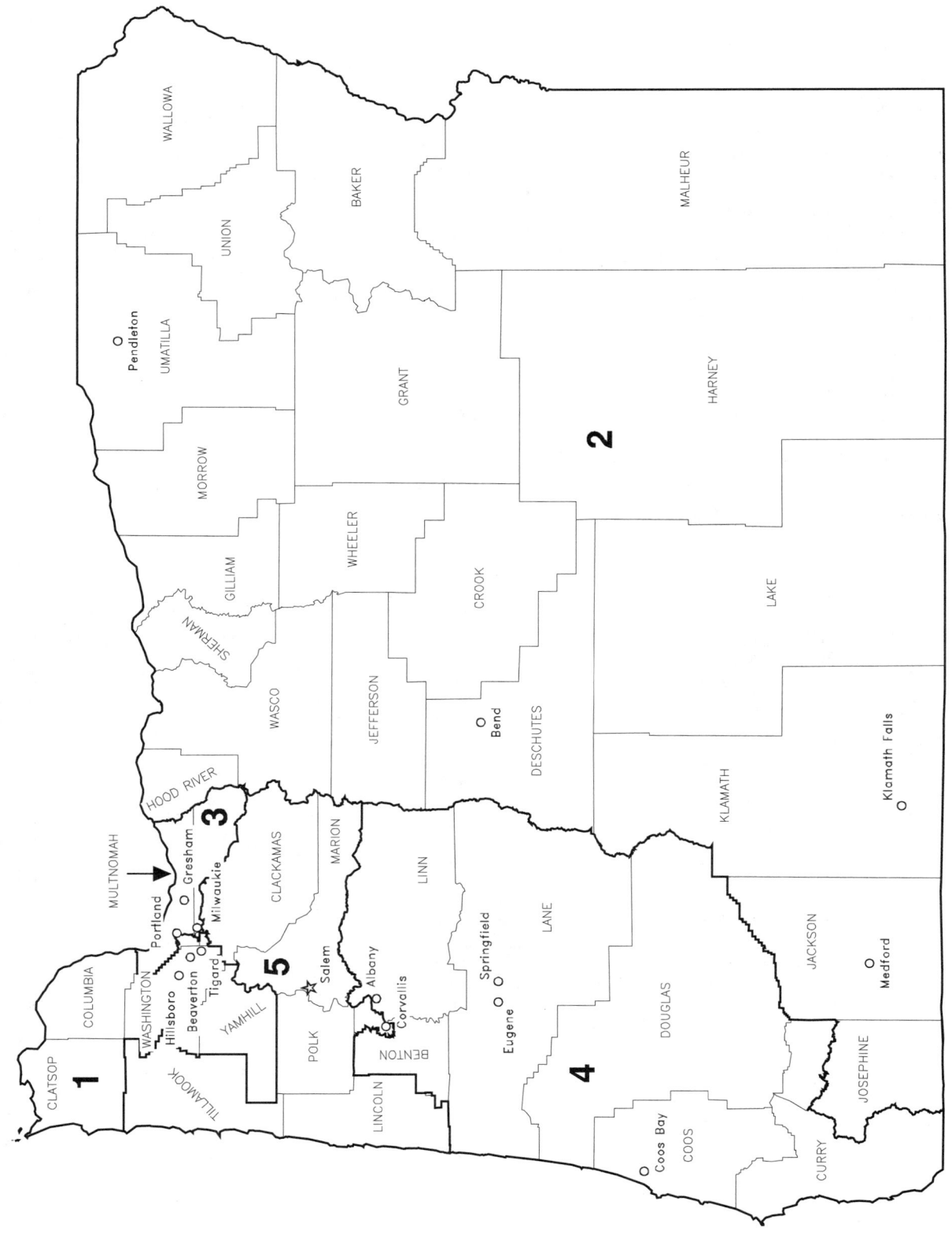

OREGON

PRESIDENT 2000

2000 Census Population	County	Total Vote	Republican	Democratic	Green (Nader)	Other	Rep.-Dem. Plurality	Percentage of Total Vote		
								Rep.	Dem.	Green
16,741	BAKER	8,258	5,618	2,195	289	156	3,423 R	68.0%	26.6%	3.5%
78,153	BENTON	38,226	15,825	19,444	2,463	494	3,619 D	41.4%	50.9%	6.4%
338,391	CLACKAMAS	162,262	77,539	76,421	6,357	1,945	1,118 R	47.8%	47.1%	3.9%
35,630	CLATSOP	16,474	6,950	8,296	939	289	1,346 D	42.2%	50.4%	5.7%
43,560	COLUMBIA	21,195	9,369	10,331	970	525	962 D	44.2%	48.7%	4.6%
62,779	COOS	29,379	15,626	11,610	1,410	733	4,016 R	53.2%	39.5%	4.8%
19,182	CROOK	8,277	5,363	2,474	258	182	2,889 R	64.8%	29.9%	3.1%
21,137	CURRY	11,513	6,551	4,090	603	269	2,461 R	56.9%	35.5%	5.2%
115,367	DESCHUTES	57,885	32,132	22,061	2,799	893	10,071 R	55.5%	38.1%	4.8%
100,399	DOUGLAS	47,220	30,294	14,193	1,768	965	16,101 R	64.2%	30.1%	3.7%
1,915	GILLIAM	1,090	679	359	37	15	320 R	62.3%	32.9%	3.4%
7,935	GRANT	3,846	3,078	589	98	81	2,489 R	80.0%	15.3%	2.5%
7,609	HARNEY	3,734	2,799	766	84	85	2,033 R	75.0%	20.5%	2.2%
20,411	HOOD RIVER	8,549	3,721	4,072	645	111	351 D	43.5%	47.6%	7.5%
181,269	JACKSON	84,796	46,052	33,153	4,207	1,384	12,899 R	54.3%	39.1%	5.0%
19,009	JEFFERSON	6,897	3,838	2,681	247	131	1,157 R	55.6%	38.9%	3.6%
75,726	JOSEPHINE	36,733	22,186	11,864	1,783	900	10,322 R	60.4%	32.3%	4.9%
63,775	KLAMATH	27,844	18,855	7,541	867	581	11,314 R	67.7%	27.1%	3.1%
7,422	LAKE	3,729	2,830	707	108	84	2,123 R	75.9%	19.0%	2.9%
322,959	LANE	152,188	61,578	78,583	10,245	1,782	17,005 D	40.5%	51.6%	6.7%
44,479	LINCOLN	21,118	8,446	10,861	1,435	376	2,415 D	40.0%	51.4%	6.8%
103,069	LINN	44,388	25,359	16,682	1,617	730	8,677 R	57.1%	37.6%	3.6%
31,615	MALHEUR	10,404	7,624	2,336	248	196	5,288 R	73.3%	22.5%	2.4%
284,834	MARION	113,334	57,443	49,430	4,679	1,782	8,013 R	50.7%	43.6%	4.1%
10,995	MORROW	3,609	2,224	1,197	87	101	1,027 R	61.6%	33.2%	2.4%
660,486	MULTNOMAH	296,685	83,677	188,441	21,048	3,519	104,764 D	28.2%	63.5%	7.1%
62,380	POLK	28,449	14,988	11,921	1,201	339	3,067 R	52.7%	41.9%	4.2%
1,934	SHERMAN	1,062	679	326	36	21	353 R	63.9%	30.7%	3.4%
24,262	TILLAMOOK	12,376	5,775	5,762	613	226	13 R	46.7%	46.6%	5.0%
70,548	UMATILLA	23,060	14,140	7,809	655	456	6,331 R	61.3%	33.9%	2.8%
24,530	UNION	12,076	7,836	3,577	436	227	4,259 R	64.9%	29.6%	3.6%
7,226	WALLOWA	4,294	3,279	836	114	65	2,443 R	76.4%	19.5%	2.7%
23,791	WASCO	10,664	5,356	4,616	513	179	740 R	50.2%	43.3%	4.8%
445,342	WASHINGTON	185,974	86,091	90,662	6,985	2,236	4,571 D	46.3%	48.7%	3.8%
1,547	WHEELER	841	584	202	27	28	382 R	69.4%	24.0%	3.2%
84,992	YAMHILL	35,539	19,193	14,254	1,486	606	4,939 R	54.0%	40.1%	4.2%
3,421,399	TOTAL	1,533,968	713,577	720,342	77,357	22,692	6,765 D	46.5%	47.0%	5.0%

OREGON

CONGRESS

CD	Year	Total Vote	Republican		Democratic		Other Vote	Rep.-Dem. Plurality	Percentage			
									Total Vote		Major Vote	
			Vote	Candidate	Vote	Candidate			Rep.	Dem.	Rep.	Dem.
1	2000	303,521	115,303	STARR, CHARLES	176,902	WU, DAVID	11,316	61,599 D	38.0%	58.3%	39.5%	60.5%
1	1998	239,496	112,827	BORDONARO, MOLLY	119,993	WU, DAVID	6,676	7,166 D	47.1%	50.1%	48.5%	51.5%
1	1996	278,604	126,146	WITT, BILL	144,588	FURSE, ELIZABETH	7,870	18,442 D	45.3%	51.9%	46.6%	53.4%
1	1994	253,989	120,846	WITT, BILL	121,147	FURSE, ELIZABETH	11,996	301 D	47.6%	47.7%	49.9%	50.1%
1	1992	294,154	140,986	MEEKER, ANTONY	152,917	FURSE, ELIZABETH	251	11,931 D	47.9%	52.0%	48.0%	52.0%
2	2000	298,907	220,086	WALDEN, GREG	78,101	PONSFORD, WALTER	720	141,985 R	73.6%	26.1%	73.8%	26.2%
2	1998	215,216	132,316	WALDEN, GREG	74,924	CAMPBELL, KEVIN M.	7,976	57,392 R	61.5%	34.8%	63.8%	36.2%
2	1996	266,056	164,062	SMITH, ROBERT F.	97,195	DUGAN, MIKE	4,799	66,867 R	61.7%	36.5%	62.8%	37.2%
2	1994	234,381	134,255	COOLEY, WES	90,822	KUPILLAS, SUE C.	9,304	43,433 R	57.3%	38.7%	59.6%	40.4%
2	1992	274,478	184,163	SMITH, ROBERT F.	90,036	FERGUSON, DENZEL	279	94,127 R	67.1%	32.8%	67.2%	32.8%
3	2000	271,161	64,128	POLLOCK, JEFFERY L.	181,049	BLUMENAUER, EARL	25,984	116,921 D	23.6%	66.8%	26.2%	73.8%
3	1998	183,351			153,889	BLUMENAUER, EARL	29,462	153,889 D		83.9%		100.0%
3	1996	247,909	65,259	BRUUN, SCOTT	165,922	BLUMENAUER, EARL	16,728	100,663 D	26.3%	66.9%	28.2%	71.8%
3	1994	222,822	43,211	HALL, EVERETT	161,624	WYDEN, RON	17,987	118,413 D	19.4%	72.5%	21.1%	78.9%
3	1992	269,879	50,235	RITTER, AL	208,028	WYDEN, RON	11,616	157,793 D	18.6%	77.1%	19.5%	80.5%
4	2000	291,065	88,950	LINDSEY, JOHN	197,998	DEFAZIO, PETER A.	4,117	109,048 D	30.6%	68.0%	31.0%	69.0%
4	1998	224,637	64,143	WEBB, STEVE J.	157,524	DEFAZIO, PETER A.	2,970	93,381 D	28.6%	70.1%	28.9%	71.1%
4	1996	269,856	76,649	NEWKIRK, JOHN D.	177,270	DEFAZIO, PETER A.	15,937	100,621 D	28.4%	65.7%	30.2%	69.8%
4	1994	238,149	78,947	NEWKIRK, JOHN D.	158,981	DEFAZIO, PETER A.	221	80,034 D	33.2%	66.8%	33.2%	66.8%
4	1992	279,299	79,733	SCHULZ, RICHARD L.	199,372	DEFAZIO, PETER A.	194	119,639 D	28.5%	71.4%	28.6%	71.4%
5	2000	275,348	118,631	BOQUIST, BRIAN J.	156,315	HOOLEY, DARLENE	402	37,684 D	43.1%	56.8%	43.1%	56.9%
5	1998	227,657	92,215	SHANNON, MARYLIN	124,916	HOOLEY, DARLENE	10,526	32,701 D	40.5%	54.9%	42.5%	57.5%
5	1996	272,636	125,409	BUNN, JIM	139,521	HOOLEY, DARLENE	7,706	14,112 D	46.0%	51.2%	47.3%	52.7%
5	1994	243,616	121,369	BUNN, JIM	114,015	WEBBER, CATHERINE	8,232	7,354 R	49.8%	46.8%	51.6%	48.4%
5	1992	272,944	97,984	SEAGRAVES, JIM	174,443	KOPETSKI, MIKE	517	76,459 D	35.9%	63.9%	36.0%	64.0%

OREGON

GENERAL AND PRIMARY ELECTIONS

2000 GENERAL ELECTIONS

President Other vote was 7,447 Libertarian (Browne); 7,063 Independent (Buchanan); 2,574 Reform (Hagelin); 2,189 Constitution (Phillips); 3,419 scattered write-in. Nader was listed on the ballot as Pacific Green.

Congress Other vote was: CD 1: 10,858 Libertarian (King), 458 scattered write-in; CD 2: 720 scattered write-in; CD 3: 15,763 Pacific Green (Arrow), 4,942 Libertarian (Knight), 4,703 Socialist (Brown), 576 scattered write-in; CD 4: 3,696 Socialist (Duemler), 421 scattered write-in; CD 5: 402 scattered write-in.

2000 PRIMARY ELECTIONS

Primary May 16, 2000

Registration (as of May 16, 2000)

Republican	657,303
Democratic	723,833
Other Parties	49,161
Non-Affiliated	377,783
TOTAL	1,808,080

OREGON

GENERAL AND PRIMARY ELECTIONS

Primary Type   Only registered Republicans could vote in their party's primary. Registered Democrats and "Non-affiliated" voters could participate in the Democratic primary.

Note: An asterisk (*) denotes incumbent. The primary was conducted entirely by mail.

	REPUBLICAN PRIMARIES			DEMOCRATIC PRIMARIES		
President	George W. Bush	292,522	83.6%	Al Gore	300,922	84.9%
	Alan Keyes	46,764	13.4%	Lyndon H. LaRouche Jr.	38,521	10.9%
	Write-in	10,545	3.0%	Write-in	15,151	4.3%
	TOTAL	349,831		TOTAL	354,594	
Congressional District 1	Charles Starr	36,779	61.4%	David Wu*	61,578	99.3%
	Alice L. Schlenker	22,893	38.2%	Write-in	459	0.7%
	Write-in	204	0.3%			
	TOTAL	59,876		TOTAL	62,037	
Congressional District 2	Greg Walden*	79,985	99.4%	Walter Ponsford	46,145	96.9%
	Write-in	506	0.6%	Write-in	1,478	3.1%
	TOTAL	80,491		TOTAL	47,623	
Congressional District 3	Jeffery L. Pollock	24,609	97.2%	Earl Blumenauer*	70,388	88.1%
	Write-in	712	2.8%	John Sweeney	9,237	11.6%
				Write-in	277	0.3%
	TOTAL	25,321		TOTAL	79,902	
Congressional District 4	John Lindsey	36,725	68.1%	Peter A. DeFazio*	78,361	99.4%
	Wendell Robinson	16,704	31.0%	Write-in	465	0.6%
	Write-in	525	1.0%			
	TOTAL	53,954		TOTAL	78,826	
Congressional District 5	Brian J. Boquist	35,450	65.0%	Darlene Hooley*	58,866	99.0%
	Aaron J. Hill	18,754	34.4%	Write-in	623	1.0%
	Write-in	374	0.7%			
	TOTAL	54,578		TOTAL	59,489	

PENNSYLVANIA

GOVERNOR
Thomas J. Ridge (R). Re-elected 1998 to a four-year term. Previously elected 1994.

SENATORS
Rick Santorum (R). Re-elected 2000 to a six-year term. Previously elected 1994.

Arlen Specter (R). Re-elected 1998 to a six-year term. Previously elected 1992, 1986, 1980.

REPRESENTATIVES
1. Robert A. Brady (D)
2. Chaka Fattah (D)
3. Robert A. Borski (D)
4. Melissa Hart (R)
5. John E. Peterson (R)
6. Tim Holden (D)
7. Curt Weldon (R)
8. James C. Greenwood (R)
9. E. G. Shuster (R)
10. Donald L. Sherwood (R)
11. Paul E. Kanjorski (D)
12. John P. Murtha (D)
13. Joseph M. Hoeffel III (D)
14. William J. Coyne (D)
15. Pat Toomey (R)
16. Joseph R. Pitts (R)
17. George W. Gekas (R)
18. Mike Doyle (D)
19. Todd Platts (R)
20. Frank R. Mascara (D)
21. Phil English (R)

POSTWAR VOTE FOR PRESIDENT

Year	Total Vote	Republican Vote	Republican Candidate	Democratic Vote	Democratic Candidate	Other Vote	Plurality	Total Vote Rep.	Total Vote Dem.	Major Vote Rep.	Major Vote Dem.
2000**	4,913,119	2,281,127	Bush, George W.	2,485,967	Gore, Al	146,025	204,840 D	46.4%	50.6%	47.9%	52.1%
1996**	4,506,118	1,801,169	Dole, Bob	2,215,819	Clinton, Bill	489,130	414,650 D	40.0%	49.2%	44.8%	55.2%
1992**	4,959,810	1,791,841	Bush, George	2,239,164	Clinton, Bill	928,805	447,323 D	36.1%	45.1%	44.5%	55.5%
1988	4,536,251	2,300,087	Bush, George	2,194,944	Dukakis, Michael S.	41,220	105,143 R	50.7%	48.4%	51.2%	48.8%
1984	4,844,903	2,584,323	Reagan, Ronald	2,228,131	Mondale, Walter F.	32,449	356,192 R	53.3%	46.0%	53.7%	46.3%
1980**	4,561,501	2,261,872	Reagan, Ronald	1,937,540	Carter, Jimmy	362,089	324,332 R	49.6%	42.5%	53.9%	46.1%
1976	4,620,787	2,205,604	Ford, Gerald R.	2,328,677	Carter, Jimmy	86,506	123,073 D	47.7%	50.4%	48.6%	51.4%
1972	4,592,106	2,714,521	Nixon, Richard M.	1,796,951	McGovern, George S.	80,634	917,570 R	59.1%	39.1%	60.2%	39.8%
1968	4,747,928	2,090,017	Nixon, Richard M.	2,259,405	Humphrey, Hubert H.	398,506	169,388 D	44.0%	47.6%	48.1%	51.9%
1964	4,822,690	1,673,657	Goldwater, Barry M.	3,130,954	Johnson, Lyndon B.	18,079	1,457,297 D	34.7%	64.9%	34.8%	65.2%
1960	5,006,541	2,439,956	Nixon, Richard M.	2,556,282	Kennedy, John F.	10,303	116,326 D	48.7%	51.1%	48.8%	51.2%
1956	4,576,503	2,585,252	Eisenhower, Dwight D.	1,981,769	Stevenson, Adlai E.	9,482	603,483 R	56.5%	43.3%	56.6%	43.4%
1952	4,580,969	2,415,789	Eisenhower, Dwight D.	2,146,269	Stevenson, Adlai E.	18,911	269,520 R	52.7%	46.9%	53.0%	47.0%
1948	3,735,348	1,902,197	Dewey, Thomas E.	1,752,426	Truman, Harry S.	80,725	149,771 R	50.9%	46.9%	52.0%	48.0%

In 2000 the other vote column includes 103,392 votes cast for Green (Nader). In 1996 the other vote column includes 430,984 votes cast for Perot. In 1992 the other vote column includes 902,667 votes cast for Perot. In 1980 the other column includes 292,921 votes for Independent (Anderson).

PENNSYLVANIA

POSTWAR VOTE FOR GOVERNOR

Year	Total Vote	Republican Vote	Republican Candidate	Democratic Vote	Democratic Candidate	Other Vote	Rep.-Dem. Plurality	Total Vote Rep.	Total Vote Dem.	Major Vote Rep.	Major Vote Dem.
1998	3,025,152	1,736,844	Ridge, Thomas J.	938,745	Itkin, Ivan	349,563	798,099 R	57.4%	31.0%	64.9%	35.1%
1994**	3,585,526	1,627,976	Ridge, Thomas J.	1,430,099	Singel, Mark S.	527,451	197,877 R	45.4%	39.9%	53.2%	46.8%
1990	3,052,760	987,516	Hafer, Barbara	2,065,244	Casey, Robert		1,077,728 D	32.3%	67.7%	32.3%	67.7%
1986	3,388,275	1,638,268	Scranton, William W.,III	1,717,484	Casey, Robert	32,523	79,216 D	48.4%	50.7%	48.8%	51.2%
1982	3,683,985	1,872,784	Thornburgh, Richard L.	1,772,353	Ertel, Allen E.	38,848	100,431 R	50.8%	48.1%	51.4%	48.6%
1978	3,741,969	1,966,042	Thornburgh, Richard L.	1,737,888	Flaherty, Peter	38,039	228,154 R	52.5%	46.4%	53.1%	46.9%
1974	3,491,234	1,578,917	Lewis, Andrew L.	1,878,252	Shapp, Milton	34,065	299,335 D	45.2%	53.8%	45.7%	54.3%
1970	3,700,060	1,542,854	Broderick, Raymond	2,043,029	Shapp, Milton	114,177	500,175 D	41.7%	55.2%	43.0%	57.0%
1966	4,050,668	2,110,349	Shafer, Raymond P.	1,868,719	Shapp, Milton	71,600	241,630 R	52.1%	46.1%	53.0%	47.0%
1962	4,378,042	2,424,918	Scranton, William W.	1,938,627	Dilworth, Richardson	14,497	486,291 R	55.4%	44.3%	55.6%	44.4%
1958	3,986,918	1,948,769	McGonigle, A. T.	2,024,852	Lawrence, David	13,297	76,083 D	48.9%	50.8%	49.0%	51.0%
1954	3,720,457	1,717,070	Wood, Lloyd H.	1,996,266	Leader, George M.	7,121	279,196 D	46.2%	53.7%	46.2%	53.8%
1950	3,540,059	1,796,119	Fine, John S.	1,710,355	Dilworth, Richardson	33,585	85,764 R	50.7%	48.3%	51.2%	48.8%
1946	3,123,994	1,828,462	Duff, James H.	1,270,947	Rice, John S.	24,585	557,515 R	58.5%	40.7%	59.0%	41.0%

In 1994 other vote was 460,269 Constitutional (Luksik); 33,602 Libertarian (Fallon); 33,235 Patriot (Holloway); 345 write-ins.

POSTWAR VOTE FOR SENATOR

Year	Total Vote	Republican Vote	Republican Candidate	Democratic Vote	Democratic Candidate	Other Vote	Rep.-Dem. Plurality	Total Vote Rep.	Total Vote Dem.	Major Vote Rep.	Major Vote Dem.
2000	4,735,504	2,481,962	Santorum, Rick	2,154,908	Klink, Ron	98,634	327,054 R	52.4%	45.5%	53.5%	46.5%
1998	2,957,772	1,814,180	Specter, Arlen	1,028,839	Lloyd, Bill	114,753	785,341 R	61.3%	34.8%	63.8%	36.2%
1994	3,513,361	1,735,691	Santorum, Rick	1,648,481	Wofford, Harris	129,189	87,210 R	49.4%	46.9%	51.3%	48.7%
1992	4,802,410	2,358,125	Specter, Arlen	2,224,966	Yeakel, Lynn	219,319	133,159 R	49.1%	46.3%	51.5%	48.5%
1991S	3,382,746	1,521,986	Thornburgh, Richard	1,860,760	Wofford, Harris		338,774 D	45.0%	55.0%	45.0%	55.0%
1988	4,366,598	2,901,715	Heinz, H. John	1,416,764	Vignola, Joseph C.	48,119	1,484,951 R	66.5%	32.4%	67.2%	32.8%
1986	3,378,226	1,906,537	Specter, Arlen	1,448,219	Edgar, Robert W.	23,470	458,318 R	56.4%	42.9%	56.8%	43.2%
1982	3,604,108	2,136,418	Heinz, H. John	1,412,965	Wecht, Cyril H.	54,725	723,453 R	59.3%	39.2%	60.2%	39.8%
1980	4,418,042	2,230,404	Specter, Arlen	2,122,391	Flaherty, Peter	65,247	108,013 R	50.5%	48.0%	51.2%	48.8%
1976	4,546,353	2,381,891	Heinz, H. John	2,126,977	Green, William J., III	37,485	254,914 R	52.4%	46.8%	52.8%	47.2%
1974	3,477,812	1,843,317	Schweiker, Richard S.	1,596,121	Flaherty, Peter	38,374	247,196 R	53.0%	45.9%	53.6%	46.4%
1970	3,644,305	1,874,106	Scott, Hugh	1,653,774	Sesler, William G.	116,425	220,332 R	51.4%	45.4%	53.1%	46.9%
1968	4,624,218	2,399,762	Schweiker, Richard S.	2,117,662	Clark, Joseph S.	106,794	282,100 R	51.9%	45.8%	53.1%	46.9%
1964	4,803,835	2,429,858	Scott, Hugh	2,359,223	Blatt, Genevieve	14,754	70,635 R	50.6%	49.1%	50.7%	49.3%
1962	4,383,475	2,134,649	Van Zandt, James E.	2,238,383	Clark, Joseph S.	10,443	103,734 D	48.7%	51.1%	48.8%	51.2%
1958	3,988,622	2,042,586	Scott, Hugh	1,929,821	Leader, George M.	16,215	112,765 R	51.2%	48.4%	51.4%	48.6%
1956	4,529,874	2,250,671	Duff, James H.	2,268,641	Clark, Joseph S.	10,562	17,970 D	49.7%	50.1%	49.8%	50.2%
1952	4,519,761	2,331,034	Martin, Edward	2,168,546	Bard, Guy Kurtz	20,181	162,488 R	51.6%	48.0%	51.8%	48.2%
1950	3,548,703	1,820,400	Duff, James H.	1,694,076	Myers, Francis J.	34,227	126,324 R	51.3%	47.7%	51.8%	48.2%
1946	3,127,860	1,853,458	Martin, Edward	1,245,338	Guffey, Joseph F.	29,064	608,120 R	59.3%	39.8%	59.8%	40.2%

The 1991 election was for a short term to fill a vacancy.

PENNSYLVANIA

Districts Established March 3, 1992

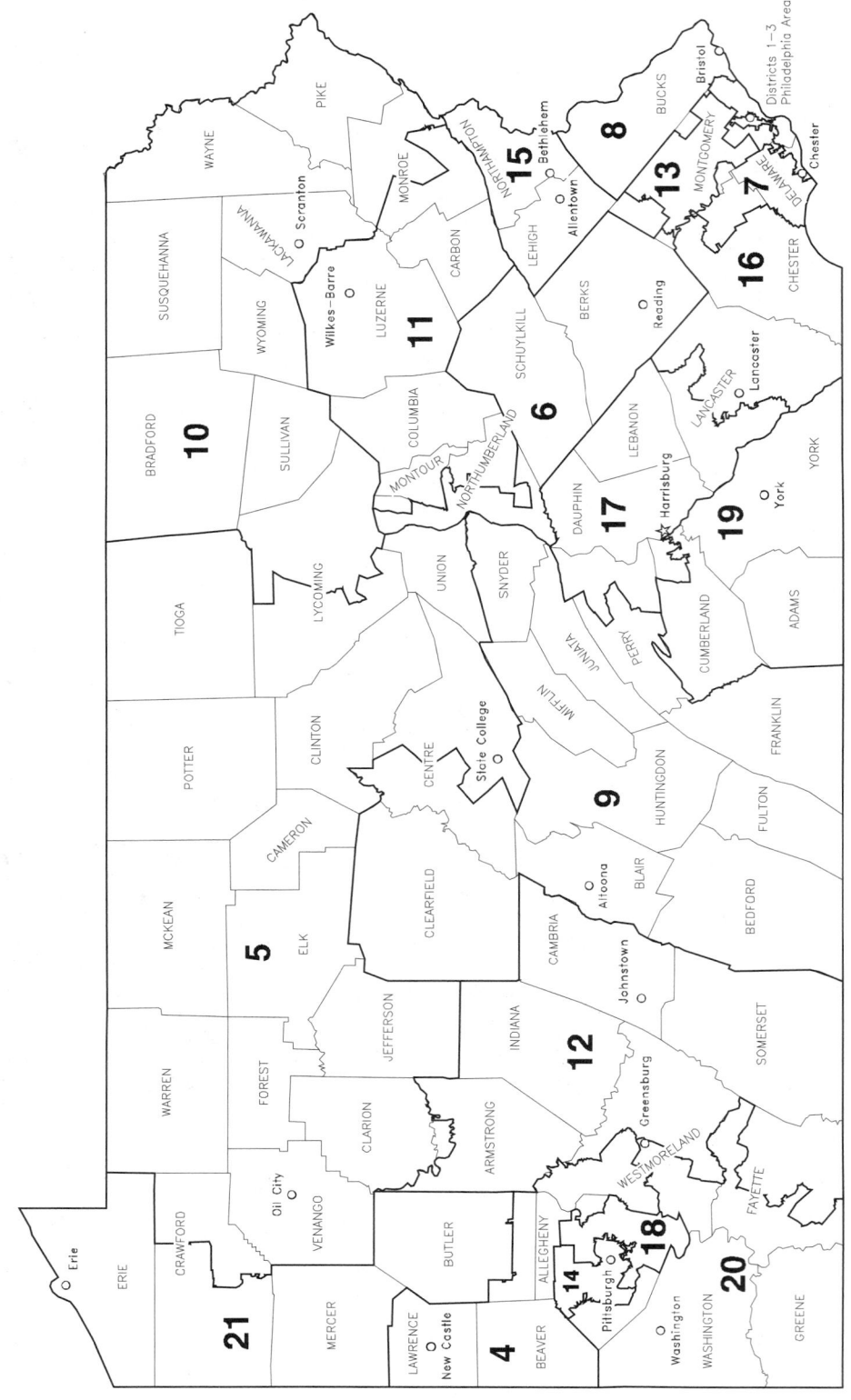

SOUTHEAST PENNSYLVANIA
CONGRESSIONAL DISTRICTS

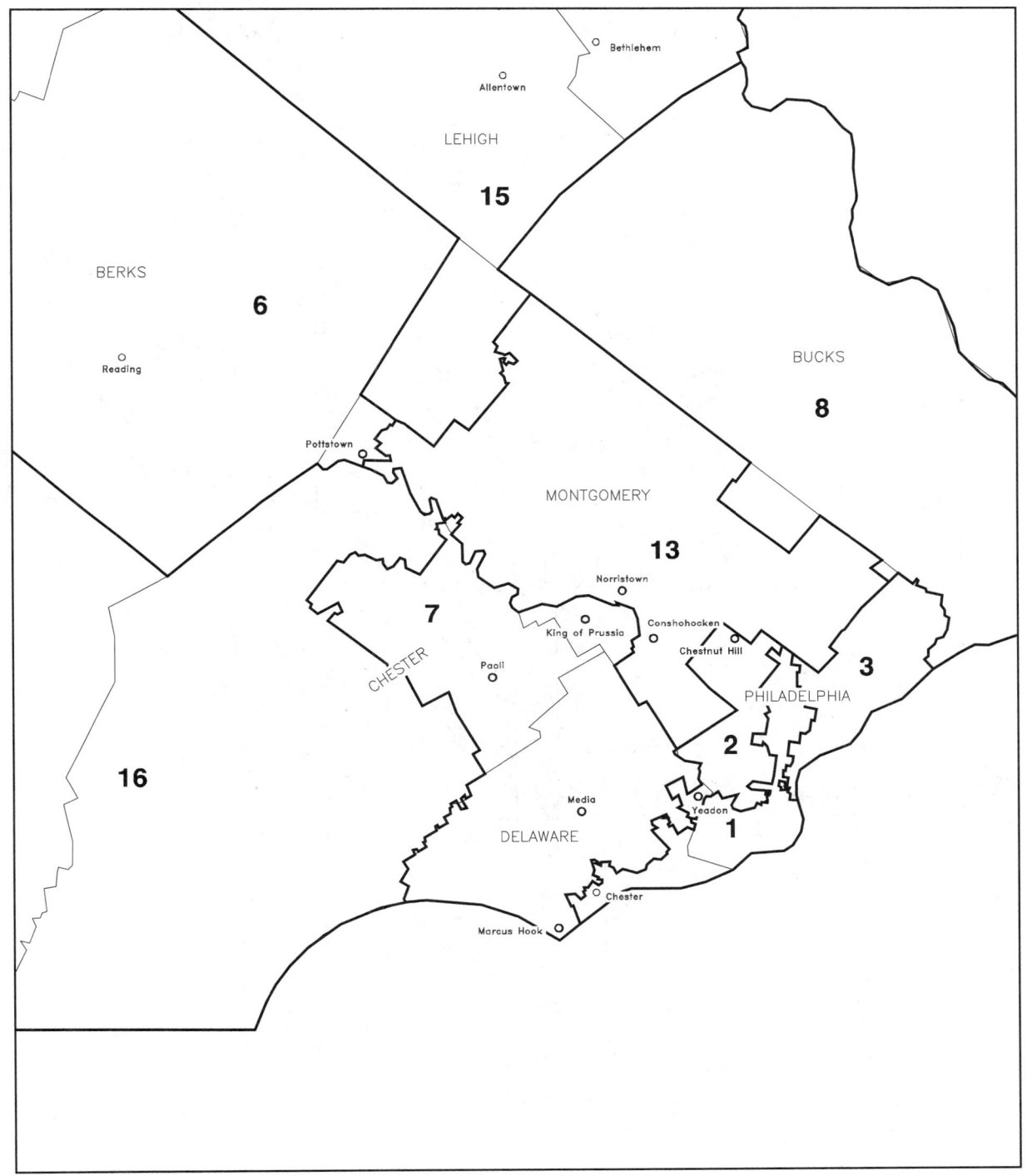

LEHIGH

15

Bethlehem

Allentown

BERKS

6

Reading

BUCKS

8

Pottstown

MONTGOMERY

13

Norristown

7

King of Prussia

Conshohocken

Chestnut Hill

3

CHESTER

Paoli

PHILADELPHIA

2

16

Media

Yeadon

1

DELAWARE

Chester

Marcus Hook

PHILADELPHIA

WARD BOUNDARIES

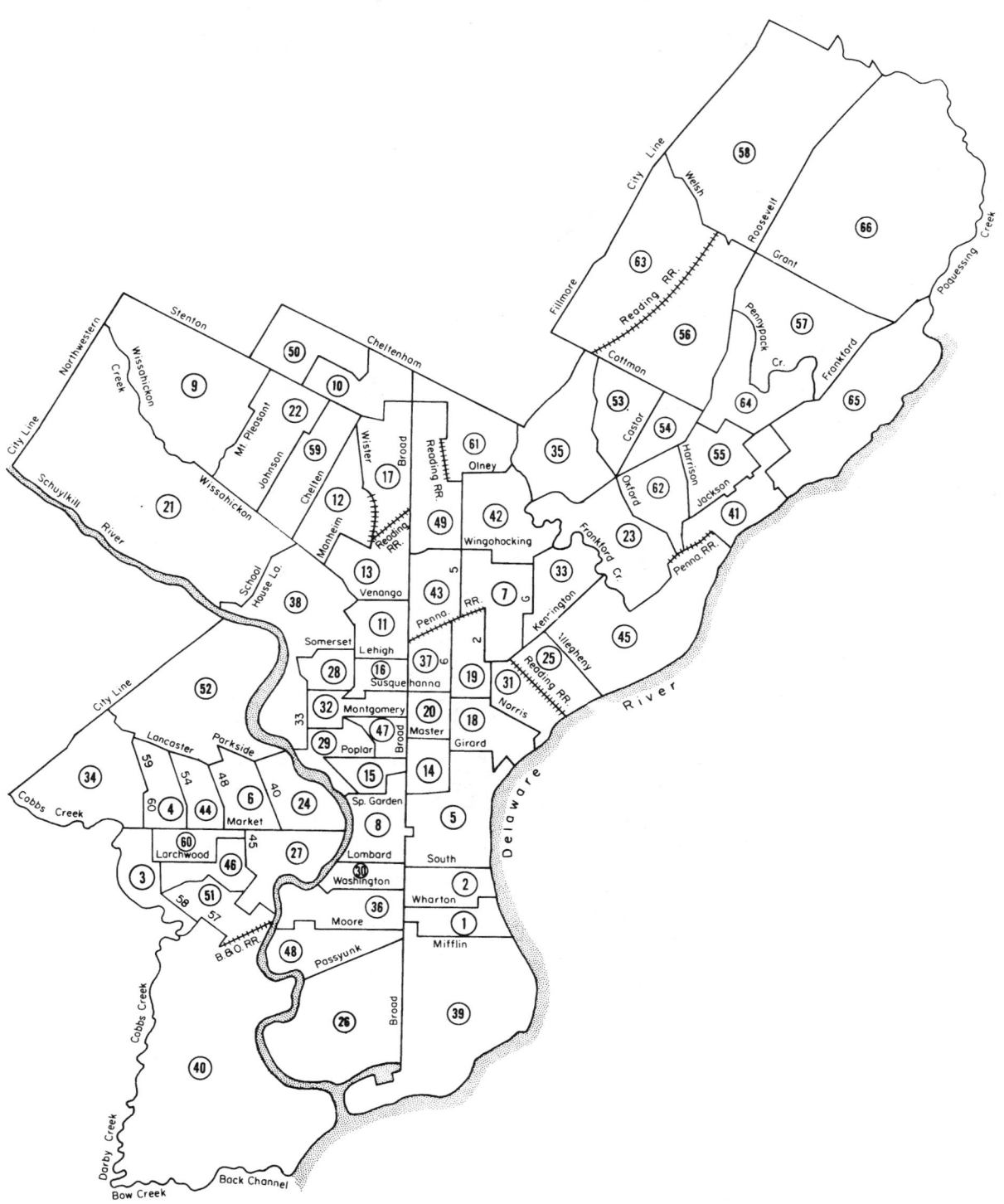

PENNSYLVANIA

PRESIDENT 2000

2000 Census Population	County	Total Vote	Republican	Democratic	Green (Nader)	Other	Rep.-Dem. Plurality	Percentage of Total Vote		
								Rep.	Dem.	Green
91,292	ADAMS	33,433	20,848	11,682	696	207	9,166 R	62.4%	34.9%	2.1%
1,281,666	ALLEGHENY	582,478	235,361	329,963	10,575	6,579	94,602 D	40.4%	56.6%	1.8%
72,392	ARMSTRONG	27,423	15,508	11,127	485	303	4,381 R	56.6%	40.6%	1.8%
181,412	BEAVER	73,593	32,491	38,925	1,450	727	6,434 D	44.1%	52.9%	2.0%
49,984	BEDFORD	19,435	13,598	5,474	265	98	8,124 R	70.0%	28.2%	1.4%
373,638	BERKS	135,163	71,273	59,150	3,494	1,246	12,123 R	52.7%	43.8%	2.6%
129,144	BLAIR	45,140	28,376	15,774	693	297	12,602 R	62.9%	34.9%	1.5%
62,761	BRADFORD	23,330	14,660	7,911	600	159	6,749 R	62.8%	33.9%	2.6%
597,635	BUCKS	263,422	121,927	132,914	6,294	2,287	10,987 D	46.3%	50.5%	2.4%
174,083	BUTLER	70,824	44,009	25,037	1,287	491	18,972 R	62.1%	35.4%	1.8%
152,598	CAMBRIA	60,286	28,001	30,308	1,369	608	2,307 D	46.4%	50.3%	2.3%
5,974	CAMERON	2,246	1,383	779	50	34	604 R	61.6%	34.7%	2.2%
58,802	CARBON	21,277	9,717	10,668	574	318	951 D	45.7%	50.1%	2.7%
135,758	CENTRE	49,538	26,172	21,409	1,623	334	4,763 R	52.8%	43.2%	3.3%
433,501	CHESTER	187,562	100,080	82,047	4,302	1,133	18,033 R	53.4%	43.7%	2.3%
41,765	CLARION	15,843	9,796	5,605	293	149	4,191 R	61.8%	35.4%	1.8%
83,382	CLEARFIELD	30,609	18,019	11,718	570	302	6,301 R	58.9%	38.3%	1.9%
37,914	CLINTON	11,994	6,064	5,521	307	102	543 R	50.6%	46.0%	2.6%
64,151	COLUMBIA	21,894	12,095	8,975	663	161	3,120 R	55.2%	41.0%	3.0%
90,366	CRAWFORD	33,321	18,858	13,250	854	359	5,608 R	56.6%	39.8%	2.6%
213,674	CUMBERLAND	88,062	54,802	31,053	1,749	458	23,749 R	62.2%	35.3%	2.0%
251,798	DAUPHIN	100,658	53,631	44,390	2,059	578	9,241 R	53.3%	44.1%	2.0%
550,864	DELAWARE	248,077	105,836	134,861	5,348	2,032	29,025 D	42.7%	54.4%	2.2%
35,112	ELK	13,578	7,347	5,754	352	125	1,593 R	54.1%	42.4%	2.6%
280,843	ERIE	112,335	49,027	59,399	2,980	929	10,372 D	43.6%	52.9%	2.7%
148,644	FAYETTE	49,532	20,013	28,152	798	569	8,139 D	40.4%	56.8%	1.6%
4,946	FOREST	2,283	1,371	843	57	12	528 R	60.1%	36.9%	2.5%
129,313	FRANKLIN	48,969	33,042	14,922	761	244	18,120 R	67.5%	30.5%	1.6%
14,261	FULTON	5,285	3,753	1,425	77	30	2,328 R	71.0%	27.0%	1.5%
40,672	GREENE	13,634	5,890	7,230	337	177	1,340 D	43.2%	53.0%	2.5%
45,586	HUNTINGDON	15,957	10,408	5,073	340	136	5,335 R	65.2%	31.8%	2.1%
89,605	INDIANA	31,401	16,799	13,667	711	224	3,132 R	53.5%	43.5%	2.3%
45,932	JEFFERSON	17,574	11,473	5,566	339	196	5,907 R	65.3%	31.7%	1.9%
22,821	JUNIATA	8,667	5,795	2,656	158	58	3,139 R	66.9%	30.6%	1.8%
213,295	LACKAWANNA	96,381	35,096	57,471	2,134	1,680	22,375 D	36.4%	59.6%	2.2%
470,658	LANCASTER	175,317	115,900	54,968	3,341	1,108	60,932 R	66.1%	31.4%	1.9%
94,643	LAWRENCE	39,640	18,060	20,593	653	334	2,533 D	45.6%	52.0%	1.6%
120,327	LEBANON	45,880	28,534	16,093	873	380	12,441 R	62.2%	35.1%	1.9%
312,090	LEHIGH	116,280	55,492	56,667	3,278	843	1,175 D	47.7%	48.7%	2.8%
319,250	LUZERNE	119,586	52,328	62,199	3,456	1,603	9,871 D	43.8%	52.0%	2.9%
120,044	LYCOMING	43,183	27,137	14,663	965	418	12,474 R	62.8%	34.0%	2.2%
45,936	MCKEAN	15,804	9,661	5,510	403	230	4,151 R	61.1%	34.9%	2.5%
120,293	MERCER	48,725	23,132	23,817	1,073	703	685 D	47.5%	48.9%	2.2%
46,486	MIFFLIN	14,614	9,400	4,835	264	115	4,565 R	64.3%	33.1%	1.8%
138,687	MONROE	46,878	23,265	21,939	1,319	355	1,326 R	49.6%	46.8%	2.8%
750,097	MONTGOMERY	332,422	145,623	177,990	6,816	1,993	32,367 D	43.8%	53.5%	2.1%
18,236	MONTOUR	6,492	3,960	2,356	132	44	1,604 R	61.0%	36.3%	2.0%
267,066	NORTHAMPTON	104,690	47,396	53,097	3,012	1,185	5,701 D	45.3%	50.7%	2.9%
94,556	NORTHUMBERLAND	33,251	18,142	13,670	956	483	4,472 R	54.6%	41.1%	2.9%
43,602	PERRY	16,071	11,184	4,459	309	119	6,725 R	69.6%	27.7%	1.9%
1,517,550	PHILADELPHIA	561,180	100,959	449,182	8,206	2,833	348,223 D	18.0%	80.0%	1.5%
46,302	PIKE	17,364	9,339	7,330	498	197	2,009 R	53.8%	42.2%	2.9%
18,080	POTTER	7,090	4,858	2,037	146	49	2,821 R	68.5%	28.7%	2.1%
150,336	SCHUYLKILL	58,300	29,841	26,215	1,713	531	3,626 R	51.2%	45.0%	2.9%
37,546	SNYDER	12,841	8,963	3,536	271	71	5,427 R	69.8%	27.5%	2.1%
80,023	SOMERSET	32,985	20,218	12,028	487	252	8,190 R	61.3%	36.5%	1.5%
6,556	SULLIVAN	3,105	1,928	1,066	91	20	862 R	62.1%	34.3%	2.9%
42,238	SUSQUEHANNA	17,271	10,226	6,481	459	105	3,745 R	59.2%	37.5%	2.7%
41,373	TIOGA	14,772	9,635	4,617	404	116	5,018 R	65.2%	31.3%	2.7%
41,624	UNION	13,175	8,523	4,209	373	70	4,314 R	64.7%	31.9%	2.8%

PENNSYLVANIA

PRESIDENT 2000

2000 Census Population	County	Total Vote	Republican	Democratic	Green (Nader)	Other	Rep.-Dem. Plurality	Percentage of Total Vote		
								Rep.	Dem.	Green
57,565	VENANGO	20,523	11,642	8,196	467	218	3,446 R	56.7%	39.9%	2.3%
43,863	WARREN	17,541	9,290	7,537	466	248	1,753 R	53.0%	43.0%	2.7%
202,897	WASHINGTON	84,441	37,339	44,961	1,442	699	7,622 D	44.2%	53.2%	1.7%
47,722	WAYNE	18,914	11,201	6,904	625	184	4,297 R	59.2%	36.5%	3.3%
369,993	WESTMORELAND	156,709	80,858	71,792	2,601	1,458	9,066 R	51.6%	45.8%	1.7%
28,080	WYOMING	11,693	6,922	4,363	344	64	2,559 R	59.2%	37.3%	2.9%
381,751	YORK	144,244	87,652	51,958	3,305	1,329	35,694 R	60.8%	36.0%	2.3%
12,281,054	TOTAL	4,913,119	2,281,127	2,485,967	103,392	42,633	204,840 D	46.4%	50.6%	2.1%

Note: The statewide totals for "Total Vote" and "Other" include 934 scattered write-in votes that are not included in the county-by-county results.

PHILADELPHIA

PRESIDENT 2000

2000 Census Population	Ward	Total Vote	Republican	Democratic	Green (Nader)	Other	Rep.-Dem. Plurality	Percentage of Total Vote		
								Rep.	Dem.	Green
	Ward 1	6,273	1,476	4,679	89	29	3,203 D	23.5%	74.6%	1.4%
	Ward 2	8,817	1,625	6,839	321	32	5,214 D	18.4%	77.6%	3.6%
	Ward 3	8,213	190	7,977	33	13	7,787 D	2.3%	97.1%	0.4%
	Ward 4	8,028	153	7,837	25	13	7,684 D	1.9%	97.6%	0.3%
	Ward 5	11,666	1,938	9,259	427	42	7,321 D	16.6%	79.4%	3.7%
	Ward 6	4,710	91	4,580	25	14	4,489 D	1.9%	97.2%	0.5%
	Ward 7	5,103	660	4,342	24	77	3,682 D	12.9%	85.1%	0.5%
	Ward 8	13,754	2,318	10,956	389	91	8,638 D	16.9%	79.7%	2.8%
	Ward 9	8,743	1,755	6,751	215	22	4,996 D	20.1%	77.2%	2.5%
	Ward 10	11,528	288	11,197	27	16	10,909 D	2.5%	97.1%	0.2%
	Ward 11	5,714	172	5,514	11	17	5,342 D	3.0%	96.5%	0.2%
	Ward 12	8,247	320	7,821	74	32	7,501 D	3.9%	94.8%	0.9%
	Ward 13	7,862	235	7,585	26	16	7,350 D	3.0%	96.5%	0.3%
	Ward 14	2,925	97	2,799	26	3	2,702 D	3.3%	95.7%	0.9%
	Ward 15	7,539	1,148	6,087	235	69	4,939 D	15.2%	80.7%	3.1%
	Ward 16	5,040	65	4,903	12	60	4,838 D	1.3%	97.3%	0.2%
	Ward 17	9,660	254	9,351	30	25	9,097 D	2.6%	96.8%	0.3%
	Ward 18	4,760	951	3,651	101	57	2,700 D	20.0%	76.7%	2.1%
	Ward 19	4,189	351	3,745	22	71	3,394 D	8.4%	89.4%	0.5%
	Ward 20	2,873	102	2,732	13	26	2,630 D	3.6%	95.1%	0.5%
	Ward 21	18,205	6,304	11,380	438	83	5,076 D	34.6%	62.5%	2.4%
	Ward 22	11,176	466	10,523	160	27	10,057 D	4.2%	94.2%	1.4%
	Ward 23	6,787	1,551	5,034	119	83	3,483 D	22.9%	74.2%	1.8%
	Ward 24	4,966	427	4,397	127	15	3,970 D	8.6%	88.5%	2.6%
	Ward 25	5,989	1,783	4,017	115	74	2,234 D	29.8%	67.1%	1.9%
	Ward 26	7,938	3,187	4,605	115	31	1,418 D	40.1%	58.0%	1.4%
	Ward 27	5,422	769	4,373	250	30	3,604 D	14.2%	80.7%	4.6%
	Ward 28	5,421	75	5,320	11	15	5,245 D	1.4%	98.1%	0.2%
	Ward 29	4,445	115	4,262	13	55	4,147 D	2.6%	95.9%	0.3%
	Ward 30	5,277	408	4,679	167	23	4,271 D	7.7%	88.7%	3.2%
	Ward 31	4,623	1,389	3,066	120	48	1,677 D	30.0%	66.3%	2.6%
	Ward 32	7,869	128	7,609	27	105	7,481 D	1.6%	96.7%	0.3%
	Ward 33	5,685	1,550	3,996	82	57	2,446 D	27.3%	70.3%	1.4%
	Ward 34	14,125	1,261	12,743	91	30	11,482 D	8.9%	90.2%	0.6%
	Ward 35	9,792	3,674	5,794	229	95	2,120 D	37.5%	59.2%	2.3%

PHILADELPHIA

PRESIDENT 2000

2000 Census Population	Ward	Total Vote	Republican	Democratic	Green (Nader)	Other	Rep.-Dem. Plurality	Rep.	Dem.	Green
	Ward 36	11,262	799	10,366	65	32	9,567 D	7.1%	92.0%	0.6%
	Ward 37	5,156	216	4,899	20	21	4,683 D	4.2%	95.0%	0.4%
	Ward 38	7,505	832	6,545	94	34	5,713 D	11.1%	87.2%	1.3%
	Ward 39	15,576	4,122	11,137	250	67	7,015 D	26.5%	71.5%	1.6%
	Ward 40	13,672	1,971	11,534	120	47	9,563 D	14.4%	84.4%	0.9%
	Ward 41	8,354	2,654	5,406	195	99	2,752 D	31.8%	64.7%	2.3%
	Ward 42	6,975	1,133	5,732	74	36	4,599 D	16.2%	82.2%	1.1%
	Ward 43	6,368	467	5,854	26	21	5,387 D	7.3%	91.9%	0.4%
	Ward 44	5,387	136	5,227	18	6	5,091 D	2.5%	97.0%	0.3%
	Ward 45	7,270	2,526	4,443	186	115	1,917 D	34.7%	61.1%	2.6%
	Ward 46	8,009	343	7,425	222	19	7,082 D	4.3%	92.7%	2.8%
	Ward 47	2,556	61	2,449	16	30	2,388 D	2.4%	95.8%	0.6%
	Ward 48	6,155	1,070	5,015	53	17	3,945 D	17.4%	81.5%	0.9%
	Ward 49	8,475	386	8,022	45	22	7,636 D	4.6%	94.7%	0.5%
	Ward 50	13,162	371	12,708	62	21	12,337 D	2.8%	96.6%	0.5%
	Ward 51	8,342	170	8,128	30	14	7,958 D	2.0%	97.4%	0.4%
	Ward 52	11,533	620	10,818	74	21	10,198 D	5.4%	93.8%	0.6%
	Ward 53	8,418	2,369	5,854	144	51	3,485 D	28.1%	69.5%	1.7%
	Ward 54	6,810	1,420	5,256	106	28	3,836 D	20.9%	77.2%	1.6%
	Ward 55	11,907	4,766	6,835	236	70	2,069 D	40.0%	57.4%	2.0%
	Ward 56	15,139	4,145	10,670	242	82	6,525 D	27.4%	70.5%	1.6%
	Ward 57	11,034	4,019	6,782	186	47	2,763 D	36.4%	61.5%	1.7%
	Ward 58	19,642	6,620	12,658	273	91	6,038 D	33.7%	64.4%	1.4%
	Ward 59	8,324	345	7,868	88	23	7,523 D	4.1%	94.5%	1.1%
	Ward 60	7,045	190	6,816	30	9	6,626 D	2.7%	96.7%	0.4%
	Ward 61	8,487	1,245	7,137	81	24	5,892 D	14.7%	84.1%	1.0%
	Ward 62	9,476	2,709	6,523	190	54	3,814 D	28.6%	68.8%	2.0%
	Ward 63	10,291	4,299	5,759	190	43	1,460 D	41.8%	56.0%	1.8%
	Ward 64	7,615	3,260	4,162	151	42	902 D	42.8%	54.7%	2.0%
	Ward 65	9,159	2,809	6,148	151	51	3,339 D	30.7%	67.1%	1.6%
	Ward 66	18,703	7,600	10,604	399	100	3,004 D	40.6%	56.7%	2.1%
1,517,550	TOTAL	561,171	100,949	449,183	8,206	2,833	348,234 D	18.0%	80.0%	1.5%

Note: Ward-by-ward results did not add to the totals certified, which were: 100,959 Republican, 449,182 Democratic, 8,206 Green, 2,833 Other.

PENNSYLVANIA

SENATOR 2000

2000 Census Population	County	Total Vote	Republican	Democratic	Other	Rep.-Dem. Plurality	Total Vote Rep.	Total Vote Dem.	Major Vote Rep.	Major Vote Dem.
91,292	ADAMS	32,746	21,621	10,177	948	11,444 R	66.0%	31.1%	68.0%	32.0%
1,281,666	ALLEGHENY	565,208	247,405	306,410	11,393	59,005 D	43.8%	54.2%	44.7%	55.3%
72,392	ARMSTRONG	27,498	15,388	11,380	730	4,008 R	56.0%	41.4%	57.5%	42.5%
181,412	BEAVER	76,089	33,609	41,419	1,061	7,810 D	44.2%	54.4%	44.8%	55.2%
49,984	BEDFORD	19,077	13,791	4,810	476	8,981 R	72.3%	25.2%	74.1%	25.9%
373,638	BERKS	130,669	78,297	48,998	3,374	29,299 R	59.9%	37.5%	61.5%	38.5%
129,144	BLAIR	44,655	30,343	12,863	1,449	17,480 R	67.9%	28.8%	70.2%	29.8%
62,761	BRADFORD	22,896	16,314	6,150	432	10,164 R	71.3%	26.9%	72.6%	27.4%
597,635	BUCKS	253,486	144,711	103,961	4,814	40,750 R	57.1%	41.0%	58.2%	41.8%
174,083	BUTLER	70,846	44,568	24,816	1,462	19,752 R	62.9%	35.0%	64.2%	35.8%
152,598	CAMBRIA	60,182	29,514	28,932	1,736	582 R	49.0%	48.1%	50.5%	49.5%
5,974	CAMERON	2,190	1,524	626	40	898 R	69.6%	28.6%	70.9%	29.1%
58,802	CARBON	19,929	10,598	8,878	453	1,720 R	53.2%	44.5%	54.4%	45.6%
135,758	CENTRE	48,449	30,002	16,706	1,741	13,296 R	61.9%	34.5%	64.2%	35.8%
433,501	CHESTER	185,119	117,092	63,259	4,768	53,833 R	63.3%	34.2%	64.9%	35.1%

PENNSYLVANIA

SENATOR 2000

2000 Census Population	County	Total Vote	Republican	Democratic	Other	Rep.-Dem. Plurality		Percentage			
								Total Vote		Major Vote	
								Rep.	Dem.	Rep.	Dem.
41,765	CLARION	15,718	9,823	5,482	413	4,341	R	62.5%	34.9%	64.2%	35.8%
83,382	CLEARFIELD	30,040	18,582	10,415	1,043	8,167	R	61.9%	34.7%	64.1%	35.9%
37,914	CLINTON	11,328	6,710	4,333	285	2,377	R	59.2%	38.3%	60.8%	39.2%
64,151	COLUMBIA	21,410	13,405	7,337	668	6,068	R	62.6%	34.3%	64.6%	35.4%
90,366	CRAWFORD	31,922	20,280	11,000	642	9,280	R	63.5%	34.5%	64.8%	35.2%
213,674	CUMBERLAND	86,435	55,799	28,080	2,556	27,719	R	64.6%	32.5%	66.5%	33.5%
251,798	DAUPHIN	98,009	54,986	40,047	2,976	14,939	R	56.1%	40.9%	57.9%	42.1%
550,864	DELAWARE	237,786	128,768	105,712	3,306	23,056	R	54.2%	44.5%	54.9%	45.1%
35,112	ELK	13,299	7,586	5,316	397	2,270	R	57.0%	40.0%	58.8%	41.2%
280,843	ERIE	107,011	58,302	46,726	1,983	11,576	R	54.5%	43.7%	55.5%	44.5%
148,644	FAYETTE	47,730	19,342	27,502	886	8,160	D	40.5%	57.6%	41.3%	58.7%
4,946	FOREST	2,249	1,406	786	57	620	R	62.5%	34.9%	64.1%	35.9%
129,313	FRANKLIN	47,971	33,541	13,594	836	19,947	R	69.9%	28.3%	71.2%	28.8%
14,261	FULTON	5,156	3,761	1,311	84	2,450	R	72.9%	25.4%	74.2%	25.8%
40,672	GREENE	13,964	5,935	7,636	393	1,701	D	42.5%	54.7%	43.7%	56.3%
45,586	HUNTINGDON	15,660	11,185	3,910	565	7,275	R	71.4%	25.0%	74.1%	25.9%
89,605	INDIANA	31,143	17,651	12,761	731	4,890	R	56.7%	41.0%	58.0%	42.0%
45,932	JEFFERSON	17,283	11,370	5,361	552	6,009	R	65.8%	31.0%	68.0%	32.0%
22,821	JUNIATA	8,532	5,912	2,407	213	3,505	R	69.3%	28.2%	71.1%	28.9%
213,295	LACKAWANNA	89,593	40,520	47,363	1,710	6,843	D	45.2%	52.9%	46.1%	53.9%
470,658	LANCASTER	169,907	119,519	47,600	2,788	71,919	R	70.3%	28.0%	71.5%	28.5%
94,643	LAWRENCE	39,267	17,672	21,026	569	3,354	D	45.0%	53.5%	45.7%	54.3%
120,327	LEBANON	43,983	28,324	14,517	1,142	13,807	R	64.4%	33.0%	66.1%	33.9%
312,090	LEHIGH	110,161	63,025	45,148	1,988	17,877	R	57.2%	41.0%	58.3%	41.7%
319,250	LUZERNE	109,623	55,549	51,613	2,461	3,936	R	50.7%	47.1%	51.8%	48.2%
120,044	LYCOMING	40,668	28,773	11,034	861	17,739	R	70.8%	27.1%	72.3%	27.7%
45,936	MCKEAN	14,398	9,804	4,304	290	5,500	R	68.1%	29.9%	69.5%	30.5%
120,293	MERCER	46,103	23,157	22,191	755	966	R	50.2%	48.1%	51.1%	48.9%
46,486	MIFFLIN	14,091	9,768	4,021	302	5,747	R	69.3%	28.5%	70.8%	29.2%
138,687	MONROE	44,000	25,524	17,351	1,125	8,173	R	58.0%	39.4%	59.5%	40.5%
750,097	MONTGOMERY	320,628	174,512	140,507	5,609	34,005	R	54.4%	43.8%	55.4%	44.6%
18,236	MONTOUR	6,406	4,309	1,927	170	2,382	R	67.3%	30.1%	69.1%	30.9%
267,066	NORTHAMPTON	98,686	53,853	42,965	1,868	10,888	R	54.6%	43.5%	55.6%	44.4%
94,556	NORTHUMBERLAND	31,133	19,029	11,208	896	7,821	R	61.1%	36.0%	62.9%	37.1%
43,602	PERRY	15,781	11,118	4,124	539	6,994	R	70.5%	26.1%	72.9%	27.1%
1,517,550	PHILADELPHIA	526,625	121,433	398,756	6,436	277,323	D	23.1%	75.7%	23.3%	76.7%
46,302	PIKE	16,321	9,856	6,138	327	3,718	R	60.4%	37.6%	61.6%	38.4%
18,080	POTTER	6,896	5,043	1,694	159	3,349	R	73.1%	24.6%	74.9%	25.1%
150,336	SCHUYLKILL	57,038	34,175	21,184	1,679	12,991	R	59.9%	37.1%	61.7%	38.3%
37,546	SNYDER	12,511	9,217	2,909	385	6,308	R	73.7%	23.3%	76.0%	24.0%
80,023	SOMERSET	32,791	19,028	13,129	634	5,899	R	58.0%	40.0%	59.2%	40.8%
6,556	SULLIVAN	3,015	2,046	897	72	1,149	R	67.9%	29.8%	69.5%	30.5%
42,238	SUSQUEHANNA	16,946	11,205	5,344	397	5,861	R	66.1%	31.5%	67.7%	32.3%
41,373	TIOGA	14,423	10,194	3,847	382	6,347	R	70.7%	26.7%	72.6%	27.4%
41,624	UNION	12,920	9,041	3,468	411	5,573	R	70.0%	26.8%	72.3%	27.7%
57,565	VENANGO	20,262	11,846	7,867	549	3,979	R	58.5%	38.8%	60.1%	39.9%
43,863	WARREN	15,978	9,973	5,565	440	4,408	R	62.4%	34.8%	64.2%	35.8%
202,897	WASHINGTON	83,384	36,908	42,934	3,542	6,026	D	44.3%	51.5%	46.2%	53.8%
47,722	WAYNE	17,623	11,762	5,526	335	6,236	R	66.7%	31.4%	68.0%	32.0%
369,993	WESTMORELAND	152,527	80,010	70,201	2,316	9,809	R	52.5%	46.0%	53.3%	46.7%
28,080	WYOMING	11,461	7,856	3,356	249	4,500	R	68.5%	29.3%	70.1%	29.9%
381,751	YORK	138,282	88,792	46,093	3,397	42,699	R	64.2%	33.3%	65.8%	34.2%
12,281,054	TOTAL	4,735,504	2,481,962	2,154,908	98,634	327,054	R	52.4%	45.5%	53.5%	46.5%

Note: The statewide totals for "Total Vote" and "Other" include 388 scattered write-in votes that are not included in the county-by-county results.

PHILADELPHIA

SENATOR 2000

2000 Census Population	County		Total Vote	Republican	Democratic	Other	Rep.-Dem. Plurality		Rep.	Dem.	Rep.	Dem.
									Total Vote		Major Vote	
	Ward	1	5,999	1,569	4,357	73	2,788	D	26.2%	72.6%	26.5%	73.5%
	Ward	2	8,176	1,693	6,160	323	4,467	D	20.7%	75.3%	21.6%	78.4%
	Ward	3	7,837	333	7,453	51	7,120	D	4.2%	95.1%	4.3%	95.7%
	Ward	4	7,435	258	7,133	44	6,875	D	3.5%	95.9%	3.5%	96.5%
	Ward	5	10,577	2,330	7,921	326	5,591	D	22.0%	74.9%	22.7%	77.3%
	Ward	6	4,394	158	4,190	46	4,032	D	3.6%	95.4%	3.6%	96.4%
	Ward	7	4,750	671	4,009	70	3,338	D	14.1%	84.4%	14.3%	85.7%
	Ward	8	12,749	2,785	9,626	338	6,841	D	21.8%	75.5%	22.4%	77.6%
	Ward	9	8,225	1,914	6,159	152	4,245	D	23.3%	74.9%	23.7%	76.3%
	Ward	10	11,001	442	10,511	48	10,069	D	4.0%	95.5%	4.0%	96.0%
	Ward	11	5,309	235	5,024	50	4,789	D	4.4%	94.6%	4.5%	95.5%
	Ward	12	7,730	479	7,160	91	6,681	D	6.2%	92.6%	6.3%	93.7%
	Ward	13	7,346	335	6,952	59	6,617	D	4.6%	94.6%	4.6%	95.4%
	Ward	14	2,607	129	2,462	16	2,333	D	4.9%	94.4%	5.0%	95.0%
	Ward	15	7,028	1,448	5,437	143	3,989	D	20.6%	77.4%	21.0%	79.0%
	Ward	16	4,707	118	4,507	82	4,389	D	2.5%	95.8%	2.6%	97.4%
	Ward	17	9,125	364	8,711	50	8,347	D	4.0%	95.5%	4.0%	96.0%
	Ward	18	4,387	983	3,322	82	2,339	D	22.4%	75.7%	22.8%	77.2%
	Ward	19	3,872	333	3,478	61	3,145	D	8.6%	89.8%	8.7%	91.3%
	Ward	20	2,715	142	2,546	27	2,404	D	5.2%	93.8%	5.3%	94.7%
	Ward	21	16,754	7,335	9,154	265	1,819	D	43.8%	54.6%	44.5%	55.5%
	Ward	22	10,459	795	9,552	112	8,757	D	7.6%	91.3%	7.7%	92.3%
	Ward	23	6,375	1,799	4,494	82	2,695	D	28.2%	70.5%	28.6%	71.4%
	Ward	24	4,406	359	3,976	71	3,617	D	8.1%	90.2%	8.3%	91.7%
	Ward	25	5,326	2,214	3,032	80	818	D	41.6%	56.9%	42.2%	57.8%
	Ward	26	7,348	3,362	3,931	55	569	D	45.8%	53.5%	46.1%	53.9%
	Ward	27	4,755	857	3,707	191	2,850	D	18.0%	78.0%	18.8%	81.2%
	Ward	28	5,456	123	5,291	42	5,168	D	2.3%	97.0%	2.3%	97.7%
	Ward	29	4,202	151	3,994	57	3,843	D	3.6%	95.0%	3.6%	96.4%
	Ward	30	5,168	547	4,492	129	3,945	D	10.6%	86.9%	10.9%	89.1%
	Ward	31	4,219	1,627	2,541	51	914	D	38.6%	60.2%	39.0%	61.0%
	Ward	32	7,376	186	7,066	124	6,880	D	2.5%	95.8%	2.6%	97.4%
	Ward	33	5,268	1,780	3,419	69	1,639	D	33.8%	64.9%	34.2%	65.8%
	Ward	34	13,396	1,536	11,765	95	10,229	D	11.5%	87.8%	11.5%	88.5%
	Ward	35	9,442	4,159	5,165	118	1,006	D	44.0%	54.7%	44.6%	55.4%
	Ward	36	10,660	931	9,638	91	8,707	D	8.7%	90.4%	8.8%	91.2%
	Ward	37	4,895	223	4,637	35	4,414	D	4.6%	94.7%	4.6%	95.4%
	Ward	38	6,906	1,010	5,814	82	4,804	D	14.6%	84.2%	14.8%	85.2%
	Ward	39	14,455	4,572	9,787	96	5,215	D	31.6%	67.7%	31.8%	68.2%
	Ward	40	12,948	2,345	10,493	110	8,148	D	18.1%	81.0%	18.3%	81.7%
	Ward	41	7,685	3,126	4,447	112	1,321	D	40.7%	57.9%	41.3%	58.7%
	Ward	42	6,583	1,266	5,243	74	3,977	D	19.2%	79.6%	19.4%	80.6%
	Ward	43	6,084	468	5,573	43	5,105	D	7.7%	91.6%	7.7%	92.3%
	Ward	44	4,888	211	4,649	28	4,438	D	4.3%	95.1%	4.3%	95.7%
	Ward	45	6,698	2,939	3,629	130	690	D	43.9%	54.2%	44.7%	55.3%
	Ward	46	7,623	485	7,005	133	6,520	D	6.4%	91.9%	6.5%	93.5%
	Ward	47	2,476	87	2,355	34	2,268	D	3.5%	95.1%	3.6%	96.4%
	Ward	48	5,874	1,275	4,560	39	3,285	D	21.7%	77.6%	21.9%	78.1%
	Ward	49	8,143	519	7,556	68	7,037	D	6.4%	92.8%	6.4%	93.6%
	Ward	50	12,484	595	11,825	64	11,230	D	4.8%	94.7%	4.8%	95.2%
	Ward	51	7,886	274	7,559	53	7,285	D	3.5%	95.9%	3.5%	96.5%
	Ward	52	10,895	918	9,882	95	8,964	D	8.4%	90.7%	8.5%	91.5%
	Ward	53	7,938	2,993	4,841	104	1,848	D	37.7%	61.0%	38.2%	61.8%
	Ward	54	6,454	1,844	4,534	76	2,690	D	28.6%	70.3%	28.9%	71.1%
	Ward	55	11,032	5,816	5,083	133	733	R	52.7%	46.1%	53.4%	46.6%
	Ward	56	14,335	5,182	8,980	173	3,798	D	36.1%	62.6%	36.6%	63.4%
	Ward	57	10,396	4,893	5,399	104	506	D	47.1%	51.9%	47.5%	52.5%
	Ward	58	18,338	8,193	9,960	185	1,767	D	44.7%	54.3%	45.1%	54.9%
	Ward	59	8,280	551	7,651	78	7,100	D	6.7%	92.4%	6.7%	93.3%
	Ward	60	6,668	242	6,391	35	6,149	D	3.6%	95.8%	3.6%	96.4%

PHILADELPHIA

SENATOR 2000

2000 Census Population	Ward	Total Vote	Republican	Democratic	Other	Rep.-Dem. Plurality		Total Vote		Major Vote	
								Rep.	Dem.	Rep.	Dem.
	Ward 61	7,998	1,515	6,407	76	4,892	D	18.9%	80.1%	19.1%	80.9%
	Ward 62	9,002	3,458	5,440	104	1,982	D	38.4%	60.4%	38.9%	61.1%
	Ward 63	10,078	5,068	4,904	106	164	R	50.3%	48.7%	50.8%	49.2%
	Ward 64	6,916	3,719	3,122	75	597	R	53.8%	45.1%	54.4%	45.6%
	Ward 65	8,496	3,373	5,020	103	1,647	D	39.7%	59.1%	40.2%	59.8%
	Ward 66	17,464	9,583	7,675	206	1,908	R	54.9%	43.9%	55.5%	44.5%
1,517,550	TOTAL	526,497	121,223	398,756	6,518	277,533	D	23.0%	75.7%	23.3%	76.7%

Note: Ward-by-ward results did not add to the vote totals certified, which were: 121,433 Republican, 398,756 Democratic, 6,436 Other.

PENNSYLVANIA

CONGRESS

CD	Year	Total Vote	Republican Vote	Republican Candidate	Democratic Vote	Democratic Candidate	Other Vote	Rep.-Dem. Plurality		Total Vote Rep.	Total Vote Dem.	Major Vote Rep.	Major Vote Dem.
1	2000	169,541	19,920	KUSH, STEVEN N.	149,621	BRADY, ROBERT A.		129,701	D	11.7%	88.3%	11.7%	88.3%
1	1998	95,848	15,898	HARRISON, WILLIAM M.	77,788	BRADY, ROBERT A.	2,162	61,890	D	16.6%	81.2%	17.0%	83.0%
1	1996	165,945	20,734	CELLA, JAMES D.	145,210	FOGLIETTA, THOMAS M.	1	124,476	D	12.5%	87.5%	12.5%	87.5%
1	1994	122,264	22,595	GORDON, ROGER F.	99,669	FOGLIETTA, THOMAS M.		77,074	D	18.5%	81.5%	18.5%	81.5%
1	1992	185,591	35,419	SNYDER, CRAIG	150,172	FOGLIETTA, THOMAS M.		114,753	D	19.1%	80.9%	19.1%	80.9%
2	2000	183,694			180,021	FATTAH, CHAKA	3,673	180,021	D		98.0%		100.0%
2	1998	118,764	16,001	MULLIGAN, ANNE MARIE	102,763	FATTAH, CHAKA		86,762	D	13.5%	86.5%	13.5%	86.5%
2	1996	191,937	23,047	MURPHY, LARRY G.	168,887	FATTAH, CHAKA	3	145,840	D	12.0%	88.0%	12.0%	88.0%
2	1994	140,377	19,824	WATSON, LAWRENCE R.	120,553	FATTAH, CHAKA		100,729	D	14.1%	85.9%	14.1%	85.9%
2	1992	213,927	47,906	HOLLIN, LARRY	164,355	BLACKWELL, LUCIEN E.	1,666	116,449	D	22.4%	76.8%	22.6%	77.4%
3	2000	189,871	59,343	DOUGHERTY, CHARLES F.	130,528	BORSKI, ROBERT A.		71,185	D	31.3%	68.7%	31.3%	68.7%
3	1998	111,660	45,390	DOUGHERTY, CHARLES F.	66,270	BORSKI, ROBERT A.		20,880	D	40.7%	59.3%	40.7%	59.3%
3	1996	175,801	54,681	MCCOLGAN, JOSEPH M.	121,120	BORSKI, ROBERT A.		66,439	D	31.1%	68.9%	31.1%	68.9%
3	1994	147,911	55,209	HASHER, JAMES C.	92,702	BORSKI, ROBERT A.		37,493	D	37.3%	62.7%	37.3%	62.7%
3	1992	221,971	86,787	DOUGHERTY, CHARLES F.	130,828	BORSKI, ROBERT A.	4,356	44,041	D	39.1%	58.9%	39.9%	60.1%
4	2000	246,467	145,390	HART, MELISSA	100,995	VAN HORNE, TERRY E.	82	44,395	R	59.0%	41.0%	59.0%	41.0%
4	1998	161,685	58,485	TURZAI, MIKE	103,183	KLINK, RON	17	44,698	D	36.2%	63.8%	36.2%	63.8%
4	1996	222,167	79,448	ADAMETZ, PAUL T.	142,621	KLINK, RON	98	63,173	D	35.8%	64.2%	35.8%	64.2%
4	1994	185,630	66,509	PEGLOW, ED	119,115	KLINK, RON	6	52,606	D	35.8%	64.2%	35.8%	64.2%
4	1992	237,922	48,484	JOHNSTON, GORDON R.	186,684	KLINK, RON	2,754	138,200	D	20.4%	78.5%	20.6%	79.4%
5	2000	172,517	147,570	PETERSON, JOHN E.			24,947	147,570	R	85.5%		100.0%	
5	1998	117,323	99,502	PETERSON, JOHN E.			17,821	99,502	R	84.8%		100.0%	
5	1996	193,003	116,303	PETERSON, JOHN E.	76,627	RUDY, RUTH C.	73	39,676	R	60.3%	39.7%	60.3%	39.7%
5	1994	145,431	145,335	*CLINGER, WILLIAM F.			96	145,335	R	99.9%		100.0%	
5	1992	188,911	188,911	*CLINGER, WILLIAM F.				188,911	R	100.0%		100.0%	
6	2000	211,313	71,227	KOPEL, THOMAS G.	140,084	HOLDEN, TIM	2	68,857	D	33.7%	66.3%	33.7%	66.3%
6	1998	139,953	54,579	MECKLEY, JOHN	85,374	HOLDEN, TIM		30,795	D	39.0%	61.0%	39.0%	61.0%
6	1996	196,729	80,061	LEINBACH, CHRISTIAN Y.	115,193	HOLDEN, TIM	1,475	35,132	D	40.7%	58.6%	41.0%	59.0%
6	1994	158,633	68,610	LEVERING, FRED	90,023	HOLDEN, TIM		21,413	D	43.3%	56.7%	43.3%	56.7%
6	1992	208,006	99,694	JONES, JOHN E.	108,312	HOLDEN, TIM		8,618	D	47.9%	52.1%	47.9%	52.1%

PENNSYLVANIA

CONGRESS

CD	Year	Total Vote	Republican Vote	Republican Candidate	Democratic Vote	Democratic Candidate	Other Vote	Rep.-Dem. Plurality	Total Vote Rep.	Total Vote Dem.	Major Vote Rep.	Major Vote Dem.
7	2000	266,256	172,569	WELDON, CURT	93,687	LENNON, PETER A.		78,882 R	64.8%	35.2%	64.8%	35.2%
7	1998	166,411	119,491	WELDON, CURT	46,920	D'URSO, MARTIN J.		72,571 R	71.8%	28.2%	71.8%	28.2%
7	1996	246,666	165,087	WELDON, CURT	79,875	INNELLI, JOHN F.	1,704	85,212 R	66.9%	32.4%	67.4%	32.6%
7	1994	197,325	137,480	WELDON, CURT	59,845	NICHOLS, SARA		77,635 R	69.7%	30.3%	69.7%	30.3%
7	1992	273,898	180,648	WELDON, CURT	91,623	DALY, FRANK	1,627	89,025 R	66.0%	33.5%	66.3%	33.7%
8	2000	260,710	154,090	GREENWOOD, JAMES C.	100,617	STROUSE, RONALD L.	6,003	53,473 R	59.1%	38.6%	60.5%	39.5%
8	1998	148,200	93,697	GREENWOOD, JAMES C.	48,320	TUTHILL, BILL	6,183	45,377 R	63.2%	32.6%	66.0%	34.0%
8	1996	226,322	133,749	GREENWOOD, JAMES C.	79,856	MURRAY, JOHN P.	12,717	53,893 R	59.1%	35.3%	62.6%	37.4%
8	1994	167,174	110,499	GREENWOOD, JAMES C.	44,559	MURRAY, JOHN P.	12,116	65,940 R	66.1%	26.7%	71.3%	28.7%
8	1992	249,538	129,593	GREENWOOD, JAMES C.	114,095	KOSTMAYER, PETER H.	5,850	15,498 R	51.9%	45.7%	53.2%	46.8%
9	2000	185,466	184,401	*SHUSTER, E. G.			1,065	184,401 R	99.4%		100.0%	
9	1998	126,027	125,409	*SHUSTER, E. G.			618	125,409 R	99.5%		100.0%	
9	1996	192,822	142,105	SHUSTER, E. G.	50,650	KEMMLER, MONTE	67	91,455 R	73.7%	26.3%	73.7%	26.3%
9	1994	147,203	146,688	*SHUSTER, E. G.			515	146,688 R	99.7%		100.0%	
9	1992	182,406	182,406	*SHUSTER, E. G.				182,406 R	100.0%		100.0%	
10	2000	237,435	124,830	SHERWOOD, DON	112,580	CASEY, PATRICK	25	12,250 R	52.6%	47.4%	52.6%	47.4%
10	1998	173,056	84,275	SHERWOOD, DON	83,760	CASEY, PATRICK	5,021	515 R	48.7%	48.4%	50.2%	49.8%
10	1996	208,540	124,670	MCDADE, JOSEPH M.	75,536	CULLEN, JOE	8,334	49,134 R	59.8%	36.2%	62.3%	37.7%
10	1994	162,890	106,992	MCDADE, JOSEPH M.	50,635	SCHREFFLER, DANIEL J.	5,263	56,357 R	65.7%	31.1%	67.9%	32.1%
10	1992	209,548	189,414	*MCDADE, JOSEPH M.			20,134	189,414 R	90.4%		100.0%	
11	2000	198,665	66,699	URBAN, STEPHEN A.	131,948	KANJORSKI, PAUL E.	18	65,249 D	33.6%	66.4%	33.6%	66.4%
11	1998	133,065	44,123	URBAN, STEPHEN A.	88,933	KANJORSKI, PAUL E.	9	44,810 D	33.2%	66.8%	33.2%	66.8%
11	1996	188,609	60,339	URBAN, STEPHEN A.	128,258	KANJORSKI, PAUL E.	12	67,919 D	32.0%	68.0%	32.0%	68.0%
11	1994	153,277	51,295	PODOLAK, J. ANDREW	101,966	KANJORSKI, PAUL E.	16	50,671 D	33.5%	66.5%	33.5%	66.5%
11	1992	206,987	68,112	FESCINA, MICHAEL A.	138,875	KANJORSKI, PAUL E.		70,763 D	32.9%	67.1%	32.9%	67.1%
12	2000	205,448	56,575	CHOBY, BILL	145,538	MURTHA, JOHN P.	3,335	88,963 D	27.5%	70.8%	28.0%	72.0%
12	1998	146,780	46,239	HOLLOWAY, TIMOTHY E.	100,528	MURTHA, JOHN P.	13	54,289 D	31.5%	68.5%	31.5%	68.5%
12	1996	195,481	58,643	CHOBY, BILL	136,815	MURTHA, JOHN P.	23	78,172 D	30.0%	70.0%	30.0%	70.0%
12	1994	171,005	53,147	CHOBY, BILL	117,825	MURTHA, JOHN P.	33	64,678 D	31.1%	68.9%	31.1%	68.9%
12	1992	166,916			166,916	MURTHA, JOHN P.		166,916 D		100.0%		100.0%
13	2000	276,751	126,501	GREENLEAF, STEWART J.	146,026	HOEFFEL, JOSEPH M.	4,224	19,525 D	45.7%	52.8%	46.4%	53.6%
13	1998	184,490	85,915	FOX, JON D.	95,105	HOEFFEL, JOSEPH M.	3,470	9,190 D	46.6%	51.6%	47.5%	52.5%
13	1996	245,979	120,304	FOX, JON D.	120,220	HOEFFEL, JOSEPH M.	5,455	84 R	48.9%	48.9%	50.0%	50.0%
13	1994	194,788	96,254	FOX, JON D.	88,073	MEZVINSKY, MARJORIE M.	10,461	8,181 R	49.4%	45.2%	52.2%	47.8%
13	1992	253,997	126,312	FOX, JON D.	127,685	MEZVINSKY, MARJORIE M.		1,373 D	49.7%	50.3%	49.7%	50.3%
14	2000	147,749			147,533	COYNE, WILLIAM J.	216	147,533 D		99.9%		100.0%
14	1998	137,736	52,745	RAVOTTI, BILL	83,355	COYNE, WILLIAM J.	1,636	30,610 D	38.3%	60.5%	38.8%	61.2%
14	1996	202,578	78,921	RAVOTTI, BILL	122,922	COYNE, WILLIAM J.	735	44,001 D	39.0%	60.7%	39.1%	60.9%
14	1994	164,210	53,221	CLARK, JOHN R.	105,310	COYNE, WILLIAM J.	5,679	52,089 D	32.4%	64.1%	33.6%	66.4%
14	1992	229,038	61,311	KING, BYRON W.	165,633	COYNE, WILLIAM J.	2,094	104,322 D	26.8%	72.3%	27.0%	73.0%
15	2000	222,184	118,307	TOOMEY, PAT	103,864	O'BRIEN, ED	13	14,443 R	53.2%	46.7%	53.3%	46.7%
15	1998	148,706	81,755	TOOMEY, PAT	66,930	AFFLERBACH, ROY C.	21	14,825 R	55.0%	45.0%	55.0%	45.0%
15	1996	200,363	82,803	KILBANKS, BOB	109,812	MCHALE, PAUL	7,748	27,009 D	41.3%	54.8%	43.0%	57.0%
15	1994	150,909	71,602	YEAGER, JIM	72,073	MCHALE, PAUL	7,234	471 D	47.4%	47.8%	49.8%	50.2%
15	1992	213,324	99,520	RITTER, DONALD L.	111,419	MCHALE, PAUL	2,385	11,899 D	46.7%	52.2%	47.2%	52.8%
16	2000	242,589	162,403	PITTS, JOSEPH R.	80,177	YORCZYK, ROBERT S.	9	82,226 R	66.9%	33.1%	66.9%	33.1%
16	1998	136,085	95,979	PITTS, JOSEPH R.	40,092	YORCZYK, ROBERT S.	14	55,887 R	70.5%	29.5%	70.5%	29.5%
16	1996	209,602	124,511	PITTS, JOSEPH R.	78,598	BLAINE, JAMES G.	6,493	45,913 R	59.4%	37.5%	61.3%	38.7%
16	1994	157,455	109,759	WALKER, ROBERT S.	47,680	CHERTOK, BILL	16	62,079 R	69.7%	30.3%	69.7%	30.3%
16	1992	212,564	137,823	WALKER, ROBERT S.	74,741	PETERS, ROBERT		63,082 R	64.8%	35.2%	64.8%	35.2%

PENNSYLVANIA

CONGRESS

CD	Year	Total Vote	Republican		Democratic		Other Vote	Rep.-Dem. Plurality	Percentage			
			Vote	Candidate	Vote	Candidate			Total Vote		Major Vote	
									Rep.	Dem.	Rep.	Dem.
17	2000	232,460	166,236	GEKAS, GEORGE W.	66,190	HERRMANN, LESLYE HESS	34	100,046 R	71.5%	28.5%	71.5%	28.5%
17	1998	115,107	114,931	GEKAS, GEORGE W.			176	114,931 R	99.8%		100.0%	
17	1996	208,616	150,678	GEKAS, GEORGE W.	57,911	KETTL, PAUL	27	92,767 R	72.2%	27.8%	72.2%	27.8%
17	1994	133,975	133,788	GEKAS, GEORGE W.			187	133,788 R	99.9%		100.0%	
17	1992	216,039	150,158	GEKAS, GEORGE W.	65,881	STURGES, BILL		84,277 R	69.5%	30.5%	69.5%	30.5%
18	2000	224,956	68,798	STEPHENS, CRAIG C.	156,131	DOYLE, MIKE	27	87,333 D	30.6%	69.4%	30.6%	69.4%
18	1998	145,337	46,945	WALKER, DICK	98,363	DOYLE, MIKE	29	51,418 D	32.3%	67.7%	32.3%	67.7%
18	1996	214,990	86,829	FAWCETT, DAVID B.	120,410	DOYLE, MIKE	7,751	33,581 D	40.4%	56.0%	41.9%	58.1%
18	1994	185,750	83,881	MCCARTY, JOHN	101,784	DOYLE, MIKE	85	17,903 D	45.2%	54.8%	45.2%	54.8%
18	1992	254,329	154,024	SANTORUM, RICK	96,655	PECORA, FRANK A.	3,650	57,369 R	60.6%	38.0%	61.4%	38.6%
19	2000	232,622	168,722	PLATTS, TODD	61,538	SANDERS, JEFF	2,362	107,184 R	72.5%	26.5%	73.3%	26.7%
19	1998	142,489	96,284	GOODLING, WILLIAM F.	40,674	ROPP, LINDA G.	5,531	55,610 R	67.6%	28.5%	70.3%	29.7%
19	1996	208,963	130,716	GOODLING, WILLIAM F.	74,944	CHRONISTER, SCOTT L.	3,303	55,772 R	62.6%	35.9%	63.6%	36.4%
19	1994	125,117	124,496	GOODLING, WILLIAM F.			621	124,496 R	99.5%		100.0%	
19	1992	217,587	98,599	GOODLING, WILLIAM F.	74,798	KILKER, PAUL V.	44,190	23,801 R	45.3%	34.4%	56.9%	43.1%
20	2000	225,463	80,312	DAVIS, RONALD J.	145,131	MASCARA, FRANK R.	20	64,819 D	35.6%	64.4%	35.6%	64.4%
20	1998	98,075			97,885	MASCARA, FRANK R.	190	97,885 D		99.8%		100.0%
20	1996	210,402	97,004	MCCORMICK, MIKE	113,394	MASCARA, FRANK R.	4	16,390 D	46.1%	53.9%	46.1%	53.9%
20	1994	179,419	84,156	MCCORMICK, MIKE	95,251	MASCARA, FRANK R..	12	11,095 D	46.9%	53.1%	46.9%	53.1%
20	1992	226,489	111,591	TOWNSEND, BILL	114,898	MURPHY, AUSTIN J.		3,307 D	49.3%	50.7%	49.3%	50.7%
21	2000	222,190	135,164	ENGLISH, PHIL	87,018	FLITTER, MARC A.	8	48,146 R	60.8%	39.2%	60.8%	39.2%
21	1998	149,115	94,518	ENGLISH, PHIL	54,591	KLEMENS, LARRY	6	39,927 R	63.4%	36.6%	63.4%	36.6%
21	1996	210,888	106,875	ENGLISH, PHIL	104,004	DINICOLA, RONALD A.	9	2,871 R	50.7%	49.3%	50.7%	49.3%
21	1994	180,829	89,439	ENGLISH, PHIL	84,796	LEAVENS, BILL	6,594	4,643 R	49.5%	46.9%	51.3%	48.7%
21	1992	221,531	150,729	RIDGE, THOMAS J.	70,802	HARKINS, JOHN C.		79,927 R	68.0%	32.0%	68.0%	32.0%

* An asterisk in the congressional table indicates that a candidate had the endorsement of more than one party.

PENNSYLVANIA

GENERAL AND PRIMARY ELECTIONS

2000 GENERAL ELECTIONS

President
Other vote was 16,023 Reform (Buchanan); 14,428 Constitution (Phillips); 11,248 Libertarian (Browne); 934 scattered write-in.

Senator
Other vote was 45,775 Libertarian (Featherman); 28,382 Constitution (Searer); 24,089 Reform (Domske); 388 scattered write-in.

Congress
Other vote was: CD 2: 3,673 Libertarian (Krawchuk); CD 4: 82 scattered write-in; CD 5: 13,857 Green (Belitskus), 11,020 Libertarian (Martin), 70 scattered write-in; CD 6: 2 scattered write-in; CD 8: 5,394 Reform (Holmen), 609 scattered write-in; CD 9: 1,065 scattered write-in; CD 10: 25 scattered write-in; CD 11: 18 scattered write-in; CD 12: 3,324 Reform (O'Neil), 11 scattered write-in; CD 13: 4,224 Libertarian (Cavanaugh); CD 14; 216 scattered write-in; CD 15: 13 scattered write-in; CD 16: 9 scattered write-in; CD 17: 34 scattered write-in; CD 18: 27 scattered write-in; CD 19: 2,234 Constitution (Paoletta), 128 scattered write-in; CD 20: 20 scattered write-in; CD 21: 8 scattered write-in.

PENNSYLVANIA

GENERAL AND PRIMARY ELECTIONS

2000 PRIMARY ELECTIONS

Primary	April 4, 2000		

Registration
(as of April 2000)

Republican	3,161,402
Democratic	3,633,822
Libertarian	27,891
Constitution	9,322
Other	695,062
TOTAL	7,527,499

Primary Type   Closed—Only registered Democrats and Republicans could vote in their party's primary.

Note: An asterisk (*) denotes incumbent.

	REPUBLICAN PRIMARIES			DEMOCRATIC PRIMARIES		
President	George W. Bush	472,398	72.5%	Al Gore	525,306	74.2%
	John McCain	145,719	22.4%	Bill Bradley	146,797	20.7%
	Steve Forbes	16,162	2.5%	Lyndon H. LaRouche Jr.	32,047	4.5%
	Gary Bauer	8,806	1.4%	Write-in	3,840	0.5%
	Alan Keyes (write-in)	7,100	1.1%			
	Write-in	1,624	0.2%			
	TOTAL	651,809		TOTAL	707,990	
Senator	Rick Santorum*	545,687	99.6%	Ron Klink	299,219	40.7%
	Write-in	2,305	0.4%	Allyson Y. Schwartz	194,783	26.5%
				Tom Foley	184,003	25.0%
				Bob Rovner	28,031	3.8%
				Murray Levin	18,903	2.6%
				Phil Berg	9,636	1.3%
				Write-in	686	0.1%
	TOTAL	547,992		TOTAL	735,261	
Congressional District 1	Steven N. Kush	4,585	100.0%	Robert A. Brady*	28,333	77.4%
				Andrew J. Carn	6,346	17.3%
				Timothy Hannah	1,943	5.3%
	TOTAL	4,585		TOTAL	36,622	
Congressional District 2	No Republican candidate			Chaka Fattah*	46,582	100.0%
				TOTAL	46,582	
Congressional District 3	Charles F. Dougherty	9,945	100.0%	Robert A. Borski*	25,439	100.0%
	TOTAL	9,945		TOTAL	25,439	
Congressional District 4	Melissa Hart	24,142	98.8%	Terry E. Van Horne	14,862	23.5%
	Write-in	290	1.2%	Matthew T. Mangino	9,580	15.2%
				Jerry Hodge	9,022	14.3%
				Jim Rooker	8,226	13.0%
				Jack Machek	6,680	10.6%
				Joe Bellissimo	6,318	10.0%
				Royal Hart	5,519	8.7%
				Jim Schmitt	2,921	4.6%
				Write-in	57	0.1%
	TOTAL	24,432		TOTAL	63,185	
Congressional District 5	John E. Peterson*	34,482	99.9%	No Democratic candidate filed for the primary.		
	Write-in	33	0.1%	There were 453 scattered write-in votes.		
	TOTAL	34,515				
Congressional District 6	Thomas G. Kopel	19,861	100.0%	Tim Holden*	21,610	100.0%
	TOTAL	19,861		TOTAL	21,610	
Congressional District 7	Curt Weldon*	44,672	100.0%	Peter A. Lennon	10,785	100.0%
	TOTAL	44,672		TOTAL	10,785	
Congressional District 8	Jim Greenwood*	25,170	67.2%	Ronald L. Strouse	13,591	99.8%
	Tom Lingenfelter	12,278	32.8%	Write-in	27	0.2%
	Write-in	10				
	TOTAL	37,458		TOTAL	13,618	

PENNSYLVANIA

GENERAL AND PRIMARY ELECTIONS

	REPUBLICAN PRIMARIES			DEMOCRATIC PRIMARIES		
Congressional District 9	Bud Shuster*	37,252	99.6%	*No Democratic candidate filed for the primary.*		
	Write-in	153	0.4%	*There were 1,579 write-in votes cast,*		
	TOTAL	37,405		*1,180 for Republican Bud Shuster, who ran*		
				in the November general election with		
				the Democratic nomination.		
Congressional District 10	Don Sherwood*	33,933	99.8%	Pat Casey	24,210	82.2%
	Write-in	75	0.2%	Francis McHale	5,196	17.6%
				Write-in	61	0.2%
	TOTAL	34,008		TOTAL	29,467	
Congressional District 11	Stephen A. Urban	15,520	99.8%	Paul E. Kanjorski*	27,985	99.9%
	Write-in	27	0.2%	Write-in	20	0.1%
	TOTAL	15,547		TOTAL	28,005	
Congressional District 12	Bill Choby	23,630	99.7%	John P. Murtha*	40,484	99.9%
	Write-in	69	0.3%	Write-in	50	0.1%
	TOTAL	23,699		TOTAL	40,534	
Congressional District 13	Stewart J. Greenleaf	24,623	57.2%	Joseph M. Hoeffel*	20,749	100.0%
	John Coffey	18,427	42.8%			
	TOTAL	43,050		TOTAL	20,749	
Congressional District 14	*No Republican candidate filed for the primary.*			William J. Coyne*	44,187	99.9%
	There were 61 scattered write-in votes.			Write-in	24	0.1%
				TOTAL	44,211	
Congressional District 15	Pat Toomey*	21,487	100.0%	Ed O'Brien	18,093	99.9%
	Write-in	6		Write-in	10	0.1%
	TOTAL	21,493		TOTAL	18,103	
Congressional District 16	Joseph R. Pitts*	34,781	100.0%	Bob Yorczyk	9,517	100.0%
	Write-in	10		Write-in	4	
	TOTAL	34,791		TOTAL	9,521	
Congressional District 17	George W. Gekas*	45,221	99.9%	Leslye Hess Herrmann	14,356	99.9%
	Write-in	65	0.1%	Write-in	21	0.1%
	TOTAL	45,286		TOTAL	14,377	
Congressional District 18	Craig C. Stephens	15,311	99.8%	Mike Doyle*	47,827	99.9%
	Write-in	29	0.2%	Write-in	52	0.1%
	TOTAL	15,340		TOTAL	47,879	
Congressional District 19	Todd Platts	21,448	33.3%	Jeff Sanders	11,670	52.9%
	Al Masland	18,674	29.0%	John J. Moran II	10,057	45.6%
	Dick Stewart	11,973	18.6%	Write-in	325	1.5%
	Charlie Gerow	8,314	12.9%			
	Christopher B. Reilly	3,948	6.1%			
	Write-in	15				
	TOTAL	64,372		TOTAL	22,052	
Congressional District 20	Ronald J. Davis	16,038	99.8%	Frank R. Mascara*	47,462	99.9%
	Write-in	39	0.2%	Write-in	27	0.1%
	TOTAL	16,077		TOTAL	47,489	
Congressional District 21	Phil English*	31,058	100.0%	Marc A. Flitter	24,465	100.0%
	Write-in	1		Write-in	3	
	TOTAL	31,059		TOTAL	24,468	

RHODE ISLAND

GOVERNOR
Lincoln C. Almond (R). Re-elected 1998 to a four-year term. Previously elected 1994.

SENATORS
Lincoln Chafee (R). Elected 2000 to a six-year term. Previously appointed to complete the term of his late father, John Chafee, beginning Nov. 4, 1999.

Jack Reed (D). Elected 1996 to a six-year term.

REPRESENTATIVES
1. Patrick J. Kennedy (D)   2. James R. Langevin (D)

POSTWAR VOTE FOR PRESIDENT

		Republican		Democratic				Total Vote		Major Vote	
Year	Total Vote	Vote	Candidate	Vote	Candidate	Other Vote	Plurality	Rep.	Dem.	Rep.	Dem.
2000**	409,047	130,555	Bush, George W.	249,508	Gore, Al	28,984	118,953 D	31.9%	61.0%	34.4%	65.6%
1996**	390,284	104,683	Dole, Bob	233,050	Clinton, Bill	52,551	128,367 D	26.8%	59.7%	31.0%	69.0%
1992**	453,477	131,601	Bush, George	213,299	Clinton, Bill	108,577	81,698 D	29.0%	47.0%	38.2%	61.8%
1988	404,620	177,761	Bush, George	225,123	Dukakis, Michael S.	1,736	47,362 D	43.9%	55.6%	44.1%	55.9%
1984	410,492	212,080	Reagan, Ronald	197,106	Mondale, Walter F.	1,306	14,974 R	51.7%	48.0%	51.8%	48.2%
1980**	416,072	154,793	Reagan, Ronald	198,342	Carter, Jimmy	62,937	43,549 D	37.2%	47.7%	43.8%	56.2%
1976	411,170	181,249	Ford, Gerald R.	227,636	Carter, Jimmy	2,285	46,387 D	44.1%	55.4%	44.3%	55.7%
1972	415,808	220,383	Nixon, Richard M.	194,645	McGovern, George S.	780	25,738 R	53.0%	46.8%	53.1%	46.9%
1968	385,000	122,359	Nixon, Richard M.	246,518	Humphrey, Hubert H.	16,123	124,159 D	31.8%	64.0%	33.2%	66.8%
1964	390,091	74,615	Goldwater, Barry M.	315,463	Johnson, Lyndon B.	13	240,848 D	19.1%	80.9%	19.1%	80.9%
1960	405,535	147,502	Nixon, Richard M.	258,032	Kennedy, John F.	1	110,530 D	36.4%	63.6%	36.4%	63.6%
1956	387,609	225,819	Eisenhower, Dwight D.	161,790	Stevenson, Adlai E.		64,029 R	58.3%	41.7%	58.3%	41.7%
1952	414,498	210,935	Eisenhower, Dwight D.	203,293	Stevenson, Adlai E.	270	7,642 R	50.9%	49.0%	50.9%	49.1%
1948	327,702	135,787	Dewey, Thomas E.	188,736	Truman, Harry S.	3,179	52,949 D	41.4%	57.6%	41.8%	58.2%

In 2000 the other vote column includes 25,052 votes cast for Green (Nader). In 1996 the other vote column includes 43,723 votes cast for Perot. In 1992 the other vote column includes 105,045 votes cast for Perot. In 1980 the other column includes 59,819 votes for Independent (Anderson).

RHODE ISLAND

POSTWAR VOTE FOR GOVERNOR

Year	Total Vote	Republican Vote	Republican Candidate	Democratic Vote	Democratic Candidate	Other Vote	Rep.-Dem. Plurality	Total Vote Rep.	Total Vote Dem.	Major Vote Rep.	Major Vote Dem.
1998	306,445	156,180	Almond, Lincoln C.	129,105	York, Myrth	21,160	27,075 R	51.0%	42.1%	54.7%	45.3%
1994**	361,377	171,194	Almond, Lincoln C.	157,361	York, Myrth	32,822	13,833 R	47.4%	43.5%	52.1%	47.9%
1992	425,026	145,590	Leonard, Elizabeth Ann	261,484	Sundlun, Bruce G.	17,952	115,894 D	34.3%	61.5%	35.8%	64.2%
1990	356,672	92,177	DiPrete, Edward	264,411	Sundlun, Bruce G.	84	172,234 D	25.8%	74.1%	25.8%	74.2%
1988	400,516	203,550	DiPrete, Edward	196,936	Sundlun, Bruce G.	30	6,614 R	50.8%	49.2%	50.8%	49.2%
1986	322,724	208,822	DiPrete, Edward	104,508	Sundlun, Bruce G.	9,394	104,314 R	64.7%	32.4%	66.6%	33.4%
1984	408,375	245,059	DiPrete, Edward	163,311	Solomon, Anthony J.	5	81,748 R	60.0%	40.0%	60.0%	40.0%
1982	337,259	79,602	Marzullo, Vincent	247,208	Garrahy, J. Joseph	10,449	167,606 D	23.6%	73.3%	24.4%	75.6%
1980	405,916	106,729	Cianci, Vincent A.	299,174	Garrahy, J. Joseph	13	192,445 D	26.3%	73.7%	26.3%	73.7%
1978	314,363	96,596	Almond, Lincoln	197,386	Garrahy, J. Joseph	20,381	100,790 D	30.7%	62.8%	32.9%	67.1%
1976	398,683	178,254	Taft, James L.	218,561	Garrahy, J. Joseph	1,868	40,307 D	44.7%	54.8%	44.9%	55.1%
1974	321,660	69,224	Nugent, James W.	252,436	Noel, Philip W.		183,212 D	21.5%	78.5%	21.5%	78.5%
1972	412,866	194,315	DeSimone, Herbert F.	216,953	Noel, Philip W.	1,598	22,638 D	47.1%	52.5%	47.2%	52.8%
1970	346,342	171,549	DeSimone, Herbert F.	173,420	Licht, Frank	1,373	1,871 D	49.5%	50.1%	49.7%	50.3%
1968	383,725	187,958	Chafee, John H.	195,766	Licht, Frank	1	7,808 D	49.0%	51.0%	49.0%	51.0%
1966	332,064	210,202	Chafee, John H.	121,862	Hobbs, Horace E.		88,340 R	63.3%	36.7%	63.3%	36.7%
1964	391,668	239,501	Chafee, John H.	152,165	Gallogly, Edward P.	2	87,336 R	61.1%	38.9%	61.1%	38.9%
1962	327,506	163,952	Chafee, John H.	163,554	Notte, John A.		398 R	50.1%	49.9%	50.1%	49.9%
1960	401,362	174,044	Del Sesto, Christopher	227,318	Notte, John A.		53,274 D	43.4%	56.6%	43.4%	56.6%
1958	346,780	176,505	Del Sesto, Christopher	170,275	Roberts, Dennis J.		6,230 R	50.9%	49.1%	50.9%	49.1%
1956	383,919	191,604	Del Sesto, Christopher	192,315	Roberts, Dennis J.		711 D	49.9%	50.1%	49.9%	50.1%
1954	328,670	137,131	Lewis, Dean J.	189,595	Roberts, Dennis J.	1,944	52,464 D	41.7%	57.7%	42.0%	58.0%
1952	409,689	194,102	Archambault, Raoul	215,587	Roberts, Dennis J.		21,485 D	47.4%	52.6%	47.4%	52.6%
1950	296,809	120,684	Lachapelle, E. T.	176,125	Roberts, Dennis J.		55,441 D	40.7%	59.3%	40.7%	59.3%
1948	323,863	124,441	Ruerat, Albert P.	198,056	Pastore, John O.	1,366	73,615 D	38.4%	61.2%	38.6%	61.4%
1946	275,341	126,456	Murphy, John G.	148,885	Pastore, John O.		22,429 D	45.9%	54.1%	45.9%	54.1%

The term of office of Rhode Island's Governor was increased to four from two years effective with the 1994 election.

POSTWAR VOTE FOR SENATOR

Year	Total Vote	Republican Vote	Republican Candidate	Democratic Vote	Democratic Candidate	Other Vote	Rep.-Dem. Plurality	Total Vote Rep.	Total Vote Dem.	Major Vote Rep.	Major Vote Dem.
2000	391,537	222,588	Chafee, Lincoln	161,023	Weygand, Bob	7,926	61,565 R	56.8%	41.1%	58.0%	42.0%
1996	363,378	127,368	Mayer, Nancy	230,676	Reed, John F.	5,334	103,308 D	35.1%	63.5%	35.6%	64.4%
1994	345,388	222,856	Chafee, John H.	122,532	Kushner, Linda J.		100,324 R	64.5%	35.5%	64.5%	35.5%
1990	364,062	138,947	Schneider, Claudine	225,105	Pell, Claiborne	10	86,158 D	38.2%	61.8%	38.2%	61.8%
1988	397,996	217,273	Chafee, John H.	180,717	Licht, Richard A.	6	36,556 R	54.6%	45.4%	54.6%	45.4%
1984	395,285	108,492	Leonard, Barbara	286,780	Pell, Claiborne	13	178,288 D	27.4%	72.6%	27.4%	72.6%
1982	342,779	175,495	Chafee, John H.	167,283	Michaelson, Julius C.	1	8,212 R	51.2%	48.8%	51.2%	48.8%
1978	305,618	76,061	Reynolds, James G.	229,557	Pell, Claiborne		153,496 D	24.9%	75.1%	24.9%	75.1%
1976	398,906	230,329	Chafee, John H.	167,665	Lorber, Richard P.	912	62,664 R	57.7%	42.0%	57.9%	42.1%
1972	413,432	188,990	Chafee, John H.	221,942	Pell, Claiborne	2,500	32,952 D	45.7%	53.7%	46.0%	54.0%
1970	341,222	107,351	McLaughlin, John	230,469	Pastore, John O.	3,402	123,118 D	31.5%	67.5%	31.8%	68.2%
1966	324,173	104,838	Briggs, Ruth M.	219,331	Pell, Claiborne	4	114,493 D	32.3%	67.7%	32.3%	67.7%
1964	386,322	66,715	Lagueux, Ronald R.	319,607	Pastore, John O.		252,892 D	17.3%	82.7%	17.3%	82.7%
1960	399,983	124,408	Archambault, Raoul	275,575	Pell, Claiborne		151,167 D	31.1%	68.9%	31.1%	68.9%
1958	344,519	122,353	Ewing, Bayard	222,166	Pastore, John O.		99,813 D	35.5%	64.5%	35.5%	64.5%
1954	326,624	132,970	Sundlun, Walter I.	193,654	Green, Theodore F.		60,684 D	40.7%	59.3%	40.7%	59.3%
1952	410,978	185,850	Ewing, Bayard	225,128	Pastore, John O.		39,278 D	45.2%	54.8%	45.2%	54.8%
1950S	297,909	114,184	Levy, Austin T.	183,725	Pastore, John O.		69,541 D	38.3%	61.7%	38.3%	61.7%
1948	320,420	130,262	Hazard, Thomas P.	190,158	Green, Theodore F.		59,896 D	40.7%	59.3%	40.7%	59.3%
1946	273,528	122,780	Dyer, W. Gurnee	150,748	McGrath, J. Howard		27,968 D	44.9%	55.1%	44.9%	55.1%

The 1950 election was for a short term to fill a vacancy.

RHODE ISLAND

Districts Established May 22, 1992

Woonsocket

1

PROVIDENCE

Pawtucket

North Providence

Providence

Cranston

Warwick

BRISTOL

Bristol

2

KENT

NEWPORT (PT)

NEWPORT (PART)

NEWPORT (PT)

NEWPORT (PART)

WASHINGTON

Kingston

Newport

Westerly

2

NEW SHOREHAM

RHODE ISLAND

PRESIDENT 2000

2000 Census Population	County	Total Vote	Republican	Democratic	Green (Nader)	Other	Rep.-Dem. Plurality	Percentage of Total Vote		
								Rep.	Dem.	Green
50,648	BRISTOL	23,252	8,375	13,424	1,283	170	5,049 D	36.0%	57.7%	5.5%
167,090	KENT	73,414	25,291	43,265	4,140	718	17,974 D	34.4%	58.9%	5.6%
85,433	NEWPORT	37,796	14,258	20,790	2,427	321	6,532 D	37.7%	55.0%	6.4%
621,602	PROVIDENCE	218,160	61,378	142,469	12,352	1,961	81,091 D	28.1%	65.3%	5.7%
123,546	WASHINGTON	56,161	21,253	29,560	4,850	498	8,307 D	37.8%	52.6%	8.6%
1,048,319	TOTAL	409,047	130,555	249,508	25,052	3,932	118,953 D	31.9%	61.0%	6.1%

Note: The statewide totals for "Total Vote" and "Other" include 264 scattered write-in votes that are not included in the county-by-county results.

2000 Census Population	City/Town	Total Vote	Republican	Democratic	Green (Nader)	Other	Rep.-Dem. Plurality	Rep.	Dem.	Green
16,819	BARRINGTON	9,071	3,864	4,585	556	66	721 D	42.6%	50.5%	6.1%
22,469	BRISTOL TOWN	9,519	3,065	5,914	459	81	2,849 D	32.2%	62.1%	4.8%
15,796	BURRILLVILLE	5,870	2,228	3,211	354	77	983 D	38.0%	54.7%	6.0%
18,928	CENTRAL FALLS	3,478	611	2,750	91	26	2,139 D	17.6%	79.1%	2.6%
7,859	CHARLESTOWN	3,625	1,456	1,780	359	30	324 D	40.2%	49.1%	9.9%
33,668	COVENTRY	14,488	5,111	8,415	807	155	3,304 D	35.3%	58.1%	5.6%
79,269	CRANSTON	33,608	10,420	21,204	1,701	283	10,784 D	31.0%	63.1%	5.1%
31,840	CUMBERLAND	14,538	5,129	8,521	776	112	3,392 D	35.3%	58.6%	5.3%
12,948	EAST GREENWICH	6,468	3,039	2,961	414	54	78 R	47.0%	45.8%	6.4%
48,688	EAST PROVIDENCE	19,268	5,072	13,033	1,011	152	7,961 D	26.3%	67.6%	5.2%
6,045	EXETER	2,658	1,097	1,298	235	28	201 D	41.3%	48.8%	8.8%
4,274	FOSTER	2,081	827	1,049	188	17	222 D	39.7%	50.4%	9.0%
9,948	GLOCESTER	4,297	1,765	2,167	317	48	402 D	41.1%	50.4%	7.4%
7,836	HOPKINTON	3,133	1,274	1,575	237	47	301 D	40.7%	50.3%	7.6%
5,622	JAMESTOWN	3,347	1,224	1,789	304	30	565 D	36.6%	53.5%	9.1%
28,195	JOHNSTON	13,666	4,054	9,013	493	106	4,959 D	29.7%	66.0%	3.6%
20,898	LINCOLN	10,229	3,850	5,733	572	74	1,883 D	37.6%	56.0%	5.6%
3,593	LITTLE COMPTON	2,118	930	987	174	27	57 D	43.9%	46.6%	8.2%
17,334	MIDDLETOWN	7,079	2,794	3,825	405	55	1,031 D	39.5%	54.0%	5.7%
16,361	NARRAGANSETT	8,007	2,753	4,447	758	49	1,694 D	34.4%	55.5%	9.5%
26,475	NEWPORT CITY	9,892	3,312	5,833	673	74	2,521 D	33.5%	59.0%	6.8%
1,010	NEW SHOREHAM	1,036	320	594	107	15	274 D	30.9%	57.3%	10.3%
26,326	NORTH KINGSTOWN	12,922	5,385	6,461	953	123	1,076 D	41.7%	50.0%	7.4%
32,411	NORTH PROVIDENCE	14,961	4,015	10,190	631	125	6,175 D	26.8%	68.1%	4.2%
10,618	NORTH SMITHFIELD	5,383	2,054	2,956	329	44	902 D	38.2%	54.9%	6.1%
72,958	PAWTUCKET	21,397	4,598	15,429	1,142	228	10,831 D	21.5%	72.1%	5.3%
17,149	PORTSMOUTH	8,826	3,703	4,549	509	65	846 D	42.0%	51.5%	5.8%
173,618	PROVIDENCE CITY	43,410	7,669	31,979	3,364	398	24,310 D	17.7%	73.7%	7.7%
7,222	RICHMOND	3,025	1,125	1,591	274	35	466 D	37.2%	52.6%	9.1%
10,324	SCITUATE	5,073	2,346	2,340	336	51	6 R	46.2%	46.1%	6.6%
20,613	SMITHFIELD	9,061	3,433	5,000	552	76	1,567 D	37.9%	55.2%	6.1%
27,921	SOUTH KINGSTOWN	11,822	4,050	6,290	1,404	78	2,240 D	34.3%	53.2%	11.9%
15,260	TIVERTON	6,534	2,295	3,807	362	70	1,512 D	35.1%	58.3%	5.5%
11,360	WARREN	4,662	1,446	2,925	268	23	1,479 D	31.0%	62.7%	5.7%
85,808	WARWICK	39,358	12,741	23,948	2,283	386	11,207 D	32.4%	60.8%	5.8%
22,966	WESTERLY	9,933	3,793	5,524	523	93	1,731 D	38.2%	55.6%	5.3%
5,085	WEST GREENWICH	2,363	1,035	1,140	171	17	105 D	43.8%	48.2%	7.2%
29,581	WEST WARWICK	10,737	3,365	6,801	465	106	3,436 D	31.3%	63.3%	4.3%
43,224	WOONSOCKET	11,840	3,307	7,894	495	144	4,587 D	27.9%	66.7%	4.2%
1,048,319	TOTAL	409,047	130,555	249,508	25,052	3,932	118,953 D	31.9%	61.0%	6.1%

Note: The statewide totals for "Total Vote" and "Other" include 264 scattered write-in votes that are not included in the city/town results.

RHODE ISLAND

SENATOR 2000

2000 Census Population	County	Total Vote	Republican	Democratic	Other	Rep.-Dem. Plurality		Percentage			
								Total Vote		Major Vote	
								Rep.	Dem.	Rep.	Dem.
50,648	BRISTOL	22,113	13,537	8,163	413	5,374	R	61.2%	36.9%	62.4%	37.6%
167,090	KENT	71,581	44,714	25,593	1,274	19,121	R	62.5%	35.8%	63.6%	36.4%
85,433	NEWPORT	35,716	22,673	12,307	736	10,366	R	63.5%	34.5%	64.8%	35.2%
621,602	PROVIDENCE	208,246	108,904	95,193	4,149	13,711	R	52.3%	45.7%	53.4%	46.6%
123,546	WASHINGTON	53,697	32,760	19,767	1,170	12,993	R	61.0%	36.8%	62.4%	37.6%
1,048,319	TOTAL	391,537	222,588	161,023	7,926	61,565	R	56.8%	41.1%	58.0%	42.0%

Note: The statewide totals for "Total Vote" and "Other" include 184 scattered write-in votes that are not included in the county-by-county returns.

	City/Town										
16,819	BARRINGTON	8,661	5,984	2,543	134	3,441	R	69.1%	29.4%	70.2%	29.8%
22,469	BRISTOL TOWN	9,001	5,068	3,764	169	1,304	R	56.3%	41.8%	57.4%	42.6%
15,796	BURRILLVILLE	5,655	3,469	2,023	163	1,446	R	61.3%	35.8%	63.2%	36.8%
18,928	CENTRAL FALLS	3,157	1,231	1,875	51	644	D	39.0%	59.4%	39.6%	60.4%
7,859	CHARLESTOWN	3,494	2,275	1,130	89	1,145	R	65.1%	32.3%	66.8%	33.2%
33,668	COVENTRY	14,077	8,281	5,461	335	2,820	R	58.8%	38.8%	60.3%	39.7%
79,269	CRANSTON	32,753	18,227	13,952	574	4,275	R	55.6%	42.6%	56.6%	43.4%
31,840	CUMBERLAND	14,160	8,107	5,803	250	2,304	R	57.3%	41.0%	58.3%	41.7%
12,948	EAST GREENWICH	6,210	4,437	1,699	74	2,738	R	71.4%	27.4%	72.3%	27.7%
48,688	EAST PROVIDENCE	18,554	8,787	9,450	317	663	D	47.4%	50.9%	48.2%	51.8%
6,045	EXETER	2,586	1,741	780	65	961	R	67.3%	30.2%	69.1%	30.9%
4,274	FOSTER	2,017	1,377	570	70	807	R	68.3%	28.3%	70.7%	29.3%
9,948	GLOCESTER	4,168	2,595	1,453	120	1,142	R	62.3%	34.9%	64.1%	35.9%
7,836	HOPKINTON	3,061	1,965	979	117	986	R	64.2%	32.0%	66.7%	33.3%
5,622	JAMESTOWN	3,199	2,179	953	67	1,226	R	68.1%	29.8%	69.6%	30.4%
28,195	JOHNSTON	13,356	6,828	6,280	248	548	R	51.1%	47.0%	52.1%	47.9%
20,898	LINCOLN	9,992	6,243	3,577	172	2,666	R	62.5%	35.8%	63.6%	36.4%
3,593	LITTLE COMPTON	2,065	1,417	607	41	810	R	68.6%	29.4%	70.0%	30.0%
17,334	MIDDLETOWN	6,582	4,208	2,234	140	1,974	R	63.9%	33.9%	65.3%	34.7%
16,361	NARRAGANSETT	7,594	4,435	3,009	150	1,426	R	58.4%	39.6%	59.6%	40.4%
26,475	NEWPORT CITY	9,119	5,511	3,435	173	2,076	R	60.4%	37.7%	61.6%	38.4%
1,010	NEW SHOREHAM	1,005	692	287	26	405	R	68.9%	28.6%	70.7%	29.3%
26,326	NORTH KINGSTOWN	12,455	7,797	4,459	199	3,338	R	62.6%	35.8%	63.6%	36.4%
32,411	NORTH PROVIDENCE	14,592	7,488	6,857	247	631	R	51.3%	47.0%	52.2%	47.8%
10,618	NORTH SMITHFIELD	5,209	3,278	1,829	102	1,449	R	62.9%	35.1%	64.2%	35.8%
72,958	PAWTUCKET	20,226	9,963	9,812	451	151	R	49.3%	48.5%	50.4%	49.6%
17,149	PORTSMOUTH	8,481	5,631	2,694	156	2,937	R	66.4%	31.8%	67.6%	32.4%
173,618	PROVIDENCE CITY	39,290	17,140	21,267	883	4,127	D	43.6%	54.1%	44.6%	55.4%
7,222	RICHMOND	2,869	1,798	999	72	799	R	62.7%	34.8%	64.3%	35.7%
10,324	SCITUATE	4,971	3,331	1,528	112	1,803	R	67.0%	30.7%	68.6%	31.4%
20,613	SMITHFIELD	8,790	5,118	3,523	149	1,595	R	58.2%	40.1%	59.2%	40.8%
27,921	SOUTH KINGSTOWN	11,203	6,867	4,090	246	2,777	R	61.3%	36.5%	62.7%	37.3%
15,260	TIVERTON	6,270	3,727	2,384	159	1,343	R	59.4%	38.0%	61.0%	39.0%
11,360	WARREN	4,451	2,485	1,856	110	629	R	55.8%	41.7%	57.2%	42.8%
85,808	WARWICK	38,610	24,875	13,156	579	11,719	R	64.4%	34.1%	65.4%	34.6%
22,966	WESTERLY	9,430	5,190	4,034	206	1,156	R	55.0%	42.8%	56.3%	43.7%
5,085	WEST GREENWICH	2,277	1,554	667	56	887	R	68.2%	29.3%	70.0%	30.0%
29,581	WEST WARWICK	10,407	5,567	4,610	230	957	R	53.5%	44.3%	54.7%	45.3%
43,224	WOONSOCKET	11,356	5,722	5,394	240	328	R	50.4%	47.5%	51.5%	48.5%
1,048,319	TOTAL	391,537	222,588	161,023	7,926	61,565	R	56.8%	41.1%	58.0%	42.0%

Note: The statewide totals for "Total Vote" and "Other" include 184 scattered write-in votes that are not included in the city/town returns.

RHODE ISLAND

CONGRESS

CD	Year	Total Vote	Republican Vote	Republican Candidate	Democratic Vote	Democratic Candidate	Other Vote	Rep.-Dem. Plurality	Total Vote Rep.	Total Vote Dem.	Major Vote Rep.	Major Vote Dem.
1	2000	185,163	61,522	CABRAL, STEPHEN	123,442	KENNEDY, PATRICK J.	199	61,920 D	33.2%	66.7%	33.3%	66.7%
1	1998	138,895	38,460	SANTA, RONALD G.	92,788	KENNEDY, PATRICK J.	7,647	54,328 D	27.7%	66.8%	29.3%	70.7%
1	1996	175,428	49,199	CICIONE, GIOVANNI D.	121,781	KENNEDY, PATRICK J.	4,448	72,582 D	28.0%	69.4%	28.8%	71.2%
1	1994	165,901	76,069	VIGILANTE, KEVIN	89,832	KENNEDY, PATRICK J.		13,763 D	45.9%	54.1%	45.9%	54.1%
1	1992	194,089	135,982	MACHTLEY, RONALD K.	48,092	CARLIN, DAVID R.	10,015	87,890 R	70.1%	24.8%	73.9%	26.1%
2	2000	198,964	27,932	TINGLE, ROBERT G.	123,805	LANGEVIN, JAMES R.	47,227	95,873 D	14.0%	62.2%	18.4%	81.6%
2	1998	154,053	38,170	MATSON, JOHN O.	110,917	WEYGAND, ROBERT A.	4,966	72,747 D	24.8%	72.0%	25.6%	74.4%
2	1996	184,322	58,458	WILD, RICHARD E.	118,827	WEYGAND, ROBERT A.	7,037	60,369 D	31.7%	64.5%	33.0%	67.0%
2	1994	176,007	56,348	ELLIOT, A. JOHN	119,659	REED, JOHN F.		63,311 D	32.0%	68.0%	32.0%	68.0%
2	1992	204,413	49,998	BELL, JAMES W.	144,450	REED, JOHN F.	9,965	94,452 D	24.5%	70.7%	25.7%	74.3%

RHODE ISLAND

GENERAL AND PRIMARY ELECTIONS

2000 GENERAL ELECTIONS

President Other vote was 2,273 Reform (Buchanan); 742 Libertarian (Browne); 271 Natural Law (Hagelin); 199 Workers World (Moorehead); 97 Constitution (Phillips); 52 Socialist (McReynolds); 34 Socialist Workers (Harris); 264 scattered write-in.

Senator Other vote was 4,107 Reform (Young); 3,635 Independent (Proulx); 184 scattered write-in.

Congress Other vote was: CD 1: 199 scattered write-in; CD 2: 42,625 Conscience for Congress (Driver), 4,536 Green (Hayes), 66 scattered write-in.

2000 PRIMARY ELECTIONS

Primary March 7, 2000 (President)
September 12, 2000 (Congress)

Registration (as of Sept. 12, 2000) 634,300 Party registration totals traditionally have been kept only at the local level.

Primary Type Modified—Registered Democrats and Republicans could vote only in their party's primary. Unaffiliated voters could vote in either party's primary if they were willing to become a member of that party.

Note: An asterisk (*) denotes incumbent.

REPUBLICAN PRIMARIES			DEMOCRATIC PRIMARIES		
President John McCain	21,754	60.2%	Al Gore	26,801	56.9%
George W. Bush	13,170	36.4%	Bill Bradley	19,000	40.4%
Alan Keyes	923	2.6%	Uncommitted	844	1.8%
Uncommitted	114	0.3%	Lyndon H. LaRouche Jr.	199	0.4%
Steve Forbes	89	0.2%	Write-In	235	0.5%
Gary Bauer	35	0.1%			
Orrin G. Hatch	35	0.1%			
Write-In	23	0.1%			
TOTAL	36,143		TOTAL	47,079	

RHODE ISLAND

GENERAL AND PRIMARY ELECTIONS

	REPUBLICAN PRIMARIES			DEMOCRATIC PRIMARIES		
Senator	Lincoln D. Chafee*	2,221	100.0%	Robert A. Weygand	51,769	57.5%
				Richard A. Licht	38,281	42.5%
	TOTAL	2,221		TOTAL	90,050	
Congressional District 1	Stephen Cabral	645	100.0%	Patrick J. Kennedy*	32,865	100.0%
	TOTAL	645		TOTAL	32,865	
Congressional District 2	Robert G. Tingle	775	100.0%	James R. Langevin	22,955	47.2%
				Kathleen Coyne-McCoy	14,219	29.3%
				Angel Taveras	5,803	11.9%
				Kevin J. McAllister	5,633	11.6%
	TOTAL	775		TOTAL	48,610	

SOUTH CAROLINA

GOVERNOR
James H. Hodges (D). Elected 1998 to a four-year term.

SENATORS
Ernest F. Hollings (D). Re-elected 1998 to a six-year term. Previously elected 1992, 1986, 1980, 1974, 1968 and in 1966 to fill out term vacated by the death of Senator Olin D. Johnston (D).

Strom Thurmond (R). Re-elected 1996 to a six-year term. Previously elected 1990, 1984, 1978, 1972, 1966, 1960 and in 1956 to fill out term vacated by his own resignation in April 1956; had been elected to this term in 1954 as an Independent Democrat. Changed party affiliation from Democrat to Republican in September 1964.

REPRESENTATIVES
1. Henry Brown (R)
2. Floyd Spence (R)
3. Lindsey Graham (R)
4. Jim DeMint (R)
5. John Spratt (D)
6. James E. Clyburn (D)

POSTWAR VOTE FOR PRESIDENT

| | | Republican | | Democratic | | Other | | Percentage | | | |
| | Total | | | | | | | Total Vote | | Major Vote | |
Year	Vote	Vote	Candidate	Vote	Candidate	Vote	Plurality	Rep.	Dem.	Rep.	Dem.
2000**	1,382,717	785,937	Bush, George W.	565,561	Gore, Al	31,219	220,376 R	56.8%	40.9%	58.2%	41.8%
1996**	1,151,689	573,458	Dole, Bob	506,283	Clinton, Bill	71,948	67,175 R	49.8%	44.0%	53.1%	46.9%
1992**	1,202,527	577,507	Bush, George	479,514	Clinton, Bill	145,506	97,993 R	48.0%	39.9%	54.6%	45.4%
1988	986,009	606,443	Bush, George	370,554	Dukakis, Michael S.	9,012	235,889 R	61.5%	37.6%	62.1%	37.9%
1984	968,529	615,539	Reagan, Ronald	344,459	Mondale, Walter F.	8,531	271,080 R	63.6%	35.6%	64.1%	35.9%
1980**	894,071	441,841	Reagan, Ronald	430,385	Carter, Jimmy	21,845	11,456 R	49.4%	48.1%	50.7%	49.3%
1976	802,583	346,149	Ford, Gerald R.	450,807	Carter, Jimmy	5,627	104,658 D	43.1%	56.2%	43.4%	56.6%
1972	673,960	477,044	Nixon, Richard M.	186,824	McGovern, George S.	10,092	290,220 R	70.8%	27.7%	71.9%	28.1%
1968**	666,978	254,062	Nixon, Richard M.	197,486	Humphrey, Hubert H.	215,430	38,632 R	38.1%	29.6%	56.3%	43.7%
1964	524,779	309,048	Goldwater, Barry M.	215,723	Johnson, Lyndon B.	8	93,325 R	58.9%	41.1%	58.9%	41.1%
1960	386,688	188,558	Nixon, Richard M.	198,129	Kennedy, John F.	1	9,571 D	48.8%	51.2%	48.8%	51.2%
1956**	300,583	75,700	Eisenhower, Dwight D.	136,372	Stevenson, Adlai E.	88,511	47,863 D	25.2%	45.4%	35.7%	64.3%
1952	341,087	168,082	Eisenhower, Dwight D.	173,004	Stevenson, Adlai E.	1	4,922 D	49.3%	50.7%	49.3%	50.7%
1948**	142,571	5,386	Dewey, Thomas E.	34,423	Truman, Harry S.	102,762	68,184 SR	3.8%	24.1%	13.5%	86.5%

In 2000 the other vote column includes 20,200 votes cast for Green (Nader). In 1996 the other vote column includes 64,386 votes cast for Perot. In 1992 the other vote column includes 138,872 votes cast for Perot. In 1980 the other column includes 14,153 votes for Independent (Anderson). In 1968 other vote was Independent (Wallace). In 1956 other vote was 88,509 Independent (Uncommitted States Rights) and 2 scattered. In 1948 other vote was 102,607 States Rights; 154 Progressive and 1 Socialist.

SOUTH CAROLINA

POSTWAR VOTE FOR GOVERNOR

Year	Total Vote	Republican Vote	Republican Candidate	Democratic Vote	Democratic Candidate	Other Vote	Rep.-Dem. Plurality	Total Vote Rep.	Total Vote Dem.	Major Vote Rep.	Major Vote Dem.
1998	1,070,869	484,088	Beasley, David	570,070	Hodges, James H.	16,711	85,982 D	45.2%	53.2%	45.9%	54.1%
1994	933,850	470,756	Beasley, David	447,002	Theodore, Nick A.	16,092	23,754 R	50.4%	47.9%	51.3%	48.7%
1990	760,965	528,831	Campbell, Carroll	212,034	Mitchell, Theo	20,100	316,797 R	69.5%	27.9%	71.4%	28.6%
1986	753,751	384,565	Campbell, Carroll	361,325	Daniel, Mike	7,861	23,240 R	51.0%	47.9%	51.6%	48.4%
1982	671,625	202,806	Workman, W. D.	468,819	Riley, Richard W.		266,013 D	30.2%	69.8%	30.2%	69.8%
1978	627,182	236,946	Young, Edward L.	384,898	Riley, Richard W.	5,338	147,952 D	37.8%	61.4%	38.1%	61.9%
1974	523,199	266,109	Edwards, James B.	248,938	Dorn, W. J. Bryan	8,152	17,171 R	50.9%	47.6%	51.7%	48.3%
1970	484,857	221,233	Watson, Albert W.	250,551	West, John C.	13,073	29,318 D	45.6%	51.7%	46.9%	53.1%
1966	439,942	184,088	Rogers, Joseph O.	255,854	McNair, Robert E.		71,766 D	41.8%	58.2%	41.8%	58.2%
1962	253,721	—		253,704	Russell, Donald S.	17	253,704 D		100.0%		100.0%
1958	77,740	—		77,714	Hollings, Ernest F.	26	77,714 D		100.0%		100.0%
1954	214,212	—		214,204	Timmerman, George B.	8	214,204 D		100.0%		100.0%
1950	50,642	—		50,633	Byrnes, James F.	9	50,633 D		100.0%		100.0%
1946	26,520	—		26,520	Thurmond, Strom		26,520 D		100.0%		100.0%

POSTWAR VOTE FOR SENATOR

Year	Total Vote	Republican Vote	Republican Candidate	Democratic Vote	Democratic Candidate	Other Vote	Plurality	Total Vote Rep.	Total Vote Dem.	Major Vote Rep.	Major Vote Dem.
1998	1,068,367	488,132	Inglis, Robert D.	562,791	Hollings, Ernest F.	17,444	74,659 D	45.7%	52.7%	46.4%	53.6%
1996	1,161,372	619,859	Thurmond, Strom	510,951	Close, Elliott Springs	30,562	108,908 R	53.4%	44.0%	54.8%	45.2%
1992	1,180,438	554,175	Hartnett, Thomas F.	591,030	Hollings, Ernest F.	35,233	36,855 D	46.9%	50.1%	48.4%	51.6%
1990	750,716	482,032	Thurmond, Strom	244,112	Cunningham, Bob	24,572	237,920 R	64.2%	32.5%	66.4%	33.6%
1986	737,962	262,886	McMaster, Henry D.	465,500	Hollings, Ernest F.	9,576	202,614 D	35.6%	63.1%	36.1%	63.9%
1984	965,130	644,815	Thurmond, Strom	306,982	Purvis, Melvin	13,333	337,833 R	66.8%	31.8%	67.7%	32.3%
1980	870,594	257,946	Mays, Marshall T.	612,554	Hollings, Ernest F.	94	354,608 D	29.6%	70.4%	29.6%	70.4%
1978	632,852	351,733	Thurmond, Strom	281,119	Ravenel, Charles D.		70,614 R	55.6%	44.4%	55.6%	44.4%
1974	512,397	146,645	Bush, Gwenyfred	356,126	Hollings, Ernest F.	9,626	209,481 D	28.6%	69.5%	29.2%	70.8%
1972	672,246	426,601	Thurmond, Strom	245,457	Zeigler, Eugene N.	188	181,144 R	63.5%	36.5%	63.5%	36.5%
1968	652,855	248,780	Parker, Marshall	404,060	Hollings, Ernest F.	15	155,280 D	38.1%	61.9%	38.1%	61.9%
1966	436,252	271,297	Thurmond, Strom	164,955	Morrah, Bradley		106,342 R	62.2%	37.8%	62.2%	37.8%
1966S	435,822	212,032	Parker, Marshall	223,790	Hollings, Ernest F.		11,758 D	48.7%	51.3%	48.7%	51.3%
1962	312,647	133,930	Workman, W. D.	178,712	Johnston, Olin D.	5	44,782 D	42.8%	57.2%	42.8%	57.2%
1960	330,266		—	330,164	Thurmond, Strom	102	330,164 D		100.0%		100.0%
1956	279,845	49,695	Crawford, Leon P.	230,150	Johnston, Olin D.		180,455 D	17.8%	82.2%	17.8%	82.2%
1956S	251,907		—	251,907	Thurmond, Strom		251,907 D		100.0%		100.0%
1954**	227,232		—	83,525	Brown, Edgar A.	143,707	59,919 ID		36.8%		100.0%
1950	50,277		—	50,240	Johnston, Olin D.	37	50,240 D		99.9%		100.0%
1948	141,006	5,008	Gerald, J. Bates	135,998	Maybank, Burnet R.		130,990 D	3.6%	96.4%	3.6%	96.4%

One each of the 1966 and 1956 elections was for a short term to fill a vacancy. In 1954 Strom Thurmond polled 143,444 votes as an Independent Democratic write-in candidate (63.1% of the total vote) and won the election with a 59,919-vote plurality.

SOUTH CAROLINA

Districts Established May 31, 1994

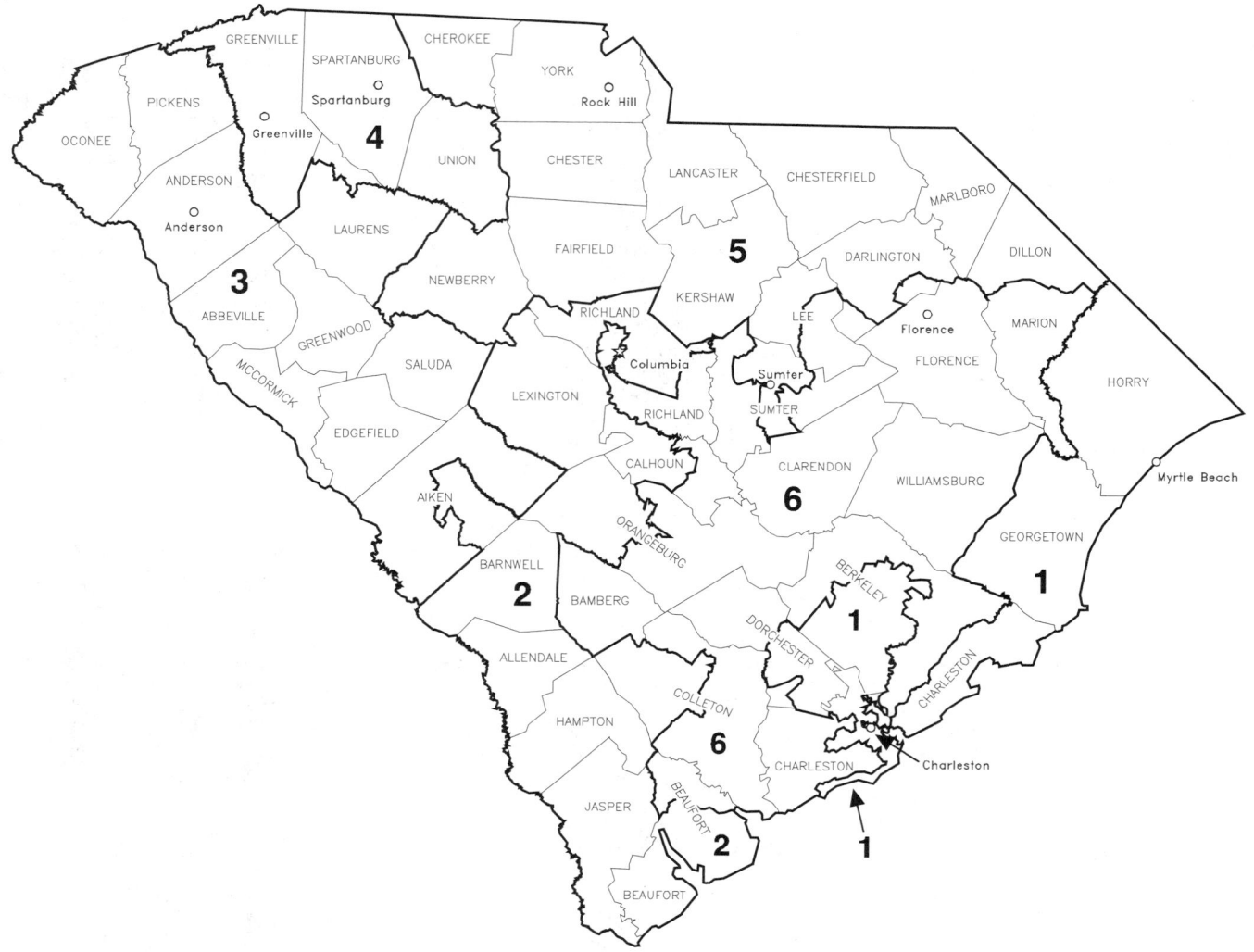

SOUTH CAROLINA

PRESIDENT 2000

2000 Census Population	County	Total Vote	Republican	Democratic	Green (Nader)	Other	Rep.-Dem. Plurality	Percentage of Total Vote		
								Rep.	Dem.	Green
26,167	ABBEVILLE	8,374	4,450	3,766	66	92	684 R	53.1%	45.0%	0.8%
142,552	AIKEN	50,782	33,203	16,409	676	494	16,794 R	65.4%	32.3%	1.3%
11,211	ALLENDALE	3,340	967	2,338	17	18	1,371 D	29.0%	70.0%	0.5%
165,740	ANDERSON	56,681	35,827	19,606	777	471	16,221 R	63.2%	34.6%	1.4%
16,658	BAMBERG	5,551	2,047	3,451	19	34	1,404 D	36.9%	62.2%	0.3%
23,478	BARNWELL	8,276	4,521	3,661	43	51	860 R	54.6%	44.2%	0.5%
120,937	BEAUFORT	44,148	25,561	17,487	846	254	8,074 R	57.9%	39.6%	1.9%
142,651	BERKELEY	43,316	24,796	17,707	464	349	7,089 R	57.2%	40.9%	1.1%
15,185	CALHOUN	6,373	3,216	3,063	60	34	153 R	50.5%	48.1%	0.9%
309,969	CHARLESTON	111,476	58,229	49,520	2,631	1,096	8,709 R	52.2%	44.4%	2.4%
52,537	CHEROKEE	16,323	9,900	6,138	144	141	3,762 R	60.7%	37.6%	0.9%
34,068	CHESTER	10,432	4,986	5,242	98	106	256 D	47.8%	50.2%	0.9%
42,768	CHESTERFIELD	12,526	6,266	6,111	105	44	155 R	50.0%	48.8%	0.8%
32,502	CLARENDON	11,290	5,186	5,999	64	41	813 D	45.9%	53.1%	0.6%
38,264	COLLETON	13,390	6,767	6,449	104	70	318 R	50.5%	48.2%	0.8%
67,394	DARLINGTON	21,863	11,290	10,253	166	154	1,037 R	51.6%	46.9%	0.8%
30,722	DILLON	8,990	3,975	4,930	46	39	955 D	44.2%	54.8%	0.5%
96,413	DORCHESTER	33,641	20,734	12,168	476	263	8,566 R	61.6%	36.2%	1.4%
24,595	EDGEFIELD	8,834	4,760	3,950	65	59	810 R	53.9%	44.7%	0.7%
23,454	FAIRFIELD	8,398	3,011	5,263	70	54	2,252 D	35.9%	62.7%	0.8%
125,761	FLORENCE	41,437	23,678	17,157	394	208	6,521 R	57.1%	41.4%	1.0%
55,797	GEORGETOWN	20,351	10,535	9,445	270	101	1,090 R	51.8%	46.4%	1.3%
379,616	GREENVILLE	140,293	92,714	43,810	2,388	1,381	48,904 R	66.1%	31.2%	1.7%
66,271	GREENWOOD	20,860	12,193	8,139	263	265	4,054 R	58.5%	39.0%	1.3%
21,386	HAMPTON	7,759	2,798	4,896	39	26	2,098 D	36.1%	63.1%	0.5%
196,629	HORRY	71,265	40,300	29,113	1,405	447	11,187 R	56.5%	40.9%	2.0%
20,678	JASPER	6,469	2,414	3,646	134	275	1,232 D	37.3%	56.4%	2.1%
52,647	KERSHAW	19,677	11,911	7,428	211	127	4,483 R	60.5%	37.7%	1.1%
61,351	LANCASTER	20,705	11,676	8,782	161	86	2,894 R	56.4%	42.4%	0.8%
69,567	LAURENS	20,410	12,102	7,920	213	175	4,182 R	59.3%	38.8%	1.0%
20,119	LEE	6,642	2,675	3,899	32	36	1,224 D	40.3%	58.7%	0.5%
216,014	LEXINGTON	83,081	58,095	22,830	1,444	712	35,265 R	69.9%	27.5%	1.7%
9,958	MCCORMICK	3,661	1,704	1,896	38	23	192 D	46.5%	51.8%	1.0%
35,466	MARION	12,149	4,687	7,358	53	51	2,671 D	38.6%	60.6%	0.4%
28,818	MARLBORO	7,883	2,699	5,060	52	72	2,361 D	34.2%	64.2%	0.7%
36,108	NEWBERRY	12,372	7,492	4,428	210	242	3,064 R	60.6%	35.8%	1.7%
66,215	OCONEE	23,575	15,364	7,571	451	189	7,793 R	65.2%	32.1%	1.9%
91,582	ORANGEBURG	32,734	12,657	19,802	170	105	7,145 D	38.7%	60.5%	0.5%
110,757	PICKENS	34,582	24,681	8,927	606	368	15,754 R	71.4%	25.8%	1.8%
320,677	RICHLAND	115,421	49,675	62,701	2,277	768	13,026 D	43.0%	54.3%	2.0%
19,181	SALUDA	6,891	4,098	2,682	56	55	1,416 R	59.5%	38.9%	0.8%
253,791	SPARTANBURG	83,553	52,114	29,559	1,150	730	22,555 R	62.4%	35.4%	1.4%
104,646	SUMTER	30,672	15,915	14,365	270	122	1,550 R	51.9%	46.8%	0.9%
29,881	UNION	10,589	5,768	4,662	90	69	1,106 R	54.5%	44.0%	0.8%
37,217	WILLIAMSBURG	11,331	4,524	6,723	46	38	2,199 D	39.9%	59.3%	0.4%
164,614	YORK	54,351	33,776	19,251	840	484	14,525 R	62.1%	35.4%	1.5%
4,012,012	TOTAL	1,382,717	785,937	565,561	20,200	11,019	220,376 R	56.8%	40.9%	1.5%

SOUTH CAROLINA

CONGRESS

CD	Year	Total Vote	Republican		Democratic		Other Vote	Rep.-Dem. Plurality	Percentage			
									Total Vote		Major Vote	
			Vote	Candidate	Vote	Candidate			Rep.	Dem.	Rep.	Dem.
1	2000	231,446	139,597	BROWN, HENRY	82,622	BRACK, ANDY	9,227	56,975 R	60.3%	35.7%	62.8%	37.2%
1	1998	130,071	118,414	SANFORD, MARK			11,657	118,414 R	91.0%		100.0%	
1	1996	143,693	138,467	SANFORD, MARK			5,226	138,467 R	96.4%		100.0%	
1	1994	147,471	97,803	SANFORD, MARK	47,769	BARBER, ROBERT	1,899	50,034 R	66.3%	32.4%	67.2%	32.8%
1	1992	184,549	121,938	RAVENEL, ARTHUR	59,908	OBERST, BILL	2,703	62,030 R	66.1%	32.5%	67.1%	32.9%
2	2000	270,976	154,338	SPENCE, FLOYD	110,672	FREDERICK, JANE	5,966	43,666 R	57.0%	40.8%	58.2%	41.8%
2	1998	206,763	119,583	SPENCE, FLOYD	84,864	FREDERICK, JANE	2,316	34,719 R	57.8%	41.0%	58.5%	41.5%
2	1996	176,289	158,229	SPENCE, FLOYD			18,060	158,229 R	89.8%		100.0%	
2	1994	133,592	133,307	SPENCE, FLOYD			285	133,307 R	99.8%		100.0%	
2	1992	169,670	148,667	SPENCE, FLOYD			21,003	148,667 R	87.6%		100.0%	
3	2000	221,621	150,176	GRAHAM, LINDSEY	67,174	BRIGHTHARP, GEORGE L.	4,271	83,002 R	67.8%	30.3%	69.1%	30.9%
3	1998	129,449	129,047	GRAHAM, LINDSEY			402	129,047 R	99.7%		100.0%	
3	1996	189,530	114,273	GRAHAM, LINDSEY	73,417	DORN, DEBBIE	1,840	40,856 R	60.3%	38.7%	60.9%	39.1%
3	1994	150,068	90,123	GRAHAM, LINDSEY	59,932	BRYAN, JAMES E.	13	30,191 R	60.1%	39.9%	60.1%	39.9%
3	1992	194,864	75,660	BLAND, JAMES L.	119,119	DERRICK, BUTLER	85	43,459 D	38.8%	61.1%	38.8%	61.2%
4	2000	189,051	150,436	DEMINT, JIM			38,615	150,436 R	79.6%		100.0%	
4	1998	182,550	105,264	DEMINT, JIM	73,314	REESE, GLENN	3,972	31,950 R	57.7%	40.2%	58.9%	41.1%
4	1996	194,812	138,165	INGLIS, ROBERT D.	54,126	CURRY, DARRELL E.	2,521	84,039 R	70.9%	27.8%	71.9%	28.1%
4	1994	149,176	109,626	INGLIS, ROBERT D.	39,396	FOWLER, JERRY	154	70,230 R	73.5%	26.4%	73.6%	26.4%
4	1992	198,410	99,879	INGLIS, ROBERT D.	94,182	PATTERSON, ELIZABETH J.	4,349	5,697 R	50.3%	47.5%	51.5%	48.5%
5	2000	215,838	85,247	GULLICK, CARL	126,877	SPRATT, JOHN	3,714	41,630 D	39.5%	58.8%	40.2%	59.8%
5	1998	164,267	66,299	BURKHOLD, MIKE	95,105	SPRATT, JOHN	2,863	28,806 D	40.4%	57.9%	41.1%	58.9%
5	1996	179,971	81,455	BIGHAM, LARRY	97,335	SPRATT, JOHN	1,181	15,880 D	45.3%	54.1%	45.6%	54.4%
5	1994	148,363	70,967	BIGHAM, LARRY	77,311	SPRATT, JOHN	85	6,344 D	47.8%	52.1%	47.9%	52.1%
5	1992	183,086	70,866	HORNE, WILLIAM T.	112,031	SPRATT, JOHN	189	41,165 D	38.7%	61.2%	38.7%	61.3%
6	2000	192,380	50,005	ELLISON, VINCE	138,053	CLYBURN, JAMES E.	4,322	88,048 D	26.0%	71.8%	26.6%	73.4%
6	1998	160,576	41,421	MCLEOD, GARY	116,507	CLYBURN, JAMES E.	2,648	75,086 D	25.8%	72.6%	26.2%	73.8%
6	1996	173,080	51,974	MCLEOD, GARY	120,132	CLYBURN, JAMES E.	974	68,158 D	30.0%	69.4%	30.2%	69.8%
6	1994	138,923	50,259	MCLEOD, GARY	88,635	CLYBURN, JAMES E.	29	38,376 D	36.2%	63.8%	36.2%	63.8%
6	1992	184,871	64,149	CHASE, JOHN R.	120,647	CLYBURN, JAMES E.	75	56,498 D	34.7%	65.3%	34.7%	65.3%

SOUTH CAROLINA

GENERAL AND PRIMARY ELECTIONS

2000 GENERAL ELECTIONS

President Other vote was 4,876 Libertarian (Browne); 3,519 Reform (Buchanan); 1,682 Constitution (Phillips); 942 Natural Law (Hagelin). Nader was listed on the ballot under the designation United Citizens.

Congress Other vote was: CD 1: 6,010 Libertarian (Woolsey), 3,177 Reform/Natural Law (Batchelder), 40 scattered write-in; CD 2: 3,622 Libertarian (Moultrie), 2,273 Natural Law (Taylor), 71 scattered write-in; CD 3: 3,116 Libertarian (Banks), 1,122 Natural Law (Klein), 33 scattered write-in; (of the 67,174 votes received by Democrat Brightharp, 2,254 were on the United Citizens line); CD 4: 16,532 Constitution (Adams), 12,757 Libertarian (Bishop), 6,210 United Citizens/Reform (Ashy), 2,640 Natural Law (Walters), 476 scattered write-in; CD 5: 3,665 Libertarian (Campbell), 49 scattered write-in; CD 6: 2,339 Natural Law (Nevins), 1,934 Libertarian (Hines), 49 scattered write-in.

SOUTH CAROLINA

GENERAL AND PRIMARY ELECTIONS

2000 PRIMARY ELECTIONS

Primary	February 19, 2000 (President)	**Registration** 2,096,679 No Party Registration
	June 13, 2000 (Congress)	(as of May 30, 2000)
Primary Runoff	June 27, 2000 (Congress)	

Primary Type Open—Any registered voter could vote in either the Democratic or Republican primary, although if they voted in one party's primary they could not vote in a primary runoff of the other party.

Note: An asterisk (*) denotes incumbent. The names of unopposed candidates do not appear on the primary ballot; therefore, no votes are cast for these candidates.

	REPUBLICAN PRIMARIES			DEMOCRATIC PRIMARIES	
President	George W. Bush	305,998	53.4%	No Democratic Primary	
	John McCain	239,964	41.9%		
	Alan Keyes	25,996	4.5%		
	Gary Bauer	618	0.1%		
	Steve Forbes	449	0.1%		
	Orrin G. Hatch	76			
	TOTAL	573,101			
Congressional District 1	Henry Brown	22,072	43.6%	Andy Brack	Unopposed
	Buck Limehouse	17,171	33.9%		
	Van Jenerette	4,269	8.4%		
	Wheeler Tillman	2,627	5.2%		
	Mike Seekings	2,470	4.9%		
	Charlie Thompson	1,998	3.9%		
	TOTAL	50,607			
	PRIMARY RUNOFF				
	Henry Brown	21,631	54.6%		
	Buck Limehouse	17,990	45.4%		
	TOTAL	39,621			
Congressional District 2	Floyd D. Spence*	Unopposed		Jane Frederick	Unopposed
Congressional District 3	Lindsey Graham*	Unopposed		George Brightharp	Unopposed
Congressional District 4	Jim DeMint*	41,851	77.3%	No Democratic candidate	
	Franklin D. Raddish	12,279	22.7%		
	TOTAL	54,130			
Congressional District 5	Carl Gullick	Unopposed		John Spratt*	Unopposed
Congressional District 6	Vince Ellison	Unopposed		James E. Clyburn*	Unopposed

SOUTH DAKOTA

GOVERNOR
William J. Janklow (R). Re-elected 1998 to a four-year term. Previously elected 1994, 1982, 1978.

SENATORS
Thomas A. Daschle (D). Re-elected 1998 to a six-year term. Previously elected 1992, 1986.

Tim Johnson (D). Elected 1996 to a six-year term.

REPRESENTATIVE
At-Large. John Thune (R)

POSTWAR VOTE FOR PRESIDENT

Year	Total Vote	Republican Vote	Republican Candidate	Democratic Vote	Democratic Candidate	Other Vote	Plurality	Total Vote Rep.	Total Vote Dem.	Major Vote Rep.	Major Vote Dem.
2000	316,269	190,700	Bush, George W.	118,804	Gore, Al	6,765	71,896 R	60.3%	37.6%	61.6%	38.4%
1996**	323,826	150,543	Dole, Bob	139,333	Clinton, Bill	33,950	11,210 R	46.5%	43.0%	51.9%	48.1%
1992**	336,254	136,718	Bush, George	124,888	Clinton, Bill	74,648	11,830 R	40.7%	37.1%	52.3%	47.7%
1988	312,991	165,415	Bush, George	145,560	Dukakis, Michael S.	2,016	19,855 R	52.8%	46.5%	53.2%	46.8%
1984	317,867	200,267	Reagan, Ronald	116,113	Mondale, Walter F.	1,487	84,154 R	63.0%	36.5%	63.3%	36.7%
1980**	327,703	198,343	Reagan, Ronald	103,855	Carter, Jimmy	25,505	94,488 R	60.5%	31.7%	65.6%	34.4%
1976	300,678	151,505	Ford, Gerald R.	147,068	Carter, Jimmy	2,105	4,437 R	50.4%	48.9%	50.7%	49.3%
1972	307,415	166,476	Nixon, Richard M.	139,945	McGovern, George S.	994	26,531 R	54.2%	45.5%	54.3%	45.7%
1968	281,264	149,841	Nixon, Richard M.	118,023	Humphrey, Hubert H.	13,400	31,818 R	53.3%	42.0%	55.9%	44.1%
1964	293,118	130,108	Goldwater, Barry M.	163,010	Johnson, Lyndon B.		32,902 D	44.4%	55.6%	44.4%	55.6%
1960	306,487	178,417	Nixon, Richard M.	128,070	Kennedy, John F.		50,347 R	58.2%	41.8%	58.2%	41.8%
1956	293,857	171,569	Eisenhower, Dwight D.	122,288	Stevenson, Adlai E.		49,281 R	58.4%	41.6%	58.4%	41.6%
1952	294,283	203,857	Eisenhower, Dwight D.	90,426	Stevenson, Adlai E.		113,431 R	69.3%	30.7%	69.3%	30.7%
1948	250,105	129,651	Dewey, Thomas E.	117,653	Truman, Harry S.	2,801	11,998 R	51.8%	47.0%	52.4%	47.6%

In 1996 the other vote column includes 31,250 votes cast for Perot. In 1992 the other vote column includes 73,295 votes cast for Perot. In 1980 the other column includes 21,431 votes for Independent (Anderson).

SOUTH DAKOTA

POSTWAR VOTE FOR GOVERNOR

Year	Total Vote	Republican Vote	Republican Candidate	Democratic Vote	Democratic Candidate	Other Vote	Rep.-Dem. Plurality	Total Vote Rep.	Total Vote Dem.	Major Vote Rep.	Major Vote Dem.
1998	260,187	166,621	Janklow, William J.	85,473	Hunhoff, Bernie	8,093	81,148 R	64.0%	32.9%	66.1%	33.9%
1994	311,613	172,515	Janklow, William J.	126,273	Beddow, Jim	12,825	46,242 R	55.4%	40.5%	57.7%	42.3%
1990	256,723	151,198	Mickelson, George S.	105,525	Samuelson, Bob L.		45,673 R	58.9%	41.1%	58.9%	41.1%
1986	294,441	152,543	Mickelson, George S.	141,898	Herseth, R. Lars		10,645 R	51.8%	48.2%	51.8%	48.2%
1982	278,562	197,426	Janklow, William J.	81,136	O'Connor, Michael J.		116,290 R	70.9%	29.1%	70.9%	29.1%
1978	259,795	147,116	Janklow, William J.	112,679	McKellips, Roger		34,437 R	56.6%	43.4%	56.6%	43.4%
1974**	278,228	129,077	Olson, John E.	149,151	Kneip, Richard F.		20,074 D	46.4%	53.6%	46.4%	53.6%
1972	308,177	123,165	Thompson, Carveth	185,012	Kneip, Richard F.		61,847 D	40.0%	60.0%	40.0%	60.0%
1970	239,963	108,347	Farrar, Frank	131,616	Kneip, Richard F.		23,269 D	45.2%	54.8%	45.2%	54.8%
1968	276,906	159,646	Farrar, Frank	117,260	Chamberlin, Robert		42,386 R	57.7%	42.3%	57.7%	42.3%
1966	228,214	131,710	Boe, Nils A.	96,504	Chamberlin, Robert		35,206 R	57.7%	42.3%	57.7%	42.3%
1964	290,570	150,151	Boe, Nils A.	140,419	Lindley, John F.		9,732 R	51.7%	48.3%	51.7%	48.3%
1962	256,120	143,682	Gubbrud, Archie M.	112,438	Herseth, Ralph		31,244 R	56.1%	43.9%	56.1%	43.9%
1960	304,625	154,530	Gubbrud, Archie M.	150,095	Herseth, Ralph		4,435 R	50.7%	49.3%	50.7%	49.3%
1958	258,281	125,520	Saunders, Phil	132,761	Herseth, Ralph		7,241 D	48.6%	51.4%	48.6%	51.4%
1956	292,017	158,819	Foss, Joe J.	133,198	Herseth, Ralph		25,621 R	54.4%	45.6%	54.4%	45.6%
1954	236,255	133,878	Foss, Joe J.	102,377	Martin, Ed C.		31,501 R	56.7%	43.3%	56.7%	43.3%
1952	289,515	203,102	Anderson, Sigurd	86,413	Iverson, Sherman A.		116,689 R	70.2%	29.8%	70.2%	29.8%
1950	253,316	154,254	Anderson, Sigurd	99,062	Robbie, Joseph		55,192 R	60.9%	39.1%	60.9%	39.1%
1948	245,372	149,883	Mickelson, George	95,489	Volz, Harold J.		54,394 R	61.1%	38.9%	61.1%	38.9%
1946	162,292	108,998	Mickelson, George	53,294	Haeder, Richard		55,704 R	67.2%	32.8%	67.2%	32.8%

The term of office of South Dakota's Governor was increased from two to four years effective with the 1974 election.

POSTWAR VOTE FOR SENATOR

Year	Total Vote	Republican Vote	Republican Candidate	Democratic Vote	Democratic Candidate	Other Vote	Rep.-Dem. Plurality	Total Vote Rep.	Total Vote Dem.	Major Vote Rep.	Major Vote Dem.
1998	262,111	95,431	Schmidt, Ron	162,884	Daschle, Thomas A.	3,796	67,453 D	36.4%	62.1%	36.9%	63.1%
1996	324,487	157,954	Pressler, Larry	166,533	Johnson, Tim		8,579 D	48.7%	51.3%	48.7%	51.3%
1992	334,495	108,733	Haar, Charlene	217,095	Daschle, Thomas A.	8,667	108,362 D	32.5%	64.9%	33.4%	66.6%
1990	258,976	135,682	Pressler, Larry	116,727	Muenster, Ted	6,567	18,955 R	52.4%	45.1%	53.8%	46.2%
1986	295,830	143,173	Abdnor, James	152,657	Daschle, Thomas A.		9,484 D	48.4%	51.6%	48.4%	51.6%
1984	315,713	235,176	Pressler, Larry	80,537	Cunningham, George V.		154,639 R	74.5%	25.5%	74.5%	25.5%
1980	327,478	190,594	Abdnor, James	129,018	McGovern, George S.	7,866	61,576 R	58.2%	39.4%	59.6%	40.4%
1978	255,599	170,832	Pressler, Larry	84,767	Barnett, Don		86,065 R	66.8%	33.2%	66.8%	33.2%
1974	278,884	130,955	Thorsness, Leo K.	147,929	McGovern, George S.		16,974 D	47.0%	53.0%	47.0%	53.0%
1972	306,386	131,613	Hirsch, Robert W.	174,773	Abourezk, James		43,160 D	43.0%	57.0%	43.0%	57.0%
1968	279,912	120,951	Gubbrud, Archie M.	158,961	McGovern, George S.		38,010 D	43.2%	56.8%	43.2%	56.8%
1966	227,080	150,517	Mundt, Karl E.	76,563	Wright, Donn H.		73,954 R	66.3%	33.7%	66.3%	33.7%
1962	254,319	126,861	Bottum, Joe H.	127,458	McGovern, George S.		597 D	49.9%	50.1%	49.9%	50.1%
1960	305,442	160,181	Mundt, Karl E.	145,261	McGovern, George S.		14,920 R	52.4%	47.6%	52.4%	47.6%
1956	290,622	147,621	Case, Francis	143,001	Holum, Kenneth		4,620 R	50.8%	49.2%	50.8%	49.2%
1954	235,745	135,071	Mundt, Karl E.	100,674	Holum, Kenneth		34,397 R	57.3%	42.7%	57.3%	42.7%
1950	251,362	160,670	Case, Francis	90,692	Engel, John A.		69,978 R	63.9%	36.1%	63.9%	36.1%
1948	242,833	144,084	Mundt, Karl E.	98,749	Engel, John A.		45,335 R	59.3%	40.7%	59.3%	40.7%

SOUTH DAKOTA

One At Large

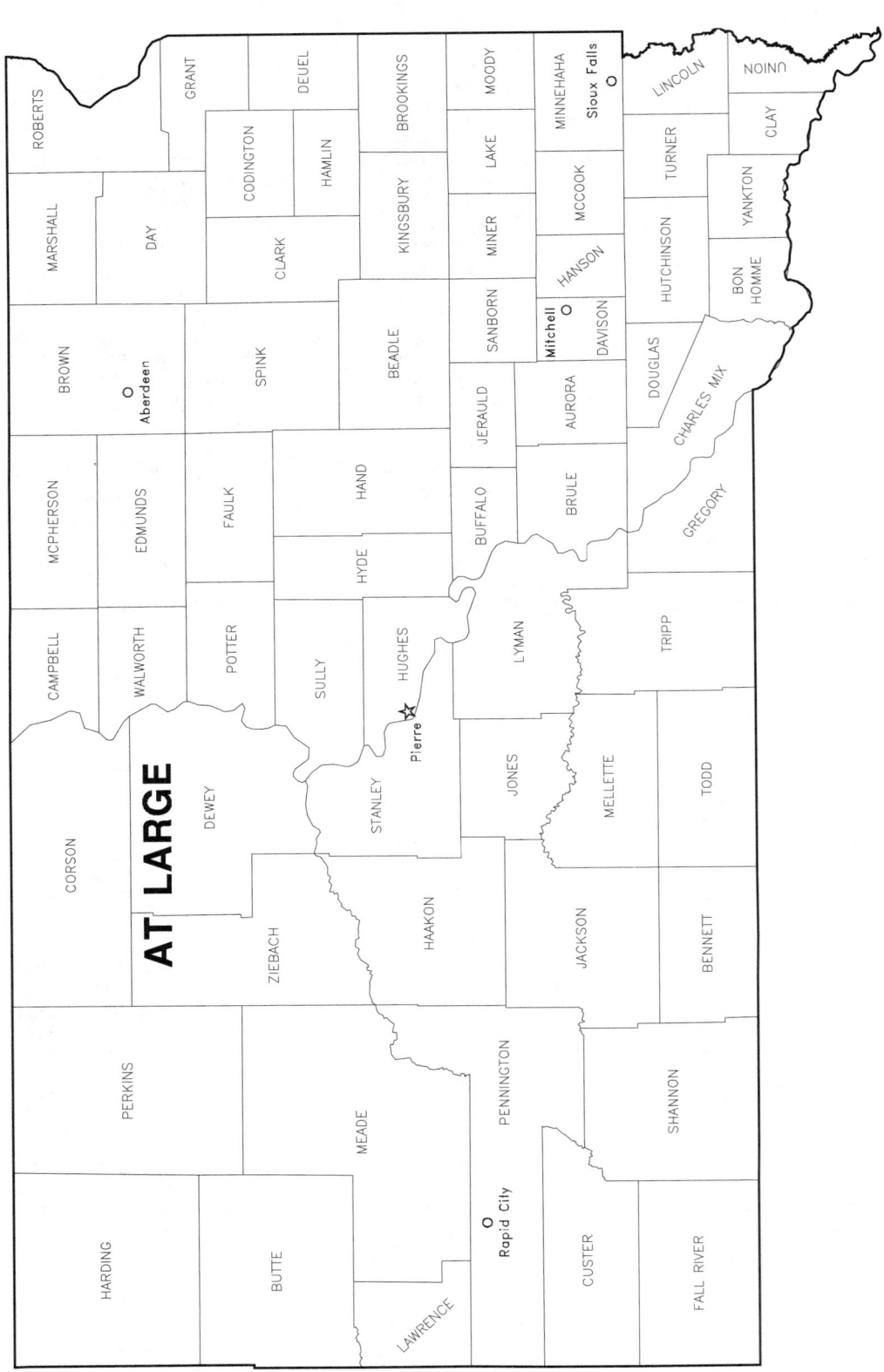

SOUTH DAKOTA

PRESIDENT 2000

2000 Census Population	County	Total Vote	Republican	Democratic	Green (Nader)	Other	Rep.-Dem. Plurality	Rep.	Dem.	Green
3,058	AURORA	1,413	847	513		53	334 R	59.9%	36.3%	
17,023	BEADLE	7,739	4,347	3,216		176	1,131 R	56.2%	41.6%	
3,574	BENNETT	1,116	712	377		27	335 R	63.8%	33.8%	
7,260	BON HOMME	3,139	1,901	1,162		76	739 R	60.6%	37.0%	
28,220	BROOKINGS	10,984	6,212	4,546		226	1,666 R	56.6%	41.4%	
35,460	BROWN	16,556	9,060	7,173		323	1,887 R	54.7%	43.3%	
5,364	BRULE	2,167	1,268	818		81	450 R	58.5%	37.7%	
2,032	BUFFALO	408	140	256		12	116 D	34.3%	62.7%	
9,094	BUTTE	3,689	2,760	840		89	1,920 R	74.8%	22.8%	
1,782	CAMPBELL	917	739	147		31	592 R	80.6%	16.0%	
9,350	CHARLES MIX	3,579	2,205	1,300		74	905 R	61.6%	36.3%	
4,143	CLARK	2,108	1,272	791		45	481 R	60.3%	37.5%	
13,537	CLAY	5,105	2,363	2,638		104	275 D	46.3%	51.7%	
25,897	CODINGTON	11,138	6,718	4,192		228	2,526 R	60.3%	37.6%	
4,181	CORSON	1,243	629	549		65	80 R	50.6%	44.2%	
7,275	CUSTER	3,573	2,495	955		123	1,540 R	69.8%	26.7%	
18,741	DAVISON	7,528	4,445	2,936		147	1,509 R	59.0%	39.0%	
6,267	DAY	3,197	1,623	1,492		82	131 R	50.8%	46.7%	
4,498	DEUEL	2,224	1,245	926		53	319 R	56.0%	41.6%	
5,972	DEWEY	1,681	761	880		40	119 D	45.3%	52.3%	
3,458	DOUGLAS	1,709	1,311	363		35	948 R	76.7%	21.2%	
4,367	EDMUNDS	1,986	1,257	676		53	581 R	63.3%	34.0%	
7,453	FALL RIVER	3,429	2,185	1,133		111	1,052 R	63.7%	33.0%	
2,640	FAULK	1,329	904	388		37	516 R	68.0%	29.2%	
7,847	GRANT	3,830	2,235	1,475		120	760 R	58.4%	38.5%	
4,792	GREGORY	2,257	1,487	718		52	769 R	65.9%	31.8%	
2,196	HAAKON	1,129	938	164		27	774 R	83.1%	14.5%	
5,540	HAMLIN	2,723	1,731	923		69	808 R	63.6%	33.9%	
3,741	HAND	2,031	1,419	565		47	854 R	69.9%	27.8%	
3,139	HANSON	1,421	944	457		20	487 R	66.4%	32.2%	
1,353	HARDING	731	650	64		17	586 R	88.9%	8.8%	
16,481	HUGHES	7,534	5,188	2,212		134	2,976 R	68.9%	29.4%	
8,075	HUTCHINSON	3,625	2,497	1,052		76	1,445 R	68.9%	29.0%	
1,671	HYDE	835	592	218		25	374 R	70.9%	26.1%	
2,930	JACKSON	1,040	687	319		34	368 R	66.1%	30.7%	
2,295	JERAULD	1,122	624	468		30	156 R	55.6%	41.7%	
1,193	JONES	664	509	137		18	372 R	76.7%	20.6%	
5,815	KINGSBURY	2,727	1,612	1,049		66	563 R	59.1%	38.5%	
11,276	LAKE	5,154	2,724	2,331		99	393 R	52.9%	45.2%	
21,802	LAWRENCE	9,406	6,327	2,797		282	3,530 R	67.3%	29.7%	
24,131	LINCOLN	10,556	6,546	3,844		166	2,702 R	62.0%	36.4%	
3,895	LYMAN	1,386	875	482		29	393 R	63.1%	34.8%	
5,832	MCCOOK	2,631	1,610	965		56	645 R	61.2%	36.7%	
2,904	MCPHERSON	1,417	1,073	295		49	778 R	75.7%	20.8%	
4,576	MARSHALL	2,079	1,097	939		43	158 R	52.8%	45.2%	
24,253	MEADE	9,366	6,870	2,267		229	4,603 R	73.4%	24.2%	
2,083	MELLETTE	733	495	222		16	273 R	67.5%	30.3%	
2,884	MINER	1,266	724	523		19	201 R	57.2%	41.3%	
148,281	MINNEHAHA	61,369	33,428	27,042		899	6,386 R	54.5%	44.1%	
6,595	MOODY	2,735	1,361	1,318		56	43 R	49.8%	48.2%	
88,565	PENNINGTON	36,557	24,696	11,123		738	13,573 R	67.6%	30.4%	
3,363	PERKINS	1,614	1,237	297		80	940 R	76.6%	18.4%	
2,693	POTTER	1,494	1,112	356		26	756 R	74.4%	23.8%	
10,016	ROBERTS	4,074	2,237	1,700		137	537 R	54.9%	41.7%	
2,675	SANBORN	1,268	767	468		33	299 R	60.5%	36.9%	
12,466	SHANNON	1,953	252	1,667		34	1,415 D	12.9%	85.4%	
7,454	SPINK	3,284	1,957	1,274		53	683 R	59.6%	38.8%	
2,772	STANLEY	1,381	955	402		24	553 R	69.2%	29.1%	
1,556	SULLY	871	633	209		29	424 R	72.7%	24.0%	
9,050	TODD	1,494	478	993		23	515 D	32.0%	66.5%	

SOUTH DAKOTA

PRESIDENT 2000

2000 Census Population	County	Total Vote	Republican	Democratic	Green (Nader)	Other	Rep.-Dem. Plurality	Percentage of Total Vote		
								Rep.	Dem.	Green
6,430	TRIPP	2,765	1,909	799		57	1,110 R	69.0%	28.9%	
8,849	TURNER	4,004	2,514	1,414		76	1,100 R	62.8%	35.3%	
12,584	UNION	5,772	3,265	2,358		149	907 R	56.6%	40.9%	
5,974	WALWORTH	2,553	1,758	721		74	1,037 R	68.9%	28.2%	
21,652	YANKTON	8,740	4,904	3,596		240	1,308 R	56.1%	41.1%	
2,519	ZIEBACH	721	384	314		23	70 R	53.3%	43.6%	
754,844	TOTAL	316,269	190,700	118,804		6,765	71,896 R	60.3%	37.6%	

Note: No votes were tallied for Nader in South Dakota. He did not qualify for the ballot and write-in votes were not allowed.

SOUTH DAKOTA

CONGRESS

CD	Year	Total Vote	Republican		Democratic		Other Vote	Rep.-Dem. Plurality	Percentage			
									Total Vote		Major Vote	
			Vote	Candidate	Vote	Candidate			Rep.	Dem.	Rep.	Dem.
AL	2000	314,761	231,083	THUNE, JOHN	78,321	HOHN, CURT	5,357	152,762 R	73.4%	24.9%	74.7%	25.3%
AL	1998	258,590	194,157	THUNE, JOHN	64,433	MOSER, JEFF		129,724 R	75.1%	24.9%	75.1%	24.9%
AL	1996	323,203	186,393	THUNE, JOHN	119,547	WEILAND, RICK	17,263	66,846 R	57.7%	37.0%	60.9%	39.1%
AL	1994	305,922	112,054	BERKHOUT, JAN	183,036	JOHNSON, TIM	10,832	70,982 D	36.6%	59.8%	38.0%	62.0%
AL	1992	332,902	89,375	TIMMER, JOHN	230,070	JOHNSON, TIM	13,457	140,695 D	26.8%	69.1%	28.0%	72.0%
AL	1990	257,298	83,484	FRANKENFELD, DON	173,814	JOHNSON, TIM		90,330 D	32.4%	67.6%	32.4%	67.6%
AL	1988	311,916	88,157	VOLK, DAVID	223,759	JOHNSON, TIM		135,602 D	28.3%	71.7%	28.3%	71.7%
AL	1986	289,723	118,261	BELL, DALE	171,462	JOHNSON, TIM		53,201 D	40.8%	59.2%	40.8%	59.2%
AL	1984	316,222	134,821	BELL, DALE	181,401	DASCHLE, THOMAS A.		46,580 D	42.6%	57.4%	42.6%	57.4%
AL	1982	275,652	133,530	ROBERTS, CLINT	142,122	DASCHLE, THOMAS A.		8,592 D	48.4%	51.6%	48.4%	51.6%

SOUTH DAKOTA

GENERAL AND PRIMARY ELECTIONS

2000 GENERAL ELECTIONS

President   Other vote was 3,322 Reform (Buchanan); 1,781 Independent (Phillips); 1,662 Libertarian (Browne).

Congress   Other vote was 5,357 Libertarian (Lerohl).

2000 PRIMARY ELECTIONS

Primary	June 6, 2000	**Registration** (active registrants as of May 22, 2000)	Republican	215,938
			Democratic	174,758
			Libertarian	968
			Reform	97
			Other	55,170
			TOTAL	446,931

SOUTH DAKOTA

GENERAL AND PRIMARY ELECTIONS

Primary Type   Closed-Only registered Democrats and Republican could vote in their party's primary.

Note: An asterisk (*) denotes incumbent. The names of unopposed candidates do not appear on the primary ballot; therefore, no votes are cast for these candidates. The threshold to avoid a primary runoff in congressional and gubernatorial primaries is 35 percent of the vote.

	REPUBLICAN PRIMARIES			DEMOCRATIC PRIMARIES		
President	George W. Bush	35,418	78.2%	No Democratic Primary		
	John McCain	6,228	13.8%			
	Alan Keyes	3,478	7.7%			
	James Attia	155	0.3%			
	TOTAL	45,279				
Congressional At-large	John Thune*	Unopposed		Curt Hohn	12,827	56.1%
				Steve Sandven	8,333	36.4%
				Raymond Earl Osloond	1,715	7.5%
				TOTAL	22,875	

TENNESSEE

GOVERNOR
Don Sundquist (R). Re-elected 1998 to a four-year term. Previously elected 1994.

SENATORS
Bill Frist (R). Re-elected 2000 to a six-year term. Previously elected 1994.

Fred Thompson (R). Re-elected 1996 to a six-year term. Previously elected 1994 to fill out the remaining two years of the term vacated when Senator Albert Gore, Jr. (D) resigned to become Vice President.

REPRESENTATIVES
1. Bill Jenkins (R)
2. John J. Duncan, Jr. (R)
3. Zach Wamp (R)
4. Van Hilleary (R)
5. Bob Clement (D)
6. Bart Gordon (D)
7. Ed Bryant (R)
8. John Tanner (D)
9. Harold E. Ford Jr. (D)

POSTWAR VOTE FOR PRESIDENT

| | | Republican | | Democratic | | Other | | Percentage | | | |
| | | | | | | | | Total Vote | | Major Vote | |
Year	Total Vote	Vote	Candidate	Vote	Candidate	Vote	Plurality	Rep.	Dem.	Rep.	Dem.
2000**	2,076,181	1,061,949	Bush, George W.	981,720	Gore, Al	32,512	80,229 R	51.1%	47.3%	52.0%	48.0%
1996**	1,894,105	863,530	Dole, Bob	909,146	Clinton, Bill	121,429	45,616 D	45.6%	48.0%	48.7%	51.3%
1992**	1,982,638	841,300	Bush, George	933,521	Clinton, Bill	207,817	92,221 D	42.4%	47.1%	47.4%	52.6%
1988	1,636,250	947,233	Bush, George	679,794	Dukakis, Michael S.	9,223	267,439 R	57.9%	41.5%	58.2%	41.8%
1984	1,711,994	990,212	Reagan, Ronald	711,714	Mondale, Walter F.	10,068	278,498 R	57.8%	41.6%	58.2%	41.8%
1980**	1,617,616	787,761	Reagan, Ronald	783,051	Carter, Jimmy	46,804	4,710 R	48.7%	48.4%	50.1%	49.9%
1976	1,476,345	633,969	Ford, Gerald R.	825,879	Carter, Jimmy	16,497	191,910 D	42.9%	55.9%	43.4%	56.6%
1972	1,201,182	813,147	Nixon, Richard M.	357,293	McGovern, George S.	30,742	455,854 R	67.7%	29.7%	69.5%	30.5%
1968**	1,248,617	472,592	Nixon, Richard M.	351,233	Humphrey, Hubert H.	424,792	47,800 R	37.8%	28.1%	57.4%	42.6%
1964	1,143,946	508,965	Goldwater, Barry M.	634,947	Johnson, Lyndon B.	34	125,982 D	44.5%	55.5%	44.5%	55.5%
1960	1,051,792	556,577	Nixon, Richard M.	481,453	Kennedy, John F.	13,762	75,124 R	52.9%	45.8%	53.6%	46.4%
1956	939,404	462,288	Eisenhower, Dwight D.	456,507	Stevenson, Adlai E.	20,609	5,781 R	49.2%	48.6%	50.3%	49.7%
1952	892,553	446,147	Eisenhower, Dwight D.	443,710	Stevenson, Adlai E.	2,696	2,437 R	50.0%	49.7%	50.1%	49.9%
1948	550,283	202,914	Dewey, Thomas E.	270,402	Truman, Harry S.	76,967	67,488 D	36.9%	49.1%	42.9%	57.1%

In 2000 the other vote column includes 19,781 votes cast for Green (Nader). In 1996 the other vote column includes 105,918 votes cast for Perot. In 1992 the other vote column includes 199,968 votes cast for Perot. In 1980 the other column includes 35,991 votes for Independent (Anderson). In 1968 other vote was American (Wallace).

TENNESSEE

POSTWAR VOTE FOR GOVERNOR

Year	Total Vote	Republican Vote	Candidate	Democratic Vote	Candidate	Other Vote	Rep.-Dem. Plurality	Total Vote Rep.	Total Vote Dem.	Major Vote Rep.	Major Vote Dem.
1998	976,236	669,973	Sundquist, Don	287,750	Hooker, John J.	18,513	382,223 R	68.6%	29.5%	70.0%	30.0%
1994	1,487,130	807,104	Sundquist, Don	664,252	Bredesen, Phil	15,774	142,852 R	54.3%	44.7%	54.9%	45.1%
1990	790,441	289,348	Henry, Dwight	480,885	McWherter, Ned	20,208	191,537 D	36.6%	60.8%	37.6%	62.4%
1986	1,210,339	553,449	Dunn, Winfield	656,602	McWherter, Ned	288	103,153 D	45.7%	54.2%	45.7%	54.3%
1982	1,238,927	737,963	Alexander, Lamar	500,937	Tyree, Randy	27	237,026 R	59.6%	40.4%	59.6%	40.4%
1978	1,189,695	661,959	Alexander, Lamar	523,495	Butcher, Jake	4,241	138,464 R	55.6%	44.0%	55.8%	44.2%
1974	1,040,714	455,467	Alexander, Lamar	576,833	Blanton, Ray	8,414	121,366 D	43.8%	55.4%	44.1%	55.9%
1970	1,108,247	575,777	Dunn, Winfield	509,521	Hooker, John J.	22,949	66,256 R	52.0%	46.0%	53.1%	46.9%
1966**	656,566		—	532,998	Ellington, Buford	123,568	532,998 D		81.2%		100.0%
1962**	621,064	100,190	Patty, Hubert D.	315,648	Clement, Frank G.	205,226	215,458 D	16.1%	50.8%	24.1%	75.9%
1958**	432,545	35,938	Wall, Thomas P.	248,874	Ellington, Buford	147,733	212,936 D	8.3%	57.5%	12.6%	87.4%
1954**	322,586		—	281,291	Clement, Frank G.	41,295	281,291 D		87.2%		100.0%
1952	806,771	166,377	Witt, R. Beecher	640,290	Clement, Frank G.	104	473,913 D	20.6%	79.4%	20.6%	79.4%
1950	236,194		—	184,437	Browning, Gordon	51,757	184,437 D		78.1%		100.0%
1948	543,881	179,957	Acuff, Roy	363,903	Browning, Gordon	21	183,946 D	33.1%	66.9%	33.1%	66.9%
1946	229,456	73,222	Lowe, W. O.	149,937	McCord, Jim Nance	6,297	76,715 D	31.9%	65.3%	32.8%	67.2%

The term of office of Tennessee's Governor was increased from two to four years effective with the 1954 election. In 1958 Jim Nance McCord (Independent) received 136,399 votes (31.5% of the total vote) and ran second. In 1962 other vote was 203,765 William R. Anderson (Independent) who ran second; 1,441 E. B. Bowles (Independent) and 20 scattered. In 1966 other vote was 64,602 H. L. Crawford (Independent); 50,221 Charles Moffett (Independent); 8,407 Charles G. Vick (Independent) and 338 scattered.

POSTWAR VOTE FOR SENATOR

Year	Total Vote	Republican Vote	Candidate	Democratic Vote	Candidate	Other Vote	Rep.-Dem. Plurality	Total Vote Rep.	Total Vote Dem.	Major Vote Rep.	Major Vote Dem.
2000	1,928,613	1,255,444	Frist, Bill	621,152	Clark, Jeff	52,017	634,292 R	65.1%	32.2%	66.9%	33.1%
1996	1,778,664	1,091,554	Thompson, Fred	654,937	Gordon, Houston	32,173	436,617 R	61.4%	36.8%	62.5%	37.5%
1994	1,480,391	834,226	Frist, Bill	623,164	Sasser, James R.	23,001	211,062 R	56.4%	42.1%	57.2%	42.8%
1994S	1,465,862	885,998	Thompson, Fred	565,930	Cooper, Jim	13,934	320,068 R	60.4%	38.6%	61.0%	39.0%
1990	783,922	233,703	Hawkins, William R.	530,898	Gore, Albert, Jr.	19,321	297,195 D	29.8%	67.7%	30.6%	69.4%
1988	1,567,181	541,033	Anderson, Bill	1,020,061	Sasser, James R.	6,087	479,028 D	34.5%	65.1%	34.7%	65.3%
1984	1,648,064	557,016	Ashe, Victor	1,000,607	Gore, Albert, Jr.	90,441	443,591 D	33.8%	60.7%	35.8%	64.2%
1982	1,259,785	479,642	Beard, Robin L.	780,113	Sasser, James R.	30	300,471 D	38.1%	61.9%	38.1%	61.9%
1978	1,157,094	642,644	Baker, Howard H., Jr.	466,228	Eskind, Jane	48,222	176,416 R	55.5%	40.3%	58.0%	42.0%
1976	1,432,046	673,231	Brock, William E.	751,180	Sasser, James R.	7,635	77,949 D	47.0%	52.5%	47.3%	52.7%
1972	1,164,195	716,539	Baker, Howard H., Jr.	440,599	Blanton, Ray	7,057	275,940 R	61.5%	37.8%	61.9%	38.1%
1970	1,097,041	562,645	Brock, William E.	519,858	Gore, Albert	14,538	42,787 R	51.3%	47.4%	52.0%	48.0%
1966	866,961	483,063	Baker, Howard H., Jr.	383,843	Clement, Frank G.	55	99,220 R	55.7%	44.3%	55.7%	44.3%
1964	1,064,018	493,475	Kuykendall, Daniel H.	570,542	Gore, Albert	1	77,067 D	46.4%	53.6%	46.4%	53.6%
1964S	1,091,093	517,330	Baker, Howard H., Jr.	568,905	Bass, Ross	4,858	51,575 D	47.4%	52.1%	47.6%	52.4%
1960	828,519	234,053	Frazier, A. Bradley	594,460	Kefauver, Estes	6	360,407 D	28.2%	71.7%	28.2%	71.8%
1958	401,666	76,371	Atkins, Hobart F.	317,324	Gore, Albert	7,971	240,953 D	19.0%	79.0%	19.4%	80.6%
1954	356,094	106,971	Wall, Thomas P.	249,121	Kefauver, Estes	2	142,150 D	30.0%	70.0%	30.0%	70.0%
1952	735,219	153,479	Atkins, Hobart F.	545,432	Gore, Albert	36,308	391,953 D	20.9%	74.2%	22.0%	78.0%
1948	499,218	166,947	Reece, B. Carroll	326,142	Kefauver, Estes	6,129	159,195 D	33.4%	65.3%	33.9%	66.1%
1946	218,714	57,238	Ladd, William B.	145,654	McKellar, Kenneth	15,822	88,416 D	26.2%	66.6%	28.2%	71.8%

One of the 1994 and 1964 elections was for a short term to fill a vacancy.

TENNESSEE

Districts Established May 7, 1992

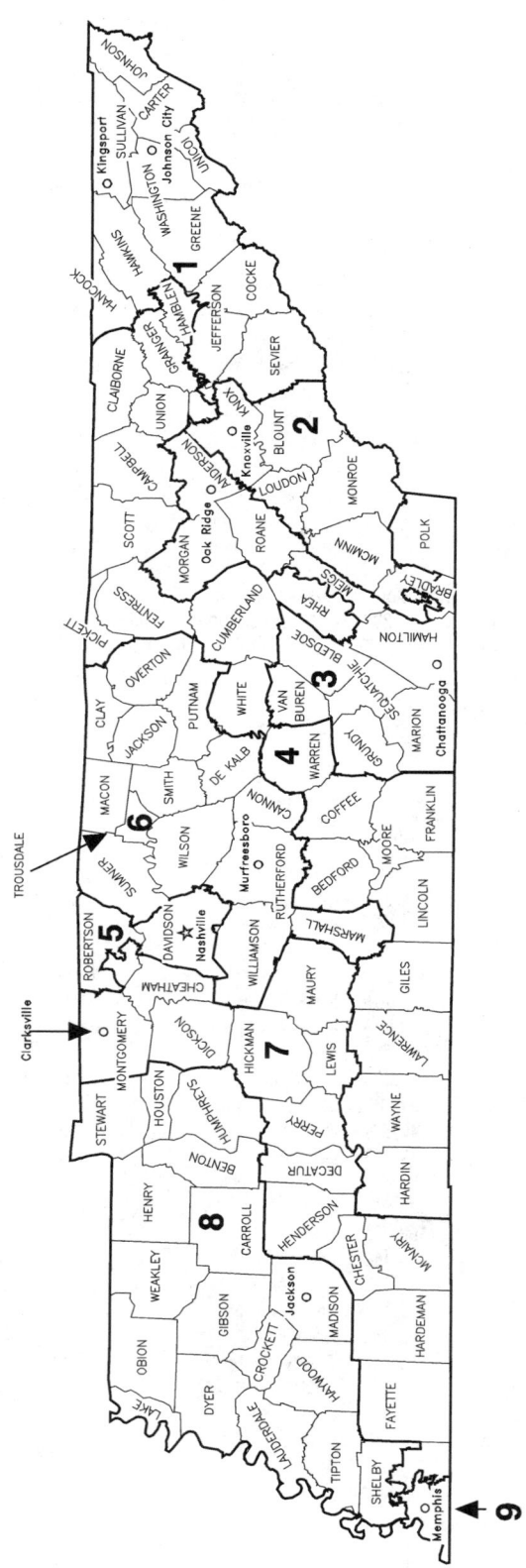

TENNESSEE

PRESIDENT 2000

2000 Census Population	County	Total Vote	Republican	Democratic	Green (Nader)	Other	Rep.-Dem. Plurality	Percentage of Total Vote		
								Rep.	Dem.	Green
71,330	ANDERSON	28,779	14,688	13,556	316	219	1,132 R	51.0%	47.1%	1.1%
37,586	BEDFORD	12,207	5,911	6,136	80	80	225 D	48.4%	50.3%	0.7%
16,537	BENTON	6,311	2,484	3,700	62	65	1,216 D	39.4%	58.6%	1.0%
12,367	BLEDSOE	4,196	2,380	1,756	35	25	624 R	56.7%	41.8%	0.8%
105,823	BLOUNT	40,662	25,273	14,688	379	322	10,585 R	62.2%	36.1%	0.9%
87,965	BRADLEY	29,443	20,167	8,768	271	237	11,399 R	68.5%	29.8%	0.9%
39,854	CAMPBELL	12,421	5,784	6,492	74	71	708 D	46.6%	52.3%	0.6%
12,826	CANNON	4,697	1,924	2,697	45	31	773 D	41.0%	57.4%	1.0%
29,475	CARROLL	10,827	5,465	5,239	65	58	226 R	50.5%	48.4%	0.6%
56,742	CARTER	19,102	12,111	6,724	157	110	5,387 R	63.4%	35.2%	0.8%
35,912	CHEATHAM	12,616	6,356	6,062	139	59	294 R	50.4%	48.1%	1.1%
15,540	CHESTER	5,728	3,487	2,192	25	24	1,295 R	60.9%	38.3%	0.4%
29,862	CLAIBORNE	9,000	5,023	3,841	60	76	1,182 R	55.8%	42.7%	0.7%
7,976	CLAY	3,442	1,468	1,931	19	24	463 D	42.6%	56.1%	0.6%
33,565	COCKE	10,239	6,185	3,872	93	89	2,313 R	60.4%	37.8%	0.9%
48,014	COFFEE	17,788	8,788	8,741	151	108	47 R	49.4%	49.1%	0.8%
14,532	CROCKETT	5,440	2,676	2,705	42	17	29 D	49.2%	49.7%	0.8%
46,802	CUMBERLAND	19,017	10,994	7,644	223	156	3,350 R	57.8%	40.2%	1.2%
569,891	DAVIDSON	208,588	84,117	120,508	2,920	1,043	36,391 D	40.3%	57.8%	1.4%
11,731	DECATUR	4,370	2,046	2,278	22	24	232 D	46.8%	52.1%	0.5%
17,423	DE KALB	6,265	2,411	3,765	63	26	1,354 D	38.5%	60.1%	1.0%
43,156	DICKSON	15,556	7,016	8,332	120	88	1,316 D	45.1%	53.6%	0.8%
37,279	DYER	11,841	6,282	5,425	88	46	857 R	53.1%	45.8%	0.7%
28,806	FAYETTE	11,529	6,402	5,037	44	46	1,365 R	55.5%	43.7%	0.4%
16,625	FENTRESS	6,029	3,417	2,529	28	55	888 R	56.7%	41.9%	0.5%
39,270	FRANKLIN	14,691	6,560	7,828	190	113	1,268 D	44.7%	53.3%	1.3%
48,152	GIBSON	17,137	8,286	8,663	101	87	377 D	48.4%	50.6%	0.6%
29,447	GILES	10,066	4,377	5,527	79	83	1,150 D	43.5%	54.9%	0.8%
20,659	GRAINGER	6,194	3,746	2,361	46	41	1,385 R	60.5%	38.1%	0.7%
62,909	GREENE	20,816	12,540	7,909	185	182	4,631 R	60.2%	38.0%	0.9%
14,332	GRUNDY	4,596	1,553	2,970	37	36	1,417 D	33.8%	64.6%	0.8%
58,128	HAMBLEN	19,699	11,824	7,564	181	130	4,260 R	60.0%	38.4%	0.9%
307,896	HAMILTON	120,379	66,605	51,708	1,290	776	14,897 R	55.3%	43.0%	1.1%
6,786	HANCOCK	2,075	1,343	690	17	25	653 R	64.7%	33.3%	0.8%
28,105	HARDEMAN	8,803	3,729	4,953	38	83	1,224 D	42.4%	56.3%	0.4%
25,578	HARDIN	8,782	4,951	3,735	49	47	1,216 R	56.4%	42.5%	0.6%
53,563	HAWKINS	17,098	10,071	6,753	147	127	3,318 R	58.9%	39.5%	0.9%
19,797	HAYWOOD	6,478	2,554	3,887	20	17	1,333 D	39.4%	60.0%	0.3%
25,522	HENDERSON	8,399	5,153	3,166	46	34	1,987 R	61.4%	37.7%	0.5%
31,115	HENRY	12,309	5,944	6,093	125	147	149 D	48.3%	49.5%	1.0%
22,295	HICKMAN	7,264	2,914	4,239	58	53	1,325 D	40.1%	58.4%	0.8%
8,088	HOUSTON	3,127	993	2,081	16	37	1,088 D	31.8%	66.5%	0.5%
17,929	HUMPHREYS	6,681	2,387	4,205	65	24	1,818 D	35.7%	62.9%	1.0%
10,984	JACKSON	4,754	1,384	3,304	36	30	1,920 D	29.1%	69.5%	0.8%
44,294	JEFFERSON	14,087	8,657	5,226	121	83	3,431 R	61.5%	37.1%	0.9%
17,499	JOHNSON	5,657	3,740	1,813	54	50	1,927 R	66.1%	32.0%	1.0%
382,032	KNOX	150,586	86,851	60,969	1,772	994	25,882 R	57.7%	40.5%	1.2%
7,954	LAKE	2,224	781	1,419	11	13	638 D	35.1%	63.8%	0.5%
27,101	LAUDERDALE	7,618	3,329	4,224	27	38	895 D	43.7%	55.4%	0.4%
39,926	LAWRENCE	14,470	7,613	6,643	98	116	970 R	52.6%	45.9%	0.7%
11,367	LEWIS	4,420	2,037	2,281	63	39	244 D	46.1%	51.6%	1.4%
31,340	LINCOLN	10,659	5,435	5,060	72	92	375 R	51.0%	47.5%	0.7%
39,086	LOUDON	16,406	10,266	5,905	132	103	4,361 R	62.6%	36.0%	0.8%
49,015	MCMINN	16,600	10,155	6,142	142	161	4,013 R	61.2%	37.0%	0.9%
24,653	MCNAIRY	8,989	4,897	4,003	47	42	894 R	54.5%	44.5%	0.5%
20,386	MACON	6,491	3,366	3,059	30	36	307 R	51.9%	47.1%	0.5%
91,837	MADISON	33,930	17,862	15,781	173	114	2,081 R	52.6%	46.5%	0.5%
27,776	MARION	10,250	4,651	5,441	74	84	790 D	45.4%	53.1%	0.7%
26,767	MARSHALL	9,359	4,105	5,107	94	53	1,002 D	43.9%	54.6%	1.0%
69,498	MAURY	23,400	11,930	11,127	207	136	803 R	51.0%	47.6%	0.9%

TENNESSEE

PRESIDENT 2000

2000 Census Population	County	Total Vote	Republican	Democratic	Green (Nader)	Other	Rep.-Dem. Plurality	Percentage of Total Vote		
								Rep.	Dem.	Green
11,086	MEIGS	3,390	1,797	1,555	12	26	242 R	53.0%	45.9%	0.4%
38,961	MONROE	13,003	7,514	5,327	78	84	2,187 R	57.8%	41.0%	0.6%
134,768	MONTGOMERY	39,044	19,644	18,818	359	223	826 R	50.3%	48.2%	0.9%
5,740	MOORE	2,301	1,145	1,107	27	22	38 R	49.8%	48.1%	1.2%
19,757	MORGAN	6,162	3,144	2,921	39	58	223 R	51.0%	47.4%	0.6%
32,450	OBION	12,440	6,168	6,056	99	117	112 R	49.6%	48.7%	0.8%
20,118	OVERTON	7,496	2,875	4,507	46	68	1,632 D	38.4%	60.1%	0.6%
7,631	PERRY	2,866	1,165	1,650	28	23	485 D	40.6%	57.6%	1.0%
4,945	PICKETT	2,239	1,281	939	12	7	342 R	57.2%	41.9%	0.5%
16,050	POLK	5,594	2,907	2,574	46	67	333 R	52.0%	46.0%	0.8%
62,315	PUTNAM	22,438	11,248	10,785	228	177	463 R	50.1%	48.1%	1.0%
28,400	RHEA	9,772	5,900	3,722	74	76	2,178 R	60.4%	38.1%	0.8%
51,910	ROANE	21,326	11,345	9,575	211	195	1,770 R	53.2%	44.9%	1.0%
54,433	ROBERTSON	20,164	9,675	10,249	148	92	574 D	48.0%	50.8%	0.7%
182,023	RUTHERFORD	62,182	33,445	27,360	1,024	353	6,085 R	53.8%	44.0%	1.6%
21,127	SCOTT	6,615	3,579	2,967	31	38	612 R	54.1%	44.9%	0.5%
11,370	SEQUATCHIE	3,887	2,169	1,648	37	33	521 R	55.8%	42.4%	1.0%
71,170	SEVIER	25,365	16,734	8,208	259	164	8,526 R	66.0%	32.4%	1.0%
897,472	SHELBY	336,755	141,756	190,404	2,860	1,735	48,648 D	42.1%	56.5%	0.8%
17,712	SMITH	7,348	2,384	4,884	42	38	2,500 D	32.4%	66.5%	0.6%
12,370	STEWART	4,782	1,826	2,870	50	36	1,044 D	38.2%	60.0%	1.0%
153,048	SULLIVAN	55,727	33,482	21,354	520	371	12,128 R	60.1%	38.3%	0.9%
130,449	SUMNER	50,477	27,601	22,118	482	276	5,483 R	54.7%	43.8%	1.0%
51,271	TIPTON	16,552	10,070	6,300	96	86	3,770 R	60.8%	38.1%	0.6%
7,259	TROUSDALE	2,945	950	1,966	15	14	1,016 D	32.3%	66.8%	0.5%
17,667	UNICOI	6,429	3,780	2,566	40	43	1,214 R	58.8%	39.9%	0.6%
17,808	UNION	5,821	3,199	2,564	30	28	635 R	55.0%	44.0%	0.5%
5,508	VAN BUREN	2,131	845	1,255	8	23	410 D	39.7%	58.9%	0.4%
38,276	WARREN	13,131	5,552	7,378	105	96	1,826 D	42.3%	56.2%	0.8%
107,198	WASHINGTON	37,942	22,579	14,769	375	219	7,810 R	59.5%	38.9%	1.0%
16,842	WAYNE	5,306	3,370	1,859	43	34	1,511 R	63.5%	35.0%	0.8%
34,895	WEAKLEY	11,844	6,106	5,570	91	77	536 R	51.6%	47.0%	0.8%
23,102	WHITE	7,775	3,525	4,135	58	57	610 D	45.3%	53.2%	0.7%
126,638	WILLIAMSON	58,429	38,901	18,745	536	247	20,156 R	66.6%	32.1%	0.9%
88,809	WILSON	35,916	18,844	16,561	308	203	2,283 R	52.5%	46.1%	0.9%
5,689,283	TOTAL	2,076,181	1,061,949	981,720	19,781	12,731	80,229 R	51.1%	47.3%	1.0%

TENNESSEE

SENATOR 2000

2000 Census Population	County	Total Vote	Republican	Democratic	Other	Rep.-Dem. Plurality	Percentage			
							Total Vote		Major Vote	
							Rep.	Dem.	Rep.	Dem.
71,330	ANDERSON	26,653	18,188	7,692	773	10,496 R	68.2%	28.9%	70.3%	29.7%
37,586	BEDFORD	10,722	6,683	3,934	105	2,749 R	62.3%	36.7%	62.9%	37.1%
16,537	BENTON	6,079	3,071	2,862	146	209 R	50.5%	47.1%	51.8%	48.2%
12,367	BLEDSOE	4,035	2,636	1,312	87	1,324 R	65.3%	32.5%	66.8%	33.2%
105,823	BLOUNT	37,969	28,536	7,876	1,557	20,660 R	75.2%	20.7%	78.4%	21.6%
87,965	BRADLEY	28,751	22,264	5,945	542	16,319 R	77.4%	20.7%	78.9%	21.1%
39,854	CAMPBELL	10,538	6,480	3,864	194	2,616 R	61.5%	36.7%	62.6%	37.4%
12,826	CANNON	4,221	2,393	1,705	123	688 R	56.7%	40.4%	58.4%	41.6%
29,475	CARROLL	10,070	6,513	3,391	166	3,122 R	64.7%	33.7%	65.8%	34.2%
56,742	CARTER	17,997	13,497	4,115	385	9,382 R	75.0%	22.9%	76.6%	23.4%

TENNESSEE

SENATOR 2000

2000 Census Population	County	Total Vote	Republican	Democratic	Other	Rep.-Dem. Plurality		Percentage			
								Total Vote		Major Vote	
								Rep.	Dem.	Rep.	Dem.
35,912	CHEATHAM	11,788	7,967	3,359	462	4,608	R	67.6%	28.5%	70.3%	29.7%
15,540	CHESTER	5,208	3,702	1,383	123	2,319	R	71.1%	26.6%	72.8%	27.2%
29,862	CLAIBORNE	8,072	5,530	2,344	198	3,186	R	68.5%	29.0%	70.2%	29.8%
7,976	CLAY	2,636	1,514	1,088	34	426	R	57.4%	41.3%	58.2%	41.8%
33,565	COCKE	8,604	6,557	1,795	252	4,762	R	76.2%	20.9%	78.5%	21.5%
48,014	COFFEE	16,284	10,188	5,920	176	4,268	R	62.6%	36.4%	63.2%	36.8%
14,532	CROCKETT	5,011	3,282	1,661	68	1,621	R	65.5%	33.1%	66.4%	33.6%
46,802	CUMBERLAND	17,566	12,322	4,693	551	7,629	R	70.1%	26.7%	72.4%	27.6%
569,891	DAVIDSON	194,598	117,611	68,424	8,563	49,187	R	60.4%	35.2%	63.2%	36.8%
11,731	DECATUR	4,044	2,423	1,574	47	849	R	59.9%	38.9%	60.6%	39.4%
17,423	DE KALB	5,361	2,948	2,252	161	696	R	55.0%	42.0%	56.7%	43.3%
43,156	DICKSON	13,886	8,463	5,307	116	3,156	R	60.9%	38.2%	61.5%	38.5%
37,279	DYER	11,308	7,449	3,691	168	3,758	R	65.9%	32.6%	66.9%	33.1%
28,806	FAYETTE	10,729	6,959	3,575	195	3,384	R	64.9%	33.3%	66.1%	33.9%
16,625	FENTRESS	5,275	3,684	1,455	136	2,229	R	69.8%	27.6%	71.7%	28.3%
39,270	FRANKLIN	13,661	7,670	5,655	336	2,015	R	56.1%	41.4%	57.6%	42.4%
48,152	GIBSON	16,149	10,021	5,843	285	4,178	R	62.1%	36.2%	63.2%	36.8%
29,447	GILES	9,015	5,059	3,663	293	1,396	R	56.1%	40.6%	58.0%	42.0%
20,659	GRAINGER	5,724	4,019	1,549	156	2,470	R	70.2%	27.1%	72.2%	27.8%
62,909	GREENE	18,464	13,867	4,230	367	9,637	R	75.1%	22.9%	76.6%	23.4%
14,332	GRUNDY	4,348	2,008	2,275	65	267	D	46.2%	52.3%	46.9%	53.1%
58,128	HAMBLEN	18,927	13,727	4,750	450	8,977	R	72.5%	25.1%	74.3%	25.7%
307,896	HAMILTON	117,710	78,652	36,733	2,325	41,919	R	66.8%	31.2%	68.2%	31.8%
6,786	HANCOCK	1,725	1,320	352	53	968	R	76.5%	20.4%	78.9%	21.1%
28,105	HARDEMAN	7,108	4,076	2,760	272	1,316	R	57.3%	38.8%	59.6%	40.4%
25,578	HARDIN	8,037	5,561	2,374	102	3,187	R	69.2%	29.5%	70.1%	29.9%
53,563	HAWKINS	15,815	11,203	4,226	386	6,977	R	70.8%	26.7%	72.6%	27.4%
19,797	HAYWOOD	5,930	3,063	2,792	75	271	R	51.7%	47.1%	52.3%	47.7%
25,522	HENDERSON	7,689	5,757	1,771	161	3,986	R	74.9%	23.0%	76.5%	23.5%
31,115	HENRY	11,266	6,669	4,386	211	2,283	R	59.2%	38.9%	60.3%	39.7%
22,295	HICKMAN	6,810	3,772	2,920	118	852	R	55.4%	42.9%	56.4%	43.6%
8,088	HOUSTON	2,691	1,168	1,512	11	344	D	43.4%	56.2%	43.6%	56.4%
17,929	HUMPHREYS	6,344	2,997	3,225	122	228	D	47.2%	50.8%	48.2%	51.8%
10,984	JACKSON	3,698	1,585	2,038	75	453	D	42.9%	55.1%	43.7%	56.3%
44,294	JEFFERSON	13,199	9,788	3,068	343	6,720	R	74.2%	23.2%	76.1%	23.9%
17,499	JOHNSON	5,240	4,014	1,059	167	2,955	R	76.6%	20.2%	79.1%	20.9%
382,032	KNOX	140,835	101,551	35,185	4,099	66,366	R	72.1%	25.0%	74.3%	25.7%
7,954	LAKE	1,441	738	682	21	56	R	51.2%	47.3%	52.0%	48.0%
27,101	LAUDERDALE	7,124	4,031	3,006	87	1,025	R	56.6%	42.2%	57.3%	42.7%
39,926	LAWRENCE	12,951	8,197	4,618	136	3,579	R	63.3%	35.7%	64.0%	36.0%
11,367	LEWIS	4,252	2,334	1,761	157	573	R	54.9%	41.4%	57.0%	43.0%
31,340	LINCOLN	9,641	5,756	3,670	215	2,086	R	59.7%	38.1%	61.1%	38.9%
39,086	LOUDON	14,780	10,694	3,672	414	7,022	R	72.4%	24.8%	74.4%	25.6%
49,015	MCMINN	16,161	11,521	4,281	359	7,240	R	71.3%	26.5%	72.9%	27.1%
24,653	MCNAIRY	8,503	5,764	2,666	73	3,098	R	67.8%	31.4%	68.4%	31.6%
20,386	MACON	5,491	3,601	1,815	75	1,786	R	65.6%	33.1%	66.5%	33.5%
91,837	MADISON	33,057	22,254	10,273	530	11,981	R	67.3%	31.1%	68.4%	31.6%
27,776	MARION	9,884	5,592	4,126	166	1,466	R	56.6%	41.7%	57.5%	42.5%
26,767	MARSHALL	8,761	5,246	3,302	213	1,944	R	59.9%	37.7%	61.4%	38.6%
69,498	MAURY	22,578	13,997	8,252	329	5,745	R	62.0%	36.5%	62.9%	37.1%
11,086	MEIGS	3,203	2,088	1,043	72	1,045	R	65.2%	32.6%	66.7%	33.3%
38,961	MONROE	12,655	8,520	3,831	304	4,689	R	67.3%	30.3%	69.0%	31.0%
134,768	MONTGOMERY	36,740	24,382	11,560	798	12,822	R	66.4%	31.5%	67.8%	32.2%
5,740	MOORE	2,010	1,267	683	60	584	R	63.0%	34.0%	65.0%	35.0%
19,757	MORGAN	5,766	3,615	2,069	82	1,546	R	62.7%	35.9%	63.6%	36.4%
32,450	OBION	9,380	6,002	3,202	176	2,800	R	64.0%	34.1%	65.2%	34.8%
20,118	OVERTON	6,022	3,001	2,938	83	63	R	49.8%	48.8%	50.5%	49.5%
7,631	PERRY	2,427	1,294	1,085	48	209	R	53.3%	44.7%	54.4%	45.6%
4,945	PICKETT	1,993	1,346	624	23	722	R	67.5%	31.3%	68.3%	31.7%
16,050	POLK	5,479	3,211	2,176	92	1,035	R	58.6%	39.7%	59.6%	40.4%

TENNESSEE

SENATOR 2000

2000 Census Population	County	Total Vote	Republican	Democratic	Other	Rep.-Dem. Plurality		Percentage			
								Total Vote		Major Vote	
								Rep.	Dem.	Rep.	Dem.
62,315	PUTNAM	21,003	13,418	6,987	598	6,431	R	63.9%	33.3%	65.8%	34.2%
28,400	RHEA	8,491	6,136	2,224	131	3,912	R	72.3%	26.2%	73.4%	26.6%
51,910	ROANE	20,159	13,646	5,988	525	7,658	R	67.7%	29.7%	69.5%	30.5%
54,433	ROBERTSON	18,868	12,135	6,461	272	5,674	R	64.3%	34.2%	65.3%	34.7%
182,023	RUTHERFORD	58,460	39,497	16,947	2,016	22,550	R	67.6%	29.0%	70.0%	30.0%
21,127	SCOTT	5,272	3,695	1,523	54	2,172	R	70.1%	28.9%	70.8%	29.2%
11,370	SEQUATCHIE	3,761	2,560	1,147	54	1,413	R	68.1%	30.5%	69.1%	30.9%
71,170	SEVIER	23,761	18,237	4,198	1,326	14,039	R	76.8%	17.7%	81.3%	18.7%
897,472	SHELBY	308,202	171,249	126,721	10,232	44,528	R	55.6%	41.1%	57.5%	42.5%
17,712	SMITH	6,033	2,927	3,027	79	100	D	48.5%	50.2%	49.2%	50.8%
12,370	STEWART	4,458	2,212	2,133	113	79	R	49.6%	47.8%	50.9%	49.1%
153,048	SULLIVAN	53,032	38,463	13,527	1,042	24,936	R	72.5%	25.5%	74.0%	26.0%
130,449	SUMNER	47,840	32,919	13,943	978	18,976	R	68.8%	29.1%	70.2%	29.8%
51,271	TIPTON	15,916	10,933	4,593	390	6,340	R	68.7%	28.9%	70.4%	29.6%
7,259	TROUSDALE	2,506	1,248	1,195	63	53	R	49.8%	47.7%	51.1%	48.9%
17,667	UNICOI	5,376	3,986	1,291	99	2,695	R	74.1%	24.0%	75.5%	24.5%
17,808	UNION	4,978	3,454	1,471	53	1,983	R	69.4%	29.6%	70.1%	29.9%
5,508	VAN BUREN	1,720	986	712	22	274	R	57.3%	41.4%	58.1%	41.9%
38,276	WARREN	12,286	7,096	4,882	308	2,214	R	57.8%	39.7%	59.2%	40.8%
107,198	WASHINGTON	35,220	25,481	8,856	883	16,625	R	72.3%	25.1%	74.2%	25.8%
16,842	WAYNE	4,504	3,236	1,236	32	2,000	R	71.8%	27.4%	72.4%	27.6%
34,895	WEAKLEY	11,340	6,936	4,240	164	2,696	R	61.2%	37.4%	62.1%	37.9%
23,102	WHITE	7,735	4,505	3,069	161	1,436	R	58.2%	39.7%	59.5%	40.5%
126,638	WILLIAMSON	55,976	44,850	9,768	1,358	35,082	R	80.1%	17.5%	82.1%	17.9%
88,809	WILSON	33,627	22,781	10,095	751	12,686	R	67.7%	30.0%	69.3%	30.7%
5,689,283	TOTAL	1,928,613	1,255,444	621,152	52,017	634,292	R	65.1%	32.2%	66.9%	33.1%

TENNESSEE

CONGRESS

CD	Year	Total Vote	Republican		Democratic		Other Vote	Rep.-Dem. Plurality		Percentage			
			Vote	Candidate	Vote	Candidate				Total Vote		Major Vote	
										Rep.	Dem.	Rep.	Dem.
1	2000	157,848	157,828	JENKINS, BILL			20	157,828	R	100.0%		100.0%	
1	1998	99,689	68,904	JENKINS, BILL	30,710	WHITE, KAY C.	75	38,194	R	69.1%	30.8%	69.2%	30.8%
1	1996	181,708	117,676	JENKINS, BILL	58,657	SMITH, KAY C.	5,375	59,019	R	64.8%	32.3%	66.7%	33.3%
1	1994	141,227	102,947	QUILLEN, JAMES H.	34,691	CHRISTIAN, J. CARR	3,589	68,256	R	72.9%	24.6%	74.8%	25.2%
1	1992	170,158	114,797	QUILLEN, JAMES H.	47,809	CHRISTIAN, J. CARR	7,552	66,988	R	67.5%	28.1%	70.6%	29.4%
2	2000	209,485	187,154	DUNCAN, JOHN J., Jr.			22,331	187,154	R	89.3%		100.0%	
2	1998	102,502	90,860	DUNCAN, JOHN J., Jr.			11,642	90,860	R	88.6%		100.0%	
2	1996	213,574	150,953	DUNCAN, JOHN J., Jr.	61,020	SMITH, STEPHEN	1,601	89,933	R	70.7%	28.6%	71.2%	28.8%
2	1994	142,482	128,937	DUNCAN, JOHN J., Jr.			13,545	128,937	R	90.5%		100.0%	
2	1992	205,401	148,377	DUNCAN, JOHN J., Jr.	52,887	GOODALE, TROY	4,137	95,490	R	72.2%	25.7%	73.7%	26.3%
3	2000	218,940	139,840	WAMP, ZACH	75,785	CALLAWAY, WILLIAM L.	3,315	64,055	R	63.9%	34.6%	64.9%	35.1%
3	1998	113,786	75,100	WAMP, ZACH	37,144	LEWIS, JAMES M., Jr.	1,542	37,956	R	66.0%	32.6%	66.9%	33.1%
3	1996	201,444	113,408	WAMP, ZACH	85,714	JOLLY, CHARLES N.	2,322	27,694	R	56.3%	42.5%	57.0%	43.0%
3	1994	161,853	84,583	WAMP, ZACH	73,839	BUTTON, RANDY	3,431	10,744	R	52.3%	45.6%	53.4%	46.6%
3	1992	216,533	102,763	WAMP, ZACH	105,693	LLOYD, MARILYN	8,077	2,930	D	47.5%	48.8%	49.3%	50.7%

TENNESSEE

CONGRESS

CD	Year	Total Vote	Republican		Democratic		Other Vote	Rep.-Dem. Plurality	Percentage			
									Total Vote		Major Vote	
			Vote	Candidate	Vote	Candidate			Rep.	Dem.	Rep.	Dem.
4	2000	203,210	133,622	HILLEARY, VAN	67,165	DUNAWAY, DAVID H.	2,423	66,457 R	65.8%	33.1%	66.5%	33.5%
4	1998	105,479	62,829	HILLEARY, VAN	42,627	COOPER, JERRY W.	23	20,202 R	59.6%	40.4%	59.6%	40.4%
4	1996	178,063	103,091	HILLEARY, VAN	73,331	STEWART, MARK	1,641	29,760 R	57.9%	41.2%	58.4%	41.6%
4	1994	143,976	81,539	HILLEARY, VAN	60,489	WHORLEY, JEFF	1,948	21,050 R	56.6%	42.0%	57.4%	42.6%
4	1992	154,511	50,340	JOHNSON, DALE	98,984	COOPER, JIM	5,187	48,644 D	32.6%	64.1%	33.7%	66.3%
5	2000	205,933	50,386	SCOTT, STAN	149,277	CLEMENT, BOB	6,270	98,891 D	24.5%	72.5%	25.2%	74.8%
5	1998	90,102			74,611	CLEMENT, BOB	15,491	74,611 D		82.8%		100.0%
5	1996	193,783	46,201	EDMONDSON, STEVEN L.	140,264	CLEMENT, BOB	7,318	94,063 D	23.8%	72.4%	24.8%	75.2%
5	1994	159,304	61,692	OSBORNE, JOHN	95,953	CLEMENT, BOB	1,659	34,261 D	38.7%	60.2%	39.1%	60.9%
5	1992	187,590	49,417	STONE, TOM	125,233	CLEMENT, BOB	12,940	75,816 D	26.3%	66.8%	28.3%	71.7%
6	2000	271,899	97,169	CHARLES, DAVID	168,861	GORDON, BART	5,869	71,692 D	35.7%	62.1%	36.5%	63.5%
6	1998	137,436	62,277	MASSEY, WALT	75,055	GORDON, BART	104	12,778 D	45.3%	54.6%	45.3%	54.7%
6	1996	195,249	62,277	GILL, STEVE	123,846	GORDON, BART	9,126	61,569 D	31.9%	63.4%	33.5%	66.5%
6	1994	179,699	88,759	GILL, STEVE	90,933	GORDON, BART	7	2,174 D	49.4%	50.6%	49.4%	50.6%
6	1992	212,428	86,289	BLACKBURN, MARSHA	120,177	GORDON, BART	5,962	33,888 D	40.6%	56.6%	41.8%	58.2%
7	2000	245,649	171,056	BRYANT, ED	71,587	SIMS, RICHARD P.	3,006	99,469 R	69.6%	29.1%	70.5%	29.5%
7	1998	91,980	91,503	BRYANT, ED			477	91,503 R	99.5%		100.0%	
7	1996	213,088	136,643	BRYANT, ED	73,629	TROTTER, DON	2,816	63,014 R	64.1%	34.6%	65.0%	35.0%
7	1994	170,383	102,587	BRYANT, ED	65,851	BYRD, HAROLD	1,945	36,736 R	60.2%	38.6%	60.9%	39.1%
7	1992	202,866	125,101	SUNDQUIST, DON	72,062	DAVIS, DAVID R.	5,703	53,039 R	61.7%	35.5%	63.5%	36.5%
8	2000	198,080	54,929	YANCY, BILLY	143,127	TANNER, JOHN	24	88,198 D	27.7%	72.3%	27.7%	72.3%
8	1998	76,825			76,803	TANNER, JOHN	22	76,803 D		100.0%		100.0%
8	1996	183,898	55,024	WATSON, TOM	123,681	TANNER, JOHN	5,193	68,657 D	29.9%	67.3%	30.8%	69.2%
8	1994	153,538	55,573	MORRIS, NEAL R.	97,951	TANNER, JOHN	14	42,378 D	36.2%	63.8%	36.2%	63.8%
8	1992	163,432			136,852	TANNER, JOHN	26,580	136,852 D		83.7%		100.0%
9	2000	143,334			143,298	FORD, HAROLD E., Jr.	36	143,298 D		100.0%		100.0%
9	1998	95,782	18,078	BURDIKOFF, CLAUDE	75,428	FORD, HAROLD E., Jr.	2,276	57,350 D	18.9%	78.7%	19.3%	80.7%
9	1996	190,414	70,951	DEBERRY, ROD	116,345	FORD, HAROLD E., Jr.	3,118	45,394 D	37.3%	61.1%	37.9%	62.1%
9	1994	164,040	69,226	DEBERRY, ROD	94,805	FORD, HAROLD E.	9	25,579 D	42.2%	57.8%	42.2%	57.8%
9	1992	212,755	60,606	BLACK, CHARLES L.	123,276	FORD, HAROLD E.	28,873	62,670 D	28.5%	57.9%	33.0%	67.0%

TENNESSEE

GENERAL AND PRIMARY ELECTIONS

2000 GENERAL ELECTIONS

President Other vote was 4,284 Libertarian (Browne); 4,250 Reform (Buchanan); 1,606 Independent (Brown); 1,015 Independent (Phillips); 613 Reform (Hagelin); 535 Independent (Venson); 428 scattered write-in. All of these candidates, including Nader, were listed as Independent, with partisan designations, where applicable, indicated in parentheses.

Senator Other vote was 25,815 Green (Burrell); 10,004 Independent (Johnson); 8,416 Independent (Watson); 4,388 Independent (Ownby); 3,135 Independent (Kinstle); 259 scattered write-in. All of these candidates were listed as Independent, including Burrell, whose partisan designation was indicated in parentheses.

Congress Other vote was: CD 1: 20 scattered write-in; CD 2: 22,304 Libertarian (Rowland), 27 scattered write-in; CD 3: 3,235 Libertarian (Austin), 80 scattered write-in; CD 4: 2,418 Independent (Lyons), 5 scattered write-in; CD 5:

TENNESSEE

GENERAL AND PRIMARY ELECTIONS

Congress (cont.)   6,268 Libertarian (Carew), 2 scattered write-in; CD 6: 4,685 Libertarian (Coffer), 1,184 scattered write-in; CD 7: 2,941 Libertarian (Solee), 65 scattered write-in; CD 8: 24 scattered write-in; CD 9: 36 scattered write-in. All of these candidates were listed as Independent, with partisan designations, where applicable, indicated in parentheses.

2000 PRIMARY ELECTIONS

Primary   March 14, 2000   (President)   **Registration**   3,176,984   No Party Registration
August 3, 2000   (Congress)   (as of Aug. 3, 2000)

Primary Type   Open—Any registered voter could vote in either the Democratic or Republican primary.

Note: An asterisk (*) denotes incumbent.

	REPUBLICAN PRIMARIES			DEMOCRATIC PRIMARIES		
President	George W. Bush	193,166	77.0%	Al Gore	198,264	92.1%
	John McCain	36,436	14.5%	Bill Bradley	11,323	5.3%
	Alan Keyes	16,916	6.7%	Uncommitted	4,407	2.0%
	Uncommitted	1,623	0.6%	Lyndon H. LaRouche Jr.	1,031	0.5%
	Gary Bauer	1,305	0.5%	Write-in	178	0.1%
	Steve Forbes	1,018	0.4%			
	Orrin G. Hatch	252	0.1%			
	Write-in	75				
	TOTAL	250,791		TOTAL	215,203	
Senator	Bill Frist*	186,882	99.8%	Jeff Clark	64,851	34.2%
	Write-in	345	0.2%	John Jay Hooker	64,041	33.8%
				Mary Taylor-Shelby	28,604	15.1%
				Shannon Wood	25,372	13.4%
				James Looney	6,354	3.4%
				Write-in	218	0.1%
	TOTAL	187,227		TOTAL	189,440	
Congressional District 1	Bill Jenkins*	24,440	99.7%	No Democratic candidate		
	Write-in	64	0.3%			
	TOTAL	24,504				
Congressional District 2	John J. "Jimmy" Duncan Jr.*	27,450	100.0%	No Democratic candidate		
	Write-in	5				
	TOTAL	27,455				
Congressional District 3	Zach Wamp*	25,129	99.3%	William L. Callaway	17,148	98.0%
	Write-in	185	0.7%	Write-in	350	2.0%
	TOTAL	25,314		TOTAL	17,498	
Congressional District 4	Van Hilleary*	21,192	99.8%	David H. Dunaway	14,563	63.9%
	Write-in	46	0.2%	Jack Jennings	8,203	36.0%
				Write-in	29	0.1%
	TOTAL	21,238		TOTAL	22,795	
Congressional District 5	Stan Scott	6,160	100.0%	Bob Clement*	20,414	100.0%
				Write-in	9	
	TOTAL	6,160		TOTAL	20,423	
Congressional District 6	David Charles	11,680	54.0%	Bart Gordon*	31,546	99.7%
	Eleanor Gibbs	9,915	45.9%	Write-in	87	0.3%
	Write-in	23	0.1%			
	TOTAL	21,618		TOTAL	31,633	
Congressional District 7	Ed Bryant*	29,755	99.9%	Richard P. Sims	11,834	57.6%
	Write-in	16	0.1%	Bob Hatton	8,703	42.3%
				Write-in	22	0.1%
	TOTAL	29,771		TOTAL	20,559	
Congressional District 8	Bill Yancy	12,062	100.0%	John Tanner*	32,078	86.7%
	Write-in	1		Marvin Williams	4,914	13.3%
				Write-in	11	
	TOTAL	12,063		TOTAL	37,003	
Congressional District 9	No Republican candidate			Harold E. Ford Jr.*	33,280	99.8%
				Write-in	52	0.2%
				TOTAL	33,332	

TEXAS

GOVERNOR
Rick Perry (R). Assumed office Dec. 21, 2000, following the resignation of president-elect George W. Bush.

SENATORS
Kay Bailey Hutchison (R). Re-elected 2000 to a six-year term. Previously elected 1994 and in a special election June 5, 1993, to fill out the remaining year and a half of the term vacated when Senator Lloyd Bentsen (D) resigned to become Secretary of the Treasury.

Phil Gramm (R). Re-elected 1996 to a six-year term. Previously elected 1990, 1984.

REPRESENTATIVES
1. Max Sandlin (D)
2. Jim Turner (D)
3. Sam Johnson (R)
4. Ralph M. Hall (D)
5. Pete Sessions (R)
6. Joe L. Barton (R)
7. John Culberson (R)
8. Kevin Brady (R)
9. Nick Lampson (D)
10. Lloyd Doggett (D)
11. Chet Edwards (D)
12. Kay Granger (R)
13. William M. Thornberry (R)
14. Ron Paul (R)
15. Ruben Hinojosa (D)
16. Silvestre Reyes (D)
17. Charles W. Stenholm (D)
18. Sheila Jackson-Lee (D)
19. Larry Combest (R)
20. Charlie Gonzalez (D)
21. Lamar Smith (R)
22. Thomas D. DeLay (R)
23. Henry Bonilla (R)
24. Martin Frost (D)
25. Ken Bentsen (D)
26. Dick Armey (R)
27. Solomon P. Ortiz (D)
28. Ciro D. Rodriguez (D)
29. Gene Green (D)
30. Eddie B. Johnson (D)

POSTWAR VOTE FOR PRESIDENT

Year	Total Vote	Republican Vote	Candidate	Democratic Vote	Candidate	Other Vote	Plurality	Total Vote Rep.	Total Vote Dem.	Major Vote Rep.	Major Vote Dem.
2000**	6,407,637	3,799,639	Bush, George W.	2,433,746	Gore, Al	174,252	1,365,893 R	59.3%	38.0%	61.0%	39.0%
1996**	5,611,644	2,736,167	Dole, Bob	2,459,683	Clinton, Bill	415,794	276,484 R	48.8%	43.8%	52.7%	47.3%
1992**	6,154,018	2,496,071	Bush, George	2,281,815	Clinton, Bill	1,376,132	214,256 R	40.6%	37.1%	52.2%	47.8%
1988	5,427,410	3,036,829	Bush, George	2,352,748	Dukakis, Michael S.	37,833	684,081 R	56.0%	43.3%	56.3%	43.7%
1984	5,397,571	3,433,428	Reagan, Ronald	1,949,276	Mondale, Walter F.	14,867	1,484,152 R	63.6%	36.1%	63.8%	36.2%
1980**	4,541,636	2,510,705	Reagan, Ronald	1,881,147	Carter, Jimmy	149,784	629,558 R	55.3%	41.4%	57.2%	42.8%
1976	4,071,884	1,953,300	Ford, Gerald R.	2,082,319	Carter, Jimmy	36,265	129,019 D	48.0%	51.1%	48.4%	51.6%
1972	3,471,281	2,298,896	Nixon, Richard M.	1,154,289	McGovern, George S.	18,096	1,144,607 R	66.2%	33.3%	66.6%	33.4%
1968**	3,079,216	1,227,844	Nixon, Richard M.	1,266,804	Humphrey, Hubert H.	584,568	38,960 D	39.9%	41.1%	49.2%	50.8%
1964	2,626,811	958,566	Goldwater, Barry M.	1,663,185	Johnson, Lyndon B.	5,060	704,619 D	36.5%	63.3%	36.6%	63.4%
1960	2,311,084	1,121,310	Nixon, Richard M.	1,167,567	Kennedy, John F.	22,207	46,257 D	48.5%	50.5%	49.0%	51.0%
1956	1,955,168	1,080,619	Eisenhower, Dwight D.	859,958	Stevenson, Adlai E.	14,591	220,661 R	55.3%	44.0%	55.7%	44.3%
1952	2,075,946	1,102,878	Eisenhower, Dwight D.	969,228	Stevenson, Adlai E.	3,840	133,650 R	53.1%	46.7%	53.2%	46.8%
1948	1,249,577	303,467	Dewey, Thomas E.	824,235	Truman, Harry S.	121,875	520,768 D	24.3%	66.0%	26.9%	73.1%

In 2000 the other vote column includes 137,994 votes cast for Green (Nader). In 1996 the other vote column includes 378,537 votes cast for Perot. In 1992 the other vote column includes 1,354,781 votes cast for Perot. In 1980 the other column includes 111,613 votes for Independent (Anderson). In 1968 other vote was 584,269 American (Wallace) and 299 scattered.

TEXAS

POSTWAR VOTE FOR GOVERNOR

Year	Total Vote	Republican Vote	Republican Candidate	Democratic Vote	Democratic Candidate	Other Vote	Rep.-Dem. Plurality	Total Vote Rep.	Total Vote Dem.	Major Vote Rep.	Major Vote Dem.
1998	3,738,483	2,551,454	Bush, George W.	1,165,444	Mauro, Garry	21,585	1,386,010 R	68.2%	31.2%	68.6%	31.4%
1994	4,396,242	2,350,994	Bush, George W.	2,016,928	Richards, Ann	28,320	334,066 R	53.5%	45.9%	53.8%	46.2%
1990	3,892,746	1,826,431	Williams, Clayton	1,925,670	Richards, Ann	140,645	99,239 D	46.9%	49.5%	48.7%	51.3%
1986	3,441,460	1,813,779	Clements, William P.	1,584,515	White, Mark	43,166	229,264 R	52.7%	46.0%	53.4%	46.6%
1982	3,191,091	1,465,937	Clements, William P.	1,697,870	White, Mark	27,284	231,933 D	45.9%	53.2%	46.3%	53.7%
1978	2,369,764	1,183,839	Clements, William P.	1,166,979	Hill, John	18,946	16,860 R	50.0%	49.2%	50.4%	49.6%
1974**	1,654,984	514,725	Granberry, Jim	1,016,334	Briscoe, Dolph	123,925	501,609 D	31.1%	61.4%	33.6%	66.4%
1972	3,410,128	1,534,060	Grover, Henry C.	1,633,970	Briscoe, Dolph	242,098	99,910 D	45.0%	47.9%	48.4%	51.6%
1970	2,235,847	1,037,723	Eggers, Paul W.	1,197,726	Smith, Preston	398	160,003 D	46.4%	53.6%	46.4%	53.6%
1968	2,916,509	1,254,333	Eggers, Paul W.	1,662,019	Smith, Preston	157	407,686 D	43.0%	57.0%	43.0%	57.0%
1966	1,425,861	368,025	Kennerly, T. E.	1,037,517	Connally, John B.	20,319	669,492 D	25.8%	72.8%	26.2%	73.8%
1964	2,544,753	661,675	Crichton, Jack	1,877,793	Connally, John B.	5,285	1,216,118 D	26.0%	73.8%	26.1%	73.9%
1962	1,569,181	715,025	Cox, Jack	847,036	Connally, John B.	7,120	132,011 D	45.6%	54.0%	45.8%	54.2%
1960	2,250,718	612,963	Steger, William M.	1,637,755	Daniel, Price		1,024,792 D	27.2%	72.8%	27.2%	72.8%
1958	789,133	94,098	Mayer, Edwin S.	695,035	Daniel, Price		600,937 D	11.9%	88.1%	11.9%	88.1%
1956	1,828,161	271,088	Bryant, William R.	1,433,051	Daniel, Price	124,022	1,161,963 D	14.8%	78.4%	15.9%	84.1%
1954	636,892	66,154	Adams, Tod R.	569,533	Shivers, Allan	1,205	503,379 D	10.4%	89.4%	10.4%	89.6%
1952	1,881,202		—	1,844,530	Shivers, Allan	36,672	1,844,530 D		98.1%		100.0%
1950	394,747	39,737	Currie, Ralph W.	355,010	Shivers, Allan		315,273 D	10.1%	89.9%	10.1%	89.9%
1948	1,208,860	177,399	Lane, Alvin H.	1,024,160	Jester, Beauford	7,301	846,761 D	14.7%	84.7%	14.8%	85.2%
1946	378,744	33,231	Nolte, Eugene	345,513	Jester, Beauford		312,282 D	8.8%	91.2%	8.8%	91.2%

The term of office of Texas' Governor was increased from two to four years effective with the 1974 election.

POSTWAR VOTE FOR SENATOR

Year	Total Vote	Republican Vote	Republican Candidate	Democratic Vote	Democratic Candidate	Other Vote	Rep.-Dem. Plurality	Total Vote Rep.	Total Vote Dem.	Major Vote Rep.	Major Vote Dem.
2000	6,276,652	4,082,091	Hutchison, Kay Bailey	2,030,315	Kelly, Gene	164,246	2,051,776 R	65.0%	32.3%	66.8%	33.2%
1996	5,527,441	3,027,680	Gramm, Phil	2,428,776	Morales, Victor M.	70,985	598,904 R	54.8%	43.9%	55.5%	44.5%
1994	4,279,940	2,604,218	Hutchison, Kay Bailey	1,639,615	Fisher, Richard	36,107	964,603 R	60.8%	38.3%	61.4%	38.6%
1993S	1,765,254	1,188,716	Hutchison, Kay Bailey	576,538	Krueger, Robert		612,178 R	67.3%	32.7%	67.3%	32.7%
1990	3,822,157	2,302,357	Gramm, Phil	1,429,986	Parmer, Hugh	89,814	872,371 R	60.2%	37.4%	61.7%	38.3%
1988	5,323,606	2,129,228	Boulter, Beau	3,149,806	Bentsen, Lloyd	44,572	1,020,578 D	40.0%	59.2%	40.3%	59.7%
1984	5,319,178	3,116,348	Gramm, Phil	2,202,557	Doggett, Lloyd	273	913,791 R	58.6%	41.4%	58.6%	41.4%
1982	3,103,167	1,256,759	Collins, James M.	1,818,223	Bentsen, Lloyd	28,185	561,464 D	40.5%	58.6%	40.9%	59.1%
1978	2,312,540	1,151,376	Tower, John G.	1,139,149	Krueger, Robert	22,015	12,227 R	49.8%	49.3%	50.3%	49.7%
1976	3,874,516	1,636,370	Steelman, Alan	2,199,956	Bentsen, Lloyd	38,190	563,586 D	42.2%	56.8%	42.7%	57.3%
1972	3,413,903	1,822,877	Tower, John G.	1,511,985	Sanders, Barefoot	79,041	310,892 R	53.4%	44.3%	54.7%	45.3%
1970	2,231,671	1,035,794	Bush, George	1,194,069	Bentsen, Lloyd	1,808	158,275 D	46.4%	53.5%	46.5%	53.5%
1966	1,493,182	842,501	Tower, John G.	643,855	Carr, Waggoner	6,826	198,646 R	56.4%	43.1%	56.7%	43.3%
1964	2,603,856	1,134,337	Bush, George	1,463,958	Yarborough, Ralph	5,561	329,621 D	43.6%	56.2%	43.7%	56.3%
1961S	886,091	448,217	Tower, John G.	437,874	Blakley, William A.		10,343 R	50.6%	49.4%	50.6%	49.4%
1960	2,253,784	926,653	Tower, John G.	1,306,625	Johnson, Lyndon B.	20,506	379,972 D	41.1%	58.0%	41.5%	58.5%
1958	787,128	185,926	Whittenburg, Roy [See note below]	587,030	Yarborough, Ralph	14,172	401,104 D	23.6%	74.6%	24.1%	75.9%
1957S	957,298						D				
1954	636,475	94,131	Watson, Carlos G.	539,319	Johnson, Lyndon B.	3,025	445,188 D	14.8%	84.7%	14.9%	85.1%
1952	1,895,192		—	1,895,192	Daniel, Price		1,895,192 D		100.0%		100.0%
1948	1,061,563	349,665	Porter, Jack	702,985	Johnson, Lyndon B.	8,913	353,320 D	32.9%	66.2%	33.2%	66.8%
1946	380,681	43,750	Sells, Murray C.	336,931	Connally, Tom		293,181 D	11.5%	88.5%	11.5%	88.5%

The June 1993 election was for a short term to fill a vacancy; the vote above was for the runoff special election. The May 1961 and April 1957 elections were for short terms to fill vacancies. Though neither vote was held with official party designations, the 1961 vote above was a runoff contest between unofficial party candidates. In 1957 there was a single ballot without a runoff and Ralph Yarborough polled 364,605 votes (38.1% of the total vote) and won the election with a 73,802 plurality.

TEXAS

Districts Established August 29, 1991

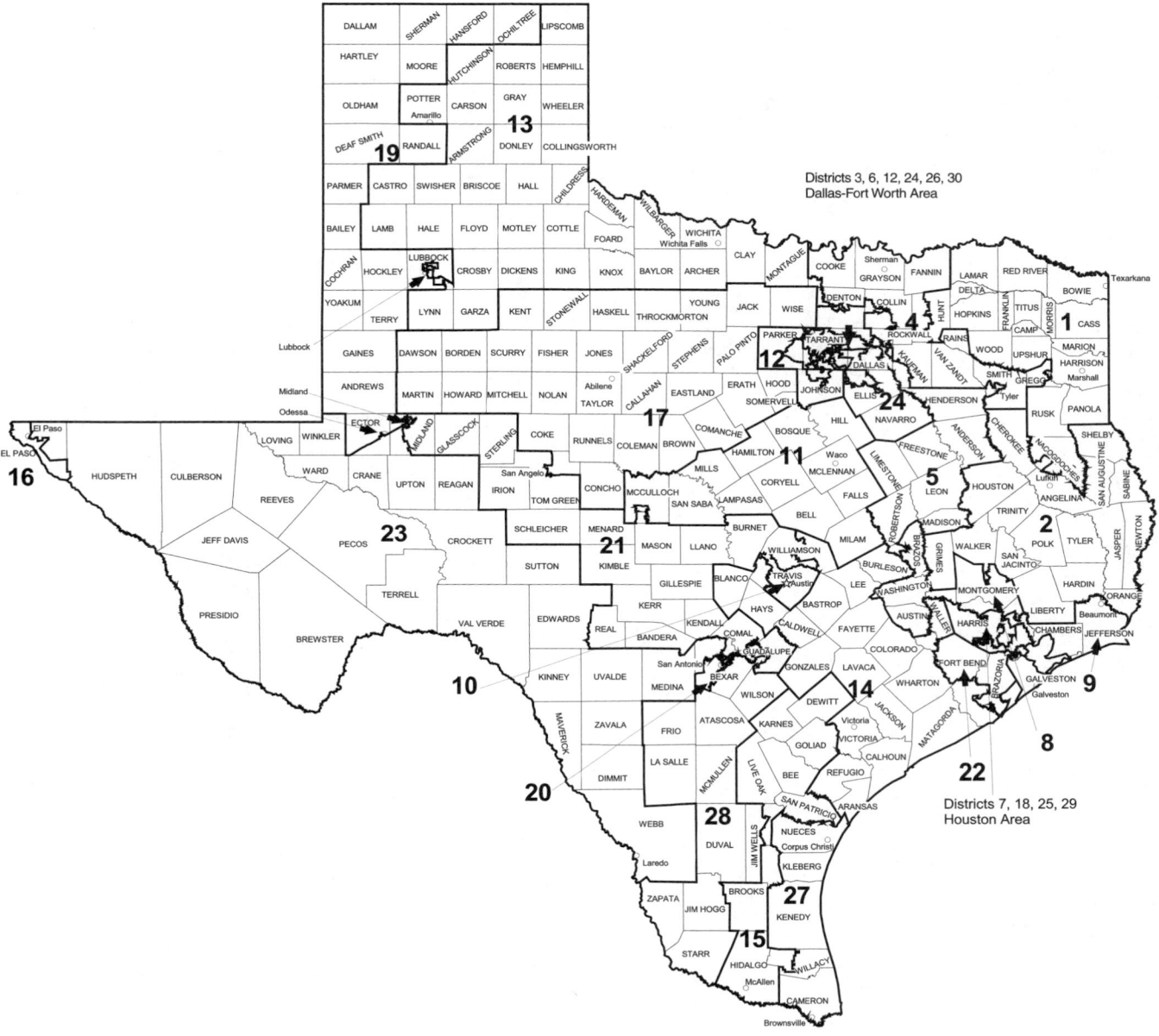

Districts 3, 6, 12, 24, 26, 30
Dallas-Fort Worth Area

Districts 7, 18, 25, 29
Houston Area

Note: Texas districts were established originally in 1991. In August 1996 a U.S. district court redrew boundaries for 13 districts located in the Houston and Dallas-Fort Worth areas. The new lines for those areas are shown in the detail maps on pages 414 and 415.

HOUSTON METROPOLITAN AREA

CONGRESSIONAL DISTRICTS

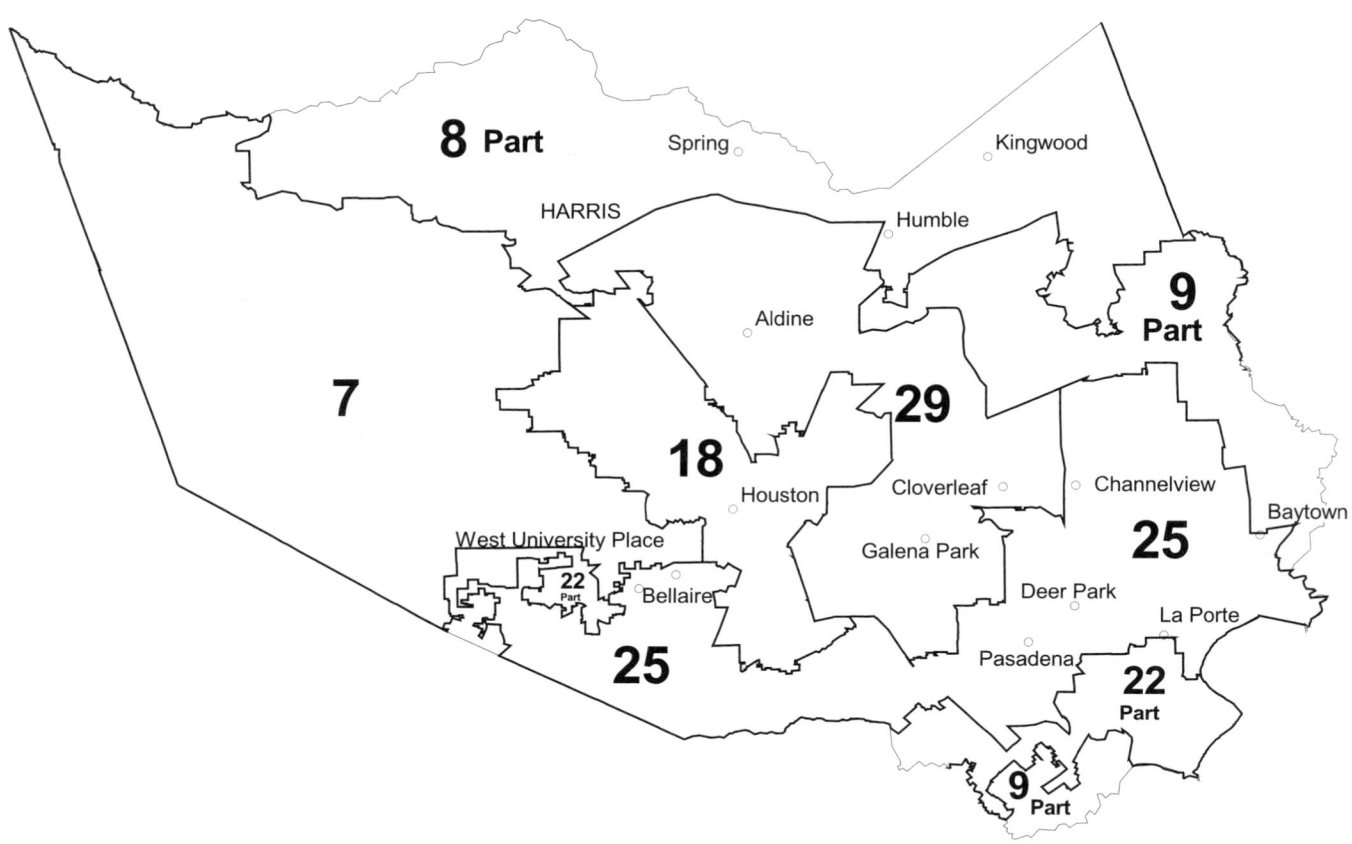

DALLAS-FORT WORTH METROPOLITAN AREA

CONGRESSIONAL DISTRICTS

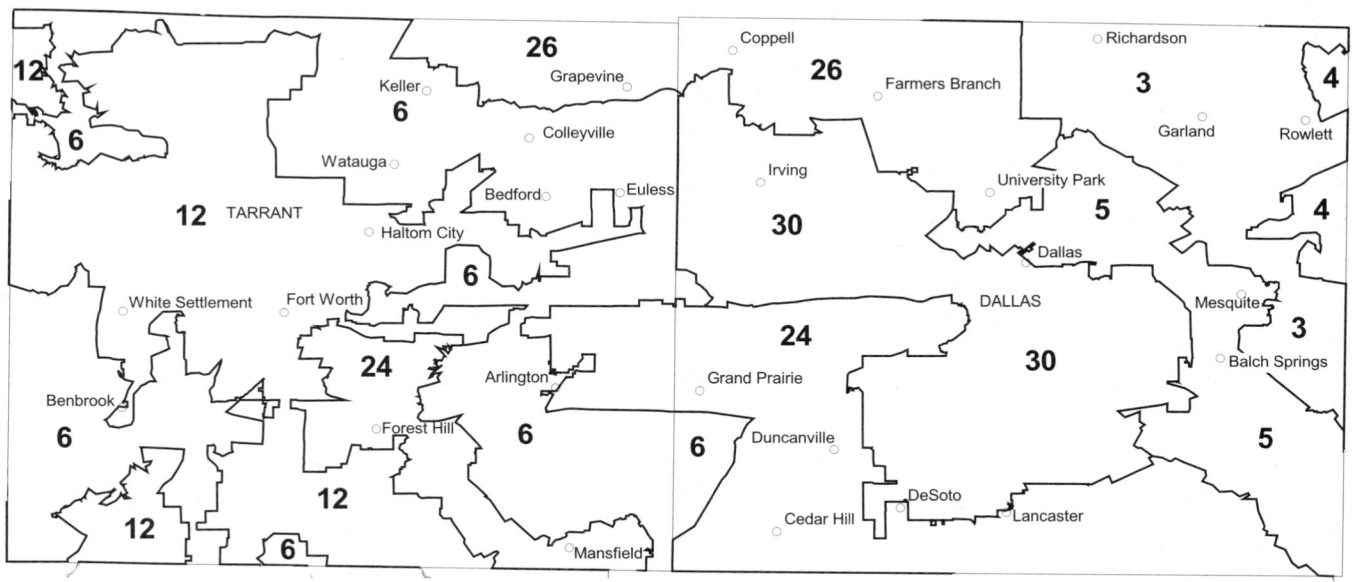

TEXAS

PRESIDENT 2000

2000 Census Population	County	Total Vote	Republican	Democratic	Green (Nader)	Other	Rep.-Dem. Plurality	Percentage of Total Vote		
								Rep.	Dem.	Green
55,109	ANDERSON	15,080	9,835	5,041	131	73	4,794 R	65.2%	33.4%	0.9%
13,004	ANDREWS	4,024	3,091	876	28	29	2,215 R	76.8%	21.8%	0.7%
80,130	ANGELINA	26,974	16,648	9,957	245	124	6,691 R	61.7%	36.9%	0.9%
22,497	ARANSAS	8,247	5,390	2,637	182	38	2,753 R	65.4%	32.0%	2.2%
8,854	ARCHER	3,997	2,951	993	36	17	1,958 R	73.8%	24.8%	0.9%
2,148	ARMSTRONG	938	772	150	11	5	622 R	82.3%	16.0%	1.2%
38,628	ATASCOSA	10,746	6,231	4,322	130	63	1,909 R	58.0%	40.2%	1.2%
23,590	AUSTIN	9,227	6,661	2,407	112	47	4,254 R	72.2%	26.1%	1.2%
6,594	BAILEY	2,090	1,589	488	6	7	1,101 R	76.0%	23.3%	0.3%
17,645	BANDERA	7,273	5,613	1,426	157	77	4,187 R	77.2%	19.6%	2.2%
57,733	BASTROP	18,308	10,310	6,973	871	154	3,337 R	56.3%	38.1%	4.8%
4,093	BAYLOR	1,984	1,285	663	26	10	622 R	64.8%	33.4%	1.3%
32,359	BEE	8,330	4,429	3,795	66	40	634 R	53.2%	45.6%	0.8%
237,974	BELL	63,291	41,208	21,011	728	344	20,197 R	65.1%	33.2%	1.2%
1,392,931	BEXAR	412,726	215,613	185,158	9,790	2,165	30,455 R	52.2%	44.9%	2.4%
8,418	BLANCO	3,767	2,777	811	140	39	1,966 R	73.7%	21.5%	3.7%
729	BORDEN	353	283	62	5	3	221 R	80.2%	17.6%	1.4%
17,204	BOSQUE	6,770	4,745	1,930	65	30	2,815 R	70.1%	28.5%	1.0%
89,306	BOWIE	30,320	18,325	11,662	238	95	6,663 R	60.4%	38.5%	0.8%
241,767	BRAZORIA	80,019	53,445	24,883	1,212	479	28,562 R	66.8%	31.1%	1.5%
152,415	BRAZOS	46,941	32,864	12,359	1,351	367	20,505 R	70.0%	26.3%	2.9%
8,866	BREWSTER	3,580	1,867	1,349	306	58	518 R	52.2%	37.7%	8.5%
1,790	BRISCOE	772	544	224	1	3	320 R	70.5%	29.0%	0.1%
7,976	BROOKS	2,431	556	1,854	14	7	1,298 D	22.9%	76.3%	0.6%
37,674	BROWN	12,920	9,609	3,138	125	48	6,471 R	74.4%	24.3%	1.0%
16,470	BURLESON	5,866	3,542	2,235	60	29	1,307 R	60.4%	38.1%	1.0%
34,147	BURNET	13,232	9,286	3,557	292	97	5,729 R	70.2%	26.9%	2.2%
32,194	CALDWELL	9,425	5,216	3,872	266	71	1,344 R	55.3%	41.1%	2.8%
20,647	CALHOUN	6,563	3,724	2,766	43	30	958 R	56.7%	42.1%	0.7%
12,905	CALLAHAN	4,896	3,656	1,174	34	32	2,482 R	74.7%	24.0%	0.7%
335,227	CAMERON	62,057	27,800	33,214	699	344	5,414 D	44.8%	53.5%	1.1%
11,549	CAMP	3,784	2,121	1,625	31	7	496 R	56.1%	42.9%	0.8%
6,516	CARSON	2,742	2,216	480	29	17	1,736 R	80.8%	17.5%	1.1%
30,438	CASS	11,019	6,295	4,618	68	38	1,677 R	57.1%	41.9%	0.6%
8,285	CASTRO	2,354	1,607	727	7	13	880 R	68.3%	30.9%	0.3%
26,031	CHAMBERS	9,806	6,769	2,888	111	38	3,881 R	69.0%	29.5%	1.1%
46,659	CHEROKEE	14,537	9,599	4,755	122	61	4,844 R	66.0%	32.7%	0.8%
7,688	CHILDRESS	2,126	1,506	602	11	7	904 R	70.8%	28.3%	0.5%
11,006	CLAY	4,637	3,112	1,460	39	26	1,652 R	67.1%	31.5%	0.8%
3,730	COCHRAN	1,171	807	344	11	9	463 R	68.9%	29.4%	0.9%
3,864	COKE	1,515	1,137	355	14	9	782 R	75.0%	23.4%	0.9%
9,235	COLEMAN	3,578	2,687	853	27	11	1,834 R	75.1%	23.8%	0.8%
491,675	COLLIN	175,420	128,179	42,884	3,195	1,162	85,295 R	73.1%	24.4%	1.8%
3,206	COLLINGSWORTH	1,415	974	429	6	6	545 R	68.8%	30.3%	0.4%
20,390	COLORADO	7,249	4,913	2,229	84	23	2,684 R	67.8%	30.7%	1.2%
78,021	COMAL	32,748	24,599	7,131	787	231	17,468 R	75.1%	21.8%	2.4%
14,026	COMANCHE	5,022	3,334	1,636	33	19	1,698 R	66.4%	32.6%	0.7%
3,966	CONCHO	1,103	818	268	10	7	550 R	74.2%	24.3%	0.9%
36,363	COOKE	13,469	10,128	3,153	124	64	6,975 R	75.2%	23.4%	0.9%
74,978	CORYELL	15,087	10,321	4,493	202	71	5,828 R	68.4%	29.8%	1.3%
1,904	COTTLE	757	502	241	3	11	261 R	66.3%	31.8%	0.4%
3,996	CRANE	1,654	1,246	387	16	5	859 R	75.3%	23.4%	1.0%
4,099	CROCKETT	1,398	924	467	2	5	457 R	66.1%	33.4%	0.1%
7,072	CROSBY	2,002	1,270	705	23	4	565 R	63.4%	35.2%	1.1%
2,975	CULBERSON	1,012	413	577	12	10	164 D	40.8%	57.0%	1.2%
6,222	DALLAM	1,744	1,385	341	11	7	1,044 R	79.4%	19.6%	0.6%
2,218,899	DALLAS	613,039	322,345	275,308	11,671	3,715	47,037 R	52.6%	44.9%	1.9%
14,985	DAWSON	4,839	3,337	1,463	17	22	1,874 R	69.0%	30.2%	0.4%
18,561	DEAF SMITH	4,984	3,687	1,240	27	30	2,447 R	74.0%	24.9%	0.5%
5,327	DELTA	1,900	1,143	726	16	15	417 R	60.2%	38.2%	0.8%

TEXAS

PRESIDENT 2000

2000 Census Population	County	Total Vote	Republican	Democratic	Green (Nader)	Other	Rep.-Dem. Plurality	Percentage of Total Vote		
								Rep.	Dem.	Green
432,976	DENTON	146,790	102,171	40,144	3,430	1,045	62,027 R	69.6%	27.3%	2.3%
20,013	DE WITT	6,183	4,541	1,570	53	19	2,971 R	73.4%	25.4%	0.9%
2,762	DICKENS	881	589	284	3	5	305 R	66.9%	32.2%	0.3%
10,248	DIMMIT	3,753	1,032	2,678	20	23	1,646 D	27.5%	71.4%	0.5%
3,828	DONLEY	1,719	1,333	360	18	8	973 R	77.5%	20.9%	1.0%
13,120	DUVAL	5,030	1,010	3,990	22	8	2,980 D	20.1%	79.3%	0.4%
18,297	EASTLAND	6,414	4,531	1,774	56	53	2,757 R	70.6%	27.7%	0.9%
121,123	ECTOR	32,901	22,893	9,425	378	205	13,468 R	69.6%	28.6%	1.1%
2,162	EDWARDS	937	663	261	6	7	402 R	70.8%	27.9%	0.6%
111,360	ELLIS	37,307	26,091	10,629	377	210	15,462 R	69.9%	28.5%	1.0%
679,622	EL PASO	145,042	57,574	83,848	2,840	780	26,274 D	39.7%	57.8%	2.0%
33,001	ERATH	11,115	8,126	2,804	129	56	5,322 R	73.1%	25.2%	1.2%
18,576	FALLS	5,715	3,239	2,417	33	26	822 R	56.7%	42.3%	0.6%
31,242	FANNIN	10,340	6,074	4,102	110	54	1,972 R	58.7%	39.7%	1.1%
21,804	FAYETTE	9,387	6,658	2,542	132	55	4,116 R	70.9%	27.1%	1.4%
4,344	FISHER	1,872	968	884	11	9	84 R	51.7%	47.2%	0.6%
7,771	FLOYD	2,420	1,830	580	8	2	1,250 R	75.6%	24.0%	0.3%
1,622	FOARD	556	286	263	5	2	23 R	51.4%	47.3%	0.9%
354,452	FORT BEND	123,509	73,567	47,569	1,953	420	25,998 R	59.6%	38.5%	1.6%
9,458	FRANKLIN	3,472	2,420	1,018	22	12	1,402 R	69.7%	29.3%	0.6%
17,867	FREESTONE	6,641	4,247	2,316	46	32	1,931 R	64.0%	34.9%	0.7%
16,252	FRIO	4,128	1,774	2,317	23	14	543 D	43.0%	56.1%	0.6%
14,467	GAINES	3,459	2,691	723	23	22	1,968 R	77.8%	20.9%	0.7%
250,158	GALVESTON	92,983	50,397	40,020	2,150	416	10,377 R	54.2%	43.0%	2.3%
4,872	GARZA	1,770	1,302	454	8	6	848 R	73.6%	25.6%	0.5%
20,814	GILLESPIE	9,920	8,096	1,511	220	93	6,585 R	81.6%	15.2%	2.2%
1,406	GLASSCOCK	571	528	39	3	1	489 R	92.5%	6.8%	0.5%
6,928	GOLIAD	3,392	2,108	1,233	27	24	875 R	62.1%	36.4%	0.8%
18,628	GONZALES	6,069	4,092	1,877	72	28	2,215 R	67.4%	30.9%	1.2%
22,744	GRAY	8,185	6,732	1,376	40	37	5,356 R	82.2%	16.8%	0.5%
110,595	GRAYSON	39,940	25,596	13,647	484	213	11,949 R	64.1%	34.2%	1.2%
111,379	GREGG	38,433	26,739	11,244	324	126	15,495 R	69.6%	29.3%	0.8%
23,552	GRIMES	6,802	4,197	2,450	98	57	1,747 R	61.7%	36.0%	1.4%
89,023	GUADALUPE	30,567	21,499	8,311	545	212	13,188 R	70.3%	27.2%	1.8%
36,602	HALE	9,110	6,868	2,158	45	39	4,710 R	75.4%	23.7%	0.5%
3,782	HALL	1,446	966	472	6	2	494 R	66.8%	32.6%	0.4%
8,229	HAMILTON	3,376	2,447	878	27	24	1,569 R	72.5%	26.0%	0.8%
5,369	HANSFORD	2,088	1,874	198	12	4	1,676 R	89.8%	9.5%	0.6%
4,724	HARDEMAN	1,557	976	566	10	5	410 R	62.7%	36.4%	0.6%
48,073	HARDIN	17,836	11,962	5,595	185	94	6,367 R	67.1%	31.4%	1.0%
3,400,578	HARRIS	974,822	529,159	418,267	22,994	4,402	110,892 R	54.3%	42.9%	2.4%
62,110	HARRISON	22,970	13,834	8,878	164	94	4,956 R	60.2%	38.7%	0.7%
5,537	HARTLEY	2,031	1,645	359	16	11	1,286 R	81.0%	17.7%	0.8%
6,093	HASKELL	2,927	1,488	1,401	23	15	87 R	50.8%	47.9%	0.8%
97,589	HAYS	34,317	20,170	11,387	2,451	309	8,783 R	58.8%	33.2%	7.1%
3,351	HEMPHILL	1,474	1,203	251	13	7	952 R	81.6%	17.0%	0.9%
73,277	HENDERSON	25,627	16,607	8,704	201	115	7,903 R	64.8%	34.0%	0.8%
569,463	HIDALGO	101,050	38,301	61,390	968	391	23,089 D	37.9%	60.8%	1.0%
32,321	HILL	10,735	7,054	3,524	100	57	3,530 R	65.7%	32.8%	0.9%
22,716	HOCKLEY	6,745	5,250	1,419	41	35	3,831 R	77.8%	21.0%	0.6%
41,100	HOOD	17,505	12,429	4,704	239	133	7,725 R	71.0%	26.9%	1.4%
31,960	HOPKINS	10,910	7,076	3,692	82	60	3,384 R	64.9%	33.8%	0.8%
23,185	HOUSTON	8,236	5,308	2,833	51	44	2,475 R	64.4%	34.4%	0.6%
33,627	HOWARD	9,548	6,668	2,744	75	61	3,924 R	69.8%	28.7%	0.8%
3,344	HUDSPETH	922	514	380	15	13	134 R	55.7%	41.2%	1.6%
76,596	HUNT	24,466	16,177	7,857	283	149	8,320 R	66.1%	32.1%	1.2%
23,857	HUTCHINSON	9,351	7,443	1,796	59	53	5,647 R	79.6%	19.2%	0.6%
1,771	IRION	793	624	162	2	5	462 R	78.7%	20.4%	0.3%
8,763	JACK	2,974	2,107	822	26	19	1,285 R	70.8%	27.6%	0.9%
14,391	JACKSON	4,856	3,365	1,446	33	12	1,919 R	69.3%	29.8%	0.7%

TEXAS

PRESIDENT 2000

2000 Census Population	County	Total Vote	Republican	Democratic	Green (Nader)	Other	Rep.-Dem. Plurality	Percentage of Total Vote		
								Rep.	Dem.	Green
35,604	JASPER	11,742	7,071	4,533	87	51	2,538 R	60.2%	38.6%	0.7%
2,207	JEFF DAVIS	1,060	708	283	46	23	425 R	66.8%	26.7%	4.3%
252,051	JEFFERSON	86,909	40,320	45,409	796	384	5,089 D	46.4%	52.2%	0.9%
5,281	JIM HOGG	2,157	623	1,512	9	13	889 D	28.9%	70.1%	0.4%
39,326	JIM WELLS	12,023	4,498	7,418	73	34	2,920 D	37.4%	61.7%	0.6%
126,811	JOHNSON	38,726	26,202	11,778	513	233	14,424 R	67.7%	30.4%	1.3%
20,785	JONES	6,048	4,080	1,899	50	19	2,181 R	67.5%	31.4%	0.8%
15,446	KARNES	4,308	2,638	1,617	25	28	1,021 R	61.2%	37.5%	0.6%
71,313	KAUFMAN	23,063	15,290	7,455	207	111	7,835 R	66.3%	32.3%	0.9%
23,743	KENDALL	11,073	8,788	1,901	286	98	6,887 R	79.4%	17.2%	2.6%
414	KENEDY	228	106	119	2	1	13 D	46.5%	52.2%	0.9%
859	KENT	536	346	185		5	161 R	64.6%	34.5%	
43,653	KERR	19,228	14,637	4,002	463	126	10,635 R	76.1%	20.8%	2.4%
4,468	KIMBLE	1,666	1,313	328	15	10	985 R	78.8%	19.7%	0.9%
356	KING	137	120	14		3	106 R	87.6%	10.2%	
3,379	KINNEY	1,444	932	486	16	10	446 R	64.5%	33.7%	1.1%
31,549	KLEBERG	9,194	4,526	4,481	131	56	45 R	49.2%	48.7%	1.4%
4,253	KNOX	1,576	947	617	8	4	330 R	60.1%	39.1%	0.5%
48,499	LAMAR	15,430	9,775	5,553	99	3	4,222 R	63.4%	36.0%	0.6%
14,709	LAMB	4,598	3,451	1,114	15	18	2,337 R	75.1%	24.2%	0.3%
17,762	LAMPASAS	6,214	4,526	1,569	78	41	2,957 R	72.8%	25.2%	1.3%
5,866	LA SALLE	2,014	731	1,266	5	12	535 D	36.3%	62.9%	0.2%
19,210	LAVACA	7,546	5,288	2,171	53	34	3,117 R	70.1%	28.8%	0.7%
15,657	LEE	5,536	3,699	1,733	76	28	1,966 R	66.8%	31.3%	1.4%
15,335	LEON	6,326	4,362	1,893	46	25	2,469 R	69.0%	29.9%	0.7%
70,154	LIBERTY	20,077	12,458	7,311	199	109	5,147 R	62.1%	36.4%	1.0%
22,051	LIMESTONE	7,075	4,212	2,768	57	38	1,444 R	59.5%	39.1%	0.8%
3,057	LIPSCOMB	1,294	1,072	206	9	7	866 R	82.8%	15.9%	0.7%
12,309	LIVE OAK	4,004	2,828	1,114	35	27	1,714 R	70.6%	27.8%	0.9%
17,044	LLANO	8,627	6,295	2,143	142	47	4,152 R	73.0%	24.8%	1.6%
67	LOVING	156	124	29	1	2	95 R	79.5%	18.6%	0.6%
242,628	LUBBOCK	76,008	56,054	18,469	1,042	443	37,585 R	73.7%	24.3%	1.4%
6,550	LYNN	2,084	1,507	562	7	8	945 R	72.3%	27.0%	0.3%
8,205	MCCULLOCH	2,920	2,084	794	29	13	1,290 R	71.4%	27.2%	1.0%
213,517	MCLENNAN	68,789	43,955	23,462	1,032	340	20,493 R	63.9%	34.1%	1.5%
851	MCMULLEN	439	358	77	4		281 R	81.5%	17.5%	0.9%
12,940	MADISON	3,623	2,333	1,241	27	22	1,092 R	64.4%	34.3%	0.7%
10,941	MARION	3,930	2,039	1,852	31	8	187 R	51.9%	47.1%	0.8%
4,746	MARTIN	1,949	1,520	415	6	8	1,105 R	78.0%	21.3%	0.3%
3,738	MASON	1,801	1,352	417	18	14	935 R	75.1%	23.2%	1.0%
37,957	MATAGORDA	12,459	7,584	4,696	141	38	2,888 R	60.9%	37.7%	1.1%
47,297	MAVERICK	9,229	3,143	5,995	53	38	2,852 D	34.1%	65.0%	0.6%
39,304	MEDINA	12,873	8,590	4,025	171	87	4,565 R	66.7%	31.3%	1.3%
2,360	MENARD	990	642	334	9	5	308 R	64.8%	33.7%	0.9%
116,009	MIDLAND	39,740	31,514	7,534	475	217	23,980 R	79.3%	19.0%	1.2%
24,238	MILAM	8,269	4,706	3,429	84	50	1,277 R	56.9%	41.5%	1.0%
5,151	MILLS	2,314	1,738	548	14	14	1,190 R	75.1%	23.7%	0.6%
9,698	MITCHELL	2,574	1,708	837	20	9	871 R	66.4%	32.5%	0.8%
19,117	MONTAGUE	7,330	4,951	2,256	66	57	2,695 R	67.5%	30.8%	0.9%
293,768	MONTGOMERY	106,213	80,600	23,286	1,825	502	57,314 R	75.9%	21.9%	1.7%
20,121	MOORE	5,290	4,201	1,040	24	25	3,161 R	79.4%	19.7%	0.5%
13,048	MORRIS	4,889	2,381	2,455	31	22	74 D	48.7%	50.2%	0.6%
1,426	MOTLEY	642	514	118	5	5	396 R	80.1%	18.4%	0.8%
59,203	NACOGDOCHES	19,799	13,145	6,204	387	63	6,941 R	66.4%	31.3%	2.0%
45,124	NAVARRO	13,890	8,358	5,366	105	61	2,992 R	60.2%	38.6%	0.8%
15,072	NEWTON	4,990	2,423	2,503	38	26	80 D	48.6%	50.2%	0.8%
15,802	NOLAN	5,312	3,337	1,874	60	41	1,463 R	62.8%	35.3%	1.1%
313,645	NUECES	97,326	49,906	45,349	1,574	497	4,557 R	51.3%	46.6%	1.6%
9,006	OCHILTREE	2,962	2,687	251	19	5	2,436 R	90.7%	8.5%	0.6%
2,185	OLDHAM	774	659	108	6	1	551 R	85.1%	14.0%	0.8%

TEXAS

PRESIDENT 2000

2000 Census Population	County	Total Vote	Republican	Democratic	Green (Nader)	Other	Rep.-Dem. Plurality	Percentage of Total Vote		
								Rep.	Dem.	Green
84,966	ORANGE	29,654	17,325	11,887	290	152	5,438 R	58.4%	40.1%	1.0%
27,026	PALO PINTO	9,118	5,690	3,263	86	79	2,427 R	62.4%	35.8%	0.9%
22,756	PANOLA	9,074	5,975	3,011	50	38	2,964 R	65.8%	33.2%	0.6%
88,495	PARKER	33,225	23,651	8,878	485	211	14,773 R	71.2%	26.7%	1.5%
10,016	PARMER	2,744	2,274	447	15	8	1,827 R	82.9%	16.3%	0.5%
16,809	PECOS	4,303	2,700	1,539	44	20	1,161 R	62.7%	35.8%	1.0%
41,133	POLK	18,994	11,746	6,877	259	112	4,869 R	61.8%	36.2%	1.4%
113,546	POTTER	25,376	17,629	7,242	362	143	10,387 R	69.5%	28.5%	1.4%
7,304	PRESIDIO	1,757	618	1,064	65	10	446 D	35.2%	60.6%	3.7%
9,139	RAINS	3,333	2,049	1,225	34	25	824 R	61.5%	36.8%	1.0%
104,312	RANDALL	41,790	33,921	7,209	448	212	26,712 R	81.2%	17.3%	1.1%
3,326	REAGAN	1,255	959	282	6	8	677 R	76.4%	22.5%	0.5%
3,047	REAL	1,490	1,146	316	16	12	830 R	76.9%	21.2%	1.1%
14,314	RED RIVER	5,202	2,941	2,219	19	23	722 R	56.5%	42.7%	0.4%
13,137	REEVES	3,176	1,273	1,872	22	9	599 D	40.1%	58.9%	0.7%
7,828	REFUGIO	2,921	1,721	1,172	22	6	549 R	58.9%	40.1%	0.8%
887	ROBERTS	549	472	72	3	2	400 R	86.0%	13.1%	0.5%
16,000	ROBERTSON	6,369	3,007	3,283	41	38	276 D	47.2%	51.5%	0.6%
43,080	ROCKWALL	17,652	13,666	3,642	231	113	10,024 R	77.4%	20.6%	1.3%
11,495	RUNNELS	4,046	3,020	969	31	26	2,051 R	74.6%	23.9%	0.8%
47,372	RUSK	16,633	11,611	4,841	112	69	6,770 R	69.8%	29.1%	0.7%
10,469	SABINE	4,591	2,764	1,753	40	34	1,011 R	60.2%	38.2%	0.9%
8,946	SAN AUGUSTINE	3,805	2,116	1,636	34	19	480 R	55.6%	43.0%	0.9%
22,246	SAN JACINTO	7,714	4,623	2,946	103	42	1,677 R	59.9%	38.2%	1.3%
67,138	SAN PATRICIO	18,699	10,599	7,840	179	81	2,759 R	56.7%	41.9%	1.0%
6,186	SAN SABA	2,333	1,691	618	12	12	1,073 R	72.5%	26.5%	0.5%
2,935	SCHLEICHER	1,173	826	338	4	5	488 R	70.4%	28.8%	0.3%
16,361	SCURRY	5,326	4,060	1,193	45	28	2,867 R	76.2%	22.4%	0.8%
3,302	SHACKELFORD	1,347	1,066	264	9	8	802 R	79.1%	19.6%	0.7%
25,224	SHELBY	9,005	5,692	3,227	55	31	2,465 R	63.2%	35.8%	0.6%
3,186	SHERMAN	1,163	998	144	11	10	854 R	85.8%	12.4%	0.9%
174,706	SMITH	60,624	43,320	16,470	548	286	26,850 R	71.5%	27.2%	0.9%
6,809	SOMERVELL	2,918	2,120	752	37	9	1,368 R	72.7%	25.8%	1.3%
53,597	STARR	8,464	1,911	6,505	19	29	4,594 D	22.6%	76.9%	0.2%
9,674	STEPHENS	3,291	2,425	811	32	23	1,614 R	73.7%	24.6%	1.0%
1,393	STERLING	659	520	132	3	4	388 R	78.9%	20.0%	0.5%
1,693	STONEWALL	799	496	294	7	2	202 R	62.1%	36.8%	0.9%
4,077	SUTTON	1,540	1,063	468	6	3	595 R	69.0%	30.4%	0.4%
8,378	SWISHER	2,501	1,612	856	20	13	756 R	64.5%	34.2%	0.8%
1,446,219	TARRANT	472,389	286,921	173,758	8,808	2,902	113,163 R	60.7%	36.8%	1.9%
126,555	TAYLOR	43,020	31,701	10,504	589	226	21,197 R	73.7%	24.4%	1.4%
1,081	TERRELL	477	243	219	7	8	24 R	50.9%	45.9%	1.5%
12,761	TERRY	4,054	2,910	1,108	18	18	1,802 R	71.8%	27.3%	0.4%
1,850	THROCKMORTON	842	608	228	4	2	380 R	72.2%	27.1%	0.5%
28,118	TITUS	8,103	4,995	3,008	65	35	1,987 R	61.6%	37.1%	0.8%
104,010	TOM GREEN	34,626	24,733	9,288	454	151	15,445 R	71.4%	26.8%	1.3%
812,280	TRAVIS	301,263	141,235	125,526	31,243	3,259	15,709 R	46.9%	41.7%	10.4%
13,779	TRINITY	5,297	3,093	2,142	40	22	951 R	58.4%	40.4%	0.8%
20,871	TYLER	7,116	4,236	2,775	65	40	1,461 R	59.5%	39.0%	0.9%
35,291	UPSHUR	12,808	8,448	4,180	116	64	4,268 R	66.0%	32.6%	0.9%
3,404	UPTON	1,273	982	266	11	14	716 R	77.1%	20.9%	0.9%
25,926	UVALDE	8,420	4,855	3,436	36	93	1,419 R	57.7%	40.8%	0.4%
44,856	VAL VERDE	11,474	6,223	5,056	129	66	1,167 R	54.2%	44.1%	1.1%
48,140	VAN ZANDT	17,891	12,383	5,245	141	122	7,138 R	69.2%	29.3%	0.8%
84,088	VICTORIA	27,408	18,787	8,176	215	230	10,611 R	68.5%	29.8%	0.8%
61,758	WALKER	14,374	9,076	4,943	274	81	4,133 R	63.1%	34.4%	1.9%
32,663	WALLER	10,858	5,686	5,046	95	31	640 R	52.4%	46.5%	0.9%
10,909	WARD	3,874	2,534	1,256	58	26	1,278 R	65.4%	32.4%	1.5%
30,373	WASHINGTON	11,809	8,645	2,996	133	35	5,649 R	73.2%	25.4%	1.1%
193,117	WEBB	31,571	13,076	18,120	256	119	5,044 D	41.4%	57.4%	0.8%

TEXAS

PRESIDENT 2000

2000 Census Population	County	Total Vote	Republican	Democratic	Green (Nader)	Other	Rep.-Dem. Plurality	Percentage of Total Vote		
								Rep.	Dem.	Green
41,188	WHARTON	13,426	8,455	4,838	103	30	3,617 R	63.0%	36.0%	0.8%
5,284	WHEELER	2,389	1,787	579	15	8	1,208 R	74.8%	24.2%	0.6%
131,664	WICHITA	42,713	27,802	14,108	518	285	13,694 R	65.1%	33.0%	1.2%
14,676	WILBARGER	4,577	3,138	1,356	43	40	1,782 R	68.6%	29.6%	0.9%
20,082	WILLACY	5,062	1,789	3,218	24	31	1,429 D	35.3%	63.6%	0.5%
249,967	WILLIAMSON	95,935	65,041	26,591	3,486	817	38,450 R	67.8%	27.7%	3.6%
32,408	WILSON	11,698	7,509	3,997	130	62	3,512 R	64.2%	34.2%	1.1%
7,173	WINKLER	2,043	1,468	556	5	14	912 R	71.9%	27.2%	0.2%
48,793	WISE	16,368	11,234	4,830	185	119	6,404 R	68.6%	29.5%	1.1%
36,752	WOOD	13,884	9,810	3,893	128	53	5,917 R	70.7%	28.0%	0.9%
7,322	YOAKUM	2,465	1,911	531	10	13	1,380 R	77.5%	21.5%	0.4%
17,943	YOUNG	6,954	5,022	1,843	46	43	3,179 R	72.2%	26.5%	0.7%
12,182	ZAPATA	2,616	953	1,638	11	14	685 D	36.4%	62.6%	0.4%
11,600	ZAVALA	3,391	751	2,616	14	10	1,865 D	22.1%	77.1%	0.4%
20,851,820	TOTAL	6,407,637	3,799,639	2,433,746	137,994	36,258	1,365,893 R	59.3%	38.0%	2.2%

Note: A blank in a candidate's column in a particular county indicates that no votes were cast for that candidate.

HARRIS COUNTY

PRESIDENT 2000

Ward	Total Vote	Republican	Democratic	Green (Nader)	Other	Rep.-Dem. Plurality	Percentage of Total Vote		
							Rep.	Dem.	Green
R.D. 126	58,043	42,626	14,036	1,153	228	28,590 R	73.4%	24.2%	2.0%
R.D. 127	52,348	39,245	11,830	1,021	252	27,415 R	75.0%	22.6%	2.0%
R.D. 128	29,975	14,211	15,310	351	103	1,099 D	47.4%	51.1%	1.2%
R.D. 129	56,750	39,756	15,343	1,370	281	24,413 R	70.1%	27.0%	2.4%
R.D. 130	70,837	52,865	16,295	1,370	307	36,570 R	74.6%	23.0%	1.9%
R.D. 131	33,418	7,487	25,398	427	106	17,911 D	22.4%	76.0%	1.3%
R.D. 132	45,647	18,154	25,523	1,739	231	7,369 D	39.8%	55.9%	3.8%
R.D. 133	50,743	35,085	13,865	1,522	271	21,220 R	69.1%	27.3%	3.0%
R.D. 134	38,234	20,833	15,726	1,484	191	5,107 R	54.5%	41.1%	3.9%
R.D. 135	57,675	40,358	15,883	1,179	255	24,475 R	70.0%	27.5%	2.0%
R.D. 136	52,716	38,255	12,796	1,392	273	25,459 R	72.6%	24.3%	2.6%
R.D. 137	34,290	15,269	15,995	2,746	280	726 D	44.5%	46.6%	8.0%
R.D. 138	31,495	14,611	15,838	886	160	1,227 D	46.4%	50.3%	2.8%
R.D. 139	27,686	6,137	21,209	270	70	15,072 D	22.2%	76.6%	1.0%
R.D. 140	18,342	7,364	10,688	213	77	3,324 D	40.1%	58.3%	1.2%
R.D. 141	36,083	10,431	25,286	276	90	14,855 D	28.9%	70.1%	0.8%
R.D. 142	30,518	5,922	24,264	247	85	18,342 D	19.4%	79.5%	0.8%
R.D. 143	19,314	6,943	12,043	257	71	5,100 D	35.9%	62.4%	1.3%
R.D. 144	33,382	20,918	11,500	776	188	9,418 R	62.7%	34.4%	2.3%
R.D. 145	17,731	6,964	10,304	380	83	3,340 D	39.3%	58.1%	2.1%
R.D. 146	39,523	11,478	27,410	529	106	15,932 D	29.0%	69.4%	1.3%
R.D. 147	28,078	6,905	20,524	545	104	13,619 D	24.6%	73.1%	1.9%
R.D. 148	22,554	8,864	12,463	1,093	134	3,599 D	39.3%	55.3%	4.8%
R.D. 149	37,493	20,343	16,253	756	141	4,090 R	54.3%	43.3%	2.0%
R.D. 150	51,501	37,941	12,361	954	245	25,580 R	73.7%	24.0%	1.9%
3,400,578 TOTAL	974,376	528,965	418,143	22,936	4,332	110,822 R	54.3%	42.9%	2.4%

Note: The Harris County vote was certified as follows: 529,159 Republican; 418,267 Democratic; 22,994 Green; 4,402 Other.

TEXAS

SENATOR 2000

2000 Census Population	County	Total Vote	Republican	Democratic	Other	Rep.-Dem. Plurality		Percentage			
								Total Vote		Major Vote	
								Rep.	Dem.	Rep.	Dem.
55,109	ANDERSON	14,947	10,304	4,452	191	5,852	R	68.9%	29.8%	69.8%	30.2%
13,004	ANDREWS	3,942	3,117	758	67	2,359	R	79.1%	19.2%	80.4%	19.6%
80,130	ANGELINA	26,704	16,970	9,353	381	7,617	R	63.5%	35.0%	64.5%	35.5%
22,497	ARANSAS	8,099	5,858	2,056	185	3,802	R	72.3%	25.4%	74.0%	26.0%
8,854	ARCHER	3,940	3,052	837	51	2,215	R	77.5%	21.2%	78.5%	21.5%
2,148	ARMSTRONG	906	767	124	15	643	R	84.7%	13.7%	86.1%	13.9%
38,628	ATASCOSA	10,547	6,762	3,570	215	3,192	R	64.1%	33.8%	65.4%	34.6%
23,590	AUSTIN	9,106	6,953	2,025	128	4,928	R	76.4%	22.2%	77.4%	22.6%
6,594	BAILEY	2,026	1,623	386	17	1,237	R	80.1%	19.1%	80.8%	19.2%
17,645	BANDERA	7,190	5,876	1,062	252	4,814	R	81.7%	14.8%	84.7%	15.3%
57,733	BASTROP	18,053	11,095	5,954	1,004	5,141	R	61.5%	33.0%	65.1%	34.9%
4,093	BAYLOR	1,779	1,206	552	21	654	R	67.8%	31.0%	68.6%	31.4%
32,359	BEE	8,174	4,740	3,331	103	1,409	R	58.0%	40.8%	58.7%	41.3%
237,974	BELL	61,018	42,472	17,644	902	24,828	R	69.6%	28.9%	70.7%	29.3%
1,392,931	BEXAR	406,208	244,639	149,064	12,505	95,575	R	60.2%	36.7%	62.1%	37.9%
8,418	BLANCO	3,657	2,875	621	161	2,254	R	78.6%	17.0%	82.2%	17.8%
729	BORDEN	343	274	63	6	211	R	79.9%	18.4%	81.3%	18.7%
17,204	BOSQUE	6,700	4,890	1,700	110	3,190	R	73.0%	25.4%	74.2%	25.8%
89,306	BOWIE	29,838	19,843	9,664	331	10,179	R	66.5%	32.4%	67.2%	32.8%
241,767	BRAZORIA	79,268	56,312	21,405	1,551	34,907	R	71.0%	27.0%	72.5%	27.5%
152,415	BRAZOS	46,226	34,737	10,040	1,449	24,697	R	75.1%	21.7%	77.6%	22.4%
8,866	BREWSTER	3,373	1,896	1,161	316	735	R	56.2%	34.4%	62.0%	38.0%
1,790	BRISCOE	738	535	197	6	338	R	72.5%	26.7%	73.1%	26.9%
7,976	BROOKS	2,354	663	1,637	54	974	D	28.2%	69.5%	28.8%	71.2%
37,674	BROWN	12,797	9,896	2,729	172	7,167	R	77.3%	21.3%	78.4%	21.6%
16,470	BURLESON	5,759	3,687	1,974	98	1,713	R	64.0%	34.3%	65.1%	34.9%
34,147	BURNET	13,104	9,757	2,911	436	6,846	R	74.5%	22.2%	77.0%	23.0%
32,194	CALDWELL	9,276	5,656	3,289	331	2,367	R	61.0%	35.5%	63.2%	36.8%
20,647	CALHOUN	6,449	3,863	2,491	95	1,372	R	59.9%	38.6%	60.8%	39.2%
12,905	CALLAHAN	4,812	3,723	1,001	88	2,722	R	77.4%	20.8%	78.8%	21.2%
335,227	CAMERON	60,175	31,806	26,958	1,411	4,848	R	52.9%	44.8%	54.1%	45.9%
11,549	CAMP	3,663	2,177	1,451	35	726	R	59.4%	39.6%	60.0%	40.0%
6,516	CARSON	2,680	2,205	443	32	1,762	R	82.3%	16.5%	83.3%	16.7%
30,438	CASS	10,844	6,690	4,040	114	2,650	R	61.7%	37.3%	62.3%	37.7%
8,285	CASTRO	2,253	1,590	639	24	951	R	70.6%	28.4%	71.3%	28.7%
26,031	CHAMBERS	9,697	7,046	2,511	140	4,535	R	72.7%	25.9%	73.7%	26.3%
46,659	CHEROKEE	14,359	9,892	4,317	150	5,575	R	68.9%	30.1%	69.6%	30.4%
7,688	CHILDRESS	2,044	1,546	484	14	1,062	R	75.6%	23.7%	76.2%	23.8%
11,006	CLAY	4,517	3,202	1,265	50	1,937	R	70.9%	28.0%	71.7%	28.3%
3,730	COCHRAN	1,113	802	284	27	518	R	72.1%	25.5%	73.8%	26.2%
3,864	COKE	1,459	1,104	320	35	784	R	75.7%	21.9%	77.5%	22.5%
9,235	COLEMAN	3,431	2,684	707	40	1,977	R	78.2%	20.6%	79.2%	20.8%
491,675	COLLIN	172,954	138,238	30,655	4,061	107,583	R	79.9%	17.7%	81.8%	18.2%
3,206	COLLINGSWORTH	1,335	950	369	16	581	R	71.2%	27.6%	72.0%	28.0%
20,390	COLORADO	7,091	5,115	1,891	85	3,224	R	72.1%	26.7%	73.0%	27.0%
78,021	COMAL	32,434	25,668	5,769	997	19,899	R	79.1%	17.8%	81.6%	18.4%
14,026	COMANCHE	4,879	3,309	1,521	49	1,788	R	67.8%	31.2%	68.5%	31.5%
3,966	CONCHO	1,054	824	212	18	612	R	78.2%	20.1%	79.5%	20.5%
36,363	COOKE	13,307	10,574	2,553	180	8,021	R	79.5%	19.2%	80.6%	19.4%
74,978	CORYELL	14,895	10,982	3,635	278	7,347	R	73.7%	24.4%	75.1%	24.9%
1,904	COTTLE	712	479	224	9	255	R	67.3%	31.5%	68.1%	31.9%
3,996	CRANE	1,535	1,179	331	25	848	R	76.8%	21.6%	78.1%	21.9%
4,099	CROCKETT	1,352	936	401	15	535	R	69.2%	29.7%	70.0%	30.0%
7,072	CROSBY	1,933	1,296	622	15	674	R	67.0%	32.2%	67.6%	32.4%
2,975	CULBERSON	804	401	377	26	24	R	49.9%	46.9%	51.5%	48.5%
6,222	DALLAM	1,676	1,396	265	15	1,131	R	83.3%	15.8%	84.0%	16.0%
2,218,899	DALLAS	605,123	357,695	232,222	15,206	125,473	R	59.1%	38.4%	60.6%	39.4%
14,985	DAWSON	4,429	3,244	1,120	65	2,124	R	73.2%	25.3%	74.3%	25.7%
18,561	DEAF SMITH	4,897	3,734	1,093	70	2,641	R	76.3%	22.3%	77.4%	22.6%
5,327	DELTA	1,831	1,192	622	17	570	R	65.1%	34.0%	65.7%	34.3%

TEXAS

SENATOR 2000

2000 Census Population	County	Total Vote	Republican	Democratic	Other	Rep.-Dem. Plurality		Percentage			
								Total Vote		Major Vote	
								Rep.	Dem.	Rep.	Dem.
432,976	DENTON	144,740	109,883	30,541	4,316	79,342	R	75.9%	21.1%	78.3%	21.7%
20,013	DE WITT	5,993	4,622	1,305	66	3,317	R	77.1%	21.8%	78.0%	22.0%
2,762	DICKENS	842	576	257	9	319	R	68.4%	30.5%	69.1%	30.9%
10,248	DIMMIT	3,323	1,135	2,102	86	967	D	34.2%	63.3%	35.1%	64.9%
3,828	DONLEY	1,645	1,366	267	12	1,099	R	83.0%	16.2%	83.6%	16.4%
13,120	DUVAL	4,926	1,076	3,800	50	2,724	D	21.8%	77.1%	22.1%	77.9%
18,297	EASTLAND	6,329	4,673	1,535	121	3,138	R	73.8%	24.3%	75.3%	24.7%
121,123	ECTOR	32,726	23,993	8,130	603	15,863	R	73.3%	24.8%	74.7%	25.3%
2,162	EDWARDS	793	631	155	7	476	R	79.6%	19.5%	80.3%	19.7%
111,360	ELLIS	36,904	27,618	8,635	651	18,983	R	74.8%	23.4%	76.2%	23.8%
679,622	EL PASO	141,986	67,451	70,103	4,432	2,652	D	47.5%	49.4%	49.0%	51.0%
33,001	ERATH	10,969	8,444	2,367	158	6,077	R	77.0%	21.6%	78.1%	21.9%
18,576	FALLS	5,383	3,300	2,017	66	1,283	R	61.3%	37.5%	62.1%	37.9%
31,242	FANNIN	10,219	6,658	3,396	165	3,262	R	65.2%	33.2%	66.2%	33.8%
21,804	FAYETTE	9,249	6,992	2,098	159	4,894	R	75.6%	22.7%	76.9%	23.1%
4,344	FISHER	1,813	990	806	17	184	R	54.6%	44.5%	55.1%	44.9%
7,771	FLOYD	2,314	1,819	476	19	1,343	R	78.6%	20.6%	79.3%	20.7%
1,622	FOARD	539	305	231	3	74	R	56.6%	42.9%	56.9%	43.1%
354,452	FORT BEND	122,078	78,957	41,098	2,023	37,859	R	64.7%	33.7%	65.8%	34.2%
9,458	FRANKLIN	3,358	2,426	886	46	1,540	R	72.2%	26.4%	73.2%	26.8%
17,867	FREESTONE	6,539	4,412	2,054	73	2,358	R	67.5%	31.4%	68.2%	31.8%
16,252	FRIO	3,877	1,849	1,942	86	93	D	47.7%	50.1%	48.8%	51.2%
14,467	GAINES	3,359	2,637	663	59	1,974	R	78.5%	19.7%	79.9%	20.1%
250,158	GALVESTON	91,987	55,754	34,145	2,088	21,609	R	60.6%	37.1%	62.0%	38.0%
4,872	GARZA	1,588	1,227	335	26	892	R	77.3%	21.1%	78.6%	21.4%
20,814	GILLESPIE	9,802	8,340	1,172	290	7,168	R	85.1%	12.0%	87.7%	12.3%
1,406	GLASSCOCK	557	518	33	6	485	R	93.0%	5.9%	94.0%	6.0%
6,928	GOLIAD	3,250	2,096	1,100	54	996	R	64.5%	33.8%	65.6%	34.4%
18,628	GONZALES	5,901	4,279	1,511	111	2,768	R	72.5%	25.6%	73.9%	26.1%
22,744	GRAY	8,137	6,868	1,195	74	5,673	R	84.4%	14.7%	85.2%	14.8%
110,595	GRAYSON	39,407	28,251	10,491	665	17,760	R	71.7%	26.6%	72.9%	27.1%
111,379	GREGG	37,932	28,034	9,409	489	18,625	R	73.9%	24.8%	74.9%	25.1%
23,552	GRIMES	6,681	4,505	2,013	163	2,492	R	67.4%	30.1%	69.1%	30.9%
89,023	GUADALUPE	30,014	22,729	6,551	734	16,178	R	75.7%	21.8%	77.6%	22.4%
36,602	HALE	9,013	6,958	1,932	123	5,026	R	77.2%	21.4%	78.3%	21.7%
3,782	HALL	1,281	891	384	6	507	R	69.6%	30.0%	69.9%	30.1%
8,229	HAMILTON	3,332	2,493	796	43	1,697	R	74.8%	23.9%	75.8%	24.2%
5,369	HANSFORD	2,038	1,854	165	19	1,689	R	91.0%	8.1%	91.8%	8.2%
4,724	HARDEMAN	1,444	967	462	15	505	R	67.0%	32.0%	67.7%	32.3%
48,073	HARDIN	17,552	11,982	5,260	310	6,722	R	68.3%	30.0%	69.5%	30.5%
3,400,578	HARRIS	942,257	564,027	355,253	22,977	208,774	R	59.9%	37.7%	61.4%	38.6%
62,110	HARRISON	22,589	14,692	7,612	285	7,080	R	65.0%	33.7%	65.9%	34.1%
5,537	HARTLEY	1,986	1,668	298	20	1,370	R	84.0%	15.0%	84.8%	15.2%
6,093	HASKELL	2,452	1,533	899	20	634	R	62.5%	36.7%	63.0%	37.0%
97,589	HAYS	34,036	22,508	9,328	2,200	13,180	R	66.1%	27.4%	70.7%	29.3%
3,351	HEMPHILL	1,425	1,213	197	15	1,016	R	85.1%	13.8%	86.0%	14.0%
73,277	HENDERSON	25,368	17,430	7,581	357	9,849	R	68.7%	29.9%	69.7%	30.3%
569,463	HIDALGO	92,333	41,436	49,159	1,738	7,723	D	44.9%	53.2%	45.7%	54.3%
32,321	HILL	10,616	7,514	2,942	160	4,572	R	70.8%	27.7%	71.9%	28.1%
22,716	HOCKLEY	6,652	5,336	1,220	96	4,116	R	80.2%	18.3%	81.4%	18.6%
41,100	HOOD	17,241	12,944	3,974	323	8,970	R	75.1%	23.0%	76.5%	23.5%
31,960	HOPKINS	10,660	7,418	3,076	166	4,342	R	69.6%	28.9%	70.7%	29.3%
23,185	HOUSTON	7,949	5,428	2,412	109	3,016	R	68.3%	30.3%	69.2%	30.8%
33,627	HOWARD	9,466	6,828	2,485	153	4,343	R	72.1%	26.3%	73.3%	26.7%
3,344	HUDSPETH	776	473	261	42	212	R	61.0%	33.6%	64.4%	35.6%
76,596	HUNT	24,141	17,384	6,293	464	11,091	R	72.0%	26.1%	73.4%	26.6%
23,857	HUTCHINSON	9,256	7,711	1,442	103	6,269	R	83.3%	15.6%	84.2%	15.8%
1,771	IRION	751	610	133	8	477	R	81.2%	17.7%	82.1%	17.9%
8,763	JACK	2,873	2,060	771	42	1,289	R	71.7%	26.8%	72.8%	27.2%
14,391	JACKSON	4,658	3,391	1,240	27	2,151	R	72.8%	26.6%	73.2%	26.8%

TEXAS

SENATOR 2000

2000 Census Population	County	Total Vote	Republican	Democratic	Other	Rep.-Dem. Plurality		Percentage			
								Total Vote		Major Vote	
								Rep.	Dem.	Rep.	Dem.
35,604	JASPER	11,566	7,011	4,404	151	2,607	R	60.6%	38.1%	61.4%	38.6%
2,207	JEFF DAVIS	987	718	212	57	506	R	72.7%	21.5%	77.2%	22.8%
252,051	JEFFERSON	85,473	42,217	42,103	1,153	114	R	49.4%	49.3%	50.1%	49.9%
5,281	JIM HOGG	2,020	647	1,337	36	690	D	32.0%	66.2%	32.6%	67.4%
39,326	JIM WELLS	11,704	4,914	6,619	171	1,705	D	42.0%	56.6%	42.6%	57.4%
126,811	JOHNSON	38,350	28,086	9,498	766	18,588	R	73.2%	24.8%	74.7%	25.3%
20,785	JONES	5,717	4,029	1,580	108	2,449	R	70.5%	27.6%	71.8%	28.2%
15,446	KARNES	4,177	2,856	1,255	66	1,601	R	68.4%	30.0%	69.5%	30.5%
71,313	KAUFMAN	22,777	16,389	6,074	314	10,315	R	72.0%	26.7%	73.0%	27.0%
23,743	KENDALL	10,956	9,255	1,359	342	7,896	R	84.5%	12.4%	87.2%	12.8%
414	KENEDY	188	100	83	5	17	R	53.2%	44.1%	54.6%	45.4%
859	KENT	490	315	167	8	148	R	64.3%	34.1%	65.4%	34.6%
43,653	KERR	19,032	15,224	3,243	565	11,981	R	80.0%	17.0%	82.4%	17.6%
4,468	KIMBLE	1,630	1,331	270	29	1,061	R	81.7%	16.6%	83.1%	16.9%
356	KING	127	103	21	3	82	R	81.1%	16.5%	83.1%	16.9%
3,379	KINNEY	1,279	957	300	22	657	R	74.8%	23.5%	76.1%	23.9%
31,549	KLEBERG	8,975	4,986	3,793	196	1,193	R	55.6%	42.3%	56.8%	43.2%
4,253	KNOX	1,502	964	522	16	442	R	64.2%	34.8%	64.9%	35.1%
48,499	LAMAR	15,179	10,303	4,768	108	5,535	R	67.9%	31.4%	68.4%	31.6%
14,709	LAMB	4,434	3,428	966	40	2,462	R	77.3%	21.8%	78.0%	22.0%
17,762	LAMPASAS	6,138	4,747	1,261	130	3,486	R	77.3%	20.5%	79.0%	21.0%
5,866	LA SALLE	1,861	732	1,091	38	359	D	39.3%	58.6%	40.2%	59.8%
19,210	LAVACA	7,428	5,454	1,882	92	3,572	R	73.4%	25.3%	74.3%	25.7%
15,657	LEE	5,377	3,752	1,528	97	2,224	R	69.8%	28.4%	71.1%	28.9%
15,335	LEON	6,182	4,406	1,697	79	2,709	R	71.3%	27.5%	72.2%	27.8%
70,154	LIBERTY	19,825	13,058	6,453	314	6,605	R	65.9%	32.5%	66.9%	33.1%
22,051	LIMESTONE	6,990	4,382	2,504	104	1,878	R	62.7%	35.8%	63.6%	36.4%
3,057	LIPSCOMB	1,247	1,073	158	16	915	R	86.0%	12.7%	87.2%	12.8%
12,309	LIVE OAK	3,875	2,871	960	44	1,911	R	74.1%	24.8%	74.9%	25.1%
17,044	LLANO	8,553	6,526	1,852	175	4,674	R	76.3%	21.7%	77.9%	22.1%
67	LOVING	140	116	20	4	96	R	82.9%	14.3%	85.3%	14.7%
242,628	LUBBOCK	75,007	58,484	14,725	1,798	43,759	R	78.0%	19.6%	79.9%	20.1%
6,550	LYNN	2,008	1,519	470	19	1,049	R	75.6%	23.4%	76.4%	23.6%
8,205	MCCULLOCH	2,759	2,128	589	42	1,539	R	77.1%	21.3%	78.3%	21.7%
213,517	MCLENNAN	68,013	47,216	19,400	1,397	27,816	R	69.4%	28.5%	70.9%	29.1%
851	MCMULLEN	393	334	55	4	279	R	85.0%	14.0%	85.9%	14.1%
12,940	MADISON	3,585	2,427	1,105	53	1,322	R	67.7%	30.8%	68.7%	31.3%
10,941	MARION	3,709	2,089	1,581	39	508	R	56.3%	42.6%	56.9%	43.1%
4,746	MARTIN	1,816	1,454	308	54	1,146	R	80.1%	17.0%	82.5%	17.5%
3,738	MASON	1,765	1,357	373	35	984	R	76.9%	21.1%	78.4%	21.6%
37,957	MATAGORDA	12,199	8,034	3,967	198	4,067	R	65.9%	32.5%	66.9%	33.1%
47,297	MAVERICK	8,190	3,095	4,838	257	1,743	D	37.8%	59.1%	39.0%	61.0%
39,304	MEDINA	13,110	9,204	3,620	286	5,584	R	70.2%	27.6%	71.8%	28.2%
2,360	MENARD	930	658	262	10	396	R	70.8%	28.2%	71.5%	28.5%
116,009	MIDLAND	39,230	32,191	6,317	722	25,874	R	82.1%	16.1%	83.6%	16.4%
24,238	MILAM	8,123	4,923	3,072	128	1,851	R	60.6%	37.8%	61.6%	38.4%
5,151	MILLS	2,220	1,712	489	19	1,223	R	77.1%	22.0%	77.8%	22.2%
9,698	MITCHELL	2,406	1,697	676	33	1,021	R	70.5%	28.1%	71.5%	28.5%
19,117	MONTAGUE	7,232	5,238	1,869	125	3,369	R	72.4%	25.8%	73.7%	26.3%
293,768	MONTGOMERY	105,009	83,611	19,236	2,162	64,375	R	79.6%	18.3%	81.3%	18.7%
20,121	MOORE	5,224	4,264	894	66	3,370	R	81.6%	17.1%	82.7%	17.3%
13,048	MORRIS	4,822	2,535	2,237	50	298	R	52.6%	46.4%	53.1%	46.9%
1,426	MOTLEY	623	512	106	5	406	R	82.2%	17.0%	82.8%	17.2%
59,203	NACOGDOCHES	19,512	13,930	5,176	406	8,754	R	71.4%	26.5%	72.9%	27.1%
45,124	NAVARRO	13,729	8,770	4,782	177	3,988	R	63.9%	34.8%	64.7%	35.3%
15,072	NEWTON	4,837	2,342	2,423	72	81	D	48.4%	50.1%	49.2%	50.8%
15,802	NOLAN	5,241	3,555	1,584	102	1,971	R	67.8%	30.2%	69.2%	30.8%
313,645	NUECES	95,384	55,925	37,403	2,056	18,522	R	58.6%	39.2%	59.9%	40.1%
9,006	OCHILTREE	2,900	2,636	231	33	2,405	R	90.9%	8.0%	91.9%	8.1%
2,185	OLDHAM	753	646	98	9	548	R	85.8%	13.0%	86.8%	13.2%

TEXAS

SENATOR 2000

2000 Census Population	County	Total Vote	Republican	Democratic	Other	Rep.-Dem. Plurality		Percentage			
								Total Vote		Major Vote	
								Rep.	Dem.	Rep.	Dem.
84,966	ORANGE	29,279	17,495	11,268	516	6,227	R	59.8%	38.5%	60.8%	39.2%
27,026	PALO PINTO	9,006	6,047	2,781	178	3,266	R	67.1%	30.9%	68.5%	31.5%
22,756	PANOLA	8,951	6,118	2,737	96	3,381	R	68.3%	30.6%	69.1%	30.9%
88,495	PARKER	32,919	25,092	7,169	658	17,923	R	76.2%	21.8%	77.8%	22.2%
10,016	PARMER	2,689	2,272	396	21	1,876	R	84.5%	14.7%	85.2%	14.8%
16,809	PECOS	4,158	2,727	1,339	92	1,388	R	65.6%	32.2%	67.1%	32.9%
41,133	POLK	18,557	12,225	5,985	347	6,240	R	65.9%	32.3%	67.1%	32.9%
113,546	POTTER	23,211	16,646	6,022	543	10,624	R	71.7%	25.9%	73.4%	26.6%
7,304	PRESIDIO	1,509	573	859	77	286	D	38.0%	56.9%	40.0%	60.0%
9,139	RAINS	3,209	2,195	973	41	1,222	R	68.4%	30.3%	69.3%	30.7%
104,312	RANDALL	41,487	34,932	5,930	625	29,002	R	84.2%	14.3%	85.5%	14.5%
3,326	REAGAN	1,139	937	178	24	759	R	82.3%	15.6%	84.0%	16.0%
3,047	REAL	1,410	1,136	250	24	886	R	80.6%	17.7%	82.0%	18.0%
14,314	RED RIVER	4,869	2,895	1,931	43	964	R	59.5%	39.7%	60.0%	40.0%
13,137	REEVES	3,030	1,366	1,602	62	236	D	45.1%	52.9%	46.0%	54.0%
7,828	REFUGIO	2,862	1,879	951	32	928	R	65.7%	33.2%	66.4%	33.6%
887	ROBERTS	541	475	60	6	415	R	87.8%	11.1%	88.8%	11.2%
16,000	ROBERTSON	6,284	3,172	3,018	94	154	R	50.5%	48.0%	51.2%	48.8%
43,080	ROCKWALL	17,423	14,496	2,592	335	11,904	R	83.2%	14.9%	84.8%	15.2%
11,495	RUNNELS	3,903	3,134	719	50	2,415	R	80.3%	18.4%	81.3%	18.7%
47,372	RUSK	16,212	11,823	4,149	240	7,674	R	72.9%	25.6%	74.0%	26.0%
10,469	SABINE	4,466	2,693	1,694	79	999	R	60.3%	37.9%	61.4%	38.6%
8,946	SAN AUGUSTINE	3,677	2,086	1,540	51	546	R	56.7%	41.9%	57.5%	42.5%
22,246	SAN JACINTO	7,566	4,856	2,604	106	2,252	R	64.2%	34.4%	65.1%	34.9%
67,138	SAN PATRICIO	18,341	11,254	6,823	264	4,431	R	61.4%	37.2%	62.3%	37.7%
6,186	SAN SABA	2,290	1,764	492	34	1,272	R	77.0%	21.5%	78.2%	21.8%
2,935	SCHLEICHER	1,095	854	230	11	624	R	78.0%	21.0%	78.8%	21.2%
16,361	SCURRY	5,183	4,040	1,059	84	2,981	R	77.9%	20.4%	79.2%	20.8%
3,302	SHACKELFORD	1,285	1,063	207	15	856	R	82.7%	16.1%	83.7%	16.3%
25,224	SHELBY	8,859	5,870	2,886	103	2,984	R	66.3%	32.6%	67.0%	33.0%
3,186	SHERMAN	1,032	895	124	13	771	R	86.7%	12.0%	87.8%	12.2%
174,706	SMITH	60,297	44,744	14,734	819	30,010	R	74.2%	24.4%	75.2%	24.8%
6,809	SOMERVELL	2,779	2,087	660	32	1,427	R	75.1%	23.7%	76.0%	24.0%
53,597	STARR	7,674	1,957	5,583	134	3,626	D	25.5%	72.8%	26.0%	74.0%
9,674	STEPHENS	3,253	2,487	712	54	1,775	R	76.5%	21.9%	77.7%	22.3%
1,393	STERLING	607	517	80	10	437	R	85.2%	13.2%	86.6%	13.4%
1,693	STONEWALL	755	478	270	7	208	R	63.3%	35.8%	63.9%	36.1%
4,077	SUTTON	1,414	1,063	345	6	718	R	75.2%	24.4%	75.5%	24.5%
8,378	SWISHER	2,456	1,620	808	28	812	R	66.0%	32.9%	66.7%	33.3%
1,446,219	TARRANT	467,099	313,435	143,191	10,473	170,244	R	67.1%	30.7%	68.6%	31.4%
126,555	TAYLOR	42,862	34,052	8,023	787	26,029	R	79.4%	18.7%	80.9%	19.1%
1,081	TERRELL	431	235	187	9	48	R	54.5%	43.4%	55.7%	44.3%
12,761	TERRY	3,915	3,016	837	62	2,179	R	77.0%	21.4%	78.3%	21.7%
1,850	THROCKMORTON	805	602	201	2	401	R	74.8%	25.0%	75.0%	25.0%
28,118	TITUS	7,939	5,181	2,670	88	2,511	R	65.3%	33.6%	66.0%	34.0%
104,010	TOM GREEN	34,146	26,362	7,148	636	19,214	R	77.2%	20.9%	78.7%	21.3%
812,280	TRAVIS	295,119	164,748	100,895	29,476	63,853	R	55.8%	34.2%	62.0%	38.0%
13,779	TRINITY	5,177	3,232	1,871	74	1,361	R	62.4%	36.1%	63.3%	36.7%
20,871	TYLER	6,977	4,204	2,659	114	1,545	R	60.3%	38.1%	61.3%	38.7%
35,291	UPSHUR	12,579	8,625	3,764	190	4,861	R	68.6%	29.9%	69.6%	30.4%
3,404	UPTON	1,190	919	251	20	668	R	77.2%	21.1%	78.5%	21.5%
25,926	UVALDE	8,167	5,149	2,853	165	2,296	R	63.0%	34.9%	64.3%	35.7%
44,856	VAL VERDE	11,141	6,576	4,324	241	2,252	R	59.0%	38.8%	60.3%	39.7%
48,140	VAN ZANDT	17,611	12,838	4,508	265	8,330	R	72.9%	25.6%	74.0%	26.0%
84,088	VICTORIA	26,341	19,030	6,923	388	12,107	R	72.2%	26.3%	73.3%	26.7%
61,758	WALKER	14,190	9,915	3,950	325	5,965	R	69.9%	27.8%	71.5%	28.5%
32,663	WALLER	10,758	6,190	4,430	138	1,760	R	57.5%	41.2%	58.3%	41.7%
10,909	WARD	3,781	2,622	1,063	96	1,559	R	69.3%	28.1%	71.2%	28.8%
30,373	WASHINGTON	11,685	9,000	2,531	154	6,469	R	77.0%	21.7%	78.1%	21.9%
193,117	WEBB	30,808	15,147	14,837	824	310	R	49.2%	48.2%	50.5%	49.5%

TEXAS

SENATOR 2000

2000 Census Population	County	Total Vote	Republican	Democratic	Other	Rep.-Dem. Plurality		Percentage			
								Total Vote		Major Vote	
								Rep.	Dem.	Rep.	Dem.
41,188	WHARTON	13,287	8,964	4,182	141	4,782	R	67.5%	31.5%	68.2%	31.8%
5,284	WHEELER	2,309	1,817	480	12	1,337	R	78.7%	20.8%	79.1%	20.9%
131,664	WICHITA	42,341	29,912	11,671	758	18,241	R	70.6%	27.6%	71.9%	28.1%
14,676	WILBARGER	4,444	3,248	1,142	54	2,106	R	73.1%	25.7%	74.0%	26.0%
20,082	WILLACY	4,861	2,218	2,525	118	307	D	45.6%	51.9%	46.8%	53.2%
249,967	WILLIAMSON	94,721	70,036	20,829	3,856	49,207	R	73.9%	22.0%	77.1%	22.9%
32,408	WILSON	11,518	8,086	3,187	245	4,899	R	70.2%	27.7%	71.7%	28.3%
7,173	WINKLER	2,014	1,514	477	23	1,037	R	75.2%	23.7%	76.0%	24.0%
48,793	WISE	16,145	11,807	4,016	322	7,791	R	73.1%	24.9%	74.6%	25.4%
36,752	WOOD	13,734	10,215	3,308	211	6,907	R	74.4%	24.1%	75.5%	24.5%
7,322	YOAKUM	2,455	1,988	435	32	1,553	R	81.0%	17.7%	82.0%	18.0%
17,943	YOUNG	6,758	5,056	1,623	79	3,433	R	74.8%	24.0%	75.7%	24.3%
12,182	ZAPATA	2,447	1,012	1,384	51	372	D	41.4%	56.6%	42.2%	57.8%
11,600	ZAVALA	3,198	581	2,568	49	1,987	D	18.2%	80.3%	18.5%	81.5%
20,851,820	TOTAL	6,276,652	4,082,091	2,030,315	164,246	2,051,776	R	65.0%	32.3%	66.8%	33.2%

HARRIS COUNTY

SENATOR 2000

Ward	Total Vote	Republican	Democratic	Other	Rep.-Dem. Plurality		Percentage			
							Total Vote		Major Vote	
							Rep.	Dem.	Rep.	Dem.
R.D. 126	56,452	44,189	11,174	1,089	33,015	R	78.3%	19.8%	79.8%	20.2%
R.D. 127	50,821	40,177	9,712	932	30,465	R	79.1%	19.1%	80.5%	19.5%
R.D. 128	28,983	14,869	13,667	447	1,202	R	51.3%	47.2%	52.1%	47.9%
R.D. 129	55,067	41,599	12,225	1,243	29,374	R	75.5%	22.2%	77.3%	22.7%
R.D. 130	68,676	54,409	12,922	1,345	41,487	R	79.2%	18.8%	80.8%	19.2%
R.D. 131	32,171	9,312	22,319	540	13,007	D	28.9%	69.4%	29.4%	70.6%
R.D. 132	43,983	21,185	21,246	1,552	61	D	48.2%	48.3%	49.9%	50.1%
R.D. 133	49,210	37,080	10,793	1,337	26,287	R	75.4%	21.9%	77.5%	22.5%
R.D. 134	36,896	23,003	12,518	1,375	10,485	R	62.3%	33.9%	64.8%	35.2%
R.D. 135	55,883	41,975	12,761	1,147	29,214	R	75.1%	22.8%	76.7%	23.3%
R.D. 136	51,354	40,373	9,677	1,304	30,696	R	78.6%	18.8%	80.7%	19.3%
R.D. 137	33,051	17,148	13,318	2,585	3,830	R	51.9%	40.3%	56.3%	43.7%
R.D. 138	30,367	15,828	13,615	924	2,213	R	52.1%	44.8%	53.8%	46.2%
R.D. 139	26,730	7,529	18,824	377	11,295	D	28.2%	70.4%	28.6%	71.4%
R.D. 140	17,542	7,921	9,273	348	1,352	D	45.2%	52.9%	46.1%	53.9%
R.D. 141	34,894	11,337	23,157	400	11,820	D	32.5%	66.4%	32.9%	67.1%
R.D. 142	29,496	6,820	22,287	389	15,467	D	23.1%	75.6%	23.4%	76.6%
R.D. 143	18,378	7,477	10,539	362	3,062	D	40.7%	57.3%	41.5%	58.5%
R.D. 144	32,303	22,007	9,510	786	12,497	R	68.1%	29.4%	69.8%	30.2%
R.D. 145	16,942	7,507	8,967	468	1,460	D	44.3%	52.9%	45.6%	54.4%
R.D. 146	38,126	13,047	24,520	559	11,473	D	34.2%	64.3%	34.7%	65.3%
R.D. 147	26,970	8,292	18,068	610	9,776	D	30.7%	67.0%	31.5%	68.5%
R.D. 148	21,596	9,917	10,640	1,039	723	D	45.9%	49.3%	48.2%	51.8%
R.D. 149	36,140	21,908	13,426	806	8,482	R	60.6%	37.1%	62.0%	38.0%
R.D. 150	49,937	38,936	10,003	998	28,933	R	78.0%	20.0%	79.6%	20.4%
3,400,578 TOTAL	941,968	563,845	355,161	22,962	208,684	R	59.9%	37.7%	61.4%	38.6%

Note: The Harris County vote was certified as follows: 564,027 Republican; 355,253 Democratic; 22,977 Other.

TEXAS

CONGRESS

CD	Year	Total Vote	Republican Vote	Republican Candidate	Democratic Vote	Democratic Candidate	Other Vote	Rep.-Dem. Plurality		Total Vote Rep.	Total Vote Dem.	Major Vote Rep.	Major Vote Dem.
1	2000	211,848	91,912	WILLINGHAM, NOBLE	118,157	SANDLIN, MAX	1,779	26,245	D	43.4%	55.8%	43.8%	56.2%
1	1998	135,979	55,191	BOERNER, DENNIS	80,788	SANDLIN, MAX		25,597	D	40.6%	59.4%	40.6%	59.4%
1	1996	199,170	93,105	MERRITT, ED	102,697	SANDLIN, MAX	3,368	9,592	D	46.7%	51.6%	47.6%	52.4%
1	1994	156,392	63,911	BLANKENSHIP, MIKE	86,480	CHAPMAN, JAMES L.	6,001	22,569	D	40.9%	55.3%	42.5%	57.5%
1	1992	152,209			152,209	CHAPMAN, JAMES L.		152,209	D		100.0%		100.0%
2	2000	178,830			162,891	TURNER, JIM	15,939	162,891	D		91.1%		100.0%
2	1998	139,589	56,891	BABIN, BRIAN	81,556	TURNER, JIM	1,142	24,665	D	40.8%	58.4%	41.1%	58.9%
2	1996	196,971	89,838	BABIN, BRIAN	102,908	TURNER, JIM	4,225	13,070	D	45.6%	52.2%	46.6%	53.4%
2	1994	153,780	66,071	PETERSON, DONNA	87,709	WILSON, CHARLES		21,638	D	43.0%	57.0%	43.0%	57.0%
2	1992	211,350	92,176	PETERSON, DONNA	118,625	WILSON, CHARLES	549	26,449	D	43.6%	56.1%	43.7%	56.3%
3	2000	261,897	187,486	JOHNSON, SAM	67,233	ZACHARY, BILLY WAYNE	7,178	120,253	R	71.6%	25.7%	73.6%	26.4%
3	1998	116,978	106,690	JOHNSON, SAM			10,288	106,690	R	91.2%		100.0%	
3	1996			JOHNSON, SAM		*			R				
4	2000	241,878	91,574	NEWTON, JON	145,887	HALL, RALPH M.	4,417	54,313	D	37.9%	60.3%	38.6%	61.4%
4	1998	144,080	58,954	LOHMEYER, JIM	82,989	HALL, RALPH M.	2,137	24,035	D	40.9%	57.6%	41.5%	58.5%
4	1996	207,177	71,065	HALL, JERRY RAY	132,126	HALL, RALPH M.	3,986	61,061	D	34.3%	63.8%	35.0%	65.0%
4	1994	168,947	67,267	BRIDGES, DAVID L.	99,303	HALL, RALPH M.	2,377	32,036	D	39.8%	58.8%	40.4%	59.6%
4	1992	220,333	83,875	BRIDGES, DAVID L.	128,008	HALL, RALPH M.	8,450	44,133	D	38.1%	58.1%	39.6%	60.4%
5	2000	185,958	100,487	SESSIONS, PETE	82,629	COGGINS, REGINA MONTOYA	2,842	17,858	R	54.0%	44.4%	54.9%	45.1%
5	1998	110,667	61,714	SESSIONS, PETE	48,073	MORALES, VICTOR M.	880	13,641	R	55.8%	43.4%	56.2%	43.8%
5	1996			SESSIONS, PETE		*			R				
6	2000	252,741	222,685	BARTON, JOE L.			30,056	222,685	R	88.1%		100.0%	
6	1998	154,886	112,957	BARTON, JOE L.	40,112	BOOTHE, BEN B.	1,817	72,845	R	72.9%	25.9%	73.8%	26.2%
6	1996			BARTON, JOE L.		*			R				
7	2000	248,593	183,712	CULBERSON, JOHN	60,694	SELL, JEFF	4,187	123,018	R	73.9%	24.4%	75.2%	24.8%
7	1998	118,946	111,010	ARCHER, W. R.			7,936	111,010	R	93.3%		100.0%	
7	1996			ARCHER, W. R.		*			R				
8	2000	255,216	233,848	BRADY, KEVIN			21,368	233,848	R	91.6%		100.0%	
8	1998	132,948	123,372	BRADY, KEVIN			9,576	123,372	R	92.8%		100.0%	
8	1996	51,370	51,370	BRADY/FONTENOT				51,370	R	100.0%		100.0%	
9	2000	219,816	87,165	WILLIAMS, PAUL	130,143	LAMPSON, NICK	2,508	42,978	D	39.7%	59.2%	40.1%	59.9%
9	1998	135,162	49,107	COTTAR, TOM	86,055	LAMPSON, NICK		36,948	D	36.3%	63.7%	36.3%	63.7%
9	1996	112,095	52,870	STOCKMAN, STEVE	59,225	LAMPSON, NICK		6,355	D	47.2%	52.8%	47.2%	52.8%
10	2000	240,831			203,628	DOGGETT, LLOYD	37,203	203,628	D		84.6%		100.0%
10	1998	136,282			116,127	DOGGETT, LLOYD	20,155	116,127	D		85.2%		100.0%
10	1996	234,991	97,204	DOGGETT, TERESA	132,066	DOGGETT, LLOYD	5,721	34,862	D	41.4%	56.2%	42.4%	57.6%
10	1994	201,986	80,382	BAYLOR, A. JO	113,738	DOGGETT, LLOYD	7,866	33,356	D	39.8%	56.3%	41.4%	58.6%
10	1992	261,892	68,646	SPIRO, HERBERT	177,233	PICKLE, JAKE	16,013	108,587	D	26.2%	67.7%	27.9%	72.1%
11	2000	192,918	85,546	FARLEY, RAMSEY	105,782	EDWARDS, CHET	1,590	20,236	D	44.3%	54.8%	44.7%	55.3%
11	1998	86,303			71,142	EDWARDS, CHET	15,161	71,142	D		82.4%		100.0%
11	1996	175,935	74,549	MATHIS, JAY	99,990	EDWARDS, CHET	1,396	25,441	D	42.4%	56.8%	42.7%	57.3%
11	1994	129,543	52,876	BROYLES, JAMES W.	76,667	EDWARDS, CHET		23,791	D	40.8%	59.2%	40.8%	59.2%
11	1992	178,032	58,033	BROYLES, JAMES W.	119,999	EDWARDS, CHET		61,966	D	32.6%	67.4%	32.6%	67.4%

TEXAS

CONGRESS

CD	Year	Total Vote	Republican Vote	Republican Candidate	Democratic Vote	Democratic Candidate	Other Vote	Rep.-Dem. Plurality	Percentage Total Vote Rep.	Dem.	Major Vote Rep.	Dem.
12	2000	187,916	117,739	GRANGER, KAY	67,612	GREENE, MARK	2,565	50,127 R	62.7%	36.0%	63.5%	36.5%
12	1998	107,741	66,740	GRANGER, KAY	39,084	HALL, TOM	1,917	27,656 R	61.9%	36.3%	63.1%	36.9%
12	1996	170,204	98,349	GRANGER, KAY	69,859	PARMER, HUGH	1,996	28,490 R	57.8%	41.0%	58.5%	41.5%
12	1994	140,331	43,959	ANDERSON, ERNEST J.	96,372	GEREN, PETE		52,413 D	31.3%	68.7%	31.3%	68.7%
12	1992	199,924	74,432	HOBBS, DAVID	125,492	GEREN, PETE		51,060 D	37.2%	62.8%	37.2%	62.8%
13	2000	174,475	117,995	THORNBERRY, WILLIAM M.	54,343	CLINESMITH, CURTIS	2,137	63,652 R	67.6%	31.1%	68.5%	31.5%
13	1998	119,466	81,141	THORNBERRY, WILLIAM M.	37,027	HARMON, MARK	1,298	44,114 R	67.9%	31.0%	68.7%	31.3%
13	1996	173,627	116,098	THORNBERRY, WILLIAM M.	56,066	SILVERMAN, SAMUEL B.	1,463	60,032 R	66.9%	32.3%	67.4%	32.6%
13	1994	143,389	79,466	THORNBERRY, WILLIAM M.	63,923	SARPALIUS, BILL		15,543 R	55.4%	44.6%	55.4%	44.6%
13	1992	195,406	77,514	BOULTER, BEAU	117,892	SARPALIUS, BILL		40,378 D	39.7%	60.3%	39.7%	60.3%
14	2000	230,059	137,370	PAUL, RON	92,689	SNEARY, LOY		44,681 R	59.7%	40.3%	59.7%	40.3%
14	1998	152,863	84,459	PAUL, RON	68,014	SNEARY, LOY	390	16,445 R	55.3%	44.5%	55.4%	44.6%
14	1996	195,699	99,961	PAUL, RON	93,200	MORRIS, CHARLES "LEFTY	2,538	6,761 R	51.1%	47.6%	51.8%	48.2%
14	1994	154,968	68,793	DEATS, JIM	86,175	LAUGHLIN, GREG		17,382 D	44.4%	55.6%	44.4%	55.6%
14	1992	199,671	54,412	GARZA, HUMBERTO J.	135,930	LAUGHLIN, GREG	9,329	81,518 D	27.3%	68.1%	28.6%	71.4%
15	2000	120,448			106,570	HINOJOSA, RUBEN	13,878	106,570 D		88.5%		100.0%
15	1998	82,178	34,221	HAUGHEY, TOM	47,957	HINOJOSA, RUBEN		13,736 D	41.6%	58.4%	41.6%	58.4%
15	1996	138,594	50,914	HAUGHEY, TOM	86,347	HINOJOSA, RUBEN	1,333	35,433 D	36.7%	62.3%	37.1%	62.9%
15	1994	104,366	41,119	HAUGHEY, TOM	61,527	DE LA GARZA, ELIGIO	1,720	20,408 D	39.4%	59.0%	40.1%	59.9%
15	1992	142,900	56,549	HAUGHEY, TOM	86,351	DE LA GARZA, ELIGIO		29,802 D	39.6%	60.4%	39.6%	60.4%
16	2000	135,650	40,921	POWER, DANIEL S.	92,649	REYES, SILVESTRE	2,080	51,728 D	30.2%	68.3%	30.6%	69.4%
16	1998	76,767			67,486	REYES, SILVESTRE	9,281	67,486 D		87.9%		100.0%
16	1996	127,784	35,271	LEDESMA, RICK	90,260	REYES, SILVESTRE	2,253	54,989 D	27.6%	70.6%	28.1%	71.9%
16	1994	87,224	37,409	ORTIZ, BOBBY	49,815	COLEMAN, RONALD		12,406 D	42.9%	57.1%	42.9%	57.1%
16	1992	128,601	61,870	TABERSKI, CHIP	66,731	COLEMAN, RONALD		4,861 D	48.1%	51.9%	48.1%	51.9%
17	2000	204,430	72,535	CLEMENTS, DARRELL	120,670	STENHOLM, CHARLES W.	11,225	48,135 D	35.5%	59.0%	37.5%	62.5%
17	1998	140,685	63,700	IZZARD, RUDY	75,367	STENHOLM, CHARLES W.	1,618	11,667 D	45.3%	53.6%	45.8%	54.2%
17	1996	192,994	91,429	IZZARD, RUDY	99,678	STENHOLM, CHARLES W.	1,887	8,249 D	47.4%	51.6%	47.8%	52.2%
17	1994	155,605	72,108	BOONE, PHIL	83,497	STENHOLM, CHARLES W.		11,389 D	46.3%	53.7%	46.3%	53.7%
17	1992	206,171	69,958	SADOWSKI, JEANNIE	136,213	STENHOLM, CHARLES W.		66,255 D	33.9%	66.1%	33.9%	66.1%
18	2000	172,378	38,191	LEVY, BOB	131,857	JACKSON-LEE, SHEILA	2,330	93,666 D	22.2%	76.5%	22.5%	77.5%
18	1998	91,267			82,091	JACKSON-LEE, SHEILA	9,176	82,091 D		89.9%		100.0%
18	1996			*		JACKSON-LEE, SHEILA		D				
19	2000	185,898	170,319	COMBEST, LARRY			15,579	170,319 R	91.6%		100.0%	
19	1998	129,428	108,266	COMBEST, LARRY	21,162	BLANKENSHIP, SIDNEY		87,104 R	83.6%	16.4%	83.6%	16.4%
19	1996	195,226	156,910	COMBEST, LARRY	38,316	SAWYER, JOHN W.		118,594 R	80.4%	19.6%	80.4%	19.6%
19	1994	120,641	120,641	COMBEST, LARRY				120,641 R	100.0%		100.0%	
19	1992	209,382	162,057	COMBEST, LARRY	47,325	MOSER, TERRY L.		114,732 R	77.4%	22.6%	77.4%	22.6%
20	2000	122,574			107,487	GONZALEZ, CHARLIE	15,087	107,487 D		87.7%		100.0%
20	1998	79,713	28,347	WALKER, JAMES	50,356	GONZALEZ, CHARLIE	1,010	22,009 D	35.6%	63.2%	36.0%	64.0%
20	1996	138,409	47,616	WALKER, JAMES	88,190	GONZALEZ, HENRY B.	2,603	40,574 D	34.4%	63.7%	35.1%	64.9%
20	1994	96,149	36,035	COLYER, CARL B.	60,114	GONZALEZ, HENRY B.		24,079 D	37.5%	62.5%	37.5%	62.5%
20	1992	103,755			103,755	GONZALEZ, HENRY B.		103,755 D		100.0%		100.0%
21	2000	330,878	251,049	SMITH, LAMAR	73,326	GREEN, JIM	6,503	177,723 R	75.9%	22.2%	77.4%	22.6%
21	1998	180,608	165,047	SMITH, LAMAR			15,561	165,047 R	91.4%		100.0%	
21	1996	269,307	205,830	SMITH, LAMAR	60,338	WHARTON, GORDON H.	3,139	145,492 R	76.4%	22.4%	77.3%	22.7%
21	1994	184,075	165,595	SMITH, LAMAR			18,480	165,595 R	90.0%		100.0%	
21	1992	264,653	190,979	SMITH, LAMAR	62,827	GADDY, JAMES M.	10,847	128,152 R	72.2%	23.7%	75.2%	24.8%

TEXAS

CONGRESS

CD	Year	Total Vote	Republican		Democratic		Other Vote	Rep.-Dem. Plurality	Percentage			
									Total Vote		Major Vote	
			Vote	Candidate	Vote	Candidate			Rep.	Dem.	Rep.	Dem.
22	2000	256,267	154,662	DELAY, THOMAS D.	92,645	MATRANGA, JO ANN	8,960	62,017 R	60.4%	36.2%	62.5%	37.5%
22	1998	134,720	87,840	DELAY, THOMAS D.	45,386	KEMP, HILL	1,494	42,454 R	65.2%	33.7%	65.9%	34.1%
22	1996			DELAY, THOMAS D.		*		R				
23	2000	201,754	119,679	BONILLA, HENRY	78,274	GARZA, ISIDRO, JR.	3,801	41,405 R	59.3%	38.8%	60.5%	39.5%
23	1998	114,720	73,177	BONILLA, HENRY	40,281	JONES, CHARLIE URBINA	1,262	32,896 R	63.8%	35.1%	64.5%	35.5%
23	1996	163,839	101,332	BONILLA, HENRY	59,596	JONES, CHARLES P.	2,911	41,736 R	61.8%	36.4%	63.0%	37.0%
23	1994	117,916	73,815	BONILLA, HENRY	44,101	RIOS, ROLANDO L.		29,714 R	62.6%	37.4%	62.6%	37.4%
23	1992	166,347	98,259	BONILLA, HENRY	63,797	BUSTAMANTE, ALBERT G.	4,291	34,462 R	59.1%	38.4%	60.6%	39.4%
24	2000	166,948	61,235	WRIGHT, JAMES "BRYNDAN"	103,152	FROST, MARTIN	2,561	41,917 D	36.7%	61.8%	37.3%	62.7%
24	1998	97,992	40,105	TERRY, SHAWN	56,321	FROST, MARTIN	1,566	16,216 D	40.9%	57.5%	41.6%	58.4%
24	1996			*		FROST, MARTIN		D				
25	2000	176,522	68,010	SUDAN, PHIL	106,112	BENTSEN, KEN	2,400	38,102 D	38.5%	60.1%	39.1%	60.9%
25	1998	101,269	41,848	SANCHEZ, JOHN M.	58,591	BENTSEN, KEN	830	16,743 D	41.3%	57.9%	41.7%	58.3%
25	1996	51,288	21,892	MCKENNA, DOLLY MADISON	29,396	BENTSEN, KEN		7,504 D	42.7%	57.3%	42.7%	57.3%
26	2000	295,272	214,025	ARMEY, DICK	75,601	LOVE, STEVE	5,646	138,424 R	72.5%	25.6%	73.9%	26.1%
26	1998	136,514	120,332	ARMEY, DICK			16,182	120,332 R	88.1%		100.0%	
26	1996			ARMEY, DICK		*		R				
27	2000	161,072	54,660	AHUMADA, PAT	102,088	ORTIZ, SOLOMON P.	4,324	47,428 D	33.9%	63.4%	34.9%	65.1%
27	1998	97,398	34,284	STONE, EROL A.	61,638	ORTIZ, SOLOMON P.	1,476	27,354 D	35.2%	63.3%	35.7%	64.3%
27	1996	150,600	50,964	GARDNER, JOE	97,350	ORTIZ, SOLOMON P.	2,286	46,386 D	33.8%	64.6%	34.4%	65.6%
27	1994	110,018	44,693	STONE, EROL A.	65,325	ORTIZ, SOLOMON P.		20,632 D	40.6%	59.4%	40.6%	59.4%
27	1992	156,844	66,853	KIMBROUGH, JAY	87,022	ORTIZ, SOLOMON P.	2,969	20,169 D	42.6%	55.5%	43.4%	56.6%
28	2000	138,260			123,104	RODRIGUEZ, CIRO D.	15,156	123,104 D		89.0%		100.0%
28	1998	79,353			71,849	RODRIGUEZ, CIRO D.	7,504	71,849 D		90.5%		100.0%
28	1996	146,135	34,191	CUDE, MARK L.	110,148	TEJEDA, FRANK	1,796	75,957 D	23.4%	75.4%	23.7%	76.3%
28	1994	104,375	28,777	SLATTER, DAVID C.	73,986	TEJEDA, FRANK M.	1,612	45,209 D	27.6%	70.9%	28.0%	72.0%
28	1992	140,585			122,457	TEJEDA, FRANK M.	18,128	122,457 D		87.1%		100.0%
29	2000	115,475	29,606	VU, JOE	84,665	GREEN, GENE	1,204	55,059 D	25.6%	73.3%	25.9%	74.1%
29	1998	47,631			44,179	GREEN, GENE	3,452	44,179 D		92.8%		100.0%
29	1996			*		GREEN, GENE		D				
30	2000	118,961			109,163	JOHNSON, EDDIE B.	9,798	109,163 D		91.8%		100.0%
30	1998	79,752	21,338	KELLEHER, CARRIE	57,603	JOHNSON, EDDIE B.	811	36,265 D	26.8%	72.2%	27.0%	73.0%
30	1996			*		JOHNSON, EDDIE B.		D				

Note: A federal district court in August 1996 redrew the lines in 13 districts and ordered they hold open primaries Nov. 5, 1996, with candidates from all parties running on the same ballot. In 10 of the districts—3, 5, 6, 7, 18, 22, 24, 26, 29 and 30—a candidate received a majority in the November voting and was elected. In three districts—8, 9 and 25— there was a Dec. 10, 1996, runoff election between the top two finishers in November, regardless of party. Results from these 13 districts for 1992 and 1994 are not included in the table because the district lines were no longer comparable. Results from these earlier years can be found in *America Votes 21*.

TEXAS

GENERAL AND PRIMARY ELECTIONS

2000 GENERAL ELECTIONS

President Other vote was 23,160 Libertarian (Browne); 12,394 Independent (Buchanan); 567 write-in (Phillips); 74 write-in (Wright); 63 write-in (McReynolds).

Senator Other vote was 91,448 Green (Sandage); 72,798 Libertarian (Ruwart).

Congress Other vote was: CD 1: 1,779 Libertarian (Carr); CD 2: 15,939 Libertarian (Dye); CD 3: 7,178 Libertarian (Flores); CD 4: 4,417 Libertarian (Turner); CD 5: 2,842 Libertarian (Ashby); CD 6: 30,056 Libertarian (Brady); CD 7: 4,182 Libertarian (Parks), 5 write-in (Skone-Palmer); CD 8: 21,368 Libertarian (Guillory); CD 9: 2,508 Libertarian (Knipp); CD 10: 37,203 Libertarian (Davis); CD 11: 1,590 Libertarian (Swanstrom); CD 12: 2,565 Libertarian (Clay); CD 13: 2,137 Libertarian (Clardy); CD 15: 13,167 Libertarian (Jones), 711 write-in (Cantu); CD 16: 2,080 Libertarian (Moser); CD 17: 11,180 Libertarian (Monde), 45 write-in (Julia); CD 18: 2,330 Libertarian (Nankervis); CD 19: 15,579 Libertarian (Turnbow); CD 20: 15,087 Libertarian (De Pena); CD 21: 6,503 Libertarian (Steinbrecher); CD 22: 5,577 Independent (Schneider), 3,383 Libertarian (Probst); CD 23: 3,801 Libertarian (Blunt); CD 24: 2,561 Libertarian (Worthington); CD 25: 2,400 Libertarian (Messina); CD 26: 5,646 Libertarian (Badagnani); CD 27: 4,324 Libertarian (Bunch); CD 28: 15,156 Libertarian (Stallknecht); CD 29: 1,204 Libertarian (Dittmar); CD 30: 9,798 Libertarian (Rush).

2000 PRIMARY ELECTIONS

Primary March 14, 2000
Primary Runoff April 11, 2000

Registration 11,612,761 No Party Registration
(as of March 14, 2000)

Primary Type Open—Any registered voter could vote in the primary of either party, although if they voted in the primary of one party they could not vote in the runoff of the other party.

Note: An asterisk (*) denotes incumbent.

REPUBLICAN PRIMARIES			DEMOCRATIC PRIMARIES		
President					
George W. Bush	986,416	87.5%	Al Gore	631,428	80.2%
John McCain	80,082	7.1%	Bill Bradley	128,564	16.3%
Alan Keyes	43,518	3.9%	Lyndon H. LaRouche Jr.	26,898	3.4%
Uncommitted	9,570	0.8%			
Steve Forbes	2,865	0.3%			
Gary Bauer	2,189	0.2%			
Orrin G. Hatch	1,324	0.1%			
Charles Bass Urban	793	0.1%			
TOTAL	1,126,757		TOTAL	786,890	
Senator					
Kay Bailey Hutchison*	955,033	100.0%	Gene Kelly	220,531	35.7%
			Charles Gandy	140,636	22.8%
			Don Clark	139,243	22.5%
			Bobby Wightman	83,643	13.5%
			H. Gerald Bintliff	33,979	5.5%
TOTAL	955,033		TOTAL	618,032	
			PRIMARY RUNOFF		
			Gene Kelly	143,366	58.4%
			Charles Gandy	101,984	41.6%
			TOTAL	245,350	
Congressional District 1	Noble Willingham	14,619	57.2%	Max Sandlin*	56,207	84.6%
	John Lawrence	10,919	42.8%	B. D. Blount	10,265	15.4%
	TOTAL	25,538		TOTAL	66,472	
Congressional District 2	No Republican candidate			Jim Turner*	65,446	100.0%
				TOTAL	65,446	

TEXAS

GENERAL AND PRIMARY ELECTIONS

	REPUBLICAN PRIMARIES			DEMOCRATIC PRIMARIES		
Congressional District 3	Sam Johnson*	40,802	93.5%	Billy Wayne Zachary	6,031	100.0%
	J. A. Gonnell	2,843	6.5%			
	TOTAL	43,645		TOTAL	6,031	
Congressional District 4	Jon Newton	21,791	54.5%	Ralph M. Hall*	16,403	100.0%
	Mark D. Peterman	18,164	45.5%			
	TOTAL	39,955		TOTAL	16,403	
Congressional District 5	Pete Sessions*	26,179	100.0%	Regina Montoya Coggins	18,368	68.1%
				Gary L. Harrison	8,619	31.9%
	TOTAL	26,179		TOTAL	26,987	
Congressional District 6	Joe L. Barton*	51,664	100.0%	No Democratic candidate		
	TOTAL	51,664				
Congressional District 7	John Culberson	23,894	37.7%	Jeff Sell	3,828	100.0%
	Peter Wareing	16,837	26.6%			
	Cathy McConn	8,488	13.4%			
	Mark Brewer	4,865	7.7%			
	Wallace Henley	4,649	7.3%			
	Ron Kapche	3,107	4.9%			
	Gene Hsiao	1,063	1.7%			
	Susan Malfer	411	0.6%			
	TOTAL	63,314		TOTAL	3,828	
	PRIMARY RUNOFF					
	John Culberson	29,968	60.0%			
	Peter Wareing	20,017	40.0%			
	TOTAL	49,985				
Congressional District 8	Kevin Brady*	61,252	100.0%	No Democratic candidate		
	TOTAL	61,252				
Congressional District 9	Paul Williams	19,886	100.0%	Nick Lampson*	27,457	100.0%
	TOTAL	19,886		TOTAL	27,457	
Congressional District 10	Charles Moritz	19,889	59.1%	Lloyd Doggett*	31,638	100.0%
	Jerry J. Mikus Jr.	11,002	32.7%			
	Ronnie "Reeferseed" Gjemre	2,759	8.2%			
	TOTAL	33,650		TOTAL	31,638	

Charles Moritz withdrew from the race after the primary, and there was no Republican candidate on the general election ballot.

	REPUBLICAN PRIMARIES			DEMOCRATIC PRIMARIES		
Congressional District 11	Rodney Geer	14,537	40.6%	Chet Edwards*	28,053	100.0%
	Ramsey Farley	14,171	39.6%			
	Rob Curnock	7,078	19.8%			
	TOTAL	35,786		TOTAL	28,053	
	PRIMARY RUNOFF					
	Ramsey Farley	8,385	61.2%			
	Rodney Geer	5,315	38.8%			
	TOTAL	13,700				
Congressional District 12	Kay Granger*	32,382	100.0%	Mark Greene	9,495	76.2%
				Prentiss Bryant Davis	2,964	23.8%
	TOTAL	32,382		TOTAL	12,459	
Congressional District 13	William M. "Mac" Thornberry*	30,867	91.5%	Curtis Clinesmith	18,805	100.0%
	David G. Morris	2,863	8.5%			
	TOTAL	33,730		TOTAL	18,805	
Congressional District 14	Ron Paul*	37,892	100.0%	Loy Sneary	28,318	100.0%
	TOTAL	37,892		TOTAL	28,318	
Congressional District 15	No Republican candidate			Ruben Hinojosa*	46,247	73.5%
				Diana Rivera-Martinez	12,710	20.2%
				Mel Buentello Hawkins	3,928	6.2%
				TOTAL	62,885	
Congressional District 16	Daniel S. Power	9,602	100.0%	Silvestre Reyes*	20,169	100.0%
	TOTAL	9,602		TOTAL	20,169	

TEXAS

	REPUBLICAN PRIMARIES			DEMOCRATIC PRIMARIES		
Congressional District 17	Darrell Clements	15,167	51.6%	Charles W. Stenholm*	36,753	100.0%
	Shane Hunt	14,248	48.4%			
	TOTAL	29,415		TOTAL	36,753	
Congressional District 18	Bob Levy	5,234	54.1%	Sheila Jackson-Lee*	16,067	100.0%
	Elmer L. Zoch	4,437	45.9%			
	TOTAL	9,671		TOTAL	16,067	
Congressional District 19	Larry Combest*	64,433	100.0%	No Democratic candidate		
	TOTAL	64,433		TOTAL		
Congressional District 20	No Republican candidate			Charles A. Gonzalez*	22,213	100.0%
				TOTAL	22,213	
Congressional District 21	Lamar Smith*	90,924	100.0%	Jim Green	12,381	100.0%
	TOTAL	90,924		TOTAL	12,381	
Congressional District 22	Tom DeLay*	41,901	83.3%	Jo Ann Matranga	4,833	51.3%
	Michael "Fjet" Fjetland	8,385	16.7%	Virginia Stogner	4,590	48.7%
	TOTAL	50,286		TOTAL	9,423	
Congressional District 23	Henry Bonilla*	25,231	100.0%	Isidro Garza Jr.	43,424	69.6%
				Joseph P. Sullivan	18,937	30.4%
	TOTAL	25,231		TOTAL	62,361	
Congressional District 24	James "Bryndan" Wright	5,551	32.9%	Martin Frost*	18,892	100.0%
	Bill Payne	4,369	25.9%			
	Cynthia Newman	3,837	22.7%			
	Mac Warren	3,135	18.6%			
	TOTAL	16,892		TOTAL	18,892	
	PRIMARY RUNOFF					
	James "Bryndan" Wright	2,240	62.0%			
	Bill Payne	1,371	38.0%			
	TOTAL	3,611				
Congressional District 25	Phil Sudan	11,658	51.3%	Ken Bentsen*	9,455	100.0%
	Tom Reiser	11,060	48.7%			
	TOTAL	22,718		TOTAL	9,455	
Congressional District 26	Dick Armey*	48,179	87.6%	Steve Love	6,128	100.0%
	Larry K. Thompson	6,806	12.4%			
	TOTAL	54,985		TOTAL	6,128	
Congressional District 27	Pat Ahumada	13,652	100.0%	Solomon P. Ortiz*	36,569	100.0%
	TOTAL	13,652		TOTAL	36,569	
Congressional District 28	No Republican candidate			Ciro D. Rodriguez*	37,110	100.0%
				TOTAL	37,110	
Congressional District 29	Joe Vu	3,960	51.8%	Gene Green*	9,673	100.0%
	Allen H. Goforth	3,685	48.2%			
	TOTAL	7,645		TOTAL	9,673	
Congressional District 30	No Republican candidate			Eddie Bernice Johnson*	20,119	100.0%
				TOTAL	20,119	

UTAH

GOVERNOR
Mike Leavitt (R). Re-elected 2000 to a four-year term. Previously elected 1996, 1992.

SENATORS
Robert F. Bennett (R). Re-elected 1998 to a six-year term. Previously elected 1992.

Orrin G. Hatch (R). Re-elected 2000 to a six-year term. Previously elected 1994, 1988, 1982, 1976.

REPRESENTATIVES
1. James V. Hansen (R) 2. Jim Matheson (D) 3. Christopher B. Cannon (R)

POSTWAR VOTE FOR PRESIDENT

		Republican		Democratic		Other		Total Vote		Major Vote	
Year	Total Vote	Vote	Candidate	Vote	Candidate	Vote	Plurality	Rep.	Dem.	Rep.	Dem.
2000**	770,754	515,096	Bush, George W.	203,053	Gore, Al	52,605	312,043 R	66.8%	26.3%	71.7%	28.3%
1996**	665,629	361,911	Dole, Bob	221,633	Clinton, Bill	82,085	140,278 R	54.4%	33.3%	62.0%	38.0%
1992**	743,999	322,632	Bush, George	183,429	Clinton, Bill	237,938	119,232 R	43.4%	24.7%	63.8%	36.2%
1988	647,008	428,442	Bush, George	207,343	Dukakis, Michael S.	11,223	221,099 R	66.2%	32.0%	67.4%	32.6%
1984	629,656	469,105	Reagan, Ronald	155,369	Mondale, Walter F.	5,182	313,736 R	74.5%	24.7%	75.1%	24.9%
1980**	604,222	439,687	Reagan, Ronald	124,266	Carter, Jimmy	40,269	315,421 R	72.8%	20.6%	78.0%	22.0%
1976	541,198	337,908	Ford, Gerald R.	182,110	Carter, Jimmy	21,180	155,798 R	62.4%	33.6%	65.0%	35.0%
1972	478,476	323,643	Nixon, Richard M.	126,284	McGovern, George S.	28,549	197,359 R	67.6%	26.4%	71.9%	28.1%
1968	422,568	238,728	Nixon, Richard M.	156,665	Humphrey, Hubert H.	27,175	82,063 R	56.5%	37.1%	60.4%	39.6%
1964	401,413	181,785	Goldwater, Barry M.	219,628	Johnson, Lyndon B.		37,843 D	45.3%	54.7%	45.3%	54.7%
1960	374,709	205,361	Nixon, Richard M.	169,248	Kennedy, John F.	100	36,113 R	54.8%	45.2%	54.8%	45.2%
1956	333,995	215,631	Eisenhower, Dwight D.	118,364	Stevenson, Adlai E.		97,267 R	64.6%	35.4%	64.6%	35.4%
1952	329,554	194,190	Eisenhower, Dwight D.	135,364	Stevenson, Adlai E.		58,826 R	58.9%	41.1%	58.9%	41.1%
1948	276,306	124,402	Dewey, Thomas E.	149,151	Truman, Harry S.	2,753	24,749 D	45.0%	54.0%	45.5%	54.5%

In 2000 the other vote column includes 35,850 votes cast for Green (Nader). In 1996 the other vote column includes 66,461 votes cast for Perot. In 1992 the other vote column includes 203,400 votes cast for Perot who came in second. In 1980 the other column includes 30,284 votes for Independent (Anderson).

UTAH

POSTWAR VOTE FOR GOVERNOR

Year	Total Vote	Republican		Democratic		Other Vote	Plurality	Percentage			
								Total Vote		Major Vote	
		Vote	Candidate	Vote	Candidate			Rep.	Dem.	Rep.	Dem.
2000	761,806	424,837	Leavitt, Michael O.	321,979	Orton, Bill	14,990	102,858 R	55.8%	42.3%	56.9%	43.1%
1996	671,879	503,693	Leavitt, Mike	156,616	Bradley, Jim	11,570	347,077 R	75.0%	23.3%	76.3%	23.7%
1992**	762,549	321,713	Leavitt, Mike	177,181	Hanson, Stewart	263,655	65,960 R	42.2%	23.2%	64.5%	35.5%
1988**	649,114	260,462	Bangerter, Norman H.	249,321	Wilson, Ted	139,331	11,141 R	40.1%	38.4%	51.1%	48.9%
1984	629,619	351,792	Bangerter, Norman H.	275,669	Owens, Wayne	2,158	76,123 R	55.9%	43.8%	56.1%	43.9%
1980	600,019	266,578	Wright, Bob	330,974	Matheson, Scott M.	2,467	64,396 D	44.4%	55.2%	44.6%	55.4%
1976	539,649	248,027	Romney, Vernon B.	280,706	Matheson, Scott M.	10,916	32,679 D	46.0%	52.0%	46.9%	53.1%
1972	476,447	144,449	Strike, Nicholas L.	331,998	Rampton, Calvin L.		187,549 D	30.3%	69.7%	30.3%	69.7%
1968	421,012	131,729	Buehner, Carl W.	289,283	Rampton, Calvin L.		157,554 D	31.3%	68.7%	31.3%	68.7%
1964	398,256	171,300	Melich, Mitchell	226,956	Rampton, Calvin L.		55,656 D	43.0%	57.0%	43.0%	57.0%
1960	371,489	195,634	Clyde, George D.	175,855	Barlocker, W. A.		19,779 R	52.7%	47.3%	52.7%	47.3%
1956**	332,889	127,164	Clyde, George D.	111,297	Romney, L. C.	94,428	15,867 R	38.2%	33.4%	53.3%	46.7%
1952	327,704	180,516	Lee, J. Bracken	147,188	Glade, Earl J.		33,328 R	55.1%	44.9%	55.1%	44.9%
1948	275,067	151,253	Lee, J. Bracken	123,814	Maw, Herbert B.		27,439 R	55.0%	45.0%	55.0%	45.0%

In 1992 other vote was 255,753 Independent (Cook); 3,593 Populist (Gum); 1,492 American (Van Horn); 1,158 Socialist Workers (Garcia); 917 Independent (Metzger-Agin); 729 Independent American (Richins) and 13 scattered; Cook finished second. In 1988 other vote was 136,651 Independent (Cook); 1,661 Libertarian (Burton) and 1,019 American (Pedersen). In 1956 other vote was Independent (Lee).

POSTWAR VOTE FOR SENATOR

Year	Total Vote	Republican		Democratic		Other Vote	Rep.-Dem. Plurality	Percentage			
								Total Vote		Major Vote	
		Vote	Candidate	Vote	Candidate			Rep.	Dem.	Rep.	Dem.
2000	769,704	504,803	Hatch, Orrin G.	242,569	Howell, Scott N.	22,332	262,234 R	65.6%	31.5%	67.5%	32.5%
1998	494,909	316,652	Bennett, Robert F.	163,172	Leckman, Scott	15,085	153,480 R	64.0%	33.0%	66.0%	34.0%
1994	519,323	357,297	Hatch, Orrin G.	146,938	Shea, Patrick A.	15,088	210,359 R	68.8%	28.3%	70.9%	29.1%
1992	758,479	420,069	Bennett, Robert F.	301,228	Owens, Wayne	37,182	118,841 R	55.4%	39.7%	58.2%	41.8%
1988	640,702	430,089	Hatch, Orrin G.	203,364	Moss, Brian H.	7,249	226,725 R	67.1%	31.7%	67.9%	32.1%
1986	435,111	314,608	Garn, E. J.	115,523	Oliver, Craig	4,980	199,085 R	72.3%	26.6%	73.1%	26.9%
1982	530,802	309,332	Hatch, Orrin G.	219,482	Wilson, Ted	1,988	89,850 R	58.3%	41.3%	58.5%	41.5%
1980	594,298	437,675	Garn, E. J.	151,454	Berman, Dan	5,169	286,221 R	73.6%	25.5%	74.3%	25.7%
1976	540,108	290,221	Hatch, Orrin G.	241,948	Moss, Frank E.	7,939	48,273 R	53.7%	44.8%	54.5%	45.5%
1974	420,642	210,299	Garn, E. J.	185,377	Owens, Wayne	24,966	24,922 R	50.0%	44.1%	53.1%	46.9%
1970	374,303	159,004	Burton, Laurence J.	210,207	Moss, Frank E.	5,092	51,203 D	42.5%	56.2%	43.1%	56.9%
1968	419,262	225,075	Bennett, Wallace F.	192,168	Weilenmann, Milton	2,019	32,907 R	53.7%	45.8%	53.9%	46.1%
1964	397,384	169,562	Wilkinson, Ernest L.	227,822	Moss, Frank E.		58,260 D	42.7%	57.3%	42.7%	57.3%
1962	318,411	166,755	Bennett, Wallace F.	151,656	King, David S.		15,099 R	52.4%	47.6%	52.4%	47.6%
1958**	291,311	101,471	Watkins, Arthur V.	112,827	Moss, Frank E.	77,013	11,356 D	34.8%	38.7%	47.4%	52.6%
1956	330,381	178,261	Bennett, Wallace F.	152,120	Hopkin, Alonzo F.		26,141 R	54.0%	46.0%	54.0%	46.0%
1952	327,033	177,435	Watkins, Arthur V.	149,598	Granger, Walter K.		27,837 R	54.3%	45.7%	54.3%	45.7%
1950	264,440	142,427	Bennett, Wallace F.	121,198	Thomas, Elbert D.	815	21,229 R	53.9%	45.8%	54.0%	46.0%
1946	197,399	101,142	Watkins, Arthur V.	96,257	Murdock, Abe		4,885 R	51.2%	48.8%	51.2%	48.8%

In 1958 other vote was Independent (Lee).

UTAH

Districts Established January 1, 1992

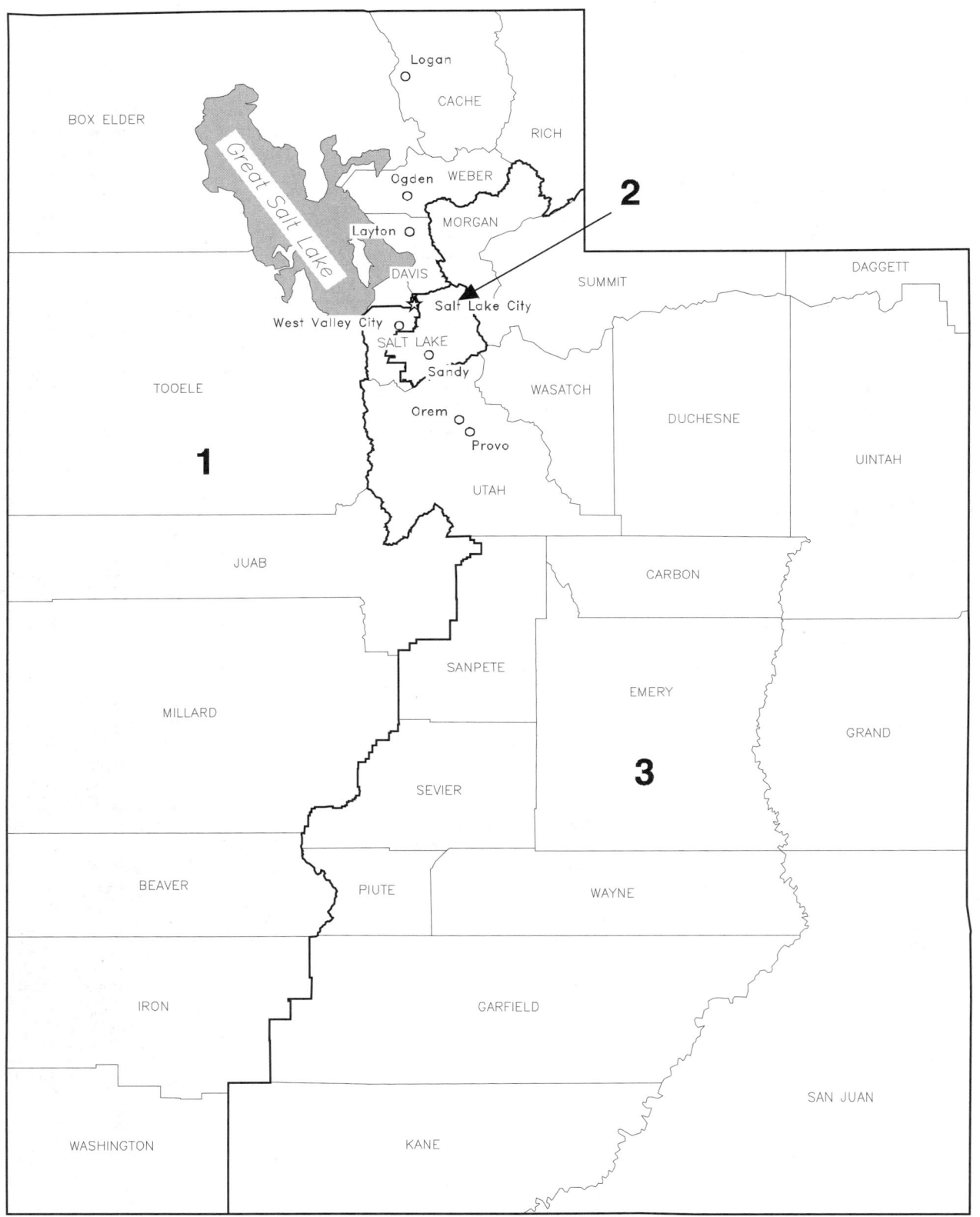

UTAH

PRESIDENT 2000

2000 Census Population	County	Total Vote	Republican	Democratic	Green (Nader)	Other	Rep.-Dem. Plurality	Percentage of Total Vote		
								Rep.	Dem.	Green
6,005	BEAVER	2,252	1,653	541	38	20	1,112 R	73.4%	24.0%	1.7%
42,745	BOX ELDER	15,483	12,288	2,555	326	314	9,733 R	79.4%	16.5%	2.1%
91,391	CACHE	33,142	25,920	5,170	1,511	541	20,750 R	78.2%	15.6%	4.6%
20,422	CARBON	7,384	3,758	3,298	213	115	460 R	50.9%	44.7%	2.9%
921	DAGGETT	435	317	104	9	5	213 R	72.9%	23.9%	2.1%
238,994	DAVIS	87,855	64,375	18,845	2,891	1,744	45,530 R	73.3%	21.5%	3.3%
14,371	DUCHESNE	4,546	3,622	779	76	69	2,843 R	79.7%	17.1%	1.7%
10,860	EMERY	4,398	3,243	958	81	116	2,285 R	73.7%	21.8%	1.8%
4,735	GARFIELD	1,968	1,719	178	43	28	1,541 R	87.3%	9.0%	2.2%
8,485	GRAND	3,614	1,822	1,158	540	94	664 R	50.4%	32.0%	14.9%
33,779	IRON	12,594	10,106	1,789	341	358	8,317 R	80.2%	14.2%	2.7%
8,238	JUAB	2,785	2,023	619	60	83	1,404 R	72.6%	22.2%	2.2%
6,046	KANE	2,802	2,254	387	102	59	1,867 R	80.4%	13.8%	3.6%
12,405	MILLARD	4,775	3,850	696	73	156	3,154 R	80.6%	14.6%	1.5%
7,129	MORGAN	3,171	2,464	553	80	74	1,911 R	77.7%	17.4%	2.5%
1,435	PIUTE	781	626	133	10	12	493 R	80.2%	17.0%	1.3%
1,961	RICH	903	736	152	10	5	584 R	81.5%	16.8%	1.1%
898,387	SALT LAKE	307,258	171,585	107,576	21,252	6,845	64,009 R	55.8%	35.0%	6.9%
14,413	SAN JUAN	4,744	2,721	1,838	107	78	883 R	57.4%	38.7%	2.3%
22,763	SANPETE	7,430	5,781	1,211	153	285	4,570 R	77.8%	16.3%	2.1%
18,842	SEVIER	7,077	5,763	1,046	125	143	4,717 R	81.4%	14.8%	1.8%
29,736	SUMMIT	12,121	6,168	4,601	1,156	196	1,567 R	50.9%	38.0%	9.5%
40,735	TOOELE	12,480	7,807	4,001	387	285	3,806 R	62.6%	32.1%	3.1%
25,224	UINTAH	8,397	6,733	1,387	132	145	5,346 R	80.2%	16.5%	1.6%
368,536	UTAH	120,256	98,255	16,445	2,732	2,824	81,810 R	81.7%	13.7%	2.3%
15,215	WASATCH	5,675	3,819	1,476	259	121	2,343 R	67.3%	26.0%	4.6%
90,354	WASHINGTON	32,461	25,481	5,465	714	801	20,016 R	78.5%	16.8%	2.2%
2,509	WAYNE	1,225	953	202	58	12	751 R	77.8%	16.5%	4.7%
196,533	WEBER	62,742	39,254	19,890	2,371	1,227	19,364 R	62.6%	31.7%	3.8%
2,233,169	TOTAL	770,754	515,096	203,053	35,850	16,755	312,043 R	66.8%	26.3%	4.7%

UTAH

GOVERNOR 2000

2000 Census Population	County	Total Vote	Republican	Democratic	Other	Rep.-Dem. Plurality	Percentage			
							Total Vote		Major Vote	
							Rep.	Dem.	Rep.	Dem.
6,005	BEAVER	2,228	1,396	798	34	598 R	62.7%	35.8%	63.6%	36.4%
42,745	BOX ELDER	15,292	9,910	5,107	275	4,803 R	64.8%	33.4%	66.0%	34.0%
91,391	CACHE	32,671	23,949	8,264	458	15,685 R	73.3%	25.3%	74.3%	25.7%
20,422	CARBON	7,284	2,566	4,630	88	2,064 D	35.2%	63.6%	35.7%	64.3%
921	DAGGETT	423	246	175	2	71 R	58.2%	41.4%	58.4%	41.6%
238,994	DAVIS	86,629	54,324	30,972	1,333	23,352 R	62.7%	35.8%	63.7%	36.3%
14,371	DUCHESNE	4,533	2,597	1,857	79	740 R	57.3%	41.0%	58.3%	41.7%
10,860	EMERY	4,447	2,493	1,867	87	626 R	56.1%	42.0%	57.2%	42.8%
4,735	GARFIELD	1,911	1,224	629	58	595 R	64.1%	32.9%	66.1%	33.9%
8,485	GRAND	3,503	1,630	1,771	102	141 D	46.5%	50.6%	47.9%	52.1%
33,779	IRON	12,379	8,472	3,450	457	5,022 R	68.4%	27.9%	71.1%	28.9%
8,238	JUAB	2,728	1,524	1,134	70	390 R	55.9%	41.6%	57.3%	42.7%
6,046	KANE	2,739	1,881	760	98	1,121 R	68.7%	27.7%	71.2%	28.8%
12,405	MILLARD	4,728	2,862	1,733	133	1,129 R	60.5%	36.7%	62.3%	37.7%
7,129	MORGAN	3,163	1,862	1,243	58	619 R	58.9%	39.3%	60.0%	40.0%

UTAH

GOVERNOR 2000

2000 Census Population	County	Total Vote	Republican	Democratic	Other	Rep.-Dem. Plurality		Percentage			
								Total Vote		Major Vote	
								Rep.	Dem.	Rep.	Dem.
1,435	PIUTE	757	536	211	10	325	R	70.8%	27.9%	71.8%	28.2%
1,961	RICH	898	553	341	4	212	R	61.6%	38.0%	61.9%	38.1%
898,387	SALT LAKE	304,963	141,698	157,564	5,701	15,866	D	46.5%	51.7%	47.3%	52.7%
14,413	SAN JUAN	4,730	2,213	2,424	93	211	D	46.8%	51.2%	47.7%	52.3%
22,763	SANPETE	7,355	4,498	2,596	261	1,902	R	61.2%	35.3%	63.4%	36.6%
18,842	SEVIER	6,974	4,858	1,971	145	2,887	R	69.7%	28.3%	71.1%	28.9%
29,736	SUMMIT	11,904	4,914	6,819	171	1,905	D	41.3%	57.3%	41.9%	58.1%
40,735	TOOELE	12,312	6,318	5,804	190	514	R	51.3%	47.1%	52.1%	47.9%
25,224	UINTAH	8,224	5,026	3,018	180	2,008	R	61.1%	36.7%	62.5%	37.5%
368,536	UTAH	118,467	79,626	36,202	2,639	43,424	R	67.2%	30.6%	68.7%	31.3%
15,215	WASATCH	5,627	2,895	2,662	70	233	R	51.4%	47.3%	52.1%	47.9%
90,354	WASHINGTON	31,837	21,693	9,059	1,085	12,634	R	68.1%	28.5%	70.5%	29.5%
2,509	WAYNE	1,183	733	450		283	R	62.0%	38.0%	62.0%	38.0%
196,533	WEBER	61,917	32,340	28,468	1,109	3,872	R	52.2%	46.0%	53.2%	46.8%
2,233,169	TOTAL	761,806	424,837	321,979	14,990	102,858	R	55.8%	42.3%	56.9%	43.1%

UTAH

SENATOR 2000

2000 Census Population	County	Total Vote	Republican	Democratic	Other	Rep.-Dem. Plurality		Percentage			
								Total Vote		Major Vote	
								Rep.	Dem.	Rep.	Dem.
6,005	BEAVER	2,264	1,704	507	53	1,197	R	75.3%	22.4%	77.1%	22.9%
42,745	BOX ELDER	15,504	11,931	3,138	435	8,793	R	77.0%	20.2%	79.2%	20.8%
91,391	CACHE	33,111	25,874	6,427	810	19,447	R	78.1%	19.4%	80.1%	19.9%
20,422	CARBON	7,347	3,644	3,526	177	118	R	49.6%	48.0%	50.8%	49.2%
921	DAGGETT	418	300	112	6	188	R	71.8%	26.8%	72.8%	27.2%
238,994	DAVIS	87,677	63,009	22,575	2,093	40,434	R	71.9%	25.7%	73.6%	26.4%
14,371	DUCHESNE	4,555	3,517	927	111	2,590	R	77.2%	20.4%	79.1%	20.9%
10,860	EMERY	4,465	3,234	1,146	85	2,088	R	72.4%	25.7%	73.8%	26.2%
4,735	GARFIELD	1,970	1,679	247	44	1,432	R	85.2%	12.5%	87.2%	12.8%
8,485	GRAND	3,559	1,920	1,439	200	481	R	53.9%	40.4%	57.2%	42.8%
33,779	IRON	12,516	9,806	2,182	528	7,624	R	78.3%	17.4%	81.8%	18.2%
8,238	JUAB	2,776	1,980	687	109	1,293	R	71.3%	24.7%	74.2%	25.8%
6,046	KANE	2,787	2,212	472	103	1,740	R	79.4%	16.9%	82.4%	17.6%
12,405	MILLARD	4,774	3,761	834	179	2,927	R	78.8%	17.5%	81.8%	18.2%
7,129	MORGAN	3,189	2,412	680	97	1,732	R	75.6%	21.3%	78.0%	22.0%
1,435	PIUTE	748	605	136	7	469	R	80.9%	18.2%	81.6%	18.4%
1,961	RICH	881	710	169	2	541	R	80.6%	19.2%	80.8%	19.2%
898,387	SALT LAKE	307,177	168,029	130,329	8,819	37,700	R	54.7%	42.4%	56.3%	43.7%
14,413	SAN JUAN	4,768	2,957	1,681	130	1,276	R	62.0%	35.3%	63.8%	36.2%
22,763	SANPETE	7,444	5,622	1,459	363	4,163	R	75.5%	19.6%	79.4%	20.6%
18,842	SEVIER	7,076	5,730	1,158	188	4,572	R	81.0%	16.4%	83.2%	16.8%
29,736	SUMMIT	12,011	5,905	5,739	367	166	R	49.2%	47.8%	50.7%	49.3%
40,735	TOOELE	12,477	7,895	4,190	392	3,705	R	63.3%	33.6%	65.3%	34.7%
25,224	UINTAH	8,329	6,434	1,622	273	4,812	R	77.2%	19.5%	79.9%	20.1%
368,536	UTAH	120,015	95,524	21,189	3,302	74,335	R	79.6%	17.7%	81.8%	18.2%
15,215	WASATCH	5,689	3,842	1,714	133	2,128	R	67.5%	30.1%	69.2%	30.8%
90,354	WASHINGTON	32,334	24,403	6,329	1,602	18,074	R	75.5%	19.6%	79.4%	20.6%
2,509	WAYNE	1,181	920	255	6	665	R	77.9%	21.6%	78.3%	21.7%
196,533	WEBER	62,662	39,244	21,700	1,718	17,544	R	62.6%	34.6%	64.4%	35.6%
2,233,169	TOTAL	769,704	504,803	242,569	22,332	262,234	R	65.6%	31.5%	67.5%	32.5%

UTAH
CONGRESS

CD	Year	Total Vote	Republican Vote	Republican Candidate	Democratic Vote	Democratic Candidate	Other Vote	Rep.-Dem. Plurality	Total Vote Rep.	Total Vote Dem.	Major Vote Rep.	Major Vote Dem.
1	2000	261,805	180,591	HANSEN, JAMES V.	71,229	COLLINWOOD, KATHLEEN	9,985	109,362 R	69.0%	27.2%	71.7%	28.3%
1	1998	162,085	109,708	HANSEN, JAMES V.	49,307	BEIERLEIN, STEVE	3,070	60,401 R	67.7%	30.4%	69.0%	31.0%
1	1996	219,779	150,126	HANSEN, JAMES V.	65,866	SANDERS, GREGORY J.	3,787	84,260 R	68.3%	30.0%	69.5%	30.5%
1	1994	162,618	104,954	HANSEN, JAMES V.	57,664	CORAY, BOBBIE		47,290 R	64.5%	35.5%	64.5%	35.5%
1	1992	245,254	160,037	HANSEN, JAMES V.	68,712	HOLT, RON	16,505	91,325 R	65.3%	28.0%	70.0%	30.0%
2	2000	259,601	107,114	SMITH, DEREK W.	145,021	MATHESON, JIM	7,466	37,907 D	41.3%	55.9%	42.5%	57.5%
2	1998	177,641	93,718	COOK, MERRILL	77,198	ESKELSEN, LILY	6,725	16,520 R	52.8%	43.5%	54.8%	45.2%
2	1996	236,321	129,963	COOK, MERRILL	100,283	ANDERSON, ROSS	6,075	29,680 R	55.0%	42.4%	56.4%	43.6%
2	1994	186,585	85,507	WALDHOLTZ, ENID GREEN	66,911	SHEPHERD, KAREN	34,167	18,596 R	45.8%	35.9%	56.1%	43.9%
2	1992	252,969	118,307	GREENE, ENID	127,738	SHEPHERD, KAREN	6,924	9,431 D	46.8%	50.5%	48.1%	51.9%
3	2000	237,348	138,943	CANNON, CHRISTOPHER B.	88,547	DUNN, DONALD	9,858	50,396 R	58.5%	37.3%	61.1%	38.9%
3	1998	131,123	100,830	CANNON, CHRISTOPHER B.			30,293	100,830 R	76.9%		100.0%	
3	1996	207,715	106,220	CANNON, CHRISTOPHER B.	98,178	ORTON, BILL	3,317	8,042 R	51.1%	47.3%	52.0%	48.0%
3	1994	155,146	61,839	THOMPSON, DIXIE	91,505	ORTON, BILL	1,802	29,666 D	39.9%	59.0%	40.3%	59.7%
3	1992	229,061	84,019	HARRINGTON, RICHARD R.	135,029	ORTON, BILL	10,013	51,010 D	36.7%	58.9%	38.4%	61.6%

UTAH
GENERAL AND PRIMARY ELECTIONS

2000 GENERAL ELECTIONS

President   Other vote was 9,319 Reform (Buchanan); 3,616 Libertarian (Browne); 2,709 Independent American (Phillips); 763 Natural Law (Hagelin); 186 Socialist Workers (Harris); 161 Unaffiliated (Youngkeit); 1 write-in (Kunzler).

Governor   Other vote was 14,990 Independent American (Friedbaum).

Senator   Other vote was 11,938 Independent American (Bowen); 10,394 Libertarian (Dexter).

Congress   Other vote was: CD 1: 5,131 Independent American (Anderson), 3,151 Libertarian (Seely), 1,703 Natural Law (Frandsen); CD 2: 4,704 Independent American (Bangerter), 2,165 Libertarian (Pixton), 597 Unaffiliated (Voris); CD 3: 5,436 Independent American (Lehman), 3,570 Libertarian (Burton), 852 Natural Law (Tolpinrud).

2000 PRIMARY ELECTIONS

Primary   March 10, 2000   (President)   **Registration**   1,118,041   No Statewide Party
June 27, 2000   (Congress)   (as of June 27, 2000)   Registration

Primary Type   Open—Any registered voter could vote in either the Democratic or Republican primary.

Note: An asterisk (*) denotes incumbent. Candidates in Utah are usually nominated by convention. It is up to each party to determine the percentage of the convention vote that is needed to force a primary.

UTAH

GENERAL AND PRIMARY ELECTIONS

	REPUBLICAN PRIMARIES			DEMOCRATIC PRIMARIES		
President	George W. Bush	57,617	63.3%	Al Gore	12,527	79.9%
	Alan Keyes	19,367	21.3%	Bill Bradley	3,160	20.1%
	John McCain	12,784	14.0%			
	Steve Forbes	859	0.9%			
	Gary Bauer	426	0.5%			
	TOTAL	91,053		TOTAL	15,687	
Governor	Mike O. Leavitt*	122,289	61.8%	Bill Orton	Nominated by convention	
	Glen P. Davis	75,719	38.2%			
	TOTAL	198,008				
Senator	Orrin G. Hatch*	Nominated by convention		Scott N. Howell	Nominated by convention	
Congressional District 1	James V. Hansen*	Nominated by convention		Kathleen Collinwood	Nominated by convention	
Congressional District 2	Derek W. Smith	37,494	58.9%	Jim Matheson	Nominated by convention	
	Merrill Cook*	26,199	41.1%			
	TOTAL	63,693				
Congressional District 3	Christopher B. Cannon*	Nominated by convention		Donald Dunn	Nominated by convention	

VERMONT

GOVERNOR

Howard B. Dean (D). Re-elected 2000 to a two-year term. Previously elected 1998, 1996, 1994, 1992. Had been elected Lt. Governor 1990 and became Governor August 1991 upon the death of Richard A. Snelling (R).

SENATORS

James M. Jeffords (R). Re-elected 2000 to a six-year term. Previously elected 1994, 1988. Announced his switch in party affiliation from Republican to Independent May 24, 2001, effective June 5, 2001.

Patrick J. Leahy (D). Re-elected 1998 to a six-year term. Previously elected 1992, 1986, 1980, 1974.

REPRESENTATIVE

At-Large. Bernard Sanders (I)

POSTWAR VOTE FOR PRESIDENT

Year	Total Vote	Republican Vote	Republican Candidate	Democratic Vote	Democratic Candidate	Other Vote	Plurality	Total Vote Rep.	Total Vote Dem.	Major Vote Rep.	Major Vote Dem.
2000**	294,308	119,775	Bush, George W.	149,022	Gore, Al	25,511	29,247 D	40.7%	50.6%	44.6%	55.4%
1996**	258,449	80,352	Dole, Bob	137,894	Clinton, Bill	40,203	57,542 D	31.1%	53.4%	36.8%	63.2%
1992**	289,701	88,122	Bush, George	133,592	Clinton, Bill	67,987	45,470 D	30.4%	46.1%	39.7%	60.3%
1988	243,328	124,331	Bush, George	115,775	Dukakis, Michael S.	3,222	8,556 R	51.1%	47.6%	51.8%	48.2%
1984	234,561	135,865	Reagan, Ronald	95,730	Mondale, Walter F.	2,966	40,135 R	57.9%	40.8%	58.7%	41.3%
1980**	213,299	94,628	Reagan, Ronald	81,952	Carter, Jimmy	36,719	12,676 R	44.4%	38.4%	53.6%	46.4%
1976	187,765	102,085	Ford, Gerald R.	80,954	Carter, Jimmy	4,726	21,131 R	54.4%	43.1%	55.8%	44.2%
1972	186,947	117,149	Nixon, Richard M.	68,174	McGovern, George S.	1,624	48,975 R	62.7%	36.5%	63.2%	36.8%
1968	161,404	85,142	Nixon, Richard M.	70,255	Humphrey, Hubert H.	6,007	14,887 R	52.8%	43.5%	54.8%	45.2%
1964	163,089	54,942	Goldwater, Barry M.	108,127	Johnson, Lyndon B.	20	53,185 D	33.7%	66.3%	33.7%	66.3%
1960	167,324	98,131	Nixon, Richard M.	69,186	Kennedy, John F.	7	28,945 R	58.6%	41.3%	58.6%	41.4%
1956	152,978	110,390	Eisenhower, Dwight D.	42,549	Stevenson, Adlai E.	39	67,841 R	72.2%	27.8%	72.2%	27.8%
1952	153,557	109,717	Eisenhower, Dwight D.	43,355	Stevenson, Adlai E.	485	66,362 R	71.5%	28.2%	71.7%	28.3%
1948	123,382	75,926	Dewey, Thomas E.	45,557	Truman, Harry S.	1,899	30,369 R	61.5%	36.9%	62.5%	37.5%

In 2000 the other vote column includes 20,374 votes cast for Green (Nader). In 1996 the other vote column includes 31,024 votes cast for Perot. In 1992 the other vote column includes 65,991 votes cast for Perot. In 1980 the other column includes 31,761 votes for Independent (Anderson).

VERMONT

POSTWAR VOTE FOR GOVERNOR

Year	Total Vote	Republican Vote	Republican Candidate	Democratic Vote	Democratic Candidate	Other Vote	Rep.-Dem. Plurality	Percentage Total Vote Rep.	Percentage Total Vote Dem.	Percentage Major Vote Rep.	Percentage Major Vote Dem.
2000	293,473	111,359	Dwyer, Ruth	148,059	Dean, Howard B.	34,055	36,700 D	37.9%	50.5%	42.9%	57.1%
1998	218,120	89,726	Dwyer, Ruth	121,425	Dean, Howard B.	6,969	31,699 D	41.1%	55.7%	42.5%	57.5%
1996	254,648	57,161	Gropper, John L.	179,544	Dean, Howard B.	17,943	122,383 D	22.4%	70.5%	24.1%	75.9%
1994	212,046	40,292	Kelley, David F.	145,661	Dean, Howard B.	26,093	105,369 D	19.0%	68.7%	21.7%	78.3%
1992	285,728	65,837	McClaughry, John	213,523	Dean, Howard B.	6,368	147,686 D	23.0%	74.7%	23.6%	76.4%
1990	211,422	109,540	Snelling, Richard A.	97,321	Welch, Peter	4,561	12,219 R	51.8%	46.0%	53.0%	47.0%
1988	243,130	105,319	Bernhardt, Michael	134,594	Kunin, Madeleine M.	3,253	29,275 D	43.3%	55.4%	43.9%	56.1%
1986**	196,716	75,162	Smith, Peter	92,379	Kunin, Madeleine M.	29,175	17,217 D	38.2%	47.0%	44.9%	55.1%
1984	233,753	113,264	Easton, John J.	116,938	Kunin, Madeleine M.	3,551	3,674 D	48.5%	50.0%	49.2%	50.8%
1982	169,251	93,111	Snelling, Richard A.	74,394	Kunin, Madeleine M.	1,746	18,717 R	55.0%	44.0%	55.6%	44.4%
1980	210,381	123,229	Snelling, Richard A.	77,363	Diamond, J. Jerome	9,789	45,866 R	58.6%	36.8%	61.4%	38.6%
1978	124,482	78,181	Snelling, Richard A.	42,482	Granai, Edwin C.	3,819	35,699 R	62.8%	34.1%	64.8%	35.2%
1976	185,929	99,268	Snelling, Richard A.	75,262	Hackel, Stella B.	11,399	24,006 R	53.4%	40.5%	56.9%	43.1%
1974	141,156	53,672	Kennedy, Walter L.	79,842	Salmon, Thomas P.	7,642	26,170 D	38.0%	56.6%	40.2%	59.8%
1972	189,237	82,491	Hackett, Luther F.	104,533	Salmon, Thomas P.	2,213	22,042 D	43.6%	55.2%	44.1%	55.9%
1970	153,528	87,458	Davis, Deane C.	66,028	O'Brien, Leo	42	21,430 R	57.0%	43.0%	57.0%	43.0%
1968	161,089	89,387	Davis, Deane C.	71,656	Daley, John J.	46	17,731 R	55.5%	44.5%	55.5%	44.5%
1966	136,262	57,577	Snelling, Richard A.	78,669	Hoff, Philip H.	16	21,092 D	42.3%	57.7%	42.3%	57.7%
1964	164,199	57,576	Foote, Ralph A.	106,611	Hoff, Philip H.	12	49,035 D	35.1%	64.9%	35.1%	64.9%
1962	121,422	60,035	Keyser, F. Ray	61,383	Hoff, Philip H.	4	1,348 D	49.4%	50.6%	49.4%	50.6%
1960	164,632	92,861	Keyser, F. Ray	71,755	Niquette, Russell F.	16	21,106 R	56.4%	43.6%	56.4%	43.6%
1958	123,728	62,222	Stafford, Robert T.	61,503	Leddy, Bernard J.	3	719 R	50.3%	49.7%	50.3%	49.7%
1956	153,809	88,379	Johnson, Joseph B.	65,420	Branon, E. Frank	10	22,959 R	57.5%	42.5%	57.5%	42.5%
1954	114,360	59,778	Johnson, Joseph B.	54,554	Branon, E. Frank	28	5,224 R	52.3%	47.7%	52.3%	47.7%
1952	150,862	78,338	Emerson, Lee E.	60,051	Larrow, Robert W.	12,473	18,287 R	51.9%	39.8%	56.6%	43.4%
1950	87,155	64,915	Emerson, Lee E.	22,227	Moran, J. Edward	13	42,688 R	74.5%	25.5%	74.5%	25.5%
1948	120,183	86,394	Gibson, Ernest W., Jr.	33,588	Ryan, Charles F.	201	52,806 R	71.9%	27.9%	72.0%	28.0%
1946	72,044	57,849	Gibson, Ernest W., Jr.	14,096	Coburn, Berthold	99	43,753 R	80.3%	19.6%	80.4%	19.6%

In 1986, in the absence of a majority for any candidate, the State Legislature elected Madeleine M. Kunin to a two-year term.

POSTWAR VOTE FOR SENATOR

Year	Total Vote	Republican Vote	Republican Candidate	Democratic Vote	Democratic Candidate	Other Vote	Rep.-Dem. Plurality	Percentage Total Vote Rep.	Percentage Total Vote Dem.	Percentage Major Vote Rep.	Percentage Major Vote Dem.
2000	288,500	189,133	Jeffords, James M.	73,352	Flanagan, Ed	26,015	115,781 R	65.6%	25.4%	72.1%	27.9%
1998	214,036	48,051	Tuttle, Fred H.	154,567	Leahy, Patrick J.	11,418	106,516 D	22.4%	72.2%	23.7%	76.3%
1994	211,672	106,505	Jeffords, James M.	85,868	Backus, Jan	19,299	20,637 R	50.3%	40.6%	55.4%	44.6%
1992	285,739	123,854	Douglas, James H.	154,762	Leahy, Patrick J.	7,123	30,908 D	43.3%	54.2%	44.5%	55.5%
1988	240,111	163,203	Jeffords, James M.	71,469	Gray, William	5,439	91,736 R	68.0%	29.8%	69.5%	30.5%
1986	196,532	67,798	Snelling, Richard A.	124,123	Leahy, Patrick J.	4,611	56,325 D	34.5%	63.2%	35.3%	64.7%
1982	168,003	84,450	Stafford, Robert T.	79,340	Guest, James A.	4,213	5,110 R	50.3%	47.2%	51.6%	48.4%
1980	209,124	101,421	Ledbetter, Stewart M.	104,176	Leahy, Patrick J.	3,527	2,755 D	48.5%	49.8%	49.3%	50.7%
1976	189,060	94,481	Stafford, Robert T.	85,682	Salmon, Thomas P.	8,897	8,799 R	50.0%	45.3%	52.4%	47.6%
1974	142,772	66,223	Mallary, Richard W.	70,629	Leahy, Patrick J.	5,920	4,406 D	46.4%	49.5%	48.4%	51.6%
1972S	71,348	45,888	Stafford, Robert T.	23,842	Major, Randolph T.	1,618	22,046 R	64.3%	33.4%	65.8%	34.2%
1970	154,899	91,198	Prouty, Winston L.	62,271	Hoff, Philip H.	1,430	28,927 R	58.9%	40.2%	59.4%	40.6%
1968**	157,375	157,154	Aiken, George D.		—	221	157,154 R	99.9%		100.0%	
1964	164,350	87,879	Prouty, Winston L.	76,457	Fayette, Frederick J.	14	11,422 R	53.5%	46.5%	53.5%	46.5%
1962	121,571	81,241	Aiken, George D.	40,134	Johnson, W. Robert	196	41,107 R	66.8%	33.0%	66.9%	33.1%
1958	124,442	64,900	Prouty, Winston L.	59,536	Fayette, Frederick J.	6	5,364 R	52.2%	47.8%	52.2%	47.8%
1956	155,289	103,101	Aiken, George D.	52,184	O'Shea, Bernard G.	4	50,917 R	66.4%	33.6%	66.4%	33.6%
1952	154,052	111,406	Flanders, Ralph E.	42,630	Johnston, Allan R.	16	68,776 R	72.3%	27.7%	72.3%	27.7%
1950	89,171	69,543	Aiken, George D.	19,608	Bigelow, James E.	20	49,935 R	78.0%	22.0%	78.0%	22.0%
1946	73,340	54,729	Flanders, Ralph E.	18,594	McDevitt, Charles P.	17	36,135 R	74.6%	25.4%	74.6%	25.4%

The January 1972 election was for a short term to fill a vacancy. In 1968 the Republican candidate won both major party nominations.

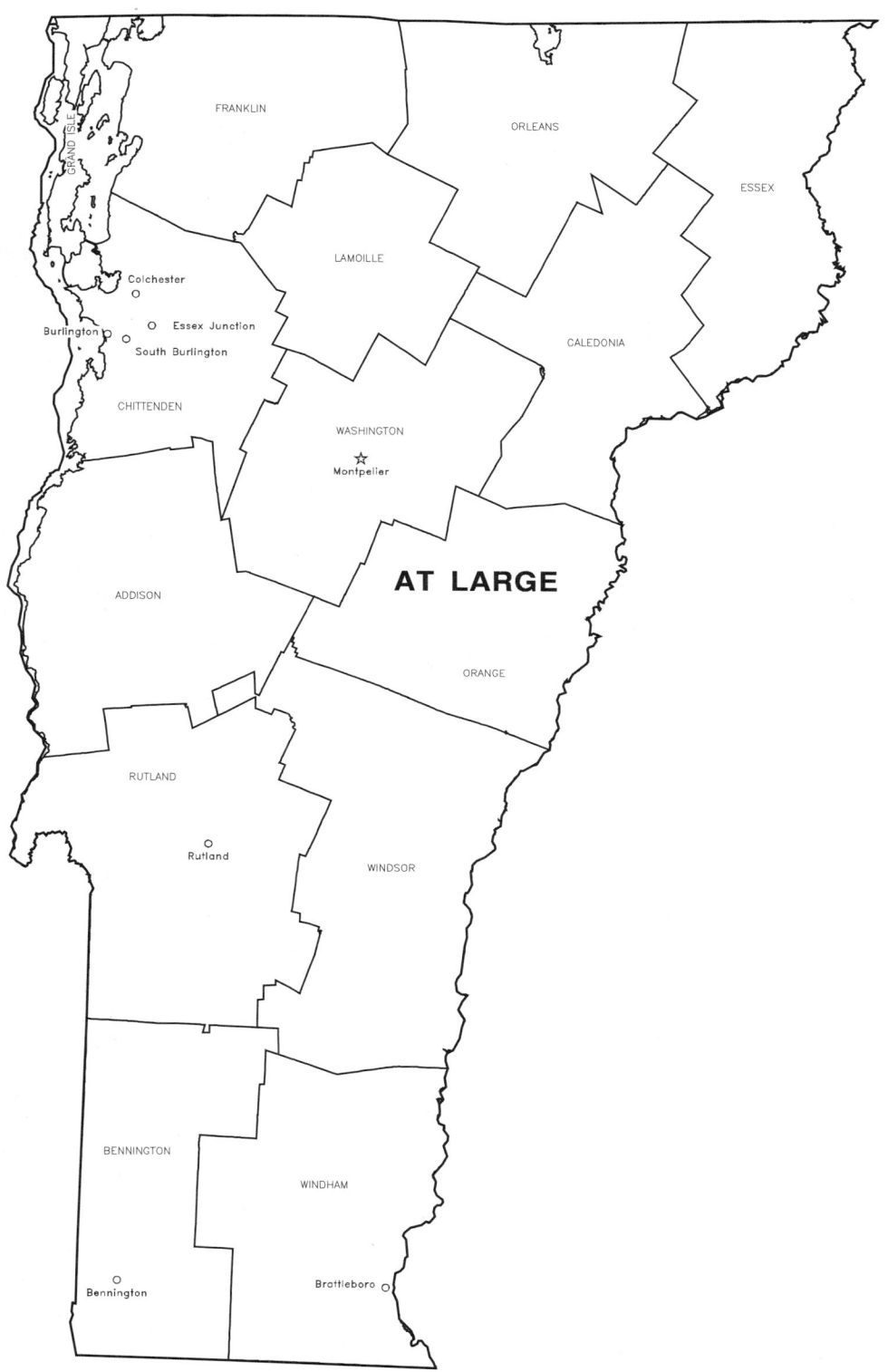

VERMONT

One At Large

GRAND ISLE

FRANKLIN

ORLEANS

ESSEX

LAMOILLE

Colchester

Essex Junction

Burlington

South Burlington

CALEDONIA

CHITTENDEN

WASHINGTON

Montpelier

AT LARGE

ADDISON

ORANGE

RUTLAND

Rutland

WINDSOR

BENNINGTON

WINDHAM

Bennington

Brattleboro

VERMONT

PRESIDENT 2000

2000 Census Population	County	Total Vote	Republican	Democratic	Green (Nader)	Other	Rep.-Dem. Plurality		Percentage of Total Vote		
									Rep.	Dem.	Green
35,974	ADDISON	17,427	6,953	8,936	1,207	331	1,983	D	39.9%	51.3%	6.9%
36,994	BENNINGTON	17,677	7,284	9,021	1,112	260	1,737	D	41.2%	51.0%	6.3%
29,702	CALEDONIA	13,641	6,746	5,859	771	265	887	R	49.5%	43.0%	5.7%
146,571	CHITTENDEN	72,017	26,105	39,156	5,769	987	13,051	D	36.2%	54.4%	8.0%
6,459	ESSEX	2,892	1,564	1,129	133	66	435	R	54.1%	39.0%	4.6%
45,417	FRANKLIN	19,194	8,395	9,514	823	462	1,119	D	43.7%	49.6%	4.3%
6,901	GRAND ISLE	3,638	1,550	1,835	174	79	285	D	42.6%	50.4%	4.8%
23,233	LAMOILLE	11,246	4,456	5,676	878	236	1,220	D	39.6%	50.5%	7.8%
28,226	ORANGE	14,695	6,858	6,694	888	255	164	R	46.7%	45.6%	6.0%
26,277	ORLEANS	12,132	5,799	5,472	564	297	327	R	47.8%	45.1%	4.6%
63,400	RUTLAND	29,362	13,546	13,990	1,355	471	444	D	46.1%	47.6%	4.6%
58,039	WASHINGTON	29,749	11,448	15,281	2,433	587	3,833	D	38.5%	51.4%	8.2%
44,216	WINDHAM	21,491	7,358	11,319	2,475	339	3,961	D	34.2%	52.7%	11.5%
57,418	WINDSOR	29,147	11,713	15,140	1,792	502	3,427	D	40.2%	51.9%	6.1%
608,827	TOTAL	294,308	119,775	149,022	20,374	5,137	29,247	D	40.7%	50.6%	6.9%

	City/Town										
9,291	BARRE CITY	3,801	1,676	1,895	156	74	219	D	44.1%	49.9%	4.1%
7,602	BARRE TOWN	4,072	2,099	1,778	122	73	321	R	51.5%	43.7%	3.0%
15,737	BENNINGTON	6,677	2,384	3,745	446	102	1,361	D	35.7%	56.1%	6.7%
12,005	BRATTLEBORO	5,480	1,486	3,128	770	96	1,642	D	27.1%	57.1%	14.1%
38,889	BURLINGTON	18,069	4,273	10,961	2,596	239	6,688	D	23.6%	60.7%	14.4%
16,986	COLCHESTER	7,383	2,989	3,876	404	114	887	D	40.5%	52.5%	5.5%
4,604	DERBY	2,176	1,012	1,028	75	61	16	D	46.5%	47.2%	3.4%
18,626	ESSEX	9,603	4,344	4,632	490	137	288	D	45.2%	48.2%	5.1%
10,367	HARTFORD	4,702	1,957	2,462	211	72	505	D	41.6%	52.4%	4.5%
5,015	JERICHO	2,818	1,145	1,469	173	31	324	D	40.6%	52.1%	6.1%
5,448	LYNDON	2,199	1,136	922	97	44	214	R	51.7%	41.9%	4.4%
4,180	MANCHESTER	2,186	1,081	975	115	15	106	R	49.5%	44.6%	5.3%
8,183	MIDDLEBURY	3,472	1,067	2,095	268	42	1,028	D	30.7%	60.3%	7.7%
9,479	MILTON	4,032	1,971	1,864	132	65	107	R	48.9%	46.2%	3.3%
8,035	MONTPELIER	4,473	1,265	2,576	573	59	1,311	D	28.3%	57.6%	12.8%
5,139	MORRISTOWN	2,272	898	1,182	140	52	284	D	39.5%	52.0%	6.2%
5,791	NORTHFIELD	2,315	988	1,130	137	60	142	D	42.7%	48.8%	5.9%
4,853	RANDOLPH	2,261	991	1,062	155	53	71	D	43.8%	47.0%	6.9%
4,090	RICHMOND	2,180	825	1,165	159	31	340	D	37.8%	53.4%	7.3%
5,309	ROCKINGHAM	2,291	747	1,308	187	49	561	D	32.6%	57.1%	8.2%
17,292	RUTLAND CITY	7,334	3,003	3,916	297	118	913	D	40.9%	53.4%	4.0%
4,038	RUTLAND TOWN	2,314	1,244	976	75	19	268	R	53.8%	42.2%	3.2%
6,944	SHELBURNE	4,100	1,656	2,145	263	36	489	D	40.4%	52.3%	6.4%
15,814	SOUTH BURLINGTON	7,901	2,995	4,393	427	86	1,398	D	37.9%	55.6%	5.4%
9,078	SPRINGFIELD	4,415	1,720	2,386	230	79	666	D	39.0%	54.0%	5.2%
7,650	ST. ALBANS CITY	2,669	1,045	1,466	105	53	421	D	39.2%	54.9%	3.9%
5,086	ST. ALBANS TOWN	2,434	1,075	1,216	94	49	141	D	44.2%	50.0%	3.9%
7,571	ST. JOHNSBURY	3,005	1,472	1,308	159	66	164	R	49.0%	43.5%	5.3%
2,548	SWANTON	2,478	1,065	1,302	70	41	237	D	43.0%	52.5%	2.8%
4,915	WATERBURY	2,469	919	1,360	142	48	441	D	37.2%	55.1%	5.8%
7,650	WILLISTON	4,384	1,839	2,273	221	51	434	D	41.9%	51.8%	5.0%
6,561	WINOOSKI	2,530	806	1,520	149	55	714	D	31.9%	60.1%	5.9%
3,232	WOODSTOCK	1,897	770	996	115	16	226	D	40.6%	52.5%	6.1%

VERMONT

GOVERNOR 2000

2000 Census Population	County	Total Vote	Republican	Democratic	Other	Rep.-Dem. Plurality		Percentage Total Vote Rep.	Dem.	Major Vote Rep.	Dem.
35,974	ADDISON	17,394	6,097	9,388	1,909	3,291	D	35.1%	54.0%	39.4%	60.6%
36,994	BENNINGTON	17,559	7,658	8,312	1,589	654	D	43.6%	47.3%	48.0%	52.0%
29,702	CALEDONIA	13,623	6,389	5,399	1,835	990	R	46.9%	39.6%	54.2%	45.8%
146,571	CHITTENDEN	71,661	22,425	41,599	7,637	19,174	D	31.3%	58.0%	35.0%	65.0%
6,459	ESSEX	2,879	1,671	891	317	780	R	58.0%	30.9%	65.2%	34.8%
45,417	FRANKLIN	19,194	8,815	8,318	2,061	497	R	45.9%	43.3%	51.5%	48.5%
6,901	GRAND ISLE	3,648	1,596	1,659	393	63	D	43.8%	45.5%	49.0%	51.0%
23,233	LAMOILLE	11,284	4,164	5,577	1,543	1,413	D	36.9%	49.4%	42.7%	57.3%
28,226	ORANGE	14,691	6,514	6,905	1,272	391	D	44.3%	47.0%	48.5%	51.5%
26,277	ORLEANS	12,136	6,004	4,403	1,729	1,601	R	49.5%	36.3%	57.7%	42.3%
63,400	RUTLAND	29,309	12,551	13,039	3,719	488	D	42.8%	44.5%	49.0%	51.0%
58,039	WASHINGTON	29,695	10,437	14,935	4,323	4,498	D	35.1%	50.3%	41.1%	58.9%
44,216	WINDHAM	21,384	7,245	11,085	3,054	3,840	D	33.9%	51.8%	39.5%	60.5%
57,418	WINDSOR	29,016	9,793	16,549	2,674	6,756	D	33.8%	57.0%	37.2%	62.8%
608,827	TOTAL	293,473	111,359	148,059	34,055	36,700	D	37.9%	50.5%	42.9%	57.1%
	City/Town										
9,291	BARRE CITY	3,792	1,579	1,725	488	146	D	41.6%	45.5%	47.8%	52.2%
7,602	BARRE TOWN	4,067	2,052	1,607	408	445	R	50.5%	39.5%	56.1%	43.9%
15,737	BENNINGTON	6,608	2,457	3,574	577	1,117	D	37.2%	54.1%	40.7%	59.3%
12,005	BRATTLEBORO	5,459	1,197	3,271	991	2,074	D	21.9%	59.9%	26.8%	73.2%
38,889	BURLINGTON	17,907	3,616	11,611	2,680	7,995	D	20.2%	64.8%	23.7%	76.3%
16,986	COLCHESTER	7,340	2,636	3,983	721	1,347	D	35.9%	54.3%	39.8%	60.2%
4,604	DERBY	2,180	1,111	804	265	307	R	51.0%	36.9%	58.0%	42.0%
18,626	ESSEX	9,564	3,726	4,972	866	1,246	D	39.0%	52.0%	42.8%	57.2%
10,367	HARTFORD	4,665	1,418	2,863	384	1,445	D	30.4%	61.4%	33.1%	66.9%
5,015	JERICHO	2,814	990	1,615	209	625	D	35.2%	57.4%	38.0%	62.0%
5,448	LYNDON	2,198	1,026	835	337	191	R	46.7%	38.0%	55.1%	44.9%
4,180	MANCHESTER	2,166	1,064	879	223	185	R	49.1%	40.6%	54.8%	45.2%
8,183	MIDDLEBURY	3,442	812	2,234	396	1,422	D	23.6%	64.9%	26.7%	73.3%
9,479	MILTON	4,022	1,805	1,851	366	46	D	44.9%	46.0%	49.4%	50.6%
8,035	MONTPELIER	4,460	1,002	2,687	771	1,685	D	22.5%	60.2%	27.2%	72.8%
5,139	MORRISTOWN	2,264	781	1,183	300	402	D	34.5%	52.3%	39.8%	60.2%
5,791	NORTHFIELD	2,305	862	1,162	281	300	D	37.4%	50.4%	42.6%	57.4%
4,853	RANDOLPH	2,239	850	1,176	213	326	D	38.0%	52.5%	42.0%	58.0%
4,090	RICHMOND	2,179	687	1,291	201	604	D	31.5%	59.2%	34.7%	65.3%
5,309	ROCKINGHAM	2,279	772	1,280	227	508	D	33.9%	56.2%	37.6%	62.4%
17,292	RUTLAND CITY	7,322	2,756	3,838	728	1,082	D	37.6%	52.4%	41.8%	58.2%
4,038	RUTLAND TOWN	2,322	1,272	836	214	436	R	54.8%	36.0%	60.3%	39.7%
6,944	SHELBURNE	4,061	1,187	2,557	317	1,370	D	29.2%	63.0%	31.7%	68.3%
15,814	SOUTH BURLINGTON	7,883	2,500	4,633	750	2,133	D	31.7%	58.8%	35.0%	65.0%
9,078	SPRINGFIELD	4,427	1,368	2,672	387	1,304	D	30.9%	60.4%	33.9%	66.1%
7,650	ST. ALBANS CITY	2,676	1,038	1,351	287	313	D	38.8%	50.5%	43.4%	56.6%
5,086	ST. ALBANS TOWN	2,441	1,081	1,067	293	14	R	44.3%	43.7%	50.3%	49.7%
7,571	ST. JOHNSBURY	2,972	1,356	1,213	403	143	R	45.6%	40.8%	52.8%	47.2%
2,548	SWANTON	2,466	1,178	1,036	252	142	R	47.8%	42.0%	53.2%	46.8%
4,915	WATERBURY	2,467	808	1,377	282	569	D	32.8%	55.8%	37.0%	63.0%
7,650	WILLISTON	4,364	1,647	2,295	422	648	D	37.7%	52.6%	41.8%	58.2%
6,561	WINOOSKI	2,533	833	1,432	268	599	D	32.9%	56.5%	36.8%	63.2%
3,232	WOODSTOCK	1,889	637	1,083	169	446	D	33.7%	57.3%	37.0%	63.0%

VERMONT

SENATOR 2000

2000 Census Population	County	Total Vote	Republican	Democratic	Other	Rep.-Dem. Plurality		Percentage			
								Total Vote		Major Vote	
								Rep.	Dem.	Rep.	Dem.
35,974	ADDISON	17,170	11,696	4,185	1,289	7,511	R	68.1%	24.4%	73.6%	26.4%
36,994	BENNINGTON	17,185	11,413	4,447	1,325	6,966	R	66.4%	25.9%	72.0%	28.0%
29,702	CALEDONIA	13,331	8,545	3,164	1,622	5,381	R	64.1%	23.7%	73.0%	27.0%
146,571	CHITTENDEN	70,420	45,839	19,380	5,201	26,459	R	65.1%	27.5%	70.3%	29.7%
6,459	ESSEX	2,784	1,793	646	345	1,147	R	64.4%	23.2%	73.5%	26.5%
45,417	FRANKLIN	18,971	12,805	4,796	1,370	8,009	R	67.5%	25.3%	72.8%	27.2%
6,901	GRAND ISLE	3,609	2,373	936	300	1,437	R	65.8%	25.9%	71.7%	28.3%
23,233	LAMOILLE	11,093	7,174	2,698	1,221	4,476	R	64.7%	24.3%	72.7%	27.3%
28,226	ORANGE	14,414	8,777	3,249	2,388	5,528	R	60.9%	22.5%	73.0%	27.0%
26,277	ORLEANS	11,928	7,879	2,695	1,354	5,184	R	66.1%	22.6%	74.5%	25.5%
63,400	RUTLAND	28,818	20,421	5,837	2,560	14,584	R	70.9%	20.3%	77.8%	22.2%
58,039	WASHINGTON	29,279	19,479	7,538	2,262	11,941	R	66.5%	25.7%	72.1%	27.9%
44,216	WINDHAM	20,943	11,786	6,803	2,354	4,983	R	56.3%	32.5%	63.4%	36.6%
57,418	WINDSOR	28,555	19,153	6,978	2,424	12,175	R	67.1%	24.4%	73.3%	26.7%
608,827	TOTAL	288,500	189,133	73,352	26,015	115,781	R	65.6%	25.4%	72.1%	27.9%
	City/Town										
9,291	BARRE CITY	3,731	2,514	960	257	1,554	R	67.4%	25.7%	72.4%	27.6%
7,602	BARRE TOWN	3,992	2,893	833	266	2,060	R	72.5%	20.9%	77.6%	22.4%
15,737	BENNINGTON	6,472	4,118	1,921	433	2,197	R	63.6%	29.7%	68.2%	31.8%
12,005	BRATTLEBORO	5,359	2,792	2,008	559	784	R	52.1%	37.5%	58.2%	41.8%
38,889	BURLINGTON	17,438	9,419	6,567	1,452	2,852	R	54.0%	37.7%	58.9%	41.1%
16,986	COLCHESTER	7,256	4,971	1,872	413	3,099	R	68.5%	25.8%	72.6%	27.4%
4,604	DERBY	2,138	1,469	476	193	993	R	68.7%	22.3%	75.5%	24.5%
18,626	ESSEX	9,419	6,570	2,045	804	4,525	R	69.8%	21.7%	76.3%	23.7%
10,367	HARTFORD	4,563	2,995	1,209	359	1,786	R	65.6%	26.5%	71.2%	28.8%
5,015	JERICHO	2,778	1,920	630	228	1,290	R	69.1%	22.7%	75.3%	24.7%
5,448	LYNDON	2,134	1,375	517	242	858	R	64.4%	24.2%	72.7%	27.3%
4,180	MANCHESTER	2,142	1,552	423	167	1,129	R	72.5%	19.7%	78.6%	21.4%
8,183	MIDDLEBURY	3,386	2,139	1,058	189	1,081	R	63.2%	31.2%	66.9%	33.1%
9,479	MILTON	3,947	2,694	941	312	1,753	R	68.3%	23.8%	74.1%	25.9%
8,035	MONTPELIER	4,400	2,874	1,239	287	1,635	R	65.3%	28.2%	69.9%	30.1%
5,139	MORRISTOWN	2,243	1,461	564	218	897	R	65.1%	25.1%	72.1%	27.9%
5,791	NORTHFIELD	2,282	1,570	551	161	1,019	R	68.8%	24.1%	74.0%	26.0%
4,853	RANDOLPH	2,216	1,355	412	449	943	R	61.1%	18.6%	76.7%	23.3%
4,090	RICHMOND	2,157	1,446	525	186	921	R	67.0%	24.3%	73.4%	26.6%
5,309	ROCKINGHAM	2,238	1,334	698	206	636	R	59.6%	31.2%	65.6%	34.4%
17,292	RUTLAND CITY	7,241	5,113	1,644	484	3,469	R	70.6%	22.7%	75.7%	24.3%
4,038	RUTLAND TOWN	2,284	1,702	379	203	1,323	R	74.5%	16.6%	81.8%	18.2%
6,944	SHELBURNE	4,035	2,982	840	213	2,142	R	73.9%	20.8%	78.0%	22.0%
15,814	SOUTH BURLINGTON	7,742	5,344	1,923	475	3,421	R	69.0%	24.8%	73.5%	26.5%
9,078	SPRINGFIELD	4,377	2,940	1,076	361	1,864	R	67.2%	24.6%	73.2%	26.8%
7,650	ST. ALBANS CITY	2,612	1,669	751	192	918	R	63.9%	28.8%	69.0%	31.0%
5,086	ST. ALBANS TOWN	2,392	1,633	613	146	1,020	R	68.3%	25.6%	72.7%	27.3%
7,571	ST. JOHNSBURY	2,918	1,843	741	334	1,102	R	63.2%	25.4%	71.3%	28.7%
2,548	SWANTON	2,448	1,616	657	175	959	R	66.0%	26.8%	71.1%	28.9%
4,915	WATERBURY	2,444	1,699	542	203	1,157	R	69.5%	22.2%	75.8%	24.2%
7,650	WILLISTON	4,309	3,047	939	323	2,108	R	70.7%	21.8%	76.4%	23.6%
6,561	WINOOSKI	2,466	1,487	791	188	696	R	60.3%	32.1%	65.3%	34.7%
3,232	WOODSTOCK	1,856	1,349	380	127	969	R	72.7%	20.5%	78.0%	22.0%

VERMONT

CONGRESS

CD	Year	Total Vote	Republican		Democratic		Other Vote	Rep.-Dem. Plurality	Percentage			
									Total Vote		Major Vote	
			Vote	Candidate	Vote	Candidate			Rep.	D or I	Rep.	Dem.
AL	2000	283,366	51,977	KERIN, KAREN ANN	14,918	*DIAMONDSTONE, PETE	216,471	144,141 I	18.3%	69.2%		
AL	1998	215,133	70,740	CANDON, MARK			144,393	65,663 I	32.9%	63.4%		
AL	1996	254,706	83,021	SWEETSER, SUSAN W.	23,830	LONG, JACK	147,855	57,657 I	32.6%	55.2%		
AL	1994	211,449	98,523	CARROLL, JOHN			112,926	6,979 I	46.6%	49.9%		
AL	1992	281,626	86,901	PHILBIN, TIMOTHY	22,279	YOUNG, LEWIS E.	172,446	75,823 I	30.9%	57.8%		
AL	1990	209,856	82,938	SMITH, PETER	6,315	SANDOVAL, DOLORES	120,603	34,584 I	39.5%	56.0%		
AL	1988	240,131	98,937	SMITH, PETER	45,330	POIRIER, PAUL N	95,864	53,607 R	41.2%	18.9%	68.6%	31.4%
AL	1986	188,954	168,403	*JEFFORDS, JAMES M.			20,551	168,403 R	89.1%		100.0%	
AL	1984	226,297	148,025	JEFFORDS, JAMES M.	60,360	POLLINA, ANTHONY	17,912	87,665 R	65.4%	26.7%	71.0%	29.0%
AL	1982	164,951	114,191	JEFFORDS, JAMES M.	38,296	KAPLAN, MARK A.	12,464	75,895 R	69.2%	23.2%	74.9%	25.1%
AL	1980	194,697	154,274	JEFFORDS, JAMES M.			40,423	154,274 R	79.2%		100.0%	
AL	1978	120,502	90,688	JEFFORDS, JAMES M.	23,228	DIETZ, S. MARIE	6,586	67,460 R	75.3%	19.3%	79.6%	20.4%
AL	1976	184,783	124,458	JEFFORDS, JAMES M.	60,202	*BURGESS, JOHN A.	123	64,256 R	67.4%	32.6%	67.4%	32.6%
AL	1974	140,899	74,561	JEFFORDS, JAMES M.	56,342	*CAIN, FRANCIS J.	9,996	74,561 R	52.9%	40.0%	57.0%	43.0%
AL	1972	186,028	120,924	MALLARY, RICHARD W.	65,062	MEYER, WILLIAM H.	42	55,862 R	65.0%	35.0%	65.0%	35.0%
AL	1970	152,557	103,806	STAFFORD, ROBERT T.	44,415	O'SHEA, BERNARD G.	4,336	59,391 R	68.0%	29.1%	70.0%	30.0%
AL	1968	157,133	156,956	*STAFFORD, ROBERT T.			177	156,956 R	99.9%		100.0%	
AL	1966	135,748	89,097	STAFFORD, ROBERT T.	46,643	RYAN, WILLIAM J.	8	42,454 R	65.6%	34.4%	65.6%	34.4%
AL	1964	163,452	92,252	STAFFORD, ROBERT T.	71,193	O'SHEA, BERNARD G.	7	21,059 R	56.4%	43.6%	56.4%	43.6%
AL	1962	121,381	68,822	STAFFORD, ROBERT T.	52,535	RAYNOLDS, HAROLD	24	16,287 R	56.7%	43.3%	56.7%	43.3%
AL	1960	166,035	94,905	STAFFORD, ROBERT T.	71,111	MEYER, WILLIAM H.	19	23,794 R	57.2%	42.8%	57.2%	42.8%
AL	1958	122,702	59,536	ARTHUR, HAROLD J.	63,131	MEYER, WILLIAM H.	35	3,595 D	48.5%	51.5%	48.5%	51.5%
AL	1956	154,536	103,736	PROUTY, WINSTON L.	50,797	ST. AMOUR, CAMILLE	3	52,939 R	67.1%	32.9%	67.1%	32.9%
AL	1954	114,289	70,143	PROUTY, WINSTON L.	44,141	BOYLAN, JOHN J.	5	26,002 R	61.4%	38.6%	61.4%	38.6%
AL	1952	153,060	109,871	PROUTY, WINSTON L.	43,187	COMINGS, HERBERT B.	2	66,684 R	71.8%	28.2%	71.8%	28.2%
AL	1950	88,851	65,248	PROUTY, WINSTON L.	22,709	COMINGS, HERBERT B.	894	42,539 R	73.4%	25.6%	74.2%	25.8%
AL	1948	121,968	74,076	PLUMLEY, CHARLES A.	47,767	READY, ROBERT W.	125	26,309 R	60.7%	39.2%	60.8%	39.2%
AL	1946	73,066	46,985	PLUMLEY, CHARLES A.	26,056	CALDBECK, MATTHEW J.	25	20,929 R	64.3%	35.7%	64.3%	35.7%

**Seat was won in 1990, 1992, 1994, 1996, 1998 and 2000 by an independent candidate, Bernard Sanders. "Other" Vote for those years includes that for Sanders and other minor party candidates. However, plurality and percent of total vote figures compare the Republican candidate and Sanders only. For earlier years the comparison is between the Republican and Democratic candidates. An asterisk (*) indicates that a candidate received votes from another party.

Pete Diamondstone received 5.3 percent of the vote in 2000, as the candidate of the Democratic and Liberty Union parties. In the 1990s, Democratic candidates received the following shares of the total vote: Jack Long, 9.4 percent in 1996; Lewis E. Young, 7.9 percent in 1992; Dolores Sandoval, 3.0 percent in 1990.

VERMONT

GENERAL AND PRIMARY ELECTIONS

2000 GENERAL ELECTIONS

President Other vote was 2,192 Reform (Buchanan); 1,044 Vermont Grassroots (Lane); 784 Libertarian (Browne); 219 Natural Law (Hagelin); 161 Liberty Union (McReynolds); 153 Constitution (Phillips); 70 Socialist Workers (Harris); 514 scattered write-in. Nader was listed on the ballot as Progressive/Green.

Governor Other vote was 28,116 Progressive (Pollina); 2,148 Independent (Stannard); 1,359 Vermont Grassroots (Williams); 1,054 Independent (Christian); 785 Libertarian (Macia); 337 Liberty Union (Gottlieb); 256 scattered write-in.

Senator Other vote was 10,079 Constitution (Russell); 5,366 Independent (Hubbard); 4,889 Vermont Grassroots (Greer); 3,843 Libertarian (Douglas); 1,477 Liberty Union (Levy); 361 scattered write-in.

VERMONT

GENERAL AND PRIMARY ELECTIONS

Congress   Other vote was 196,118 Independent (Sanders); 11,816 Independent (Skrill); 4,799 Vermont Grassroots (Rogers); 2,978 Libertarian (Krymkowski); 760 scattered write-in.

2000 PRIMARY ELECTIONS

Primary   March 7, 2000   (President)   **Registration**   408,421   No Party Registration
September 12, 2000   (Congress)   (as of Sept. 12, 2000)

Primary Type   Open—Any registered voter could vote in the primary of either party.

Note: An asterisk (*) denotes incumbent.

	REPUBLICAN PRIMARIES			DEMOCRATIC PRIMARIES		
President	John McCain	49,045	60.3%	Al Gore	26,774	54.3%
	George W. Bush	28,741	35.3%	Bill Bradley	21,629	43.9%
	Alan Keyes	2,164	2.7%	Lyndon H. LaRouche Jr.	355	0.7%
	Steve Forbes	616	0.8%	Write-in	525	1.1%
	Gary Bauer	293	0.4%			
	Write-in	496	0.6%			
	TOTAL	81,355		TOTAL	49,283	
Governor	Ruth Dwyer	46,611	57.9%	Howard Dean*	31,366	84.4%
	William Meub	33,105	41.1%	Brian Pearl	4,357	11.7%
	Write-in	855	1.1%	Write-in	1,446	3.9%
	TOTAL	80,571		TOTAL	37,169	
Senator	Jim Jeffords*	60,234	77.8%	Ed Flanagan	17,440	49.2%
	Rick Hubbard	15,991	20.7%	Jan Backus	16,444	46.4%
	Write-in	1,204	1.6%	Write-in	1,533	4.3%
	TOTAL	77,429		TOTAL	35,417	
Congressional At-large	Karen Ann Kerin	47,632	92.5%	Pete Diamondstone	20,539	90.9%
	Bernard Sanders (write-in)	895	1.7%	Bernard Sanders (write-in)	1,337	5.9%
	Write-in	2,981	5.8%	Write-in	710	3.1%
	TOTAL	51,508		TOTAL	22,586	

VIRGINIA

GOVERNOR
James S. Gilmore III (R). Elected 1997 to a four-year term.

SENATORS
George F. Allen (R). Elected 2000 to a six-year term.

John Warner (R). Re-elected 1996 to a six-year term. Previously elected 1990, 1984, 1978.

REPRESENTATIVES
1. JoAnn S. Davis (R)
2. Edward L. Schrock (R)
3. Robert C. Scott (D)
4. Norman Sisisky (D)
5. Virgil H. Goode Jr. (I)
6. Robert W. Goodlatte (R)
7. Eric I. Cantor (R)
8. James P. Moran (D)
9. Frederick C. Boucher (D)
10. Frank R. Wolf (R)
11. Thomas M. Davis (R)

POSTWAR VOTE FOR PRESIDENT

Year	Total Vote	Republican Vote	Republican Candidate	Democratic Vote	Democratic Candidate	Other Vote	Plurality	Percentage Total Vote Rep.	Percentage Total Vote Dem.	Percentage Major Vote Rep.	Percentage Major Vote Dem.
2000**	2,739,447	1,437,490	Bush, George W.	1,217,290	Gore, Al	84,667	220,200 R	52.5%	44.4%	54.1%	45.9%
1996**	2,416,642	1,138,350	Dole, Bob	1,091,060	Clinton, Bill	187,232	47,290 R	47.1%	45.1%	51.1%	48.9%
1992**	2,558,665	1,150,517	Bush, George	1,038,650	Clinton, Bill	369,498	111,867 R	45.0%	40.6%	52.6%	47.4%
1988	2,191,609	1,309,162	Bush, George	859,799	Dukakis, Michael S.	22,648	449,363 R	59.7%	39.2%	60.4%	39.6%
1984	2,146,635	1,337,078	Reagan, Ronald	796,250	Mondale, Walter F.	13,307	540,828 R	62.3%	37.1%	62.7%	37.3%
1980**	1,866,032	989,609	Reagan, Ronald	752,174	Carter, Jimmy	124,249	237,435 R	53.0%	40.3%	56.8%	43.2%
1976	1,697,094	836,554	Ford, Gerald R.	813,896	Carter, Jimmy	46,644	22,658 R	49.3%	48.0%	50.7%	49.3%
1972	1,457,019	988,493	Nixon, Richard M.	438,887	McGovern, George S.	29,639	549,606 R	67.8%	30.1%	69.3%	30.7%
1968**	1,361,491	590,319	Nixon, Richard M.	442,387	Humphrey, Hubert H.	328,785	147,932 R	43.4%	32.5%	57.2%	42.8%
1964	1,042,267	481,334	Goldwater, Barry M.	558,038	Johnson, Lyndon B.	2,895	76,704 D	46.2%	53.5%	46.3%	53.7%
1960	771,449	404,521	Nixon, Richard M.	362,327	Kennedy, John F.	4,601	42,194 R	52.4%	47.0%	52.8%	47.2%
1956	697,978	386,459	Eisenhower, Dwight D.	267,760	Stevenson, Adlai E.	43,759	118,699 R	55.4%	38.4%	59.1%	40.9%
1952	619,689	349,037	Eisenhower, Dwight D.	268,677	Stevenson, Adlai E.	1,975	80,360 R	56.3%	43.4%	56.5%	43.5%
1948	419,256	172,070	Dewey, Thomas E.	200,786	Truman, Harry S.	46,400	28,716 D	41.0%	47.9%	46.1%	53.9%

In 2000 the other vote column includes 59,398 votes cast for Green (Nader). In 1996 the other vote column includes 159,861 votes cast for Perot. In 1992 the other vote column includes 348,639 votes cast for Perot. In 1980 the other column includes 95,418 votes for Independent (Anderson). In 1968 other vote was 321,833 American Independent (Wallace); 4,671 Socialist Labor; 1,680 Peace and Freedom and 601 Prohibition.

VIRGINIA

POSTWAR VOTE FOR GOVERNOR

Year	Total Vote	Republican Vote	Republican Candidate	Democratic Vote	Democratic Candidate	Other Vote	Plurality	Percentage Total Vote Rep.	Percentage Total Vote Dem.	Percentage Major Vote Rep.	Percentage Major Vote Dem.
1997	1,736,314	969,062	Gilmore, James S., III	738,971	Beyer, Donald S., Jr.	28,281	230,091 R	55.8%	42.6%	56.7%	43.3%
1993	1,793,916	1,045,319	Allen, George F.	733,527	Terry, Mary Sue	15,070	311,792 R	58.3%	40.9%	58.8%	41.2%
1989	1,789,078	890,195	Coleman, J. Marshall	896,936	Wilder, L. Douglas	1,947	6,741 D	49.8%	50.1%	49.8%	50.2%
1985	1,343,243	601,652	Durrette, Wyatt B.	741,438	Baliles, Gerald L.	153	139,786 D	44.8%	55.2%	44.8%	55.2%
1981	1,420,611	659,398	Coleman, J. Marshall	760,357	Robb, Charles S.	856	100,959 D	46.4%	53.5%	46.4%	53.6%
1977	1,250,940	699,302	Dalton, John	541,319	Howell, Henry	10,319	157,983 R	55.9%	43.3%	56.4%	43.6%
1973**	1,035,495	525,075	Godwin, Mills E.	—		510,420	14,972 R	50.7%		100.0%	
1969	915,764	480,869	Holton, Linwood	415,695	Battle, William C.	19,200	65,174 R	52.5%	45.4%	53.6%	46.4%
1965	562,789	212,207	Holton, Linwood	269,526	Godwin, Mills E.	81,056	57,319 D	37.7%	47.9%	44.1%	55.9%
1961	394,490	142,567	Pearson, H. Clyde	251,861	Harrison, Albertis	62	109,294 D	36.1%	63.8%	36.1%	63.9%
1957	517,655	188,628	Dalton, Ted	326,921	Almond, J. Lindsay	2,106	138,293 D	36.4%	63.2%	36.6%	63.4%
1953	414,025	183,328	Dalton, Ted	226,998	Stanley, Thomas B.	3,699	43,670 D	44.3%	54.8%	44.7%	55.3%
1949	262,350	71,991	Johnson, Walter	184,772	Battle, John S.	5,587	112,781 D	27.4%	70.4%	28.0%	72.0%
1945	168,783	52,386	Landreth, S. Floyd	112,355	Tuck, William M.	4,042	59,969 D	31.0%	66.6%	31.8%	68.2%

In 1973 other vote was 510,103 Independent (Howell) and 317 scattered.

POSTWAR VOTE FOR SENATOR

Year	Total Vote	Republican Vote	Republican Candidate	Democratic Vote	Democratic Candidate	Other Vote	Plurality	Percentage Total Vote Rep.	Percentage Total Vote Dem.	Percentage Major Vote Rep.	Percentage Major Vote Dem.
2000*	2,718,301	1,420,460	Allen, George F.	1,296,093	Robb, Charles S.	1,748	124,367 R	52.3%	47.7%	52.3%	47.7%
1996	2,354,715	1,235,744	Warner, John W.	1,115,982	Warner, Mark R.	2,989	119,762 R	52.5%	47.4%	52.5%	47.5%
1994	2,057,463	882,213	North, Oliver L.	938,376	Robb, Charles S.	236,874	56,163 D	42.9%	45.6%	48.5%	51.5%
1990	1,083,690	876,782	Warner, John	—		206,908	876,782 R	80.9%		100.0%	
1988	2,068,897	593,652	Dawkins, Maurice A.	1,474,086	Robb, Charles S.	1,159	880,434 D	28.7%	71.2%	28.7%	71.3%
1984	2,007,487	1,406,194	Warner, John	601,142	Harrison, Edythe C.	151	805,052 R	70.0%	29.9%	70.1%	29.9%
1982	1,415,622	724,571	Trible, Paul	690,839	Davis, Richard	212	33,732 R	51.2%	48.8%	51.2%	48.8%
1978	1,222,256	613,232	Warner, John	608,511	Miller, Andrew P.	513	4,721 R	50.2%	49.8%	50.2%	49.8%
1976**	1,557,500	—		596,009	Zumwalt, Elmo R.	961,491	294,769 I		38.3%		100.0%
1972	1,396,268	718,337	Scott, William L.	643,963	Spong, William B.	33,968	74,374 R	51.4%	46.1%	52.7%	47.3%
1970**	946,751	145,031	Garland, Ray	295,057	Rawlings, George C.	506,663	211,576 I	15.3%	31.2%	33.0%	67.0%
1966	733,879	245,681	Ould, James P.	429,855	Spong, William B.	58,343	184,174 D	33.5%	58.6%	36.4%	63.6%
1966S	729,839	272,804	Traylor, Lawrence M.	389,028	Byrd, Harry Flood, Jr.	68,007	116,224 D	37.4%	53.3%	41.2%	58.8%
1964	928,363	176,624	May, Richard A.	592,260	Byrd, Harry Flood	159,479	415,636 D	19.0%	63.8%	23.0%	77.0%
1960	622,820		—	506,169	Robertson, A. Willis	116,651	506,169 D		81.3%		100.0%
1958	457,640		—	317,221	Byrd, Harry Flood	140,419	317,221 D		69.3%		100.0%
1954	306,510		—	244,844	Robertson, A. Willis	61,666	244,844 D		79.9%		100.0%
1952	543,516		—	398,677	Byrd, Harry Flood	144,839	398,677 D		73.4%		100.0%
1948	386,178	118,546	Woods, Robert	253,865	Robertson, A. Willis	13,767	135,319 D	30.7%	65.7%	31.8%	68.2%
1946	252,863	77,005	Parsons, Lester S.	163,960	Byrd, Harry Flood	11,898	86,955 D	30.5%	64.8%	32.0%	68.0%
1946S	248,962	72,253	Woods, Robert	169,680	Robertson, A. Willis	7,029	97,427 D	29.0%	68.2%	29.9%	70.1%

One each of the 1966 and 1946 elections was for a short term to fill a vacancy. In 1970 Harry Flood Byrd, Jr., the Independent candidate, polled 506,633 votes (53.5% of the total vote) and won the election with a 211,576 plurality. In 1976 Harry Flood Byrd, Jr., polled 890,778 votes as an Independent candidate (57.2% of the total vote) and won the election with a 294,769 plurality. In the 1970 and 1976 elections Byrd's plurality is listed. In other elections, the plurality is the difference between the Republican and Democratic vote.

VIRGINIA

Districts Established February 11, 1998

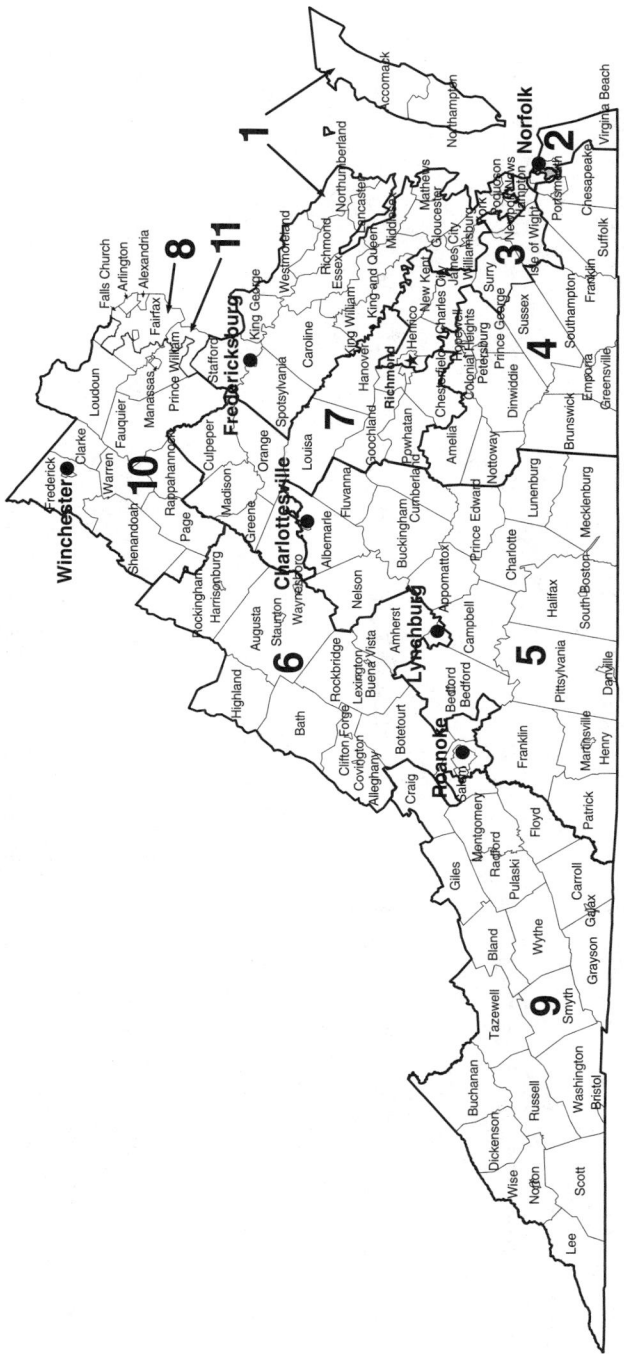

VIRGINIA

PRESIDENT 2000

2000 Census Population	County	Total Vote	Republican	Democratic	Green (Nader)	Other	Rep.-Dem. Plurality	Percentage of Total Vote		
								Rep.	Dem.	Green
38,305	ACCOMACK	11,925	6,352	5,092	220	261	1,260 R	53.3%	42.7%	1.8%
79,236	ALBEMARLE	36,846	18,291	16,255	2,043	257	2,036 R	49.6%	44.1%	5.5%
12,926	ALLEGHANY	5,123	2,808	2,214	62	39	594 R	54.8%	43.2%	1.2%
11,400	AMELIA	4,788	2,947	1,754	40	47	1,193 R	61.5%	36.6%	0.8%
31,894	AMHERST	11,712	6,660	4,812	135	105	1,848 R	56.9%	41.1%	1.2%
13,705	APPOMATTOX	5,927	3,654	2,132	62	79	1,522 R	61.7%	36.0%	1.0%
189,453	ARLINGTON	83,559	28,555	50,260	3,952	792	21,705 D	34.2%	60.1%	4.7%
65,615	AUGUSTA	25,271	17,744	6,643	527	357	11,101 R	70.2%	26.3%	2.1%
5,048	BATH	2,210	1,311	822	35	42	489 R	59.3%	37.2%	1.6%
60,371	BEDFORD COUNTY	26,149	17,224	8,160	376	389	9,064 R	65.9%	31.2%	1.4%
6,871	BLAND	2,688	1,759	851	42	36	908 R	65.4%	31.7%	1.6%
30,496	BOTETOURT	13,840	8,867	4,627	207	139	4,240 R	64.1%	33.4%	1.5%
18,419	BRUNSWICK	5,997	2,561	3,387	28	21	826 D	42.7%	56.5%	0.5%
26,978	BUCHANAN	9,856	3,867	5,745	65	179	1,878 D	39.2%	58.3%	0.7%
15,623	BUCKINGHAM	5,454	2,738	2,561	96	59	177 R	50.2%	47.0%	1.8%
51,078	CAMPBELL	20,327	13,162	6,659	236	270	6,503 R	64.8%	32.8%	1.2%
22,121	CAROLINE	8,351	3,873	4,314	102	62	441 D	46.4%	51.7%	1.2%
29,245	CARROLL	11,001	7,142	3,638	126	95	3,504 R	64.9%	33.1%	1.1%
6,926	CHARLES CITY	3,066	1,023	1,981	31	31	958 D	33.4%	64.6%	1.0%
12,472	CHARLOTTE	4,994	2,855	2,017	43	79	838 R	57.2%	40.4%	0.9%
259,903	CHESTERFIELD	110,951	69,924	38,638	1,646	743	31,286 R	63.0%	34.8%	1.5%
12,652	CLARKE	5,284	2,883	2,166	195	40	717 R	54.6%	41.0%	3.7%
5,091	CRAIG	2,493	1,580	851	39	23	729 R	63.4%	34.1%	1.6%
34,262	CULPEPER	12,244	7,440	4,364	253	187	3,076 R	60.8%	35.6%	2.1%
9,017	CUMBERLAND	3,507	1,974	1,405	35	93	569 R	56.3%	40.1%	1.0%
16,395	DICKENSON	7,226	3,122	3,951	85	68	829 D	43.2%	54.7%	1.2%
24,533	DINWIDDIE	9,136	4,959	4,001	74	102	958 R	54.3%	43.8%	0.8%
9,989	ESSEX	3,831	1,995	1,750	59	27	245 R	52.1%	45.7%	1.5%
969,749	FAIRFAX COUNTY	413,775	202,181	196,501	12,201	2,892	5,680 R	48.9%	47.5%	2.9%
55,139	FAUQUIER	23,481	14,456	8,296	570	159	6,160 R	61.6%	35.3%	2.4%
13,874	FLOYD	5,739	3,423	1,957	244	115	1,466 R	59.6%	34.1%	4.3%
20,047	FLUVANNA	8,706	4,962	3,431	252	61	1,531 R	57.0%	39.4%	2.9%
47,286	FRANKLIN COUNTY	18,829	11,225	7,145	303	156	4,080 R	59.6%	37.9%	1.6%
59,209	FREDERICK	22,392	14,574	7,158	483	177	7,416 R	65.1%	32.0%	2.2%
16,657	GILES	6,820	3,574	3,004	137	105	570 R	52.4%	44.0%	2.0%
34,780	GLOUCESTER	13,699	8,718	4,553	225	203	4,165 R	63.6%	33.2%	1.6%
16,863	GOOCHLAND	8,777	5,378	3,197	139	63	2,181 R	61.3%	36.4%	1.6%
17,917	GRAYSON	6,852	4,236	2,467	102	47	1,769 R	61.8%	36.0%	1.5%
15,244	GREENE	5,412	3,375	1,774	194	69	1,601 R	62.4%	32.8%	3.6%
11,560	GREENSVILLE	3,906	1,565	2,314	13	14	749 D	40.1%	59.2%	0.3%
37,355	HALIFAX	14,072	7,732	5,963	110	267	1,769 R	54.9%	42.4%	0.8%
86,320	HANOVER	41,585	28,614	12,044	711	216	16,570 R	68.8%	29.0%	1.7%
262,300	HENRICO	114,252	62,887	48,645	1,893	827	14,242 R	55.0%	42.6%	1.7%
57,930	HENRY	21,463	11,870	8,898	234	461	2,972 R	55.3%	41.5%	1.1%
2,536	HIGHLAND	1,437	942	453	32	10	489 R	65.6%	31.5%	2.2%
29,728	ISLE OF WIGHT	12,950	7,587	5,162	123	78	2,425 R	58.6%	39.9%	0.9%
48,102	JAMES CITY	24,492	14,628	9,090	639	135	5,538 R	59.7%	37.1%	2.6%
6,630	KING AND QUEEN	2,859	1,423	1,387	33	16	36 R	49.8%	48.5%	1.2%
16,803	KING GEORGE	5,852	3,590	2,070	132	60	1,520 R	61.3%	35.4%	2.3%
13,146	KING WILLIAM	5,769	3,547	2,125	74	23	1,422 R	61.5%	36.8%	1.3%
11,567	LANCASTER	5,455	3,411	1,937	88	19	1,474 R	62.5%	35.5%	1.6%
23,589	LEE	8,748	4,551	4,031	79	87	520 R	52.0%	46.1%	0.9%
169,599	LOUDOUN	75,653	42,453	30,938	1,665	597	11,515 R	56.1%	40.9%	2.2%
25,627	LOUISA	10,096	5,461	4,309	222	104	1,152 R	54.1%	42.7%	2.2%
13,146	LUNENBURG	4,591	2,510	2,026	33	22	484 R	54.7%	44.1%	0.7%
12,520	MADISON	5,027	2,940	1,844	148	95	1,096 R	58.5%	36.7%	2.9%
9,207	MATHEWS	4,609	2,951	1,499	88	71	1,452 R	64.0%	32.5%	1.9%
32,380	MECKLENBURG	11,654	6,600	4,797	104	153	1,803 R	56.6%	41.2%	0.9%
9,932	MIDDLESEX	4,689	2,844	1,671	84	90	1,173 R	60.7%	35.6%	1.8%
83,629	MONTGOMERY	27,160	13,991	11,720	1,222	227	2,271 R	51.5%	43.2%	4.5%

VIRGINIA

PRESIDENT 2000

2000 Census Population	County	Total Vote	Republican	Democratic	Green (Nader)	Other	Rep.-Dem. Plurality		Percentage of Total Vote		
									Rep.	Dem.	Green
14,445	NELSON	6,145	2,913	2,907	273	52	6	R	47.4%	47.3%	4.4%
13,462	NEW KENT	6,114	3,934	2,055	81	44	1,879	R	64.3%	33.6%	1.3%
13,093	NORTHAMPTON	4,892	2,299	2,340	108	145	41	D	47.0%	47.8%	2.2%
12,259	NORTHUMBERLAND	5,605	3,362	2,118	97	28	1,244	R	60.0%	37.8%	1.7%
15,725	NOTTOWAY	5,492	2,870	2,460	46	116	410	R	52.3%	44.8%	0.8%
25,881	ORANGE	10,483	5,991	4,126	236	130	1,865	R	57.1%	39.4%	2.3%
23,177	PAGE	7,996	5,089	2,726	143	38	2,363	R	63.6%	34.1%	1.8%
19,407	PATRICK	7,385	4,901	2,254	101	129	2,647	R	66.4%	30.5%	1.4%
61,745	PITTSYLVANIA	24,255	15,760	7,834	207	454	7,926	R	65.0%	32.3%	0.9%
22,377	POWHATAN	9,711	6,820	2,708	122	61	4,112	R	70.2%	27.9%	1.3%
19,720	PRINCE EDWARD	6,363	3,214	2,922	115	112	292	R	50.5%	45.9%	1.8%
33,047	PRINCE GEORGE	10,900	6,579	4,182	97	42	2,397	R	60.4%	38.4%	0.9%
280,813	PRINCE WILLIAM	100,511	52,788	44,745	1,927	1,051	8,043	R	52.5%	44.5%	1.9%
35,127	PULASKI	12,697	7,089	5,255	207	146	1,834	R	55.8%	41.4%	1.6%
6,983	RAPPAHANNOCK	3,513	1,850	1,462	161	40	388	R	52.7%	41.6%	4.6%
8,809	RICHMOND COUNTY	2,949	1,784	1,076	44	45	708	R	60.5%	36.5%	1.5%
85,778	ROANOKE COUNTY	42,817	25,740	16,141	681	255	9,599	R	60.1%	37.7%	1.6%
20,808	ROCKBRIDGE	7,827	4,522	2,953	248	104	1,569	R	57.8%	37.7%	3.2%
67,725	ROCKINGHAM	23,994	17,482	5,834	539	139	11,648	R	72.9%	24.3%	2.2%
30,308	RUSSELL	10,792	5,065	5,442	102	183	377	D	46.9%	50.4%	0.9%
23,403	SCOTT	9,335	5,535	3,552	85	163	1,983	R	59.3%	38.1%	0.9%
35,075	SHENANDOAH	14,452	9,636	4,420	294	102	5,216	R	66.7%	30.6%	2.0%
33,081	SMYTH	11,740	6,580	4,836	131	193	1,744	R	56.0%	41.2%	1.1%
17,482	SOUTHAMPTON	6,714	3,293	3,359	44	18	66	D	49.0%	50.0%	0.7%
90,395	SPOTSYLVANIA	35,021	20,739	13,455	586	241	7,284	R	59.2%	38.4%	1.7%
92,446	STAFFORD	34,246	20,731	12,596	657	262	8,135	R	60.5%	36.8%	1.9%
6,829	SURRY	3,230	1,313	1,845	29	43	532	D	40.7%	57.1%	0.9%
12,504	SUSSEX	3,906	1,745	2,006	41	114	261	D	44.7%	51.4%	1.0%
44,598	TAZEWELL	16,344	8,655	7,227	162	300	1,428	R	53.0%	44.2%	1.0%
31,584	WARREN	11,166	6,335	4,313	260	258	2,022	R	56.7%	38.6%	2.3%
51,103	WASHINGTON	20,222	12,064	7,549	288	321	4,515	R	59.7%	37.3%	1.4%
16,718	WESTMORELAND	6,026	2,932	2,922	88	84	10	R	48.7%	48.5%	1.5%
40,123	WISE	13,310	6,504	6,412	160	234	92	R	48.9%	48.2%	1.2%
27,599	WYTHE	10,225	6,539	3,462	132	92	3,077	R	64.0%	33.9%	1.3%
56,297	YORK	24,583	15,312	8,622	480	169	6,690	R	62.3%	35.1%	2.0%
	City/Town										
128,283	ALEXANDRIA	55,199	19,043	33,633	2,094	429	14,590	D	34.5%	60.9%	3.8%
6,299	BEDFORD CITY	2,441	1,269	1,078	38	56	191	R	52.0%	44.2%	1.6%
17,367	BRISTOL	6,279	3,495	2,646	89	49	849	R	55.7%	42.1%	1.4%
6,349	BUENA VISTA	1,975	980	941	27	27	39	R	49.6%	47.6%	1.4%
45,049	CHARLOTTESVILLE	13,224	4,034	7,762	1,196	232	3,728	D	30.5%	58.7%	9.0%
199,184	CHESAPEAKE	74,585	39,684	33,578	732	591	6,106	R	53.2%	45.0%	1.0%
4,289	CLIFTON FORGE	1,532	613	868	25	26	255	D	40.0%	56.7%	1.6%
16,897	COLONIAL HEIGHTS	7,782	5,519	2,100	123	40	3,419	R	70.9%	27.0%	1.6%
6,303	COVINGTON	2,214	966	1,168	24	56	202	D	43.6%	52.8%	1.1%
48,411	DANVILLE	18,307	9,427	8,221	168	491	1,206	R	51.5%	44.9%	0.9%
5,665	EMPORIA	2,080	938	1,116	17	9	178	D	45.1%	53.7%	0.8%
21,498	FAIRFAX CITY	9,556	4,762	4,361	352	81	401	R	49.8%	45.6%	3.7%
10,377	FALLS CHURCH	5,593	2,131	3,109	285	68	978	D	38.1%	55.6%	5.1%
8,346	FRANKLIN CITY	3,191	1,393	1,763	25	10	370	D	43.7%	55.2%	0.8%
19,279	FREDERICKSBURG	6,681	2,935	3,360	326	60	425	D	43.9%	50.3%	4.9%
6,837	GALAX	2,213	1,160	996	42	15	164	R	52.4%	45.0%	1.9%
146,437	HAMPTON	47,887	19,561	27,490	563	273	7,929	D	40.8%	57.4%	1.2%
40,468	HARRISONBURG	9,958	5,741	3,482	641	94	2,259	R	57.7%	35.0%	6.4%
22,354	HOPEWELL	6,978	3,749	3,024	73	132	725	R	53.7%	43.3%	1.0%
6,867	LEXINGTON	2,140	957	1,048	103	32	91	D	44.7%	49.0%	4.8%

VIRGINIA

PRESIDENT 2000

2000 Census Population	City/Town	Total Vote	Republican	Democratic	Green (Nader)	Other	Rep.-Dem. Plurality		Percentage of Total Vote		
									Rep.	Dem.	Green
65,269	LYNCHBURG	23,506	12,518	10,374	441	173	2,144	R	53.3%	44.1%	1.9%
35,135	MANASSAS	12,410	6,752	5,262	230	166	1,490	R	54.4%	42.4%	1.9%
10,290	MANASSAS PARK	2,580	1,460	1,048	51	21	412	R	56.6%	40.6%	2.0%
15,416	MARTINSVILLE	5,694	2,560	3,048	59	27	488	D	45.0%	53.5%	1.0%
180,150	NEWPORT NEWS	57,825	27,006	29,779	722	318	2,773	D	46.7%	51.5%	1.2%
234,403	NORFOLK	61,946	21,920	38,221	1,153	652	16,301	D	35.4%	61.7%	1.9%
3,904	NORTON	1,530	639	867	20	4	228	D	41.8%	56.7%	1.3%
33,740	PETERSBURG	11,062	2,109	8,751	117	85	6,642	D	19.1%	79.1%	1.1%
11,566	POQUOSON	5,861	4,271	1,448	93	49	2,823	R	72.9%	24.7%	1.6%
100,565	PORTSMOUTH	35,455	12,628	22,286	348	193	9,658	D	35.6%	62.9%	1.0%
15,859	RADFORD	4,448	2,190	2,063	172	23	127	R	49.2%	46.4%	3.9%
197,790	RICHMOND CITY	65,926	20,265	42,717	2,425	519	22,452	D	30.7%	64.8%	3.7%
94,911	ROANOKE CITY	33,442	14,630	17,920	603	289	3,290	D	43.7%	53.6%	1.8%
24,747	SALEM	10,770	6,188	4,348	181	53	1,840	R	57.5%	40.4%	1.7%
23,853	STAUNTON	8,514	4,878	3,324	278	34	1,554	R	57.3%	39.0%	3.3%
63,677	SUFFOLK	24,661	11,836	12,471	199	155	635	D	48.0%	50.6%	0.8%
425,257	VIRGINIA BEACH	149,771	83,674	62,268	2,370	1,459	21,406	R	55.9%	41.6%	1.6%
19,520	WAYNESBORO	7,102	4,084	2,737	233	48	1,347	R	57.5%	38.5%	3.3%
11,998	WILLIAMSBURG	3,725	1,777	1,724	188	36	53	R	47.7%	46.3%	5.0%
23,585	WINCHESTER	7,886	4,314	3,318	209	45	996	R	54.7%	42.1%	2.7%
7,078,515	TOTAL	2,739,447	1,437,490	1,217,290	59,398	25,269	220,200	R	52.5%	44.4%	2.2%

VIRGINIA

SENATOR 2000

2000 Census Population	County	Total Vote	Republican	Democratic	Other	Rep.-Dem. Plurality		Percentage			
								Total Vote		Major Vote	
								Rep.	Dem.	Rep.	Dem.
38,305	ACCOMACK	11,423	6,027	5,396		631	R	52.8%	47.2%	52.8%	47.2%
79,236	ALBEMARLE	36,341	17,503	18,807	31	1,304	D	48.2%	51.8%	48.2%	51.8%
12,926	ALLEGHANY	5,152	2,855	2,297		558	R	55.4%	44.6%	55.4%	44.6%
11,400	AMELIA	4,737	3,076	1,661		1,415	R	64.9%	35.1%	64.9%	35.1%
31,894	AMHERST	11,551	6,661	4,888	2	1,773	R	57.7%	42.3%	57.7%	42.3%
13,705	APPOMATTOX	5,943	3,639	2,304		1,335	R	61.2%	38.8%	61.2%	38.8%
189,453	ARLINGTON	82,562	27,871	54,651	40	26,780	D	33.8%	66.2%	33.8%	66.2%
65,615	AUGUSTA	24,910	17,269	7,639	2	9,630	R	69.3%	30.7%	69.3%	30.7%
5,048	BATH	2,153	1,366	787		579	R	63.4%	36.6%	63.4%	36.6%
60,371	BEDFORD COUNTY	25,284	16,868	8,415	1	8,453	R	66.7%	33.3%	66.7%	33.3%
6,871	BLAND	2,599	1,759	840		919	R	67.7%	32.3%	67.7%	32.3%
30,496	BOTETOURT	13,791	8,830	4,960	1	3,870	R	64.0%	36.0%	64.0%	36.0%
18,419	BRUNSWICK	6,178	2,660	3,502	16	842	D	43.1%	56.7%	43.2%	56.8%
26,978	BUCHANAN	9,547	3,928	5,619		1,691	D	41.1%	58.9%	41.1%	58.9%
15,623	BUCKINGHAM	5,376	2,815	2,560	1	255	R	52.4%	47.6%	52.4%	47.6%
51,078	CAMPBELL	19,966	12,897	7,069		5,828	R	64.6%	35.4%	64.6%	35.4%
22,121	CAROLINE	8,221	3,936	4,285		349	D	47.9%	52.1%	47.9%	52.1%
29,245	CARROLL	10,673	6,919	3,754		3,165	R	64.8%	35.2%	64.8%	35.2%
6,926	CHARLES CITY	3,037	1,054	1,983		929	D	34.7%	65.3%	34.7%	65.3%
12,472	CHARLOTTE	5,042	2,955	2,087		868	R	58.6%	41.4%	58.6%	41.4%
259,903	CHESTERFIELD	111,310	69,712	41,524	74	28,188	R	62.6%	37.3%	62.7%	37.3%
12,652	CLARKE	5,196	2,921	2,275		646	R	56.2%	43.8%	56.2%	43.8%
5,091	CRAIG	2,485	1,611	873	1	738	R	64.8%	35.1%	64.9%	35.1%
34,262	CULPEPER	12,024	7,605	4,416	3	3,189	R	63.2%	36.7%	63.3%	36.7%
9,017	CUMBERLAND	3,486	2,003	1,483		520	R	57.5%	42.5%	57.5%	42.5%

VIRGINIA

SENATOR 2000

2000 Census Population	County	Total Vote	Republican	Democratic	Other	Rep.-Dem. Plurality		Percentage			
								Total Vote		Major Vote	
								Rep.	Dem.	Rep.	Dem.
16,395	DICKENSON	7,123	3,308	3,815		507	D	46.4%	53.6%	46.4%	53.6%
24,533	DINWIDDIE	9,038	5,081	3,957		1,124	R	56.2%	43.8%	56.2%	43.8%
9,989	ESSEX	3,778	2,004	1,774		230	R	53.0%	47.0%	53.0%	47.0%
969,749	FAIRFAX COUNTY	410,475	196,827	213,311	337	16,484	D	48.0%	52.0%	48.0%	52.0%
55,139	FAUQUIER	23,402	14,457	8,932	13	5,525	R	61.8%	38.2%	61.8%	38.2%
13,874	FLOYD	5,761	3,606	2,154	1	1,452	R	62.6%	37.4%	62.6%	37.4%
20,047	FLUVANNA	8,596	4,991	3,605		1,386	R	58.1%	41.9%	58.1%	41.9%
47,286	FRANKLIN COUNTY	18,522	11,568	6,953	1	4,615	R	62.5%	37.5%	62.5%	37.5%
59,209	FREDERICK	22,088	14,766	7,320	2	7,446	R	66.9%	33.1%	66.9%	33.1%
16,657	GILES	6,717	3,687	3,027	3	660	R	54.9%	45.1%	54.9%	45.1%
34,780	GLOUCESTER	13,490	8,216	5,274		2,942	R	60.9%	39.1%	60.9%	39.1%
16,863	GOOCHLAND	8,732	5,321	3,411		1,910	R	60.9%	39.1%	60.9%	39.1%
17,917	GRAYSON	6,642	4,164	2,478		1,686	R	62.7%	37.3%	62.7%	37.3%
15,244	GREENE	5,375	3,386	1,989		1,397	R	63.0%	37.0%	63.0%	37.0%
11,560	GREENSVILLE	3,850	1,606	2,244		638	D	41.7%	58.3%	41.7%	58.3%
37,355	HALIFAX	13,777	7,514	6,263		1,251	R	54.5%	45.5%	54.5%	45.5%
86,320	HANOVER	41,295	28,077	13,209	9	14,868	R	68.0%	32.0%	68.0%	32.0%
262,300	HENRICO	114,821	62,143	52,580	98	9,563	R	54.1%	45.8%	54.2%	45.8%
57,930	HENRY	20,856	11,895	8,959	2	2,936	R	57.0%	43.0%	57.0%	43.0%
2,536	HIGHLAND	1,452	952	499	1	453	R	65.6%	34.4%	65.6%	34.4%
29,728	ISLE OF WIGHT	13,115	7,318	5,782	15	1,536	R	55.8%	44.1%	55.9%	44.1%
48,102	JAMES CITY	24,488	13,379	11,088	21	2,291	R	54.6%	45.3%	54.7%	45.3%
6,630	KING AND QUEEN	2,832	1,494	1,338		156	R	52.8%	47.2%	52.8%	47.2%
16,803	KING GEORGE	5,880	3,473	2,397	10	1,076	R	59.1%	40.8%	59.2%	40.8%
13,146	KING WILLIAM	5,846	3,629	2,211	6	1,418	R	62.1%	37.8%	62.1%	37.9%
11,567	LANCASTER	5,482	3,323	2,156	3	1,167	R	60.6%	39.3%	60.6%	39.4%
23,589	LEE	8,329	4,678	3,651		1,027	R	56.2%	43.8%	56.2%	43.8%
169,599	LOUDOUN	74,979	43,009	31,862	108	11,147	R	57.4%	42.5%	57.4%	42.6%
25,627	LOUISA	10,010	5,688	4,320	2	1,368	R	56.8%	43.2%	56.8%	43.2%
13,146	LUNENBURG	4,647	2,552	2,095		457	R	54.9%	45.1%	54.9%	45.1%
12,520	MADISON	4,954	3,010	1,943	1	1,067	R	60.8%	39.2%	60.8%	39.2%
9,207	MATHEWS	4,582	2,844	1,738		1,106	R	62.1%	37.9%	62.1%	37.9%
32,380	MECKLENBURG	11,351	6,642	4,709		1,933	R	58.5%	41.5%	58.5%	41.5%
9,932	MIDDLESEX	4,618	2,777	1,841		936	R	60.1%	39.9%	60.1%	39.9%
83,629	MONTGOMERY	26,741	13,774	12,964	3	810	R	51.5%	48.5%	51.5%	48.5%
14,445	NELSON	6,182	3,110	3,068	4	42	R	50.3%	49.6%	50.3%	49.7%
13,462	NEW KENT	6,171	3,929	2,238	4	1,691	R	63.7%	36.3%	63.7%	36.3%
13,093	NORTHAMPTON	4,809	2,121	2,688		567	D	44.1%	55.9%	44.1%	55.9%
12,259	NORTHUMBERLAND	5,651	3,439	2,209	3	1,230	R	60.9%	39.1%	60.9%	39.1%
15,725	NOTTOWAY	5,504	2,912	2,592		320	R	52.9%	47.1%	52.9%	47.1%
25,881	ORANGE	10,415	6,052	4,363		1,689	R	58.1%	41.9%	58.1%	41.9%
23,177	PAGE	8,189	5,360	2,821	8	2,539	R	65.5%	34.4%	65.5%	34.5%
19,407	PATRICK	6,957	4,597	2,357	3	2,240	R	66.1%	33.9%	66.1%	33.9%
61,745	PITTSYLVANIA	23,436	15,357	8,079		7,278	R	65.5%	34.5%	65.5%	34.5%
22,377	POWHATAN	9,656	6,767	2,888	1	3,879	R	70.1%	29.9%	70.1%	29.9%
19,720	PRINCE EDWARD	6,541	3,236	3,305		69	D	49.5%	50.5%	49.5%	50.5%
33,047	PRINCE GEORGE	10,988	6,687	4,290	11	2,397	R	60.9%	39.0%	60.9%	39.1%
280,813	PRINCE WILLIAM	97,825	52,783	45,023	19	7,760	R	54.0%	46.0%	54.0%	46.0%
35,127	PULASKI	12,703	7,270	5,432	1	1,838	R	57.2%	42.8%	57.2%	42.8%
6,983	RAPPAHANNOCK	3,515	1,936	1,576	3	360	R	55.1%	44.8%	55.1%	44.9%
8,809	RICHMOND COUNTY	2,854	1,774	1,080		694	R	62.2%	37.8%	62.2%	37.8%
85,778	ROANOKE COUNTY	42,384	25,082	17,292	10	7,790	R	59.2%	40.8%	59.2%	40.8%
20,808	ROCKBRIDGE	7,798	4,581	3,217		1,364	R	58.7%	41.3%	58.7%	41.3%
67,725	ROCKINGHAM	23,959	17,475	6,481	3	10,994	R	72.9%	27.1%	72.9%	27.1%
30,308	RUSSELL	10,665	5,348	5,316	1	32	R	50.1%	49.8%	50.2%	49.8%
23,403	SCOTT	8,994	5,662	3,331	1	2,331	R	63.0%	37.0%	63.0%	37.0%
35,075	SHENANDOAH	14,525	9,800	4,703	22	5,097	R	67.5%	32.4%	67.6%	32.4%
33,081	SMYTH	11,390	6,858	4,532		2,326	R	60.2%	39.8%	60.2%	39.8%
17,482	SOUTHAMPTON	6,861	3,285	3,569	7	284	D	47.9%	52.0%	47.9%	52.1%
90,395	SPOTSYLVANIA	34,862	20,308	14,510	44	5,798	R	58.3%	41.6%	58.3%	41.7%

VIRGINIA

SENATOR 2000

2000 Census Population	County	Total Vote	Republican	Democratic	Other	Rep.-Dem. Plurality		Percentage			
								Total Vote		Major Vote	
								Rep.	Dem.	Rep.	Dem.
92,446	STAFFORD	34,117	20,163	13,908	46	6,255	R	59.1%	40.8%	59.2%	40.8%
6,829	SURRY	3,185	1,322	1,863		541	D	41.5%	58.5%	41.5%	58.5%
12,504	SUSSEX	3,999	1,774	2,225		451	D	44.4%	55.6%	44.4%	55.6%
44,598	TAZEWELL	15,543	8,602	6,941		1,661	R	55.3%	44.7%	55.3%	44.7%
31,584	WARREN	10,993	6,645	4,347	1	2,298	R	60.4%	39.5%	60.5%	39.5%
51,103	WASHINGTON	19,595	12,315	7,278	2	5,037	R	62.8%	37.1%	62.9%	37.1%
16,718	WESTMORELAND	6,049	2,970	3,078	1	108	D	49.1%	50.9%	49.1%	50.9%
40,123	WISE	12,962	6,770	6,192		578	R	52.2%	47.8%	52.2%	47.8%
27,599	WYTHE	10,394	6,704	3,674	16	3,030	R	64.5%	35.3%	64.6%	35.4%
56,297	YORK	24,617	14,207	10,374	36	3,833	R	57.7%	42.1%	57.8%	42.2%
	City/Town										
128,283	ALEXANDRIA	54,846	18,624	36,107	115	17,483	D	34.0%	65.8%	34.0%	66.0%
6,299	BEDFORD CITY	2,379	1,218	1,161		57	R	51.2%	48.8%	51.2%	48.8%
17,367	BRISTOL	6,239	3,706	2,528	5	1,178	R	59.4%	40.5%	59.4%	40.6%
6,349	BUENA VISTA	1,955	1,024	931		93	R	52.4%	47.6%	52.4%	47.6%
45,049	CHARLOTTESVILLE	13,206	4,012	9,177	17	5,165	D	30.4%	69.5%	30.4%	69.6%
199,184	CHESAPEAKE	74,994	38,833	36,120	41	2,713	R	51.8%	48.2%	51.8%	48.2%
4,289	CLIFTON FORGE	1,510	616	894		278	D	40.8%	59.2%	40.8%	59.2%
16,897	COLONIAL HEIGHTS	7,865	5,521	2,334	10	3,187	R	70.2%	29.7%	70.3%	29.7%
6,303	COVINGTON	2,198	995	1,203		208	D	45.3%	54.7%	45.3%	54.7%
48,411	DANVILLE	17,518	9,152	8,365	1	787	R	52.2%	47.8%	52.2%	47.8%
5,665	EMPORIA	2,054	986	1,068		82	D	48.0%	52.0%	48.0%	52.0%
21,498	FAIRFAX CITY	9,462	4,677	4,777	8	100	D	49.4%	50.5%	49.5%	50.5%
10,377	FALLS CHURCH	5,532	1,988	3,528	16	1,540	D	35.9%	63.8%	36.0%	64.0%
8,346	FRANKLIN CITY	3,236	1,363	1,871	2	508	D	42.1%	57.8%	42.1%	57.9%
19,279	FREDERICKSBURG	6,711	2,809	3,889	13	1,080	D	41.9%	57.9%	41.9%	58.1%
6,837	GALAX	2,148	1,162	986		176	R	54.1%	45.9%	54.1%	45.9%
146,437	HAMPTON	48,105	19,149	28,892	64	9,743	D	39.8%	60.1%	39.9%	60.1%
40,468	HARRISONBURG	9,903	5,735	4,144	24	1,591	R	57.9%	41.8%	58.1%	41.9%
22,354	HOPEWELL	6,759	3,832	2,927		905	R	56.7%	43.3%	56.7%	43.3%
6,867	LEXINGTON	2,078	901	1,177		276	D	43.4%	56.6%	43.4%	56.6%
65,269	LYNCHBURG	23,604	12,421	11,147	36	1,274	R	52.6%	47.2%	52.7%	47.3%
35,135	MANASSAS	12,100	6,866	5,233	1	1,633	R	56.7%	43.2%	56.7%	43.3%
10,290	MANASSAS PARK	2,527	1,497	1,029	1	468	R	59.2%	40.7%	59.3%	40.7%
15,416	MARTINSVILLE	5,710	2,693	3,009	8	316	D	47.2%	52.7%	47.2%	52.8%
180,150	NEWPORT NEWS	57,998	26,099	31,830	69	5,731	D	45.0%	54.9%	45.1%	54.9%
234,403	NORFOLK	62,513	21,717	40,753	43	19,036	D	34.7%	65.2%	34.8%	65.2%
3,904	NORTON	1,527	741	785	1	44	D	48.5%	51.4%	48.6%	51.4%
33,740	PETERSBURG	10,679	2,423	8,255	1	5,832	D	22.7%	77.3%	22.7%	77.3%
11,566	POQUOSON	5,839	3,920	1,909	10	2,011	R	67.1%	32.7%	67.2%	32.8%
100,565	PORTSMOUTH	35,824	12,571	23,208	45	10,637	D	35.1%	64.8%	35.1%	64.9%
15,859	RADFORD	4,386	2,146	2,240		94	D	48.9%	51.1%	48.9%	51.1%
197,790	RICHMOND CITY	65,193	20,211	44,966	16	24,755	D	31.0%	69.0%	31.0%	69.0%
94,911	ROANOKE CITY	32,865	14,696	18,165	4	3,469	D	44.7%	55.3%	44.7%	55.3%
24,747	SALEM	10,646	6,011	4,631	4	1,380	R	56.5%	43.5%	56.5%	43.5%
23,853	STAUNTON	8,389	4,642	3,740	7	902	R	55.3%	44.6%	55.4%	44.6%
63,677	SUFFOLK	24,287	11,535	12,744	8	1,209	D	47.5%	52.5%	47.5%	52.5%
425,257	VIRGINIA BEACH	150,197	80,946	69,132	119	11,814	R	53.9%	46.0%	53.9%	46.1%
19,520	WAYNESBORO	6,993	4,070	2,920	3	1,150	R	58.2%	41.8%	58.2%	41.8%
11,998	WILLIAMSBURG	3,651	1,587	2,064		477	D	43.5%	56.5%	43.5%	56.5%
23,585	WINCHESTER	7,756	4,265	3,490	1	775	R	55.0%	45.0%	55.0%	45.0%
7,078,515	TOTAL	2,718,301	1,420,460	1,296,093	1,748	124,367	R	52.3%	47.7%	52.3%	47.7%

VIRGINIA

CONGRESS

CD	Year	Total Vote	Republican Vote	Republican Candidate	Democratic Vote	Democratic Candidate	Other Vote	Rep.-Dem. Plurality	Total Vote Rep.	Total Vote Dem.	Major Vote Rep.	Major Vote Dem.
1	2000	263,014	151,344	DAVIS, JO ANN S.	97,399	DAVIES, LAWRENCE	14,271	53,945 R	57.5%	37.0%	60.8%	39.2%
1	1998	100,057	76,474	BATEMAN, HERBERT H.			23,583	76,474 R	76.4%		100.0%	
1	1996	167,235	165,574	BATEMAN, HERBERT H.			1,661	165,574 R	99.0%		100.0%	
1	1994	192,496	142,930	BATEMAN, HERBERT H.	45,173	SINCLAIR, MARY F.	4,393	97,757 R	74.3%	23.5%	76.0%	24.0%
1	1992	232,051	133,537	BATEMAN, HERBERT H.	89,814	FOX, ANDREW H.	8,700	43,723 R	57.5%	38.7%	59.8%	40.2%
2	2000	188,329	97,856	SCHROCK, EDWARD L.	90,328	WAGNER, JODY	145	7,528 R	52.0%	48.0%	52.0%	48.0%
2	1998	72,091			67,975	PICKETT, OWEN B.	4,116	67,975 D		94.3%		100.0%
2	1996	163,996	57,586	TATE, JOHN F.	106,215	PICKETT, OWEN B.	195	48,629 D	35.1%	64.8%	35.2%	64.8%
2	1994	137,802	56,375	CHAPMAN, J. L.	81,372	PICKETT, OWEN B.	55	24,997 D	40.9%	59.0%	40.9%	59.1%
2	1992	177,133	77,797	CHAPMAN, J. L.	99,253	PICKETT, OWEN B.	83	21,456 D	43.9%	56.0%	43.9%	56.1%
3	2000	140,753			137,527	SCOTT, ROBERT C.	3,226	137,527 D		97.7%		100.0%
3	1998	63,354			48,129	SCOTT, ROBERT C.	15,225	48,129 D		76.0%		100.0%
3	1996	144,418	25,781	HOLLAND, ELSIE G.	118,603	SCOTT, ROBERT C.	34	92,822 D	17.9%	82.1%	17.9%	82.1%
3	1994	136,620	28,080	WARD, THOMAS E.	108,532	SCOTT, ROBERT C.	8	80,452 D	20.6%	79.4%	20.6%	79.4%
3	1992	168,473	35,780	JENKINS, DANIEL	132,432	SCOTT, ROBERT C.	261	96,652 D	21.2%	78.6%	21.3%	78.7%
4	2000	191,895			189,787	SISISKY, NORMAN	2,108	189,787 D		98.9%		100.0%
4	1998	66,579			64,563	SISISKY, NORMAN	2,016	64,563 D		97.0%		100.0%
4	1996	203,666	43,516	ZEVGOLIS, ANTHONY J.	160,100	SISISKY, NORMAN	50	116,584 D	21.4%	78.6%	21.4%	78.6%
4	1994	186,755	71,678	SWEET, A. GEORGE	115,055	SISISKY, NORMAN	22	43,377 D	38.4%	61.6%	38.4%	61.6%
4	1992	215,960	68,286	ZEVGOLIS, A. J.	147,649	SISISKY, NORMAN	25	79,363 D	31.6%	68.4%	31.6%	68.4%
5	2000	212,705			65,387	BOYD, JOHN, JR.	147,318	77,925 I		30.7%		
5	1998	73,882			73,097	GOODE, VIRGIL H., Jr.	785	73,097 D		98.9%		100.0%
5	1996	197,923	70,869	LANDRITH, GEORGE C.	120,323	GOODE, VIRGIL H., Jr.	6,731	49,454 D	35.8%	60.8%	37.1%	62.9%
5	1994	178,897	83,555	LANDRITH, GEORGE C.	95,308	PAYNE, L. F.	34	11,753 D	46.7%	53.3%	46.7%	53.3%
5	1992	193,084	60,030	HURLBURT, W. A.	133,031	PAYNE, L. F.	23	73,001 D	31.1%	68.9%	31.1%	68.9%
6	2000	154,483	153,338	GOODLATTE, ROBERT W.			1,145	153,338 R	99.3%		100.0%	
6	1998	128,730	89,177	GOODLATTE, ROBERT W.	39,487	BOWERS, DAVID A.	66	49,690 R	69.3%	30.7%	69.3%	30.7%
6	1996	199,361	133,576	GOODLATTE, ROBERT W.	61,485	GREY, JEFFREY W.	4,300	72,091 R	67.0%	30.8%	68.5%	31.5%
6	1994	126,644	126,455	GOODLATTE, ROBERT W.			189	126,455 R	99.9%		100.0%	
6	1992	212,087	127,309	GOODLATTE, ROBERT W.	84,618	MUSSELWHITE, STEPHEN A.	160	42,691 R	60.0%	39.9%	60.1%	39.9%
7	2000	287,891	192,652	CANTOR, ERIC I.	94,935	STEWART, WARREN A.	304	97,717 R	66.9%	33.0%	67.0%	33.0%
7	1998	97,889	77,044	BLILEY, THOMAS J.			20,845	77,044 R	78.7%		100.0%	
7	1996	252,505	189,644	BLILEY, THOMAS J.	51,206	SLAYTON, RODERIC H.	11,655	138,438 R	75.1%	20.3%	78.7%	21.3%
7	1994	210,632	176,941	BLILEY, THOMAS J.			33,691	176,941 R	84.0%		100.0%	
7	1992	255,375	211,618	BLILEY, THOMAS J.			43,757	211,618 R	82.9%		100.0%	
8	2000	259,199	88,262	MILLER, DEMARIS H.	164,178	MORAN, JAMES P.	6,759	75,916 D	34.1%	63.3%	35.0%	65.0%
8	1998	146,287	48,352	MILLER, DEMARIS H.	97,545	MORAN, JAMES P.	390	49,193 D	33.1%	66.7%	33.1%	66.9%
8	1996	229,421	64,562	OTEY, JOHN E.	152,334	MORAN, JAMES P.	12,525	87,772 D	28.1%	66.4%	29.8%	70.2%
8	1994	202,673	79,568	MCSLARROW, KYLE E.	120,281	MORAN, JAMES P.	2,824	40,713 D	39.3%	59.3%	39.8%	60.2%
8	1992	247,126	102,717	MCSLARROW, KYLE E.	138,542	MORAN, JAMES P.	5,867	35,825 D	41.6%	56.1%	42.6%	57.4%
9	2000	196,855	59,335	OSBORNE, MICHAEL D. "OZ	137,488	BOUCHER, FREDERICK C.	32	78,153 D	30.1%	69.8%	30.1%	69.9%
9	1998	143,126	55,918	BARTA, J.A. "JOE	87,163	BOUCHER, FREDERICK C.	45	31,245 D	39.1%	60.9%	39.1%	60.9%
9	1996	189,077	58,055	MULDOON, PATRICK C.	122,908	BOUCHER, FREDERICK C.	8,114	64,853 D	30.7%	65.0%	32.1%	67.9%
9	1994	175,024	72,133	FAST, S. H.	102,876	BOUCHER, FREDERICK C.	15	30,743 D	41.2%	58.8%	41.2%	58.8%
9	1992	211,295	77,985	WEDDLE, L. GARRETT	133,284	BOUCHER, FREDERICK C.	26	55,299 D	36.9%	63.1%	36.9%	63.1%

VIRGINIA

CONGRESS

CD	Year	Total Vote	Republican Vote	Republican Candidate	Democratic Vote	Democratic Candidate	Other Vote	Rep.-Dem. Plurality	Total Vote Rep.	Total Vote Dem.	Major Vote Rep.	Major Vote Dem.
10	2000	283,637	238,817	WOLF, FRANK R.			44,820	238,817 R	84.2%		100.0%	
10	1998	144,755	103,648	WOLF, FRANK R.	36,476	BROOKS, CORNELL W.	4,631	67,172 R	71.6%	25.2%	74.0%	26.0%
10	1996	235,013	169,266	WOLF, FRANK R.	59,145	WEINBERG, ROBERT L.	6,602	110,121 R	72.0%	25.2%	74.1%	25.9%
10	1994	175,531	153,311	WOLF, FRANK R.			22,220	153,311 R	87.3%		100.0%	
10	1992	227,191	144,471	WOLF, FRANK R.	75,775	VICKERY, RAYMOND E.	6,945	68,696 R	63.6%	33.4%	65.6%	34.4%
11	2000	242,968	150,395	DAVIS, THOMAS M., III	83,455	CORRIGAN, MIKE	9,118	66,940 R	61.9%	34.3%	64.3%	35.7%
11	1998	112,111	91,603	DAVIS, THOMAS M., III			20,508	91,603 R	81.7%		100.0%	
11	1996	216,482	138,758	DAVIS, THOMAS M., III	74,701	HORTON, THOMAS J.	3,023	64,057 R	64.1%	34.5%	65.0%	35.0%
11	1994	185,680	98,216	DAVIS, THOMAS M., III	84,104	BYRNE, LESLIE L.	3,360	14,112 R	52.9%	45.3%	53.9%	46.1%
11	1992	228,272	103,119	BUTLER, HENRY N.	114,172	BYRNE, LESLIE L.	10,981	11,053 D	45.2%	50.0%	47.5%	52.5%

Note: The seat for the Virginia 5th District was won in 2000 by Virgil H. Goode Jr., an independent candidate, who was elected in 1996 and 1998 as a Democrat. Goode won in 2000 with 67.4 percent of the vote and a 77,925-vote plurality over the runner-up, the Democratic candidate.

VIRGINIA

GENERAL AND PRIMARY ELECTIONS

2000 GENERAL ELECTIONS

President   Other vote was 15,198 Libertarian (Browne); 5,455 Reform (Buchanan); 1,809 Constitution (Phillips); 171 write-in (Hagelin); 2,636 scattered write-in.

Senator   Other vote was 1,748 scattered write-in.

Congress   Other vote was: CD 1: 9,652 Independent (Wood), 4,082 Independent (Billings), 537 scattered write-in; CD 2: 145 scattered write-in; CD 3: 3,226 scattered write-in; CD 4: 2,108 scattered write-in; CD 5: 143,312 Independent (Goode), 3,936 Independent (Spence), 70 scattered write-in; CD 6: 1,145 scattered write-in; CD 7: 304 scattered write-in; CD 8: 3,483 Independent (Crickenberger), 2,805 Independent (Herron), 471 scattered write-in; CD 9: 32 scattered write-in; CD 10: 28,107 Independent (Brown), 16,031 Independent (Rossi), 682 scattered write-in; CD 11: 4,774 Independent (McBride), 4,059 Independent (Levy), 285 scattered write-in.

2000 PRIMARY ELECTIONS

Primary   February 29, 2000   (President)   **Registration**   3,908,929   No Party Registration
June 13, 2000   (Congress)   (as of April 3, 2000)

Primary Type   Open-Any registered voter could vote in the primary of either party.

Note: An asterisk (*) denotes incumbent. The state parties and local party committees have the option of holding a primary or nominating candidates by convention. If a primary has been called and only one candidate files to run in it, then no primary is held.

VIRGINIA

GENERAL AND PRIMARY ELECTIONS

	REPUBLICAN PRIMARIES			DEMOCRATIC PRIMARIES	
President	George W. Bush	350,588	52.8%	No Democratic Primary	
	John McCain	291,488	43.9%		
	Alan Keyes	20,356	3.1%		
	Gary Bauer	852	0.1%		
	Steve Forbes	809	0.1%		
	TOTAL	664,093			
Senator	George F. Allen	Unopposed		Charles S. Robb*	Unopposed
Congressional District 1	Jo Ann S. Davis	14,274	35.2%	Lawrence Davies	Nominated by convention
	Paul C. Jost	12,171	30.0%		
	Michael I. Rothfeld	8,932	22.0%		
	Robert L. Cunningham	2,686	6.6%		
	Philip G. Short	2,535	6.2%		
	TOTAL	40,598			
Congressional District 2	Edward L. Schrock		Unopposed	Jody Wagner	Nominated by convention
Congressional District 3	No Republican candidate			Robert C. Scott*	Unopposed
Congressional District 4	No Republican candidate			Norman Sisisky*	Unopposed
Congressional District 5	No Republican candidate			John Boyd Jr.	Nominated by convention
Congressional District 6	Robert W. Goodlatte*	Nominated by convention			No Democratic candidate
Congressional District 7	Eric I. Cantor	20,902	50.3%	Warren A. Stewart	Nominated by convention
	Stephen H. Martin	20,639	49.7%		
	TOTAL	41,541			
Congressional District 8	Demaris H. Miller	Nominated by convention		James P. Moran*	Nominated by convention
Congressional District 9	Michael D. "Oz" Osborne	Nominated by convention		Rick Boucher*	Nominated by convention
Congressional District 10	Frank R. Wolf*		Unopposed		No Democratic candidate
Congressional District 11	Thomas M. Davis III*		Unopposed	Mike Corrigan	Nominated by convention

WASHINGTON

GOVERNOR
Gary Locke (D). Re-elected 2000 to a four-year term. Previously elected 1996.

SENATORS
Maria Cantwell (D). Elected 2000 to a six-year term.

Patty Murray (D). Re-elected 1998 to a six-year term. Previously elected 1992.

REPRESENTATIVES
1. Jay Inslee (D)
2. Rick Larsen (D)
3. Brian Baird (D)
4. Richard Hastings (R)
5. George Nethercutt (R)
6. Norman D. Dicks (D)
7. Jim McDermott (D)
8. Jennifer Dunn (R)
9. Adam Smith (D)

POSTWAR VOTE FOR PRESIDENT

Year	Total Vote	Republican Vote	Republican Candidate	Democratic Vote	Democratic Candidate	Other Vote	Plurality	Total Vote Rep.	Total Vote Dem.	Major Vote Rep.	Major Vote Dem.
2000**	2,487,433	1,108,864	Bush, George W.	1,247,652	Gore, Al	130,917	138,788 D	44.6%	50.2%	47.1%	52.9%
1996**	2,253,837	840,712	Dole, Bob	1,123,323	Clinton, Bill	289,802	282,611 D	37.3%	49.8%	42.8%	57.2%
1992**	2,288,230	731,234	Bush, George	993,037	Clinton, Bill	563,959	261,803 D	32.0%	43.4%	42.4%	57.6%
1988	1,865,253	903,835	Bush, George	933,516	Dukakis, Michael S.	27,902	29,681 D	48.5%	50.0%	49.2%	50.8%
1984	1,883,910	1,051,670	Reagan, Ronald	807,352	Mondale, Walter F.	24,888	244,318 R	55.8%	42.9%	56.6%	43.4%
1980**	1,742,394	865,244	Reagan, Ronald	650,193	Carter, Jimmy	226,957	215,051 R	49.7%	37.3%	57.1%	42.9%
1976	1,555,534	777,732	Ford, Gerald R.	717,323	Carter, Jimmy	60,479	60,409 R	50.0%	46.1%	52.0%	48.0%
1972	1,470,847	837,135	Nixon, Richard M.	568,334	McGovern, George S.	65,378	268,801 R	56.9%	38.6%	59.6%	40.4%
1968	1,304,281	588,510	Nixon, Richard M.	616,037	Humphrey, Hubert H.	99,734	27,527 D	45.1%	47.2%	48.9%	51.1%
1964	1,258,556	470,366	Goldwater, Barry M.	779,881	Johnson, Lyndon B.	8,309	309,515 D	37.4%	62.0%	37.6%	62.4%
1960	1,241,572	629,273	Nixon, Richard M.	599,298	Kennedy, John F.	13,001	29,975 R	50.7%	48.3%	51.2%	48.8%
1956	1,150,889	620,430	Eisenhower, Dwight D.	523,002	Stevenson, Adlai E.	7,457	97,428 R	53.9%	45.4%	54.3%	45.7%
1952	1,102,708	599,107	Eisenhower, Dwight D.	492,845	Stevenson, Adlai E.	10,756	106,262 R	54.3%	44.7%	54.9%	45.1%
1948	905,058	386,314	Dewey, Thomas E.	476,165	Truman, Harry S.	42,579	89,851 D	42.7%	52.6%	44.8%	55.2%

In 2000 the other vote column includes 103,002 votes cast for Green (Nader). In 1996 the other vote column includes 201,003 votes cast for Perot. In 1992 the other vote column includes 541,780 votes cast for Perot. In 1980 the other column includes 185,073 votes for Independent (Anderson).

WASHINGTON

POSTWAR VOTE FOR GOVERNOR

Year	Total Vote	Republican Vote	Republican Candidate	Democratic Vote	Democratic Candidate	Other Vote	Rep.-Dem. Plurality	Total Vote Rep.	Total Vote Dem.	Major Vote Rep.	Major Vote Dem.
2000	2,469,852	980,060	Carlson, John	1,441,973	Locke, Gary	47,819	461,913 D	39.7%	58.4%	40.5%	59.5%
1996	2,237,030	940,538	Craswell, Ellen	1,296,492	Locke, Gary		355,954 D	42.0%	58.0%	42.0%	58.0%
1992	2,270,826	1,086,216	Eikenberry, Ken	1,184,315	Lowry, Mike	295	98,099 D	47.8%	52.2%	47.8%	52.2%
1988	1,874,929	708,481	Williams, Bob	1,166,448	Gardner, Booth		457,967 D	37.8%	62.2%	37.8%	62.2%
1984	1,888,987	881,994	Spellman, John D.	1,006,993	Gardner, Booth		124,999 D	46.7%	53.3%	46.7%	53.3%
1980	1,730,896	981,083	Spellman, John D.	749,813	McDermott, James A.		231,270 R	56.7%	43.3%	56.7%	43.3%
1976	1,546,382	687,039	Spellman, John D.	821,797	Ray, Dixy Lee	37,546	134,758 D	44.4%	53.1%	45.5%	54.5%
1972	1,472,542	747,825	Evans, Daniel J.	630,613	Rosellini, Albert D.	94,104	117,212 R	50.8%	42.8%	54.3%	45.7%
1968	1,265,355	692,378	Evans, Daniel J.	560,262	O'Connell, John J.	12,715	132,116 R	54.7%	44.3%	55.3%	44.7%
1964	1,250,274	697,256	Evans, Daniel J.	548,692	Rosellini, Albert D.	4,326	148,564 R	55.8%	43.9%	56.0%	44.0%
1960	1,215,748	594,122	Andrews, Lloyd J.	611,987	Rosellini, Albert D.	9,639	17,865 D	48.9%	50.3%	49.3%	50.7%
1956	1,128,977	508,041	Anderson, Emmett T.	616,773	Rosellini, Albert D.	4,163	108,732 D	45.0%	54.6%	45.2%	54.8%
1952	1,078,497	567,822	Langlie, Arthur B.	510,675	Mitchell, Hugh B.		57,147 R	52.6%	47.4%	52.6%	47.4%
1948	883,141	445,958	Langlie, Arthur B.	417,035	Wallgren, Mon C.	20,148	28,923 R	50.5%	47.2%	51.7%	48.3%

POSTWAR VOTE FOR SENATOR

Year	Total Vote	Republican Vote	Republican Candidate	Democratic Vote	Democratic Candidate	Other Vote	Rep.-Dem. Plurality	Total Vote Rep.	Total Vote Dem.	Major Vote Rep.	Major Vote Dem.
2000	2,461,379	1,197,208	Gorton, Slade	1,199,437	Cantwell, Maria	64,734	2,229 D	48.6%	48.7%	50.0%	50.0%
1998	1,888,561	785,377	Smith, Linda	1,103,184	Murray, Patty		317,807 D	41.6%	58.4%	41.6%	58.4%
1994	1,700,173	947,821	Gorton, Slade	752,352	Sims, Ron		195,469 R	55.7%	44.3%	55.7%	44.3%
1992	2,219,162	1,020,829	Chandler, Rod	1,197,973	Murray, Patty	360	177,144 D	46.0%	54.0%	46.0%	54.0%
1988	1,848,542	944,359	Gorton, Slade	904,183	Lowry, Mike		40,176 R	51.1%	48.9%	51.1%	48.9%
1986	1,337,367	650,931	Gorton, Slade	677,471	Adams, Brock	8,965	26,540 D	48.7%	50.7%	49.0%	51.0%
1983S	1,213,307	672,326	Evans, Daniel J.	540,981	Lowry, Mike		131,345 R	55.4%	44.6%	55.4%	44.6%
1982	1,368,476	332,273	Jewett, Doug	943,655	Jackson, Henry M.	92,548	611,382 D	24.3%	69.0%	26.0%	74.0%
1980	1,728,369	936,317	Gorton, Slade	792,052	Magnuson, Warren G.		144,265 R	54.2%	45.8%	54.2%	45.8%
1976	1,491,111	361,546	Brown, George M.	1,071,219	Jackson, Henry M.	58,346	709,673 D	24.2%	71.8%	25.2%	74.8%
1974	1,007,847	363,626	Metcalf, Jack	611,811	Magnuson, Warren G.	32,410	248,185 D	36.1%	60.7%	37.3%	62.7%
1970	1,066,807	170,790	Elicker, Charles W.	879,385	Jackson, Henry M.	16,632	708,595 D	16.0%	82.4%	16.3%	83.7%
1968	1,236,063	435,894	Metcalf, Jack	796,183	Magnuson, Warren G.	3,986	360,289 D	35.3%	64.4%	35.4%	64.6%
1964	1,213,088	337,138	Andrews, Lloyd J.	875,950	Jackson, Henry M.		538,812 D	27.8%	72.2%	27.8%	72.2%
1962	943,229	446,204	Christensen, Richard G.	491,365	Magnuson, Warren G.	5,660	45,161 D	47.3%	52.1%	47.6%	52.4%
1958	886,822	278,271	Bantz, William B.	597,040	Jackson, Henry M.	11,511	318,769 D	31.4%	67.3%	31.8%	68.2%
1956	1,122,217	436,652	Langlie, Arthur B.	685,565	Magnuson, Warren G.		248,913 D	38.9%	61.1%	38.9%	61.1%
1952	1,058,735	460,884	Cain, Harry P.	595,288	Jackson, Henry M.	2,563	134,404 D	43.5%	56.2%	43.6%	56.4%
1950	744,783	342,464	Williams, Walter	397,719	Magnuson, Warren G.	4,600	55,255 D	46.0%	53.4%	46.3%	53.7%
1946	660,342	358,847	Cain, Harry P.	298,683	Mitchell, Hugh B.	2,812	60,164 R	54.3%	45.2%	54.6%	45.4%

The 1983 election was for a short term to fill a vacancy.

460

WASHINGTON

Districts Established February 12, 1992

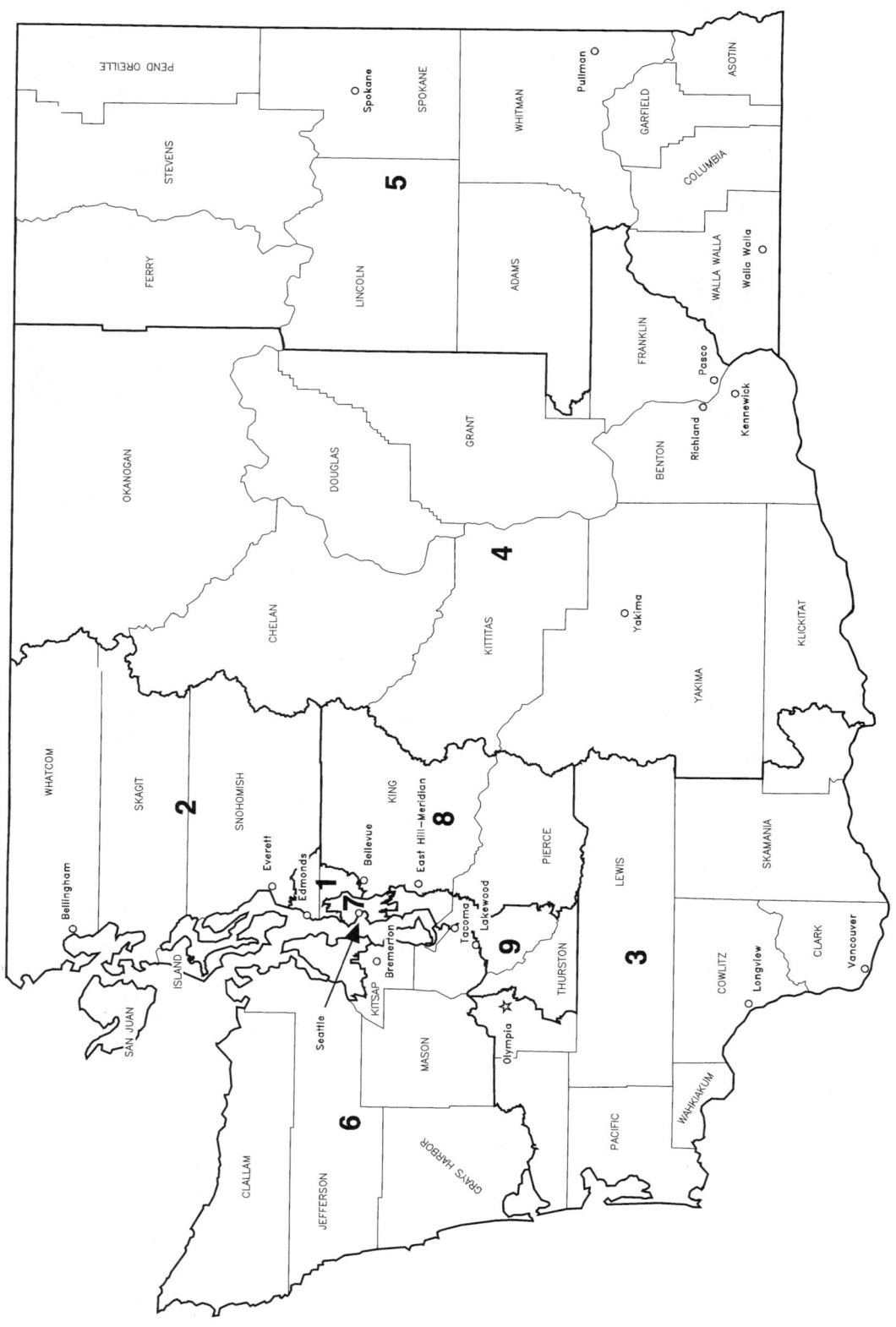

SEATTLE/PUGET SOUND AREA
CONGRESSIONAL DISTRICTS

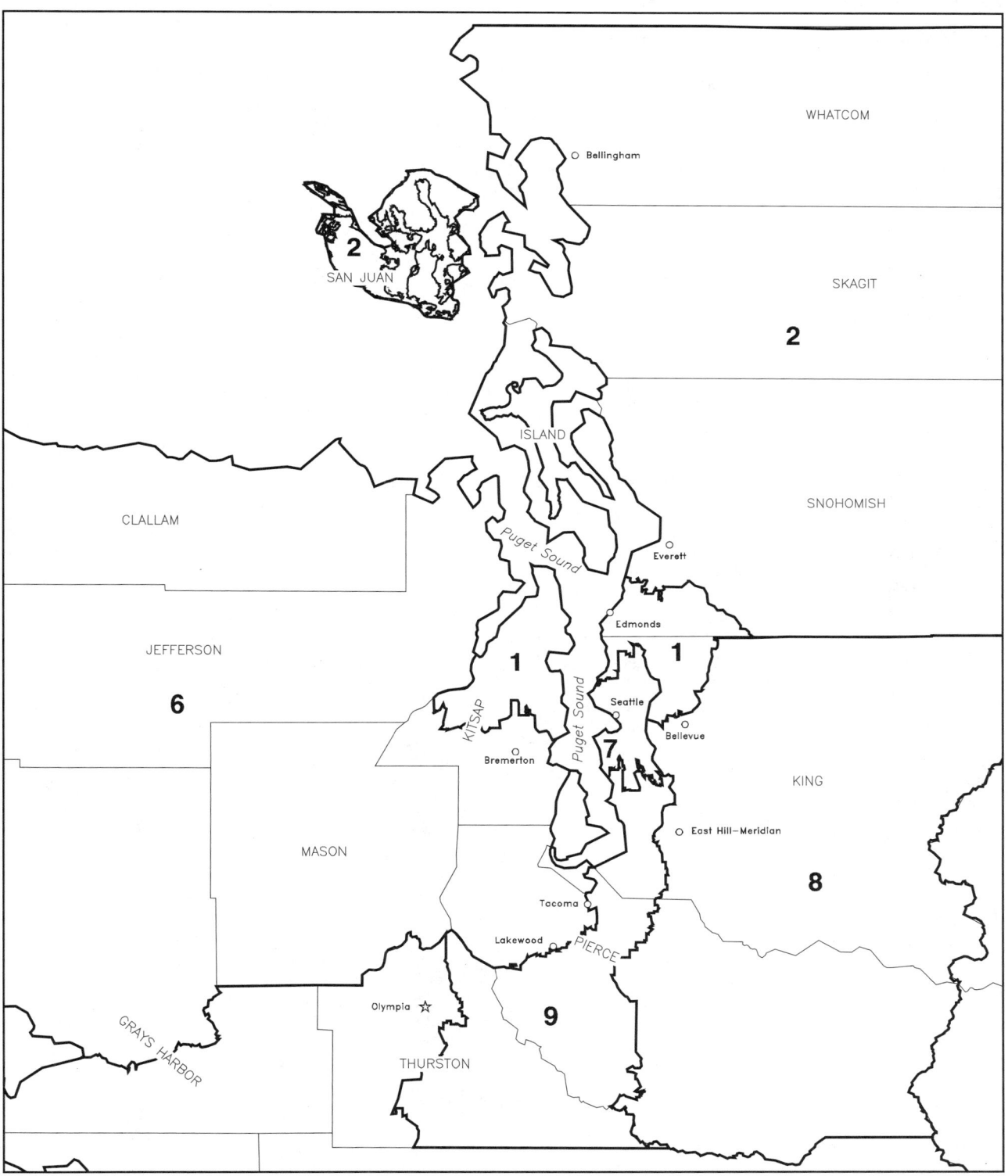

WASHINGTON

PRESIDENT 2000

2000 Census Population	County	Total Vote	Republican	Democratic	Green (Nader)	Other	Rep.-Dem. Plurality	Percentage of Total Vote		
								Rep.	Dem.	Green
16,428	ADAMS	4,974	3,440	1,406	85	43	2,034 R	69.2%	28.3%	1.7%
20,551	ASOTIN	7,985	4,909	2,736	215	125	2,173 R	61.5%	34.3%	2.7%
142,475	BENTON	59,779	38,367	19,512	1,102	798	18,855 R	64.2%	32.6%	1.8%
66,616	CHELAN	26,517	16,980	8,412	850	275	8,568 R	64.0%	31.7%	3.2%
64,525	CLALLAM	32,232	16,251	13,779	1,603	599	2,472 R	50.4%	42.7%	5.0%
345,238	CLARK	135,544	67,219	61,767	5,140	1,418	5,452 R	49.6%	45.6%	3.8%
4,064	COLUMBIA	2,107	1,523	515	45	24	1,008 R	72.3%	24.4%	2.1%
92,948	COWLITZ	36,962	16,873	18,233	1,429	427	1,360 D	45.6%	49.3%	3.9%
32,603	DOUGLAS	12,855	8,512	3,822	339	182	4,690 R	66.2%	29.7%	2.6%
7,260	FERRY	3,038	1,896	932	117	93	964 R	62.4%	30.7%	3.9%
49,347	FRANKLIN	13,614	8,594	4,653	210	157	3,941 R	63.1%	34.2%	1.5%
2,397	GARFIELD	1,329	982	300	35	12	682 R	73.9%	22.6%	2.6%
74,698	GRANT	23,798	15,830	7,073	528	367	8,757 R	66.5%	29.7%	2.2%
67,194	GRAYS HARBOR	25,972	11,225	13,304	1,059	384	2,079 D	43.2%	51.2%	4.1%
71,558	ISLAND	33,004	16,408	14,778	1,484	334	1,630 R	49.7%	44.8%	4.5%
25,953	JEFFERSON	15,833	6,095	8,281	1,241	216	2,186 D	38.5%	52.3%	7.8%
1,737,034	KING	794,196	273,171	476,700	37,383	6,942	203,529 D	34.4%	60.0%	4.7%
231,969	KITSAP	102,596	46,427	50,302	4,607	1,260	3,875 D	45.3%	49.0%	4.5%
33,362	KITTITAS	14,086	7,727	5,516	644	199	2,211 R	54.9%	39.2%	4.6%
19,161	KLICKITAT	8,159	4,557	3,062	396	144	1,495 R	55.9%	37.5%	4.9%
68,600	LEWIS	29,986	18,565	9,891	980	550	8,674 R	61.9%	33.0%	3.3%
10,184	LINCOLN	5,197	3,546	1,417	160	74	2,129 R	68.2%	27.3%	3.1%
49,405	MASON	22,480	10,257	10,876	1,029	318	619 D	45.6%	48.4%	4.6%
39,564	OKANOGAN	14,798	9,384	4,335	722	357	5,049 R	63.4%	29.3%	4.9%
20,984	PACIFIC	9,519	4,042	4,895	447	135	853 D	42.5%	51.4%	4.7%
11,732	PEND OREILLE	5,438	3,076	1,973	234	155	1,103 R	56.6%	36.3%	4.3%
700,820	PIERCE	268,427	118,431	138,249	8,749	2,998	19,818 D	44.1%	51.5%	3.3%
14,077	SAN JUAN	8,407	3,005	4,426	875	101	1,421 D	35.7%	52.6%	10.4%
102,979	SKAGIT	45,221	22,163	20,432	2,070	556	1,731 R	49.0%	45.2%	4.6%
9,872	SKAMANIA	4,249	2,151	1,753	252	93	398 R	50.6%	41.3%	5.9%
606,024	SNOHOMISH	250,967	109,615	129,612	9,023	2,717	19,997 D	43.7%	51.6%	3.6%
417,939	SPOKANE	172,112	89,299	74,604	6,250	1,959	14,695 R	51.9%	43.3%	3.6%
40,066	STEVENS	17,999	11,299	5,560	700	440	5,739 R	62.8%	30.9%	3.9%
207,355	THURSTON	97,422	39,924	50,467	5,792	1,239	10,543 D	41.0%	51.8%	5.9%
3,824	WAHKIAKUM	1,973	1,033	803	97	40	230 R	52.4%	40.7%	4.9%
55,180	WALLA WALLA	21,365	13,304	7,188	624	249	6,116 R	62.3%	33.6%	2.9%
166,814	WHATCOM	73,757	34,287	34,033	4,502	935	254 R	46.5%	46.1%	6.1%
40,740	WHITMAN	16,237	9,003	6,509	530	195	2,494 R	55.4%	40.1%	3.3%
222,581	YAKIMA	67,299	39,494	25,546	1,454	805	13,948 R	58.7%	38.0%	2.2%
5,894,121	TOTAL	2,487,433	1,108,864	1,247,652	103,002	27,915	138,788 D	44.6%	50.2%	4.1%

WASHINGTON

GOVERNOR 2000

2000 Census Population	County	Total Vote	Republican	Democratic	Other	Rep.-Dem. Plurality		Percentage			
								Total Vote		Major Vote	
								Rep.	Dem.	Rep.	Dem.
16,428	ADAMS	4,946	2,629	2,250	67	379	R	53.2%	45.5%	53.9%	46.1%
20,551	ASOTIN	7,911	3,070	4,718	123	1,648	D	38.8%	59.6%	39.4%	60.6%
142,475	BENTON	59,302	29,245	28,892	1,165	353	R	49.3%	48.7%	50.3%	49.7%
66,616	CHELAN	26,345	14,970	10,984	391	3,986	R	56.8%	41.7%	57.7%	42.3%
64,525	CLALLAM	31,762	13,795	17,128	839	3,333	D	43.4%	53.9%	44.6%	55.4%
345,238	CLARK	132,844	57,464	71,998	3,382	14,534	D	43.3%	54.2%	44.4%	55.6%
4,064	COLUMBIA	2,098	1,116	950	32	166	R	53.2%	45.3%	54.0%	46.0%
92,948	COWLITZ	36,518	14,589	20,919	1,010	6,330	D	40.0%	57.3%	41.1%	58.9%
32,603	DOUGLAS	12,835	7,454	5,149	232	2,305	R	58.1%	40.1%	59.1%	40.9%
7,260	FERRY	3,013	1,624	1,254	135	370	R	53.9%	41.6%	56.4%	43.6%
49,347	FRANKLIN	13,922	6,832	6,757	333	75	R	49.1%	48.5%	50.3%	49.7%
2,397	GARFIELD	1,330	646	644	40	2	R	48.6%	48.4%	50.1%	49.9%
74,698	GRANT	23,695	13,673	9,491	531	4,182	R	57.7%	40.1%	59.0%	41.0%
67,194	GRAYS HARBOR	25,961	9,566	15,817	578	6,251	D	36.8%	60.9%	37.7%	62.3%
71,558	ISLAND	32,658	14,381	17,736	541	3,355	D	44.0%	54.3%	44.8%	55.2%
25,953	JEFFERSON	15,738	5,628	9,712	398	4,084	D	35.8%	61.7%	36.7%	63.3%
1,737,034	KING	785,807	250,103	522,229	13,475	272,126	D	31.8%	66.5%	32.4%	67.6%
231,969	KITSAP	102,927	42,358	58,603	1,966	16,245	D	41.2%	56.9%	42.0%	58.0%
33,362	KITTITAS	14,000	7,262	6,423	315	839	R	51.9%	45.9%	53.1%	46.9%
19,161	KLICKITAT	7,999	3,468	4,278	253	810	D	43.4%	53.5%	44.8%	55.2%
68,600	LEWIS	29,744	16,422	12,545	777	3,877	R	55.2%	42.2%	56.7%	43.3%
10,184	LINCOLN	5,182	2,984	2,083	115	901	R	57.6%	40.2%	58.9%	41.1%
49,405	MASON	22,289	9,473	12,319	497	2,846	D	42.5%	55.3%	43.5%	56.5%
39,564	OKANOGAN	14,666	8,559	5,626	481	2,933	R	58.4%	38.4%	60.3%	39.7%
20,984	PACIFIC	9,406	3,643	5,519	244	1,876	D	38.7%	58.7%	39.8%	60.2%
11,732	PEND OREILLE	5,375	2,590	2,621	164	31	D	48.2%	48.8%	49.7%	50.3%
700,820	PIERCE	266,983	113,633	148,450	4,900	34,817	D	42.6%	55.6%	43.4%	56.6%
14,077	SAN JUAN	8,306	2,684	5,385	237	2,701	D	32.3%	64.8%	33.3%	66.7%
102,979	SKAGIT	45,052	19,990	24,191	871	4,201	D	44.4%	53.7%	45.2%	54.8%
9,872	SKAMANIA	4,034	1,656	2,148	230	492	D	41.1%	53.2%	43.5%	56.5%
606,024	SNOHOMISH	249,945	102,993	142,196	4,756	39,203	D	41.2%	56.9%	42.0%	58.0%
417,939	SPOKANE	171,992	69,848	99,492	2,652	29,644	D	40.6%	57.8%	41.2%	58.8%
40,066	STEVENS	17,833	9,871	7,426	536	2,445	R	55.4%	41.6%	57.1%	42.9%
207,355	THURSTON	96,466	35,404	58,915	2,147	23,511	D	36.7%	61.1%	37.5%	62.5%
3,824	WAHKIAKUM	1,951	770	1,112	69	342	D	39.5%	57.0%	40.9%	59.1%
55,180	WALLA WALLA	21,185	9,936	10,869	380	933	D	46.9%	51.3%	47.8%	52.2%
166,814	WHATCOM	72,674	28,861	42,313	1,500	13,452	D	39.7%	58.2%	40.5%	59.5%
40,740	WHITMAN	16,058	6,676	9,113	269	2,437	D	41.6%	56.8%	42.3%	57.7%
222,581	YAKIMA	69,100	34,194	33,718	1,188	476	R	49.5%	48.8%	50.4%	49.6%
5,894,121	TOTAL	2,469,852	980,060	1,441,973	47,819	461,913	D	39.7%	58.4%	40.5%	59.5%

WASHINGTON

SENATOR 2000

2000 Census Population	County	Total Vote	Republican	Democratic	Other	Rep.-Dem. Plurality		Percentage			
								Total Vote		Major Vote	
								Rep.	Dem.	Rep.	Dem.
16,428	ADAMS	4,937	3,542	1,328	67	2,214	R	71.7%	26.9%	72.7%	27.3%
20,551	ASOTIN	7,896	4,917	2,789	190	2,128	R	62.3%	35.3%	63.8%	36.2%
142,475	BENTON	59,323	40,314	17,858	1,151	22,456	R	68.0%	30.1%	69.3%	30.7%
66,616	CHELAN	26,229	17,958	7,758	513	10,200	R	68.5%	29.6%	69.8%	30.2%
64,525	CLALLAM	31,852	17,470	13,202	1,180	4,268	R	54.8%	41.4%	57.0%	43.0%
345,238	CLARK	132,423	69,265	58,971	4,187	10,294	R	52.3%	44.5%	54.0%	46.0%
4,064	COLUMBIA	2,096	1,590	467	39	1,123	R	75.9%	22.3%	77.3%	22.7%
92,948	COWLITZ	36,499	19,191	16,271	1,037	2,920	R	52.6%	44.6%	54.1%	45.9%
32,603	DOUGLAS	11,992	8,554	3,177	261	5,377	R	71.3%	26.5%	72.9%	27.1%
7,260	FERRY	3,026	1,918	996	112	922	R	63.4%	32.9%	65.8%	34.2%
49,347	FRANKLIN	13,874	9,190	4,445	239	4,745	R	66.2%	32.0%	67.4%	32.6%
2,397	GARFIELD	1,323	1,013	284	26	729	R	76.6%	21.5%	78.1%	21.9%
74,698	GRANT	23,651	16,361	6,768	522	9,593	R	69.2%	28.6%	70.7%	29.3%
67,194	GRAYS HARBOR	25,754	13,386	11,449	919	1,937	R	52.0%	44.5%	53.9%	46.1%
71,558	ISLAND	32,702	17,249	14,676	777	2,573	R	52.7%	44.9%	54.0%	46.0%
25,953	JEFFERSON	15,722	6,647	8,647	428	2,000	D	42.3%	55.0%	43.5%	56.5%
1,737,034	KING	783,056	306,251	459,605	17,200	153,354	R	39.1%	58.7%	40.0%	60.0%
231,969	KITSAP	102,572	49,786	49,627	3,159	159	R	48.5%	48.4%	50.1%	49.9%
33,362	KITTITAS	14,026	8,104	5,598	324	2,506	R	57.8%	39.9%	59.1%	40.9%
19,161	KLICKITAT	7,976	4,511	3,214	251	1,297	R	56.6%	40.3%	58.4%	41.6%
68,600	LEWIS	29,778	19,904	8,843	1,031	11,061	R	66.8%	29.7%	69.2%	30.8%
10,184	LINCOLN	5,206	3,718	1,379	109	2,339	R	71.4%	26.5%	72.9%	27.1%
49,405	MASON	22,250	11,118	10,268	864	850	R	50.0%	46.1%	52.0%	48.0%
39,564	OKANOGAN	14,727	10,006	4,253	468	5,753	R	67.9%	28.9%	70.2%	29.8%
20,984	PACIFIC	9,368	4,674	4,348	346	326	R	49.9%	46.4%	51.8%	48.2%
11,732	PEND OREILLE	5,430	3,226	1,994	210	1,232	R	59.4%	36.7%	61.8%	38.2%
700,820	PIERCE	265,510	129,674	127,644	8,192	2,030	R	48.8%	48.1%	50.4%	49.6%
14,077	SAN JUAN	8,310	3,362	4,729	219	1,367	D	40.5%	56.9%	41.6%	58.4%
102,979	SKAGIT	44,937	24,047	19,628	1,262	4,419	R	53.5%	43.7%	55.1%	44.9%
9,872	SKAMANIA	4,068	2,132	1,717	219	415	R	52.4%	42.2%	55.4%	44.6%
606,024	SNOHOMISH	249,390	119,339	123,111	6,940	3,772	D	47.9%	49.4%	49.2%	50.8%
417,939	SPOKANE	171,426	93,633	73,565	4,228	20,068	R	54.6%	42.9%	56.0%	44.0%
40,066	STEVENS	17,911	11,489	5,792	630	5,697	R	64.1%	32.3%	66.5%	33.5%
207,355	THURSTON	96,503	42,804	50,436	3,263	7,632	D	44.4%	52.3%	45.9%	54.1%
3,824	WAHKIAKUM	1,932	1,105	762	65	343	R	57.2%	39.4%	59.2%	40.8%
55,180	WALLA WALLA	21,193	13,528	7,249	416	6,279	R	63.8%	34.2%	65.1%	34.9%
166,814	WHATCOM	71,348	36,144	33,308	1,896	2,836	R	50.7%	46.7%	52.0%	48.0%
40,740	WHITMAN	16,097	9,281	6,516	300	2,765	R	57.7%	40.5%	58.8%	41.2%
222,581	YAKIMA	69,066	40,807	26,765	1,494	14,042	R	59.1%	38.8%	60.4%	39.6%
5,894,121	TOTAL	2,461,379	1,197,208	1,199,437	64,734	2,229	D	48.6%	48.7%	50.0%	50.0%

WASHINGTON

CONGRESS

CD	Year	Total Vote	Republican Vote	Republican Candidate	Democratic Vote	Democratic Candidate	Other Vote	Rep.-Dem. Plurality	Total Vote Rep.	Total Vote Dem.	Major Vote Rep.	Major Vote Dem.
1	2000	285,636	121,823	MCDONALD, DAN	155,820	INSLEE, JAY	7,993	33,997 D	42.6%	54.6%	43.9%	56.1%
1	1998	226,473	99,910	WHITE, RICK	112,726	INSLEE, JAY	13,837	12,816 D	44.1%	49.8%	47.0%	53.0%
1	1996	264,135	141,948	WHITE, RICK	122,187	COOPERSMITH, JEFF		19,761 R	53.7%	46.3%	53.7%	46.3%
1	1994	194,664	100,554	WHITE, RICK	94,110	CANTWELL, MARIA		6,444 R	51.7%	48.3%	51.7%	48.3%
1	1992	271,278	113,897	NELSON, GARY	148,844	CANTWELL, MARIA	8,537	34,947 D	42.0%	54.9%	43.3%	56.7%
2	2000	293,180	134,660	KOSTER, JOHN	146,617	LARSEN, RICK	11,903	11,957 D	45.9%	50.0%	47.9%	52.1%
2	1998	224,901	124,125	METCALF, JACK	100,776	CAMMERMEYER, GRETHE		23,349 R	55.2%	44.8%	55.2%	44.8%
2	1996	256,944	124,655	METCALF, JACK	122,728	QUIGLEY, KEVIN	9,561	1,927 R	48.5%	47.8%	50.4%	49.6%
2	1994	196,526	107,430	METCALF, JACK	89,096	SPANEL, HARRIET A.		18,334 R	54.7%	45.3%	54.7%	45.3%
2	1992	255,926	107,365	METCALF, JACK	133,207	SWIFT, AL	15,354	25,842 D	42.0%	52.0%	44.6%	55.4%
3	2000	282,664	114,861	MATSON, TRENT R.	159,428	BAIRD, BRIAN	8,375	44,567 D	40.6%	56.4%	41.9%	58.1%
3	1998	220,219	99,855	BENTON, DON	120,364	BAIRD, BRIAN		20,509 D	45.3%	54.7%	45.3%	54.7%
3	1996	245,347	123,117	SMITH, LINDA	122,230	BAIRD, BRIAN		887 R	50.2%	49.8%	50.2%	49.8%
3	1994	192,634	100,188	SMITH, LINDA	85,826	UNSOELD, JOLENE	6,620	14,362 R	52.0%	44.6%	53.9%	46.1%
3	1992	246,644	108,583	FISKE, PAT	138,043	UNSOELD, JOLENE	18	29,460 D	44.0%	56.0%	44.0%	56.0%
4	2000	235,104	143,259	HASTINGS, RICHARD	87,585	DAVIS, JIM	4,260	55,674 R	60.9%	37.3%	62.1%	37.9%
4	1998	176,090	121,684	HASTINGS, RICHARD	43,043	PROSS, GORDON ALLEN	11,363	78,641 R	69.1%	24.4%	73.9%	26.1%
4	1996	205,149	108,647	HASTINGS, RICHARD	96,502	LOCKE, RICK		12,145 R	53.0%	47.0%	53.0%	47.0%
4	1994	174,026	92,828	HASTINGS, RICHARD	81,198	INSLEE, JAY		11,630 R	53.3%	46.7%	53.3%	46.7%
4	1992	209,604	103,028	HASTINGS, RICHARD	106,556	INSLEE, JAY	20	3,528 D	49.2%	50.8%	49.2%	50.8%
5	2000	251,214	144,038	NETHERCUTT, GEORGE	97,703	KEEFE, TOM	9,473	46,335 R	57.3%	38.9%	59.6%	40.4%
5	1998	193,258	110,040	NETHERCUTT, GEORGE	73,545	LYONS, BRAD	9,673	36,495 R	56.9%	38.1%	59.9%	40.1%
5	1996	236,784	131,618	NETHERCUTT, GEORGE	105,166	OLSON, JUDY		26,452 R	55.6%	44.4%	55.6%	44.4%
5	1994	216,131	110,057	NETHERCUTT, GEORGE	106,074	FOLEY, THOMAS S.		3,983 R	50.9%	49.1%	50.9%	49.1%
5	1992	246,413	110,443	SONNELAND, JOHN	135,965	FOLEY, THOMAS S.	5	25,522 D	44.8%	55.2%	44.8%	55.2%
6	2000	254,713	79,215	LAWRENCE, BOB	164,853	DICKS, NORMAN D.	10,645	85,638 D	31.1%	64.7%	32.5%	67.5%
6	1998	209,599	66,291	LAWRENCE, BOB	143,308	DICKS, NORMAN D.		77,017 D	31.6%	68.4%	31.6%	68.4%
6	1996	235,910	71,337	TINSLEY, BILL	155,467	DICKS, NORMAN D.	9,106	84,130 D	30.2%	65.9%	31.5%	68.5%
6	1994	180,802	75,322	GREGG, BENJAMIN	105,480	DICKS, NORMAN D.		30,158 D	41.7%	58.3%	41.7%	58.3%
6	1992	238,182	66,664	PHILLIPS, LAURI J.	152,933	DICKS, NORMAN D.	18,585	86,269 D	28.0%	64.2%	30.4%	69.6%
7	2000	265,809			193,470	MCDERMOTT, JIM	72,339	193,470 D		72.8%		100.0%
7	1998	207,542			183,076	MCDERMOTT, JIM	24,466	183,076 D		88.2%		100.0%
7	1996	259,094	49,341	KLESCHEN, FRANK	209,753	MCDERMOTT, JIM		160,412 D	19.0%	81.0%	19.0%	81.0%
7	1994	197,444	49,091	HARRIS, KEITH	148,353	MCDERMOTT, JIM		99,262 D	24.9%	75.1%	24.9%	75.1%
7	1992	283,992	54,149	HAMPSON, GLENN C.	222,604	MCDERMOTT, JIM	7,239	168,455 D	19.1%	78.4%	19.6%	80.4%
8	2000	294,468	183,255	DUNN, JENNIFER	104,944	BEHRENS-BENEDICT, HEIDI	6,269	78,311 R	62.2%	35.6%	63.6%	36.4%
8	1998	226,910	135,539	DUNN, JENNIFER	91,371	BEHRENS-BENEDICT, HEIDI		44,168 R	59.7%	40.3%	59.7%	40.3%
8	1996	261,031	170,691	DUNN, JENNIFER	90,340	LITTLE, DAVE		80,351 R	65.4%	34.6%	65.4%	34.6%
8	1994	184,574	140,409	DUNN, JENNIFER	44,165	WYRICK, JIM		96,244 R	76.1%	23.9%	76.1%	23.9%
8	1992	258,188	155,874	DUNN, JENNIFER	87,611	TAMBLYN, GOERGE O.	14,703	68,263 R	60.4%	33.9%	64.0%	36.0%
9	2000	219,623	76,766	VANCE, CHRIS	135,452	SMITH, ADAM	7,405	58,686 D	35.0%	61.7%	36.2%	63.8%
9	1998	173,056	61,108	TABER, RON	111,948	SMITH, ADAM		50,840 D	35.3%	64.7%	35.3%	64.7%
9	1996	209,867	99,199	TATE, RANDY	105,236	SMITH, ADAM	5,432	6,037 D	47.3%	50.1%	48.5%	51.5%
9	1994	150,284	77,833	TATE, RANDY	72,451	KREIDLER, MIKE		5,382 R	51.8%	48.2%	51.8%	48.2%
9	1992	212,931	91,910	VON REICHBAUER, PETER	110,902	KREIDLER, MIKE	10,119	18,992 D	43.2%	52.1%	45.3%	54.7%

WASHINGTON

GENERAL AND PRIMARY ELECTIONS

2000 GENERAL ELECTIONS

President Other vote was 13,135 Libertarian (Browne); 7,171 Freedom (Buchanan); 2,927 Natural Law (Hagelin); 1,989 Constitutiton (Phillips); 1,729 Workers World (Moorehead); 660 Socialist (McReynolds); 304 Socialist Workers (Harris).

Governor Other vote was 47,819 Libertarian (LePage).

Senator Other vote was 64,734 Libertarian (Jared).

Congress Other vote was: CD 1: 7,993 Libertarian (Newman); CD 2: 7,672 Libertarian (Andrews), 4,231 Natural Law (Johnson); CD 3: 8,375 Libertarian (Lewis); CD 4: 4,260 Libertarian (Krauss); CD 5: 9,473 Libertarian (Holmes); CD 6: 10,645 Libertarian (Bennett); CD 7: 52,142 Green (Szwaja), 20,197 Libertarian (Grus); CD 8: 6,269 Libertarian (McIlroy); CD 9: 7,405 Libertarian (Wright).

2000 PRIMARY ELECTIONS

Primary February 29, 2000 (President) **Registration** 3,224,762 No Party Registration
September 19, 2000   (Congress) (as of Sept. 19, 2000)

Primary Type Open—For each office, candidates ran on a single, multi-party ballot and the primary was open to all registered voters. The nominations went to the candidate with the highest vote in each party, providing the winner received at least 1 percent of the total votes cast for that office. In the presidential primary, there were separate Democratic and Republican ballots, as well as an unaffiliated ballot. The totals below marked "All Ballots" include the unaffiliated ballots.

Note: An asterisk (*) denotes incumbent. The party identification of candidates is indicated in parentheses.

2000 PRIMARIES

President	Republican	George W. Bush	284,053	57.8%
		John McCain	191,101	38.9%
		Alan Keyes	11,753	2.4%
		Steve Forbes	1,749	0.4%
		Gary Bauer	1,469	0.3%
		Orrin G. Hatch	1,023	0.2%
		TOTAL	491,148	
	Republican (All Ballots)	George W. Bush	402,287	48.3%
		John McCain	399,980	48.0%
		Alan Keyes	21,122	2.5%
		Steve Forbes	5,136	0.6%
		Gary Bauer	2,870	0.3%
		Orrin G. Hatch	2,263	0.3%
		TOTAL	833,658	
	Democratic	Al Gore	202,456	68.2%
		Bill Bradley	93,375	31.4%
		Lyndon H. LaRouche Jr.	1,170	0.4%
		TOTAL	297,001	
	Democratic (All Ballots)	Al Gore	310,406	65.3%
		Bill Bradley	162,725	34.2%
		Lyndon H. LaRouche Jr.	2,576	0.5%
		TOTAL	475,707	

WASHINGTON

GENERAL AND PRIMARY ELECTIONS

2000 PRIMARIES

			Overall Percentage	Republican Percentage	Democratic Percentage
Governor	Gary Locke (D)*	701,929	54.3%		96.1%
	John Carlson (R)	446,142	34.5%	82.7%	
	Harold Hochstatter (R)	93,467	7.2%	17.3%	
	Meta Heller (D)	28,578	2.2%		3.9%
	Steve W. LePage (Libertarian)	22,186	1.7%		
	GRAND TOTAL	1,292,302			
	Republican Total	539,609			
	Democratic Total	730,507			
Senator	Slade Gorton (R)*	560,787	43.6%	93.3%	
	Maria Cantwell (D)	472,609	36.7%		70.6%
	Deborah Senn (D)	168,110	13.1%		25.1%
	Warren E. Hanson (R)	17,782	1.4%	3.0%	
	Jeff Jared (Libertarian)	16,247	1.3%		
	Barbara Lampert (D)	15,150	1.2%		2.3%
	Robert Tilden Medley (D)	14,009	1.1%		2.1%
	Ken McCandless (R)	12,089	0.9%	2.0%	
	June Riggs (R)	10,455	0.8%	1.7%	
	GRAND TOTAL	1,287,238			
	Republican Total	601,113			
	Democratic Total	669,878			
Congressional District 1	Jay Inslee (D)*	80,362	55.6%		100.0%
	Dan McDonald (R)	60,303	41.7%	100.0%	
	Bruce Newman (Libertarian)	3,950	2.7%		
	TOTAL	144,615			
	Republican Total	60,303			
	Democratic Total	80,362			
Congressional District 2	John Koster (R)	72,244	49.1%	100.0%	
	Rick Larsen (D)	68,315	46.4%		100.0%
	Stuart Andrews (Libertarian)	4,274	2.9%		
	Glen S. Johnson (Natural Law)	2,412	1.6%		
	TOTAL	147,245			
	Republican Total	72,244			
	Democratic Total	68,315			
Congressional District 3	Brian Baird (D)*	81,240	56.2%		100.0%
	Trent R. Matson (R)	58,077	40.2%	100.0%	
	Erne Lewis (Libertarian)	5,332	3.7%		
	TOTAL	144,649			
	Republican Total	58,077			
	Democratic Total	81,240			
Congressional District 4	Richard "Doc" Hastings (R)*	79,683	60.8%	93.6%	
	Jim Davis (D)	42,337	32.3%		100.0%
	Gordon Allen Pross (R)	5,420	4.1%	6.4%	
	Fred D. Krauss (Libertarian)	3,684	2.8%		
	TOTAL	131,124			
	Republican Total	85,103			
	Democratic Total	42,337			
Congressional District 5	George Nethercutt (R)*	64,341	45.4%	69.4%	
	Tom Keefe (D)	30,263	21.4%		66.0%
	Richard Clear (R)	28,373	20.0%	30.6%	
	Tom Flynn (D)	15,609	11.0%		34.0%
	Greg Holmes (Libertarian)	3,129	2.2%		
	TOTAL	141,715			
	Republican Total	92,714			
	Democratic Total	45,872			

WASHINGTON

GENERAL AND PRIMARY ELECTIONS

2000 PRIMARIES

			Overall Percentage	Republican Percentage	Democratic Percentage
Congressional District 6	Norm Dicks (D)*	103,131	66.0%		100.0%
	Bob Lawrence (R)	38,817	24.9%	83.1%	
	William Edward Chovil (R)	7,882	5.0%	16.9%	
	John Bennett (Libertarian)	6,311	4.0%		
	TOTAL	156,141			
	Republican Total	46,699			
	Democratic Total	103,131			
Congressional District 7	Jim McDermott (D)*	94,450	77.9%		
	Joe Szwaja (Green)	16,214	13.4%		
	Joel Grus (Libertarian)	10,546	8.7%		
	No Republican candidate was listed on the primary ballot.				
	TOTAL	121,210			
	Democratic Total	94,450			
Congressional District 8	Jennifer Dunn (R)*	89,133	60.8%	100.0%	
	Heidi Behrens-Benedict (D)	54,449	37.1%		100.0%
	Bernard McIlroy (Libertarian)	3,059	2.1%		
	TOTAL	146,641			
	Republican Total	89,133			
	Democratic Total	54,449			
Congressional District 9	Adam Smith (D)*	70,901	59.8%		100.0%
	Chris Vance (R)	34,861	29.4%	78.9%	
	Gary Snell (R)	9,322	7.9%	21.1%	
	Jonathan V. Wright (Libertarian)	3,569	3.0%		
	TOTAL	118,653			
	Republican Total	44,183			
	Democratic Total	70,901			

WEST VIRGINIA

GOVERNOR
Bob Wise (D). Elected 2000 to a four-year term.

SENATORS
Robert C. Byrd (D). Re-elected 2000 to a six-year term. Previously elected 1994, 1988, 1982, 1976, 1970, 1964, 1958.

John D. Rockefeller (D). Re-elected 1996 to a six-year term. Previously elected 1990, 1984.

REPRESENTATIVES
1. Alan B. Mollohan (D) 2. Shelley Moore Capito (R) 3. Nick J. Rahall (D)

POSTWAR VOTE FOR PRESIDENT

| | | Republican | | Democratic | | Other | | Percentage | | | |
| | | | | | | | | Total Vote | | Major Vote | |
Year	Total Vote	Vote	Candidate	Vote	Candidate	Vote	Plurality	Rep.	Dem.	Rep.	Dem.
2000**	648,124	336,475	Bush, George W.	295,497	Gore, Al	16,152	40,978 R	51.9%	45.6%**	53.2%	46.8%
1996**	636,459	233,946	Dole, Bob	327,812	Clinton, Bill	74,701	93,866 D	36.8%	51.5%	41.6%	58.4%
1992**	683,762	241,974	Bush, George	331,001	Clinton, Bill	110,787	89,027 D	35.4%	48.4%	42.2%	57.8%
1988	653,311	310,065	Bush, George	341,016	Dukakis, Michael S.	2,230	30,951 D	47.5%	52.2%	47.6%	52.4%
1984	735,742	405,483	Reagan, Ronald	328,125	Mondale, Walter F.	2,134	77,358 R	55.1%	44.6%	55.3%	44.7%
1980**	737,715	334,206	Reagan, Ronald	367,462	Carter, Jimmy	36,047	33,256 D	45.3%	49.8%	47.6%	52.4%
1976	750,964	314,760	Ford, Gerald R.	435,914	Carter, Jimmy	290	121,154 D	41.9%	58.0%	41.9%	58.1%
1972	762,399	484,964	Nixon, Richard M.	277,435	McGovern, George S.		207,529 R	63.6%	36.4%	63.6%	36.4%
1968	754,206	307,555	Nixon, Richard M.	374,091	Humphrey, Hubert H.	72,560	66,536 D	40.8%	49.6%	45.1%	54.9%
1964	792,040	253,953	Goldwater, Barry M.	538,087	Johnson, Lyndon B.		284,134 D	32.1%	67.9%	32.1%	67.9%
1960	837,781	395,995	Nixon, Richard M.	441,786	Kennedy, John F.		45,791 D	47.3%	52.7%	47.3%	52.7%
1956	830,831	449,297	Eisenhower, Dwight D.	381,534	Stevenson, Adlai E.		67,763 R	54.1%	45.9%	54.1%	45.9%
1952	873,548	419,970	Eisenhower, Dwight D.	453,578	Stevenson, Adlai E.		33,608 D	48.1%	51.9%	48.1%	51.9%
1948	748,750	316,251	Dewey, Thomas E.	429,188	Truman, Harry S.	3,311	112,937 D	42.2%	57.3%	42.4%	57.6%

In 2000 the other vote column includes 10,680 votes cast for Green (Nader). In 1996 the other vote column includes 71,639 votes cast for Perot. In 1992 the other vote column includes 108,829 votes cast for Perot. In 1980 the other column includes 31,691 votes for Independent (Anderson).

POSTWAR VOTE FOR GOVERNOR

| | | Republican | | Democratic | | Other | Rep.-Dem. | Percentage | | | |
| | | | | | | | | Total Vote | | Major Vote | |
Year	Total Vote	Vote	Candidate	Vote	Candidate	Vote	Plurality	Rep.	Dem.	Rep.	Dem.
2000	648,047	305,926	Underwood, Cecil H.	324,822	Wise, Bob	17,299	18,896 D	47.2%	50.1%	48.5%	51.5%
1996	628,559	324,518	Underwood, Cecil H.	287,870	Pritt, Charlotte	16,171	36,648 R	51.6%	45.8%	53.0%	47.0%
1992	657,193	240,390	Benedict, Cleveland K.	368,302	Caperton, Gaston	48,501	127,912 D	36.6%	56.0%	39.5%	60.5%
1988	649,593	267,172	Moore, Arch A.	382,421	Caperton, Gaston		115,249 D	41.1%	58.9%	41.1%	58.9%
1984	741,502	394,937	Moore, Arch A.	346,565	See, Clyde M.		48,372 R	53.3%	46.7%	53.3%	46.7%
1980	742,150	337,240	Moore, Arch A.	401,863	Rockefeller, John D.	3,047	64,623 D	45.4%	54.1%	45.6%	54.4%
1976	749,270	253,420	Underwood, Cecil H.	495,661	Rockefeller, John D.	189	242,241 D	33.8%	66.2%	33.8%	66.2%
1972	774,279	423,817	Moore, Arch A.	350,462	Rockefeller, John D.		73,355 R	54.7%	45.3%	54.7%	45.3%
1968	743,845	378,315	Moore, Arch A.	365,530	Sprouse, James M.		12,785 R	50.9%	49.1%	50.9%	49.1%
1964	788,582	355,559	Underwood, Cecil H.	433,023	Smith, Hulett C.		77,464 D	45.1%	54.9%	45.1%	54.9%
1960	827,420	380,665	Neely, Harold E.	446,755	Barron, W. W.		66,090 D	46.0%	54.0%	46.0%	54.0%
1956	817,623	440,502	Underwood, Cecil H.	377,121	Mollohan, Robert H.		63,381 R	53.9%	46.1%	53.9%	46.1%
1952	882,527	427,629	Holt, Rush D.	454,898	Marland, William C.		27,269 D	48.5%	51.5%	48.5%	51.5%
1948	768,061	329,309	Boreman, Herbert	438,752	Patteson, Okey L.		109,443 D	42.9%	57.1%	42.9%	57.1%

WEST VIRGINIA

POSTWAR VOTE FOR SENATOR

| | | Republican | | Democratic | | Other | Rep.-Dem. | Percentage | | | |
| | Total | | | | | | | Total Vote | | Major Vote | |
Year	Vote	Vote	Candidate	Vote	Candidate	Vote	Plurality	Rep.	Dem.	Rep.	Dem.
2000	603,477	121,635	Gallaher, David T.	469,215	Byrd, Robert C.	12,627	347,580 D	20.2%	77.8%	20.6%	79.4%
1996	595,614	139,088	Burks, Betty A.	456,526	Rockefeller, John D.		317,438 D	23.4%	76.6%	23.4%	76.6%
1994	420,936	130,441	Klos, Stan	290,495	Byrd, Robert C.		160,054 D	31.0%	69.0%	31.0%	69.0%
1990	404,305	128,071	Yoder, John	276,234	Rockefeller, John D.		148,163 D	31.7%	68.3%	31.7%	68.3%
1988	634,547	223,564	Wolfe, M. Jay	410,983	Byrd, Robert C.		187,419 D	35.2%	64.8%	35.2%	64.8%
1984	722,212	344,680	Raese, John R.	374,233	Rockefeller, John D.	3,299	29,553 D	47.7%	51.8%	47.9%	52.1%
1982	565,314	173,910	Benedict, Cleveland K.	387,170	Byrd, Robert C.	4,234	213,260 D	30.8%	68.5%	31.0%	69.0%
1978	493,351	244,317	Moore, Arch A.	249,034	Randolph, Jennings		4,717 D	49.5%	50.5%	49.5%	50.5%
1976	566,790		—	566,423	Byrd, Robert C.	367	566,423 D		99.9%		100.0%
1972	731,841	245,531	Leonard, Louise	486,310	Randolph, Jennings		240,779 D	33.5%	66.5%	33.5%	66.5%
1970	445,623	99,658	Dodson, Elmer H.	345,965	Byrd, Robert C.		246,307 D	22.4%	77.6%	22.4%	77.6%
1966	491,216	198,891	Love, Francis J.	292,325	Randolph, Jennings		93,434 D	40.5%	59.5%	40.5%	59.5%
1964	761,087	246,072	Benedict, Cooper P.	515,015	Byrd, Robert C.		268,943 D	32.3%	67.7%	32.3%	67.7%
1960	828,292	369,935	Underwood, Cecil H.	458,355	Randolph, Jennings	2	88,420 D	44.7%	55.3%	44.7%	55.3%
1958	644,917	263,172	Revercomb, Chapman	381,745	Byrd, Robert C.		118,573 D	40.8%	59.2%	40.8%	59.2%
1958S	630,677	256,510	Hoblitzell, John D.	374,167	Randolph, Jennings		117,657 D	40.7%	59.3%	40.7%	59.3%
1956S	805,174	432,123	Revercomb, Chapman	373,051	Marland, William C.		59,072 R	53.7%	46.3%	53.7%	46.3%
1954	593,329	268,066	Sweeney, Tom	325,263	Neely, Matthew M.		57,197 D	45.2%	54.8%	45.2%	54.8%
1952	876,573	406,554	Revercomb, Chapman	470,019	Kilgore, Harley M.		63,465 D	46.4%	53.6%	46.4%	53.6%
1948	763,888	328,534	Revercomb, Chapman	435,354	Neely, Matthew M.		106,820 D	43.0%	57.0%	43.0%	57.0%
1946	542,768	269,617	Sweeney, Tom	273,151	Kilgore, Harley M.		3,534 D	49.7%	50.3%	49.7%	50.3%

One of the 1958 elections and the 1956 election were for short terms to fill vacancies.

WEST VIRGINIA

Districts Established October 17, 1991

WEST VIRGINIA

PRESIDENT 2000

2000 Census Population	County	Total Vote	Republican	Democratic	Green (Nader)	Other	Rep.-Dem. Plurality	Percentage of Total Vote		
								Rep.	Dem.	Green
15,557	BARBOUR	6,051	3,411	2,503	89	48	908 R	56.4%	41.4%	1.5%
75,905	BERKELEY	23,010	13,619	8,797	414	180	4,822 R	59.2%	38.2%	1.8%
25,535	BOONE	9,141	3,353	5,656	84	48	2,303 D	36.7%	61.9%	0.9%
14,702	BRAXTON	5,328	2,529	2,719	47	33	190 D	47.5%	51.0%	0.9%
25,447	BROOKE	9,405	4,195	4,678	228	304	483 D	44.6%	49.7%	2.4%
96,784	CABELL	32,216	16,440	14,896	605	275	1,544 R	51.0%	46.2%	1.9%
7,582	CALHOUN	2,615	1,425	1,112	63	15	313 R	54.5%	42.5%	2.4%
10,330	CLAY	3,582	1,887	1,617	50	28	270 R	52.7%	45.1%	1.4%
7,403	DODDRIDGE	2,816	1,955	773	68	20	1,182 R	69.4%	27.5%	2.4%
47,579	FAYETTE	14,619	5,897	8,371	239	112	2,474 D	40.3%	57.3%	1.6%
7,160	GILMER	2,740	1,560	1,092	66	22	468 R	56.9%	39.9%	2.4%
11,299	GRANT	4,534	3,571	891	39	33	2,680 R	78.8%	19.7%	0.9%
34,453	GREENBRIER	12,808	6,866	5,627	235	80	1,239 R	53.6%	43.9%	1.8%
20,203	HAMPSHIRE	6,097	3,879	2,069	97	52	1,810 R	63.6%	33.9%	1.6%
32,667	HANCOCK	13,472	6,458	6,249	329	436	209 R	47.9%	46.4%	2.4%
12,669	HARDY	4,514	2,816	1,621	44	33	1,195 R	62.4%	35.9%	1.0%
68,652	HARRISON	26,578	12,948	13,009	427	194	61 D	48.7%	48.9%	1.6%
28,000	JACKSON	11,518	6,341	4,937	166	74	1,404 R	55.1%	42.9%	1.4%
42,190	JEFFERSON	14,378	7,045	6,860	359	114	185 R	49.0%	47.7%	2.5%
200,073	KANAWHA	76,670	36,809	38,524	948	389	1,715 D	48.0%	50.2%	1.2%
16,919	LEWIS	6,134	3,606	2,355	114	59	1,251 R	58.8%	38.4%	1.9%
22,108	LINCOLN	7,464	3,389	3,939	84	52	550 D	45.4%	52.8%	1.1%
37,710	LOGAN	14,439	5,334	8,927	88	90	3,593 D	36.9%	61.8%	0.6%
27,329	MCDOWELL	7,303	2,348	4,845	67	43	2,497 D	32.2%	66.3%	0.9%
56,598	MARION	22,873	9,972	12,315	418	168	2,343 D	43.6%	53.8%	1.8%
35,519	MARSHALL	13,498	6,859	6,000	316	323	859 R	50.8%	44.5%	2.3%
25,957	MASON	11,223	5,972	4,963	195	93	1,009 R	53.2%	44.2%	1.7%
62,980	MERCER	18,875	10,206	8,347	227	95	1,859 R	54.1%	44.2%	1.2%
27,078	MINERAL	9,782	6,180	3,341	186	75	2,839 R	63.2%	34.2%	1.9%
28,253	MINGO	10,043	3,866	6,049	74	54	2,183 D	38.5%	60.2%	0.7%
81,866	MONONGALIA	27,367	13,595	12,603	942	227	992 R	49.7%	46.1%	3.4%
14,583	MONROE	5,139	2,940	2,094	78	27	846 R	57.2%	40.7%	1.5%
14,943	MORGAN	5,772	3,639	1,939	148	46	1,700 R	63.0%	33.6%	2.6%
26,562	NICHOLAS	8,579	4,359	4,059	111	50	300 R	50.8%	47.3%	1.3%
47,427	OHIO	17,964	9,607	7,653	390	314	1,954 R	53.5%	42.6%	2.2%
8,196	PENDLETON	3,221	1,996	1,172	37	16	824 R	62.0%	36.4%	1.1%
7,514	PLEASANTS	3,208	1,884	1,267	26	31	617 R	58.7%	39.5%	0.8%
9,131	POCAHONTAS	3,467	1,970	1,392	69	36	578 R	56.8%	40.1%	2.0%
29,334	PRESTON	10,439	6,607	3,515	209	108	3,092 R	63.3%	33.7%	2.0%
51,589	PUTNAM	20,426	12,173	7,891	251	111	4,282 R	59.6%	38.6%	1.2%
79,220	RALEIGH	24,061	12,587	11,047	299	128	1,540 R	52.3%	45.9%	1.2%
28,262	RANDOLPH	9,542	5,248	4,028	199	67	1,220 R	55.0%	42.2%	2.1%
10,343	RITCHIE	3,812	2,717	1,024	47	24	1,693 R	71.3%	26.9%	1.2%
15,446	ROANE	5,625	3,172	2,332	95	26	840 R	56.4%	41.5%	1.7%
12,999	SUMMERS	4,713	2,304	2,299	81	29	5 R	48.9%	48.8%	1.7%
16,089	TAYLOR	5,712	3,124	2,473	82	33	651 R	54.7%	43.3%	1.4%
7,321	TUCKER	3,346	1,935	1,319	50	42	616 R	57.8%	39.4%	1.5%
9,592	TYLER	3,928	2,582	1,214	80	52	1,368 R	65.7%	30.9%	2.0%
23,404	UPSHUR	8,123	5,165	2,770	130	58	2,395 R	63.6%	34.1%	1.6%
42,903	WAYNE	16,241	7,993	7,940	182	126	53 R	49.2%	48.9%	1.1%
9,719	WEBSTER	3,308	1,484	1,764	35	25	280 D	44.9%	53.3%	1.1%
17,693	WETZEL	6,288	3,239	2,849	104	96	390 R	51.5%	45.3%	1.7%
5,873	WIRT	2,382	1,518	818	21	25	700 R	63.7%	34.3%	0.9%
87,986	WOOD	33,857	20,428	12,664	582	183	7,764 R	60.3%	37.4%	1.7%
25,708	WYOMING	7,878	3,473	4,289	66	50	816 D	44.1%	54.4%	0.8%
1,808,344	TOTAL	648,124	336,475	295,497	10,680	5,472	40,978 R	51.9%	45.6%	1.6%

WEST VIRGINIA

GOVERNOR 2000

2000 Census Population	County	Total Vote	Republican	Democratic	Other	Rep.-Dem. Plurality		Percentage			
								Total Vote		Major Vote	
								Rep.	Dem.	Rep.	Dem.
15,557	BARBOUR	6,071	2,900	3,052	119	152	D	47.8%	50.3%	48.7%	51.3%
75,905	BERKELEY	22,933	12,221	10,045	667	2,176	R	53.3%	43.8%	54.9%	45.1%
25,535	BOONE	9,194	2,865	6,193	136	3,328	D	31.2%	67.4%	31.6%	68.4%
14,702	BRAXTON	5,322	1,848	3,419	55	1,571	D	34.7%	64.2%	35.1%	64.9%
25,447	BROOKE	9,432	4,317	4,908	207	591	D	45.8%	52.0%	46.8%	53.2%
96,784	CABELL	32,226	15,661	15,190	1,375	471	R	48.6%	47.1%	50.8%	49.2%
7,582	CALHOUN	2,632	1,124	1,411	97	287	D	42.7%	53.6%	44.3%	55.7%
10,330	CLAY	3,619	1,420	2,115	84	695	D	39.2%	58.4%	40.2%	59.8%
7,403	DODDRIDGE	2,845	1,878	906	61	972	R	66.0%	31.8%	67.5%	32.5%
47,579	FAYETTE	14,674	5,520	8,746	408	3,226	D	37.6%	59.6%	38.7%	61.3%
7,160	GILMER	2,744	1,231	1,418	95	187	D	44.9%	51.7%	46.5%	53.5%
11,299	GRANT	4,470	3,453	957	60	2,496	R	77.2%	21.4%	78.3%	21.7%
34,453	GREENBRIER	12,806	6,443	5,896	467	547	R	50.3%	46.0%	52.2%	47.8%
20,203	HAMPSHIRE	6,072	3,648	2,245	179	1,403	R	60.1%	37.0%	61.9%	38.1%
32,667	HANCOCK	12,831	5,660	6,926	245	1,266	D	44.1%	54.0%	45.0%	55.0%
12,669	HARDY	4,444	2,991	1,377	76	1,614	R	67.3%	31.0%	68.5%	31.5%
68,652	HARRISON	26,585	11,606	14,417	562	2,811	D	43.7%	54.2%	44.6%	55.4%
28,000	JACKSON	11,542	5,157	6,155	230	998	D	44.7%	53.3%	45.6%	54.4%
42,190	JEFFERSON	14,221	6,598	6,772	851	174	D	46.4%	47.6%	49.3%	50.7%
200,073	KANAWHA	76,609	30,571	43,312	2,726	12,741	D	39.9%	56.5%	41.4%	58.6%
16,919	LEWIS	6,167	2,686	3,368	113	682	D	43.6%	54.6%	44.4%	55.6%
22,108	LINCOLN	7,495	2,841	4,498	156	1,657	D	37.9%	60.0%	38.7%	61.3%
37,710	LOGAN	14,725	5,889	8,692	144	2,803	D	40.0%	59.0%	40.4%	59.6%
27,329	MCDOWELL	7,354	3,570	3,723	61	153	D	48.5%	50.6%	49.0%	51.0%
56,598	MARION	22,708	9,207	13,078	423	3,871	D	40.5%	57.6%	41.3%	58.7%
35,519	MARSHALL	13,544	6,406	6,832	306	426	D	47.3%	50.4%	48.4%	51.6%
25,957	MASON	11,290	4,512	6,569	209	2,057	D	40.0%	58.2%	40.7%	59.3%
62,980	MERCER	18,858	9,786	8,728	344	1,058	R	51.9%	46.3%	52.9%	47.1%
27,078	MINERAL	9,762	5,525	4,022	215	1,503	R	56.6%	41.2%	57.9%	42.1%
28,253	MINGO	10,124	4,286	5,737	101	1,451	D	42.3%	56.7%	42.8%	57.2%
81,866	MONONGALIA	27,220	12,673	13,089	1,458	416	D	46.6%	48.1%	49.2%	50.8%
14,583	MONROE	5,148	2,721	2,301	126	420	R	52.9%	44.7%	54.2%	45.8%
14,943	MORGAN	5,635	3,240	2,219	176	1,021	R	57.5%	39.4%	59.4%	40.6%
26,562	NICHOLAS	8,652	3,366	5,144	142	1,778	D	38.9%	59.5%	39.6%	60.4%
47,427	OHIO	17,996	9,690	7,833	473	1,857	R	53.8%	43.5%	55.3%	44.7%
8,196	PENDLETON	3,160	1,834	1,285	41	549	R	58.0%	40.7%	58.8%	41.2%
7,514	PLEASANTS	3,216	1,886	1,286	44	600	R	58.6%	40.0%	59.5%	40.5%
9,131	POCAHONTAS	3,460	1,692	1,654	114	38	R	48.9%	47.8%	50.6%	49.4%
29,334	PRESTON	10,445	6,231	3,920	294	2,311	R	59.7%	37.5%	61.4%	38.6%
51,589	PUTNAM	20,585	9,969	9,991	625	22	D	48.4%	48.5%	49.9%	50.1%
79,220	RALEIGH	24,102	12,072	11,435	595	637	R	50.1%	47.4%	51.4%	48.6%
28,262	RANDOLPH	9,562	4,071	5,219	272	1,148	D	42.6%	54.6%	43.8%	56.2%
10,343	RITCHIE	3,831	2,524	1,210	97	1,314	R	65.9%	31.6%	67.6%	32.4%
15,446	ROANE	5,674	2,505	2,988	181	483	D	44.1%	52.7%	45.6%	54.4%
12,999	SUMMERS	4,730	2,459	2,145	126	314	R	52.0%	45.3%	53.4%	46.6%
16,089	TAYLOR	5,863	2,690	2,991	182	301	D	45.9%	51.0%	47.4%	52.6%
7,321	TUCKER	3,375	1,630	1,661	84	31	D	48.3%	49.2%	49.5%	50.5%
9,592	TYLER	3,950	2,921	960	69	1,961	R	73.9%	24.3%	75.3%	24.7%
23,404	UPSHUR	8,187	4,333	3,669	185	664	R	52.9%	44.8%	54.1%	45.9%
42,903	WAYNE	16,204	7,103	8,787	314	1,684	D	43.8%	54.2%	44.7%	55.3%
9,719	WEBSTER	3,334	1,084	2,204	46	1,120	D	32.5%	66.1%	33.0%	67.0%
17,693	WETZEL	6,353	3,292	2,962	99	330	R	51.8%	46.6%	52.6%	47.4%
5,873	WIRT	2,387	1,261	1,099	27	162	R	52.8%	46.0%	53.4%	46.6%
87,986	WOOD	33,813	19,474	13,673	666	5,801	R	57.6%	40.4%	58.8%	41.2%
25,708	WYOMING	7,866	3,385	4,390	91	1,005	D	43.0%	55.8%	43.5%	56.5%
1,808,344	TOTAL	648,047	305,926	324,822	17,299	18,896	D	47.2%	50.1%	48.5%	51.5%

WEST VIRGINIA

SENATOR 2000

2000 Census Population	County	Total Vote	Republican	Democratic	Other	Rep.-Dem. Plurality		Percentage			
								Total Vote		Major Vote	
								Rep.	Dem.	Rep.	Dem.
15,557	BARBOUR	5,892	1,123	4,698	71	3,575	D	19.1%	79.7%	19.3%	80.7%
75,905	BERKELEY	19,564	6,344	12,857	363	6,513	D	32.4%	65.7%	33.0%	67.0%
25,535	BOONE	9,005	1,057	7,824	124	6,767	D	11.7%	86.9%	11.9%	88.1%
14,702	BRAXTON	4,898	797	4,051	50	3,254	D	16.3%	82.7%	16.4%	83.6%
25,447	BROOKE	8,113	1,261	6,719	133	5,458	D	15.5%	82.8%	15.8%	84.2%
96,784	CABELL	30,898	6,618	23,559	721	16,941	D	21.4%	76.2%	21.9%	78.1%
7,582	CALHOUN	2,550	506	1,981	63	1,475	D	19.8%	77.7%	20.3%	79.7%
10,330	CLAY	3,508	620	2,827	61	2,207	D	17.7%	80.6%	18.0%	82.0%
7,403	DODDRIDGE	2,761	698	2,003	60	1,305	D	25.3%	72.5%	25.8%	74.2%
47,579	FAYETTE	13,451	2,112	11,098	241	8,986	D	15.7%	82.5%	16.0%	84.0%
7,160	GILMER	2,634	460	2,085	89	1,625	D	17.5%	79.2%	18.1%	81.9%
11,299	GRANT	3,939	1,419	2,480	40	1,061	D	36.0%	63.0%	36.4%	63.6%
34,453	GREENBRIER	12,545	2,440	9,750	355	7,310	D	19.4%	77.7%	20.0%	80.0%
20,203	HAMPSHIRE	5,908	1,850	3,925	133	2,075	D	31.3%	66.4%	32.0%	68.0%
32,667	HANCOCK	11,705	1,976	9,520	209	7,544	D	16.9%	81.3%	17.2%	82.8%
12,669	HARDY	4,223	917	3,259	47	2,342	D	21.7%	77.2%	22.0%	78.0%
68,652	HARRISON	26,187	3,684	22,041	462	18,357	D	14.1%	84.2%	14.3%	85.7%
28,000	JACKSON	11,265	2,690	8,337	238	5,647	D	23.9%	74.0%	24.4%	75.6%
42,190	JEFFERSON	12,386	3,481	8,648	257	5,167	D	28.1%	69.8%	28.7%	71.3%
200,073	KANAWHA	68,551	15,140	51,885	1,526	36,745	D	22.1%	75.7%	22.6%	77.4%
16,919	LEWIS	6,061	899	4,965	197	4,066	D	14.8%	81.9%	15.3%	84.7%
22,108	LINCOLN	7,282	1,440	5,693	149	4,253	D	19.8%	78.2%	20.2%	79.8%
37,710	LOGAN	11,964	1,426	10,401	137	8,975	D	11.9%	86.9%	12.1%	87.9%
27,329	MCDOWELL	7,100	519	6,370	211	5,851	D	7.3%	89.7%	7.5%	92.5%
56,598	MARION	21,831	2,813	18,708	310	15,895	D	12.9%	85.7%	13.1%	86.9%
35,519	MARSHALL	11,414	2,255	8,925	234	6,670	D	19.8%	78.2%	20.2%	79.8%
25,957	MASON	11,042	2,033	8,686	323	6,653	D	18.4%	78.7%	19.0%	81.0%
62,980	MERCER	16,596	4,159	12,071	366	7,912	D	25.1%	72.7%	25.6%	74.4%
27,078	MINERAL	9,639	2,321	7,167	151	4,846	D	24.1%	74.4%	24.5%	75.5%
28,253	MINGO	8,930	1,059	7,809	62	6,750	D	11.9%	87.4%	11.9%	88.1%
81,866	MONONGALIA	26,619	4,360	21,321	938	16,961	D	16.4%	80.1%	17.0%	83.0%
14,583	MONROE	5,065	1,202	3,745	118	2,543	D	23.7%	73.9%	24.3%	75.7%
14,943	MORGAN	4,966	1,765	3,155	46	1,390	D	35.5%	63.5%	35.9%	64.1%
26,562	NICHOLAS	8,436	1,438	6,835	163	5,397	D	17.0%	81.0%	17.4%	82.6%
47,427	OHIO	16,010	3,187	12,460	363	9,273	D	19.9%	77.8%	20.4%	79.6%
8,196	PENDLETON	2,997	711	2,260	26	1,549	D	23.7%	75.4%	23.9%	76.1%
7,514	PLEASANTS	3,072	601	2,435	36	1,834	D	19.6%	79.3%	19.8%	80.2%
9,131	POCAHONTAS	3,361	569	2,718	74	2,149	D	16.9%	80.9%	17.3%	82.7%
29,334	PRESTON	10,250	1,982	8,040	228	6,058	D	19.3%	78.4%	19.8%	80.2%
51,589	PUTNAM	18,354	5,192	12,813	349	7,621	D	28.3%	69.8%	28.8%	71.2%
79,220	RALEIGH	23,687	4,769	18,166	752	13,397	D	20.1%	76.7%	20.8%	79.2%
28,262	RANDOLPH	9,300	1,567	7,513	220	5,946	D	16.8%	80.8%	17.3%	82.7%
10,343	RITCHIE	3,717	874	2,759	84	1,885	D	23.5%	74.2%	24.1%	75.9%
15,446	ROANE	5,461	1,267	4,069	125	2,802	D	23.2%	74.5%	23.7%	76.3%
12,999	SUMMERS	4,612	830	3,651	131	2,821	D	18.0%	79.2%	18.5%	81.5%
16,089	TAYLOR	5,689	983	4,627	79	3,644	D	17.3%	81.3%	17.5%	82.5%
7,321	TUCKER	3,286	511	2,718	57	2,207	D	15.6%	82.7%	15.8%	84.2%
9,592	TYLER	3,820	803	2,939	78	2,136	D	21.0%	76.9%	21.5%	78.5%
23,404	UPSHUR	7,286	1,601	5,562	123	3,961	D	22.0%	76.3%	22.4%	77.6%
42,903	WAYNE	13,959	2,855	10,953	151	8,098	D	20.5%	78.5%	20.7%	79.3%
9,719	WEBSTER	3,252	347	2,847	58	2,500	D	10.7%	87.5%	10.9%	89.1%
17,693	WETZEL	5,695	1,109	4,508	78	3,399	D	19.5%	79.2%	19.7%	80.3%
5,873	WIRT	2,244	530	1,683	31	1,153	D	23.6%	75.0%	23.9%	76.1%
87,986	WOOD	33,095	7,374	25,007	714	17,633	D	22.3%	75.6%	22.8%	77.2%
25,708	WYOMING	7,402	1,091	6,089	222	4,998	D	14.7%	82.3%	15.2%	84.8%
1,808,344	TOTAL	603,477	121,635	469,215	12,627	347,580	D	20.2%	77.8%	20.6%	79.4%

WEST VIRGINIA

CONGRESS

CD	Year	Total Vote	Republican		Democratic		Other Vote	Rep.-Dem. Plurality	Percentage			
			Vote	Candidate	Vote	Candidate			Total Vote		Major Vote	
									Rep.	Dem.	Rep.	Dem.
1	2000	194,771			170,974	MOLLOHAN, ALAN B.	23,797	170,974 D		87.8%		100.0%
1	1998	124,114			105,101	MOLLOHAN, ALAN B.	19,013	105,101 D		84.7%		100.0%
1	1996	171,334			171,334	MOLLOHAN, ALAN B.		171,334 D		100.0%		100.0%
1	1994	146,767	43,590	RILEY, SALLY R.	103,177	MOLLOHAN, ALAN B.		59,587 D	29.7%	70.3%	29.7%	70.3%
1	1992	172,924			172,924	MOLLOHAN, ALAN B.		172,924 D		100.0%		100.0%
2	2000	224,315	108,769	CAPITO, SHELLEY MOORE	103,003	HUMPHREYS, JIM	12,543	5,766 R	48.5%	45.9%	51.4%	48.6%
2	1998	136,153	29,136	KAY, SALLY ANNE	99,357	WISE, ROBERT E.	7,660	70,221 D	21.4%	73.0%	22.7%	77.3%
2	1996	205,484	63,933	MORRIS, GREG	141,551	WISE, ROBERT E.		77,618 D	31.1%	68.9%	31.1%	68.9%
2	1994	142,448	51,691	CRAVOTTA, SAMUEL A.	90,757	WISE, ROBERT E.		39,066 D	36.3%	63.7%	36.3%	63.7%
2	1992	203,090	59,102	CRAVOTTA, SAMUEL A.	143,988	WISE, ROBERT E.		84,886 D	29.1%	70.9%	29.1%	70.9%
3	2000	160,786			146,807	RAHALL, NICK J.	13,979	146,807 D		91.3%		100.0%
3	1998	91,010			78,814	RAHALL, NICK J.	12,196	78,814 D		86.6%		100.0%
3	1996	145,550			145,550	RAHALL, NICK J.		145,550 D		100.0%		100.0%
3	1994	117,349	42,382	WALDMAN, BEN	74,967	RAHALL, NICK J.		32,585 D	36.1%	63.9%	36.1%	63.9%
3	1992	186,291	64,012	WALDMAN, BEN	122,279	RAHALL, NICK J.		58,267 D	34.4%	65.6%	34.4%	65.6%

WEST VIRGINIA

GENERAL AND PRIMARY ELECTIONS

2000 GENERAL ELECTIONS

President   3,169 Reform (Buchanan); 1,912 Libertarian (Browne); 367 Natural Law (Hagelin); 23 write-in (Phillips); 1 write-in (Strickland).

Governor   Other vote was 10,416 Mountain (Giardina); 5,548 Libertarian (Myers); 1,301 Natural Law (Ashelman); 34 write-in (Davis).

Senator   Other vote was 12,627 Libertarian (Whelan).

Congress   Other vote was: CD 1: 23,797 Libertarian (Kerr); CD 2: 12,543 Libertarian (Brown); CD 3: 13,979 Libertarian (Robinson).

2000 PRIMARY ELECTIONS

Primary   May 9, 2000

Registration (as of May 2, 2000)	Republican	291,151
	Democratic	634,560
	Libertarian	645
	Other	84,924
	TOTAL	1,011,280

Primary Type   Only registered Democrats could vote in the Democratic primary. Registered Republicans and those with no party registration could vote in the Republican primary.

Note: An asterisk (*) denotes incumbent.

WEST VIRGINIA

GENERAL AND PRIMARY ELECTIONS

	REPUBLICAN PRIMARIES			DEMOCRATIC PRIMARIES		
President	George W. Bush	87,050	79.6%	Al Gore	182,403	72.0%
	John McCain	14,121	12.9%	Bill Bradley	46,710	18.4%
	Alan Keyes	5,210	4.8%	Angus Wheeler McDonald	19,374	7.6%
	Steve Forbes	1,733	1.6%	Lyndon H. LaRouche Jr.	4,823	1.9%
	Gary Bauer	1,290	1.2%			
	TOTAL	109,404		TOTAL	253,310	
Governor	Cecil H. Underwood*	87,910	81.0%	Bob Wise	174,202	63.1%
	Joseph Oliverio	11,590	10.7%	Jim Lees	101,774	36.9%
	Donna H. McCase	5,902	5.4%			
	Larry Eugene Butcher	3,117	2.9%			
	TOTAL	108,519		TOTAL	275,976	
Senator	David T. Gallaher	42,446	52.0%	Robert C. Byrd*	251,438	100.0%
	Garry P. Adkins	39,254	48.0%			
	TOTAL	81,700		TOTAL	251,438	
Congressional District 1	No Republican candidate			Alan B. Mollohan*	79,036	100.0%
				TOTAL	79,036	
Congressional District 2	Shelley Moore Capito	33,667	100.0%	Jim Humphreys	37,810	43.3%
				Martha Yeager Walker	22,985	26.3%
				Ken Hechler	21,451	24.5%
				Beth Taylor	5,141	5.9%
	TOTAL	33,667		TOTAL	87,387	
Congressional District 3	No Republican candidate			Nick J. Rahall II*	87,959	100.0%
				TOTAL	87,959	

WISCONSIN

GOVERNOR
Scott McCallum (R). Became governor Feb. 2, 2001, on resignation of Tommy G. Thompson to become U.S. Secretary of Health and Human Services.

SENATORS
Russell D. Feingold (D). Re-elected 1998 to a six-year term. Previously elected 1992.

Herbert H. Kohl (D). Re-elected 2000 to a six-year term. Previously elected 1994, 1988.

REPRESENTATIVES
1. Paul Ryan (R)
2. Tammy Baldwin (D)
3. Ron Kind (D)
4. Gerald D. Kleczka (D)
5. Thomas M. Barrett (D)
6. Thomas E. Petri (R)
7. David R. Obey (D)
8. Mark Green (R)
9. F. James Sensenbrenner (R)

POSTWAR VOTE FOR PRESIDENT

Year	Total Vote	Republican Vote	Candidate	Democratic Vote	Candidate	Other Vote	Plurality	Total Vote Rep.	Total Vote Dem.	Major Vote Rep.	Major Vote Dem.
2000**	2,598,607	1,237,279	Bush, George W.	1,242,987	Gore, Al	118,341	5,708 D	47.6%	47.8%	49.9%	50.1%
1996**	2,196,169	845,029	Dole, Bob	1,071,971	Clinton, Bill	279,169	226,942 D	38.5%	48.8%	44.1%	55.9%
1992**	2,531,114	930,855	Bush, George	1,041,066	Clinton, Bill	559,193	110,211 D	36.8%	41.1%	47.2%	52.8%
1988	2,191,608	1,047,499	Bush, George	1,126,794	Dukakis, Michael S.	17,315	79,295 D	47.8%	51.4%	48.2%	51.8%
1984	2,211,689	1,198,584	Reagan, Ronald	995,740	Mondale, Walter F.	17,365	202,844 R	54.2%	45.0%	54.6%	45.4%
1980**	2,273,221	1,088,845	Reagan, Ronald	981,584	Carter, Jimmy	202,792	107,261 R	47.9%	43.2%	52.6%	47.4%
1976	2,104,175	1,004,987	Ford, Gerald R.	1,040,232	Carter, Jimmy	58,956	35,245 D	47.8%	49.4%	49.1%	50.9%
1972	1,852,890	989,430	Nixon, Richard M.	810,174	McGovern, George S.	53,286	179,256 R	53.4%	43.7%	55.0%	45.0%
1968	1,691,538	809,997	Nixon, Richard M.	748,804	Humphrey, Hubert H.	132,737	61,193 R	47.9%	44.3%	52.0%	48.0%
1964	1,691,815	638,495	Goldwater, Barry M.	1,050,424	Johnson, Lyndon B.	2,896	411,929 D	37.7%	62.1%	37.8%	62.2%
1960	1,729,082	895,175	Nixon, Richard M.	830,805	Kennedy, John F.	3,102	64,370 R	51.8%	48.0%	51.9%	48.1%
1956	1,550,558	954,844	Eisenhower, Dwight D.	586,768	Stevenson, Adlai E.	8,946	368,076 R	61.6%	37.8%	61.9%	38.1%
1952	1,607,370	979,744	Eisenhower, Dwight D.	622,175	Stevenson, Adlai E.	5,451	357,569 R	61.0%	38.7%	61.2%	38.8%
1948	1,276,800	590,959	Dewey, Thomas E.	647,310	Truman, Harry S.	38,531	56,351 D	46.3%	50.7%	47.7%	52.3%

In 2000 the other vote column includes 94,070 votes cast for Green (Nader). In 1996 the other vote column includes 227,339 votes cast for Perot. In 1992 the other vote column includes 544,479 votes cast for Perot. In 1980 the other column includes 160,657 votes for Independent (Anderson).

WISCONSIN

POSTWAR VOTE FOR GOVERNOR

Year	Total Vote	Republican Vote	Republican Candidate	Democratic Vote	Democratic Candidate	Other Vote	Rep.-Dem. Plurality	Total Vote Rep.	Total Vote Dem.	Major Vote Rep.	Major Vote Dem.
1998	1,756,014	1,047,716	Thompson, Tommy G.	679,553	Garvey, Edward R.	28,745	368,163 R	59.7%	38.7%	60.7%	39.3%
1994	1,563,835	1,051,326	Thompson, Tommy G.	482,850	Chvala, Chuck	29,659	568,476 R	67.2%	30.9%	68.5%	31.5%
1990	1,379,727	802,321	Thompson, Tommy G.	576,280	Loftus, Thomas	1,126	226,041 R	58.2%	41.8%	58.2%	41.8%
1986	1,526,960	805,090	Thompson, Tommy G.	705,578	Earl, Anthony S.	16,292	99,512 R	52.7%	46.2%	53.3%	46.7%
1982	1,580,344	662,838	Kohler, Terry J.	896,812	Earl, Anthony S.	20,694	233,974 D	41.9%	56.7%	42.5%	57.5%
1978	1,500,996	816,056	Dreyfus, Lee S.	673,813	Schreiber, Martin J.	11,127	142,243 R	54.4%	44.9%	54.8%	45.2%
1974	1,181,976	497,195	Dyke, William D.	628,639	Lucey, Patrick J.	56,142	131,444 D	42.1%	53.2%	44.2%	55.8%
1970**	1,343,160	602,617	Olson, Jack B.	728,403	Lucey, Patrick J.	12,140	125,786 D	44.9%	54.2%	45.3%	54.7%
1968	1,689,738	893,463	Knowles, Warren P.	791,100	LaFollette, Bronson C.	5,175	102,363 R	52.9%	46.8%	53.0%	47.0%
1966	1,170,173	626,041	Knowles, Warren P.	539,258	Lucey, Patrick J.	4,874	86,783 R	53.5%	46.1%	53.7%	46.3%
1964	1,694,887	856,779	Knowles, Warren P.	837,901	Reynolds, John W.	207	18,878 R	50.6%	49.4%	50.6%	49.4%
1962	1,265,900	625,536	Kuehn, Philip G.	637,491	Reynolds, John W.	2,873	11,955 D	49.4%	50.4%	49.5%	50.5%
1960	1,728,009	837,123	Kuehn, Philip G.	890,868	Nelson, Gaylord A.	18	53,745 D	48.4%	51.6%	48.4%	51.6%
1958	1,202,219	556,391	Thomson, Vernon W.	644,296	Nelson, Gaylord A.	1,532	87,905 D	46.3%	53.6%	46.3%	53.7%
1956	1,557,788	808,273	Thomson, Vernon W.	749,421	Proxmire, William	94	58,852 R	51.9%	48.1%	51.9%	48.1%
1954	1,158,666	596,158	Kohler, Walter J.	560,747	Proxmire, William	1,761	35,411 R	51.5%	48.4%	51.5%	48.5%
1952	1,615,214	1,009,171	Kohler, Walter J.	601,844	Proxmire, William	4,199	407,327 R	62.5%	37.3%	62.6%	37.4%
1950	1,138,148	605,649	Kohler, Walter J.	525,319	Thompson, Carl W.	7,180	80,330 R	53.2%	46.2%	53.6%	46.4%
1948	1,266,139	684,839	Rennebohm, Oscar	558,497	Thompson, Carl W.	22,803	126,342 R	54.1%	44.1%	55.1%	44.9%
1946	1,040,444	621,970	Goodland, Walter	406,499	Hoan, Daniel W.	11,975	215,471 R	59.8%	39.1%	60.5%	39.5%

The term of office of Wisconsin's Governor was increased from two to four years effective with the 1970 election.

POSTWAR VOTE FOR SENATOR

Year	Total Vote	Republican Vote	Republican Candidate	Democratic Vote	Democratic Candidate	Other Vote	Rep.-Dem. Plurality	Total Vote Rep.	Total Vote Dem.	Major Vote Rep.	Major Vote Dem.
2000	2,540,083	940,744	Gillespie, John	1,563,238	Kohl, Herbert H.	36,101	622,494 D	37.0%	61.5%	37.6%	62.4%
1998	1,760,836	852,272	Neumann, Mark W.	890,059	Feingold, Russell D.	18,505	37,787 D	48.4%	50.5%	48.9%	51.1%
1994	1,565,628	636,989	Welch, Robert T.	912,662	Kohl, Herbert H.	15,977	175,673 D	40.7%	58.3%	41.1%	58.9%
1992	2,455,124	1,129,599	Kasten, Robert W.	1,290,662	Feingold, Russell D.	34,863	161,063 D	46.0%	52.6%	46.7%	53.3%
1988	2,168,190	1,030,440	Engeleiter, Susan	1,128,625	Kohl, Herbert H.	9,125	98,185 D	47.5%	52.1%	47.7%	52.3%
1986	1,483,174	754,573	Kasten, Robert W.	702,963	Garvey, Edward R.	25,638	51,610 R	50.9%	47.4%	51.8%	48.2%
1982	1,544,981	527,355	McCallum, Scott	983,311	Proxmire, William	34,315	455,956 D	34.1%	63.6%	34.9%	65.1%
1980	2,204,202	1,106,311	Kasten, Robert W.	1,065,487	Nelson, Gaylord A.	32,404	40,824 R	50.2%	48.3%	50.9%	49.1%
1976	1,935,183	521,902	York, Stanley	1,396,970	Proxmire, William	16,311	875,068 D	27.0%	72.2%	27.2%	72.8%
1974	1,199,495	429,327	Petri, Thomas E.	740,700	Nelson, Gaylord A.	29,468	311,373 D	35.8%	61.8%	36.7%	63.3%
1970	1,338,967	381,297	Erickson, John E.	948,445	Proxmire, William	9,225	567,148 D	28.5%	70.8%	28.7%	71.3%
1968	1,654,861	633,910	Leonard, Jerris	1,020,931	Nelson, Gaylord A.	20	387,021 D	38.3%	61.7%	38.3%	61.7%
1964	1,673,776	780,116	Renk, Wilbur N.	892,013	Proxmire, William	1,647	111,897 D	46.6%	53.3%	46.7%	53.3%
1962	1,260,168	594,846	Wiley, Alexander	662,342	Nelson, Gaylord A.	2,980	67,496 D	47.2%	52.6%	47.3%	52.7%
1958	1,194,678	510,398	Steinle, Roland J.	682,440	Proxmire, William	1,840	172,042 D	42.7%	57.1%	42.8%	57.2%
1957S	772,620	312,931	Kohler, Walter J.	435,985	Proxmire, William	23,704	123,054 D	40.5%	56.4%	41.8%	58.2%
1956	1,523,356	892,473	Wiley, Alexander	627,903	Maier, Henry W.	2,980	264,570 R	58.6%	41.2%	58.7%	41.3%
1952	1,605,228	870,444	McCarthy, Joseph R.	731,402	Fairchild, Thomas E.	3,382	139,042 R	54.2%	45.6%	54.3%	45.7%
1950	1,116,135	595,283	Wiley, Alexander	515,539	Fairchild, Thomas E.	5,313	79,744 R	53.3%	46.2%	53.6%	46.4%
1946	1,014,594	620,430	McCarthy, Joseph R.	378,772	McMurray, Howard J.	15,392	241,658 R	61.2%	37.3%	62.1%	37.9%

The August 1957 election was for a short term to fill a vacancy.

WISCONSIN

Districts Established May 12, 1992

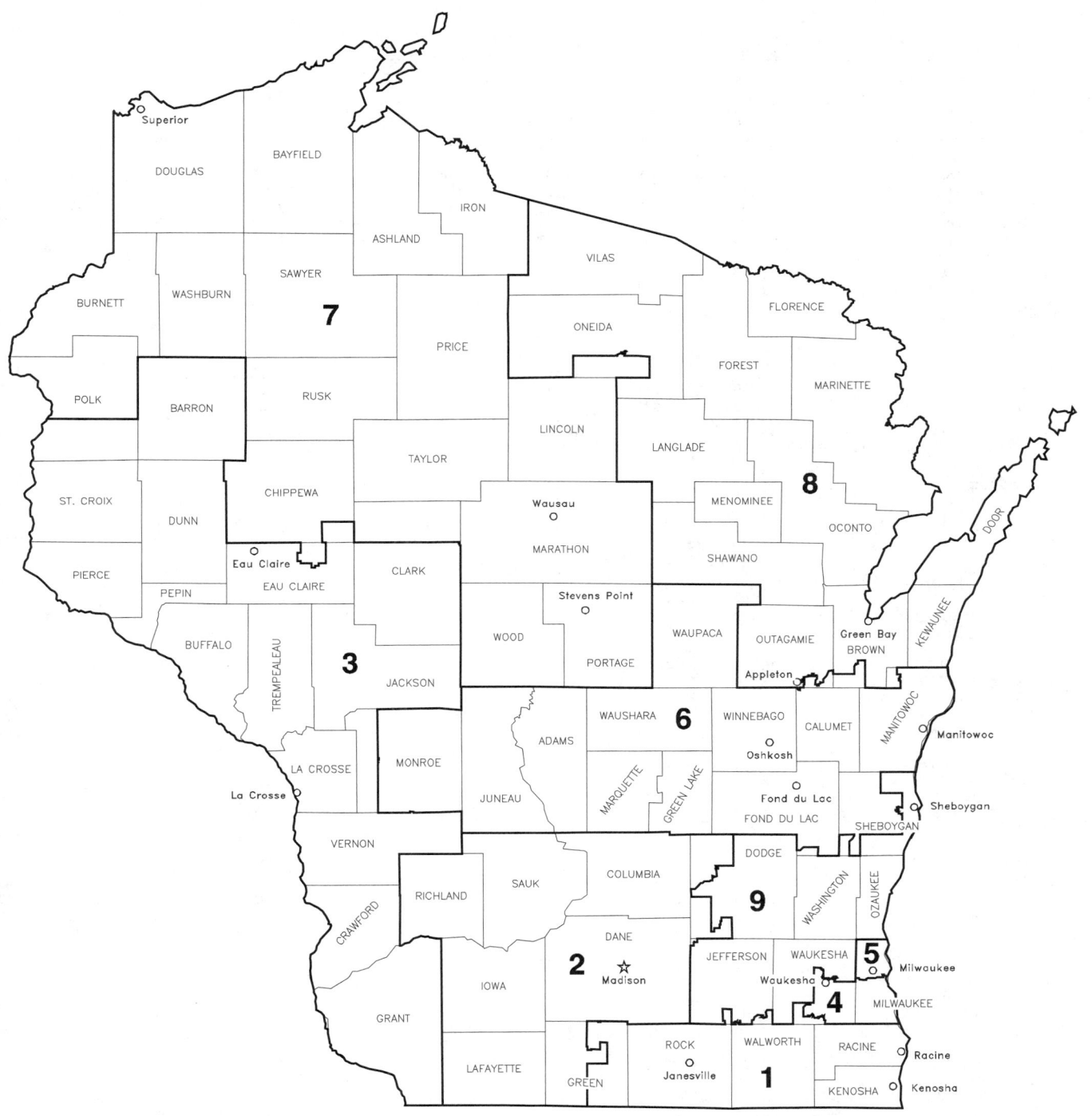

WISCONSIN

PRESIDENT 2000

2000 Census Population	County	Total Vote	Republican	Democratic	Green (Nader)	Other	Rep.-Dem. Plurality	Percentage of Total Vote		
								Rep.	Dem.	Green
18,643	ADAMS	9,116	3,920	4,826	217	153	906 D	43.0%	52.9%	2.4%
16,866	ASHLAND	7,890	3,038	4,356	440	56	1,318 D	38.5%	55.2%	5.6%
44,963	BARRON	19,904	9,848	8,928	1,009	119	920 R	49.5%	44.9%	5.1%
15,013	BAYFIELD	8,259	3,266	4,427	511	55	1,161 D	39.5%	53.6%	6.2%
226,778	BROWN	107,769	54,258	49,096	3,311	1,104	5,162 R	50.3%	45.6%	3.1%
13,804	BUFFALO	6,641	3,038	3,237	316	50	199 D	45.7%	48.7%	4.8%
15,674	BURNETT	8,151	3,967	3,626	499	59	341 R	48.7%	44.5%	6.1%
40,631	CALUMET	19,947	10,837	8,202	658	250	2,635 R	54.3%	41.1%	3.3%
55,195	CHIPPEWA	26,173	12,835	12,102	973	263	733 R	49.0%	46.2%	3.7%
33,557	CLARK	14,149	7,461	5,931	521	236	1,530 R	52.7%	41.9%	3.7%
52,468	COLUMBIA	25,587	11,987	12,636	790	174	649 D	46.8%	49.4%	3.1%
17,243	CRAWFORD	7,394	3,024	4,005	309	56	981 D	40.9%	54.2%	4.2%
426,526	DANE	232,739	75,790	142,317	13,030	1,602	66,527 D	32.6%	61.1%	5.6%
85,897	DODGE	37,701	21,684	14,580	1,098	339	7,104 R	57.5%	38.7%	2.9%
27,961	DOOR	15,220	7,810	6,560	709	141	1,250 R	51.3%	43.1%	4.7%
43,287	DOUGLAS	21,706	6,930	13,593	975	208	6,663 D	31.9%	62.6%	4.5%
39,858	DUNN	19,330	8,911	9,172	1,109	138	261 D	46.1%	47.4%	5.7%
93,142	EAU CLAIRE	47,875	20,921	24,078	2,461	415	3,157 D	43.7%	50.3%	5.1%
5,088	FLORENCE	2,405	1,528	816	48	13	712 R	63.5%	33.9%	2.0%
97,296	FOND DU LAC	46,589	26,548	18,181	1,389	471	8,367 R	57.0%	39.0%	3.0%
10,024	FOREST	4,716	2,404	2,158	126	28	246 R	51.0%	45.8%	2.7%
49,597	GRANT	21,956	10,240	10,691	858	167	451 D	46.6%	48.7%	3.9%
33,647	GREEN	15,276	6,790	7,863	493	130	1,073 D	44.4%	51.5%	3.2%
19,105	GREEN LAKE	9,107	5,451	3,301	282	73	2,150 R	59.9%	36.2%	3.1%
22,780	IOWA	10,541	4,221	5,842	429	49	1,621 D	40.0%	55.4%	4.1%
6,861	IRON	3,507	1,734	1,620	134	19	114 R	49.4%	46.2%	3.8%
19,100	JACKSON	8,417	3,670	4,380	290	77	710 D	43.6%	52.0%	3.4%
74,021	JEFFERSON	36,099	19,204	15,203	1,361	331	4,001 R	53.2%	42.1%	3.8%
24,316	JUNEAU	10,218	4,910	4,813	297	198	97 R	48.1%	47.1%	2.9%
149,577	KENOSHA	63,709	28,891	32,429	1,852	537	3,538 D	45.3%	50.9%	2.9%
20,187	KEWAUNEE	10,084	4,883	4,670	388	143	213 R	48.4%	46.3%	3.8%
107,120	LA CROSSE	55,559	24,327	28,455	2,272	505	4,128 D	43.8%	51.2%	4.1%
16,137	LAFAYETTE	7,263	3,336	3,710	185	32	374 D	45.9%	51.1%	2.5%
20,740	LANGLADE	9,721	5,125	4,199	261	136	926 R	52.7%	43.2%	2.7%
29,641	LINCOLN	14,239	6,727	6,664	509	339	63 R	47.2%	46.8%	3.6%
82,887	MANITOWOC	38,824	19,358	17,667	1,301	498	1,691 R	49.9%	45.5%	3.4%
125,834	MARATHON	58,374	28,883	26,546	2,021	924	2,337 R	49.5%	45.5%	3.5%
43,384	MARINETTE	19,921	10,535	8,676	504	206	1,859 R	52.9%	43.6%	2.5%
15,832	MARQUETTE	7,194	3,522	3,437	195	40	85 R	49.0%	47.8%	2.7%
4,562	MENOMINEE	1,233	225	949	47	12	724 D	18.2%	77.0%	3.8%
940,164	MILWAUKEE	433,537	163,491	252,329	13,953	3,764	88,838 D	37.7%	58.2%	3.2%
40,899	MONROE	16,335	8,217	7,460	489	169	757 R	50.3%	45.7%	3.0%
35,634	OCONTO	16,596	8,706	7,260	437	193	1,446 R	52.5%	43.7%	2.6%
36,776	ONEIDA	18,891	9,512	8,339	805	235	1,173 R	50.4%	44.1%	4.3%
160,971	OUTAGAMIE	75,742	39,460	32,735	2,583	964	6,725 R	52.1%	43.2%	3.4%
82,317	OZAUKEE	47,751	31,155	15,030	1,235	331	16,125 R	65.2%	31.5%	2.6%
7,213	PEPIN	3,664	1,631	1,854	152	27	223 D	44.5%	50.6%	4.1%
36,804	PIERCE	17,962	8,169	8,559	1,076	158	390 D	45.5%	47.7%	6.0%
41,319	POLK	19,762	9,557	8,961	1,084	160	596 R	48.4%	45.3%	5.5%
67,182	PORTAGE	33,760	13,214	17,942	2,143	461	4,728 D	39.1%	53.1%	6.3%
15,822	PRICE	7,930	4,136	3,413	313	68	723 R	52.2%	43.0%	3.9%
188,831	RACINE	88,865	44,014	41,563	2,436	852	2,451 R	49.5%	46.8%	2.7%
17,924	RICHLAND	8,293	3,994	3,837	388	74	157 R	48.2%	46.3%	4.7%
152,307	ROCK	70,404	27,467	40,472	1,980	485	13,005 D	39.0%	57.5%	2.8%
15,347	RUSK	7,366	3,758	3,161	346	101	597 R	51.0%	42.9%	4.7%
63,155	ST. CROIX	29,954	15,240	13,077	1,369	268	2,163 R	50.9%	43.7%	4.6%
55,225	SAUK	25,653	11,586	13,035	858	174	1,449 D	45.2%	50.8%	3.3%
16,196	SAWYER	7,767	3,972	3,333	398	64	639 R	51.1%	42.9%	5.1%
40,664	SHAWANO	17,603	9,548	7,335	532	188	2,213 R	54.2%	41.7%	3.0%
112,646	SHEBOYGAN	55,201	29,648	23,569	1,487	497	6,079 R	53.7%	42.7%	2.7%

WISCONSIN

PRESIDENT 2000

2000 Census Population	County	Total Vote	Republican	Democratic	Green (Nader)	Other	Rep.-Dem. Plurality	Percentage of Total Vote		
								Rep.	Dem.	Green
19,680	TAYLOR	8,992	5,278	3,254	318	142	2,024 R	58.7%	36.2%	3.5%
27,010	TREMPEALEAU	12,168	5,002	6,678	409	79	1,676 D	41.1%	54.9%	3.4%
28,056	VERNON	13,044	5,684	6,577	676	107	893 D	43.6%	50.4%	5.2%
21,033	VILAS	12,322	6,958	4,706	557	101	2,252 R	56.5%	38.2%	4.5%
93,759	WALWORTH	40,458	22,982	15,492	1,582	402	7,490 R	56.8%	38.3%	3.9%
16,036	WASHBURN	8,045	3,912	3,695	380	58	217 R	48.6%	45.9%	4.7%
117,493	WASHINGTON	61,412	41,162	18,115	1,563	572	23,047 R	67.0%	29.5%	2.5%
360,767	WAUKESHA	203,734	133,105	64,319	4,864	1,446	68,786 R	65.3%	31.6%	2.4%
51,731	WAUPACA	22,804	12,980	8,787	822	215	4,193 R	56.9%	38.5%	3.6%
23,154	WAUSHARA	10,248	5,571	4,239	310	128	1,332 R	54.4%	41.4%	3.0%
156,763	WINNEBAGO	76,080	38,330	33,983	2,963	804	4,347 R	50.4%	44.7%	3.9%
75,555	WOOD	35,761	17,803	15,936	1,384	638	1,867 R	49.8%	44.6%	3.9%
5,363,675	TOTAL	2,598,607	1,237,279	1,242,987	94,070	24,271	5,708 D	47.6%	47.8%	3.6%

WISCONSIN

SENATOR 2000

2000 Census Population	County	Total Vote	Republican	Democratic	Other	Rep.-Dem. Plurality	Percentage			
							Total Vote		Major Vote	
							Rep.	Dem.	Rep.	Dem.
18,643	ADAMS	8,874	2,994	5,752	128	2,758 D	33.7%	64.8%	34.2%	65.8%
16,866	ASHLAND	7,247	1,650	5,470	127	3,820 D	22.8%	75.5%	23.2%	76.8%
44,963	BARRON	18,774	7,214	11,395	165	4,181 D	38.4%	60.7%	38.8%	61.2%
15,013	BAYFIELD	7,840	2,010	5,772	58	3,762 D	25.6%	73.6%	25.8%	74.2%
226,778	BROWN	105,657	44,493	59,789	1,375	15,296 D	42.1%	56.6%	42.7%	57.3%
13,804	BUFFALO	6,008	1,934	4,014	60	2,080 D	32.2%	66.8%	32.5%	67.5%
15,674	BURNETT	7,580	2,970	4,486	124	1,516 D	39.2%	59.2%	39.8%	60.2%
40,631	CALUMET	19,365	9,740	9,410	215	330 R	50.3%	48.6%	50.9%	49.1%
55,195	CHIPPEWA	25,842	7,957	17,426	459	9,469 D	30.8%	67.4%	31.3%	68.7%
33,557	CLARK	13,748	4,803	8,739	206	3,936 D	34.9%	63.6%	35.5%	64.5%
52,468	COLUMBIA	25,197	8,746	16,043	408	7,297 D	34.7%	63.7%	35.3%	64.7%
17,243	CRAWFORD	7,067	2,034	4,949	84	2,915 D	28.8%	70.0%	29.1%	70.9%
426,526	DANE	228,216	51,948	171,946	4,322	119,998 D	22.8%	75.3%	23.2%	76.8%
85,897	DODGE	37,304	17,204	19,588	512	2,384 D	46.1%	52.5%	46.8%	53.2%
27,961	DOOR	15,019	6,425	8,372	222	1,947 D	42.8%	55.7%	43.4%	56.6%
43,287	DOUGLAS	21,257	4,350	16,481	426	12,131 D	20.5%	77.5%	20.9%	79.1%
39,858	DUNN	18,051	5,835	11,867	349	6,032 D	32.3%	65.7%	33.0%	67.0%
93,142	EAU CLAIRE	46,813	13,908	32,043	862	18,135 D	29.7%	68.4%	30.3%	69.7%
5,088	FLORENCE	2,192	1,067	1,106	19	39 D	48.7%	50.5%	49.1%	50.9%
97,296	FOND DU LAC	45,864	20,964	24,336	564	3,372 D	45.7%	53.1%	46.3%	53.7%
10,024	FOREST	4,369	1,133	3,194	42	2,061 D	25.9%	73.1%	26.2%	73.8%
49,597	GRANT	20,806	7,470	13,099	237	5,629 D	35.9%	63.0%	36.3%	63.7%
33,647	GREEN	15,050	4,585	10,264	201	5,679 D	30.5%	68.2%	30.9%	69.1%
19,105	GREEN LAKE	8,962	4,576	4,276	110	300 R	51.1%	47.7%	51.7%	48.3%
22,780	IOWA	10,185	3,074	7,019	92	3,945 D	30.2%	68.9%	30.5%	69.5%
6,861	IRON	3,275	1,059	2,195	21	1,136 D	32.3%	67.0%	32.5%	67.5%
19,100	JACKSON	8,161	2,449	5,631	81	3,182 D	30.0%	69.0%	30.3%	69.7%
74,021	JEFFERSON	35,582	15,800	19,284	498	3,484 D	44.4%	54.2%	45.0%	55.0%
24,316	JUNEAU	9,748	4,114	5,542	92	1,428 D	42.2%	56.9%	42.6%	57.4%
149,577	KENOSHA	60,979	20,613	39,332	1,034	18,719 D	33.8%	64.5%	34.4%	65.6%
20,187	KEWAUNEE	9,959	4,472	5,357	130	885 D	44.9%	53.8%	45.5%	54.5%
107,120	LA CROSSE	54,684	16,199	37,730	755	21,531 D	29.6%	69.0%	30.0%	70.0%
16,137	LAFAYETTE	7,002	2,280	4,687	35	2,407 D	32.6%	66.9%	32.7%	67.3%
20,740	LANGLADE	9,329	3,301	5,931	97	2,630 D	35.4%	63.6%	35.8%	64.2%
29,641	LINCOLN	14,059	3,767	9,980	312	6,213 D	26.8%	71.0%	27.4%	72.6%

WISCONSIN

SENATOR 2000

2000 Census Population	County	Total Vote	Republican	Democratic	Other	Rep.-Dem. Plurality		Percentage			
								Total Vote		Major Vote	
								Rep.	Dem.	Rep.	Dem.
82,887	MANITOWOC	37,771	15,826	21,323	622	5,497	D	41.9%	56.5%	42.6%	57.4%
125,834	MARATHON	57,734	18,612	38,294	828	19,682	D	32.2%	66.3%	32.7%	67.3%
43,384	MARINETTE	19,131	8,357	10,546	228	2,189	D	43.7%	55.1%	44.2%	55.8%
15,832	MARQUETTE	7,047	3,031	3,968	48	937	D	43.0%	56.3%	43.3%	56.7%
4,562	MENOMINEE	1,158	207	922	29	715	D	17.9%	79.6%	18.3%	81.7%
940,164	MILWAUKEE	424,996	120,373	299,236	5,387	178,863	D	28.3%	70.4%	28.7%	71.3%
40,899	MONROE	15,720	5,945	9,555	220	3,610	D	37.8%	60.8%	38.4%	61.6%
35,634	OCONTO	16,353	7,372	8,796	185	1,424	D	45.1%	53.8%	45.6%	54.4%
36,776	ONEIDA	18,233	6,043	11,736	454	5,693	D	33.1%	64.4%	34.0%	66.0%
160,971	OUTAGAMIE	74,264	38,564	34,719	981	3,845	R	51.9%	46.8%	52.6%	47.4%
82,317	OZAUKEE	47,244	24,908	21,848	488	3,060	R	52.7%	46.2%	53.3%	46.7%
7,213	PEPIN	3,363	990	2,325	48	1,335	D	29.4%	69.1%	29.9%	70.1%
36,804	PIERCE	16,937	6,100	10,398	439	4,298	D	36.0%	61.4%	37.0%	63.0%
41,319	POLK	18,354	7,443	10,631	280	3,188	D	40.6%	57.9%	41.2%	58.8%
67,182	PORTAGE	32,742	9,574	22,520	648	12,946	D	29.2%	68.8%	29.8%	70.2%
15,822	PRICE	7,439	2,455	4,939	45	2,484	D	33.0%	66.4%	33.2%	66.8%
188,831	RACINE	87,771	33,637	53,167	967	19,530	D	38.3%	60.6%	38.8%	61.2%
17,924	RICHLAND	7,677	3,012	4,608	57	1,596	D	39.2%	60.0%	39.5%	60.5%
152,307	ROCK	69,395	20,232	48,149	1,014	27,917	D	29.2%	69.4%	29.6%	70.4%
15,347	RUSK	6,962	2,353	4,484	125	2,131	D	33.8%	64.4%	34.4%	65.6%
63,155	ST. CROIX	28,758	12,242	15,547	969	3,305	D	42.6%	54.1%	44.1%	55.9%
55,225	SAUK	25,327	8,433	16,519	375	8,086	D	33.3%	65.2%	33.8%	66.2%
16,196	SAWYER	7,328	3,183	4,078	67	895	D	43.4%	55.6%	43.8%	56.2%
40,664	SHAWANO	17,003	7,910	8,914	179	1,004	D	46.5%	52.4%	47.0%	53.0%
112,646	SHEBOYGAN	54,486	22,987	30,914	585	7,927	D	42.2%	56.7%	42.6%	57.4%
19,680	TAYLOR	8,785	2,998	5,514	273	2,516	D	34.1%	62.8%	35.2%	64.8%
27,010	TREMPEALEAU	11,550	3,415	8,007	128	4,592	D	29.6%	69.3%	29.9%	70.1%
28,056	VERNON	12,540	4,216	8,213	111	3,997	D	33.6%	65.5%	33.9%	66.1%
21,033	VILAS	12,067	4,717	7,172	178	2,455	D	39.1%	59.4%	39.7%	60.3%
93,759	WALWORTH	39,956	18,077	20,959	920	2,882	D	45.2%	52.5%	46.3%	53.7%
16,036	WASHBURN	7,641	2,982	4,577	82	1,595	D	39.0%	59.9%	39.4%	60.6%
117,493	WASHINGTON	60,481	33,091	26,722	668	6,369	R	54.7%	44.2%	55.3%	44.7%
360,767	WAUKESHA	201,209	105,901	93,306	2,002	12,595	R	52.6%	46.4%	53.2%	46.8%
51,731	WAUPACA	22,118	12,281	9,669	168	2,612	R	55.5%	43.7%	55.9%	44.1%
23,154	WAUSHARA	9,828	4,865	4,840	123	25	R	49.5%	49.2%	50.1%	49.9%
156,763	WINNEBAGO	75,009	33,519	40,200	1,290	6,681	D	44.7%	53.6%	45.5%	54.5%
75,555	WOOD	35,641	11,755	23,418	468	11,663	D	33.0%	65.7%	33.4%	66.6%
5,363,675	TOTAL	2,540,083	940,744	1,563,238	36,101	622,494	D	37.0%	61.5%	37.6%	62.4%

WISCONSIN

CONGRESS

			Republican		Democratic		Other	Rep.-Dem.	Percentage			
		Total							Total Vote		Major Vote	
CD	Year	Vote	Vote	Candidate	Vote	Candidate	Vote	Plurality	Rep.	Dem.	Rep.	Dem.
1	2000	266,791	177,612	RYAN, PAUL D.	88,885	THOMAS, JEFFREY C.	294	88,727 R	66.6%	33.3%	66.6%	33.4%
1	1998	189,946	108,475	RYAN, PAUL D.	81,164	SPOTTSWOOD, LYDIA C.	307	27,311 R	57.1%	42.7%	57.2%	42.8%
1	1996	232,801	118,408	NEUMANN, MARK W.	114,148	SPOTTSWOOD, LYDIA C.	245	4,260 R	50.9%	49.0%	50.9%	49.1%
1	1994	169,855	83,937	NEUMANN, MARK W.	82,817	BARCA, PETER W.	3,101	1,120 R	49.4%	48.8%	50.3%	49.7%
1	1992	256,280	104,352	NEUMANN, MARK W.	147,495	ASPIN, LES	4,433	43,143 D	40.7%	57.6%	41.4%	58.6%
2	2000	318,380	154,632	SHARPLESS, JOHN	163,534	BALDWIN, TAMMY	214	8,902 D	48.6%	51.4%	48.6%	51.4%
2	1998	221,693	103,528	MUSSER, JOSEPHINE W.	116,377	BALDWIN, TAMMY	1,788	12,849 D	46.7%	52.5%	47.1%	52.9%
2	1996	269,374	154,557	KLUG, SCOTT L.	110,467	SOGLIN, PAUL R.	4,350	44,090 R	57.4%	41.0%	58.3%	41.7%
2	1994	193,249	133,734	KLUG, SCOTT L.	55,406	HECHT, THOMAS C.	4,109	78,328 R	69.2%	28.7%	70.7%	29.3%
2	1992	292,898	183,366	KLUG, SCOTT L.	108,291	DEER, ADA E.	1,241	75,075 R	62.6%	37.0%	62.9%	37.1%
3	2000	272,212	97,741	TULLY, SUSAN	173,505	KIND, RON	966	75,764 D	35.9%	63.7%	36.0%	64.0%
3	1998	179,448	51,001	BRECHLER, TROY A.	128,256	KIND, RON	191	77,255 D	28.4%	71.5%	28.5%	71.5%
3	1996	234,650	112,146	HARSDORF, JAMES E.	121,967	KIND, RON	537	9,821 D	47.8%	52.0%	47.9%	52.1%
3	1994	160,313	89,338	GUNDERSON, STEVEN	65,758	STOWER, HARVEY	5,217	23,580 R	55.7%	41.0%	57.6%	42.4%
3	1992	260,335	146,903	GUNDERSON, STEVEN	108,664	SACIA, PAUL	4,768	38,239 R	56.4%	41.7%	57.5%	42.5%
4	2000	269,265	101,811	RIENER, TIM	163,622	KLECZKA, GERALD D.	3,832	61,811 D	37.8%	60.8%	38.4%	61.6%
4	1998	182,701	76,666	REYNOLDS, TOM	105,841	KLECZKA, GERALD D.	194	29,175 D	42.0%	57.9%	42.0%	58.0%
4	1996	233,284	98,438	REYNOLDS, TOM	134,470	KLECZKA, GERALD D.	376	36,032 D	42.2%	57.6%	42.3%	57.7%
4	1994	174,689	78,225	REYNOLDS, TOM	93,789	KLECZKA, GERALD D.	2,675	15,564 D	44.8%	53.7%	45.5%	54.5%
4	1992	263,803	84,872	COOK, JOSEPH L.	173,482	KLECZKA, GERALD D.	5,449	88,610 D	32.2%	65.8%	32.9%	67.1%
5	2000	223,852	49,296	SMITH, JONATHAN	173,893	BARRETT, THOMAS M.	663	124,597 D	22.0%	77.7%	22.1%	77.9%
5	1998	154,861	33,506	MELVIN, JACK	121,129	BARRETT, THOMAS M.	226	87,623 D	21.6%	78.2%	21.7%	78.3%
5	1996	192,569	47,384	MELOTIK, PAUL D.	141,179	BARRETT, THOMAS M.	4,006	93,795 D	24.6%	73.3%	25.1%	74.9%
5	1994	140,640	51,145	HOLLINGSHEAD, STEPHEN B.	87,806	BARRETT, THOMAS M.	1,689	36,661 D	36.4%	62.4%	36.8%	63.2%
5	1992	234,176	71,085	HAMMERSMITH, DONALDA A.	162,344	BARRETT, THOMAS M.	747	91,259 D	30.4%	69.3%	30.5%	69.5%
6	2000	275,605	179,205	PETRI, THOMAS E.	96,125	FLAHERTY, DAN	275	83,080 R	65.0%	34.9%	65.1%	34.9%
6	1998	155,669	144,144	PETRI, THOMAS E.			11,525	144,144 R	92.6%		100.0%	
6	1996	231,719	169,213	PETRI, THOMAS E.	55,377	LINDSKOOG, AL	7,129	113,836 R	73.0%	23.9%	75.3%	24.7%
6	1994	119,987	119,384	PETRI, THOMAS E.			603	119,384 R	99.5%		100.0%	
6	1992	272,137	143,875	PETRI, THOMAS E.	128,232	LAUTENSCHLAGER, PEGGY A.	30	15,643 R	52.9%	47.1%	52.9%	47.1%
7	2000	273,460	100,264	CRONIN, SEAN	173,007	OBEY, DAVID R.	189	72,743 D	36.7%	63.3%	36.7%	63.3%
7	1998	190,865	75,049	WEST, SCOTT	115,613	OBEY, DAVID R.	203	40,564 D	39.3%	60.6%	39.4%	60.6%
7	1996	240,898	103,365	WEST, SCOTT	137,428	OBEY, DAVID R.	105	34,063 D	42.9%	57.0%	42.9%	57.1%
7	1994	178,921	81,706	WEST, SCOTT	97,184	OBEY, DAVID R.	31	15,478 D	45.7%	54.3%	45.7%	54.3%
7	1992	257,982	91,772	VANNES, DALE R.	166,200	OBEY, DAVID R.	10	74,428 D	35.6%	64.4%	35.6%	64.4%
8	2000	283,294	211,388	GREEN, MARK	71,575	REICH, DEAN	331	139,813 R	74.6%	25.3%	74.7%	25.3%
8	1998	205,974	112,418	GREEN, MARK	93,441	JOHNSON, JAY	115	18,977 R	54.6%	45.4%	54.6%	45.4%
8	1996	249,157	119,398	PROSSER, DAVID	129,551	JOHNSON, JAY	208	10,153 D	47.9%	52.0%	48.0%	52.0%
8	1994	179,460	114,319	ROTH, TOBY	65,065	GRUSZYNSKI, STAN	76	49,254 R	63.7%	36.3%	63.7%	36.3%
8	1992	273,532	191,704	ROTH, TOBY	81,792	HELMS, CATHERINE L.	36	109,912 R	70.1%	29.9%	70.1%	29.9%
9	2000	323,455	239,498	SENSENBRENNER, F. JAMES	83,720	CLAWSON, MIKE	237	155,778 R	74.0%	25.9%	74.1%	25.9%
9	1998	192,318	175,533	SENSENBRENNER, F. JAMES			16,785	175,533 R	91.3%		100.0%	
9	1996	265,875	197,910	SENSENBRENNER, F. JAMES	67,740	BRENHOLT, FLOYD	225	130,170 R	74.4%	25.5%	74.5%	25.5%
9	1994	141,953	141,617	SENSENBRENNER, F. JAMES			336	141,617 R	99.8%		100.0%	
9	1992	276,787	192,898	SENSENBRENNER, F. JAMES	77,362	BUXTON, INGRID K.	6,527	115,536 R	69.7%	28.0%	71.4%	28.6%

WISCONSIN

GENERAL AND PRIMARY ELECTIONS

2000 GENERAL ELECTIONS

President   Other vote 11,471 Reform (Buchanan); 6,640 Libertarian (Browne); 2,042 Constitution (Phillips); 1,063 Workers World (Moorehead); 853 Reform (Hagelin); 306 Socialist Workers (Harris); 1,896 scattered write-in.

Senator   Other vote was 21,348 Libertarian (Peterson); 9,555 Independent (Hem); 4,296 Constitution (Raymond); 902 scattered write-in.

Congress   Other vote was: CD 1: 294 scattered write-in; CD 2: 214 scattered write-in; CD 3: 966 scattered write-in; CD 4: 3,705 Libertarian (Rajnovic), 127 scattered write-in; CD 5: 663 scattered write-in; CD 6: 275 scattered write-in; CD 7: 189 scattered write-in; CD 8: 331 scattered write-in; CD 9: 237 scattered write-in.

2000 PRIMARY ELECTIONS

Primary   April 4, 2000   (President)   No Statewide Registration
                September 12, 2000   (Congress)

Primary Type   Open—Any registered voter could vote in the primary of either party in municipalities where registration is required. Elsewhere, a voter must merely be a resident of voting age.

Note: An asterisk (*) denotes incumbent.

	REPUBLICAN PRIMARIES			DEMOCRATIC PRIMARIES		
President	George W. Bush	343,292	69.2%	Al Gore	328,682	88.5%
	John McCain	89,684	18.1%	Bill Bradley	32,560	8.8%
	Alan Keyes	48,919	9.9%	Uninstructed Delegation	4,105	1.1%
	Steve Forbes	5,505	1.1%	Lyndon H. LaRouche Jr.	3,743	1.0%
	Uninstructed Delegation	3,452	0.7%	Write-in	2,106	0.6%
	Gary Bauer	1,813	0.4%			
	Orrin G. Hatch	1,712	0.3%			
	Write-in	1,392	0.3%			
	TOTAL	495,769		TOTAL	371,196	
Senator	John Gillespie	135,364	68.0%	Herbert H. Kohl*	184,920	89.8%
	Bill Lorge	41,026	20.6%	Jim Sigl	20,858	10.1%
	Marc Gumz	21,698	10.9%	Write-in	203	0.1%
	Write-in	851	0.4%			
	TOTAL	198,939		TOTAL	205,981	
Congressional District 1	Paul D. Ryan*	15,915	99.9%	Jeffrey C. Thomas	9,859	60.4%
	Write-in	15	0.1%	John Graf	6,459	39.6%
				Write-in	12	0.1%
	TOTAL	15,930		TOTAL	16,330	
Congressional District 2	John Sharpless	18,344	99.8%	Tammy Baldwin*	25,467	99.5%
	Write-in	37	0.2%	Write-in	128	0.5%
	TOTAL	18,381		TOTAL	25,595	
Congressional District 3	Susan Tully	23,921	99.8%	Ron Kind*	22,192	99.8%
	Write-in	45	0.2%	Write-in	50	0.2%
	TOTAL	23,966		TOTAL	22,242	
Congressional District 4	Tim Riener	4,513	70.7%	Gerald D. Kleczka*	12,765	99.4%
	Roman R. Blenski	1,859	29.1%	Write-in	73	0.6%
	Write-in	15	0.2%			
	TOTAL	6,387		TOTAL	12,838	
Congressional District 5	Jonathan Smith	3,172	99.3%	Thomas M. Barrett*	11,082	99.5%
	Write-in	21	0.7%	Write-in	55	0.5%
	TOTAL	3,193		TOTAL	11,137	

WISCONSIN

GENERAL AND PRIMARY ELECTIONS

	REPUBLICAN PRIMARIES			DEMOCRATIC PRIMARIES		
Congressional District 6	Tom Petri*	31,113	86.8%	Dan Flaherty	10,607	99.9%
	John L. Moder	4,713	13.2%	Write-in	12	0.1%
	Write-in	11				
	TOTAL	35,837		TOTAL	10,619	
Congressional District 7	Sean Cronin	15,948	99.8%	David R. Obey*	29,099	99.9%
	Write-in	38	0.2%	Write-in	42	0.1%
	TOTAL	15,986		TOTAL	29,141	
Congressional District 8	Mark Green*	63,726	99.9%	Dean Reich	30,792	99.7%
	Write-in	95	0.1%	Write-in	103	0.3%
	TOTAL	63,821		TOTAL	30,895	
Congressional District 9	F. James Sensenbrenner Jr.*	20,295	99.7%	Mike Clawson	6,949	99.9%
	Write-in	70	0.3%	Write-in	4	0.1%
	TOTAL	20,365		TOTAL	6,953	

WYOMING

GOVERNOR
Jim Geringer (R). Re-elected 1998 to a four-year term. Previously elected 1994.

SENATORS
Michael B. Enzi (R). Elected 1996 to a six-year term.

Craig Thomas (R). Elected 2000 to a six-year term. Previously elected 1994.

REPRESENTATIVE
At-Large. Barbara Cubin (R)

POSTWAR VOTE FOR PRESIDENT

Year	Total Vote	Republican Vote	Republican Candidate	Democratic Vote	Democratic Candidate	Other Vote	Plurality	Total Vote Rep.	Total Vote Dem.	Major Vote Rep.	Major Vote Dem.
2000**	218,351	147,947	Bush, George W.	60,481	Gore, Al	9,923	87,466 R	67.8%	27.7%	71.0%	29.0%
1996**	211,571	105,388	Dole, Bob	77,934	Clinton, Bill	28,249	27,454 R	49.8%	36.8%	57.5%	42.5%
1992**	200,598	79,347	Bush, George	68,160	Clinton, Bill	53,091	11,187 R	39.6%	34.0%	53.8%	46.2%
1988	176,551	106,867	Bush, George	67,113	Dukakis, Michael S.	2,571	39,754 R	60.5%	38.0%	61.4%	38.6%
1984	188,968	133,241	Reagan, Ronald	53,370	Mondale, Walter F.	2,357	79,871 R	70.5%	28.2%	71.4%	28.6%
1980**	176,713	110,700	Reagan, Ronald	49,427	Carter, Jimmy	16,586	61,273 R	62.6%	28.0%	69.1%	30.9%
1976	156,343	92,717	Ford, Gerald R.	62,239	Carter, Jimmy	1,387	30,478 R	59.3%	39.8%	59.8%	40.2%
1972	145,570	100,464	Nixon, Richard M.	44,358	McGovern, George S.	748	56,106 R	69.0%	30.5%	69.4%	30.6%
1968	127,205	70,927	Nixon, Richard M.	45,173	Humphrey, Hubert H.	11,105	25,754 R	55.8%	35.5%	61.1%	38.9%
1964	142,716	61,998	Goldwater, Barry M.	80,718	Johnson, Lyndon B.		18,720 D	43.4%	56.6%	43.4%	56.6%
1960	140,782	77,451	Nixon, Richard M.	63,331	Kennedy, John F.		14,120 R	55.0%	45.0%	55.0%	45.0%
1956	124,127	74,573	Eisenhower, Dwight D.	49,554	Stevenson, Adlai E.		25,019 R	60.1%	39.9%	60.1%	39.9%
1952	129,253	81,049	Eisenhower, Dwight D.	47,934	Stevenson, Adlai E.	270	33,115 R	62.7%	37.1%	62.8%	37.2%
1948	101,425	47,947	Dewey, Thomas E.	52,354	Truman, Harry S.	1,124	4,407 D	47.3%	51.6%	47.8%	52.2%

In 2000 the other vote column includes 4,625 votes cast for Green (Nader). In 1996 the other vote column includes 25,928 votes cast for Perot. In 1992 the other vote column includes 51,263 votes cast for Perot. In 1980 the other column includes 12,072 votes for Independent (Anderson).

POSTWAR VOTE FOR GOVERNOR

Year	Total Vote	Republican Vote	Republican Candidate	Democratic Vote	Democratic Candidate	Other Vote	Rep.-Dem. Plurality	Total Vote Rep.	Total Vote Dem.	Major Vote Rep.	Major Vote Dem.
1998	174,888	97,235	Geringer, Jim	70,754	Vinich, John P.	6,899	26,481 R	55.6%	40.5%	57.9%	42.1%
1994	200,990	118,016	Geringer, Jim	80,747	Karpan, Kathy	2,227	37,269 R	58.7%	40.2%	59.4%	40.6%
1990	160,109	55,471	Mead, Mary	104,638	Sullivan, Mike		49,167 D	34.6%	65.4%	34.6%	65.4%
1986	164,720	75,841	Simpson, Peter	88,879	Sullivan, Mike		13,038 D	46.0%	54.0%	46.0%	54.0%
1982	168,555	62,128	Morton, Warren A.	106,427	Herschler, Ed		44,299 D	36.9%	63.1%	36.9%	63.1%
1978	137,567	67,595	Ostlund, John C.	69,972	Herschler, Ed		2,377 D	49.1%	50.9%	49.1%	50.9%
1974	128,386	56,645	Jones, Dick	71,741	Herschler, Ed		15,096 D	44.1%	55.9%	44.1%	55.9%
1970	118,257	74,249	Hathaway, Stan	44,008	Rooney, John J.		30,241 R	62.8%	37.2%	62.8%	37.2%
1966	120,873	65,624	Hathaway, Stan	55,249	Wilkerson, Ernest		10,375 R	54.3%	45.7%	54.3%	45.7%
1962	119,268	64,970	Hansen, Clifford P.	54,298	Gage, Jack R.		10,672 R	54.5%	45.5%	54.5%	45.5%
1958	112,537	52,488	Simpson, Milward L.	55,070	Hickey, J. J.	4,979	2,582 D	46.6%	48.9%	48.8%	51.2%
1954	111,438	56,275	Simpson, Milward L.	55,163	Jack, William		1,112 R	50.5%	49.5%	50.5%	49.5%
1950	96,959	54,441	Barrett, Frank A.	42,518	McIntyre, John J.		11,923 R	56.1%	43.9%	56.1%	43.9%
1946	81,353	38,333	Wright, Earl	43,020	Hunt, Lester C.		4,687 D	47.1%	52.9%	47.1%	52.9%

WYOMING

POSTWAR VOTE FOR SENATOR

Year	Total Vote	Republican Vote	Republican Candidate	Democratic Vote	Democratic Candidate	Other Vote	Rep.-Dem. Plurality	Total Vote Rep.	Total Vote Dem.	Major Vote Rep.	Major Vote Dem.
2000	213,659	157,622	Thomas, Craig	47,087	Logan, Mel	8,950	110,535 R	73.8%	22.0%	77.0%	23.0%
1996	211,077	114,116	Enzi, Michael B.	89,103	Karpan, Kathy	7,858	25,013 R	54.1%	42.2%	56.2%	43.8%
1994	201,710	118,754	Thomas, Craig	79,287	Sullivan, Mike	3,669	39,467 R	58.9%	39.3%	60.0%	40.0%
1990	157,632	100,784	Simpson, Alan K.	56,848	Helling, Kathy		43,936 R	63.9%	36.1%	63.9%	36.1%
1988	180,964	91,143	Wallop, Malcolm	89,821	Vinich, John P.		1,322 R	50.4%	49.6%	50.4%	49.6%
1984	186,898	146,373	Simpson, Alan K.	40,525	Ryan, Victor A.		105,848 R	78.3%	21.7%	78.3%	21.7%
1982	167,191	94,725	Wallop, Malcolm	72,466	McDaniel, Rodger		22,259 R	56.7%	43.3%	56.7%	43.3%
1978	133,364	82,908	Simpson, Alan K.	50,456	Whitaker, Raymond B.		32,452 R	62.2%	37.8%	62.2%	37.8%
1976	155,368	84,810	Wallop, Malcolm	70,558	McGee, Gale		14,252 R	54.6%	45.4%	54.6%	45.4%
1972	142,067	101,314	Hansen, Clifford P.	40,753	Vinich, Mike		60,561 R	71.3%	28.7%	71.3%	28.7%
1970	120,486	53,279	Wold, John S.	67,207	McGee, Gale		13,928 D	44.2%	55.8%	44.2%	55.8%
1966	122,689	63,548	Hansen, Clifford P.	59,141	Roncalio, Teno		4,407 R	51.8%	48.2%	51.8%	48.2%
1964	141,670	65,185	Wold, John S.	76,485	McGee, Gale		11,300 D	46.0%	54.0%	46.0%	54.0%
1962S	119,372	69,043	Simpson, Milward L.	50,329	Hickey, J. J.		18,714 R	57.8%	42.2%	57.8%	42.2%
1960	138,550	78,103	Thomson, E. Keith	60,447	Whitaker, Ray		17,656 R	56.4%	43.6%	56.4%	43.6%
1958	114,157	56,122	Barrett, Frank A.	58,035	McGee, Gale		1,913 D	49.2%	50.8%	49.2%	50.8%
1954	112,252	54,407	Harrison, William H.	57,845	O'Mahoney, Joseph C.		3,438 D	48.5%	51.5%	48.5%	51.5%
1952	130,097	67,176	Barrett, Frank A.	62,921	O'Mahoney, Joseph C.		4,255 R	51.6%	48.4%	51.6%	48.4%
1948	101,480	43,527	Robertson, Edward V.	57,953	Hunt, Lester C.		14,426 D	42.9%	57.1%	42.9%	57.1%
1946	81,557	35,714	Henderson, Harry B.	45,843	O'Mahoney, Joseph C.		10,129 D	43.8%	56.2%	43.8%	56.2%

The 1962 election was for a short term to fill a vacancy.

WYOMING

One At Large

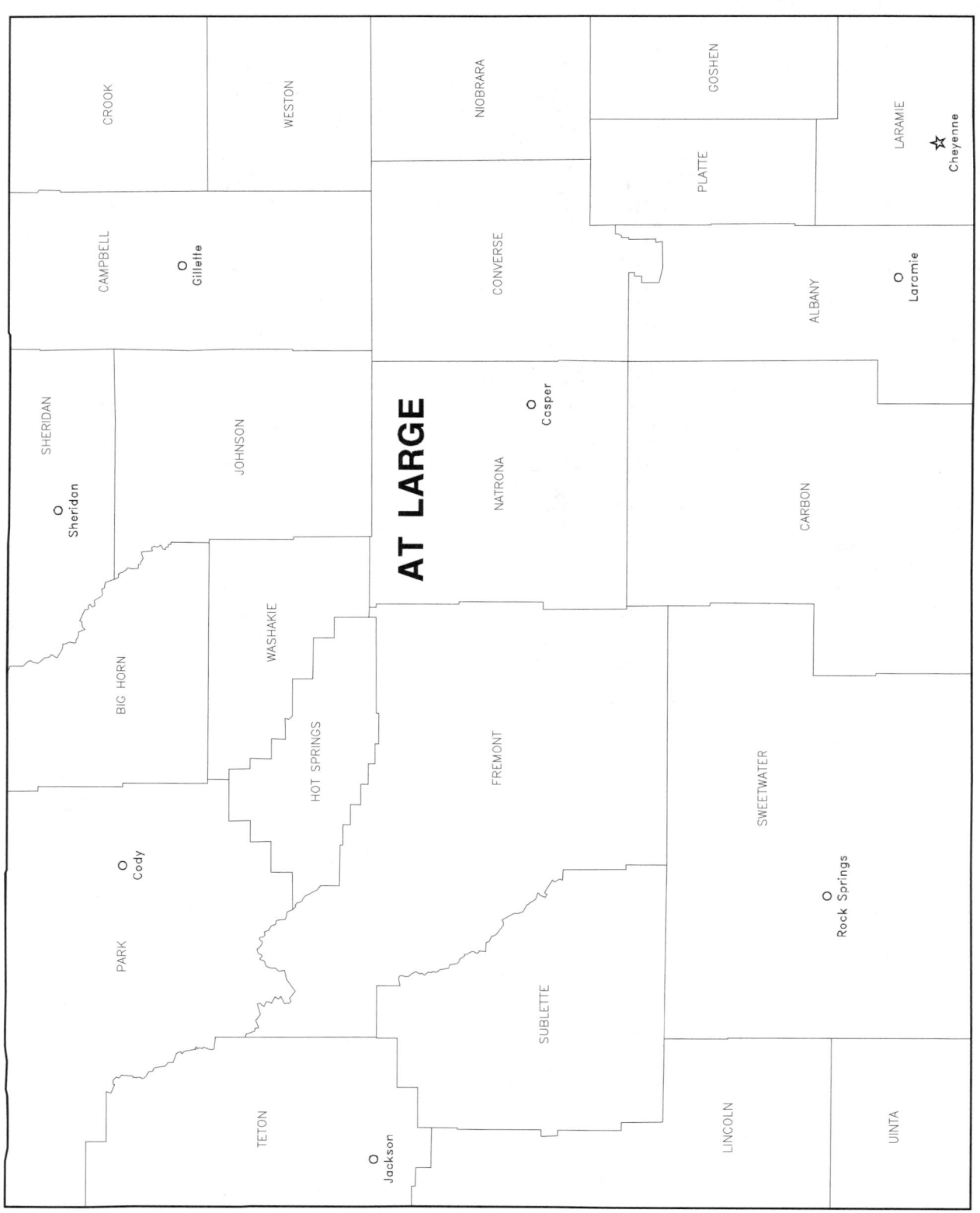

WYOMING

PRESIDENT 2000

2000 Census Population	County	Total Vote	Republican	Democratic	Green (Nader)	Other	Rep.-Dem. Plurality	Percentage of Total Vote		
								Rep.	Dem.	Green
32,014	ALBANY	14,151	7,814	5,069	988	280	2,745 R	55.2%	35.8%	7.0%
11,461	BIG HORN	4,918	3,720	1,004	40	154	2,716 R	75.6%	20.4%	0.8%
33,698	CAMPBELL	12,540	10,203	1,967	86	284	8,236 R	81.4%	15.7%	0.7%
15,639	CARBON	6,968	4,498	2,206	105	159	2,292 R	64.6%	31.7%	1.5%
12,052	CONVERSE	5,175	3,919	1,076	32	148	2,843 R	75.7%	20.8%	0.6%
5,887	CROOK	2,738	2,289	361	32	56	1,928 R	83.6%	13.2%	1.2%
35,804	FREMONT	15,444	10,560	4,172	304	408	6,388 R	68.4%	27.0%	2.0%
12,538	GOSHEN	5,520	3,922	1,439	27	132	2,483 R	71.1%	26.1%	0.5%
4,882	HOT SPRINGS	2,352	1,733	544	13	62	1,189 R	73.7%	23.1%	0.6%
7,075	JOHNSON	3,550	2,886	555	33	76	2,331 R	81.3%	15.6%	0.9%
81,607	LARAMIE	35,323	21,797	12,162	608	756	9,635 R	61.7%	34.4%	1.7%
14,573	LINCOLN	6,845	5,415	1,184	83	163	4,231 R	79.1%	17.3%	1.2%
66,533	NATRONA	28,388	18,439	8,646	590	713	9,793 R	65.0%	30.5%	2.1%
2,407	NIOBRARA	1,127	888	190	16	33	698 R	78.8%	16.9%	1.4%
25,786	PARK	12,836	9,884	2,424	227	301	7,460 R	77.0%	18.9%	1.8%
8,807	PLATTE	4,373	2,925	1,249	69	130	1,676 R	66.9%	28.6%	1.6%
26,560	SHERIDAN	12,236	8,424	3,330	208	274	5,094 R	68.8%	27.2%	1.7%
5,920	SUBLETTE	3,216	2,624	458	47	87	2,166 R	81.6%	14.2%	1.5%
37,613	SWEETWATER	15,691	9,425	5,521	222	523	3,904 R	60.1%	35.2%	1.4%
18,251	TETON	10,431	5,454	4,019	764	194	1,435 R	52.3%	38.5%	7.3%
19,742	UINTA	7,418	5,469	1,650	76	223	3,819 R	73.7%	22.2%	1.0%
8,289	WASHAKIE	4,051	3,138	806	29	78	2,332 R	77.5%	19.9%	0.7%
6,644	WESTON	3,060	2,521	449	26	64	2,072 R	82.4%	14.7%	0.8%
493,782	TOTAL	218,351	147,947	60,481	4,625	5,298	87,466 R	67.8%	27.7%	2.1%

Note: The votes cast for Nader were write-ins.

WYOMING

SENATOR 2000

2000 Census Population	County	Total Vote	Republican	Democratic	Other	Rep.-Dem. Plurality	Percentage			
							Total Vote		Major Vote	
							Rep.	Dem.	Rep.	Dem.
32,014	ALBANY	13,768	8,884	4,106	778	4,778 R	64.5%	29.8%	68.4%	31.6%
11,461	BIG HORN	4,771	3,972	598	201	3,374 R	83.3%	12.5%	86.9%	13.1%
33,698	CAMPBELL	11,996	10,005	1,557	434	8,448 R	83.4%	13.0%	86.5%	13.5%
15,639	CARBON	6,878	4,775	1,791	312	2,984 R	69.4%	26.0%	72.7%	27.3%
12,052	CONVERSE	5,180	4,125	887	168	3,238 R	79.6%	17.1%	82.3%	17.7%
5,887	CROOK	2,740	2,330	316	94	2,014 R	85.0%	11.5%	88.1%	11.9%
35,804	FREMONT	15,203	11,293	3,299	611	7,994 R	74.3%	21.7%	77.4%	22.6%
12,538	GOSHEN	5,221	4,014	1,036	171	2,978 R	76.9%	19.8%	79.5%	20.5%
4,882	HOT SPRINGS	2,191	1,769	359	63	1,410 R	80.7%	16.4%	83.1%	16.9%
7,075	JOHNSON	3,232	2,828	316	88	2,512 R	87.5%	9.8%	89.9%	10.1%
81,607	LARAMIE	34,844	24,230	9,314	1,300	14,916 R	69.5%	26.7%	72.2%	27.8%
14,573	LINCOLN	6,801	5,519	1,075	207	4,444 R	81.1%	15.8%	83.7%	16.3%
66,533	NATRONA	27,926	20,274	6,312	1,340	13,962 R	72.6%	22.6%	76.3%	23.7%
2,407	NIOBRARA	1,085	929	120	36	809 R	85.6%	11.1%	88.6%	11.4%
25,786	PARK	12,731	10,421	1,890	420	8,531 R	81.9%	14.8%	84.6%	15.4%
8,807	PLATTE	4,346	3,263	874	209	2,389 R	75.1%	20.1%	78.9%	21.1%
26,560	SHERIDAN	12,177	8,803	2,729	645	6,074 R	72.3%	22.4%	76.3%	23.7%
5,920	SUBLETTE	2,696	2,265	329	102	1,936 R	84.0%	12.2%	87.3%	12.7%
37,613	SWEETWATER	15,510	10,072	4,728	710	5,344 R	64.9%	30.5%	68.1%	31.9%
18,251	TETON	9,919	6,443	2,949	527	3,494 R	65.0%	29.7%	68.6%	31.4%
19,742	UINTA	7,484	5,613	1,544	327	4,069 R	75.0%	20.6%	78.4%	21.6%
8,289	WASHAKIE	3,883	3,209	568	106	2,641 R	82.6%	14.6%	85.0%	15.0%
6,644	WESTON	3,077	2,586	390	101	2,196 R	84.0%	12.7%	86.9%	13.1%
493,782	TOTAL	213,659	157,622	47,087	8,950	110,535 R	73.8%	22.0%	77.0%	23.0%

WYOMING

CONGRESS

CD	Year	Total Vote	Republican Vote	Republican Candidate	Democratic Vote	Democratic Candidate	Other Vote	Rep.-Dem. Plurality	Percentage Total Vote Rep.	Dem.	Major Vote Rep.	Dem.
AL	2000	212,312	141,848	CUBIN, BARBARA	60,638	GREEN, MICHAEL ALLEN	9,826	81,210 R	66.8%	28.6%	70.1%	29.9%
AL	1998	174,219	100,687	CUBIN, BARBARA	67,399	FARRIS, SCOTT	6,133	33,288 R	57.8%	38.7%	59.9%	40.1%
AL	1996	209,983	116,004	CUBIN, BARBARA	85,724	MAXFIELD, PETE	8,255	30,280 R	55.2%	40.8%	57.5%	42.5%
AL	1994	196,197	104,426	CUBIN, BARBARA	81,022	SCHUSTER, BOB	10,749	23,404 R	53.2%	41.3%	56.3%	43.7%
AL	1992	196,977	113,882	THOMAS, CRAIG	77,418	HERSCHLER, JON	5,677	36,464 R	57.8%	39.3%	59.5%	40.5%
AL	1990	158,055	87,078	THOMAS, CRAIG	70,977	MAXFIELD, PETE		16,101 R	55.1%	44.9%	55.1%	44.9%
AL	1988	177,651	118,350	CHENEY, RICHARD	56,527	SHARRATT, BRYAN	2,774	61,823 R	66.6%	31.8%	67.7%	32.3%
AL	1986	159,787	111,007	CHENEY, RICHARD	48,780	GILMORE, RICK		62,227 R	69.5%	30.5%	69.5%	30.5%
AL	1984	187,904	138,234	CHENEY, RICHARD	45,857	MCFADDEN, HUGH B.	3,813	92,377 R	73.6%	24.4%	75.1%	24.9%
AL	1982	159,277	113,236	CHENEY, RICHARD	46,041	HOMMEL, THEODORE H.		67,195 R	71.1%	28.9%	71.1%	28.9%
AL	1980	169,699	116,361	CHENEY, RICHARD	53,338	ROGERS, JIM		63,023 R	68.6%	31.4%	68.6%	31.4%
AL	1978	129,377	75,855	CHENEY, RICHARD	53,522	BAGLEY, BILL		22,333 R	58.6%	41.4%	58.6%	41.4%
AL	1976	151,868	66,147	HART, LARRY	85,721	RONCALIO, TENO		19,574 D	43.6%	56.4%	43.6%	56.4%
AL	1974	126,933	57,499	STROOCK, TOM	69,434	RONCALIO, TENO		11,935 D	45.3%	54.7%	45.3%	54.7%
AL	1972	146,299	70,667	KIDD, WILLIAM	75,632	RONCALIO, TENO		4,965 D	48.3%	51.7%	48.3%	51.7%
AL	1970	116,304	57,848	ROBERTS, HARRY	58,456	RONCALIO, TENO		608 D	49.7%	50.3%	49.7%	50.3%
AL	1968	123,313	77,363	WOLD, JOHN S.	45,950	LINFORD, VELMA		31,413 R	62.7%	37.3%	62.7%	37.3%
AL	1966	119,426	62,984	HARRISON, WILLIAM H.	56,442	CHRISTIAN, AL		6,542 R	52.7%	47.3%	52.7%	47.3%
AL	1964	139,175	68,482	HARRISON, WILLIAM H.	70,693	RONCALIO, TENO		2,211 D	49.2%	50.8%	49.2%	50.8%
AL	1962	116,474	71,489	HARRISON, WILLIAM H.	44,985	MANKUS, LOUIS A.		26,504 R	61.4%	38.6%	61.4%	38.6%
AL	1960	134,331	70,241	HARRISON, WILLIAM H.	64,090	ARMSTRONG, H. T	6,151	6,151 R	52.3%	47.7%	52.3%	47.7%
AL	1958	111,780	59,894	THOMSON, E. KEITH	51,886	WHITAKER, RAY		8,008 R	53.6%	46.4%	53.6%	46.4%
AL	1956	120,128	69,903	THOMSON, E. KEITH	50,225	O'CALLAGHAN, JERRY		19,678 R	58.2%	41.8%	58.2%	41.8%
AL	1954	108,771	61,111	THOMSON, E. KEITH	47,660	TULLY, SAM		13,451 R	56.2%	43.8%	56.2%	43.8%
AL	1952	126,720	76,161	HARRISON, WILLIAM H.	50,559	ROSE, ROBERT R		25,602 R	60.1%	39.9%	60.1%	39.9%
AL	1950	93,348	50,865	HARRISON, WILLIAM H.	42,483	CLARK, JOHN B.		8,382 R	54.5%	45.5%	54.5%	45.5%
AL	1948	97,464	50,218	BARRETT, FRANK A.	47,246	FLANNERY, L. G.		2,972 R	51.5%	48.5%	51.5%	48.5%
AL	1946	79,438	44,482	BARRETT, FRANK A.	34,956	MCINTYRE, JOHN J.		9,526 R	56.0%	44.0%	56.0%	44.0%

WYOMING

GENERAL AND PRIMARY ELECTIONS

2000 GENERAL ELECTIONS

President Other vote was 2,724 Reform (Buchanan); 1,443 Libertarian (Browne); 720 Independent (Phillips); 411 Natural Law (Hagelin). The write-in vote for Nader was tallied at Nader's request, and was not included in the certified returns.

Senator Other vote was 8,950 Libertarian (Dawson).

Congress Other vote was 6,411 Libertarian (Stock); 3,415 Natural Law (Raymond).

2000 PRIMARY ELECTIONS

Primary August 22, 2000

Registration (as of Aug. 18, 2000)

Republican	124,030
Democratic	61,169
Libertarian	202
Other Parties	19
Other	20,685
TOTAL	206,105

WYOMING

GENERAL AND PRIMARY ELECTIONS

Primary Type — Only registered Democrats and Republicans could vote in their party's primary, although on primary day any new voter could register in the party of their choice and any previously registered voter could participate in another party's primary by changing their registration to that party.

Note: An asterisk (*) denotes incumbent.

	REPUBLICAN PRIMARIES			DEMOCRATIC PRIMARIES		
Senator	Craig Thomas*	68,132	100.0%	Mel Logan	16,530	64.6%
				Sheldon Sumey	9,062	35.4%
	TOTAL	68,132		TOTAL	25,592	
Congressional At-large	Barbara Cubin*	54,946	77.8%	Michael Allen Green	14,219	53.1%
	Larry Jay Herdt	10,148	14.4%	Leonard D. Munker	12,555	46.9%
	Dino Wenino	5,515	7.8%			
	TOTAL	70,609		TOTAL	26,774	

DISTRICT OF COLUMBIA

DELEGATE

Eleanor Holmes Norton (D). Re-elected 2000 to a two-year term. Previously elected 1998, 1996, 1994, 1992, 1990.

POSTWAR VOTE FOR PRESIDENT

Year	Total Vote	Republican		Democratic		Other Vote	Plurality	Percentage			
								Total Vote		Major Vote	
		Vote	Candidate	Vote	Candidate			Rep.	Dem.	Rep.	Dem.
2000**	201,894	18,073	Bush, George W.	171,923	Gore, Al	11,898	153,850 D	9.0%	85.2%	9.5%	90.5%
1996**	185,726	17,339	Dole, Bob	158,220	Clinton, Bill	10,167	140,881 D	9.3%	85.2%	9.9%	90.1%
1992**	227,572	20,698	Bush, George	192,619	Clinton, Bill	14,255	171,921 D	9.1%	84.6%	9.7%	90.3%
1988	192,877	27,590	Bush, George	159,407	Dukakis, Michael S.	5,880	131,817 D	14.3%	82.6%	14.8%	85.2%
1984	211,288	29,009	Reagan, Ronald	180,408	Mondale, Walter F.	1,871	151,399 D	13.7%	85.4%	13.9%	86.1%
1980**	175,237	23,545	Reagan, Ronald	131,113	Carter, Jimmy	20,579	107,568 D	13.4%	74.8%	15.2%	84.8%
1976	168,830	27,873	Ford, Gerald R.	137,818	Carter, Jimmy	3,139	109,945 D	16.5%	81.6%	16.8%	83.2%
1972	163,421	35,226	Nixon, Richard M.	127,627	McGovern, George S.	568	92,401 D	21.6%	78.1%	21.6%	78.4%
1968	170,578	31,012	Nixon, Richard M.	139,566	Humphrey, Hubert H.		108,554 D	18.2%	81.8%	18.2%	81.8%
1964**	198,597	28,801	Goldwater, Barry M.	169,796	Johnson, Lyndon B.		140,995 D	14.5%	85.5%	14.5%	85.5%

In 2000 the other vote column includes 10,576 votes cast for Green (Nader). In 1996 the other vote column includes 3,611 votes cast for Perot. In 1992 the other vote column includes 9,681 votes cast for Perot. In 1980 the other column includes 16,337 votes for Independent (Anderson). Under the 23rd Amendment to the Constitution, the District of Columbia became entitled to choose Electors beginning with the 1964 election.

POSTWAR VOTE FOR DELEGATE

Year	Total Vote	Republican		Democratic		Other Vote	Rep.-Dem. Plurality	Percentage			
								Total Vote		Major Vote	
		Vote	Candidate	Vote	Candidate			Rep.	Dem.	Rep.	Dem.
2000	175,631	10,258	Wolterbeek, Edward	158,824	Norton, Eleanor Holmes	6,549	148,566 D	5.8%	90.4%	6.1%	93.9%
1998	136,359	8,610	Wolterbeek, Edward	122,228	Norton, Eleanor Holmes	5,221	113,618 D	6.3%	89.6%	6.6%	93.4%
1996	149,998	11,306	Simonds, Sprague	134,996	Norton, Eleanor Holmes	3,696	123,690 D	7.5%	90.0%	7.7%	92.3%
1994	173,664	13,828	Saltz, Donald	154,988	Norton, Eleanor Holmes	4,848	141,160 D	8.0%	89.2%	8.2%	91.8%
1992	196,754	20,108	Emerson, Susan	166,808	Norton, Eleanor Holmes	9,838	146,700 D	10.2%	84.8%	10.8%	89.2%
1990	159,627	41,999	Singleton, Harry M.	98,442	Norton, Eleanor Holmes	19,186	56,443 D	26.3%	61.7%	29.9%	70.1%
1988	170,933	22,936	Reed, William	121,817	Fauntroy, Walter E.	26,180	98,881 D	13.4%	71.3%	15.8%	84.2%
1986	126,855	17,643	King, Mary L. H.	101,604	Fauntroy, Walter E.	7,608	83,961 D	13.9%	80.1%	14.8%	85.2%
1984**	161,771		—	154,583	Fauntroy, Walter E.	7,188	154,583 D		95.6%		100.0%
1982	112,543	17,242	West, John	93,422	Fauntroy, Walter E.	1,879	76,180 D	15.3%	83.0%	15.6%	84.4%
1980	151,046	21,245	Roehr, Robert J.	112,339	Fauntroy, Walter E.	17,462	91,094 D	14.1%	74.4%	15.9%	84.1%
1978	96,306	11,677	Champion, Jackson R.	76,557	Fauntroy, Walter E.	8,072	64,880 D	12.1%	79.5%	13.2%	86.8%
1976	159,790	21,699	Hall, Daniel L.	123,464	Fauntroy, Walter E.	14,627	101,765 D	13.6%	77.3%	14.9%	85.1%
1974	104,014	9,166	Phillips, William R.	66,337	Fauntroy, Walter E.	28,511	57,171 D	8.8%	63.8%	12.1%	87.9%
1972	159,612	39,487	Chin-Lee, William	95,300	Fauntroy, Walter E.	24,825	55,813 D	24.7%	59.7%	29.3%	70.7%
1971 S	116,635	29,249	Nevius, John A.	68,166	Fauntroy, Walter E.	19,220	38,917 D	25.1%	58.4%	30.0%	70.0%

In 1984 the Democratic candidate was also the nominee of the Republican and Statehood parties. The 1971 election was held in March for a short term to the end of the 92nd Congress.

DISTRICT OF COLUMBIA

DISTRICT OF COLUMBIA

PRESIDENT 2000

2000 Census Population	Ward	Total Vote	Republican	Democratic	Green (Nader)	Other	Rep.-Dem. Plurality	Percentage of Total Vote		
								Rep.	Dem.	Green
80,014	Ward 1	24,981	1,707	20,526	2,542	206	18,819 D	6.8%	82.2%	10.2%
82,845	Ward 2	27,063	4,070	20,638	2,091	264	16,568 D	15.0%	76.3%	7.7%
79,566	Ward 3	35,191	7,508	24,451	2,922	310	16,943 D	21.3%	69.5%	8.3%
71,393	Ward 4	28,497	1,037	26,553	787	120	25,516 D	3.6%	93.2%	2.8%
65,548	Ward 5	24,553	785	23,136	519	113	22,351 D	3.2%	94.2%	2.1%
65,457	Ward 6	25,239	2,202	21,477	1,371	189	19,275 D	8.7%	85.1%	5.4%
64,704	Ward 7	22,136	477	21,361	228	70	20,884 D	2.2%	96.5%	1.0%
61,537	Ward 8	13,920	251	13,524	95	50	13,273 D	1.8%	97.2%	0.7%
	Federal Ballots	314	36	257	21		221 D	11.5%	81.8%	6.7%
572,059	TOTAL	201,894	18,073	171,923	10,576	1,322	153,850 D	9.0%	85.2%	5.2%

Note: The ward populations provided by the District of Columbia total 571,059. The official Census Bureau 2000 population for the district is 572,059.

DISTRICT OF COLUMBIA

GENERAL ELECTIONS

2000 GENERAL ELECTIONS

President   Other vote was 669 Libertarian (Browne); 114 Socialist Workers (Harris); 539 scattered write-in.

Delegate   Other vote was 4,594 Libertarian (Kampia); 1,419 Socialist Workers (Manuel); 536 scattered write-in.